THERAPYED'S
National Physical Therapy Examination Review & Study Guide

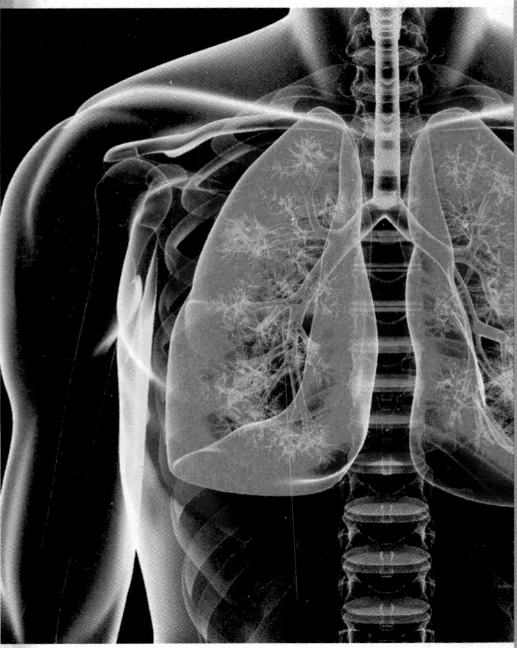

SUSAN B. O'SULLIVAN, PT, EdD
Professor Emerita
Department of Physical Therapy
College of Health Sciences
University of Massachusetts Lowell
Lowell, Massachusetts

RAYMOND P. SIEGELMAN, PT, DPT, MS
President Emeritus
TherapyEd
Boston, Massachusetts

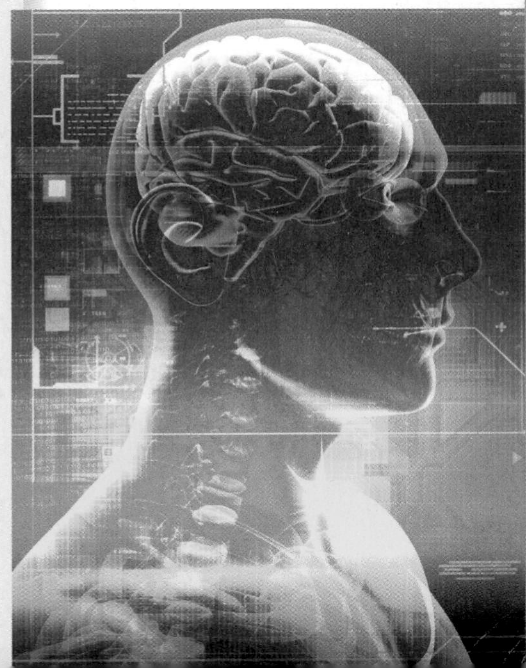

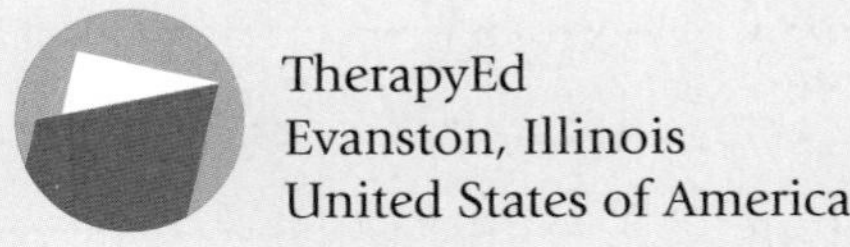

TherapyEd
Evanston, Illinois
United States of America

Library of Congress Control Number: 96-78846

ISBN: 978-0-9904162-4-1

The authors and contributors have made a faithful attempt to include relevant summaries of current physical therapy practice and other information at the time of publication. It is recognized that recommended practices, drug therapies, equipment, devices, governmental regulations, administrative procedures and other protocols and factors may change or be open to other interpretations. Therapists should take responsibility for updating their knowledge of technological advances, new information or conclusions available through publications, research, new regulations or guidelines.

The publisher disclaims any liability or loss incurred as a result of direct or indirect use of this book. Use of this book does not guarantee successful passage of the National Physical Therapy Examination.

Copies of this book and software may be obtained from:
TherapyEd
500 Davis Street, Suite 512
Evanston, IL 60201
Telephone (888) 369-0743 or (847) 328-5361
Fax (847) 328-5049
www.TherapyEd.com

Preface

One of the final hurdles for physical therapists to become licensed to practice in the United States is successful completion of the National Physical Therapy Examination (NPTE). This exam often requires candidates to combine basic physical therapy knowledge with clinical experience in order to interpret, evaluate, or solve problems that may occur in clinical situations. In order to protect the public, licensing boards use NPTE results as the main resource to determine whether a candidate has demonstrated minimal standards necessary for safe and effective practice.

Founded in 1988, TherapyEd offers Examination Preparatory Courses and/or Review & Study Guides for physical therapists, physical therapist assistants, occupational therapists, occupational therapy assistants, and speech-language pathologists. The physical therapist and physical therapist assistant courses help exam candidates assess their strengths and weaknesses vis-à-vis NPTE expectations and help shape and focus their preparation. Building on the years of experience of both the organization and the authors and contributors, the *National Physical Therapy Examination Review & Study Guide* provides a comprehensive content review, practice tests, critical reasoning rationales, strategies for study, and review and licensure information. Practice tests help familiarize therapists with the format and type of questions to expect on the national exam.

The *Review & Study Guide* is an ongoing project that is updated every year. The authors encourage and appreciate the feedback we have received from our many readers over the years. It is our hope that all exam candidates who use this book receive good news about their results and go on to reap the rewards of patient care and contribute to the development of physical therapy in the United States and throughout the world.

Table of Contents

Contributors

Jaqueline Banker, PT, DPT, OCS
Institute of Higher Learning
Brooks Rehabilitation
Jacksonville, Florida

Thomas Bianco, PT, MSPT
President
Sensible Ergonomic Solutions
Wilbraham, Massachusetts

Jason Beneciuk, PT, DPT, PhD, MPH, FAAOMPT
Residency and Fellowship Scholarly Mentor
Institute of Higher Learning
Brooks Rehabilitation
Jacksonville, Florida

Suzanne Robben Brown, PT, PhD
Mesa, Arizona

Tava Buck, PT, DPT, OCS
Institute of Higher Learning
Brooks Rehabilitation
Jacksonville, Florida

John Carlos, Jr., PT, PhD
Professor Emeritus
Department of Physical Therapy
Andrews University
Berrien Springs, Michigan

Sean Collins, PT, ScD, CCS
Professor and Chair of Physical Therapy
Plymouth State University
Plymouth, New Hampshire

Timothy Dellwo, PT, DPT, OCS
Institute of Higher Learning
Brooks Rehabilitation
Jacksonville, Florida

Gerard J. Dybel, PT, ScD, GCS
Associate Professor
Department of Physical Therapy
College of Health Sciences
University of Massachusetts, Lowell
Lowell, Massachusetts

William Farina, PT, DPT, MBA, FACHE
Principal
Terapia Consulting, LLC
Groton, Massachusetts

Rita P. Fleming-Castaldy, PhD, OTL, FAOTA
Associate Professor
Occupational Therapy Program
University of Scranton
Scranton, Pennsylvania

Lauren Clark, PT, DPT, OCS
Institute of Higher Learning
Brooks Rehabilitation
Jacksonville, Florida

Brittany Comer, PT, DPT, OCS
Institute of Higher Learning
Brooks Rehabilitation
Jacksonville, Florida

Suzanne M. Giuffre, PT, EdD
Associate Professor and Program Director
Doctor of Physical Therapy Program
Cleveland State University
Cleveland, Ohio

Kari Inda, OTR, PhD
Professor
Occupational Therapy Department Chairperson
Mount Mary College
Milwaukee, Wisconsin

Christopher J. Ivey, PT, MPT, MS, OCS, SCS, ATC
Assistant Professor
University of Saint Augustine for Health Sciences
San Marcos, California

Linda Kahn-D'Angelo, PT, ScD
Professor
Department of Physical Therapy
College of Health Sciences
Lowell, Massachusetts

Edward Kane, PT, PhD, SCS, ATC
Professor
University of Saint Augustine for Health Sciences
San Marcos, California

Steven M. Laslovich, PT, DPT, CPed
Assistant Professor
University of Saint Augustine for Health Sciences
San Marcos, California

L. Vincent Lepak III, PT, DPT, MPH, CWS
Assistant Professor
Division of Rehabilitation Sciences
University of Oklahoma Health Sciences Center
Tulsa, Oklahoma

Karen A. Leyva, PT, DPT, OCS
Instructor
University of Saint Augustine for Health Sciences
San Marcos, California

Kelly Macauley, PT, DPT, GCS, CCS
Assistant Professor
Department of Physical Therapy
MGH Institute of Health Professions
Boston, Massachusetts

Susan B. O'Sullivan, PT, EdD
Professor Emerita
Department of Physical Therapy
College of Health Sciences
University of Massachusetts Lowell
Lowell, Massachusetts

Elizabeth Oakley, PT, DHSc, MSPT
Associate Professor
Department of Physical Therapy
Andrews University
Berrien Springs, Michigan

Raine Osborne, PT, DPT, OCS, FAAOMPT
Program Coordinator
Orthopedic Residency Program
Brooks Institute of Higher Learning
Brooks Rehabilitation
Jacksonville, Florida

Robert Rowe, PT, DPT, DMT, MHS, FAAOMPT
Director
Brooks Institute of Higher Learning
Brooks Rehabilitation
Jacksonville, Florida

Renata Salvatori, PT, DPT, OCS, FAAOMPT
Faculty Member
Orthopedic Residency Program Coordinator and OMPT Fellowship Programs
Brooks Institute of Higher Learning
Brooks Rehabilitation
Jacksonville, Florida

Lois S. Siegelman, MS, FACHE
Healthcare Consultant
Boston, Massachusetts

Raymond P. Siegelman, PT, DPT, MS
President Emeritus
TherapyEd
Boston, Massachusetts

Laura Smith, PT, PhD, DPT, OCS, MTC, FAAOMPT
Assistant Professor
Department of Physical Therapy
Coordinator, Orthopedic Post Professional Residency and Certificate Program
University of Michigan-Flint
Flint, Michigan

Julie Ann Starr, PT, DPT, MS, CCS
Clinical Associate Professor
Physical Therapy Program
Department of Rehabilitation Sciences
Sargent College of Health and Rehabilitation Sciences
Boston University
Boston, Massachusetts

Thomas Sutlive, PT, PhD, OCS
Associate Professor
Doctoral Program in Physical Therapy
U.S. Army—Baylor University
San Antonio, Texas

James A Viti, PT, DPT, MHSc, OHC, MTC, FAAOMPT
Assistant Professor
University of Saint Augustine for Health Sciences
Saint Augustine, Florida

 Acknowledgments

Harjeet Singh
Head: U.S. Operations
Spearhead Group
Bear, Delaware

Ruth Ann Cassidy
President and Creative Director
Zographix, Inc.
Roseville, California

Crystal Clifton
Director
Progressive Publishing Services
Emigsville, Pennsylvania

Christine Becker
Project Manager
Progressive Publishing Services
Emigsville, Pennsylvania

Introduction

RAYMOND P. SIEGELMAN

Review>Practice>Motivate>Analyze>Apply

Purpose of This Book and Software

The *National Physical Therapy Examination Review & Study Guide* is designed to help physical therapist candidates prepare for the National Physical Therapy Examination (NPTE). Each chapter is presented in an easy-to-read outline format. Specific chapters focus on musculoskeletal, neuromuscular, cardiovascular, pulmonary, lymphatic, integumentary, metabolic, endocrine, gastrointestinal and genitourinary systems as well as other aspects of physical therapy practice. Relevant anatomy, kinesiology and pathophysiology of different diagnostic categories are briefly reviewed. Important medical, pharmacological and surgical interventions are also identified. Each chapter reviews the elements of physical therapy practice, including examination, evaluation of data, determination of an appropriate diagnosis, prognosis, plan of care, interventions and reevaluation of interventions selected. Additional chapters focus on the professional roles assumed by the physical therapist: consultant, administrator, educator and researcher. Chapters on pediatrics, geriatrics, therapeutic exercise, research and evidence-based practice, biophysical agents and functional devices are also included.

It is vital for candidates to master the elements of physical therapy practice in order to apply the information to clinical situations. This book was developed to help you organize and focus your review efficiently and effectively. However, you may elect to pursue a more in-depth review of topics, terms or procedures by referring to our recommended references.

The practice-exam software will help you assess your understanding of particular content areas and your ability to apply this knowledge to real-world situations. The practice exam format simulates the actual NPTE format, with a question counter and running clock on the top of the screen to help you keep track of your progress. The software also allows you to go back to questions you would like to review. Simulated exam breaks are included. When you are finished, the computer program will analyze your results and provide feedback to help you focus on areas for additional study. The software also allows creation of specialized tests emphasizing particular content areas, reasoning subtypes and so on.

At the back of the text are the question explanations along with critical reasoning rationales to help you understand how the answers were derived. Reading and interpreting these practice questions will also help prepare you for the various forms of multiple-choice questions you may encounter on the actual NPTE.

It is important to note that although these challenging practice tests are designed to help you diagnose the strengths and weaknesses of your academic and clinical preparation, they should not be used to measure minimal entry-level competency or predict your score on the NPTE.

Introduction

What Is the Procedure for Obtaining a License?

Licensure of health care practitioners protects the public from unsafe practices. In the United States and its territories, all physical therapists require a license to practice. Licensure is a function of state or territorial governments, not the federal government. It should be noted that physical therapist employees of the federal government are exempt from state regulation. However, a valid license in at least one state or jurisdiction is usually required by federal employers, such as the military or Public Health Service.

All jurisdictions require candidates to complete the NPTE successfully to obtain a license, but because the United States is made up of numerous states and governing entities, each state may have different requirements for you to become eligible to take the NPTE. Different states may also have different practice restrictions after you have passed the NPTE. These requirements can even differ within the same state, according to whether you graduated from a program accredited by the Commission on Accreditation in Physical Therapy Education (CAPTE). The CAPTE no longer accredits baccalaureate degree programs. In the United States, all candidates must have graduated from an entry-level master's or doctoral program or an equivalent international program. Each state has sovereignty over physical therapy licensure and regulation. Contact the individual licensing board in your jurisdiction to obtain applications and information about requirements and procedures.

Jurisprudence Examination

Some states require candidates to pass a separate examination concerning the rules, regulations, and laws governing physical therapy practice in that state. Licensed therapists who wish to obtain a license when moving to another state may have to pass a jurisprudence examination if it is required by that state. The Federation of State Boards of Physical Therapy (FSBPT) administers some, but not all, jurisprudence exams.

Fees

All states require a fee to apply for and renew a license. There are separate fees to sit for the NPTE. Fees vary widely and can change yearly.

Special Accommodation

1. Candidates with documented current disabilities can apply to their jurisdiction for special accommodation during the NPTE.
2. Medical or health conditions that may require a snack, water, medications, visual aids, a reader, extra time, wheelchair placement and so on may be considered. Pregnancy without complications is not considered a disability by the ADA.
3. English as a second language is not considered a disability. No dictionaries or extra time will be granted.
4. Test anxiety and technophobia are not considered disabilities.
5. All accommodations must be approved at least 15 days before the exam date.
6. If special accommodation is denied, the jurisdiction may have an appeal process.

Other Requirements and Issues

Tests of English Language Proficiency. Various tests of spoken, written or comprehended English may be required if English is not your first language. Standards and requirements differ from state to state. Personal interviews may also be required.

Fingerprinting, FBI Check, Vaccination, Malpractice Insurance. One or more of these may be required by some jurisdictions.

Credentials Evaluation. Currently, most states require physical therapists educated outside of the United States who graduated from programs not accredited by CAPTE to submit transcripts and other credentials to approved agencies for evaluation. Credentials often include course content, credit hours, grades earned and degrees granted. This process is required to establish eligibility to take the NPTE.

Supervised Practice Period. Some states may require therapists educated outside of the United States to undergo a period of supervised practice after successfully completing the NPTE. Permanent license is not granted until this supervised practice period is successfully completed.

Temporary License. Some states grant a temporary license to candidates eligible to take the NPTE. This temporary license allows the individual to practice under the supervision of a licensed therapist before taking and passing the NPTE. In some states, this temporary license may be revoked if a candidate fails the NPTE. As of 2012, only two states extend this temporary license if the candidate applies to retake the examination. In some states, if a temporary license is not offered, a physical therapist may *not* practice in that state until all requirements for licensure have been satisfied. In other states without a temporary license provision, applicants who have filed to take the exam may be allowed to practice under supervision of a licensed therapist. Therefore, it is prudent for you to keep current on the rules and regulations of the state(s) in which you wish to practice.

Transfer of Scores to Other Jurisdictions. All jurisdictions use the criterion-referenced grading method, which standardizes exam scoring and allows transfer of passing scores. The Federation of State Boards of Physical Therapy (FSBPT) is responsible for score transfer (www.fsbpt.org). For a fee, you may transfer your scores online or download the Score Transfer Request Form and mail the completed form to the FSBPT. If you maintain a license, you should not have to retake the NPTE if you move to a different state. However, if you are unlicensed, let your license lapse, or never took the examination, you will have to take the NPTE when seeking a license in that jurisdiction.

Retaking the Examination. Candidates may take the NPTE exam up to three times per 12-month period, which is the limit set by the FSBPT. After six attempts without passing, a lifetime ban on further testing is imposed. Candidates who incur two very low scores of 400 or less will also incur a lifetime ban. A candidate never takes the same form of an exam he or she had previously taken. Some states allow only three opportunities to take the NPTE in total. If you fail, the state may impose a stipulation that you show evidence of remedial work or study before retaking the NPTE. The state licensure board has an obligation to protect the public from practitioners who do not demonstrate competency.

License Renewal. After 1, 2 or 3 years, a license must be renewed for a physical therapist to continue practicing. Renewal notices are sent out by the state or territory in which the therapist is practicing. Sometimes, renewal simply involves paying the fee and returning the form. However, some states require verification of continuing education units. If you fail to notify the state of a change of address or e-mail address and do not receive a renewal notice, fail to respond to renewal in a timely manner or do not meet other requirements, your license could lapse. It is illegal to practice without a valid license. The state may require that a number of conditions be met to reinstate a lapsed license. One condition might include retaking the NPTE even if you had previously passed the exam. *Inform the board of any change of address. Do not let your license lapse!*

Continuing Education or Active Practice. Many states require the physical therapist to acquire a specific number of continuing education units (CEUs) to renew a license. Documentation, approval and reporting of CEUs vary from state to state. Some states require evidence of continuing active practice to renew. The FSBPT and the American Physical Therapy Association (APTA) are exploring alternative means to ascertain continued competency.

Endorsement. With a valid license in one state or jurisdiction, a physical therapist may apply to another state for a "license by endorsement." All criteria established by the new state must be met. This can include taking a jurisprudence exam for that state, attending interviews, providing letters of recommendation, taking English competency exams, attending AIDS awareness training and accruing CEUs. Contact the licensure board in the state where licensure by endorsement is sought to get information and applications. Start the process early; it can take months.

How Is the NPTE Developed?

The FSBPT is the organization that develops and owns the NPTE. The exam is based on a survey of practice conducted periodically by the FSBPT, from which the "blueprint" for the exam is developed. Numerous clinicians, educators and others contribute questions to the NPTE. Questions are designed to test knowledge and problem-solving skills that reflect current clinical practice and entry-level competency (defined as the first 6 months of practice). Various content experts and clinicians review the questions (item reviewers). Finally, the FSBPT committees and psychometricians fine-tune the questions and construct the final exam blueprint. The APTA or the individual state licensing boards do not develop, oversee or administer the NPTE.

Each examination adheres closely to the blueprint to fairly and comprehensively assess a candidate's competency to practice. The blueprint imparts a degree of stability, consistency, and continuity between different forms of the exam. However, each exam is a unique document with its own mix of questions. Questions are referenced to physical therapy textbooks in common use (a list of textbooks is available at www.fsbpt.org) and are not derived from a specific textbook or point of view. Terminology is consistent with that used in the *Guide to Physical Therapist Practice* and other commonly used texts.

NPTE Security Agreement

Each candidate who takes the NPTE must accept the NPTE Security Agreement. In part, this agreement states that it is illegal and unethical to recall (memorize) and share NPTE questions or solicit questions from candidates who have taken the exam. The FSBPT will continue to prosecute individuals who violate the security agreement.

What Areas Does the Exam Cover?

The exam places great emphasis on patient examination, evaluation, plan of care and interventions for a variety of patient/client problems. The exam also covers topics that are peripheral to direct patient care, often including professional roles in research, evidence-based practice, teaching/learning, ethical decision-making, communication, administration and other supporting activities. The exam is very comprehensive. Ensure that your preparation reflects the composition of the current exam. Naturally, not every item or sub-item listed here is covered in each examination. The NPTE currently consists of 250 questions, but only 200 questions count for your score. The additional 50 questions are used by the FSBPT to check their validity for future use. The content outline is based on the 200 questions that are scored.

The following information has been adapted from the NPTE Content Outline Federation of State Boards of Physical Therapy (effective 2013–2017). The use of category and domain designations is specific to the TherapyEd practice exams, and is used for the purposes of reporting your results.

Category A

Physical Therapy Examination: 50–56 Questions, or about 26.5% of the NPTE

- Tests and measures and their applications, including outcome measures and current best evidence
- Anatomy and physiology related to tests and measures
- Ultrasound imaging [musculoskeletal only]
- Movement analysis for all systems except Domain 5 (including rib cage excursion [pulmonary], friction, pressure, shear and scar mobility [integumentary only])
- Joint biomechanics and applications
- Physiological response of genitourinary system to tests and measures

Category A: Number of Questions by System

Domain I. Cardiovascular/Pulmonary and Lymphatic	10 questions
Domain II. Musculoskeletal/ Connective Tissue	22 questions
Domain III. Neuromuscular (CNS, PNS, ANS)	17 questions
Domain IV. Integumentary	3 questions
Domain V. Metabolic/Endocrine	0 questions
Domain VI. Gastrointestinal	0 questions
Domain VII. Genitourinary	1 question
Domain VIII. System Interactions	0 questions
Domain IX. Nonsystem	0 questions

Category B

Foundations for Evaluation, Differential Diagnosis and Prognosis: 65 Questions, or 32.5% of the NPTE

- Pathophysiology related to diseases/conditions or where primary impact is on more than one system in order to establish and carry out a plan of care, including prognosis
- Differential diagnosis related to diseases/conditions or where primary impact is on more than one system
- Diagnostic imaging
- Medical procedures and tests/surgical management
- Lab values
- Impact of comorbidities or coexisting conditions on patient/client management (e.g., dementia and arthritis)
- Pharmacological management
  - Psychological and psychiatric conditions that impact patient/client management (e.g., schizophrenia, depression)

Category B: Number of Questions by System

Domain I. Cardiovascular/Pulmonary and Lymphatic	12 questions
Domain II. Musculoskeletal/Connective Tissue	18 questions
Domain III. Neuromuscular (CNS, PNS, ANS)	15 questions
Domain IV. Integumentary	4 questions
Domain V. Metabolic/Endocrine	5 questions
Domain VI. Gastrointestinal	2 questions
Domain VII. Genitourinary	2 questions
Domain VIII. System Interactions	7 questions
Domain IX. Nonsystem	0 questions

Category C

Interventions: 57 Questions, or 28.5% of the NPTE

- PT interventions and their application for health promotion, rehabilitation and performance according to current best evidence
- Anatomy and physiology related to PT interventions, ADLs, and environmental factors
- Complications or secondary effects of PT or medical interventions
- Motor control and motor learning (neuromuscular system only)
- Positioning for reflux prevention, bowel programs (gastrointestinal system)
- Biofeedback, bladder programs and pelvic floor retraining (genitourinary system)

Category C: Number of Questions by System

Domain I. Cardiovascular/Pulmonary and Lymphatic	11 questions
Domain II. Musculoskeletal/Connective tissue	21 questions
Domain III. Neuromuscular (CNS, PNS, ANS)	18 questions
Domain IV. Integumentary	3 questions
Domain V. Metabolic/Endocrine	2 questions
Domain VI. Gastrointestinal	1 question
Domain VII. Genitourinary	1 question
Domain VIII. System interactions	0 questions
Domain IX. Nonsystem	0 questions

Category D

Equipment, Devices and Therapeutic Modalities: 12 Questions, or 6% of the NPTE

Equipment and devices	5 questions
Therapeutic modalities	7 questions

- Applications, adjustments, indications, precautions, contraindications of assistive, adaptive, protective, supportive, prosthetic and orthotic devices
- Applications, indications, precautions, contraindications for therapeutic modalities
- Thermal modalities
  - Iontophoresis
  - Electrotherapy
  - Phonophoresis
- Mechanical modalities (e.g., traction and motion devices [CPM])
  - Ultrasound
  - Biofeedback
  - Pressure differential modalities (e.g., intermittent compression)
  - Electromagnetic radiation (diathermy)

Category D: Number of Questions by System

Domain I. Cardiovascular/Pulmonary and Lymphatic	0 questions
Domain II. Musculoskeletal and Connective tissue	0 questions
Domain III. Neuromuscular (CNS, PNS, ANS)	0 questions
Domain IV. Integumentary	0 questions
Domain V. Metabolic/Endocrine	0 questions
Domain VI. Gastrointestinal	0 questions
Domain VII. Genitourinary	0 questions
Domain VIII. System interactions	0 questions
Domain IX. Nonsystem	12 questions

Category E

Research and Evidence-Based Practice; Safety, Protection and Professional Responsibilities: 13 Questions, or 6.5% of the NPTE

Research and evidence-based practice	4 questions
Safety and protection	5 questions
Professional responsibilities	4 questions

- Factors influencing safety and injury prevention
- Function and precautions related to IV lines, tubes, catheters and monitoring devices
- Emergency preparedness (CPR, first aid, disaster response)
- Infection control (isolation and sterile techniques, standard/universal precautions)
- Signs/symptoms of neglect or psychological, physical or sexual abuse
- Standards of documentation
- Patient/client rights (e.g., HIPAA, ADA, IDEA)
  - Human resources legal issues (e.g., sexual harassment, OSHA matters)
  - Roles and responsibilities of PTA and other health care professionals
  - Roles and responsibilities of support staff
  - Research design and interpretation (e.g., quantitative, qualitative, hierarchy of evidence)
  - Measurement science (e.g., reliability, validity)
- Statistics, including t-test, chi-square, ANOVA, correlation coefficient, likelihood ratio
- Data collection techniques such as surveys or observation

Category E: Number of Questions by System

Domain I. Cardiovascular/Pulmonary and Lymphatic	0 questions
Domain II. Musculoskeletal and Connective tissue	0 questions
Domain III. Neuromuscular (CNS, PNS, ANS)	0 questions
Domain IV. Integumentary	0 questions
Domain V. Metabolic/Endocrine	0 questions
Domain VI. Gastrointestinal	0 questions
Domain VII. Genitourinary	0 questions
Domain VIII. System Interactions	0 questions
Domain IX. Nonsystem	13 questions

What Is the Procedure for Taking the Exam?

To start the process of preparing for the exam, contact the licensing agency in the state or jurisdiction in which you wish to apply for a license. Return the completed application to the appropriate agency. If you are eligible, the FSBPT will send you an "Authorization to Test" letter. Once you are eligible, you should receive information about how to contact Prometric to establish your test location. You may contact the FSBPT Examination Services by phone at (703)739-9420 to check on the status of your application or inquire about other general information. Note that you are *not* required to take the exam in the state where you seek a license. You may take the NPTE in any Prometric Center in the United States. (See Box A for an outline of these steps.)

Determine the exam site for your exam. If it is necessary to travel the day before and seek lodging, make arrangements in advance. Plan to arrive at the exam site early. You *must* arrive at least 30 minutes *before* your scheduled examination. Bring a map or use GPS (you can also get directions at www.2test.com), know the traffic patterns (including rush hour times) and bring money to cover possible parking fees.

BOX A ◐ Procedure for Registering for the Exam

1. Contact the appropriate board or agency in the jurisdiction (state, district, territory) where you seek a license once you are eligible to take the exam.
2. Complete the application materials. If you are or will soon be a new graduate, your academic program must certify your eligibility. Do this as soon as possible.
3. Register for the exam at the FSBPT website (www.fsbpt.org) as soon as you can. The registration deadline is 30 days prior to the exam date you wish to take. There is a fee.
4. If the jurisdiction approves your eligibility, they must notify the FSBPT no later than 15 days prior to the scheduled exam. If the jurisdiction does not notify the FSBPT in time, you will not get an "Authorization to Test" letter for the exam date you requested.
5. If you receive an "Authorization to Test" letter, you will be instructed to contact Prometric to schedule the site where you wish to take the NPTE.
6. You do not have to take the exam in the jurisdiction where you seek a license. You may take it at any Prometric Center in another jurisdiction. Contact Prometric at www.prometric/fsbpt.com. Do this as soon as possible after receiving the "Authorization to Test" letter. Some sites may fill up rapidly, and you may have to choose alternative sites that involve travel or overnight stays.

Test Dates

Fixed NPTE (Physical Therapist) Dates for 2017

There are generally five testing dates per year. Dates for 2017 are:

January 26, 2017 (Thursday)
April 26, 2017 (Wednesday)
July 18, 2017 (Tuesday)
July 19, 2017 (Wednesday)
October 25, 2017 (Wednesday)

Go to www.fsbpt.org for time table to submit application.

Candidates with documented disabilities may receive special accommodation during the exam. Special seating, extra time, a reader and other considerations are possible. Any special accommodation must be approved in advance by the licensing board.

Prometric personnel will orient you regarding exam procedures. A tutorial before the exam should familiarize you with keyboard commands and other functions. We urge you to take the tutorial and ask for clarification of any detail before the start of the exam. If you are dissatisfied with the lighting, seating, ability to read the computer screen, noise levels or other factors, request a change to another computer cubicle *before* the exam starts. Contact Prometric personnel immediately if there is any computer malfunction.

Test-Taking Strategies

The exam is divided into sections of 50 questions each. The sections are balanced in terms of the content covered on the exam blueprint. Once you have completed a section and you take a break, you may not go back to any questions in that section. However, before you complete any section, you may review marked questions and change answers, if you wish. The computer screen shows a running clock of your remaining time to complete the exam. There will be a scheduled break of 15 minutes when the clock is stopped. During other breaks, the clock will run. You may also choose not to take a break. If you complete the exam before the allocated time, you may leave early.

During the exam, you may electronically mark questions you have skipped or wish to review at a later time. We do not recommend skipping questions. Answer each question to the best of your ability. Use educated guesses if you must. Guessing is not penalized. If time permits, use the computer review commands to return to previously marked items. Answers may be changed if necessary. If in doubt, stick with your original choice. Return to the marked questions before you exit each section. Once you exit a section of the exam, you cannot return to that section.

Time management is crucial. There are 250 items to answer in a 5-hour period not counting breaks. This amounts to a time allotment of just over 1 minute per question. You must complete an average of 50 questions per hour to finish all of the examination questions. When you have completed the first 50 questions, check the running clock on the computer screen. Have you completed them in an hour or less? If not, you must increase your pace or you may not get to answer all of the questions. Check again at questions #100 and #150. Some people prefer to check the computer clock at the end of each hour and note the number of questions answered. Either way, pace yourself properly.

Also keep in mind that during the third hour of the examination, reading skills tend to deteriorate and it may take longer to process each question. If English is your second language, you should think in English when answering questions. Otherwise, it may be very difficult to finish the examination on time, and this could also cause interpretation errors.

What should you do if there are only 2 minutes left and you have not answered all of the questions? Do not leave anything blank. Quickly choose answers for each question, even if you have not had a chance to read them all. Since there is no penalty for entering incorrect answers, you may be lucky and get a few correct! Over the years, many candidates have been unsuccessful on the NPTE because of failure to budget their time properly.

Once the exam has begun, communicate only with Prometric personnel. An innocent remark to a nearby test-taker or a glance at another computer screen might be mistaken for an attempt to cheat. Candidates attempting to cheat can face serious consequences. Trying to obtain a physical therapy license by fraudulent means is a crime. Don't even think about doing it.

BOX B Test Center Procedures

1. Check in at least 30 minutes prior to the exam. When you arrive at the exam site, visit the restroom before you check in. The whole examination procedure can last up to 6 hours. You may use the restroom during breaks.
2. Remember to bring proper identification and your "Authorization to Test" letter, since you will not be allowed to take the exam without either of them. Two forms of identification are required. One must be a government-issued photo ID such as a passport or driver's license. Another can be an ID preprinted with your name and signature, such as a credit card. Social Security cards are not accepted. IDs will be scanned. Your first and last names on the IDs must be the same as on the "Authorization to Test" letter. If there is any problem with the IDs, you will not be allowed to take the exam. All fees will be forfeited, and you will have to reschedule for the next fixed date. Photocopies of identification are not acceptable.
3. You will be fingerprinted and photographed. All testing sessions are videotaped. If you leave the testing room for any reason (e.g,, to visit the restroom), you will be fingerprinted again.
4. You may request a dry erase board to make notes. You may not bring in your own scratch paper. The boards will be collected when you leave the testing center.
5. Personal items such as eyeglasses, contacts and medications are allowed. Some comfort items such as tissues or mints may be allowed.
6. Earplugs are not permitted. Prometric will supply sound-dampening headphones upon request. Keep in mind that background noise may be distracting.
7. A locker will be provided for personal items. The locker cannot be accessed during the exam.
8. Wear multilayer clothing to stay comfortable in various room temperatures. Jackets with pockets, "hoodie" sweatshirts, hats or scarves are not permitted. If you remove a sweater or outer shirt, you must wrap it around your waist. These items cannot be placed on the back of a chair or elsewhere in the testing room. If you must wear a head covering for health or religious reasons, you must receive approval before the testing date. Prometric personnel cannot grant approval on site.
9. No electronic devices of any kind (such as cell phones, MP3 players or digital watches) are allowed in the testing room. They must be put in the locker.
10. Eat a good meal before taking the exam. Food or drink is officially not allowed at the computer cubicle during the examination. At some centers, water may be available in the reception area, or you may keep your own drink there.
11. You may not talk or read aloud during the exam.

How Is the NPTE Graded, and How Are Scores Reported?

The FSBPT employs criterion-referenced performance standards. Using this system, a test score is interpreted in terms of an individual's mastery of a specified content domain. A passing criterion or standard is established by the FSBPT for each examination. A candidate must reach or exceed the designated cut score of competency to pass the exam. The cut score represents the minimal acceptable level of exam performance consistent with safe and effective practice expected of physical therapists. A panel of physical therapy content experts establishes the passing score after screening questions for performance characteristics and bias. The examinee's performance is not compared with the performance of others who took the same test. Each form of the NPTE has its own criterion-referenced passing grade, and these may vary from exam to exam. Grading on a curve, using a fixed percentage and using the number of questions answered correctly are methods that are NOT used to determine passing scores.

Reporting of grades to candidates can be confusing. Scaled scores, rather than the absolute number of questions answered correctly (raw score), are reported to candidates. The scaled scoring range is from 200 to 800, with 600 always reflecting the cut score. For example, if the passing raw score is determined to be 149 out of 200 questions for an exam, this would equal a scaled score of 600. If a candidate achieved a score of 600 or better, the state licensing board would notify the candidate of his or her success and issue a license provided that all other conditions were satisfied. A change in the scaling procedure in 2013 may result in some higher scaled scores with some even reaching the 800 level.

Some states still convert the passing scaled score to another system based on the number 70 or 75.

Your score can be reported as being above or below the number 70 or 75. This does not mean that you scored above or below 70% or 75% or correctly or incorrectly answered 70 or 75 questions. It is merely an arbitrary numbering system used to denote a pass/fail line.

Planning Your Exam Review

After you have completed your entry-level physical therapy education, you bring all of your academic and clinical experiences to the table in preparation for the NPTE. Four to 6 weeks of structured independent review should be adequate. More time might be necessary for candidates who are not native English speakers or for candidates who were not educated through an APTA-accredited program.

Candidates with learning disabilities might require more preparation time because the processing of information may be slower. Most candidates probably do not need to take a lengthy refresher/remedial course. However, a Licensure Examination Preparatory course, such as the type offered since 1988 by TherapyEd, can be quite helpful. Extensive student feedback has indicated that this type of preparation course, when used in combination with this text, is an effective tool to provide information about current exam expectations and trends. The course manual and additional means of self-assessment provide even more focus and direction for exam preparation.

Please show respect for the examination process. Procrastination, skimpy review, and lack of understanding about the nature of the NPTE could lead to disappointing results. The expenses incurred to retake the examination, along with the potential loss of income because of failure to obtain a license, are significant. If you are unsuccessful, your self-esteem may take a mighty blow.

Discipline. About a month or two before your scheduled exam, establish a routine and spend 6 days per week reviewing material. Set up realistic and potentially achievable short-term goals as to what you wish to accomplish each day. Take 1 day off per week to pursue interests other than physical therapy. Give yourself a break! When you are reviewing, however, allot 2 to 3 hours of uninterrupted study time each day. Study in a quiet and well-lit space. Do not study when you are tired or ill. If you work during the week, weekends may give you more flexibility and time for review.

If you break your routine, add compensatory time. Answer the computer-based sample questions as a means of diagnosing strengths and weaknesses. Trying to memorize hundreds of sample questions and rationales is not a satisfactory means of preparation. Practice questions serve as templates for a multitude of item possibilities and primarily serve as diagnostic tools. You must review basic physical therapy knowledge and be able to apply that knowledge to a variety of problems, settings, circumstances and situations. Some individuals may benefit from small group study sessions.

Although the review is for the purpose of passing the NPTE, we have received feedback through the years that this retrospective overview of one's physical therapy education has helped to sharpen and focus many aspects of clinical practice as well.

Analysis of Strengths and Weaknesses

A "shotgun" approach to exam preparation is not the best way to use your time. Try to form a composite picture of your physical therapy education and experiences.

Academic Program. Even accredited physical therapist programs can vary widely in terms of the quantity and quality of the content covered. Many programs are superb. Others may have problems with curricula or faculty. There could be a lack of emphasis on content that might be important for the NPTE. Be sure to request a copy of your school's report on performance of previous classes on the exam according to the exam blueprint. Some information is available at the FSBPT website.

Consider which content areas were presented in a comprehensive manner and which areas left something to be desired. Were there any gaps in your basic preparation that may be emphasized on the NPTE? Will this require you to spend more time gathering or reviewing information in these areas? Were academic standards poorly enforced, were grades inflated, or were some marginal students given social promotions to help enhance their self-esteem or the status of the program? Your study plan should compensate for weaknesses in your academic program, since the NPTE conforms to a standard outside the academic setting.

Classroom Performance. Generally, strong classroom performers with good English skills should fare well on the NPTE *as long as they take the time to prepare properly*. Students who performed marginally in their program, whose basic physical therapy education program lacked rigor or whose English skills are not well developed are often disappointed when they receive NPTE results.

Clinical Experiences/Affiliations. If the range of clinical experiences was limited in terms of settings, patient populations, types of treatments or degree of responsibility, exam candidates may have difficulty answering questions that require the application of clinical knowledge or judgment. For example, an exam candidate with no clinical exposure in such areas as pediatrics, cardiac rehabilitation or wound or burn care may have difficulty in reaching conclusions requiring systems review, evaluation, outcome projection or interventions in these areas. Many NPTE questions require an amalgam of clinical experience and academic knowledge to solve problems. Selected use of the *Guide to Physical Therapist Practice* may prove helpful in areas of deficient clinical preparation. Specific practice patterns, examinations, goals, interventions and outcomes may be delineated.

Analysis of Sample Question Results. At appropriate times, you should attempt to answer the practice questions in the simulated exams in the accompanying software. The computer scoring will assist you in identifying content areas, domains and critical reasoning categories in which your performance was sufficient and those areas that need more work. This analysis can serve as a basis for structuring further study and review. After taking the exams, be sure to read the rationale and critical reasoning strategies for the practice exam questions in the *Review & Study Guide*.

Based on your personal analysis, write down areas of weakness and try to rank order them in terms of which areas might require the most remedial work. Set priorities based on the Content Outline, *Guide to Physical Therapist Practice*, Second Edition, and expectations of the examination. Keep in mind that the NPTE emphasis is primarily on entry-level knowledge and judgment.

Levels of Question Difficulty

The NPTE attempts to ascertain how a candidate deals with a variety of different situations to determine how the applicant would function in the role of a physical therapist in a clinical setting. Most of the questions require problem solving at the upper levels of cognitive functioning (see Box C: Levels of NPTE Exam Questions).

BOX C ▶ Levels of NPTE Exam Questions

Question Level and Description

1. Knowledge

Recall of basic information such as characteristics of diagnoses, spinal cord level functionality, wheelchair measurements, shapes of joints, and so on.

Relevance to the NPTE

A solid knowledge foundation of all information related to entry-level PT practice is required to answer various scenarios proposed on NPTE questions.

It is highly unlikely that any NPTE questions are solely at this level. Ready recall of this information is needed in order to help solve advanced-level questions.

(Continued)

BOX C ◗ Levels of NPTE Exam Questions (*Continued*)

NPTE Exam Preparation Strategy

A strong commitment to studying is needed to remember all the relevant information acquired during PT entry-level education. This is a short-term goal of about 2 months. Fortunately, this *Review & Study Guide* (and the Course Manual, if you took a TherapyEd prep course) provides extensive information in an outline format to make your review easier.

2. Comprehension

Understanding of basic information to determine significance, consequences or implications. For example, the impact of a tenodesis grasp on function or the possible consequences of using aquatic therapy for a group of patients with multiple sclerosis.

Relevance to the NPTE

The NPTE is not a matching test. Therefore, you must do more than recall information to succeed on the exam; you must have a firm grasp of content to understand the nuances and meaning of the questions. This may be the "who, what, where, when and how" of the question.

NPTE Exam Preparation Strategy

When reviewing foundational knowledge, think about why this information might be important. Studying with a peer/study group and explaining to the group the relevance, significance, consequences and implications of the study material may help you master it. Having a family member or friend quiz you on basic information may help you determine your ability to "think on your feet." Don't enter the test without strong comprehension abilities in all major areas of PT practice.

3. Application

Use of information and application of rules, procedures or theories to new situations. For example, how to apply ergonomic principles to modify a work station for someone with bilateral carpal tunnel syndrome.

Relevance to the NPTE

The NPTE requires one to integrate knowledge and comprehension as well as competencies developed during clinical experiences in order to best answer a practice scenario. Many NPTE questions should be at this level, since a main goal of the exam is to assess the candidate's ability to respond competently to different situations.

NPTE Exam Preparation Strategy

If your knowledge and comprehension are solid in all major domains of the exam as put forth in this *Review & Study Guide*, take one of the computer-based practice exams that accompany this text. The challenging questions follow the format of the NPTE. Use your results to determine areas of academic, clinical and reasoning strengths and weaknesses.

4. Analysis

Recognition of interrelationships between principles and interpretation or evaluation of data presented. For example, the most beneficial focus for discharge planning sessions for a parent and an adolescent with acquired traumatic brain injury.

Relevance to the NPTE

The NPTE assumes that test-takers have mastery and comprehension of entry-level knowledge and can apply it competently in diverse situations. Therefore, expect to analyze and respond to ambiguous situations. Direct "textbook answers" may not apply, which causes problems for some concrete thinkers. Many items are at this level, since the main objective of the exam is to determine competency in complex practice or ethical situations. In other words, practice your ability to think "outside of the box" in order to solve problems in real-world situations.

NPTE Exam Preparation Strategy

Use the analyses of the practice exams to reflect on your reasoning and judgment. Critically review the explanations for each question that you struggled with. Use peer or study groups to help determine gaps in analyses of exam questions. Ascertain what actions to take regarding deficiencies in critical reasoning skills to adequately prepare for the complexities of the NPTE.

Modified and adapted with permission from Fleming-Castaldy, R: National Occupational Therapy Certification Examination Review & Study Guide, 5th ed.

BOX D General Strategies for Answering NPTE Items

- Read the exam item carefully but quickly before selecting a response.
- Read the exam item for key words that set a priority.
- Use knowledge of medical terminology to decipher unknown words using prefixes, suffixes and root words.
- Employ relevant clinical experience. Do not call on unusual or atypical cases.
- Apply clinical reasoning skills to determine the relevance of the information in the question (diagnosis, setting, intervention, theoretical principles).
- Check the answer to see whether it is theoretically, diagnostically and developmentally consistent with the item scenario.
- Choose patient/client-centered actions that focus on the emotional well-being of the person, if they are relevant to the question.
- Eliminate choices that contain contraindications (unless asked for a contraindication) or unsafe options.
- Use both your academic knowledge and clinical judgment to support your answer.
- Work rapidly but accurately. Time management is an important criterion for success.
- The NPTE is a 5-hour exam. Fight fatigue and eye strain.
- Exam boredom can be a factor, especially after you have answered 200 questions, with 50 more to go. Losing interest in reading and answering questions can cost you points.

Methods of Reading Multiple-Choice Questions

Carefully read the stem of each question. What is the focus of the question? Think about the information, using your knowledge as well as your judgment. Then read each choice carefully. Begin the process by eliminating one option at a time. Every time you are able to rationalize eliminating an incorrect option, the odds of answering the question correctly increase dramatically. Be careful; sometimes options have some correct information that does not apply to the question asked. If the stem of the question is long or involved, you might wish to read the options first. This may help you focus better on the relevance of the information presented.

As the exam progresses, your reading skills may tend to deteriorate. You may have to rest your eyes for a minute or stand up and walk away from the computer screen for a short time. If your mind is no longer processing information properly, you may answer questions incorrectly that you normally would get right. Stop and rest for a few moments until you can refocus on the question. You might have to take a longer break after you complete a section.

Strategies for Answering Multiple-Choice Questions

1. Look for opposites in the list of options. These are the extremes of a concept, such as positive/negative, inversion/eversion, hypoglycemia/hyperglycemia or spasticity/flaccidity. Examine opposites first. If you cannot eliminate both of them immediately, there is a good chance that one is the correct answer. If you can eliminate both opposites right away, the chances drop to 50/50 for selecting the correct response from the remaining two choices.
2. Identify choices that are so similar that it is difficult to choose between them. These may be choices that say the same thing in slightly different ways. If you cannot discriminate between them, it is possible that both are incorrect. For example, if one option in a question is "the primary muscle of inspiration" and another choice in the same question is "the diaphragm," they both say the same thing and need to be eliminated. Sometimes a choice that is

unique but not far-fetched merits greater consideration than others.

3. Identify clues in the stem that may be helpful in focusing your thoughts. For example, a question presents a recently discharged patient who can transfer independently but cannot ambulate independently for more than 20 feet. Your judgment should lead you to conclude that the patient is probably homebound. A response requiring outpatient management, use of a therapeutic pool, or elaborate therapeutic exercise equipment might be inappropriate.
4. Look for key words or phrases in the stem. If you see **best, most important, first,** or **primary,** you will need to set priorities. All of the choices could correctly answer the question; however, you must go through a process of rank ordering and elimination to reach the best option. Try to eliminate any obvious, unrealistic choices first, and work backward toward what you consider to be the top priority.
5. Look for overlapping facts in the options. If you ascertain that a fact or statement in one option is incorrect, and you see the same fact or statement in another option, both choices can be eliminated. For example, given a patient problem, two options in the question are (1) pallor and diaphoresis and (2) tachycardia and diaphoresis. If you determine that diaphoresis is never a sign of the problem, then you can automatically eliminate both choices (1) and (2).
6. Identify options that are crucial for the survival or safety of the patient. These always receive a high priority. You should give less credibility to responses that provide false reassurance to the patient, are overly optimistic or do not address the patient's or family's feelings. Also give less credibility to responses in which the therapist gives away decision-making capability or responsibility to other health care workers. Consider abdicating responsibility only if there is a medical situation outside of the scope of practice for physical therapists, or if the therapist does not possess the skills to treat a particular type of patient problem.
7. Look for negative words or phrases in the stem. Phrases and words such as **least important, not, contraindicated,** and other negatives denote that you must search for an answer that is false, unacceptable, low priority, or contraindicated. Negative words are often in bold type. If you consider each choice as either *true* or *false* relative to the scenario presented, you should end up with three *trues* and one *false,* and therefore be able to answer the question. The false choice would be the correct answer if you categorized everything appropriately. These types of negative questions are becoming much less common on the NPTE with the possible exception of questions related to contraindications.

BOX E Strategy Review for Answering Multiple-Choice Items

- Identify the question theme. What is the question really asking?
- Avoid "reading into" the question. Don't make up a story. Read the question, and nothing but the question.
- Identify choices that are equally plausible. If two choices say basically the same thing, eliminate both.
- Carefully consider opposites. If you cannot eliminate both right away, one may be the correct answer.
- More than one choice may correctly answer the question. Choose the one that is *most* correct.
- In most cases, select positive, active choices rather than passive, negative ones.
- When changing an answer, make sure you have a good reason to eliminate your original choice, and an even better reason to make a new choice. Don't let second-guessing talk you out of the correct answer.

Adapted from Fleming-Castaldy, R; National Occupational Therapy Review & Study Guide, 5th ed.

8. Don't look for a particular pattern of answers that would cause you to alter a choice you believe to be correct. For instance, do not eliminate a correct choice because you chose the same letter or number choice as a response in the item immediately preceding the one you are currently answering. Questions are selected and randomly placed in the exam. Don't look for or think about answer patterns.
9. Don't overanalyze a question. Read the question at face value. Don't go outside of the gist of the information in the stem of the question to reach a conclusion. Sufficient information should be available. Adding your own hypothetical conditions to the situation presented could lead you in the wrong direction.
10. Some questions may present graphic or visual representations with an accompanying question. These may include x-rays; wounds; ECG readouts; therapists performing various tests, measures, or interventions; or depictions of patients with impairments such as scoliosis or amputations. A useful strategy for these types of questions is to look at the choices first. With the choices in mind, look at the graphic representation next, and finally look at the question. Looking at the choices first may help you focus on the aspect of the graphic representation that may be most relevant to answer the question.

Final Review

A review consisting of *just* answering or memorizing sample questions is often unsatisfactory, since the sample questions in the accompanying computer software are not actual NPTE questions. These questions are meant to be used for diagnostic or learning purposes. Although some questions on the NPTE may seem similar to the practice questions, the NPTE questions may have entirely different answers. You most likely will also encounter some questions on the actual NPTE that have a different focus than the practice exam questions.

Your final review should refocus on the areas that are emphasized on the NPTE and that you have identified as areas of personal weakness. You may wish to retake the practice exams, if time permits.

The Day Before the Exam

The day before the examination, make sure you have gathered all necessary documents, materials, medications, eyeglasses and personal items you may need. It will heighten your anxiety to look for these things on the day of the exam. Do not use medications such as antihistamines or muscle relaxants, drink alcohol or use other substances that may affect your alertness. Do not "cram" or stay up late the night before, reviewing material. Do not go to a party the night before the exam. (After it's over, okay!) Try to get a good night's sleep. On the day of the test, eat a meal before the exam. You may not have the opportunity to eat again for many hours. Finally, allow extra time to arrive at the test site in case travel is delayed.

Expect to be a little nervous. Prometric personnel are trained to put you at ease and explain what will happen. However, if you are unrealistic in your expectations at the testing site, Prometric personnel may react negatively to your demands. This will not put you in the proper frame of mind to take the NPTE. Also, if you are overly anxious, your ability to process questions and recall information could be impaired. Anxiety can also lead you to dwell more on the consequences of the exam rather than the questions presented. Practice relaxation strategies you find helpful. If you have disciplined yourself to review material thoroughly, you should feel confident, and there is more likelihood of a positive outcome.

The Role of Critical Reasoning in Your Performance

Critical reasoning is an important part of NPTE preparation. At this moment, you have achieved a certain level of critical reasoning skill that has helped you succeed in academic and clinical arenas. Critical reasoning skills are the foundation for how we analyze the situations we encounter in everyday life. We often do not acknowledge how important this implicit skill is for exam success.

It is important to define critical reasoning and why you should spend time focusing your attention on this process. Critical reasoning is a decision-making process by which one uses one's knowledge, skills, experience and logic to draw conclusions about everyday situations. When this process is used judiciously, it is undertaken with purpose, clarity, accuracy and thoroughness. It is the foundation by which individuals draw conclusions about their world and what one determines to be true.

How does this relate to the NPTE, and why should you be concerned about it? The NPTE provides opportunities for you to demonstrate how well you can reason out challenging clinical, ethical, administrative or other circumstances with the 250 questions you will need to answer for the exam. Each question will require you to draw on your knowledge, skills and experiences to arrive at a correct conclusion. The way you arrive at a correct conclusion is primarily by using critical reasoning.

Some individuals erroneously believe that the NPTE tests only your ability to recall facts that are readily found in books. Although factual knowledge is important and provides a foundation for the exam, the NPTE also tests your ability to evaluate challenging circumstances correctly and to make prudent

Table 1

Critical Reasoning Self-Assessment Questions

OBSERVED EXAM DIFFICULTY	REASONING CHALLENGE	NPTE EXAM PREPARATION STRATEGY
Do You: - Have difficulty with taking specific information and applying it to larger populations? - Selecting incorrect answers because you don't know how to generalize your knowledge?	Inductive	When studying a specific content area, think about how to apply the information you are reviewing to a diversity of situations. Use a reflective "what if" stance to think about how this information may be generalized to a broader context. This can be a fun and effective study group activity.
Do you: - Prefer to follow your instincts rather than the guidelines that a protocol may provide? - Select incorrect answers because you are unfamiliar with established practice standards or major theoretical approaches?	Deductive	When studying, be sure to master all major concepts, laws, rules and accepted principles that guide PT practice. Carefully review all frames of reference, practice guidelines and intervention protocols and procedures. Review the APTA Code of Ethics and Guidelines for Professional Conduct.
Do You: - Tend to misinterpret information provided and make poor judgments and apply inadequately conceived assumptions about it? - Select incorrect answers because you misjudged the effects of a clinical condition on functional performance?	Analytical	Obtain knowledge of all major clinical conditions, their symptoms, diagnostic testing and criteria, anticipated sequelae and expected outcomes. This information is extensively reviewed in this text to help you make accurate judgments and correct assumptions about the potential impact of a clinical condition on functional performance. Review potential adverse effects (red flags in this text) and common errors associated with training.
Do You: - Have difficulty with thinking about how clinical conditions and practice situations may evolve over time? - Assume information is valid when it is not true? - Select incorrect answers because you have difficulty deciding the best course of action in a practice scenario?	Inferential	When studying clinical conditions, think about how the presentation of these conditions may sometimes vary from textbook descriptions. Use the knowledge and experience you acquired during your clinical education experiences to assess the trustworthiness of your assumptions. Study guidelines and models developed from evidence-based practice to develop a solid foundation on how to decide the best course of action.
Do you: - Feel anxious when you have questions that are ambiguous and you cannot find answers to them in a textbook? - Rely on protocols and guidelines more than gut instinct? - Select incorrect answers because you become overwhelmed by questions that present ethical dilemmas?	Evaluative	When reviewing specific content, think about the practice ambiguities and ethical dilemmas you observed during your clinical education experiences related to these areas. Review the APTA Code of Ethics and Guidelines for Professional Conduct and practice applying this information to determine a correct course of action using practice examples and case studies.

This table was adapted with permission from Dr. Kari Inda, from a table published in Fleming-Castaldy, R: National Occupational Therapy Certification Exam: Review & Study Guide, 5th ed. TherapyEd, 2009, p. x.

decisions about the situations described in each question. The exam often moves beyond simple recall of knowledge and facts to contextualized clinical information. This means that you will be given clinical scenarios in which you will need to draw conclusions about a patient's symptoms, diagnosis, response to therapy and expected outcomes. You must draw on your knowledge to take your reasoning to the next level application of information.

One should be aware of critical reasoning processes and skills (see Table 1). The following section helps you become aware of the different skills involved in the process of critical reasoning, and how NPTE success is, in part, tied to these processes.

Subskills of Critical Reasoning

There are five subskills of critical reasoning that underlie the foundation for good critical reasoning skill. They are based on expert consensus of many critical thinking experts and reported by Peter and Noreen Facione (1990a, 1990b, 2006), who describe the skills used in reasoning out challenging circumstances. These skills include **inductive reasoning, deductive reasoning, analysis, inference,** and **evaluation**.

Inductive Reasoning

Inductive reasoning is the process of reasoning in which the assumptions of an argument are believed to endorse the conclusion, but do not guarantee it. It starts with reasoning in specific situations and then moves to more generalized situations. It may start with observations about a specific situation and then require one to draw conclusions about larger circumstances.

For example, if we observe a patient who experienced a stroke demonstrating dysarthria, we might conclude that all patients with stroke have dysarthria. We know that this is, in fact, not true. Inductive reasoning skill was used to draw this conclusion because we took observations from a specific situation and applied them to a larger, more global assumption. Recognizing that inductive reasoning can be flawed is an important part of successful exam performance. Inductive reasoning is an important skill clinically, because it helps us to examine all possible options in a clinical situation and determine the most reasonable action. It is used in diagnostic thinking, where we form assumptions about what to expect from a diagnosis as it evolves over time.

Deductive Reasoning

Deductive reasoning is the process of reasoning whereby one draws conclusions based on facts, laws, rules or accepted principles. It is the reverse thinking process of inductive reasoning, whereby the individual starts with larger circumstances and theories and applies them to specific situations.

For example, if we read the *Physical Therapy Guide for Professional Conduct,* which states that fraudulent billing for therapy services is unethical, we could reasonably conclude that when we witness therapist A in a clinic billing for services for patient B that did not occur, therapist A is acting unethically. Here the circumstance started with a global principle and was applied to a specific circumstance.

However, deductive reasoning also has its flaws. Sometimes individuals make erroneous assumptions about the premises of a theory and then apply this error in thinking to the specific circumstance. If we start with a premise that all patients enjoy physical therapy, then patients B, C, and D all will enjoy physical therapy. Can we say this for sure? Of course not! This is a type of flawed premise that leads to a faulty conclusion. We must be sure that our deductive reasoning begins with sound theory and known principles.

Deductive reasoning is important to physical therapists because it helps them apply rules and laws, without necessitating independent judgment for the situation. This is especially beneficial when applying protocols for treatment approaches (e.g., functional electrical stimulation, assuming one is following a published protocol) or research guidelines (e.g., how to carry out correlational analysis of an array of data).

Analysis

Analytical reasoning or analysis is defined as the process of interpreting the meaning of information as well as relationships within the information presented, and then making assumptions or judgments about that information. Information presented in the form of graphs, charts, tables and pictures encourages analytical reasoning skills, because one must interpret the information and determine what it means. Other times, information is presented in such a manner that one must make a "mental chart" of the information.

Popular questions that test one's analytical reasoning contain descriptors assigned to a group, with the key features of the group given in part. This leaves the test-taker to make assumptions about what is true about the whole group based on the information provided. Questions of this nature tend to place groups of people into categories, and the test-taker must determine the characteristics of each group, based on limited information. These questions tend to frustrate people. Nonetheless, analytical reasoning is a necessary evil!

In physical therapy practice, analytical reasoning is important because it helps one to interpret an ECG strip or determine the diagnosis when analyzing the x-ray of a patient with a "Scotty dog" fracture in the spine (What is the significance?). Often, questions of this nature provide a host of symptoms, and the test-taker must determine the diagnosis (categorization of information). We also use analytical reasoning to give definitions to symptoms we are reading about (How can we describe this symptom?). Overall, analytical reasoning helps us to examine ideas and concepts and the relationships between them.

Inference

Inference or inferential reasoning is the process of drawing conclusions or making logical judgments based on concepts, assumptions and evidence, rather than direct observations. Questions that ask you to determine what is best, most important or most beneficial often test your inferential reasoning ability. Questions of this nature also ask you to determine what is believed to be true, even though you cannot be 100% sure.

Inferential reasoning skills are used in clinical situations when a physical therapist must determine what symptoms to expect from a diagnosis or what is the likely functional result from a disease process or disorder. Because we cannot be 100% sure about the nature of a disease and all its possible symptoms, we must infer this information based on our knowledge and experiences. This is an important skill for a physical therapist to possess.

Pitfalls to inferential reasoning commonly occur when we fail to consider all the information presented or use faulty logic to determine what may occur in certain situations. An example of this might be a physical therapist who determines that it is most appropriate for a patient with T12 paraplegia to focus on strengthening upper trapezius and levator scapulae muscles in preparation for ambulation with crutches, rather than triceps and lower trapezius muscles. Here, the therapist did not consider the nature of the task at hand (ambulation with crutches) or tie the muscle functions with the use of crutches for ambulation. Hasty decisions can lead to suboptimal treatment planning with patients.

Evaluation

Evaluation and evaluative reasoning is a process by which one weighs the merits of an argument for its validity and the inherent value of the argument itself. Here, the individual determines whether an argument "holds water," whether there is value to be found in the argument itself, and what value one can assign to it.

Individuals make value judgments all the time. We are often unaware of the thought processes involved. Every day, we evaluate ideas that are presented to us, sometimes in the form of a news story or a discussion with a friend. We tend to judge the merits and value of the information we receive. However, a good evaluative thinker listens with a skeptical ear, determining how truthful the information is and how much value one should assign to that information. Accepting information at face value can be a pitfall because we are not considering the possibility that there is more information to be heard that may complete the story.

There are also times where we may have to make difficult decisions in areas that have no clear-cut answers. In physical therapy practice, we may be faced with dilemmas that pose a challenge for the correct course of action. Pay close attention to questions with the picture of the cogwheels next to them because they will help you to identify questions that pose difficult clinical and ethical situations and require evaluative reasoning.

An example of such a dilemma is a situation in which a therapist is working with a patient who becomes short of breath. The therapist must determine whether to immediately notify the physician, document the symptoms or continue with the treatment session as planned. It is also helpful to know whether shortness of breath is an expected symptom, given the patient's medical history and past response to treatment. This information helps guide the therapist's thinking about a correct course of action. Nonetheless, these types of situations are not clear-cut, and require the therapist to evaluate the circumstances, weigh the information presented and determine a correct course of action, given his or her knowledge and experience.

Pitfalls in evaluative reasoning involve assigning great value to information that has little value to the situation, not assigning enough value to highly valuable information and not using principles and guidelines that are put into place to help guide one's thinking (such as the Code of Ethics and *Guide to Professional Conduct*).

Summary of Reasoning Skills

You are encouraged to pay particular attention to the five types of critical reasoning listed with each practice question in the simulated examination section. The following five symbols have been assigned to help you key into areas that may be weaknesses:

 = inductive reasoning

 = deductive reasoning

 = analysis

 = inference

 = evaluation

As you complete the simulated examination items, pay attention to any patterns that emerge. Are you particularly weak in a certain area of reasoning? Often, individuals are stronger in certain areas of reasoning than others. Our skill in reasoning ability comes from not only our knowledge, but also our day-to-day experiences. If you notice that you have a weakness in a certain area of reasoning, do not despair. Being aware of the issue is a good first step. The next section will help you to determine your next course of action.

Introduction

Critical Reasoning Challenge

In order to solve problems and understand the reasoning process, use the following checklist to dissect the sample questions. This training activity helps you mentally address the items in the checklist. Not all items are relevant and a mental "not applicable" ("NA") can be inserted. The answers and explanations to the exam questions on the software are organized in this way. Given the time constraints of the NPTE, it is not practical to use this 14-point checklist for each question on the actual exam. However, the reasoning framework will carry over. If you focus and organize your thoughts, reasoning and success will follow!

NPTE Exam Question Checklist

1. What domain and category does this question represent?
   Domains:
   - Cardiovascular, Pulmonary and Lymphatic Systems
   - Musculoskeletal System
   - Neuromuscular and Nervous System
   - Integumentary System
   - Other Systems (Metabolic/Endocrine/Gastrointestinal/Genitourinary)
   - System Interactions
   - Nonsystem

   Categories:
   - PT Examination
   - Evaluation, Differential Diagnosis and Prognosis
   - Interventions
   - Equipment and Devices
   - Therapeutic Modalities
   - Safety and Protection
   - Professional Responsibilities
   - Research and Evidence-Based Practice
2. What is the diagnosis or condition of the patient/client?
3. What age is the client (if relevant)?
4. What deficit(s) or problem(s) does the client have?
5. How does the deficit or problem affect the client's function?
6. What is the setting for treatment? (e.g., inpatient, outpatient, early intervention, school)
7. What **KEY WORDS** indicate importance or priority? (e.g., **BEST, MOST, NEXT, INITIAL, GREATEST BENEFIT**)
8. What information is needed to answer the question? (e.g., type or stage of condition/disease, examination tools, treatment techniques, knowledge of statistics, lab values, type of equipment or modality)
9. Is any information in the question stem irrelevant or included only as a distracter?
10. Give a rationale for why Choice #1 is correct or why it should be eliminated.
11. Give a rationale for why Choice #2 is correct or why it should be eliminated.
12. Give a rationale for why Choice #3 is correct or why it should be eliminated.
13. Give a rationale for why Choice #4 is correct or why it should be eliminated.
14. What type of critical reasoning subtype is needed to answer this question?
    - Inductive
    - Deductive
    - Analysis
    - Inference
    - Evaluation

Use the checklist to solve the following challenges. Answers appear at the end of this Introduction.

Critical Reasoning Challenge #1

A patient has experienced long-term lumbar pain and is diagnosed with degenerative joint disease (DJD) of the lumbar facet joints. The patient complains of numbness, paresthesias, and weakness of the bilateral lower extremities that increase with extended positions or walking greater than 100 feet. Pain persists for hours after assuming a resting position. The patient reports the ability to ride a stationary bike for 30 minutes without any problems. Physical therapy intervention should include:

Choice 1	Increasing cardiovascular endurance with walking for 30 minutes, twice a day.
Choice 2	Limiting extended spinal positions and improving the dynamic control of the trunk musculature.
Choice 3	Back extension strengthening throughout the entire ROM.
Choice 4	Traction and limitation of weight-bearing positions.

Critical Reasoning Challenge #2

A patient sustained a fracture of the proximal humerus, which has healed well. Upon examination, the therapist notes limitation in active shoulder flexion. The scapula protracts, elevates and upwardly rotates early and elevates excessively when the patient attempts to lift the arm. The **NEXT** thing the therapist should do is:

Choice 1 Passive shoulder flexion and glenohumeral accessory mobility testing.

Choice 2 Manual muscle test of serratus anterior and rhomboids.

Choice 3 Manual resistance exercises for the supraspinatus and infraspinatus.

Choice 4 Large amplitude oscillations performed at the end-range of joint play for the glenohumeral inferior and posterior capsule.

Improving Your Critical Reasoning Skills

Critical reasoning is not learned or improved in a quick lesson or by simply reading basic definitions. It requires practice with items that test these skill areas and provide feedback on your performance. The good news is that you already have this information contained in this study guide! Each practice question in the book has an accompanying rationale for the correct and incorrect choices. Additionally, each question has an explanation about the subskill of critical reasoning and the knowledge or skill required to arrive at a correct conclusion. Paying attention to these areas will help you to build your knowledge and experiences with critical reasoning skills and prepare you for the NPTE and all its challenges.

After you receive the results of your flash drive practice test, refer back to your incorrect responses. This may help you uncover a pattern in the types of questions you are answering incorrectly, as related to a subskill of critical reasoning. Do you notice that you have difficulty with certain types of questions, such as those that encourage evaluative or inferential reasoning? This will help you to identify a potential area for improvement and an area to help base study strategies. Once you have identified a weakness in critical reasoning, take some time to reflect on why this is so. Look again at Table 1.

Other Courses of Action. This study guide was designed to help you to identify potential weak areas and prepare you to succeed on the NPTE. More detailed information about critical reasoning is beyond the scope and focus of this book. However, if you would like additional information about critical reasoning and practice with questions that test critical thinking and reasoning skills, the following resources may help you practice honing these skill areas:

- **Insight Assessment, Inc.** www.insightassessment.com. Offers periodic free mini-tests with rationales for correct and incorrect answers. Also offers resources that discuss the various types of reasoning.
- Nosich, G. M. (2001). *Learning to Think Things Through: A Guide to Critical Thinking in the Curriculum*, 2nd ed. Prentice Hall. A handy guide to help students engage in critical thinking.

Reasoning References

Facione P (2006). *Critical Thinking: What It Is and Why It Counts.* Millbrae, CA: The California Academic Press.

Facione P (1990a). *Critical Thinking: A Statement of Expert Consensus for Purposes of Educational Assessment and Instruction: Research Findings and Recommendations.* Newark, DE: The American Psychological Association. ERIC Document Reproduction Service. No. ED 315423.

Facione P (1990b). *Critical Thinking: A Statement of Expert Consensus for Purposes of Educational Assessment and Instruction* ("Executive Summary: The Delphi Report"). Millbrae, CA: The California Academic Press.

Facione NC & Facione PA (2006). *The Health Sciences Reasoning Test HSRT: Test Manual 2006 Edition.* Millbrae, CA: The California Academic Press.

Retaking the Examination

Remember, most candidates are successful the first time! If you receive bad news about your NPTE results, life goes on, but gets a bit more complicated. You might lose your temporary license if your state or jurisdiction has granted you one. If applicable, your visa to work as a physical therapist in the United States may be revoked. In two states you may retain a temporary license if you reapply to take the NPTE. If you are working as a physical therapist, you could lose your job, or you might continue to work, albeit with a different title, responsibilities or salary until you pass the examination. If you have accepted a future position and fail to get a license, your employer might opt not to save the position for you. Undoubtedly, you will experience various emotions, which could include frustration, anger, depression, low self-esteem and embarrassment.

What can be done? You can go online or download the Performance Feedback Request Form from the FSBPT. This report lists your score by Content area, Body Systems and Section of the exam. The number of items correct and a percentage are given for each subsection. The current cost is $90 plus a $3 credit card fee. No personal checks are accepted. Due to examination security rules, you will not be able to access or revisit your actual examination. You may contact www.fsbpt.org, or call (703) 739-9420.

Our advice is not to dwell on past failures. Carefully evaluate your performance. Think about areas on the previous exam with which you had some difficulty. Were there any gaps in your academic or clinical knowledge? Did you find it difficult to make decisions and answer questions requiring clinical judgment or analysis? Were your English language skills inadequate?

Focus on the next exam. Reinstitute a program of disciplined study. Consider taking a preparation course if you had not previously attended one. We have found that candidates who retake the exam without adjusting their behaviors or correcting deficiencies wind up with the same disappointing results. There is no magic potion that helps you pass the exam. It is your responsibility to demonstrate competency to practice. Take a positive and determined outlook. Approach the next examination with self-confidence.

Useful Web Links

www.fsbpt.org: information on licensure, the NPTE and the role of the FSBPT, as well as addresses and links to state physical therapy boards.

www.fsbpt.net/pt: transfer of exam scores and other related information.

www.2test.com: locations of Prometric Testing Centers.

www.apta.org: information on the profession, policies regarding the role of the physical therapist and resources in selected areas of practice.

www.TherapyEd.com: information on examination preparatory courses as well as materials for physical and occupational therapists and assistants.

Answers to Critical Reasoning Challenge #1 (answers are in bold)

1. What domain and category does this question represent?
   Domains:
   - Cardiovascular, Pulmonary and Lymphatic Systems
   - **Musculoskeletal System**
   - Neuromuscular and Nervous System
   - Integumentary System
   - Other Systems (Metabolic/Endocrine/Gastrointestinal/Genitourinary)
   - System Interactions
   - Nonsystem

   Categories:
   - PT Examination
   - Evaluation, Differential Diagnosis and Prognosis
   - **Interventions**
   - Equipment and Devices
   - Therapeutic Modalities
   - Safety and Protection
   - Professional Responsibilities
   - Research and Evidence-Based Practice
2. What is the diagnosis or condition of the patient/client?
   DJD of lumbar facet joints. Spinal stenosis?
3. What age is the client (if relevant)?
   NA
4. What deficit(s) or problem(s) does the client have?
   Pain, numbness, paresthesias both LEs.
5. How does the deficit or problem affect the client's function?
   Cannot walk >100 feet.
6. What is the setting for treatment? (e.g., inpatient, outpatient, early intervention, school)
   NA
7. What KEY WORDS indicate importance or priority? (e.g., BEST, MOST, NEXT, INITIAL, GREATEST BENEFIT)
   Intervention

8. What information is needed to answer the question? (e.g., type or stage of condition/disease, examination tools, treatment techniques, knowledge of statistics, lab values, type of equipment or modality)
Need to limit trunk extension with spinal stenosis.
9. Is any information in the question stem irrelevant or included only as a distracter?
No.
10. Give a rationale for why Choice #1 is correct or why it should be eliminated.
Intervention does not deal with pain, numbness and paresthesia. Patient cannot walk > 100 feet. How could they walk for 30 minutes bid?
ELIMINATE.
11. Give a rationale for why Choice #2 is correct or why it should be eliminated.
Trunk extension exacerbates symptoms. Dynamic trunk control to limit extension is best intervention for spinal stenosis.
CORRECT.
12. Give a rationale for why Choice #3 is correct or why it should be eliminated.
Back extension exacerbates symptoms.
ELIMINATE.
13. Give a rationale for why Choice #4 is correct or why it should be eliminated.
Limiting weight bearing and traction are of little help in addressing the major problems and alleviating symptoms.
ELIMINATE.
14. What type of critical reasoning subtype is needed to answer this question?
Inductive
Deductive
Analysis
Inference
Evaluation
This type of reasoning requires one to be a "forward thinker" and determine the best course of action for future functioning.

Answers to Critical Reasoning Challenge #2

1. What domain and category does this question represent?
Domains:
Cardiovascular, Pulmonary and Lymphatic Systems
Musculoskeletal System
Neuromuscular and Nervous System
Integumentary System
Other Systems (Metabolic/Endocrine/Gastrointestinal/Genitourinary)
System Interactions
Nonsystem
Categories:
PT Examination
Evaluation, Differential Diagnosis and Prognosis
Interventions
Equipment and Devices
Therapeutic Modalities
Safety and Protection
Professional Responsibilities
Research and Evidence-Based Practice
2. What is the diagnosis or condition of the patient/client?
Proximal fracture of the humerus.
3. What age is the client (if relevant)?
NA
4. What deficit(s) or problem(s) does the client have?
Limitations in active shoulder flexion. Scapula protracts, elevates and upwardly rotates early.
5. How does the deficit or problem affect the client's function?
Possible ADL limitations.
6. What is the setting for treatment? (e.g., inpatient, outpatient, early intervention, school)
NA
7. What KEY WORDS indicate importance or priority? (e.g., BEST, MOST, NEXT, INITIAL, GREATEST BENEFIT)
NEXT
8. What information is needed to answer the question? (e.g., type or stage of condition/disease, examination tools, treatment techniques, knowledge of statistics, lab values, type of equipment or modality)
Reasons for shoulder AROM limitations after humeral fracture. Examination approaches for shoulder AROM limitations. How to perform glenohumeral accessory mobility testing.
9. Is any information in the question stem irrelevant or included only as a distracter?
No.
10. Give a rationale for why Choice #1 is correct or why it should be eliminated.
Therapist should perform passive shoulder flexion and glenohumeral accessory mobility testing to determine the tissue at fault and proceed from this point.
CORRECT.
11. Give a rationale for why Choice #2 is correct or why it should be eliminated.
Weak serratus anterior would result in retraction of the scapula and possible winging. Rhomboids are downward rotators of the scapula, which does not match the patient presentation.
ELIMINATE.
12. Give a rationale for why Choice #3 is correct or why it should be eliminated.
This is a treatment approach for weakness of the rotator cuff. Information provided does not indicate rotator cuff weakness. There is not enough

information to begin treatment. Further evaluation must be done to determine the tissue at fault. ELIMINATE.

13. Give a rationale for why Choice #4 is correct or why it should be eliminated.
This treatment is appropriate for capsular restrictions. There is not enough information to begin treatment. Further evaluation must be done to determine the tissue at fault.
ELIMINATE.

14. What type of critical reasoning subtype is needed to answer this question?
Inductive
Deductive
Analysis
Inference
Evaluation
Based on the diagnosis, the examiner has to determine the next course of action. This requires clinical judgment, an inductive reasoning skill.

1

Musculoskeletal Physical Therapy

ROBERT ROWE

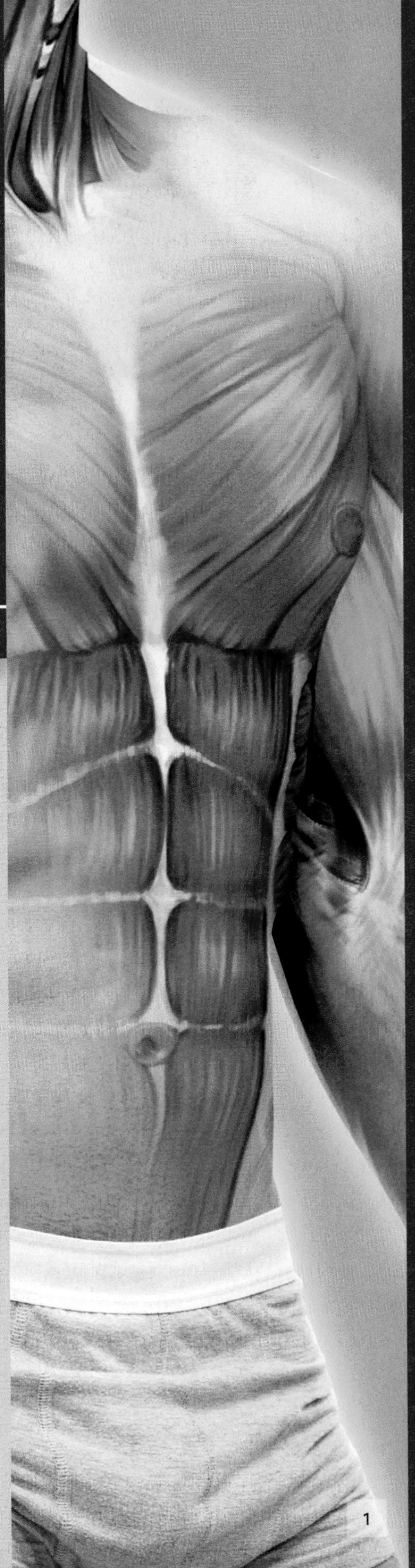

Chapter Outline

Anatomy and Biomechanics of the Musculoskeletal System

General Principles of Biomechanics

1. Levers. Rotations of a rigid surface about an axis. There are three types of levers.
   a. First-class lever occurs when two forces are applied on either side of an axis.
      (1) The effort is the force that attempts to cause movement.
      (2) The resistance is the force that opposes movement.
      (3) Example in human body is the contraction of triceps at elbow joint.
   b. Second-class lever occurs when two forces are applied on one side of an axis.
      (1) Resistance lies between the effort force and the axis of rotation.
      (2) Few examples in human body (toe raises).
   c. Third-class lever occurs when two forces are applied on one side of an axis.
      (1) The effort force lies closer to the axis than the resistance force.
      (2) Most muscles in the human body are third-class levers (elbow flexion).
2. Selected kinematics.
   a. Arthrokinematics is defined as the movement between joint surfaces.
   b. Three motions describe the movement of one joint surface on another.
      (1) Roll consists of one joint surface rolling on another, such as a tire rolling on the road (e.g., movement between the femoral and tibial articular surfaces of knee).
      (2) Glide consists of a pure translatory motion of one surface gliding on another, as when a braked wheel skids (e.g., movement of the joint surface of the proximal phalanx at the head of the metacarpal bone of the hand).
      (3) Spin consists of a rotation of the movable component of the joint (e.g., movement between joint surfaces of radial head with humerus).
      (4) Combinations of all three motions can occur at joints (e.g., between joint surfaces of humerus and scapula of shoulder).
   c. Osteokinematics: movement between two bones.
   d. Convex-concave rule describes relationship between arthrokinematics and osteokinematics.
      (1) When a convex surface is moving on a fixed concave surface, the convex surface moves opposite to the direction of the shaft of the bony lever.
      (2) When a concave surface moves on a fixed convex surface, the concave articulating surface moves in the same direction as the bony lever (see Table 1-1).
      (3) In the spine, the convex rule applies at the atlanto-occipital joint. Below the second vertebra, the concave rule applies.
3. Capsular positions.
   a. Resting or loose-packed position (see Table 1-2).
      (1) Joint position where capsule and other soft tissues are in most relaxed position.
      (2) Minimal joint surface contact.
      (3) May perform joint play and mobilization techniques in this joint position.
   b. Close-packed position (see Table 1-2).
      (1) Joint position where capsule and other soft tissues are maximally tensed.
      (2) Maximal contact between joint surfaces.
      (3) Joint play and mobilization cannot be properly performed in this position.
   c. Selected capsular patterns (see Table 1-3).
   d. End-feels.
      (1) Normal physiological end-feel.
         (a) Soft: occurs with soft tissue approximation.
         (b) Firm: capsular and ligamentous stretching.
         (c) Hard: when bone and/or cartilage meet.
      (2) Pathological end-feel.
         (a) Boggy: edema, joint swelling.
         (b) Firm with decreased elasticity: fibrosis of soft tissues.
         (c) Rubbery: muscle spasm.
         (d) Empty: loose, then very hard; associated with muscle guarding or patient avoiding painful part of range.
         (e) Hypermobility: end-feel at a later time than on opposite side.
   e. Grading of accessory joint movement.
      (1) Accessory joint movement or joint play is graded to assess arthrokinematic motion of the joint and/or when it is impractical or impossible to measure joint motion with a goniometer (see Table 1-4).
      (2) Although interrater reliability is poor, intrarater reliability is acceptable.
      (3) Data gleaned provides clinician with more specific data on source of patient's problem.

Table 1-1

Concave-Convex Rule Application

ARTICULATION	FUNCTION	MOVING COMPONENT OF ARTICULATION	RELATIONSHIP OF CONVEX/CONCAVE RULE
Fingers	Flexion/extension	Distal phalanx	Concave moving on Convex
Metacarpal-phalangeal	Abduction/adduction	Proximal phalanx	Concave moving on Convex
Wrist	Flexion/extension	Capitate, scaphoid, lunate, triquetrum	Convex moving on Concave
		Trapezoid	Concave moving on Convex
Radioulnar			
Distal	Pronation/supination	Radius	Concave moving on Convex
Proximal	Pronation/supination	Radius	Convex moving on Concave
Humeroradial	Flexion/extension	Radius	Concave moving on Convex
Humeroulnar	Flexion/extension	Ulna	Concave moving on Convex
Glenohumeral	All movements	Humerus	Convex moving on Concave
Sternoclavicular	Elevation/depression	Clavicle	Convex moving on Concave
	Protraction/retraction	Clavicle	Concave moving on Convex
Acromioclavicular	All movements	Scapula	Concave moving on Convex
Toes	Flexion/extension	Distal phalanx	Concave moving on Convex
Metatarsal-phalangeal	Abduction/adduction	Proximal phalanx	Concave moving on Convex
Ankle/Foot			
Subtalar	All movements	Navicular, cuneiform	Concave moving on Convex
	Inversion/eversion	Cuboid, calcaneus	Convex moving on Concave
Talocrural	Dorsal/plantar flexion	Talus	Convex moving on Concave
Tibiofibular	All movements	Fibular head	Concave moving on Convex
Knee	All movements	Tibia	Concave moving on Convex
Hip	All movements	Femur	Convex moving on Concave
Temporomandibular	All movements	Mandible	Convex moving on Concave

Adapted from Kaltenborn FM: Manual Mobilization of the Extremity Joints, 4th ed. FM Kaltenborn, 1989.

Table 1-2

Joint Positions

ARTICULATIONS	RESTING POSITION	CLOSE-PACKED POSITION
Vertebral	Midway between flexion and extension	Maximal extension
Temporomandibular	Jaw slightly open (freeway space)	Maximal retrusion (mouth closed with teeth clenched) or maximal anterior position mouth maximally opened
Sternoclavicular	Arm resting by side	Arm maximally elevated
Acromioclavicular	Arm resting by side	Arm abducted 90°
Glenohumeral	55°–70° abduction; 30° horizontal adduction; neutral rotation	Maximum abduction and ER
Elbow		
Humeroulnar	70° flexion and 10° supination	Full extension and supination
Humeroradial	Full extension and supination	90° flexion and 5° supination
Forearm		
Proximal radioulnar	70° flexion and 35° supination	5° supination and full extension
Distal radioulnar	10° supination	5° supination
Radio/ulnocarpal	Neutral with slight ulnar deviation	Full extension with radial deviation
Hand		
Midcarpal	Neutral with slight flexion and ulnar deviation	Full extension
Carpometacarpal (2–5)	Midway between flexion/and extension, mid flexion, and mid extension	Full opposition
Trapeziometacarpal	Midway between flexion/extension and between abduction/adduction	Full opposition
Metacarpophalangeal (MCP)	First MCP joint: slight flexion MCP joints 2–5: slight flexion with ulnar deviation	First MCP joint: full extension MCP joints 2–5: full flexion
Interphalangeal (IP)	Proximal IP joints: 10° flexion Distal IP joints: 30° flexion	Full extension

(*Continued*)

Table 1-2

Joint Positions (Continued)

ARTICULATIONS	RESTING POSITION	CLOSE-PACKED POSITION
Hip	30° flexion, 30° abduction, and slight lateral rotation	✓Ligamentous: full extension, abduction, and internal rotation 9q → lcuk Bony: 90° flexion, slight abduction, and slight ER Full extension and ER
Knee	25° flexion	
Ankle/Foot		Full dorsiflexion
Talocrural	Mid inversion/eversion and 10° plantar flexion	Full inversion
Subtalar	Midway between extremes of range of motion with 10° plantar flexion	Full supination
Midtarsal	Midway between extremes of range of motion with 10° plantar flexion	Full supination
Tarsometatarsal	Midway between supination and pronation	
Toes		Full extension
Metatarsophalangeal	Neutral (extension 10°)	Full extension
Interphalangeal	Slight flexion	

Adapted from Hertling DH, Kessler RM: Management of Common Musculoskeletal Disorders: Physical Therapy Principals and Methods, 3rd ed. Lippincott, 1996.

Table 1-3

Capsular Patterns

ARTICULATIONS	RELATIVE LIMITATIONS OF MOVEMENT
Temporomandibular	Limited mouth opening
Upper cervical spine (occiput–C2)	
Occipitoatlantal joint	Forward flexion limited greater than extension
Atlantoatlantal joint	Limitation with rotation
Lower cervical spine (C3–T2)	Limitation of all motions except flexion (side-bending and rotation equally limited and both greater than extension)
Glenohumeral	Greater limitation of ER, followed by abduction and internal rotation
Sternoclavicular	Full elevation limited; pain at extreme range of motion
Acromioclavicular	Full elevation limited; pain at extreme range of motion
Humeroulnar	Loss of flexion more so than extension
Humeroradial	Loss of flexion more so than extension
Proximal radioulnar	Limitation: pronation = supination
Distal radioulnar	Limitation: pronation = supination
Wrist	Limitation: flexion = extension
Midcarpal	Limitation: equal all directions
Trapeziometacarpal	Limitation: abduction more so than extension
Carpometacarpals II–V	Equally restricted all directions
Upper extremity digits	Limitation: flexion > extension
Thoracic Spine	Limitation of side-bending and rotation > loss of extension > flexion
Lumbar spine	Marked and equal limitation of side-bending and rotation; loss of extension > flexion
Sacroiliac, symphysis pubis, sacrococcygeal	Pain when joints are stressed
Hip	Limited flexion/internal rotation; some limitation of abduction; no or little limitation of adduction and ER
Knee	Flexion grossly limited; slight limitation of extension
Tibiofibular (Proximal & Distal)	Pain when joint is stressed
Talocrural	Loss of plantarflexion greater than dorsiflexion
Talocalcaneal (subtalar)	Increasing limitations of varus; joint fixed in valgus (inversion > eversion)
Midtarsal	Supination > pronation (limited dorsiflexion, plantar flexion, adduction, and medial rotation)
First metatarsophalangeal	Marked limitation of extension; slight limitation of flexion
Metatarsophalangeal (II–V)	Variable; tend toward flexion restrictions
Interphalangeal	Tend toward extension restrictions

Adapted from Hertling DH, Kessler RM: Management of Common Musculoskeletal Disorders: Physical Therapy Principles and Methods, 3rd ed. 1996.

Table 1-4

Manual Grading of Accessory Joint Motion

ASSESSED GRADE OF MOVEMENT	CLASSIFICATION OF JOINT
0	Ankylosed
1	Considerable hypomobility
2	Slight hypomobility
3	Normal
4	Slight hypermobility
5	Considerable hypermobility
6	Unstable

Adapted from Grieve GP: Mobilization of the Spine: A Primary Handbook of Clinical Method, 5th ed. Churchill Livingstone, 1991.

4. Muscle substitutions.
   a. Occur when muscles have become shortened/lengthened, weakened, lost endurance, developed impaired coordination, or paralyzed.
   b. Stronger muscles compensate for loss of motion.
   c. Common muscle substitutions:
      (1) Use of scapular stabilizers to initiate shoulder motion when shoulder abductors are weakened.
      (2) Use of lateral trunk muscles or tensor fascia latae (TFL) when hip abductors are weak.
      (3) Use of passive finger flexion by contraction of wrist extensors when finger flexors are weak (tenodesis).
      (4) Use of long head of biceps, coracobrachialis, and anterior deltoid when pectoralis major is weak.
      (5) Use of lower back extensors, adductor magnus, and quadratus lumborum when hip extensors are weak.
      (6) Use of lower abdominal, lower obliques, hip adductors, and latissimus dorsi when hip flexors are weak.

Functional Anatomy and Biomechanics

Figures 1-1, 1-2, 1-3, and 1-4.

1. Shoulder region.
   a. Osteology (humerus, scapula, and clavicle).
      (1) Humerus (see Figure 1-5).
         (a) Proximal end of humerus is approximately half a spheroid.
         (b) Articular surface is covered by hyaline cartilage.
         (c) Head is retroverted 20°–30°.
         (d) Longitudinal axis of head is 135° from axis of neck.
      (2) Scapula.
         (a) Large, flat triangular bone that sits over second to seventh ribs.
         (b) Costal surface and a dorsal surface.
         (c) Three angles: medial, superior, and lateral.
         (d) Lateral angle bears glenoid fossa, which faces anteriorly, laterally, and superiorly.
            - Pear shape of fossa allows for freer range of motion (ROM) in abduction and flexion.
            - Concave shape receives convex humeral head.
            - Orientation of the glenoid fossa places true abduction at 30° anterior to frontal plane.
      (3) Clavicle.
         (a) Extends laterally and links manubrium to acromion.
         (b) Connects shoulder complex to axial skeleton.
   b. Arthrology (glenohumeral, sternoclavicular, acromioclavicular, and scapulothoracic).
      (1) Glenohumeral joint.
         (a) Convex humeral head articulates with concave glenoid fossa.
         (b) Glenoid fossa very shallow.
      (2) Sternoclavicular joint.
         (a) Convex (superior/inferior) and concave (anterior/posterior) articulates with reciprocal shape of sternum.
         (b) Both articulations covered with fibrocartilage.
      (3) Acromioclavicular joint.
         (a) A plane joint with relatively flat surfaces.
      (4) Scapulothoracic joint.
         (a) A "clinical" articulation.
   c. Muscles (depressors, elevators, protractors, retractors, internal rotators, external rotators, flexors, abductors, adductors, and extensors) (see Table 1-5).
   d. Noncontractile structures (acromioclavicular, trapezoid, conoid, and sternoclavicular ligament, subacromial bursa, shoulder capsule, glenoid labrum and associated nerves and vessels).
      (1) Capsule.
         (a) Attaches medially to glenoid margin, glenoid labrum, coracoid process.
         (b) Attaches laterally to humeral anatomical neck and descends approximately 1 cm on the shaft.
         (c) Supported by tendons of supraspinatus, infraspinatus, teres minor, subscapularis, and long head of triceps below.
         (d) Inferiorly capsule is least supported and most lax.

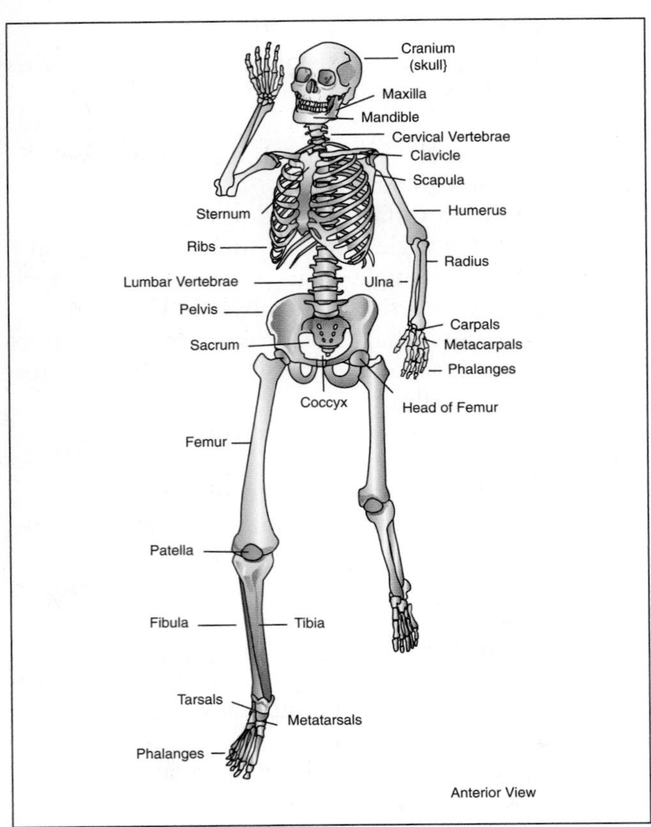

Figure 1-1 **Skeletal system—anterior view.**

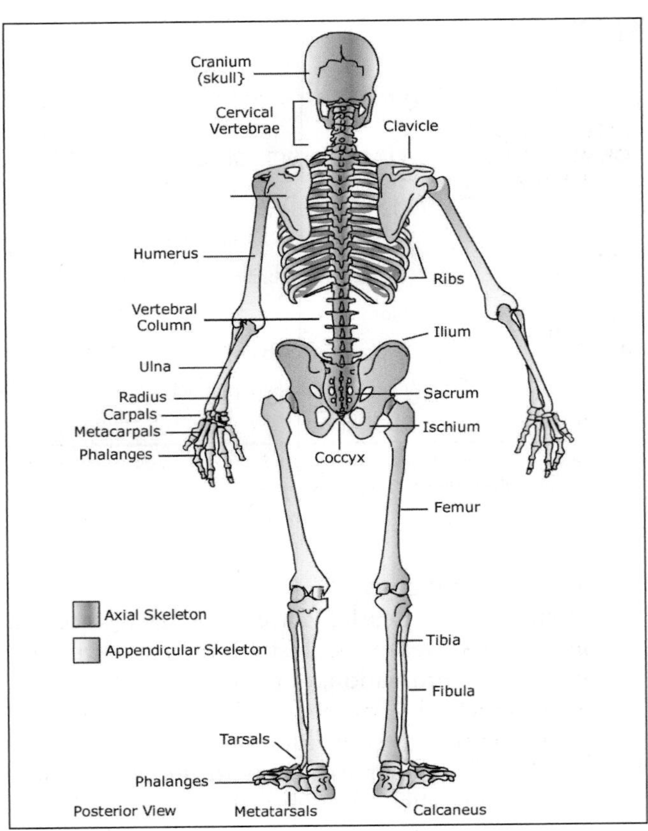

Figure 1-2 **Skeletal system—posterior view.**

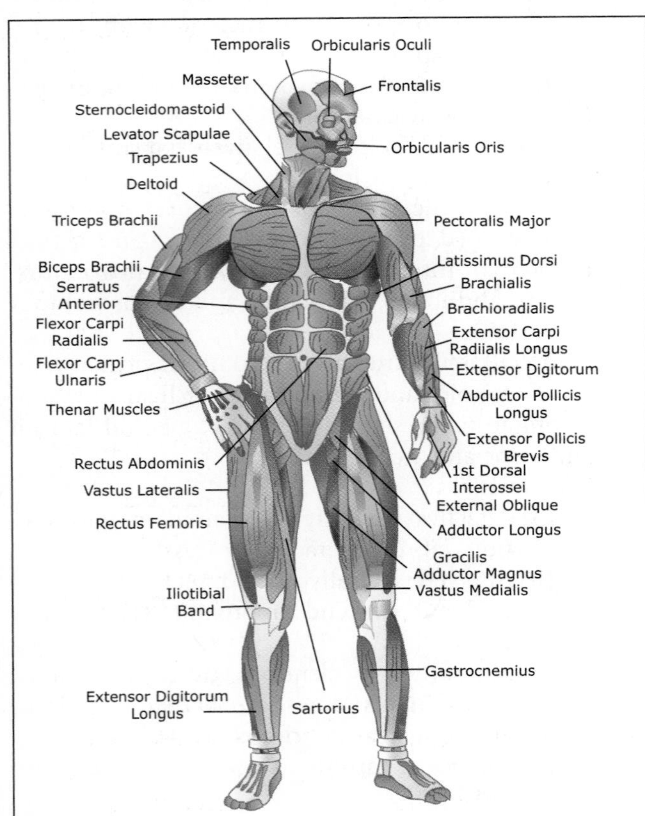

Figure 1-3 **Muscular system—anterior view.**

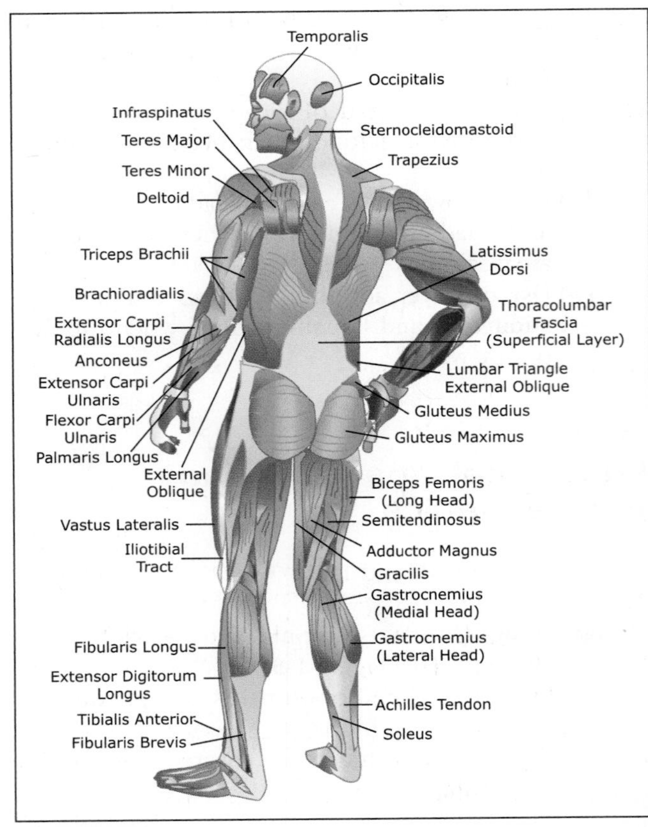

Figure 1-4 **Muscular system—posterior view.**

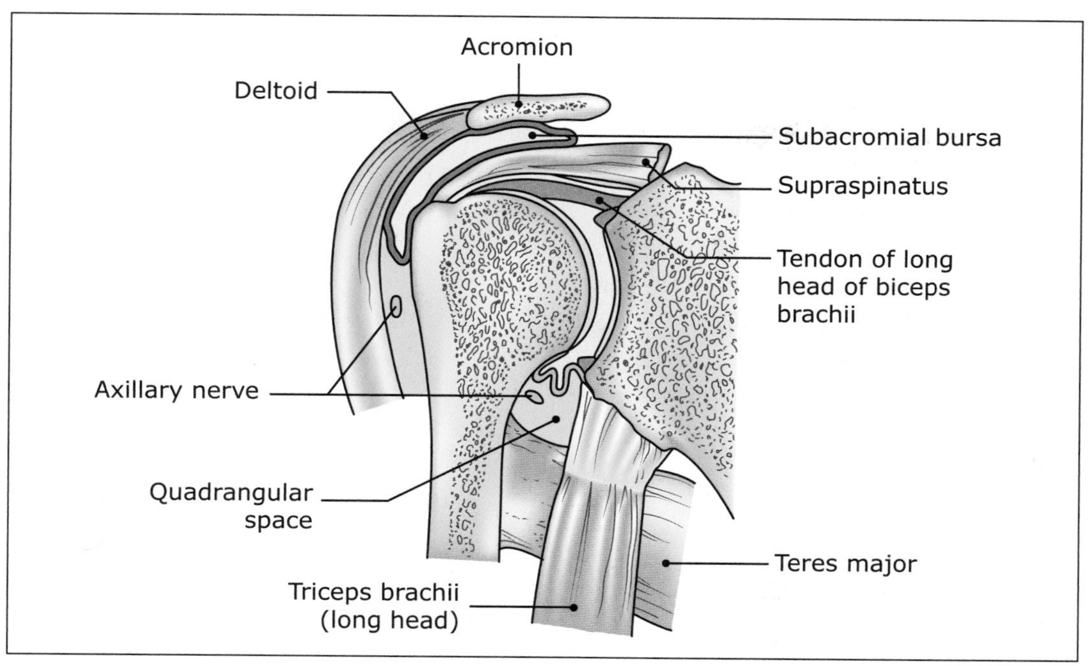

Figure 1-5 **Coronal section of shoulder.**

Table 1-5

Shoulder Girdle and Upper Extremity Muscular and Neurological Screening

ACTION TO BE TESTED	MUSCLES	MYOTOMES	REFLEXES	CORD SEGMENT	NERVES
Neck flexion Neck extension Neck rotation Neck lateral bending	Sternocleidomastoid, trapezius, other deep neck muscles			C1–C4	Cervical spinal accessory
Shoulder shrug, scapular upward rotation	Upper trapezius	C4		C1–C4	Spinal accessory
Shoulder horizontal adduction	Pect. major/minor			C5–C8, T1	Medial/lateral pectoral
Scapular downward rotation	Pectoralis minor			C8–T1	Medial pectoral
Shoulder protraction, scapular upward rotation	Serratus anterior			C5–C7	Long thoracic
Scapular elevation, downward rotation	Levator scapula			C5	Dorsal scapular
Scapular adduction, elevation, downward rotation	Rhomboids			C4–C5	Dorsal scapular
Shoulder abduction	Supraspinatus			C4–C6	Suprascapular
Shoulder lateral rotation	Infraspinatus			C4–C6	Suprascapular
Shoulder medial rotation, adduction	Latissimus dorsi, teres major, and subscapularis			C5–C8	Subscapular and thoracodorsal
Shoulder abduction, flexion, extension	Deltoid	C5		C5–C6	Axillary
Shoulder lateral rotation	Teres minor			C4–C5	Axillary
Elbow flexion, forearm supination	Biceps brachii	C6	C5	C5–C6	Musculocutaneous
Shoulder flexion, adduction	Coracobrachialis			C6–C7	Musculocutaneous

(*Continued*)

Table 1-5

Shoulder Girdle and Upper Extremity Muscular and Neurological Screening (Continued)

ACTION TO BE TESTED	MUSCLES	MYOTOMES	REFLEXES	CORD SEGMENT	NERVES
Elbow flexion	Brachialis			C5–C6	Musculocutaneous
4th and 5th digit DIP flexion	Flexor digitorum (ulnar part)			C7–T1	Ulnar profundus
Wrist ulnar flexion	Flexor carpi ulnaris	C7		C7–T1	Ulnar
Thumb adduction	Adductor pollicis			C8–T1	Ulnar
5th digit abduction	Abductor digiti			C8–T1	Ulnar quinti
5th digit opposition	Opponens digiti			C7–T1	Ulnar quinti
5th digit MCP flexion	Flexor digiti quinti			C7–T1	Ulnar brevis
2nd–5th digit MCP flexion, adduction, abduction	Interossei	T1		C8–T1	Ulnar
Forearm pronation	Pronator teres, pronator quadratus			C6–C7	Median
Wrist radial flexion	Flexor carpi radialis			C6–C7	Median
Wrist flexion	Palmaris longus			C7–T1	Median
2nd–5th digit proximal IP flexion	Flexor digitorum sublimis			C7–T1	Median
Thumb IP flexion	Flexor pollicis longus			C7–T1	Median
2nd–3rd digit distal IP flexion	Flexor digitorum			C7–T1	Median profundus (radial part)
Thumb abduction	Abductor pollicis brevis			C6–T1	Median
Thumb MCP flexion	Flexor pollicis brevis			C6–T1	Median/ulnar
Thumb opposition	Opponens pollicis			C8–T1	Median
2nd–5th digit MCP flexion, IP extension	Lumbricals			C8–T1	Median/ulnar
Elbow flexion	Brachioradialis		C6	C5–C6	Radial
Elbow extension	Triceps brachii, anconeus		C7	C6–C8	Radial
Wrist radial extension	Extensor carpi radialis			C6–C8	Radial
2nd–5th digit MCP, IP extension	Extensor digitorum communis extensor digiti quinti proprius			C6–C8	Radial
Wrist ulnar extension	Extensor carpi ulnaris			C6–C8	Radial
Forearm supination	Supinator			C5–C6	Radial
Thumb MCP abduction	Abductor pollicis longus	C8		C7–C8	Radial
Thumb extension	Extensor pollicis longus/ brevis			C6–C8	Radial
2nd digit extension	Extensor indicis proprius			C6–C8	Radial

Adapted from Chusid JG: Correlative Neuroanatomy and Functional Neurology. Lange Medical Publications, 1970; Kendall FP, McCreary EK, Provance PG: Muscles Testing and Function, 4th ed. Williams & Wilkins, 1993.

(2) Ligaments.

(a) Coracohumeral ligament.

- Base of coracoid process to greater and lesser tubercle of humerus.
- Primary function to reinforce biceps tendon, reinforce superior capsule, and prevent caudal dislocation of humerus. Taut with external rotation (ER).

(b) Coracoacromial ligament.

- Strong triangular ligament runs from coracoid to acromion.
- Not a "true" ligament; connects two points of same bone.

(c) Glenohumeral ligaments.

- Three bands (superior, middle, and inferior) located on anterior glenohumeral joint.
- Reinforce anterior glenohumeral capsule.

(d) Transverse humeral ligament.
- Broad band passing over top of bicipital groove.
- Acts as a retinaculum for long biceps tendon.

(3) Labrum.
(a) Glenoid labrum is a fibrocartilaginous ring that deepens glenoid fossa.
(b) Attached to capsule superiorly and inferiorly as well as to the long head of the biceps tendon superiorly.
(c) Internal surface covered with articular cartilage, which is thicker peripherally and thinner centrally.
(d) Aids in lubrication, as in meniscus of knee, and serves to protect the bone.

(4) Bursae.
(a) Multiple bursae found within this region.
(b) Primary bursa involved with pathology is subacromial bursa between deltoid and capsule. Also runs under acromion and coracoacromial ligament and between the supraspinatus tendon.

e. Shoulder biomechanics.
(1) Glenohumeral joint arthrokinematics/osteokinematics.
(a) Occurs in opposite directions. With elevation of humerus, head of humerus moves in an inferior direction because of convex moving on concave.
(b) Rolling-gliding occurs during elevation of the humerus, so that the instantaneous center of rotation varies considerably during the complete range.
(c) At approximately 75° of elevation, ER (conjunct rotation) occurs, preventing compression of greater tubercle against the acromion.

(2) Scapulothoracic and glenohumeral rhythm (scapulohumeral rhythm) is the ratio of movement of the glenohumeral with the scapulothoracic joint.
(a) With 180° of abduction, there is a 2:1 ratio of movement between the two joints.
(b) First 30°–60° of elevation occurs mainly in the glenohumeral joint.
(c) 120° of movement occurs at glenohumeral joint.
(d) 60° of movement occurs at scapulothoracic joint.

(3) Requirements of full elevation.
(a) Scapular stabilization.
(b) Inferior glide of humerus.
(c) ER of humerus.
(d) Rotation of the clavicle at sternoclavicular joint.
(e) Scapular abduction and lateral rotation of acromioclavicular joint.
(f) Straightening of thoracic kyphosis.

2. Elbow region.

a. Osteology and arthrology (ulnohumeral, radiohumeral, superior, and inferior radioulnar).
(1) Humeroulnar joint (see Figure 1-6).
(a) Distal end humerus (trochlea) articulates with proximal end of ulna.
(b) Trochlea and trochlear notch face anteriorly at a 45° angle, allowing space between ulna and humerus during flexion.

(2) Humeroradial joint.
(a) Distal end humerus (capitulum) articulates with concave oval facet of proximal radius.

(3) Proximal radioulnar joint.
(a) Radial head is ovoid and cone-shaped.
(b) Medial radius articulates with radial notch (of ulna).

(4) Distal radioulnar joint.
(a) Convex ulna articulates with concave radius (opposite to proximal articulation of these two bones).

b. Muscles (flexors, extensors, supinators, and pronators) (see Table 1-5).

c. Noncontractile structures (medial collateral ligament, radial collateral ligament, annular ligament, elbow capsule, associated bursae, nerves, and vessels).
(1) Capsule.
(a) Encloses entire elbow joint complex. It is thin, both anteriorly and posteriorly. Continuous medially with ulnar collateral ligament and laterally with radial collateral ligament.

(2) Ligaments.
(a) Ulnar collateral.
- Ligament is triangular shaped consisting of three parts.
- Reinforces humeroulnar joint medially.

(b) Radial collateral.
- Ligament is fan shaped and runs from lateral epicondyle of humerus to annular ligament.
- Reinforces humeroradial joint laterally.

(c) Annular.
- An osteofibrous ring attached to medial ulna and encircles radial head.
- Cone shaped, inner surface is lined with fibrocartilage.
- Protects radial head, especially in semiflexion, where it is very unstable. Taut in extremes of pronation and supination.

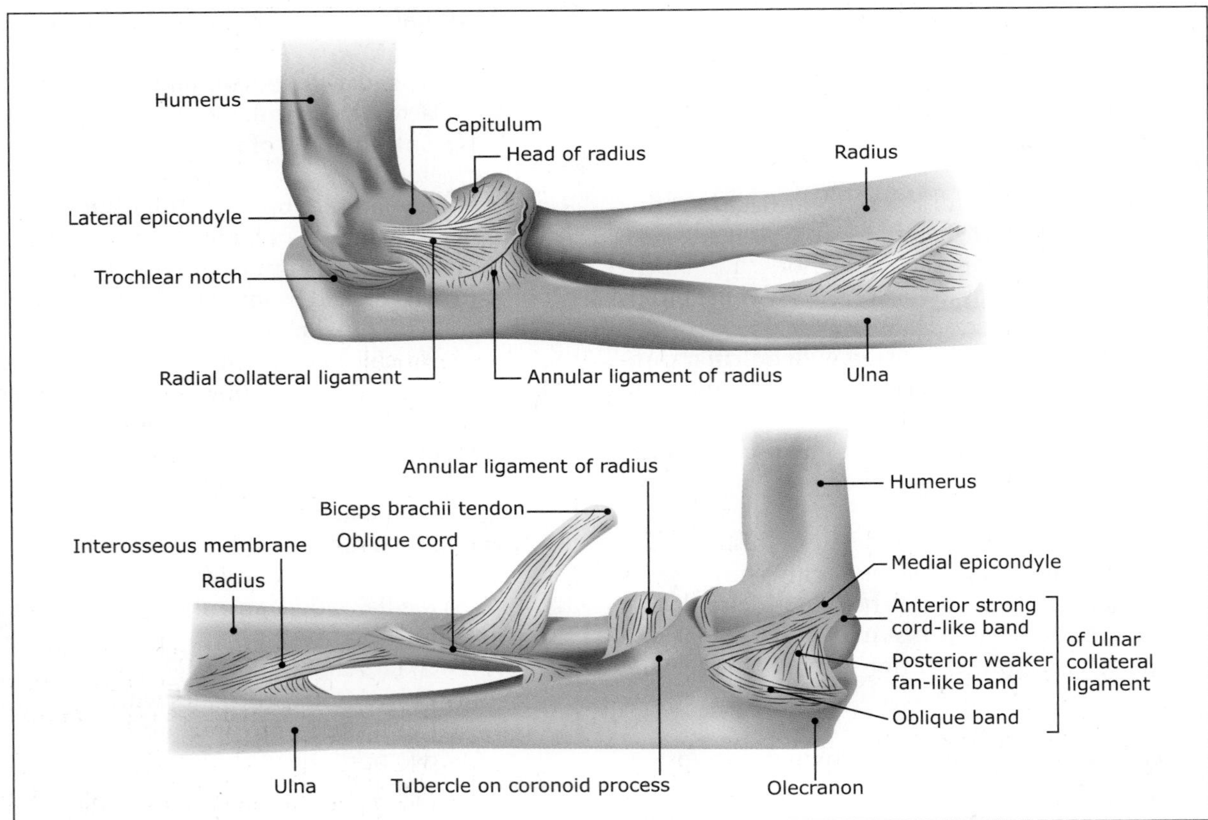

Figure 1-6 **Elbow: lateral view.**

(d) Quadrate.
- Extends from radial notch (ulna) to the neck of radius.
- Reinforces inferior joint capsule, maintains radial head in opposition to ulna, limits amount of spin in supination and pronation.

(e) Distal radioulnar.
- Anterior radioulnar ligament: primarily strengthens capsule.
- Posterior radioulnar ligament: primarily strengthens capsule.

(3) Bursa.

(a) Olecranon bursa located on posterior aspect of elbow over olecranon process.

(4) Blood supply.

(a) Elbow joint receives blood supply from brachial artery, anterior ulnar recurrent artery, posterior ulnar recurrent artery, radial recurrent artery, and middle collateral branch of the deep brachial artery.

(5) Elbow joint stability.

(a) Elbow joint complex possesses significant inherent stability.

(b) Main contributor to bony stability is articulation between the trochlea (humerus) and trochlear fossa (ulna).

(c) Medial collateral ligament provides strong resistance to valgus forces.

(d) Resistance of lateral collateral ligament to varus forces is minimal, due to its attachment to another soft tissue structure (annular ligament).

(e) Functionally, this relationship is beneficial, since functional activities place tensile forces medially and compressive forces laterally. Therefore, the lateral ligament does not have to be as strong as the medial ligament.

d. Elbow biomechanics.

(1) Conjunct rotations.

(a) Ulna pronates slightly with extension. Ulna supinates slightly with flexion.

(b) Proximal ulna glides medially during extension and laterally during flexion.

(c) Flexion/extension of elbow is accompanied by a screw-home mechanism with conjunct rotation of ulna. Ulna externally rotates (or supinates) during elbow flexion and internally rotates (or pronates) during elbow extension.

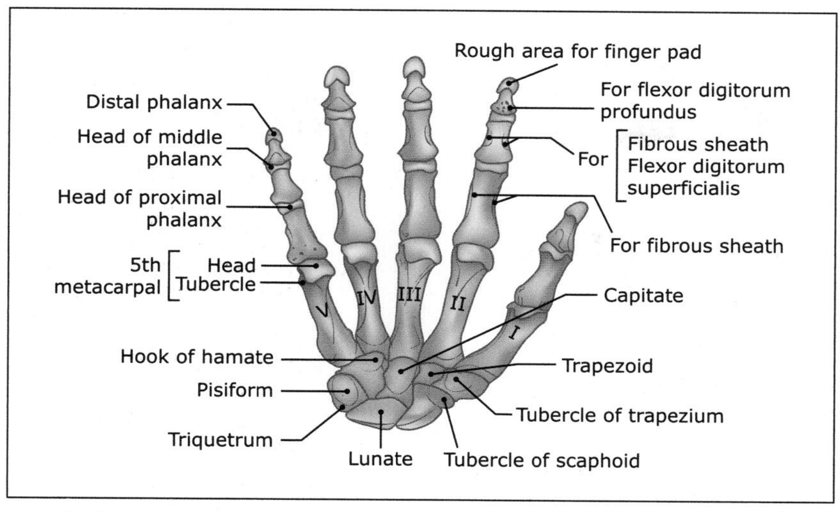

Figure 1-7 **Bones of the hand.**

3. Wrist and hand region.
   a. Osteology (radius, ulna, carpals, metacarpals, and phalanges) (see Figure 1-7).
      (1) Radius is biconcave relative to carpals.
      (2) Ulna is convex at its distal end relative to the triquetrum.
      (3) Proximal aspect of proximal row is biconvex. Distal aspect of proximal row is concave at lunate/capitate and triquetrum/hamate articulations. Scaphoid is convex anterior/posterior and concave medial/lateral relative to trapezium/trapezoid. Capitate is convex and articulates with concavities of scaphoid, hamate, and trapezoid.
      (4) Metacarpal heads are biconvex, and bases are generally flat relative to distal row of carpals.
      (5) Phalanges' proximal ends are mostly biconcave, with a ridge running down the center, dividing it into two surfaces. Distal end is pulley-shaped, and mostly biconvex, with a groove running through the center.
   b. Arthrology (radiocarpal, midcarpal, carpometacarpal, metacarpophalangeal [MCP], and interphalangeal [IP]).
      (1) Dorsal radiocarpal: limits flexion, pronation, and possibly radial deviation.
      (2) Radiate: stabilizes hand for any impact.
      (3) Radiocarpal joint.
         (a) Convex scaphoid and lunate articulate with concave radius.
      (4) Midcarpal joint.
         (a) Articulation between four proximal and four distal carpal bones is known as midcarpal joint.
         (b) Functional rather than anatomical joint.
         (c) Can be divided into middle pillar (lunate and triquetrum with capitate and hamate) and lateral pillar (scaphoid with trapezoid and trapezium).
      (5) Carpometacarpal (CMC) joint.
         (a) First CMC (thumb) is a saddle articulation with trapezium being convex in medial/lateral direction and concave in anterior/posterior direction.
         (b) First metacarpal is opposite in shape to trapezium.
         (c) The second through fifth CMC joints are essentially flat between bases of metacarpals and distal row of carpals.
      (6) Metacarpalphalangeal (MCP) joints consist of convex metacarpals with concave proximal phalanges.
      (7) Proximal interphalangeal (PIP) joints consist of convex distal aspects proximal phalanges with concave proximal aspect of middle phalanges. Same orientation exists at distal interphalangeal (DIP) joints.
   c. Muscles (wrist flexors, wrist extensors, radial deviators, ulnar deviators, extrinsic finger flexors, extrinsic finger extensors, and intrinsic finger muscles) (see Table 1-5).
   d. Noncontractile structures (volar carpal, radiocarpal, collateral, and palmar ligaments; extensor hood; associated capsules; volar plate; nerves; and vessels).
      (1) Ligaments.
         (a) Fingers (see Figure 1-8).
            - Collaterals: run separately from lateral condyle to distal phalanx and lateral volar plate at each MP, PIP, and DIP joint. All fibers tighten with flexion and volar fibers tighten with extension.

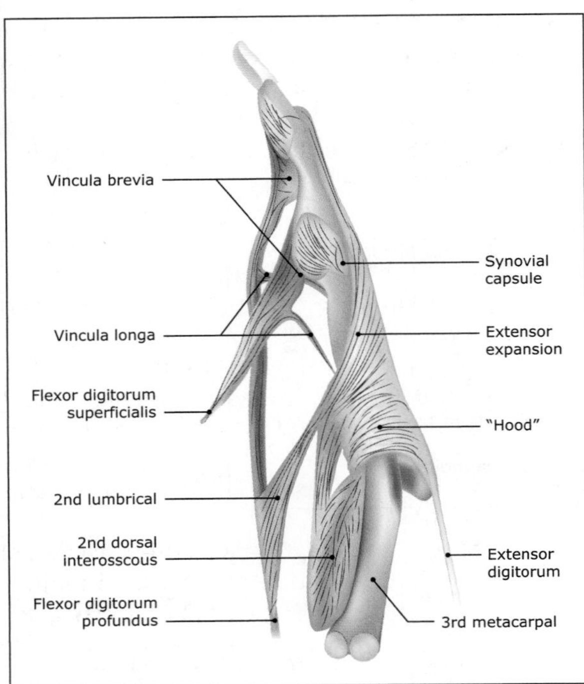

Figure 1-8 **Dissection of the third digit.**

- Accessory: run from condylar head to volar plate.
- Transverse: present at MCP joints. Provide stability linking MCP joints and providing reinforcement to anterior capsule.

(b) Wrist.
- Radial collateral: limits ulnar deviation.
- Ulnar collateral: limits radial deviation.
- Palmar ulnocarpal: limits extension and supination.
- Palmar radiocarpal: limits extension and supination through knuckles.

(2) Extensor hood.
(a) Fibrous mechanism on the dorsum of each finger that is a fibrous expansion of the extensor digitorum tendon.
(b) Its purpose is to assist with extension of the PIP and DIP joints.

(3) Capsule.
(a) Fingers.
- MCP, PIP, and DIP joints all have fibrous capsules that are strong but lax and supported by ligaments.

(b) Wrist.
- Radiocarpal joint shares fibrous capsule (which is thicker palmarly and dorsally) with midcarpal joint, but usually has its own synovial membrane.

(4) Volar plate.
(a) Present on palmar aspect of the MCP, PIP, and DIP joints. Thickening of capsule. Functions to increase articular surface during extension and protect joint volarly. Volar plate more mobile at MCP than at IPs.

(5) Nerves.
(a) Ulnar innervates hypothenar region (palmarly and dorsally), fifth digit, and medial half of fourth digit.
(b) Median nerve innervates remainder of palmar surface not innervated by ulnar nerve and dorsal portions of second, third, and lateral half of fourth digit from DIP joint to tip of finger.
(c) Radial nerve innervates remainder of dorsum of hand not innervated by ulnar or median nerves.

(6) Blood supply from ulna and radial arteries. Merge to form palmar arch and then send digital branches that run up medial and lateral aspects of each digit.

e. Hand and wrist biomechanics.
(1) Hand.
(a) PIPs and DIPs.
- During flexion digits rotate radially to enhance grasp and opposition.

(b) MCPs.
- During flexion digits rotate radially to enhance grasp and opposition.

(c) First CMC.
- Due to position of trapezium (anteriorly and medially rotated relative to other carpals) plane of flexion/extension is perpendicular to other digits.
- During flexion/extension it is concave moving on convex.
- During abduction/adduction, it is convex moving on concave.
- During flexion and abduction, the first metacarpal rotates ulnarly.
- During extension and adduction, the first metacarpal rotates radially.

(2) Wrist.
(a) Flexion. Proximal aspect of scaphoid/lunate glide dorsally relative to radius.
(b) Extension. Proximal aspect of scaphoid/lunate glide ventrally relative to radius.
(c) Radial deviation. Proximal row glides ulnarly. Proximal surface of scaphoid rotates palmarly.
(d) Ulnar deviation. Proximal row glides radially as a unit.

4. Hip region.
a. Osteology (femur and acetabulum of pelvis) (see Figure 1-9).
(1) Femur.
(a) Head is two-thirds of a sphere with a depression at its center called the fovea capitis femoris.
(b) Head is oriented superiorly, anteriorly, and medially.

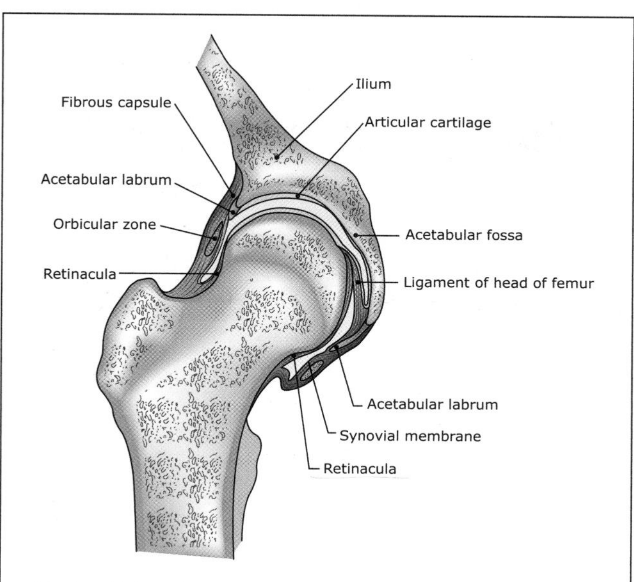

Figure 1-9 Hip joint osteology: anterior view.

(c) Articular cartilage covers entire head, except for fovea capitis.
(d) Angle of inclination normally 115°–125°.
- Coxa valga is angle > 125°.
- Coxa vara is angle < 115°.

(e) Femoral neck angles anteriorly 10°–15° from frontal plane to form anterior antetorsion angle.
- Anteversion: considered excessive if anterior antetorsion angle > 25°–30°.
- Retroversion: considered excessive if anterior antetorsion angle < 10°.

(2) Acetabulum.
(a) Acetabulum faces laterally, inferiorly, and anteriorly.
(b) Made of union between ischium, ilium, and pubis bones.
(c) Acetabular fossa: center of acetabulum, which is nonarticulating and filled with fat pad for shock absorption.
(d) Acetabulum is not completely covered with cartilage. Lined with a horseshoe-shaped articular cartilage with interruption inferiorly forming acetabular notch.

b. Arthrology (coxofemoral).
(1) Synovial joint.
(2) Convex femoral head articulates with concave acetabulum.
(3) Very stable joint due to bony anatomy as well as strength of ligaments and capsule.

c. Muscles (flexors, extensors, adductors, abductors, internal rotators [IRs], and external rotators [ERs]) (see Table 1-6).

d. Noncontractile structures (capsule, labrum, bursae, iliofemoral ligament, ischiofemoral ligament, pubofemoral ligament, and associated nerves and vessels) (see Figure 1-10).
(1) Capsule is strong and dense, and encloses the entire joint.
(2) Labrum.
(a) Triangular shaped, made up of a fibrocartilaginous ring, thickest superiorly.
(b) Attaches to bony rim of acetabulum, bridging acetabular notch.
(c) Serves to deepen acetabulum.
(d) Inner surface is lined with articular cartilage, and outer surface connects to joint capsule.

(3) Ligaments.
(a) Iliofemoral ligament ("Y" or ligament of Bigelow).
- Two bands, both starting from anterior inferior iliac spine (AIIS). Medial running to distal intertrochanteric line. Lateral running to proximal aspect of intertrochanteric line.
- Very strong.
- Both bands taut with extension and ER. Superior band taut with adduction. Inferior band taut with abduction.

(b) Pubofemoral ligament.
- Runs from iliopectineal eminence, superior rami of pubis, obturator crest, and obturator membrane, laterally blending with capsule; inserts into same point as medial iliofemoral ligament.
- Taut with extension, ER, and abduction.

(c) Ischiofemoral ligament.
- Runs from ischium and posterior acetabulum, superiorly and laterally, blending with zona articularis, and attaching to greater trochanter.
- Taut with medial rotation, abduction, and extension.

(d) Zona orbicularis.
- Runs in a circular pattern around femoral neck.
- Has no bony attachments, but helps to hold head of femur in acetabulum.

(e) Inguinal ligament.
- 12–14 cm long, running from anterior superior iliac spine (ASIS) medially and inferiorly, attaching to pubic tubercle.
- Forms tunnel for muscles, arteries, veins, and nerves.

(4) Bursae.
(a) Subtendinous iliac, located between hip and os pubis.
(b) Iliopectineal between tendons of psoas major, iliacus, and capsule. Lies close to femoral nerve.

Table 1-6

Pelvic Girdle and Lower Extremity Muscular and Neurological Screening

ACTION TO BE TESTED	MUSCLES	MYOTOMES	REFLEXES	CORD SEGMENT	NERVES
Hip flexion	Iliopsoas	L2	L4	L1–L3	Femoral
Hip flexion, abduction, lateral rotation	Sartorius	L2		L2–L3	Femoral
Knee extension	Quadriceps femoris	L3		L2–L4	Femoral
Hip adduction	Pectineus, adductor longus			L2–L3	Obturator
Hip adduction	Adductor brevis			L2–L4	Obturator
Hip adduction	Gracilis			L2–L4	Obturator
Hip abduction, flexion, medial rotation	Gluteus medius, minimus	L5		L4–S1	Superior gluteal
Hip flexion, abduction, medial rotation	Tensor fascia lata			L4–L5	Superior gluteal
Hip lateral rotation	Piriformis			L5–S1	Sacral plexus
Hip extension, lateral rotation	Gluteus maximus			L4–S2	Inferior gluteal
Hip lateral rotation	Obturator internus			L5–S1	Sacral plexus
Hip lateral rotation	Gemelli, quadratus femoris			L4–S1	Sacral plexus
Hip extension, knee flexion, leg lateral rotation	Biceps femoris			L5–S2	Sciatic
Hip extension, knee flexion	Semitendinosus		L5	L5–S2	Sciatic
Leg medial rotation	Semimembranosus			L5–S2	Sciatic
Ankle dorsiflexion	Tibialis anterior	L4		L4–L5	Deep fibular
2nd–5th digit MTP extension	Extensor digitorum longus			L4–S1	Deep fibular
Great toe MTP extension	Extensor hallucis longus	L5		L4–S1	Deep fibular
Foot eversion	Fibularis longus/brevis	S1		L5–S1	Superior fibular
Leg medial rotation	Popliteus			L4–S1	Tibial
Foot inversion	Tibialis posterior	S1	S1	L5–S2	Tibial
Ankle plantar flexion	Gastrocnemius/soleus		S1	L5–S2	Tibial
2nd–5th digit DIP flexion	Flexor digitorum longus			L5–S2	Tibial
Great toe IP flexion	Flexor hallucis longus			L5–S2	Tibial
2nd–5th digit PIP flexion	Flexor digitorum brevis			L5–S1	Medial plantar
Great toe MTP flexion	Flexor hallucis brevis			L5–S2	Medial plantar
Toe adduction/abduction	Dorsal/plantar interossei			S1–S2	Lateral plantar
Pelvic floor control	Perineals and sphincters			S2–S4	Pudendal

Adapted from Chusid JG: Correlative Neuroanatomy and Functional Neurology, Lange Medical Publications, 1970; Kendall FP, McCreary EK, Provance PG: Muscles Testing and Function, 4th ed. Williams & Wilkins, 1993.

(c) Ischiofemoral between ischial tuberosity and gluteus maximus. May cause pain in sciatic distribution.

(d) Deep trochanteric between gluteus maximus and posterior lateral greater trochanter. May cause pain with hip flexion and internal rotation due to compression of gluteus maximus.

(e) Superficial trochanteric located over greater trochanter.

(5) Innervation of hip joint comes from femoral, obturator, sciatic, and superior gluteal nerves.

(6) Blood supply.

(a) Medial and lateral femoral circumflex supplies proximal femur.

(b) Femoral head is supplied by a small branch off obturator artery.

(c) Acetabulum is supplied by branches from superior and inferior gluteal arteries.

(7) Hip biomechanics.

(a) Coxofemoral joint arthrokinematics/osteokinematics occur in opposite directions due to relationship of convex femoral head moving within concave acetabulum.

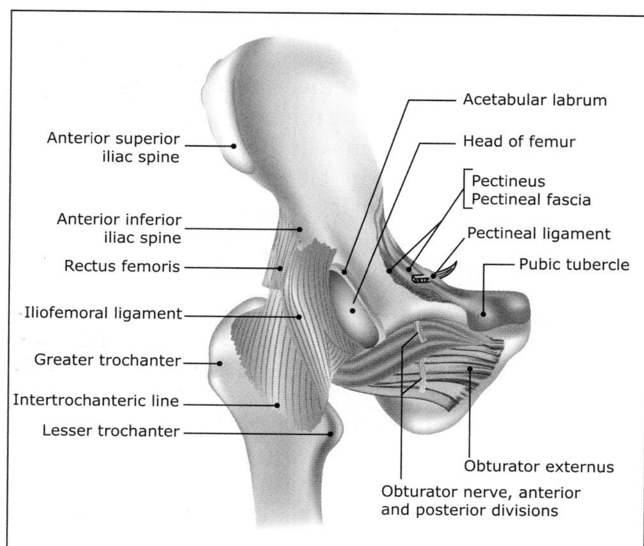

Figure 1-10 **Hip joint: ligament and muscular attachments.**

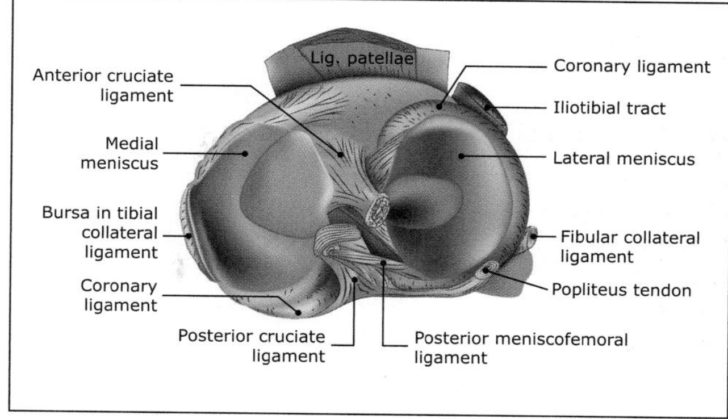

Figure 1-11 **Knee: coronal view.**

5. Knee region.
   a. Osteology (femur, tibia, fibula, and patella) (see Figure 1-11).
      (1) Femur.
         (a) Femoral condyles are convex in anterior/posterior and medial/lateral planes. Both femoral condyles are spiral, but lateral one has a longer surface area and medial one descends further inferiorly.
      (2) Tibia.
         (a) Medial tibial condyle is biconcave, has a larger surface area and is more stable, and therefore less mobile.
         (b) Lateral tibial condyle is convex anterior/posterior and concave medial/lateral. Smaller surface area, more circular, and less stable, therefore more mobile.
         (c) Both tibial surfaces are raised where they border intercondylar area.
      (3) Patella.
         (a) A vertical ridge divides patella into a larger and smaller medial part. Patella can further be divided by two faint horizontal ridges that divide it into its facets.
   b. Arthrology (tibiofemoral, patellofemoral, and proximal tibiofibular).
      (1) Proximal tibiofibular joint.
         (a) Oval tibial facet is flat or slightly convex. Fibular head has an oval, slightly concave to flat surface.
      (2) Tibiofemoral joint.
         (a) Synovial hinge joint with two degrees of freedom. Minimal bony stability thus relies on capsule, ligaments, and muscles.
      (3) Patellofemoral joint.
         (a) Patella articular surface is adapted to patellar surface of femur. An oblique groove running inferiorly and laterally is the guiding mechanism on femur for patellar tracking. Patellar surface of femur is concave transversely and convex sagittally, creating its saddle (sellar) shape.
   c. Muscles (flexors, tibial rotators, and extensors) (see Table 1-6).
   d. Noncontractile structures (medial collateral ligament, lateral collateral ligament, anterior cruciate ligament, posterior cruciate ligament, menisci, capsule, bursae and associated nerves and vessels).
      (1) Capsule.
         (a) Tibiofemoral capsule is a fibrous sleeve attached to distal femur and proximal tibia. Inner wall is covered by a synovium. Shaped as a cylinder with a posterior invagination, which posteriorly divides cavity into medial and lateral halves. Anterior surface has a window cut out for patella.
         (b) Proximal tibiofibular joint has a fibrous capsule, which is continuous with knee joint capsule 10% of time.
      (2) Ligaments (see Figure 1-12).
         (a) Tibiofemoral and patellofemoral joints (knee joint proper).
            - Medial collateral ligament (MCL): runs from medial aspect of medial femoral condyle to upper end of tibia. Posterior fibers blend with capsule. Runs oblique anteriorly and inferiorly. Taut in extension and slackened in flexion. Prevents ER and provides stability against valgus forces. Runs in same direction as anterior cruciate ligament.
            - Lateral collateral ligament (LCL): runs from lateral femoral condyle to head of fibula. Free of any capsular attachment.

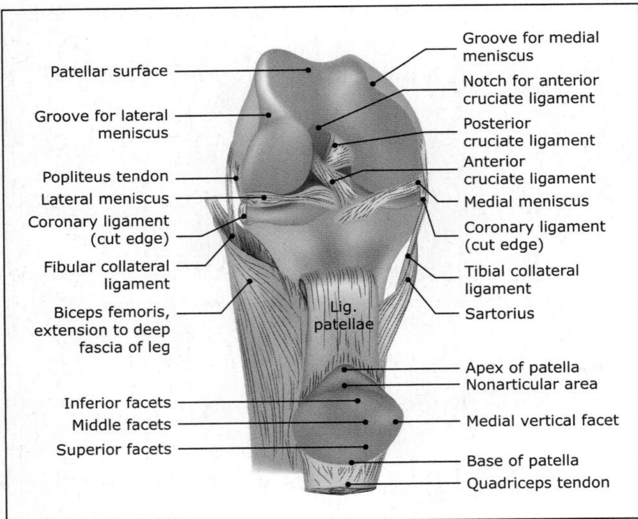

Figure 1-12 **Knee: anterior view, cutaway.**

Runs oblique inferiorly and posteriorly in same direction as posterior cruciate ligament. Taut in extension and slackened in flexion. Prevents ER and provides stability against varus forces.

- Anterior cruciate ligament (ACL): attaches to anterior intercondylar fossa of tibia and to femur at medial aspect of lateral condyle. Runs oblique superiorly and laterally. Extracapsular, but more correctly a thickening of the capsule. Checks forward gliding of tibia on femur and limits internal rotation of tibia during flexion as it twists around posterior cruciate ligament.
- Posterior cruciate ligament (PCL): attaches to posterior intercondylar fossa of tibia and on lateral surface of femoral medial condyle. Runs oblique medially and anteriorly-superiorly. Checks posterior displacement of tibia on femur.
- Meniscofemoral ligament runs with PCL: attaches below posterior horn of lateral meniscus. Has common insertion into lateral aspect of medial condyle. Occasionally a similar ligament exists medially.
- Oblique popliteal ligament: inserts into expansion from tendon of semimembranosus. It partially blends with capsule. Forms floor of popliteal fossa and is in contact with popliteal anterior artery. Strengthens posteromedial capsule.
- Arcuate popliteal ligament: Y-shaped and commonly described as having two bands (medial and lateral). Stem attaches to fibular head. Medial band attaches to posterior border of intercondylar area of tibia. Lateral band extends to lateral epicondyle of femur. Strengthens posterolateral capsule.
- Transverse ligament: connects lateral and medial meniscus anteriorly.
- Meniscopatellar ligament: runs from inferolateral edges of patella to lateral borders of each meniscus. Pulls menisci forward with extension.
- Alar fold: runs from lateral borders of patella to medial and lateral aspects of femoral condyles. Keeps patella in contact with femur.

(b) Infrapatellar fold: formed by attachments of patella fat pad and tendons via a fibroadipose band lying in intercondylar notch. Acts as stop gap as it is compressed by patella tendon in full flexion.

(c) Proximal tibiofibular joint ligaments.
- Anterior tibiofibular ligament: located on anterior aspect of joint. Reinforces capsule anteriorly.
- Posterior tibiofibular ligament: located on posterior aspect of joint. Reinforces capsule posteriorly.

(3) Menisci.

(a) Medial meniscus.
- Medial meniscus is large, C-shaped, and fairly stable. Laterally, it is firmly attached to MCL and fibrous capsule. Other structures that attach to the medial meniscus are semimembranosus muscle and medial meniscopatellar ligament.

(b) Lateral meniscus.
- Smaller than medial meniscus and more circular. Structures that attach to lateral meniscus include popliteus muscle, lateral meniscopatellar ligament, and meniscofemoral ligament. Lateral meniscus is separated from LCL and lateral capsule by popliteus muscle tendon.

(c) Function of menisci.
- Deepens fossa of tibia.
- Increases congruency of tibia and femur.
- Provides stability to tibiofemoral joint.
- Provides shock absorption and lubrication to knee.
- Reduces friction during movement.
- Improves weight distribution.

(d) Movement of menisci.
- Menisci follow tibia with flexion/extension and femoral condyles with internal/ER.
- Medial meniscus moves a total of 6 mm while lateral moves 12 mm. With isolated tibial rotation, the menisci move opposite; e.g., with tibial IR, the medial

meniscus moves anteriorly and the lateral meniscus moves posteriorly.

- Meniscal motion is also influenced by soft tissue structures. Medial meniscus is pulled posteriorly (flexion) by semimembranosus muscle and ACL. Pulled anteriorly (extension) by medial meniscopatellar ligament. Held firm by attachment to MCL and fibrous capsule.
- Lateral meniscus pulled posteriorly (flexion) by popliteus muscle and anteriorly (extension) by lateral meniscopatellar ligament and meniscofemoral ligament.

(4) Bursae.
(a) Prepatellar, between skin and anterior distal patella.
(b) Superficial infrapatellar, anterior to ligamentum patella.
(c) Deep infrapatellar, between posterior ligamentum patella and anterior tibial tuberosity.
(d) Suprapatellar, between patella and tibia femoral joint.
(e) Popliteal, posterior knee often connected to synovial cavity.
(f) Semimembranosus, between muscle and femoral condyle.
(g) Gastrocnemius, one for each head. Medial bursa usually communicates with semimembranosus bursa.
(h) Pes anserine bursa, between pes anserine and MCL.

(5) Blood supply comes from descending branch from lateral circumflex femoral branch of the deep femoral artery. Genicular branches of popliteal artery and recurrent branches of anterior tibial artery.

(6) Articular innervation is provided by obturator, femoral, tibial, and common fibular nerves.

e. Biomechanics knee joint proper.

(1) Arthrokinematics/osteokinematics.
(a) Movements of femoral condyles during flexion and extension.

- Condyles roll and glide simultaneously (only way that posterior dislocation of femoral condyle can be avoided). Initially, movement is pure rolling and ends in pure gliding. For medial condyle, pure rolling occurs during first 10°–15° of flexion. For lateral condyle, 20° of flexion.
- During flexion, femoral condyles roll posteriorly; ACL becomes taut, causing condyles to glide anteriorly.
- During extension, femoral condyles roll anteriorly; PCL becomes taut, causing condyles to glide posteriorly.

(b) During walking, normal range of knee flexion is approximately 15°. We are essentially using pure rolling of femur on tibia.

(2) Conjunct rotations.
(a) During flexion at 10°–15°, ACL tightens, causing femur to glide anteriorly, then 5° further, rolling occurs on lateral condyle, causing a conjunct medial rotation of tibia.
(b) During extension, PCL causes femur to glide posteriorly, while condyles roll anteriorly 10°–15°. Then a further 5° of rolling occurs anteriorly on lateral side, causing a medial femoral rotation or a lateral rotation of tibia as a conjunct rotation with extension.
(c) "Screw home" mechanism describes the 5° of tibial ER, which occurs during terminal knee extension.

- Occurs as closed-chain internal femoral rotation during weight bearing to provide increased stability of knee joint during weight-bearing activities. Can also occur as open-chain external tibial rotation.
- Lateral or ER of tibia occurs as knee moves toward terminal extension, due to anatomical relationship of surfaces of tibia and femur.
- Unlocking occurs through action of popliteus. Open-chain unlocking occurs primarily with popliteal action.

(d) Causes for screw home mechanism.

- Lateral femoral condyle glides more freely on lateral convex (anterior-posterior) facet of tibia. Causes greater tibial motion in posterior direction on lateral side.
- Medial femoral condyle has a longer articular surface than lateral condyle. During femoral rolling, more motion occurs on lateral side (20°) than on medial side (10°–15°).
- Medial meniscus is attached to MCL, which tightens during extension. Medial meniscus stops gliding, while lateral meniscus continues to glide forward. Creates internal rotation of femur, which is same as ER of tibia.
- Twisted cruciate ligaments create ER force on tibia, while preventing an internal rotation.
- Lateral angle of pull of quadriceps muscle creates ER of tibia.

f. Biomechanics proximal tibiofibular joint.

(1) Dorsiflexion of talocrural joint.
(a) Fibular head glides superiorly and posteriorly. Fibular shaft rotates externally.

(2) Plantar flexion of talocrural joint.
(a) Fibular head glides inferiorly and anteriorly. Fibular shaft rotates internally.

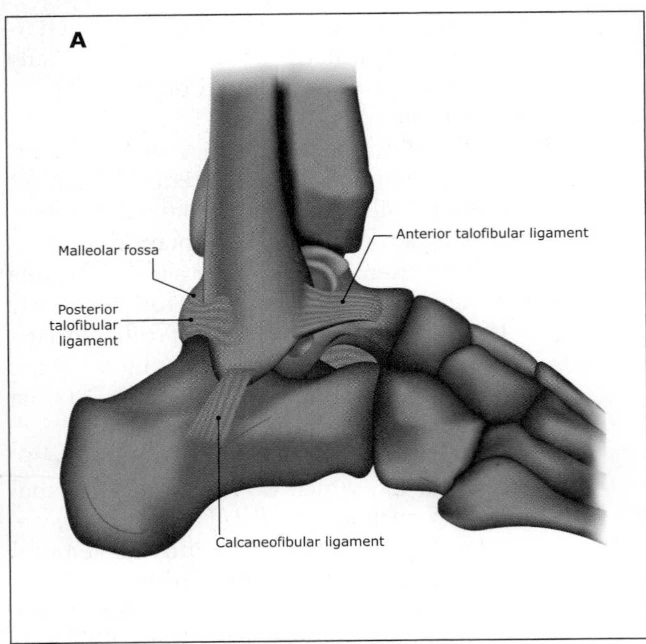

Figure 1-13a **Ankle: lateral view.**

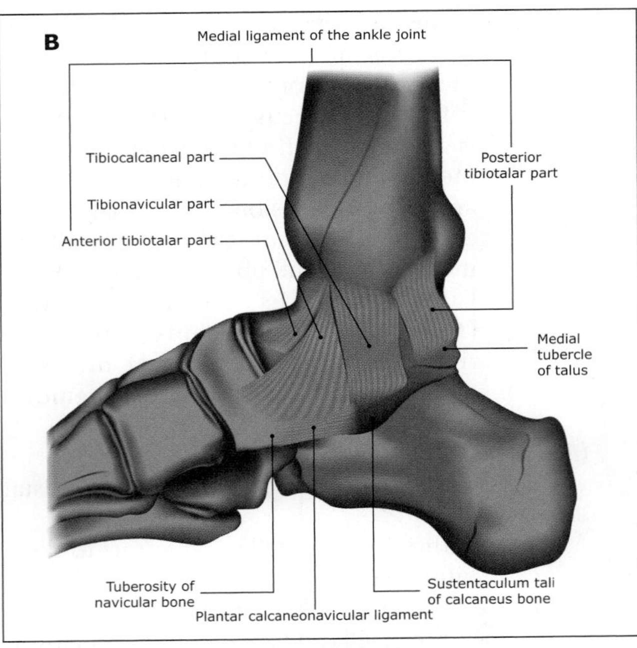

Figure 1-13b **Ankle: medial view.**

6. Foot and ankle region.
   a. Osteology and arthrology (talocrural, subtalar, talocalcaneonavicular, calcaneocuboid, transverse tarsal, tarsometatarsal, metatarsophalangeal, and interphalangeal) (see Figures 1-13 and 1-14).
      (1) Talocrural joint.
         (a) Ankle mortise formed by three components: distal end of tibia and its medial malleolus, lateral malleolus of fibula and inferior transverse tibiofibular ligament, and trochlear surface of talus.
         (b) Three articulations involved in the talocrural joint: tibiofibular, tibiotalar, and fibulotalar.
         (c) Transversely (medial/lateral), trochlear surface is gently concave. Trochlear surface is wedge shaped, wider anteriorly than posteriorly.
         (d) Laterally, talus is triangular shaped and concave in superior/inferior direction, and convex in anterior/posterior direction. Articulates with reciprocally curved fibula. Medial part of trochlear surface is comparatively flat and articulates with distal end of tibia, which is also flat.
      (2) Subtalar joint.
         (a) Two separate articulations: anterior and posterior talocalcaneal.
            - Posterior talocalcaneal articulation (subtalar joint proper): posterior superior articulation is convex in anterior/posterior direction, and concave in medial/lateral direction. This articulates with

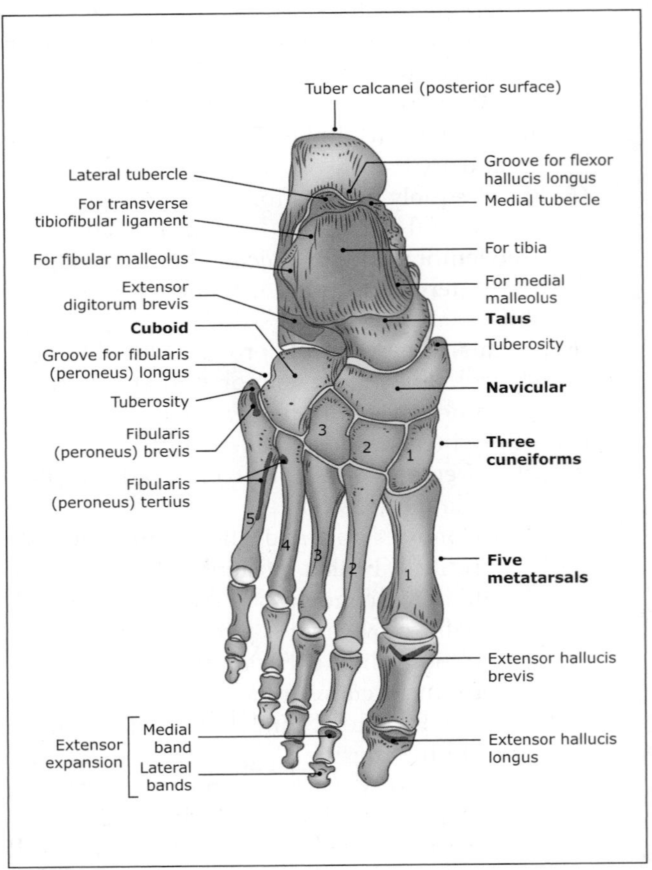

Figure 1-14 **Foot: dorsal view.**

reciprocally curved posterior part of inferior surface of talus.
- Anterior talocalcaneal articulation consists of obliquely oriented surfaces of biconvex inferior surface of neck and head of talus, resting on the biconcave anterior surface of calcaneus. Anterior talocalcaneal articulation, when described functionally, also includes posterior surface of navicular bone, which articulates with head of talus. Joint is properly referred to as talocalcaneonavicular joint.

(3) Talonavicular joint.
(a) Biconvex head of talus articulates with biconcavity, formed by posterior navicular surfaces and upper edge of plantar calcaneonavicular ligament.

(4) Calcaneocuboid joint.
(a) Anterior calcaneus is concave medial/lateral and convex superior/inferior. Posterior cuboid is concave superior/inferior and convex medial/lateral. Bony prominence on inferior/medial surface of cuboid articulates with inferior surface of calcaneus, making saddle shape deeper. Cuboid is key to lateral arch.

(5) Tarsometatarsal joints.
(a) Proximally, three cuneiforms medially and cuboid laterally. Distally bases of five metatarsals. First metatarsal (MT) is largest and strongest, second MT is longest. Third MT articulates primarily with the third cuneiform. Fourth and fifth MT articulate with cuboid.

(6) Cuneonavicular joint.
(a) Biconvex anterior surface of navicular has three facets to articulate with concave posterior surfaces of three cuneiform bones.

(7) Metatarsalphalangeal joint.
(a) Metatarsal heads are convex and proximal phalanges are concave.

(8) Interphalangeal joints.
(a) Same as fingers of hand.

b. Muscles (ankle plantarflexors, ankle dorsiflexors, everters, inverters, and intrinsics) (see Table 1-6).

c. Noncontractile structures (deltoid ligament, anterior talofibular, posterior talofibular, calcaneofibular, calcaneonavicular [spring ligament], interosseous, bifurcate ligament, plantaraponeurosis, long plantar ligament, and short plantar ligament, capsule, bursae, fascia, nerves, and vessels).

(1) Capsule.
(a) Talocrural joint. Fibrous capsule lined with synovial membrane strengthened by collateral, anterior, and posterior ligaments. Thin anteriorly and posteriorly and thickened laterally.
(b) Subtalar joint. Posterior articulation has an independent capsule with synovial membrane. Anterior articulation has capsule with synovial membrane that includes talonavicular joint.
(c) Talonavicular joint. Fibrous capsule with synovial lining is shared with anterior subtalar joint.
(d) Calcaneocuboid. Independent fibrous capsule with synovial membrane independent from other tarsal articulations.
(e) Tarsometatarsal (three capsular cavities):
- First MT with medial cuneiform.
- Second and third cuneiform capsule is continuous with intercuneiform and cuneonavicular joint cavity.
- Third cuneiform with base of fourth MT capsule encloses fourth MT with cuboid and third cuneiform.

(f) Cuneonavicular. Continuous with those of intercuneiform and cuneocuboid joints, as is its synovial cavity. Capsule is connected to second and third cuneometatarsal joints between second and fourth metatarsal bones.
(g) Metatarsalphalangeal joint. Fibrous capsule present for each articulation.
(h) Interphalangeal joints. Fibrous capsule present for each articulation.

(2) Ligaments.
(a) Talocrural joint.
- Medial collateral ligament (deep fibers): anterior talotibial ligament and posterior talotibial ligament.
- Medial collateral ligament (superficial fibers): deltoid ligament.
- Lateral collateral ligament: anterior talofibular ligament, calcaneofibular ligament, posterior talofibular ligament.

(b) Subtalar joint.
- Interosseous talocalcaneal ligament: two fibrous bands taut with eversion.
- Lateral talocalcaneal ligament.
- Posterior talocalcaneal ligament.
- Medial talocalcaneal ligament.

(c) Talonavicular joint.
- Plantar calcaneonavicular ligament (spring ligament).
- Dorsal talonavicular ligament.

(d) Calcaneocuboid joint.
- Medial band of the bifurcate ligament (lateral calcaneonavicular ligament).
- Medial calcaneocuboid (lateral band of the bifurcated ligament).
- Long plantar ligament (superficial plantar calcaneocuboid).
- Plantar calcaneocuboid (short plantar).

(e) Tarsometatarsal joint.
- Medially, dorsal ligament runs from medial cuneiform to base of second MT.
- Laterally, dorsal ligaments with straight fibers from middle cuneiform to second MT, lateral cuneiform to third MT, cruciate fibers from lateral cuneiform to second MT, and middle cuneiform to third MT.

(f) Cuneonavicular joint.
- Three dorsal cuneonavicular ligaments, one attached to each cuneiform.
- Plantar ligaments have similar attachments and receive slips from tendons of posterior tibialis muscle.

(g) Metatarsalphalangeal (MTP) joint. Plantar ligaments and collateral ligaments present.

(h) Interphalangeal joints. Plantar ligaments and collateral ligaments present.

(3) Plantar fascia.

(a) Also known as plantar aponeurosis.

(b) A broad, dense band of longitudinally arranged collagen fibers that can be divided into three components, running from medial calcaneus to phalanges.

(c) Fascia tightens with dorsiflexion of MTP joints as occurs during push off. Known as "windlass effect." Tightening of this fascia causes supination of calcaneus and inversion of subtalar joint, creating a rigid lever for push off.

(4) Bursa.

(a) Posterior calcaneal bursa.

(b) Retrocalcaneal bursa.

(5) Blood supply comes from malleolar rami of anterior tibial and fibular arteries.

(6) Articular innervation comes from deep fibular and tibial nerves.

d. Ankle and foot biomechanics.

(1) Talocrural joint.

(a) Conjunct rotations.
- Talus rotates medially 30° from dorsiflexion to plantar flexion. Also slight side-to-side gliding, rotation, and abduction/adduction are permitted when foot is plantar flexed.

(b) Arthrokinematics/osteokinematics.
- Open chain: During plantar flexion talus describes anterior glide on mortise with slight medial rotation or adduction. Dorsiflexion occurs as reciprocally opposite motion.
- Closed chain: During plantar flexion tibia glides posteriorly on talus with slight lateral rotation. Dorsiflexion occurs as a reciprocally opposite motion.

(2) Subtalar joint.

(a) Joint axes.
- Oblique axis extends from posterior, plantar, and lateral to anterior, dorsal, and medial. Joint is oriented obliquely, with the average at 42° from the horizontal and 16° from midline of foot.
- Variances in joint axis are fairly common.
- With a high inclination of axis, movement at subtalar joint is increased in transverse plane and decreased in frontal plane.
- With a low inclination of axis joint will be more frontal plane dominant, leading to greater calcaneal pronation/supination.

(b) Conjunct rotation.
- Calcaneus can move in many directions, due to its multiple articulations. Like a ship in the waves—rotation around a vertical axis, tilts medially and laterally, glides anteriorly and posteriorly.

(c) Arthrokinematics/osteokinematics.
- Occurs in same direction when mobilizing calcaneus on a fixed talus. Subtalar joint represents the purest triplanar movement.
- Open chain: During inversion, calcaneus moves into adduction, supination, and plantar flexion on fixed talus. Eversion occurs as a reciprocally opposite motion.
- Closed chain: During inversion, supination of calcaneus (talus guides laterally) with abduction and dorsiflexion of talus. Produces ER of tibia. Eversion occurs as a reciprocally opposite motion. Produces internal rotation of tibia.

(3) Talonavicular joint.

(a) Arthrokinematics/osteokinematics.
- Arthokinematics and osteokinematics occur in same direction when mobilizing navicular on a fixed talus. Rotational movements of midtarsal joint allow forefoot to twist on rearfoot. Talus and navicular rotate in opposite directions.
- Open chain: During inversion, navicular plantar flexes, adducts, and externally rotates on talus. Eversion occurs as a reciprocally opposite motion.
- Closed chain: During inversion, navicular plantar flexes (talus glides dorsally on navicular), adducts (talus abducts), and internally rotates. Eversion occurs as a reciprocally opposite motion.

(4) MTPs and PIPs same as fingers.

7. Spine.
   a. General function of the vertebral column.
      (1) Support for head and internal organs.
      (2) Stable attachment for all soft tissues, extremities, rib cage, and pelvis.
      (3) Protection of internal organs and spinal cord.
      (4) Attenuates forces from above and below.
   b. Components of the vertebral column.
      (1) Consists of 24 freely movable and 9 fused bones.
      (2) Divided into five distinct regions (cervical, thoracic, lumbar, sacral, and coccygeal).
   c. Osteology.
      (1) Typical vertebra (vertebral body, pedicles, lamina which includes superior and inferior articular processes or facets, transverse processes, and the spinous process).
      (2) Regional variations.
         (a) Cervical: two atypical (atlas and axis) which allow for increase active range of motion (AROM) in rotation without compressing the spinal cord), uncinate processes, and transverse foramen.
            - Vertebral body is rectangular shaped.
            - Uncinate joints (joints of von Luschka) found at C3–C7 limit lateral cervical movement.
         (b) Costotransverse and costovertebral: articulations between rib and transverse process and vertebral body respectively.
         (c) Thoracic: demifacets for articulation with the ribs. Vertebral body is heart shaped. Prominent spinous processes are angled following "Rules of 3."
            - Rules of 3: spinous process of T1–T3 even with transverse process of same level vertebra; T4–T6 spinous processes are found one-half level below transverse processes of same level; T7–T9 spinous processes are one full level below transverse process of same level; T10 is full level below; T11 is one-half level below; and T12 is level.
         (d) Lumbar: vertebra larger than other regions and body is kidney shaped. Very prominent spinous processes (see Figures 1-15 and 1-16).
         (e) Sacrum is wedge shaped, both anteriorly/posteriorly and inferiorly/superiorly. Made of five fused vertebrae.
         (f) Ilium is made up of three fused bones (ischium, ilium, and pubis). Shape varies widely among people, with significant difference in shape between men and women.
   d. Arthrology.
      (1) Atypical joints.
         (a) Atlanto-occipital joint: synovial articulation between occiput and C1. Also known as "yes" joint, since much of head nodding motion comes from this articulation.
         (b) Atlanto-axial joint: nonsynovial articulation between dens of C2 and anterior arch of C1.

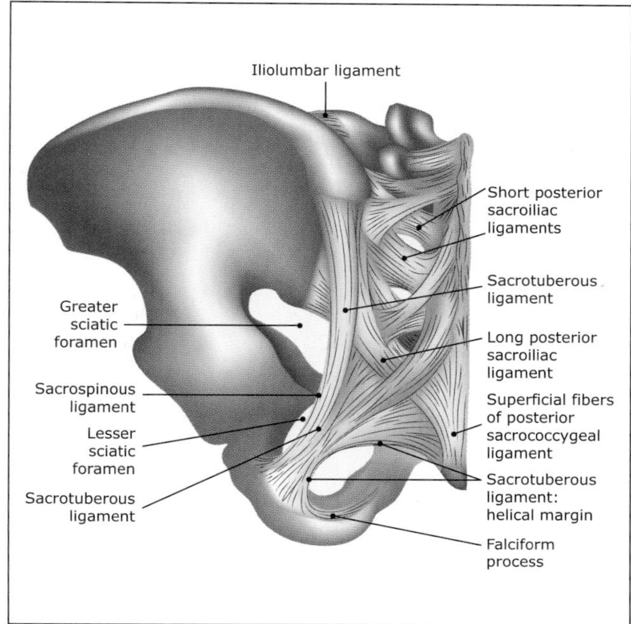

Figure 1-15 Half of pelvis and 5th lumbar vertebra.

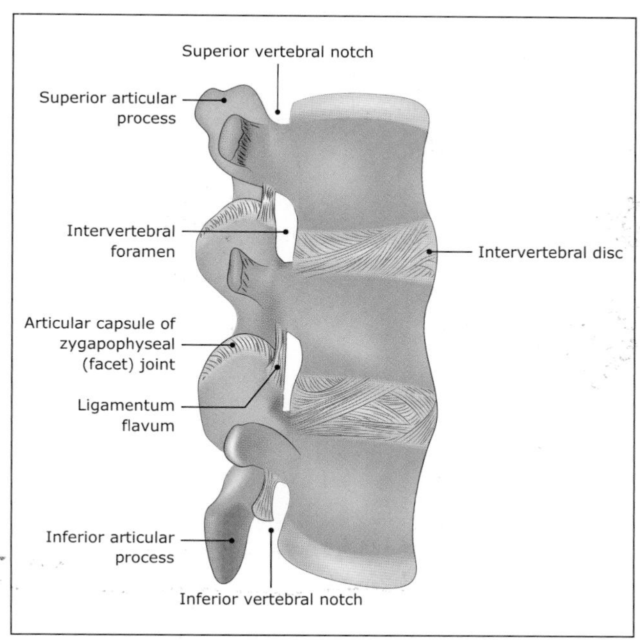

Figure 1-16 Lumbar vertebra.

Known as "no" joint, since much of head rotation comes from this articulation.

(2) Apophyseal or facet joints which guide movement of spine. Synovial/diarthrodial joints with capsule and synovial membrane. Composed of superior and inferior articulatory processes of adjacent vertebrae. In lumbar region, facet surfaces may be flat or curved. In cervical and thoracic regions, surfaces are generally flat.

(3) Intervertebral joints between intervertebral disc and adjacent superior and inferior vertebral bodies. Allow movement between vertebral bodies and transmit loads from one vertebral segment to another.

(4) Sacroiliac joint (SIJ): composed of auricular-shaped joint surfaces of sacrum and ilium. Diarthrosis/synarthrosis (syndesmosis) combination. Ilial articulation is primarily convex and covered with a thin layer of fibrocartilage. Sacral articulation is primarily concave and covered with hyaline cartilage. SI joints attenuate forces from trunk and lower extremities.

e. Fibroadipose meniscoid.
  (1) Structure composed of dense connective tissue and adipose tissue.
  (2) Found at superior and inferior aspects of facet joints.
  (3) Protects cartilage of facet surface during extremes in motion.

f. Muscles (see Table 1-7).

g. Intervertebral disc/endplate.
  (1) Annulus fibrosis/fibrosus.
    (a) Concentric layers or lamellae composed of collagen (type II) and fibrocartilage. 65% water.
    (b) Outer one-third of annulus is innervated by branches from sinovertebral nerve.
    (c) Functions to sustain compressive, torsional, shearing, and distraction loads.
  (2) Nucleus pulposis/pulposus.
    (a) Gel with imbibing capabilities composed of water and proteoglycans with a minimal amount of collagen (type I). 70%–90% water.
    (b) Avascular and aneural structure.
    (c) Makes up 20%–33% height of vertebral column.
    (d) Functions to sustain compressive, torsional, shearing, and distraction loads.
  (3) Vertebral endplate.
    (a) Structure continuous with annulus and nucleus. Sits inside ring apophysis of vertebral body.
    (b) Composed of proteoglycans, collagen, and water as well as both fibrocartilage (on side closest to disc) and hyaline cartilage (on side closest to vertebral body).
    (c) Functions to provide passive diffusion of nutrients.

h. Other noncontractile soft tissues.
  (1) Ligaments.
    (a) Alar ligament.
    (b) Tectorial membrane.

Table 1-7

Trunk and Ribcage Muscular and Neurological Screening

ACTION TO BE TESTED	MUSCLES	CORD SEGMENT	NERVES
Inspiration	Diaphragm Levator costarum, external intercostals, anterior Internal intercostals	C3–C5 T1–T12	Phrenic Intercostal
Forced expiration	Internal obliques, transverse abdominis, external obliques, posterior internal intercostals, rectus abdominis	T7–L1 T7–T12 T1–T12 T7–T12	Intercostal Intercostal Intercostal Intercostal
Spine extension	Erector spinae, transversospinalis, interspinales, rotatores intertransversarii	T1–T12, L1–L5, S1–S3	
Spine flexion	Rectus abdominis/external obliques, internal obliques, psoas minor	T7–T12 T7–L1 L1	Intercostal Intercostal Lumbar plexus
Spine lateral flexion (hip hiking in reverse)	Quadratus lumborum	T12–L3	Lumbar plexus
Spine rotation	Rotators, internal/external obliques, intertransversarii, transversospinalis	as above	

Adapted from Chusid JG: Correlative Neuroanatomy and Functional Neurology. Lange Medical Publications, 1970; Kendall FP, McCreary EK, Provance PG: Muscles Testing and Function, 4th ed. Williams & Wilkins, 1993.

(c) Anterior longitudinal ligament.
(d) Posterior longitudinal ligament.
(e) Ligamentum flavum.
(f) Interspinous ligament.
(g) Supraspinous ligament.
(h) Transforaminal ligaments.
(i) Costotransverse ligament (superior, posterior, and lateral).
(j) Iliolumbar ligament.
(k) Posterior sacroiliac ligaments (short, transverse, and long).
(l) Anterior sacroiliac ligament.
(m) Sacrotuberous ligament.
(n) Posterior interosseous ligament (SIJ).

(2) Capsules.
(a) Facet joint: assist ligaments in providing limitation of motion and stability of spine. Strongest in the thoracolumbar and cervicothoracic regions.
(b) Sacroiliac joints: synovial capsule present in surrounding joint, which is very prominent anteriorly; posteriorly, it is lost within posterior interosseous ligament.

(3) Thoracolumbar fascia.
(a) Provides stability of vertebral column when a force is applied.
(b) Acts as a corset when tension is created by contraction of abdominals, gluteals, and lumbar muscles.

i. Nerves. 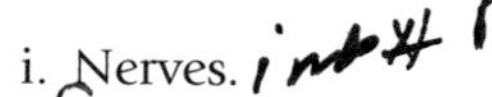

(1) Dorsal roots transmit sensory fibers to spinal cord and ventral roots; mainly transmit motor fibers from spinal cord to spinal nerve.
(2) Spinal nerves are connected centrally to spinal cord by a dorsal and ventral root, which join to become the spinal nerve in the intervertebral foramen. Spinal nerve divides into dorsal and ventral rami.
(a) Dorsal rami innervate structures on posterior trunk.
(b) Ventral rami.
- Cervical ventral rami form cervical and brachial plexuses (see Figures 1-17 and 1-18).
- Thoracic ventral rami innervate anterior structures of trunk within thoracic region.
- Lumbar ventral rami form lumbar and lumbosacral plexuses (see Figures 1-19 and 1-20).

(3) Spinal nerves in various sections of spine.
(a) Cervical: spinal nerves come out at the level above its associated vertebra.
(b) Thoracic/lumbar: spinal nerves come out at level below its associated vertebra.
(4) Spinal cord terminates approximately at level of L1–L2 disc.

j. Spinal biomechanics.
(1) Arthrokinematics.
(a) Flexion: upper facets glide anteroproximally and tilt forward.

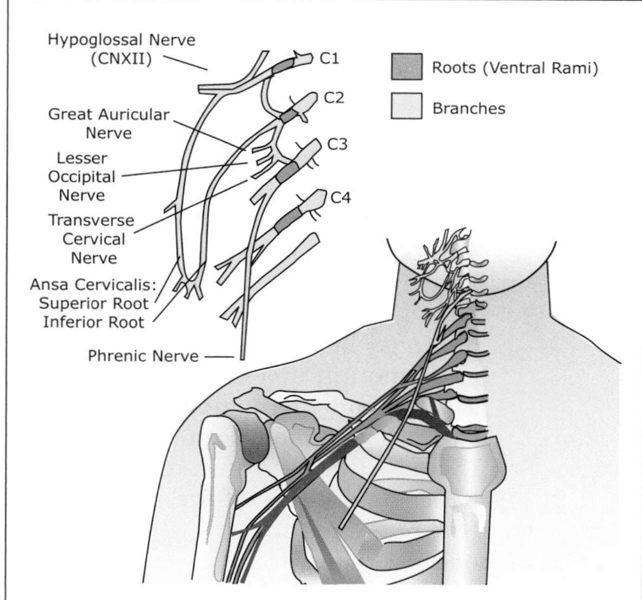

Figure 1-17 **Cervical plexus.**

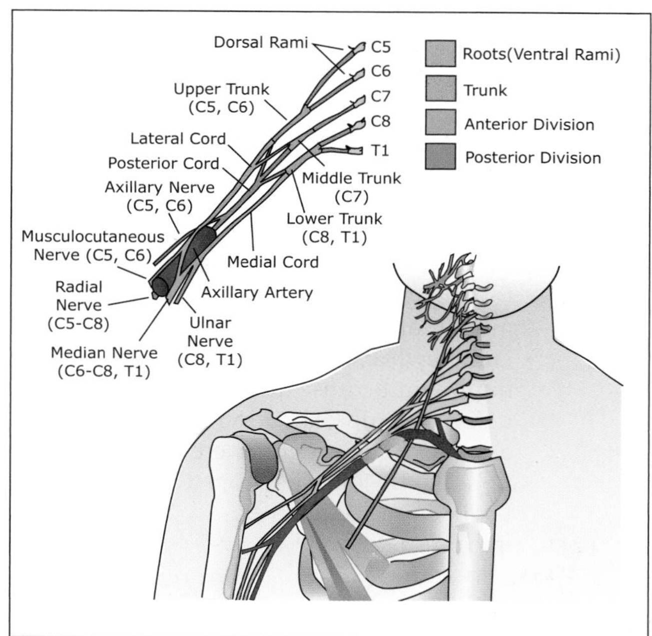

Figure 1-18 **Brachial plexus.**

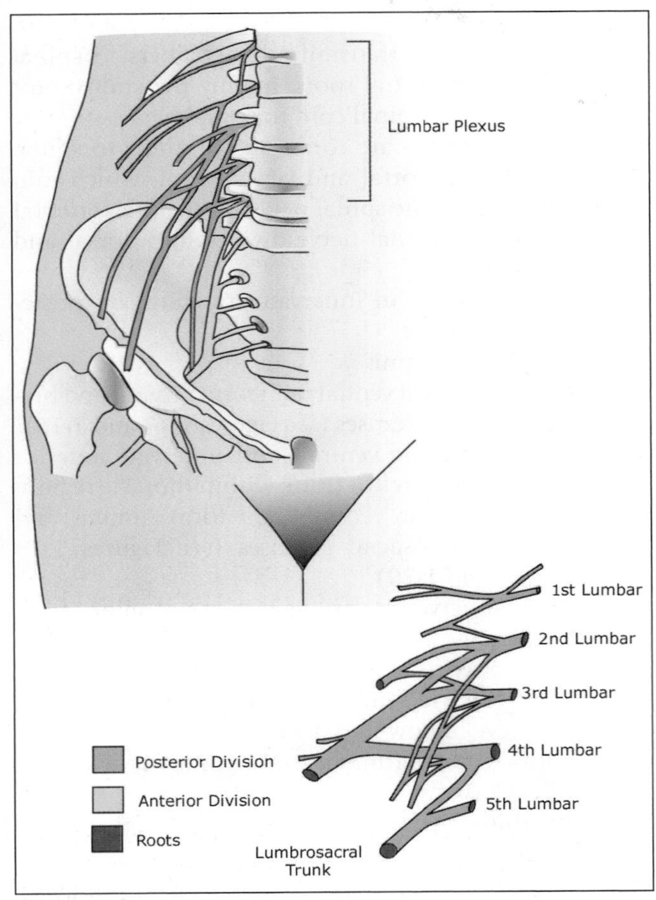

Figure 1-19 **Lumbar plexus.**

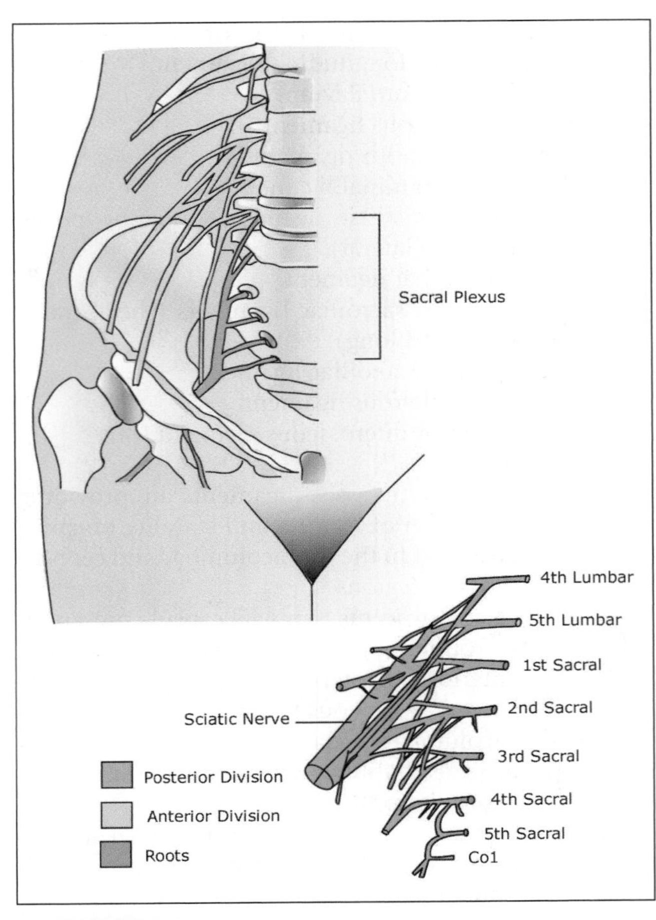

Figure 1-20 **Sacral plexus.**

(b) Extension: upper facets move downward, slightly posterior, and tilt backward.

(c) Side-bending: when side-bending right, upper facet moves down and slightly anterior. Left facet moves upward and slightly posterior. Both facets move to the left.

(d) Rotation.

(e) Cervical: right rotation causes facets on right to glide down and back, causing approximation of facet joints on right.

(f) Lumbar/thoracic: very little, but clinically important because this motion causes separation and approximation of the facet joints; e.g., if L3 rotates right, there is separation at right L3–L4 joint and approximation at left L3–L4 joint.

(2) Coupled motions.

(a) Cervical.

- Side-bending and rotation occur in same direction from C2–C7, regardless of whether spine is in neutral/extension or flexion. When occiput side bends, C1 rotates in opposite direction.

(b) Lumbar/thoracic.

- Neutral/extension: lumbar segments will side bend and rotate in opposite directions; e.g., side bend right results in segment rotating left.
- Flexion: lumbar segments will side bend and rotate in the same direction.
- This coupling described above is a very basic interpretation. In reality, there are significant variations in coupling motions between individuals. Coupling motion may depend on whether a side bend or rotation is done first. Direction of spinal segmental coupling should always be checked with each patient prior to performing a manual technique.

(3) Lumbopelvic rhythm.

(a) During flexion, spine (primarily lumbar spine) goes through 60°–70° of motion and then pelvis will rotate anteriorly to allow more movement, eventually followed by flexion of hips.

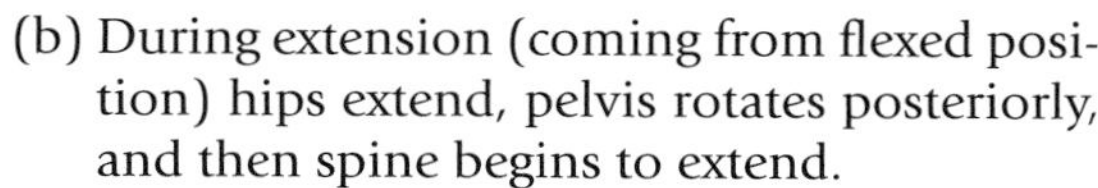

(b) During extension (coming from flexed position) hips extend, pelvis rotates posteriorly, and then spine begins to extend.

(4) Sacroiliac joint osteokinematics.

(a) Motion limited, but during gait movements takes place in multiple planes.

(b) Nutation and counternutation: coupling movement that occurs between sacrum and ilium during gait.

- Nutation: describes a movement that involves flexion of sacrum and posterior rotation of ilium.
- Counternutation: describes a movement that involves extension of sacrum and anterior rotation of ilium.

8. Temporomandibular joint (TMJ).

a. Functional anatomy. A bilateral articulation between mandible and cranium (craniomandibular joint).

b. Arthrology.

(1) Synovial joint with articular surfaces covered by dense fibrous connective tissue rather than hyaline cartilage.

(2) Articular disc composed of dense fibrous connective tissue without blood vessels or nerves in pressure bearing areas.

(3) Discal ligaments function to restrict movement in sagittal plane.

(4) Superior retrodiscal lamina (superior stratum) composed of elastic connective tissue; counteracts forward pull of superior lateral pterygoid muscle on articular disc.

(5) Retrodiscal pad consists of loose neurovascular connective tissue.

c. Joint movement.

(1) Combination of hinge axis rotation in disc condyle complex and sliding movement of the upper joint.

(2) Functional range of opening is 40 mm, with 25 mm of rotation and 15 mm of translatory glide.

Physical Therapy Examination

Patient/Client History (or Interview), Systems Review, and Tests and Measures

1. Patient/client history.

a. Gather information to develop a hypothetical diagnosis, which dictates flow of examination. Delineate any precautions and/or contraindications when performing components of examination (see Table 1-8).

b. Components of history.

(1) Demographics: age, gender, diagnosis and referral (if appropriate), hand dominance, etc.

(2) Social and family history.

(3) Current condition(s)/chief complaint.

(4) General health status.

(5) Social health.

(6) Employment/work.

(7) Growth and development.

(8) Living environment.

(9) Functional status and activity level.

(10) Medical/surgical history, including previous treatment and review of systems.

2. Systems review.

a. Components of system review (see Table 1-9).

(1) Musculoskeletal.

(2) Neuromuscular.

(3) Cardiopulmonary.

(4) Integumentary systems.

b. Determine whether identified condition(s) are comorbidity(ies) and/or complicating factor(s).

c. Determine whether a referral to an additional health care provider is appropriate, and if so, make the referral.

3. Tests and measures.

a. Gather specific data regarding patient/client. Choosing specific components as well as order of exam will be dictated by history.

b. Components that may be a part of tests and measures include:

(1) Anthropometric characteristics.

(2) Postural alignment and position (see Table 1-10, Figure 1-21).

(a) Dynamic.

(b) Static.

(3) Range of motion (see Tables 1-11 and 1-12).

(a) AROM.

(b) Passive range of motion (PROM).

(c) Flexibility testing.

(4) Muscle performance: resisted tests, manual muscle testing, muscle tension (see Table 1-13).

(5) Motor function.

(6) Cranial and peripheral nerve integrity.

(7) Reflex integrity.

(8) Sensory integrity.

(9) Joint integrity and mobility.

(10) Pain.

(11) Assistive and adaptive devices.

Table 1-8

Questions Related to Specific Areas of Dysfunction	
AREA OF DYSFUNCTION	**RELATED QUESTIONS**
Shoulder	Do you have pain raising your arm up, and if so, at what part of the range does that occur? Have you ever dislocated your shoulder? Do you have pain sleeping on your shoulder at night?
Elbow	Have you recently changed your activities? Have you recently changed the type of tools you use at work or the instruments you use for recreational activities?
Hand	Have you been doing more or different work with your hands than the usual, such as typing, sewing, gardening, etc.?
Cervical	Do you have dizziness when looking overhead? Have you had any previous motor vehicle accidents with resulting neck injury? How many pillows do you use at night?
TMJ	Do you have any popping or clicking in the TMJ? Do you have pain trying to eat specific foods? Does your jaw ever get stuck open or closed?
Thoracic	Do you have pain with breathing? Have you had a recent upper respiratory infection?
Lumbar	Have you had any changes in your ability to urinate or have a bowel movement? Do you have any symptoms such as pain, tingling, burning, etc. in either of your legs?
Sacroiliac	Did you fall onto your buttocks? Did you step off a curb and experience pain? Do you have pain with walking and/or sustained postures?
Hip	Do you have pain in your groin? Do you have stiffness in the morning that feels better with movement?
Knee	Does your knee "pop"? Does your knee ever give way and/or lock? Did your knee swell as soon as you were injured or did the swelling come later?
Ankle/Foot	Have you ever sprained your ankle, and if so, how many times? Do you have pain in your foot when you first try to step out of bed in the morning?

Table 1-9

Summary of Symptoms Observed in Common and Uncommon Dysfunctions	
DYSFUNCTION	**SYMPTOMS OBSERVED**
Degenerative joint disease/osteoarthritis	Pain and stiffness upon rising Pain eases through the morning (4–5 hours) Pain increases with repetitive bending activities Constant awareness of discomfort with episodes of exacerbation Describes pain as more soreness and nagging
Facet joint dysfunction	Stiff upon rising; pain eases within an hour Loss of motion accompanied by pain Patient will describe pain as sharp with certain movements Movement in pain-free range usually reduces symptoms Stationary positions increase symptoms
Discal, with nerve root compromise	No pain in reclined or semireclined position Pain increases with increasing weight-bearing activities Describes pain as shooting, burning, or stabbing Patient may describe altered strength or ability to perform ADLs
Spinal stenosis	Pain is related to position Flexed positions decrease pain, and extended positions increase pain Describes symptoms as a numbness, tightness, or cramping Walking for any distance brings on symptoms Pain may persist for hours after assuming a resting position
Vascular claudication	Pain is consistent in all spinal positions Pain is brought on by physical exertion Pain is relieved promptly with rest (1–5 minutes) Pain is described as a numbness Patient usually has decreased or absent pulses
Neoplastic disease	Patient describes pain as gnawing, intense, or penetrating Pain is not resolved by changes in position, time of day, or activity level Pain will wake the patient

Table 1-10

Effects of Forward Head Posture on the Spine, TMJ, and Associated Soft Tissue Structures

STRUCTURE	POSTURE CHANGES
Cranium	Extended on upper cervical spine
Mandible	Elevated and retruded
TMJ	Posterior close-packed position
Maxillomandibular relationship	Increased freeway space with significant posterior intercuspation
Hyoid	Elevated (suprahyoids shorten, infrahyoids lengthen)
Tongue	Drops to the floor of mouth
Upper cervical spine	Extended (can compress neurovascular structures)
Middle and lower cervical spine	Lordosis decreased (flexed positioning)
First and second ribs	Elevated
Scalenes, suboccipital, sternocleidomastoids, longus colli, upper trapezius, levator scapulae	Shorten
Pectoralis major and minor	Shorten, creating rounded shoulder position
Scapular stabilizers, rectus capitis anterior	Stretched
Longus capitis	Stretched suboccipital region, shorten C2–C6

Adapted from Darnell MA: Proposed chronology of events for forward head posture. Journal of Craniomandibular Practice, 1983, 1(4): 50–54.

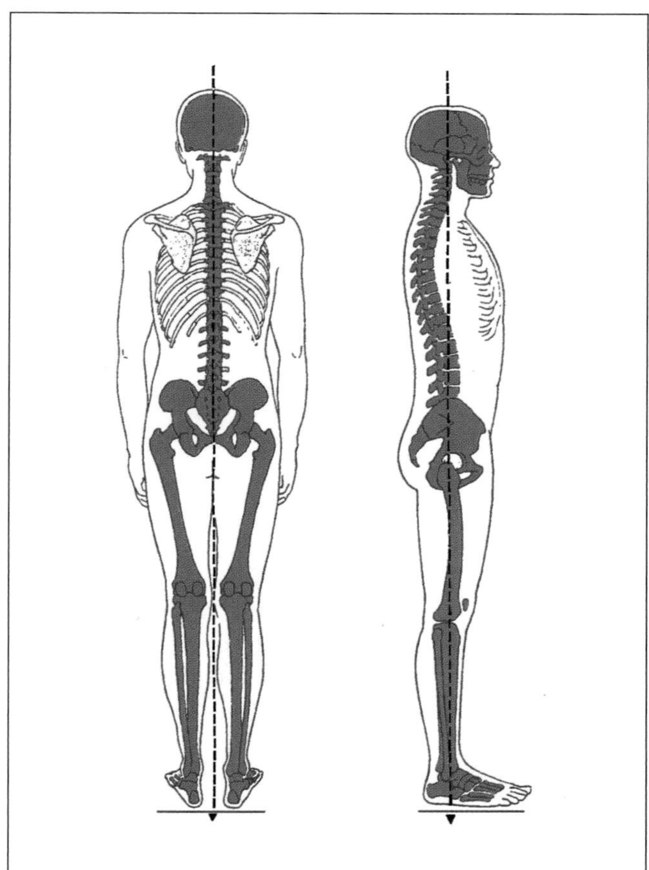

Figure 1-21 **Vertical line of gravity.**

(12) Orthotic, protective, and supportive devices.
(13) Ergonomics and body mechanics.
(14) Self-care and home management.
(15) Gait, locomotion, and balance.
(16) Work, community, and leisure integration or reintegration.
(17) Special tests (see specifics for each joint/region).

4. Diagnostic testing.
   a. Diagnostic tests are utilized for correlation with history and tests and measures to determine patient's primary physical therapy diagnosis as well as identify any medical conditions that may be contributing factors or comorbidities.
   b. If further diagnostic tests are warranted and/or beneficial, make appropriate referral or recommendation.
   c. Most common types of diagnostic testing for musculoskeletal dysfunctions include imaging, laboratory tests, and electrodiagnostic testing.
   d. Imaging (see Appendix 1M).
      (1) Plain film radiograph (x-rays).
         (a) X-rays are used to demonstrate bony tissues. Beams pass through the tissues resulting in varying shades of gray on film depending on density of tissue it passed through. The more dense the structure (bone), the whiter the structure will appear on the film.
         (b) Readily available, relatively inexpensive, and shows bony anatomy very well.
         (c) Negative is patient exposure to radiation.

Table 1-11

Extremity Range of Motion

JOINT	FLEXION/ EXTENSION	ABDUCTION/ ADDUCTION	EXTERNAL/ INTERNAL ROTATION	HORIZONTAL ADDUCTION	SUPINATION/ PRONATION	RADIAL/ ULNAR DEVIATION	PLANTAR-FLEXION/ DORSIFLEXION
Shoulder	160–180/50–60	170–180/50–75	80–90/60–100	130/45			
Elbow	140–150/0–10				90/80–90		
Wrist	80–90/70–90					15/30–45	
MCP	85–90/30–45						
PIP	100–115/0						
DIP	80–90/20						
1st CMC	45–50	60–70/30					
1st MCP	50–55/0						
1st IP	85–90/0–5						
Hip	110–120/10–15	30–50/30	40–60/30–40				
Knee	135/0–15		30–40/20–30				
Ankle					45–60/15–30		50/20
2nd–5th MTP	40/40						
1st MTP	45/70						
1st IP	90/0						
2nd–5th PIP	35/0						
2nd–5th DIP	60/30						

Table 1-12

Spine Range of Motion

REGION	FLEXION/EXTENSION	SIDE-BENDING	ROTATION	OPENING	PROTRUSION/ RETRUSION	LATERAL DEVIATION
Cervical	80–90/70	20–45	70–90			
Thoracic	20–45/25–45	20–40	35–50			
Lumbar	40–60/20–35	15–20	3–18			
TMJ				35–50 mm	3–6 mm/3–4 mm	10–15 mm

(d) Requires two different projections, since structures may be superimposed on each other, making it difficult to identify pathology with one view. Typical views are anterior-posterior and lateral, although other views may be used.

(e) Used for viewing dysfunction and/or disease of bones. Does not demonstrate soft tissues well or at all.

(2) Computed tomography (CT) scan.

(a) Uses plain film x-ray slices that are enhanced by a computer to improve resolution. It is multiplanar so can image in any plane; therefore, tissue can be viewed from multiple directions.

(b) Typically used to assess complex fractures as well as facet dysfunction, disc disease, or stenosis of the spinal canal or intervertebral foramen. CT demonstrates better quality and better visualization of bony structures than plain films. CT also demonstrates soft tissue structures, although not as well as MRI.

(c) Fairly expensive, and patient is exposed to radiation.

(3) Discography.

(a) Radiopaque dye is injected into the disc to identify abnormalities within the disc (annulus or nucleus). The needle is inserted into the disc with the assistance of radiography (fluoroscopy).

Table 1-13

Muscle Grading			
Normal	N	5/5	Lift or hold against gravity with maximal resistance.
Good +	G+	4+/5	Good grades include lifting or holding against gravity with moderate to minimal resistance.
Good	G	4/5	
Good –	G–	4–/5	
Fair +	F+	3+/5	Fair grades include lifting or holding against gravity without resistance.
Fair	F	3/5	
Fair –	F–	3–/5	Some assistance may be required to complete the motion in the minus category.
Poor +	P+	2+/5	Poor grades include movement with gravity eliminated.
Poor	P	2/5	
Poor –	P–	2–/5	Some assistance may be required to complete the motion in the minus category.
Trace	T	1/5	Muscle contraction can be seen or felt. No movement is produced.
Zero	0	0/5	No contraction is seen or felt.

Adapted from Kendall FP, McCreary EK, Provance PG: Muscles Testing and Function, 4th ed. Williams & Wilkins, 1993.

(b) Not commonly used. Requires a high level of skill and proper equipment to perform. Fairly specific technique to identify internal disc disruptions of the nucleus and/or annulus.
(c) Expensive, may be painful, and since it is invasive, there is a risk of infection.

(4) Magnetic resonance imaging (MRI).
(a) Uses magnetic fields rather than radiation.
(b) Offers excellent visualization of tissue anatomy. Utilizes two types of images: T1 demonstrates fat within the tissues and is typically used to assess bony anatomy, while T2 suppresses fat and demonstrates tissues with high water content. T2 is used to assess soft tissue structures.
(c) Fairly expensive, and patients with claustrophobia do not tolerate this test well. Quality of open MRI is inferior to closed. May not be able to use with patients who have metallic implants.

(5) Arthrography.
(a) Invasive technique that injects water-soluble dye into area and is observed with a radiograph. Dye is observed as it surrounds tissues, demonstrating the anatomy where fluid moves within joint.
(b) Typically used to identify abnormalities within joints such as tendon ruptures.
(c) Expensive and carries risks since it is invasive.

(6) Bone scans (osteoscintigraphy).
(a) Chemicals laced with radioactive tracers are injected.
(b) Isotope settles in areas where there is a high metabolic activity of bone.
(c) Radiograph is taken to demonstrate any "hot spots" of increased metabolic activity.
(d) Patients with dysfunctions, such as rheumatoid arthritis, possible stress fractures, bone cancer, infection within bone, often receive a bone scan, since these dysfunctions increase metabolic activity of bone in the affected regions.

(7) Diagnostic ultrasound.
(a) Utilizes transmission of high-frequency sound waves, similar to therapeutic ultrasound.
(b) Limited by contrast resolution, small viewing field, how deep it penetrates, and poor penetration of bone. Interpretation of data is subjective, so results depend on skill of operator.
(c) Provides real-time dynamic images and can assess soft tissue dysfunctions.
(d) No known harmful effects at this time.

(8) Myelography.
(a) Invasive technique using water-soluble dye. Dye is visualized as it passes through vertebral canal to observe anatomy within region.
(b) Seldom used due to side effects versus MRI or CT scan, which provide as good, if not better, information. Very expensive, since it often involves a hospital stay overnight.
(c) Traditionally used for diagnostic assessment of the discs and stenosis. May still be beneficial to identify stenosis.

e. Laboratory tests.
   (1) Laboratory tests are typically used to screen patients, assist with making a diagnosis, or for monitoring.
   (2) Since many patients with musculoskeletal dysfunction present with other medical pathology, it is important to monitor clinical laboratory findings.
   (3) Multiple tests available that fall into the following categories.
      (a) Blood tests.
      (b) Serum chemistries.
      (c) Immunological tests.
      (d) Pulmonary function tests.
      (e) Arterial blood gases.
      (f) Fluid analysis.
f. Electrodiagnostic testing (also refer to Chapter 2: Neuromuscular Physical Therapy).
   (1) Electroneuromyography (ENMG) and nerve conduction velocity (NCV) tests are commonly used to assess and/or monitor musculoskeletal conditions.

Special Tests of the Upper Extremity

1. Shoulder special tests.
   a. Yergason's test.
      (1) Tests for integrity of transverse ligament; may also identify bicipital tendonosis/tendonopathy.
      (2) Patient sitting with shoulder in neutral stabilized against trunk, elbow at 90°, and forearm pronated. Resist supination of forearm and ER of shoulder.
      (3) Tendon of biceps long head will "pop out" of groove. May also reproduce pain in long head of biceps tendon.
      (4) Sensitivity (SN) 74%; Specificity (SP) 58%; Positive Likelihood Ratio (+LR) 1.76; Negative Likelihood Ratio (–LR) 0.45.
   b. Speed's test (biceps straight arm).
      (1) Identifies bicipital tendonosis/tendonopathy.
      (2) Patient sitting or standing with upper limb in full extension and forearm supinated. Resist shoulder flexion. May also place shoulder in 90° flexion and push upper limb into extension, causing an eccentric contraction of the biceps.
      (3) Reproduces symptoms (pain) in long head of biceps tendon.
      (4) SN 90%; SP 13.8%.
   c. Neer's impingement test (see Figure 1-22).
      (1) For impingement of soft tissue structures of shoulder complex (long head of biceps and supraspinatus tendon).
      (2) Patient sitting and shoulder is passively, internally rotated, then fully abducted.
      (3) Reproduces symptoms of pain within shoulder region.
      (4) SN 88.7%; SP 30.5%.
   d. Supraspinatus (empty can) test (see Figure 1-23).
      (1) Identifies tear and/or impingement of supraspinatus tendon or possible suprascapular nerve neuropathy.
      (2) Patient sitting with shoulder at 90° and no rotation. Resist shoulder abduction. Then place shoulder in "empty can" position, which is internal rotation and 30° forward (horizontal adduction) and resist abduction. Differentiate whether pain is present between two positions.
      (3) Reproduces pain in supraspinatus tendon and/or weakness while in "empty can" position.
      (4) SN and SP not available.
   e. Drop arm test.
      (1) Identifies tear and/or full rupture of rotator cuff.
      (2) Patient sitting with shoulder passively abducted to 120°. Patient instructed slowly to bring arm down to side. Guard patient's arm from falling in case it gives way.
      (3) Patient unable to lower arm back down to side.
      (4) SN 7.8%; SP 97.2%; (+LR) 2.79; (–LR) 0.95.
   f. Posterior internal impingement test.
      (1) Identifies an impingement between rotator cuff and greater tuberosity or posterior glenoid and labrum.
      (2) Patient supine. Move shoulder into 90° abduction, maximum ER, and 15°–20° horizontal adduction.
      (3) Reproduction of pain in posterior shoulder during test.
      (4) SN and SP not available.
   g. Clunk test (see Figure 1-24).
      (1) Identifies a glenoid labrum tear.
      (2) Patient supine, with shoulder in full abduction. Push humeral head anterior while rotating humerus externally.
      (3) Audible "clunk" is heard while performing test.
      (4) SN and SP not available.
   h. Anterior apprehension sign.
      (1) Identifies past history of anterior shoulder dislocation.
      (2) Patient supine, with shoulder in 90° abduction. Slowly take shoulder into ER.
      (3) Patient does not allow and/or does not like shoulder to move in direction to simulate anterior dislocation.
      (4) SN and SP not available.
   i. Posterior apprehension sign.
      (1) Identifies past history of posterior shoulder dislocation.
      (2) Patient supine with shoulder abducted 90° (in plane of scapula) with scapula stabilized by table. Place a posterior force through shoulder

via force on patient's elbow while simultaneously moving shoulder into medial rotation and horizontal adduction.

(3) Patient does not allow and/or does not like shoulder to move in direction to simulate posterior dislocation.

(4) SN and SP not available.

j. Acromioclavicular (AC) shear test.

(1) Identifies dysfunction of AC joint (such as arthritis, separation).

(2) Patient sitting with arm resting at side. Examiner clasps hands and places heel of one hand on spine of scapula and heel of other hand on clavicle. Squeeze hands together, causing compression of AC joint.

(3) Reproduces pain in AC joint.

(4) SN and SP not available.

k. Adson's test (see Figure 1-25).

(1) Identifies pathology of structures that pass through thoracic inlet.

(2) Patient sitting. Find radial pulse of extremity being tested. Rotate head toward extremity being tested, and then extend and externally rotate the shoulder while extending the head.

(3) Neurological and/or vascular symptoms (disappearance of pulse) will be reproduced in upper extremity.

(4) SN and SP not available.

l. Costoclavicular syndrome (military brace) test.

(1) Identifies pathology of structures that pass through thoracic inlet.

(2) Patient sitting. Find radial pulse of the extremity being tested. Move involved shoulder down and back.

(3) Neurological and/or vascular symptoms (disappearance of pulse) will be reproduced in upper extremity.

(4) SN and SP not available.

m. Wright (hyperabduction) test.

(1) Identifies pathology of structures that pass through thoracic inlet.

(2) Patient sitting. Find radial pulse of extremity being tested. Move shoulder into maximal abduction and ER. Taking deep breath and rotating head opposite to side being tested may accentuate symptoms.

(3) Neurological and/or vascular symptoms (disappearance of pulse) will be reproduced in upper extremity.

(4) SN and SP not available.

n. Roos elevated arm test.

(1) Identifies pathology of structures that pass through thoracic inlet.

(2) Patient standing, with shoulders fully externally rotated, 90° abducted, and slightly horizontally abducted. Elbows flexed to 90° and patient opens/closes hands for 3 minutes slowly.

(3) Neurological and/or vascular symptoms (disappearance of pulse) will be reproduced in upper extremity.

(4) SN and SP not available.

o. Upper limb tension tests (see Table 1-14).

(1) Evaluation of peripheral nerve compression.

(2) Neurological symptoms will be reproduced in upper extremity.

p. Hawkins-Kennedy (impingement) test.

(1) Identifies subacromial impingement.

(2) The examiner places the patient's shoulder into 90° of shoulder flexion with the elbow flexed

Table 1-14

Neurodynamic Tension Tests: Upper Limb Tension Test (ULTT)

	ULTT1 *(MEDIAN AND ANTERIOR INTEROSSEOUS NERVE BIAS)*	ULTT2 *(MEDIAN, AXILLARY, AND MUSCULOCUTANEOUS NERVE BIAS)*	ULTT3 *(RADIAL NERVE BIAS)*	ULTT4 *(ULNAR NERVE BIAS)*
Shoulder	Depression and abduction (110°)	Depression and abduction (10°)	Depression and abduction (10°)	Depression and abduction (10° to 90°) with hand to ear (waiter's position)
Elbow	Extension	Extension	Extension	Flexion
Forearm	Supination	Supination	Pronation	Supination
Wrist	Extension	Extension	Flexion and ulnar deviation	Extension and radial deviation
Fingers and thumb	Extension	Extension	Flexion	Extension
Shoulder		Lateral rotation	Medial rotation	Lateral rotation
Cervical Spine	Contralateral side flexion	Contralateral side flexion	Contralateral side flexion	Contralateral side flexion

Adapted from Magee D: Orthopedic Physical Assessment, 3rd ed. Saunders 1997, p 148.

to 90°. The therapist then passively, internally rotates the patient's arm.

(3) If the patient has pain with internal rotation, the test is considered positive.

(4) SN 92.1%; SP 25%; (+LR) 1.23; (−LR) 0.32.

q. Allen's maneuver.

(1) Identifies the presence of thoracic outlet syndrome (TOS).

(2) The test is best performed with the patient in a relaxed, sitting position. The arm to be tested should be in 90° of abduction and full ER. The elbow should be in 90° of flexion. The patient rotates the head to the side opposite the arm being tested while the examiner palpates the radial pulse. The examiner can also palpate the radial pulse continuously as the patient moves from having the arm in a neutral position as the patient moves the arm and head into the end position of the test.

(3) The test is considered positive if the radial pulse becomes diminished or absent after rotation of the head.

(4) SN and SP not available.

r. Active compression (labrum).

(1) Identifies the presence of a labral tear or acromioclavicular lesion.

(2) Sitting or standing. The patient is instructed to place the shoulder into 90° of flexion and 10° of adduction. Next, the arm is actively, internally rotated so the thumb is pointing downward. The instructor then applies an inferior directed force (into shoulder extension), first with the thumb pointing down and a second time with the thumb pointing up.

(3) Test is considered positive for an acromioclavicular lesion if the patient has localized pain in the acromioclavicular joint with the thumb pointing down and a decrease in pain with the thumb pointing up (supinates the forearm). Test is considered positive for a labral tear if the patient reports a painful clicking in the joint with the thumb pointed down, which is reduced or eliminated when the patient resists the inferior force with the thumb up (supinates the forearm).

(4) Acromioclavicular lesions SN 41%–100%; SP 95%–97%; (+LR) 8.2–33.3; (−LR) −0.62. Labral tear SN 63%–100%; SP 73%–98%; (+LR) 2.3–50.0; (−LR) 0.0–0.51.

s. Rent sign.

(1) Identifies a torn rotator cuff or rotator cuff impingement.

(2) Patient seated with arm relaxed and examiner stands to the rear of the patient. Examiner palpates anterior to the anterior edge of the acromion with one hand while holding the patient's flexed elbow with the other. Examiner passively extends the shoulder while slowly rotating the shoulder into external and internal rotation.

(3) The greater tuberosity will be prominent and a depression of about 1 finger width will be felt if a rotator cuff tear is present.

(4) SN 91%–96%; SP 75%–97%.

t. Crank test (see Figure 1-26).

(1) Test is used to evaluate the different glenohumeral ligaments or identify anterior shoulder instability. May also be used to identify a labral tear.

(2) Patient standing, the examiner places the distal hand on the subject's elbow and the proximal hand on the subject's proximal humerus and then passively elevates the subjects shoulder to 160° in the scapular plane. With the distal hand, the examiner applies a load along the long axis of the humerus while the proximal hand externally and internally rotates the humerus.

(3) The test is considered positive if pain with or without a click is present in the shoulder.

(4) SN 90%; SP 85%.

u. Biceps load 2.

(1) Identifies the presence of glenohumeral labral tears (SLAP lesion).

(2) Supine. The examiner brings the patient's shoulder into 120° abduction, maximal ER, 90° of elbow flexion, and forearm supination. The examiner holds onto the patient's wrist with one hand and stabilizes the elbow with the second hand. The patient is then instructed to perform elbow flexion against the examiner's resistance.

(3) The test is considered positive if symptoms increase during the resisted biceps contraction.

(4) SN 89.7%; SP 96.9%; (+LR) 30; (−LR) 0.10.

v. Bear hug test.

(1) Identifies for presence of a subscapularis tear.

(2) Patient sitting or standing with their hand placed on the opposite shoulder with the elbow anterior to the body. The examiner then applies an ER force while the patient attempts to maintain the hand on the shoulder.

(3) Test is considered positive if patient cannot hold the hand against the shoulder as examiner applies an ER force.

(4) SN 60%; SP 92%; (+LR) 7.5; (−LR) 0.43.

w. Belly compression test.

(1) Identifies a subscapularis lesion—especially for patients who cannot medially rotate the shoulder enough to take it behind the back.

(2) Patient sitting or standing and the examiner places a hand on the abdomen so that the he

or she can feel how much pressure the patient is applying to the abdomen. The patient places his or her hand of the shoulder being tested on the examiner's hand and pushes as hard as he or she can into the stomach. The patient also attempts to bring the elbow forward in the scapular plane causing greater medial shoulder rotation.

(3) Test is positive if the patient is unable to maintain the pressure on the examiner's hand while moving the elbow forward or if the patient extends the shoulder.

(4) SN 40%; SP 98%.

x. Horizontal adduction (acromioclavicular joint) test.

(1) Identifies the presence of AC joint dysfunction or subacromial impingement.

(2) The examiner should stand behind the patient on the side being tested. Grasp the patient's arm just distal to the elbow and passively flex the patient's shoulder to 90°. Then maximally adduct the patient's shoulder (bring it across their body toward the other shoulder).

(3) A positive test is considered if the patient reports pain during the adduction motion or localized pain in the acromioclavicular joint.

(4) SN 82%; SP 27.7%.

2. Elbow special tests.

a. Ligament instability tests (medial and lateral stability).

(1) Identifies ligament laxity or restriction.

(2) Patient sitting or supine. Entire upper limb is supported and stabilized and elbow placed in 20°–0° of flexion. Valgus force placed through elbow tests ulnar collateral ligament. Varus force placed through elbow tests radial collateral ligament.

(3) Primary finding is laxity, but pain may be noted as well.

(4) SN and SP not available.

b. Lateral epicondylitis and epicondylopathy ("tennis elbow") test (see Figure 1-27).

(1) Identifies lateral epicondylopathy (although the test name is "epicondylitis," it is assessing for what is currently referred to as an epicondylosis/epicondylopathy).

(2) Patient sitting with elbow in 90° flexion and supported/stabilized. Resist wrist extension, wrist radial deviation, and forearm pronation with fingers fully flexed (fist) simultaneously.

(3) Reproduces pain at lateral epicondyle.

(4) SN and SP not available.

c. Medial epicondylitis ("golfer's elbow") test.

(1) Identifies medial epicondylopathy (although the test name is "epicondylitis," it is assessing for what is currently referred to as an epicondylosis/epicondylopathy).

(2) Patient sitting with elbow in 90° flexion and supported/stabilized. Passively supinate forearm, extend elbow, and extend wrist.

(3) Reproduces pain at medial epicondyle.

(4) SN and SP not available.

d. Tinel's sign.

(1) Identifies dysfunction of ulnar nerve at olecranon.

(2) Tap region where the ulnar nerve passes through cubital tunnel.

(3) Reproduces a tingling sensation in ulnar distribution.

(4) SN and SP not available.

e. Pronator teres syndrome test.

(1) Identifies a median nerve entrapment within pronator teres.

(2) Patient sitting with elbow in 90° flexion and supported/stabilized. Resist forearm pronation and elbow extension simultaneously.

(3) Reproduces a tingling or paresthesia within median nerve distribution.

(4) SN and SP not available.

f. Elbow flexion test.

(1) Identifies the presence of cubital tunnel syndrome.

(2) Patient supine. Performed bilaterally with the shoulder in full ER and the elbow actively held in maximal flexion with wrist extension for one minute.

(3) Positive if pain is present at the medial aspect of the elbow and numbness and tingling in the ulnar distribution on the involved side.

(4) SN 75%; SP 99%.

3. Wrist and hand special tests.

a. Finkelstein's test (see Figure 1-28).

(1) Identifies de Quervain's tenosynovitis (paratendonitis of the abductor pollicis longus and/or extensor pollicis brevis).

(2) Patient makes fist with thumb within confines of fingers. Passively move wrist into ulnar deviation.

(3) Reproduces pain in wrist. Often painful with no pathology, so compare to uninvolved side.

(4) SN 81%; SP 50%.

b. Bunnel-Littler test.

(1) Identifies tightness in structures surrounding the MCP joints.

(2) MCP joint is stabilized in slight extension while PIP joint is flexed. Then MCP joint is flexed and PIP joint is flexed.

(3) Differentiates between a tight capsule and tight intrinsic muscles. If flexion is limited in both cases, capsule is tight. If more PIP flexion

with MCP flexion, then intrinsic muscles are tight.
(4) SN and SP not available.

c. Tight retinacular test (see Figure 1-29).
(1) Identifies tightness around proximal interphalangeal joint.
(2) PIP is stabilized in neutral while DIP is flexed. Then PIP is flexed and DIP is flexed.
(3) Differentiates between a tight capsule and tight retinacular ligaments. If flexion is limited in both cases, capsule is tight. If more DIP flexion with PIP flexion, then retinacular ligaments are tight.
(4) SN and SP not available.

d. Ligamentous instability tests (medial and lateral stability).
(1) Identifies ligament laxity or restriction.
(2) Fingers are supported and stabilized. Valgus and varus forces applied to PIP joints all digits. Repeated at DIP joints.
(3) Primary finding is laxity, but pain may be noted as well.
(4) SN and SP not available.

e. Froment's sign.
(1) Identifies ulnar nerve dysfunction.
(2) Patient grasps paper between first and second digits of hand. Pull paper out and look for IP flexion of thumb, which is compensation due to weakness of adductor pollicis.
(3) Patient unable to perform test without compensating may indicate ulnar nerve dysfunction.
(4) SN and SP not available.

f. Tinel's sign.
(1) Identifies carpal tunnel compression of median nerve.
(2) Tap region where median nerve passes through carpal tunnel.
(3) Reproduces tingling and/or paresthesia into hand following median nerve distribution.
(4) SN and SP not available.

g. Phalen's test (see Figure 1-30).
(1) Identifies carpal tunnel compression of median nerve.
(2) Patient maximally flexes both wrists holding them against each other for 1 minute.
(3) Reproduces tingling and/or paresthesia into hand following median nerve distribution.
(4) SN 77%; SP 40%.

h. Two-point discrimination test.
(1) Identifies level of sensory innervation within hand that correlates with functional ability to perform certain tasks involving grasp.
(2) Patient sitting with hand stabilized. Using a caliper, two-point discriminator, or paper clip, apply device to palmar aspect of fingers to assess patient's ability to distinguish between two points of testing device. Record smallest difference that patient can sense two separate points.
(3) Normal amount that can be discriminated is generally less than 6 mm.
(4) SN 64%; SP 64%.

i. Allen's test (see Figure 1-31).
(1) Identifies vascular compromise.
(2) Identify radial and ulnar arteries at wrist. Have patient open/close fingers quickly several times and then make a closed fist. Compress the ulnar artery and have patient open hand. Observe palm of hand and then release the compression on artery and observe for vascular filling. Perform same procedure with radial artery.
(3) Positive finding will present by abnormal filling of blood within hand during test. Under normal circumstances, there is a change in color from white to normal appearance on palm of hand.
(4) SN 73%; SP 97%.

j. Flick test.
(1) Identifies carpal tunnel syndrome.
(2) With patient sitting or standing, patient moves hand like shaking down a thermometer.
(3) Patient performs the shaking motion to reduce the symptoms in the wrist.
(4) SN 90%; SP 30%.

Special Tests of the Lower Extremity

1. Hip special tests.

a. Patrick's (FABER) test (see Figure 1-32).
(1) Identifies dysfunction of hip, such as mobility restriction.
(2) Patient lies supine. Passively flex, abduct, and externally rotate test leg so that foot is resting just above knee on opposite leg. Slowly lower testing leg down toward table surface.
(3) Positive test when involved knee is unable to assume relaxed position and/or reproduction of painful symptoms.
(4) SN 60%; SP 18%; (+LR) 0.73; (−LR) 2.2.

b. Grind (Scouring) test (see Figure 1-33).
(1) Identifies degenerative joint disease (DJD) of hip joint.
(2) Patient supine with hip in 90° flexion and knee maximally flexed. Place compressive load into femur via knee joint, thereby loading hip joint.
(3) May reproduce pain within hip joint and refer pain to the knee and elsewhere.
(4) SN 62%; SP 75%; (+LR) 2.54; (−LR) 0.51.

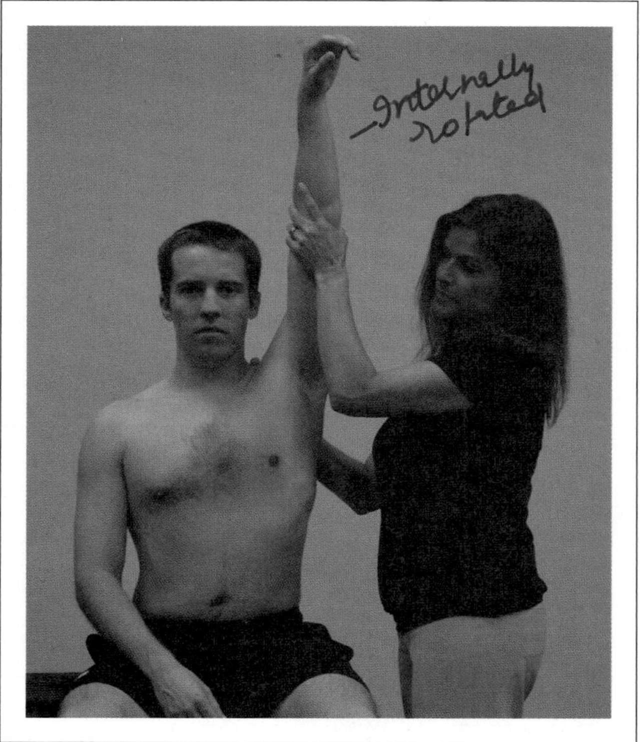

Figure 1-22 **Neer's test.**

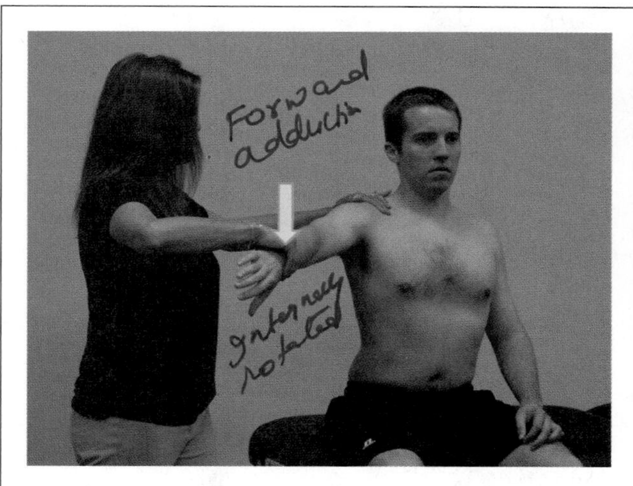

Figure 1-23 **Supraspinatus (empty can) test.**

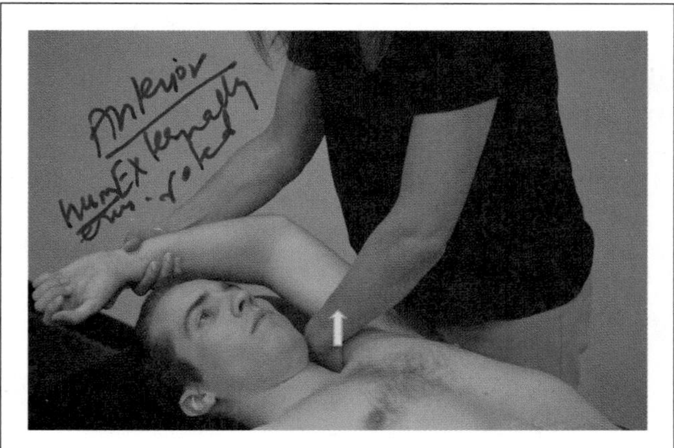

Figure 1-24 **Clunk test.**

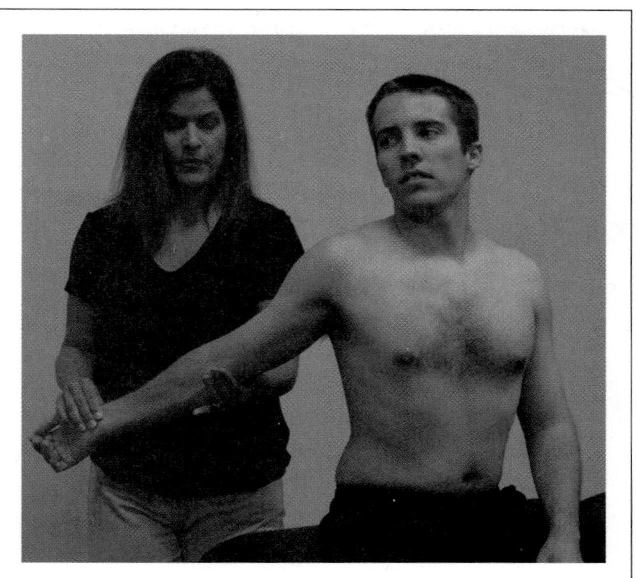

Figure 1-25 **Adson's test.**

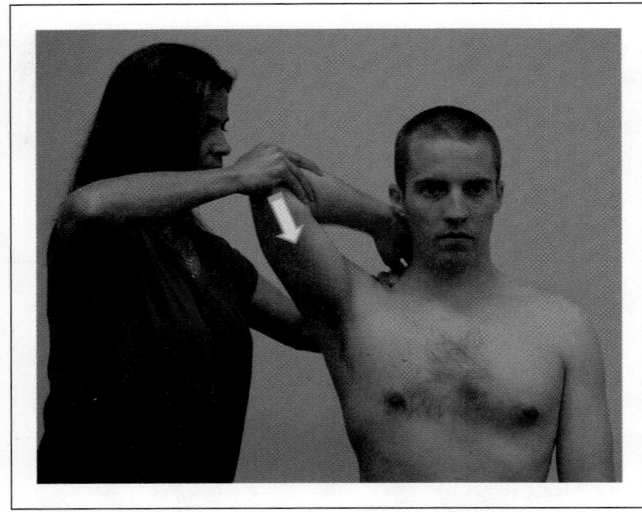

Figure 1-26 Crank test.

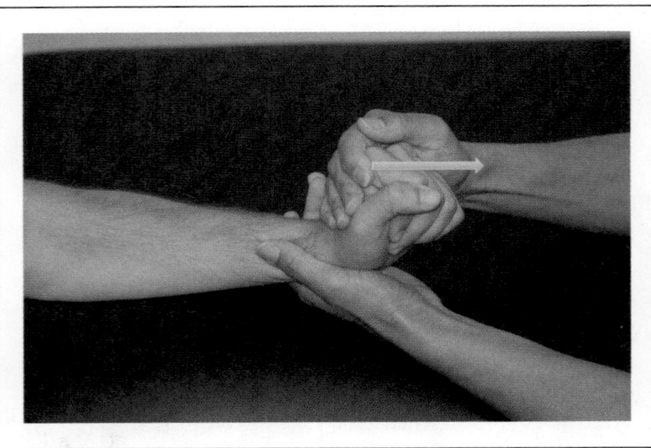

Figure 1-27 Lateral epicondylitis and epicondylopathy ("tennis elbow") test.

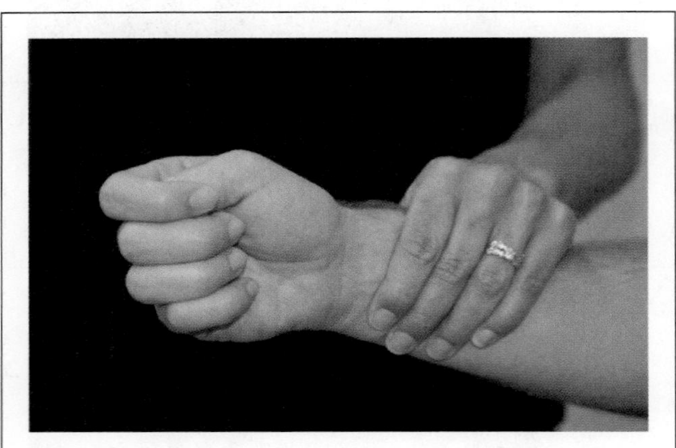

Figure 1-28a Finkelstein's test; start position.

Figure 1-28b Finkelstein's test; passive movement into ulnar deviation.

Figure 1-29a Tight retinacular test.

Figure 1-29b Tight retinacular test.

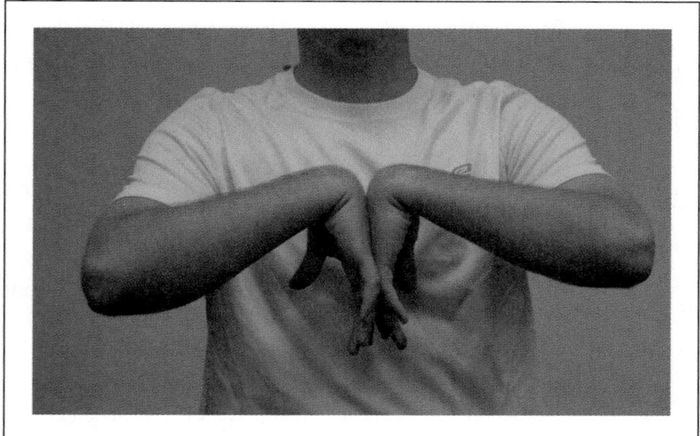

Figure 1-30 Phalen's test.

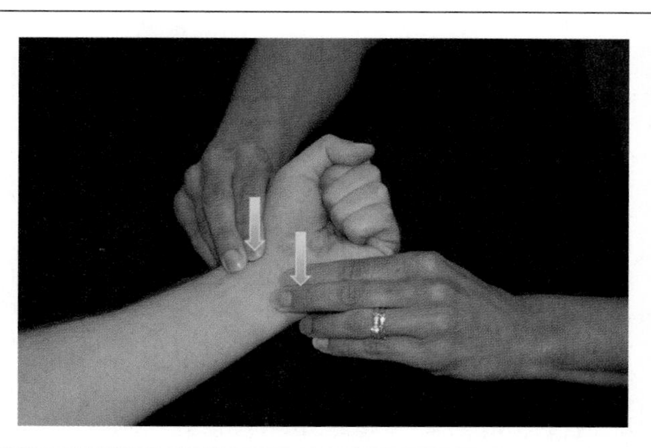

Figure 1-31a Allen test; compress ulnar and radial arteries.

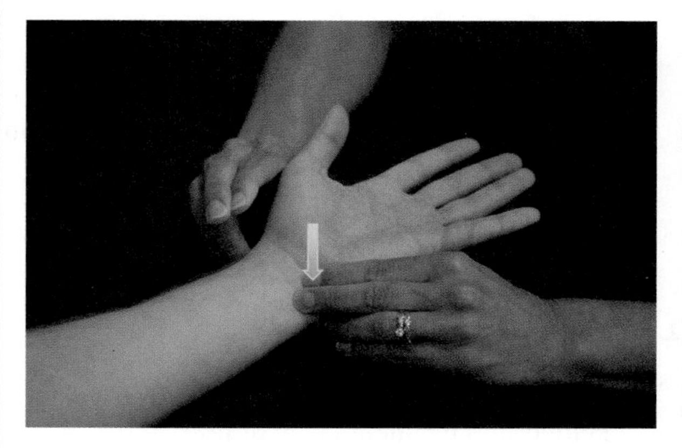

Figure 1-31b Allen test; compress ulnar artery.

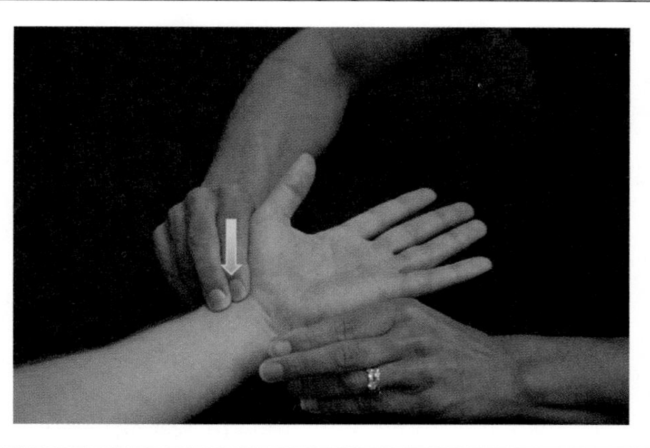

Figure 1-31c Allen test; compress radial artery.

c. Trendelenburg sign (see Figure 1-34).
   (1) Identifies weakness of gluteus medius or unstable hip.
   (2) Patient standing and asked to stand on one leg (flex opposite knee). Observe pelvis of stance leg.
   (3) Positive when ipsilateral pelvis drops when lower limb support is removed while standing.
   (4) SN 23%; SP 94%; (+LR) 3.64; (–LR) 0.82.
d. Thomas test (see Figure 1-35).
   (1) Identifies tightness of hip flexors.
   (2) Patient supine with one hip and knee maximally flexed to chest and held there. Opposite limb is kept straight on table. Observe whether hip flexion occurs on straight leg as opposite limb is flexed.
   (3) Weakness of test is that it does not differentiate between tightness in iliacus versus psoas major.
   (4) Positive if straight limb's hip flexes and/or patient is unable to remain flat on table when opposite limb is flexed.
   (5) SN and SP not available.
e. Ober's test (see Figures 1-36 and 1-37).
   (1) Identifies tightness of tensor fascia lata and/or iliotibial band.
   (2) Patient lying on side, with lower limb flexed at hip and knee. Passively extend and abduct testing hip with knee flexed to 90°. Modified Ober's test starts with knee extended. Slowly lower uppermost limb and observe if it goes below the horizontal or reaches table.
   (3) Positive if uppermost limb is unable to go below the horizontal or rest on table.
   (4) SN and SP not available.
f. Ely's test (see Figure 1-38).
   (1) Identifies tightness of rectus femoris.
   (2) Patient prone, with knee of testing limb flexed. Observe hip of testing limb.
   (3) Positive if hip of testing limb flexes.
   (4) SN and SP not available.
g. 90–90 hamstring test.
   (1) Identifies tightness of hamstrings.
   (2) Patient supine with hip and knee of testing limb supported in 90° flexion. Passively extend knee of testing limb until a barrier is encountered.
   (3) Positive if knee is unable to reach 10° from neutral position (lacking 10° of extension).
   (4) SN and SP not available.
h. Piriformis test.
   (1) Identifies piriformis syndrome.
   (2) Patient supine, with foot of test leg passively placed lateral to opposite limb's knee. Testing hip is adducted. Observe position of testing knee relative to opposite knee.
   (3) Positive if testing knee is unable to pass over resting knee, and/or reproduction of pain in buttock, and/or along sciatic nerve distribution.
   (4) SN and SP not available.
i. Leg length test.
   (1) Identifies true leg length discrepancy.
   (2) Patient supine, with pelvis balanced/aligned with lower limbs and trunk. Measure distance from ASIS to lateral malleolus or medial malleolus on each limb several times for consistency and compare results. Unequal girth of the thigh musculature (left versus right) can skew results if using medial malleolus landmark.
   (3) A difference in lengths between two limbs identifies a true leg length discrepancy. This test will determine whether the limb discrepancy is true or functional. True discrepancy is caused by an anatomical difference in bone lengths (either tibia or femur). Functional discrepancies are not anatomical in origin, and are the result of compensation due to abnormal position or posture, such as pronation of a foot or pelvic obliquity.
   (4) SN and SP not available.
j. Craig's test.
   (1) Identifies abnormal femoral antetorsion angle.
   (2) Patient prone with knee flexed to 90°. Palpate greater trochanter and slowly move hip through internal/ER. When greater trochanter feels most lateral, stop and measure the angle of leg relative to a line perpendicular with table surface.
   (3) Based on findings, patient may have an anteverted or retroverted hip. Normal angle is between 8° and 15° hip internal rotation. Less than 8° indicates a retroverted hip, and greater than 15° indicates an anteverted hip.
   (4) SN and SP not available.
k. FADDIR/FADIR test (flexion, adduction, internal rotation; see Figure 1-39).
   (1) Identifies anterior-superior impingement, iliopsoas tendonopathy, and anterior labral tears.
   (2) Patient in supine and the involved lower extremity is taken from full passive hip flexion, abduction, and ER into a flexed, adducted, and internally rotated position.
   (3) Positive test is reproduction of pain with or without click.
   (4) SN 78%; SP 10%; (+LR) 0.86; (–LR) 2.3.

2. Knee special tests.
   a. Collateral ligament instability tests (medial and lateral stability).
      (1) Identifies ligament laxity or restriction.
      (2) Patient is supine. Entire lower limb is supported and stabilized and knee placed in 20°–30° of flexion. Valgus force placed through knee tests

medial collateral ligament. Varus force placed through knee tests lateral collateral ligament.
   (3) Primary finding is laxity, but pain may be noted as well.
   (4) Valgus at 30° with pain (+LR) 2.3; (−LR) 0.30; Valgus at 30° with laxity (+LR) 1.8; (−LR) 0.20.

b. Lachman stress test (see Figure 1-40).
   (1) Indicates integrity of anterior cruciate ligament.
   (2) Patient supine, with testing knee flexed 20°–30°. Stabilize femur and passively try to glide tibia anterior.
   (3) Positive finding is excessive anterior glide of tibia.
   (4) SN 48%–100%; SP 46%–100%.

c. Pivot shift (anterolateral rotary instability).
   (1) Indicates integrity of anterior cruciate ligament.
   (2) Patient supine, with testing knee in extension, hip flexed and abducted 30° with slight internal rotation. Hold knee with one hand and foot with other hand. Place valgus force through knee and flex knee.
   (3) Positive finding is ligament laxity as indicated by tibia relocating during the test. As knee is flexed, the tibia clunks backward at approximately 30°–40°. The tibia at beginning of test was subluxed, and then was reduced by pull of iliotibial band as knee was flexed.
   (4) SN 16%–93%; SP 89%–100%.

d. Posterior sag test.
   (1) Indicates integrity of posterior cruciate ligament.
   (2) Patient supine with testing hip flexed to 45° and knee flexed to 90°. Observe to see whether tibia "sags" posteriorly in this position.
   (3) Positive finding is sag of tibia relative to femur.
   (4) SN 78.9%; SP 100%.

e. Posterior drawer test.
   (1) Indicates integrity of posterior cruciate ligament.
   (2) Patient supine and testing hip flexed to 45° and knee flexed to 90°. Passively glide tibia posteriorly following the joint plane.
   (3) Positive finding is excessive posterior glide.
   (4) SN 89.5%; SP 98.2%.

f. Reverse Lachman.
   (1) Indicates integrity of posterior cruciate ligament.
   (2) Patient prone with knees flexed to 30°. Stabilize femur and passively try to glide tibia posterior.
   (3) Positive finding is ligament laxity.
   (4) SN and SP not available.

g. McMurray's test (see Figure 1-41).
   (1) Identifies meniscal tears.
   (2) Patient supine, with testing knee in maximal flexion. Passively, internally rotate and extend the knee. This tests lateral meniscus. Test medial meniscus with same procedure, except rotate tibia into lateral rotation.
   (3) Positive finding is reproduction of click and/or pain in knee joint.
   (4) Medial SN 64.7%; SP 93.2%; Lateral SN 51.6%; SP 93.5%.

h. Apley test (see Figure 1-42).
   (1) Helps differentiate between meniscal tears and ligamentous lesions.
   (2) Patient prone, with testing knee flexed to 90°. Stabilize patient's thigh to table with your knee. Passively distract the knee joint, then slowly rotate tibia internally and externally. Next, apply a compressive load to knee joint and again slowly rotate tibia internally and externally.
   (3) Pain or decreased motion during compression indicates a meniscal dysfunction. If pain or increased motion occurs during the distraction, then it is most likely a ligamentous dysfunction.
   (4) (+LR) 1.8; (−LR) 0.89.

i. Hughston's plica test.
   (1) Identifies dysfunction of the plica.
   (2) Patient is supine and testing knee is flexed with tibia internally rotated. Passively glide the patella medially, while palpating the medial femoral condyle. Feel for popping as you passively flex and extend the knee.
   (3) Positive finding is pain and/or "popping" noted during the test.
   (4) SN acute 23%; subacute 33%; chronic 89.8%.

j. Patellar apprehension test.
   (1) Indicates past history of patella dislocation.
   (2) Patient supine, with patella passively glided laterally.
   (3) Patient does not allow and/or does not like patella to move in lateral direction to simulate subluxation/dislocation.
   (4) (+LR) 8.3; (−LR) 0.0.

k. Clarke's sign.
   (1) Indicates patellofemoral dysfunction.
   (2) Patient supine, with knee in extension resting on table. Push posterior on superior pole of patella, then ask patient to perform an active contraction of the quadriceps muscle.
   (3) Pain is produced in knee as a result of the test.
   (4) (+LR) 1.94; (−LR) 0.69.

l. Ballotable patella (patellar tap test).
   (1) Indicates infrapatellar effusion.
   (2) Patient supine, with knee in extension resting on table. Apply a soft tap over the central patella.
   (3) Positive finding is perception of the patella floating ("dancing patella" sign).
   (4) (+LR) 1.6; (−LR) 0.30.

m. Fluctuation test.
  (1) Indicates knee joint effusion.
  (2) Patient supine, with knee in extension resting on table. Place one hand over suprapatellar pouch and other over anterior aspect of knee joint. Alternate pushing down with one hand at a time.
  (3) Positive finding is fluctuation (movement) of fluid noted during the test.
  (4) SN and SP not available.

n. Q-angle measurement.
  (1) Measurement of angle between the quadriceps muscle and the patellar tendon.
  (2) Normal is 13° for men and 18° for women.
  (3) Angles less than or greater than normal may be indicative of knee dysfunction and/or biomechanical dysfunctions within the lower limb.
  (4) SN and SP not available.

o. Noble compression test (see Figure 1-43).
  (1) Identifies whether distal iliotibial (IT) band friction syndrome is present.
  (2) Patient supine, with hip flexed to 45° and knee flexed to 90°. Apply pressure to lateral femoral epicondyle then extend knee.
  (3) Reproduces same pain over lateral femoral condyle. Patient will complain of pain over lateral femoral epicondyle at approximately 30° flexion.
  (4) SN and SP not available.

p. Tinel's sign.
  (1) Identifies dysfunction of common fibular nerve posterior to fibular head following common fibular nerve distribution.
  (2) Tap region where common fibular nerve passes through posterior to fibular head.
  (3) Reproduces tingling and/or paresthesia into leg.
  (4) SN and SP not available.

q. Wilson test.
  (1) Identifies osteochondritis dissecans of the medial femoral condyle.
  (2) Patient sitting on edge of table. Patient actively extends knee with medial rotation of tibia.
  (3) Positive if pain is present at 30° with medial rotation but no pain at 30° with lateral tibial rotation.
  (4) SN and SP not available.

3. Ankle and foot special tests.

a. Neutral subtalar positioning.
  (1) Examination identifies abnormal rearfoot to forefoot positioning.
  (2) Patient prone, with foot over edge of table. Palpate dorsal aspect of talus on both sides with one hand, and grasp lateral forefoot with other hand. Gently dorsiflex foot until resistance is felt, then gently move foot through arc of supination and pronation.
  (3) Neutral position is point at which you feel foot fall off easier to one side or other. At this point, compare rearfoot to forefoot and rearfoot to leg.
  (4) SN and SP not available.

b. Anterior drawer test.
  (1) Identifies ligamentous instability (particularly anterior talofibular ligament).
  (2) Patient supine, with heel just off edge of table in 20° plantar flexion. Stabilize lower leg and grasp foot. Pull talus anterior.
  (3) Positive finding if talus has excessive anterior glide and/or pain is noted.
  (4) SN 78%; SP 75%.

c. Talar tilt.
  (1) Identifies ligamentous instability (particularly calcaneofibular ligament).
  (2) Patient side-lying, with knee slightly flexed and ankle in neutral. Move foot into adduction testing calcaneofibular ligament and into abduction testing deltoid ligament.
  (3) Positive finding if excessive adduction or abduction occurs and/or pain is noted.
  (4) SN 67%; SP 75%.

d. Thompson's test (see Figure 1-44).
  (1) Evaluates integrity of the Achilles' tendon.
  (2) Patient prone, with foot off edge of table. Squeeze calf muscles.
  (3) No movement of foot while squeezing calf indicates positive finding of lack of integrity.
  (4) SN 40%; SP unknown.

e. Tinel's sign.
  (1) Identifies dysfunction of posterior tibial nerve posterior to the medial malleolus or deep fibular nerve anterior to talocrural joint.
  (2) Patient supine with foot supported on the table. Tap over region of posterior tibial nerve as it passes posterior to medial malleolus. Tap over region of deep fibular nerve as it passes under dorsal retinaculum (anterior to ankle joint).
  (3) Reproduces tingling and/or paresthesia into the respective nerve distributions.
  (4) SN 58%; SP unknown.

f. Morton's test.
  (1) Identifies stress fracture or neuroma in forefoot.
  (2) Patient supine, with foot supported on table. Grasp around metatarsal heads and squeeze.
  (3) Positive finding is pain in forefoot.
  (4) SN and SP not available.

g. Kleiger test.
  (1) Identifies integrity of the distal tibiofibular syndesmosis.
  (2) Patient is seated on the edge of the table with knee flexed to 90°. Examiner applies an ER force to the foot while holding tibia in neutral position.

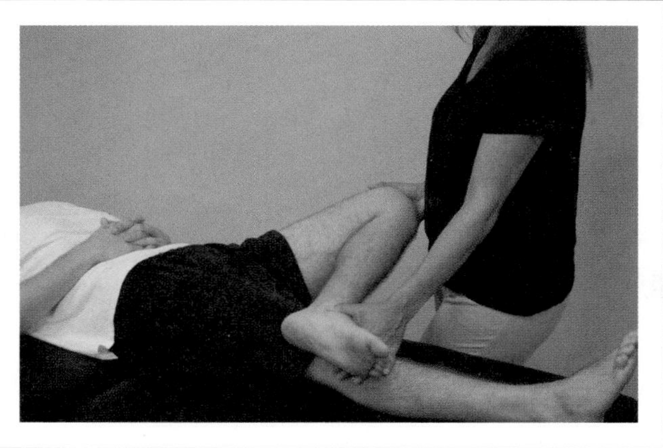

Figure 1-32 Patrick's (FABER) test.

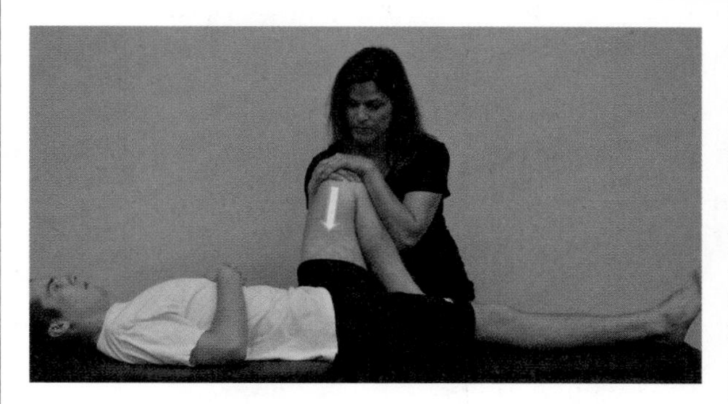

Figure 1-33 Grind (Scouring) test.

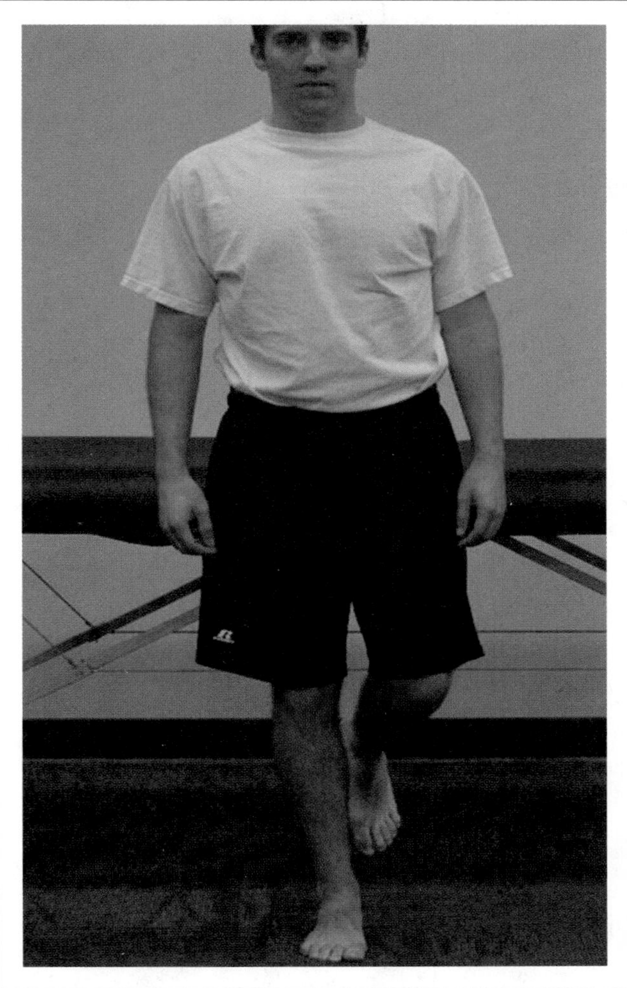

Figure 1-34a Trendelenburg sign; negative test.

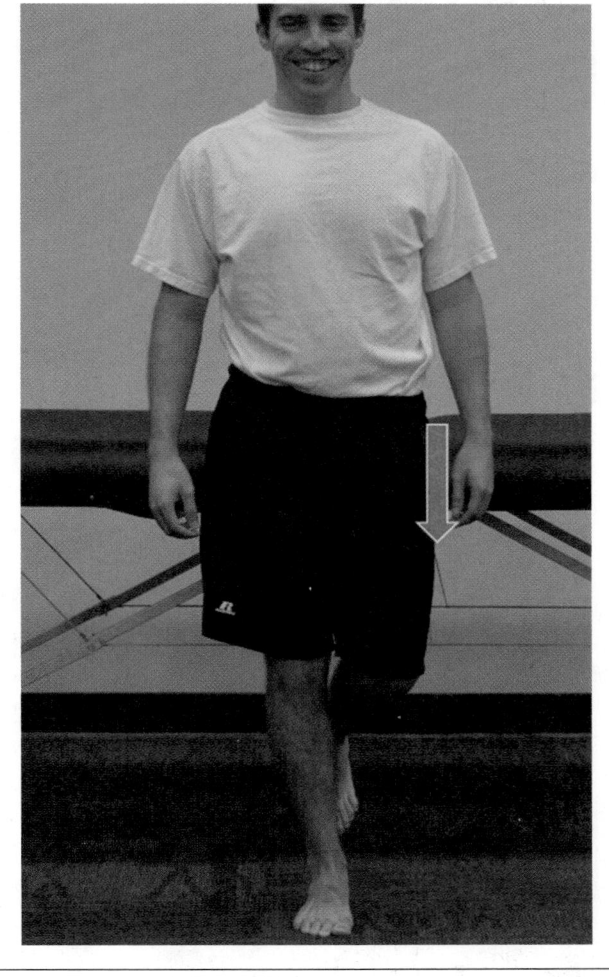

Figure 1-34b Trendelenburg sign; positive test; dropped pelvis.

Figure 1-35a Thomas test; negative.

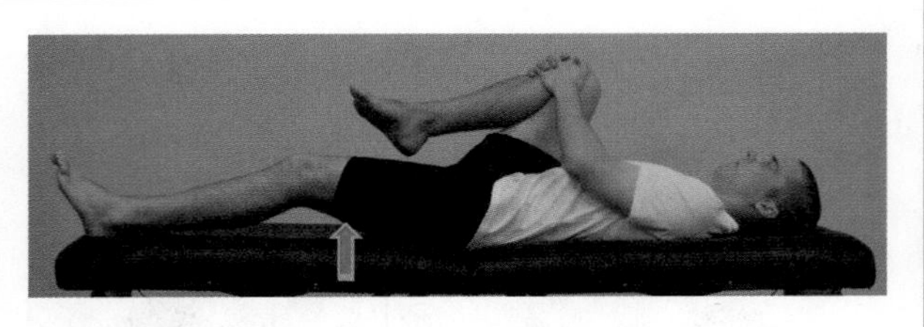

Figure 1-35b Thomas test; positive.

Figure 1-36 Ober test.

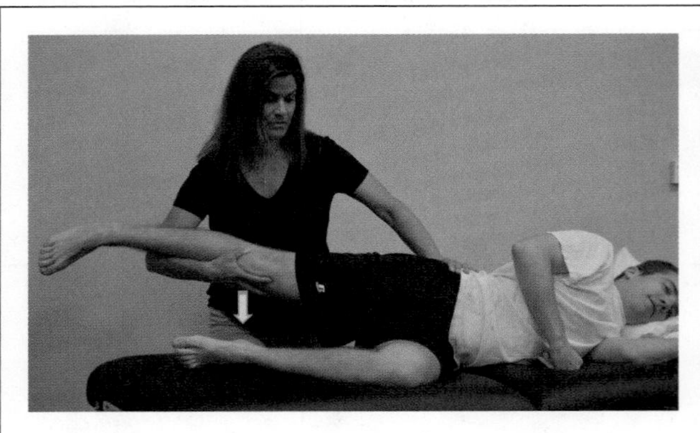

Figure 1-37 Modified Ober test.

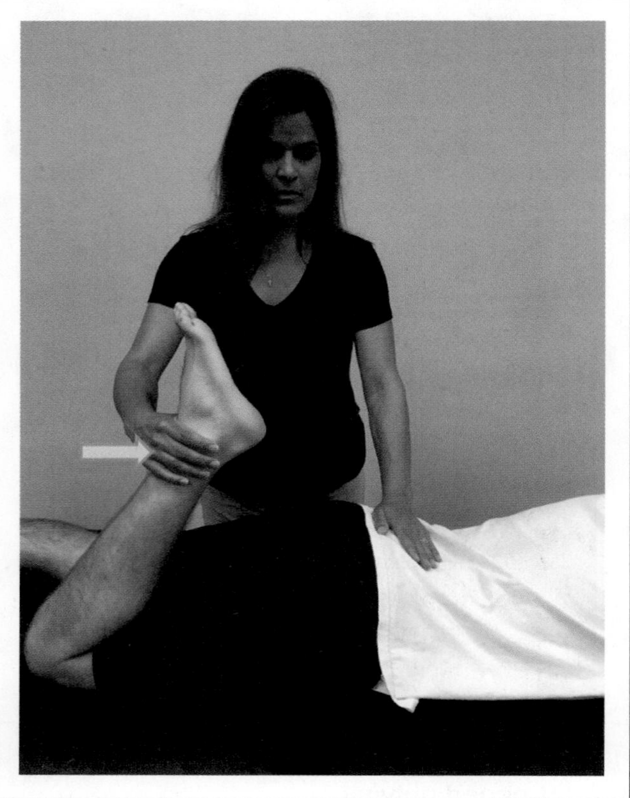

Figure 1-38a Ely's test; negative.

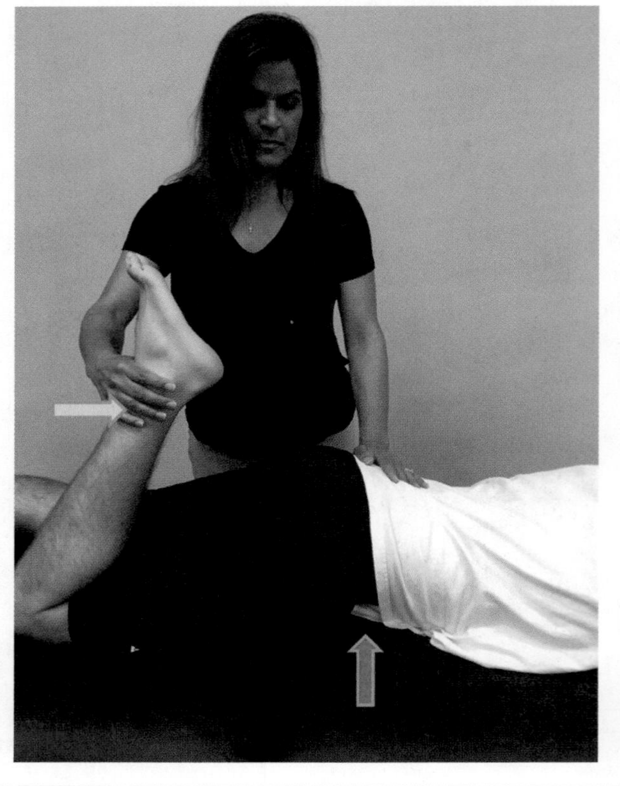

Figure 1-38b Ely's test; positive.

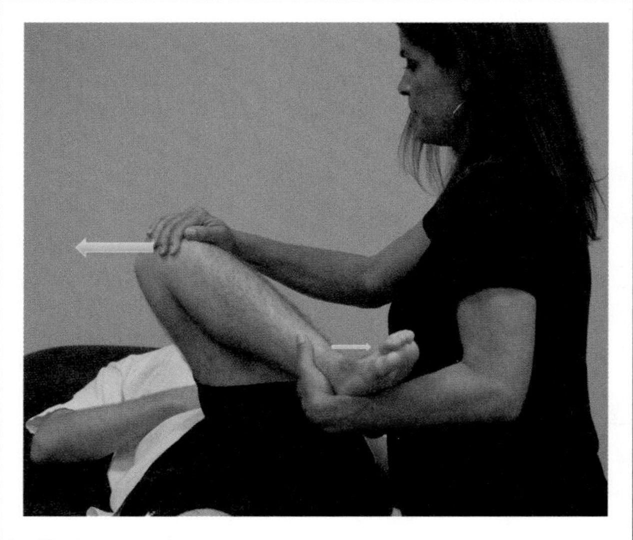

Figure 1-39 **FADDIR/FADIR test.**

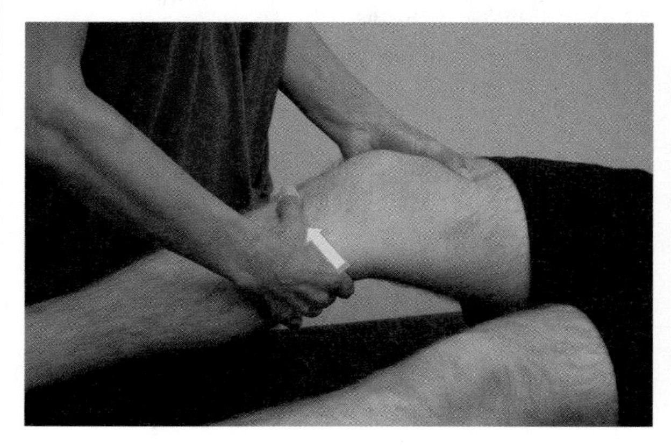

Figure 1-40 **Lachman stress test.**

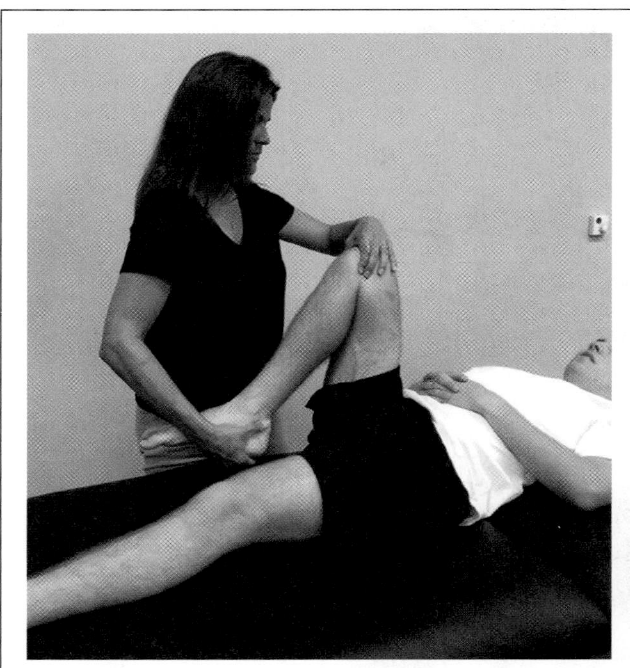

Figure 1-41a **McMurray's test; knee flexion.**

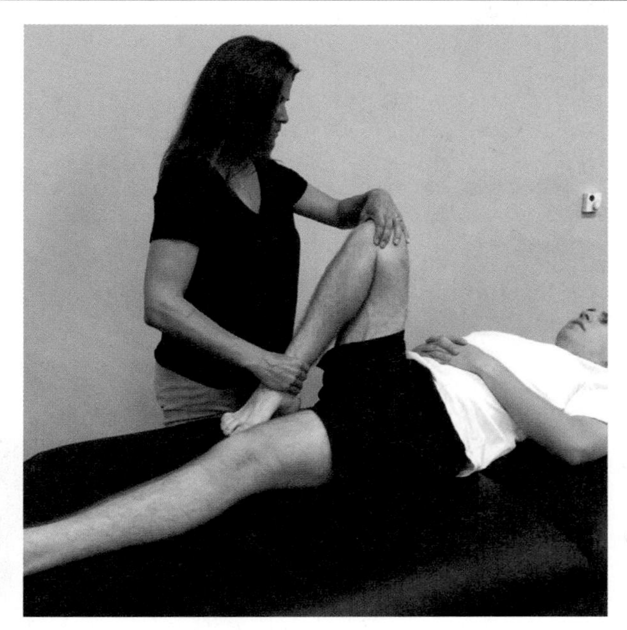

Figure 1-41b **McMurray's test; tibial internal rotation.**

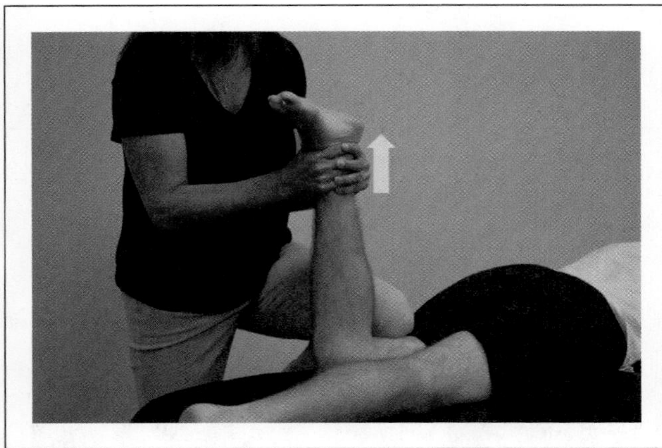

Figure 1-42a Apley test; distraction.

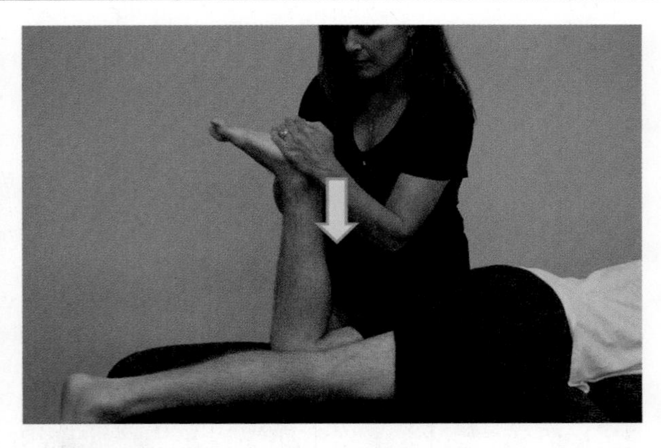

Figure 1-42b Apley test; compression.

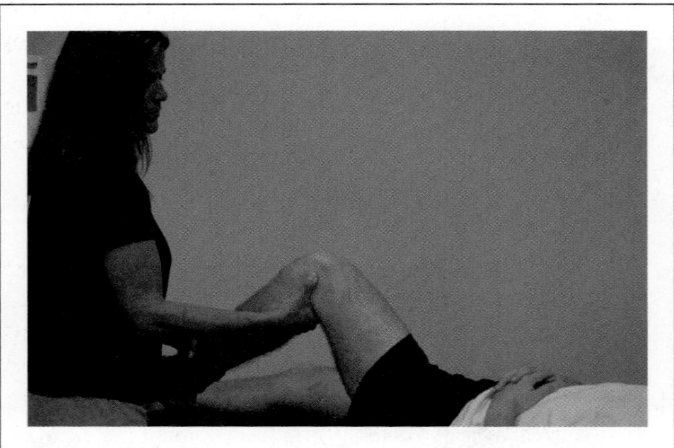

Figure 1-43a Noble compression test; hip and knee flexion.

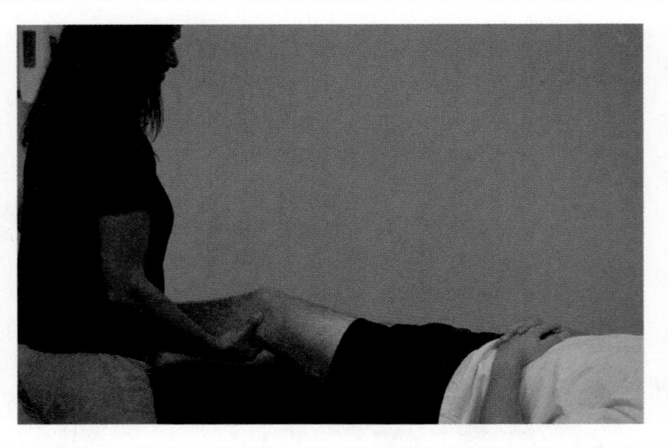

Figure 1-43b Noble compression test; knee extension and pressure.

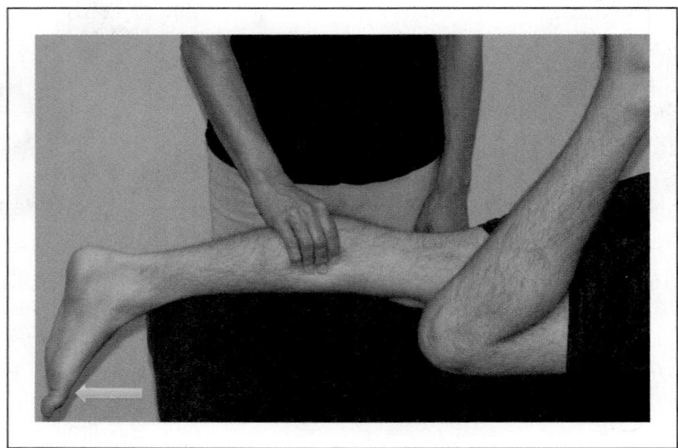

Figure 1-44 Thompson's test.

(3) Positive if symptoms or visible joint gapping are reproduced.
(4) SN and SP not available.

h. Windlass.
(1) Identifies windlass effect of plantar fascia.
(2) Weight-bearing test. Patient stands on step with toes positioned over the edge of the step and equal weight bearing. The examiner then passively extends the patient's first MTP joint. Non–weight-bearing test. The patient is seated in non–weight-bearing position with the knee flexed to 90°. The examiner stabilizes the ankle and passively extends the patient's first MTP joint.
(3) A positive test is the reproduction of plantar surface symptoms. (In a non–weight-bearing test, the symptoms occur at the end of range of motion.)
(4) SN 100%; SP 32%.

Special Tests of the Spine, Pelvis, and Temporomandibular Joint

Peat x

1. Cervical special tests.
a. Vertebral artery test.
(1) Assesses the integrity of the vertebrobasilar vascular system.
(2) Patient supine, with head supported over end of table, eyes open.
(a) Passively extend head and neck, hold for 30 seconds. If no symptoms, progress to passive rotation and side-bending with extension in both directions. Hold each position for 30 seconds.
(b) Causes reduction of the lumen of the vertebral artery (VA), resulting in decreased blood flow of the intracranial VA of the contralateral side.
(c) Symptoms include dizziness, nausea, syncope, dysarthria, dysphagia, and disturbances of hearing or vision, paresis or paralysis of patients with vertebral basilar infarction (VBI).
(3) Patient should be continuously monitored for any change in symptoms during entire test.
(4) Performing mobilization/manipulation within cervical region without performing this test beforehand would be considered, by most, to be a breach in standard of care even if current evidence demonstrates statistical limitations of this test.
(5) SN and SP not available.

b. Flexion rotation test.
(1) Identifies cervical contributions to headache.
(2) Patient supine, passively perform maximal flexion of the cervical spine then fully rotate the head in each direction.
(3) Positive finding is reproduction of headache symptoms or a loss of 10° range of motion from one side.
(4) SN 86%; SP 20%.

c. Transverse ligament stress test.
(1) Identifies integrity of transverse ligament.
(2) Patient supine, with head supported on table. Glide C1 anterior. Should be firm end-feel.
(3) Positive findings: soft end-feel, dizziness, nystagmus, lump sensation in throat, nausea.
(4) SN and SP not available.

d. Anterior shear test.
(1) Assesses integrity of upper cervical spine ligaments and capsules.
(2) Patient supine, with head supported on table. Glide C2–7 anterior. Should be firm end-feel.
(3) Laxity of ligaments is positive finding, as well as dizziness, nystagmus, a lump sensation in the throat, nausea.
(4) SN and SP not available.

e. Foraminal compression (Spurling's test).
(1) Identifies dysfunction (typically compression) of cervical nerve root.
(2) Patient sitting, with head side bent toward uninvolved side. Apply pressure through head straight down. Repeat with head side bent toward involved side.
(3) Positive finding is pain and/or paresthesia in dermatomal pattern for involved nerve root.
(4) SN 39%; SP 92%.

f. Maximum cervical compression test.
(1) Identifies compression of neural structures at intervertebral foramen and/or facet dysfunction.
(2) Patient sitting. Passively move head into side-bending and rotation toward nonpainful side, followed by extension. Repeat this toward painful side.
(3) Be careful since this is very similar to vertebral artery test.
(4) Positive finding is pain and/or paresthesia in dermatomal pattern for involved nerve root, or localized pain in neck if facet dysfunction.
(5) SN and SP not available.

g. Distraction test.
 (1) Indicates compression of neural structures at the intervertebral foramen or facet joint dysfunction.
 (2) Patient sitting with head passively distracted.
 (3) Positive finding is a decrease in symptoms in neck (facet condition) or a decrease in upper limb pain (neurological condition).
 (4) SN 40%; SP 100%.

h. Shoulder abduction test.
 (1) Indicates compression of neural structures within intervertebral foramen.
 (2) Patient sitting and asked to place one hand on top of their head. Repeat with opposite hand.
 (3) Positive finding is a decrease in symptoms into upper limb.
 (4) SN 43%; SP 80%.

i. Lhermitte's sign (see Figure 1-45).
 (1) Identifies dysfunction of spinal cord and/or an upper motor neuron lesion.
 (2) Patient long sitting on table. Passively flex patient's head and one hip, while keeping knee in extension. Repeat with other hip.
 (3) Positive finding is pain down the spine and into the upper or lower limbs.
 (4) SN 3%; SP 80%.

j. Alar ligament test.
 (1) Identifies integrity of the alar ligament.
 (2) Patient seated, passively, slightly flex the upper cervical spine and apply a firm pincer grip to the C2 spinous process. Palpate movement at C2 during passive upper cervical side-bending and/or rotation.
 (3) Positive finding is an inability to palpate C2 moving in conjunction with C1.
 (4) SN and SP not available.

k. Modified sharp purser test.
 (1) Identifies integrity of the transverse ligament.
 (2) Patient seated, passively, slightly flex the upper cervical spine and apply a firm pincer grip to the C2 spinous process. Apply a posterior translation and extension force through the forehead while assessing for excessive linear translation or reproduction of myelopathic symptoms.
 (3) Positive findings include myelopathic symptoms with upper cervical flexion or a decrease in symptoms or excessive translation during the posterior translation.
 (4) SN 69%; SP 96%.

l. TOS tests (see shoulder special tests).

m. Upper limb tension tests (see Table 1-14).

2. Thoracic special tests.

a. Rib springing.
 (1) Evaluates rib mobility.
 (2) Patient prone. Begin at upper ribs applying a posterior/anterior force through each rib progressively working through entire rib cage. Following prone test, position patient side-lying and repeat. Be careful with springing the eleventh and twelfth ribs, since they have no anterior attachments and therefore are less stable.
 (3) Positive finding is pain, excessive motion of rib, or restriction of rib.
 (4) SN and SP not available.

b. Thoracic springing.
 (1) Evaluates intervertebral joint mobility in thoracic spine.
 (2) Patient prone. Apply posterior/anterior glides/springs to transverse processes of thoracic vertebra. Remember that the spinous process and transverse process of the same vertebra may not be at the same level in the thoracic region.
 (3) Positive finding is pain, excessive movement, and/or restricted movement.
 (4) SN and SP not available.

3. Lumbar special tests.

a. Slump test (see Figure 1-46).
 (1) Identifies dysfunction of neurological structures supplying the lower limb.
 (2) Patient sitting on edge of table with knees flexed. Patient slump-sits, while maintaining neutral position of head and neck. The following progression is then followed.
  (a) Passively flex patient's head and neck. If no reproduction of symptoms, move on to next step.
  (b) Passively extend one of patient's knees. If no reproduction of symptoms, move on to next step.
  (c) Passively dorsiflex ankle of limb with extended knee.
  (d) Repeat flow with opposite leg.
 (3) Positive finding is reproduction of pathological neurological symptoms.
 (4) SN 83%; SP 55%.

b. Lasegue's test (straight leg raising) (see Table 1-15).
 (1) Identifies dysfunction of neurological structures that supply lower limb.
 (2) Patient supine, with legs resting on table. Passively flex hip of one leg with knee extended until patient complains of shooting pain into lower limb. Slowly lower limb until pain subsides, then passively dorsiflex foot.
 (3) Positive finding is reproduction of pathological neurological symptoms when foot is dorsiflexed.
 (4) SN 97%; SP 57%.

c. Femoral nerve traction test.
 (1) Identifies compression of femoral nerve anywhere along its course.

Table 1-15

Lower Extremity Neurotension Tests						
VERSION OF SLR	**POSITION OF HIP**	**POSITION OF KNEE**	**POSITION OF ANKLE**	**POSITION OF FOOT**	**POSITION OF TOES**	**NERVE BIAS**
SLR	Flexion and Abduction	Extension	Dorsiflexion	N/A	N/A	Sciatic and Tibial Nerves
SLR2	Flexion	Extension	Dorsiflexion	Eversion	Extension	Tibial Nerve
SLR3	Flexion	Extension	Dorsiflexion	Inversion	N/A	Sural Nerve
SLR4	Flexion and Internal Rotation	Extension	Plantarflexion	Inversion	N/A	Common Fibular Nerve
SLR5 (Well Leg)	Flexion	Extension	Dorsiflexion	N/A	N/A	Spinal Nerve Root

Adapted from Magee D: Orthopedic Physical Assessment, 5th ed.

(2) Patient lies on nonpainful side with trunk in neutral, head flexed slightly, and lower limb's hip and knee flexed. Passively extend hip while knee of painful limb is in extension. If no reproduction of symptoms, flex knee of painful leg.
(3) Positive finding is neurological pain in anterior thigh.
(4) SN 84%; SP not available.

d. Valsalva's maneuver.
(1) Patient sitting. Instruct patient to take a deep breath and hold while they "bear down" as if having a bowel movement.
(2) Increases pressure in middle ear and in the chest. Used when bracing to lift heavy objects.
(3) Can be used to identify a space-occupying lesion. Positive finding is increased low back pain or neurological symptoms into lower extremity.
(4) SN 22%; SP 94%.

e. Prone instability test
(1) Tests instability of the lumbar spine.
(2) Patient prone with torso resting on the plinth and legs off the edge with feet supported on the ground. Apply PA springing throughout the lumbar spine until a painful segment(s) is identified.
(3) Instruct the patient to lift their legs a few inches off the ground then perform spring testing again on the painful segment(s).
(4) Positive finding is decreased pain during PA springing with the legs raised compared to when the feet were supported on the ground.
(5) SN 61%, SP 57%.

f. Quadrant test.
(1) Identifies compression of neural structures at the intervertebral foramen and facet dysfunction.
(2) Patient standing.
(a) Intervertebral foramen: cue patient into side-bending left, rotation left, and extension to maximally close intervertebral foramen on the left. Repeat on other side.
(b) Facet dysfunction: cue patient into side-bending left, rotation right, and extension to maximally compress facet joint on left. Repeat on other side.
(3) Positive finding is pain and/or paresthesia in the dermatomal pattern for the involved nerve root, or localized pain if facet dysfunction.
(4) SN 70%; SP not available.

g. Stork standing test (see Figure 1-47).
(1) Identifies spondylolisthesis.
(2) Patient standing on one leg. Cue patient into trunk extension. Repeat with opposite leg on ground.
(3) Positive finding is pain in low back with ipsilateral leg on ground.
(4) SN and SP not available.

h. McKenzie's side glide test.
(1) Differentiates between scoliotic curvature versus neurological dysfunction causing abnormal curvature (lateral shift) of trunk.
(2) Test is performed if lateral shift of trunk is noted. Patient standing. Stand on side of patient so that upper trunk is shifted toward you. Place your shoulders into patient's upper trunk and wrap your arms around patient's pelvis. Stabilize upper trunk and pull pelvis, to bring pelvis and trunk into proper alignment.
(3) Positive test is reproduction of neurological symptoms as alignment of trunk is corrected.
(4) SN and SP not available.

i. Bicycle (van Gelderen's test).
(1) Differentiates between intermittent claudication and spinal stenosis.
(2) Patient seated on stationary bicycle. Patient rides bike while sitting erect. Time how long the patient can ride at a set pace/speed. After a

sufficient rest period, have patient ride bike at same speed while in a slumped position.

(3) Determination is based on length of time patient can ride bike in sitting upright versus sitting slumped. If pain is related to spinal stenosis, patient should be able to ride bike longer while slumped.

(4) SN and SP not available.

j. Well straight leg raise.

(1) Identifies herniated nucleus pulposis or neural tension/radiculopathy.

(2) Patient supine with head, neck, and torso in neutral, maintain knee extension and neutral dorsiflexion and lift the leg to the point of symptom provocation.

(3) Perform on the contralateral, non-involved lower extremity.

(4) Positive finding is reproduction of low back pain during the straight leg raise of the non-involved lower extremity.

(5) SN 43%; SP 97%.

4. Sacroiliac joint (SIJ) special tests (see Table 1-16).

a. Gillet's test (see Figure 1-48).

(1) Assessing posterior movement of the ilium relative to the sacrum.

(2) Patient standing. Place thumb of the hand under posterior superior iliac spine (PSIS) of limb to be tested and place the other thumb on center of sacrum at same level as thumb under PSIS. Ask patient to flex hip and knee of limb being tested as if bringing the knee to the chest. Assess movement of PSIS via comparison of positions of the thumbs. Make sure eyes are level with thumbs. PSIS should move in an inferior direction.

(3) Positive finding is no identified movement of PSIS as compared to sacrum.

(4) SN 43%; SP 68%.

b. Ipsilateral anterior rotation test.

(1) Assessing anterior movement of ilium relative to sacrum.

(2) Place thumb under PSIS of limb to be tested, and place the other thumb on center of sacrum, at same level as thumb under PSIS. Ask patient to extend hip of limb being tested. Assess movement of PSIS via comparison of positions of thumbs. Make sure eyes are level with thumbs. PSIS should move in a superior direction.

(3) Positive finding is no identified movement of PSIS compared to sacrum.

(4) SN and SP not available.

c. Gaenslen's test.

(1) Identifies SIJ dysfunction.

(2) Patient side-lying at edge of table while holding bottom leg in maximal hip and knee flexion (knee to chest). Standing behind patient, passively extend hip of uppermost limb. This places stress on SIJ associated with uppermost limb.

(3) Positive finding is pain in SIJ.

(4) SN 53%; SP 71%.

d. Long sitting (supine to sit) test (see Figure 1-49).

(1) Identifies dysfunction of SIJ that may be cause of functional leg length discrepancy.

(2) Patient supine with correct alignment of trunk, pelvis, and lower limbs. Stand at edge of table near patient's feet, palpating the medial malleoli to assess symmetry (one longer than other). Have patient come into long sitting position, and once again assess leg length, making a comparison between supine and long sitting.

Table 1-16

Positions/Activities that Precipitate SI Dysfunction

TYPE OF DYSFUNCTION	ACTIVITIES THAT PRECIPITATE DYSFUNCTION
Anterior torsion of innominate	Squatting/lifting/lowering Pregnancy Hip at 90° with axial loading Golfing/batting/tennis
Posterior torsion of innominate	Vertical thrust onto extended LE Sprint starting position Fall onto ischial tuberosity Unilateral standing
Sacral dysfunction	Long-term postural abnormalities Fall onto sacrum/coccyx Carrying a load during ambulation Trauma during childbirth Loss of balance during ambulation Sitting combined with rotation and lifting

(3) Abnormal finding is reversal in limb lengths between supine and long sitting.
(4) SN 44%; SP 64%.

e. Goldthwait's test (see Figure 1-50).
(1) Differentiates between dysfunction in lumbar spine versus SIJ.
(2) Patient supine with examiner's fingers between spinous processes of lumbar spine. With the other hand, passively perform a straight leg raise.
(3) If pain presents prior to palpation of movement in lumbar segments, dysfunction is related to SIJ.
(4) SN and SP not available.

f. Side-lying iliac compression test.
(1) Identifies SIJ dysfunction.
(2) Patient lies in side-lying position with painful side up and baseline symptoms are gathered. Examiner places hands on the iliac crest and applies force through the ilium in the downward direction. The examiner may hold the position for 30 seconds and apply continued force.
(3) A positive test reproduces the patient's chief complaint.
(4) SN 69%; SP 69%.

g. Supine iliac gapping.
(1) Identifies SIJ dysfunction.
(2) Patient lies in supine position and baseline symptoms are gathered. Examiner crosses arms and places each hand on the medial aspect of the patient's ASIS and applies a posterior and lateral force. The examiner may hold the position for 30 seconds and apply continued force.
(3) Positive finding is reproduction of patient's chief complaint.
(4) SN 60%; SP 81%.

5. TMJ special tests.
a. TMJ compression.
(1) Evaluates for pain with compression of the retrodiscal tissues.
(2) Patient sitting or supine. Support/stabilize patient's head with one hand. With other hand, push mandible superior, causing a compressive load to the TMJ.
(3) Positive finding is pain in TMJ.
(4) SN and SP not available.

Assessment of Normal Gait Pattern

1. Divided into two phases of gait (stance phase and swing phase) (see Figure 11-1).
a. Stance phase is subdivided into initial contact, foot flat, midstance, heel off, and preswing (see Table 1-17).
(1) Initial contact: heel strikes the ground and the limb prepares to absorb the ground reaction forces.
(2) Foot flat: as the limb is being loaded, the individual makes a subconscious decision regarding the ability to tolerate the loading, and may compensate as necessary.
(3) Midstance: the foot fully flattens and the trunk is aligned over the stance leg.
(4) Heel off: the weight distribution shifts from the entire foot to the forefoot.
(5) Preswing: as the toe takes on the final contact of the stance phase, the force is accelerated to provide momentum for propulsion.

b. Swing phase is subdivided into initial swing, midswing, and terminal swing (see Table 1-18).
(1) Initial swing: the foot loses contact with the ground and accelerates forward.
(2) Midswing: the limb transitions from acceleration to deceleration.
(3) Terminal swing: the limb decelerates and prepares for heel strike.

c. Typical coupling patterns throughout the lower kinematic chain are presented in Table 1-19.
d. Lower kinematic chain compensations are presented in Table 1-20.

Arthritic Conditions

1. Degenerative joint disease (DJD); degenerative osteoarthritis (OA)/osteoarthrosis (see Table 1-9).
a. A degenerative process of varied etiology, which includes mechanical changes, diseases, and/or joint trauma.
b. Characterized by degeneration of articular cartilage, with hypertrophy of subchondral bone and joint capsule of weight-bearing joints.
c. Many different medications are used to control pain, including corticosteroids and nonsteroidal anti-inflammatory drugs (NSAIDs). Glucocorticoids are injected into joints that are inflamed and not responsive to NSAIDs. For mild pain without inflammation, acetaminophen may be used.
d. Diagnostic tests utilized: plain film imaging demonstrates characteristic findings of OA (diminished joint space, decreased height of articular cartilage, presence of osteophytes) and lab tests help to rule out other disorders such as rheumatoid arthritis (RA).
e. Clinical examination assists in confirming diagnosis.
f. Physical therapy goals, outcomes, and interventions.
(1) Joint protection strategies.
(2) Maintain/improve joint mechanics and connective tissue functions.

Figure 1-45 **Lhermitte's sign.**

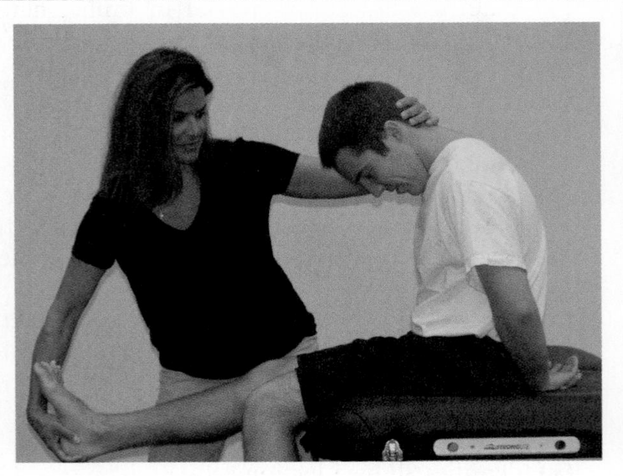

Figure 1-46 **Slump test.**

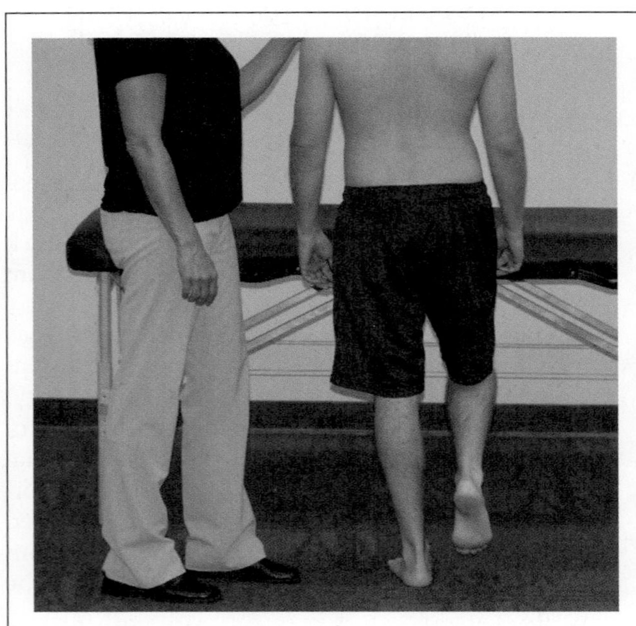

Figure 1-47a **Stork standing test; standing on one leg.**

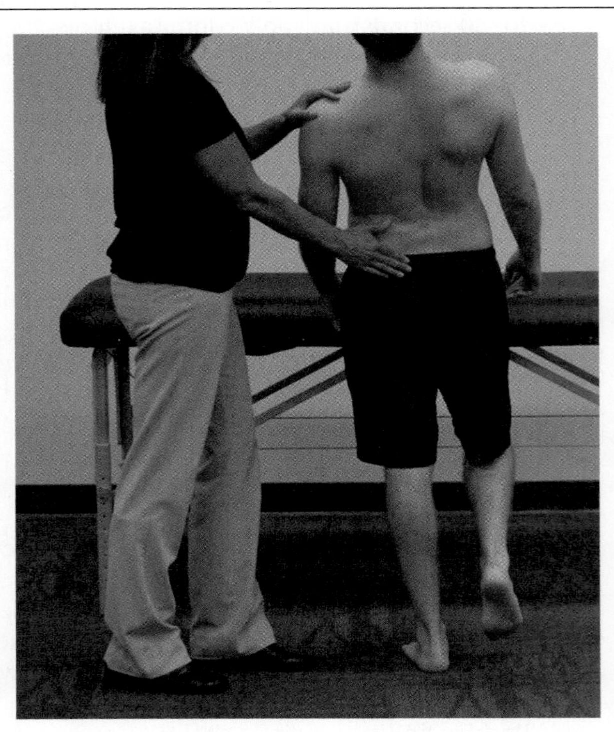

Figure 1-47b **Stork standing test; trunk extension.**

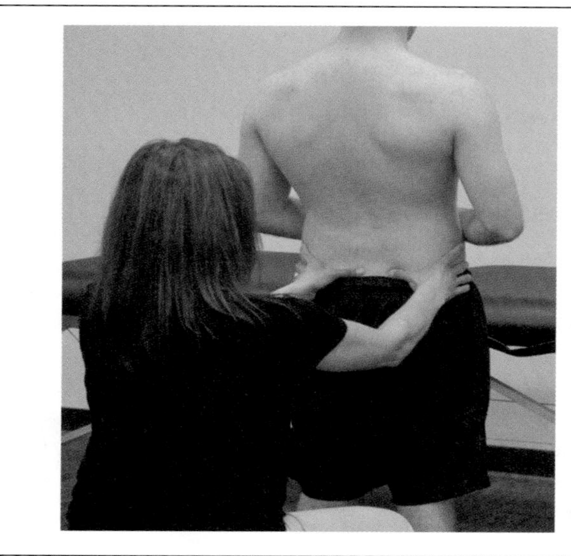

Figure 1-48a Gillet's test; hand position.

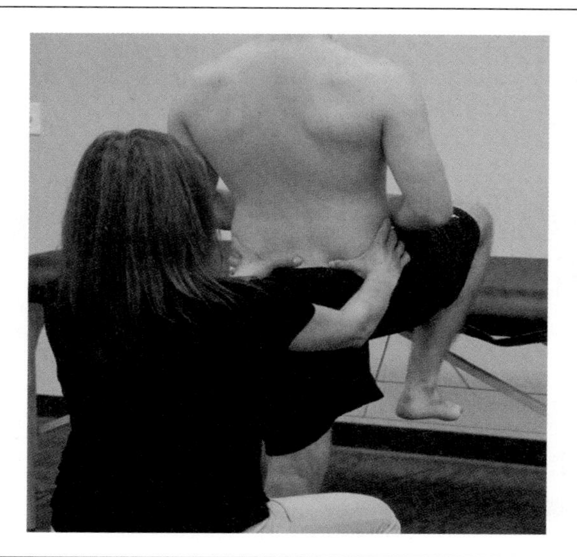

Figure 1-48b Gillet's test; hip and knee flexion.

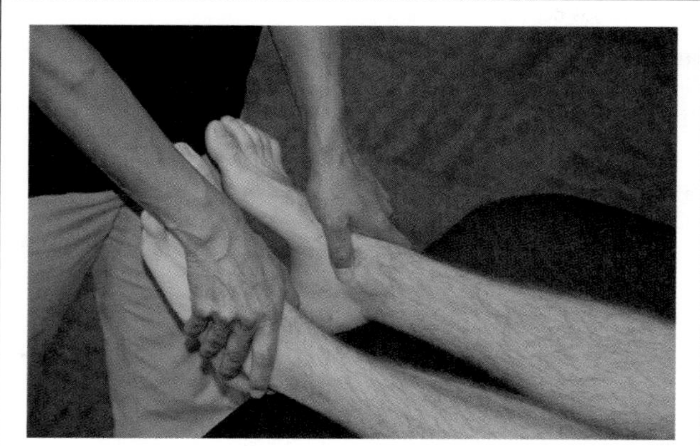

Figure 1-49a Long sitting (supine to sit) test; initial hand position.

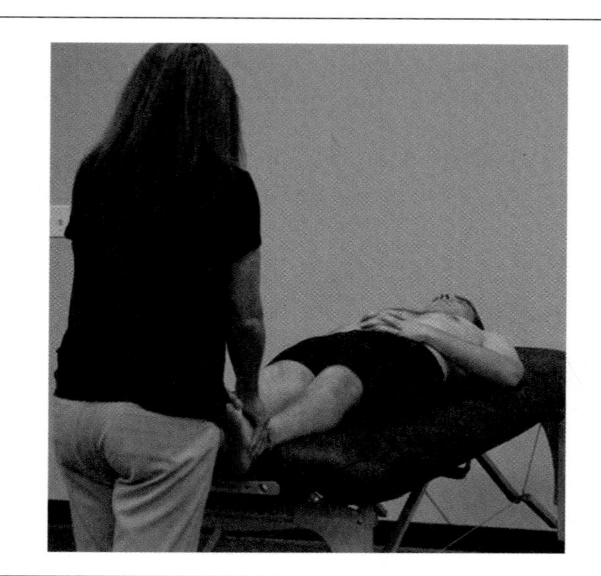

Figure 1-49b Long sitting (supine to sit) test.

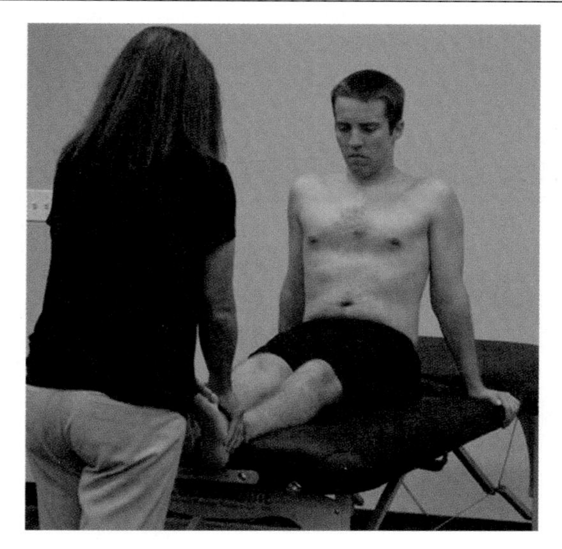

Figure 1-49c Long sitting (supine to sit) test.

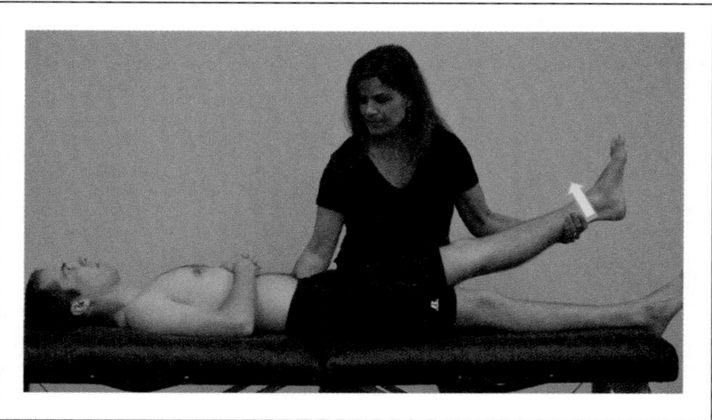

Figure 1-50 Goldthwait's test.

Table 1-17

Summary of Joint Motions at the Hip, Knee, Tibia, Foot, and Ankle During the Stance Phase of Gait

HIP

	KINEMATIC MOTION	KINETIC MOTION	
PHASE		EXTERNAL FORCES	INTERNAL FORCES
Heel strike	20° to 40° of hip flexion moving toward extension	Reaction force in front of joint; flexion moment moving toward extension; forward pelvic rotation	Gluteus maximus and hamstrings working eccentrically to resist flexion moment
	Slight adduction and lateral rotation		Erector spinae working eccentrically to resist forward bend
Foot flat	Hip moving into extension, adduction, medial rotation	Flexion moment	Gluteus maximus and hamstrings contracting concentrically to bring hip into extension
Midstance	Moving through neutral position Pelvis rotating posteriorly	Reaction force posterior to hip joint; extension moment	Iliopsoas activity continuing
Toe-off	Moving toward 10° extension, abduction, lateral rotation	Decrease of extension moment	Adductor magnus working eccentrically to control or stabilize pelvis Iliopsoas activity continuing

KNEE AND TIBIA

	KINEMATIC MOTION		KINETIC MOTION	
PHASE	KNEE	TIBIA	EXTERNAL FORCES	INTERNAL FORCES
Heel strike	In full extension before heel contact; flexing as heel strikes floor	Slight lateral rotation	Rapidly increasing reaction forces behind knee joint, causing flexion moment	Quadriceps femoris contracting eccentrically to control rapid knee flexion and to prevent buckling
Foot flat	In 20° flexion moving toward extension	Medial rotation	Flexion moment	After foot is flat, quadriceps femoris activity, becoming concentric to bring femur over tibia
Midstance	In 15° flexion moving toward extension	Lateral rotation	Reaction forces moving anterior to joint extension moment	Gastrocnemius beginning to work concentrically to start knee flexion
Toe-off	Moving from near full extension to 40° flexion	Lateral rotation	Reaction forces moving posterior to joint as knee flexes, flexion moment	Quadriceps femoris contracting eccentrically

FOOT AND ANKLE

	KINEMATIC MOTION		KINETIC MOTION	
PHASE	FOOT	ANKLE	EXTERNAL FORCES	INTERNAL FORCES
Heel strike	Supination (rigid) at heel contact	Moving into plantar flexion	Reaction forces behind joint axis; plantar flexion moment at heel strike	Dorsiflexors (tibialis anterior, extensor digitorum longus, and extensor hallucis longus) contracting eccentrically to slow plantar flexion
Foot flat	Pronation, adapting to support surface	Plantar flexion to dorsiflexion over a fixed foot	Maximum plantar flexion moment; reaction forces beginning to shift anterior, producing a dorsiflexion moment	Plantar flexor muscles (gastrocsoleus and peroneal muscles), activated to control dorsiflexion of the tibia and fibula over a fixed foot, contracting eccentrically

Table 1-17

Summary of Joint Motions at the Hip, Knee, Tibia, Foot, and Ankle During the Stance Phase of Gait (Continued)

Midstance	Neutral	3° of dorsiflexion	Slight dorsiflexion moment	Plantar flexor muscles (gastrocsoleus and peroneal muscles), activated to control dorsiflexion of the tibia and fibula over a fixed foot, contracting eccentrically
Heel-off	Supination as foot becomes rigid for push-off	15° dorsiflexion toward plantar flexion	Maximal dorsiflexion moment	Plantar flexor muscles beginning to contract concentrically to prepare for push-off
Toe-off	Supination	20° plantar flexion	Dorsiflexion moment	Plantar flexor muscles at peak activity but becoming inactive as foot leaves ground

Adapted from Giallonardo LM: Gait. In Myers RS (ed.): Saunders Manual of Physical Therapy Practice, Saunders, 1995, pp 1108–1109.

Table 1-18

Summary of Joint Motion and Forces During Swing Phase: Acceleration to Midswing and Midswing to Deceleration

	ACCELERATION TO MIDSWING		MIDSWING TO DECELERATION	
JOINT	KINEMATIC MOTION	KINETIC MOTION	KINEMATIC MOTION	KINETIC MOTION
Hip	Slight flexion (0° to 15°) moving at 30° flexion and lateral rotation to neutral	Hip flexors working concentrically to bring limb through; contralateral gluteus medius concentrically contracting to maintain pelvis position	Continued flexion at about 30° to 40°	Gluteus maximus contracting eccentrically to slow hip flexion
Knee	30° to 60° knee flexion and lateral rotation of tibia moving toward neutral	Hamstrings concentrically contracting	Moving to near full extension and slight lateral tibial rotation	Quadriceps femoris contracting concentrically and hamstrings contracting eccentrically
Ankle and foot	20° dorsiflexion and slight pronation	Dorsiflexors contracting concentrically	Ankle in neutral; foot in slight supination	Dorsiflexors contracting isometrically

Adapted from Giallonardo LM: Gait. In Myers RS (ed.): Saunders Manual of Physical Therapy Practice, Saunders, 1995, p 1110.

(3) Implementation of aerobic capacity/endurance conditioning or reconditioning, such as aquatic programs.

2. Rheumatoid conditions.

a. Ankylosing spondylitis (Marie-Strümpell disease, Bechterew's disease, rheumatoid spondylitis) (see Table 1-21).

(1) Progressive inflammatory disorder of unknown etiology that initially affects axial skeleton.

(2) Initial onset (usually mid and low back pain for 3 months or greater) before fourth decade of life.

(3) First symptoms include mid and low back pain, morning stiffness, and sacroiliitis.

(4) Results in kyphotic deformity of the cervical and thoracic spine and a decrease in lumbar lordosis.

(5) Degeneration of peripheral and costovertebral joints may be observed in advanced stages.

(6) Affects men three times more often than women.

(7) Medications: NSAIDs, such as aspirin, are used to reduce inflammation and pain. Corticosteroid therapy or medications to suppress immune system may be used to control various symptoms. Cytotoxic drugs (drugs that block cell growth) may be used in people who do not respond well to corticosteroids or who are dependent on high doses of corticosteroids.

Table 1-19

Typical Coupling Patterns Throughout the Lower Kinematic Chain	
Lumbar Spine	Lumbar spine flexion is coupled with ilial posterior rotation. Lumbar spine extension is coupled with ilial anterior rotation.
Pelvis	During unilateral ilial posterior rotation, the ilium simultaneously moves in the direction of an outflare, causing ER of the acetabulum (i.e., the hip joint), leading to hip ER.
Femur	ER of the femur causes ER of the tibia.
Tibia	Tibial ER is coupled with an upward glide of the talus and supination of the foot.
Fibula	Supination of the foot is coupled with cranial and anterior glide of the fibula head.

Table 1-20

Lower Kinematic Chain Compensations*,**

REGION	TRUE LEG LENGTH DISCREPANCY ON THE RIGHT
Lumbar Spine	Side bent right. Rotated left.
Pelvis	Right ilium rotated posteriorly.
Femur	Right femur adducted and in ER at hip joint. Right femur in relative extension at hip joint.
Tibia	ER of right tibia.
Fibula	Fibular head glides cranially and anteriorly.
Ankle/Foot	Supination of right foot. Talus rotated externally and glides upwardly.

*Describes the potential functional compensational movements that may be seen in a patient with a leg length discrepancy.

**Individuals may not demonstrate some or any of the compensations for the related conditions listed above. The functional compensations described above are commonly seen, but must be assessed for each patient to determine if they are truly present.

Table 1-21

Differential Diagnosis of Ankylosing Spondylitis and Spinal Stenosis

	ANKYLOSING SPONDYLITIS	SPINAL STENOSIS
History	Morning stiffness Male predominance Sharp pain → ache Bilateral sacroiliac pain may refer to posterior thigh	Intermittent aching pain Pain may refer to both legs with walking (neurogenic intermittent claudication)
Active movements	Restricted	May be normal
Passive movements	Restricted	May be normal
Resisted isometric movements	Normal (in beginning of disorder)	Normal
Posture	Flexed posture of entire spine	Flexed posture of lumbar spine
Special tests	None	Bicycle test of van Gelderen may be positive; Stoop test may be positive
Reflexes	Normal (in beginning of disorder)	May be affected in long-standing cases
Sensory deficit	None (in beginning of disorder)	Usually temporary
Diagnostic imaging	Plain films are diagnostic	Computed tomography scans are diagnostic

Adapted from Magee D: Orthopedic Physical Assessment, 3rd ed. Saunders 1997, p 359.

Tumor necrosis factor (TNF) inhibitors have been shown to improve some symptoms of ankylosing spondylitis.

(8) Diagnostic tests utilized: HLA-B27 antigen may be helpful, but not diagnostic by itself.

(9) Clinical examination will assist in confirming diagnosis.

(10) Physical therapy goals, outcomes, and interventions.

(a) Implementation of flexibility exercises for trunk to maintain/improve normal joint motion and length of muscles in all directions, especially extension.

(b) Implementation of aerobic capacity/endurance conditioning or reconditioning such as aquatic programs.

(c) Implementation of relaxation activities to maintain/improve respiratory function.

- Breathing strategies to maintain/improve vital capacity.

b. Gout.

(1) Genetic disorder of purine metabolism, characterized by elevated serum uric acid (hyperuricemia). Uric acid changes into crystals and deposits into peripheral joints and other tissues (e.g., kidneys).

(2) Most frequently observed at knee and great toe of foot.
(3) Medications: NSAIDS (specifically indomethacin), COX-2 inhibitors (cardiac side effects may limit use), colchicine, corticosteroids, adrenocorticotropic hormone (ACTH), allopurinol, probenecid, and sulfinpyrazone.
(4) Diagnostic tests utilized: lab tests identify monosodium urate crystals in synovial fluid and/or connective tissue samples.
(5) Clinical examination assists in confirming diagnosis.
(6) Physical therapy goals, outcomes, and interventions.
 (a) Patient/client education for injury prevention and reduction of involved joint(s).
 (b) Early identification of condition, with fast implementation of intervention, is very important.

c. Psoriatic arthritis.
(1) Chronic, erosive inflammatory disorder of unknown etiology, associated with psoriasis.
(2) Erosive degeneration usually occurs in joints of digits as well as axial skeleton.
(3) Both sexes are affected equally.
(4) Medications: acetaminophen for pain, NSAIDs, corticosteroids, disease-modifying antirheumatic drugs (DMARDs) can slow the progression of psoriatic arthritis, and biological response modifiers (BRMs) such as Enbrel (etanercept) are a newly developed class of medicines.
(5) Diagnostic tests utilized: lab tests are not useful except to rule out rheumatoid arthritis.
(6) Clinical examination assists in confirming diagnosis.
(7) Physical therapy goals, outcomes, and interventions.
 (a) Joint protection strategies.
 (b) Maintain/improve joint mechanics and connective tissue functions.
 (c) Implementation of aerobic capacity/endurance conditioning or reconditioning, such as aquatic programs.

d. Rheumatoid arthritis (RA).
(1) Chronic systemic disorder of unknown etiology, usually involving a symmetrical pattern of dysfunction in synovial tissues and articular cartilage of joints of hands, wrists, elbows, shoulders, knees, ankles, and feet.
(2) Metacarpophalangeal (MCP) and proximal interphalangeal (PIP) joints are usually affected, with characteristic pannus formation (inflammatory granulation tissue that covers joint surface), ulnar drift, and volar subluxation of MCP joints; ulnar drift observed at PIPs in severe forms. Distal interphalangeal (DIP) joints are usually spared. Other deformities include swan neck and boutonnière deformities and Bouchard's nodes (excessive bone formation on dorsal aspect of PIP joints).
(3) Women have two to three times greater incidence than men.
(4) Juvenile rheumatoid arthritis (JRA) onset prior to age 16, with complete remission in 75% of children.
(5) Pharmacological management varies with disease progression, and may include gold compounds and antirheumatic drugs (DMARDs) (e.g., hydroxychloroquine and methotrexate) early. NSAIDs (e.g., ibuprofen), immunosuppressive agents (e.g., cyclosporine, azathioprine, and mycophenolate), or cortico-steroids are commonly prescribed for long-term management.
(6) Diagnostic tests: plain film imaging demonstrating symmetrical involvement within joints as well as laboratory testing. Positive test findings include increased white blood cell count and erythrocyte sedimentation rate. Hemoglobin and hematocrit tests will show anemia, and rheumatoid factor will be elevated.
(7) Clinical examination assists in confirming diagnosis.
(8) Physical therapy goals, outcomes, and interventions.
 (a) Joint protection strategies.
 (b) Maintain/improve joint mechanics and connective tissue functions.
 (c) Implementation of aerobic capacity and endurance conditioning or reconditioning, such as aquatic programs.

Skeletal and Soft Tissue Conditions

1. Osteoporosis.
 a. A metabolic disease that depletes bone mineral density/mass, predisposing individual to fracture.
 b. Affects women 10 times more frequently than men.
 c. Common sites of fracture include thoracic and lumbar spine, femoral neck, proximal humerus, proximal tibia, pelvis, and distal radius.
 d. Primary or postmenopausal osteoporosis is directly related to a decrease in estrogen production.
 e. Senile osteoporosis occurs due to a decrease in bone cell activity secondary to genetics or acquired abnormalities.
 f. Medications: calcium, vitamin D, estrogen, calcitonin, and biophosphonates.

g. Diagnostic tests utilized: CT scan to assess bone density. Single and dual photon absorptiometry are also used, but very expensive.
h. Clinical examination will assist in confirming diagnosis.
i. Physical therapy goals, outcomes, and interventions.
   (1) Joint/bone protection strategies.
   (2) Maintain/improve joint mechanics and connective tissue functions.
   (3) Implementation of aerobic capacity/endurance conditioning or reconditioning, such as aquatic programs.

2. Osteomalacia.
   a. Characterized by decalcification of bones due to vitamin D deficiency.
   b. Symptoms include severe pain, fractures, weakness, and deformities.
   c. Medications: calcium, vitamin D, and vitamin D injections in the form of calciferol (vitamin D2).
   d. Diagnostic tests: plain films, lab tests (urinalysis and blood work), bone scan, and bone biopsy if warranted.
   e. Clinical examination assists in confirming diagnosis.
   f. Physical therapy goals, outcomes, and interventions.
      (1) Joint/bone protection strategies.
      (2) Maintain/improve joint mechanics and connective tissue functions.
      (3) Implementation of aerobic capacity/endurance conditioning or reconditioning, such as aquatic programs.

3. Osteomyelitis.
   a. An inflammatory response within bone caused by an infection.
   b. Usually caused by *Staphylococcus aureus*, but could be another organism.
   c. More common in children and immunosuppressed adults than healthy adults; more common in males than females.
   d. Medical treatment consists of antibiotics. Proper nutrition is important as well. Surgery may be indicated if infection spreads to joints.
   e. Diagnostic tests utilized: lab tests for infection and possibly a bone biopsy.
   f. Clinical examination will assist in confirming diagnosis.
   g. Physical therapy goals, outcomes, and interventions.
      (1) Joint/bone protection strategies and cast care.
      (2) Maintain/improve joint mechanics and connective tissue functions.

4. Myofascial pain syndrome.
   a. Characterized by clinical entity known as a "trigger point," which is a focal point of irritability found within a muscle. Trigger point can be identified as a taut, palpable band within the muscle.
   b. Trigger points may be active or latent. Active trigger points are tender to palpation and have a characteristic referral pattern of pain when provoked. Latent trigger points are palpable taut bands that are not tender to palpation, but can be converted into an active trigger point.
   c. Onset is hypothesized to sudden overload, overstretching, and/or repetitive/sustained muscle activities.
   d. Medical intervention may include dry needling (aka intramuscular manual therapy) and/or injection of analgesic, possibly combined with a corticosteroid.
   e. Diagnosis is made by clinical assessment, with no diagnostic tests available.
   f. Clinical examination will assist in confirming diagnosis.
   g. Physical therapy goals, outcomes, and interventions.
      (1) Implementation of flexibility exercises to maintain/improve normal joint motion and length of muscles.
      (2) Implementation of manual therapy for maintenance of normal joint mechanics.
         (a) Soft tissue/massage techniques and joint oscillations to reduce pain and/or muscle guarding.
         (b) Biomechanical faults caused by joint restrictions should be corrected with joint mobilization to the specific restrictions identified during the examination.
         (c) Use of "spray and stretch" technique.
         (d) Utilization of dry needling.
         (e) Cryotherapy, thermotherapy, hydrotherapy, sound agents, and transcutaneous electrical nerve stimulation (TENS) for symptomatic relief of pain.
         (f) Desensitization of trigger point with manual pressure.
      (3) Implementation of strength, power, and endurance exercises.
         (a) Active assistive, active, and resistive exercises.
         (b) Task-specific performance training.

5. Tendonosis/tendonopathy.
   a. Common tendon dysfunction whose cause and pathogenesis are poorly understood. Often referred to as tendonitis; however, there is no inflammatory response noted.
   b. Common in many tendons throughout body (supraspinatus, common extensor tendon of elbow, patella, Achilles' tendon).
   c. Histological characteristics include hypercellularity, hypervascularity, no indication of inflammatory

infiltrates, and poor organization and loosening of collagen fibrils.
d. Medications: acetaminophen, NSAIDs, and/or steroid injection.
e. Diagnostic tests utilized: possibly MRI.
f. Clinical examination assists in confirming diagnosis. Specific special tests are available to assist with making diagnosis within each region/joint.
g. Physical therapy goals, outcomes, and interventions.
(1) Implementation of flexibility exercises to maintain/improve normal joint motion and length of muscles.
(2) Implementation of manual therapy for maintenance of normal joint mechanics.
(a) Soft tissue/massage techniques and joint oscillations to reduce pain and/or muscle guarding.
(b) Biomechanical faults caused by joint restrictions should be corrected with joint mobilization to the specific restrictions identified during the examination.
(3) Endurance and strengthening exercise with initial emphasis on eccentric phase of exercise.
(4) Implementation of aerobic capacity/endurance conditioning or reconditioning.
(5) Application of thermal agents for pain reduction.
(a) Cryotherapy, thermotherapy, hydrotherapy, and sound agents.
(6) Patient/client education and training/retraining for instrumental activities of daily living (IADLs).
(a) Household chores, yard work, shopping, caring for dependents, and home maintenance.

6. Bursitis.
a. Inflammation of bursa secondary to overuse, trauma, gout, or infection.
b. Signs and symptoms of bursitis.
(1) Pain with rest.
(2) PROM and AROM are limited due to pain, but not in a capsular pattern.
c. Medications: acetaminophen, NSAIDs, and/or steroid injection.
d. Clinical examination assists in confirming diagnosis.
e. Physical therapy goals, outcomes, and interventions.
(1) Implementation of flexibility exercises to maintain/improve normal joint motion and length of muscles.
(2) Implementation of manual therapy for maintenance of normal joint mechanics.
(a) Soft tissue/massage techniques and joint oscillations to reduce pain and/or muscle guarding.
(b) Biomechanical faults caused by joint restrictions should be corrected with joint mobilization to the specific restrictions identified during the examination.
(3) Implementation of aerobic capacity/endurance conditioning or reconditioning.
(4) Application of thermal agents for pain reduction, edema reduction, and muscle performance.
(a) Cryotherapy, thermotherapy, hydrotherapy, and sound agents.
(5) Patient/client education and training/retraining for IADLs.
(a) Household chores, yard work, shopping, caring for dependents, and home maintenance.

7. Muscle strains.
a. Inflammatory response within a muscle following a traumatic event that caused microtearing of the musculotendinous fibers.
b. Pain and tenderness within that muscle.
c. Seen within muscles throughout the body.
d. Medications: acetaminophen and/or NSAIDs.
e. Diagnostic tests utilized: MRI if necessary.
f. Clinical examination will assist in confirming diagnosis.
g. Physical therapy goals, outcomes, and interventions.
(1) Implementation of flexibility exercises to maintain/improve normal joint motion and length of muscles.
(2) Implementation of manual therapy for maintenance of normal joint mechanics.
(a) Soft tissue/massage techniques and joint oscillations to reduce pain and/or muscle guarding.
(b) Biomechanical faults caused by joint restrictions should be corrected with joint mobilization to the specific restrictions identified during the examination.
(3) Implementation of aerobic capacity/endurance conditioning or reconditioning.
(4) Application of thermal agents for pain reduction, edema reduction, and muscle performance.
(a) Cryotherapy, thermotherapy, hydrotherapy, and sound agents.
(5) Patient/client education and training/retraining for IADLs.
(a) Household chores, yard work, shopping, caring for dependents, and home maintenance.

8. Myositis ossificans.
a. Painful condition of abnormal calcification within a muscle belly.
b. Usually precipitated by direct trauma that results in hematoma and calcification of the muscle.

c. Can also be induced by early mobilization and stretching, with aggressive physical therapy following trauma to muscle.
d. Most frequent locations are quadriceps, brachialis, and biceps brachii muscles.
e. Medications: acetaminophen and/or NSAIDs.
f. Surgical care is warranted only in patients with nonhereditary myositis ossificans, and only after maturation of the lesion (6–24 months). Surgery is indicated when lesions mechanically interfere with joint movement or impinge on nerves.
g. Diagnostic tests utilized: imaging (plain films, CT scan, and/or MRI).
h. Clinical examination assists in confirming diagnosis.
i. Physical therapy goals, outcomes, and interventions.
   (1) Implementation of flexibility exercises to maintain/improve normal joint motion and length of muscles. Avoid being overly aggressive with muscle flexibility exercises, which may worsen condition.
   (2) Implementation of manual therapy for maintenance of normal joint mechanics.
      (a) Soft tissue/massage techniques and joint oscillations to reduce pain and/or muscle guarding. Avoid aggressive soft tissue/massage techniques, which may worsen condition.
      (b) Biomechanical faults caused by joint restrictions should be corrected with joint mobilization to the specific restrictions identified during the examination.
   (3) Implementation of aerobic capacity/endurance conditioning or reconditioning, such as aquatic programs.

9. Complex regional pain syndrome (CRPS).
a. Formerly referred to as reflex sympathetic dystrophy (RSD).
b. Etiology largely unknown, but thought to be related to trauma. Can affect upper and lower extremities, trunk, head, and neck.
c. Results in dysfunction of sympathetic nervous system to include pain, circulation, and vasomotor disturbances.
d. Two types of CRPS.
   (1) CRPS I is frequently triggered by tissue injury; term describes all patients with the above symptoms, but with no underlying nerve injury.
   (2) Patients with CRPS II experience the same symptoms, but their cases are clearly associated with a nerve injury.
e. Medical intervention may include sympathetic nerve block, surgical sympathectomy, spinal cord stimulation, intrathecal drug pumps.
f. Medications: multiple forms including topical analgesic drugs that act locally on painful nerves, skin, and muscles; antiseizure drugs; antidepressants, corticosteroids, and opioids.
g. Long-term changes include muscle wasting, trophic skin changes, decreased bone density, decreased proprioception, loss of muscle strength from disuse, and joint contractures.
h. Diagnostic tests utilized: none.
i. Clinical examination will assist in confirming diagnosis.
j. Physical therapy goals, outcomes, and interventions.
   (1) Patient/client education for injury prevention and reduction.
   (2) Desensitization activities that focus on return to work/school/home activities.
   (3) Implementation of flexibility exercises to maintain/improve normal joint motion and length of muscles.
   (4) Electrical stimulation (TENS) for pain relief.

10. Paget's disease (osteitis deformans).
a. Etiology is largely unknown, but thought to be linked to a type of viral infection along with environmental factors.
b. Considered to be a metabolic bone disease involving abnormal osteoclastic and osteoblastic activity.
c. Results in spinal stenosis, facet arthropathy, and possible spinal fracture.
d. Primary medical intervention is drug therapy, such as acetaminophen for pain control. Drugs such as calcitonin and etidronate disodium may be beneficial, since they limit osteoclast activity.
e. Diagnostic tests utilized: plain film imaging identifies bony changes. Lab tests look for increased levels of serum alkaline phosphatase and urinary hydroxyproline.
f. Clinical examination assists in confirming diagnosis.
g. Physical therapy goals, outcomes, and interventions.
   (1) Joint/bone protection strategies should be taught to patient.
   (2) Maintain/improve joint mechanics and connective tissue functions.
   (3) Implementation of aerobic capacity/endurance conditioning or reconditioning, such as aquatic programs.

11. Torticollis.
a. Spasm and/or tightness of sternocleidomastoid (SCM) muscle, with varied etiology.
b. Dysfunction observed is side-bending toward and rotation away from the affected SCM.
c. Medications: acetaminophen, muscle relaxants, and/or NSAIDs.

d. Diagnostic tests utilized: none.
e. Physical therapy goals, outcomes, and interventions.
(1) Implementation of flexibility exercises to maintain/improve normal joint motion and length of muscles.
(2) Implementation of manual therapy for maintenance of normal joint mechanics.
(a) Soft tissue/massage techniques and joint oscillations to reduce pain and/or muscle guarding.
(b) Biomechanical faults caused by joint restrictions should be corrected with joint mobilization to the specific restrictions identified during the examination.

Upper Extremity Disorders

1. Shoulder conditions (see Tables 1-22, 1-23, and 1-24).
a. Glenohumeral subluxation and dislocation.
(1) Most dislocations (95%) occur in anterior-inferior direction.
(2) Anterior-inferior dislocation occurs when abducted upper extremity is forcefully, externally rotated, causing tearing of inferior glenohumeral ligament, anterior capsule, and occasionally glenoid labrum.
(3) Posterior dislocations are rare and occur with multidirectional laxity of glenohumeral joint.

Table 1-22

Differential Diagnosis of Rotator Cuff Degeneration, Frozen Shoulder, Atraumatic Instability, and Cervical Spondylosis

	ROTATOR CUFF LESIONS	FROZEN SHOULDER	ATRAUMATIC INSTABILITY	CERVICAL SPONDYLOSIS
History	Age 30–50 years Pain and weakness after eccentric load	Age 45+ (insidious type) Insidious onset or after trauma or surgery Functional restriction of lateral rotation, abduction, and medial rotation Normal bone and soft-tissue outlines	Age 10–35 years Pain and instability with activity No history of trauma	Age 50+ years Acute or chronic
Observation	Normal bone and soft tissue outlines Protective shoulder hike may be seen	Normal bone and soft-tissue outlines	Normal bone and soft-tissue outlines	Minimal or no cervical spine movement Torticollis may be present
Active movement	Weakness of abduction or rotation, or both Crepitus may be present	Restricted ROM Shoulder hiking	Full or excessive ROM	Limited ROM with pain
Passive movement	Pain if impingement occurs	Limited ROM, especially in lateral rotation, abduction, flexion, and medial rotation (capsular pattern)	Normal or excessive ROM	Limited ROM (symptoms may be exacerbated)
Resisted isometric movement	Pain and weakness on abduction and lateral rotation	Normal, when arm by side	Normal	Normal, except if nerve root compressed Myotome may be affected
Special tests	Drop-arm test positive Empty can test positive	None	Load and shift test positive Apprehension test positive Relocation test positive Augmentation tests positive	Spurling's test positive Distraction test positive ULTT positive Shoulder abduction test positive
Sensory function and reflexes	Not affected	Not affected	Anterior or posterior pain	Dermatomes affected Reflexes affected
Palpation	Tender over rotator cuff	Not painful unless capsule is stretched	Negative	Tender over appropriate vertebra or facet
Diagnostic imaging	Radiography: upward displacement of humeral head; acromial spurring MRI diagnostic	Radiography: negative Arthrography: decreased capsular size		Radiography: narrowing osteophytes

MRI = magnetic resonance imaging; ROM = range of motion; ULTT = upper limb tension test

Table 1-23

Differential Diagnosis of Shoulder Pathology

PATHOLOGY	SYMPTOMS
External primary impingement (stage I)	Intermittent mild pain with overhead activities Over age 35
External primary impingement (stage II)	Mild to moderate pain with overhead activities or strenuous activities
External primary impingement (stage III)	Pain at rest or with activities Night pain may occur Scapular or rotator cuff weakness is noted
Rotator cuff tears (full thickness)	Classic night pain Weakness noted predominantly in abduction and lateral rotators Loss of motion
Adhesive capsulitis (idiopathic frozen shoulder)	Inability to perform activities of daily living owing to loss of motion Loss of motion may be perceived as weakness
Anterior instability (with or without external secondary impingement)	Apprehension to mechanical shifting limits activities Slipping, popping, or sliding may present as suitable instability Apprehension usually associated with horizontal abduction and lateral rotation Anterior or posterior pain may be present Weak scapular stabilizers
Posterior instability	Slipping or popping of the humerus out the back This may be associated with forward flexion and medial rotation while the shoulder is under a compressive load
Multidirectional instability	Looseness of shoulder in all directions This may be most pronounced while carrying luggage or turning over while asleep Pain may or may not be present

Modified from Maughon TS, Andrews JR: The subjective evaluation of the shoulder in the athlete. In Andrews JR, Wilk KE (eds): The Athlete's Shoulder. Churchill-Livingstone, 1994, p 36.

Table 1-24

Signs and Symptoms of Possible Peripheral Nerve Involvement

Spinal accessory nerve	Inability to abduct arm beyond 90° Pain in shoulder on abduction
Long thoracic nerve	Pain on flexing fully extended arm Inability to flex fully extended arm Winging starts at 90° forward flexion
Suprascapular nerve	Increased pain on forward shoulder flexion Shoulder weakness (partial loss of humeral control) Pain increases with scapular abduction Pain increases with cervical rotation to opposite side
Axillary (circumflex) nerve	Inability to abduct arm with neutral rotation

(4) Posterior dislocation occurs with horizontal adduction and internal rotation of glenohumeral joint.

(5) Complications may include compression fracture of posterior humeral head (Hill-Sachs lesion), tearing of superior glenoid labrum from anterior (front) to posterior (back) (aka SLAP [superior labrum, anterior to posterior] lesion), an avulsion of anteroinferior capsule and ligaments associated with glenoid rim (Bankart's lesion), and bruising of axillary nerve.

(6) Following surgical repair for dislocation/chronic subluxation, patients should avoid apprehension position (flexion to 90° or greater, horizontal abduction to 90° or greater, and ER to 80°).

(7) Diagnostic tests utilized: plain film imaging, CT scan, and/or MRI.

(8) Diagnosis made by clinical examination. Apprehension tests will be positive.

(9) Medications.
   (a) Acetaminophen for pain.
   (b) NSAIDs for pain and/or inflammation.

(10) Physical therapy goals, outcomes, and interventions.
   (a) Physical therapy intervention is varied, depending on specific patient problems and whether surgery is performed.
   (b) Biomechanical faults caused by joint restrictions should be corrected with joint mobilization to the specific restrictions identified during the examination.

(c) Restoration of normal shoulder mechanics via strengthening/endurance/coordination exercises that focus on regaining dynamic scapulothoracic, glenohumeral stabilization, and muscular reeducation.

b. Instability.

(1) Divided into two categories: traumatic (common in young throwing athletes) and atraumatic (individuals with congenitally loose connective tissue around the shoulder).

(2) Characterized by popping/clicking and repeated dislocation/subluxation of the glenohumeral joint.

(3) Unstable injuries require surgery to reattach the labrum to the glenoid. Bankart's lesions require surgery.

(4) Diagnosis made by clinical examination by comparing results of patient history with the AROM, PROM, resistive tests, and palpation. MRI arthrograms are very effective in identifying labral tears.

(5) Medications.

(a) Acetaminophen for pain.

(b) NSAIDS for pain and/or inflammation.

(6) Physical therapy goals, outcomes, and interventions.

(a) Physical therapy intervention emphasizes return of function without pain.

(b) Functional training and restoration of muscle imbalances using exercise to normalize strength, endurance, coordination, and flexibility.

(c) Biomechanical faults caused by joint restrictions should be corrected with joint mobilization to the specific restrictions identified during the examination.

(d) For patients requiring surgery, the shoulder is usually kept in a sling for 3–4 weeks. After 6 weeks, more sports-specific training can be done, although full fitness may take 3–4 months.

c. Labral tears.

(1) Glenoid labrum injuries are classified as either superior (toward the top of the glenoid socket) or inferior (toward the bottom of the glenoid socket). A SLAP lesion is a tear of the rim above the middle of the socket that may also involve the biceps tendon. A tear of the rim below the middle of the glenoid socket is called a Bankart's lesion and also involves the inferior glenohumeral ligament. Tears of the glenoid labrum may often occur with other shoulder injuries, such as a dislocated shoulder.

(2) Characterized by the following signs and symptoms.

(a) Shoulder pain that cannot be localized to a specific point.

(b) Pain is made worse by overhead activities or when the arm is held behind the back.

(c) Weakness.

(d) Instability in the shoulder.

(e) Pain on resisted flexion of the biceps (bending the elbow against resistance).

(f) Tenderness over the front of the shoulder.

(3) Unstable injuries require surgery to reattach the labrum to the glenoid. Bankart's lesions require surgery.

(4) Diagnosis made by clinical examination, through comparing results of AROM, PROM, resistive tests, and palpation. MRI arthrograms are very effective in identifying labral tears. The "gold" standard for identifying a labral tear is through arthroscopic surgery of the shoulder.

(5) Medications.

(a) Acetaminophen for pain.

(b) NSAIDS for pain and/or inflammation.

(6) Physical therapy goals, outcomes, and interventions.

(a) Physical therapy intervention emphasizes return of function without pain.

(b) Functional training and restoration of muscle imbalances using exercise to normalize strength, endurance, coordination, and flexibility.

(c) Any underlying causes that contributed to the injury such as shoulder instability should be addressed.

(d) Biomechanical faults caused by joint restrictions should be corrected with joint mobilization to the specific restrictions identified during the examination.

(e) Following surgery, the shoulder is usually kept in a sling for 3–4 weeks. After 6 weeks, more sports-specific training can be done, although full fitness may take 3–4 months.

d. TOS (see Table 1-25).

(1) Compression of neurovascular bundle (brachial plexus, subclavian artery and vein, vagus and phrenic nerves, and the sympathetic trunk) in thoracic outlet between bony and soft tissue structures.

(2) Compression occurs when size or shape of thoracic outlet is altered.

(3) Common areas of compression:

(a) Superior thoracic outlet.

(b) Scalene triangle.

(c) Between clavicle and first rib.

(d) Between pectoralis minor and thoracic wall.

(4) Surgery may be performed to remove a cervical rib or a release of anterior and/or middle scalene muscle.

Table 1-25

Differential Diagnosis of Cervical Facet Syndrome, Cervical Spinal Nerve Lesion, and Thoracic Outlet Syndrome			
SIGNS AND SYMPTOMS	**CERVICAL SPINAL NERVE**	**CERVICAL FACET SYNDROME**	**THORACIC OUTLET SYNDROME**
Referred Pain	Yes	Common	Possible
Pain on hyperextension and rotation of cervical spine	Yes—typically symptoms increase.	Yes—typically sharp localized pain at joint (often without increased referral of symptoms)	No
Spine stiffness	Possible	Yes	Possible—typically more muscular as compared to joint stiffness.
Paresthesia	Yes	Not likely, but possible.	Possible
Reflexes	May be affected	Not affected	May be affected
Muscle guarding	Yes	Yes	Yes
Tension tests	Positive	Typically not positive	May be positive
Pallor and coolness	No	No	Possible—primarily in hands.
Muscle weakness	Possible	No	Not early (later smaller muscles)
Muscle fatigue and cramps	No	No	Possible

Adapted from Magee D: Orthopedic Physical Assessment, 3rd ed. Saunders 1997, p 148.

(5) Diagnostic tests utilized: plain film imaging to identify abnormal bony anatomy and MRI to identify abnormal soft tissue anatomy. Electrodiagnostic test to assess nerve dysfunction.

(6) Clinical examination including the following special tests will be useful to make diagnosis.
   (a) Adson's test.
   (b) Roos test.
   (c) Wright test.
   (d) Costoclavicular test.

(7) Medications.
   (a) Acetaminophen for pain.
   (b) NSAIDs for pain and/or inflammation.

(8) Physical therapy goals, outcomes, and interventions.
   (a) Physical therapy intervention varies, depending on the exact cause.
   (b) Includes postural reeducation.
   (c) Functional training and restoration of muscle imbalances using exercise to normalize strength, endurance, coordination, and flexibility.
   (d) Biomechanical faults caused by joint restrictions should be corrected with joint mobilization to the specific restrictions identified during the examination.
   (e) Manipulations (typically first rib articulation) to diminish pain and soft tissue guarding.

e. Acromioclavicular and sternoclavicular joint disorders.

(1) Mechanism of injury is a fall onto shoulder, with upper extremity adducted, or a collision with another individual during a sporting event.

(2) Traditionally, degree of injury is graded from first to third degree. Rockwood classification scale uses grades from I to IV, with grades IV–VI as variations of the traditional grade III.

(3) Upper extremity is positioned in neutral with use of sling in acute phase. Avoid shoulder elevation during the acute phase of healing.

(4) Diagnostic tests utilized: plain film imaging.

(5) Clinical examination including the following special tests will be useful to make diagnosis.
   (a) Shear test.

(6) Surgical repair is rare, due to tendency of acromioclavicular joint degeneration following the repair.

(7) Medications.
   (a) Acetaminophen for pain.
   (b) NSAIDs for pain and/or inflammation.

(8) Physical therapy goals, outcomes, and interventions.
   (a) Emphasize return of function without pain.
   (b) Functional training and restoration of muscle imbalances using exercise to normalize strength, endurance, coordination, and flexibility.
   (c) Manual therapy techniques to AC and SC joints and surrounding connective tissues, such as soft tissue/massage, joint oscillations, and mobilizations to normalize soft tissue and joint biomechanics.

f. Subacromial/subdeltoid bursitis.

(1) Subacromial and subdeltoid bursae (which may be continuous) have a close relationship to

rotator cuff tendons, making them susceptible to overuse.

(2) They can also become impinged beneath the acromial arch.

(3) Diagnosis made by clinical examination. Differentiate from contractile condition by comparing results of AROM, PROM, and resistive tests.

(4) Medications.

(a) Acetaminophen for pain.

(b) NSAIDs for pain and/or inflammation.

(5) Physical therapy goals, outcomes, and interventions.

(a) Refer to intervention for general bursitis/tendonitis/tendonosis.

g. Rotator cuff tendonosis/tendonopathy.

(1) Tendons of rotator cuff are susceptible to tendonitis due to relatively poor blood supply near insertion of muscles.

(2) Results from mechanical impingement of the distal attachment of the rotator cuff on the anterior acromion and/or coracoacromial ligament with repetitive overhead activities.

(3) Diagnostic tests utilized: MRI may be used, but sometimes not sensitive enough for accurate assessment.

(4) Clinical examination including the following special tests will be useful to make diagnosis.

(a) Supraspinatus test.

(b) Neer's impingement test.

(5) Medications.

(a) Acetaminophen for pain.

(b) NSAIDs for pain and/or inflammation.

(6) Physical therapy goals, outcomes, and interventions.

(a) Refer to intervention for general bursitis/tendonitis/tendonosis.

h. Impingement syndrome.

(1) Characterized by soft tissue inflammation of the shoulder from impingement against the acromion with repetitive overhead AROM.

(2) Diagnostic tests utilized: arthrogram or MRI.

(3) Clinical examination including the following special tests will be useful to make diagnosis.

(a) Neer's impingement test.

(b) Supraspinatus test.

(c) Drop arm test.

(4) Surgical repair of shoulder impingement. The patient should avoid shoulder elevation greater than 90°.

(5) Medications.

(a) Acetaminophen for pain.

(b) NSAIDs for pain and/or inflammation.

(6) Physical therapy goals, outcomes, and interventions.

(a) Restoration of posture.

(b) Correction of muscle imbalances and biomechanical faults using strengthening, endurance, coordination, and flexibility exercises to gain restoration of normal function.

(c) Biomechanical faults caused by joint restrictions should be corrected with joint mobilization to the specific restrictions identified during the examination.

i. Internal (posterior) impingement.

(1) Characterized by an irritation between the rotator cuff and greater tuberosity or posterior glenoid and labrum.

(2) Often seen in athletes performing overhead activities. Pain commonly noted in posterior shoulder.

(3) Diagnostic tests utilized: None.

(4) Clinical examination including posterior internal impingement test helps to identify this condition.

(5) Medications.

(a) Acetaminophen for pain.

(b) NSAIDs for pain and/or inflammation.

(6) Physical therapy goals, outcomes, and interventions.

(a) Correction of muscle imbalances and biomechanical faults using strengthening, endurance, coordination, and flexibility exercises to gain restoration of normal function.

(b) Biomechanical faults caused by joint restrictions should be corrected with joint mobilization to the specific restrictions identified during the examination.

j. Bicipital tendonosis/tendonopathy.

(1) Most commonly an inflammation of the long head of the biceps.

(2) Results from mechanical impingement of the proximal tendon, between the anterior acromion and the bicipital groove of the humerus.

(3) Diagnostic tests utilized: MRI may be used, but sometimes not sensitive enough for accurate assessment.

(4) Clinical examination including the following special tests will be useful to make diagnosis.

(a) Speed's test.

(5) Medications.

(a) Acetaminophen for pain.

(b) NSAIDs for pain and/or inflammation.

(6) Physical therapy goals, outcomes, and interventions.

(a) Refer to intervention for general bursitis/tendonosis/tendonopathy.

k. Proximal humeral fractures.

(1) Humeral neck fractures frequently occur with a fall onto an outstretched upper extremity

among older osteoporotic women. Generally does not require immobilization or surgical repair, since it is a fairly stable fracture.

(2) Greater tuberosity fractures are more common in middle-aged and elder adults. Usually related to a fall onto the shoulder, and does not require immobilization for healing.

(3) Diagnostic tests utilized: plain film imaging.

(4) Medications.

(a) Acetaminophen for pain.

(b) NSAIDs for pain and/or inflammation.

(5) Physical therapy goals, outcomes, and interventions.

(a) Physical therapy intervention emphasizes return of function without pain.

(b) Functional training and restoration of muscle imbalances using exercise to normalize strength, endurance, coordination, and flexibility.

(c) Biomechanical faults caused by joint restrictions should be corrected with joint mobilization to the specific restrictions identified during the examination.

(d) Early PROM is important in preventing capsular adhesions.

l. Adhesive capsulitis (frozen shoulder) (see Tables 1-23, 1-24, and Appendix 1J).

(1) Characterized by a restriction in shoulder motion as a result of inflammation and fibrosis of the shoulder capsule, usually due to disuse following injury or repetitive microtrauma.

(2) Restriction follows a capsular pattern of limitation:

(a) Greatest limitation in ER, followed by abduction and flexion, and least restricted in internal rotation.

(3) Commonly seen in association with diabetes mellitus.

(4) Diagnosis made by clinical examination by comparing results of AROM, PROM, resistive tests, and palpation.

(5) Medications.

(a) Acetaminophen for pain.

(b) NSAIDs for pain and/or inflammation.

(6) Physical therapy goals, outcomes, and interventions.

(a) Physical therapy intervention emphasizes return of function without pain.

(b) Functional training and restoration of muscle imbalances using exercise to normalize strength, endurance, coordination, and flexibility.

(c) Biomechanical faults caused by joint restrictions should be corrected with joint mobilization to the specific restrictions identified during the examination.

2. Elbow conditions.

a. Elbow contractures.

(1) Loss of motion in capsular pattern (loss of flexion greater than extension).

(2) Loss of motion in noncapsular pattern as the result of a loose body in the joint, ligamentous sprain, and/or complex regional pain syndrome.

(3) Diagnosis made by clinical examination by comparing results of AROM, PROM, resistive tests, and palpation.

(4) Medications.

(a) Acetaminophen for pain.

(b) NSAIDs for pain and/or inflammation.

(5) Physical therapy goals, outcomes, and interventions.

(a) Biomechanical faults caused by joint restrictions should be corrected with joint mobilization to the specific restrictions identified during the examination.

(b) Soft tissue/massage techniques, modalities, flexibility exercises, and functional exercises, including strengthening, endurance, and coordination.

(c) Splinting may be an effective adjunct to physical therapy management in regaining loss of motion for capsular restrictions.

b. Lateral epicondylosis/epicondylopathy ("tennis elbow").

(1) Most often a chronic degenerative condition of the extensor carpi radialis brevis tendon (ECRB) at its proximal attachment to the lateral epicondyle of the humerus.

(2) Onset is gradual, usually the result of sports activities or occupations that require repetitive wrist extension or strong grip with the wrist extended, resulting in overloading the ECRB.

(3) Must rule out involvement or relationship to cervical spine condition.

(4) Clinical examination including lateral epicondylitis and epicondylopathy tests helps to identify this condition.

(5) Medications.

(a) Acetaminophen for pain.

(b) NSAIDs for pain and/or inflammation.

(6) Physical therapy goals, outcomes, and interventions.

(a) Correction of muscle imbalances and biomechanical faults using strengthening, endurance, coordination, and flexibility exercises to gain restoration of normal function.

(b) Endurance and strengthening exercise with initial emphasis on eccentric phase of exercise.

(c) Biomechanical faults caused by joint restrictions should be corrected with joint mobilization to the specific restrictions identified during the examination.
(d) Education regarding prevention.
(e) Cryotherapy, thermotherapy, hydrotherapy, sound agents, and TENS for symptomatic relief of pain.
(f) Counterforce bracing is frequently used to reduce forces along the ECRB.

c. Medial epicondylosis/epicondylopathy ("golfer's elbow").
(1) Usually a degenerative condition of the pronator teres and flexor carpi radialis tendons at their attachment to the medial epicondyle of the humerus.
(2) Occurs with overuse in sports, such as baseball pitching, driving golf swings, swimming, or occupations that require a strong hand grip and excessive pronation of the forearm.
(3) Diagnostic tests utilized: none.
(4) Clinical examination including medial epicondylitis test helps to identify this condition.
(5) Physical therapy goals, outcomes, and interventions.
(a) Intervention is similar to lateral epicondylitis and epicondylopathy.

d. Distal humeral fractures.
(1) Complications can include loss of motion, myositis ossificans, malalignment, neurovascular compromise, ligamentous injury, and CRPS.
(2) Supracondylar fractures must be examined quickly for neurovascular status due to high number of neurological (typically radial nerve involvement) and vascular structures that pass through this region (may lead to Volkmann's ischemia). In youth, it is important to assess growth plate as well. These fractures have a high incidence of malunion.
(3) Lateral epicondyle fractures are fairly common in young people and typically require an open reduction internal fixation (ORIF) to ensure absolute alignment.
(4) Diagnostic tests utilized: plain film imaging.
(5) Medications.
(a) Acetaminophen for pain.
(b) NSAIDs for pain and/or inflammation.
(6) Physical therapy goals, outcomes, and interventions.
(a) Physical therapy intervention includes pain reduction and limiting the inflammatory response following trauma and/or surgery.
(b) Improving flexibility of shortened structures, strengthening, and training to restore functional use of UE.

e. Osteochondrosis of humeral capitellum.
(1) Osteochondritis dissecans affects central and/or lateral aspect of capitellum or radial head. An osteochondral bone fragment becomes detached from articular surface, forming a loose body in joint. Caused by repetitive compressive forces between radial head and humeral capitellum. Occurs in adolescents between 12 and 15 years of age.
(2) Panner's disease is a localized avascular necrosis of capitellum leading to loss of subchondral bone, with fissuring and softening of articular surfaces of radiocapitellar joint. Etiology is unknown, but occurs in children age 10 or younger.
(3) Diagnostic tests utilized: plain film imaging.
(4) Medications.
(a) Acetaminophen for pain.
(b) NSAIDs for pain and/or inflammation.
(5) Physical therapy goals, outcomes, and interventions.
(a) Physical therapy intervention includes rest with avoidance of any throwing or upper extremity-loading activities (e.g., gymnastics).
(b) When patient is pain-free, initiate flexibility and strengthening/endurance/coordination exercises.
(c) During late phases of rehabilitation, a program to slowly increase load on joint is initiated. If symptoms persist, surgical intervention is necessary.
(d) After surgery, initial focus of rehabilitation is to minimize pain and swelling using modalities. Flexibility exercises are begun immediately following surgery.
(e) Thereafter, a progressive strengthening program is initiated.
(f) Biomechanical faults caused by joint restrictions should be corrected with joint mobilization to the specific restrictions identified during the examination.

f. Ulnar collateral ligament injuries.
(1) Occurs as result of repetitive valgus stresses to medial elbow with overhead throwing.
(2) Clinical signs include pain along medial elbow at distal insertion of ligament. In some cases, paresthesias are reported in ulnar nerve distribution with positive Tinel's sign.
(3) Diagnostic tests utilized: MRI.
(4) Clinical examination including medial ligament instability test helps to identify this condition.
(5) Medications.
(a) Acetaminophen for pain.
(b) NSAIDs for pain and/or inflammation.

(6) Physical therapy goals, outcomes, and interventions.
(a) Initial intervention includes rest and pain management.
(b) After resolution of pain and inflammation, strengthening exercises that focus on elbow flexors are initiated. Taping can also be used for protection during return to activities.

g. Nerve entrapments.
(1) Ulnar nerve entrapment.
(a) Various causes including direct trauma at the cubital tunnel, traction due to laxity at medial aspect of elbow, compression due to a thickened retinaculum or hypertrophy of flexor carpi ulnaris muscle, recurrent subluxation or dislocation, and DJD that affects the cubital tunnel.
(b) Clinical findings include medial elbow pain, paresthesias in ulnar distribution, and a positive Tinel's sign.
(2) Median nerve entrapment.
(a) Occurs within pronator teres muscle and under superficial head of flexor digitorum superficialis with repetitive gripping activities required in occupations (e.g., electricians) and with leisure time activities (e.g., tennis).
(b) Clinical signs include an aching pain with weakness of forearm muscles and positive Tinel's sign, with paresthesias in median nerve distribution.
(3) Radial nerve entrapment.
(a) Entrapment of distal branches (posterior interosseous nerve) occurs within radial tunnel (radial tunnel syndrome) as result of overhead activities and throwing.
(b) Clinical signs include lateral elbow pain that can be confused with lateral epicondylitis and epicondylopathy, pain over supinator muscle, and paresthesias in a radial nerve distribution. Tinel's sign may be positive.
(4) Diagnostic tests utilized: electrodiagnostic tests.
(5) Clinical examination helps to identify this condition.
(6) Medications.
(a) Acetaminophen for pain.
(b) NSAIDs for pain and/or inflammation.
(c) Neurontin for neuropathic pain.
(7) Physical therapy goals, outcomes, and interventions.
(a) Early intervention includes rest, avoiding exacerbating activities, use of NSAIDs, modalities, and soft tissue/massage techniques to reduce inflammation and pain.
(b) If abnormal neurotension is present, neurodynamic mobilization may be indicated.
(c) Protective padding and night splints to maintain slackened position of involved nerves.
(d) With reduction in pain and paresthesias, rehabilitation program should focus on strengthening/endurance/coordination exercise of involved muscles to achieve muscle balance between agonists and antagonists, normal flexibility of shortened structures, and normalization of strength/endurance/coordination.
(e) Intervention should also include functional training, patient education, and self-management techniques.

h. Elbow dislocations.
(1) Posterior dislocations account for most dislocations occurring at elbow.
(a) Posterior dislocations are defined by position of olecranon relative to the humerus.
(b) Posterolateral dislocations are most common and occur as the result of elbow hyperextension from a fall on the outstretched upper extremity.
(c) Posterior dislocations frequently cause avulsion fractures of medial epicondyle secondary to traction pull of medial collateral ligament.
(2) Anterior and radial head dislocations account for only 1%–2% of all elbow dislocations.
(3) With a complete dislocation, ulnar collateral ligament will rupture, with possible rupture of anterior capsule, lateral collateral ligament, brachialis muscle, and/or wrist flexor and extensor muscles.
(4) Clinical signs include rapid swelling, severe pain at the elbow, and a deformity with the olecranon pushed posteriorly.
(5) Diagnostic tests utilized: plain film imaging.
(6) Medications.
(a) Acetaminophen for pain.
(b) NSAIDs for pain and/or inflammation.
(7) Physical therapy goals, outcomes, and interventions.
(a) Initial intervention includes reduction of the dislocation.
(b) If elbow is stable, there is an initial phase of immobilization, followed by rehabilitation focusing on regaining flexibility within limits of stability and strengthening.
(c) If elbow is not stable, surgery is indicated.

3. Wrist and hand conditions.

a. Carpal tunnel syndrome (repetitive stress syndrome).
(1) Compression of the median nerve at the carpal tunnel of the wrist due to inflammation of the flexor tendons and/or median nerve.

(2) Commonly occurs as result of repetitive wrist motions or gripping, with pregnancy, diabetes, and rheumatoid arthritis.
(3) Must rule out potential of cervical spine dysfunction, TOS, or peripheral nerve entrapment that mimics this condition.
(4) Diagnostic tests utilized: electrodiagnostic testing.
(5) Common clinical findings include exacerbation of burning, tingling, pins and needles, and numbness into median nerve distribution at night, and a positive Tinel's sign and/or Phalen's test. Long-term compression causes atrophy and weakness of thenar muscles and lateral two lumbricals.
(6) Medications.
   (a) Acetaminophen for pain.
   (b) NSAIDs for pain and/or inflammation.
(7) Physical therapy goals, outcomes, and interventions.
   (a) Biomechanical faults caused by joint restrictions should be corrected with joint mobilization to the specific restrictions identified during the examination.
   (b) Soft tissue/massage techniques, modalities, flexibility exercises, and functional exercises including strengthening, endurance, and coordination.

b. de Quervain's tenosynovitis.
(1) Inflammation of extensor pollicis brevis and abductor pollicis longus tendons at first dorsal compartment.
(2) Results from repetitive microtrauma or as a complication of swelling during pregnancy.
(3) Diagnostic tests utilized: MRI, but usually not necessary to make diagnosis.
(4) Clinical signs include: pain at anatomical snuffbox, swelling, decreased grip and pinch strength, positive Finkelstein's test (which places tendons on a stretch).
(5) Medications.
   (a) Acetaminophen for pain.
   (b) NSAIDs for pain and/or inflammation.
(6) Physical therapy goals, outcomes, and interventions.
   (a) Biomechanical faults caused by joint restrictions should be corrected with joint mobilization to the specific restrictions identified during the examination.
   (b) Soft tissue/massage techniques, modalities, flexibility exercises, and functional exercises including strengthening, endurance, and coordination.

c. Colles' fracture.
(1) Most common wrist fracture, resulting from a fall onto an outstretched upper extremity (UE). These fractures are immobilized for 5–8 weeks. Complication of median nerve compression can occur with excessive edema.
(2) Characteristic "dinner fork" deformity of wrist and hand results from dorsal or posterior displacement of distal fragment of radius, with a radial shift of wrist and hand.
(3) Diagnostic tests utilized: plain film imaging.
(4) Complications may include loss of motion, decreased grip strength, CRPS, and carpal tunnel syndrome.
(5) Medications.
   (a) Acetaminophen for pain.
   (b) NSAIDs for pain and/or inflammation.
(6) Physical therapy goals, outcomes, and interventions.
   (a) Early physical therapy intervention that focuses on normalizing flexibility is paramount to functional recovery of wrist and hand.
   (b) Biomechanical faults caused by joint restrictions should be corrected with joint mobilization to the specific restrictions identified during the examination.
   (c) Soft tissue/massage techniques, modalities, flexibility exercises, and functional exercises including strengthening, endurance, and coordination.

d. Smith's fracture.
(1) Similar to Colles' fracture, except distal fragment of radius dislocates in a volar direction, causing a characteristic "garden spade" deformity.
(2) Diagnostic tests utilized: plain film imaging.
(3) Medications.
   (a) Acetaminophen for pain.
   (b) NSAIDs for pain and/or inflammation.
(4) Physical therapy goals, outcomes, and interventions.
   (a) Intervention is similar to Colles' fracture.

e. Scaphoid fracture.
(1) Results from a fall onto outstretched UE in a younger person. Most commonly fractured carpal.
(2) Diagnostic tests utilized: plain film imaging.
(3) Complications include a high incidence of avascular necrosis of the proximal fragment of the scaphoid secondary to poor vascular supply. Carpals are immobilized for 4–8 weeks.
(4) Medications.
   (a) Acetaminophen for pain.
   (b) NSAIDs for pain and/or inflammation.
(5) Physical therapy goals, outcomes, and interventions.
   (a) Early intervention includes maintenance of flexibility of distal and proximal joints while

UE is casted. Later intervention emphasizes strengthening, stretching, and joint and soft tissue mobilizations to regain full functional use of wrist and hand.

f. Dupuytren's contracture.
   (1) Observed as banding on palm and digit flexion contractures, resulting from contracture of palmar fascia that adheres to skin.
   (2) Affects men more often than women.
   (3) Contracture usually affects the metacarpophalangeal (MCP) and proximal interphalangeal (PIP) joints of fourth and fifth digits in nondiabetic individuals and affects third and fourth digits most often in individuals with diabetes.
   (4) Medications.
      (a) Acetaminophen for pain.
      (b) NSAIDs for pain and/or inflammation.
   (5) Physical therapy goals, outcomes, and interventions.
      (a) Physical therapy intervention includes flexibility exercise to prevent further contracture and splint fabrication/application.
      (b) Once contracture is under control, promote restoration of normal hand function through functional exercises.
      (c) Physical therapy intervention following surgery includes wound management, edema control, and progression of functional exercise.

g. Boutonnière deformity.
   (1) Results from rupture of central tendinous slip of extensor hood.
   (2) Observed deformity is extension of MCP and distal interphalangeal (DIP) with flexion of PIP.
   (3) Commonly occurs following trauma, or in rheumatoid arthritis with degeneration of the central extensor tendon.
   (4) Medications.
      (a) Acetaminophen for pain.
      (b) NSAIDs for pain and/or inflammation.
   (5) Physical therapy goals, outcomes, and interventions.
      (a) Physical therapy intervention includes edema management, flexibility exercises of involved and uninvolved joints, splinting or taping, and functional strengthening/endurance/coordination exercises.

h. Swan neck deformity.
   (1) Results from contracture of intrinsic muscles with dorsal subluxation of lateral extensor tendons.
   (2) Observed deformity is flexion of MCP and DIP with extension of PIP.
   (3) Commonly occurs following trauma, or with rheumatoid arthritis following degeneration of lateral extensor tendons.
   (4) Diagnostic tests utilized: plain film imaging, but may not be necessary.
   (5) Medications.
      (a) Acetaminophen for pain.
      (b) NSAIDs for pain and/or inflammation.
   (6) Physical therapy goals, outcomes, and interventions.
      (a) Physical therapy intervention includes edema management, flexibility exercises of involved and uninvolved joints, splinting or taping, and functional strengthening/endurance/coordination exercises.

i. Ape hand deformity
   (1) Observed as thenar muscle wasting, with first digit moving dorsally until it is in line with second digit.
   (2) Results from median nerve dysfunction.
   (3) Diagnostic tests utilized: electrodiagnostic testing.
   (4) Medications.
      (a) Acetaminophen for pain.
      (b) NSAIDs for pain and/or inflammation.
   (5) Physical therapy goals, outcomes, and interventions.
      (a) Physical therapy intervention includes edema management, flexibility exercises of involved and uninvolved joints, splinting or taping, and functional strengthening/endurance/coordination exercises.

j. Mallet finger
   (1) Rupture or avulsion of extensor tendon at its insertion into distal phalanx of digit.
   (2) Observed deformity is flexion of DIP joint.
   (3) Usually occurs from trauma, forcing distal phalanx into a flexed position.
   (4) Diagnostic tests utilized: possibly MRI.
   (5) Medications.
      (a) Acetaminophen for pain.
      (b) NSAIDs for pain and/or inflammation.
   (6) Physical therapy goals, outcomes, and interventions.
      (a) Physical therapy intervention includes edema management, flexibility exercises of involved and uninvolved joints, splinting or taping, and functional strengthening/endurance/coordination exercises.

k. Gamekeeper's thumb.
   (1) A sprain/rupture of ulnar collateral ligament of MCP joint of first digit.
   (2) Results in medial instability of thumb.
   (3) Frequently occurs during a fall while skiing, when increasing forces are placed on thumb through ski pole. Immobilized for 6 weeks.
   (4) Diagnostic tests utilized: possibly MRI.
   (5) Medications.
      (a) Acetaminophen for pain.
      (b) NSAIDs for pain and/or inflammation.

(6) Physical therapy goals, outcomes, and interventions.
(a) Physical therapy intervention includes edema management, flexibility exercises of involved and uninvolved joints, splinting or taping, and functional strengthening/endurance/coordination exercises.

l. Boxer's fracture.
(1) Fracture of neck of fifth metacarpal.
(2) Frequently sustained during a fight, or from punching a wall in anger or frustration.
(3) Casted for 2–4 weeks.
(4) Diagnostic tests utilized: plain film imaging.
(5) Medications.
(a) Acetaminophen for pain.
(b) NSAIDs for pain and/or inflammation.
(6) Physical therapy goals, outcomes, and interventions.
(a) Physical therapy intervention includes edema management, flexibility exercise initially at uninvolved joints, followed by involved joints after sufficient healing has occurred.
(b) Initiation of functional strengthening/endurance/coordination occurs when flexibility is restored.

Lower Extremity Conditions

1. Hip conditions (see Appendices 1D and 1L).
a. Avascular necrosis (AVN) of the hip (osteonecrosis).
(1) Multiple etiologies resulting in an impaired blood supply to the femoral head.
(2) Hip ROM is decreased in flexion, internal rotation, and abduction.
(3) Diagnostic tests utilized: plain film imaging, bone scans, CT, and/or MRI may be utilized.
(4) Symptoms include pain in the groin and/or thigh, and tenderness with palpation at the hip joint.
(5) Coxalgic gait.
(6) Medications.
(a) Acetaminophen for pain.
(b) NSAIDs for pain and/or inflammation.
(c) Corticosteroids contraindicated since they may be causative factor. Patient taking steroids for some other condition should have dose decreased.
(7) Physical therapy goals, outcomes, and interventions.
(a) Joint/bone protection strategies.
(b) Maintain/improve joint mechanics and connective tissue functions.
(c) Implementation of aerobic capacity/endurance conditioning or reconditioning such as aquatic programs.
(d) Postsurgical intervention includes regaining functional flexibility, improving strength/endurance/coordination, and gait training.

b. Coxa vara and coxa valga.
(1) Angle of femoral neck with shaft of femur is $< 115°$; coxa vara results.
(2) Angle of femoral neck with shaft of femur is $> 125°$; coxa valga results.
(3) Coxa vara usually results from a defect in ossification of head of femur. Coxa vara and coxa valga may result from necrosis of femoral head occurring with septic arthritis.
(4) Diagnostic tests utilized: plain film imaging.
(5) Physical therapy goals, outcomes, and interventions.
(a) Maintain/improve joint mechanics and connective tissue functions.

c. Trochanteric bursitis.
(1) An inflammation of deep trochanteric bursa from a direct blow, irritation by iliotibial band (ITB), and biomechanical/gait abnormalities causing repetitive microtrauma.
(2) This condition is common in patients with rheumatoid arthritis.
(3) Diagnostic tests utilized: none.
(4) Diagnosis made by clinical examination. Differentiate from contractile condition by comparing results of AROM, PROM, and resistive tests.
(5) Medications.
(a) Acetaminophen for pain.
(b) NSAIDs for pain and/or inflammation.
(6) Physical therapy goals, outcomes, and interventions.
(a) Refer to intervention for general bursitis/tendonitis/tendonosis.

d. Iliotibial band tightness/friction disorder.
(1) Etiology: tight ITB, abnormal gait patterns.
(2) Results in inflammation of trochanteric bursa.
(3) Noble compression test is positive when friction is introduced over the lateral femoral condyle during knee extension. Ober's test will also demonstrate tightness in ITB.
(4) Medications.
(a) Acetaminophen for pain.
(b) NSAIDs for pain and/or inflammation.
(5) Physical therapy goals, outcomes, and interventions.
(a) Reduction of pain and inflammation utilizing modalities, soft tissue techniques, and manual therapy techniques such as soft tissue/massage and joint oscillations.

(b) Correction of muscle imbalances and biomechanical faults using strengthening, endurance, coordination, and flexibility (ITB, hamstrings, quadriceps, and hip flexors) exercises to gain restoration of normal function.

(c) Biomechanical faults caused by joint restrictions should be corrected with joint mobilization to the specific restrictions identified during the examination.

(d) Gait training and patient education regarding the selection of running shoes and running surfaces. Orthoses may be fabricated.

e. Piriformis syndrome.

(1) Piriformis muscle is an external rotator of hip and can become overworked with excessive pronation of foot, causing abnormal femoral internal rotation. Considered a tonic muscle that is active with motion of sacroiliac joint, particularly sacrum.

(2) Tightness or spasm of piriformis muscle can result in compression of sciatic nerve and/or sacroiliac dysfunction.

(3) Diagnostic tests utilized: possibly electrodiagnostic tests for sciatic nerve.

(4) Signs and symptoms include:

(a) Restriction in internal rotation.

(b) Pain with palpation of piriformis muscle.

(c) Referral of pain to posterior thigh.

(d) Weakness in ER, positive piriformis test.

(e) Uneven sacral base.

(5) Perform lower extremity biomechanical examination to determine if abnormal biomechanics are the cause. Must rule out involvement of lumbar spine and/or sacroiliac joint.

(6) Medications.

(a) Acetaminophen for pain.

(b) NSAIDs for pain and/or inflammation.

(c) Neurontin for neuropathic pain.

(7) Physical therapy goals, outcomes, and interventions.

(a) Reduction of pain utilizing modalities and manual therapy techniques, such as soft tissue/massage to piriformis muscle.

(b) Joint oscillations to hip or pelvis to inhibit pain.

(c) Correction of muscle imbalances and biomechanical faults using strengthening, endurance, coordination, and flexibility exercises to gain restoration of normal function.

(d) Restore muscle balance and patient education regarding protection of the sacroiliac joint (e.g., instruction not to step off a curb onto the dysfunctional lower extremity).

(e) Correction of biomechanical faults may include orthoses or orthotic devices for feet.

2. Knee conditions.

a. Ligament sprains (see Appendix 1G).

(1) Four major ligaments may be involved (anterior cruciate [ACL], posterior cruciate [PCL], medial collateral [MCL], and lateral collateral [LCL]).

(2) Injury to the ligaments may result in a single plane or rotary instability.

(a) ACL laxity may result in single plane anterior instability.

(b) PCL laxity may result in single plane posterior instability.

(c) ACL and MCL laxity may result in anteromedial rotary instability.

(d) ACL and LCL laxity may result in anterolateral rotary instability.

(e) PCL and MCL laxity may result in posteromedial rotary instability.

(f) PCL and LCL laxity may result in posterolateral rotary instability.

(3) Classification of injury.

(a) First degree, resulting in little or no instability.

(b) Second degree, resulting in minimal to moderate instability.

(c) Third degree, resulting in extreme instability.

(4) "Unhappy triad" includes injury to the MCL, ACL, and the medial meniscus, resulting from a combination of valgum, flexion, and ER forces applied to knee when the foot is planted.

(5) Diagnostic tests utilized: MRI. Difficult to visualize complete ACL on MRI, so often read incorrectly as partially torn even if normal.

(6) Refer to knee special tests that help to identify ligamentous instabilities of knee joint.

(7) Reconstruction frequently involves a combination of intra-articular and extra-articular procedures.

(8) Medications.

(a) Acetaminophen for pain.

(b) NSAIDs for pain and/or inflammation.

(9) Physical therapy goals, outcomes, and interventions.

(a) Physical therapy intervention is varied depending on whether the patient undergoes a surgical procedure, as well as type of surgery performed.

(b) Reduction of pain and inflammation utilizing modalities, soft tissue techniques, and manual therapy techniques such as oscillations.

(c) Postoperatively, continuous passive motion (CPM) devices may be used to promote flexibility of the joint.

(d) Correction of muscle imbalances and biomechanical faults using strengthening, endurance, coordination, and flexibility exercises to gain restoration of normal function.
(e) Biomechanical faults caused by joint restrictions should be corrected with joint mobilization to the specific restrictions identified during the examination.
(f) Progression to functional training based on patient's occupation and/or recreational goals.

b. Meniscal injuries (see Appendix 1C).
(1) Result from a combination of forces to include tibiofemoral joint flexion, compression, and rotation, which places abnormal shear stresses on the meniscus.
(2) Symptoms include lateral and/or medial joint pain, effusion, joint popping, knee giving way during walking, limitation in flexibility of knee joint, and joint locking.
(3) Diagnostic tests utilized: MRI typically done, but not always sensitive enough to confirm tear.
(4) Clinical examination including the following special tests will be useful to make diagnosis.
(a) McMurray's test.
(b) Apley test.
(5) Medications.
(a) Acetaminophen for pain.
(b) NSAIDs for pain and/or inflammation.
(6) Physical therapy goals, outcomes, and interventions.
(a) Reduction of pain and inflammation utilizing modalities, soft tissue/massage techniques to surrounding muscles, and manual therapy techniques, such as joint oscillations to inhibit pain.
(b) Correction of muscle imbalances and biomechanical faults using strengthening, endurance, coordination, and flexibility exercises to gain restoration of normal function.
(c) Biomechanical faults caused by joint restrictions should be corrected with joint mobilization to the specific restrictions identified during the examination.
(d) Progression to functional training based on patient's occupation and/or recreational goals.

c. Patellofemoral conditions.
(1) Abnormal patella positions.
(a) Patella alta.
- Malalignment in which patella tracks superiorly in femoral intercondylar notch.
- May result in chronic patellar subluxation.
- Positive camel back sign (two bumps over anterior knee region instead of typical one). Two bumps, since patella rides high within femoral condyles, creating a superior bump with tibial tuberosity forming second bump inferiorly.

(b) Patella baja.
- Malalignment in which patella tracks inferiorly in femoral intercondylar notch.
- Results in restricted knee extension with abnormal cartilaginous wearing, resulting in DJD.

(c) Lateral patellar tracking.
- Could result if there is an increase in "Q angle" with a tendency for lateral subluxation or dislocation.

(d) Diagnostic tests utilized: plain film imaging including "sunrise" view.
(e) Physical therapy goals, outcomes, and interventions.
- Regaining functional strength of structures surrounding knee, particularly vastus medialis oblique (VMO) muscle, regain normal flexibility of ITB and hamstrings, orthoses (if appropriate), and patellar bracing/taping.

(2) Patellofemoral pain syndrome (PFPS).
(a) Common dysfunction that may occur on its own or in conjunction with other entities. May have been caused by trauma or by congenital/developmental dysfunction.
(b) May be interrelated with chondromalacia patellae and/or patella tendonitis.
(c) Common result is an abnormal patellofemoral tracking leading to abnormal patellofemoral stress.
(d) Occasionally, surgery is indicated.
(e) Diagnostic tests utilized: possibly MRI to rule out other dysfunctions.
(f) Medications.
- Acetaminophen for pain.
- NSAIDs for pain and/or inflammation.

(g) Physical therapy goals, outcomes, and interventions.
- Patellofemoral (McConnell) taping is helpful to inhibit pain during rehabilitation.
- Patella mobilization indicated with restrictions of patella glides (e.g., if patella is in a lateral glide position and has decreased medial glide, perform a medial glide joint mobilization to the patella).

- Correction of muscle imbalances and biomechanical faults using strengthening, endurance, coordination, and flexibility exercises to gain restoration of normal function.
- *Don't use quadriceps sets, single-leg raise flexion, and isolated quadriceps exercises for patellofemoral pain* (White N, et al. Phys Ther. 2015).

(3) Patellar tendonosis/tendonopathy ("jumper's knee").
(a) This is a degenerative condition of the patellar tendon, typically of the deep aspect of the tendon.
(b) May be related to overload and/or jumping related activities/sports.
(c) May also be interrelated to patellofemoral dysfunction.
(d) Diagnosis made by clinical examination.
(e) Medications.
- Acetaminophen for pain.
- NSAIDs for pain and/or inflammation.
- Corticosteroid injection or by mouth.

(f) Physical therapy goals, outcomes, and interventions.
- Refer to intervention for general tendonosis/tendonopathy.

d. Pes anserine bursitis.
(1) Typically caused by overuse or a contusion.
(2) Must be differentiated from tendonitis.
(3) Diagnosis made by clinical examination. Differentiate from contractile condition by comparing results of AROM, PROM, and resistive tests.
(4) Medications.
(a) Acetaminophen for pain.
(b) NSAIDs for pain and/or inflammation.
(c) Corticosteroid injection or by mouth.
(5) Physical therapy goals, outcomes, and interventions.

e. Fractures involving knee joint.
(1) Femoral condyle.
(a) Medial femoral most often involved due to its anatomical design.
(b) Numerous etiological factors include trauma, shearing, impacting, and avulsion forces.
(c) Common mechanism of injury is a fall, with knee subjected to a shearing force.
(2) Tibial plateau.
(a) Common mechanism of injury is a combination of valgum and compression forces to knee when knee is in a flexed position.
(b) Often occurs in conjunction with a medial collateral ligamentous injury.
(3) Epiphyseal plate.
(a) Mechanism of injury is frequently a weight-bearing torsional stress.
(b) Presents more frequently in adolescents where an ACL injury would occur in an adult.
(4) Patella.
(a) Most common mechanism of injury is a direct blow to patella due to a fall.
(5) Diagnostic tests utilized: plain film imaging most likely, unless complex fracture, which would benefit from CT.
(6) Medications.
(a) Acetaminophen for pain.
(b) NSAIDs for pain and/or inflammation.
(7) Physical therapy goals, outcomes, and interventions.
(a) Physical therapy intervention emphasizes return of function without pain.

3. Conditions of the lower leg.

a. Anterior compartment syndrome (ACS).
(1) Increased compartmental pressure resulting in a local ischemic condition.
(2) Multiple etiologies; direct trauma, fracture, overuse, and/or muscle hypertrophy.
(3) Symptoms of chronic or exertional compartment syndrome are produced by exercise or exertion and described as a deep, cramping feeling.
(4) Symptoms of acute ACS are produced by sudden trauma causing swelling within the compartment.
(5) Diagnosis made by clinical examination.
(6) Acute ACS is considered a medical emergency and requires immediate surgical intervention with fasciotomy.

b. Anterior tibial periostitis (shin splints).
(1) Musculotendinous overuse condition.
(2) Three common etiologies:
(a) Abnormal biomechanical alignment.
(b) Poor conditioning.
(c) Improper training methods.
(3) Muscles involved include anterior tibialis and extensor hallucis longus.
(4) Pain elicited with palpation of lateral tibia and anterior compartment.
(5) Diagnosis made by clinical examination.
(6) Medications.
(a) Acetaminophen for pain.
(b) NSAIDS for pain and/or inflammation.
(7) Physical therapy goals, outcomes, and interventions.
(a) Correction of muscle imbalances and biomechanical faults using strengthening, endurance, and coordination exercises.

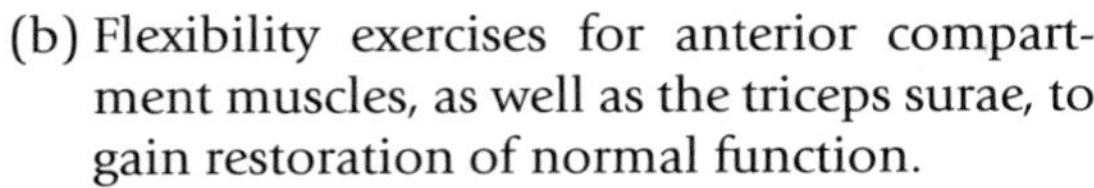

(b) Flexibility exercises for anterior compartment muscles, as well as the triceps surae, to gain restoration of normal function.

c. Medial tibial stress syndrome.

(1) Overuse injury of the posterior tibialis and/or the medial soleus, resulting in periosteal inflammation at the muscular attachments.

(2) Etiology is thought to be excessive pronation.

(3) Pain elicited with palpation of the distal posteromedial border of the tibia.

(4) Diagnosis made by clinical examination.

(5) Medications.

(a) Acetaminophen for pain.

(b) NSAIDs for pain and/or inflammation.

(6) Physical therapy goals, outcomes, and interventions.

(a) Correction of muscle imbalances and biomechanical faults using strengthening, endurance, and coordination exercises.

(b) Flexibility exercises for anterior compartment muscles as well as the triceps surae to gain restoration of normal function.

d. Stress fractures.

(1) Overuse injury resulting most often in microfracture of the tibia or fibula.

(2) 49% of all stress fractures involve the tibia, and 10% involve the fibula.

(3) Three common etiologies: abnormal biomechanical alignment, poor conditioning, and improper training methods.

(4) Diagnostic tests utilized: plain film imaging and bone scan.

(5) Medications.

(a) Acetaminophen for pain.

(b) NSAIDs for pain and/or inflammation.

(6) Physical therapy goals, outcomes, and interventions.

(a) Correction of muscle imbalances and biomechanical faults using strengthening, endurance, and coordination exercises.

(b) Flexibility exercises for anterior compartment muscles as well as the triceps surae to gain restoration of normal function.

4. Foot and ankle conditions.

a. Ligament sprains (see Appendix 1K).

(1) 95% of all ankle sprains involve lateral ligaments.

(2) With lateral sprains, foot is plantar flexed and inverted at time of injury.

(3) The most common grading system is as follows:

(a) Grade I: no loss of function, with minimal tearing of the anterior talofibular ligament.

(b) Grade II: some loss of function, with partial disruption of the anterior talofibular and calcaneofibular ligaments.

(c) Grade III: complete loss of function, with complete tearing of the anterior talofibular and calcaneofibular ligaments, with partial tear of the posterior talofibular ligament.

(4) Diagnostic tests utilized: MRI if necessary.

(5) Instability is evaluated using anterior drawer and talar tilt special tests.

(6) Medications.

(a) Acetaminophen for pain.

(b) NSAIDs for pain and/or inflammation.

(7) Physical therapy goals, outcomes, and interventions.

(a) Physical therapy intervention is varied, depending on whether the patient undergoes a surgical procedure as well as type of surgery that is performed.

(b) Reduction of pain and inflammation utilizing modalities, soft tissue techniques, and manual therapy techniques, such as oscillations.

(c) Correction of muscle imbalances and biomechanical faults using strengthening, endurance, coordination, and flexibility exercises to gain restoration of normal function.

(d) Biomechanical faults caused by joint restrictions should be corrected with joint mobilization to the specific restrictions identified during the examination.

(e) Progression to functional training based on patient's occupation and/or recreational goals.

b. Achilles' tendonosis/tendonopathy (see Appendix 1I).

(1) This is a degenerative condition of the Achilles' tendon.

(2) Clinical examination including Thompson's test helps to identify this condition.

(3) Medications.

(a) Acetaminophen for pain.

(b) NSAIDs for pain and/or inflammation.

(c) Corticosteroid injection or by mouth.

(4) Physical therapy goals, outcomes, and interventions.

(a) Refer to intervention for general bursitis/tendonitis/tendonosis.

c. Fractures of foot and ankle.

(1) Unimalleolar involves the medial or lateral malleolus.

(2) Bimalleolar involves the medial and lateral malleoli.

(3) Trimalleolar involves the medial and lateral malleoli, and the posterior tubercle of the distal tibia.

(4) Diagnostic tests utilized: plain film imaging.
(a) Growth plate fractures are a concern, since bone growth can be affected. Types III and IV fractures, according to the Salter Harris classification, are of most concern and can have a high complication rate (see Table 1-26).
(5) Medications.
(a) Acetaminophen for pain.
(b) NSAIDs for pain and/or inflammation.
(6) Physical therapy goals, outcomes, and interventions.
(a) Physical therapy intervention emphasizes return of function without pain.
(b) Functional training and restoration of muscle imbalances using exercise to normalize strength, endurance, coordination, and flexibility.
(c) Early PROM is important in preventing capsular adhesions.

d. Tarsal tunnel syndrome.
(1) Entrapment of the posterior tibial nerve or one of its branches within the tarsal tunnel.
(2) Over/excessive pronation, overuse problems resulting in tendonitis of the long flexor and posterior tibialis tendon, and trauma may compromise space in the tarsal tunnel.
(3) Symptoms include pain, numbness, and paresthesias along the medial ankle to the plantar surface of the foot.
(4) Diagnostic tests utilized: electrodiagnostic tests.
(5) Positive Tinel's sign at the tarsal tunnel.
(6) Medications.
(a) Acetaminophen for pain.
(b) NSAIDs for pain and/or inflammation.
(c) Neurontin for neuropathic pain.
(7) Physical therapy goals, outcomes, and interventions.
(a) Intervention includes the use of orthoses to maintain neutral alignment of the foot.
(b) If abnormal neurotension is present, neurodynamic mobilization may be indicated.

e. Flexor hallucis tendonopathy.
(1) Identified as a tendonitis in the acute stage, or can present as a chronic tendonosis. Commonly seen in ballet performers.

Table 1-26

Salter-Harris Fracture Classification

TYPE	ANATOMICAL DEFORMITY	COMMON CAUSE	GENERAL PROGNOSIS	MEDICAL MANAGEMENT
I	Entire epiphysis	Caused by shearing, torsion, or avulsion forces.	Good, with very few complications to growth of the bone.	Relocated if necessary, and immobilized with cast.
II	Entire epiphysis and portion of the metaphysis	Usually caused by a shear or avulsion with angular force. Most common type.	May cause decreased bone growth, but typically minimal, so limited negative impact on long term function.	Relocated and immobilized with cast.
III	Portion of the epiphysis	Typically occurs when the growth plate is partially fused. Rare, but most commonly occurs to the distal tibia in adolescents.	This type of fracture may lead to long-term problems secondary to the fracture, crossing the physis and extending into the articular surface of the bone. Even with this potential, the prognosis is typically favorable, since these fractures rarely result in significant deformity.	Relocated and immobilized. Occasionally requires surgical intervention (e.g., ORIF). A specific fracture known as the Tillaux fracture (a Type III fracture of the distal tibia) has a particularly poor prognosis.
IV	Portion of the epiphysis and portion of the metaphysis	Similar to Type III. Most commonly seen in the distal humerus.	Since this fracture interferes with the cartilage growth, it may lead to premature focal fusion of the involved bone causing deformity of the joint.	Generally, surgery (e.g., ORIF) is necessary to restore alignment. Prognosis is correlated to quality of alignment achieved.
V	Nothing "broken off"; compression injury of the epiphyseal plate	This is caused by a compression or crush injury of the epiphyseal plate, with no associated epiphyseal or metaphyseal fracture.	Type V fractures are associated with growth disturbances at the physis, and generally will have a poor functional prognosis.	These are usually found "after the fact," so no immediate intervention is provided. If it is identified acutely, patient is placed on non-weight-bearing protocols.

(2) Medications.
(a) Acetaminophen for pain.
(b) NSAIDs for pain and/or inflammation.
(c) Corticosteroid injection or by mouth.
(3) Physical therapy goals, outcomes, and interventions.
(a) Refer to intervention for general bursitis/tendonitis/tendonosis.

f. Pes cavus (hollow foot).
(1) Numerous etiologies to include genetic predisposition, neurological disorders resulting in muscle imbalances, and contracture of soft tissues.
(2) Deformity observed includes an increased height of longitudinal arches, dropping of anterior arch, metatarsal heads lower than hindfoot, plantar flexion and splaying of forefoot, and claw toes.
(3) Function is limited due to altered arthrokinematics, reducing ability to absorb forces through foot.
(4) Diagnosis made by clinical examination including thorough biomechanical lower quarter exam.
(5) Physical therapy goals, outcomes, and interventions.
(a) Intervention includes patient education emphasizing limitation of high impact sports (e.g., long-distance running and ballet), use of proper footwear, and fitting for orthoses.

g. Equinus.
(1) Etiology can include congenital bone deformity, neurological disorders such as cerebral palsy, contracture of gastrocnemius and/or soleus muscles, trauma, or inflammatory disease.
(2) Deformity observed: plantar flexed foot.
(3) Compensation secondary to limited dorsiflexion includes subtalar or midtarsal pronation.
(4) Diagnosis made by clinical examination, including thorough biomechanical lower quarter exam.
(5) Physical therapy goals, outcomes, and interventions.
(a) Physical therapy intervention includes flexibility exercises of shortened structures within foot, joint mobilization to joint restrictions identified in examination, strengthening to intrinsic and extrinsic foot muscles, and orthotic management.

h. Hallux valgus.
(1) Etiology is varied to include biomechanical malalignment (excessive pronation), ligamentous laxity, heredity, weak muscles, and footwear that is too tight.
(2) Deformity observed: a medial deviation of head of first metatarsal from midline of body; metatarsal and base of proximal first phalanx move medially, while distal phalanx then moves laterally.
(3) Normal metatarsophalangeal angle is 8°–20°.
(4) Diagnosis made by clinical examination, including thorough biomechanical lower quarter exam.
(5) Physical therapy goals, outcomes, and interventions.
(a) Early orthotic fitting and patient education.
(b) Later management requires surgery, followed by flexibility exercises to restore normal function, strengthening exercises, and possible joint mobilization to identified restrictions.

i. Metatarsalgia.
(1) Etiologies.
(a) Mechanical: tight triceps surae group and/or Achilles' tendon, collapse of transverse arch, short first ray, pronation of forefoot.
(b) Structural changes in transverse arch, possibly leading to vascular and/or neural compromise in tissues of forefoot.
(c) Changes in footwear.
(2) Complaint frequently heard is pain at first and second metatarsal heads after long periods of weight bearing.
(3) Diagnosis made by clinical examination including thorough biomechanical lower quarter exam.
(4) Medications.
(a) Acetaminophen for pain.
(b) NSAIDs for pain and/or inflammation.
(c) Neurontin for neuropathic pain.
(5) Physical therapy goals, outcomes, and interventions.
(a) Intervention includes correction of biomechanical abnormality (improving flexibility of triceps surae), modalities to decrease pain.
(b) Prescription and/or creation of orthoses.
(c) Patient education regarding selection of footwear.

j. Charcot-Marie-Tooth disease.
(1) Peroneal muscular atrophy that affects motor and sensory nerves.
(2) May begin in childhood or adulthood.
(3) Initially affects muscles in lower leg and foot, but eventually progresses to muscles of hands and forearm.
(4) Slowly progressive disorder with varying degrees of involvement, depending on degree of genetic dominance.

(5) Diagnostic tests utilized: electrodiagnostic tests.
(6) Diagnosis made by clinical examination including thorough biomechanical lower quarter exam.
(7) Medications.
(a) Acetaminophen for pain.
(b) NSAIDs for pain and/or inflammation.
(c) Neurontin for neuropathic pain.
(8) Physical therapy goals, outcomes, and interventions.
(a) No specific treatment to prevent, since it is an inherited disorder.
(b) Physical therapy intervention centers on preventing contractures/skin breakdown and maximizing patient's functional capacity to perform activities.
(c) Patient education and training regarding braces and ambulatory assistive devices.

k. Plantar fasciitis (see Appendix 1F).
(1) Etiology is usually mechanical.
(a) Chronic irritation of plantar fascia from excessive pronation.
(b) Limited ROM of first MTP and talocrural joint.
(c) Tight triceps surae.
(d) Acute injury from excessive loading of foot.
(e) Rigid cavus foot.
(2) Results in microtears at attachment of plantar fascia.
(3) Diagnostic tests utilized: none.
(4) Diagnosis made by clinical examination including thorough biomechanical lower quarter exam. Differentiated from tarsal tunnel syndrome by a negative Tinel's sign.
(5) Medications.
(a) Acetaminophen for pain.
(b) NSAIDs for pain and/or inflammation.
(c) Corticosteroid injection or by mouth.
(6) Physical therapy goals, outcomes, and interventions.
(a) Physical therapy intervention includes regaining proper mechanical alignment.
(b) Modalities to reduce pain and inflammation.
(c) Flexibility of the plantar fascia for the pes cavus foot.
(d) Careful flexibility exercises for triceps surae.
(e) Joint mobilization to identified restrictions.
(f) Night splints.
(g) Strengthening of invertors of foot.
(h) Patient education regarding selection of footwear, and orthotic fitting.

l. Forefoot/rearfoot deformities.
(1) Rearfoot varus (subtalar varus, calcaneal varus).
(a) Etiology: abnormal mechanical alignment of tibia, shortened rearfoot soft tissues, or malunion of calcaneus.
(b) Deformity observed: rigid inversion of calcaneus when subtalar joint is in neutral position.
(c) Diagnosis made by clinical examination including thorough biomechanical lower quarter exam.
(d) Physical therapy goals, outcomes, and interventions.
- Regaining proper mechanical alignment.
- Improving flexibility of shortened soft tissues.
- Orthotic fitting and patient education regarding selection of footwear.

(2) Rearfoot valgus.
(a) Etiology: abnormal mechanical alignment of the knee (genu valgum), or tibial valgus.
(b) Deformity observed: eversion of calcaneus with a neutral subtalar joint.
(c) Due to increased mobility of hindfoot, fewer musculoskeletal problems develop from this deformity than with rearfoot varus.
(d) Diagnosis made by clinical examination, including thorough biomechanical lower quarter exam.
(e) Physical therapy goals, outcomes, and interventions.
- Regaining proper mechanical alignment.
- Improving flexibility of shortened soft tissues.
- Orthotic fitting and patient education regarding selection of footwear.

(3) Forefoot varus.
(a) Etiology: congenital abnormal deviation of head and neck of talus.
(b) Deformity observed: inversion of forefoot when subtalar joint is in neutral.
(c) Diagnosis made by clinical examination, including thorough biomechanical lower quarter exam.
(d) Physical therapy goals, outcomes, and interventions.
- Regaining proper mechanical alignment.
- Improving flexibility of shortened soft tissues.
- Orthotic fitting and patient education regarding selection of footwear.

(4) Forefoot valgus.
(a) Etiology: congenital abnormal development of head and neck of talus.
(b) Deformity observed: eversion of forefoot when the subtalar joint is in neutral.
(c) Diagnosis made by clinical examination, including thorough biomechanical lower quarter exam.

(d) Physical therapy goals, outcomes, and interventions.
- Regaining proper mechanical alignment.
- Improving flexibility of shortened soft tissues.
- Orthotic fitting and patient education regarding selection of footwear.

Spinal Conditions (see also Appendices 1E and 1H)

1. Muscle strain.
   a. May be related to sudden trauma, chronic or sustained overload, or abnormal muscle biomechanics secondary to faulty function (abnormal joint or muscle biomechanics).
   b. Commonly will resolve without intervention, but if trauma is too great or if related to chronic etiology, patient will benefit from intervention.
   c. Diagnosis made by clinical examination through comparing results of flexibility (AROM/PROM), resistive tests, and palpation.
   d. Medications.
      (1) Acetaminophen for pain.
      (2) NSAIDs for pain and/or inflammation.
      (3) Corticosteroid injection or by mouth.
      (4) Muscle relaxants; e.g., as Flexeril (cyclobenzaprine) or Valium (diazepam).
      (5) Trigger point injections.
   e. Physical therapy goals, outcomes, and interventions.
      (1) Biomechanical faults caused by joint restrictions should be corrected with joint mobilization.
      (2) Patient education regarding the elimination of harmful positions and postural reeducation.
      (3) Spinal manipulation for pain inhibition is generally indicated for this condition.
2. Spinal or intervertebral stenosis (see Table 1-22).
   a. Etiology: congenital narrow spinal canal or intervertebral foramen, coupled with hypertrophy of the spinal lamina and ligamentum flavum or facets, as the result of age-related degenerative processes or disease.
   b. Results in vascular and/or neural compromise.
   c. Signs and symptoms (see Table 1-9).
      (1) Bilateral pain and paresthesia in back, buttocks, thighs, calves, and feet.
      (2) Pain decreases in spinal flexion, increases in extension.
      (3) Pain increases with walking.
      (4) Pain relieved with prolonged rest.
   d. Diagnostic tests utilized: imaging including plain films, MRI, and/or CT scan. Occasionally, myelography is helpful.
   e. Clinical examination, including bicycle (van Gelderen's test), helps identify this condition and differentiate it from intermittent claudication.
   f. Medications.
      (1) Acetaminophen for pain.
      (2) NSAIDs for pain and/or inflammation.
      (3) Corticosteroid injection or by mouth.
      (4) Muscle relaxants.
      (5) Trigger point injections.
   g. Physical therapy goals, outcomes, and interventions.
      (1) Biomechanical faults caused by joint restrictions should be corrected with joint mobilization to the specific restrictions identified during the examination.
      (2) Perform flexion-based exercise and exercises that promote dynamic stability throughout the trunk and pelvis.
      (3) Avoid extension and/or other positions that narrow the spinal canal or intervertebral foramen (i.e., extension, ipsilateral side-bending, and ipsilateral rotation).
      (4) Manual and/or mechanical traction.
         (a) Traction.
         - Cervical spine positioned at 15° of flexion to provide the optimum intervertebral foraminal opening.
         - Contraindications include joint hypermobility, pregnancy, rheumatoid arthritis, Down syndrome, or any other systemic disease that affects ligamentous integrity.
3. Disc conditions.
   a. Internal disc disruption (see Table 1-9).
      (1) Internal structure of disc annulus is disrupted; however, external structures remain normal. Most common in lumbar region.
      (2) Symptoms include constant deep, achy pain, and increased pain with movement. No objective neurological findings, although patient may have referred pain in lower extremity.
      (3) Regular CT or myelogram will not demonstrate any abnormal findings. Can be diagnosed by CT discogram or an MRI.
      (4) Clinical examination helps to identify this condition.
      (5) Medications.
         (a) Acetaminophen for pain.
         (b) NSAIDs for pain and/or inflammation.
         (c) Muscle relaxants.
         (d) Trigger point injections.
         (e) Corticosteroid injection or by mouth.
      (6) Physical therapy goals, outcomes, and interventions.
         (a) Biomechanical faults caused by joint restrictions should be corrected with joint

mobilization to the specific restrictions identified during the examination.
(b) Spinal manipulation may be contraindicated for this condition.
(c) Patient education regarding proper body mechanics, positions to avoid, limiting repetitive bending and twisting movements, limiting upper extremity overhead and sitting activities, and carrying heavy loads.

b. Posterolateral bulge/herniation.
(1) Most commonly observed disc disorder of lumbar spine due to three structural deficiencies:
(a) Posterior disc is narrower in height than anterior disc.
(b) Posterior longitudinal ligament is not as strong and only centrally located in lumbar spine.
(c) Posterior lamellae of annulus are thinner.
(2) Etiology: overstretching and/or tearing of annular rings, vertebral endplate and/or ligamentous structures, from high compressive forces or repetitive microtrauma.
(3) Results in loss of strength, radicular pain, paresthesia and inability to perform activities of daily living.
(4) Diagnostic tests utilized: MRI.
(5) Clinical examination helps to identify this condition.
(6) Medications.
(a) Acetaminophen for pain.
(b) NSAIDs for pain and/or inflammation.
(c) Muscle relaxants.
(d) Trigger point injections.
(e) Corticosteroid injection or by mouth.
(7) Physical therapy goals, outcomes, and interventions.
(a) Exercise program to promote dynamic stability throughout trunk and pelvis and to provide optimal stimulus for regeneration of disc.
(b) Positional gapping for 10 minutes to increase space within region of space occupying lesion. If left posterolateral lumbar is herniation present:
- Have patient side-lying on right side, with pillow under right trunk (accentuating trunk side-bending right).
- Flex both hips and knees.
- Rotate trunk to left (or pelvis to right).
- Patient can be taught to perform this at home.

(c) Spinal manipulation may be contraindicated for this condition, particularly at the level of the herniation.
(d) Patient education regarding proper body mechanics, positions to avoid, limiting repetitive bending and twisting movements, limiting upper extremity overhead and sitting activities, and carrying heavy loads.
(e) Manual and/or mechanical traction.
- Traction: cervical spine positioned at 15° of flexion to provide the optimum intervertebral foraminal opening.
- Contraindications include joint hypermobility, pregnancy, rheumatoid arthritis, Down syndrome, or any other systemic disease that affects ligamentous integrity.
- Efficacy of traction for intervention of disc conditions is currently under scrutiny.

c. Central posterior bulge/herniation.
(1) More commonly observed in the cervical spine but can also be seen in the lumbar spine.
(2) Etiology: overstretching and/or tearing of annular rings, vertebral endplate, and/or ligamentous structures (posterior longitudinal ligament) from high compressive forces and/or long-term postural malalignment.
(3) Results in loss of strength, radicular pain, paresthesia, inability to perform activities of daily living, and possible compression of the spinal cord. Patient exhibits central nervous system symptoms, e.g., hyperreflexia and a positive Babinski reflex.
(4) Diagnostic tests utilized: MRI.
(5) Clinical examination helps to identify this condition.
(6) Medications.
(a) Acetaminophen for pain.
(b) NSAIDs for pain and/or inflammation.
(c) Muscle relaxants.
(d) Trigger point injections.
(e) Corticosteroid injection or by mouth.
(7) Physical therapy goals, outcomes, and interventions.
- Refer to posterolateral intervention above.

d. Anterior bulge/herniation is very rare due to structural integrity of anterior intervertebral disc.

4. Facet joint conditions.
a. Degenerative joint disease (DJD) (see Tables 1-9 and 1-21).
(1) Etiology: Part of normal aging process due to weight-bearing properties of facets and intervertebral joints (see Table 1-9).
(2) Results in bone hypertrophy, capsular fibrosis, hypermobility or hypomobility of joint, and proliferation of synovium.
(3) Symptoms include reduction in mobility of the spine, pain, and possible impingement of associated nerve root, resulting in loss of strength and paresthesias.

(4) Diagnostic tests utilized: plain film imaging.
(5) Clinical examination including lumbar quadrant test helps to identify this condition.
(6) Medications.
  (a) Acetaminophen for pain.
  (b) NSAIDs for pain and/or inflammation.
  (c) Muscle relaxants.
  (d) Trigger point injections.
  (e) Corticosteroid injection or by mouth.
(7) Physical therapy goals, outcomes, and interventions.
  (a) Exercise program to promote dynamic stability throughout trunk and pelvis and to provide optimal stimulus for regeneration of facet cartilage and/or capsule.
  (b) Biomechanical faults caused by joint restrictions should be corrected with joint mobilization to the specific restrictions identified during the examination.
  (c) Spinal manipulation may be useful.

b. Facet entrapment (acute locked back).
(1) Caused by abnormal movement of fibroadipose meniscoid in facet during extension (from flexion). Meniscoid does not properly reenter joint cavity and bunches up, becoming a space-occupying lesion, which distends capsule and causes pain.
(2) Flexion is most comfortable for patient, and extension increases pain.
(3) Clinical examination, including lumbar quadrant test, helps to identify this condition.
(4) Medications.
  (a) Acetaminophen for pain.
  (b) NSAIDs for pain and/or inflammation.
  (c) Muscle relaxants.
  (d) Trigger point injections.
  (e) Corticosteroid injection or by mouth.
(5) Physical therapy goals, outcomes, and interventions.
  (a) Positional facet joint gapping and/or manipulation are appropriate treatments.

5. Acceleration/deceleration injuries of cervical spine.
a. Formerly known as "whiplash."
b. Occurs when excess shear and tensile forces are exerted on cervical structures.
c. Structures injured may include facets/articular processes, facet joint capsules, ligaments, disc, anterior/posterior muscles, fracture to odontoid process and spinous processes, TMJ, sympathetic chain ganglia, spinal and cranial nerves.
d. Signs and symptoms.
(1) Early include headaches, neck pain, limited flexibility, reversal of lower cervical lordosis and decrease in upper cervical kyphosis, vertigo, change in vision and hearing, irritability to noise and light, dysesthesias of face and bilateral upper extremities, nausea, difficulty swallowing, and emotional lability.
(2) Late include chronic head and neck pain, limitation in flexibility, TMJ dysfunction, limited tolerance to ADLs, disequilibrium, anxiety, and depression.

e. Common clinical findings include postural changes, excessive muscle guarding with soft tissue fibrosis, segmental hypermobility, and gradual development of restricted segmental motion, cranial and caudal to the injury (segmental hypomobility).
f. Diagnostic tests utilized: plain film imaging, CT, and/or MRI.
g. Clinical examination helps to identify this condition.
h. Medications.
(1) Acetaminophen for pain.
(2) NSAIDs for pain and/or inflammation.
(3) Muscle relaxants.
(4) Trigger point injections.
(5) Corticosteroid injection or by mouth.

i. Physical therapy goals, outcomes, and interventions.
(1) Spinal manipulation is generally indicated.
(2) Correction of muscle imbalances and biomechanical faults using strengthening, endurance, coordination, and flexibility exercises to gain restoration of normal function.
(3) Biomechanical faults caused by joint restrictions should be corrected with joint mobilization to the specific restrictions identified during the examination.
(4) Progression to functional training based on patient's occupation and/or recreational goals.
(5) Patient education regarding the elimination of harmful positions and postural reeducation.
(6) Manual and/or mechanical traction.
  (a) Traction.
  - Cervical spine positioned at 15° of flexion to provide the optimum intervertebral foraminal opening.
  - Contraindications include joint hypermobility, pregnancy, rheumatoid arthritis, Down syndrome, or any other systemic disease that affects ligamentous integrity.

6. Hypermobile spinal segments.
a. An abnormal increase in ROM at a joint due to insufficient soft tissue control (i.e., ligamentous, discal, muscle, or a combination of all three).
b. Diagnostic tests utilized: plain film imaging, particularly dynamic flexion/extension views.
c. Clinical examination helps to identify this condition.

d. Medications.
(1) Acetaminophen for pain.
(2) NSAIDs for pain and/or inflammation.
(3) Muscle relaxants.
(4) Trigger point injections.
(5) Sclerosing injections.
(6) Corticosteroid injection or by mouth.
e. Physical therapy goals, outcomes, and interventions.
(1) Pain reduction modalities to reduce irritability of structures.
(2) Passive ROM within a normal range of movement.
(3) Passive stabilization with corsets, splints, casts, tape, and collars.
(4) Increase strength/endurance/coordination, especially in the multifidus, abdominals, extensors, and gluteals, which control posture.
(5) Regain muscle balance.
(6) Patient education regarding postural reeducation, limiting excessive overloading, limiting sustained activities, and limiting end range postures.

7. Sacroiliac joint (SIJ) conditions.
a. Cause and specific pathology is unknown. Since this is a joint, it may become inflamed, develop degenerative changes, or develop abnormal movement patterns.
b. Anatomically and functionally, SIJ is closely related to lumbar spine, so a thorough examination of both regions is indicated if a patient presents with pain in either.
c. Diagnostic tests utilized: plain film imaging and possibly MRI. Occasionally, double-blind injections may be used to assist in making the diagnosis (first injection is provocative in nature, and second injection is analgesic). If increased "same" pain with first injection and decreased pain following second injection, joint is determined to be pathological.
d. Clinical examination, including the following special tests, will be useful to make diagnosis.
(1) Gillet's test.
(2) Ipsilateral anterior rotation test.
(3) Gaenslen's test.
(4) Long-sitting (supine to sit) test.
(5) Goldthwait's test.
e. Medications.
(1) Acetaminophen for pain.
(2) NSAIDs for pain and/or inflammation.
(3) Muscle relaxants.
(4) Trigger point injections.
(5) Corticosteroid injection or by mouth.
f. Physical therapy goals, outcomes, and interventions.
(1) Spinal manipulation such as SIJ gapping is generally indicated to inhibit pain, reduce muscle guarding, and restore normal joint motion.
(2) Correction of muscle imbalances throughout pelvis using strengthening, endurance, coordination, and flexibility exercises to gain restoration of normal function.
(3) Biomechanical faults caused by joint restrictions should be corrected with joint mobilization to the specific restrictions identified during the examination.
(4) Patient education regarding the elimination of harmful positions and postural reeducation.
(5) Sacroiliac belts may be useful in some patients.

8. Repetitive/cumulative trauma to back.
a. Disorders of the nerves, soft tissues, and bones precipitated or aggravated by repeated exertions or movements of the back, occurring most often in the workplace.
b. Repetitive trauma disorders account for 48% of all reported occupational diseases.
c. Diagnosis is difficult, with up to 85% of back pain nondiagnosed.
d. Typically causes one of the conditions previously listed above: muscle, disc, and/or joint impairment.
e. Vocational factors that contribute to back pain include physically heavy static work postures, lifting, frequent bending and twisting, repetitive work, and vibration.
f. Chronic disability may be reduced by enrollment in a work-conditioning program, including patient education, aerobic exercises, general strengthening, and functional stability exercises that promote endurance for work-related activities.
g. Clinical examination helps to identify this condition.
h. Intervention should focus on prevention, consisting of education. If this phenomenon leads to a condition listed above, follow the specific intervention associated with that condition.

9. Other conditions affecting the spine (see Table 1-9).
a. Bone tumors.
(1) May be primary or metastatic.
(a) Primary tumors include multiple myeloma (the most common primary bone tumor), Ewing's sarcoma, malignant lymphoma, chondrosarcoma, osteosarcoma, and chondromas.
(b) Metastatic bone cancer has primary sites in lung, prostate, breast, kidney, and thyroid.
(c) Patient history should always include questions about a prior episode of cancer.
(d) Signs and symptoms include pain that is unvarying and progressive, is not relieved with rest or analgesics, and is more pronounced at night.
(e) Diagnostic tests utilized: plain film imaging, CT, and/or MRI as well as laboratory tests.

b. Visceral tumors.
   (1) Esophageal cancer symptomatology may include pain radiating to the back, pain with swallowing, dysphagia, and weight loss.
   (2) Pancreatic cancer symptomatology includes a deep, gnawing pain that may radiate from the chest to the back.
   (3) Diagnostic tests utilized: plain film imaging, CT, and/or MRI as well as laboratory tests.

c. Gastrointestinal conditions.
   (1) Acute pancreatitis may manifest itself as mid-epigastric pain radiating through to the back.
   (2) Cholecystitis may present with abrupt, severe abdominal pain and right upper quadrant tenderness, nausea, vomiting, and fever.
   (3) Diagnostic tests utilized: plain film imaging, CT, and/or MRI as well as laboratory tests.

d. Cardiovascular and pulmonary conditions.
   (1) Heart and lung disorders can refer pain to chest, back, neck, jaw, and upper extremity.
   (2) Abdominal aortic aneurysm (AAA) usually appears as nonspecific lumbar pain.
   (3) Diagnostic tests utilized: plain film imaging, CT, and/or MRI as well as laboratory tests.
   (4) Will be identified as pain during examination of abdominal region.

e. Urological and gynecological conditions.
   (1) Kidney, bladder, ovary, and uterus disorders can refer pain to the trunk, pelvis, and thighs.
   (2) Diagnostic tests utilized: plan film imaging, CT, and/or MRI as well as other laboratory tests.

f. See Figure 1-51.

10. Temporomandibular joint conditions.
   a. Common signs and symptoms include joint noise (i.e., clicking, popping, and/or crepitation), joint

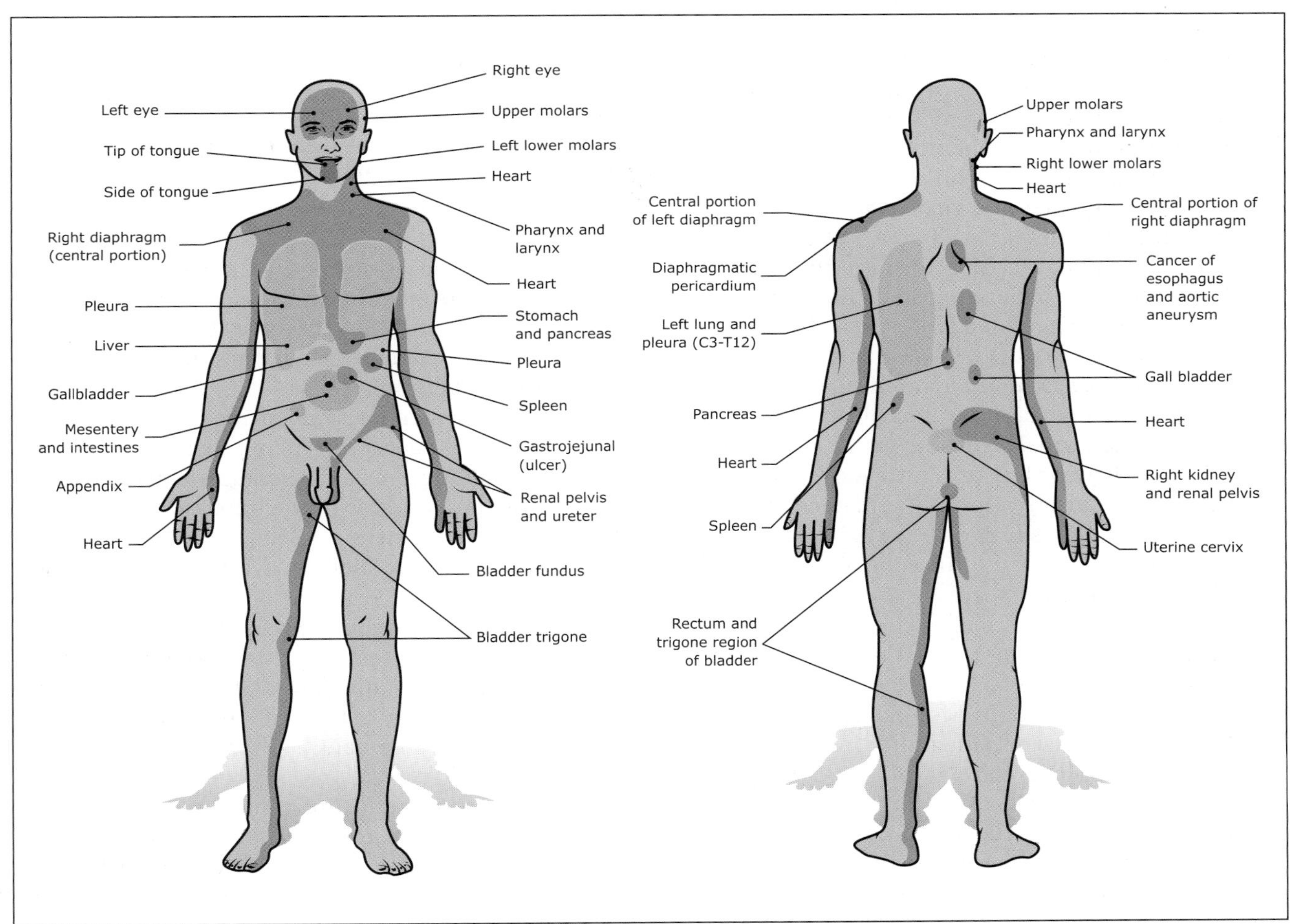

Figure 1-51 Pain referred from viscera.

From Rothstein, J, Roy, S, and Wolf, S: Rehabilitation Specialist's Handbook, 4th ed., Philadelphia, F A Davis, pg 412, 413, with permission.

locking, limited flexibility of jaw, lateral deviation of mandible during depression or elevation of mandible, decreased strength/endurance of muscles of mastication, tinnitus, headaches, forward head posture, and pain with movement of mandible.

b. Cervical spine must be thoroughly examined due to close biomechanical and functional relationships between TMJ and the cervical region. Many patients with a TMJ condition have a component of cervical dysfunction.

c. Dysfunctions fall into three diagnostic categories.
   (1) DJD, such as OA or RA in TMJ (refer to OA and RA for causes, characteristic findings, diagnostic methods, medical and physical therapy intervention).
   (2) Myofascial pain is most common form of temporomandibular dysfunction (TMD), which is discomfort or pain in muscles controlling jaw function, as well as neck and shoulder muscles (refer to myofascial pain syndrome for causes, characteristic findings, diagnostic methods, medical and physical therapy intervention).
   (3) Internal derangement of joint, meaning a dislocated jaw, displaced articular disc, or injury to condyle.
      (a) Loss of functional mobility may result from increased activity in muscles of mastication due to stress and anxiety.
      (b) Causes.
         - Trauma: leading to joint edema, capsulitis, hypomobility/hypermobility, or abnormal function of ligaments, capsule, and/or muscles.
         - Congenital anatomical anomalies: change in shape of palate.
         - Abnormal function, such as repeatedly chewing ice or hard candy, paranormal breathing (mouth breather), forward head posture.
      (c) Diagnostic tests utilized: plain film imaging and/or MRI if necessary.
      (d) Clinical examination helps to identify this condition.
      (e) Medications.
         - Acetaminophen for pain.
         - NSAIDs for pain and/or inflammation.
         - Muscle relaxants.
         - Trigger point injections.
         - Corticosteroid injection or by mouth.
      (f) Physical therapy goals, outcomes, and interventions.
         - Postural reeducation regarding regaining the normal anterior-posterior curves and left-right symmetry of the spine.
         - Modalities for reduction of pain and inflammation.
         - Biofeedback to minimize effects of stress and/or anxiety.
         - Joint mobilization if restriction in TMJ is present. Primary glide is inferior, which gaps joint, stretches the capsule, and allows relocation of anteriorly displaced disc.
         - Flexibility and muscle-strengthening exercises (e.g., Rocabado's jaw opening while maintaining the tongue in contact with the palate and isometric mandibular exercises).
         - Patient education (e.g., foods to avoid, maintaining proper postural alignment).
         - Night splints may be prescribed by the dentist to maintain resting jaw position.
         - Educate patient regarding resting position of tongue on hard palate.
         - It is critical to normalize the cervical spine posture before the patient receives any permanent dental procedures and/or appliances.

Pediatric Orthopedic Conditions

1. Torsional conditions.
   a. Toeing in/out.
      (1) Foot progression angle (gait angle) is the angle made by the foot with respect to a straight line plotted in the direction the child is walking.
      (2) It can be normal in children with combined torsional deformity.
         (a) + sign denotes out-toeing angle
         (b) – sign denote in-toeing angle.
      (3) Thigh–foot angle is the angle between axis of the foot and axis of thigh measured with child prone and knees at 90°.
         (a) The angle describes the degrees of tibial torsion.
      (4) Toeing in (pigeon-toed) is common in W sitting (hips and knees bent in front of the body) and is caused by three types of deformity depending on the age of the child including metatarsus adductus, internal tibial torsion, and increased femoral anteversion.
      (5) Metatarsus adductus is the most common congenital foot deformity; greater occurrence in females and more common on left side.
         (a) The most common cause is intrauterine packing.
         (b) There are two types, including rigid and flexible.

(c) Rigid form results in a medial subluxation of tarsometatarsal joints.
(d) Hindfoot slightly in valgus with navicular lateral to head of talus.
(e) Flexible form is observed as adduction of all five metatarsals at the tarsometatarsal joints.
- Diagnosis through clinical exam.
- Treatment includes stretching exercises and casting if needed.
- Surgical option is release of abductor hallucis tendon.
- Strengthening and regaining proper alignment of the foot (use of orthoses).
- 85%–90% of cases identified at birth resolve without treatment by 1 year.

(6) Internal tibial torsion is the most common cause of in-toeing.
(a) There is a high complication rate with osteotomy of tibia and is associated with W sitting.
(7) Increased femoral anteversion.
(a) The femoral neck angles anteriorly 10°–15° from the frontal plane to form anterior antetorsion angle.
(b) It is considered excessive if angle is > 25°–30° and is associated with W sitting.
(8) Toeing-out is less common and can be caused by: femoral retroversion, external tibial torsion, and flat feet.
(a) The femoral neck angles anteriorly 10°–15° from the frontal plane to form anterior antetorsion angle.
- It is considered excessive if anterior antetorsion angle < 10°.

(b) External tibial torsion correction has a high complication rate with surgery.

2. Talipes equinovarus (clubfoot).
a. Etiology: postural or talipes equinovarus.
(1) Postural from intrauterine malposition.
(a) Abnormal development of the head and neck of talus, due to hereditary or neuromuscular disorders.
(b) Observation: plantar flexed, adducted and inverted foot (postural).
b. Talipes equinovarus: plantar flexion at talocrural joint.
(1) Inversion at subtalar, talocalcaneal, talonavicular, and calcaneocuboid joints.
(2) Supination at midtarsal joints.
c. Diagnosis: at birth and can be detected with prenatal ultrasound.
(1) Thorough biomechanical lower quarter exam.
(2) Affected foot is a half size smaller and less mobile. The calf muscles will be smaller.
(3) 50% can be affected bilaterally.
d. Physical therapy goals, outcomes, and interventions.
(1) Postural condition: manipulation followed by casting or splinting (Ponseti method).
(2) Following casting, stretching is important. Orthoses (Denis-Browne splints) throughout the day for up to 3 months and then at night for up to 3 years.
(3) Talipes equinovarus (non-postural) requires surgical intervention to correct deformity followed by casting or splinting.
(a) Achilles' tenotomy may be necessary.

3. Angular conditions.
a. Genu valgum: excessive lateral tibial torsion, referred to as knock-knees; excessive lateral patellar positioning.
b. Genu varum: excessive medial tibial torsion, referred to as bowlegs.
c. Excessive medial patellar positioning; pigeon-toed orientation of the feet.
d. Age norms.
(1) Genu varum is normal in newborn and infants.
(2) Maximal varum present at 6–12 months of age.
(3) Lower limbs gradually straighten with a zero tibiofemoral angle by 18–24 months.
(4) Knees gradually drift into valgus and is maximal around 3–4 years with an average lateral tibiofemoral angle of 12°.
(5) Genu valgum spontaneously corrects by age 7 to the adult alignment of lower limbs.
(6) 8° of valgum in females and 7° in the male.
e. Diagnosis: plain film imaging consisting of standing long films (AP and lateral).
(1) Clinical examination.
f. Physical therapy goals, outcomes, and interventions: decreased loading of knee while maintaining strength and endurance.

4. Hip dysplasia.
a. Etiology: abnormality in the size, shape, orientation, or organization of the femoral head, acetabulum, or both.
(1) Can result in subluxations or dislocation.
b. Risk factors: females > males, breech position, family history of hip dysplasia, low levels of amniotic fluid, swaddling an infant too tightly.
c. Diagnosis: US screening after 4 weeks.
(1) Radiographs for infants 4–6 months can be used to assess the hips, monitor development after treatment, and assess long term outcomes.
(2) Clinical/physical exam: Barlow test, Ortolani test, Limited hip abduction, Galeazzi sign, Klisic sign.
d. Treatment: Pavlik harness current gold standard treatment.

(1) Maintain the hip in flexion and abduction position to maintain femoral head in acetabulum; recommendation for time frame varies. 85%-95% success rate with use in newborns to 6 months.
(2) Closed reduction under anesthesia followed by spica cast for 12 weeks for children 6 months to 2 years.
(3) Open reduction under anesthesia followed by spica cast for 6-12 weeks for children older than 2 years.

e. Physical therapy goals, outcomes, and interventions.
(1) Moderate resistance exercise program, delay deformities, and maximize function and patient education.

5. Transient synovitis in children.

a. Etiology: acute onset of sudden hip pain in children ages 3–10.
(1) Transient inflammation of the synovium of the hip.

b. Diagnosis: clinical exam shows decreased hip abduction and internal rotation.
(1) Biopsy, ultrasonography shows effusion that causes bulging of the anterior joint capsule.

c. Signs and symptoms.
(1) Unilateral hip or groin pain.
(2) Less common medial thigh or knee pain.
(3) Crying at night.
(4) Antalgic limp.
(5) Pain not common.
(6) Recent history of upper respiratory tract infection.

d. Treatment: NSAIDs, rest while healing; lasts about 7-10 days.

6. Legg-Calvé-Perthes disease.

a. Etiology: blood supply interrupted to the femoral head.
(1) Age of onset between 2–13 years.
(2) Four times greater incidence in males than females.

b. Diagnosis: MRI showing positive bony crescent sign.
(1) Clinical exam.
(a) Characteristic psoatic limp due to weakness of psoas major; moves in ER, flexion, and adduction.
(b) Gradual onset of aching pain at hip, thigh, and knee.
(c) AROM limited in abduction and extension (collapse of subchondral bone at femoral neck/head).

c. Treatment: medications include acetaminophen for pain, NSAIDs for pain and/or inflammation.
(1) Cast for 4–6 weeks, surgery if necessary.

d. Physical therapy goals, outcomes, and interventions.
(1) Joint/bone protection strategies.
(2) Maintain/improve joint mechanics and connective tissue functions.
(3) Implementation of aerobic capacity/endurance conditioning activities or reconditioning such as aquatic programs.
(4) Postsurgical interventions: regaining functional flexibility; improving strength, endurance, coordination, and gait training.

7. Slipped capital femoral epiphysis.

a. Etiology: most common hip disorder observed in adolescents of unknown etiology.
(1) Femoral head is displaced posteriorly and inferiorly in relation to the femoral neck and within the confines of the acetabulum.
(2) Onset in males 10–17 years, with average onset at 13 years.
(3) Onset in females 8–15 years, with average onset at 11 years.
(4) Two times greater incident in males than females.

b. Diagnosis based on clinical examination.
(1) AROM restricted in abduction, flexion, and internal rotation.
(2) Patient describes pain as vague at knee, thigh, and hip.
(3) In chronic conditions, may demonstrate a Trendelenburg gait.
(4) Plain film imaging shows positive displacement of upper femoral epiphysis.

c. Treatment: operative internal fixation—prevention of complications such as avascular necrosis.
(1) Medications: acetaminophen for pain, NSAIDs for pain and inflammation.

d. Physical therapy goals, outcomes, and interventions.
(1) Joint/bone protection strategies.
(2) Maintain/improve joint mechanics and connective tissue functions.
(3) Implementation of aerobic capacity/endurance conditioning or reconditioning.
(4) Postsurgical intervention includes regaining functional flexibility; improving strength, endurance, coordination, and gait training.

8. Tendon lengthening conditions.

a. Osgood-Schlatter disease.
(1) Etiology: mechanical dysfunction resulting in traction apophysitis of the tibial tubercle at the patellar tendon insertion.
(2) Diagnosis: plain film findings demonstrate irregularities of the epiphyseal line and/or clinical examination.
(3) Treatment.

(a) Medications: acetaminophen for pain, NSAIDs for pain and inflammation.
(b) Occasionally surgery is indicated.
(4) Physical therapy goals, outcomes, and interventions.
(a) Modify activities to prevent excessive stress to irritated site.
(b) Flexibility is important especially for prevention.

b. Sever's disease (calcaneal apophysitis).
(1) Etiology: most common cause of heel pain in growing children, occurs before or during peak growth spurt.
(a) Caused by repetitive microtrauma due to increased traction by the Achilles tendon on its insertion site.
(b) Bilateral involvement in 60% of cases.
(2) Diagnosis based on plain film imaging.
(3) Treatment: NSAIDs; temporary cessation of running, jumping activities, heel lifts/heel cups.
(4) Physical therapy goals, outcomes, and interventions.
(a) Stretching and strengthening exercises.

c. Sinding-Larsen Johannson's disease.
(1) Etiology: traction apophysitis at the patella-patellar tendon junction, overuse injury due to repeated stresses, can occur after significant growth spurt and/or increase in activity.
(2) Diagnosis based on plain film imaging and/or, clinical examination.
(3) Treatment includes NSAIDs, temporary cessation of activity.
(4) Physical therapy goals, outcomes, and interventions.
(a) Stretching and strengthening exercise.
(b) Activity modification.

9. Growing pains (benign nocturnal pains of childhood).
a. Etiology is unknown but could be due to muscular fatigue, poor posture, stress, etc.
(1) No evidence linking growing pains and growing.
(2) Can affect 20% of children most likely between ages 3–5 and 8–11.
b. Diagnosis based on clinical exam.
(1) Increased pain at night, typically bilateral leg pain.
(2) Not associated with redness, temperature, swelling, and tenderness.
c. Treatment primarily related to managing the pain.

10. Osteochondritis dissecans.
a. Etiology: occurs in adolescents between ages of 12–15 years.
(1) Most common is a separation of articular cartilage from underlying bone (osteochondral fracture), usually involving medial femoral condyle near intercondylar notch.
(2) Can also be observed less frequently at femoral head and talar dome.
(3) Osteochondritis of humeral capitellum affects central and/or lateral aspect of capitellum or radial head. Osteochondral bone fragment becomes detached from articular surface, forming a loose body in the joint. Caused by repetitive compressive forces.
b. Diagnosis based on plain film imaging or CT scan to identify defect and/or clinical examination.
c. Treatment: if fracture is displaced, surgical intervention required.
(1) Medications: acetaminophen and/or NSAIDs.
d. Physical therapy goals, outcomes, and interventions.
(1) Rest and avoidance of aggravating factors.
(2) Joint/bone protection strategies.
(3) Correct biomechanical faults.
(4) Implementation of flexibility, strengthening, endurance, and coordination exercises to maintain/improve normal joint motion and length of muscles.
(5) Implementation of aerobic capacity/endurance conditioning or reconditioning.
(6) Implementation of strength, power, and endurance exercises to increase load on joints in late phases of rehabilitation.

11. Panner's disease.
a. Etiology: Localized avascular necrosis of capitellum leading to loss of subchondral bone, with fissuring and softening of articular surfaces of radiocapitellar joint.
(1) Unknown etiology but occurs in children age 10 or younger.
b. Diagnosis based on plain film imaging or CT scan to identify defect and/or clinical examination.

12. Leg length discrepancies.
a. Etiology: congenital disorders of bones, muscles, or joints.
(1) Disuses or overuse of the bones, muscles, or joints caused by illness or disease.
(2) Disease such as bone cancer.
(3) Traumatic injuries, such as severe fractures that damage growth plates.
b. Diagnosis based on clinical exam.
(1) Leg length test: patient supine with pelvis balanced/aligned with lower limbs and trunk. Measure distance from ASIS to lateral malleolus or medial malleolus on each limb three times. Will determine true or functional limb discrepancy.
c. Treatment: noninvasive therapy and/or shoe inserts.
(1) Invasive: surgical.

d. Physical therapy goals, outcomes and interventions.
   (1) Biomechanical corrections.

13. Scoliosis.
   a. Etiology: structural and nonstructural, both of unknown etiology.
      (1) Structural is an irreversible lateral curvature of the spine with a rotational component.
      (2) Nonstructural is a reversible lateral curvature of spine without a rotational component which straightens as individual flexes the spine.
   b. Diagnosis: plain film imaging—full length Cobb's method.
      (1) CT and/or MRI to rule out other associated conditions.
      (2) Clinical examination.
   c. Treatment.
      (1) Conservative.
         (a) Degree of curvature less than 25°.
      (2) Bracing.
         (a) Degree curvature 25°–45°.
      (3) Surgery with placement of Harrington rod instrumentation.
         (a) Curvature greater than 45°.
   d. Physical therapy goals, outcomes, and interventions.
      (1) Flexibility exercises to maintain/improve normal joint motion and length of muscles throughout trunk and pelvis.
      (2) Implementation of strength, power, and endurance exercises.
      (3) Patient education.

14. Pes planus (flat foot).
   a. Etiology: can include genetic predisposition, muscle weakness, ligamentous laxity, paralysis, excessive pronation, trauma, or disease.
      (1) Normal in infant and toddler feet and develop around 2–3 years.
   b. Diagnosis based on clinical examination.
      (1) Biomechanical lower quarter exam.
         (a) Reduction in height of medial longitudinal arch.
         (b) Decreased ability of foot to provide a rigid lever for push off during gait due to altered arthrokinematics.
   c. Physical therapy goals, outcomes, and interventions.
      (1) Patient education.
      (2) Postural corrections.
      (3) Use of proper footwear and orthotic fitting.

15. Congenital muscular torticollis.
   a. Spasm and/or tightness of SCM muscle.
   b. Etiology: Fibrosis related to birth trauma; breech births, forceps birth, vacuum extraction, or C-section; restrictive intrauterine environment; genetic predisposition; cervical-vertebral abnormalities.
   c. Observation: side-bending toward and rotation away from the affected SCM.
   d. Diagnosis based on clinical exam and plain film imaging to rule out cervical spine abnormality or tumor.
   e. Treatment.
      (1) Medications: acetaminophen, muscle relaxants and/or NSAIDs.
      (2) Physical therapy and positioning techniques.
      (3) Splinting in older children (> 4 months) with continued head tilt.
   f. Physical therapy goals, outcomes, and interventions.
      (1) Flexibility exercises to maintain/improve normal joint motion and length of muscles.
      (2) Manual therapy including soft tissue/massage techniques and/or joint oscillations for maintenance and to reduce pain and/or muscle guarding.
      (3) Therapeutic exercises.
      (4) Education to parents on positioning.
      (5) Good prognosis; poor if left untreated.

16. Spasmodic torticollis.
   a. Movement disorder with CNS pathology.

17. Plagiocephaly (flat head syndrome).
   a. Etiology: development of a flat spot on the back or side of the head as the skull is soft and malleable and can be misshapen easily.
      (1) No lasting harmful effects on the infant.
   b. Diagnosis: clinical examination.
   c. Treatment: repositioning techniques, parent education, use of helmet.

18. Arthrogryposis multiplex congenita.
   a. Etiology: congenital deformity of skeleton and soft tissues, characterized by limitation in joint motion and a "sausage-like" appearance of limbs.
      (1) Nonprogressive contractures.
      (2) Intelligence develops normally.
   b. Diagnosis: plain films and/or clinical examination.
   c. Treatment.
      (1) Ongoing communication with patient and family.
   d. Physical therapy goals, outcomes, and interventions.
      (1) Joint/bone protection strategies.
      (2) Maintain/improve joint mechanics and connective tissue functions.
      (3) Implementation of aerobic capacity/endurance conditioning or reconditioning.
      (4) Patient education regarding adaptive devices, assistive devices, orthotic devices, and supportive devices.
      (5) Implementation of flexibility, coordination, endurance, and strength exercises.

19. Osteogenesis imperfecta.
    a. Etiology: inherited disorder transmitted by autosomal dominant gene.
        (1) Characterized by abnormal collagen synthesis leading to imbalance between bone deposition and reabsorption.
        (2) Cortical and cancellous bones become very thin, leading to fractures and deformity of weight-bearing bones.
    b. Diagnosis: bone scan and plain films to show old fractures and deformities; serological testing; clinical examination.
    c. Treatment.
        (1) Medications: calcium, vitamin D, estrogen, calcitonin, and bisphosphonates.
    d. Physical therapy goals, outcomes, and interventions.
        (1) Joint/bone protection strategies.
        (2) Maintain/improve joint mechanics and connective tissue functions.
        (3) Implement of aerobic capacity/endurance conditioning or reconditioning.
            (a) Aquatic therapy.
20. Spondylolisthesis.
    a. Etiology: congenitally defective pars interarticularis.
        (1) Spondylolysis is a fracture of the pars interarticularis with positive "Scotty dog" on oblique radiographic view of the spine.
        (2) Spondylolisthesis is the actual anterior or posterior slippage of one vertebra on another, following bilateral fracture of pars interarticularis.
        (3) Can be graded from grade 1 (25% slippage) to 4 (100% slippage).
    b. Diagnosis: plain films; oblique views to see fracture, lateral views to see slippage.
        (1) Clinical examination: Stork test.
    c. Treatment.
        (1) Medication.
            (a) Acetaminophen for pain.
            (b) NSAIDs for pain and/or inflammation.
            (c) Corticosteroid injection or by mouth.
            (d) Muscle relaxants.
    d. Physical Therapy goals, outcomes, and interventions.
        (1) Correct biomechanical faults caused by joint restriction.
        (2) Dynamic stabilization exercises for the trunk with emphasis on abdominals.
        (3) Avoid extension and/or other positions that cause stress to defect.
        (4) Patient education on positioning and postural education.
        (5) Orthoses if needed.
        (6) Spinal manipulation is contraindicated.

Orthopedic Surgical Repairs

1. Surgical repairs of upper extremity.
    a. Rotator cuff tears.
        (1) Usually degenerative and occur over time, with impingement of supraspinatus tendon between greater tuberosity and acromion.
        (2) Signs and symptoms include:
            (a) Significant reduction of AROM into abduction.
            (b) No reduction of PROM.
            (c) Drop arm test is positive.
            (d) Poor scapulothoracic and glenohumeral rhythm.
        (3) Diagnostic tests utilized: arthrogram traditionally had been the "gold standard" test. MRI may be done, but may not be as sensitive.
        (4) Physical therapy goals, outcomes, and interventions.
            (a) Rehabilitation is initiated, following a period of immobilization with surgical intervention.
            (b) Physical therapy intervention emphasizes return of normal strength/endurance/coordination of muscles, joint mechanics, flexibility (AROM/PROM), and scapulothoracic and glenohumeral rhythm with overhead function.
    b. Tendon injuries and repairs of the hand.
        (1) Flexor tendon repairs.
            (a) First 3–4 weeks, distal extremity is immobilized with a protective splint, with wrist and digits flexed. Rubber band traction is applied to maintain interphalangeal joints in 30°–50° of passive flexion.
            (b) Physical therapy goals, outcomes, and interventions.
                - Patient can perform resisted extension and passive flexion within constraints of splint. AROM to tolerance is initiated at 4 weeks.
                - Goal is to manage all soft tissues through wound-healing phases by providing collagen remodeling, which preserves free tendon gliding.
                - Early intervention consists of wound management, edema control, and passive exercises.
                - Active extension exercises are initiated first, followed by flexion.
                - Resistive and functional exercises are introduced when full AROM is achieved.
        (2) Extensor tendon repairs.
            (a) Distal repairs are immobilized such that the distal interphalangeal joints are in neutral for 6–8 weeks.

(b) Physical therapy goals, outcomes, and interventions.
- AROM is initiated at 6 weeks, with proximal interphalangeal joints in neutral.
- Goal is to manage all soft tissues through wound-healing phases by providing collagen remodeling, which preserves free tendon gliding.
- Early intervention consists of wound management, edema control, and passive exercises.
- Active extension exercises are initiated first, followed by flexion.
- Resistive and functional exercises are introduced when full AROM is achieved.

(c) Proximal repairs are immobilized, with the wrist and digital joints in extension for 4 weeks.

(d) Physical therapy goals, outcomes, and interventions.
- Early AROM/PROM in flexion with metacarpophalangeal joint in extension. At 6 weeks, full AROM is initiated into flexion and extension.

2. Surgical repairs of lower extremity.

a. Total hip replacement/arthroplasty (THR).

(1) This information may vary, depending on surgical procedure and/or MD preference/protocol. Must be familiar with postoperative protocol for each patient relative to procedure and/or MD.

(2) Cemented versus noncemented.

(a) Cemented hips can tolerate full weight bearing immediately following surgery.

(b) Cement may crack with aging, causing a loosening of prosthesis. Noncemented technique is more stressful on bones during the surgical procedure.

(c) Noncemented procedures are typically used with younger and/or more active individuals. Cemented technique may be better for individuals with fragile bones, or for those who will benefit from immediate ability to weight bear; e.g., those with dementia or significant debilitation.

(3) Bed positioning with a wedge to prevent adduction.

(4) Patient should avoid the position of hip flexion > 90° with adduction and internal rotation. Partial weight bearing (PWB) to tolerance is initiated on the second postsurgery day, using crutches or a walker with typical surgical procedures.

(5) Physical therapy goals, outcomes, and interventions.

(a) Physical therapy interventions focus on bed mobility, transitional movements, ambulation, and return to premorbid activities of daily living.

b. Open reduction internal fixation (ORIF) following femoral fracture.

(1) Patient will typically be non–weight-bearing for 1–2 weeks, using crutches or a walker. Thereafter, the patient will be PWB as tolerated.

(2) Physical therapy goals, outcomes, and interventions.

(a) Physical therapy interventions focus on bed mobility, transitional movements, ambulation, and return to premorbid activities of daily living. Important to note that guidelines/precautions can vary significantly (see Table 1-27).

c. Total knee replacements/arthroplasty (TKR).

(1) TKR surgery is typically performed as a result of severe DJD of the knee joint, which has led to pain and impaired function.

(2) Physical therapy goals, outcomes, and interventions.

(a) Goals of early rehabilitation (1–3 weeks) include muscle reeducation, soft tissue mobilization, lymphedema reduction, initiation of PROM, AROM, and reduction of postsurgical swelling. *Don't use continuous passive motion machines for postoperative management of patients following uncomplicated total knee replacement* (White N, et al. Phys Ther. 2015).

(b) Goals of the second phase of rehabilitation include regaining endurance, coordination, and strength of the muscles surrounding the knee. Functional activities include progressive ambulation stair climbing, as well as transitional training based on healing and the type of prosthesis used.

(c) Goals and outcomes of the last phase of rehabilitation include returning the patient to premorbid activities of daily living. Functional and endurance training and proprioceptive exercises are introduced during this phase.

(d) The weight-bearing status of patients with a cemented prosthesis is at the level of the patient's tolerance. Patients with cementless prostheses are progressed according to the time frame for fracture healing. Weight bearing is 25% at 1–7 weeks, 50% by week 8, 75% by week 10, and 100% without an assistive device by week 12.

(e) Avoidance of forceful mobilization and PROM into flexion > 90° is important because of the mechanical restraints of the prosthesis.

(f) Biomechanical faults caused by joint restrictions should be corrected with joint

Table 1-27

Total Hip Replacement Guidelines/Precautions

ACTIVITY	CEMENTED	CEMENTLESS	
Internal rotation of hip joint	Do not perform for 3–6 months.	Do not perform for 3–6 months.	
Adduction of hip joint	Do not perform for 3–6 months.	Do not perform for 3–6 months.	
Flexion of hip joint beyond 90°	Do not perform for 3–6 months.	Do not perform for 3–6 months.	
Ambulation	Partial weight bearing (PWB) for approximately 3 weeks. Begin ambulation with cane at week 4 postop. Begin transition to full weight bearing at week 5.	Varies from weight bearing as tolerated (WBAT) to touch-down weight bearing (TDWB), based on the surgeon's philosophy and the surgical approach.	
		WBAT (WB as Tolerated)	**TDWB (Touch Down)**
		Partial weight bearing (PWB) for approximately 3 weeks. Begin ambulation with cane at week 4 postop. Begin transition to full weight bearing at week 6.	Progress to ⅓ weight bearing at week 6. Progress to ⅔ weight bearing at week 8. Progress to full weight bearing at week 10 with walker. Begin transition to cane at week 12. Progress to no assistive device when safe and no Trendelenberg gait.
Isometric exercise	Immediately postop as tolerated by the patient.	Immediately postop as tolerated by the patient.	
Active exercise	Initiation is variable between weeks 1 through 4, depending on the surgeon's guidelines.	Initiation is variable between weeks 1 through 4, depending on surgeon's guidelines.	

Table 1-28

Total Knee Replacement Guidelines/Precautions

ACTIVITY	CEMENTED	CEMENTLESS	
Range of motion	0°–90° within 2 weeks 0°–120° within 3–4 weeks	0°–90° within 2 weeks 0°–120° within 3–4 weeks	
Ambulation	Weight bearing as tolerated with walker immediately postop. Ambulation with cane at week 3. Transition to full weight bearing at week 4.	Varies from weight bearing as tolerated (WBAT) to touch-down weight bearing (TDWB) based on surgeon's philosophy and surgical approach.	
		WBAT	**TDWB**
		Weight bearing as tolerated with walker immediately postop. Ambulation with cane at week 5–6. Transition to full weight bearing at week 6.	Touch down weight bearing with walker immediately postop. Weight bearing as tolerated with walker at week 6. Ambulation with cane at week 8–10. Transition to full weight bearing at week 10.
Isometric and active exercise	Immediately postop	Immediately postop	
Resisted exercise	Begin at week 2–3	Begin at week 2–3	

mobilization to the specific restrictions identified during the examination. Important to note that guidelines/precautions can vary significantly (see Table 1-28).

d. Ligamentous repairs of knee.
   (1) Six phases of rehabilitation are followed with ACL and PCL reconstructive surgery. Note that protocols may vary.
   (2) Anterior cruciate ligament reconstruction (see Table 1-29).
      (a) Immediately following surgery, a continuous passive motion (CPM) unit is utilized, with PROM from 0°–70° of flexion.
      (b) Motion is increased to 0°–120° by the sixth week.
      (c) Reconstruction is usually protected with a hinged brace set at 20°–70° of flexion initially.
      (d) Patient is non–weight bearing for approximately one week.

Table 1-29

Hamstring versus Patella Tendon Graft for ACL Reconstruction	
HAMSTRING GRAFTS	**PATELLA TENDON GRAFTS**
Pros	
1. Typically fewer symptoms postoperatively.	1. Better at maintaining graft tension postoperatively.
2. Greater return to preinjury level of activity.	2. Typically less expensive.
3. Typically allows earlier rehabilitation.	3. Faster healing time.
Cons	
1. Typically more expensive.	1. Increased potential for anterior knee pain and later patellofemoral osteoarthrosis.
2. Believed to be more technically difficult procedure.	2. Increased potential for knee extension deficit.
3. Rehabilitation can be more difficult (i.e., slower).	3. Potential delay in rehabilitation secondary to more atrophy of quadriceps.

(e) Weight-bearing progresses as tolerated to full weight bearing.

(f) Patient is weaned from brace between the second and fourth weeks.

(3) Posterior cruciate ligament reconstruction.

(a) Generally similar to ACL repair, except patient is often initially in hinged brace at 0° during ambulation.

(4) Physical therapy goals, outcomes, and interventions following ACL and PCL surgical repairs.

(a) Six phases of rehabilitation are as follows: preoperative, maximum protection, controlled motion, moderate protection, minimum protection, and return to activity.

(b) Specific interventions.

- Soft tissue/massage techniques to quadriceps and hamstring muscles to reduce muscle guarding.
- Joint oscillations to inhibit joint pain and muscle guarding.
- Correction of muscle imbalances and biomechanical faults using strengthening, endurance, coordination, and flexibility exercises to gain restoration of normal function.
- Biomechanical faults caused by joint restrictions should be corrected with joint mobilization to the specific restrictions identified during the examination.
- Progression to functional training based on patient's occupation and/or recreational goals.

e. Lateral retinacular release.

(1) Typically performed as a result of patellofemoral pain syndrome (PFPS). Purpose of procedure is to restore normal tracking of the patella during contraction of the quadriceps muscle.

(2) Physical therapy goals, outcomes, and interventions.

(a) Intervention should emphasize closed kinetic chain exercises to strengthen quadriceps muscle and regain dynamic balance of all structures (contractile and noncontractile) surrounding knee.

(b) Normalize the flexibility of the hamstrings, triceps surae, and ITB will help restore mechanical alignment.

(c) Mobilization of patella is important to maintain nutrition and decrease the likelihood of adhesions.

f. Meniscal arthroscopy.

(1) Partial meniscectomy.

(a) PWB as tolerated when full knee extension is obtained.

(b) Physical therapy goals, outcomes, and interventions.

- Initial goals focus on edema/effusion control.
- AROM is urged after surgical day 1.
- Isotonic and isokinetic strengthening by day 3.
- Jogging on the ball of the foot or toes is recommended to decrease the loading of the knee joint.

(2) Repairs.

(a) Rehabilitation protocols vary.

(b) Rehabilitation begins within 3–10 days of the procedure.

- Patient is placed in a knee brace. The brace is locked in extension during ambulation with crutches. Weight bearing is to tolerance.
- Knee flexion is gradually increased to 90°.

(c) Physical therapy goals, outcomes, and interventions.

- Soft tissue/massage techniques to quadriceps and hamstring muscles to reduce muscle guarding.

- Joint oscillations to inhibit joint pain and muscle guarding.
- Correction of muscle imbalances and biomechanical faults using strengthening, endurance, coordination, and flexibility exercises to gain restoration of normal function.
- Biomechanical faults caused by joint restrictions should be corrected with joint mobilization to the specific restrictions identified during the examination.
- Progression to functional training, based on patient's occupation and/or recreational goals.

3. Surgical repairs of spine.
   a. Rehabilitation varies according to the type of surgery performed.
   b. A back protection program and early mobilization exercises should be initiated prior to surgery.
   c. Patients should avoid prolonged sitting, heavy lifting, and long car trips for approximately 3 months.
   d. Repetitive bending with twisting should always be avoided.
   e. With microdiscectomies, rehabilitation time is decreased because the fibers of the annulus fibrosus are not damaged.
   f. With laminectomy/discectomy, early movement and activation of paraspinal musculature (especially multifidus) is necessary.
   g. Multilevel vertebra fusion:
      (1) Typically requires 6 weeks of trunk immobility with bracing.
      (2) Once brace is removed and movement is allowed, important to regain as much normal/functional movement as possible, while restoring functional activation of muscles.
      (3) With combined anterior/posterior surgical approach, bracing is seldom used.
   h. With Harrington rod placement for idiopathic scoliosis, rehabilitation goals focus on early mobilization in bed and effective coughing.
      (1) The patient can begin ambulation between the fourth and seventh postoperative days.
      (2) The patient should avoid heavy lifting and excessive twisting and bending.
   i. Physical therapy goals, outcomes, and interventions following surgical interventions.
      (1) Soft tissue/massage techniques to paraspinal muscles to reduce muscle guarding.
      (2) Joint oscillations to inhibit joint pain and muscle guarding.
      (3) Correction of muscle imbalances using strengthening, endurance, coordination, and flexibility exercises to gain restoration of normal function. Make sure that multifidus function is restored.
      (4) Must develop dynamic stabilization for muscles of trunk and pelvis during all functional activities.
      (5) Biomechanical faults caused by joint restrictions should be corrected with joint mobilization to the specific restrictions identified during the examination.
      (6) Progression to functional training based on patient's occupation and/or recreational goals.

Interventions for Patients/Clients with Musculoskeletal Conditions

Interventions for Patients/Clients with Acute Conditions

1. Acute phase.
   a. Immobilization with limited (1–2 days) bed rest. Use of braces, slings, corsets, cervical collars, assistive devices, and taping (see Table 1-30).
   b. Control inflammatory response (rest, ice, compression, elevation [RICE]).
      (1) Physical agents: ice and electric stimulation.
      (2) Compression and elevation to reduce and prevent effusion and swelling.
      (3) NSAIDs.
      (4) Rest/relaxation to reduce pain.
      (5) Soft tissue/massage techniques.
   c. Assisted movement of injured tissues.
   d. Joint oscillations (grades I and II) for pain relief.
   e. Therapeutic exercise.
      (1) Dose of 40%–60% of one repetition maximum (i.e., high repetition with low resistance) to stimulate regeneration of tissue and revascularization.
      (2) Exercise should be nontraumatic, meaning no pain and/or increased edema as a result of the exercise.
   f. Educate patient/client on joint protection strategies.
2. Subacute phase.
   a. Avoidance of continued irritation and repetitive trauma.
      (1) Modify activities at home/work/recreation.
      (2) Modify use of equipment or type of equipment at home/work/recreation.

Table 1-30

Musculoskeletal Practice Patterns	
Pattern 4A	Primary prevention/risk reduction for skeletal demineralization
Pattern 4B	Impaired posture
Pattern 4C	Impaired muscle performance
Pattern 4D	Impaired joint mobility, motor function, muscle performance, and range of motion associated with connective tissue dysfunction
Pattern 4E	Impaired joint mobility, motor function, muscle performance, and range of motion associated with localized inflammation
Pattern 4F	Impaired joint mobility, motor function, muscle performance, range of motion, and reflex integrity associated with spinal disorders
Pattern 4G	Impaired joint mobility, muscle performance, and range of motion associated with fracture
Pattern 4H	Impaired joint mobility, motor function, muscle performance, and range of motion associated with joint arthroplasty
Pattern 4I	Impaired joint mobility, motor function, muscle performance, and range of motion associated with bony or soft tissue surgery
Pattern 4J	Impaired motor function, muscle performance, range of motion, gait, locomotion, and balance associated with amputation

Adapted from Practice Patterns. American Physical Therapy Association, 2014. Note: On the APTA website, each practice pattern includes:
- Inclusion criteria: risk factors or consequences of pathology/pathophysiology; impairments of body functions and structures, activity limitations, or participation restrictions
- Exclusion or Multiple-Pattern Classification
- Examination: relevant tests and measures
- Evaluation, Diagnosis, and Prognosis (including Plan of Care) factors
- Intervention categories

(3) Correct biomechanical faults, such as leg length discrepancy, abnormal foot biomechanics, abnormal throwing motion.

b. Joint mobilization.
c. Continued therapeutic exercise, including flexibility/endurance/coordination exercise.
d. Postural reeducation.
e. Biomechanical education.

3. Functional restoration phase.
   a. Maintain or return to optimum level of patient function.
   b. Normalize flexibility of joints and related soft tissues.
   c. Restore loading capacity of connective tissues to normal strength.
   d. Functional strengthening exercises.
   e. Functional stabilization of the involved joint/region.

Interventions for Patients/Clients with a Chronic Condition

1. Determine possible causative factors.
   a. Abnormal remodeling of injured tissues (see Table 1-30).
   b. Chronic low-grade inflammation due to repetitive stresses of tissues.
2. Reduce stresses to tissues.
   a. Identify/eliminate the magnitude of loading.
   b. Identify/eliminate direction of forces.
   c. Identify and eliminate any biomechanical barriers that are preventing healing; e.g., leg length discrepancy.
   d. Patient education regarding protection of joints and associated soft tissues.
3. Regain structural integrity.
   a. Improving flexibility.
   b. Postural reeducation.
   c. Increasing tissue's capacity to tolerate loading.
   d. Functional strengthening, endurance, and coordination exercises.
4. Resume optimal patient function and prevention of reoccurrence.
   a. Patient education regarding causative factors in dysfunction.
   b. Work conditioning.

Specific Interventions

1. Soft tissue/myofascial techniques.
   a. Aid in reduction of metabolites from muscle, reactivating a muscle that has not been functioning secondary to guarding and ischemia, revascularization of muscle, and also decrease guarding in a muscle.
   b. Autonomic: stimulation of skin and superficial fascia to facilitate a decrease in muscle tension.
   c. Mechanical: movement of skin, fascia, and muscle causes histological and mechanical changes to occur in soft tissues to produce improved mobility and function (e.g., acupressure and osteopathic mechanical stretching techniques).
   d. Goals: decrease pain, edema, and muscle spasm, increase metabolism and cutaneous temperature, stretch tight muscles and other soft tissues, improve circulation, strengthen weak muscles, and mobilize joint restrictions.
   e. Indications: patients with soft tissue and joint restriction that results in pain and limits ADLs.

f. Contraindications.
   (1) Absolute: soft tissue breakdown, infection, cellulitis, inflammation, and/or neoplasm.
   (2) Relative: hypermobility, and sensitivity.
g. Traditional massage techniques, such as effleurage and petrissage.
h. Functional massage.
   (1) Three techniques used to assist in reactivation of a debilitated muscle and/or to increase vascularity to a muscle.
      (a) Soft tissue without motion.
         • Traditional technique; however, hands do not slide over skin; instead, they stay in contact with skin while hands and skin move together over the muscle.
         • Direction of force is parallel to muscle fibers, and total stroke time should be 5–7 seconds.
      (b) Soft tissue with passive pumping.
         • Place muscle in shortened position and with one hand place tension on muscle parallel to muscle fibers.
         • Other hand passively lengthens muscle and simultaneously gradually releases tension of hand in contact with muscle.
      (c) Soft tissue with active pumping.
         • Place muscle in lengthened position, and with one hand place tension on muscle perpendicular to muscle fibers.
         • Other hand guides limb as patient actively shortens muscle. As muscle shortens, gradually release tension of hand in contact with muscle.
i. Transverse friction massage.
   (1) Used to initiate an acute inflammatory response for a tissue that is in metabolic stasis, such as a tendonosis.
   (2) Involved tendon is briskly massaged in a transverse fashion (perpendicular to the direction of the fibers).
   (3) Performed for 5–10 minutes and tends to be very uncomfortable for the patient.
j. Movement approaches require the patient to actively participate in treatment. Examples include:
   (1) Feldenkrais.
      (a) Facilitates development of normal movement patterns.
      (b) The practitioner uses skillful, supportive, gentle hands to create a sense of safety, maintain supportive contact, while introducing new movement possibilities in small, easily available increments.
   (2) Muscle energy techniques.
      (a) Include voluntary contraction in a precisely controlled direction, at varying levels of intensity, against an applied counterforce from the clinician.
      (b) Purpose is to gain motion that is limited by restrictions of the neuromuscular system.
      (c) Modification of proprioceptive neuromuscular facilitation (PNF) technique.
   (3) PNF hold-relax-contract technique.
      (a) Antagonist of the shortened muscle is contracted to achieve reciprocal inhibition and increased range.
      (b) Refer to Chapter 2: Neuromuscular Physical Therapy for details.

2. Articulatory techniques.
   a. Joint oscillation.
      (1) Inhibit pain and/or muscle guarding.
      (2) Lubricate joint surfaces.
      (3) Provide nutrition to the joint structures.
      (4) Maitland suggests that grades III and IV oscillations are beneficial to stretch tight connective tissues.
      (5) Grades of movement as described by Maitland (see Figure 1-52).
         (a) Five grades of joint play in neutral.
            • Grade I oscillations are small amplitude at the beginning of the range of joint play.
            • Grade II oscillations are large amplitude at the midrange of joint play.
            • Grade III oscillations are large amplitude at the end range of joint play.
            • Grade IV oscillations are small amplitude at the end range of joint play.
            • Grade V is a manipulation of high velocity and low amplitude to the anatomical endpoint of a joint. Technically, this is not an oscillation, since it is a single movement rather than a repetitive movement.
         (b) Indications for use of oscillation grades, per Maitland.
            • Grades I and II are used to improve joint lubrication/nutrition, as well as decrease pain and muscle guarding.

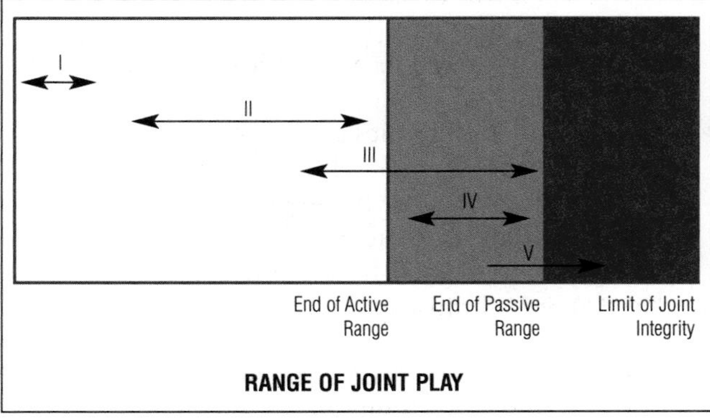

Figure 1-52 Grades of movement.
Adapted from Grieve GP: Mobilization of the Spine: A Primary Handbook of Clinical Method, 5th ed. Churchill Livingstone, 1991.

- Grades III and IV are used to stretch tight muscles, capsules, and ligaments.
- Grade V is used to regain normal joint mechanics, as well as decrease pain and muscle guarding.

(6) Contraindications.
(a) Absolute: joint ankylosis, malignancy involving bone, diseases that affect the integrity of ligaments (RA and Down syndrome), arterial insufficiency, and active inflammatory and/or infective process.
(b) Relative: arthrosis (DJD), metabolic bone disease (osteoporosis, Paget's disease, and tuberculosis), hypermobility, total joint replacement, pregnancy, spondylolisthesis, use of steroids, and radicular symptoms.

b. Joint mobilization (nonthrust).
(1) To stretch/lengthen/deform collagen and normalize the arthrokinematic glide of joint structures.
(2) Grades of translatoric glide, as described by Kaltenborn.
(a) Grade I.
- "Loosening" translatoric glide.
- Movement is a very small amplitude traction force.
- Used to relieve pain and/or decompress a joint during joint glides, performed within examination or intervention.

(b) Grade II.
- "Tightening" translatoric glide.
- Movement takes up slack in tissues surrounding joint.
- Used to alleviate pain, assess joint play, and/or reduce muscle guarding.

(c) Grade III.
- "Stretching" translatoric glide.
- Movement stretches the tissues crossing joint.
- Used to assess end-feel, or to increase movement (stretch tissue).

(3) Traction: manual, mechanical, and self or auto traction.
(a) Vertebral bodies separating.
(b) Distraction and gliding of facet joints.
(c) Tensing of the ligamentous structures of the spinal segment.
(d) Intervertebral foramen widening.
(e) Spinal muscles stretching.
(4) Contraindications.
(a) Absolute: joint ankylosis, malignancy involving bone, diseases that affect the integrity of ligaments (RA and Down syndrome), arterial insufficiency, and active inflammatory and/or infective process.
(b) Relative: arthrosis (DJD), metabolic bone disease (osteoporosis, Paget's disease, and tuberculosis), hypermobility, total joint replacement, pregnancy, spondylolisthesis, use of steroids, and radicular symptoms.

c. Manipulation (thrust).
(1) Inhibit pain and/or muscle guarding.
(2) Improve translatoric glide in cases of joint dysfunction due to restriction.
(3) Health care practitioners who commonly perform manipulative thrusts include physical therapists, osteopaths, chiropractors, and medical doctors.
(4) Types of manipulations.
(a) Generalized.
- Fairly forceful, long lever techniques intended to include as many vertebral segments as possible.
- More commonly performed by chiropractic practitioners.

(b) Specific.
- Aimed at having an effect on either a specific segment or only a few vertebral segments.
- Uses minimal force with short lever arms.
- Often includes "locking" techniques based on biomechanics to ensure that a specific vertebral segment receives the manipulative thrust.
- More commonly performed by physical therapists.

(c) Mid-range.
- Very gentle, short lever arm techniques.
- Barrier is created in mid-range by specific positioning of patient as well as creating tautness in surrounding soft tissues.
- More commonly performed by osteopathic practitioners.

(5) Contraindications.
(a) Absolute: joint ankylosis, malignancy involving bone, diseases that affect the integrity of ligaments (RA and Down syndrome), arterial insufficiency, and active inflammatory and/or infective process.
(b) Relative: arthrosis (DJD), metabolic bone disease (osteoporosis, Paget's disease, and tuberculosis), hypermobility, total joint replacement, pregnancy, spondylolisthesis, use of steroids, and radicular symptoms.
(6) Common mistakes in performing a thrust manipulation.
(a) Not communicating clearly with the patient regarding the technique.
(b) Taking too long to properly position the patient.

(c) Not performing the "trial" thrust prior to the actual thrust.
(d) Not allowing the person to "bottom out" with their breath prior to performing the thrust.
(e) Taking up the slack while the patient exhales and then letting off with pressure prior to the thrust.
(f) Velocity too slow.
(g) Amplitude too great.
(7) Suggested algorithm to perform a manipulation.
(a) Consider indications and contraindications.
(b) Explain the intentions and implications regarding manipulation to the patient.
(c) Describe the actual technique to the patient.
(d) Place patient into position and assess for patient comfort.
(e) Perform a prethrust force into the range to determine patient tolerance.
(f) Ask patient to inhale and then exhale. Take up the slack into the range as they exhale.
(g) When they reach the end of exhalation, perform the thrust.
(h) Specific thoughts for thrusting the cervical region.
(i) Perform vertebrobasilar testing when performing manipulations to cervical segments.
(j) Consider performing thrusts to thoracic region to attain the result that was sought after for the cervical thrust.
(k) Headaches in the cervical region are a common indication for thrusts, but are also a contraindication. Query female patients regarding birth control combined with smoking since this may be a cause for vascular accidents. Consider that headaches frequently precede a cerebrovascular accident.

3. Neural tissue mobilization.
a. Movement of neural structures to regain normal mobility.
b. Tension tests for upper and lower extremities (i.e., dural stretch test).
(1) Movement of soft tissues that may be restricting neural structures (e.g., cross friction massage for adhesions of the radial nerve to the humerus at a fracture site).
(2) Indications: used for patients who have some type of restriction in neural mobility, anywhere along the course of the nerve.
(3) Postural reeducation: to open up the intervertebral foramen, and decrease tension to tissues.
(4) Contraindications: extreme pain and/or increase in abnormal neurological signs.
c. Perform assessment with neurotension testing.
d. Determine whether managing irritated or nonirritated neurologic tissue.
(1) Irritated tissue.
(a) Utilize grade II mobilizations (based on Maitland scale); should be nonpainful.
(2) Nonirritated tissue.
(a) Utilize grade III mobilizations (based on Maitland scale) to engage the barrier but remain nonpainful.

4. Therapeutic exercise for musculoskeletal conditions.
a. Therapeutic exercise is indicated to:
(1) Decrease muscle guarding.
(2) Decrease pain.
(3) Increase vascularity of tissue.
(4) Promote regeneration and/or speed up recovery of connective tissues, such as cartilage, tendons, ligaments, capsules, intervertebral discs.
(5) Mobilize restricted tissue to increase flexibility.
(6) Increase endurance of muscle.
(7) Increase coordination of muscle.
(8) Increase strength of muscle.
(9) Sensitize muscles to minimize joints going into excessive range in cases of hypermobility.
(10) Develop dynamic stability and functional movement patterns, allowing for optimal function within the environment.
b. Home exercise program for patients/clients with musculoskeletal conditions.
(1) Patient's home program will consist of exercises to reinforce clinical program.
(2) Necessary to perform enough repetitions for desired physiological effect on appropriate tissues, as well as to develop coordination and endurance in order to promote dynamic stability within functional patterns.
c. See Chapter 9: Therapeutic Exercise Foundations.

5. Dry needling.
a. Also referred to as intramuscular manual therapy (IMT).
b. Utilized to break up trigger points in myofascial pain syndrome.
c. A solid filiform needle is inserted into the trigger point (within the muscle).

Manual Therapy Approaches in Rehabilitation

1. All approaches provide a philosophical basis, subjective evaluation, objective examination, a diagnosis, and a plan of care.
2. Approaches can be divided into three categories.
a. Physician generated.
(1) Mennell believed the joint is the dysfunctional unit.

(2) Osteopaths suggest that any component of the somatic system is responsible for dysfunction.
(3) Cyriax contends that dysfunction is due to interplay between contractile and noncontractile tissues.

b. Physical therapist generated.
(1) McKenzie feels that postural factors precipitate discal dysfunction. Treatment emphasizes the use of extension exercises.
(2) Maitland proposes that the subjective evaluation should be integrated with objective measures to determine the dysfunctional area.
(3) Kaltenborn believes that abnormal joint mobility and soft tissue changes account for dysfunction.

c. Chiropractic generated.
(1) Focus is to restore normal joint function through soft tissue and joint manipulation. Chiropractors believe that restoration of normal biomechanical function affects other systems of the body as well, thus improving the state of health in many ways.

Relevant Pharmacology

1. Nonsteroidal anti-inflammatory drugs (NSAIDs).
   a. Most commonly prescribed medication for pain relief for musculoskeletal dysfunction.
   b. Examples include ibuprofen (Motrin), naproxen sodium (Aleve), salsalate (Discalced), and indomethacin (Indocin).
   c. Provide analgesic, anti-inflammatory, and antipyretic capabilities.
   d. Adverse side effects could include gastrointestinal irritation, fluid retention, renal or liver problems, and prolonged bleeding.
   e. COX-2 inhibitors have decreased gastrointestinal irritation, but rofecoxib (Vioxx) was withdrawn from the market secondary to its relationship with heart-related conditions. Other COX-2 inhibitors such as colecoxib (Celebrex) and valdecoxib (Bextra) are being evaluated for their safety and possible association with heart-related conditions.
2. Muscle relaxants.
   a. Commonly prescribed for skeletal muscle spasm.
   b. Examples include cyclobenzaprine HCl (Flexeril), methocarbamol (Robaxin), and carisoprodol (Soma).
   c. Act on the central nervous system to reduce skeletal muscle tone by depressing the internuncial neurons of the brain stem and spinal cord.
   d. Adverse side effects could include drowsiness, lethargy, ataxia, and decreased alertness.
3. Nonnarcotic analgesics.
   a. Prescribed when NSAIDs are contraindicated.
   b. Examples include acetaminophen (Tylenol).
   c. Act on the central nervous system to alter response to pain, and have antipyretic capabilities.
   d. Adverse side effects are negligible when taken in recommended doses. Excessive amounts of acetaminophen may lead to liver disease or acute liver shutdown.

Psychosocial Considerations

1. Malingering (symptom magnification syndrome).
   a. Defined as a behavioral response where displays of symptoms control the life of the patient, leading to functional disability.
   b. There may be psychological advantages to illness.
      (1) The patient may feel protected from the threatening world.
      (2) Uncertainty or fear about the future.
      (3) Social gain.
      (4) Reduces stressors.
   c. Therapist needs to recognize symptoms and respond to the patient.
      (1) Tests to evaluate malingering back pain may include Hoover test, Burn's test, and Waddell's signs.
         (a) Hoover test involves the therapist's evaluation of the amount of pressure the patient's heels place on the therapist's hands when the patient is asked to raise one lower extremity while in a supine position.
         (b) Burn's test requires the patient to kneel and bend over a chair to touch the floor.
         (c) Waddell's signs evaluate tenderness, simulation tests, distraction tests, regional disturbances, and overreaction. Waddell's scores can be predictive of functional outcome.
      (2) Functional capacity evaluations are used to evaluate psychosocial as well as physical components of disability.
      (3) Emphasize regaining functional outcomes, not pain reduction.
2. Secondary gain.
   a. Usually some type of financial gain for staying ill.
      (1) Workers' compensation.
      (2) Larger settlement for injury claims.
   b. Frequently seen in clinics that manage industrial injuries.
   c. May not want to return to work for various reasons associated with the work environment; e.g., stress, disliking coworkers.

APPENDIX 1A

Selected Musculoskeletal Outcome Measures

Table 1A-1

BODY STRUCTURE AND FUNCTION MEASURES	REFERENCES
Disabilities of the Arm, Shoulder and Hand Outcome Measure (DASH)	• Beaton DE, Davis AM, Hudak P, McConnell S. The DASH (Disabilities of the Arm, Shoulder and Hand) Outcome Measure: What do we know about it now? Br J Hand Ther. 2001; 6(4): 109–118. • Beaton DE, Katz JN, Fossel AH, et al. Measuring the whole or the parts? Validity, reliability & responsiveness of the disabilities of the arm, shoulder, and hand outcome measure in different regions of the upper extremity. J Hand Ther. 2001; 14(2): 128. • Bot SDM, Terwee CB, van der Windt DAWN, et al. Clinimetric evaluation of shoulder disability questionnaires: A systematic review of the literature. Ann Rheum Dis. 2004; 63(4): 335. • Available online at: http://www.dash.iwh.on.ca/
Fear Avoidance Behavior Questionnaire (FABQ)	• Waddell G, Newton M, Henderson I, Somerville D, Main CJ. A Fear-Avoidance Beliefs Questionnaire (FABQ) and the role of fear-avoidance beliefs in chronic low back pain and disability. Pain. 1993; 52(2): 157–168. • Available online at: http://www.udel.edu/PT/PT%20Clinical%20Services/journalclub/caserounds/05_06/mar06/FABQ1.pdf
Global Rating of Change (GRC)	• Kamper SJ, Maher CG, Mackay G. Global rating of change scales: a review of strengths and weaknesses and considerations for design. J Man Manip Ther. 2009;17(3): 163–170. • Available online at: http://academic.regis.edu/clinicaleducation/pdf's/Knee_Pain_GROC.pdf
Joint Motion	• Norkin C, White J. Measurement of Joint Motion, 4th ed. FA Davis, Philadelphia, 2009.
Knee Injury and Osteoarthritis Outcome Score (KOOS)	• Roos R, Roos H, Lohmander L, Ekdahl C, Beynnon B. Knee Injury and Osteoarthritis Outcome Score Development of a Self-Administered Outcome Measure. JOSPT. 1998; 78(2): 88–96. • Available online at: http://www.koos.nu/
Lower Extremity Functional Scale (LEFS)	• Wang Y-C, Hart DL, Stratford PW, Mioduski JE. Clinical Interpretation of a Lower-Extremity Functional Scale-derived computerized adaptive test. Phys Ther. 2009; 89(9): 957. • Lin CW, Moseley AM, Refshauge KM, Bundy AC. The Lower Extremity Functional Scale has good clinimetric properties in people with ankle fracture. Phys Ther. 2009; 89(6): 580. • Binkley JM, Stratford PW, Lott SA, Riddle DL. The Lower Extremity Functional Scale (LEFS): Scale development, measurement properties, and clinical application. Phys Ther. 1999; 79(4): 371.

(*Continued*)

Table 1A-1 (*Continued*)

BODY STRUCTURE AND FUNCTION MEASURES	REFERENCES
Manual Muscle Test (MMT)	• Hislop HJ, Montgomery J. Daniels and Worthingham's Muscle Testing: Techniques of Manual Examination, 8th ed. Saunders (Elsevier), Philadelphia, Muscle Testing and Function with Posture and Pain, 5th ed. Lippincott Williams & Wilkins, Baltimore. 2005. • Kendall F, McCreary E, Provance P, et al. Muscles Test
Neck Disability Index (NDI)	• McDermid J, Walton D, Avery S, Blanchard A, Etruw E, McAlpine C, Goldsmith C. Measurement Properties of the Neck Disability Index: A Systematic Review. JOSPT. 2009; 39(5): 400–416.
Oswestry Disability Index (ODI)	• Fairbank J, Pynsent P. The Oswestry Disability Index. SPINE. 2000; 25(22): 2940–2953.
Pain Catastrophizing Scale (PCS)	• Osman A, Barrios F, Gutierrez P, Kopper B, Merrifield T, Grittman L. The Pain Catastrophizing Scale: Further Psychometric Evaluation with Adult Samples. Jour Behavioral Med. 2000; 23(4): 351–365. • Available online at: http://sullivan-painresearch.mcgill.ca/pdf/pcs/PCSManual_English.pdf
Patient Specific Functional Scale (PSFS)	• Westaway M, Stratford P, Binkley J. The Patient-Specific Functional Scale: Validation of Its Use in Persons With Neck Dysfunction. JOSPT. 1998; 27(5): 331–338.
Penn Shoulder Scale (PSS)	• Leggin B, Michener L, Shaffer M, Brenneman S, Iannotti J, Williams G. The Penn Shoulder Score: Reliability and Validity. JOSPT.2006; 36(3): 138–149. • Available online at: http://www.eliterehabsolutions.com/pdfs/PENN%20SHOULDER%20SCORE.pdf
Subgroups for Targeted Treatment (STarT)	• Hill J, Whitehurst D, Lewis M, Bryan S, Dunn K, Foster N, Konstantinou K, Main C, Mason E, Somerville S, Sowden G, Vohora K, Hay E. Comparison of stratified primary care management for low back pain with current best practice (STarT Back): a randomised controlled trial. The Lancet. 2011; 378(9802): 1560–1571.
Tampa Scale for Kinesiophobia (TSK)	• Swinkels-Meewisse IEJ, Swinkels R, Verbeek A, Vlaeyen J, Oostendorp R. Psychometric properties of the Tampa Scale for kinesiophobia and the fear-avoidance beliefs questionnaire in acute low back pain. Manual Therapy. 2003; 8(1): 29–36.
Western Ontario and McMaster Universities Osteoarthritis Index (WOMAC)	• McConnell S, Kolopack P, Davis A. The Western Ontario and McMaster Universities Osteoarthritis Index (WOMAC): A Review of Its Utility and Measurement Properties. Arthritis Care & Research. 2001; 45: 453–461. • Available online at: http://www.hss.edu/files/New_patient_Hip_WOMAC.PDF
Western Ontario Shoulder Instability Index (WOSI)	• Kirley A, Griffin S, McLintock H, Ng L. The Development and Evaluation of a Disease-Specific Quality of Life Measurement Tool for Shoulder Instability. Amer Jour Sports Med. 1998; 26(6): 764–771.
Whiplash Disability Questionnaire (WDQ)	• Willis C, Niere K, Hoving J, Green S, O'Leary E, Buchbinder R. Reproducibility and responsiveness of the Whiplash Disability Questionnaire. Pain. 2004; 110: 681–688.

APPENDIX 1B
Grades of Evidence

Table 1B-1

GRADES OF RECOMMENDATION BASED ON	STRENGTH OF EVIDENCE
A Strong evidence	A preponderance of Level I and/or Level II studies support the recommendation. This must include at least one Level I study.
B Moderate evidence	A single, high-quality, randomized controlled trial or a preponderance of Level II studies support the recommendation.
C Weak evidence	A single Level II study or a preponderance of Level III and IV studies, including statements of consensus by content experts support the recommendation.
D Conflicting evidence	Higher-quality studies conducted on this topic disagree on conclusions. The recommendation is based on these conflicting studies.
E Theoretical/foundational evidence	A preponderance of evidence from animal or cadaver studies, from conceptual models/ principles, or from basic sciences/bench research support this conclusion.
F Expert opinion	Best practice based on the clinical experience of the guidelines development team.

Adapted from Knee Pain and Mobility Impairments: Meniscal and Articular Cartilage Lesions. Clinical Practice Guidelines Linked to the International Classification of Functioning, Disability, and Health from the Orthopaedic Section of the American Physical Therapy Association, Summary of Recommendations. JOSPT 6(40): A30, 2010.

APPENDIX 1C

Meniscal and Articular Cartilage Lesions

Clinical Course (C)

Knee pain and mobility impairments associated with meniscal and articular cartilage tears can be the result of a contact or noncontact incident. This can result in damage to one or more structures. Clinicians should assess for impairments in range of motion, motor control, strength, and endurance of the limb associated with the identified meniscal or articular cartilage pathology or following meniscal or chondral surgery.

Risk Factors: Meniscus (C)

Clinicians should consider age and greater time from injury as predisposing factors for having a meniscal injury. Patients who participated in high-level sports or had increased knee laxity after an ACL injury are more likely to have late meniscal surgery.

Risk Factors: Articular Cartilage (C)

Clinicians should consider the patient's age and presence of a meniscal tear for the odds of having a chondral lesion subsequent to an ACL injury. Greater patient age and longer time from initial ACL injury are predictive factors of the severity of chondral lesions. Time from initial ACL injury is significantly associated with the number of chondral lesions.

Diagnosis/Classification (C)

Knee pain, mobility impairments, and effusion are useful clinical findings for classifying a patient with knee pain and mobility disorders into the following International Statistical Classification of Diseases and Related Health Problems (ICD) categories: tear of the meniscus and tear of the articular cartilage.

Differential Diagnosis (C)

Clinicians should consider diagnostic classifications associated with serious pathological conditions or psychosocial factors when the patient's reported activity limitations or impairments of body function and structure are not consistent with those presented in the diagnosis/classification section of this guideline, or, when the patient's symptoms are not resolving with interventions aimed at normalization of the patient's impairments of body function.

Examination: Outcome Measures (C)

Clinicians should use a validated, patient-reported outcome measure, a general health questionnaire, and a validated activity scale for patients with knee pain and mobility impairments. These tools are useful for identifying a patient's baseline status relative to pain, function, and disability and for monitoring changes in the patient's status throughout the course of treatment.

Examination: Activity Limitation Measures (C)

Clinicians should utilize easily reproducible physical performance measures, such as single-limb hop tests, 6-Minute Walk Test, or timed up-and-go test, to assess activity limitation and participation restrictions associated with their patient's knee pain or mobility impairments and to assess the changes in the patient's level of function over the episode of care.

Interventions: Progressive Knee Motion (C)

Clinicians may utilize early progressive knee motion following knee meniscal and articular cartilage surgery.

Interventions: Progressive Weight Bearing (D)

There are conflicting opinions regarding the best use of progressive weight bearing for patients with meniscal repairs or chondral lesions.

Interventions: Progressive Return to Activity—Meniscus (C)

Clinicians may utilize early progressive return to activity following knee meniscal repair surgery.

Interventions: Progressive Return to Activity—Articular Cartilage (E)

Clinicians may need to delay return to activity, depending on the type of articular cartilage surgery.

Interventions: Supervised Rehabilitation (D)

There are conflicting opinions regarding the best use of clinic-based programs for patients following arthroscopic meniscectomy to increase quadriceps strength and functional performance.

Interventions: Therapeutic Exercises (B)

Clinicians should consider strength training and functional exercise to increase quadriceps and hamstrings strength, quadriceps endurance, and functional performance following meniscectomy.

Interventions: Neuromuscular Electrical Stimulation (B)

Neuromuscular electrical stimulation can be used with patients following meniscal or chondral injuries to increase quadriceps muscle strength.

Adapted from Knee Pain and Mobility Impairments: Meniscal and Articular Cartilage Lesions. Clinical Practice Guidelines Linked to the International Classification of Functioning, Disability, and Health from the Orthopaedic Section of the American Physical Therapy Association, Summary of Recommendations. JOSPT 6(40): A30, 2010.

APPENDIX 1D

Hip Pain and Mobility Deficits/Hip Osteoarthritis

Pathoanatomical Features (B)

Clinicians should assess for impairments in mobility of the hip joint and strength of the surrounding muscles, especially the hip abductor muscles, when a patient presents with hip pain.

Risk Factors (A)

Clinicians should consider age, hip developmental disorders, and previous hip joint injury as risk factors for hip osteoarthritis.

Diagnosis/Classification (A)

Moderate lateral or anterior hip pain during weight bearing, in adults over the age of 50 years, with morning stiffness less than 1 hour, with limited hip internal rotation and hip flexion by more than 15° when comparing the painful to the nonpainful side are useful clinical findings to classify a patient with hip pain into the International Statistical Classification of Diseases and Related Health Problems (ICD).

Differential Diagnosis (E)

Clinicians should consider diagnostic classifications other than osteoarthritis of the hip when the patient's history, reported activity limitations, or impairments of body function and structure are not consistent with those presented in the diagnosis/classification section of this guideline, or when the patient's symptoms do not diminish with interventions aimed at normalization of the patient's impairments of body function.

Examination: Outcome Measures (A)

Clinicians should use validated functional outcome measures, such as the Western Ontario and McMaster Universities Osteoarthritis Index, the Lower Extremity Functional Scale, and the Harris Hip Score before and after interventions intended to alleviate the impairments of body function and structure, activity limitations, and participation restrictions associated with hip osteoarthritis.

Examination: Activity Limitation and Participation Restriction Measures (A)

Clinicians should utilize easily reproducible physical performance measures, such as the 6-minute walk, self-paced walk, stair measure, and timed up-and-go tests to assess activity limitation and participation restrictions associated with their patient's hip pain, and to assess changes in the patient's level of function over the episode of care.

Interventions: Patient Education (B)

Clinicians should consider the use of patient education to teach activity modification, exercise, weight reduction when overweight, and methods of unloading the arthritic joints.

Interventions: Functional, Gait, and Balance Training (C)

Functional, gait, and balance training, including the use of assistive devices such as canes, crutches, and walkers, can be used in patients with hip osteoarthritis to improve function associated with weight-bearing activities.

Interventions: Manual Therapy (B)

Clinicians should consider the use of manual therapy procedures to provide short-term pain relief and improve hip mobility and function in patients with mild hip osteoarthritis.

Interventions: Flexibility, Strengthening, and Endurance Exercises (B)

Clinicians should consider the use of flexibility, strengthening, and endurance exercises in patients with hip osteoarthritis.

Adapted from Hip Pain and Mobility Deficits—Hip Osteoarthritis. Clinical Practice Guidelines Linked to the International Classification of Functioning, Disability, and Health from the Orthopaedic Section of the American Physical Therapy Association, Summary of Recommendations. JOSPT 4(39): A18, 2009.

APPENDIX 1E

Neck Pain

Pathoanatomical Features (E)

Although the cause of neck pain may be associated with degenerative processes or pathology identified during diagnostic imaging, the tissue causing a patient's neck pain is most often unknown. Thus, clinicians should assess for impaired function of muscle, connective, and nerve tissues associated with the identified pathological tissues when a patient presents with neck pain.

Risk Factors (B)

Clinicians should consider age greater than 40, coexisting low back pain, a long history of neck pain, cycling as a regular activity, loss of strength in the hands, worrisome attitude, poor quality of life, and less vitality as predisposing factors for the development of chronic neck pain.

Diagnosis/Classification (B)

Neck pain, without symptoms or signs of serious medical or psychological conditions, associated with (1) motion limitations in the cervical and upper thoracic regions, (2) headaches, and (3) referred or radiating pain into an upper extremity are useful clinical findings for classifying a patient into one of the following International Statistical Classification of Diseases and Related Health Problems (ICD) categories: cervicalgia, pain in thoracic spine, headaches, cervicocranial syndrome, sprain and strain of cervical spine, spondylosis with radiculopathy, and cervical disc disorder with radiculopathy; and the associated International Classification of Functioning, Disability, and Health (ICF) impairment-based category neck pain. The following physical examination measures may be useful in classifying a patient in the ICF impairment-based category of neck pain with mobility impairments and the associated ICD categories of cervicalgia or pain in thoracic spine:

- Cervical active range of motion.
- Cervical and thoracic segmental mobility.

The following physical examination measures may be useful in classifying a patient in the ICF impairment-based category of neck pain with headaches and the associated ICD categories of headaches or cervicocranial syndrome:

- Cervical active range of motion.
- Cervical segmental mobility.
- Cranial cervical flexion test.

The following physical examination measures may be useful in classifying a patient in the ICF impairment-based category of neck pain with movement coordination impairments, and the associated ICD category of sprain and strain of cervical spine:

- Cranial cervical flexion test.
- Deep neck flexor endurance.

The following physical examination measures may be useful in classifying a patient in the ICF impairment-based category of neck pain with radiating pain, and the associated ICD categories of spondylosis with radiculopathy or cervical disc disorder with radiculopathy:

- Upper limb tension test
- Spurling's test
- Distraction test

Differential Diagnosis (B)

Clinicians should consider diagnostic classifications associated with serious pathological conditions or psychosocial factors when the patient's reported activity limitations or impairments of body function and structure are not consistent with those presented in the diagnosis/classification section of this guideline, or, when the patient's symptoms are not resolving with interventions aimed at normalization of the patient's impairments of body function.

Examination: Outcome Measures (A)

Clinicians should use validated self-report questionnaires, such as the Neck Disability Index and the Patient-Specific Functional Scale for patients with neck pain. These tools are useful for identifying a patient's baseline status relative to pain, function, and disability, as well as for monitoring a change in patient's status throughout the course of treatment.

Examination: Activity Limitation Measures (F)

Clinicians should utilize easily reproducible activity limitation and participation restriction measures associated with their patient's neck pain to assess changes in the patient's level of function over the episode of care.

Interventions: Cervical Mobilization/Manipulation (A)

Clinicians should consider utilizing cervical manipulation and mobilization procedures, thrust and non-thrust, to reduce neck pain and headache. Combining cervical manipulation and mobilization with exercise is more effective for reducing neck pain, headache, and disability than manipulation and mobilization alone.

Interventions: Thoracic Mobilization/Manipulation (C)

Thoracic spine thrust manipulation can be used for patients with primary complaints of neck pain. Thoracic spine thrust manipulation can also be used for reducing pain and disability in patients with neck and neck-related arm pain.

Interventions: Stretching Exercises (C)

Flexibility exercises can be used for patients with neck symptoms. Examination and targeted flexibility exercises for the following muscles are suggested by the authors: anterior/medial/posterior scalenes, upper trapezius, levator scapulae, pectoralis minor, and pectoralis major.

Interventions: Coordination, Strengthening, and Endurance Exercises (A)

Clinicians should consider the use of coordination, strengthening, and endurance exercises to reduce neck pain and headache.

Interventions: Centralization Procedures and Exercises (C)

Specific repeated movements or procedures to promote centralization are not more beneficial in reducing disability than other forms of interventions.

Interventions: Upper Quarter and Nerve Mobilization Procedures (B)

Clinicians should consider the use of upper quarter and nerve mobilization procedures to reduce pain and disability in patients with neck and arm pain.

Interventions: Traction (B)

Clinicians should consider the use of mechanical intermittent cervical traction, combined with other interventions such as manual therapy and strengthening exercises, for reducing pain and disability in patients with neck and neck-related arm pain.

Interventions: Patient Education and Counseling (A)

To improve the recovery in patients with whiplash-associated disorder, clinicians should (1) educate the patient that early return to normal, nonprovocative preaccident activities is important, and (2) provide reassurance to the patient that good prognosis and full recovery commonly occurs.

Adapted from Neck Pain. Clinical Practice Guidelines Linked to the International Classification of Functioning, Disability, and Health from the Orthopaedic Section of the American Physical Therapy Association, Summary of Recommendations. JOSPT 9(38): A28–A29, 2008.

APPENDIX 1F

Heel Pain/Plantar Fasciitis

Risk Factors (B)

Clinicians should assess the presence of limited ankle dorsiflexion range of motion, high body mass index in nonathletic individuals, running, and work-related weight-bearing activities—particularly under conditions with poor shock absorption—as risk factors for the development of heel pain/plantar fasciitis.

Diagnosis/Classification (B)

Physical therapists should diagnose the International Classification of Diseases (ICD) category of plantar fasciitis and the associated International Classification of Functioning, Disability, and Health Resources (ICF) impairment-based category of heel pain using the following history and physical examination findings:

- Plantar medial heel pain: most noticeable with initial steps after a period of inactivity but also worse following prolonged weight bearing.
- Heel pain precipitated by a recent increase in weight-bearing activity.
- Pain with palpation of the proximal insertion of the plantar fascia.
- Positive windlass test.
- Negative tarsal tunnel tests.
- Limited active and passive talocrural joint dorsiflexion range of motion.
- Abnormal Foot Posture Index score.
- High body mass index in nonathletic individuals.

Differential Diagnosis (C)

Clinicians should assess for diagnostic classifications other than heel pain/plantar fasciitis, including spondyloarthritis, fat-pad atrophy, and proximal plantar fibroma, when the individual's reported activity limitations or impairments of body function and structure are not consistent with those presented in the Diagnosis/Classification section of this guideline, or when the individual's symptoms are not resolving with interventions aimed at normalization of the individual's impairments of body function.

Examination: Outcome Measures (A)

Clinicians should use the Foot and Ankle Ability Measure (FAAM), the Foot Health Status Questionnaire (FHSQ), or the Foot Function Index (FFI) and may use the computer-adaptive version of the Lower Extremity Functional Scale (LEFS) as validated self-report questionnaires before and after interventions intended to alleviate the physical impairments, activity limitations, and participation restrictions associated with heel pain/plantar fasciitis.

Examination: Activity Limitation and Participation Restriction Measures (F)

Clinicians should utilize easily reproducible performance-based measures of activity limitation and participation restriction measures to assess changes in the patient's level of function associated with heel pain/plantar fasciitis over the episode of care.

Examination: Physical Impairment Measures (B)

When evaluating a patient with heel pain/plantar fasciitis over an episode of care, assessment of impairment of body function should include measures of pain with initial steps after a period of inactivity and pain with palpation of the proximal insertion of the plantar fascia, and may include measures of active and passive ankle dorsiflexion range of motion and body mass index in nonathletic individuals.

Interventions: Manual Therapy (A)

Clinicians should use manual therapy procedures, consisting of joint and soft tissue mobilization, to treat relevant lower extremity joint mobility and calf flexibility deficits and to decrease pain and improve function in individuals with heel pain/plantar fasciitis.

Interventions: Stretching (A)

Clinicians should use plantar fascia–specific and gastrocnemius/soleus stretching to provide short-term (1 week to 4 months) pain relief for individuals with heel pain/plantar fasciitis. Heel pads may be used to increase the benefits of stretching.

Interventions: Taping (A)

Clinicians should use antipronation taping for immediate (up to 3 weeks) pain reduction and improved function for individuals with heel pain/plantar fasciitis. Additionally, clinicians may use elastic therapeutic tape applied to the gastrocnemius and plantar fascia for short-term (1 week) pain reduction.

Interventions: Foot Orthoses (A)

Clinicians should use foot orthoses, either prefabricated or custom fabricated/fitted, to support the medial longitudinal arch and cushion the heel in individuals with heel pain/plantar fasciitis to reduce pain and improve function for short-term (2 weeks) to long-term (1 year) periods, especially in those individuals who respond positively to antipronation taping techniques.

Interventions: Night Splints (A)

Clinicians should prescribe a 1- to 3-month program of night splints for individuals with heel pain/plantar fasciitis who consistently have pain with the first step in the morning.

Interventions: Physical Agents (D)

Electrotherapy: Clinicians should use manual therapy, stretching, and foot orthoses instead of electrotherapeutic modalities, to promote intermediate and long-term (1 to 6 months) improvements in clinical outcomes for individuals with heel pain/plantar fasciitis. Clinicians may or may not use iontophoresis with dexamethasone or acetic acid to provide short-term (2 to 4 weeks) pain relief and improved function.

Low-Level Laser (C)

Clinicians may use low-level laser therapy to reduce pain and activity limitations in individuals with heel pain/plantar fasciitis.

Phonophoresis (C)

Clinicians may use phonophoresis with ketoprofen gel to reduce pain in individuals with heel pain/plantar fasciitis.

Ultrasound (C)

The use of ultrasound cannot be recommended for individuals with heel pain/plantar fasciitis.

Interventions: Footwear (C)

To reduce pain in individuals with heel pain/plantar fasciitis, clinicians may prescribe (1) a rocker-bottom shoe construction in conjunction with a foot orthosis and (2) shoe rotation during the workweek for those who stand for long periods.

Interventions: Education and Counseling for Weight Loss (E)

Clinicians may provide education and counseling on exercise strategies to gain or maintain optimal lean body mass in individuals with heel pain/plantar fasciitis. Clinicians may also refer individuals to an appropriate health care practitioner to address nutrition issues.

Interventions: Therapeutic Exercise and Neuromuscular Reeducation (F)

Clinicians may prescribe strengthening exercises and movement training for muscles that control pronation and attenuate forces during weight-bearing activities.

Interventions: Dry Needling (F)

The use of trigger point dry needling cannot be recommended for individuals with heel pain/plantar fasciitis.

Adapted from Heel Pain, Plantar Fasciitis. Clinical Practice Guidelines Linked to the International Classification of Functioning, Disability, and Health from the Orthopaedic Section of the American Physical Therapy Association, Summary of Recommendations. JOSPT 4(38): A2–A3, 2014.

APPENDIX 1G

Knee Ligament Sprains

Risk Factors (B)

Clinicians should consider the shoe-surface interaction, increased body mass index, narrow femoral notch width, increased joint laxity, preovulatory phase of the menstrual cycle in females, combined loading pattern, and strong quadriceps predisposing activation during eccentric contractions as predisposing factors for the risk of sustaining a non-contact anterior cruciate ligament (ACL) injury.

Diagnosis/Classification (A)

Passive knee instability, joint pain, joint effusion, and movement coordination impairments are useful clinical findings for classifying a patient with knee instability into the following International Statistical Classification of Diseases and Related Health Problems (ICD) categories: Sprain and strain involving collateral ligament of knee, Sprain and strain involving cruciate ligament of knee, Injury to multiple structures of knee; and the associated International Classification of Functioning, Disability, and Health (ICF) impairment-based category of knee instability.

Differential Diagnosis (B)

Clinicians should consider diagnostic classifications associated with serious pathological conditions or psychosocial factors when the patient's reported activity limitations or impairments of body function and structure are not consistent with those presented in the diagnosis/classification section of this guideline or when the patient's symptoms are not resolving with interventions aimed at normalization of the patient's impairments of body function.

Examination: Outcome Measures (A)

Clinicians should use a validated patient-reported outcome measure with a general health questionnaire, along with a validated activity scale for patients with knee stability and movement coordination impairments. These tools are useful for identifying a patient's baseline status relative to pain, function, and disability and for monitoring changes in the patient's status throughout the course of treatment.

Examination: Activity Limitation Measures (C)

Clinicians should utilize easily reproducible physical performance measures, such as single-limb hop tests, to assess activity limitation and participation restriction associated with their patient's knee stability and movement coordination impairments, to assess the changes in the patient's level of function over the episode of care, and to classify and screen knee stability and movement coordination.

Interventions: Continuous Passive Motion (C)

Clinicians can consider using passive motion in the immediate postoperative period to decrease postoperative pain.

Intervention: Early Weight Bearing (C)

Early weight bearing can be used for patients following ACL reconstruction without incurring detrimental effects on stability or function.

Interventions: Knee Bracing (C)

The use of functional knee bracing appears to be more beneficial than not using a brace in patients with ACL deficiency.

(B).

The use of immediate postoperative knee bracing appears to be no more beneficial than not using a brace in patients following ACL reconstruction.

(D).

Conflicting evidence exists for the use of functional knee bracing in patients following ACL reconstruction. Knee bracing can be used for patients with acute PCL injuries, severe MCL injuries, or PLC injuries.

Interventions: Immediate versus Delayed Mobilization (B)

Clinicians should consider the use of immediate mobilization following ACL reconstruction to increase range of motion, reduce pain, and limit adverse change to soft tissue structures.

Interventions: Cryotherapy (C)

Clinicians should consider the use of cryotherapy to reduce postoperative knee pain immediately post-ACL reconstruction.

Interventions: Supervised Rehabilitation (B)

Clinicians should consider the use of exercises as part of the in-clinic program, supplemented by a prescribed home-based program supervised by a physical therapist in patients with knee stability and movement coordination impairments.

Intervention: Therapeutic Exercises (A)

Clinicians should consider the use of non–weight-bearing (open chain) exercises in conjunction with weight-bearing (closed-chain) exercises in patients with knee stability and movement coordination impairments.

Interventions: Neuromuscular Electrical Stimulation (B)

Neuromuscular electrical stimulation can be used with patients following ACL reconstruction to increase quadriceps muscle strength.

Interventions: Neuromuscular Reeducation (B)

Clinician should consider the use of neuromuscular training as a supplementary program to strength training in patients with knee stability and movement coordination impairments.

Interventions: "Accelerated" Rehabilitation (B)

Rehabilitation that emphasizes early restoration of knee extension and early weight-bearing activity appears safe for patients with ACL reconstruction. No evidence exists to determine the efficacy and/or safety of early return to sports.

Interventions: Eccentric Strengthening (B)

Clinicians should consider the use of an eccentric exercise ergometer in patients following ACL reconstruction to increase muscle strength and functional performance. Clinicians should consider the use of eccentric squat program in patients with PCL injury to increase muscle strength and functional performance.

Adapted from Knee Ligament Sprains. Clinical Practice Guidelines Linked to the International Classification of Functioning, Disability, and Health from the Orthopaedic Section of the American Physical Therapy Association, Summary of Recommendations. JOSPT 4(40): A31–32, 2010.

APPENDIX 1H

Low Back Pain

Risk Factors (B)

Current literature does not support a definitive cause for initial episodes of low back pain. Risk factors are multifactorial, population specific, and only weakly associated with the development of low back pain.

Clinical Course (E)

The clinical course of low back pain can be described as acute, subacute, recurrent, or chronic. Given the high prevalence of recurrent and chronic low back pain and the associated costs, clinicians should place high priority on interventions that prevent (1) recurrences and (2) the transition to chronic low back pain.

Diagnosis/Classification (B)

Low back pain, without symptoms or signs of serious medical or psychological conditions, associated with clinical findings of (1) mobility impairment in the thoracic, lumbar, or sacroiliac regions, (2) referred or radiating pain into a lower extremity, and (3) generalized pain, is useful for classifying a patient with low back pain into the following International Statistical Classification of Diseases and Related Health Problems (ICD) categories: low back pain, lumbago, lumbosacral segmental/somatic dysfunction, low back strain, spinal instabilities, flatback syndrome, lumbago due to displacement of intervertebral disc, lumbago with sciatica, and the associated International Classification of Functioning, Disability, and Health (ICF) impairment-based category of low back pain and the following corresponding impairments of body function:

- Acute or subacute low back pain with mobility deficits.
- Acute, subacute, or chronic low back pain with movement coordination impairments.
- Acute low back pain with related (referred) lower extremity pain.
- Acute, subacute, or chronic low back pain with radiating pain.
- Acute or subacute low back pain with related cognitive or affective tendencies.
- Chronic low back pain with related generalized pain.

The ICD diagnosis of lumbosacral segmental/somatic dysfunction and the associated ICF diagnosis of acute low back pain with mobility deficits are made with a reasonable level of certainty when the patient presents with the following clinical findings:

- Acute low back, buttock, or thigh pain (duration of 1 month or less).
- Restricted lumbar range of motion and segmental mobility.

- Low back and low back–related lower extremity symptoms reproduced with provocation of the involved lower thoracic, lumbar, or sacroiliac segments.

The ICD diagnosis of lumbosacral segmental/somatic dysfunction and the associated ICF diagnosis of subacute low back pain with mobility deficits are made with a reasonable level of certainty when the patient presents with the following clinical findings:

- Subacute, unilateral low back, buttock, or thigh pain.
- Symptoms reproduced with end-range spinal motions and provocation of the involved lower thoracic, lumbar, or sacroiliac segments.
- Presence of thoracic, lumbar, pelvic girdle, or hip active, segmental, or accessory mobility deficits.

The ICD diagnosis of spinal instabilities and the associated ICF diagnosis of acute low back pain with movement coordination impairments are made with a reasonable level of certainty when the patient presents with the following clinical findings:

- Acute exacerbation of recurring low back pain and associated (referred) lower extremity pain.
- Symptoms produced with initial to mid-range spinal movements and provocation of the involved lumbar segment(s).
- Movement coordination impairments of the lumbopelvic region with low back flexion and extension movements.

The ICD diagnosis of spinal instabilities and the associated ICF diagnosis of subacute low back pain with movement coordination impairments are made with a reasonable level of certainty when the patient presents with the following clinical findings:

- Subacute exacerbation of recurring low back pain and associated (referred) lower extremity pain.
- Symptoms produced with mid-range motions that worsen with end-range movements or positions and provocation of the involved lumbar segment(s).
- Lumbar segmental hypermobility may be present.
- Mobility deficits of the thorax and pelvic/hip regions may be present.
- Diminished trunk or pelvic-region muscle strength and endurance.
- Movement coordination impairments while performing self-care/home management activities.

The ICD diagnosis of spinal instabilities and the associated ICF diagnosis of chronic low back pain with movement coordination impairments are made with a reasonable level of certainty when the patient presents with the following clinical findings:

- Chronic, recurring low back pain and associated (referred) lower extremity pain.
- Presence of 1 or more of the following:
  - Low back and/or low back–related lower extremity pain that worsens with sustained end-range movements or positions.
  - Lumbar hypermobility with segmental motion assessment.
  - Mobility deficits of the thorax and lumbopelvic/hip regions.
  - Diminished trunk or pelvic-region muscle strength and endurance.
  - Movement coordination impairments while performing community/work-related recreational or occupational activities.

The ICD diagnosis of flatback syndrome, or lumbago due to displacement of intervertebral disc, and the associated ICF diagnosis of acute low back pain with related (referred) lower extremity pain are made with a reasonable level of certainty when the patient presents with the following clinical findings:

- Low back pain, commonly associated with referred buttock, thigh, or leg pain, that worsens with flexion activities and sitting.
- Low back and lower extremity pain that can be centralized and diminished with positioning, manual procedures, and/or repeated movements.
- Lateral trunk shift, reduced lumbar lordosis, limited lumbar extension mobility, and clinical findings associated with the subacute or chronic low back pain with movement coordination impairments category are commonly present.

The ICD diagnosis of lumbago with sciatica and the associated ICF diagnosis of acute low back pain with radiating pain are made with a reasonable level of certainty when the patient presents with the following clinical findings:

- Acute low back pain with associated radiating pain in the involved lower extremity.
- Lower extremity paresthesias, numbness, and weakness may be reported.
- Symptoms are reproduced or aggravated with initial to mid-range spinal mobility, lower-limb tension/straight leg raising, and/or slump tests.
- Signs of nerve root involvement (sensory, strength, or reflex deficits) may be present.

It is common for the symptoms and impairments of body function in patients who have acute low back pain with radiating pain to also be present in patients who have acute low back pain with related (referred) lower extremity pain.

The ICD diagnosis of lumbago with sciatica and the associated ICF diagnosis of subacute low back pain with radiating pain are made with a reasonable level of certainty when the patient presents with the following clinical findings:

- Subacute, recurring mid-back and/or low back pain with associated radiating pain and potential sensory, strength, or reflex deficits in the involved lower extremity.
- Symptoms are reproduced or aggravated with mid-range and worsen with end-range lower-limb tension/straight leg raising and/ or slump tests.

The ICD diagnosis of lumbago with sciatica and the associated ICF diagnosis of chronic low back pain with radiating pain are made with a reasonable level of certainty when the patient presents with the following clinical findings:

- Chronic, recurring mid-back and/or low back pain with associated radiating pain and potential sensory, strength, or reflex deficits in the involved lower extremity.
- Symptoms are reproduced or aggravated with sustained end-range lower-limb tension/straight leg raising and/or slump tests.

The ICD diagnosis of low back pain/low back strain/ lumbago and the associated ICF diagnosis of acute or subacute low back pain with related cognitive or affective tendencies are made with a reasonable level of certainty when the patient presents with the following clinical findings:

- Acute or subacute low back and/or low back–related lower extremity pain.
- Presence of 1 or more of the following:
  - Two positive responses to Primary Care Evaluation of Mental Disorders for depressive symptoms.
  - High scores on the Fear-Avoidance Beliefs Questionnaire and behavior consistent with an individual who has excessive anxiety or fear.
  - High scores on the Pain Catastrophizing Scale and cognitive processes consistent with individuals with high helplessness, rumination, or pessimism about low back pain.

The ICD diagnosis of low back pain/low back strain/ lumbago and the associated ICF diagnosis of chronic low back pain with related generalized pain are made with a reasonable level of certainty when the patient presents with the following clinical findings:

- Low back and/or low back–related lower extremity pain with symptom duration for longer than 3 months.
- Generalized pain not consistent with other impairment-based classification criteria presented in these clinical guidelines.
- Presence of depression, fear-avoidance beliefs, and/ or pain catastrophizing.

Differential Diagnosis (A)

Clinicians should consider diagnostic classifications associated with serious medical conditions or psychosocial factors and initiate referral to the appropriate medical practitioner when (1) the patient's clinical findings are suggestive of serious medical or psychological pathology, (2) the reported activity limitations or impairments of body function and structure are not consistent with those presented in the diagnosis/classification section of these guidelines, or (3) the patient's symptoms are not resolving with interventions aimed at normalization of the patient's impairments of body function.

Examination: Outcome Measures (A)

Clinicians should use validated self-report questionnaires, such as the Oswestry Disability Index and the Roland-Morris Disability Questionnaire. These tools are useful for identifying a patient's baseline status relative to pain, function, and disability and for monitoring a change in a patient's status throughout the course of treatment.

Examination: Activity Limitation and Participation Restriction Measures (F)

Clinicians should routinely assess activity limitation and participation restriction through validated performance-based measures. Changes in the patient's level of activity limitation and participation restriction should be monitored with these same measures over the course of treatment.

Interventions: Manual Therapy (A)

Clinicians should consider utilizing thrust manipulative procedures to reduce pain and disability in patients with mobility deficits and acute low back and back-related buttock or thigh pain. Thrust manipulative and nonthrust mobilization procedures can also be used to improve spine and hip mobility and reduce pain and disability in patients with subacute and chronic low back and back-related lower extremity pain.

Interventions: Trunk Coordination, Strengthening, and Endurance Exercises (A)

Clinicians should consider utilizing trunk coordination, strengthening, and endurance exercises to reduce low back pain and disability in patients with subacute and chronic low back pain with movement coordination impairments and in patients post-lumbar microdiscectomy.

Interventions: Centralization and Directional Preference Exercises and Procedures (A)

Clinicians should consider utilizing repeated movements, exercises, or procedures to promote centralization to reduce symptoms in patients with acute low back pain with related (referred) lower extremity pain. Clinicians should consider using repeated exercises in a specific direction determined by treatment response to improve mobility and reduce symptoms in patients with acute, subacute, or chronic low back pain with mobility deficits.

Interventions: Flexion Exercises (C)

Clinicians can consider flexion exercises, combined with other interventions such as manual therapy, strengthening exercises, nerve mobilization procedures, and progressive walking, for reducing pain and disability in older patients with chronic low back pain with radiating pain.

Interventions: Lower-Quarter Nerve Mobilization Procedures (C)

Clinicians should consider utilizing lower-quarter nerve mobilization procedures to reduce pain and disability in patients with subacute and chronic low back pain and radiating pain.

Interventions: Traction (D)

There is conflicting evidence for the efficacy of intermittent lumbar traction for patients with low back pain. There is preliminary evidence that a subgroup of patients with signs of nerve root compression along with peripheralization of symptoms or a positive crossed straight leg raise will benefit from intermittent lumbar traction in the prone position. There is moderate evidence that clinicians should not utilize intermittent or static lumbar traction for reducing symptoms in patients with acute or subacute, nonradicular low back pain or in patients with chronic low back pain.

Interventions: Patient Education and Counseling (B)

Clinicians should not utilize patient education and counseling strategies that either directly or indirectly increase the perceived threat or fear associated with low back pain, such as education and counseling strategies that (1) promote extended bed-rest or (2) provide in-depth, pathoanatomical explanations for the specific cause of the patient's low back pain. Patient education and counseling strategies for patients with low back pain should emphasize (1) the promotion of the understanding of the anatomical/structural strength inherent in the human spine, (2) the neuroscience that explains pain perception, (3) the overall favorable prognosis of low back pain, (4) the use of active pain coping strategies that decrease fear and catastrophizing, (5) the early resumption of normal or vocational activities, even when still experiencing pain, and (6) the importance of improvement in activity levels, not just pain relief.

Interventions: Progressive Endurance Exercise and Fitness Activities (A)

Clinicians should consider (1) moderate- to high-intensity exercise for patients with chronic low back pain without generalized pain, and (2) incorporating progressive, low-intensity, submaximal fitness and endurance activities into the pain management and health promotion strategies for patients with chronic low back pain with generalized pain.

Adapted from Low Back Pain. Clinical Practice Guidelines Linked to the International Classification of Functioning, Disability, and Health from the Orthopaedic Section of the American Physical Therapy Association, Summary of Recommendations. JOSPT 4(42): A44–A46, 2012.

APPENDIX 11

Achilles' Tendonitis

Risk Factors (B)

For specific groups of individuals, clinicians should consider abnormal ankle dorsiflexion range of motion, abnormal subtalar joint range of motion, decreased ankle plantar flexion strength, increased foot pronation, and abnormal tendon structure as intrinsic risk factors associated with Achilles' tendinopathy. Obesity, hypertension, hyperlipidemia, and diabetes are medical conditions associated with Achilles' tendinopathy. Clinicians should also consider training errors, environmental factors, and faulty equipment as extrinsic risk factors associated with Achilles tendinopathy.

Diagnosis/Classification (C)

Self-reported localized pain and perceived stiffness in the Achilles' tendon following a period of inactivity (i.e., sleep, prolonged sitting), lessens with an acute bout of activity and may increase after the activity. Symptoms are frequently accompanied with Achilles' tendon tenderness, a positive arc sign, and positive findings on the Royal London Hospital test. These signs and symptoms are useful clinical findings for classifying a patient with ankle pain into the ICD category of Achilles' bursitis or tendinitis and the associated ICF impairment-based category of Achilles' pain, stiffness, and muscle power deficits.

Differential Diagnosis (F)

Clinicians should consider diagnostic classifications other than Achilles' tendinopathy when the patient's reported activity limitations or impairments of body function and structure are not consistent with those presented in the diagnosis/classification section of this guideline, or, when the patient's symptoms are not resolving with interventions aimed at normalization of the patient's impairments of body function.

Examination: Outcome Measures (A)

Clinicians should incorporate validated functional outcome measures, such as the Victorian Institute of Sport Assessment and the Foot and Ankle Ability Measure. These should be utilized before and after interventions intended to alleviate the impairments of body function and structure, activity limitations, and participation restrictions associated with Achilles' tendinopathy.

Examination: Activity Limitation and Participation Restriction Measures (B)

When evaluating functional limitations over an episode of care for those with Achilles' tendinopathy, measures of activity limitation and participation restriction can include objective and reproducible assessment of the ability to walk, descend stairs, perform unilateral heel raises, single-limb hop, and participate in recreational activity.

Examination: Physical Impairment Measures (B)

When evaluating physical impairment over an episode of care for those with Achilles' tendinopathy, one should consider measuring dorsiflexion range of motion, subtalar joint range of motion, plantar flexion strength and endurance, static arch height, forefoot alignment, and pain with palpation.

Interventions: Eccentric Loading (A)

Clinicians should consider implementing an eccentric loading program to decrease pain and improve function in patients with midportion Achilles' tendinopathy.

Interventions: Low-Level Laser Therapy (B)

Clinicians should consider the use of low-level laser therapy to decrease pain and stiffness in patients with Achilles' tendinopathy.

Interventions: Iontophoresis (B)

Clinicians should consider the use of iontophoresis with dexamethasone to decrease pain and improve function in patients with Achilles' tendinopathy.

Interventions: Stretching (C)

Stretching exercises can be used to reduce pain and improve function in patients who exhibit limited dorsiflexion range of motion with Achilles' tendinopathy.

Interventions: Foot Orthoses (C)

A foot orthosis can be used to reduce pain and alter ankle and foot kinematics while running in patients with Achilles' tendinopathy.

Interventions: Manual Therapy (F)

Soft tissue mobilization can be used to reduce pain and improve mobility and function in patients with Achilles' tendinopathy.

Interventions: Taping (F)

Taping may be used in an attempt to decrease strain on the Achilles' tendon in patients with Achilles' tendinopathy.

Interventions: Heel Lifts (D)

Contradictory evidence exists for the use of heel lifts in patients with Achilles' tendinopathy.

Interventions: Night Splints (C)

Night splints are not beneficial in reducing pain when compared to eccentric exercise for patients with Achilles' tendinopathy.

Adapted from Achilles' Tendonitis. Clinical Practice Guidelines Linked to the International Classification of Functioning, Disability, and Health from the Orthopaedic Section of the American Physical Therapy Association, Summary of Recommendations. JOSPT 9(40): A21, 2010.

APPENDIX 1J

Adhesive Capsulitis

Pathoanatomical Features (E)

Clinicians should assess for impairments in the capsuloligamentous complex and musculotendinous structures surrounding the shoulder complex when a patient presents with shoulder pain and mobility deficits (adhesive capsulitis). The loss of passive motion in multiple planes, particularly ER with the arm at the side and in varying degrees of shoulder abduction, is a significant finding that can be used to guide treatment planning.

Risk Factors (C)

Clinicians should recognize that (1) patients with diabetes mellitus and thyroid disease are at risk for developing adhesive capsulitis, and (2) adhesive capsulitis is more prevalent in individuals who are 40 to 65 years of age, female, and have had a previous episode of adhesive capsulitis in the contralateral arm.

Clinical Course (B)

Clinicians should recognize that adhesive capsulitis occurs as a continuum of pathology characterized by a staged progression of pain and mobility deficits and that, at 12 to 18 months, mild to moderate mobility deficits and pain may persist, though many patients report minimal to no disability.

Diagnosis/Classification (F)

Clinicians should recognize that patients with adhesive capsulitis present with a gradual and progressive onset of pain and loss of active and passive shoulder motion in both elevation and rotation. Utilizing the evaluation and intervention components described in these guidelines will assist clinicians in medical screening, differential evaluation of common shoulder musculoskeletal disorders, diagnosing tissue irritability levels, and planning intervention strategies for patients with shoulder pain and mobility deficits.

Differential Diagnosis (F)

Clinicians should consider diagnostic classifications other than adhesive capsulitis when the patient's reported activity limitations or impairments of body function and structure are not consistent with the diagnosis/classification section of these guidelines, or when the patient's symptoms are not resolving with interventions aimed at normalization of the patient's impairments of body function.

Examination – Outcome Measures (A)

Clinicians should use validated functional outcome measures, such as the DASH, the ASES, or the SPADI. These should be utilized before and after interventions intended to alleviate the impairments of body function and structure, activity limitations, and participation restrictions associated with adhesive capsulitis.

Examination – Activity Limitation and Participation Restriction Measures (A)

Clinicians should utilize easily reproducible activity limitation and participation restriction measures associated with their patient's shoulder pain to assess the changes in the patient's level of shoulder function over the episode of care.

Examination – Physical Impairment Measures (E)

Clinicians should measure pain, active shoulder ROM, and passive shoulder ROM to assess the key impairments of body function and body structures in patients with adhesive capsulitis. Glenohumeral joint accessory motion may be assessed to determine translational glide loss.

Intervention – Corticosteroid Injections (A)

Intra-articular corticosteroid injections combined with shoulder mobility and stretching exercise are more effective in providing short-term (4–6 weeks) pain relief and improved function compared to shoulder mobility and stretching exercises alone.

Interventions – Patient Education (B)

Clinicians should utilize patient education that (1) describe the natural course of the disease, (2) promotes activity modification to encourage functional, pain-free ROM, and (3) matches the intensity of stretching to the patient's current level of irritability.

Interventions – Modalities (C)

Clinicians may utilize shortwave diathermy, ultrasound, or electrical stimulation combined with mobility and stretching exercises to reduce pain and improve shoulder ROM in patients with adhesive capsulitis.

Interventions – Joint Mobilization (C)

Clinicians may utilize joint mobilization procedures primarily directed to the glenohumeral joint to reduce pain and increase motion and function in patients with adhesive capsulitis.

Interventions – Translational Manipulation (C)

Clinicians may utilize translational manipulation under anesthesia directed to the glenohumeral joint in patients with adhesive capsulitis who are not responding to conservative interventions.

Interventions – Stretching Exercises (B)

Clinicians should instruct patients with adhesive capsulitis in stretching exercises. The intensity of the exercises should be determined by the patient's tissue irritability level.

Adapted from Adhesive Capsulitis. Clinical Practice Guidelines Linked to the International Classification of Functioning, Disability, and Health from the Orthopaedic Section of the American Physical Therapy Association, Summary of Recommendations. JOSPT 5(43): A26, 2013.

Figure 1M-23 AP Radiographic View of Left Ankle Showing Oblique Fibular Fracture with Deltoid Ligament Tear (Weber C Injury):

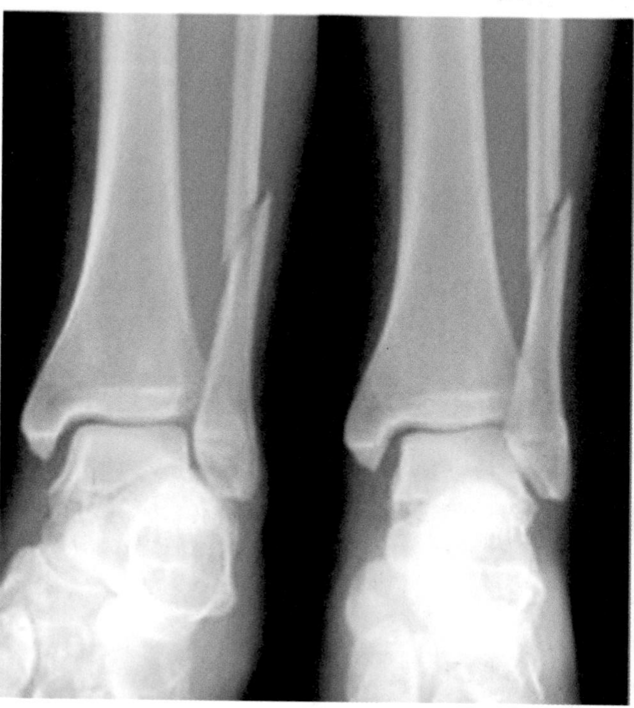

Figure 1M-24 AP Radiographic View of Right Ankle Medial Malleolus Fracture:

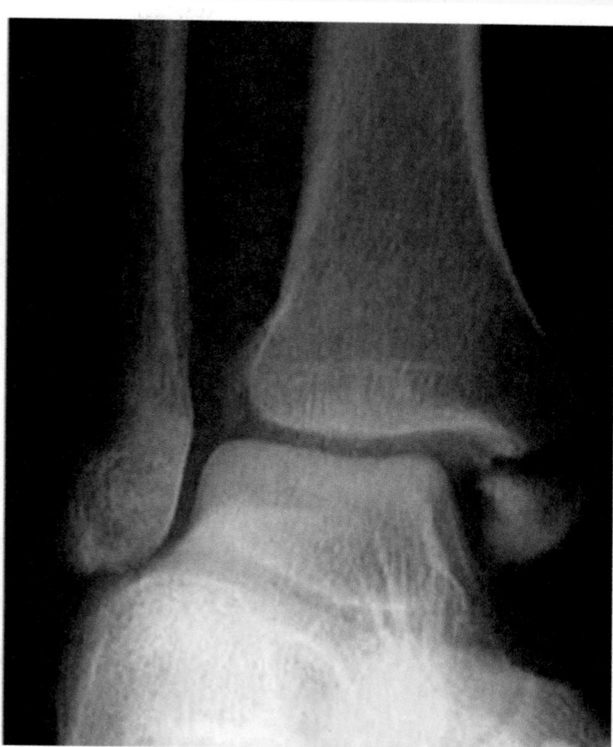

Figure 1M-25 Maisonneuve Fracture. AP Radiographic image showing abduction (eversion) injury to left ankle (image on left). Forces were transmitted through the syndesmosis, exiting through proximal fibula (arrow seen on lateral view at right):

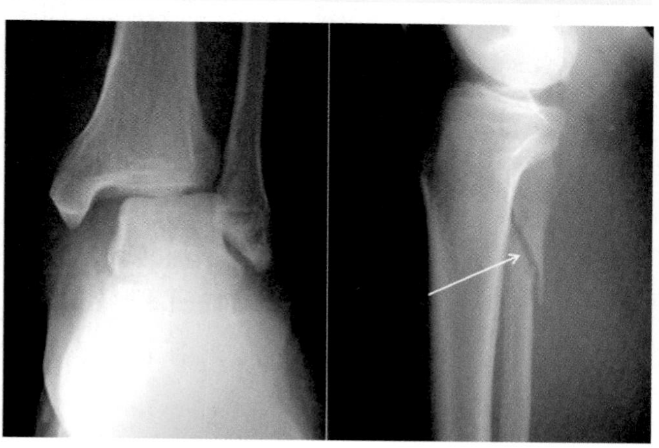

Figure 1M-26 Lateral Radiographic View Showing Shrapnel in Leg, Ankle and Foot:

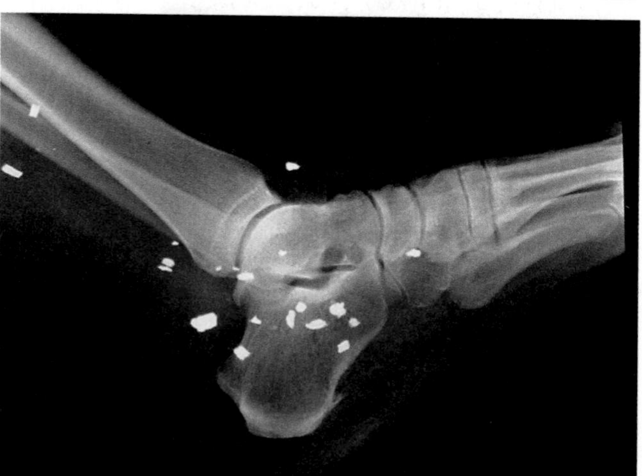

From: https://commons.wikimedia.org/wiki/File:Korean_War_shrapnel_ankle_X-ray.jpg

Figure 1M-27 Lateral Radiographic View of Right Foot Showing Jones' Fracture (base of 5th metatarsal):

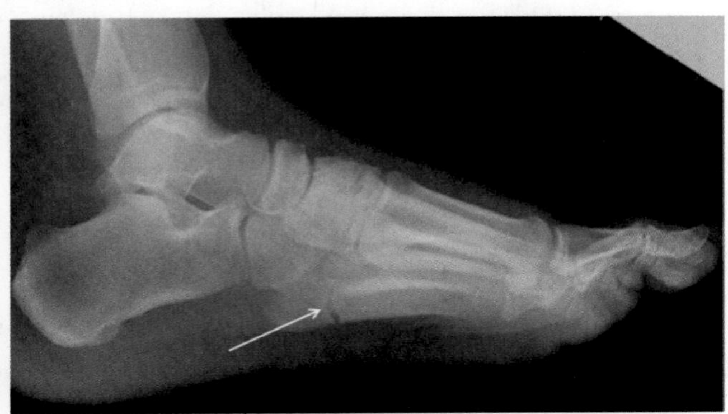

Figure 1M-28 T1 MRI (left image) and T2 MRI (right image) of Torn Achilles Tendon:

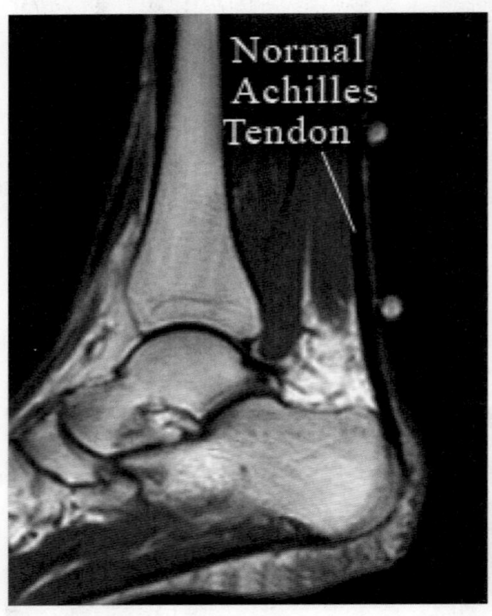

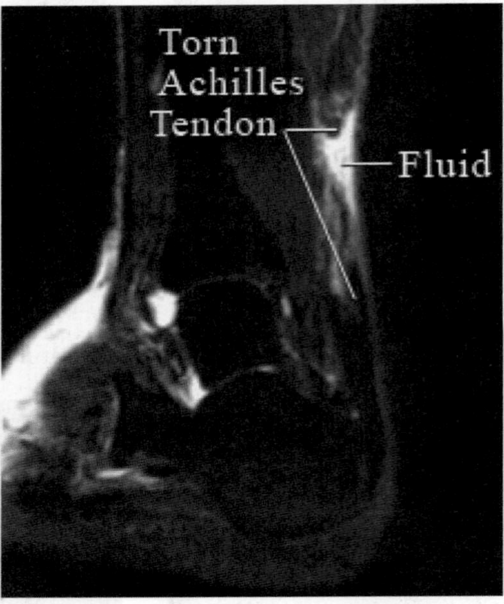

Figure 1M-29 Coronal T1 MRI of Talar Dome Osteochondral Defect:

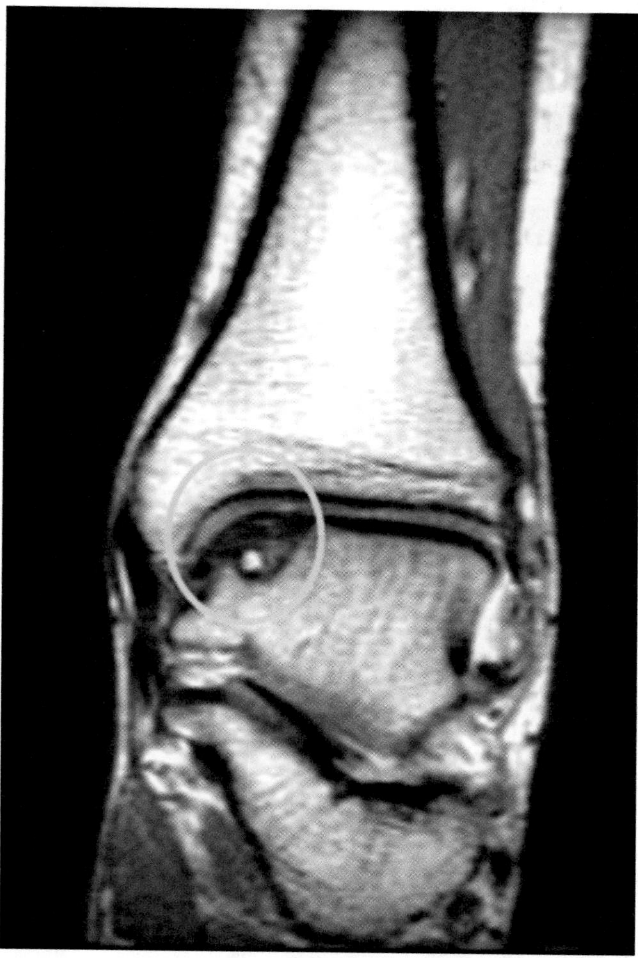

Figure 1M-30 Coronal T1 MRI (left image) and Axial T2 MRI (right image) of Posterior Tibial Tendonitis (arrow):

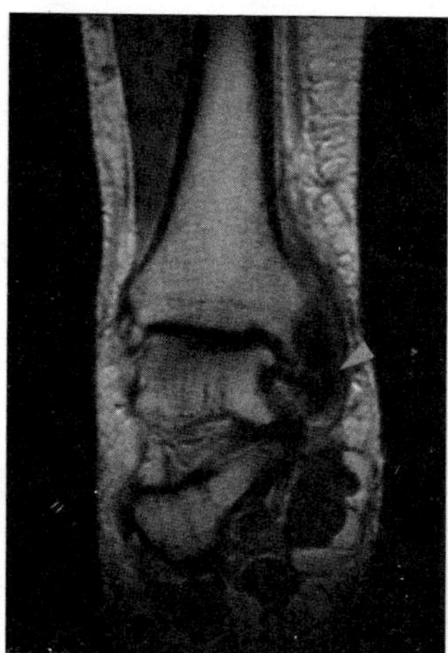

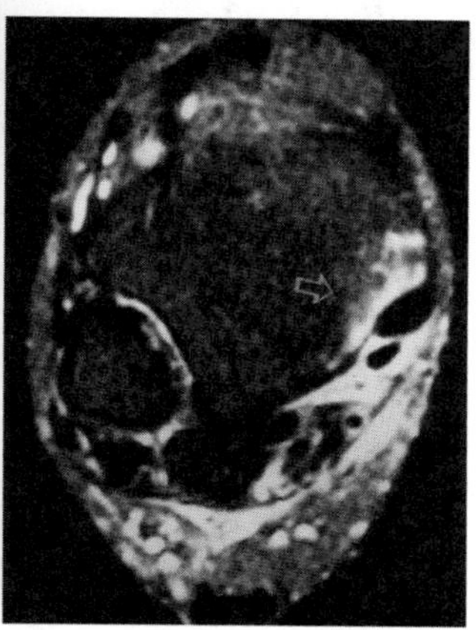

Figure 1M-31 AP Radiographic View of Normal Foot:

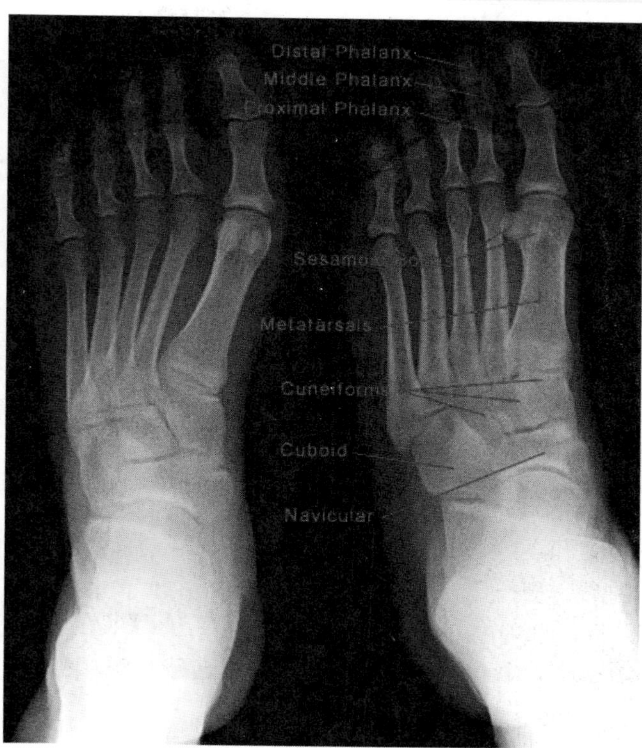

Figure 1M-32 Full Body Bone Scan of Insufficiency Rib Fractures:

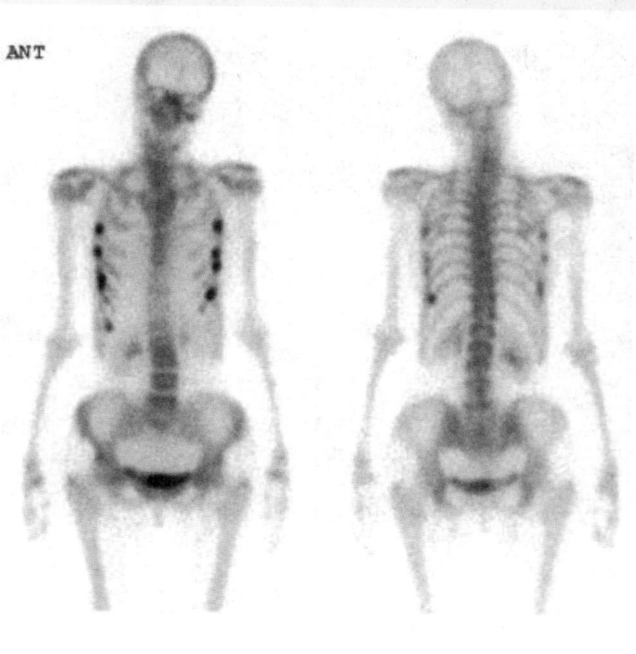

Chapter 1 MS

Ultrasound Images

Figure 1M-33 Ultrasound Image of Muscles of the Anterolateral Abdominal Wall:

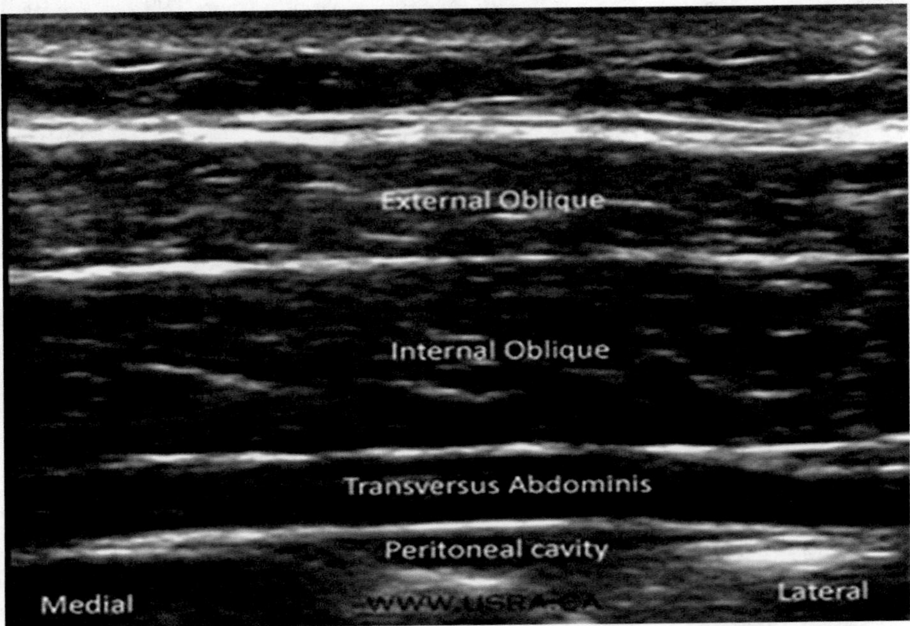

From: http://www.usra.ca/tapscan.php

Figure 1M-34 Lateral Ultrasound Image of Achilles tendon rupture:

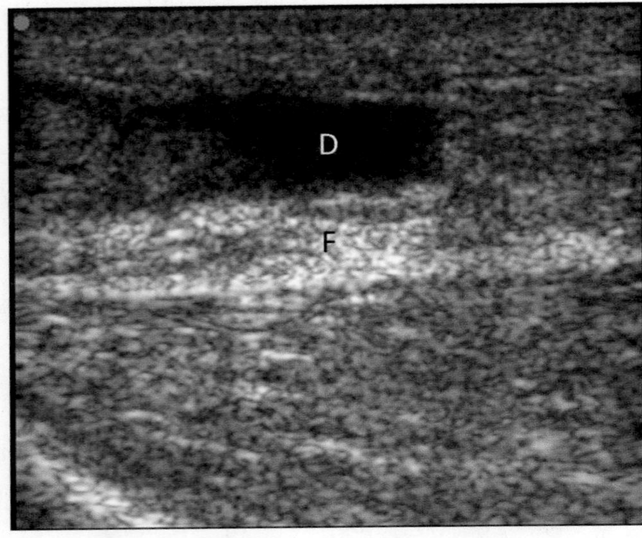

Dark, anechoic area is the palpable defect (D). White, hyperechoic area just below the defect is the fascia/tendon sheath separating the deep compartment muscles/tendons from the superficial muscles (F). Proximal segment is to the right on this image; distal segment is to the left.

Figure 1M-35 AP Ultrasound Image of Partially Denervated Infraspinatus Muscle:

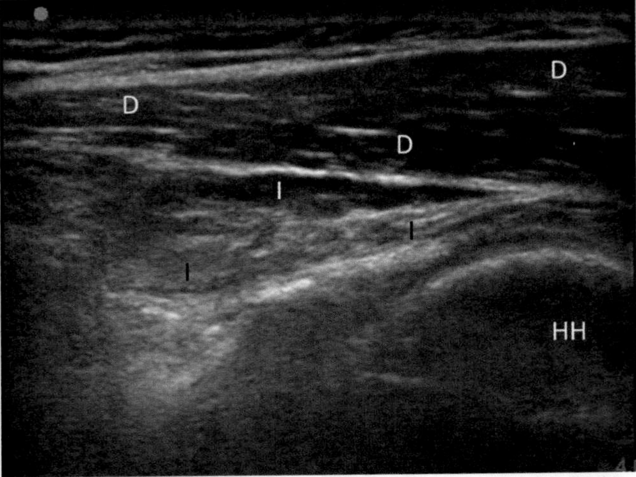

I = the infraspinatus muscle. Since the muscle is mostly denervated as confirmed by EMG, most of the infraspinatus appears hyperechoic (white or light). The darker, hypoechoic area is the posterior deltoid muscle (D).
HH = The posterior aspect of the head of the humerus.

Review Questions

Musculoskeletal Physical Therapy

1. Which motion at the glenohumeral joint has the greatest limitation if the diagnosis is adhesive capsulitis?

2. When considering the concave-convex rule, to which joints in the spine does the concave rule apply?

3. Which special test when applied to the ankle/foot is BEST used to identify ligamentous instability of the calcaneofibular ligament?

4. What are the major differences in diagnostic characteristics and pattern of joint dysfunction between osteoarthritis and rheumatoid arthritis?

5. Based on Clinical Practice Guidelines for Knee Ligament Sprain, which intervention has the strongest overall evidence for effectiveness?

6. Following a total hip replacement, in the acute phase, which positions should be avoided in bed positioning and activities involving bed mobility?

7. For an anteriorly displaced articular disc at the TMJ, what is the primary joint mobilization technique?

2

Neuromuscular Physical Therapy

SUSAN B. O'SULLIVAN

Chapter Outline

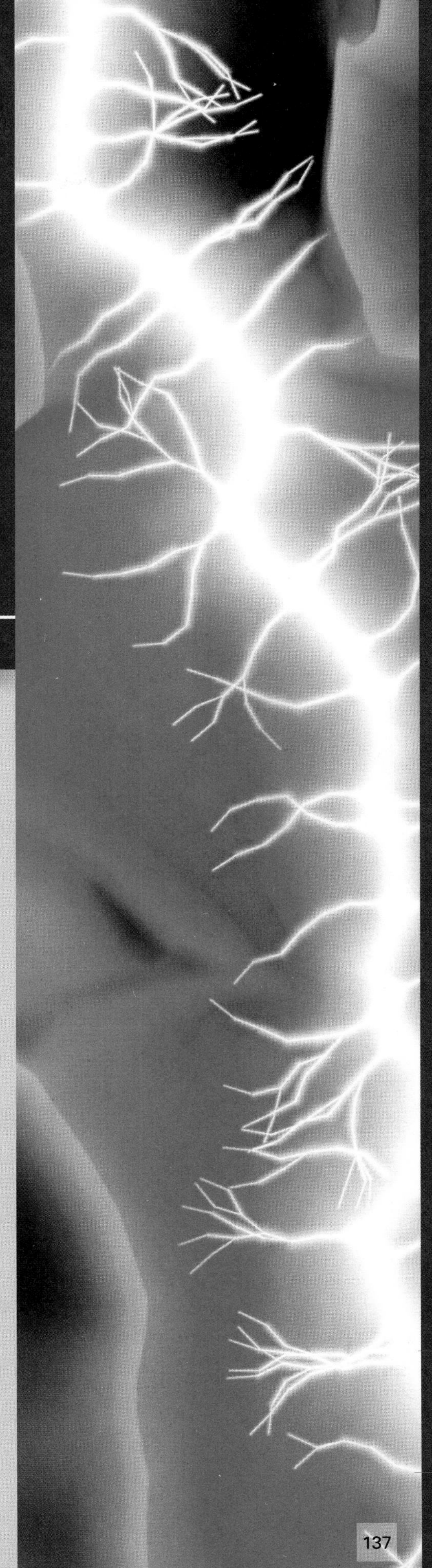

Chapter 2 NM

Anatomy and Physiology of the Nervous System

Brain

1. Cerebral hemispheres (telencephalon) (see Figure 2-1).
   a. Convolutions of gray matter composed of gyri (crests) and sulci (fissures).
      (1) Lateral central fissure (fissure of Sylvius) separates temporal lobe from frontal and parietal lobes.
      (2) Longitudinal cerebral fissure separates the two hemispheres.
      (3) Central sulcus separates the frontal lobe from the parietal lobe.
   b. Paired hemispheres, consisting of six lobes on each side: frontal, parietal, temporal, occipital, insular, limbic.
      (1) Frontal lobe.
         (a) Precentral gyrus: primary motor cortex for voluntary muscle activation.
         (b) Prefrontal cortex: controls emotions and judgments.
         (c) Broca's area: controls motor aspects of speech.
      (2) Parietal lobe.
         (a) Postcentral gyrus: primary sensory cortex for integration of sensation.
         (b) Receives fibers conveying touch, proprioceptive, pain and temperature sensations from opposite side of body.

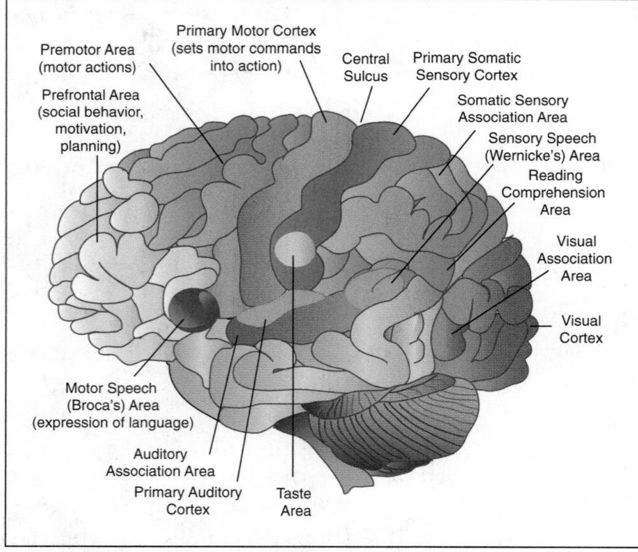

Figure 2-1 Functional areas of the brain.

      (3) Temporal lobe.
         (a) Primary auditory cortex: receives/processes auditory stimuli.
         (b) Associative auditory cortex: processes auditory stimuli.
         (c) Wernicke's area: language comprehension.
      (4) Occipital lobe.
         (a) Primary visual cortex: receives/processes visual stimuli.
         (b) Visual association cortex: processes visual stimuli.
      (5) Insula.
         (a) Deep within lateral sulcus, associated with visceral functions.
      (6) Limbic system.
         (a) Consists of the limbic lobe (cingulate, parahippocampal and subcallosal gyri), hippocampal formation, amygdaloid nucleus, hypothalamus and anterior nucleus of thalamus.
         (b) Phylogenetically oldest part of the brain, concerned with instincts and emotions contributing to preservation of the individual.
         (c) Basic functions include feeding, aggression, emotions, and endocrine aspects of sexual response.
   c. White matter: myelinated nerve fibers located centrally.
      (1) Transverse (commissural) fibers: interconnect the two hemispheres, including the corpus callosum (the largest), anterior commissure, and hippocampal commissure.
      (2) Projection fibers: connect cerebral hemispheres with other portions of the brain and spinal cord.
      (3) Association fibers: connect different portions of the cerebral hemispheres, allowing cortex to function as an integrated whole.
   d. Basal ganglia (BG).
      (1) Masses of gray matter deep within the cerebral hemispheres, including the striatum (caudate nucleus, nucleus accumbens, putamen), globus pallidus (external segment, internal segment), subthalamic nucleus and substantia nigra (compact part, reticular part). The term *lenticular nucleus* refers to the putamen and globus pallidus.
      (2) Forms an associated motor system (extrapyramidal system) with other nuclei in the subthalamus and the midbrain.
      (3) Multiple circuits exist in the BG.
         (a) Oculomotor circuit (caudate loop): originates in frontal and supplementary motor

eye fields; projects to caudate; functions with saccadic eye movements.

(b) Motor loop (putamen loop): originates in precentral motor and postcentral somatosensory areas; projects to and excites putamen neurons; putamen cells inhibit globus pallidus neurons, which in turn boosts activity in the ventral lateral nucleus and supplemental motor area; functions to scale amplitude and velocity of movements; reinforces selected pattern, suppresses conflicting patterns; preparatory for movement (i.e., motor set, anticipatory movement).

(c) Limbic circuit: originates in prefrontal and limbic areas of cortex; to BG; to prefrontal cortex; functions to organize behaviors (executive functions, problem solving, motivation) and for procedural learning.

2. Diencephalon.

a. Thalamus.

(1) Sensory nuclei: integrate and relay sensory information from body, face, retina, cochlea, and taste receptors to cerebral cortex and subcortical regions; smell (olfaction) is the exception.

(2) Motor nuclei: relay motor information from cerebellum and globus pallidus to precentral motor cortex.

(3) Other nuclei: assist in integration of visceral and somatic functions.

b. Subthalamus: involved in control of several functional pathways for sensory, motor, and reticular function.

c. Hypothalamus.

(1) Integrates and controls the functions of the autonomic nervous system and the neuroendocrine system.

(2) Maintains body homeostasis: regulates body temperature, eating, water balance, anterior pituitary function/sexual behavior, and emotion.

d. Epithalamus.

(1) Habenular nuclei: integrate olfactory, visceral, and somatic afferent pathways.

(2) Pineal gland: secretes hormones that influence the pituitary gland and several other organs; influences circadian rhythm.

3. Brainstem.

a. Midbrain (mesencephalon).

(1) Connects pons to cerebrum; superior peduncle connects midbrain to cerebellum.

(2) Contains cerebral peduncles (two lateral halves), each divided into an anterior part or basis (crus cerebri and substantia nigra) and a posterior part (tegmentum).

(3) Tegmentum contains all ascending tracts and some descending tracts; the red nucleus receives fibers from the cerebellum; is the origin for the rubrospinal tract, important for coordination; contains cranial nerve nuclei: oculomotor and trochlear.

(4) Substantia nigra is a large motor nucleus connecting with the basal ganglia and cortex; it is important in motor control and muscle tone.

(5) Superior colliculus is an important relay station for vision and visual reflexes; the inferior colliculus is an important relay station for hearing and auditory reflexes.

(6) Periaqueductal gray contains endorphin-producing cells (important for the suppression of pain) and descending autonomic tracts.

b. Pons.

(1) Connects the medulla oblongata to the midbrain, allowing passage of important ascending and descending tracts.

(2) Anterior basal part acts as a bridge to cerebellum (middle cerebellar peduncle).

(3) Midline raphe nuclei project widely and are important for modulating pain and controlling arousal.

(4) Tegmentum contains several important cranial nerve nuclei: abducens, trigeminal, facial, vestibulocochlear.

c. Medulla oblongata.

(1) Connects spinal cord with pons.

(2) Contains relay nuclei of dorsal columns (gracilis and cuneatus); fibers cross to give rise to medial lemniscus.

(3) Inferior cerebellar peduncle relays dorsal spinocerebellar tract to cerebellum.

(4) Corticospinal tracts cross (decussate) in pyramids.

(5) Medial longitudinal fasciculus arises from vestibular nuclei and extends throughout brainstem and upper cervical spinal cord; important for control of head movements and gaze stabilization (vestibular-ocular reflex).

(6) Olivary nuclear complex connects cerebellum to brainstem and is important for voluntary movement control.

(7) Contains several important cranial nerve nuclei: hypoglossal, dorsal nucleus of vagus and vestibulocochlear.

(8) Contains important centers for vital functions: cardiac, respiratory, and vasomotor centers.

4. Cerebellum.

a. Located behind dorsal pons and medulla in posterior fossa.

b. Structure.

(1) Joined to brainstem by three pairs of peduncles: superior, middle, and inferior.

(2) Comprises two hemispheres and midline vermis; cerebellar cortex, underlying white matter; and four paired deep nuclei.
(3) Archicerebellum (flocculonodular lobe) connects with vestibular system and is concerned with equilibrium and regulation of muscle tone; helps coordinate vestibulo-ocular reflex.
(4) Paleocerebellum (rostral cerebellum, anterior lobe; also known as spinocerebellum) receives input from proprioceptive pathways and is concerned with modifying muscle tone and synergistic actions of muscles; it is important in maintenance of posture and voluntary movement control.
(5) Neocerebellum (cerebellar hemisphere, posterior lobe; also known as pontocerebellum); receives input from corticopontocerebellar tracts and olivocerebellar fibers; it is concerned with the smooth coordination of voluntary movements; ensures accurate force, direction, and extent of movement. Important for motor learning, sequencing of movements, and visually triggered movements. May have a role in assisting cognitive function and mental imagery.

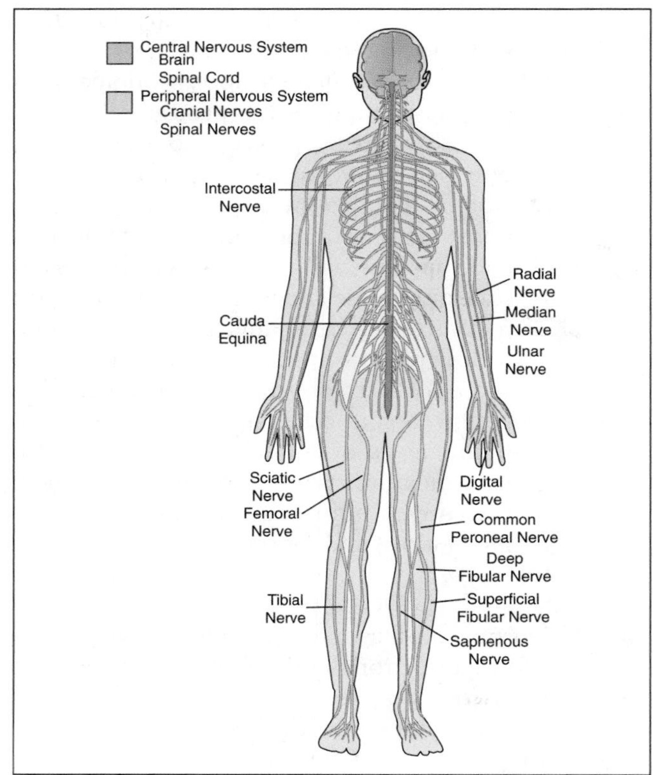

Figure 2-2 **Overview of nervous system.**

Spinal Cord

1. General structure (see Figure 2-2).
   a. Cylindrical mass of nerve tissue extending from the foramen magnum in the skull continuous with the medulla to the lower border of the first lumbar vertebra in the conus medullaris.
   b. Divided into 30 segments—8 cervical, 12 thoracic, 5 lumbar, 5 sacral—and a few coccygeal segments.
2. Central gray matter. Two anterior (ventral) and two posterior (dorsal) horns united by gray commissure with central canal (Figure 2-3).
   a. Anterior horns contain cell bodies that give rise to efferent (motor) neurons: alpha motor neurons to affect muscles and gamma motor neurons to affect muscle spindles.
   b. Posterior horns contain afferent (sensory) neurons with cell bodies located in the dorsal root ganglia.
   c. Two enlargements (cervical and lumbosacral) for origins of nerves of upper and lower extremities.
   d. Lateral horn is found in thoracic and upper lumbar segments for preganglionic fibers of the autonomical nervous system.
3. White matter. Anterior (ventral), lateral, and posterior (dorsal) white columns or funiculi.
   a. Ascending fiber systems (sensory pathways).
      (1) Dorsal columns/medial lemniscal system: convey sensations of proprioception, vibration,

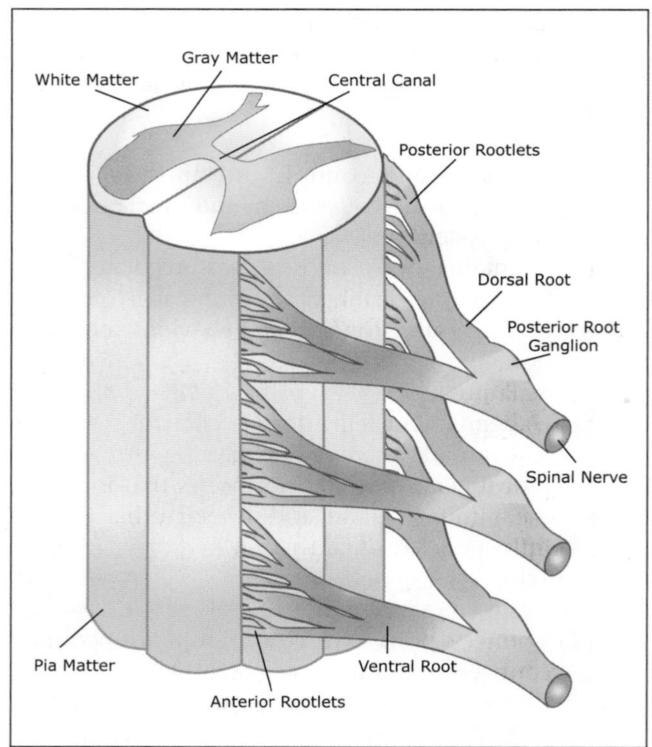

Figure 2-3 **Spinal cord: Anterior cross section.**

and tactile discrimination; divided into fasciculus cuneatus (upper extremity tracts, laterally located) and fasciculus gracilis (lower extremity tracts, medially located); neurons ascend to medulla where fibers cross (lemniscal decussation) to form medial lemniscus; ascend to thalamus and then to somatosensory cortex.

(2) Spinothalamic tracts: convey sensations of pain and temperature (lateral spinothalamic tract), and crude touch (anterior spinothalamic tract); tracts ascend one or two ipsilateral spinal cord segments (Lissauer's tract), synapse and cross in spinal cord to opposite side and ascend in ventrolateral spinothalamic system.

(3) Spinocerebellar tracts: convey proprioception information from muscle spindles, Golgi tendon organs, and touch and pressure receptors to cerebellum for control of voluntary movements; dorsal spinocerebellar tract ascends to ipsilateral inferior cerebellar peduncle, and ventrospinocerebellar tract ascends to contralateral and ipsilateral superior cerebellar peduncle.

(4) Spinoreticular tracts: convey deep and chronic pain to reticular formation of brainstem via diffuse, polysynaptic pathways.

b. Descending fiber systems (motor pathways).

(1) Corticospinal tracts: arise from primary motor cortex, descend in brainstem, cross in medulla (pyramidal decussation), via lateral corticospinal tract to ventral gray matter (anterior horn cells); 10% of fibers do not cross and travel in anterior corticospinal tract to cervical and upper thoracic segments; important for voluntary motor control.

(2) Vestibulospinal tracts: arise from vestibular nucleus and descend to spinal cord in lateral (uncrossed) and medial (crossed and uncrossed) vestibulospinal tracts; important for control of muscle tone, antigravity muscles, and postural reflexes.

(3) Rubrospinal tracts: arise in contralateral red nucleus and descend in lateral white columns to spinal gray; assist in motor function.

(4) Reticulospinal system: arises in the reticular formation of the brainstem and descends (crossed and uncrossed) in ventral and lateral columns, terminates both on dorsal gray (modifies transmission of sensation, especially pain) and on ventral gray (influences gamma motor neurons and spinal reflexes).

(5) Tectospinal tract: arises from superior colliculus (midbrain) and descends to ventral gray; assists in head-turning responses to visual stimuli.

4. Autonomic nervous system (ANS).

a. Concerned with innervations of involuntary structures: smooth muscle, heart, glands; helps maintain homeostasis (constant internal body environment).

b. Two divisions: sympathetic and parasympathetic; both have afferent and efferent nerve fibers; preganglionic and postganglionic fibers.

(1) Sympathetic (thoracolumbar division, T1–L2): prepares body for fight or flight, emergency responses; increases heart rate and blood pressure, constricts peripheral blood vessels, and redistributes blood; inhibits peristalsis (Figure 2-4).

(2) Parasympathetic (craniosacral division, CN III, VII, IX, X; pelvic nerves): conserves and restores homeostasis; slows heart rate and reduces blood pressure; increases peristalsis and glandular activity (Figure 2-5).

c. Autonomic plexuses: cardiac, pulmonary, celiac (solar), hypogastric, pelvic.

d. Modulated by brain centers.

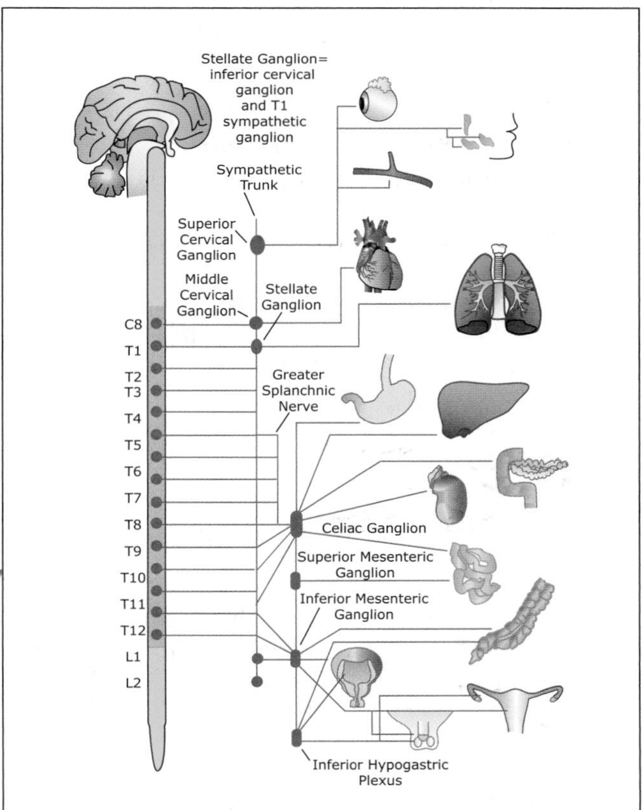

Figure 2-4 **ANS-sympathetic division.**

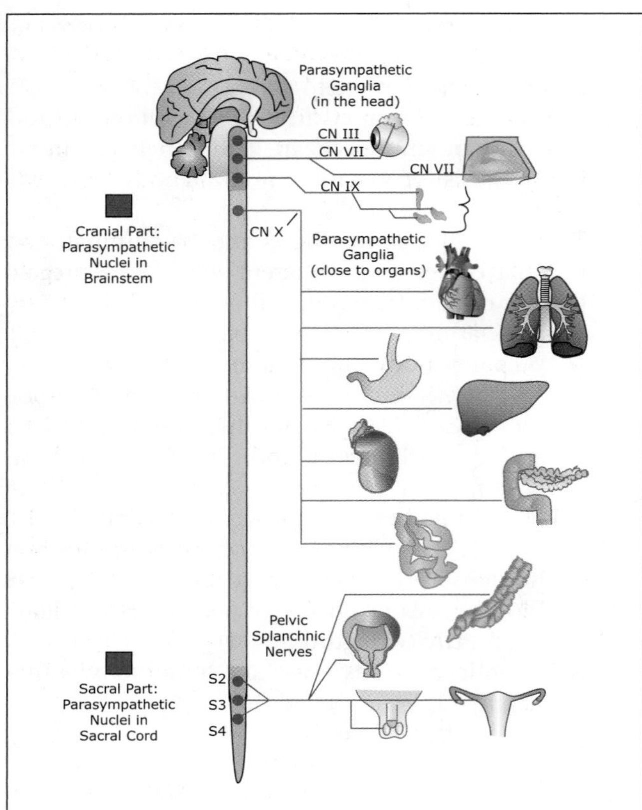

Figure 2-5 **ANS-parasympathetic division.**

(1) Descending autonomic system: arises from control centers in hypothalamus and lower brainstem (cardiac, respiratory, vasomotor) and projects to preganglionic ANS segments in thoracolumbar (sympathetic) and craniosacral (parasympathetic) segments.

(2) Cranial nerves: visceral afferent sensations via glossopharyngeal and vagus nerves; efferent outflow via oculomotor, facial, glossopharyngeal, and vagus nerves.

CNS Support Structures

1. Bony structure.
   a. Skull (cranium): rigid bony chamber that contains the brain and facial skeleton, with an opening (foramen magnum) at its base.
2. Meninges. Three membranes that envelop the brain.
   a. Dura mater: outer, tough, fibrous membrane attached to inner surface of cranium; forms falx and tentorium.
   b. Arachnoid: delicate, vascular membrane.
   c. Subarachnoid space: formed by arachnoid and pia mater, contains cerebrospinal fluid (CSF) and cisterns, major arteries.
   d. Pia mater: thin, vascular membrane that covers the brain surface; forms tela choroidea of ventricles.
3. Ventricles.
   a. Four cavities or ventricles that are filled with CSF and communicate with each other and with the spinal cord canal.
   b. Lateral ventricles: large, irregularly shaped with anterior (frontal), posterior (occipital), and inferior (temporal) horns; communicates with third ventricle through foramen of Monro.
   c. Third ventricle: located posterior and deep between the two thalami; third ventricle communicates with fourth ventricle through cerebral aqueduct.
   d. Fourth ventricle: pyramid-shaped cavity located in pons and medulla; foramina (openings) of Luschka and Magendie communicate with fourth ventricle through subarachnoid space.
4. Cerebrospinal fluid (CSF).
   a. Provides mechanical support (cushions brain), controls brain excitability by regulating ionic composition, aids in exchange of nutrients and waste products.
   b. Produced in choroid plexuses in ventricles.
5. Blood-brain barrier.
   a. Selective restriction of blood-borne substances from entering the CNS.
   b. Associated with capillary endothelial cells.
6. Blood supply.
   a. Brain is 2% of body weight with a circulation of 18% of total blood volume.
   b. Carotid system: internal carotid arteries arise off common carotids and branch to form anterior and middle cerebral arteries; supplies a large area of brain and many deep structures.
   c. Vertebrobasilar system: vertebral arteries arise off subclavian arteries and unite to form the basilar artery; this vessel bifurcates into two posterior cerebral arteries; supplies the brainstem, cerebellum, occipital lobe, and parts of thalamus.
   d. Circle of Willis: formed by anterior communicating artery, connecting the two anterior cerebral arteries and the posterior communicating artery, connecting each posterior and middle cerebral artery (Figure 2-6).
   e. Venous drainage: includes cerebral veins and dural venous sinuses.
   f. See Neurological Dysfunction, Cerebrovascular Accident for a discussion of specific stroke syndromes (characteristic signs and symptoms associated with occlusion of specific cerebral vessels).

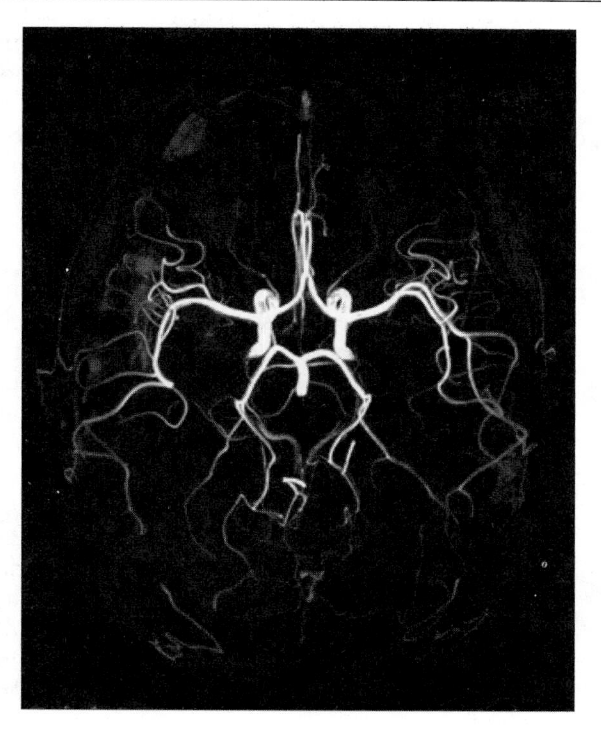

Figure 2-6 **MRI of circle of Willis and other cerebral arteries.**

Neurons

1. Structure.
   a. Neurons vary in size and complexity.
      (1) Cell bodies (genetic center) with dendrites (receptive surface area to receive information via synapses).
      (2) Axons conduct impulses away from the cell body (one-way conduction).
      (3) Synapses allow communication between neurons; chemical neurotransmitters are released (chemical synapses) or electrical signals pass directly from cell to cell (electrical synapses).
   b. Neuron groupings and types.
      (1) Nuclei are compact groups of nerve cell bodies; in the peripheral nervous system, these groups are called ganglia.
      (2) Projection neurons carry impulses to other parts of the CNS.
      (3) Interneurons are short relay neurons.
      (4) Axon bundles are called tracts or fasciculi; in the spinal cord, collections of tracts are called columns or funiculi.
   c. Neuroglia: support cells that do not transmit signals; important for myelin and neuron production; maintenance of K+ levels and reuptake of neurotransmitters after neural transmission at synapses.
2. Function. Neuronal signaling.
   a. Resting membrane potential: positive on outside, negative on inside (about –70 mV).
   b. Action potential: increased permeability of Na+ and influx into cell with outflow of K+ results in polarity changes (inside to about +35 mV) and depolarization; generation of an action potential is all-or-none.
   c. Conduction velocity is proportional to axon diameter; the largest myelinated fibers conduct the fastest.
   d. Repolarization results from activation of K+ channels.
   e. Myelinated axons: many axons are covered with myelin with small gaps (nodes of Ranvier) where myelin is absent; the action potential jumps from one node to the next, termed *saltatory conduction;* myelin functions to increase speed of conduction and conserve energy.
   f. Nerve fiber types.
      (1) A fibers: large, myelinated, fast-conducting.
         (a) Alpha: proprioception, somatic motor.
         (b) Beta: touch, pressure.
         (c) Gamma: motor to muscle spindles.
         (d) Delta: pain, temperature, touch.
      (2) B fibers: small, myelinated, conduct less rapidly; preganglionic autonomic.
      (3) C fibers: smallest, unmyelinated, slowest conducting.
         (a) Dorsal root: pain, reflex responses.
         (b) Sympathetic: postganglionic sympathetics.

Peripheral Nervous System

1. Peripheral nerve (lower motor neuron [LMN]) (see Figure 2-1).
   a. Motor (efferent) fibers originate from motor nuclei (cranial nerves) or anterior horn cells (spinal nerves).
   b. Sensory (afferent) fibers originate in cells outside of brainstem or spinal cord with sensory ganglia (cranial nerves) or dorsal root ganglia (spinal nerves) (Figure 2-7).
   c. Autonomic nervous system fibers: sympathetic fibers at thoracolumbar spinal segments and parasympathetic fibers at craniosacral segments.
2. Cranial nerves (CN).
   a. Twelve pairs of cranial nerves; all nerves are distributed to the head and neck, except CN X, which is distributed to the thorax and abdomen (Table 2-1).

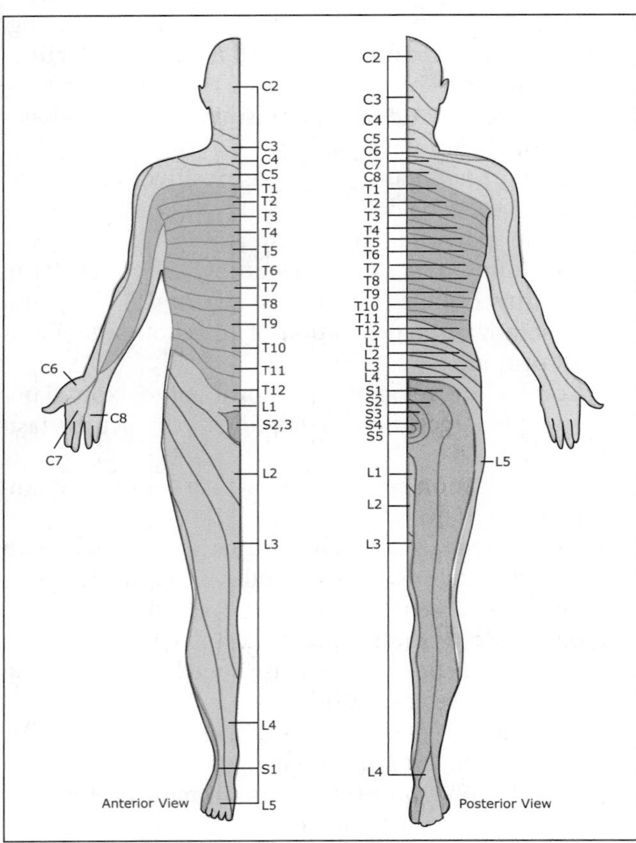

Figure 2-7 Dermatomes.

b. CN I, II, and VIII are pure sensory, carry special senses of smell, vision, hearing, and equilibrium.
c. CN III, IV, and VI are pure motor, controlling eye movements and pupillary constriction.
d. CN XI and XII are pure motor, innervating sternocleidomastoid, trapezius, and tongue.
e. CN V, VII, IX, and X are mixed motor and sensory; involved in chewing (V), facial expression (VII), swallowing (IX, X), vocal sounds (X); sensations from head (V, VII, IX), alimentary tract, heart, vessels, and lungs (IX, X), and taste (VII, IX, X).
f. CN III, VII, IX, and X carry parasympathetic fibers of ANS; involved in control of smooth muscles of inner eye (III); salivatory and lacrimal glands (VII); parotid gland (IX); muscles of heart, lung, and bowel (X).

3. Spinal nerves.
   a. 31 pairs of spinal nerves; spinal nerves are divided into groups (8 cervical, 12 thoracic, 5 lumbar, 5 sacral, and 1 coccygeal) and correspond to vertebral segments; each has a ventral root and a dorsal root.
   b. Ventral (anterior) root: efferent (motor) fibers to voluntary muscles (alpha motor neurons, gamma motor neurons), and to viscera, glands, and smooth muscles (preganglionic ANS fibers).
   c. Dorsal (posterior) root: afferent (sensory) fibers from sensory receptors from skin, joints, and muscles; each dorsal root possesses a dorsal root ganglion (cell bodies of sensory neurons); there is no dorsal root for C1.
   d. The term *dermatome* refers to a specific segmental skin area innervated by sensory spinal axons; the term *myotome* refers to the skeletal muscles innervated by motor axons in a given spinal root. A motor unit consists of the alpha motor neuron and the muscle fibers it innervates.
   e. Nerve roots exit from the vertebral column through the intervertebral foramina.
      (1) In the cervical spine, numbered roots exit horizontally above the corresponding vertebral body, with C8 exiting below C7 and above T1.
      (2) In the thoracic, lumbar, and sacral spine, the roots exit below the corresponding vertebral body.
      (3) Spinal cord ends at the level of L1; in the lumbosacral region, the nerve roots descend almost vertically below the cord to form the cauda equina (horse's tail).
   f. After emerging from the intervertebral foramen, each spinal nerve divides into a large anterior ramus (supplying the muscles and skin of the anterolateral body wall and limbs) and a small posterior ramus (supplying the muscles and skin of the back); each ramus contains motor and sensory fibers.
   g. The anterior rami join at the root of the limbs to form nerve plexuses. The cervical and brachial plexuses are at the root of the upper limbs; the lumbar and sacral plexuses are at the root of the lower limbs.
      (1) The cervical plexus arises from C1 through C4 nerve roots. The brachial plexus arises from C5 through T1 nerve roots that split into anterior and posterior divisions, redistributing fibers into three cords (lateral, posterior, and medial) and finally into the peripheral nerves that supply the upper extremity.
      (2) The lumbar plexus arises from T12 through L4 nerve roots. The sacral plexus arises from L4 through S3 nerve roots. Nerve fibers from both are redistributed into the peripheral nerves that supply the lower extremity.
      (3) Refer to Table 1-5 (Shoulder Girdle and Upper Extremity Muscular and Neurological Screening), Table 1-6 (Pelvic Girdle and Lower

Table 2-1

Examination of Cranial Nerve Integrity

NERVE	FUNCTION	TEST	POSSIBLE ABNORMAL FINDINGS
I Olfactory	Smell	Test sense of smell on each side: use common, nonirritating odors; close off other nostril	Anosmia (inability to detect smells), seen with frontal lobe lesions
II Optic	Vision	Test visual acuity	Blindness, myopia (impaired far vision); presbyopia (impaired near vision)
		Central: Snellen eye chart; test each eye separately by covering other eye; test at distance of 20 feet	
		Visual fields: test peripheral vision by confrontation	Visual field defects: (homonymous hemianopsia)
II, III Optic and Oculomotor	Pupillary reflexes	Test pupillary reactions (constriction) by shining light in eye; if abnormal, test near reaction	Absence of pupillary constriction
		Examine pupillary size/shape	Anisocoria (unequal pupils); Horner's syndrome, CN III paralysis
III, IV, VI Oculomotor, Trochlear, and Abducens	Extraocular movements	Test extraocular movements in each of six directions	Strabismus (eye deviates from normal conjugate position). Impaired eye movements
	CN III: turns eye up, down, in	Observe position of eye	Strabismus: eye pulled outward by CN VI; eye cannot look upward, downward, inward movements
	Elevates eyelid	Test pursuit eye movement	May see ptosis, pupillary dilation
	CN IV: turns adducted eye down	Test pursuit eye movement	Eye cannot look down when eye is adducted
	CN VI: turns eye out	Observe position of eye	Esotropia (eye pulled inward)
		Test pursuit eye movement	Eye cannot look out
V Trigeminal	Sensory: face	Test pain, light touch sensations: forehead, cheeks, jaw (eyes closed)	Loss of facial sensations, numbness with CN V lesion
	Sensory: cornea	Test corneal reflex: touch lightly with wisp of cotton	Loss of corneal reflex ipsilaterally (blinking in response to corneal touch)
	Motor: temporal and masseter muscles	Palpate muscles; have patient clench teeth, hold against resistance	Weakness, wasting of muscles of mastication
			Deviation of jaw when opened to ipsilateral side
VII Facial	Facial expression	Test motor function facial muscles: raise eyebrows, frown, show teeth, smile, close eyes tightly, puff out both cheeks	Paralysis ipsilateral facial muscles: inability to close eye, droop in corner of mouth, difficulty with speech articulation; peripheral nerve injury (PNI) CN VII Bell's palsy; CNS facial paralysis stroke V
VIII Vestibulocochlear (Acoustic)	Vestibular function	Test balance: vestibulospinal function	Vertigo, dysequilibrium
	Test eye-head coordination: vestibular ocular reflex (VOR)	Gaze instability with head rotations	Nystagmus (constant, involuntary cyclical movement of the eyeball)
	Cochlear function	Test auditory acuity	Deafness, impaired hearing, tinnitus
		Test for lateralization (Weber's test): place vibrating tuning fork on top of head, mid position; check if sound heard in one ear, or equally in both	Unilateral conductive loss: sound lateralized to impaired ear Sensorineural loss: sound heard in good ear
		Compare air and bone conduction (Rinne's test): place vibrating tuning fork on mastoid bone, then close to ear canal; sound heard longer through air than bone	Conductive loss: sound heard through bone is equal to or longer than air
			Sensorineural loss: sound heard longer through air
IX/X Glossopharyngeal and Vagus	Phonation	Listen to voice quality	Dysphonia: hoarseness denotes vocal cord paralysis; nasal quality denotes palatal weakness
	Swallowing	Examine for difficulty in swallowing	Dysphagia

(*Continued*)

Table 2-1

Examination of Cranial Nerve Integrity (Continued)

NERVE	FUNCTION	TEST	POSSIBLE ABNORMAL FINDINGS
IX/X Glossopharyngeal and Vagus	Palatal, pharynx control	Have patient say "ah"; observe motion of soft palate (elevates) and position of uvula (remains midline)	Paralysis: palate fails to elevate (lesion of CN X); asymmetrical elevation: unilateral paralysis
	Gag reflex	Stimulate back of throat lightly on each side	Absent reflex: lesion of CN IX; possibly CN X
XI Accessory	Muscle function	Examine bulk, strength	Atrophy, fasciculations, weakness (PNI):
	Trapezius muscle	Test shoulder elevation and shoulder flexion above 90°	Inability to shrug ipsilateral shoulder; shoulder droops
	Sternocleidomastoid	Test head rotation to contralateral side Turn head to each side against resistance	Inability to turn head to contralateral side
XII Hypoglossal	Tongue movements	Listen to patient's articulation Examine resting position of tongue Examine tongue movements (move side-to-side, protrude)	Dysarthria (lesions of CN X or CN XII) Atrophy or fasciculations of tongue Impaired movements, deviation to weak side on protrusion

Key: CN = cranial nerve; CNS = central nervous system; PNI = peripheral nerve injury

Extremity Muscular and Neurological Screening), and Table 1-7 (Trunk and Ribcage Muscular and Neurological Screening).

Spinal Level Reflexes

Involuntary responses to stimuli; basic, specific, and predictable; dependent on intact neural pathway (reflex arc); reflexes may be monosynaptic or polysynaptic (involving interneurons); provides basis for unconscious motor function and basic defense mechanisms.

1. Stretch (myotatic) reflexes.
   a. Stimulus: muscle stretch.
   b. Reflex arc: afferent Ia fiber from muscle spindle to alpha motor neurons projecting back to muscle of origin (monosynaptic).
   c. Functions for maintenance of muscle tone, support agonist muscle contraction, and provide feedback about muscle length.
   d. Clinically, sensitivity of the stretch reflex and intactness of spinal cord segment are tested by applying stretch to the deep tendons.
   e. Reciprocal inhibition: via an inhibitory interneuron, the same stretch stimulus inhibits the antagonist muscle.
   f. Reciprocal innervation: describes the effects of a stretch stimulus on agonist (autogenic facilitation), antagonist (reciprocal inhibition), and synergistic muscles (facilitation).
2. Inverse stretch (myotatic) reflex.
   a. Stimulus: muscle contraction.
   b. Reflex arc: afferent Ib fiber from Golgi tendon organ via inhibitory interneuron to muscle of origin (polysynaptic).
   c. Functions to provide agonist inhibition, diminution of force of agonist contraction, stretch-protection reflex.
3. Gamma reflex loop.
   a. Stretch reflex forms part of this loop.
   b. Allows muscle tension to come under control of descending pathways (reticulospinal, vestibulospinal, and others).
   c. Descending pathways excite gamma motor neurons, causing contraction of muscle spindle, and in turn increased stretch sensitivity and increased rate of firing from spindle afferents; impulses are then conveyed to alpha motor neurons.
4. Flexor (withdrawal) reflex.
   a. Stimulus: cutaneous sensory stimuli.
   b. Reflex arc: cutaneous receptors via interneurons to largely flexor muscles; multisegmental response involving groups of muscles (polysynaptic).
   c. Functions as a protective withdrawal mechanism to remove body part from harmful stimuli.
5. Crossed extension reflex.
   a. Stimulus: noxious stimuli and reciprocal action of antagonists; flexors of one side are excited, causing extensors on same side to be inhibited; opposite responses occur in opposite limb.
   b. Reflex arc: cutaneous and muscle receptors diverging to many spinal cord motor neurons on same and opposite side (polysynaptic).
   c. Function: coordinates reciprocal limb activities such as gait.

Neurological Examination: History, Systems Review, Tests, and Measures

Patient Interview

1. Presenting symptoms. Onset, progression, nature of symptoms, patient's insight into medical condition.
2. Past medical history. Other diagnoses, surgeries, health factors.
3. Social history. Current living situation, family/social support, education level, employment, lifestyle, risk factors.

Examine Level of Consciousness

1. Determine orientation to person, place, and time (oriented ×3).
2. Determine response to stimuli.
   a. Purposeful, nonpurposeful, no response.
   b. Verbal, tactile, simple commands.
   c. Painful stimuli: pinch, pinprick.
3. Determine level of consciousness (arousal).
   a. Alertness: alert patient responds appropriately; can open eyes, look at examiner, respond fully and appropriately to stimuli.
   b. Lethargy: patient appears drowsy; can open eyes and look at examiner, respond to questions, but falls asleep easily.
   c. Obtundation: patient can open eyes, look at examiner, but responds slowly and is confused; demonstrates decreased alertness and interest in environment.
   d. Stupor: patient can be aroused from sleep only with painful stimuli; verbal responses are slow or absent; patient returns to unresponsive state when stimuli are removed; demonstrates minimal awareness of self and environment.
   e. Coma: a state of unconsciousness from which patient cannot be aroused, eyes remain closed; no response to external stimuli or environment.
   f. Unresponsive vigilance (vegetative) state: a state characterized by the return of sleep/wake cycles, normalization of vegetative functions (respiration, heart rate, blood pressure, digestion) and lack of cognitive responsiveness (can be aroused but is unaware). Persistent vegetative state: a state lasting > 1 year for traumatic brain injury (TBI) and > 3 months for anoxic brain injury.
   g. Minimally conscious state (MCS): a state characterized by severely altered consciousness with minimal but definite evidence of self or environmental awareness.
4. Glasgow Coma Scale (GCS) (Teasdale and Jennette, 1974).
   a. Relates consciousness to three elements of response: eye opening, motor response, and verbal response.
   b. Scoring range from 3 to 15; severe brain injury (scores 1–8); moderate brain injury (scores 9–12); minor brain injury (scores 13–15).

Examine Cognitive Function

1. Memory.
   a. Immediate recall: name three items previously presented after a brief interval (i.e., 5 minutes).
   b. Recent memory (short-term): recall of recent events (i.e., What did you have for breakfast?).
   c. Remote memory (long-term): recall of past events (i.e., Where were you born? Where did you grow up?).
2. Attention.
   a. Length of attention span: digit span retention test (i.e., ability to recall seven numbers in order presented).
   b. Ability to attend to task without redirection (sustained attention); determine time on task, frequency of redirection.
   c. Ability to shift attention from one task to another (divided attention); assess ability of dual task control; assess also for perseveration (mental inertia): getting stuck on a task.
   d. Ability to stay on task in presence of detractors (focused attention); assess impact of environmental versus internal detractors.
   e. Ability to follow commands: one- or two-step, multilevel commands.
3. Emotional responses/behaviors.
   a. Safety, judgment: impulsivity and lack of inhibition.
   b. Affect, mood: irritability, agitation, depression, and withdrawal.
   c. Frustration tolerance.
   d. Self-centeredness (egocentricity).
   e. Insight into disability.
   f. Ability to follow rules of social conduct.
   g. Ability to tolerate criticism.
4. Higher-level cognitive abilities.
   a. Judgment, problem solving.
   b. Abstract reasoning.
   c. Fund of general knowledge: current events, ability to learn new information, generalize learning to new situations.

d. Calculation: serial 7 test (count backward from 100 by 7s).
e. Sequencing: ability to order components of cognitive or functional task; assess if cueing is necessary, frequency of cues.

5. Mini-Mental State Examination (MMSE) (Folstein, Flostein, and McHugh, 1975).
   a. Brief screening test for cognitive dysfunction.
   b. Includes screening items for orientation, registration, attention and calculation, recall and language.
   c. Maximum score is 30; 21–24 indicates mild cognitive impairment, 16–20 indicates moderate impairment, 15 or less indicates severe impairment.
6. Cognitive scale: Rancho Los Amigos Levels of Cognitive Function (LOCF) (Hagen et al., 1979).
   a. Assesses cognitive recovery from TBI.
   b. Includes eight levels of behavior: No response (I), decreased response levels (II and III), confused levels (IV, V, and VI), appropriate (automatic, purposeful) levels (VII and VIII).
   c. Delineates emerging behaviors; patients may plateau at any level.

Examine Speech and Communication

1. Expressive function.
   a. Examine fluency of speech, speech production.
   b. Nonfluent aphasia (Broca's motor aphasia, expressive aphasia).
      (1) A central language disorder in which speech is typically awkward, restricted, interrupted, and produced with effort.
      (2) The result of a lesion involving the third frontal convolution of the left hemisphere (Broca's area).
   c. Verbal apraxia: impairment of volitional articulatory control secondary to a cortical, dominant hemisphere lesion.
   d. Dysarthria: impairment of speech production resulting from damage to the central or peripheral nervous system; causes weakness, paralysis, or incoordination of the motor-speech system (respiration, articulation, phonation, and movements of jaw and tongue).
2. Receptive function.
   a. Examine comprehension.
   b. Fluent aphasia (Wernicke's aphasia, receptive aphasia).
      (1) A central language disorder in which spontaneous speech is preserved and flows smoothly, while auditory comprehension is impaired.
   c. The result of a lesion in the posterior first temporal gyrus of the left hemisphere (Wernicke's area).
3. Global aphasia.
   a. Severe aphasia.
   b. Examine for marked impairments in comprehension and production of language.
4. Nonverbal communication.
   a. Examine ability to read and write.
   b. Use of gestures, symbols, and pictographs.

Examine Cranial Nerves

1. See Table 2-1.

Examine Vital Signs

1. Determine heart rate (HR), blood pressure (BP).
   a. Examine for any irregularities in pulse: bounding, thready (fine, barely perceptible).
   b. Examine for decrease or increase in blood pressure. See Table 3-4, American Heart Association (AHA) Blood Pressure Definitions.
   c. Examine for changes in response to activity: normally, HR increases in direct proportion to intensity of exercise; SBP increases, while DBP remains the same or decreases moderately (a widening of pulse pressure).
   d. With increasing intracranial pressures, examine for changes in HR and BP that occur late.
2. Examine respiratory rate (RR), depth, rhythm, and characteristics of inspiratory and expiratory phases.
   a. Cheyne-Stokes respiration: a period of apnea lasting 10–60 seconds followed by gradually increasing depth and frequency of respirations; accompanies depression of frontal lobe and diencephalic dysfunction.
   b. Hyperventilation: increased rate and depth of respirations; accompanies dysfunction of lower midbrain and pons.
   c. Apneustic breathing: abnormal respiration marked by prolonged inspiration; accompanies damage to upper pons.
3. Examine temperature.
   a. Elevation may indicate infection, damage to hypothalamus or brainstem.

Examine for CNS Infection or Meningeal Irritation

1. Signs are global, not focal.
2. Neck mobility.
   a. Patient is positioned in supine, flex neck to chest.
   b. Positive sign: neck pain, with limitation and guarding of head flexion due to spasm of posterior neck muscles; can result from meningeal inflammation, arthritis, or neck injury.

3. Kernig's sign.
   a. Patient is positioned in supine; flex hip and knee fully to chest, and then extend knee.
   b. Positive sign: causes pain and increased resistance to extending the knee due to spasm of hamstring; when bilateral, suggests meningeal irritation.
4. Brudzinski's sign.
   a. Patient is positioned in supine; flex neck to chest.
   b. Positive sign: causes flexion of hips and knees (drawing up); suggests meningeal irritation.
5. Irritability.
6. Slowed mental function.
   a. Examine for persistent headache, increased in head-down position.
   b. May progress to delirium, lethargy, and coma.
7. Altered vital signs.
   a. Examine for increased HR and RR, fever; fluctuating BP.
8. Generalized weakness.

Examine for Increased Intracranial Pressure Secondary to Cerebral Edema and Brain Herniation

1. Altered level of consciousness.
   a. Progresses from restlessness and confusion to decreasing level of consciousness, unresponsiveness, and coma.
2. Altered vital signs.
   a. Examine for increased BP; widening pulse pressure and slowing of pulse; irregular respirations including periods of apnea, Cheyne-Stokes respirations; elevated temperature.
3. Headache.
4. Vomiting.
   a. Secondary to irritation of vagal nuclei, CN X.
5. Pupillary changes (CN III signs).
   a. Examine for ipsilateral dilation of pupil (unequal pupils), slowed reaction to light progressing to fixed, dilated pupils (a poor prognostic sign).
6. Papilledema at entrance to eye.
7. Progressive impairment of motor function.
   a. Examine for weakness, hemiplegia, positive Babinski response, decorticate or decerebrate rigidity.
8. Seizure activity.

Examine Autonomic Nervous System Function

1. See Table 2-2.

Table 2-2

Autonomic Nervous System Functions

SYMPATHETIC NERVOUS SYSTEM	PARASYMPATHETIC NERVOUS SYSTEM
Activated in stressful situations, producing an arousal reaction (fight or flight)	Results in conservation and restoration of body energy and homeostasis (system balance)
Effects are widespread	Effects are localized and short-acting
Inhibits salivation and tearing	Stimulates salivation and tearing
Dilates pupils (mydriasis)	Constricts pupils
Accelerates heart rate and output	Slows heart rate
Constricts or dilates blood flow in skeletal muscles	Dilates blood vessels in gut
Constricts blood flow to skin and viscera	
Relaxes airways	Constricts airways
Stimulates secretion of epinephrine and norepinephrine from adrenal medulla	
Decreases peristalsis, intestinal motility; inhibits digestion	Stimulates pancreas to release insulin and digestive enzymes Stimulates digestion
Increases sweating	
Stimulates glucose production and release	
Relaxes urinary bladder	Stimulates urinary bladder to contract

Examine Sensory Function

1. Subjective.
   a. Ask patient to describe (map out areas) where sensation does not feel normal; provide sensory clues.
2. Topographical organization.
   a. Use sensory dermatome chart.
3. Testing considerations.
   a. Document key sensory systems: test superficial and proprioceptive sensations first, then combined (cortical) sensations. See Table 2-3.
   b. Ensure that patient comprehends instructions and can communicate responses.
   c. Occlude vision: consider barrier method (use a piece of paper to block vision) versus blindfolding the patient.
   d. Apply stimulus in random, unpredictable order; avoid summation.
   e. To assess responses, always pose a choice (e.g., hot or cold).
   f. Examine for objective manifestations: withdrawal, wincing, blinking.
   g. Consider skin condition (calluses, scars) for areas of desensitivity.
   h. Look for signs of repetitive trauma, skin lesions.
4. Evaluation and documentation.
   a. Determine whether the patient can readily distinguish one sensation from another.
   b. Determine the sensory threshold, the lightest stimulus perceived.
   c. Determine the degree and location of deficits (dermatome mapping).
   d. Determine the patient's subjective feelings, level of awareness of sensory losses.
   e. Determine functional impact of sensory losses.

Examine Perceptual Function

1. Testing considerations.
   a. Suspect perceptual dysfunction if patient has difficulty with functional mobility skills or activities of daily living for reasons that cannot be accounted for by specific sensory, motor, or comprehension deficits.
   b. Rule out specific sensory and motor loss, language impairment, hearing loss, or visual disturbance as cause of loss of function.
   c. Rule out psychological/emotional and cognitive factors.
2. Test for homonymous hemianopsia.
   a. Loss of half of visual field in each eye, contralateral to the side of a cerebral hemisphere lesion.
   b. Slowly bring two fingers from behind head into the patient's visual field while asking the patient to gaze straight ahead; the patient indicates when and where the fingers first appear.
3. Examine for body scheme/body image disorders.
   a. Body scheme disorder (somatognosia): have patient identify body parts or their relationship to each other.

Table 2-3

Examination of Sensory Integrity*

Test Superficial Sensations	
Pain	Test sharp/dull sensation in response to sharp/dull stimuli with paper clip.
Temperature	Test hot/cold sensation in response to hot/cold stimuli with test tubes filled with hot or cold water.
Touch	Test touch/nontouch in response to slight touch stimulus (cotton ball) or no touch.
Test Proprioceptive (Deep) Sensations	
Joint position sense:	Test ability to perceive joint position at rest in response to your positioning the patient's limb (up or down, in or out).
Kinesthesia (movement sense)	Test ability to perceive movement in response to your moving the patient's limb; patient can duplicate movement with opposite limb or give a verbal report.
Vibration sense (pallesthesia)	Test proprioceptive pathways by applying vibrating tuning fork or pressure only (sham vibration) on bony areas.
Test Combined (Cortical) Sensations (Use a sample of two or three from this group.)	
Stereognosis	Test ability to identify familiar objects placed in the hand by manipulation and touch.
Tactile localization	Test ability to identify location of a touch stimulus on the body by verbal report or pointing.
Two-point discrimination	Test ability to recognize one or two blunt points applied to the skin simultaneously; determine minimal distance on skin where two points can still be distinguished in millimeters using an aesthesiometer (the two tips must be applied simultaneously).
Barognosis	Test ability to identify similar size/shaped objects placed in the hand with different gradations of weight.
Graphesthesia	Test ability to identify numbers, letters, or symbols traced on skin, typically the hand.
Bilateral simultaneous stimulation	Test ability to identify simultaneous touch on the two sides/segments of the body.

*All tests are with vision occluded.

b. Visual spatial neglect (unilateral neglect): determine whether patient ignores one side of the body and stimuli coming from that side.
c. Right/left discrimination disorder: have patient identify right and left sides of his or her own body and your body.
d. Anosognosia: severe denial, neglect or lack of awareness of severity of condition; determine whether patient shows severe impairments in neglect and body scheme.

4. Examine for spatial relations syndrome.
   a. Figure-ground discrimination: have patient pick out an object from an array of objects (e.g., brake from rest of wheelchair).
   b. Form constancy: have patient pick out an object from an array of similarly shaped but different-sized objects (e.g., large block from group of blocks).
   c. Spatial relations: have patient duplicate a pattern of two or three blocks.
   d. Position in space: have patient demonstrate different limb positions (e.g., put your arm overhead; put your foot underneath the chair).
   e. Topographical disorientation: determine whether patient can navigate a familiar route on his or her own (e.g., travel from room to physical therapy clinic).
   f. Depth and distance imperceptions: determine whether patient can judge depth and distance (e.g., navigate stairs, sit down in chair).
   g. Vertical disorientation: determine whether patient can accurately identify when something is upright (e.g., hold a cane, ask patient when it is vertical; ask patient to determine whether own body is vertical).
5. Examine for agnosia.
   a. Inability to recognize familiar objects with one sensory modality while retaining ability to recognize same object with other sensory modalities.
   b. Subject doesn't recognize an object (clock) by sight, but can recognize it by sound (ticking).
6. Examine for apraxia.
   a. Inability to perform voluntary, learned movements in the absence of loss of sensation, strength, coordination, attention, or comprehension; represents a breakdown in the conceptual system or motor production system or both.
   b. Ideomotor apraxia: patient cannot perform the task on command, but can do the task when left on own.
   c. Ideational apraxia: patient cannot perform the task at all, either on command or on own.

Examine Motor Function

1. Examine muscle bulk, firmness (see Tables 2-4 and 2-5).
   a. Determine whether there is atrophy.
      (1) Determine whether atrophy is due to denervation, disuse, or primary atrophy.
      (2) The presence of persistent fasciculations suggests neurogenic injury.
      (3) Examine by inspection, palpation, and girth measurement.
   b. Check muscle firmness, tenderness, and reactivity.
2. Examine muscle tone.
   a. Use passive range of motion (PROM) to assess muscle stretch reflexes and responsiveness to passive elongation.
   b. Flaccidity (absent tone), hypotonia (decreased tone).
      (1) Seen in segmental/LMN lesions: nerve roots and peripheral nerve injury.
      (2) Seen initially after suprasegmental/upper motor neuron (UMN) lesions (i.e., brief period of spinal shock in spinal cord injuries, cerebral shock in stroke). There is decreased or no resistance to PROM.
   c. Spasticity (spastic hypertonia).
      (1) Seen in suprasegmental/UMN lesions.
      (2) There is increased resistance to PROM; determine whether increasing the speed increases the resistance (spasticity is velocity-dependent) (Table 2-6).
      (3) Examine for additional signs of spastic hypertonia.
         (a) Clasp-knife response: marked resistance to PROM suddenly gives way.
         (b) Clonus: maintained stretch stimulus produces a cyclical, spasmodic contraction; common in plantar flexors, also seen in wrist flexors and jaw.
         (c) Hyperactive cutaneous reflexes, positive Babinski response: dorsiflexion of great toe with fanning of other toes in response to stroking up the lateral side of the sole of the foot; indicative of corticospinal (pyramidal) tract disruption.
         (d) Hyperreflexia: increased deep tendon reflexes (DTRs).
         (e) Some degree of muscle weakness is usually present.
      (4) Modified Ashworth Scale: six grades are used for grading spasticity:
         0—No increase in muscle tone.
         1—Slight increase in muscle tone, minimal resistance at end of ROM.
         1+—Slight increase in muscle tone, minimal resistance through less than half of ROM.
         2—More marked increase in muscle tone, through most of ROM, affected part easily moved.
         3—Considerable increase in muscle tone, passive movement difficult.
         4—Affected part rigid in flexion or extension.
   d. Rigidity: increased resistance to PROM that is independent of the velocity of movement.

Table 2-4

Differential Diagnosis: Comparison of Major Types of Central Nervous System Disorders

LOCATION OF LESION	CEREBRAL CORTEX CORTICOSPINAL TRACTS	BASAL GANGLIA: SUBCORTICAL GRAY	CEREBELLUM	SPINAL CORD
Disorder	Stroke	Parkinsonism	Cerebellar lesion: tumor, stroke	SCI: trauma, complete incomplete
Sensation	Impaired or absent, depending on lesion location; contralateral sensory loss	Not affected	Not affected	Impaired or absent below
Tone	Hypertonia/spasticity; clasp-knife phenomena present; spasticity is velocity-dependent; with cerebral shock, may see initial flaccidity	Leadpipe rigidity: uniform increased resistance to movement; cogwheel rigidity: rachet-like resistance to movement; rigidity is not velocity-dependent	Normal or may be decreased	Hypertonia/spasticity below the level of the lesion; initial flaccidity: spinal shock
Reflexes	Increased hyperreflexia	Normal or may be decreased	Normal or may be decreased	Increased hyperreflexia
Strength	Contralateral weakness or paralysis: hemiplegia	Slowness of movement	Normal or weak: asthenia	Impaired or absent below the level of the lesion: paraplegia or tetraplegia
Bulk	Normal: acute; disuse atrophy: chronic	Normal or disuse atrophy	Normal	Disuse atrophy
Involuntary Movements	Spasms	Resting tremor	None	Spasms
Voluntary Movements	Dyssynergic: abnormal timing, coactivation, activation, fatigability	Bradykinesia/akinesia slowness, lack of spontaneous and automatic movements	Ataxia: intention tremor dysdiadochokinesia, dysmetria, dyssynergia nystagmus	Intact: above level of lesion
Postural	Impaired or absent, depends on lesion location	Impaired: stooped	Impaired: truncal ataxia, dysequilibrium	Impaired below level of lesion
Gait	Impaired: gait deficits due to abnormal synergies, spasticity, timing deficits	Impaired: shuffling, festinating gait	Impaired: ataxic gait deficits, wide-based, unsteady	Impaired or absent: depends on level of lesion

(1) Rigidity seen in basal ganglia/nigrostriatal disorders: increased resistance to passive movement in agonist and antagonist muscle.

(2) Rigidity can be leadpipe (uniform throughout the range) or cogwheel (interrupted by a series of jerks).

(3) Associated with Parkinson's disease, resting tremor, bradykinesia; strength is affected with immobility and deconditioning.

e. Decerebrate rigidity/posturing.

(1) Seen in comatose patients with brainstem lesions between the superior colliculus and the vestibular nucleus.

(2) Results in increased tone and sustained posturing in rigid extension of all four limbs and trunk/neck.

f. Decorticate rigidity/posturing.

(1) Seen in comatose patients with lesions above the superior colliculus.

(2) Results in increased tone and sustained posturing of upper limbs in flexion and the lower limbs in extension.

g. Opisthotonos.

(1) Prolonged, severe spasm of muscles, causing the head, back, and heels to arch backward; arms and hands are held rigidly flexed.

(2) Seen in severe meningitis, tetanus, epilepsy, and strychnine poisoning.

h. Use active ROM, active movement control to assess tone in automatic postural adjustments.

(1) Check stiffness of limbs and trunk in maintaining posture against gravity.

Table 2-5

Differential Diagnosis: Comparison of Upper Motor Neuron (UMN) and Lower Motor Neuron (LMN) Syndromes

	UMN LESION	LMN LESION
Location of Lesion	Central nervous system	Peripheral nervous system
Structures Involved	Cortex, brainstem, corticospinal tracts, spinal cord	SC: anterior horn cell, spinal roots, peripheral nerves CN: cranial nerves
Disorders	Stroke, traumatic brain injury, spinal cord injury	Polio, Guillain-Barré, PNI, peripheral neuropathy, radiculopathy
Tone	Increased: hypertonia Velocity-dependent	Decreased or absent: hypotonia, flaccidity Not velocity dependent
Reflexes	Increased: hyperreflexia, clonus Exaggerated cutaneous and autonomic reflexes: + Babinski response	Decreased or absent: hyporeflexia Cutaneous reflexes decreased or absent
Involuntary Movements	Muscle spasms: flexor or extensor	With denervation: fasciculations
Strength	Stroke: weakness or paralysis on one side of the body Corticospinal lesions: contralateral if above decussation in medulla, ipsilateral if below Spinal cord lesions: bilateral loss below level of lesion	Limited distribution: segmental or focal pattern Root-innervated pattern
Muscle Bulk	Variable, disuse atrophy	Neurogenic atrophy: rapid, focal, severe wasting
Voluntary Movements	Impaired or absent: dyssynergic patterns, obligatory synergies	Weak or absent if nerve interrupted

Key: CN = cranial nerve; PNI = peripheral nerve injury; SC = spinal cord

(2) Examine for abnormal movements: are movements restricted, are they performed with great effort, are there limitations in voluntary movements?

i. Evaluation and documentation.
 (1) Determine which body parts and joints have abnormal tone.
 (2) Determine whether asymmetries exist, upper extremities versus lower extremities, axial (trunk) versus appendicular (limbs), distal versus proximal.
 (3) Describe the character of the resistance (e.g., velocity-dependent versus uniform, clasp-knife, leadpipe, cogwheel).
 (4) Describe the effects of tone on active movements, posture, and functional activities.

3. Examine reflexes (see Table 2-7).
 a. Reflex categories.
  (1) Deep tendon reflexes: normally occurring reflexes in response to stretch of muscle.
  (2) Superficial cutaneous reflexes: normally occurring reflexes in response to noxious stimulus (light scratch) applied to skin.
  (3) Primitive spinal reflexes.
  (4) Midbrain/cortical reactions.
 b. Reflex Scoring Scale (Capute) for primitive/spinal and tonic/brainstem reflexes:
  0—absent.
  1+—Tone change; no visible movement of extremities.
  2+—Visible movement of extremities.
  3+—Exaggerated, full movement of extremities.
  4+—Obligatory and sustained movement, lasting for > 30 seconds.

4. Examine muscle performance. Strength, power, and endurance.
 a. Determine/document: relative strength/peak power, ability to initiate/accelerate contraction, control torque output at varying speeds.
 b. Methods: patient's self-report, manual muscle test (MMT), dynamometry, muscle performance tests, physical capacity tests, technology-assisted analyses, timed activity tests.
 c. Observe muscle strength, power, and endurance during functional activities (e.g., basic and instrumental activities of daily living, functional mobility skills).
 d. Decreased strength: paresis (weakness) or paralysis (loss of voluntary motion).
  (1) Cerebrovascular accident: hemiparesis or hemiplegia.
  (2) Spinal cord injury: paraplegia or tetraplegia (quadriplegia).
  (3) Traumatic brain injury: any level or degree possible.
 e. Clinical issues with strength testing (standard MMT): patients with CNS, UMN lesions.
  (1) Passive restraint: soft tissue changes restrict ability to move (e.g., contractures).

Table 2-6

Typical Patterns of Spasticity in Upper Motor Neuron Syndrome

UPPER LIMBS	ACTIONS	MUSCLES AFFECTED
Scapula	Retraction, downward rotation	Rhomboids
Shoulder	Adduction and internal rotation, depression	Pectoralis major, latissimus dorsi, teres major, subscapularis
Elbow	Flexion	Biceps, brachialis, brachioradialis
Forearm	Pronation	Pronator teres, pronator quadratus
Wrist	Flexion, adduction	F. carpi radialis
Hand	Finger flexion, clenched fist Thumb adducted in palm	F. dig. profundus/sublimis, Add. pollicis brevis, F. pollicis brevis
LOWER LIMBS		
Pelvis	Retraction (hip hiking)	Quadratus lumborum
Hip	Adduction (scissoring) Internal rotation Extension	Add. longus/brevis Add. magnus, gracilis Gluteus maximus
Knee	Extension	Quadriceps
Foot and ankle	Plantarflexion Inversion Equinovarus Toes claw (MP ext., PIP flex, DIP ext.) Toes curl (PIP, DIP flex)	Gastrocsoleus Tibialis posterior Long toe flexors Ext. hallucis longus Peroneus longus
Hip and knee (prolonged sitting posture)	Flexion Sacral sitting	Iliopsoas Rectus femoris, pectineus Hamstrings
Trunk	Lateral flexion with concavity rotation	Rotators Internal/external obliques
COG forward (prolonged sitting posture)	Excessive forward flexion Forward head	Rectus abdominis, external obliques Psoas minor

The form and intensity of spasticity may vary greatly, depending upon the CNS lesion site and extent of damage. The degree of spasticity can fluctuate within each individual (i.e., due to body position, level of excitation, sensory stimulation, and voluntary effort). Spasticity predominates in antigravity muscles (i.e., the flexors of the upper extremity and the extensors of the lower extremity). If left untreated, spasticity can result in movement deficiencies, subsequent contractures, degenerative joint changes, and deformity.

Adapted from Mayer NH, Esquenazi A, Childers MK. Common patterns of clinical motor dysfunction. Muscle and Nerve 6:S21, 1997.

(2) Active restraint: spastic muscles restrict ability to move.

(3) Abnormal synergistic activity, inappropriate coactivation of muscles.

(4) Recruitment problems: abnormal type II fiber recruitment.

(5) Abnormal reflex activity: restricts ability to move.

(6) Isokinetic dynamometry: patients with UMN syndrome (i.e., stroke) typically demonstrate decreased torque development with increased problems at higher speeds, decreased limb excursion, extended time to peak torque development, extended time peak torque held, increased time intervals between reciprocal contractions, and changes on "supposedly normal" extremities.

f. Clinical issues with strength testing: patients with PNS, LMN lesions.

(1) With myopathies: see proximal weakness of extremities.

(2) With neuropathies: see distal weakness of extremities.

(3) Some conditions produce decremental strength losses (e.g., myasthenia gravis).

Table 2-7

Examination of Reflexes

Deep Tendon Reflexes (DTRs)	Tap directly on tendon: stretch stimulus produces contraction of agonist muscle with corresponding quick movement Reflexes commonly tested: jaw reflex, trigeminal CN V; biceps, C5–C6; triceps, C7–C8; brachioradialis, C5–C6; hamstrings, L5–S3; quadriceps (knee jerk, patellar), L2–4; Achilles (ankle jerk), S1–2 Scoring: 0 absent reflex; 1+ decreased response; 2+ normal response; 3+ exaggerated; 4+ hyperactive DTRs: may be abnormal in CNS lesions (hyporeflexia, hyperreflexia) or PNS lesions (hyporeflexia)
Superficial Cutaneous Reflexes	
Plantar Reflex (S1–2, tibial nerve):	Stroking of the lateral sole of foot from calcaneus to base of fifth metatarsal and medially across metatarsal heads produces plantar flexion of the toes Occurs in neurologically intact individual
Positive Babinski Response	Stroking of the lateral sole of foot from calcaneus to base of fifth metatarsal and medially across metatarsal heads produces dorsiflexion of the great toe and fanning (abduction) of the four lesser toes Seen in patients with corticospinal lesions
Abdominal Reflexes (T6–L1)	Lateral to medial scratching of skin (toward umbilicus) in each of four quadrants produces deviation of the umbilicus toward the stimulus Occurs in neurologically intact individual Loss of abdominal reflexes is a sign of corticospinal lesions
Cremasteric Reflex (L1–L2)	Stroking of skin of the proximal and medial thigh produces elevation of the testicle (neurologically intact individuals) Absent in spinal cord injury and corticospinal lesions
Primitive/Spinal Reflexes	Present developmentally in normal infants (see Chapter 7) and in some patients with brain injury
Flexor Withdrawal	Noxious stimulus (pinprick) to sole of foot produces toe extension, dorsiflexion of the foot, and flexion of entire LE
Crossed Extension Reflex	Noxious stimulus to sole of foot produces flexion of stimulated leg, then extension with adduction of opposite leg
Traction	Stretch stimulus from grasping the forearm and pulling produces total flexion response of the UE
Grasp	Maintained pressure to palm of hand (palmar grasp) or ball of foot (plantar grasp) produces maintained flexion of fingers or toes
Tonic/Brainstem Reflexes	Present developmentally in normal infants (see Chapter 7) and in some patients with brain injury
Asymmetrical Tonic Neck (ATNR)	Rotation of the head to one side produces flexion of the skull limbs and extension of the jaw limbs
Symmetrical Tonic Neck (STNR)	Flexion of the head produces flexion of the UEs with extension of the LEs Extension of the head produces extension of the UEs and flexion of the LEs
Positive Supporting	Contact to the ball of the foot in the standing position produces rigid extension (co-contraction) of the LEs
Associated Reactions	Strong voluntary movement in one body segment produces involuntary movement in another resting extremity

LE = lower extremity; UE = upper extremity

5. Examine for fatigue.
   a. Fatigue is the failure to generate the required or expected force during sustained or repeated contractions.
      (1) Fatigue is protective: guards against overwork and injury.
      (2) Fatigue is task-dependent.
      (3) Sources of fatigue.
         (a) CNS/central fatigue: seen in multiple sclerosis, amyotrophic lateral sclerosis, chronic fatigue syndrome.
         (b) Neural/myoneural junction: seen in multiple sclerosis, postpolio syndrome, Guillain-Barré syndrome, myasthenia gravis.
         (c) Muscle contractile failure: metabolic changes at the level of the muscle (e.g., depleted Ca^{2+} stores) seen in muscular dystrophy.
   b. Determine/document.
      (1) Source of fatigue.
      (2) Frequency and severity of fatigue episodes.
      (3) Threshold for fatigue: level of exercise that cannot be sustained indefinitely.
         (a) Onset is typically gradual, not abrupt.
         (b) Dependent on the intensity and duration of activity attempted.
      (4) Factors that influence fatigue: health status, environmental temperature, stress.
      (5) Level of functional performance: independence, modified dependence, dependence, level of assistance, assistive devices.
      (6) Episodes of exhaustion: limit of endurance beyond which no further performance is possible.
      (7) Overwork weakness or injury: prolonged decrease in absolute strength and endurance due to excessive activity of partially denervated muscle. Common in postpolio syndrome, Duchenne's muscular dystrophy.
      (8) Test and measures.
         (a) Modified Fatigue Impact Scale (MFIS): subjective scale that includes three subscales

assessing the impact of fatigue on physical, cognitive, and psychosocial function.

(b) Isokinetic dynamometry, electromyography (EMG): can observe decrements in force production.

6. Examine voluntary movement control.
   a. Determine/document.
      (1) Quality (synergistic organization) of muscle activation patterns.
      (2) Are movements appropriate and timely in response to stimulus or command?
      (3) Able to vary easily type of contraction pattern (i.e., isometric, concentric, eccentric)?
      (4) Are movements symmetrical?
      (5) Adequate control of multiple body segments, postural stabilization?
      (6) Assess for presence of abnormal synergy patterns: muscle synergistic patterns that are highly stereotyped and obligatory; commonly seen in UMN dysfunction (e.g., cerebrovascular accident, TBI) (Table 2-8).
7. Examine for presence of involuntary movements.
   a. Extrapyramidal disorders, basal ganglia dysfunction.
      (1) Tics: spasmodic contractions of specific muscles, commonly involving face, head, neck, or shoulder muscles.
      (2) Chorea: relatively quick twitches or "dancing" movements.
      (3) Athetosis: slow, irregular, twisting, sinuous movements, occurring especially in upper extremities.
      (4) Tremor: continuous quivering movements; rhythmic, oscillatory movement observed at rest (resting tremor).
      (5) Myoclonus: single, quick jerk.
   b. Cerebellar disorders: intention tremor occurring when voluntary movement is attempted.
   c. Cortical disorders: epileptic seizures, tonic/clonic convulsive movements.
   d. Determine/document.
      (1) Are movements extraneous and spontaneous, apparently unintended?
      (2) Part of body involved, orientation in space.
      (3) Frequency, amplitude, pattern.
      (4) Effect of triggering stimuli or changes in environment.
      (5) Methods: patient's self-report, observation/functional assessment, videotaped analysis.
8. Examine coordination.
   a. Gross motor coordination: body posture, balance, and extremity movements involving large muscle groups.
      (1) Upper extremity tests: unilateral (finger to nose); rapid alternating movements (RAM), supination/pronation; bilateral symmetrical movements (clapping, RAM), bilateral asymmetrical movements (alternate touch knee/shoulder), bilateral unrelated movements (knee pat/elbow extension).
      (2) Lower extremity tests: unilateral (heel to shin, foot tapping); bilateral symmetrical (foot tapping, alternate knee flexion/extension); bilateral asymmetrical (alternate knee flexion/extension); bilateral unrelated movements (knee flexion/extension and hip abduction/adduction).
      (3) Postural/trunk tests: whole body movements.
   b. Fine motor coordination: extremity movements concerned with use of small muscle groups.
      (1) Thumb/finger opposition (unilateral, bilateral).
      (2) Manual/finger dexterity: grasp and release.
      (3) Standardized tests and measures: Jebsen-Taylor Hand Function Test, Minnesota Rate of Manipulation Test, Purdue Pegboard.
   c. Evaluation and documentation.
      (1) Speed/rate control: Does increasing the speed of performance affect quality of motor performance?

Table 2-8

Abnormal Synergy Patterns of the Extremities Seen in Patients Following Stroke
UPPER EXTREMITY
Flexion synergy components: scapular retraction/elevation, shoulder abduction, external rotation, elbow flexion,* forearm supination, wrist and finger flexion*
Extension synergy components: scapular protraction, shoulder adduction,* internal rotation, elbow extension, forearm pronation, wrist and finger flexion
LOWER EXTREMITY
Flexion synergy components: hip flexion, abduction, external rotation, knee flexion, ankle dorsiflexion/inversion
Extension synergy components: hip extension, adduction,* internal rotation, knee extension,* ankle plantarflexion*/inversion

The form and intensity of abnormal synergy patterns may vary greatly, depending upon the CNS lesion site, extent of damage, and stage of recovery. Synergies can fluctuate due to body position (presence of reflexes), degree of spasticity, level of excitation, sensory stimulation, and voluntary effort.

*Generally the strongest components are starred.

(2) Control: Are movements precise? Are continuous and appropriate motor adjustments made if speed and direction are changed? Can movement and distance be judged following a moving target? Does occluding vision alter performance?
(3) Steadiness: Is there consistency over time? Can a position be maintained without swaying, tremors, or extra movements? Does patient fatigue rapidly?
(4) Response orientation: Does correct movement occur in response to a specific stimulus?
(5) Reaction time: Does movement occur in a reasonable amount of time?
(6) Descriptive comments/terms.
  (a) Dyssynergia: impaired ability to associate muscles together for complex movement.
  (b) Dysmetria: impaired ability to judge the distance or range of movement.
  (c) Dysdiadochokinesia: impaired ability to perform rapid alternating movements.
(7) Scoring: 0 (unable), 1 (severe impairment), 2 (moderate impairment), 3 (minimal impairment), 4 (normal performance).
(8) Methods.
  (a) Patient's self-report.
  (b) Observation/functional assessment.
  (c) Timed tests.
  (d) Videotaped analysis.

9. Examine balance.
  a. The control of relative positions of body parts by skeletal muscles, with respect to gravity and to each other.
  b. Sensory elements of balance.
    (1) Visual system: examine visual acuity, depth perception, visual field defects.
    (2) Somatosensory: examine proprioception, cutaneous sensation (touch, pressure), lower extremities and trunk, especially feet and ankles.
    (3) Vestibular: observe balance with changes in head position.
    (4) Sensory Organization Test (SOT)
      (a) Equipment: computerized moving platform (e.g., NeuroComBasic and Balance Master Systems); stopwatch.
      (b) Examines six different sensory conditions, progressing in difficulty.
        Condition 1: eyes open, stable surface (EOSS).
        Condition 2: eyes closed, stable surface (ECSS).
        Condition 3: visual conflict (sway-referenced vision using a moving surround screen or dome using force-platform surround screen), stable support.
        Condition 4: eyes open, moving surface (EOMS), using moving platform.
        Condition 5: eyes closed, moving surface (ECMS).
        Condition 6: visual conflict, moving surface.
      (c) Evaluation and documentation.
        - Record time that standing posture is maintained (30 seconds); record changes in the amount and direction of postural sway, on a scale of 1 (minimal sway) to 4 (fall).
        - Patients dependent on vision become unstable in conditions 2, 3, 5, and 6.
        - Patients dependent on surface/somatosensory inputs become unstable in conditions 4, 5, and 6.
        - Patients with vestibular loss become unstable in conditions 5 and 6.
        - Patients with sensory selection problems become unstable in conditions 3, 4, 5, and 6.
    (5) Clinical Test for Sensory Interaction in Balance (CTSIB) (Shumway-Cook and Horak, 1986): uses medium-density foam to substitute for a moving platform and a modified visual dome to substitute for a moving visual surround. Tests six conditions, similar to SOT.
    (6) Modified Clinical Test of Sensory Interaction on Balance (mCTSIB)
      (a) A simpler test that uses four different sensory conditions: eyes open and eyes closed on stable surface and on foam (EOSS, ECSS, EOFS, ECFS).
      (b) Three 30-second trials are used.
      (c) Time in balance and changes in sway are recorded. Test is stopped if patient alters position of feet (takes a step), opens eyes, or loses balance.
      (d) Patient subjective complaints are also recorded (e.g., nausea, dizziness).
  c. Motor responses to positional and movement testing.
    (1) Move or position the body; observe automatic adjustments that restore normal alignment of the head position (face vertical, mouth horizontal) (righting reactions).
    (2) Alter the body's center of mass (COM) or base of support (BOS) or both; observe automatic postural adjustments that serve to maintain body posture and balance (keep COM within the BOS).
    (3) Alter the body's COM outside of the BOS; observe the automatic adjustments of the arms (protective reaching) or legs (protective stepping) or both to extend and support the body weight in anticipation of a fall.
    (4) Testing considerations: can use a displacing manual force against the COM (a perturbation

or push) or displace the BOS using a movable surface (platform, gymnastic ball, equilibrium board).

d. Musculoskeletal elements and limits of stability (LOS).
 (1) Determine musculoskeletal strength and range of motion (ROM), lower extremities, and trunk.
 (2) Determine LOS: ability to move their COM over the BOS during self-initiated movements; can document with force plate analysis.
 (3) Determine center of alignment: location of COM within the center of the BOS; center of pressure documented using force plate analysis.
 (4) Determine availability of postural synergies (strategies) used to preserve balance.
  (a) Ankle strategy: ankle muscles (dorsiflexors and plantar flexors) maintain balance by shifting COM forward or back using a long axis of motion (lower extremity is relatively fixed).
  (b) Hip strategy: hip and lower trunk muscles maintain balance by shifting COM using hip motions (flexion or extension).
  (c) Stepping strategy: rapid steps are taken to realign COM within BOS.
 (5) Examine static balance: ability to maintain a position and response to perturbation.
  (a) Sitting: holding a steady position, arm support, no arm support.
  (b) Standing: double-limb and single-limb support.
  (c) Romberg test: patient stands with feet in normal stance position, first with eyes open, then with eyes closed; used to detect posterior column (sensory) ataxia.
  (d) Sharpened or tandem Romberg: patient stands in a tandem heel-to-toe position, first with eyes open, then eyes closed; increases sensitivity of Romberg test.
 (6) Examine dynamic balance: response to dynamic movement challenges.
  (a) Functional movement tasks: standing up and sitting down, walking, turning.
  (b) Navigation through obstacle course.
  (c) Dual-tasking: Walks While Talking test, walk and carry items, walk and complete cognitive task (count backwards by 3s from 100).
  (d) BOS challenges: sits on Swiss ball, wobble board, or dyna disc; stands on balance/wobble board, dense foam, and foam rollers.
 (7) See Table 2-9 for functional balance grades.

e. Selected Neuromuscular Outcome Measures are presented in Appendix 2A.

f. See Table 2-10 for selected functional balance and locomotion tests.

10. Examine gait and locomotion (see also Chapter 11).
 a. Gait is the manner in which a person walks, characterized by rhythm, cadence, step, stride, and speed (Guide to Physical Therapist Practice).
  (1) Kinematic gait analysis: analyzes gait characteristics and deviations.
 b. Locomotion is the ability to move from one place to another (Guide to Physical Therapist Practice). (Table 2-10.)
  (1) Timed walking test: patient is asked to walk first at preferred speed and then at maximal speed over a set distance; e.g., 10-m or 50-foot walk test. Velocity, cadence (steps/min), and stride length are calculated.
  (2) 6-Minute Walk Test (6MWT): test examines ability to walk at self-selected speed for a set time interval (also 12MWT or 2MWT). Total distance walked is measured and overall exercise tolerance is determined.

Table 2-9

Functional Balance Grades	
Normal	Patient is able to maintain steady balance without hand-hold support (static). Patient accepts maximal challenge and can shift weight easily at full range in all directions (dynamic).
Good	Patient is able to maintain balance without hand-hold support, limited postural sway (static). Patient accepts moderate challenge; able to maintain balance while picking object off floor (dynamic).
Fair	Patient is able to maintain balance with hand-hold support; may require occasional minimal assistance (static). Patient accepts minimal challenge; able to maintain balance while turning head/trunk (dynamic).
Poor	Patient requires hand-hold support and moderate to maximal assistance to maintain position (static). Patient unable to accept challenge or move without loss of balance (dynamic).
0 Absent	Patient unable to maintain balance.

From: O'Sullivan S, Schmitz T. Physical Rehabilitation, ed 6. Philadelphia, FA Davis, 2014, pg 233, with permission.

Table 2-10

Selected Functional Balance and Locomotion Tests

TEST	DESCRIPTION	SCORING
Performance-Oriented Mobility Assessment (POMA, Tinetti)	Examines balance (balance subtest, nine items including sitting, sit-to-stand, standing, standing feet together, turn 360°, sternal nudge, stand on one leg, tandem stand, reaching up, bending over, stand-to-sit, timed rising) and walking (gait subtest, eight items including gait initiation, path, turning timed walk, step over obstacles)	Maximum score is 28; patients who score < 19 are at high risk for falls; patients who score 19–24 are at moderate risk
Berg Balance Scale	Examines functional balance (14 items) including sitting unsupported, sit-to-stand, stand-to-sit, transfers; in standing: EO to EC, feet together, forward reach, pick object off floor, head turns, turning 360°, stepping up, tandem stand, stand on one leg	Uses ordinal scale with specific scoring criteria for each activity. Some items are timed. Maximum score is 56; patients who score < 45 are at high risk for falls; with scores 54–46, a 1-point drop is associated with a 6–8% increase in fall risk
Timed Up and Go (TUG)	Examines functional balance during rise from a chair, walk 3 m, turn, and return to chair. Performance on the TUG is timed	Normal intact adults can perform the test in ≤ 10 seconds; 11–20 seconds is considered normal for frail elderly or disabled patients; patients who take > 20 seconds are at increased risk for falls; patients who take > 30 seconds are at high risk
Functional Reach (FR)	Examines maximal distance a person can reach forward beyond arm's length while maintaining a fixed position in standing (single item test)	Forward reach norms: age — Men (inches) — Women (inches) 20–40 — 16.7 ± 1.9 — 14.6 ± 2.2 41–69 — 14.9 ± 2.2 — 13.8 ± 2.2 70–87 — 13.2 ± 1.6 — 10.5 ± 3.5 A score of 6 or less indicates a significant risk for falls; scores between 6–10 indicate a moderate risk for falls.
Multidirectional Reach Test (MDRT)	Examines maximal distance a person can reach forward, backward, and lateral to right and left	Backward: above average > 7.6 inches, below average < 1.6 inches; lateral: above average > 9.4 inches, below average < 3.8 inches
Five Times Sit to Stand Test	Examines sit-to-stand-to-sit transitions five times with arms crossed on chest	Test is timed using a stopwatch
Activities-Specific Balance Confidence (ABC) Scale	Examines level of confidence using percentage points; activities rated include 16 daily activities, e.g., reaching, walking (in house, outside, ramps, stairs), stepping on escalator	0–100% scoring scale with 0 being no confidence and 100% being full confidence
The Balance Evaluation Systems Test (BESTest)	A comprehensive instrument with six sections. Examines biomechanical constraints, stability limits/verticality, transitions/anticipatory, reactive, sensory integration; includes assessment of posture, gait, transfers, and balance/falls	Specific scoring criteria for each section. Uses ordinal scale, timed items, and observation
The Mini-BESTest Items are scored . . .	A shorter version of the test with 14 items	Items are scored from 0–2 with a maximum score of 28
High-Level Mobility Assessment Tool (Hi-MAT)	Examines high-level balance and mobility problems. Minimal requirement for testing is independent walking for 20 m without gait aids. Includes walking tasks, running, skipping, hopping, bounding, and stairs	Items are scored using time or distance on a 0–5 scale. Total Hi-MAT score is 54
Short Physical Performance Battery (SPPB)	Includes repeated chair stands (sit-to-stand rises), semi-tandem, tandem, and side-by-side stands as well as a timed 8 ft (2.44 meter) walk	Tests are scored in terms of time to complete: Five sit-to-stands, 10 sec in each of the standing conditions and 8 ft walk An ordinal score is given for each section. Summary ordinal score: 0 (worst performance) to 12 (best performance).
Balance Efficacy Scale (BES)	Examines level of self-confidence when performing functional tasks encountered in daily life; 18 questions are scored from 0–100% confidence; activities include getting out of chair, walking up and down flight of 10 stairs, getting out of bed, getting into and out of tub or shower, removing items from cupboard, walking on uneven ground, standing on one leg	Total score is divided by 18 to yield mean BES score; scores < 50 indicate low confidence
Dynamic Gait Index (DGI)	Examines dynamic gait (eight items) including changes in gait speed, head turns, pivot turns, obstacles, and stairs	Uses a 4-point ordinal scale; total score is 24. Scores of 22/24 indicate safe ambulation while scores <19/24 are predictive of falls in the elderly.

(*Continued*)

Table 2-10

Selected Functional Balance and Locomotion Tests (Continued)

TEST	DESCRIPTION	SCORING
Walkie-Talkie Test (Stops Walking When Talking, SWWT)	Test examines ability to talk while walking, a measure of dual task control	Test is positive if the person must stop walking in order to respond to a question
Functional Gait Assessment (FGA)	A 10-item gait assessment is based on the Dynamic Gait Index. It includes additional items on walking (ambulating backward, with narrow base of support, with eyes closed)	Items are scaled using an ordinal scale; total possible score is 30
Modified Emory Functional Ambulation Profile Scale (mEFAP)	A timed measure of walking using five environmental challenges (floor, carpet, up and go, obstacles, stairs)	Recorded time is multiplied by a factor related to use of assistive device: no assistance = × 1; AFO = × 2; single point cane = × 3; hemiwalker or quad cane = × 4; AFO + singlepoint cane = × 5; AFO + hemiwalker (or quad cane) = × 6

Review Medical Record for Diagnostic Procedures and Results

1. Radiological procedures. Skull x-rays.
   a. Delineates lesions of bone.
   b. Tomograms (tomography) are layered x-ray exposures, either vertical or horizontal.
2. Ventriculography. X-rays of skull after injection of air into lateral ventricles.
   a. Delineates ventricles, helps localize tumors.
   b. Useful with increased intracranial pressures.
3. Myelography. X-rays of spine after injection of air or dye into spinal subarachnoid space.
   a. Delineates abnormalities impinging on subarachnoid space.
   b. Complications: dye may result in meningeal irritation.
4. Cerebral angiography. X-rays of skull after injection of dye into carotid or vertebral arteries or both.
   a. Has largely been replaced by magnetic resonance angiography (see description below).
   b. Complications: invasive technique; may cause meningeal irritation, hemorrhage, vasospasm, or anaphylactic reaction to dye.
5. Computed tomography (CT). Neuroimaging technique in which narrow x-ray beams are transmitted through tissues of varying densities and precisely measured; allows cross-sections (slices) of the brain to be visualized with three-dimensional localization.
   a. Contrast agents (intravenous iodinated agents) can be used to increase diagnostic sensitivity, to detect brain abnormalities (e.g., tumor, calcifications).
   b. Useful for showing presence of abnormal changes in tissue density: areas of acute bleeding (hemorrhage in developing stroke), cerebral edema (within 3 days post stroke), and cerebral infarction (within 3–5 days' post stroke).

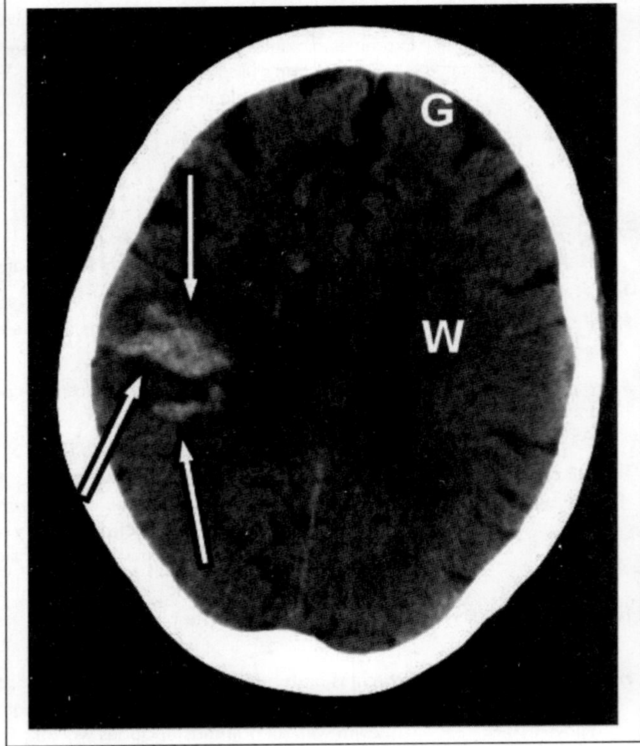

Figure 2-8 Axial CT of hemorrhagic stroke. The blood is white, with slightly darker than normal areas surrounding this, due to local brain swelling (edema). G = normal brain gray matter; W = normal brain white matter (darker on CT scans than gray matter).
From: www.radiologyinfo.org

   c. Diagnostic in acute stroke: allows administration of TPA (clot busting drug) in absence of evidence of hemorrhage within 3 hours of thromboembolic stroke.
   d. See images of CT scans in Figures 2-8 and 2-9.

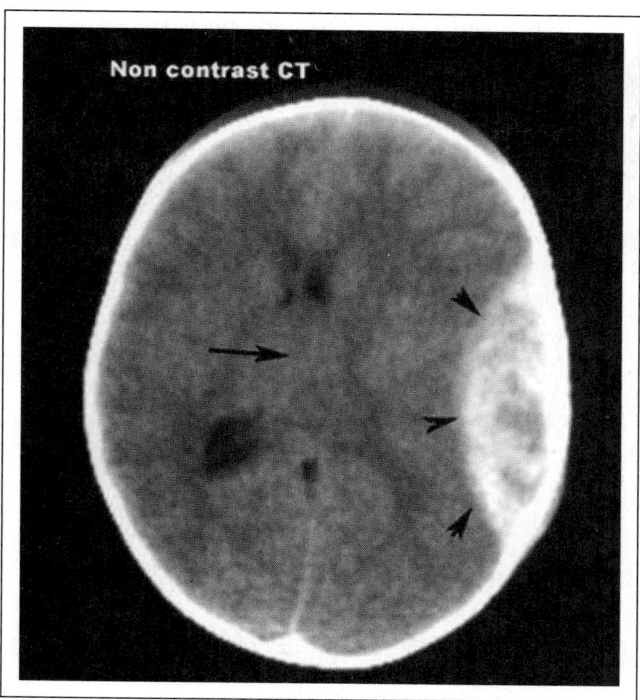

Figure 2-9 Axial CT of epidural hematoma.
Arrowheads point to the collection of blood between the skull and dura. The arrow demonstrates a shift of midline to the right.
From: www.meddean.luc.edu

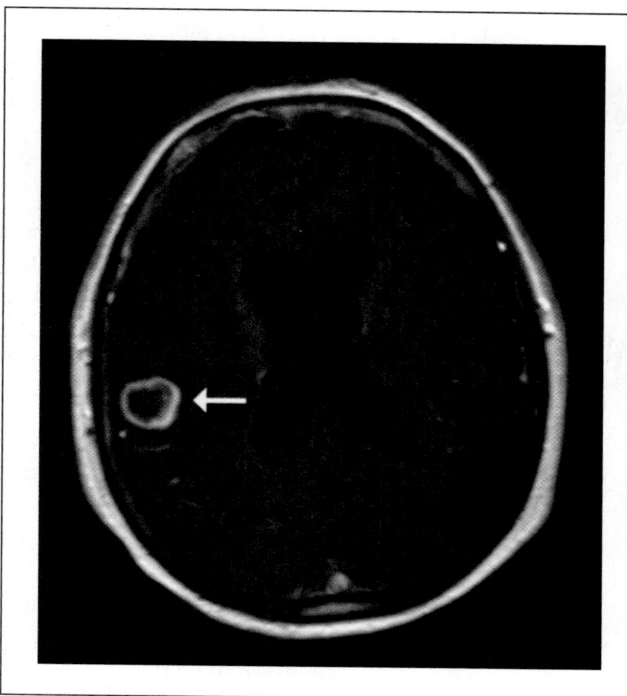

Figure 2-10 Brain metastasis.
A cross-section through a patient's brain after administration of intravenous contrast shows the contrast accumulating in the periphery of a cancerous deposit that has traveled to the brain, giving a characteristic ring-enhancing appearance.

6. Magnetic resonance imaging (MRI). Neuroimaging technique in which nuclear particles (protons and neutrons) are depicted in a strong external magnetic field; no radiation is used.
   a. Useful for superior imaging of brain, providing greater resolution of tissues and flow of blood within medium and larger arteries and veins; bone is poorly imaged.
   b. Allows three-dimensional localization with high spatial resolution.
   c. More sensitive in diagnosis of acute stroke: allows detection of cerebral edema within 30 minutes after vascular occlusion and infarction within 2 to 6 hours.
   d. Primary method of examination of tumors, demyelination, and vascular abnormalities.
   e. Magnetic resonance angiography (MRA) uses special software to create an image of the arteries in the brain; identifies vascular abnormalities similar to angiography (x-ray of the brain) with increased sensitivity and lowered risks.
   f. Contraindications: metal implants, pacemakers.
   g. See MRI brain image in Figure 2-10.
7. Positron emission tomography (PET). Neuroimaging technique in which radioisotopes are inhaled or injected and emissions are measured with a gamma-ray detector system.
   a. Allows physiological mapping; a major clinical research tool for imaging cerebral blood flow, brain metabolism.
   b. Lacks detailed resolution of CT or MRI.
8. Electroencephalography (EEG). Ongoing electrical activity of brain is recorded, appearing as periodic waves.
   a. Provides useful information about structural disease of the brain, especially when seizures are present or likely.
   b. Can assist in localization of intracranial lesions in the brain.
9. Evoked potentials/evoked responses. External visual, auditory or somatosensory stimuli are used to evoke potentials in brain; visual evoked potential (VEP), brainstem auditory evoked potential (BAEP), somatosensory evoked potential (SEP).
   a. Potentials are recorded from surface electrodes and processed by computer.

b. Delineates conduction times along these sensory pathways.
c. Detects lesions if responses are delayed or absent.

10. Echoencephalogram (ultrasound/Doppler techniques). Reflected ultrasonic waves are recorded and analyzed.
    a. Useful for imaging lumen of carotid artery and analyzing flow, detection of plaques in carotid arteries.
    b. Measures position and shifts of midline structures (e.g., tumors or hematomas).
11. Lumbar puncture (LP). Insertion of spinal needle below level of L1–2.
    a. Purposes.
        (1) Withdraw CSF for chemical analysis and cytological examination: measurement of protein, glucose, immunoglobulin content, cell count.
        (2) Measure intracranial pressures and spinal fluid dynamics.
        (3) Injection of contrast medium for radiological examination.
        (4) Injection of therapeutic agents (e.g., treatment of cancer, meningitis).
    b. Complications: severe headache caused by CSF leakage (relieved by lying down); more severe complications include infection, epidural hematoma, uncal herniation.
    c. Normal CSF.
        (1) Appearance: crystal clear and colorless.
        (2) Volume: 90–150 mL (adult); 60–100 mL (child).
        (3) Pressure: 90–180 mm H_2O (adult); 10–100 mm H_2O (child).
        (3) Normal protein: 15–45 mg/dL (adults); 15–100 mg/dL (neonates).
        (4) Elevated proteins may indicate tumors or inflammation.
    d. Pathological CSF findings.
        (1) Increased pressure occurs with intracranial tumors, abscesses, meningitis, inflammatory processes, subarachnoid hemorrhage, cerebral edema, and thrombosis of venous sinuses.
        (2) Decreased pressure occurs with leaking CSF, subarachnoid block circulatory collapse, severe dehydration.
        (3) Changes in color or appearance occur with inflammatory diseases, hemorrhage, tumors. Red blood cells (RBCs) indicate hemorrhage or traumatic tap; elevated white blood cells (WBCs) indicate significant inflammation and infection.
12. Neuromuscular diagnostic procedures.
    a. Electromyography (EMG): detects electrical activity arising from muscles, both resting state and active contraction.
        (1) Useful in diagnosing LMN disease or primary muscle disease, defects in transmission at neuromuscular junction.
        (2) Insertional activity (burst of action potentials when EMG needle is inserted into normal muscle) is increased in denervated muscle and many muscle diseases.
        (3) Number of motor unit potentials (MUPs) is decreased in LMN injury (denervated muscles); overall configurations remain normal.
        (4) Alterations in MUP configurations (increased in size and duration, polyphasic shape) occur with reinnervation of previously denervated muscles.
        (5) Spontaneous, ongoing EMG activity.
            (a) Fibrillation (spontaneous independent contractions of individual muscle fibers) evident with denervation for 1–3 weeks after losing nerve.
            (b) Fasciculations (spontaneous contractions of all or most of the fibers in a motor unit; muscle twitches that can be observed or palpated) are present with LMN disorders and denervation.
            (c) Complete LMN lesions show only fibrillation potentials; partial LMN lesions show fibrillation and fasciculation potentials.
    b. Nerve conduction velocity (NCV): conduction velocities are obtained by stimulating peripheral nerves through the skin and recording muscle and sensory nerve action potentials.
        (1) Distance between two points (conduction distance) is divided by the difference between the corresponding latencies (conduction time), expressed as meters/second (m/s).
        (2) Decreased conduction velocities are seen in peripheral neuropathies characterized by demyelination (e.g., Guillain-Barré syndrome, chronic demyelinating polyneuropathy, Charcot-Marie-Tooth disease).
        (3) Slowed conduction velocities seen with focal compression of peripheral nerve.

Neurological Dysfunction

Table 2-11

Neuromuscular Practice Patterns	
Pattern 5A	Primary Prevention/Risk Reduction for Loss of Balance and Falling
Pattern 5B	Impaired Neuromotor Development
Pattern 5C	Impaired Motor Function and Sensory Integrity Associated with Nonprogressive Disorders of the Central Nervous System—Congenital Origin or Acquired in Infancy or Childhood
Pattern 5D	Impaired Motor Function and Sensory Integrity Associated with Nonprogressive Disorders of the Central Nervous System—Acquired in Adolescence or Adulthood
Pattern 5E	Impaired Motor Function and Sensory Integrity Associated with Progressive Disorders of the Central Nervous System
Pattern 5F	Impaired Peripheral Nerve Integrity and Muscle Performance Associated with Peripheral Nerve Injury
Pattern 5G	Impaired Motor Function and Sensory Integrity Associated with Acute or Chronic Polyneuropathies
Pattern 5H	Impaired Motor Function, Peripheral Nerve Integrity, and Sensory Integrity Associated with Nonprogressive Disorders of the Spinal Cord
Pattern 5I	Impaired Arousal, Range of Motion, and Motor Control Associated with Coma, Near Coma, or Vegetative State

From APTA Guide to Physical Therapist Practice, Version 3.0. American Physical Therapy Association, Alexandria VA, 2014.
Note: On the APTA website, each practice pattern includes:

- Inclusion critera: risk factors or consequences of pathology/pathophysiology; impairments of body functions and structures, activity limitations, or participation restrictions
- Exclusion or Multiple-Pattern Classification
- Examination: relevant tests and measures
- Evaluation, Diagnosis, and Prognosis (including Plan of Care) factors
- Intervention categories

Infectious Diseases

1. Examine for signs of CNS infection, meningeal irritation.
2. Examine for signs of increased intracranial pressure.
3. Meningitis. Inflammation of the membranes of the spinal cord or brain.
   a. Etiology: can be bacterial (*Escherichia coli, Haemophilus influenzae, Streptococcus pneumoniae,* other streptococci) or viral; patients with bacterial meningitis are usually sicker with more rapid time course.
   b. Treat infective organism (bacterial meningitis) with antibacterial therapy (antibiotic, antipyretic); maintain fluid and electrolyte balance.
   c. Provide supportive symptomatic therapy, including bed positioning, PROM, skin care to prevent complications of immobility; safety measures if confusion is present.
4. Encephalitis. Severe infection and inflammation of the brain.
   a. Etiology: arboviruses, or a sequela in influenza (Reye's syndrome, eastern equine encephalitis, measles), chronic and recurrent sinusitis, otitis, or other infections; bacterial encephalitis, prion-caused disease (kuru, "mad cow" disease).
   b. Treat infective organism (bacterial encephalitis).
   c. Provide supportive symptomatic therapy.
5. Brain abscess. Infectious process in which there is a collection of pyogenic material in the brain parenchyma.
   a. Signs and symptoms: headaches, fever, brainstem compression, focal signs CN II and VI.
   b. Can be an extension of an infection (e.g., meningitis, otitis media, sinusitis, post-TBI); typically frontal or temporal lobes or cerebellum.
   c. Treat infective organism, surgical intervention.
   d. Provide supportive symptomatic therapy.
6. Acquired immunodeficiency syndrome (AIDS).
   a. Viral syndrome characterized by acquired and severe depression of cell-mediated immunity.
   b. Symptoms: wide ranging; one-third of patients exhibit CNS or PNS deficits.
      (1) AIDS dementia complex (ADC): symptoms range from confusion and memory loss to disorientation.
      (2) Motor deficits: ataxia, weakness, tremor, loss of fine motor coordination.
      (3) Peripheral neuropathy: hypersensitivity, pain, sensory loss.
   c. Treat with anti-HIV drugs (see Chapter 6).
   d. Provide palliative and supportive therapy.

Cerebrovascular Accident (CVA, Stroke)

1. Sudden, focal neurological deficit resulting from ischemic or hemorrhagic lesions in the brain (see Table 2-12).
2. Etiological categories.
   a. Cerebral thrombosis: formation or development of a blood clot or thrombus within the cerebral arteries or their branches.
   b. Cerebral embolism: traveling bits of matter (thrombi, tissue, fat, air, bacteria) that produce occlusion and infarction in the cerebral arteries.
   c. Cerebral hemorrhage: abnormal bleeding as a result of rupture of a blood vessel (extradural, subdural, subarachnoid, intracerebral).
3. Risk factors.
   a. Atherosclerosis.
   b. Hypertension.
   c. Cardiac disease (rheumatic valvular disease, endocarditis, arrhythmias, cardiac surgery).
   d. Diabetes, metabolic syndrome.
   e. Transient ischemic attacks: brief warning episodes of dysfunction (< 24 hours); a precursor of major stroke in more than one-third of patients.
4. Pathophysiology.
   a. Cerebral anoxia: lack of oxygen supply to the brain (irreversible anoxic damage to the brain begins after 4–6 minutes).
   b. Cerebral infarction: irreversible cellular damage.
   c. Cerebral edema: accumulation of fluids within brain; causes further dysfunction; elevates intracranial pressures, can result in herniation and death.
5. Neurovascular clinical syndromes. Characteristic signs and symptoms associated with occlusion of specific cerebral vessels. See Table 2-12.
   a. Internal carotid artery (ICA) syndrome: ICA arises off the common carotid artery, gives off an ophthalmic branch and terminates in the anterior cerebral artery (ACA) and middle cerebral artery (MCA); occlusions commonly produce signs and symptoms of MCA involvement with reduced levels of consciousness; ACA may also be affected; lesions involving MCA and ACA distributions may produce massive edema, brain herniation, and death.
      (1) ACA syndrome: ACA supplies anterior two-thirds of the medial cerebral cortex. Occlusions proximal to anterior communicating artery produce minimal deficits due to collateral circulation (circle of Willis).
      (2) MCA syndrome: MCA supplies lateral cerebral cortex, basal ganglia, and large portions of the internal capsule.
   b. Vertebrobasilar artery syndrome: two vertebral arteries arise off the subclavian arteries and supply the ventral surface of the medulla and the posterior inferior aspect of the cerebellum before joining to form the basilar artery at the junction of the pons and the medulla; the basilar artery supplies the ventral portion of the pons and terminates in the posterior cerebral artery (PCA). Syndromes include:
      (1) Medial medullary syndrome: occlusion of the vertebral anterior branch of the lower basilar artery.
      (2) Lateral medullary (Wallenberg's) syndrome: occlusion of vertebral, posterior inferior cerebellar, or basilar artery.
      (3) Basilar artery syndrome: produces brainstem signs and symptoms and PCA signs and symptoms; locked-in syndrome (basilar artery occlusion at the level of the pons).
      (4) Medial inferior pontine syndrome: occlusion of the paramedian branch of basilar artery.
      (5) Lateral inferior pontine syndrome: occlusion of the anterior inferior cerebellar artery.
      (6) PCA syndrome: PCA and posterior communicating arteries supply the midbrain, temporal lobe, diencephalon, and posterior third of cortex; occlusions proximal to posterior communicating artery produce minimal deficits owing to collateral circulation.
6. Sequential recovery stages.
   a. Stage 1: initial flaccidity, no voluntary movement.
   b. Stage 2: emergence of spasticity, hyperreflexia, synergies (mass patterns of movement).
   c. Stage 3: voluntary movement possible, but only in synergies; spasticity strong.
   d. Stage 4: voluntary control in isolated joint movements emerging, corresponding decline of spasticity and synergies.
   e. Stage 5: increasing voluntary control out of synergy; coordination deficits present.
   f. Stage 6: control and coordination near normal.
7. Examine.
   a. Generalized signs of increased intracranial pressure.
   b. Level of consciousness, cognitive function.
   c. Speech and communication.
      (1) Examine for aphasia with lesions of parieto-occipital cortex of dominant hemisphere (typically left hemisphere).
      (2) Examine for perceptual deficits with lesions of parietal lobe of nondominant hemisphere (typically right hemisphere).
   d. Behaviors.
      (1) Patients with lesions of the left hemisphere (right hemiplegia) are typically slow, cautious, hesitant, and insecure.

Table 2-12

Neurovascular Syndromes: Stroke

LESION LOCATION	CHARACTERISTICS	OTHER LOCALIZING FEATURES (NOT ALWAYS PRESENT)
Hemisphere lesion: cortex and internal capsule CONTRALATERAL HEMISPHERE LESION CONTRALATERAL INTERNAL CAOSYKE LESION	Contralateral hemiplegia face, UE, LE Contralateral hemisensory loss Homonymous hemianopsia *MCA syndrome:* LE more spared *ACA syndrome:* UE more spared	Impairment of consciousness Motor speech involvement—nonfluent aphasia (dominant hemisphere) Perceptual deficit (nondominant hemisphere) Loss of conjugate gaze to the opposite side Sensory ataxia Apraxia Akinetic mutism
Hemisphere lesion: primary visual cortex, occipital lobe Occipital Lobe	*PCA syndrome:* Contralateral sensory loss Involuntary movements—choreoathetosis, tremor, hemiballismus Transient contralateral hemiparesis Homonymous hemianopsia	Visual agnosia Memory defect Dyslexia Central (thalamic) pain Weber's syndrome Oculomotor n. palsy
Internal capsule lesion-posterior limb	*Lacunar (pure motor)* stroke Contralateral hemiplegia UE and LE	No aphasia Visual field deficit rare
Midbrain lesion CONTRALATERAL MINDBRAIN LESION	Contralateral hemiplegia	Contralateral CN III palsy
Pontine lesion CONTRALATERAL PONTINE LESION	*Medial inferior pontine syndrome:* Ipsilateral to lesion: Cerebellar ataxia, nystagmus Paralysis of conjugate gaze to side of lesion Diplopia Contralateral to lesion: Hemiparesis UE, LE Impaired sensation *Lateral inferior pontine syndrome:* Ipsilateral to lesion: Cerebellar: ataxia, nystagmus, vertigo Facial paralysis Paralysis of conjugate gaze to the side of the lesion Deafness, tinnitus Impaired facial sensation Contralateral to lesion: Impaired pain and temperature sensation half of body *Locked-in syndrome:* Tetraplegia Lower bulbar paralysis (CN V–XII) Mutism (anarthria) Preserved consciousness Preserved vertical eye movements and blinking	

(*Continued*)

Table 2-12

Neurovascular Syndromes: Stroke (Continued)

LESION LOCATION	CHARACTERISTICS	OTHER LOCALIZING FEATURES (NOT ALWAYS PRESENT)
Medullary lesion CONTRALATERAL MEDULLARY LESION	*Medial medullary syndrome:* Ipsilateral to lesion: paralysis of half of tongue Contralateral to lesion: Hemiplegia UE and LE Impaired sensation *Lateral medullary (Wallenberg's) syndrome:* Ipsilateral to lesion: Cerebellar symptoms (ataxia, vertigo, nystagmus) Loss of pain and temperature to face Sensory loss UE, trunk, or LE Contralateral to lesion: Loss of pain and temperature to body and face	 Horner's syndrome (miosis, ptosis, decreased sweating) Dysphagia Impaired speech

ACA = anterior cerebral artery; CN = cranial nerve; LE = lower extremity; MCA = middle cerebral artery; PCA = posterior cerebral artery; UE = upper extremity

(2) Patients with lesions of the right hemisphere (left hemiplegia) are typically impulsive, quick, indifferent; often exhibit poor judgment and safety, overestimating their abilities while underestimating their problems.

e. Sensory deficits.
  (1) Superficial, proprioceptive and combined sensations of contralateral extremities, trunk, and face.
  (2) Hearing, vision; examine for homonymous hemianopsia.
  (3) Cranial nerve function with brainstem, vertebrobasilar strokes (pseudobulbar palsy).

f. Motor function.
  (1) Presence of abnormal tone and primitive reflexes.
  (2) Spasticity (see Table 2-6).
  (3) Loss of selective movements, presence of abnormal limb synergies (see Table 2-8).
    (a) Upper extremity flexion synergy.
    (b) Upper extremity extension synergy.
    (c) Lower extremity flexion synergy.
    (d) Lower extremity extension synergy.
  (4) Presence of paresis, incoordination, motor programming deficits (apraxia).
  (5) Postural and balance deficits.
  (6) Gait: typical deficits.
    (a) Hip: poor hip position (retracted, flexed); Trendelenburg limp (weak abductors); scissoring (spastic adductors); insufficient pelvic rotation during swing.
    (b) Weak hip flexors during swing may yield circumducted gait, external rotation with adduction, backward leaning of trunk or exaggerated flexion synergy.
    (c) Knee: weak knee extensors (knee flexes during stance) may result in compensatory locking of knee in hyperextension; spastic quadriceps may also yield a hyperextended knee.
    (d) Ankle: footdrop; equinus gait (heel does not touch down); varus foot (weight is borne on lateral side of foot); or equinovarus position.
    (e) Unequal step lengths: leg does not advance through the end of stance into toe-off.
    (f) Decreased cadence, uneven timing.

g. Function: functional mobility skills (FMS), activities of daily living (ADLs).

h. Standardized tests and measures for examination of patients with stroke (see also Appendix 2A).
  (1) Fugl-Meyer Assessment of Physical Performance (FMA): provides objective criteria for scoring of movements (0, cannot perform, to 2, fully performed). Includes subtests for upper extremity function, lower extremity function, balance, sensation, ROM, and pain.
  (2) Motor Activity Log (MAL): Includes 30 items of ADL function using the more-affected arm. Performance is assessed using two scales: the Amount of Use scale and the How Well scale. Items are rated on a 0–5 ordinal scale for each.
  (3) National Institute of Stroke (NIH) Stroke Scale examines level of consciousness, visual function, facial palsy, motor arm, motor leg, limb ataxia, sensory function, best language, dysarthria, extinction, and inattention. Uses ordinal scales with specific criteria for each section.

(4) Postural Assessment Scale for Stroke Patients (PASS) provides a standardized assessment of postural control and balance in patients recovering from stroke.
(5) Stroke Impact Scale provides a brief assessment of physical and social functioning after stroke.
(6) Functional Independence Measure (FIM) is a widely used instrument that provides measurement of 18 items of physical (functional mobility and basic ADL), psychological, and social functioning (Guide for the Uniform Data Set for Medical Rehabilitation [Adult FIM] version 4.0.
(7) Functional Assessment Measure (FAM). In addition to FIM items, the FAM includes additional functional areas including community access, instrumental ADL, safety, employability, and adjustment.
(8) Stroke Impact Scale evaluates how stroke has impacted health and life. Patients respond to questions about physical problems, memory and thinking, changes in mood and emotions, communication abilities, typical daily activities at home and in the community, and participation in normal and meaningful activities.

8. Physical therapy goals, outcomes, and interventions.
   a. Monitor changes associated with recovery and inactivity.
      (1) Prevent or minimize indirect impairments/secondary complications.
         (a) Maintain ROM and prevent deformity through optimal positioning, PROM, and mobilization.
         (b) Maintain skin integrity.
         (c) Avoid traction injuries to arm, development of painful shoulder. Overhead pulleys are contraindicated for patients with poor shoulder alignment and decreased function.
         (d) Overhead pulleys are contraindicated in patients after stroke who do not have appropriate shoulder girdle alignment and function.
      (2) Teach sensory compensation strategies for sensory and perceptual losses.
      (3) Strengthen all available muscles.
   b. Promote awareness, active movement, and use of hemiplegic side (remediation-facilitation approach).
      (1) Promote normalization of tone through activities.
      (2) Promote selective movement control (out-of-synergy movements) of involved extremities; emphasize functional patterns of movement.
   c. Improve postural control, symmetry, and balance.
   d. Task-specific training.
      (1) Promote active problem-solving independence.
      (2) Focus on goal-directed tasks, functional mobility skills (e.g., rolling, supine-to-sit, sitting, sit-to-stand, transfers, wheelchair skills, and locomotion).
      (3) Focus on adapting movements to specific environmental demands.
      (4) Organize feedback inputs (knowledge of results, knowledge of performance) and practice schedules to facilitate learning.
   e. Promote independence in ADL/self-care; compensatory training as appropriate.
   f. Improve respiratory and oromotor function; promote functional cardiorespiratory endurance.
      (1) Improve chest expansion, diaphragmatic breathing pattern.
      (2) Oromotor training.
      (3) Aerobic conditioning: cycle ergometry, treadmill, or overground walking.
      (4) Monitor heart and blood pressure during exercise and progressive physical activity.
   g. Isokinetic training: useful to improve timing deficits, velocity control of movement.
   h. Locomotor training using body weight-support (BWS) and motorized treadmill training (TT).
   i. EMG—biofeedback training: useful to decrease firing in spastic muscles, increase firing in paretic muscles, and improve motor control.
   j. Functional electrical stimulation (FES): useful to stimulate muscle action, reduce spasticity, and substitute for an orthosis.
   k. Constraint-induced movement therapy (CIMT) for patients with stroke. Patients must meet minimal movement criteria of wrist and finger movement.

9. Guidelines to promote learning with hemispheric differences.
   a. Patients with left hemisphere lesions (right hemiplegia).
      (1) Develop an appropriate communication base: words, gestures, pantomime; assess level of understanding.
      (2) Give frequent feedback and support.
      (3) Do not underestimate ability to learn.
   b. Patients with right hemisphere lesions (left hemiplegia).
      (1) Use verbal cues; demonstrations or gestures may confuse patients with visuospatial deficits.
      (2) Give frequent feedback: focus on slowing down and controlling movement.
      (3) Focus on safety (patient may be impulsive).
      (4) Avoid environmental (spatial) clutter.
      (5) Do not overestimate ability to learn.

Table 2-13

Signs Associated with Localized Lesions of the Cortex

LOBE	STRUCTURE	FUNCTION	DESTRUCTIVE LESION
Frontal	**Precentral area:** Primary motor cortex	Discrete volitional movements	Contralateral paralysis and paresis (most pronounced in distal parts of limbs and lower part of face)
	Premotor area	Motor planning or praxis	Apraxia or motor planning difficulties
	Prefrontal area	Motor association area	Lost of specific motor plans
	Supplementary motor	Bilateral control of posture	Loss of bilateral control of posture
	Middle frontal gyrus	Conjugate eye movements	Transitory paralysis of conjugate eye movements to opposite side
	Motor speech area (Broca)	Language production	Nonfluent aphasia
	Prefrontal area: Dorsolateral	Motivation, problem solving	Bilateral lesions: Impaired ability to concentrate
	Orbitofrontal	Emotions, behavior	Unstable emotions; unpredictable behaviors
	Orbital Gyri (posterolateral)	Olfaction	Inability to discriminate odors
Parietal	Postcentral gyrus/Primary somatosensory area	Somesthetic sensations	Loss of contralateral stimulus location, intensity
	Secondary somatosensory area	Sensory interpretation	Tactile agnosia: astereognosis, agraphesthesia, loss of two-point discrimination, extinction
	Gustatory cortex	Taste	Impairment of taste in contralateral side of tongue
	Parietal lobe (right hemisphere)	Perceptual function	Visual-spatial disorders, body scheme disorders, apraxias, tactile and auditory perceptual disorders
Temporal	Primary auditory cortex	Hearing	Subtle decrease in hearing and ability to localize sounds, both contralaterally
	Wernicke's speech area	Language understanding and formulation; storage of auditorially presented information	Fluent aphasia
	Superior temporal Gyrus (left hemisphere)		Impairment of learning and memory
	Temporal Cortex (nondominant side)	Storage of visually presented information	Profound memory loss of recent events, no new learning
	Parahippocampal region	Recent memory	
Occipital	Primary visual cortex	Vision	Contralateral homonymous hemianopsia Impairment of vision
	Visual association cortex	Visual understanding	Visual agnosia
	Posterior multimodal area (parietal, occipital, temporal lobes)	Integrates sensory information (somatosensory, visual, auditory)	Perceptual impairment

Trauma

1. Traumatic brain injury (TBI).
   a. Etiology: mechanism of injury is contact forces to skull and rotational acceleration forces, causing varying degrees of injury to the brain.
   b. Localized lesions of the cortex (see Table 2-13).
   c. Pathophysiology.
      (1) Primary brain damage.
         (a) Diffuse axonal injury: disruption and tearing of axons and small blood vessels from shear-strain of angular acceleration; results in neuronal death and petechial hemorrhages.
         (b) Focal injury: contusions, lacerations, mass effect from hemorrhage, and edema (hematoma).
         (c) Coup-contracoup injury: injury at point of impact and opposite point of impact.
         (d) Closed or open injury (with fracture of the skull).
      (2) Secondary brain damage.
         (a) Hypoxic-ischemic injury: results from systemic problems (respiratory or cardiovascular) that compromise cerebral circulation.
         (b) Swelling/edema: can result in mass effect, with increased intracranial pressures, brain herniation (uncal, central, or tonsillar), and death.

Table 2-14

Levels of Traumatic Brain Injury (TBI)			
	MILD TBI	MODERATE TBI	SEVERE TBI
Loss of Consciousness	0–30 minutes	> 30 minutes but < 24 hours	> 24 hours
Alteration of Consciousness	brief; > 24 hrs	> 24 hours	> 24 hours
Posttraumatic Amnesia	< 1 day	> 1 but < 7 days	> 7 days
Glasgow Coma Scale	13–15	9–12	< 9
Imaging	normal	normal or abnormal	normal or abnormal

(c) Electrolyte imbalance and mass release of damaging neurotransmitters.

(3) Concussion: loss of consciousness, either temporary or permanent, resulting from injury or blow to head, with impaired functioning of the brainstem reticular activating system (RAS); may see changes in HR, RR, BP.

d. Levels of traumatic brain injury (see Table 2-14).

e. Standardized tests/outcome measures for patients with traumatic brain injury. (see also Appendix 2A.)

(1) Glasgow Coma Scale (GCS): examines eye, verbal, and motor responses; allows classification into mild (score 13–15), moderate (score 9–12), or severe (score < 8) head injury (coma).

(2) Rancho Los Amigos Levels of Cognitive Functioning (LOCF): delineates eight general cognitive and behavioral levels.

(3) Rappaport's Disability Rating Scale (DRS): classifies levels of disability using a wide range of functional behaviors.

(4) Glasgow Outcome Scale (GOS): examines cognition, behavior regulation, home management, community function, work, and leisure/recreational activities.

(5) High-Level Mobility Assessment (Hi-MAT): see previous discussion.

(6) Functional Independence Measure/Functional Assessment Measure (FIM/FAM): see previous discussion.

(7) Neurological Outcome Scale for Traumatic Brain Injury (NOS-TBI): stratifies for injury severity and demonstrates progress of TBI interventions.

(8) Assessment of Life Habits (Life-H) examines participation in ADLs, health and wellness, community function, leisure/recreational activities, life satisfaction, quality of life, work, and social activities.

(9) Coma Recovery Scale—revised: examines cognition, somatosensation, and responsiveness to auditory, visual, motor, oromotor, communication, and arousal.

(10) Moss Attention Rating Scale: examines cognition and moderate to severe problems with attention.

f. Recovery stages from diffuse axonal injury.

(1) Coma: a state of unconsciousness in which there is neither arousal nor awareness; eyes remain closed, no sleep/wake cycles.

(2) Unresponsive vigilance/vegetative state: marked by the return of sleep/wake cycles and normalization of vegetative functions (respiration, digestion, BP control); persistent vegetative state is determined if patient remains in vegetative state > 1 year after TBI.

(3) Mute responsiveness/minimally responsive: state in which patient is not vegetative and does show signs, even if intermittent, of fluctuating awareness.

(4) Confusional state: mainly a disturbance of attention mechanisms; all cognitive operations are affected, patient is unable to form new memories; may demonstrate either hypoarousal or hyperarousal.

(5) Emerging independence: confusion is clearing and some memory is possible; significant cognitive problems and limited insight remain; frequently uninhibited social behaviors.

(6) Intellectual/social competence: increasing independence, although cognitive difficulties (problem solving, reasoning) persist along with behavioral and social problems (enhancement of premorbid traits, mood swings).

(7) Patient can plateau at any stage or regress under conditions of stress or repetitive brain injury.

g. Examine.

(1) For generalized signs of increased intracranial pressure.

(2) Level of consciousness (GCS), cognitive function (LOCF), examine for disorders of learning, attention, memory, and complex information processing.

(3) Cranial nerve function.
(4) For changes in behavior: examine for inappropriate physical, verbal, sexual behaviors; poor judgment; irritability, low frustration tolerance, and aggression; impulsivity and safety issues; depressed mood; restricted affect.
(5) Speech and communication.
(6) Sensory deficits.
(7) Motor function: examine for paresis, apraxia (dyspraxia), reflexive behaviors, balance deficits, ataxia, and incoordination (cerebellar damage is common).
(8) Functional mobility skills (FMS), ADLs.
(9) Level of general deconditioning; after prolonged hospitalization (comatose, vegetative, decreased response levels), patients experience severe deconditioning and effects of prolonged immobilization (disuse atrophy, contractures and deformity, skin breakdown).

h. Physical therapy goals, outcomes, and interventions.
(1) Monitor changes associated with recovery and inactivity.
(2) Management based on decreased response levels (LOCF I–III).
(a) Maintain ROM, prevent contracture development: PROM, positioning, splinting, and serial casting.
(b) Maintain skin integrity; prevent development of decubitus ulcers through frequent position changes.
(c) Maintain respiratory status, prevent complications: postural drainage, percussion, vibration, suctioning to keep airway clear.
(d) Provide appropriate stimulation for arousal and to elicit movement and function; structure environment to enhance alertness and function.
(e) Promote early return of FMS: upright positioning for improved arousal, proper body alignment.
(3) Management based on mid-level recovery (LOCF IV–VI).
(a) Provide structure, prevent overstimulation for confused, agitated patient: closed, reduced stimulus environment, daily schedules and memory logs; relaxation techniques.
(b) Provide consistency: use team-determined behavioral modification techniques, give clear feedback, written contracts.
(c) Engage the patient in task-specific training; limit activities to familiar, well-liked ones; offer options; break down complex tasks into component parts.
(d) Provide verbal or physical assistance.
(e) Control rate of instruction; provide frequent orientation to time, place, your name, and task.
(f) Emphasize safety, behavioral management techniques.
(g) Model calm, focused behavior.
(4) Management based on high-level recovery (LOCF VII–VIII).
(a) Allow for increasing independence: wean patient from structure (closed to open environments); involve patient in decision-making.
(b) Assist patient in behavioral, cognitive, emotional reintegration: provide honest feedback, prepare for community reentry.
(c) Enhance motor learning and promote independence in functional tasks: FMS, ADLs, in real-life environments.
(d) Improve postural control, symmetry, and balance.
(e) Encourage active lifestyle, improved cardiovascular endurance.
(5) Provide emotional support, encourage socialization, behavioral control, and motivation.
(a) Reorient and reassure.
(b) Provide patient and family education.

2. Spinal cord injury (SCI).

a. Etiology: partial or complete disruption of spinal cord resulting in paralysis, sensory loss, altered autonomic and reflex activities.
(1) Traumatic causes: motor vehicle accident (most common cause of SCI), jumps and falls, diving, gunshot wounds.
(2) Mechanisms of injury: flexion (most common lumbar injury), flexion-rotation (most common cervical injury), compression, hyperextension.
(3) Spinal areas of greatest frequency of injury: C5, C7, T12, and L1.
(4) Nontraumatic causes: disc prolapse, vascular insult, cancer, infection.

b. Pathophysiology.
(1) Primary injury, interruption of blood supply.
(2) Secondary sequelae: ischemia, edema, demyelination, and necrosis of axons, progressing to scar tissue formation.

c. Classification.
(1) Level of injury: UMN injury.
(a) Lesion level indicates most distal uninvolved nerve root segment with normal function; muscles must have a grade of at least 3+/5 or fair+ function.
(b) Tetraplegia (quadriplegia): injury occurs between C1 and C8, involves all four extremities and trunk.

(c) Paraplegia: injury occurs between T1 and T12–L1, involves both lower extremities and trunk (varying levels).

(2) Degree of injury.

(a) Complete: no sensory or motor function below level of lesion.

(b) Incomplete: preservation of sensory or motor function below level of injury; spotty sensation, some muscle function.

(c) American Spinal Injury Association (ASIA) Impairment Scale.

A = Complete, no motor or sensory function is preserved in the sacral segments S4–5.

B = Incomplete: sensory but not motor function is preserved below the neurological level and includes the sacral segments S4–5.

C = Incomplete: motor function is preserved below the neurological level, and most key muscles below the neurological level have a muscle grade of less than 3.

D = Incomplete: motor function is preserved below the neurological level, and most key muscles below the neurological level have a muscle grade of 3 or more.

E = Normal: motor and sensory function is normal.

(3) Clinical Syndromes (see Table 2-15).

(a) Central cord syndrome: loss of more centrally located cervical tracts/arm function, with preservation of more peripherally located lumbar and sacral tracts/leg function; typically caused by hyperextension injuries to the cervical spine.

(b) Brown-Séquard syndrome: hemisection of spinal cord typically caused by penetration wounds (gunshot or knife) with asymmetrical symptoms.

(c) Anterior cord syndrome: damage is mainly in anterior cord, resulting in loss of motor function, pain and temperature with preservation of light touch, proprioception and position sense, typically caused by flexion injuries of the cervical spine.

(d) Posterior cord syndrome: loss of posterior columns with preservation of motor function, sense of pain and light touch; extremely rare.

(e) Cauda equina: injury below L1 results in injury to lumbar and sacral roots of peripheral nerves (LMN) with sensory loss and paralysis and some capacity for regeneration; an LMN lesion with autonomous or nonreflex bladder.

(f) Sacral sparing: sparing of tracts to sacral segments, with preservation of perianal sensation, rectal sphincter tone, or active toe flexion.

d. Examine.

(1) Vital signs.

(2) Respiratory function: action of diaphragm, respiratory muscles, intercostals; chest expansion, breathing pattern, cough, vital capacity; respiratory insufficiency or failure occurs in lesions above C4 (phrenic nerve, C3–5 innervates diaphragm).

(3) Skin condition, integrity: check areas of high pressure.

(4) Muscle tone, spasms, and DTRs.

(5) Sensation/spinal cord level of injury: check to see if sensory level corresponds to motor level of innervation (may differ in incomplete lesions).

(6) Muscle strength (MMT)/spinal cord level of injury: lowest segmental level of innervation includes muscle strength present at a fair+ grade (3+/5); use caution when doing MMT in acute phase with spinal immobilization.

(7) Functional status: full functional assessment possible only when patient is cleared for activity and active rehabilitation.

e. Standardized tests/outcome measures for patients with spinal cord injury (see also Appendix 2A).

(1) FIM/FAM. See previous discussion.

(2) Manual Muscle Test (MMT) and hand held myometry.

(3) Numeric Pain Rating Scale.

(4) Multidimensional Pain Inventory, SCI version: measures pain severity and impact in patients with SCI and pain.

(5) Modified Ashworth Scale (MAS).

(6) Penn Spasm Frequency Scale (PSFS): measures frequency of spasms/spasticity.

(7) International Standards for Neurological Classification of Spinal Cord Injury, ASIA Impairment Scale (AIS): measures motor function/strength and somatosensation.

(8) Spinal Cord Injury Independence Measure (SCIM): measures ADL, bed mobility, gait, transfers, and wheelchair skills.

(9) Walking Index for Spinal Cord Injury II (WISCI II): measures walking function in SCI patients with higher level walking ability.

(10) Wheelchair Skills Test (WST): measures upper extremity function and wheelchair mobility/skills.

(11) Craig Handicap Reporting and Assessment Technique (Chart): measures disability, community reintegration and function, quality of life.

Table 2-15

Spinal Cord Injury Syndromes

LESION	CHARACTERISTICS
Complete Cord Lesion: UMN lesion	Complete bilateral loss of all sensory modalities Bilateral loss motor function with spastic paralysis below level of lesion Loss of bladder and bowel functions with spastic bladder and bowel
Central Cord Lesion: UMN lesion	Cavitation of central cord in cervical section Loss of spinothalamic tracts with bilateral loss of pain and temperature Loss of ventral horn with bilateral loss of motor function: primarily upper extremities Preservation of proprioception and discriminatory sensation
Brown-Sequard Syndrome: UMN lesion	Hemisection of spinal cord Ipsilateral loss of dorsal columns with loss of tactile discrimination, pressure, vibration, and proprioception Ipsilateral loss of corticospinal tracts with loss of motor function and spastic paralysis below level of lesion Contralateral loss of spinothalamic tract with loss of pain and temperature below level of lesion; at lesion level, bilateral loss of pain and temperature
Anterior Cord Syndrome: UMN lesion	Loss of anterior cord Loss of lateral corticospinal tracts with bilateral loss of motor function, spastic paralysis below level of lesion Loss of spinothalamic tracts with bilateral loss of pain and temperature Preservation of dorsal columns: proprioception, kinesthesia, and vibratory sense
Posterior Cord Syndrome: UMN lesion	Loss of dorsal columns bilaterally Bilateral loss of proprioception, vibration, pressure, and epicritic sensations (stereognosis, two-point discrimination) Preservation of motor function, pain, and light touch
Cauda Equina Injury: LMN lesion Dura and arachnoid mater Conus medullaris First lumber spinal nerve Cauda equina Roots of spinal nerves Posterior root ganglion Lower limit of subarachnoid space Sacrum Filum terminale Coccygeal spinal nerve Coccyx	Loss of long nerve roots at or below L1 Variable nerve root damage (motor and sensory signs); incomplete lesions common Flaccid paralysis with no spinal reflex activity Flaccid paralysis of bladder and bowel Potential for nerve regeneration; regeneration often incomplete, slows and stops after about 1 year

LMN = lower motor neuron; UMN = upper motor neuron

f. Physical therapy goals, outcomes, and interventions.
   (1) Monitor changes associated with spinal cord injury and recovery.
      (a) Spinal shock: transient period of reflex depression and flaccidity; may last several hours or up to 24 weeks.
      (b) Spasticity/spasms: determine location and degree of tone. Examine for nociceptive stimuli that may trigger increased tone (e.g., blocked catheter, tight clothing or straps, body position, environmental temperature, infection, decubitus ulcers).
      (c) Autonomic dysreflexia (hyperreflexia): an emergency situation in which a noxious stimulus precipitates a pathological autonomic reflex with symptoms of paroxysmal hypertension, bradycardia, headache, diaphoresis (sweating), flushing, diplopia, or convulsions; examine for irritating stimuli; treat as a medical emergency, elevate head, check and empty catheter first.
      (d) Heterotopic bone formation (ectopic bone): abnormal bone growth in soft tissues; examine for early changes—soft tissue swelling, pain, erythema, generally near large joint; late changes—calcification, initial signs of ankylosis.
      (e) Deep venous thrombosis: see discussion in Chapter 3 and Appendix 3B.
   (2) Improve respiratory capacity: deep breathing exercises, strengthening exercises to respiratory muscles; assisted coughing, respiratory hygiene (postural drainage, percussion, vibration, suctioning) as needed to keep airway clear; abdominal support.
   (3) Maintain ROM, prevent contracture: PROM, positioning, splinting; selective stretching to preserve function (e.g., tenodesis grasp).
   (4) Maintain skin integrity, free of decubitus ulcers and other injury: positioning program, pressure-relieving devices (e.g., cushions, gel cushion, ankle boots), patient education: pressure relief activities (e.g., pushups) and skin inspection; provide prompt treatment of pressure sores.
   (5) Improve strength: strengthen all remaining innervated muscles; use selective strengthening during acute phase to reduce stress on spinal segments; resistive training to hypertrophy muscles.
   (6) Reorient patient to vertical position: tilt table, wheelchair; use of abdominal binder, elastic lower extremity wraps to decrease venous pooling; examine for signs and symptoms of orthostatic hypotension (lightheadedness, syncope, mental or visual blurring, sense of weakness).
   (7) Promote early return of FMS and ADLs: emphasis on independent rolling and bed mobility, assumption of sitting, transfers, sit-to-stand, and ambulation as indicated.
   (8) Improve sitting tolerance, postural control, symmetry, and balance; standing balance as indicated.
   (9) Appropriate wheelchair prescription.
      (a) Wheelchair prescription varies according to level and extent of injury. Configuring the wheelchair to provide optimal support and mobility requires an individualized prescription. Requirements below address typical needs of patients with ASIA A or B impairments.
      (b) Patients with high cervical lesions (C1–4): require electric wheelchair with tilt-in space seating or reclining seat back; microswitch or puff-and-sip controls; portable respirator may be attached.
      (c) Patients with cervical lesions, shoulder function, elbow flexion (C5): can use a manual chair with propulsion aids (e.g., projections); independent for short distances on smooth flat surfaces; may choose electric wheelchair for distances and energy conservation.
      (d) Patients with cervical lesions, radial wrist extensors (C6): manual wheelchair with friction surface hand rims; independent.
      (e) Patients with cervical lesions, triceps (C7): same as for C6, but with increased propulsion.
      (f) Patients with hand function (C8–T1 and below): manual wheelchair, standard hand rims.
      (g) Significant changes in lighter, more durable, sports-oriented chairs.
   (10) Promote wheelchair skills/independence: management of wheelchair parts, turns, propulsion on all surfaces indoors and outdoors, safe fall out of and return to wheelchair.
   (11) Locomotor training (LT) for individuals with complete injuries.
      (a) Patients with midthoracic lesions (T6–9): supervised ambulation for short distances (physiological, limited household ambulator); requires bilateral knee-ankle-foot orthoses (KAFOs) and crutches, swing-to gait pattern; requires assistance; may prefer standing devices/standing wheelchairs for physiological standing.
      (b) Patients with high lumbar lesions (T12–L3): can be independent in ambulation on all surfaces and stairs; using a swing-through or

four-point gait pattern and bilateral KAFOs and crutches. Patients may also use reciprocating gait orthoses with walker with or without FES system. Typically independent household ambulators; wheelchair use for community ambulation.

(c) Patients with low lumbar lesions (L4–5); can be independent with bilateral AFOs and crutches or canes. Typically independent community ambulators; may still use wheelchair for activities with high-endurance requirements.

(d) High rate of rejection of orthoses/ambulation in favor of wheelchair mobility and energy conservation.

(12) Neuromodulation: use of electrical stimulation to replace or improve function of a paralyzed or paretic limb; available to limited number of patients.

(a) Functional electrical stimulation (FES) is used for exercise, walking, and functional use of the UEs.

(b) Robotic devices can be used during LT to enhance stepping and promote recovery of walking ability.

(13) Locomotor training for individuals with incomplete injury.

(a) Treadmill training (TT) using body weight support (BWS).

- Indications: incomplete injuries (ASIA B, C, or D).
- Promotes spinal cord learning/activation of spinal locomotor pools.
- Uses body harness to support weight; variable levels of loading, e.g., from 35% unweighting, progressively decreasing to full loading.
- During early training therapists can manually assist with foot placement.
- High frequency (4 days/week); moderate duration (20–30 minutes); typically for 8–12 weeks.

(b) Progression: decrease BWS, increase treadmill speed, eliminate manual assistance.

(c) Progression to overground locomotor training for community ambulation.

(14) Improve cardiovascular endurance.

(a) Monitor heart rate and blood pressure during all exercise or progressive activity.

(b) Methods (complete injuries): arm crank ergometry; functional electrical stimulation–leg cycle ergometry; hybrid: arm crank ergometry and functional electrical stimulation–leg cycle ergometry; wheelchair propulsion.

(c) Precautions: individuals with tetraplegia and high-lesion paraplegia experience blunted tachycardia, lack of pressor response, and very low VO_2 peak, substantially higher variability of most responses.

(d) Trunk stabilization and skin protection important.

(e) Vascular support may be needed (elastic stockings, abdominal binder).

(f) Absolute contraindications to exercise testing and training of individuals with SCI (from American College of Sports Medicine [ACSM]).

- Autonomic dysreflexia.
- Severe or infected skin on weight-bearing surfaces.
- Symptomatic hypotension.
- Urinary tract infection.
- Unstable fracture.
- Uncontrolled hot and humid environments.
- Insufficient ROM to perform exercise task.

(15) Promote maximum independence and mobility in home and community environment; assist patient in community reintegration; ordering of proper equipment, home modification.

g. Provide psychological and emotional support, encourage socialization and motivation.

(1) Reorient and reassure.

(2) Promote independent problem solving, self-direction.

(3) Provide patient and family education. Focus on strategies to prevent skin breakdown, and maintain ROM, strength, and function.

Degenerative Disorders

1. Multiple sclerosis (MS). A chronic, progressive, demyelinating disease of the CNS affecting mostly young adults.

a. Etiology: unknown; most likely viral, autoimmune (active immune responses detected in CSF).

b. Characteristics.

(1) Demyelinating lesions (plaques) impair neural transmission, cause nerves to fatigue rapidly.

(2) Variable symptoms: lesions scattered in time and place; lesions common in pyramidal tract, dorsal columns and periventricular areas of cerebrum, cerebellar peduncles.

(3) Variable course with fluctuating periods: exacerbations (worsening of symptoms) and remissions, progressing to permanent dysfunction.

(4) Precipitating or exacerbating factors: infections, trauma, pregnancy, stress.

(5) Transient worsening of symptoms: adverse reactions to heat, hyperventilation, dehydration, fatigue.

(6) Categories of MS.

(a) Relapsing-remitting MS (RRMS): characterized by discrete attacks of neurological deficits (relapses) with either full or partial recovery (remission) in subsequent weeks or months; periods between relapses are characterized by lack of disease progression. Affects approximately 85% of cases.

(b) Primary-progressive MS (PPMS): characterized by disease progression and a deterioration in function from onset; patients may experience modest fluctuations in neurological disability but discrete attacks do not occur.

(c) Secondary-progressive MS (SPMS): characterized by an initial relapsing-remitting course, followed by a change to a progressive course with a steady decline in function, with or without continued acute attacks.

(d) Progressive-relapsing MS (PRMS): characterized by a steady deterioration in disease from onset (similar to PPMS) but with occasional acute attacks; intervals between attacks are characterized by continuing disease progression.

c. Diagnostic tests: LP/CSF, elevated gamma globulin, CT or MRI, myelogram, EEG.

d. Examine.

(1) History: symptoms, disease progression, functional deficits.

(2) Cognitive/behavioral status: mild-to-moderate cognitive impairment common; also euphoria, emotional dysregulation.

(3) Communication: dysarthria and scanning speech common; dysphasia.

(4) ROM, deformity: associated with disuse and inactivity.

(5) Sensation: sensory symptoms common; e.g., paresthesias, hyperpathia (hypersensitivity to sensory stimuli), dysesthesias (abnormal sensations), trigeminal neuralgia, Lhermitte's sign (electric shock-like sensation throughout the body produced by flexing the neck).

(6) Vision: diplopia or blurred vision common; also optic neuritis, scotoma (blind spot), nystagmus.

(7) Skin integrity and condition.

(8) Muscle tone, DTRs: spasticity and hyperreflexia are common (pyramidal tract lesions).

(9) Muscle strength and control: paresis is common; if spasticity is severe, MMT may be invalid.

(10) Coordination: ataxia is common; intention tremors, dysmetria, dysdiadochokinesia.

(11) Balance: vestibular involvement common, with vertigo, dizziness, unsteadiness, paroxysmal or sudden onset of symptoms.

(12) Gait: ataxic gait is common.

(13) Fatigue: number one complaint; common with high levels of activity and as day progresses.

(14) Respiratory status.

(15) Functional status: FMS, ADLs.

e. Standardized tests/outcome measures for patients with MS (see also Appendix 2A).

(1) Expanded Disability Status Scale (EDSS): based on eight functional central nervous system (FS) components: pyramidal, cerebellar, brain stem, sensory, bowel/bladder, visual, cerebral, and other; completed by a physician/neurologist.

(2) Modified Fatigue Impact Scale (MFIS): a self-report, 21-item measure that examines the effects of fatigue on physical, cognitive, and psychosocial functioning in people with MS.

(3) Scale for the Assessment and Rating of Ataxia (SARA): a performance based measure of ataxia that includes eight tasks (gait, stance, sitting, speech disturbances, finger chase, finger-nose, fast alternating hand movements, and heel-shin slide.

(4) Dizziness Handicap Inventory (DHI): 25 item questionnaire that examines a person's perception of disability in three subscales: physical, emotional, and functional.

(5) Functional Assessment of Multiple Sclerosis (FAMS): examines quality of life across six life domains: mobility, symptoms, emotional well-being, general contentment, thinking/fatigue, and family/social well-being.

f. Medical management.

(1) Immunosuppressant drugs: treat acute flare-ups and shorten duration of episode; adrenocorticotropic hormone (ACTH) and steroids (e.g., prednisone, dexamethasone, betamethasone, methylprednisolone).

(2) Interferon drugs: slow progression of disease, decrease symptoms (e.g., Avonex, Betaseron, Copaxone).

(3) Symptomatic management of spasticity: drugs (e.g., baclofen, diazepam [Valium], dantrolene [Dantrium]), baclofen pump, phenol block surgery.

(4) Symptomatic management of urinary problems: anticholinergic drugs.

g. Physical therapy goals, outcomes, and interventions.

(1) Monitor changes associated with disease progression; revise rehabilitation plan accordingly; develop/supervise maintenance program.

(a) Examine for signs of urinary tract infection, respiratory infection (common causes of death).

(2) Rehabilitation goals.

(a) Restorative: intensive, time-limited rehabilitation services designed to improve/stabilize patient status after a relapse.

(b) Functional maintenance: services designed to manage effects of progressive disease and prevent/minimize indirect impairments associated with disuse and inactivity.

(3) Maintain ROM, prevent contracture.

(4) Maintain skin integrity, free of decubitus ulcers and other injury.

(5) Improve respiratory function.

(6) Improve sensory awareness, sensory compensation to prevent injury; consider eye patching with diplopia.

(7) Improve strength.

(8) Improve motor control, coordination: teach tone reduction techniques, compensatory strategies, safety.

(9) Improve postural control, symmetry, and balance; teach compensatory strategies and safety, provide assistive devices for gait.

(10) Locomotor training.

(11) Promote independence in functional mobility skills and ADLs; supervise family/home health aides in assisting patient.

(12) Promote maximum mobility in home and community; provide appropriate mobility aids and adaptive equipment (wheelchair use common); anticipate changes, rate of disease progression.

(13) Teach energy conservation techniques, activity pacing.

(14) Avoid precipitating exacerbations: schedule therapy sessions during optimal times for function; minimize fatigue, establish schedule of rest and moderate exercise; avoid stressors, overheating.

h. Provide psychological and emotional support.

(1) Emphasize realistic expectations; focus on remaining abilities.

(2) Provide patient, family, and caregiver education.

(3) Teach problem-solving skills, emphasize coping skills.

2. Parkinson's disease. A chronic, progressive disease of the CNS with degeneration of dopaminergic substantia nigra neurons and nigrostriatal pathways.

a. Etiology: several different causes identified: infectious/postencephalitic, atherosclerosis, idiopathic, toxic, drug induced.

(1) Deficiency of dopamine within the basal ganglia corpus striatum with degeneration of substantia nigra.

(2) Loss of inhibitory dopamine results in excessive excitatory output from cholinergic system (acetylcholine) of basal ganglia.

b. Characteristics.

(1) Classic symptoms: rigidity (leadpipe or cogwheel), bradykinesia (hypokinesia), resting tremor (resting), impaired postural reflexes.

(2) Slowly progressive with emergence of secondary impairments and permanent dysfunction.

(3) Stages (Hoehn and Yahr classification).

I. Minimal or absent disability, unilateral symptoms.

II. Minimal bilateral or midline involvement, no balance involvement.

III. Impaired balance, some restrictions in activity.

IV. All symptoms present and severe; stands and walks only with assistance.

V. Confinement to bed or wheelchair.

c. Examine.

(1) History: symptoms, disease progression, functional deficits.

(2) Cognitive/behavioral status: intellectual impairment/dementia occurs in advanced stages; examine for memory deficits, bradyphrenia (slowing of thought processes), and depression.

(3) Communication: dysarthria, hypophonia (decreased volume) are common; mutism in advanced stages; mask-like face with infrequent blinking and expression, writing becomes progressively smaller.

(4) Oromotor control, nutritional status: dysphagia is common, problems in chewing and swallowing.

(5) Respiratory status: breathing patterns, vital capacity; decreased chest expansion common.

(6) ROM, deformity associated with disuse and inactivity: contractures common in flexors, adductors; persistent posturing in kyphosis with forward head; many patients osteoporotic with high risk of fracture.

(7) Sensation/perceptual function: examine for aching and stiffness, abnormal sensations (cramp-like sensations, poorly localized), problems in spatial organization, perception of vertical, extreme restlessness (akathisia).

(8) Vision: examine for blurring, cogwheeling eye pursuit, eye irritation from decreased blinking, decreased pupillary reflexes.

(9) Skin integrity and condition, circulatory changes: edema may occur in lower extremities; increased sweating (ANS dysfunction); decubitus ulcers in late stages.

(10) Muscle tone: examine for rigidity, including location, distribution, and symmetry between two sides of body, type (cogwheel or leadpipe).
(11) Muscle strength: weakness is associated with disuse and atrophy; assess torque output at varying speeds (isokinetics).
(12) Motor function: examine for bradykinesia (slowed movement) or akinesia (absent movement), ability to initiate movement (number of freezing episodes, precipitating factors); assess reaction time versus movement time, overall poverty of movement.
(13) For involuntary movements: examine for presence, location of tremor, precipitating factors; resting tremor common, especially pill-rolling of hands; tremors during movement may occur in advanced stages; postural tremors.
(14) Balance: impaired postural reactions are common (worse with severe rigidity of trunk, lack of trunk rotation); examine for ability to maintain static and dynamic balance, reactive adjustments and anticipatory adjustments.
(15) Gait: characterized by poverty of movements, with generalized lack of extension; festination common (an abnormal, involuntary increase in the speed of walking, often with forward acceleration, but may occur with backward progression).
(16) Functional status.
(17) Overall level of endurance: fatigue and inability to sustain performance is common, affected by stress, high effort; cardiovascular deconditioning occurs with long-standing disease.
(18) Patients on levodopa: examine for fluctuations in symptoms related to dosing (end-of-dose deterioration, on-off phenomenon, dyskinesia); common with disease progression and long-term use of levodopa (e.g., 2–3 years).

d. Standardized tests/outcome measures for patients with Parkinson's disease (see also Appendix 2A).
(1) Hoehn & Yahr Disease Stage (I, II, III, IV, and V);
(2) Unified Rating Scale for Parkinsonism (MDS-UPDRS) revision: documents the overall effects of the disease on body structure, activity, and participation.
(3) The Parkinson's Disease Questionnaire (PDQ-39) is a quality of life questionnaire that focuses on the subjective report of the impact of Parkinson's disease on daily life.
(4) Freezing of Gait Questionnaire: examines gait, freezing episodes, and community function.
(5) Parkinson's Fatigue Scale: examines fatigue and its effect on activity, participation, social function, and quality of life.

e. Medical management.
(1) Sinemet (levodopa/carbidopa) or sustained-release Sinemet: provides dopamine (crosses blood-brain barrier) and decreases effects of disease; effect is prolonged with low-protein diet. Numerous adverse effects including nausea and vomiting, orthostatic hypotension, cardiac arrhythmias, involuntary movements (dyskinesias), and psychoses and abnormal behaviors (hallucinations are common). In on-off phenomenon, patients experience sudden changes from normal function to immobility to severe dyskinetic movements.
(2) Dopamine agonist drugs: enhance the effects of Sinemet therapy (bromocriptine, pergolide mesylate).
(3) Anticholinergic drugs: for control of tremor.
(4) Amantadine: enhances dopamine release.
(5) Selegiline (deprenyl): monoamine oxidase inhibitor increases dopamine; used during early disease to slow progression.
(6) Deep brain stimulation in thalamus or subthalamic nucleus.

f. Physical therapy goals, outcomes, and interventions.
(1) Monitor changes associated with disease progression and pharmacological interventions; revise rehabilitation plan accordingly; develop/supervise maintenance program.
(2) Prevent or minimize secondary impairments associated with disuse and inactivity (see section on MS).
(3) Teach compensatory strategies to initiate movement and unlock freezing episodes, e.g., repetitive auditory stimulation/music.
(4) Improve strength: emphasis on improving overall mobility, rotational patterns (consider proprioceptive neuromuscular facilitation patterns, rhythmic initiation technique).
(5) Teach relaxation skills.
(6) Improve postural control, symmetry, and balance; teach compensatory strategies, safety.
(7) Improve gait; locomotor training.
(8) Promote independence in FMS and ADLs; supervise family/home health aides in assisting patient.
(9) Promote maximum mobility and safety in home and community, improve gait: provide appropriate aids and adaptive equipment; anticipate changes, progression of disease.
(10) Improve cardiovascular endurance.
(11) Teach energy conservation techniques, activity pacing.
(12) Provide psychological and emotional support (see section on MS).

3. Myasthenia gravis. A neuromuscular junction disorder characterized by progressive muscular weakness and fatigability on exertion.
   a. Etiology: autoimmune antibody-mediated attack on acetylcholine receptors at neuromuscular junction.
   b. Characteristics.
      (1) Muscular strength worse with continuing contraction, improved with rest.
      (2) Classified into four types: ocular myasthenia (confined to extraocular muscles), mild generalized myasthenia, severe generalized myasthenia, and crisis.
      (3) Generalized myasthenia: usually involves bulbar (extraocular, facial, and muscles of mastication) and proximal limb-girdle muscles.
      (4) Course varies: may progress from mild to severe, typically within 18 months.
      (5) Myasthenic crisis: myasthenia gravis with respiratory failure; treat as medical emergency.
   c. Examine.
      (1) Cranial nerves: examine for diplopia and ptosis; progressive dysarthria or nasal speech; difficulties in chewing and swallowing; difficulties in facial expression, drooping facial muscles.
      (2) Respiratory function: breathing difficulties, hoarse voice.
      (3) Muscle strength: proximal more involved than distal. Fatigability is characteristic of this disease; repeated muscle use results in rapid weakness.
      (4) Functional mobility skills: common difficulties with climbing stairs, rising from chair, or lifting (similar to myopathies).
      (5) EMG and repetitive nerve stimulation studies conclusive: show abnormal responses to repetitive nerve stimulation (failure of transmission, decreased EMG-recorded responses).
   d. Medical interventions.
      (1) Acetylcholinesterase inhibitors: pyridostigmine.
      (2) Corticosteroids: prednisone, methylprednisolone.
      (3) Immunosuppressants: azathioprine, intravenous immunoglobulin (IVIG).
      (4) Alternative treatments: plasmapheresis (removal of blood with filtering and separation of cellular elements from plasma); thymectomy.
   e. Physical therapy goals, outcomes, and interventions.
      (1) Monitor changes in patient's condition for complications: vital signs, respiration, swallowing.
      (2) Promote independence in FMS and ADLs.
      (3) Teach energy conservation techniques; activity pacing: promote optimal activity with rest as indicated.
      (4) Provide psychological and emotional support.

Epilepsy

1. Characteristics.
   a. A disorder characterized by recurrent seizures (repetitive abnormal electrical discharges within the brain).
   b. Symptoms.
      (1) Altered consciousness.
      (2) Altered motor activity (convulsion): characterized by involuntary contractions of muscles; tonic activity (stiffening and rigidity of muscles); clonic activity (rhythmic jerking of extremities).
      (3) Sensory phenomena: patient experiences somatosensory, visual, auditory, olfactory, gustatory, and vertiginous sensations.
      (4) Autonomic phenomena: associated with sudden attack of anxiety, tachycardia, sweating, piloerection, abnormal sensation rising up in upper abdomen and chest.
      (5) Cognitive phenomena: sudden failure of comprehension, inability to communicate, intrusion of thought, illusions, hallucinations, affective disturbances (intense feelings of fear, anger, and hate).
   c. Common causes of seizures.
      (1) Acquired brain disease or trauma: tumor, stroke.
      (2) Degenerative brain diseases: Alzheimer's dementia, amyloidosis.
      (3) Developmental brain defects.
      (4) Drug overdose: cocaine, antihistamines, cholinesterase inhibitors, methylxanthines, tricyclic antidepressants.
      (5) Drug withdrawal: alcohol, benzodiazepines.
      (6) Electrolyte disorders: hyponatremia, hypernatremia, hypoglycemia, hypomagnesemia.
      (7) Hyperthermia.
      (8) Infections; brain abscess, meningitis, neurocysticercosis.
      (9) Pregnancy complications: eclampsia.
   d. Classification of seizures.
      (1) Generalized seizures.
         (a) Tonic-clonic (grand mal): dramatic loss of consciousness, with a cry, fall, and tonic-clonic convulsions of all extremities; often with tongue biting and arrested breathing, urinary and fecal incontinence; after 2–5 minutes, contractions subside, and consciousness is gradually regained;

patient is confused, drowsy, and amnesiac about the event; full recovery may take several hours; some attacks are preceded by a brief aura.
(b) Absence seizures (petit mal): brief, almost imperceptible lapse of consciousness followed by immediate and full return to consciousness; posture is maintained, with no convulsive muscle contractions; may occur as often as a hundred times a day.
(2) Partial seizures.
(a) Simple partial seizures: focal, begin locally, limited to a portion of the body, consciousness preserved; usually has an identifiable structural cause.
(b) Focal motor: clonic activity involving a specific area of the body.
(c) Focal motor with march (Jacksonian): an orderly spread or march of clonic movements from initial muscles to involve adjacent muscles, with spread to the entire side.
(d) Temporal lobe seizure: characterized by episodic changes in behavior, with complex hallucinations; automatisms (e.g., lip smacking, chewing, pulling on clothing); altered cognitive and emotional function (e.g., sexual arousal, depression, violent behaviors); preceded by an aura.
(e) Complex partial seizures: simple partial seizures followed by impairment of consciousness.
(3) Secondarily generalized seizures: simple or complex partial seizures evolving to a generalized seizure.
(4) Status epilepticus: prolonged seizure or a series of seizures (lasting > 30 minutes) with very little recovery between attacks; may be life threatening; medical emergency (generalized status epilepticus).

2. Examine/determine.
a. Time of onset, duration, type of seizure, sequence of events, frequency, duration.
b. Patient activity at onset, presence of aura.
c. Sensory elements, motor activity: type, degree, and location of involvement.
d. Presence of tongue biting, incontinence, respiratory distress.
e. Behavioral elements, changes in mood and perception.
f. Patient responses after the seizure.

3. Medical interventions.
a. Antiepileptic medications: phenytoin (Dilantin), carbamazepine (Tegretol), phenobarbital; drugs may have significant adverse side effects.
b. Surgical intervention: lobe resection, hemispherectomy.

4. Physical therapy goals, outcomes, and interventions.
a. Protect patient from injury during seizure: remain with patient, remove potentially harmful nearby objects, loosen restrictive clothing, and do not restrain limbs.
b. Establish airway, prevent aspiration: turn head to side or side-lying position; check to see if airway is open, wait for tonic-clonic activity to subside before initiating artificial ventilation if needed.
c. Promote regular routines for physical activity and emotional health.

Cerebellar Disorders

1. Diseases/lesions of the cerebellum.
a. Hereditary ataxia, Friedreich's ataxia.
b. Neoplastic or metastatic tumors.
c. Infection.
d. Vascular: stroke.
e. Developmental: ataxic cerebral palsy, Arnold-Chiari syndrome.
f. Trauma: TBI.
g. Drugs, heavy metals.
h. Chronic alcoholism.

2. Lesions/impairments of the cerebellum. Cerebellar lesions tend to produce ipsilateral signs and symptoms.
a. Lesions of the archicerebellum (flocculonodular lobe).
(1) Central vestibular symptoms: ocular dysmetria, poor eye pursuit, dysfunctional vestibular ocular reflex (VOR), impaired eye-hand coordination.
(2) Gait and trunk ataxia: poor postural control and orientation, wide-based gait.
(3) Little change in tone or dyssynergia of extremity movements.
b. Lesions of the paleocerebellum (spinocerebellum; rostral cerebellum and anterior lobe).
(1) Hypotonia.
(2) Truncal ataxia: dysequilibrium, static postural tremor, increased sway, wide BOS, and high guard arm position. Posture worse with eyes closed, narrow BOS (Romberg, sharpened Romberg).
(3) Ataxic gait: unsteady, increased falls, uneven/decreased step length, increased step width.
c. Lesions of neocerebellum (hemisphere, posterior lobe).
(1) Intention tremor: irregular, oscillatory voluntary movements.
(2) Dysdiadochokinesia: impaired RAM.

(3) Dysmetria: hypermetria (overshooting), errors or force, direction, amplitude, rebound phenomenon (Holmes).
(4) Dyssynergia: abnormal timing (errors of velocity, onset, and stop), movement decomposition of agonist/antagonist interactions; impairments of multijoint coordination, movement sequences, complex motor tasks.
(5) Errors in timing related to perceptual tasks.

d. Additional impairments.
(1) Asthenia: generalized weakness (F to G muscle grades).
(2) Hypotonia: especially in acute cerebellar lesions, difficulty with postural control of proximal (axial) muscles.
(3) Motor learning impairments: decreased anticipatory control, feedback, and learning delays.
(4) Cognition: deficits in information procession, attention deficits.
(5) Emotional dysregulation: changes in emotional behaviors.

3. Examine.
a. Muscle strength, tone.
b. Range of motion.
c. Coordination: determine abnormalities of coordinated movement.
d. Balance: determine abnormalities of postural control and balance.
e. Gait: determine abnormalities of gait (ataxic gait).
f. Motor function: determine abnormalities of motor learning.
g. Functional status.
h. Endurance and fatigue level: fatigue is common with dysmetric patients.
i. Standardized tests/outcome measures for patients with cerebellar disorders (see previous discussions of various tests and also Appendix 2-A).
(1) Scale for Assessment and Rating of Ataxia (SARA).
(2) Dizziness Handicap Inventory (DHI).
(3) Modified Fatigue Impact Scale (MFIS).
(4) Balance tests.
(5) Functional Gait tests.
(6) Functional Independence Measure (FIM) and Functional Assessment Measure (FAM).

4. Physical therapy goals, outcomes, and interventions.
a. Goals.
(1) Improve accuracy of limb movements.
(2) Improve postural stability and dynamic postural control.
(3) Improve functional mobility and safety: transfers and gait.
(4) Stabilize VOR/vision.

b. Eye-head coordination exercise: slow head movements with visual fixation; active eye and head movements.
c. Stability exercises: use of weight-bearing postures, carefully graded resistance, and approximation to promote steady holding. Use of theraband, weights (ankle and wrist cuffs), weighted waist belts, and walkers to decrease ataxic movements.
d. Dynamic stability exercises: promote small range control, smooth reversals of movements, movement transitions, using carefully graded resistance.
e. Balance training: compensatory training/safety important.
f. Locomotor training: TT with BWS; overground and community training.
g. Therapeutic pool: water provides graded resistance, decreases ataxic movements and postural instability.
h. Coordination exercises: proprioceptive neuromuscular facilitation (PNF) patterns, ball gymnastics to promote balance.
i. Stationary bike: assists timing of reciprocal movements.
j. Motor learning strategies: low-stimulus environment (closed environment) ideal; focus on practice and repetition; distributed practice (endurance may be low).
k. Biofeedback: augmented feedback to enhance stability and postural control (i.e., balance training platform).
l. Energy conservation techniques, assistive devices as needed.

Vestibular Disorders

1. Characteristics.
a. Dizziness: sensation of lightheadedness, giddiness, faintness; increased risk of falls.
b. Vertigo: sensation of moving around in space or having objects move around a person; tends to come in attacks; if severe, accompanied by nausea and vomiting.
c. Visual changes.
(1) Nystagmus: involuntary, cyclical movement of the eyeball; e.g., horizontal, rotary.
(2) Blurred vision: gaze instability secondary to vestibular ocular reflex (VOR) dysfunction.
d. Dysequilibrium or postural instability: vestibular spinal reflex (VSR) dysfunction; ataxia, gait disturbances; increased risk of falls.
e. Anxiety, fear, depression.
f. Indirect impairments: physical deconditioning, decreased cervical ROM.

2. Etiology: unilateral vestibular disorders (UVD).
a. Trauma: vestibular symptoms seen in 30%–65% of patients with TBI.

b. Vestibular neuronitis, labyrinthitis: an acute infection with prolonged attack of symptoms, persisting for several days or several weeks; caused by viral or bacterial infection.
c. Ménière's disease: recurrent and usually progressive vestibular disease; episodic attacks may last from minutes to several hours with severe symptoms; usually associated with tinnitus, deafness, sensation of pressure/fullness within ear; etiology unknown, edema of membranous labyrinth is a consistent finding.
d. Benign paroxysmal positional vertigo (BPPV): brief attacks of vertigo and nystagmus that occur with certain head positions (lying down, turning over in bed, tilting head back); may be related to degenerative processes, mechanical impairment of peripheral vestibular system.
e. Tumor: acoustic neuroma, gliomas/brainstem, or cerebellar medulloblastoma.

3. Etiology: bilateral vestibular disorders (BVD).
   a. Toxicity: ototoxic drugs.
   b. Bilateral infection: neuritis, meningitis.
   c. Vestibular neuropathy, otosclerosis (Paget's disease).
4. Examine.
   a. History: determine type, nature, duration of symptoms, triggering stimuli/activity.
   b. VOR function: examine for nystagmus, blurred vision with head and total body movements.
   c. Sensory function.
      (1) Examine for intact vision, proprioception, especially of feet/ankles. Important for compensatory postural adjustments with vestibular losses.
      (2) Examine for sensory interaction in balance (CTSIB).
   d. VSR function: examine posture and balance; examine for instability in sitting, standing, during functional activities, and gait.
   e. Positional testing: changes in position produce symptoms, e.g., dizziness, vertigo, nystagmus.
      (1) Hallpike Dix test.
      (2) Roll test.
      (3) Sidelying test.
   f. Diagnostic testing.
      (1) Head Impulse test/Head Thrust.
      (2) Head Shaking Nystagmus test.
   g. ROM: special attention to cervical ROM.
   h. Standardized tests/outcome measures for patients with vestibular disorders (see previous discussions of various tests and also Appendix 2A).
      (1) Dizziness Handicap Inventory (DHI).
      (2) NeuroCom Sensory Organization Test (SOT).
      (3) Clinical Test for Sensory Interaction in Balance (CTSIB).
      (4) Dynamic Visual Acuity Test.
      (5) Postural stability/balance tests: e.g., Berg Balance Test, MiniBest Test, Romberg and Sharpened Romberg, Functional Reach, Activities-Specific Balance Confidence Scale.
      (6) Functional Gait tests: e.g., Dynamic Gait Index, Functional Gait Assessment, Timed Up and Go, Gait Velocity, Five Times Sit to Stand, Fukuda Stepping Test.
      (7) Vestibular Disorders Activities of Daily Living Scale (VADL): assesses self-perceived disablement in patients with vestibular impairment.
   i. Functional status: determine current level of activity.
   j. Vertebral artery compression: can produce vestibular symptoms (i.e., in supine position, extend, laterally flex, and rotate head, hold for 30 seconds; each side tested separately).
5. Medical interventions. Vestibular suppressant medications; prolonged use may delay recovery; severe cases may require ablative surgery.
6. Physical therapy goals, outcomes, and interventions.
   a. Implement safety measures: teach sensory substitution, compensatory strategies; provide ambulatory aids as indicated; e.g., cane, walker.
   b. Provide active exercises to promote vestibular adaptation (recalibration of system).
      (1) Habituation training: repetition of movements and positions that provoke dizziness and vertigo.
      (2) Gaze stability exercises.
         (a) Eye movements: side-to-side eyes on stationary target (X1 paradigm); side-to-side eyes on moving target (X2 paradigm).
         (b) Head movements up and down, side to side while maintaining eyes focused on a visual target; progressing slow to fast movements, standing to walking.
      (3) Postural stability: exercises such as sitting and standing, static and dynamic balance activities (e.g., bending forward, turning); walking, walking and turning, walking with head turns.
      (4) Emphasize functional mobility skills: community activities, activities with spatial and timing constraints.
      (5) Relaxation training: to decrease anxiety levels.
      (6) Begin conservatively, avoid excessive exacerbation of symptoms.
   c. Recovery is better, generally faster in unilateral than bilateral vestibular dysfunction.
   d. Provide psychological support and reassurance.
   e. BPPV treatment techniques.
      (1) Canalith repositioning treatment (CRT): for horizontal SCC BPPV, posterior SCC BPPV.

(2) Liberatory maneuver: for posterior SCC BPPV.
(3) Brandt-Daroff exercises: for residual or mild vertigo.

Cranial and Peripheral Nerve Disorders

1. Peripheral nerve disease/injury.
   a. Etiology: wide range of etiological factors (more than 100 distinct diseases).
   b. Basic pathological processes.
      (1) Wallerian degeneration: transection (neurotmesis) results in degeneration of the axon and myelin sheath distal to the site of axonal interruption.
         (a) Chromatolysis and repair processes occurs in nerve cell body.
         (b) Endoneurium (sheath) does not degenerate but forms a tube directing regeneration.
      (2) Segmental demyelination: axons are preserved (no wallerian degeneration); remyelination restores function (e.g., Guillain-Barré syndrome).
      (3) Axonal degeneration: degeneration of axon cylinder and myelin, progressing from distal to proximal, "dying back" of nerves (e.g., peripheral neuropathy).
   c. Terminology.
      (1) Neuropathy (peripheral neuropathy): any disease of nerves characterized by deteriorating neural function; e.g., diabetic neuropathy, alcoholic neuropathy.
         (a) Polyneuropathy: bilateral symmetrical involvement of peripheral nerves, usually legs more than arms, distal segments earlier and more involved than proximal.
         (b) Mononeuropathy: involvement of a single nerve.
      (2) Radiculopathy: involvement of nerve roots.
      (3) Traumatic nerve injury.
         (a) Neurapraxia (Class 1): injury to nerve that causes a transient loss of function (conduction block ischemia); nerve dysfunction may be rapidly reversed or persist a few weeks; e.g., compression.
         (b) Axonotmesis (Class 2): injury to nerve interrupting the axon and causing loss of function and wallerian degeneration distal to the lesion; with no disruption of the endoneurium, regeneration is possible; e.g., crush injury.
         (c) Neurotmesis (Class 3): cutting of the nerve with severance of all structures and complete loss of function; reinnervation typically fails without surgical intervention because of aberrant regeneration (failure of regenerating axon to find its terminal end).
   d. Clinical symptoms LMN syndrome (see Table 2-5).
      (1) Weakness/paresis of denervated muscle, hyporeflexia and hypotonia, (rapid) atrophy, fatigue.
      (2) Sensory loss: corresponds to motor weakness; proprioceptive losses may yield sensory ataxia; insensitivity may yield limb trauma.
      (3) Autonomic dysfunction: vasodilation and loss of vasomotor tone (dryness, warm skin, edema, orthostatic hypotension).
      (4) Hyperexcitability of remaining nerve fibers.
         (a) Sensory dysesthesias: hyperalgesia, pins and needles, numbness, tingling, burning.
         (b) Motor: fasciculations, spasms.
      (5) Muscle pain (myalgia) with inflammatory myopathies (e.g., postpolio syndrome).
   e. Diagnostic tests.
      (1) NCV studies: conduction times (motor, sensory) are slowed or complete conduction block may be evident.
      (2) EMG (motor nerve function): examine for signs of widespread denervation atrophy (spontaneous fibrillation potentials); evidence of reinnervation (low-amplitude, short-duration, polyphasic motor unit potentials).
2. Trigeminal neuralgia (tic douloureux). Neuralgia of the trigeminal nerve (CN V).
   a. Etiology: results from degeneration (etiology unknown) or compression (tortuous basilar artery or cerebellopontine tumor); occurs in older population (mean age over 50); abrupt onset.
   b. Characteristics: brief paroxysms of neurogenic pain (stabbing and/or shooting pain); reoccurring frequently.
      (1) Occurs along the distribution of the trigeminal nerve, mandibular and maxillary divisions (involvement of ophthalmic division is rare); restricted to one side of the face.
      (2) There is autonomic instability: exacerbated by stress, cold; relieved by relaxation.
   c. Examine/determine.
      (1) Pain: location, intensity.
      (2) Trigger points: light touch to face, lips, or gums will cause pain.
      (3) Triggering stimuli: extremes of heat or cold, chewing, talking, brushing teeth, movement of air across the face.
      (4) Motor function: control is normal.
   d. Medical: medications (anticonvulsants, vitamin B_{12}); alcohol injections, surgery (sectioning of nerve, permanent anesthesia).
   e. Transcutaneous electrical nerve stimulation (TENS) can be effective for pain relief.

3. Bell's palsy (facial paralysis). LMN lesion involving CN VII (facial nerve), resulting in unilateral facial paralysis.
   a. Etiology: acute inflammatory process of unknown etiology (immune or viral disease) resulting in compression of the nerve within the temporal bone.
   b. Characteristics.
      (1) Muscles of facial expression on one side are weakened or paralyzed.
      (2) Loss of control of salivation or lacrimation.
      (3) Onset is acute, with maximum severity in a few hours or days; commonly preceded by a day or two of pain behind the ear; most recover fully in several weeks or months.
      (4) Sensation is normal.
   c. Examine/determine.
      (1) Drooping of corner of mouth, eyelids that don't close.
      (2) Function of muscles of facial expression: have patient wrinkle forehead, raise eyebrows, frown, smile, close eyes tightly, puff cheeks.
      (3) Taste of the anterior two thirds of tongue.
   d. Medications: corticosteroids (prednisone); analgesics.
   e. Physical therapy goals, outcomes, and interventions.
      (1) Protect cornea (artificial tears or temporary patching) until recovery allows for eyelid closure.
      (2) Electrical stimulation to maintain tone, support function of facial muscles.
      (3) Provide active facial muscle exercises.
      (4) May require face sling to prevent overstretching of facial muscles.
      (5) Provide functional retraining: foods that can be easily eaten, chewing with opposite side.
      (6) Provide emotional support and reassurance.
4. Bulbar palsy (bulbar paralysis). Refers to weakness or paralysis of the muscles innervated by the motor nuclei of the lower brainstem, affecting the muscles of the face, tongue, larynx, and pharynx.
   a. Etiology: the result of tumors, vascular or degenerative diseases of lower cranial nerve motor nuclei (e.g., amyotrophic lateral sclerosis).
   b. Examine/determine.
      (1) Glossopharyngeal and vagal paralysis: phonation, articulation, palatal action, gag reflex, swallowing.
      (2) Changes in voice quality: dysphonia (hoarseness or nasal quality).
      (3) Bilateral involvement: severe airway restriction with dyspnea, difficulty with coughing.
      (4) Possible complications: aspiration pneumonia.
   c. Pseudobulbar palsy: bilateral dysfunction of corticobulbar innervation of brainstem nuclei; a central or UMN lesion analogous to corticospinal lesions disrupting function of anterior horn cells.
      (1) Produces similar symptoms as bulbar palsy.
      (2) Examine for hyperactive reflexes: increased jaw jerk, and snout reflex (tapping on lips produces pouting of lips).
   d. Medical/surgical treatment of underlying cause.
   e. Physical therapy goals, outcomes, and interventions.
      (1) Suctioning, oral care.
      (2) Maintenance of respiratory function, open airway.
      (3) Elevate head of bed.
      (4) Dietary changes: soft foods, liquids.
5. Guillain-Barré syndrome (GBS, acute ascending, symmetrical polyneuropathy). Polyneuritis with progressive muscular weakness that develops rapidly.
   a. Etiology: unknown; associated with an autoimmune attack, usually occurs after recovery from an infectious illness (respiratory or gastrointestinal).
   b. Characteristics.
      (1) Involves acute demyelination of both cranial and peripheral nerves (LMN disease).
      (2) Sensory loss, paresthesias (tingling, burning), pain; sensory loss is typically less than motor loss.
      (3) Motor paresis or paralysis: relative symmetrical distribution of weakness; progresses from lower extremities to upper (ascending pattern) and from distal to proximal; may produce full tetraplegia with respiratory failure.
      (4) Dysarthria, dysphagia, diplopia, and facial weakness may develop in severe cases.
      (5) Progression evolves over a few days or weeks; recovery usually slow (6 months to 2 years) and usually complete (85% of cases); some mild weakness may persist; 3% mortality.
      (6) Complications.
         (a) Respiratory impairment and failure.
         (b) Autonomic instability: tachycardia, arrhythmias, BP fluctuations.
         (c) Pain: myalgia.
         (d) Risk of pneumonia.
         (e) Prolonged hospitalizations and immobility: deep venous thrombosis, skin breakdown, contracture.
         (f) Relapse: if treatment is inadequate.
   c. Examine.
      (1) Cardiac and respiratory status, vital signs.
      (2) Cranial nerve function (VII, IX, X, XI, XII).
      (3) Motor strength (serial MMTs indicated).
      (4) Reflexes: decreased or absent tendon reflexes.

Chapter 2 NM

(5) Sensation: changes can include paresthesias, anesthesias, hyperesthesias, pain (muscle aching, burning); may have stocking and glove distribution (anesthesia of distal extremities in a pattern as if the patient were wearing long gloves and stockings).
(6) Functional status.

d. Medical.
(1) Good nursing care.
(2) Plasmapheresis.
(3) IVIG.
(4) Analgesics for relief of pain.

e. Physical therapy goals, outcomes, and interventions.
(1) Maintain respiratory function: may require endotracheal intubation, tracheotomy, and ventilation; pulmonary physical therapy.
(2) Prevent indirect impairments: PROM within pain tolerance, positioning, and skin care.
(3) Prevent injury to denervated muscles: monitor recovery; splinting, positioning.
(4) Provide muscle reeducation, moderate exercise program (active assistance and active exercise progressing to resistive), functional training as recovery progresses.
(5) Teach energy conservation techniques and activity pacing: avoid overuse and fatigue, which may prolong recovery.
(6) Improve cardiovascular fitness following prolonged bed rest and deconditioning.
(7) Provide emotional support and reassurance to patient and family.

6. Amyotrophic lateral sclerosis (ALS, "Lou Gehrig's disease"). A degenerative disease affecting both UMNs and LMNs (degeneration of anterior horn cells and descending corticobulbar and corticospinal tracts).

a. Etiology: unknown (viral/autoimmune, toxic); 5%–10% genetic (autosomal dominant).

b. Characteristics.
(1) Progressive disease, often leading to death, typically in 2–5 years; highly variable symptoms.
(a) Bulbar onset (progressive bulbar palsy).
(b) Spinal cord onset (progressive muscular atrophy).
(2) Muscular weakness that spreads over time: early onset involves limbs progressing to whole body; atrophy, cramping, muscle fasciculations, or twitching (LMN signs).
(3) Spasticity, hyperreflexia (UMN signs).
(4) Dysarthria, dysphagia, dysphonia secondary to pseudobulbar palsy and progressive bulbar palsy.
(5) Usually absence of sensory changes; small number (20%) may show sensory deficits.
(6) Autonomic dysfunction in about one-third of patients.
(7) Pain due to spasticity, cramping, postural stress syndrome, joint hypomobility, or instability.
(8) Respiratory impairments: weakness > paralysis, nocturnal difficulty, exertional dyspnea, accessory muscle use; paradoxical breathing, ventilator dependent; poor cough, clearance of secretions.
(9) Typical sparing of bowel and bladder function.
(10) Cognition is normal, similar to locked-in syndrome in cerebrovascular accident (CVA).
(11) Depression common.

c. Stages of ALS.
(1) Stage I: early disease, mild focal weakness, asymmetrical distribution; symptoms of hand cramping and fasciculations.
(2) Stage II: moderate weakness in groups of muscles, some wasting (atrophy) of muscles; modified independence with assistive devices.
(3) Stage III: severe weakness of specific muscles, increasing fatigue; mild to moderate functional limitations, ambulatory.
(4) Stage IV: severe weakness and wasting of LEs, mild weakness of UEs; moderate assistance and assistive devices required; wheelchair user.
(5) Stage V: progressive weakness with deterioration of mobility and endurance, increased fatigue, moderate to severe weakness of whole limbs and trunk; spasticity, hyperreflexia; loss of head control; maximal assist.
(6) Stage VI: bedridden, dependent ADLs, FMS; progressive respiratory distress.

d. Examine.
(1) History: varied pattern of onset.
(2) Vital signs, respiratory function.
(3) Cranial nerve function: especially lower cranial nerves (VII, IX, X, XI, XII).
(4) Motor function.
(a) Examine for atrophy, widespread weakness; a symmetrical distribution, muscle cramping and muscle twitching.
(b) Examine for spasticity, hyperreflexia.
(c) Coordination tests: manual skills.
(5) Sensory function.
(6) Gait: timed walk (10-m walk test).
(7) Functional status: monitor closely for overwork fatigue, persistent weakness following exercise or activity; e.g., keep activity log.
(8) ALS Functional Rating Scale (ALSFRS): assesses disease progression and function across 10 functional categories; scored 0 (loss of function) to 4 (normal function); 40 maximal score.

e. Medical management: there is no effective treatment for this disease.

(1) Riluzole, a glutamate antagonist, may slow progression, prolong survival, especially with bulbar-onset disease.
(2) Symptomatic relief: i.e., spasticity, pain, respiratory failure.

f. Physical therapy goals, outcomes, and interventions.
(1) Maintain respiratory function: may require airway clearance techniques, cough facilitation, breathing exercises, chest stretching, suctioning, incentive spirometry, long-term mechanical ventilation.
(2) Provide for nutritional needs: assist in management of dysphagia; may require nasogastric tube or percutaneous gastrostomy in later stages.
(3) Prevent indirect impairments: maintain activity levels as long as possible, PROM, positioning, skin care.
(4) Provide exercise program.
(a) Prevent further deconditioning and disuse atrophy while avoiding overwork damage in weakened, denervated muscle; e.g., mild resistive exercises if muscles are in good to normal ranges; active exercises or functional activities as weakness progresses.
(b) Mild aerobic exercise at submaximal levels, as appropriate.
(c) Exercise precautions: monitor fatigue levels closely; avoid overwork injury (avoid exercise if less than one-third of motor units are functioning); limited positions with decreased pulmonary function.
(d) As disease progresses, replace exercise with functional training activities.
(5) Teach energy conservation activity, pacing techniques; e.g., balance activity with rest.
(6) Maintain maximal functional independence: provide appropriate assistive devices, orthotic support, wheelchair, environmental adaptations; anticipate needs.
(7) Symptomatic treatment of pain, spasms, spasticity.
(8) Teach patient, family, caregivers all care, ADLs; assist in utilization of community resources.
(9) Provide psychological support and reassurance, maximum comfort; loss of control is an important issue.

7. Postpolio syndrome (PPS). New, slowly progressive muscle weakness occurring in individuals with a confirmed history of acute poliomyelitis; follows a stable period of functioning.

a. Etiology: unknown; possible hyperfunctioning of motor neurons, long-term overuse at high levels resulting in new denervation.

b. Characteristics:
(1) New weakness and atrophy, asymmetrical in distribution. Occurs in both initially weak and uninvolved muscles.
(2) Abnormal fatigue: may not be related to activity levels, doesn't recover easily with usual rest periods.
(3) Pain: myalgia, cramping pain, joint pain with repetitive injury, hypersensitivities.
(4) Decreased function with reduced endurance for routine activities.
(5) Slow progression, either steady or stepwise.
(6) Environmental cold intolerance.
(7) Difficulty in concentration, memory, attention; damage to reticular formation, hypothalamus, dopaminergic neurons (brain fatigue generator model).
(8) Sleep disturbances.
(9) Decreased functional mobility, aerobic capacity, labile exercise blood pressures.

c. Examine.
(1) History: confirm original acute polio illness; document onset of present symptoms, presentation, course, chronology.
(2) Motor function: strength, atrophy, muscle fatigue, muscle twitching, and cramps.
(a) Identify problem musculature, weakness found in both new muscles and muscles previously affected by polio.
(b) Identify functional contractions (fair grades or above).
(c) Look for spotty involvement, asymmetrical paralysis.
(3) ROM and deformity.
(4) Pain.
(a) Muscle pain: check tenderness to touch.
(b) Skeletal, soft tissue pain: chronic overuse, poor alignment.
(5) Sensory function: any sensory deficit is due to other etiology (sensation is unaffected in PPS).
(6) Respiratory function: examine for dyspnea, difficulty in speaking, weak cough.
(7) Functional status: functional mobility skills, activities of daily living.
(8) Endurance, activity levels: fatigue is a primary symptom.
(9) Aerobic capacity: use ergometer that involves both upper and lower extremities; e.g., Schwinn Air-Dyne, discontinuous protocol, submaximal test (ACSM recommendation).
(10) EMG to identify prior anterior horn cell (AHC) disease and new motor unit pathology. See denervation changes, fasciculations, fibrillations, increased motor unit amplitude and duration.
(11) Examine for presence of depression or anxiety.

d. Medical management.
   (1) Antidepressants: e.g., amitriptyline (Elavil), fluoxetine (Prozac).
   (2) Neurotransmitter inhibitors: decreases fatigue and sleep disorders; e.g., serotonin, norepinephrine.
e. Physical therapy goals, outcomes, and interventions.
   (1) Maintain respiratory function: teach breathing exercises, supportive cough maneuvers, postural drainage as indicated.
   (2) Teach energy conservation techniques, activity pacing: balance activity with frequent rest periods to decrease fatigue, prevent overwork damage in weakened, denervated muscle.
      (a) Teach relaxation techniques to maximize rest.
      (b) Avoid unnecessary activities to maximize important work.
   (3) Preserve or increase muscle strength.
      (a) Provide moderate exercise program (nonexhaustive exercise): modified strengthening and conditioning; use low-intensity, discontinuous nonfatiguing exercise with increased rest periods.
      (b) Caution against widespread use of strength training.
      (c) Consider pool programs: minimizes overwork, relieves pain; general body conditioning.
      (d) Foster weight control and reduction.
   (4) Aerobic conditioning: moderate to low-level training depending upon class of disease, discontinuous protocol. In severe atrophic polio, exercise is contraindicated.
   (5) Maintain or increase function: provide recommendations for lifestyle modification; minimize abnormal postures, gait deviations.
   (6) Prescribe appropriate orthoses, mobility aids (motorized cart), assistive devices, environmental modifications.
   (7) Eliminate or control pain: provide options for pain control, foster self-control.
   (8) Teach patient and family all care, activities of daily living; lifestyle modifications.
   (9) Provide psychological support and reassurance.

Pain

The sensory and emotional experience associated with actual or potential tissue damage (International Association for the Study of Pain).

1. Pain pathways/neurophysiology.
   a. Fast, localized pain (lateral pain system): transmitted over thinly myelinated A delta fibers, processed in spinal cord dorsal horn lamina (I and V), crosses to excite lateral (neo)spinothalamic tract; terminates in brainstem reticular formation and thalamus with projections to cortex; functions for localization, discrimination of pain.
   b. Slow pain (divergent pathways): transmitted over small diameter, unmyelinated C fibers; processed in spinal cord lamina (II and III -V), cross to excite anterior (paleo)spinothalamic tract; terminates in brainstem reticular formation; excites RAS, functions for diffuse arousal (protective/aversive reactions), affective and motivational aspects of pain; also terminates in thalamus with projections to cortex.
   c. Intrinsic inhibitory mechanisms.
      (1) Gate control theory: transmission of sensation at spinal cord level is controlled by balance between large fibers (A alpha, A beta) and small fibers (A delta, C); activity of large fibers at level of first synapse can block activity of small fibers and pain transmission (counterirritant theory).
      (2) Descending analgesic systems: endogenous opiates (endorphins, enkephalins) produced throughout CNS (e.g., periaqueductal gray, raphe nuclei, pituitary gland/hypothalamus, SC laminae I and II); can depress pain transmission at various sites through mechanisms of presynaptic inhibition.
2. Acute pain. Pain provoked by noxious stimulation, associated with an underlying pathology (injury or acute inflammation/disease); signs include sharp pain and sympathetic changes (increased heart rate, increased blood pressure, pupillary dilation, sweating, hyperventilation, anxiety, protective/escape behaviors).
3. Chronic pain. Pain that persists beyond the usual course of healing; symptoms present for > 6 months, for which an underlying pathology is no longer identifiable or may never have been present.
4. Classification of pain.
   a. Nociceptive pain; response to an immediate noxious stimulus (mechanical, thermal, or chemical) signaling impending tissue damage. Inflammatory pain occurs after tissue damage and increases sensitivity to pain.
   b. Neurogenic pain: pain as a result of lesions in some part of the nervous system (central or peripheral); usually accompanied by some degree of sensory deficit.
      (1) Central neurogenic pain: arises from injury or disease affecting the CNS. Pain is often burn-

ing, aching, or prickling; hyperanalgesia and allodynia.

(a) Central poststroke (thalamic) pain: continuous, intense, central pain occurring on the contralateral hemiplegic side; the result of a stroke involving the ventral posterolateral thalamus; autonomic and vasomotor dysfunction common.

(b) Traumatic brain injury.

(c) Fibromyalgia.

(2) Peripheral neurogenic pain: arises from mechanical or chemical damage to peripheral nerves; may include symptoms of paresthesia, dysesthesia, and pain.

(a) Complex regional pain syndrome I (CRPS)/ reflex sympathetic dystrophy/causalgia: a complex disorder or group of disorders that develop as a consequence of trauma affecting body part(s) and disuse. The term *regional* indicates that signs and symptoms are present throughout the limb (upper or lower limb) and not occurring in a peripheral nerve or nerve root distribution. Characterized by reflex neurogenic inflammation affecting the SNS and pain disproportionate to injury.

- Acute or early stage: diffuse, severe burning or aching pain; increases with emotional stress; allodynia (pain on light touch) and hyperpathia (increased sensitivity to normal stimuli); vasomotor instability with dusky mottling, cool skin, swelling, and edema.
- Dystrophic or middle stage: skin changes with thin, pale, cyanotic skin; cessation of hair and nail growth; hyperhidrosis; muscle atrophy and osteoporosis.
- Atrophic or late stage; decreased hypersensitivity; normal blood flow and temperature; smooth, glossy skin; severe muscles atrophy; pericapsular fibrosis; diffuse osteoporosis; development of claw hand may occur.

(b) Disorders of peripheral roots and nerves. Includes neuralgia: pain occurring along the branches of a nerve; radiculalgia: neuralgia of nerve roots: paresthesias, allodynia: with nerve injury or transection.

(c) Herpes zoster (shingles): an acute, painful mononeuropathy caused by the varicella zoster virus; characterized by vesicular eruption and marked inflammation of the posterior root ganglion of the affected spinal nerve or sensory ganglion of the cranial nerve; ventral root involvement (motor weakness) in 5%–10% of cases; infection can last from 10 days to 5 weeks; postherpetic neuralgia pain may persist for months or years.

(d) Phantom limb pain: in a limb following amputation of that limb; differentiated from far more common phantom limb sensation.

(3) Musculoskeletal pain.

(a) Fibromyalgia: widespread pain accompanied by tenderness of muscles and adjacent soft tissues, a nonarticular rheumatic disease of unknown origin.

(b) Myofascial pain syndrome (MPS): persistent, deep aching pains in muscle, nonarticular in origin; characterized by well-defined, highly sensitive tender spots (trigger points).

(c) Postural stress syndrome (PSS): postural malalignment produces chronic muscle lengthening and/or shortening and stress to soft tissues.

(d) Movement adaptation syndrome (MAS); habituated movement dysfunction leading to muscle strain and pain.

(4) Pain with psychiatric disorders (psychosomatic pain): the origin of the pain experience is due to mental or emotional disorders.

(5) Headache and craniofacial pain; e.g., temporomandibular joint (TMJ) syndrome.

(6) Referred pain: pain arising from deep visceral tissues that is felt in a body region remote from the site of pathology, resulting in tenderness and cutaneous hyperalgesia; e.g., medial left arm pain with heart attack; right subscapular pain from gallbladder attack.

5. Examination of Chronic Pain.

a. History: determine chief complaints, description of onset, mechanism of injury, localization (chronic pain is poorly localized, not well defined); nature of pain (constant, intermittent); irritating stimuli/ activities.

b. Subjective assessment using pain intensity rating scales.

(1) Simple descriptive scales: verbal report (e.g., select the words that best describe your pain).

(2) Semantic differentiation scales: McGill Pain Questionnaire.

(3) Numerical rating scales (rate pain on a scale of 1–10; e.g., 8/10).

(4) Visual analog scale (e.g., bisect line where your pain falls, from mild to severe pain).

(5) Spatial distribution of pain: using drawings to plot location, type of pain.

c. For underlying pathology (cause of pain); objective physical findings are usually not readily identified.
 (1) All systems: musculoskeletal, neurological and cardiopulmonary. Examine for muscle guarding.
 (2) Examine for autonomic changes (abnormal sympathetic activity).
d. Degree of suffering.
 (1) Verbal complaints are out of proportion to degree of underlying pathology; include emotional content.
 (2) Exhibits a stooped posture, antalgic gait.
 (3) Exhibits facial grimacing.
e. Functional changes, abnormal movements.
 (1) Examine for self-imposed limited activity; disrupted lifestyle; disuse syndrome.
 (2) Examine for avoidance of work, social interactions, or sexual activity.
f. Consequences of pain, behavioral impact, secondary gains.
 (1) Monetary benefits (malingering, insurance claims).
 (2) Sympathy and attention.
 (3) Avoidance of undesirable work.
g. Depression, anxiety.
h. Prescription drug misuse.
i. Dependence on health care system: multiple health care providers, clinical services; "shopping around" behaviors.
j. Responsiveness of pain to physiological interventions/treatments: chronic pain is often unresponsive.
k. Motivational/affective components (sick role).
 (1) Previous experience with pain.
 (2) Learned responses to pain.
 (3) Perception of control over pain.
 (4) Ethnicity/cultural aspects of pain.

6. Physical therapy goals, outcomes, and interventions.
 a. Assist patient in identifying pain behaviors, remove behavioral reinforcers, and practice well behaviors.
  (1) Establish a behavior contract: establish consistent level of activity.
  (2) Provide positive reinforcers, educational support.
  (3) Demonstrate change, allow patient to experience success.
 b. Teach coping skills.
 c. Provide relaxation training.
  (1) Progressive relaxation techniques (e.g., Jacobson's), deep breathing exercises.
  (2) Guided imagery.
  (3) Yoga.
  (4) Biofeedback.
 d. Provide direct, time-limited pain control.
  (1) TENS.
  (2) Electrotherapeutic modalities.
  (3) Heat and cold.
  (4) Manipulative procedures: soft tissue massage, mobilization.
  (5) Hydrotherapy.
  (6) Counterirritants; e.g., analgesic balms.
 e. Establish a realistic daily exercise program.
  (1) Improve overall level of conditioning: daily walking program, assistive devices as appropriate.
  (2) Improve overall functional capacity, independence in functional mobility skills, ADLs: ROM, general strengthening, postural training, motor control training.

Interventions for Patients with Neurological Dysfunction

Motor Control/Motor Learning Strategies

1. General concepts.
 a. Incorporates theories of motor control and motor learning.
 b. Consideration is given to both intrinsic neuromuscular control processes and environmental constraints.
2. Motor control strategies.
 a. General concepts—motor control.
  (1) Motor program: a set of prestructured muscle commands that, when initiated, results in the production of a coordinated movement sequence (learned task); can be carried out largely uninfluenced by peripheral feedback.
  (2) Motor plan: an overall strategy for movement; an action sequence requiring the coordination of a number of motor programs.
  (3) Feedback: afferent information sent by various sensory receptors to control centers.
   (a) Feedback updates control centers about the correctness of movement while it progresses; shapes ongoing movement.

(b) Feedback allows motor responses to be adapted to the demands of the environment.

(4) Feedforward: readies the system in advance of movement; anticipatory responses that adjust the system for incoming sensory feedback or for future movements; e.g., preparatory postural adjustments.

(5) Motor skill acquisition.

(a) Behavior is organized to achieve a goal-directed task.

(b) Active problem solving/processing is required for the development of a motor program/motor plan, motor learning; improves retention of skills.

(c) Adaptive to specific environmental demands (regulatory conditions). Closed environment: fixed, nonchanging. Open environment: variable, changing.

(6) CNS recovery/reorganization is dependent upon experience.

3. Motor learning strategies.

a. General concepts—motor learning.

(1) A change in the capability of a person to perform a skill; the result of practice or experience.

(2) Measures of motor learning include:

(a) Performance: determine overall quality of performance, level of automaticity, level of effort, speed of decision-making.

(b) Retention: the ability to demonstrate the skill after a period of no practice.

(c) Generalizability: the acquired capability to apply what has been learned to other similar tasks (transfer tests); e.g., transfers wheelchair to mat, to toilet, and to car.

(d) Resistance to contextual change: acquired capability to apply what has been learned to other environmental contexts; e.g., clinic, home, work.

(3) Feedback.

(a) Intrinsic feedback: sensory information normally acquired during performance of a task.

(b) Augmented feedback: externally presented feedback that is added to that normally acquired during task performance; e.g., verbal cueing.

(c) Knowledge of results (KR): augmented feedback about the outcome of a movement.

(d) Knowledge of performance (KP): augmented feedback about the nature of the movement produced; e.g., movement characteristics.

(e) Feedback schedules: feedback given after every trial; feedback summed (after set number of trials), fading (decreasing) or bandwidth (if responses outside a designated range).

(4) Practice.

(a) Blocked practice: practice of a single motor skill repeatedly; repetitive practice.

(b) Variable practice: practice of varied motor skills in which the performer is required to make rapid modifications of the skill in order to match the demands of the task.

(c) Random practice: practice of a group or class of motor skills in random order (no predictable order).

(d) Serial practice: practice of a group or class of motor skills in serial or predictable order.

(e) Massed practice: relatively continuous practice in which the amount of rest time is small (rest time is less than the practice time).

(f) Distributed practice: practice in which the rest time is relatively large (practice time is less than rest time).

(g) Mental practice: cognitive rehearsal of a motor skill without overt physical performance.

(5) Transfer: the effects of having previous practice of a skill or skills upon the learning of a new skill or upon performance in a new context; transfer may be either positive (assisting learning) or negative (hindering learning).

(a) Part-whole transfer: a learning technique in which a complex motor task is broken down into its component or subordinate parts for separate practice before practice of the integrated whole.

(b) Bilateral transfer: improvement in movement skill performance with one limb results from practice of similar movements with the opposite limb.

b. Strategies for effective learning (Table 2-16).

(1) Feedback given after every trial improves performance, while variable feedback improves learning and retention.

(2) Early training should focus on visual feedback (cognitive phase of learning), while later training should focus on proprioceptive feedback (associative phase of learning).

(3) Reduce extraneous environmental stimuli early in learning (e.g., closed environment), while later learning focuses on adaptation to environmental demands (e.g., open environment).

(4) Supportive feedback (reinforcement) can be used to shape behavior, motivate patient.

(5) Assist learner in recognizing/pairing intrinsic feedback with movement responses.

Table 2-16

Stages of Motor Learning and Training Strategies

COGNITIVE STAGE CHARACTERISTICS	TRAINING STRATEGIES
The learner • develops an understanding of task, *cognitive mapping* • assesses abilities, task demands • identifies stimuli, contacts memory • selects response, performs initial approximations of task • structures motor program • modifies initial responses ***"What to do"*** decision	Highlight purpose of task in functionally relevant terms. Demonstrate ideal performance of task to establish a *reference of correctness* Have patient verbalize task components and requirements. Point out similarities to other learned tasks Direct attention to critical task elements **Select appropriate feedback** • Emphasize intact sensory systems, intrinsic feedback systems • Carefully pair extrinsic feedback with intrinsic feedback • High dependence on vision: have patient watch movement • Provide ***Knowledge of Performance (KP):*** focus on errors as they become consistent; do not cue on large number of random errors • Provide ***Knowledge of Results (KR):*** focus on success of movement outcome Ask learner to evaluate performance, outcomes; identify problems, solutions Use reinforcements (praise) for correct performance and continuing motivation **Organize feedback schedule** • *Feedback* after every trial improves performance during early learning • *Variable feedback* (summed, fading, bandwidth designs) increases depth of cognitive processing, improves retention; may decrease performance initially **Organize initial practice** • Stress controlled movement to minimize errors • Provide adequate rest periods using *distributed practice* if task is complex, long, or energy costly or if learner fatigues easily, has short attention, or has poor concentration • Use manual guidance to assist as appropriate • Break complex tasks down into component parts, teach both parts and integrated whole • Use *bilateral transfer* as appropriate • Use *blocked (repeated)* practice of same task to improve performance • Use *variable practice* (serial or random practice order) of related skills to increase depth of cognitive processing and retention; may decrease performance initially • Use *mental practice* to improve performance and learning, reduce anxiety **Assess, modify arousal levels as appropriate** • High or low arousal impairs performance and learning • Avoid stressors, mental fatigue **Structure environment** • Reduce extraneous environmental stimuli, distractors to ensure attention, concentration • Emphasize closed skills initially gradually progressing to open skills
ASSOCIATED STAGE CHARACTERISTICS	**TRAINING STRATEGIES**
The learner • practices movements • refines motor program • spatial and temporal organization • decreases errors • extraneous movements Dependence on visual feedback decreases, increases for use of proprioceptive feedback; cognitive monitoring decreases ***"How to do"*** decision	**Select appropriate feedback** • Continue to provide KP; intervene when errors become consistent • Emphasize proprioceptive feedback, "feel of movement" to assist in establishing an internal reference of correctness • Continue to provide KR; stress relevance of functional outcomes • Assist learner to improve self-evaluation, decision-making skills • Facilitation techniques, guided movements are counterproductive during this stage of learning **Organize feedback schedule** • Continue to provide feedback for continuing motivation; encourage patient to self-assess achievements • Avoid excessive augmented feedback • Focus on use of variable feedback (summed, fading, bandwidth) designs to improve retention **Organize practice** • Encourage consistency of performance • Focus on variable practice order (serial or random) of related skills to improve retention **Structure environment** • Progress toward open, changing environment • Prepare the learner for home, community, work environments

(*Continued*)

Table 2-16

Stages of Motor Learning and Training Strategies (Continued)

AUTONOMOUS STAGE CHARACTERISTICS	TRAINING STRATEGIES
The learner • practices movements • continues to refine motor responses • spatial and temporal highly organized • movements are largely error-free • minimal level of cognitive monitoring ***"How to succeed"*** decision	Assess need for conscious attention, automaticity of movements **Select appropriate feedback** • Learner demonstrates appropriate self-evaluation, decision-making skills • Provide occasional feedback (KP, KR) when errors evident **Organize practice** • Stress consistency of performance in variable environments, variations of tasks (open skills) • High levels of practice (massed practice) are appropriate **Structure environment** • Vary environments to challenge learner • Ready the learner for home, community, and work environments Focus on competitive aspects of skills as appropriate; e.g., wheelchair sports

From O'Sullivan S, Schmitz T. Physical Rehabilitation. 6th ed, Philadelphia, FA Davis, 2014, pg 397–398, with permission.

(6) Provide augmented feedback: knowledge of results, knowledge of performance.
  (a) Early in learning, focus feedback on correct aspects of performance.
  (b) Later in learning, focus feedback on errors as they become consistent.
  (c) Feedback after every trial improves performance, useful during early learning.
  (d) Use variable feedback (summed, fading, bandwidth) to improve retention, increase depth of cognitive processing.
  (e) Avoid feedback dependence: reduce augmented feedback as soon as possible; foster active introspection, decision-making by learner.

(7) Establish practice schedule: use distributed practice when superior performance is desired, when motivation is low or when the learner has short attention, poor concentration, or fatigues easily.

(8) Use variable practice of a group of functional tasks rather than constant practice to improve learning (promotes retention and generalizability).

(9) Use random or serial practice order rather than blocked practice to improve learning (retention).

(10) Use mental practice to improve learning; have patient verbalize task components, requirements for performance; effective when task has a large cognitive component or to decrease fear and anxiety.

(11) Use parts to whole transfer when task is complex, has highly independent parts, or when learner has limited memory or attention, or difficulty with a particular part. Practice both the parts and the integrated whole.

(12) Limit information with learners who have attention deficits, mentally fatigue easily; focus on key task elements; give frequent rest periods.

(13) Tasks that have highly integrated components should be practiced as a whole; e.g., gait.

(14) Transfer of learning is optimized when tasks are highly similar (similar stimuli, similar responses); e.g., bilateral transfer, one arm to the other.

(15) Use guided movement early in learning, not late; most effective for slow postural or positioning tasks.

(16) Optimal arousal is necessary for optimal learning; low arousal or intense arousal yield poor performance and learning (inverted U theory).

(17) Involve learner in goal setting; task should be desirable, functionally relevant, important to learn.

Task-Specific Training Strategies

1. General concepts.
   a. Emphasis is on use of the affected body segments/limbs using task-specific activities and experiences.
      (1) Patients practice important, functional tasks essential to independence; e.g., stand up and sit down; balance, walking and stair climbing, reaching, and manipulation.
      (2) Patients practice tasks in appropriate and safe environments; focus is on anticipated environments for daily function.
      (3) Repetition and extensive practice are required, including both in-therapy and out-of-therapy time.
      (4) Progressive exercise or activity training requires monitoring of heart rate and blood pressure.

b. Patients practice under therapist's supervision and independently.
   (1) Therapists can provide initial assistance through guided movements and verbal cueing; progression is to active, independent movements as soon as possible.
   (2) Therapists serve as learning coaches, encouraging correct performance.
   (3) Exercise/activity logs help organize the patient's self-monitored practice.

c. Motor learning strategies are utilized, including *behavioral shaping techniques* that use reinforcement and reward to promote skill development.

d. Activity-based, task-oriented training effectively counteracts the effects of immobility and the development of indirect impairments such as muscle weakness and loss of flexibility. It prevents *learned nonuse* of the more involved segments while promoting recovery of the central nervous system (neuroplasticity).

e. Box 2-1 presents a summary of Functional, Task-Oriented Training Strategies.

2. Initial tasks are selected to ensure patient success and motivation (e.g., grasp and release of a cup, forward reach for upper extremity dressing).

3. Tasks are continually altered to increase the level of difficulty.
   a. Therapists target the functional requirements of the task, e.g., a reciprocal stepping pattern, dynamic equilibrium during propulsion and adaptability.

BOX 2-1 Functional, Task-Oriented Training Strategies

Emphasize early training.

- To promote use-dependent cortical plasticity and overcome learned nonuse.

Define the goal of task practice.

- Involve the patient in goal setting and decision making, thereby enhancing motivation and promoting active commitment to recovery.

Determine the activities to be practiced.

- Consider the patient's history, health status, age, interests, and experience.
- Consider the patient's abilities and strengths, recovery level, learning style, impairments, and activity limitations.
- Determine a set of activities to be practiced for each training goal.
- Select activities that are interesting, stimulating, and important to the patient.
- Choose activities with the greatest potential for patient success and intersperse more difficult tasks with easier tasks.
- Target active movements involving the more involved extremities.
- Limit use of less involved extremities; set parameters, impose time limits for use of constraints.
- Prevent or limit compensatory strategies.

Determine the parameters of practice.

- Manage fatigue, determine rest and practice times.
- Model ideal performance; establish a *reference of correctness.*
- Establish requirements for intensity, minimal number of repetitions.
- Establish practice schedule of tasks (blocked or variable); shift to variable practice as soon as possible to enhance retention.
- Determine the practice order of tasks (constant, serial, random); shift to random order as soon as possible to enhance retention.
- Control use of instructions and augmented feedback to promote learning.
- Control use of assisted or guided movements to promote initial learning; ensure the patient successfully transitions to active movements as soon as possible.

Utilize behavioral shaping techniques.

- Gradually modify the task to increase the challenge and make it progressively more difficult as patient performance improves.
- Provide immediate and explicit feedback; recognize and acknowledge small improvements in task performance.
- Emphasize positive aspects of performance.
- Avoid excessive effort and fatigue; they degrade performance and dampen motivation.

BOX 2-1 (*Continued*)

Promote problem-solving.

- Have the patient evaluate performance, identify obstacles, generate potential solutions.
- Have the patient practice the chosen movement (solution) and evaluate outcome.
- Relate successes to overall goals.

Structure the environment.

- Promote initial practice in a supportive environment, free of distractors (closed environment for highly distractible patients).
- Progress to variable practice in real-world environments (open environments).

Establish parameters for practice outside of therapy.

- Identify specific goals and strategies for unsupervised practice; maximize opportunities.
- Utilize a written behavioral contract, have the patient agree to targeted behaviors to be carried out during the day.
- Have patient document unsupervised practice using an activity log or home exercise diary.

Maintain focus on active learning.

- Minimize hands-on therapy.
- Maximize therapist's role as *training coach.*

Monitor recovery closely and document progress.

- Use sensitive, valid, and reliable functional outcome measures.

Be cautious about timetables and predictions: recovery is highly individualized and may take longer than expected.

From O'Sullivan S, Schmitz T. Improving Functional Outcomes in Physical Rehabilitation, 2nd ed. FA Davis, 2016, pg 17, with permission.

b. Verbal cueing and manual assistance are provided as needed to assist.
c. Progression is from treadmill walking to overground walking. Community ambulation skills and adaptability are targeted.

4. Locomotor training.
   a. Motorized treadmill training (TT) with partial body weight support (BWS): provides a means of early task training (e.g., for patients with stroke or incomplete spinal cord injury). The activity is continually adjusted to meet the needs of the patient and progress the activity.
      (1) Focus is on good stepping and posture.
      (2) LE movements are initially manually assisted (e.g., trunk/pelvis, LE stepping); assistance is decreased as skill and control progresses.
      (3) Treadmill speeds are increased with focus on achieving normal functional walking speeds.
      (4) Progression is from body weight support to no support (e.g., 40% to 30% to 20% to 10% to 0%).
      (5) Training is high frequency (3–5 days/week), moderate duration (20–30 minutes) and maximum tolerated intensity (speed and slope).
   b. Overground training: using BWS, progressing to no BWS.
   c. Overground training with least restrictive device (LRD) to no device, as appropriate.
   d. Strategies to vary locomotor task demands: practice walking forward, backward, side-stepping, crossed-stepping (braiding); stopping, starting, and turning on cue; head movements; step-ups, step-up and over, stair climbing, obstacles.
   e. Strategies to promote community reintegration: practice walking in open environments; altered support surface; altered speeds; curbs, ramps, walking through doorways, elevators, dual-task walking.
5. Constraint-Induced (CI) Movement Therapy.
   a. The less-affected UE is restrained by the use of a protective hand mitt.
   b. Task practice is focused on using the more affected UE.
      (1) Must meet minimum movement criteria.
      (2) Repetitive practice of functional tasks.
      (3) Shaping: a functional task is selected and is progressively made more difficult. Goal is for the participant to accomplish the task with effort.

c. Adherence-enhancing behavioral strategies are used, including use of:
   (1) Daily administration of motor activity log.
   (2) Home diary.
   (3) Problem-solving to overcome barriers to use of the more-affected UE.
   (4) Behavioral contract.
   (5) Caregiver contract.
   (6) Home skill assignment, home practice, and daily schedule.

d. Therapist provides feedback, coaching, modeling, and encouragement.

e. Training is high intensity (several hours/day), high frequency (daily) for a period of 2–3 consecutive weeks.

f. Modified CI therapy is less intense, using lower intensity and frequency over a longer period of time (e.g., 1 hour/day, 3 days/week for 8 weeks).

g. Progression is to functional skills performed in the home environment.

Remediation-Facilitation Intervention

1. General concepts.
   a. Includes guided movement, neuromuscular facilitation, sensory stimulation; exercises/activities designed to reduce specific impairments, and improve function of *involved* body segments.
   b. Goal is to enhance or improve recovery.
   c. Developmental focus: emphasis is on developmental postures/activities of movement to promote recovery and function.

2. Proprioceptive Neuromuscular Facilitation (PNF).
   a. Basic procedures for facilitation.
      (1) The facilitation of total patterns of movement promoting motor learning in synergistic muscle patterns.
      (2) Utilizes proprioceptive elements: stretch resistance, overflow, manual contacts, approximation, traction.
      (3) Utilizes motor learning principles: verbal cues, visual guidance of movement, repetition, and practice.
   b. Specific PNF techniques, new revised terminology (traditional terminology):
      (1) Rhythmic Initiation.
      (2) Rhythmic Rotation.
      (3) Stabilizing Reversals (Alternating Isometrics).
      (4) Rhythmic Stabilization.
      (5) Dynamic Reversals (Slow Reversals).
      (6) Combination of Isotonics (Agonist Reversals).
      (7) Replication (Hold-Relax-Active Motion).
      (8) Contract-Relax Active Contraction (CRAC).
      (9) Hold-Relax (HR).
      (10) Repeated Stretch (Repeated Contractions).
   c. Diagonal patterns of movement: upper extremity (UE), named for motions occurring at the proximal joint (shoulder); intermediate joint (elbow) may be straight, flexing, or extending (intermediate pivot).
      (1) Flexion-adduction-external rotation (D1F, diagonal 1 flexion) verbal cues (VC) "Close your hand, turn, and pull your arm across your face."
      (2) Extension-abduction-internal rotation (D1E, diagonal 1 extension) VC: "Open your hand, turn, and push your arm down and out."
      (3) Flexion-abduction-external rotation (D2F) VC: "Open your hand, turn, and lift your arm up and out."
      (4) Extension-adduction-internal rotation (D2E) VC: "Close your hand, turn, and pull your arm down and across your body."
   d. Diagonal patterns of movement: lower extremity (LE), named for motions occurring at the proximal joint (hip); intermediate joint (knee) may be straight, flexing or extending (intermediate pivot).
      (1) Flexion-adduction-external rotation (D1F) VC: "Bring your foot up, turn, and pull your leg up and across your body."
      (2) Extension-abduction-internal rotation (D1E) VC: "Push your foot down, turn, and push your leg down and out."
      (3) Flexion-abduction-internal rotation (D2F) VC: "Lift your foot up, turn, and lift your leg up and out."
      (4) Extension-adduction-external rotation (D2E) VC: "Push your foot down, turn, and pull your leg down and in."
   e. Diagonal patterns: head and trunk.
      (1) Sitting, chop: upper trunk flexion with rotation to right or left; lead arm moves in D1E, assist arm holds on top of wrist.
      (2) Sitting, lift: upper trunk extension with rotation to right or left; lead arm moves in D2F, assist arm holds beneath the wrist.
      (3) Supine, lower trunk flexion with rotation to right or left; knees flexing.
      (4) Supine or sitting, head and neck flexion with rotation to right or left.

3. Neurodevelopmental Treatment (NDT).
   a. Basic concepts.
      (1) Focus is on enhancing motor skills, postural control, and quality of movements through movement experiences. Accurate analysis of the patient's movement patterns is essential.
      (2) Multiple factors contribute to movement dysfunction in patients with neurological dysfunc-

tion: sensory and motor deficits (weakness, limited ROM, impaired tone and coordination).
(3) Focus is on enhancing purposeful relationship between sensory input and motor output; facilitation of normal movement and postural patterns, avoidance (inhibition) of abnormal and compensatory patterns of movement.
(4) Motor learning principles: patterns of movement can be facilitated by appropriate handling techniques, a combination of inhibition/facilitation techniques, guided movements, verbal cues, repetition, and experience in the environment.
(5) Focus is on functional skills with stimulation of critical foundational elements (task components) as well as practice of the whole task. Use of goal-directed activities.
(6) Anticipated goals and outcomes determined in partnership with the family, client, and the interdisciplinary team.

b. Techniques of treatment.
(1) Therapeutic handling: guided and assisted movements leading to active movements.
(2) Normalization of postural control through promotion of appropriate trunk alignment, ability to weight shift, perform transitional movements, and postural control.
(3) Normalization of sensory/perceptual experiences.

c. Patterns of movement.
(1) Resumption of normal functional activities that are meaningful, goal-oriented; e.g., rolling, sitting up, standing, walking; appropriate developmental activities.
(2) Improve timing and synergistic activity of selective limb movements; e.g., UE functional tasks.
(3) Integrated movements utilizing both affected and intact body segments.

4. Sensory stimulation.
a. General concepts.
(1) Indications: patients who demonstrate absent or disordered motor control, i.e., difficulty initiating movement (initial mobility) or sustaining movement (stability), who would benefit from the use of augmented feedback; most useful in the early stages of motor learning.
(2) Contraindications: patients who will not benefit from a hands-on approach, who demonstrate sufficient motor control to perform and refine a motor skill, and the ability to self-correct based on intrinsic feedback mechanisms; e.g., later stages of motor learning.
(3) Response to stimulation is dependent upon multiple factors, including level of intactness of CNS, initial central state/level of CNS arousal, type and amount of stimulation, specific activity of alpha motor neurons pool.
(4) Early use of sensory stimulation techniques should be phased out as soon as possible in favor of active control by the patient; important to avoid feedback/therapist dependence. Can serve as a bridge to active movement control.
(5) Spatial summation (multiple techniques) or temporal summation (repeated application of the same technique) may be necessary to produce the desired response in some low-level patients; e.g., sensory stimulation programs for patients in coma or early recovery following TBI.
(6) Consider cumulative effects: the total environment along with the effects of sensory stimulation techniques. Avoid bombardment (overloads the CNS).

b. Techniques.
(1) Proprioceptive stimulation techniques: quick stretch, resistance, joint approximation and traction.
(2) Tactile/somatosensory techniques: inhibitory pressure, light touch (stimulating), maintain touch (calming).
(3) Vestibular stimulation techniques: slow, repetitive rocking (calming); fast, irregular vestibular stimulation (stimulating).

Compensatory Training Approach

1. General concepts.
a. Indications: to offset or adapt to residual impairments and disabilities.
b. Focus is on early resumption of functional independence with reliance on uninvolved segments for function; e.g., functional training with an individual with complete spinal cord injury.
c. Changes are made in the patient's overall approach to tasks.
(1) Patient is made aware of movement deficiencies, alternate ways to accomplish tasks.
(2) Patient relearns functional patterns and habitual ways of moving.
(3) Patient practices functional skills in a variety of environments.

2. Issues with the compensation approach.
a. Focus on uninvolved segments to accomplish daily tasks (e.g., stroke, traumatic brain injury) may suppress recovery and contribute to *learned nonuse* of the impaired segments.

b. Focus on task specific learning may lead to the development of *splinter skills* in patients with brain damage; skills cannot be easily generalized to other tasks or environmental situations.
c. May be the only approach possible.
   (1) If no additional recovery is anticipated (e.g., complete spinal cord injury).
   (2) If severe motor deficits are present or if sensorimotor recovery has plateaued (e.g., stroke).
   (3) If patient exhibits extensive comorbidities and poor health.

3. Strategies.
   a. Simplify activities.
   b. Establish a new functional pattern; identify key task elements, residual segments available for control of movements.
   c. Repeated practice; work toward consistency, efficiency.
   d. Energy conservation and activity pacing techniques are important to ensure completion of all daily movement requirements.
   e. Adapt environment to facilitate relearning of skills, ease of movement.
      (1) Simplify; set up for optimal performance.
      (2) Use environmental adaptations to enhance performance; e.g., color code stairs, grab bars.

Note: Selected Neuromuscular Outcome Measures can be found in Appendix 2A.

APPENDIX 2A

Selected Neuromuscular Outcome Measures

Table 2A-1

Selected Outcome Measures Organized by the International Classification of Functioning, Disability, and Health (ICF) Categories

BODY STRUCTURE AND FUNCTION MEASURES	REFERENCES
Manual Muscle Test (MMT)	• Hislop HJ, Montgomery J. Daniels and Worthingham's Muscle Testing: Techniques of Manual Examination, 8th ed. Saunders (Elsevier), Philadelphia. 2007. • Kendall, F, McCreary E, Provance P, et al. Muscles Testing and Function with Posture and Pain, 5th ed. Lippincott Williams & Wilkins, Baltimore. 2005.
Joint Motion	• Norkin C, White, J. Measurement of Joint Motion, 4th ed. FA Davis, Philadelphia. 2009.
Modified Ashworth Scale	• Bohannon RW, Smith MB. Interrater reliability of a modified Ashworth scale of muscle spasticity. Phys Ther. 1987; 67: 206–207. • Blackburn M, van Vliet P, Mockett SP. Reliability of measurements obtained with the Modified Ashworth Scale in the lower extremities of people with stroke. Phys Ther. 2002; 82: 25–34.
Mini Mental State Exam (MMSE)	• Folstein MF, Folstein SE, McHugh PR. "Mini-mental state." A practical method for grading the cognitive state of patients for the clinician. J Psychiatr Res. 1975; 12(3): 189.
Dizziness Handicap Inventory (DHI)	• Jacobson GP, Newman CW. The development of the dizziness handicap inventory. Arch Otolaryngol Head Neck Surg. 1990; 16: 424–427.
CEREBROVASCULAR ACCIDENT (CVA)	
Fugl-Meyer Assessment of Motor Performance	• Fugl-Meyer AR, Jaasko L, Leyman I, et al. The post-stroke hemiplegic patient: a method for evaluation and performance. Scand J Rehabil Med. 1975; 3: 13–31. • Fugl-Meyer AR. Post-stroke hemiplegia assessment of physical properties. Scand J Rehabil Med. 1980; 63: 85–93. • Gladstone DJ, Danells CJ, Black S. The Fugl-Myer assessment of motor recovery after stroke: a critical review of its measurement properties. Neurorehabil Neural Repair. 2002; 16: 232.

(Continued)

Table 2A-1

Selected Outcome Measures Organized by the International Classification of Functioning, Disability, and Health (ICF) Categories (Continued)

BODY STRUCTURE AND FUNCTION MEASURES	REFERENCES
National Institutes of Health (NIH) Stroke Scale	• Brott T, Adams HP, Olinger CP, et al. Measurements of acute cerebral infarction: a clinical examination scale. Stroke. 1989; 20: 864–870. • Goldstein LB, Bertels C, Davis JN. Interrater reliability of the NIH stroke scale. Arch Neurol. 1989; 46: 660–662. • Heinemann A, Harvey R, McGuire JR, et al. Measurement properties of the NIH stroke scale during acute rehabilitation. Stroke. 1997; 28: 1174–1180. • The NIH Stroke Scale is available online at: http://www.ninds.nih.gov/doctors/NIH_Stroke_Scale.pdf
Postural Assessment Scale for Stroke Patients (PASS)	• Benaim C, Pérennou DA, Villy J, et al. Validation of a standardized assessment of postural control in stroke patients: the Postural Assessment Scale for Stroke Patients (PASS). Stroke. 1999; 30: 1862–1868. • Pyoria O, Talvitie U, Nyrkko H, et al. Validity of the Postural Control and Balance for Stroke Test. Physiother Res Int. 2007; 12(3): 162–174.
Motor Activity Log (MAL)	• Uswatte G, et al. The Motor Activity Log-28: assessing daily use of the hemiparetic arm after stroke. Neurology 2006: 67: 1189.
Stroke Impact Scale	• Duncan P, et al. The Stroke Impact Scale Version 2.0: Evaluation of reliability, validity, sensitivity to change. Stroke. 1999; 30: 2131–2140.
TRAUMATIC BRAIN INJURY (TBI)	
Glasgow Coma Scale (GCS)	• Jennett B, Teasdale G. Management of Head Injuries. FA Davis, Philadelphia. 1981.
Rancho Levels of Cognitive Function (LOCF)	• Hagen C, Malkmus D, Durham P. Levels of cognitive functioning. In: Rehabilitation of the Head Injured Adult: Comprehensive Physical Management. Downey, CA: Professional Staff Association of Ranchos Los Amigos Hospital. 1979.
High Level Mobility Assessment Tool (HiMat)	• Williams GP, Robertson V, Greenwood KM, et al. The high-level mobility assessment tool (HiMAT) for traumatic brain injury. Part 1: Item generation. Brain Injury. 2005; 19(11): 925–932. • Williams GP, Robertson V, Greenwood, KM et al. The high-level mobility assessment tool (HiMAT) for traumatic brain injury. Part 2: Content validity and discriminability. Brain Injury. 2005; 19(10): 833–843. • Williams GP, Greenwood KM, Robertson VJ, et al. High-Level Mobility Assessment Tool (HiMAT): Inter-rater reliability, retest reliability, and internal consistency. Phys Ther. 2006; 86: 395–400. • The HiMat is available online at: http://www.tbims.org/combi/himat/index.html
SPINAL CORD INJURY (SCI)	
ASIA Impairment Scale—Standard Neurological Classification of Spinal Cord Injury	• American Spinal Injury Association (ASIS): International Standards for Neurological Classification of Spinal Cord Injury. ASIS, Chicago. 2006. • American Spinal Injury Association (ASIS): International Standards for Neurological Classification of Spinal Cord Injury. ASIS, Atlanta. 2015. • Spinal Cord Injury Levels & Classification: www.sci-info-pages.com • Kirshblum S, Waring W. Updates for the International Standards for Neurological Classification of Spinal Cord Injury. Phys Med Rehabil Clin N Am, 2014; 25(3): 505–17. • Kirshblum S, Burns S, Biering-Sorensen, F, et al. International standards for neurological classification of spinal cord injury. J Spinal Cord Med, 2011; 34(6): 535–546.
Multidimensional Pain Inventory-Spinal Cord Version (MPI-SCI)	• Widerstrom-Noga EG, Cruz-Almeida Y, Martinez-Arizala A, Turk DC. Internal consistency, stability, and validity of the spinal cord injury version of the multidimensional pain inventory. Arch Phys Med Rehabil. 2006; 87: 516–523.
Penn Spasm Frequency Scale (PSFS)	• Adams MM, Ginis KAM, Hicks AL. The spinal cord injury spasticity evaluation tool: development and evaluation. Arch Phys Med Rehabil. 2007; 88:1185–1192. • Hsieh J, Wolfe D, Miller W, Curt A. Spasticity outcome measures in spinal cord injury: psychometric properties and clinical utility. Spinal Cord. 2008; 46: 86–95.
Quadriplegia Index of Function (QIF)	• Gresham GE, Labi ML, et al. The Quadriplegia Index of Function (QIF): sensitivity and reliability demonstrated in a study of thirty quadriplegic patients. Paraplegia. 1986; 24(1): 38–44.
Spinal Cord Independence Measure (SCIM)	• Ackerman P, Morrison SA, McDowell S, Vazquez L. Using the Spinal Cord Independence Measure III to measure functional recovery in a post-acute spinal cord injury program. Spinal Cord. 2010; 48: 380–387. • Anderson K, Aito S, Atkins M, et al. Functional recovery measures for spinal cord injury: an evidence-based review for clinical practice and research. J Spinal Cord Med. 2008; 31(2): 133–144.

Table 2A-1

Selected Outcome Measures Organized by the International Classification of Functioning, Disability, and Health (ICF) Categories (Continued)

BODY STRUCTURE AND FUNCTION MEASURES	REFERENCES
Walking Index for Spinal Cord Injury (WISCI, WISCI II)	• Dittuno PL, Ditunno JF, Jr. Walking index for spinal cord injury (WISCI II): Scale revision. Spinal Cord. 2001; 39: 654–656. • Ditunno JF, Jr., et al. Validity of the walking scale for spinal cord injury and other domains of function in a multicenter clinical trial. Neurorehabil Neural Repair. 2007; 21: 539–550.
PARKINSON'S DISEASE (PD)	
Freezing of Gait Questionnaire	• Giladi, N., Shabtai, H., et al. "Construction of freezing of gait questionnaire for patients with Parkinsonism." Parkinsonism Relat Disord. 2000; 6(3): 164–170. • Giladi, N., Tal, J., et al. "Validation of the freezing of gait questionnaire in patients with Parkinson's disease." Mov Disord. 2009; 24(5): 655–661.
Parkinson's Fatigue Scale	• Brown, et al (2005). "The Parkinson fatigue scale." Parkinsonism and related disorders. 11: 49–55. • Friedman, J et al. (2010). "Fatigue rating scales critique and recommendations by the movement disorders society task force on rating scales for parkinson's disease." Movement Disorders 25(7): 805–822.
Unified Parkinson's Disease Rating Scale (UPDRS)	• Fahn S, Elton R. Unified Parkinson's Disease Rating Scale. In: Fahn S, et al (eds): Recent Developments in Parkinson's Disease, Vol 2. Macmillan Health Care Information, Florham Park, NJ. 1987:153–167. • Unified Parkinson's Disease Rating Scale available online at: www.etas.ee/wp-content/uploads/2013/10/updrs.pdf • Goetz C, et al. Movement Disorder Society-sponsored revision of the Parkinson's Disease Rating Scale (MDS-UPDRS): Scale presentation and clinimetric testing results. Mov Disord. 2008; 23(15): 2129–2170.
MULTIPLE SCLEROSIS (MS)	
Modified Fatigue Impact Scale (mFIS)	• Fisk JD, Pontefract A, Ritvo PG, et al. The impact of fatigue on patients with multiple sclerosis. Can J Neurol Sci. 1994; 21(1): 9. • Fisk JD, Ritvo PG, Ross L, et al. Measuring the functional impact of fatigue: Initial validation of the Fatigue Impact Scale. Clin Infect Dis Suppl. 1994; 1: S79.
Expanded Disability Status Scale & Kurtzke Functional Systems Score	• Kurtzke JF. Rating neurologic impairment in multiple sclerosis: an expanded disability status scale (EDSS). Neurology. 1983; 33(11): 1444–1452.
Scale for the Assessment and Rating of Ataxia (SARA)	• Schmitz-Hubsch T, Tezenas du Montcel S, Baliko L, et al. Scale for the assessment and rating of ataxia: development of a new clinical scale. Neurology. 2006; 66(11): 1717–1720.
Functional Assessment of Multiple Sclerosis (FAMS)	• Cella DF, Dineen K, Armason B, et al. Validation of the functional assessment of multiple sclerosis quality of life instrument. Neurology. 1996; 47(1): 129–139.
ACTIVITY	
Functional Independence Measure (FIM)	• Guide for the Uniform Data Set for Medical Rehabilitation (Adult FIM) version 4.0, State University of New York at Buffalo. 1993. • Dodds TA, Martin DP, Stolov WC, et al. A validation of the functional independence measurement and its performance among rehabilitation in-patients. Arch Phys Med Rehabil. 1993; 174: 531–536. • Long WB, Sacco MJ, Coombes SS, et al. Determining normative standards for Functional Independence Measure transitions in rehabilitation. Arch Phys Med Rehabil. 1994; 75: 925–932. • The FIM is available online at: http://www.udsmr.org • email: info@udsmr.org
Functional Assessment Measure (FIM + FAM) [TBI]	• Linn RT, et al. Does the Functional Assessment Measure (FAM) extend the Functional Independence Measure (FIM™) Instrument? A Rasch analysis of stroke patients. J Outcome Measure. 1999; 3: 339. • Hall KM. The Functional Assessment Measure (FAM). J Rehabil Outcomes. 1997; 1(3): 63–65. • Hall KM, Mann N, High WM, et al. Functional measures after traumatic brain injury: Ceiling effects of FIM, FIM+FAM, DRS, and CIQ. J Head Trauma Rehabil. 1996; 11(5): 27–39.
Barthel Index (BI)	• Granger CV, Devis LS, Peters MC, et al. Stroke rehabilitation analysis of repeated Barthel Index measures. Arch Phys Med Rehabil. 1979; 60: 14–17. • Mahoney FI, Barthel DW. Functional evaluation: The Barthel Index. Maryland State Med J. 1965; 14: 61–65.
Physical Performance Test	• Reuben DB, Siu AL. An objective measure of physical function of elderly populations: The Physical Performance Test. J Am Geriatr Soc. 1990; 38: 1105.

(*Continued*)

Table 2A-1

Selected Outcome Measures Organized by the International Classification of Functioning, Disability, and Health (ICF) Categories (Continued)

BODY STRUCTURE AND FUNCTION MEASURES	REFERENCES
Disabilities of the Arm, Shoulder, and Hand Outcome Measure (DASH)	• Beaton DE, Davis AM, Hudak P, McConnell S. The DASH (Disabilities of the Arm, Shoulder and Hand) Outcome Measure: What do we know about it now? Br J Hand Ther. 2001; 6(4): 109–118. • Beaton DE, Katz JN, Fossel AH, et al. Measuring the whole or the parts? validity, reliability & responsiveness of the disabilities of the arm, shoulder, and hand outcome measure in different regions of the upper extremity. J Hand Ther. 2001; 14(2): 128. • Bot SDM, Terwee CB, van der Windt DAWM, et al. Clinimetric evaluation of shoulder disability questionnaires: A systematic review of the literature. Ann Rheum Dis. 2004; 63(4): 335. • Available online at: http://www.dash.iwh.on.ca/
Lower Extremity Functional Scale (LEFS)	• Wang Y-C, Hart DL, Stratford PW, Mioduski JE. Clinical Interpretation of a Lower-Extremity Functional Scale–derived computerized adaptive test. Phys Ther. 2009; 89(9): 957. • Lin CW, Moseley AM, Refshauge KM, Bundy AC. The Lower Extremity Functional Scale has good clinimetric properties in people with ankle fracture. Phys Ther. 2009; 89(6): 580. • Binkley JM, Stratford PW, Lott SA, Riddle DL. The Lower Extremity Functional Scale (LEFS): Scale development, measurement properties, and clinical application. Phys Ther. 1999; 79(4): 371. • Available online at: www.emoryhealthcare.org
Wheelchair Skills Test (WST)	• Kirby RL, Dupuis DJ, MacPhee AH, et al. The Wheelchair Skills Test (version 2.4): measurement properties. Arch Phys Med Rehabil. 2004; 85: 794. • Videotapes for Wheelchair Users and Wheelchair Skills Program (WSP) Version 4.1 Manual available online at: http://www.wheelchairskillsprogram.ca/eng/overview.htm • Additional online resources • The Powered Wheelchair Training Guide: www.wheelchairnet.org • The Manual Wheelchair Training Guide: www.wheelchairnet.org • A Guide to Wheelchair Selection: www.spinalcord.org
Wolf Motor Function Test (WMFT) [CVA]	• Wolf SL, Catlin PA, Ellis M, et al. Assessing Wolf Motor Function Test as outcome measure for research in patients after stroke. Stroke. 2001; 32: 1635. • Morris DM, Uswatte G, Crago JE, et al. The reliability of the Wolf Motor Function Test for assessing upper extremity function after stroke. Arch Phys Med Rehabil. 2001; 82: 750.
Motor Activity Log (MAL) [CVA]	• Wolf SL, Thompson PA, Morris DM, et al. The EXCITE trial: Attributes of the Wolf Motor Function Test in patients with subacute stroke. Neurorehabil Neural Repair. 2005; 19: 194. • Uswatte G, Taub E, Morris D, et al. The Motor Activity Log-28: Assessing daily use of the hemiparetic arm after stroke. Neurology. 2006; 67: 1189. • Van der Lee JH, Beckerman H, Knol DL, et al. Clinimetric properties of the motor activity log for the assessment of arm use in hemiparetic patients. Stroke. 2004; 35: 1410.
Berg Balance Scale (BBS)	• Berg K, Wood-Dauphinee S, Williams J, et al. Measuring balance in the elderly: preliminary development of an instrument. Physiother Can. 1989; 41: 304–311. • Berg KO, Maki B, Williams JI, et al. Clinical and laboratory measures of postural balance in an elderly population. Arch Phys Med Rehabil. 1992; 73: 1073–1080. • Berg KO, Wood-Dauphinee SL, Williams JI, et al. Measuring balance in the elderly: Validation of an instrument. Can J Public Health. 1992; 83: S7–S11. • Berg KO, Wood-Dauphinee S, Williams JI. The balance scale: reliability assessment with elderly residents and patients with an acute stroke. Scand J Rehabil Med. 1995; 27: 27–36.
The Balance Evaluation Systems Test (BESTest); Mini-BESTest	• Horak FB, Wrisley DM, Frank J. The Balance Evaluation Systems Test (BESTest) to differentiate balance deficits. Phys Ther May. 2009; 89(5): 484–498. • Franchignoni F, Horak F, Godi M, et al. Using psychometric techniques to improve the Balance Evaluation Systems Test: the mini-BESTest. J Rehabil Med. 2010; 42(4): 323–331. • King L & Horak F. On the Mini-BESTest: Scoring and the reporting of total scores. Phys Ther 2013; 93(4): 542–50.
Functional Reach (FR)	• Duncan P, et al. Functional Reach: A new clinical measure of balance. J Gerontol. 1990; 45: M192. • Duncan PW, Studenski S, Chandler J, Prescott B. Functional reach: Predictive validity in a sample of elderly male veterans. J Gerontol. 1992; 47: M93. • Weiner DK, Duncan PW, Chandler J, Studenski SA. Functional Reach: A marker of physical frailty. J Am Geriatr Soc. 1992; 40: 2–3.

Table 2A-1

Selected Outcome Measures Organized by the International Classification of Functioning, Disability, and Health (ICF) Categories (Continued)

BODY STRUCTURE AND FUNCTION MEASURES	REFERENCES
Multidirectional Functional Reach Test	• Newton R. Validity of the multi-directional reach test: A practical measure for limits of stability in older adults. J Gerontol Med Sci. 2001; 56(4): M248–M252. • Newton R. Validity of MDRT. J Gerontol. 2001; 56A.4: M248.
Modified Functional Reach (seated)	• Lynch SM, Leahy P, Barker S. Reliability of measurements obtained with a modified functional reach test in subjects with spinal cord injury. Phys Ther. 1998; 78(2): 128.
Function in Sitting Test (FIST)	• Gorman SL, Radtka S, Melnick ME, et al. Development and validation of the Function in Sitting Test in adults with acute stroke. J Neurol Phys Ther. 2010; 34(3): 150–160.
Stops Walking When Talking (SWWT)	• Lundin-Olsson L, Nyberg L, Gustafson Y. Stops walking when talking as a predictor of falls in elderly people. Lancet. 1997; 348: 617.
Timed Up & Go (TUG)	• Ng SS, Hui-Chan CW. The Timed Up & Go test: Its reliability and association with lower-limb impairments and locomotor capabilities in people with chronic stroke. Arch Phys Med Rehabil. 2005; 86: 1641–1647. • Podsiadlo D, Richardson S. The Timed "Up & Go": A test of basic functional mobility for frail elderly persons. J Am Geriatr Soc. 1992; 39: 142–148.
Performance-Oriented Mobility Assessment (POMA) (Tinetti)	• Tinetti M. Performance-oriented assessment of mobility problems in elderly patients. J Am Geriatr Soc. 1986; 34: 119–126.
Clinical Test for Sensory Interaction in Balance (CTSIB)	• Shumway-Cook A, Horak F. Assessing the influence of sensory interaction on balance. Phys Ther. 1986; 66(10): 1548–1550.
Modified Clinical Test for Sensory Integration in Balance (mCTSIB)	• Rose DJ. Fallproof: A Comprehensive Balance and Mobility Training Program, 2nd ed. Human Kinetics, Champaign, IL. 2010.
Four Square Step Test	• Dite W, Temple VA. A clinical test of stepping and change of direction to identify multiple falling older adults. Archives of Physical Medicine & Rehabilitation. 2002; 83(11): 1566–1571. • Whitney SL, Marchetti GF, Morris LO, Sparto PJ. The reliability and validity of the Four Square Step Test for people with balance deficits secondary to a vestibular disorder. Archives of Physical Medicine & Rehabilitation. 2007; 88(1): 99–104.
Functional Gait Assessment (FGA)	• Wrisley DM, Marchetti GF, Kuharsky DK, Whitney SL. Reliability, internal consistency, and validity of data obtained with the functional gait assessment. Phys Ther. 2004; 84: 906–918.
Modified Emory Functional Ambulation Profile (mEFAP)	• Baer HR, Wolf SL. Modified Emory Functional Ambulation Profile: An outcome measure for rehabilitation for post stroke gait dysfunction. Stroke. 2001; 32: 973. • Wolf SL, Catlin PA, Gage K. Establishing the reliability and validity of measurements using the Emory Functional Ambulation Profile. Phys Ther. 1999; 79: 1122. • Nelson, AJ: Functional ambulation profile. Phys Ther. 1974; 54: 1059.
Five Times Sit to Stand	• Mong Y, Tilda T, et al. 5-Repetition Sit-to-Stand Test in Subjects With Chronic Stroke: Reliability and Validity. Arch Phys Med Rehabil. 2010; 91(3): 407–413. • Lord SR, Murr SM, Chapman K, et al. Sit-to-stand performance depends on sensation, speed, balance, and psychological status in addition to strength in older people. J Gerontol A Biol Sci Med Sci. 2002; 57: 539–543.
6-Minute Walk Test	• Enright, PL, Sherrill, DL. Reference equations for the six-minute walk in healthy adults. Am J Respir Crit Care Med. 1998; 158: 1384–1387. • Liu J, Drutz C, Kumar R, et al. Use of 6-Minute Walk Test post stroke. Is there a practice effect? Arch Phys Med Rehabil. 2008; 89: 1686–1692. • Fulk GD, Echternach JL, Nof L, O'Sullivan S. Clinometric properties of the 6-Minute Walk Test in individuals undergoing rehabilitation poststroke. Physiother Theory and Pract. 2008; 24: 195–204.
Timed Walk Tests (5 m, 10 m)	• Sullivan KJ, et al: Effects of task-specific locomotor and strength training in adults who were ambulatory after stroke: Results of the STEPS randomized clinical trial. Phys Ther. 2007; 87: 1580–1602.
Dynamic Gait Index (DGI)	• Shumway-Cook A, Woollacott M. Motor Control—Translating Research into Clinical Practice, 3rd ed. Lippincott Williams & Wilkins. 2007: 395–396. • Jonsdottir J, Cattaneo D. Reliability and validity of the Dynamic Gait Index in persons with chronic stroke. Arch of Phys Med and Rehabil. 2007; 88(11): 1410–1415. • Walker ML, Austin G, Banke GM, et al. Reference group data for the Functional Gait Assessment. Phys Ther. 2007; 87(11): 1468–1477. • Wrisley D. Functional Gait Assessment Phys Ther. 2007; 84(10): Appendix.

(*Continued*)

Table 2A-1

Selected Outcome Measures Organized by the International Classification of Functioning, Disability, and Health (ICF) Categories (Continued)

BODY STRUCTURE AND FUNCTION MEASURES	REFERENCES
Observational Gait Analysis (OGA)	• Pathokinesiology Service and Physical Therapy Department: Observational Gait Analysis Handbook. Los Amigos Research and Education Institute, Inc, Downey, CA, 2001. • Perry JP and Burnfield, JM. Gait Analysis: Normal and Pathological Function, 2nd ed. Thorofare, NJ: Slack. 2010.
Activities and Balance Confidence Scale (ABC)	• Myers AM, Fletcher PC, Myers AN, et al. Discriminative and evaluative properties of the ABC Scale. J Gerontol. 1998; 53A: M287–M294. • Powell LE, Myers AM. Activities-specific Balance Confidence (ABC) Scale. J Gerontol. 1995; 50A: M28–M34. • The ABC Scale is available online at: www.healthcare.uiowa.edu
PARTICIPATION	
The MOS SF-36 Health Survey	• Anderson C, Laubscher S, Burns R. Validation of the short-form (SF-36) health survey questionnaire among stroke patients. Stroke. 1996; 27: 1812–1816. • Ware JE, Sherbourne CD. The MOS 36-Item Short-Form Health Survey (SF-36), 1: conceptual framework and item selection. Med Care. 1992; 30: 473–483. • The SF-36 Health Survey is available online at: www.rand.org
Satisfaction with Life Scale (SWLS)	• Post MW, Christel M, van Leeuwen CF, Koppenhagen SD. Validity of the Life Satisfaction questions, the Life Satisfaction Questionnaire (LiSat-9) and the Satisfaction with Life Scale (SWLS) in persons with spinal cord injury. Arch Phys Med Rehabil. 2012, doi; 10.101/j.apmr.2012.03.025
Participation Objective, Participation Subjective (POPS)	• Brown M, Dijkers MPJ, Gordon W, et al Participation Objective, Participation Subjective: A measure of participation combining outsider and insider perspectives. J Head Trauma Rehabil. 2004; 19(6): 459–481. • Mascialino G, Hirshson C, Egan M, et al. Objective and subjective assessment of long-term community integration in minority groups following traumatic brain injury. NeuroRehabilitation. 2009; 24(1): 29–36. • The POPS is available online at: http://www.tbims.org/combi/pops/Appendix%20I.doc
Impact of Participation and Autonomy (IPA)	• Cardol M, de Haan RJ, de Jong BA, et al. Psychometric properties of the impact on participation and autonomy questionnaire. Arch Phys Med Rehabil. 2001; 82(2): 210–216. • The IPA is available online at: http://www.nivel.nl/pdf/INT-IPA-E.pdf
Outpatient Physical Therapy Improvement in Assessment Log (OPTIMAL)	• Guccione AA, Mielenz TJ, Devellis RF, et al. Development and testing of a self-report instrument to measure actions: outpatient physical therapy improvement in movement assessment log (OPTIMAL). Phys Ther. 2005; 85(6): 515–530. • Optimal is available online at: http://www.apta.org
Craig Handicap Assessment and Reporting Technique (CHART)	• Walker N, Mellick D, Brooks CA, et al. Measuring participation across impairment groups using the Craig Handicap Assessment Reporting Technique. Am J Phys Med Rehabil. 2003; 82(12): 936–941. • Hall KM, Dijkers M, Whiteneck G, et al. The Craig Handicap Assessment and Reporting Technique (CHART): Metric properties and scoring. J Rehabil Outcomes Measure. 1998; 2(5): 39–49. CHART is available online at: http://www.tbims.org/combi/chart/index.html
Stroke Impact Scale (SIS)	• Duncan PW, Lai SM, Bode RK, et al. Stroke Impact Scale-16: A brief assessment of physical function. Neurology. 2003; 60(2): 291. • Duncan PW, Bode R, Lai SM, et al. Rasch analysis of a new stroke specific outcome scale: The Stroke Impact Scale. Arch Phys Med Rehabil. 2003; 84(7): 950. • The SIS is available online at: http://www.chrp.org/pdf/HSR082103_SIS_Handout.pdf

Key: TBI: traumatic brain injury; SCI: spinal cord injury; CVA: cerebrovascular accident.
For a more complete list see APTA Neurology Section Outcome Measures Recommendations, www.neuropt.org/professional-resources

Review Questions

Neuromuscular Physical Therapy

1. Which cranial nerves may play any role in vision? What findings are normal or abnormal?

2. Following a CVA primarily affecting the occipital lobe, what are the major considerations when examining the patient for perceptual deficits?

3. When examining deep tendon reflexes, what is the score reported for an obligatory and sustained response?

4. What are the characteristics in terms of communication, gait, tone, balance, and respiratory function in a patient with late Parkinson's disease (Stage IV Hoehn and Yahr)?

5. What are the initial physical therapy goals and interventions upon receiving a referral for a patient recently diagnosed with a severe vestibular disorder?

6. Following an MVA, a patient with a complete SCI at the C7 level has been admitted to a rehab facility after a lengthy stay at an acute care hospital. What are the components of the physical therapist's initial examination?

7. What is the common pattern of fatigue in many patients with multiple sclerosis?

3

Cardiovascular and Lymphatic Physical Therapy

KELLY MACAULEY AND SUSAN B. O'SULLIVAN

Chapter Outline

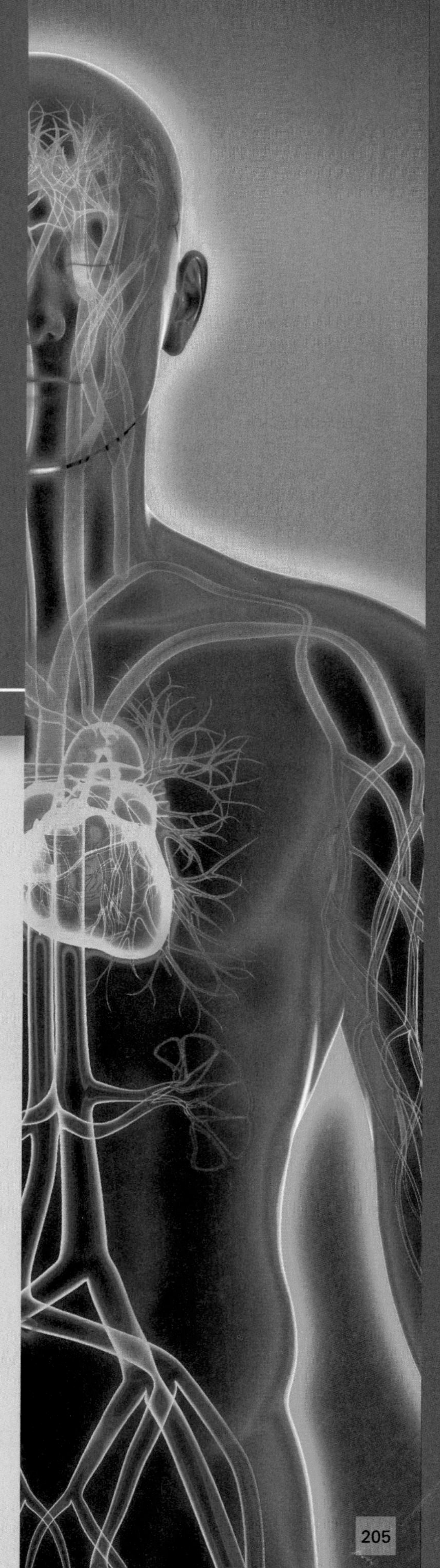

Anatomy and Physiology of the Cardiovascular System

The Heart and Circulation

1. Heart tissue.
   a. Pericardium: fibrous protective sac enclosing heart.
   b. Epicardium: inner layer of pericardium.
   c. Myocardium: heart muscle, the major portion of the heart.
   d. Endocardium: smooth lining of the inner surface and cavities of the heart.
2. Heart chambers (see Figure 3-1).
   a. Right atrium (RA): receives blood from systemic circulation, from the superior and inferior vena cavae (IVC).
   b. Right ventricle (RV): receives blood from the RA and pumps blood via the pulmonary artery to the lungs for oxygenation; the low-pressure pulmonary pump.
   c. Left atrium (LA): receives oxygenated blood from the lungs and the four pulmonary veins.

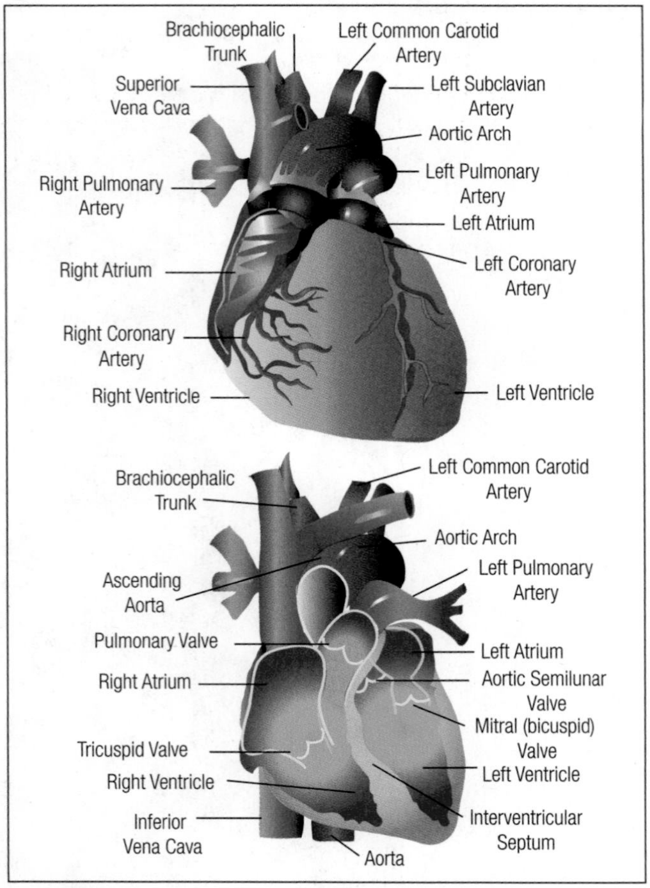

Figure 3-1 **The heart.**

   d. Left ventricle (LV): receives blood from the LA and pumps blood via the aorta throughout the entire systemic circulation; the high-pressure systemic pump. The walls of the LV are thicker and stronger than the RV and form most of the left side and apex of the heart.
3. Valves. Provide one-way flow of blood.
   a. Atrioventricular valves: prevent backflow of blood into atria during ventricular systole; anchored by chordae tendineae to papillary muscles; valves close when ventricular walls contract.
      (1) Tricuspid valve (three cusps or leaflets): right heart valve.
      (2) Bicuspid or mitral valve (two cusps or leaflets): left heart valve.
   b. Semilunar valves: prevent backflow of blood from aorta and pulmonary arteries into the ventricles during diastole.
      (1) Pulmonary valve: prevents right backflow.
      (2) Aortic valve: prevents left backflow.
4. Cardiac cycle (see Figure 3-2).
   a. The rhythmic pumping action of the heart.
   b. Systole: the period of ventricular contraction. End-systolic volume is the amount of blood in the ventricles after systole; about 50 mL.
   c. Diastole: the period of ventricular relaxation and filling of blood. End-diastolic volume is the amount of blood in the ventricles after diastole; about 120 mL.
   d. Atrial contraction (atrial kick) occurs during the last third of diastole and completes ventricular filling, comprising last 20%–30% of end diastolic volume.
5. Coronary circulation (see Figure 3-3).
   a. Arteries: arise directly from aorta near aortic valve; blood circulates to myocardium during diastole.
      (1) Right coronary artery (RCA): supplies right atrium, most of right ventricle, and in most individuals, the inferior wall of left ventricle, atrioventricular (AV) node and bundle of His; supplies the sinoatrial (SA) node 60% of the time.
      (2) Left coronary artery (LCA): supplies most of the left ventricle; has two main divisions.
         (a) Left anterior descending (LAD): supplies the left ventricle and the interventricular septum, and in most individuals, the inferior areas of the apex; it may also give off branches to the right ventricle.
         (b) Circumflex (LCx): supplies blood to the lateral and inferior walls of the left ventricle and portions of the left atrium; supplies SA node 40% of the time.

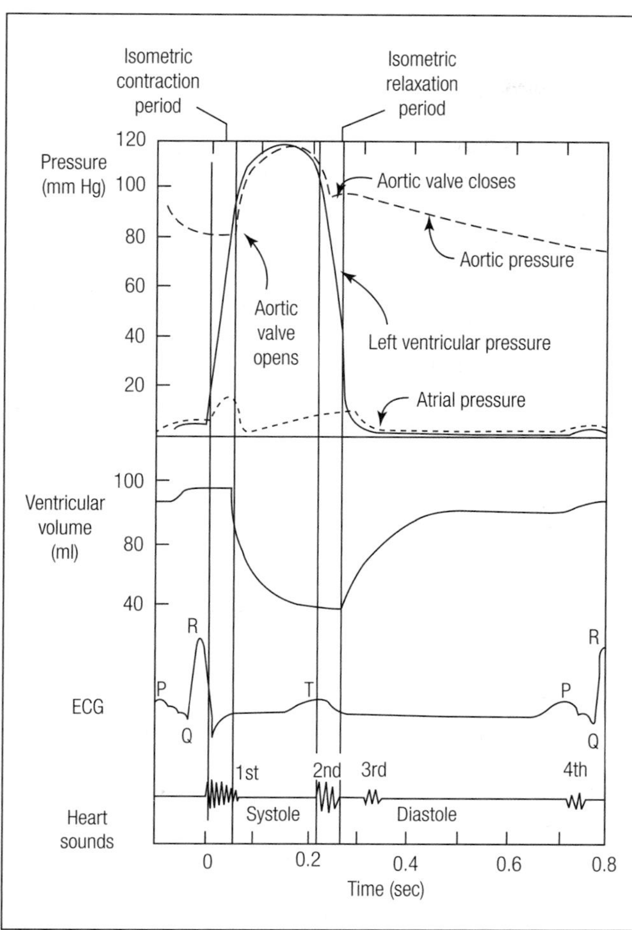

Figure 3-2 **Events of the cardiac cycle.**

b. Veins: parallel arterial system; the coronary sinus receives venous blood from the heart and empties into the right atrium.

c. Distribution of blood supply is variable from individual to individual.

d. Myocardial oxygen supply and myocardial oxygen demand (MVO_2) should be in balance in order to maintain a given activity level without ischemia.

6. Conduction (see Figure 3-4).

a. Specialized conduction tissue: allows rapid transmission of electrical impulses throughout the myocardium (normal sinus rhythm, NSR).

b. Sinoatrial (SA) node.

(1) Located at junction of superior vena cava and right atrium.

(2) Main pacemaker of the heart; initiates the impulse at rate of 60–100 beats per minute.

(3) Has sympathetic and parasympathetic innervation affecting both heart rate and strength of contraction.

c. Atrioventricular (AV) node.

(1) Located at the junction of the right atrium and the right ventricle.

(2) Has sympathetic and parasympathetic innervation.

(3) Merges with bundle of His.

(4) Intrinsic firing rate of 40–60 beats per minute.

d. Purkinje tissue.

(1) Right and left bundle branches of the AV node are located on either side of intraventricular septum.

(2) Terminate in Purkinje fibers, specialized conducting tissue spread throughout the ventricles.

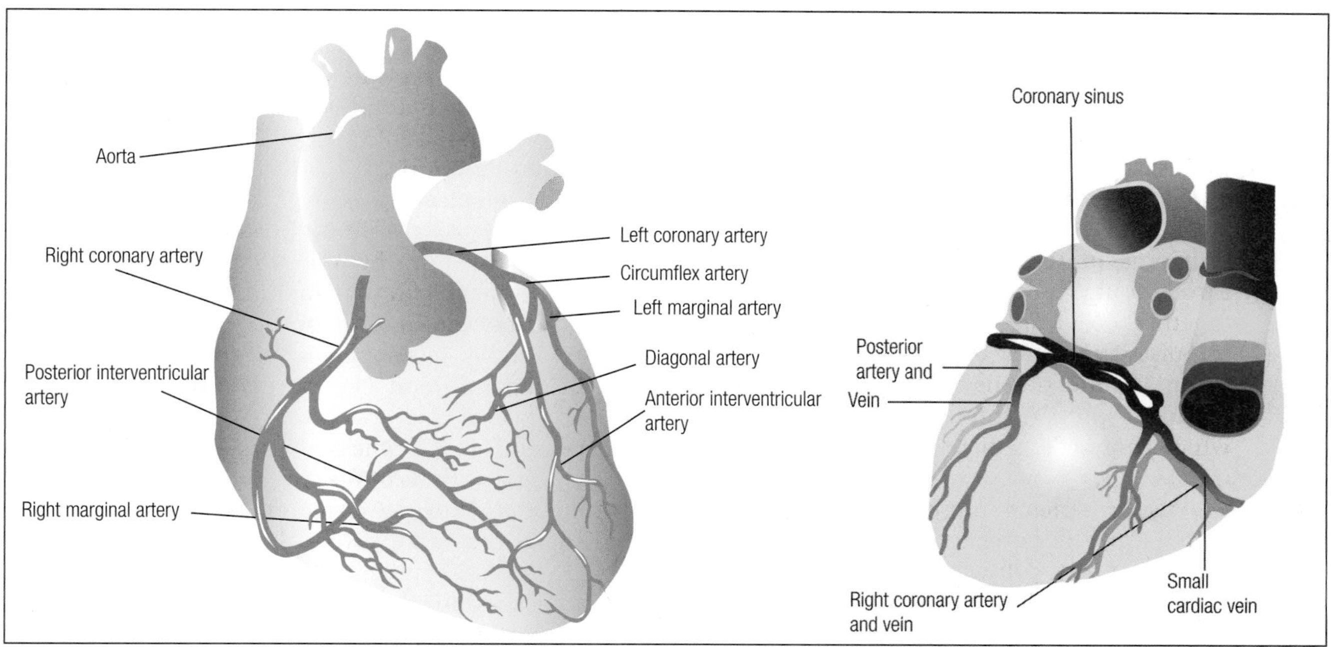

Figure 3-3 **Coronary arteries.**

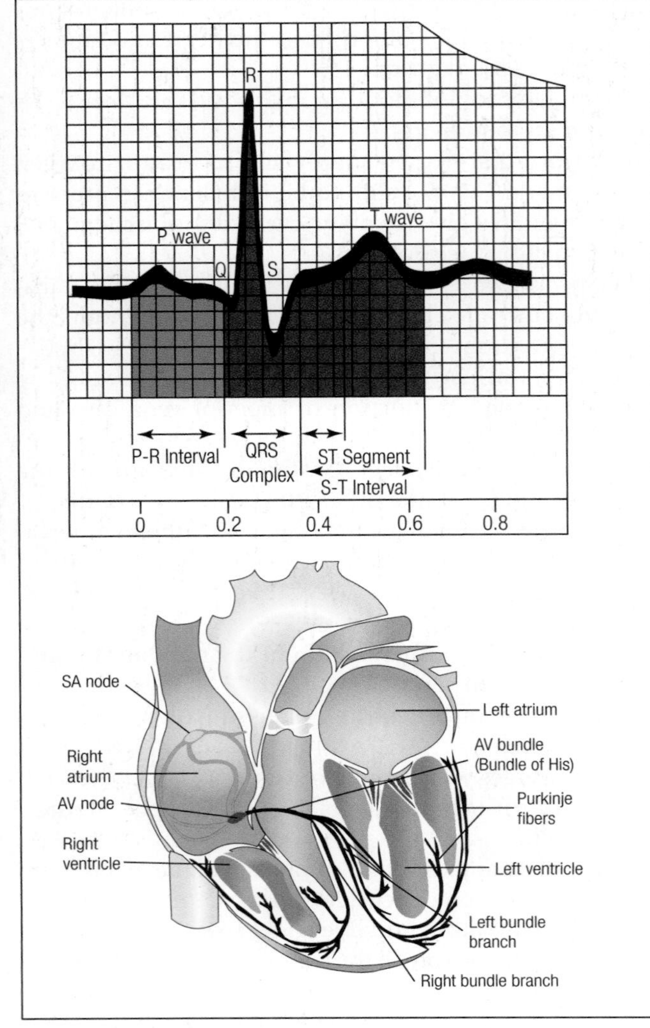

Figure 3-4 **Conduction pathways of the heart.**

(3) Intrinsic firing rate of 20–40 beats per minute.

e. Conduction of a normal heart beat (normal sinus rhythm).
   (1) Origin is in the SA node; impulse spreads throughout both atria, which contract together.
   (2) Impulse stimulates AV node, is transmitted down bundle of His to the Purkinje fibers; impulse spreads throughout the ventricles, which contract together (atrial kick).

7. Myocardial fibers.
   a. Muscle tissue: striated muscle fibers with more numerous mitochondria; exhibits rhythmicity of contraction; fibers contract as a functional unit (sliding filament theory of contraction).
   b. Myocardial metabolism is essentially aerobic, sustained by continuous O_2 delivery, from the coronary arteries.
   c. Smooth muscle tissue is found in the walls of blood vessels.

8. Hemodynamics.
   a. Stroke volume (SV): the amount of blood ejected with each myocardial contraction; normal range is 55–100 mL/beat. Influenced by:
      (1) Left ventricular end diastolic volume (LVEDV): the amount of blood left in the ventricle at the end of diastole, also known as preload. The greater the diastolic filling (preload), the greater the quantity of blood pumped (Frank-Starling law).
      (2) Contractility: the ability of the ventricle to contract.
      (3) Afterload: the force the LV must generate during systole to overcome aortic pressure to open the aortic valve.
   b. Cardiac output (CO): the amount of blood discharged from the left or right ventricle per minute.
      (1) For average adult at rest, normal range is 4–5 L per minute.
      (2) Determined by multiplying heart rate (HR) times stroke volume (SV).
      (3) Cardiac index is CO divided by body surface area; normal range is 2.5–3.5 L/min.
   c. Left ventricular end diastolic pressure (LVEDP): pressure in the left ventricle during diastole. Normal range is 5–12 mm Hg.
   d. Ejection fraction (EF): percentage of blood emptied from the ventricle during systole; a clinically useful measure of LV function.
      (1) EF = stroke volume (SV)/left ventricular end diastolic volume (LVEDV).
      (2) Normal EF averages > 55%; the lower the EF, the more impaired the LV (Lang et al 2005).
   e. Atrial filling pressure: the difference between the venous and atrial pressures.
      (1) Right atrial filling pressure is decreased during strong ventricular contraction, and atrial filling is enhanced.
      (2) Right atrial filling pressure is affected by changes in intrathoracic pressure; decreases during inspiration and increases during coughing or forced expiration.
      (3) Venous return increases when blood volume expands and decreases during hypovolemic shock.
   f. Diastolic filling time decreases with increased heart rate and with heart disease.
   g. Myocardial oxygen demand (MVO_2) represents the energy cost to the myocardium.
      (1) Clinically measured by the product of heart rate (HR) and systolic blood pressure (SBP), known as the rate pressure produce (RPP).
      (2) MVO_2 increases with activity and with HR and/or BP.

Peripheral Circulation

1. Arteries (see Figure 3-5).
   a. Transport oxygenated blood from areas of high pressure to lower pressures in the body tissues. The only exceptions are the umbilical vein (in utero) and the pulmonary veins.
   b. Arterial circulation maintained by heart pump.
   c. Influenced by elasticity and extensibility of vessel walls and by peripheral resistance, amount of blood in body.
2. Arterioles.
   a. Terminal branches of arteries that attach to capillaries.
   b. Primary site of vascular resistance.
3. Capillaries.
   a. Include small blood vessels that connect the ends of arteries (arterioles) with the beginning of veins (venules); form an anastomosing network.
   b. Function for exchange of nutrients and fluids between blood and tissues.
   c. Capillary walls are thin, permeable.
4. Veins (see Figure 3-6).
   a. Transport dark, unoxygenated blood from tissues back to the heart.
   b. Larger capacity, thinner walls than arteries, greater number.
   c. One-way valves to prevent backflow.
   d. Venous system includes both superficial and deep veins (deep veins accompany arteries, while superficial ones do not).
   e. Venous circulation is influenced by muscle contraction, gravity, respiration (increased return with inspiration), compliancy of right heart.
5. Lymphatic system (see Figure 3-7).
   a. Includes lymphatics (superficial, intermediate, and deep), lymph fluid, lymph tissues, and organs (lymph nodes, tonsils, spleen, thymus, and the thoracic duct).
   b. Drains lymph from bodily tissues and returns it to venous circulation.
   c. Lymph travels from lymphatic capillaries to lymphatic vessels to ducts to left subclavian vein. Lymphatic contraction occurs by:
      (1) Parasympathetic, sympathetic, and sensory nerve stimulation.
      (2) Contraction of adjacent muscles.
      (3) Abdominal and thoracic cavity pressure changes during normal breathing.
      (4) Mechanical stimulation of dermal tissues.
      (5) Volume changes within each lymphatic vessel.

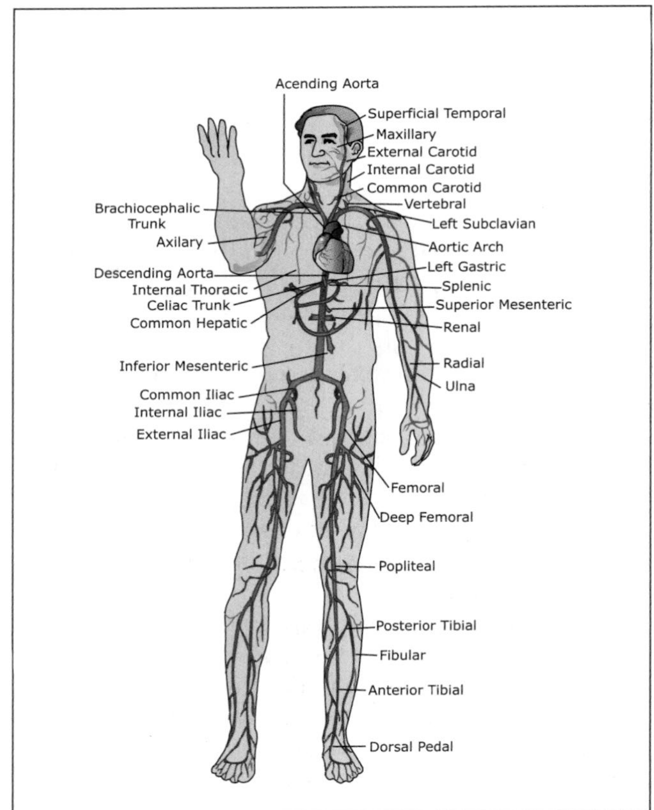

Figure 3-5 **Circulatory system: Arteries.**

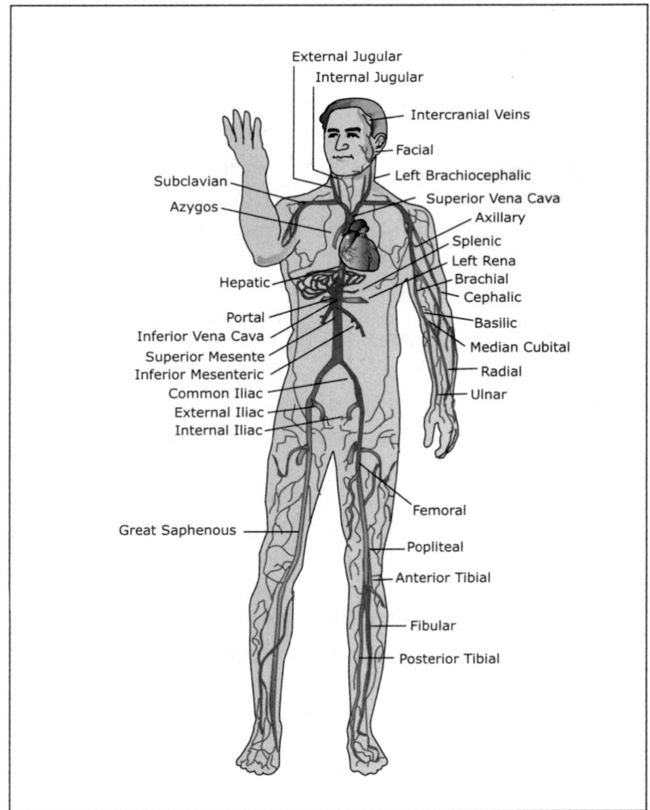

Figure 3-6 **Circulatory system: Veins.**

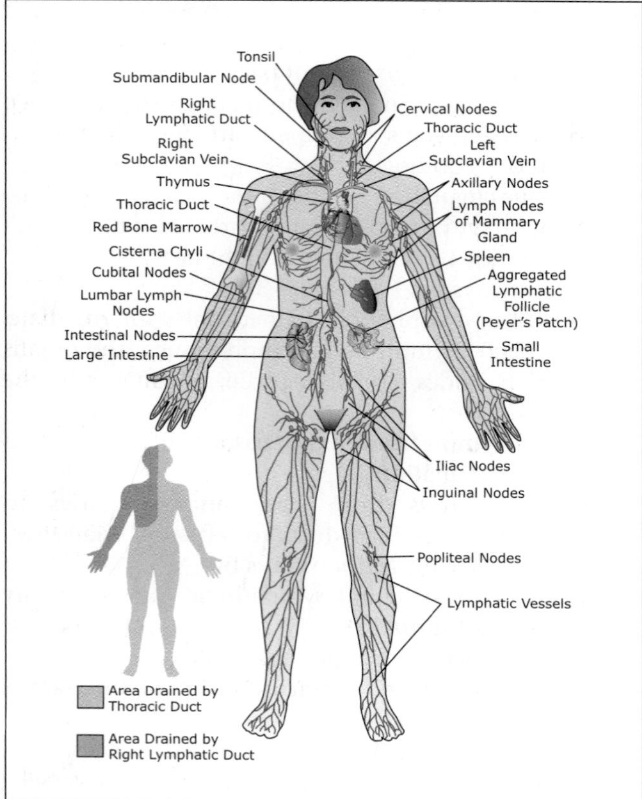

Figure 3-7 **Lymphatic system.**

d. Major lymph nodes are submaxillary, cervical, axillary, mesenteric, iliac, inguinal, popliteal, and cubital.

e. Contributes to immune system function: lymph nodes collect cellular debris and bacteria; remove excess fluid, blood waste, and protein molecules; and produce antibodies.

Neurohumeral Influences

1. Parasympathetic stimulation (cholinergic).
   a. Control located in medulla oblongata, cardioinhibitory center.
   b. Via vagus nerve (CN X), cardiac plexus; innervates the SA node, AV node and sparsely innervates myocardium; releases acetylcholine.
   c. Slows rate and force of myocardial contraction; decreases myocardial metabolism.
   d. Causes coronary artery vasoconstriction.
2. Sympathetic stimulation (adrenergic).
   a. Control located in medulla oblongata, cardioacceleratory center.
   b. Via cord segments T1–T4, upper thoracic to superior cervical chain ganglia; innervates SA node, AV node, conduction pathways, and myocytes; releases epinephrine and norepinephrine.
   c. Causes an increase in the rate and force of myocardial contraction and myocardial metabolism.
   d. Causes coronary artery vasodilation.
   e. The skin and peripheral vasculature receive only postganglionic sympathetic innervation. Causes vasoconstriction of cutaneous arteries; sympathetic inhibition must occur for vasodilation.
   f. Drugs that increase sympathetic functioning are sympathomimetics; drugs that decrease sympathetic functioning are sympatholytics.
3. Additional control mechanisms.
   a. Baroreceptors (pressoreceptors): main mechanisms controlling heart rate.
      (1) Located in walls of aortic arch and carotid sinus; via vasomotor center.
      (2) Circulatory reflex: respond to changes in blood pressure.
         (a) Increased BP results in parasympathetic stimulation, decreased rate and force of cardiac contraction; sympathetic inhibition, decreased peripheral resistance.
         (b) Decreased BP results in sympathetic stimulation, increased heart rate and blood pressure and vasoconstriction of peripheral blood vessels.
         (c) Increased right atrial pressure causes reflex acceleration of heart rate.
   b. Chemoreceptors.
      (1) Located in the carotid body.
      (2) Sensitive to changes in blood chemicals: O_2, CO_2, lactic acid.
         (a) Increased CO_2 or decreased O_2, or decreased pH (elevated lactic acid) results in an increase in heart rate.
         (b) Increased O_2 levels result in a decrease in heart rate.
   c. Body temperature.
      (1) Increased body temperature causes heart rate to increase.
      (2) Decreased body temperature causes heart rate to decrease.
   d. Ion concentrations.
      (1) Hyperkalemia: increased concentration of potassium ions decreases the rate and force of contraction, produces electrocardiographic (ECG) changes (widened PR interval and QRS, tall T waves).
      (2) Hypokalemia: decreased concentrations of potassium ions, produces ECG changes (flattened T waves, prolonged PR and QT intervals); arrhythmias, may progress to ventricular fibrillation.
      (3) Hypercalcemia: increased calcium concentration increases heart actions.
      (4) Hypocalcemia: decreased calcium concentrations depresses heart actions.

(5) Hypermagnesemia: increased magnesium is a calcium blocker which can lead to arrhythmias or cardiac arrest.
(6) Hypomagnesemia: decreased magnesium causes ventricular arrhythmias, coronary artery vasospasm, and sudden death.

4. Peripheral resistance.
   a. Increased peripheral resistance increases arterial blood volume and pressure.
   b. Decreased peripheral resistance decreases arterial blood volume and pressure.
   c. Influenced by arterial blood volume: viscosity of blood and diameter of arterioles and capillaries.

Cardiovascular Examination: History, Systems Review, Tests, and Measures

Patient Interview

1. History.
   a. Presenting symptoms. Note onset, progression, nature of symptoms, insight into medical condition, level of activity in increasing or abating the symptoms.
      (1) Chest pain, palpitations, shortness of breath.
      (2) Fatigue: generalized feeling of tiredness, weakness.
      (3) Palpitations: awareness by patient of heart rhythm abnormalities; e.g., pounding, fluttering, racing heartbeat, skipped beats.
      (4) Dizziness, syncope (transient loss of consciousness) due to inadequate cerebral blood flow.
      (5) Edema: retention of fluid in tissues; swelling, especially in dependent body parts/lower extremities; sudden weight gain.
   b. Positive risk factors (see Table 3-1).

Table 3-1

Risk Factors for Cardiovascular Disease

Non-Modifiable Risk Factors	
RISK FACTOR	**INCREASED RISK CRITERIA**
Age	Men > 45 years and women > 55 years
Family History	Cardiac event in 1st degree male relative < 55 years or 1st degree female relative < 65 years (1.5–2 fold relative risk). Risk increases further with younger age of onset, number of events, and how close genealogically the relative is.
Race	African American
Gender	Men > risk than pre-menopausal women. After menopause, the risk equalizes.
Modifiable Risk Factors	
RISK FACTOR	**GOAL TO REDUCE RISK**
Cholesterol	Total cholesterol: < 200 mg/dL LDL cholesterol: < 160 mg/dL (if low risk for cardiac disease), < 130 mg/dL (if intermediate risk for cardiac disease), < 100 mg/dL (if high risk for cardiac disease, have cardiac disease, or diabetes) HDL cholesterol: > 40 mg/dL (men) and > 50 mg/dL (women) Triglycerides: < 150 mg/dL
Diabetes	HgA1C < 7%
Diet	Low fat, salt diet with balance of vegetables, fruits, grains, and meats.
Hypertension	Systolic blood pressure < 140 mm Hg and diastolic blood pressure < 90 mm Hg (based on at least two measurements at different times)
Obesity	Body Mass Index (BMI): 18.5–24.9 kg/m2 Waist circumference: < 40 inches (men) and < 35 inches (women)
Physical inactivity	At least 30 minutes of activity, 5–7 days per week
Tobacco	Smoking cessation, regardless of time smoked, reduces risk.

Adapted from Greenland et al., 2010; World Heart Federation, American Heart Association.

c. Negative risk factors.
   (1) High serum, high-density lipoprotein (HDL) cholesterol: > 60 mg/dL.
2. Past medical history.
   a. Other diagnoses, surgeries.
   b. Medications.
3. Social history.
   a. Current living situation, family/social support.
   b. Education level, employment.
   c. Lifestyle, risk factors.
4. Quality-of-life issues.
   a. Functional mobility in home, community.
   b. Activities of daily living (ADLs); sleep.
5. Risk factors (see Table 3-1).
   a. Focus on social habits: smoking, diet.
   b. Past and present level of activity.
6. Observation and inspection of skin color for possible signs of decreased cardiac ouput and low oxygen saturation.
   a. Cyanosis: bluish color of the skin, nail beds, lips, and tongue.
   b. Pallor: washed out, absence of pink, rosy color.
   c. Diaphoresis: excess sweating and cool, clammy skin.

Physical Examination: Cardiovascular System

1. Examine pulse.
   a. Rhythmical throbbing of arterial wall as a result of each heartbeat; note rate and rhythm.
   b. Influenced by force of contraction, volume and viscosity of blood, diameter and elasticity of vessels, emotions, exercise, blood temperature, and hormones.
   c. Determine pulses; palpate for 30 seconds with regular rhythm, 1–2 minutes with irregular rhythm (Table 3-2).
      (1) Apical pulse or point of maximal impulse (PMI): patient is supine, palpate at 5th interspace, midclavicular vertical line (apex of the heart; may be displaced upward by pregnancy or high diaphragm; may be displaced laterally in congestive heart failure, cardiomyopathy, ischemic heart disease.
      (2) Radial: palpate radial artery, radial wrist at base of thumb; most common monitoring site.
      (3) Carotid: patient is lying down with head of bed elevated; palpate over carotid artery, on either side of anterior neck between sternocleidomastoid muscle and trachea.
         (a) Assess one side at a time to reduce the risk of bradycardia through stimulation of the carotid sinus baroreceptor, which produces a reflex drop in pulse rate or blood pressure.
      (4) Brachial: palpate over brachial artery, medial aspect of the antecubital fossa; used to monitor blood pressure. Best in infants.
      (5) Femoral: palpate over femoral artery in inguinal region.
      (6) Popliteal: palpate over popliteal artery, behind the knee with the knee flexed slightly.
      (7) Pedal: palpate over dorsalis pedis artery, dorsal medial aspect of foot; used to monitor lower extremity circulation.
   d. Determine heart rate (HR).
      (1) Normal HR.
         (a) Adult and teenagers: 60–100 beats per minute (bpm); 40–60 bpm in aerobically trained.
         (b) Children: 60–140 bpm.
         (c) Newborn: average is 127 bpm; normal range 90–164 bpm.
      (2) Tachycardia: > 100 bpm. Exercise commonly results in tachycardia. Compensatory tachycardia can be seen with volume loss (surgery, dehydration).
      (3) Bradycardia: < 60 bpm.
   e. Postural Tachycardia Syndrome: sustained heart rate increase ≥ 30 beats per minute within 10 minutes of standing (≥ 40 beats per minute in teenagers).
   f. Pulse abnormalities.
      (1) Irregular pulse: variations in force and frequency; may be due to arrhythmias, myocarditis.
      (2) Weak, thready pulse: may be due to low stroke volume, cardiogenic shock.
      (3) Bounding, full pulse: may be due to shortened ventricular systole and decreased peripheral pressure; aortic insufficiency.
2. Examine heart sounds.
   a. Auscultation: the process of listening for sounds within the body; stethoscope is placed directly on chest. Note intensity and quality of heart sounds.
   b. Patient position: supine.
   c. Auscultation landmarks.
      (1) Aortic valve: locate the 2nd right intercostal space at the sternal border.
      (2) Pulmonic valve: locate the 2nd left intercostal space at the sternal border.

Table 3-2

Grading Scale for Peripheral Pulses	
0	Absent pulse, not palpable
1+	Pulse diminished, barely perceptible
2+	Easily palpable, normal
3+	Full pulse, increased strength
4+	Bounding pulse

(3) Tricuspid valve: locate the 4th left intercostal space at the sternal border.
(4) Mitral valve: locate the 5th left intercostal space at the midclavical area.

d. S1 sound ("lub"): normal closure of mitral and tricuspid valves; marks beginning of systole. Decreased in first-degree heart block.

e. S2 sound ("dub"): normal closure of aortic and pulmonary valves; marks end of systole. Decreased in aortic stenosis.

f. Murmurs: extra sounds.
(1) Systolic: falls between S1 and S2. May indicate valvular disease (e.g., mitral valve prolapse) or may be normal.
(2) Diastolic: falls between S2 and S1. Usually indicates valvular disease.
(3) Grades of heart murmurs: grade 1 (softest audible murmur) to grade 6 (audible with stethoscope off the chest).
(4) Thrill: an abnormal tremor accompanying a vascular or cardiac murmur; felt on palpation.

g. Bruit: an adventitious sound or murmur (blowing sound) of arterial or venous origin; common in carotid or femoral arteries; indicative of atherosclerosis.

h. Gallop rhythm: an abnormal heart rhythm with three sounds in each cycle; resembles the gallop of a horse.
(1) S3; associated with ventricular filling; occurs soon after S2; in older individuals may be indicative of congestive (LV) heart failure.
(2) S4: associated with ventricular filling and atrial contraction; occurs just before S1. S4 is indicative of pathology; e.g., coronary heart disease (CAD), myocardial infarction (MI), aortic stenosis or chronic hypertension.

3. Examine heart rhythm.

a. Electrocardiogram (ECG): 12-lead ECG provides information about rate, rhythm, conduction, areas of ischemia, and infarct, hypertrophy, electrolyte imbalances, and systemic pathologies (COPD, cerebral T-waves, etc.)

b. Normal cardiac cycle (normal sinus rhythm) (see Figure 3-4).
(1) P wave: atrial depolarization.
(2) P-R interval: time required for impulse to travel from atria through conduction system to Purkinje fibers.
(3) QRS wave: ventricular depolarization.
(4) ST segment: beginning of ventricular repolarization.
(5) T wave: ventricular repolarization.
(6) QT interval: time for electrical systole.

c. Calculate heart rate: count number of intervals between QRS complexes in a 6-second strip and multiply by 10. With irregular heart rates, use the longest strip possible (up to 1 minute) for a more accurate assessment of heart rate.

d. Assess rhythm: regular or irregular.

e. Identify arrhythmias.
(1) Etiology: ischemic conditions of the myocardium, electrolyte imbalance, acidosis or alkalosis, hypoxemia, hypotension, emotional stress, drugs, alcohol, caffeine.
(2) Ventricular arrhythmias: originate from an ectopic focus in the ventricles (outside the normal conduction system).
(a) Significant in adversely affecting cardiac output.
(b) Premature ventricular contractions (PVCs): a premature beat arising from the ventricle; occurs occasionally in the majority of the normal population. On ECG: no P wave; a bizarre and wide QRS that is premature, followed by a long compensatory pause. Serious PVCs: > 6 per minute, paired or in sequential runs, multifocal, very early PVC (R on T phenomena).
(c) Ventricular tachycardia (VT): a run of three or more PVCs occurring sequentially; very rapid rate (150–200 bpm); may occur paroxysmally (abrupt onset); usually the result of an ischemic ventricle. On ECG: wide, bizarre QRS waves, no P waves. Seriously compromised cardiac output.
- NSVT (Non-sustained ventricular tachycardia): 3 or more consecutive beats in duration, terminating spontaneously in less than 30 seconds.
- VT (sustained ventricular tachycardia): VT > 30 seconds in duration and/or requiring termination due to hemodynamic compromise in less than 30 seconds.
(d) Ventricular fibrillation (VF): a pulseless, emergency situation requiring emergency medical treatment: cardiopulmonary resuscitation (CPR), defibrillation, medications. Characterized by chaotic activity of ventricle originating from multiple foci; unable to determine rate. On ECG: bizarre, erratic activity without QRS complexes. No effective cardiac output; clinical death within 4–6 minutes.
(3) Atrial arrhythmias (supraventricular): rapid and repetitive firing of one or more ectopic foci in the atria (outside the sinus node).
(a) On ECG, P waves are abnormal (variable in shape) or not identifiable (atrial fibrillation).
(b) Rhythm may be irregular: chronic or occurring paroxysmally.
(c) Rate: rapid with atrial tachycardia (140–250 bpm), atrial flutter (250–350 bpm); fibrillation (> 300 bpm).

(d) Cardiac output is usually maintained if rate is controlled; may precipitate ventricular failure in an abnormal heart.

(4) Atrioventricular blocks: abnormal delays or failure to conduct through normal conducting system.

(a) First-, second-, or third- (complete) degree atrioventricular blocks; bundle branch blocks.

(b) If ventricular rate is slowed, cardiac output decreased.

(c) Third degree, complete heart block is life threatening: requires medications (atropine), surgical implantation of pacemaker.

f. Determine ST segment changes.

(1) With impaired coronary perfusion (ischemia or injury), the ST segment becomes depressed.

(2) ST segment depression can be upsloping, horizontal, or downsloping.

(3) ST segment depression or elevation greater than 1 mm measured at the J point in 2 consecutive leads is considered abnormal, except in leads V2–V3. ST elevation of ≥ 2 mm in men ≥ 40 yrs, ≥ 2.5 mm in men < 40 yrs, and ≥ 1.5 mm in women (Thygesen et al, 2012).

g. ECG changes with an acute MI: acute ST elevations present in leads over the infarcted area (Prutkin 2012).

(1) Anterior wall: changes in V1–V6.

(2) Anteroseptal: changes in V1–V2.

(3) Anteroapical: changes in V3–V4.

(4) Anterolateral: changes in V5–V6, I, aVL.

(5) Lateral wall: changes in leads I and aVL.

(6) Inferior wall: II, III, aVF.

(7) Posterior wall: not seen on typical ECG, changes in V7–9.

h. Metabolic and drug influences on the ECG.

(1) Potassium levels.

(a) Hyperkalemia: widens QRS, flattens P wave, T wave becomes peaked.

(b) Hypokalemia: flattens T wave (or inverts), produces a U wave.

(2) Calcium levels.

(a) Hypercalcemia: widens QRS, shortens QT interval.

(b) Hypocalcemia: prolongs QT interval.

(3) Hypothermia: elevates ST segment; slows rhythm.

(4) Digitalis: depresses ST segment, flattens T wave (or inverts), QT shortens.

(5) Quinidine: QT lengthens, T wave flattens (or inverts), QRS lengthens.

(6) Beta blockers (e.g., propranolol [Inderal]): decreases heart rate, blunts heart rate response to exercise.

(7) Nitrates (nitroglycerin): increases heart rate.

(8) Antiarrhythmic agents: may prolong QRS and QT intervals.

i. Holter monitoring: continuous ambulatory ECG monitoring via tape recording of cardiac rhythm for up to 24 hours.

(1) Used to evaluate cardiac rhythm, transient symptoms, pacemaker function, effect of medications.

(2) Allows correlation of symptoms with activities (activity diary).

4. Examine blood pressure (BP) (see Tables 3-3 and 3-4).

a. Determine blood pressure (2003 Joint National Committee on Prevention, Detection, Evaluation, and Treatment of High Blood Pressure Guidelines).

(1) Normal adult BP: < 120 mm Hg systolic; < 80 mm Hg diastolic.

(2) Hypotension: a decrease in BP below normal; blood pressure is not adequate for normal perfusion/oxygenation of tissues. May be related to bed rest, drugs, arrhythmias, blood loss/shock, or myocardial infarction.

(3) Orthostatic hypotension: drop in BP that accompanies change from supine to standing position.

(a) Initial BP and HR assessment when patient supine, at rest for ≥ 5 minutes.

(b) Patient moves directly to standing position and repeat BP and HR assessment immediately and again at 3 minutes.

(c) A patient is orthostatic if the systolic BP drops > 20 mm Hg or if the diastolic BP drops > 10 mm Hg.

(d) Common symptoms include lightheadedness, dizziness, loss of balance, and leg weakness.

(4) Pediatric BP.

(a) Infants < 2 years (95 percentile): 106–110 mm Hg systolic; 59–63 mm Hg diastolic.

(b) Children 3–5 years: 113–116 systolic, 67–74 diastolic.

b. Mean arterial pressure (MAP): the arterial pressure within the large arteries over time; dependent upon mean blood flow and arterial compliance.

(1) Calculated by taking the sum of the systolic blood pressure (SBP) and twice the diastolic blood pressure (DBP), divided by 3.

(2) An important clinical measure in critical care.

(3) Normal MAP is 70–110 mm Hg.

5. Examine respiration.

a. Determine rate, depth of breathing.

(1) Normal adult respiratory rate (RR) is 12–20 breaths per minute.

(2) Normal newborn RR is 30–40 breaths per minute.

(3) Normal child RR is 20–30.

(4) Tachypnea: an increase in RR ≥ 22 breaths per minute.

Table 3-3

Definitions and Classification of Office Blood Pressure Levels			
CATEGORY	**SYSTOLIC**		**DIASTOLIC**
Optimal	< 120	And	< 80
Normal	120–129	And/or	80–84
High normal	130–139	And/or	85–89
Grade 1 HTN	140–159	And/or	90–99
Grade 2	160–179	And/or	100–109
Grade 3	≥ 180	And/or	≥ 110
Isolated systolic hypertension	≥ 140	And	< 90

(5) Bradypnea: a decrease of RR ≤ 10 breaths per minute.
(6) Hyperpnea: an increase in depth and rate of breathing.

b. Dyspnea: shortness of breath.
(1) Dyspnea on exertion (DOE): brought on by exercise or activity.
(2) Orthopnea: inability to breathe when in a reclining or supine position.
(3) Paroxysmal nocturnal dyspnea (PND): sudden inability to breathe occurring during sleep.
(4) Dyspnea scale (Table 3-5) (Borg, 1982).

c. Auscultation of the lungs: assess respiratory sounds.
(1) Normal breath sounds.
(2) Assess for adventitious sounds.
(a) Crackles (rales): rattling, bubbling sounds; may be due to secretions in the lungs.
(b) Wheezes (rhonchi): whistling sounds.

d. Assess cough: productive or nonproductive, strong or weak, coordinated or uncoordinated, consistency and color of any secretions.

6. Examine oxygen saturation.
a. Use pulse oximetry, an electronic device that measures the degree of saturation of hemoglobin with oxygen (SaO_2). Normal values are 95%–100% oxygen.
b. Provides an estimate of PaO_2 (partial pressure of oxygen) based on the oxyhemoglobin desaturation curve.
c. Hypoxemia: abnormally low amount of oxygen in the blood (saturation levels below 90% which corresponds to a PaO_2 of 60 mm Hg).
d. Hypoxia: low oxygen level in the tissues.
e. Anoxia: complete lack of oxygen.

Table 3-4

American Heart Association (AHA) Blood Pressure Definitions (Rosendorff et al, 2007)			
BP CATEGORY	**SYSTOLIC**		**DIASTOLIC**
Normal	< 120	And	< 80
Prehypertension	120–139	Or	80–89
Stage 1	140–159	Or	90–99
Stage 2	≥ 160	Or	≥ 100
Hypertensive Crisis	> 180	Or	≥ 110

Table 3-5

Modified Borg Dyspnea Scale (Borg 1982)	
0	Nothing at all
0.5	Very, very slight (just noticeable)
1	Very slight
2	Slight
3	Moderate
4	Somewhat severe
5	Severe
6	Severe
7	Very severe
8	Very severe
9	Very, very severe (almost maximal)
10	Maximal

7. Examine pain.
a. Chest pain may be cardiac or noncardiac in origin.
b. Ischemic cardiac pain (angina or myocardial infarction): diffuse, retrosternal pain; or a sensation of tightness, achiness, in the chest; associated with dyspnea, sweating, indigestion, dizziness, syncope, anxiety (see anginal descriptions in Acute Coronary Syndromes).
c. Rate pain using Anginal scale (Table 3-6).
d. Referred pain.
(1) Cardiac pain can refer to shoulders, back, arms, neck, or jaw.
(2) Pain referred to the back can occur from dissecting aortic aneurysm.

Table 3-6

Anginal Scale	
1+	Light, barely noticeable
2+	Moderate, bothersome
3+	Severe, very uncomfortable
4+	Most severe pain ever experienced

Physical Examination: Peripheral Vascular System

1. Examine condition of extremities.
   a. Examine for diaphoresis: excess sweating can be associated with decreased cardiac output.
   b. Examine arterial pulses: decreased or absent pulses associated with peripheral artery disease (PAD); examine bilaterally starting with most distal pulses.
      (1) Lower extremity: position patient supine, check femoral, popliteal, dorsalis pedis, posterior tibial pulses.
      (2) Upper extremity: check radial, brachial, and carotid pulses.
   c. Examine skin color.
      (1) Cyanosis: bluish color related to decreased cardiac output or cold; especially lips, fingertips, nail beds.
      (2) Pallor: absence of rosy color in light-skinned individuals, associated with decreased peripheral blood flow, PAD.
      (3) Rubor: dependent redness with PAD.
   d. Examine skin temperature.
   e. Examine for skin changes.
      (1) Clubbing: curvature of the fingernails with soft tissue enlargement at base of nail: associated with chronic oxygen deficiency, chronic pulmonary disease, or heart failure.
      (2) Trophic changes: pale, shiny, dry skin, with loss of hair is associated with PAD.
      (3) Fibrosis: tissues are thick, firm, and unyielding.
         (a) Stemmer's sign: dorsal skin folds of the toes or fingers are resistant to lifting; indicative of fibrotic changes and lymphedema.
      (4) Abnormal pigmentation, ulceration, dermatitis, gangrene is associated with PAD.
      (5) Temperature: decrease in superficial skin temperature is associated with poor arterial perfusion.
   f. Examine for pain.
      (1) Intermittent claudication (IC): pain, cramping, and lower extremity fatigue occurring during exercise and relieved by rest, associated with PAD.
      (2) IC pain is typically in calf; may also be in thigh, hips, or buttocks.
      (3) Patient may experience pain at rest with severe decrease in arterial blood supply; typically in forefoot, worse at night.
   g. Examine for edema.
      (1) Measure girth measurements using a tape measure at regular intervals, or volumetric measurements using a volumeter (useful with irregular body parts, such as hand or foot).
      (2) Pitting edema (indentation): depression is maintained when finger is pressed firmly; grading scale (see Table 3-7).
      (3) Peripheral causes of edema include chronic venous insufficiency and lymphedema.
      (4) Bilateral edema is associated with congestive heart failure.

Table 3-7

Grading Scale for Edema	
1+	Mild, barely perceptible indentation; < ¼ inch pitting
2+	Moderate, easily identified depression; returns to normal within 15 seconds; ¼–½ inch pitting
3+	Severe, depression takes 15–30 seconds to rebound; ½–1 inch pitting
4+	Very severe, depression lasts for > 30 seconds or more; > 1 inch pitting

2. Tests of peripheral venous circulation.
   a. Examine venous system before arterial; venous insufficiency can invalidate some arterial tests.
   b. Percussion test: determines competence of greater saphenous vein.
      (1) In standing, palpate one segment of vein while percussing vein approximately 20 cm higher.
      (2) If pulse wave is felt by lower hand, the intervening valves are incompetent.
   c. Trendelenburg test (retrograde filling test): determines competence of communicating veins and saphenous system.
      (1) Patient is positioned in supine with legs elevated to 60° (empties venous blood).
      (2) Tourniquet is then placed on proximal thigh (occludes venous flow in the superficial veins).
      (3) Patient is then asked to stand.
      (4) Examiner notes whether veins fill in normal pattern. Should take approximately 30 seconds.
   d. Venous filling time: Examine time necessary to refill veins after emptying.
      (1) With patient supine, passively elevate lower extremity to approximately 45° for 1 minute, then place in dependent position. Note time for veins to refill.
      (2) Delayed filling (> 15 seconds) is indicative of venous insufficiency.
   e. Doppler ultrasound: examination using an ultrasonic oscillator connected to earphones.
      (1) Determines blood flow within a vessel; useful in both venous and arterial diseases.

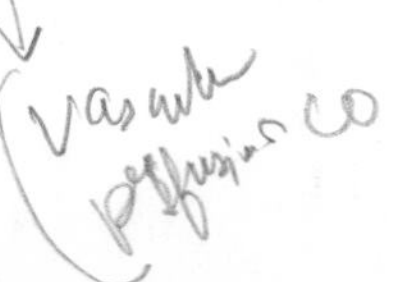

(2) Doppler probe placed over large vessel; ultrasound signal given transcutaneously; movement of blood causes an audible shift in signal frequency.
(3) Useful in locating nonpalpable pulses and measuring systolic BP in extremities.

f. Air plethysmography (APG): pneumatic device calibrated to measure patency of venous system; volume.
(1) Cuff is inflated around calf, attached to a pressure transducer and microprocessor.
(2) Occludes venous return, permits arterial inflow; recorder registers increasing volume with cuff; time to return to baseline with cuff deflation.
(3) Comparison tests performed in sitting, standing, and up onto toes.

3. Tests of peripheral arterial circulation.

a. Ankle brachial index (ABI): the ratio of lower extremity (LE) pressure divided by upper extremity (UE) pressure.
(1) Pt is positioned supine and at rest for 5 minutes.
(2) BP cuff is inflated to occlude blood flow temporarily, then deflated. Examiner listens for return of flow.
(3) Performed in UE at brachial artery; LE at posterior tibial and dorsalis pedis arteries.
(4) ABI indices (Table 3-8).
(5) ABI assists in risk stratification for cardiovascular disease: < 0.90 is associated with 2 to 4 fold increased risk for cardiovascular events and death.
(6) ABI < 0.50: increased risk of progression to severe or critical limb ischemia in 1 year.
(7) Clinically significant change in ABI is > 0.15 or > 0.10 in patients with symptoms.

b. Rubor of dependency. Examine color changes in skin during elevation of foot followed by dependency (seated, hanging position).
(1) With insufficiency, pallor develops in elevated position; reactive hyperemia (rubor of dependency) develops in dependent position.

Table 3-8

Significance of Ankle Brachial Index Values	
> 1.40	Indicates non-compliant arteries
1.00–1.40	Normal
0.91–0.99	Borderline
≤ 0.90	Abnormal
≤ 0.50	Severe arterial disease, risk for critical limb ischemia, may have pain at rest

Table 3-9

Subjective Ratings of Pain with Intermittent Claudication	
Grade I	Minimal discomfort or pain
Grade II	Moderate discomfort or pain; patient's attention can be diverted
Grade III	Intense pain; patient's attention cannot be diverted
Grade IV	Excruciating and unbearable pain

(2) Changes that take longer than 30 seconds are also indicative of arterial insufficiency.

c. Examine for intermittent claudication: exercise-induced pain or cramping in the legs that is absent at rest. Usually calf pain, but may also occur in buttock, hip, thigh, or foot.
(1) Have the patient walk on level grade, 1 mile/hour; e.g., treadmill. Test is stopped with claudicatory pain.
(2) Note time of test. Use subjective ratings of pain scale to classify degree of claudication (Table 3-9).
(3) Examine for coldness, numbness, or pallor in the legs or feet; loss of hair over anterior tibial area.
(4) Leg cramps may also result from diuretic use with hypokalemia.

4. Examine lymphatic system.

a. Palpate superficial lymph nodes: cervical, axillary, epitrochlear, superficial inguinal.

b. Examine for edema.
(1) Visual inspection: note swelling, decreased range of motion, loss of functional mobility.
(2) Measure girth.

c. Examine skin.
(1) Changes in skin texture, fibrotic tissue changes.
(2) Presence of papules, leakage, wounds.

d. Changes in function (ADL, functional mobility, sleep).

e. Paresthesias may be present.

f. Lymphangiography and lymphoscintigraphy using radioactive agents (x-ray of lymph vessels); provides information about lymph flow, lymph node uptake, and backflow.

Diagnostic Tests

1. Chest x-ray (Figure 3-8).
   a. Will reveal abnormalities of lung fluids, overall cardiac shape and size (cardiomegaly), aneurysm.
2. Myocardial perfusion imaging (Figure 3-9).

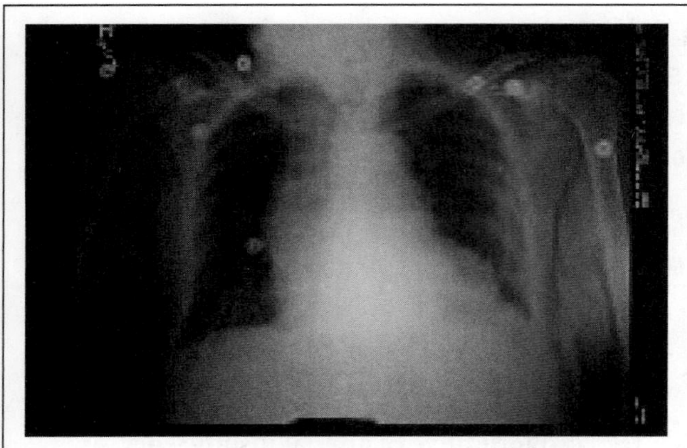

Figure 3-8 Radiographic view: Demonstrates signs of congestive heart failure.

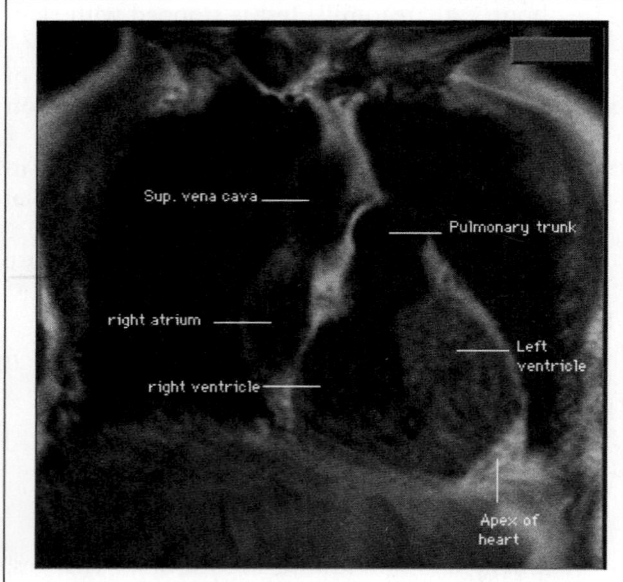

Figure 3-9 Coronal T1MRI thoracic view of normal female.

a. Used to diagnose and evaluate ischemic heart disease, myocardial infarction.
b. Thallium-201 scan: thallium (or other radioisotope) is injected into blood via IV; radioisotopes concentrate in normal tissue but not in ischemic or infarcted tissues (cold spots).
c. Used to identify myocardial blood flow, areas of stress-induced ischemia (exercise test), old infarcts.
d. Thallium stress test: used with exercise test (treadmill or bicycle ergometer); injected at peak exercise.
e. Positron emission tomography (PET); uses radioactive marker 18F-fluorodeoxyglucose (FDG).

3. Echocardiogram.
   a. Noninvasive test that uses ultrasound to assess internal structures: size of chambers, wall thickness, ejection fraction (EF), movement of valves, septum, abnormal wall movement.
4. Cardiac catheterization.
   a. Passage of a tiny tube from brachial or femoral artery through aorta into blood vessels with introduction of a contrast medium into coronary arteries and subsequent x-ray.
   b. Provides information about anatomy of heart and great vessels, ventricular and valve function, abnormal wall movements.
   c. Allows determination of ejection fraction (EF).
5. Central line (Swan-Ganz catheter).
   a. Catheter inserted through vessels into right side of heart.
   b. Measures central venous pressure (CVP), pulmonary artery pressure (PA), pulmonary capillary wedge pressures (PCWP).
6. Cardiac MRI: creates 3D images of the heart to investigate coronary arteries, aorta, pericardium, and myocardium.

Laboratory Tests and Values

1. See Table 3-10.
2. Enzyme changes associated with myocardial infarction (Thygesen et al, 2012).
   a. Rise and fall of cardiac troponin (I or T) > 99th percentile is the primary measure of myocardial infarction. It must accompany one of the following:
      (1) Symptoms of ischemia.
      (2) New or presumed new ST changes on ECG.
      (3) Development of pathological Q waves on ECG.
      (4) New loss of viable myocardium and/or new wall motion abnormality on imaging.
      (5) Evidence of intracoronary thrombus via catheterization or autopsy.
   b. Elevation of CK or CPK (serum creatine kinase or creatine phosphokinase) with concomitant elevation of CK-MB (serum creatine kinase MB) can also be assessed, but peaks between 12–24 hours.
3. Serum lipids (lipid panel, mg/dL). Used to determine coronary risk (see Table 3-1).

Table 3-10

Laboratory Tests and Values

NORMAL VALUES	CLINICAL SIGNIFICANCE
Arterial Blood Gases (ABGs)	
SpO_2 98%–100%	SaO_2 below 88%–90% usually requires supplemental O_2
PaO_2 90–100 mm Hg	↑ in hyperoxygenation ↓ in cardiac decompensation, COPD and some neuromuscular disorders
$PaCO_2$ 35–45 mm Hg	↑ in COPD, hypoventilation ↓ in hyperventilation, pregnancy, pulmonary embolism, and anxiety
pH, whole blood 7.35–7.45	< 7.35 is acidotic, > 7.45 is alkalotic ↑ in respiratory alkalosis: hyperventilation, sepsis, liver disease, fever ↑ in metabolic alkalosis: vomiting, potassium depletion, diuretics, volume depletion ↓ in respiratory acidosis: hypoventilation, COPD, respiratory depressants, myasthenia ↓ in metabolic acidosis (bicarbonate deficit): increased acids (diabetes, alcohol, starvation); renal failure, increased acid intake, and loss of alkaline body fluids
Hemostasis (Clotting/Bleeding Times)	
Prothrombin time (PT) 11–15 sec	↑ in factor X deficiency, hemorrhagic disease, cirrhosis, hepatitis drugs (warfarin)
Partial thromboplastin time (PTT) 25–40 sec	↑ in factor VIII, IX, and X deficiency
International normalized ratio (INR): Ratio of individual's PT to reference range 0.9–1.1 (ratio)	Patients with deep vein thrombosis (DVT), pulmonary embolism (PE), mechanical valves, atrial fibrillation (AF) on anticoagulation therapy will have target INRs 2–3. Patients with these conditions and/or genetic clotting disorders may have a target INR 3.5. Look for active signs of bleeding when treating these patients and use compensatory strategies to reduce fall risk.
Bleeding time 2–10 min C-reactive protein (CRP) <10 mg/L	↑ in platelet disorders, thrombocytopenia ↑ levels associated with ↑ risk of atherosclerosis > 100 mg/L associated with inflammation and infection
Complete Blood Cell Count (CBC), Adult Values	
White Blood Cells (WBCs) 4300–10,800 cells/mm³	Indicative of status of immune system ↑ in infection: bacterial, viral; inflammation, hematologic malignancy, leukemia, lymphoma, drugs (corticosteroids) ↓ in aplastic anemia, B_{12} or folate deficiency With immunosuppression: ↑ risk of infection *Physical therapy considerations:* Consider metabolic demands in presence of fever and use of mask when WBCs < 1000–2000 or Absolute Neutrophil Count (ANC) < 500–1000
Red Blood Cells (RBCs) Male: 4.6–6.2 10^6/uL Female: 4.2–5.9 10^6/uL	↑ in polycythemia ↓ in anemia
Erythrocyte sedimentation rate (ESR) Male < 15 mm/hr Female < 20 mm/hr	↑ in infection and inflammation: rheumatic or pelvic inflammatory disease, osteomyelitis used to monitor effects of treatment; e.g., RA, SLE, Hodgkin's disease
Hematocrit (Hct) % of RBC of the whole blood Male 45%–52% Female 37%–48% (age dependent)	↑ in erythrocytosis, dehydration, shock ↓ in severe anemias, acute hemorrhage *Physical therapy considerations:* Can cause ↓ exercise tolerance, ↑ fatigue, and tachycardia.
Hemoglobin (Hgb) Male: 13–18 g/dL Female: 12–16 g/dL (age dependent)	↑ polycythemia, dehydration, shock ↓ in anemias, prolonged hemorrhage, RBC destruction (cancer, sickle cell disease) *Physical therapy considerations:* Can cause ↓ exercise tolerance, ↑ fatigue, and tachycardia

(Continued)

Table 3-10

Laboratory Tests and Values (Continued)

NORMAL VALUES	CLINICAL SIGNIFICANCE
Platelet count 150,000–450,000 cells/mm³	↑ chronic leukemia, hemoconcentration ↓ thrombocytopenia, acute leukemia, aplastic anemia, cancer chemotherapy *Physical therapy considerations:* Increased risk of bleeding with low levels so monitor for hematuria, petechiae, and other signs of active bleeding. < 20,000: AROM, ADLs only 20,000–30,000: light exercise only 30,000–50,000: moderate exercise

Adapted from Hopkins T; Lab Notes, 2nd Ed. Philadelphia, FA Davis, 2009.

Cardiovascular Disease

Atherosclerosis

1. Characteristics.
   a. Disease of lipid-laden plaques (lesions) affecting moderate and large-size arteries.
   b. Thickening and narrowing of the intimal layer of the blood vessel wall from focal accumulation of lipids, platelets, monocytes, plaque, and other debris.
2. Risk factors (see Table 3-1).

Acute Coronary Syndrome (ACS) (Coronary Artery Disease)

1. Characteristics.
   a. Involves a spectrum of clinical entities ranging from angina to infarction to sudden cardiac death.
   b. An imbalance of myocardial oxygen supply and demand resulting in ischemic chest pain.
   c. Symptoms present when lumen is at least 70% occluded.
   d. Three common presentations, but may also have silent ischemia diagnosed by presence of a new pathologic Q wave on ECG. Most common in patients with diabetes, patients may have ischemia without any symptoms. Subacute occlusions may also produce no symptoms.
2. Angina pectoris.
   a. Chest pain or pressure due to ischemia; may be accompanied by Levine's sign (patient clenches fist over sternum).
   b. Represents imbalance in myocardial oxygen supply and demand; brought on by:
      (1) Increased demands on heart: exertion, emotional stress, smoking, extremes of temperature, especially cold, overeating, tachyarrhythmias.
      (2) Vasospasm: symptoms may be present at rest.
   c. Three major types of angina.
      (1) Stable angina: classic exertional angina occurring during exercise or activity; occurs at a predictable rate-pressure product, RPP (HR × BP), relieved with rest and/or nitroglycerin.
      (2) Unstable angina (preinfarction, crescendo angina): coronary insufficiency at any time without any precipitating factors or exertion. Chest pain increases in severity, frequency, and duration; refractory to treatment. Increases risk for myocardial infarction or lethal arrhythmia; pain is difficult to control.
      (3) Variant angina (Prinzmetal's angina): caused by vasospasm of coronary arteries in the absence of occlusive disease. Responds well to nitroglycerin or calcium channel blocker long term.
   d. Women more often describe sensations of discomfort, crushing, pressing, and bad ache when referring to angina.
   e. With angina, patients often describe shortness of breath, fatigue, diaphoresis, and weakness as symptoms of ACS.
   f. Older adults present more often with atypical symptoms (absence of chest pain): dyspnea, diaphoresis, nausea and vomiting, and syncope.
3. Myocardial infarction (MI) (see Figure 3-10).
   a. Prolonged ischemia, injury, and death of an area of the myocardium caused by occlusion of one or more of the coronary arteries.
   b. Precipitating factors: atherosclerotic heart disease with thrombus formation, coronary vasospasm, or embolism; cocaine use.

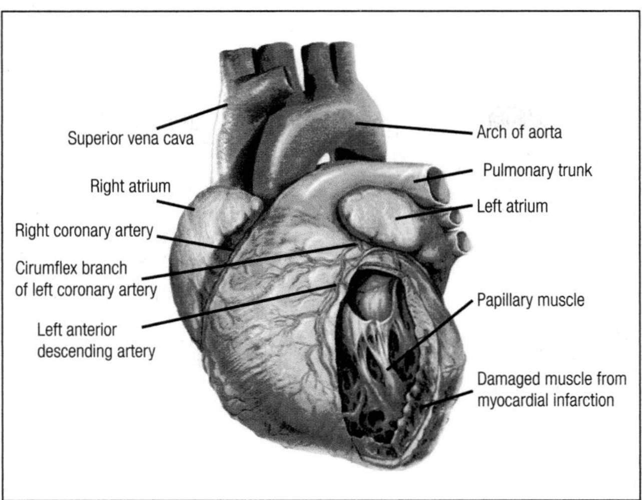

Figure 3-10 Tissue destruction in myocardial infarction.

c. Zones of infarction.
   (1) Zone of infarction: consists of necrotic, noncontractile tissue; electrically inert; on ECG, see pathological Q waves.
   (2) Zone of injury: area immediately adjacent to central zone, tissue is noncontractile, cells undergoing metabolic changes; electrically unstable; on ECG, see elevated ST segments in leads over injured area.
   (3) Zone of ischemia: outer area, cells also undergoing metabolic changes, electrically unstable; on ECG, see T wave inversion.

d. Infarction sites.
   (1) Transmural: full thickness of myocardium, which is often an ST elevated MI (STEMI) or Q wave MI.
   (2) Nontransmural: subendocardial, subepicardial, intramural infarctions. Non-ST elevated MI (NSTEMI) or non-Q wave MI.
   (3) Sites of coronary artery occlusion.
      (a) Inferior MI, right ventricle infarction, disturbances of upper conduction system: right coronary artery.
      (b) Lateral MI, ventricular ectopy: circumflex artery.
      (c) Anterior MI, disturbances of lower conduction system: left anterior descending artery.

e. Impaired ventricular function results in:
   (1) Decreased stroke volume, cardiac output and ejection fraction.
   (2) Increased end diastolic ventricular pressures.

f. Electrical instability: arrhythmias, present in injured and ischemic areas.

4. Heart failure (HF).
   a. A clinical syndrome in which the heart is unable to maintain adequate circulation of the blood to meet the metabolic needs of the body.
   b. Types of heart failure.
      (1) Left-sided heart failure (congestive heart failure, CHF): is characterized by pulmonary congestion, edema, and low cardiac output due to backup of blood from the left ventricle (LV) to the left atrium (LA) and lungs. Occurs with insult to the left ventricle from myocardial disease; excessive workload of the heart (hypertension, valvular disease or congenital defects); cardiac arrhythmias or heart damage.
      (2) Right-sided heart failure: is characterized by increased pressure load on the right ventricle (RV) with higher pulmonary vascular pressures; mitral valve disease, or chronic lung disease (cor pulmonale); produces hallmark signs of jugular vein distention and peripheral edema.
      (3) Biventricular failure: severe LV pathology producing back up into the lungs, increased PA pressure and RV signs of HF.
   c. Associated symptoms: muscle wasting, myopathies, osteoporosis.
   d. Possible clinical manifestations of heart failure (Table 3-11).
   e. Compensated heart failure: heart returns to functional status with reduced cardiac output and exercise tolerance. Control is achieved through:
      (1) Physiological compensatory mechanisms: SNS stimulation, LV hypertrophy, anaerobic metabolism, cardiac dilatation, arterial vasoconstriction.
      (2) Medical therapy.
5. Sudden death, usually due to significant ischemia or ventricular arrhythmia.

Medical and Surgical Management of Cardiovascular Disease

1. Medications.
   a. ACE Inhibitors (e.g., captopril [capoten], enalopril [vasotec], lisinopril [zestril]): inhibit conversion of angiotension I to angiotension II, decreases Na retention and peripheral vasoconstriction in order to decrease blood pressure.
   b. Angiotension II receptor blockers (ARBs) (e.g., losartan [cozaar]): blocks binder of angiotension II at the tissue/smooth muscle level, decreasing blood pressure.
   c. Nitrates (nitroglycerin): decrease preload through peripheral vasodilation, reduce myocardial oxygen demand, reduce chest discomfort (angina); may also dilate coronary arteries, improve coronary blood flow.
   d. Beta-adrenergic blocking agents (e.g., atenolol [tenormin], metoprolol [Lopressor, Toprol XL], propranolol [Inderal]): reduce myocardial demand by reducing heart rate and contractility; control arrhythmias, chest pain; reduce blood pressure.

Table 3-11

Possible Clinical Manifestations of Cardiac Failure

LEFT VENTRICULAR FAILURE	RIGHT VENTRICULAR FAILURE
Signs and symptoms of pulmonary congestion:	
Dyspnea, dry cough	Dependent edema
Orthopnea	Weight gain
Paroxysmal nocturnal dyspnea (PND)	Ascites
Pulmonary rales, wheezing	Liver engorgement (hepatomegaly)
Signs and symptoms of low cardiac output:	
Hypotension	Anorexia, nausea, bloating
Tachycardia	Cyanosis (nail beds)
Lightheadedness, dizziness	Right upper quadrant pain
Cerebral hypoxia: irritability, restlessness, confusion, impaired memory, sleep disturbances	Jugular vein distension
Fatigue, weakness	Right-sided S_3 heart sounds
Poor exercise tolerance	Murmurs of pulmonary or tricuspid insufficiency
Enlarged heart on chest x-ray	
S_3 heart sound, possibly S_4	
Murmurs of mitral or tricuspid regurgitation	

e. Calcium channel blocking agents (e.g., diltiazem [Cardizem, Procardia], amlodipine [Norvasc]): inhibit flow of calcium ions, decrease heart rate, decrease contractility, dilate coronary arteries, reduce BP, control arrhythmias, chest pain.

f. Antiarrhythmics (numerous drugs, four main classes): alter conductivity, restore normal heart rhythm, control arrhythmias, improve cardiac output (e.g., quinidine, procainamide).

g. Digitalis (cardiac glycosides): increases contractility and decreases heart rate; mainstay in the treatment of CHF (e.g., digoxin).

h. Diuretics: decrease myocardial work (reduce preload and afterload), control hypertension, (e.g., furosemide [Lasix], hydrochlorothiazide [Esidrix]).

i. Aspirin: decreases platelet aggregation; may prevent myocardial infarction.

j. Tranquilizers: decrease anxiety, sympathetic effects.

k. Hypolipidemic agents (six major cholesterol-lowering drugs): reduce serum lipid levels when diet and weight reduction are not effective, (e.g., cholestyramine [Questran], colestipol [Colestid], simvastatin [Zocor], lovastatin [Mevacor]).

2. Activity restriction.

a. Acute MI: activity can be increased once the acute MI has stopped (peak in cardiac troponin levels). Activity should be limited to 5 METs or 70% of age predicted HRmax for 4–6 weeks following MI.

b. Acute heart failure: oxygen demand should not be increased in patients in acute or decompensated heart failure. Once they have been medically managed and no longer display signs of acute decompensation, their activity can be gradually increased while monitoring hemodynamic response to activity.

3. Surgical interventions.

a. Percutaneous transluminal coronary angioplasty (PTCA): under fluoroscopy, surgical dilation of a blood vessel using a small balloon-tipped catheter inflated inside the lumen; relieves obstructed blood flow in acute angina or acute MI; results in improved coronary blood flow, improved left ventricular function, anginal relief.

b. Intravascular stents: an endoprosthesis (pliable wire mesh) implanted postangioplasty to prevent restenosis and occlusion in coronary or peripheral arteries. Often coated in medication to prevent thrombosis.

c. Coronary artery bypass graft (CABG): surgical circumvention of an obstruction in a coronary artery using an anastomosing graft (saphenous vein, internal mammary artery); multiple grafts may be necessary; results in improved coronary blood flow, improved left ventricular function, anginal relief.

d. Transplantation: used in end-stage myocardial disease; e.g., cardiomyopathy, ischemic heart disease, valvular heart disease.

(1) Heteroptics: involves leaving the natural heart and piggybacking the donor heart.

(2) Orthotopic: involves removing the diseased heart and replacing it with a donor heart.

(3) Heart and lung transplantation: involves removing both organs and replacing them with donor organs.

(4) Major problems posttransplantation are rejection, infection, complications of immunosuppressive therapy.

e. Ventricular assist device (VAD): an implanted device (accessory pump) that improves tissue perfusion and maintains cardiogenic circulation; used with severely involved patients; e.g., cardiogenic shock unresponsive to medications, severe ventricular dysfunction.

4. Thrombolytic therapy.
   a. Administered for acute myocardial infarction.
   b. Medications activate body's fibrinolytic system, dissolve clot and restore coronary blood flow, (e.g., streptokinase, tissue plasminogen activator [TPA], urokinase).

Peripheral Vascular Disease (PVD)

Arterial Disease

1. Occlusive peripheral arterial disease (PAD).
   a. Chronic, occlusive arterial disease of medium- and large-sized vessels, the result of peripheral atherosclerosis.
   b. Associated with hypertension and hyperlipidemia; patients may also have CAD, cerebrovascular disease, diabetes, metabolic syndrome, and a history of smoking.
   c. Diminished blood supply to affected extremities with pulses decreased or absent.
   d. Color: pale on elevation, dusky red on dependency.
   e. Early stages: patients exhibit intermittent claudication. Pain is described as burning, searing, aching, tightness, or cramping. Occurs regularly and predictably with walking and is relieved by rest.
   f. Late stages: patients exhibit rest pain, muscle atrophy, trophic changes (hair loss, skin and nail changes).
   g. Critical stenosis PAD: patients exhibit resting or nocturnal pain, skin ulcers, and gangrene.
   h. Affects primarily the lower extremities.
2. Thromboangiitis obliterans (Buerger's disease).
   a. Chronic, inflammatory vascular occlusive disease of small arteries and also veins.
   b. Occurs commonly in young adults, largely males, who smoke.
   c. Begins distally and progresses proximally in both upper and lower extremities.
   d. Patients exhibit paresthesias or pain, cyanotic cold extremity, diminished temperature sensation, fatigue, risk of ulceration, and gangrene.
3. Diabetic angiopathy.
   a. An inappropriate elevation of blood glucose levels and accelerated atherosclerosis.
   b. Neuropathy a major complication.
   c. Neurotrophic ulcers, may lead to gangrene and amputation.
4. Raynaud's disease or phenomenon.
   a. Episodic spasm of small arteries and arterioles.
   b. Abnormal vasoconstrictor reflex exacerbated by exposure to cold or emotional stress; tips of fingers develop pallor, cyanosis, numbness, and tingling.
   c. Affects largely females.
   d. Occlusive disease is not usually a factor.

Venous Disease

1. Varicose veins.
   a. Distended, swollen superficial veins; tortuous in appearance.
   b. May lead to varicose ulcers.
2. Venous thromboembolism (VTE).
   a. The formation of a blood clot in a deep vein that can lead to complications including deep vein thrombosis (DVT), pulmonary embolism (PE), or postthrombotic syndrome (PTS).
   b. Mortality: incidence of 10–30% within 1 month of diagnosis.
   c. Morbidity: one third experiences another VTE within 10 years.
   d. Can become chronic: postthrombotic syndrome, leads to diminished quality of life.
3. Deep vein thrombophlebitis.
   a. Clot formation and acute inflammation in a deep vein.
   b. Usually occurs in lower extremity, associated with forced immobilization (bed rest, lack of leg exercise), surgery, trauma, and hyperactivity of blood coagulation or can be unprovoked.
   c. Signs and symptoms: may be asymptomatic early; progressive inflammation with tenderness to palpation; dull ache, tightness, or pain in the calf; swelling, warmth, redness, or discoloration in the lower extremity; prominent superficial veins.
   d. Standardized risk assessment measure: use Wells Criteria Score for DVT (Table 3-12).
   e. Medical management.
      (1) Anticoagulation therapy: is used to prevent new clots from forming, prevent the existing

Table 3-12

Wells Criteria Score for DVT

CLINICAL FINDINGS	POINTS
Active cancer (treatment ongoing, or within 6 mo or palliative)	+1
Paralysis, paresis, or recent cast immobilization of the lower extremity	
Bedridden recently for 3 days or longer or major surgery within 12 weeks	
Recently bedridden for > 3 days or major surgery < 4 wk	+1
Localized tenderness along the distribution of the deep venous system	+1
Entire leg swelling	+1
Calf swelling at least 3 cm larger than asymptomatic side	+1
Pitting edema, confined to the symptomatic leg	+1
Previously documented DVT	+1
Alternative diagnosis at least as likely as DVT	+1
Total Criteria Point Count	
Clinical probability of a DVT with score:	
DVT likely	≥2
DVT unlikely	<2

Wells PS, et al. *Does this patient have deep vein thrombosis?* JAMA. 2006 Jan 11; 295(2), 199–207.

clot from getting larger, and stabilize the clot through anti-inflammatory properties (e.g., low-molecular-weight heparin [LMWH]).

(2) LMWH is contraindicated in patients at high risk for bleeding. Patients at high risk are typically treated with unfractionated heparin [UFH].

(3) Both LMWH and UFH are associated with heparin-induced thrombocytopenia (HIT) in a small percent of patients (2%–3%). HIT is associated with a paradoxical increased risk for venous and arterial thrombosis.

(4) Graded compression stockings (GCS).

f. *Don't use Homans sign to evaluate patients suspected of deep vein thrombosis (DVT)* (White N, et al. Phys Ther. 2015).

4. Pulmonary embolism.
   a. Presents abruptly with chest pain and dyspnea, also diaphoresis, cough, and apprehension; requires emergency treatment.
   b. Life threatening: 20% with acute PE die almost immediately; 40% die within 3 months.
   c. Can result in chronic thromboembolic pulmonary hypertension with reduced oxygenation and pulmonary hypertension.
   d. Can lead to right heart dysfunction and failure.
5. Chronic postthrombotic syndrome.
   a. A combination of clinical signs and symptoms that persists after an LE DVT; thrombosis resolution is incomplete.
   b. Symptoms include pain, intractable edema, limb heaviness, skin pigmentation changes, and leg ulcers.
   c. Leads to reduced quality of life and impaired functional mobility.
6. Chronic venous stasis/incompetence.
   a. Venous valvular insufficiency: from fibroelastic degeneration of valve tissue, venous dilation.
   b. Classification:
      (1) Grade I: mild aching, minimal edema, dilated superficial veins.
      (2) Grade II: increased edema, multiple dilated veins, changes in skin pigmentation.
      (3) Grade III: venous claudication, severe edema, cutaneous ulceration.

Lymphatic Disease

1. Lymphadenopathy.
   a. Enlargement of nodes, with or without tenderness.
2. Lymphedema.
   a. Chronic disorder with excessive accumulation of fluid due to obstruction of lymphatics or removal of lymph nodes.
   b. Causes swelling of the soft tissues in arms and legs.
   c. Results from mechanical insufficiency of the lymphatic system.
   d. Primary lymphedema: congenital condition with abnormal lymph node or lymph vessel formation (hypoplasia or hyperplasia).
   e. Secondary lymphedema: acquired, due to injury of one or more parts of the lymphatic system. Possible causes include:
      (1) Surgery: e.g., radical mastectomy, femoropopliteal bypass, lymph node removal.
      (2) Tumors, trauma, or infection affecting the lymph vessels.
      (3) Radiation therapy with fibrosis of tissues.
      (4) Chronic venous insufficiency.
      (5) In tropical and subtropical areas, filariasis (nematode worm larvae in the lymphatic system).
   f. Stages of lymphedema (progressive disease).
3. Acute lymphangitis.
   a. Acute bacterial infection spreading throughout lymph system.
   b. Usually streptococcal.
4. Table 3-13 presents a summary of the differential diagnoses of peripheral vascular disease.

Table 3-13

Differential Diagnosis: Peripheral Vascular Diseases

	CHRONIC ARTERIAL INSUFFICIENCY	CHRONIC VENOUS INSUFFICIENCY	CHRONIC LYMPHATIC INSUFFICIENCY
Etiology	Atherosclerosis Thrombosis Emboli Inflammatory process	Thrombophlebitis Trauma Vein obstruction (clot) Vein incompetence	Primary lymphedema Secondary lymphedema
Risk factors	Age: > 60 years Smoking Diabetes mellitus Gender: slightly higher in men Dyslipidemia Hypertension Hyperhomocysteinemia Race (African American)	Venous hypertension Varicose veins Inherited trait Gender: female Age Increased BMI Sedentary lifestyle/prolonged sitting Ligamentous laxity	Lymphadenectomy Radiation treatment Inflammatory arthritis Obesity
Signs and symptoms: determined by location and degree of vascular involvement			
Pain	Severe muscle ischemia/intermittent claudication Worse with exercise, relieved by rest Rest pain indicates severe involvement Muscle fatigue, cramping, numbness Paresthesias over time	Minimal to moderate steady pain Aching pain in lower leg with prolonged standing or sitting (dependency) Superficial pain along course of vein	Heaviness, tightness, aching, or discomfort
Location of pain	Usually calf, lower leg, or dorsum of foot May occur in thigh, hip, or buttock	Muscle compartment tenderness	Edematous limb
Vascular	Decreased or absent pulses Pallor of forefoot on elevation Dependent rubor	Venous dilatation or varicosity Edema: moderate to severe, especially after prolonged dependency	Rare complications unless severe and untreated edema
Skin changes	Pale, shiny, dry skin Loss of hair Nail changes Coolness of extremity	Hemosiderin deposition: dark, cyanotic, thickened, brown skin Lipodermatosclerosis: fibrosing of the subcutaneous tissue May lead to stasis dermatitis, cellulitis	Cutaneous fibrosis May lead to cellulitis, lymphangitis
Acute	Acute arterial obstruction: distal pain, paresthetic, pale, pulseless, sudden onset	Acute thrombophlebitis (deep venous thrombosis, DVT): calf pain, aching, edema, muscle tenderness, 50% asymptomatic	Rarely acute, usually progressive over time except with changes in pressure to limb altering flow (repeated blood pressure measurements, airplane flights)
Ulceration	May develop in toes, feet, or areas of trauma; pale or yellow to black eschar, gangrene may develop; regular in shape and may appear punched out	May develop at sides of ankles, especially medial malleolus along the course of veins; gangrene absent; painful, shallow, exudative, and have granulation tissue in the base; irregular borders	Unusual

Adapted from Bickley L, Szilagyi P. Bates Guide to Physical Examination and History Taking, 8th ed., Philadelphia, Lippincott Williams & Wilkins, 2003.

Cardiac Rehabilitation

Cardiovascular/pulmonary practice patterns are presented in Table 3-14.

Exercise Tolerance Testing

1. Exercise tolerance test (ETT, graded exercise test).
   a. Purpose: to determine physiological responses during a measured exercise stress (increasing workloads); allows the determination of functional exercise capacity of an individual and detects presence of ischemia.
      (1) Serves as a basis for exercise prescription. Symptom-limited ETT is typically administered prior to start of Phase II outpatient cardiac rehabilitation program and following cardiac rehabilitation as an outcome measure.
      (2) Used as a screening measure for CAD in asymptomatic individuals.

Table 3-14

Cardiovascular/Pulmonary Practice Patterns	
Pattern 6A	Primary prevention/risk reduction for cardiovascular/pulmonary disorders
Pattern 6B	Impaired aerobic capacity/endurance associated with deconditioning
Pattern 6C	Impaired ventilation, respiration/gas exchange, and aerobic capacity/endurance associated with airway clearance dysfunction
Pattern 6D	Impaired aerobic capacity/endurance associated with cardiovascular pump dysfunction or failure
Pattern 6E	Impaired ventilation, respiration/gas exchange associated with ventilatory pump dysfunction or failure
Pattern 6F	Impaired ventilation, respiration/gas exchange associated with respiratory failure
Pattern 6G	Impaired ventilation, respiration/gas exchange and aerobic capacity/endurance associated with respiratory failure in the neonate
Pattern 6H	Impaired circulation and anthropometric dimensions associated with lymphatic system disorder

From Practice Patterns. American Physical Therapy Association, 2014. Note: On the APTA website each practice pattern includes:
- Inclusion criteria: risk factors or consequences of pathology/pathophysiology; impairments of body functions and structures, activity limitations, or participation restrictions
- Exclusion or Multiple-Pattern Classification
- Examination: relevant tests and measures
- Evaluation, Diagnosis, and Prognosis (including Plan of Care) factors
- Intervention categories

(3) ETT with radionuclide perfusion:
  (a) A pharmacological stress test is used when patient is unable to perform a regular ETT.
  (b) Common medications used to increase cardiac demand are adenosine (increases heart rate), dobutamine (increases contractility), and persantine (vasodilates).
  (c) Imaging is used to detect decreased blood flow to myocardium.

b. Testing modes.
  (1) Treadmill and cycle ergometry (leg or arm tests) allow for precise calibration of the exercise workload.
  (2) Step test (upright or sitting) can also be used for fitness screening, healthy population.

c. ETT may be maximal or submaximal.
  (1) Maximal ETT: defined by target endpoint heart rate. Maximal ETTs should only be completed in settings with ACLS (advanced cardiac life support) trained individuals with appropriate equipment to handle abnormal responses.
    (a) Age predicted maximum heart rate.
      - 220 – age: high degree of error associated with it, especially in younger and older adults.
      - 208 – 0.7 × age: less error associated with this across different populations.
    (b) Heart-rate range (Karvonen's formula): 60%–80% (HR max – resting HR) + resting HR = target HR.
  (2) Submaximal ETT: symptom-limited or terminated at 85% of age predicted heart rate max; safe in all settings, used to evaluate the early recovery of patients after MI, coronary bypass, or coronary angioplasty.

d. Continuous ETT: workload is steadily progressed.
  (1) Step test: workload increases every 2–3 minutes, allowing the patient to reach steady state.
  (2) Ramp test: workload increased every minute so patient is not permitted to reach steady state.

e. Discontinuous (interval) ETT: allows rest in between workloads/stages; used for patients with more pronounced CAD.

f. Positive ETT: indicates myocardial oxygen supply is inadequate to meet the myocardial oxygen demand; positive for ischemia.

g. Negative ETT: indicates that at every tested physiological workload there is a balanced oxygen supply and demand.

h. False-positive ETT: test is interpreted as positive but the patient does not have ischemia.

i. False-negative ETT: test is interpreted as negative but the patient has ischemia.

j. Functional 6-Minute Walk Test (6MWT): patients walk as far as they can in 6 minutes, taking as many rests as needed. Highly correlated to other ETT, sub-max and maximal VO_2.

2. Monitoring during exercise and recovery.
  a. Patient appearance, signs and symptoms of excessive effort and exertional intolerance; examine for:
    (1) Persistent dyspnea.
    (2) Dizziness or confusion.
    (3) Anginal pain.
    (4) Severe leg claudication.
    (5) Excessive fatigue.
    (6) Pallor, cold sweat.
    (7) Ataxia, incoordination.
    (8) Pulmonary rales.
  b. Changes in HR: HR increases linearly as a function of increasing workload and oxygen uptake (VO_2), plateaus just before maximal oxygen uptake (VO_2 max).
  c. Changes in BP: systolic BP should rise with increasing workloads and VO_2; diastolic BP should remain about the same.
  d. Rate pressure product (RPP): the product of systolic BP and HR (the last two digits of a 5-digit number are dropped) is often used as an index of myocardial oxygen consumption (MVO_2).
    (1) Increased MVO_2 is the result of increased coronary blood flow.

(2) Angina is usually precipitated at a given RPP.

e. Ratings of perceived exertion (RPE): developed by Gunnar Borg. Allows subjective rating of feelings during exercise and impending fatigue. Important to use standardized instructions to reduce misinterpretation.
   (1) RPE increases linearly with increasing exercise intensity and correlates closely with exercise heart rates and work rates.
   (2) RPE has intra-user reliability over time, but not inter-user reliability. Ratings can be influenced by psychological factors, mood states, environmental conditions, exercise modes, and age.
   (3) RPE is an important measure for individuals who do not exhibit the typical rise in HR with exercise (e.g., patients on medications that depress HR, such as beta blockers).
   (4) Category scale (original Borg scale): rates exercise intensity using numbers from 6 to 20, with descriptors from very, very light (7) to somewhat hard (13) to very, very hard (19).
   (5) Category-ratio scale (Borg): rates exercise intensity using numbers from 1 to 10 with descriptors from 0 (nothing at all) to very weak (1) to moderate (3) to strong (5) to extremely strong (10).

f. Pulse oximetry: measure arterial oxygen saturation levels (SaO_2) before, during, and after exercise.

g. ECG changes with exercise: healthy individual.
   (1) Tachycardia: heart rate increase is directly proportional to exercise intensity and myocardial work.
   (2) Rate-related shortening of QT interval.
   (3) ST segment depression, upsloping, less than 1 mm.
   (4) Reduced R wave, increased Q wave.
   (5) Exertional arrhythmias: rare, single PVCs.

h. ECG changes with exercise: an individual with myocardial ischemia and CAD.
   (1) Significant tachycardia: occurs at lower intensities of exercise or with deconditioned individuals without ischemia.
   (2) Exertional arrhythmias: increased frequency of ventricular arrhythmias during exercise and/or recovery.
   (3) ST segment depression; horizontal or downsloping depression, greater than 1 mm below baseline is indicative of myocardial ischemia.

i. Delayed, abnormal responses to exercise, can occur hours later.
   (1) Prolonged fatigue.
   (2) Insomnia.
   (3) Sudden weight gain due to fluid retention.
   (4) Hypotension, especially in patients with heart failure.

3. Ambulatory monitoring (telemetry).
   a. Continuous 24-hour ECG monitoring.
   b. Allows documentation of arrhythmias and of ST segment depression or elevation, silent ischemia (if assessing via 12 leads only).

4. Transtelephonic ECG monitoring.
   a. Used to monitor patients as they exercise at home.

5. Activity levels: METs (metabolic equivalents).
   a. MET: the amount of oxygen consumed at rest (sitting); equal to 3.5 mL/kg per minute.
   b. MET levels (multiples of resting VO_2) can be directly determined during ETT: using collection and analysis of expired air; not routinely done.
   c. MET levels can be estimated during ETT during steady state exercise; the max VO_2 achieved on ETT is divided by resting VO_2; highly predictable with standardized testing modes.
   d. Can be used to predict energy expenditure during certain activities (Table 3-15).

Exercise Prescription

1. Guidelines for exercise prescription.
   a. Type (modality).
      (1) Cardiorespiratory endurance activities: walking, jogging, or cycling recommended to improve exercise tolerance; can be maintained at a constant velocity; very low interindividual variability.
      (2) Dynamic arm exercise (arm ergometry): uses a smaller muscle mass, results in lower VO_2 max (60%–70% lower) than leg ergometry; at a given workload, HR will be higher, stroke volume lower; systolic and diastolic BPs will be higher.
      (3) Other aerobic activities: swimming, cross-country skiing; less frequently used due to high interindividual variability, energy expenditure related to skill level.
      (4) Dancing, basketball, racquetball, competitive activities should not be used with high-risk, symptomatic, and low-fit individuals.
      (5) Early rehabilitation: activity is discontinuous (interval training), with frequent rest periods; progressing to continuous training. Interval training can also be incorporated in vigorous training to allow patient to work at higher percentage of VO_2 max.
      (6) Warm-up and cool-down activities.
         (a) Gradually increase or decrease the intensity of exercise, promote circulatory and muscular adjustment to exercise.
         (b) Type: low-intensity cardiorespiratory endurance activities, flexibility (ROM) exercises, functional mobility activities.

Table 3-15

Metabolic Equivalent (MET) Activity Chart

INTENSITY (70-KG PERSON)	ENDURANCE PROMOTING	ACTIVITY
1.5–2 METs	Too low in energy level	Standing, walking slowly (1 mph)
2–3 METs	Too low in energy level, unless capacity is very low	Level walking (2 mph), level bicycling (5 mph)
3–4 METs	Yes, if continuous and if target heart rate reached	Level walking (3 mph), bicycling (6 mph)
4–5 METs	Recreational activities must be continuous, lasting longer than 2 minutes	Walking (3½ mph), bicycling (8 mph)
5–6 METs	Yes	Walking at brisk pace (4 mph), bicycling (10 mph)
6–7 METs	Yes	Walking at very brisk pace (5 mph), bicycling (11 mph), swimming leisurely (20 yd/min)
7–8 METs	Yes	Jogging (5 mph), bicycling (12 mph)
8–9 METs	Yes	Running (5.5 mph), bicycling (13 mph), swimming (30 yd/min)
> 10 METs	Yes	Running 6 mph = 10 METs, 7 mph = 11.5 METs, 8 mph = 13.5 METs, 9 mph = 15 METs, 10 mph = 17 METs; swimming moderate/hard (> 40 yd/min)

Adapted from: Fox, Naughton, Gorman. Mod Concepts Cardiovas Dis 1972, 4:25. American Heart Association.

(c) Duration: 5–10 minutes.

(d) Abrupt beginning or cessation of exercise is not safe or recommended.

(7) Resistive exercises: to improve strength and endurance in clinically stable patients.

(a) Usually prescribed in later rehabilitation, after a period of aerobic conditioning.

(b) Moderate intensities are typically used (e.g., 60%–80% of 1 repetition or 10 repetition maximal voluntary contraction).

(c) Monitor responses to resistive training using rate-pressure product (incorporates BP, a safer measure).

(d) Precautions: carefully monitor BP, avoid breath holding, Valsalva's response (may dramatically increase BP and work of heart).

(e) Contraindicated for patients with: uncontrolled hypertension or arrhythmias.

(8) Relaxation training: relieves generalized muscle tension and anxiety.

(a) Usually incorporated following an aerobic training session and cool-down.

(b) Assists in successful stress management and lifestyle modification.

b. Intensity: prescribed as percentage of functional capacity revealed on ETT, within a range of 40%–85% depending upon initial level of fitness; typical training intensity is 60%–80% of functional capacity; lower training intensities may necessitate an increase in training duration; most clinicians use a combination of HR, RPE, and METs to prescribe exercise intensity (eliminates problems that may be associated with individual measures).

(1) Heart rate.

(a) Percentage of maximum heart rate achieved on ETT; without an ETT, 208 – 0.7 × age. 70%–85% HR max closely corresponds to 60%–80% of functional capacity or VO_2 max.

(b) Estimated HR max is used in cases where submaximal ETT has been given.

(c) Heart rate range or reserve (Karvonen's formula, see previous description). Can more closely approximate the relationship between HR and VO_2 max, but increased variability in patients on medications. Problems associated with use of HR alone to prescribe exercise intensity.

(d) Beta blocking: affects ability of HR to rise in response to an exercise stress.

(e) Pacemaker: can affect the ability of HR to rise in response to an exercise stress if it is fixed.

(f) Environmental extremes, heavy arm work, isometric exercise, and Valsalva may affect HR and BP responses.

(2) Rating of perceived exertion, the original Borg RPE scale (6–20).

(a) Useful along with other measures of patient effort if beta blockers or other HR suppressers are used.

(b) Problems with use of RPE alone to prescribe exercise intensity.
- Individuals with psychological problems (e.g., depression).
- Unfamiliarity with RPE scale; may affect selection of ratings.

(3) METs, or estimated energy expenditure (VO_2).
(a) 40%–85% of functional capacity (maximal METs) achieved on ETT. Without a maximal ETT, this is an estimation of workload.
(b) Problems associated with use of METs alone to prescribe exercise intensity.
- With high intensity activities (e.g., jogging), need to adopt a discontinuous work pattern: walk 5 minutes, jog 3 minutes to achieve the desired intensity.
- Varying skill level or stress of competition may affect the known metabolic cost of an activity.
- Environmental stresses (heat, cold, high humidity, altitude, wind, changes in terrain such as hills) may affect the known metabolic cost of an activity.

c. Duration.
(1) Conditioning phase may vary from 10 to 60 minutes, depending upon intensity; the higher the intensity, the shorter the duration.
(2) Average conditioning time is 20–30 minutes for moderate intensity exercise.
(3) Severely compromised individuals may benefit from multiple, short exercise sessions spaced throughout the day (e.g., 3- to 10-minute sessions).
(4) Warm-up and cool-down periods are kept constant; e.g., 5–10 minutes each.

d. Frequency.
(1) Frequency of activity is dependent upon intensity and duration; the lower the intensity, the shorter the duration, the greater the frequency.
(2) Average: three to five sessions/week for exercise at moderate intensities and duration, e.g., > 5 METs.
(3) Daily or multiple daily sessions for low intensity exercise: e.g., < 5 METs.

e. Exercise and progressive physical activity regimens require monitoring of heart rate and blood pressure.

f. Progression.
(1) Modify exercise prescription if:
(a) HR is lower than target HR for a given exercise intensity.
(b) RPE is lower (exercise is perceived as easier) for a given exercise.
(c) Symptoms of ischemia (e.g., angina) do not appear at a given exercise intensity.
(2) Rate of progression depends on age, health status, functional capacity, personal goals, preferences.
(3) As training progresses, duration is increased first, then intensity.

g. Consider reduction in exercise/activity with:
(1) Acute illness: fever, flu.
(2) Acute injury, orthopedic complications.
(3) Progression of cardiac disease: edema, weight gain, unstable angina.
(4) Overindulgence: e.g., food, caffeine, alcohol.
(5) Environmental stressors: extremes of heat, cold, humidity, air pollution.

h. Consider terminating exercise (Gibbons et al, 2002).
(1) Absolute indications.
(a) Drop in systolic blood pressure > 10 mm Hg with increased workload.
(b) Moderate to severe angina.
(c) Increasing nervous system symptoms (e.g., ataxia, dizziness, near syncope).
(d) Signs of poor perfusion.
(e) Technical difficulties in monitoring ECG or BP.
(f) Subject's desire to stop.
(g) Sustained VT.
(h) ST elevation ≥ 1.0 mm.
(2) Relative indications.
(a) ST or QRS changes (e.g., excessive ST depression) or marked axial shift.
(b) Arrhythmias other than sustained VT (e.g., multifocal PVCs, triplets, SVT, heart block, bradyarrhythmias).
(c) Fatigue, shortness of breath, wheezing, leg cramps, or claudication.
(d) Development of bundle branch block that can't be distinguished from VT.
(e) Increasing chest pain.
(f) Hypertensive response (systolic BP > 250 mm Hg or diastolic > 115 mm Hg).

i. Exercise prescription for post-PTCA (percutaneous transluminal coronary angioplasty).
(1) Wait to exercise vigorously approximately 2 weeks post-PTCA to allow inflammatory process to subside. Walking program can be initiated immediately.
(2) Use post-PTCA ETT to prescribe exercise.

j. Exercise prescription post-CABG (coronary artery bypass grafting).
(1) Limit upper extremity exercise while sternal incision is healing.
(2) Avoid lifting, pushing, pulling for 4–6 weeks postsurgery.

2. Contraindications for inpatient and outpatient cardiac rehabilitation (Box 3-1).
3. Possible effects of physical training/cardiac rehabilitation (Box-3-2).

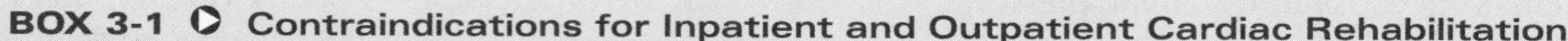

BOX 3-1 Contraindications for Inpatient and Outpatient Cardiac Rehabilitation

Absolute Contraindications

- Acute MI (within 2 days)
- Unstable angina not previously stabilized by medical therapy
- Uncontrolled cardiac arrhythmias causing symptoms or hemodynamic compromise
- Acute PE or pulmonary infarction
- Acute myocarditis or pericarditis
- Acute aortic dissection

Relative Contraindications

- Left main coronary stenosis
- Moderate stenotic valvular heart disease
- Electrolyte abnormalities
- Severe arterial hypertension
- Tachyarrhythmias or bradyarrhythmias
- Hypertrophic cardiomyopathy and other forms of outflow tract obstruction
- Mental or physical impairment leading to inability to exercise adequately
- High-degree atrioventricular block

Adapted from Gibbons et al, 2002.

BOX 3-2 Possible Effects of Physical Training/Cardiac Rehabilitation

- Decreased HR at rest and during exercise; improved HR recovery after exercise
- Increased stroke volume
- Increased myocardial oxygen supply and myocardial contractility; myocardial hypertrophy
- Improved respiratory capacity during exercise
- Improved functional capacity of exercising muscles
- Reduced body fat, increased lean body mass; successful weight reduction requires multifactorial interventions
- Decreased serum lipoproteins (cholesterol, triglycerides)
- Improved glucose tolerance
- Improved blood fibrinolytic activity and coagulability
- Improvement in measures of psychological status and functioning: self-confidence and sense of well-being
- Increased participation in exercise; improved outcomes with adherence to rehabilitation programming
  - Decreased angina in patients with CAD: anginal threshold is raised secondary to decreased myocardial oxygen consumption
  - Reduced total and cardiovascular mortality in patients following myocardial infarction
  - Decreased symptoms of heart failure, improved functional capacity in patients with left ventricular systolic dysfunction
  - Improved exercise tolerance and function in patients with cardiac transplantation

Phase 1: Inpatient Cardiac Rehabilitation (Acute)

Length of hospital stay is commonly 3–5 days for uncomplicated MI (no persistent angina, malignant arrhythmias or heart failure).

1. Exercise/activity goals and outcomes.
   a. Initiate early return to independence in activities of daily living; typically after 24 hours or until the patient is stable for 24 hours; monitor activity tolerance.
   b. Counteract deleterious effects of bed rest: reduce risk of thrombi, maintain muscle tone,

reduce orthostatic hypotension, maintain joint mobility.
   c. Help allay anxiety and depression.
   d. Provide medical surveillance.
   e. Provide patient and family education.
   f. Promote risk factor modification.
2. Exercise/activity guidelines.
   a. Program components: ADLs, selected arm and leg exercises, early supervised ambulation.
   b. Initial activities: low intensity (2–3 METs) progressing to ≥ 5 METs by discharge.
   c. Post-MI: limited to 70% max HR and/or 5 METs until 6 weeks post-MI.
   d. Short exercise sessions, two to three times a day; gradually duration is lengthened and frequency is decreased.
   e. Postsurgical patients.
      (1) Typically are progressed more rapidly than post-MI, unless there was a peri-operative MI.
      (2) Lifting activities are restricted, generally for 6 weeks.
3. Patient and family education goals.
   a. Improve understanding of cardiac disease, support risk factor modification.
   b. Teach self-monitoring procedures, warning signs of exertional intolerance; e.g., persistent dyspnea, anginal pain, dizziness.
   c. Teach concepts of energy costs, fatigue monitoring, general activity guidelines, activity pacing, energy conservation techniques; home exercise program (HEP).
   d. Provide emotional support and assist with referral to social work as needed.
4. Home exercise program (HEP).
   a. Low-risk patients may be safe candidates for unsupervised exercise at home.
      (1) Gradual increase in ambulation time: goal of 20–30 minutes, 1–2 times per day at 4–6 weeks post-MI.
      (2) Upper and lower extremity mobility exercises.
   b. Elderly, homebound patients with multiple medical problems may benefit from a home cardiac rehabilitation program.
   c. Patients should be skilled in self-monitoring procedures.
   d. Recommend family training in CPR and AED (automated external defibrillator) as indicated; emergency lifeline for some patients.

Phase 2: Outpatient Cardiac Rehabilitation (Subacute)

1. Eligible patients.
   a. MI/acute coronary syndrome.
   b. CABG.
   c. PCI.
   d. Stable angina.
   e. Heart valve surgical repair or replacement.
   f. Heart or heart/lung transplantation.
   g. Heart failure and PAD: not covered by insurance but these populations benefit from supervised exercise program.
2. Exercise/activity goals and outcomes.
   a. Improve functional capacity.
   b. Progress toward full resumption of activities of daily living, habitual and occupational activities.
   c. Promote risk-factor modification, counseling as to lifestyle changes.
   d. Encourage activity pacing, energy conservation; stress importance of taking proper rest periods.
3. Exercise/activity guidelines.
   a. Outpatient program.
      (1) Patients at risk for arrhythmias with exercise, angina, other medical problems benefit from outpatient programs with availability of ECG monitoring, trained personnel, and emergency support.
      (2) Group camaraderie and support of program participants may assist in risk-factor modification and lifestyle changes.
      (3) Frequency: 2–3 sessions/week.
      (4) Duration: 30–60 minutes with 5–10 minutes of warm-up and cool-down.
      (5) Programs may offer a single mode of training (e.g., walking) or multiple modes using a circuit training approach (e.g., treadmill, cycle ergometer, arm ergometer); strength training.
      (6) Patients are gradually weaned from continuous monitoring to spot checks and self-monitoring.
      (7) Suggested exit point: 9 MET functional capacity (5 MET capacity is needed for safe resumption of most daily activities).
   b. Strength training in Phase 2 programs.
      (1) Guidelines: after 3 weeks cardiac rehab; 5 weeks post-MI, or 8 weeks post-CABG.
      (2) Begin with use of elastic bands and light hand weights (1–3 lb).
      (3) Progress to moderate loads, 12–15 comfortable repetitions.
4. Patient and family education goals. Progression from Phase 1 goals.

Phase 3: Community Exercise Programs (Postacute, Postdischarge from Phase 2 Program)

1. Exercise/activity goals and outcomes.
   a. Improve and/or maintain functional capacity.
   b. Promote self-regulation of exercise programs.

c. Promote life-long commitment to risk-factor modification.
2. Exercise/activity guidelines.
a. Location: community centers, YMCA, or clinical facilities.
b. Entry level criteria: functional capacity of 5 METs, clinically stable angina, medically controlled arrhythmias during exercise.
c. Progression is from supervised to self-regulation of exercise.
d. Progression to 50%–85% of functional capacity, 3–4 times/week, 45 minutes or more/session.
e. Regular medical check-ups and periodic ETT generally required.
f. Utilize motivational techniques to maintain compliance with exercise programs, life-style modification.
g. Discharge typically in 6–12 months.
3. Patient and family education goals. Progression from Phase 1 goals.

Resistance Exercise Training

1. Goals and outcomes.
a. Improve muscle strength and endurance.
b. Enhance functional independence.
c. Decrease cardiac demands during daily activities.
2. Patient criteria for resistance training (American Association of Cardiovascular and Pulmonary Rehabilitation Guidelines).
a. Post-MI: resistance training permitted if remain under 70% max HR or 5 METs for 6 weeks post-MI, be cautious of Valsalva with resistance training.
b. Cardiac surgery: lower extremity resistance training can be initiated immediately, in the absence of a peri-operative MI. Upper extremity resistance training should be avoided until soft tissue and bony healing has occurred: 6–8 weeks.
c. Post-transcatheter procedure (PTCA, other): minimum of 3 weeks following procedure and 2 weeks of consistent participation in a supervised CR endurance training program.
d. No evidence of the following conditions: congestive heart failure, uncontrolled dysrhythmias, severe valvular disease, uncontrolled hypertension, and unstable symptoms.
3. Exercise prescription.
a. Start with low resistance (one set of 10–15 repetitions) and progress slowly.
b. Resistance can include:
(1) Weights, 50% or more of maximum weight used to complete one repetition (1 RM).
(2) Elastic bands.
(3) Light (1- to 5-lb) cuff and hand weights.
(4) Wall pulleys.
c. Perceived exertion (RPE–Borg Scale) should range from 11 to 13 ("light" to "somewhat hard"), but this needs to be correlated to hemodynamic response to activity.
d. Rate-pressure product should not exceed that prescribed during endurance exercise.

Exercise Prescription for Patients Requiring Special Considerations

1. Heart Failure (HF).
a. Patients demonstrate significant ventricular dysfunction, decreased cardiac output, low functional capacities.
b. Classification Systems (Table 3-16).
c. Criteria for exercise training.
(1) Compensated or chronic HF; no signs of acute HF.
(2) Exercise-induced ischemia and arrhythmias poor prognostic indicators.

Table 3-16

Classifications of Heart Failure

NEW YORK HEART ASSOCIATION STAGES	FUNCTION AND SYMPTOMS
Class I: mild HF	No limitation in physical activity (up to 6.5 METs); comfortable at rest, ordinary activity does not cause undue fatigue, palpitation, dyspnea, or anginal pain.
Class II: slight HF	Slight limitation in physical activity (up to 4.5 METs); comfortable at rest, ordinary physical activity results in fatigue, palpitation, dyspnea, or anginal pain.
Class III: marked HF	Marked limitation of physical activity (up to 3.0 METs); comfortable at rest, less than ordinary activity causes fatigue, palpitation, dyspnea, or anginal pain.
Class IV: severe HF	Unable to carry out any physical activity (1.5 METs) without discomfort; symptoms of ischemia, dyspnea, anginal pain present even at rest; increasing with exercise.
AMERICAN COLLEGE OF CARDIOLOGY FOUNDATION (ACCF)/ AMERICAN HEART ASSOCIATION (AHA) STAGES	
Stage A	At high risk for HF but without structural heart disease or symptoms of HF.
Stage B	Structural heart disease but without signs or symptoms of HF.
Stage C	Structural heart disease with prior or current symptoms of HF.
Stage D	Refractory HF requiring specialized interventions.

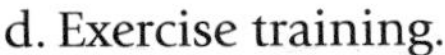

d. Exercise training.
   (1) Assess for signs of decompensation at each visit: increased SOB; sudden weight gain; increased LE edema or abdominal swelling; increased pain or fatigue; pronounced cough, lightheadedness, or dizziness.
   (2) Monitor at rest and during activity.
      (a) Use RPE that is correlated with objective measures of hemodynamic response (HR, BP, RR, SpO_2) and clinical signs of exertional intolerance.
      (b) HR response may be impaired (chronotropic incompetence).
      (c) At risk for persistent post-exercise vasodilation (and hypotension) with later stages of HF.
   (3) Use low-level, gradually progressive aerobic training.
      (a) Intensities: begin with 40%–60% functional capacity, increase as able.
      (b) Gradually increasing durations, with frequent rest periods (interval training).
      (c) Adequate warm-up and cool-down periods; may need longer than the typical 5–10 minutes.
   (4) Use caution exercising in supine or prone positions due to orthopnea.
   (5) Avoid breath holding and Valsalva's maneuver.
   (6) Respiratory muscle training. Monitoring SaO_2 via pulse oximetry is advisable in some cases.

e. Emphasis on training in energy conservation, self-monitoring techniques.

2. Cardiac transplant.
   a. Patients may present with:
      (1) Exercise intolerance due to extended inactivity and deconditioning.
      (2) Side effects from immunosuppressive drug therapy: hyperlipidemia, hypertension, obesity, diabetes, leg cramps.
      (3) Decreased lower extremity strength.
      (4) Increased fracture risk due to long-term corticosteroid use.
   b. Heart rate alone is not an appropriate measure of exercise intensity (heart is denervated and patients tend to be tachycardic). Use combination of HR, BP, RPE, METs, dyspnea scale.
   c. Use longer periods of warm-up and cool-down because the physiological responses to exercise and recovery take longer.

3. Pacemakers and automatic implantable cardioverter defibrillators (AICDs).
   a. Pacemakers are programmed to pace heart rate.
      (1) Most are demand pacemakers so that heart will increase as workload increases.
      (2) Always have a lower HR limit set, rarely have a upper limit set.
      (3) HR will not change with fixed rate pacers, which will impact activity tolerance.
   b. AICDs will deliver an electric shock if HR exceeds set limit and/or ventricular arrhythmia is detected.
   c. Should know setting for HR limits or AICD.
   d. ST segment changes may be common.
   e. Avoid UE aerobic or strengthening exercises for 4–6 weeks after implant to allow the leads to scar down.
   f. Electromagnetic signals may cause devices to fire (defibrillator), or slow down or speed up (pacemaker).

4. Diabetes.
   a. Patients demonstrate problems controlling blood glucose, with associated cardiovascular disease, renal disease, neuropathy, peripheral vascular disease, and ulceration and/or autonomic dysfunction.
   b. Exercise testing.
      (1) May need to use submaximal ETT tests; maximal tests can be precluded with autonomic neuropathy.
      (2) With PAD/peripheral neuropathy, may need to shift to arm ergometry.
   c. Exercise prescription and training. See discussion in Chapter 6 on Diabetes Mellitus.

Peripheral Vascular Disease Management

Rehabilitation Guidelines for Arterial Disease

1. Risk factor modification (see Table 3-1).
2. Limb protection.
   a. Avoid excessive strain, protection of extremities from injury, and extremes of temperature.
   b. Bed rest may be required if gangrene, ulceration, acute arterial disease are present.
3. Exercise training for patients with PAD.
   a. May result in improved functional capacity, improved peripheral blood flow via collateral circulation and muscle oxidative capacity.
   b. Consider interval training (multistage discontinuous protocol) with frequent rests.
   c. Walking program: intensity such that patient reports 1 on claudication scale within 3–5 minutes, stopping if they reach a 2 (until pain subsides),

total of 30–60 minutes (intervals as necessary), 3–5 days per week.

d. Record time of pain onset and duration.

e. Non-weight-bearing exercise (cycle ergometry, arm ergometry) may be necessary in some patients; less effective in producing a peripheral conditioning effect.

f. Well-fitting shoes essential; with insensitive feet, teach techniques of proper foot inspection and care.

g. Beta blockers for treatment of hypertension or cardiac disorders may decrease time to claudication or worsen symptoms.

h. Pentoxifylline, dipyridamole, aspirin, and warfarin may improve time to claudication.

i. High risk for CAD.

4. Lower extremity exercise.
   a. Modified Buerger-Allen exercises: postural exercises plus active plantar and dorsiflexion of the ankle; active exercises improve blood flow during and after exercise; effects less pronounced in patients with PAD.
   b. Resistive calf exercises: most effective method of increasing blood flow.
5. Medical treatment.
   a. Medications to decrease blood viscosity, prevent thrombus formation; e.g., heparin.
   b. Vasodilators: controversial.
   c. Calcium channel blockers in vasospastic disease.
6. Surgical management.
   a. Atherectomy, thromboembolectomy, laser therapy.
   b. Revascularization: angioplasty or bypass grafting.
   c. Sympathectomy: results in permanent vasodilation, improvement of blood flow to skin.
   d. Amputation when gangrene is present.

Rehabilitation Guidelines for Venous Disease

1. Venous Thromboembolism (VTE).
   a. Identification of patients who are at high risk of VTE.
      (1) Requires knowledge of signs and symptoms and risk factors.
      (2) Use standardized Risk Assessment Measure (e.g., Wells Criteria Score for DVT).
   b. Initiate preventive measures: prompt referral to physician, team members.
   c. Once therapeutic levels of medication are achieved (e.g., low molecular weight heparin), initiate ambulation and leg exercises (activation of the calf muscle pump).
   d. Bedrest is not recommended following diagnosis of VTE once acceptable levels of medication are reached unless there are significant medical concerns.
   e. Utilize mechanical compression: graded compression stockings (GCS) with at least 30 mm Hg of pressure at the ankle.
   f. A trial of intermittent pneumatic compression (IPC) may be appropriate for patients with severe postthrombotic syndrome (PTS) of the leg not adequately relieved with graded compression stockings (GCS).
   g. Mobilize patients after IVC filter placement once hemodynamically stable.
   h. Provide education to decrease risk of recurring VTE.
   i. Assess for fall risk and institute measures to reduce fall risk.
   j. See Appendix 3B.
2. Chronic venous insufficiency (CVI).
   a. Management of edema.
      (1) Positioning: extremity elevation, minimum of 18 cm above heart. Encourage patients to elevate leg as much as possible and avoid the dependent position.
      (2) Compression therapy.
         (a) Bandages (elastic, tubular); applied within 20 minutes of rising.
         (b) Paste bandages (Unna boot). Gauze impregnated with zinc oxide, gelatin, and glycerine; applied for 4–7 days (less with some wounds).
         (c) Graduated compression stockings with a pressure gradient of 30–40 mm Hg.
         (d) Compression pump therapy, used for a 1- to 2-hour session twice daily.
         (e) Red Flag: consider consequences of compression therapy to a limb with an ankle-brachial index (ABI) < 0.8 or with evidence of active cellulitis or infection.
      (3) Exercise.
         (a) Active ankle exercises: emphasis on muscle pump exercises (dorsiflexion/plantarflexion, foot circles).
         (b) Cycle ergometry in sitting or attached to foot of bed.
         (c) Early ambulation as soon as patient is able to get out of bed, three to four times/day.
   b. Patient education: meticulous skin care.
   c. Severe conditions with dermal ulceration may require surgery (ligation and vein stripping, vein grafts, valvuloplasty).

Rehabilitation Guidelines for Lymphatic Disease

1. Phase I Management: edema secondary to lymphatic dysfunction.
   a. Short-stretch compression bandages, worn 24 hours/day.

b. Manual lymph drainage (MLD) with complete decongestive therapy.
   (1) Massage and passive range of motion (PROM) to assist lymphatic flow (Vodder techniques, modifications by Asdonk, Leduc, Fodi).
   (2) Emphasis is on decongesting proximal segments first (trunk quadrant), then extremities, directing flow distal to proximal.
   (3) Compression using multilayered padding and short-stretch bandages.
      (a) Bandages have low resting pressure and high working pressure.
      (b) Bandages maintain limb after techniques applied to reduce limb.
      (c) Decongestive exercises with padding in place. Activate muscles in extremity. Work trunk and limb girdle muscles first, then limb muscles from proximal to distal. Performed with compression bandages on.
   (4) Certified specialists (certified lymphedema therapist).
c. Functional activities.
   (1) Walking program, cycling.
   (2) Water-based programs: swimming.
   (3) Tai chi and balance activities.
   (4) ADL training.
   (5) Red Flag: strenuous activities, jogging, and ballistic movements are contraindicated, as they are likely to exacerbate lymphedema.
   (6) Signs of lymph overload: discomfort, aching, or pain in proximal lymph areas (axilla or inguinal areas), change in skin color. If any of these are present, discontinue activity.
d. Meticulous skin care: hygiene, nail care.
e. Contraindicated modalities.
   (1) Ice, heat, hydrotherapy, saunas, contrast baths, paraffin; all cause vasodilation and increase lymphatic load of water.
   (2) No electrotherapeutic modalities greater than 30 Hz.
f. Compression garments at end of Phase 1.

Red Flag: excessively high pressures will occlude superficial lymph capillaries and restrict fluid absorption.

2. Phase II Management (self-management).
   a. Skin care.
   b. Compression garments.
   c. Exercise.
   d. Lymphedema bandaging at night.
   e. MLD as needed.
   f. Compression pumps: use with caution; limited benefits.

Red Flag: pressures higher than 45 mm Hg are contraindicated, as they can cause lymphatic collapse; contraindicated with soft tissue injury.

3. Education.
   a. Skin and nail care.
   b. Self-bandaging, garment care.
   c. Infection management.
   d. Maintain exercise while preventing lymph overload.
4. Specialized education for complete decongestive therapy, including manual lymphatic drainage:
   a. National Lymphedema Network: http://www.lymphnet.org.
   b. Lymphology Association of North America: http://www.clt-lana.org.
5. Surgery to assist in lymph drainage (severe cases).

Basic Life Support and Cardiopulmonary Resuscitation (CPR)

1. 2010 CPR Guidelines (see Table 3-17).
   a. Compressions come first, then focus on airway and breathing (CAB). Only exception is newborn babies.
   b. No more looking, listening, and feeling. Call 911 immediately.
   c. Push a little harder for adult CPR: at least 2 inches deep on chest.
   d. Push a little faster: about 100 compressions/min.
   e. Hands-only CPR for untrained lay rescuers.
   f. Don't stop pushing, no interruptions.

First Aid

1. External bleeding.
   a. Minor bleeding.
      (1) Usually clots within 10 minutes.
      (2) If patient/client is taking aspirin or nonsteroidal anti-inflammatory drugs (NSAIDS), clotting may take longer.
   b. Severe bleeding characteristics.
      (1) Blood spurting from a wound.
      (2) Blood fails to clot even after measures to control bleeding have been taken.
      (3) Arterial bleed: high pressure, spurting, red.
      (4) Venous bleed: low pressure, steady flow, dark red or maroon blood.
      (5) Capillary bleed: low pressure, oozing, dark red blood.
   c. Controlling external bleeding.
      (1) Use standard precautions such as wearing gloves.
      (2) Apply gauze pads using firm pressure. If no gauze available, use a clean cloth, towel, a gloved hand, or patient's own hand. If blood

Table 3-17

Summary of Key Basic Life Support (BLS) Components for Adults, Children, and Infants

COMPONENT	RECOMMENDATIONS		
	ADULTS	CHILDREN	INFANTS
Recognition	Unresponsive (all ages) No breathing, not breathing normally (e.g., only gasping)	Same as for adults	Same as for adults
CPR Sequence	CAB	CAB	CAB (ABC for neonates)
Compression Rate	At least 100/minute	Same as for adults	Same as for adults
Compression Depth	At least 2 inches (5 cm)	At least 1/3 AP depth, about 2 inches (5 cm)	At least 1/3 AP depth, about 1½ inches (4 cm)
Chest Wall Recall	Allow complete recoil between compressions, HCPs rotate compressors every 2 minutes	Same as for adults	Same as for adults
Compression Interruption	30:2 (1 or 2 rescuers)	30:2 single rescuer, 15:2 2 HCP rescuers	30:2 single rescuer, 15:2 2 HCP rescuers
Airway	Head tilt-chin lift (HCP suspected trauma: jaw thrust)	Same as for adults	Same as for adults
Compression to Ventilation Ratio (until advanced airway placed)	30:2 (1 or 2 rescuers)	30:2 single rescuer or 15:2 2 HCP rescuers	30:2 single rescuer or 15:2 2 HCP rescuers
Ventilations: when rescuer untrained or trained and not proficient	Compressions only	Compressions only	Compressions only
Ventilations with Advanced Airway (HCP)	1 breath every 6–8 seconds (8–10 breaths/min) Asynchronous with chest compressions About 1 second per breath Visible chest rise	Same as for adults	Same as for adults
Defibrillation	Attach and use AED as soon as available. Minimize interruptions in chest compressions before and after shock, resume CPR, beginning with compressions immediately after each shock	Same as for adults	Same as for adults

Key: CAB: compressions, airway, breathing; HCP: health care provider; CPR: cardiopulmonary resuscitation; AED: automatic electronic defibrillator
From 2010 American Heart Association Guidelines for CPR and ECG. Downloaded from http://circ.ahajournals.org on July 5, 2011.

soaks through, do not remove any gauze, add additional layers.

(3) Elevate the part if possible unless it is deformed or it causes significant pain when elevated.
(4) Apply a pressure bandage, such as roller gauze, over the gauze pads.
(5) If necessary, apply pressure with the heel of your hand over pressure points. The femoral artery in the groin and the brachial artery in the medial aspect of the upper arm are two such points.
(6) Monitor A, B, Cs and overall status of the patient. Administer supplemental oxygen if nearby. Seek more advanced care as necessary.

2. Internal bleeding.
   a. The possible result of a fall, blunt force trauma, or a fracture rupturing a blood vessel or organ.
   b. Severe internal bleeding may be life-threatening.
   c. Severe internal bleeding characteristics.
      (1) Ecchymosis (black and blue) in the injured area.
      (2) Body part, especially the abdomen, may be swollen, tender, and firm.
      (3) Skin may appear blue, gray, or pale and may be cool or moist.
      (4) Respiratory rate is increased.
      (5) Pulse rate is increased and weak.
      (6) Blood pressure is decreased.
      (7) Patient may be nauseated or vomit.
      (8) Patient may exhibit restlessness or anxiety.
      (9) Level of consciousness may decline.
   d. Management of internal bleeding.
      (1) If minor, follow RICE procedure: rest, ice, compression, elevation.
      (2) Major internal bleeding.

(a) Summon advanced medical personnel.
(b) Monitor A, B, Cs and vital signs.
(c) Keep the patient comfortable and quiet. Keep them from getting chilled or overheated.
(d) Reassure patient or victim.
(e) Administer supplemental oxygen if available and nearby.

3. Shock (hypoperfusion).
   a. Failure of the circulatory system to perfuse vital organs.
   b. At first, blood is shunted from the periphery to compensate.
      (1) The victim may lose consciousness as the brain is affected.
      (2) The heart rate increases, resulting in increased oxygen demand.
      (3) Organs ultimately fail when deprived of oxygen.
      (4) Heart rhythm is affected, ultimately leading to cardiac arrest and death.
   c. Types and causes of shock.
      (1) Hemorrhagic: severe internal or external bleeding.
      (2) Psychogenic: emotional stress causes blood to pool in body away from the brain.
      (3) Metabolic: loss of body fluids from heat or severe vomiting or diarrhea.
      (4) Anaphylactic: allergic reaction from drugs, food or insect stings.
      (5) Cardiogenic: MI or cardiac arrest results in pump failure.
      (6) Respiratory: respiratory illness or arrest results in insufficient oxygenation of the blood.
      (7) Septic: severe infections cause blood vessels to dilate.
      (8) Neurogenic: traumatic brain injury (TBI), spinal cord injury (SCI) or other neural trauma causes disruption of autonomic nervous system resulting in disruption of blood vessel dilation/constriction.
   d. Signs and symptoms.
      (1) Pale, gray or blue, cool skin.
      (2) Increased, weak pulse.
      (3) Increased respiratory rate.
      (4) Decreased blood pressure.
      (5) Irritability or restlessness.
      (6) Diminishing level of consciousness.
      (7) Nausea or vomiting.
   e. Care for shock.
      (1) Obtain a history if possible.
      (2) Examine the victim for airway, breathing, circulation, and bleeding.
      (3) Assess level of consciousness.
      (4) Determine skin characteristics and perform capillary refill test of finger tips.
         (a) Capillary refill test: squeeze fingernail for 2 seconds.
         (b) In healthy individuals, the nail will blanch and turn pink when pressure is released.
         (c) If nail bed does not refill and turn pink within 2 seconds, the cause could be that blood is being shunted away from the periphery to vital organs or to maintain core temperature.
      (5) Treat any specific condition if possible: control bleeding, splint a fracture, EpiPen for anaphylaxis, and so on.
      (6) Keep the victim from getting chilled or overheated.
      (7) Elevate the legs 12 inches unless there is suspected spinal injury or painful deformities of the lower extremities.
      (8) Reassure the victim and continue to monitor A, B, Cs.
      (9) Administer supplemental oxygen if nearby.
      (10) Do not give any food or drink.

APPENDIX 3A

Selected Outcome Measures for Cardiac and Pulmonary Dysfunction

Table 3A-1

OUTCOME MEASURES	REFERENCES
Chronic Respiratory Questionnaire	• Larson JL, Covey MK, Berry JK, et al: Reliability and validity of the Chronic Respiratory Disease Questionnaire. Am J Crit Care Med. 1993; 147: A350. • Guyatt GH, Berman LB, Townsend M, et al: A measure of quality of life for clinical trials in chronic lung disease. Thorax. 1987; 42: 773–778. • Jaeschke R, Singer J, Guyatt GH. Measurement of health status ascertaining the minimal clinically important difference. Controlled Clin Trials. 1989; 10: 407–415. • Guyatt GH, King DR, Feeny DH, et al: Generic and specific measurement of health-related quality of life in a clinical trial of respiratory rehabilitation. J Clin Epidemiol. 1999; 52: 187–192. • Lacasse Y, Wong E, Guyatt G. A systematic overview of the measurement properties of the Chronic Respiratory Questionnaire. Canadian Respiratory Journal. 1997; 4(3): 131–139.
St. George's Respiratory Questionnaire	• Jones PW, Quirk FH, Baveystock CM. The St. George's Respiratory Questionnaire. Resp Med. 1991; 85(suppl): 25–31. • Jones PW, Quirk FH, Baveystock CM, et al: A self-complete measure of health status for chronic airflow limitation. Am Rev Respir Dis. 1992; 145: 1321–1327.
6-Minute Walk Test	• American Thoracic Society: ATS statement: Guidelines for the Six-Minute Walk Test. Am J Respir Crit Care Med. 2002; 166: 111–117. • Guyatt GH, Townsend M, Keller J, et al: Measuring functional status in chronic lung disease: conclusions from a random control trial. Respir Med. 1991; 85(Suppl B): 17–21. • Rasekaba T, Lee A, Naughton MT, et al: The six-minute walk test: a useful metric for the cardiopulmonary patient. Internal Medicine Journal. 2009; 39: 495–501. • Casanova C, Cote CG, Marin MJ, et al: The 6-min walking distance: long-term follow up in patients with COPD. Eur Respir J. 2007; 29(3): 535–540. • Casanova C, Cote CG, Marin MJ, et al: Validation and comparison of reference equations for the 6-min walk distance test. Eur Respir J. 2008; 31: 571–578.

Table 3A-1 (*Continued*)

Walking Speed	• Fritz S, Lusardi M: White paper: Walking speed: the sixth vital sign. J Geriatr Phys Ther. 2009;32(2):46–9. Erratum in: J Geriatr Phys Ther. 2009; 32(3): 110. • Andersson M, Moberg L, Svantesson U, et al: Measuring walking speed in COPD: test-retest reliability of the 30-metre walk test and comparison with the 6-minute walk test. Prim Care Respir J. 2011; 20: 434–440. • Dolmage TE, Evans RA, Hill K, et al: The effect of pulmonary rehabilitation on critical walk speed in patients with COPD: a comparison with self-paced walks. Chest. 2012; 141(2): 413–419. • Afilalo J, Eisenberg MJ, Morin JF et al. Gait speed as an incremental predictor of mortality and major morbidity in elderly patients undergoing cardiac surgery. J Am Coll Cardiol. 2010; 56(2): 1668–1676.
10 meter Shuttle Walk Test	• Singh SJ, Morgan MDL, Hardman AE, et al: Comparison of oxygen uptake during a conventional treadmill test and the shuttle walking test in chronic airflow limitation. Eur Respir J. 1994; 7: 2016–2020. • Revill SM, Morgan MDL, Singh SJ, et al: The endurance shuttle walk: a new field test for the assessment of endurance capacity in chronic obstructive pulmonary disease. Thorax. 1999; 54: 213–222. • Singh SJ, Morgan MDL, Scott S, et al: Development of a shuttle walking test of disability in patients with chronic airways obstruction. Thorax. 1992; 47: 1019–1024. • Morales FJ, Martinez A, Mendex M, et al. A shuttle walk test for assessment of functional capacity in chronic heart failure. Am Heart J. 1999; 138(2Pt1): 291–298. • Morales FJ, Montemayor T, Martinez A. Shuttle versus six-minute walk test in the prediction of outcomes in chronic heart failure. Int J Cardiol. 2000; 76(2–3): 101–105.
BODE Index	• Celli BR, Cote CG, Marin JM, et al: The body-mass index, airflow obstruction, dyspnea, and exercise capacity index in chronic obstructive pulmonary disease. N Engl J Med. 2004; 350: 1005–1012. • Mannino DM, Buist AS: Global burden of COPD: risk factors, prevalence, and future trends. Lancet. 2007; 370: 765–773. • Cote CG, Pinto-Plata VM, Marin JM, et al: The modified BODE index: validation with mortality in COPD. Eur Respir J. 2008; 32: 1269–1274. • Martinez FJ, Han MK, Andrei AC: Longitudinal change in the BODE index predicts mortality in severe emphysema. Am J Respir Crit Care Med. 2008; 178: 491–499.
Kansas City Cardiomyopathy Questionnaire	• Garin O, Herdman M, Vialgut G et al. Assessing health related quality of life in patients with heart failure: a systematic, standardized comparison of available measures. Heart Fail Rev. 2013. • Green CP, Porter CB, Bresnahan DR, Spertus JA. Development and evaluation of the Kansas City Cardiomyopathy Questionnaire: a new health status measure for heart failure. J Am Coll Cardiol. 2000; 35(5): 1245–1255.
Inspiratory/Respiratory Muscle Training	• Cahalin LP, Arena R, Guazzi M et al. Inspiratory muscle training in heart disease and heart failure: a review of the literature with a focus on method of training and outcomes. Expert Rev Cardiovasc Ther. 2013; 11(2): 161–177. • Plentz RD, Sbruzzi G, Ribeiro RA, Ferreira JB, Dal Lago P. Inspiratory muscle training in patients with heart failure: meta-analysis of randomized trials. Arq Bras Cardiol. 2012; 99(2): 762–771.
Minnesota Living with Heart Failure Questionnaire	• Garin O, Herdman M, Vialgut G et al. Assessing health related quality of life in patients with heart failure: a systematic, standardized comparison of available measures. Heart Fail Rev. 2013. • Rector TS. Overview of the Minnesota Living with Heart Failure Questionnaire. 1/1/05. https://docs.google.com/a/umn.edu/viewer?a=v&pid=sites&srcid=dW1uLmVkdXx0bXN8Z3g6MjQxYWMzOTBkMWYwMjAwZA
Walking Impairment Questionnaire	• Jain A, Lui K, Ferrucci L et al. Declining walking impairment questionnaire scores are associated with subsequent increased mortality in peripheral artery disease. J Am Coll Cardiol. 2013; 61(17): 1820–1829. • Jain A, Lui K, Ferrucci L et al. The Walking Impairment Questionnaire stair-climbing score predicts mortality in men and women with peripheral artery disease. J Vasc Surg. 2012; 55(6): 1662–1673. • Nead KT, Zhou M, Diaz Caceres R, Olin JW, Cooke JP, Leeper NJ. Walking impairment questionnaire improves mortality risk prediction models in high-risk cohort independent of peripheral arterial disease status. Circ Cardiovasc Qual Outcomes. 2013; 6(3): 255–261.

APPENDIX 3B

Clinical Practice Guidelines: Management of Individuals with Venous Thromboembolism

Clinical Findings

VTE is the formation of a blood clot in a deep vein. Complications that can result include deep vein thrombosis (DVT), pulmonary embolism (PE), and post thrombotic syndrome (PTS). Risk of recurrence is high (as high as 5%–10% during the first 6–12 months and 10%–20% within 5 years). Thrombosis resolution is often incomplete with as many as 50% of legs affected by DVT still having residual vein thrombosis lasting years. Quality of life can be significantly affected.

Key Actions Advocated

Advocate for a culture of mobility and physical activity.

Recommendation Strength: A Strong; Evidence Quality: Level I[1]

The benefits of activity and risks of harm due to inactivity and bedrest are well established. Clinicians should advocate for mobility in all situations once therapeutic anticoagulant levels have been reached except when there is risk of harm (e.g., emboli moving through the vascular system to the pulmonary system). Early and frequent ambulation and leg exercise are key components.

Screen for risk of VTE.

Recommendation Strength: A Strong; Evidence Quality: Level I

Comprehensive screening and assessment is indicated, leading to appropriate referral. Risk factors are assessed and include previous DVT or embolism, age, active cancer or cancer treatment, severe infection, oral contraceptives, hormonal replacement therapy, pregnancy or recent birth within previous 6 weeks, immobility (bedrest, flight travel, fractures), surgery, anesthesia, critical care admission, central venous catheters, inherited thrombophilia, and obesity. Risk assessment measures should be standardized within the health care system and results should be communicated with the health care team.

[1]See Table 14-4 for a summary of levels of evidence and grades of recommendation.

Provide preventive measures for LE DVT.

Recommendation Strength: A Strong; Evidence Quality: Level I

Preventive measures should be initiated immediately, including education regarding leg exercises, ambulation, proper hydration, mechanical compression, and assessment regarding need for medication. Patients and their families and caregivers need to understand risk factors for DVT, signs and symptoms of DVT, consequences of DVT, interventions to decrease the risk of DVT, and importance of seeking prompt medical help if DVT is suspected. Follow-up monitoring regarding treatment adherence and medication issues (regimen, adverse side effects and interactions, dietary restrictions) is also important.

Recommend mechanical compression as a preventive measure for DVT.

Recommendation Strength: A Strong; Evidence quality: Level I

Mechanical compression is recommended when individuals are at moderate to high risk for LE DVT or when anticoagulation is contraindicated. This includes graded compression stockings (GCS) and can also include intermittent pneumatic compression (IPC). Fit of GCS is important as improper fit can lead to skin irritation, ulceration, or interruption of blood flow. Patients with severe peripheral neuropathy, decompensated heart failure, arterial insufficiency, dermatologic diseases, or lesions may have contraindications to selective mechanical compression modes.

Identify the likelihood of LE DVT when signs and symptoms are present.

Recommendation Strength: B Moderate; Evidence quality: Level II

Clinicians need to recognize major signs and symptoms of LE DVT: pitting edema, pain, tenderness, swelling, warmth, redness or discoloration (erythema), and prominent superficial veins. Clinicians should use a standardized tool as part of the examination process (e.g., Wells Criteria Score for DVT).

Communicate the likelihood of LE DVT and recommend further medical testing.

Recommendation Strength: A Strong; Evidence quality: Level I

Referral for further medical testing is indicated after completion of a risk assessment measure (e.g., Wells Criteria Score for DVT) prior to mobilization. Additional testing may include the D-dimer test and duplex ultrasound for patients rated as LE DVT-likely.

Verify the patient is taking an anticoagulant.

Recommendation Strength: D Theoretical/Foundational; Evidence Quality D

The clinician should verify whether the patient is taking an anticoagulant medication, what type of anticoagulant medication, and when the anticoagulant medication was initiated.

Mobilize patients who are at a therapeutic level of anticoagulation.

Recommendation Strength: A Strong; Evidence Quality: Level I

Early mobilization out-of-bed and ambulation are important in decreasing the risk of subsequent LE DVT or PE and in decreasing the risk of adverse effects of bedrest. Achieving therapeutic level of anticoagulant is key.

Recommend mechanical compression for patients with LE DVT.

Recommendation Strength: B Moderate; Evidence Quality: Level II

Compression provides secondary prevention of recurrent DVT, PE, or PTS and faster resolution of LE DVT signs and symptoms. Use of GCS at least 30 mm Hg of pressure at the ankle in combination with early ambulation is likely most effective. For patients with severe PTS of the leg not adequately relieved with GCS, a trial of IPC is suggested. Optimal mechanical compression treatment strategy has yet to be identified.

Mobilize patients after IVC filter placement once hemodynamically stable.

Recommendation Strength: P Best Practice; Evidence Quality: Level V

Clinicians should mobilize patients with IVC placement once they are hemodynamically stable and there is no bleeding at the puncture site.

Consult with medical team when a patient is not anticoagulated and without an IVC filter.

Recommendation Strength: P Best Practice; Evidence Quality: Level V

Patients who have not been anticoagulated due to contraindications or do not meet criteria for an IVC filter should not be mobilized without consultation with the primary physician or medical team.

Screen for fall risk.

Recommendation Strength: C Weak; Evidence Quality: III

Risk of falls is increased in patients who experience a major bleed as a possible complication of taking anticoagulant medication. Advanced age is also a major risk factor for falls. Clinicians should carefully screen for fall risk using standardized fall risk measures.

Recommend mechanical compression when signs and symptoms of PTS are present.

Recommendation Strength: A Strong; Evidence Quality: Level I

Mechanical compression (GCS, IPC) enhances faster resolution of LE DVT signs and symptoms and decreases PTS severity. Clinicians should assist in the development of institution-specific protocols.

Provide management strategies to prevent recurrent VTE and minimize secondary VTE complications.

Recommendation Strength: P Best Practice; Evidence Quality: V

Clinicians should monitor patients who may develop long-term consequences of VTE (e.g., LE DVT recurrence, PTS severity) and provide management strategies to improve quality of life.

Adapted from Hillegass E, et al, for the Guideline Development Group: Role of Physical Therapists in the Management of Individuals at Risk for or Diagnosed With Venous Thromboembolism: Evidence-Based Clinical Practice Guideline. PhysTher 96(2): 143–166.

Review Questions

Cardiovascular and Lymphatic Physical Therapy

1. What risk factors contribute to the development of coronary artery disease?

2. What are the expected ST segment changes following an acute myocardial infarction and with impaired coronary perfusion?

3. How would you instruct your patient regarding possible circumstances that could elicit angina pectoris?

4. When exercising a patient with diabetes and coronary artery disease who is taking beta blockers, what is the best measure to monitor exercise performance?

5. What are the goals of inpatient cardiac rehabilitation in the acute stage or Phase 1?

6. When managing edema secondary to lymphatic dysfunction, use of manual lymph drainage (MLD) emphasizes which directional principles?

4

Pulmonary Physical Therapy

JULIE ANN STARR

Chapter Outline

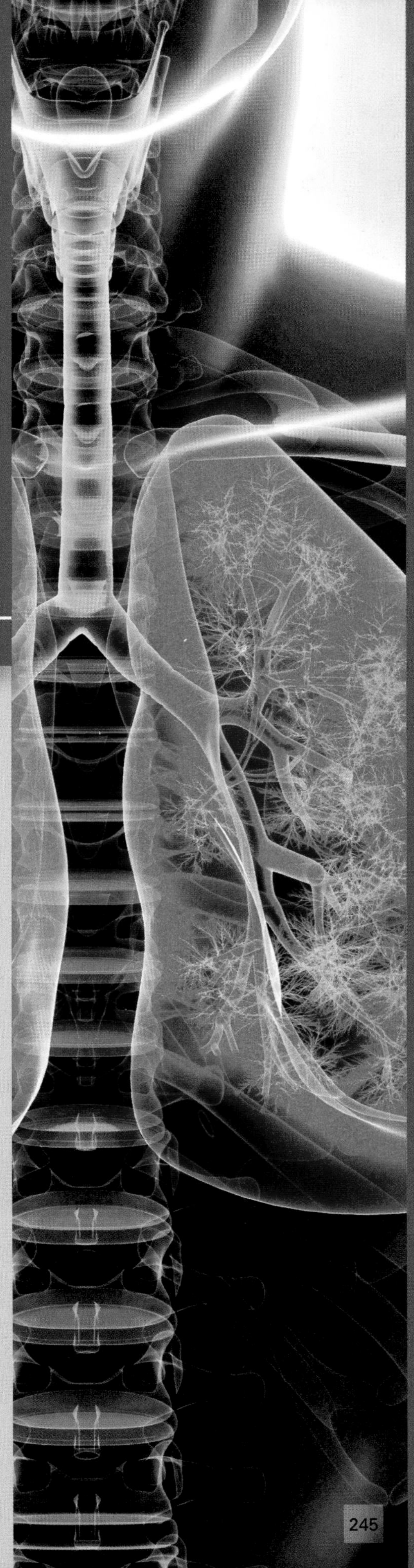

Pulmonary Anatomy and Physiology

Bony Thorax

1. Anterior border: the sternum (manubrium, body, xiphoid process).
   a. The lateral borders of the trachea run perpendicularly into the suprasternal notch.
   b. The angle of Louis (sternal angle), the bony ridge between the manubrium and body, is the point of anterior attachment of the second rib and tracheal bifurcation.
2. Lateral border: the rib cage.
   a. Ribs 1–6, termed true or costosternal ribs, have a single anterior costochondral attachment to the sternum.
   b. Ribs 7–10, termed false or costochondral ribs, share costochondral attachments before attaching anteriorly to the sternum.
   c. Ribs 11 and 12 are termed floating or costovertebral ribs, as they have no anterior attachment.
3. Posterior border.
   a. The vertebral column, from T1 through T12.
4. Shoulder girdle.
   a. Can affect the motion of the thorax.
   b. Provides attachments for accessory muscles of ventilation.

Internal Structures

1. Upper airways (see Figure 4-1).
   a. Nose or mouth: entry point into the respiratory system. The nose filters, humidifies, and warms air.
   b. Pharynx: common area used for both respiratory and digestive systems.
   c. Larynx: connects the pharynx to trachea, including the epiglottis and vocal cords.
2. Lower airways.
   a. The conducting airways, trachea to terminal bronchioles, transport air only. No gas exchange occurs.
   b. The respiratory unit: respiratory bronchioles, alveolar ducts, alveolar sacs, and alveoli. Diffusion of gas occurs through all of these structures.
3. Lung structures.
   a. Right lung divides into three lobes by the oblique and horizontal fissure lines. Each lobe divides into segments, totaling 10 segments.
   b. Left lung divides into two lobes by a single oblique fissure line. Each lobe divides into segments, totaling 8 segments.
4. Pleura.
   a. Parietal pleura covers the inner surface of the thoracic cage, diaphragm, and mediastinal border of the lung.
   b. Visceral pleura wraps the outer surface of the lung, including the fissure lines.
   c. Intrapleural space is the potential space between the two pleurae that maintains the approximation of the rib cage and lungs, allowing forces to be transmitted from one structure to another.

Muscles of Ventilation

1. Primary muscles of inspiration.
   a. Produce a normal resting tidal volume.
   b. Primary muscle of inspiration is the diaphragm. The diaphragm is made of two hemidiaphragms, each with a central tendon. When the diaphragm is at rest, the hemidiaphragms are arched high into the thorax. When the muscle contracts, the central tendon is pulled downward, flattening the dome. The result is a protrusion of the abdominal wall during inhalation.

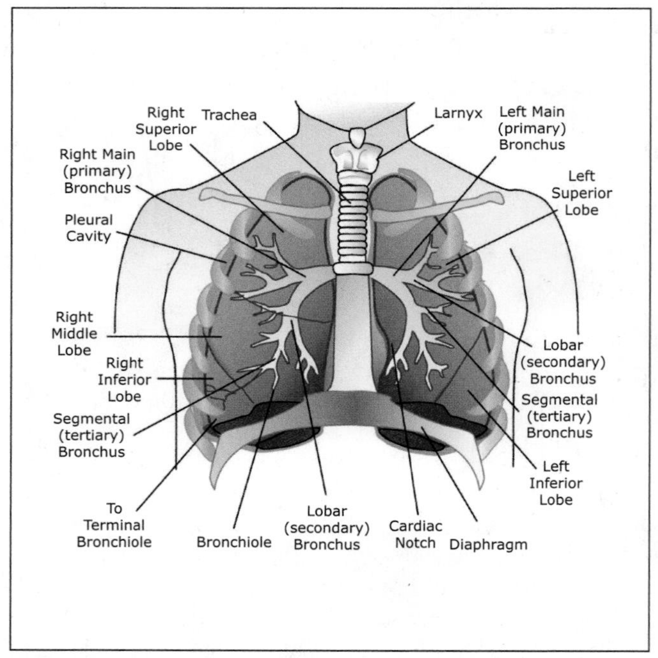

Figure 4-1 Pulmonary anatomy.

c. Additional primary muscles of inspiration are portions of the intercostals.
2. Accessory muscles of inspiration.
   a. Used when a more rapid or deeper inhalation is required or in disease states.
   b. The upper two ribs are raised by the scalenes and sternocleidomastoid. The rest of the ribs are raised by the levator costarum and serratus. By fixing the shoulder girdle, the trapezius, pectorals and serratus can become muscles of inspiration.
3. Expiratory muscles of ventilation.
   a. Resting exhalation results from a passive relaxation of the inspiratory muscles and the elastic recoil tendency of the lung. Normal abdominal tone holds the abdominal contents directly under the diaphragm, assisting the return of the diaphragm to the normal high domed position.
   b. Expiratory muscles are used when a quicker and/or fuller expiration is desired, as in exercise or in disease states. These are quadratus lumborum, portions of the intercostals, muscles of the abdomen and triangularis sterni.
4. Patients who lack abdominal musculature (e.g., spinal cord injury).
   a. Have a lower resting position of the diaphragm, decreasing inspiratory reserve.
   b. The more upright the body position, the lower the diaphragm and the lower the inspiratory capacity.
   c. The more supine the body position, the more advantageous the position of the diaphragm.
   d. An abdominal binder may be helpful in providing support to the abdominal viscera, assisting ventilation. Care must be taken not to constrict the thorax with the abdominal binder.

Mechanics of Breathing

1. Forces acting upon the rib cage.
   a. Elastic recoil of the lung parenchyma pulls the lungs and, therefore, visceral pleura, parietal pleura, and bony thorax into a position of exhalation (inward pull).
   b. Bony thorax pulls the thorax and, therefore, parietal pleura, visceral pleura and lungs into a position of inspiration (outward pull).
   c. Muscular action pulls either outward or inward, depending on the muscles used.
   d. Resting end expiratory pressure (REEP) is the point of equilibrium where these forces are balanced. Occurs at end tidal expiration.

Ventilation

1. Movement of gas in and out of the pulmonary system.
2. Volumes (see Figure 4-2).
   a. Tidal volume (TV): volume of gas inhaled (or exhaled) during a normal resting breath.
   b. Inspiratory reserve volume (IRV): volume of gas that can be inhaled beyond a normal resting tidal inhalation.
   c. Expiratory reserve volume (ERV): volume of gas that can be exhaled beyond a normal resting tidal exhalation.
   d. Residual volume (RV): volume of gas that remains in the lungs after ERV has been exhaled.
3. Capacities. Two or more lung volumes added together.
   a. Inspiratory capacity (IRV + TV): the amount of air that can be inhaled from REEP.
   b. Vital capacity (IRV + TV + ERV): the amount of air that is under volitional control; conventionally measured as forced expiratory vital capacity (FVC).
   c. Functional residual capacity (ERV + RV): the amount of air that resides in the lungs after a normal resting tidal exhalation.
   d. Total lung capacity (IRV + TV + ERV + RV): the total amount of air that is contained within the thorax during a maximum inspiratory effort.
4. Flow rates.
   a. Forced expiratory volume in 1 second (FEV_1): the amount of air exhaled during the first second of FVC. In the healthy person, at least 70% of the FVC is exhaled within the first second ($FEV_1/FVC \times 100 > 70\%$).

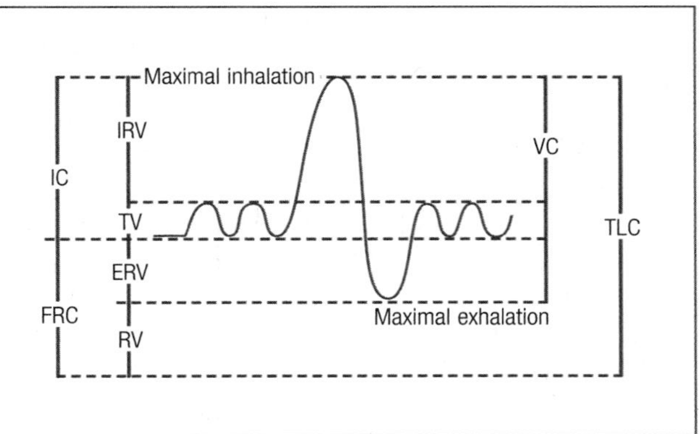

Figure 4-2 Lung volumes and capacities.
IRV = inspiratory reserve volume; TV = tidal volume; ERV = expiratory reserve volume; RV = residual volume; IC = inspiratory capacity; FRC = functional residual capacity, VC = vital capacity; TLC = total lung capacity.

From O'Sullivan S, Schmidt T: Physical Rehabilitation, 5th ed. FA Davis, 2007, p. 562, with permission.

b. Forced expiratory flow rate (FEF 25%–75%) is the slope of a line drawn between the points 25% and 75% of exhaled volume on a forced vital capacity exhalation curve. This flow rate is more specific to the smaller airways, and shows a more dramatic change with disease than FEV_1.

Respiration

1. Diffusion of gas across the alveolar-capillary membrane.
2. Arterial oxygenation. The ability of arterial blood to carry oxygen.
   a. Partial pressure of oxygen in the atmosphere (PaO_2) at sea level is 760 mm Hg (barometric pressure) × 21% = 159.6 mm Hg.
   b. Partial pressure of oxygen in the arterial blood, PaO_2, depends on the integrity of the pulmonary system, the circulatory system and the PaO_2. PaO_2 at room air is 95–100 mm Hg in a young, healthy individual. Hypoxemia: PaO_2 decreases with age, but in a young, healthy individual, mild hypoxemia would be considered at < 90. Hyperoxemia: PaO_2 > 100.
   c. Fraction of oxygen in the inspired air (FiO_2) is the percentage of oxygen in air, based on a total of 1.00. The FiO_2 of room air, approximately 21% oxygen, is written as 0.21. Supplemental oxygen increases the percentage (> 21%) of oxygen in the patient's atmosphere. Supplemental oxygen is usually prescribed when the PaO_2 falls below 55 mm Hg.
3. Alveolar ventilation. Ability to remove carbon dioxide from the pulmonary circulation and maintain pH.
   a. pH indicates the concentration of free-floating hydrogen ions within the body. Normal range for pH is 7.35–7.45.
   b. $PaCO_2$: the partial pressure of carbon dioxide within the arterial blood, in health, 35–45 mm Hg. Hypercapnea is a $PaCO_2$ > 45 mm Hg. Hypocapnea is a $PaCO_2$ < 35 mm Hg. Removal or retention of CO_2 by the respiratory system alters the pH of the body in an inverse relationship. An increase in the $PaCO_2$ decreases the body's pH. A decrease in the $PaCO_2$ raises the body's pH.
   c. HCO_3^-: amount of bicarbonate ions within the arterial blood, normally 22–28 mEq/L. Removal or retention of HCO_3^- alters the pH of the body in a direct relationship. An increase in bicarbonate ions increases the body's pH. A decrease in bicarbonate ions decreases the body's pH.

Ventilation (V_E) and Perfusion (Blood Flow or Q)

1. Optimal respiration occurs when ventilation and perfusion (blood flow to the lungs) are matched. Different ventilation and perfusion relationships exist.
2. Dead space.
   a. Anatomical (conducting airways) or physiological (diseases such as pulmonary emboli).
   b. Dead space is a space that is well ventilated, but in which no respiration (gas exchange) occurs.
3. Shunt.
   a. No respiration occurs because of a ventilation abnormality.
   b. Complete atelectasis of a respiratory unit allows the blood to travel through the pulmonary capillary without gas diffusion.
4. Effects of body position on the ventilation perfusion relationship. Gravity affects the distribution of ventilation and perfusion.
   a. Upright position.
      (1) Perfusion is gravity dependent; i.e., more pulmonary blood is found at the base of the lung in the upright position.
      (2) Ventilation. At the static point of REEP, the apical alveoli are fuller than those at the base. During the dynamic phase of inspiration, more air will be delivered to the less-filled alveoli at the bases, causing a greater change in V_E at the bases.
      (3) Ventilation perfusion ratio (V/Q ratio): the ratio of pulmonary alveolar ventilation to pulmonary capillary perfusion. In the upright position, the apices are gravity independent, with the lowest blood flow, or Q. Although relatively low, there is still more air than blood, resulting in a high V/Q ratio (dead space). Perfusion and ventilation of the middle zone of the lung are evenly matched. The bases are gravity dependent and, therefore, have the most Q. Although V_E is relatively high, there is more blood than air, resulting in a (relatively) low V/Q ratio (shunt).
   b. Other body positions. Every body position creates these zones: gravity independent, middle, and gravity dependent. The gravity-independent area of the lung, despite the position of the body, acts as dead space. The gravity-dependent area of the lung acts as a shunt. Body positions can be used for a variety of treatment goals: to drain secretions, to increase ventilation, or to optimize ventilation perfusion relationships.

Control of Ventilation

1. Receptors.
   a. Baroreceptors, chemoreceptors, irritant receptors and stretch receptors within the body assist in adjusting the ventilatory cycle by sending information to the controller.
2. Central control centers.
   a. Cortex, pons, medulla, and autonomic nervous system evaluate the receptors' information.
   b. Send a message out to the ventilatory muscles to alter the respiratory cycle in order to maintain adequate alveolar ventilation and arterial oxygenation.
3. Ventilatory muscles.
   a. Institute the changes deemed necessary by the central controllers.

Physical Therapy Examination

Patient Interview

1. Information from the patient, the patient's family, and the medical record.
2. Chief complaint.
   a. Usually involves the loss of function (decreased ability to perform activities of daily living [ADLs]) or discomfort (shortness of breath [dyspnea]).
3. Present illness.
   a. Initial onset (sudden vs. insidious) and progression of primary problem.
   b. Anything that worsens or improves condition: positions, rest, medications.
4. Review the patient's history.
   a. Occupational history. Past occupational exposures for diseases such as asbestosis, silicosis, and pneumoconiosis. Present occupational exposure to antigens within the workplace (hypersensitivity pneumonitis).
   b. Past medical history that would alter physical exam or treatment plans (e.g., heart disease, long-term steroid use).
   c. Current medications that can mask (steroids) or alter (beta blockers, bronchodilators) vital signs.
   d. Social habits.
      (1) Smoking in pack years (number of packs per day × number of years smoked).
      (2) Alcohol consumption.
      (3) Street drugs.
   e. Functional and exertional activity level during periods of wellness, as well as with present illness.
   f. Cough and sputum production. Record any changes from baseline because of present illness.
   g. Family history of pulmonary disease (e.g., cystic fibrosis).

Tests and Measures

1. Vital signs (see Table 4-1 for normal values).
   a. Temperature: normal (afebrile) 98.6°F (37°C). Core temperature increase indicates infection.
   b. Heart rate (HR): normal 60–100 bpm; tachycardia: HR > 100 bpm; bradycardia: HR < 60 bpm.
   c. Respirations.
      (1) Rate: in health is 12–20 bpm. Tachypnea is a rate > 20 bpm. Apnea means no respirations.
      (2) Rhythm: regular or irregular.
      (3) Amplitude: shallow or deep.
   d. Blood pressure.
2. Observation.
   a. Peripheral edema seen in gravity-dependent areas and jugular venous distension indicates possible heart failure. Right ventricular hypertrophy and dilation (cor pulmonale) are common sequelae to chronic lung disease.

Table 4-1

Normal Values for Infants and Adults

PARAMETER	INFANT	ADULT
Heart Rate	120 bpm	60–100 bpm
Blood Pressure	75/50 mm Hg	< 120/80 mm Hg
Respiratory Rate	40 br/min	12–20 br/min
PaO_2	75–80 mm Hg	80–100 mm Hg
$PaCO_2$	34–54 mm Hg	35–45 mm Hg
pH	7.26–7.41	7.35–7.45
Tidal Volume	20 ml	500 ml

b. Body positions. Stabilizing the shoulder girdle (e.g., sitting, hands placed on seat, arms extended, body leaning forward) places the thorax in the inspiratory position and allows the additional recruitment of muscles for inspiration (pectorals).
c. Color: cyanosis, an acute sign of hypoxemia, is a bluish tinge to nail beds and the areas around eyes and mouth.
d. Digital clubbing: a sign of chronic hypoxemia. The configuration of the distal phalanx of fingers or toes becomes bulbous.

3. Inspection and palpation.
   a. Standard precautions should be used when the therapist may come in contact with a patient's body fluids. See Box 6-1. Gloves are usually all that is needed during a routine physical exam.
   b. Neck.
      (1) Observe the trachea: it should be in midline, superior to the suprasternal notch.
      (2) Note the use of accessory muscles of ventilation.
   c. Thorax.
      (1) Changes in bony thorax (pectus excavatum, carinatum).
      (2) Observe anterior-posterior-lateral dimension. In health, there is a 1:2 ratio. With obstructive pulmonary disease, the lung recoil force is decreased, resulting in a barreled chest and an increase in the A-P dimension.
      (3) The right and left thorax should be symmetrical.
         (a) Symmetry, static and/or dynamic, may be altered by changes in the bony thorax (scoliosis, scapular immobility, pain), changes in the underlying lung and pleura (a patient with pleuritic pain or pneumothorax), or changes in the overlying skin (thoracic burn).
         (b) Thoracic excursion in health, measured at the base of the lungs from full inspiration to full expiration, is between 2 and 3 inches.
         (c) Inspect for scars, indicating potential adhesions to underlying soft tissue or surgical removal of structures within the thorax.

4. Auscultation.
   a. Intensity of inspiration and expiration is quieter at the bases than the apex.
      (1) Vesicular (normal breath sound): a soft rustling sound heard throughout all of inspiration and the beginning of expiration.
      (2) Bronchial: a more hollow, echoing sound normally found only over the right superior anterior thorax. This corresponds to an area over the right main stem bronchus. All of inspiration and most of expiration are heard with bronchial breath sounds.
      (3) Decreased: a very distant sound not normally heard over a healthy thorax; allows only some of the inspiration to be heard. Often associated with obstructive lung diseases.
   b. Adventitious (extra) sounds. According to the American Thoracic Society, there are only two adventitious breath sounds:
      (1) Crackles (also termed rales, crepitations): a crackling sound heard usually during inspiration that indicates pathology (atelectasis, fibrosis, pulmonary edema).
      (2) Wheezes: a musically pitched sound, usually heard during expiration, caused by airway obstruction (asthma, chronic obstructive pulmonary disease [COPD], foreign body aspiration). With severe airway constriction, as with croup, wheezes may be heard on inspiration as well.
   c. Vocal sounds.
      (1) Normal transmission of vocal sounds.
         (a) As with breath sounds, vocal transmission is loudest near trachea and main-stem bronchi.
         (b) Words should be intelligible, though softer and less clear at the more distal areas of the lungs.
      (2) Abnormal transmission of vocal sounds may be heard through fluid-filled areas of consolidation, cavitation lesions or pleural effusions.
         (a) Egophony is a nasal or bleating sound heard during auscultation. "E" sounds are transmitted to sound like "A."
         (b) Bronchophony, characterized by an intense, clear sound during auscultation, even at the lung bases.
         (c) Whispered pectoriloquy occurs when whispered sounds are heard clearly during auscultation.

5. Radiographic examination.
   a. Chest x-ray (CXR): a two-dimensional radiographic film to detect the presence of abnormal material (exudate, blood) or a change in pulmonary parenchyma (fibrosis, collapse).
   b. Computed tomographic (CT) scan: computer-generated picture of a cross-sectional plane of the body.
   c. Magnetic resonance imaging (MRI) (see Figure 4-3).
   d. Ventilation perfusion (V/Q) scan: matches the ventilation pattern of the lung to the perfusion pattern to identify the presence of pulmonary emboli.
   e. Fluoroscopy: continuous x-ray beam allows observation of diaphragmatic excursion.

6. Laboratory tests (see Table 4-1 for normal values).
   a. Arterial blood gas (ABG) analysis indicates the adequacy of:
      (1) Alveolar ventilation by determining pH, bicarbonate ion, and partial pressure of carbon dioxide. Table 4-2 presents the four basic conditions of acid-base balance and the $PaCO_2$, pH, and HCO_3^- values that accompany each condition.

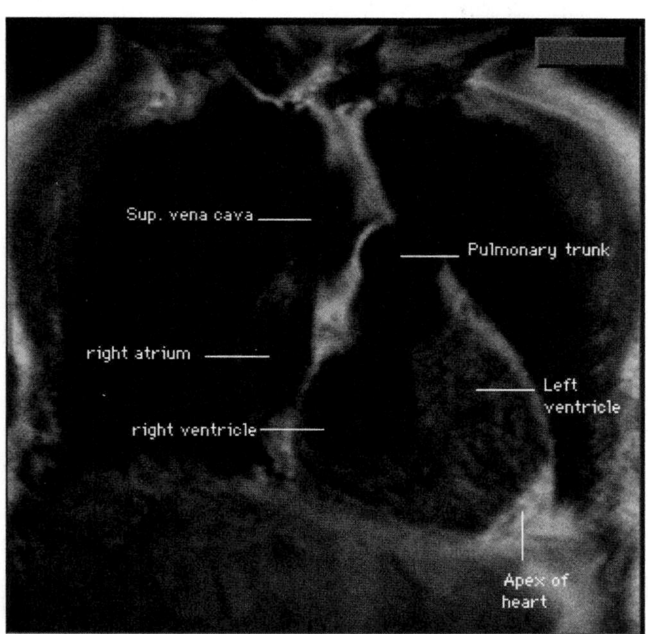

Figure 4-3 **Coronal T1 MRI thoracic view of normal female.**

(2) Arterial oxygenation by determining the partial pressure of oxygen in relation to the fraction of inspired oxygen.

b. Electrocardiogram: see Chapter 3 (Cardiovascular Physical Therapy) for discussion.

c. Sputum studies.

(1) Gram stain: immediate identification of the category of bacteria (gram-negative or gram-positive) and its appearance (e.g., pairs, chains).

(2) Culture and sensitivity: identifies the specific bacteria as well as the organism's susceptibility to various antibiotics. Results available within a few days.

(3) Cytology: reports the presence of cancer cells in sputum.

d. Pulmonary function tests (PFTs): evaluate lung volumes, capacities, and flow rates. Used to diagnose disease, monitor progression, and determine the benefits of medical management. See Figure 4-4 for changes with disease states. See Table 4-3 for classification of obstructive lung disease according to the Global Initiative for Obstructive Lung Disease (GOLD), including PFT values for each level of disease severity.

e. Blood values.

(1) White blood cell (WBC) count normal values: 4000–11,000.

(2) Hematocrit (Hct) normal values: 35%–48%.

(3) Hemoglobin (Hgb) normal values: 12–16 g/dL.

7. Bronchoscopy.

a. Endoscope used to view, biopsy, wash, suction, and/or brush the interior aspects of the tracheobronchial tree.

8. Exercise tolerance tests (ETT) (Graded Exercise Test). (See also Chapter 3, Cardiovascular Physical Therapy.)

a. Evaluates an individual's cardiopulmonary response to gradually increasing exercise.

b. Determines the presence of exercise-induced bronchospasm by testing pulmonary function, particularly FEV_1 before and after ETT.

c. Documents the need for supplemental oxygen during an exercise program by analyzing arterial blood gas values throughout the ETT. ABGs also provide a criterion for test termination. If arterial blood sampling is unavailable, pulse oximetry can be used to monitor the percent saturation of oxygen within the arterial blood. Table 4-4 presents criteria for test termination for patients with pulmonary disease.

9. See Chapter 3 Appendix: Selected Outcome Measures for Cardiac and Pulmonary Dysfunction.

Table 4-2

Interpretation of Abnormal Acid-Base Balance

TYPE	pH	$PaCO_2$	HCO_3^-	CAUSES	SIGNS AND SYMPTOMS
Respiratory alkalosis	↑	↓	WNL	Alveolar hyperventilation	Dizziness, syncope, tingling, numbness, early tetany
Respiratory acidosis	↓	↑	WNL	Alveolar hypoventilation	Early: anxiety, restlessness, dyspnea, headache Late: confusion, somnolence, coma
Metabolic alkalosis	↑	WNL	↑	Bicarbonate ingestion, vomiting, diuretics, steroids, adrenal disease	Vague symptoms: weakness, mental dullness, possibly early tetany
Metabolic acidosis	↓	WNL	↓	Diabetic, lactic, or uremic acidosis, prolonged diarrhea	Secondary hyperventilation (Kussmaul breathing), nausea, lethargy, coma

From Rothstein J, Roy S, and Wolf S: The Rehabilitation Specialist's Handbook, 3rd ed. Philadelphia, FA Davis, 2005, p. 440, with permission.

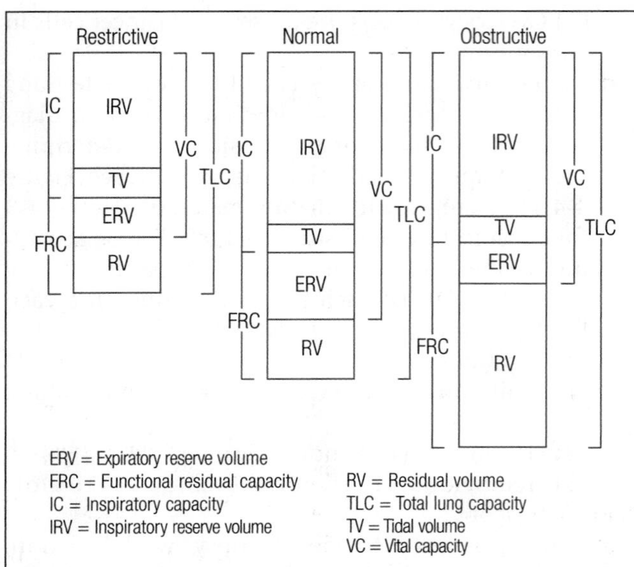

Figure 4-4 Lung volumes of a healthy pulmonary system compared with lung volumes and capacities found in restrictive and obstructive pulmonary disease.

From Rothstein J, Roy S, and Wolf S: The Rehabilitation Specialist's Handbook, 3rd ed. Philadelphia, FA Davis, 2005, p. 428, with permission.

Table 4-4

Graded Exercise Test Termination Criteria
1. Maximal shortness of breath.
2. A fall in PaO_2 of greater than 20 mm Hg or a PaO_2 less than 55 mm Hg.
3. A rise in $PaCO_2$ of greater than 10 mm Hg or a $PaCO_2$ greater than 65 mm Hg.
4. Cardiac ischemia or arrhythmias.
5. Symptoms of fatigue.
6. Increase in diastolic blood pressure readings of 20 mm Hg, systolic hypertension greater than 250 mm Hg, decrease in blood pressure with increasing workloads.
7. Leg pain.
8. Total fatigue.
9. Signs of insufficient cardiac output.
10. Reaching a ventilatory maximum.

From Brannon F, et al: Cardiopulmonary Rehabilitation: Basic Theory and Application, 3rd ed. Philadelphia, FA Davis, 1998, p. 300, with permission.

Table 4-3

Classification of Obstructive Lung Disease Outlined by the Global Initiative for Obstructive Lung Disease (GOLD) with the Addition of Functional Abilities That Correspond

STAGE	FEV_1/FVC RATIO	FEV_1	SYMPTOMS	FUNCTIONAL ABILITIES
1 Mild	< 70%	$FEV_1 \geq 80\%$ predicted	With or without chronic symptoms	Individuals may be unaware that lung function is abnormal
2 Moderate	< 70%	$50\% < FEV_1 < 80\%$ predicted	With or without chronic symptoms	Individuals typically seek medical attention because of chronic respiratory symptoms or an exacerbation of their disease
3 Severe	< 70%	$30\% < FEV_1 < 50\%$	With or without chronic symptoms	Individuals experience greater shortness of breath, reduced exercise capacity, fatigue, impact on qualitiy of life
4 Very Severe	< 70%	$FEV_1 < 30\%$ predicted or $FEV_1 < 50\%$ with chronic respiratory failure symptoms	$PaO_2 < 60$ $PaCO_2 > 50$ Cor pulmonale Increased jugular venous distension	Quality of life is very appreciably impaired and exacerbations may be life threatening

Retrieved 9/10/12 from http://www.goldcopd.org/guidelines-pocket-guide-to-copd-diagnosis.html

Physical Dysfunction/Impairments

Acute Diseases

1. Bacterial pneumonia.
   a. An intra-alveolar bacterial infection. Gram-positive bacteria is usually acquired in the community. Pneumococcal pneumonia (streptococcal) is the most common type of gram-positive pneumonia. Gram-negative bacteria usually develop in a host with underlying, chronic, debilitating conditions, severe acute illness, and recent antibiotic therapy. Gram-negative infections result in early tissue necrosis and abscess formation. Common infecting organisms: *Klebsiella, Haemophilus influenzae, Pseudomonas aeruginosa, Proteus, Serratia.*
   b. Pertinent physical findings.
      (1) Shaking chills.
      (2) Fever.
      (3) Chest pain if pleuritic involvement.
      (4) Cough becoming productive of purulent, blood-streaked or rusty sputum.
      (5) Decreased or bronchial breath sounds and/or crackles.
      (6) Tachypnea.
      (7) Increased white blood cell count.
      (8) Hypoxemia, hypocapnea initially, hypercapnea with increasing severity.
      (9) CXR confirmation of infiltrate.
2. Viral pneumonia.
   a. An interstitial or intra-alveolar inflammatory process caused by viral agents (influenza, adenovirus, cytomegalovirus, herpes, parainfluenza, respiratory syncytial virus, measles).
   b. Pertinent physical findings.
      (1) Recent history of upper respiratory infection.
      (2) Fever.
      (3) Chills.
      (4) Dry cough.
      (5) Headaches.
      (6) Decreased breath sounds and/or crackles.
      (7) Hypoxemia and hypercapnea.
      (8) Normal white blood cell count.
      (9) CXR confirmation of interstitial infiltrate.
3. Aspiration pneumonia.
   a. Aspirated material causes an acute inflammatory reaction within the lungs. Usually found in patients with impaired swallowing (dysphagia), fixed neck extension, intoxication, impaired consciousness, neuromuscular disease, recent anesthesia.
   b. Pertinent physical findings.
      (1) Symptoms begin shortly after aspiration event (hours).
      (2) Cough may be dry at the onset, progresses to produce putrid secretions.
      (3) Dyspnea.
      (4) Tachypnea.
      (5) Cyanosis.
      (6) Tachycardia.
      (7) Wheezes and crackles with decreased breath sounds.
      (8) Hypoxemia, hypercapnea in severe cases.
      (9) Chest pain over the involved area.
      (10) Fever.
      (11) WBC count shows varying degrees of leukocytosis.
      (12) CXR initially shows pneumonitis. Chronic aspiration shows necrotizing pneumonia with cavitation.
4. Tuberculosis (TB).
   a. *Mycobacterium tuberculosis* infection spread by aerosolized droplets from an untreated infected host. Incubation period: 2–10 weeks. Primary disease lasts 10 days to 2 weeks.
   b. Postprimary infection is reactivation of dormant tuberculous bacillus, which can occur years after the primary infection.
   c. Two weeks on appropriate antituberculin drugs renders the host noninfectious. During the infectious stage, the patient must be isolated from others in a negative-pressure room. Anyone entering the room must wear a protective TB mask and follow universal precautions. If the patient leaves the negative-pressure room, he or she must wear a specialized mask to keep from infecting others.
   d. Medication is taken for prolonged periods: 3–12 months.
   e. There is an increased incidence of TB in patients with HIV.
   f. Pertinent physical findings of primary disease can go unnoticed, as it causes only mild symptoms: slight nonproductive cough, low-grade fever, and possible CXR changes consistent with primary disease.
   g. Pertinent physical findings of postprimary infection.
      (1) Fever.
      (2) Weight loss.
      (3) Cough.

(4) Hilar adenopathy: enlargement of the lymph nodes surrounding the hilum.
(5) Night sweat.
(6) Crackles.
(7) Hemoptysis: blood-streaked sputum.
(8) WBC shows increased lymphocytes.
(9) CXR shows upper lobe involvement with air space densities, cavitation, pleural involvement, and parenchymal fibrosis.

5. Pneumocystis pneumonia (PCP).
   a. Pulmonary infection caused by a fungus (*Pneumocystis carinii*) in immunocompromised hosts. Most often found in patients following transplantation, neonates or patients infected with HIV.
   b. Pertinent physical findings.
      (1) Insidious progressive shortness of breath.
      (2) Nonproductive cough.
      (3) Crackles.
      (4) Weakness.
      (5) Fever.
      (6) Chest x-ray shows interstitial infiltrates.
      (7) Complete blood count (CBC) shows no evidence of infection.
6. SARS (severe acute respiratory syndrome).
   a. An atypical respiratory illness caused by a coronovirus. Initial outbreak in southern mainland China with worldwide spread to other areas such as Singapore, Toronto, Vietnam, and Hong Kong.
   b. Pertinent physical findings.
      (1) High temperature.
      (2) Dry cough.
      (3) Decreased white blood cells, decreased platelets, decreased lymphocytes.
      (4) Increased liver function tests.
      (5) Abnormal CXR with borderline breath sounds changes.
7. See Box 6-1, Standard Precautions.

Chronic Obstructive Diseases

1. Chronic obstructive pulmonary disease (COPD).
   a. According to GOLD, COPD is a disease state characterized by airflow limitation that is not fully reversible. The airflow limitation is usually both progressive and associated with an abnormal inflammatory response of the lungs to noxious particles or gases.
   b. Stages.
      (1) Stage 1 (mild).
         (a) $FEV_1/FVC < 70\%$.
         (b) $FEV_1 \geq 80\%$ predicted.
         (c) With or without chronic symptoms.
      (2) Stage 2 (moderate).
         (a) $FEV_1/FVC < 70\%$.
         (b) $50\% < FEV_1 < 80\%$ predicted.
         (c) Often with symptoms of shortness of breath with exertion.
      (3) Stage 3 (severe).
         (a) $FEV_1/FVC < 70\%$.
         (b) $30\% < FEV_1 < 50\%$.
         (c) With greater shortness of breath, decreased exercise capacity, and exacerbations of their disease.
      (4) Stage 4 (very severe).
         (a) $FEV_1/FVC < 70\%$.
         (b) $FEV_1 < 30\%$ predicted.
         (c) $FEV_1 < 50\%$ with chronic respiratory failure symptoms.
         (d) Impaired quality of life.
         (e) Exacerbations of their disease may be life threatening.
   c. Physical findings: increase in severity as the stage of disease advances.
      (1) Cough/sputum production/hemoptysis.
      (2) Dyspnea on exertion.
      (3) Breath sounds decreased with adventitious sounds.
      (4) Increased respiratory rate (RR).
      (5) Weight loss/anorexia.
      (6) Increased A-P diameter of chest wall.
      (7) Cyanosis.
      (8) Clubbing.
      (9) Postures to structurally elevate shoulder girdle.
      (10) CXR showing hyperinflation, flattened diaphragms, hyperlucency.
      (11) ABG changes of hypoxemia, hypercapnea.
      (12) PFTs showing obstructive disease, such as decreased FEV_1, decreased FVC, increased FRC and RV, and decreased FEV_1/FVC ratio.
2. Asthma.
   a. Increased reactivity of the trachea and bronchi to various stimuli (allergens, exercise, cold); reversible in nature; manifests by widespread narrowing of the airways due to inflammation, smooth muscle constriction, and increased secretions. Even during remission, some degree of airway inflammation is present.
   b. Pertinent physical findings during exacerbation.
      (1) Wheezing, possible crackles, and decreased breath sounds.
      (2) Increased secretions of variable amounts.
      (3) Dyspnea.
      (4) Increased accessory muscle use.
      (5) Anxiety.
      (6) Tachycardia.
      (7) Tachypnea.
      (8) Hypoxemia.
      (9) Hypocapnea. Responding to hypoxemia, there is an increased respiratory rate and minute ventilation. This will decrease $PaCO_2$. With severe

airway constriction, an increase in minute ventilation cannot occur and hypercapnea can be found.

(10) Cyanosis.

(11) PFTs show impaired flow rates.

(12) CXR shows hyperlucency and flattened diaphragms during exacerbation.

3. Cystic fibrosis (CF).
   a. A genetically inherited disease characterized by thickening of secretions of all exocrine glands, leading to obstruction (e.g., pancreatic, pulmonic, gastrointestinal). CF may present as an obstructive, restrictive, or mixed disease. Clinical signs include meconium ileus, frequent respiratory infections, especially *Staphylococcus aureus* and *Pseudomonas aeruginosa*, and inability to gain weight despite adequate caloric intake. Diagnosis is made postnatally by a blood test indicating trypsinogen, or later by a positive sweat electrolyte test.
   b. Pertinent physical findings with exacerbation of disease.
      (1) Onset of symptoms usually in early childhood.
      (2) Dyspnea, especially on exertion.
      (3) Productive cough.
      (4) Hypoxemia, hypercapnea.
      (5) Cyanosis.
      (6) Clubbing.
      (7) Use of accessory muscles of ventilation.
      (8) Tachypnea.
      (9) Crackles, wheezes, and/or decreased breath sounds.
      (10) Abnormal PFTs showing an obstructive pattern, restrictive pattern, or both.
      (11) CXR shows increased markings, findings of bronchiectasis, and/or pneumonitis.
4. Bronchiectasis.
   a. A chronic congenital or acquired disease characterized by abnormal dilatation of the bronchi and excessive sputum production.
   b. Pertinent physical findings.
      (1) Cough and expectoration of large amounts of mucopurulent secretions.
      (2) Frequent secondary infections.
      (3) Hemoptysis.
      (4) Crackles, decreased breath sounds.
      (5) Cyanosis.
      (6) Clubbing.
      (7) Hypoxemia.
      (8) Dyspnea.
      (9) CXR shows increased bronchial markings with interstitial changes. Bronchograms can outline bronchial dilatation, but are rarely needed.
5. Respiratory distress syndrome (RDS). Formerly known as hyaline membrane disease.
   a. Alveolar collapse in a premature infant resulting from lung immaturity, inadequate level of pulmonary surfactant.
   b. Pertinent physical findings within a few hours of birth.
      (1) Respiratory distress.
      (2) Crackles.
      (3) Tachypnea.
      (4) Hypoxemia.
      (5) Cyanosis.
      (6) Accessory muscle use.
      (7) Expiratory grunting, flaring nares.
      (8) CXR shows a classic granular pattern ("ground glass") caused by distended terminal airways and alveolar collapse.
   c. Physical therapy considerations: Increased breathing effort caused by handling a premature infant must be carefully weighed against possible benefits of physical therapy.
6. Bronchopulmonary dysplasia.
   a. An obstructive pulmonary disease, often a sequela of premature infants with respiratory distress syndrome; results from high pressures of mechanical ventilation, high fractions of inspired oxygen (FiO_2), and/or infection. Lungs show areas of pulmonary immaturity and dysfunction due to hyperinflation.
   b. Pertinent physical findings.
      (1) Hypoxemia, hypercapnea.
      (2) Crackles, wheezing, and/or decreased breath sounds.
      (3) Increased bronchial secretions.
      (4) Hyperinflation.
      (5) Frequent lower respiratory infections.
      (6) Delayed growth and development.
      (7) Cor pulmonale.
      (8) CXR shows hyperinflation, low diaphragms, atelectasis, and/or cystic changes.

Chronic Restrictive Diseases

1. Different etiologies.
   a. Typified by difficulty expanding the lungs, causing a reduction in lung volumes.
2. Restrictive disease due to alterations in lung parenchyma and pleura.
   a. Fibrotic changes within the pulmonary parenchyma or pleura due to idiopathic pulmonary fibrosis, asbestosis, radiation pneumonitis, oxygen toxicity.
   b. Pertinent physical findings.
      (1) Dyspnea.
      (2) Hypoxemia, hypocapnea (hypercapnea appears with severity).
      (3) Crackles.
      (4) Clubbing.

(5) Cyanosis.
(6) PFTs reveal a reduction in vital capacity, functional residual capacity and total lung capacity.
(7) CXR shows reduced lung volumes, diffuse interstitial infiltrates, and/or pleural thickening.

3. Restrictive disease due to alterations in the chest wall.
   a. Restricted motion of bony thorax, with diseases such as ankylosing spondylitis, arthritis, scoliosis, pectus excavatum, arthrogryposis, or the integumentary changes of the chest wall such as thoracic burns or scleroderma.
   b. Pertinent physical findings.
      (1) Shallow, rapid breathing.
      (2) Dyspnea.
      (3) Hypoxemia, hypocapnea (hypercapnea with increasing severity).
      (4) Cyanosis.
      (5) Clubbing.
      (6) Crackles.
      (7) Reduced cough effectiveness.
      (8) PFTs show reduced vital capacity, functional residual capacity, and total lung capacity.
      (9) CXR show reduced lung volumes, atelectasis.
4. Restrictive disease due to alterations in the neuromuscular apparatus.
   a. Decreased muscular strength results in an inability to expand the rib cage, seen in disease states such as multiple sclerosis, muscular dystrophy, Parkinson's disease, spinal cord injury, or cerebrovascular accident (CVA).
   b. Pertinent physical findings.
      (1) Dyspnea.
      (2) Hypoxemia, hypocapnea (hypercapnea with increasing severity).
      (3) Decreased breath sounds, crackles.
      (4) Clubbing.
      (5) Cyanosis.
      (6) Reduced cough effectiveness.
      (7) PFTs show reduced vital capacity and total lung capacity.
      (8) CXR shows reduced lung volumes, atelectasis.

Bronchogenic Carcinoma

1. A tumor that arises from the bronchial mucosa.
2. Characteristics.
   a. Smoking and occupational exposures are the most frequent causal agents.
   b. Cell types: small cell carcinoma (oat cell), and non–small cell carcinoma (squamous cell, adenocarcinoma, and large cell undifferentiated).
   c. Secondary changes due to the tumor: obstruction or compression of an airway, blood vessel, or nerve.
   d. Local metastases in the pleura, chest wall, mediastinal structures. Common distant metastases in lymph nodes, liver, bone, brain, and adrenals.
3. Pertinent physical findings with pulmonary involvement.
   a. Unexplained weight loss.
   b. Hemoptysis.
   c. Dyspnea.
   d. Weakness.
   e. Fatigue.
   f. Wheezing.
   g. Pneumonia with productive cough due to airway compression.
   h. Hoarseness with compression of the laryngeal nerve.
   i. Atelectasis or bacterial pneumonia with nonproductive cough due to airway obstruction.
4. Management of bronchogenic cancer.
   a. Chemotherapy.
   b. Radiation therapy.
   c. Surgical resection if possible.
5. Physical therapy considerations.
   a. Pneumonias that develop behind a completely obstructed bronchus cannot be cleared with physical therapy techniques. Hold treatment until palliative therapy reduces tumor size and relieves bronchial obstruction.
   b. Possible fractures from thoracic bone metastasis with chest compressive maneuvers and coughing.
   c. Ecchymosis (bruising) in patients with low platelet count.
   d. Fatigue that restricts necessary activities.

Trauma

1. Rib fracture, flail chest.
   a. Fracture of the ribs, usually due to blunt trauma. Flail chest is two or more fractures in two or more adjacent ribs.
   b. Pertinent physical findings.
      (1) Shallow breathing.
      (2) Splinting due to pain (especially with deep inspiration or cough).
      (3) Crepitation may be felt during the ventilatory cycle over fracture site.
      (4) Paradoxical movement of a flail section during the ventilatory cycle (inspiration, the flail section is pulled inward; exhalation, the flail moves outward).
      (5) Confirmation by CXR.
2. Pleural injury.
   a. Pneumothorax.
      (1) Air in the pleural space, usually through a lacerated visceral pleura from a rib fracture or ruptured bullae.

(2) Pertinent physical findings all increase with severity of injury.
  (a) Chest pain.
  (b) Dyspnea.
  (c) Tracheal and mediastinal shift away from injured side.
  (d) Absent or decreased breath sounds.
  (e) Increased tympany with mediate percussion.
  (f) Cyanosis.
  (g) Respiratory distress.
  (h) Confirmation by CXR.

b. Hemothorax.
  (1) Blood in the pleural space, usually from a laceration of the parietal pleura.
  (2) Pertinent physical findings increase with severity of injury.
    (a) Chest pain.
    (b) Dyspnea.
    (c) Tracheal and mediastinal shift away from side of injury.
    (d) Absent or decreased breath sounds.
    (e) Cyanosis.
    (f) Respiratory distress.
    (g) Confirmation by CXR.
    (h) Possible signs of blood loss.

3. Lung contusion.
  a. Blood and edema within the alveoli and interstitial space due to blunt chest trauma with or without rib fractures.
  b. Pertinent physical findings increase with severity of injury.
    (1) Cough with hemoptysis.
    (2) Dyspnea.
    (3) Decreased breath sounds and/or crackles.
    (4) Cyanosis.
    (5) Confirmation by CXR of ill-defined patchy densities.

Other Pulmonary Conditions

1. Pulmonary edema.
  a. Excessive seepage of fluid from the pulmonary vascular system into the interstitial space; may eventually cause alveolar edema.
    (1) Cardiogenic: results from increased pressure in pulmonary capillaries associated with left ventricular failure, aortic valvular disease, or mitral valvular disease.
    (2) Non-cardiogenic: results from increased permeability of the alveolar capillary membranes due to inhalation of toxic fumes, hypervolemia, narcotic overdose, or adult respiratory distress syndrome (ARDS).
  b. Pertinent physical findings.
    (1) Crackles.
    (2) Tachypnea.
    (3) Dyspnea.
    (4) Hypoxemia.
    (5) Peripheral edema if cardiogenic.
    (6) Cough with pink, frothy secretions.
    (7) CXR shows increased vascular markings, hazy opacities in gravity-dependent areas of the lung in a typical butterfly pattern. Atelectasis is possible if the surfactant lining is removed by alveolar edema.

2. Pulmonary emboli.
  a. A thrombus from the peripheral venous circulation becomes embolic and lodges in the pulmonary circulation. Small emboli do not necessarily cause infarction.
  b. Pertinent physical findings without infarction.
    (1) History consistent with pulmonary emboli: deep vein thrombosis, oral contraceptives, recent abdominal or hip surgery, polycythemia, prolonged bed rest.
    (2) Sudden onset of dyspnea.
    (3) Tachycardia.
    (4) Hypoxemia.
    (5) Cyanosis.
    (6) Auscultatory findings may be normal or show crackles and decreased breath sounds.
    (7) Ventilation-perfusion scan showing perfusion defects with concomitant normal ventilation.
  c. Added pertinent physical findings consistent with pulmonary infarction.
    (1) Chest pain.
    (2) Hemoptysis.
    (3) CXR shows decreased vascular markings, high diaphragm, pulmonary infiltrate, and/or pleural effusion.

3. Pleural effusion.
  a. Excessive fluid between the visceral and parietal pleura, caused mainly by increased pleural permeability to proteins from inflammatory diseases (pneumonia, rheumatoid arthritis, systemic lupus), neoplastic disease, increased hydrostatic pressure within pleural space (congestive heart failure), decrease in osmotic pressure (hypoproteinemia), peritoneal fluid within the pleural space (ascites, cirrhosis), or interference of pleural reabsorption from a tumor invading pleural lymphatics.
  b. Pertinent physical findings.
    (1) Decreased breath sounds over effusion; bronchial breath sounds around the perimeter. Pleural friction rub may be possible with inflammatory process.
    (2) Mediastinal shift away from large effusion.
    (3) Breathlessness with large effusions.

(4) CXR shows fluid in the pleural space in gravity-dependent areas of the thorax if > 300 mL.
(5) Pain and fever only if the pleural fluid is infected (empyema).

4. Atelectasis.
   a. Collapsed or airless alveolar unit, caused by hypoventilation secondary to pain during the ventilatory cycle (pleuritis, postoperative pain, or rib fracture), internal bronchial obstruction (aspiration, mucus plugging), external bronchial compression (tumor or enlarged lymph nodes), low tidal volumes (narcotic overdose, inappropriately low ventilator settings), or neurologic insult.
   b. Pertinent physical findings.
      (1) Decreased breath sounds.
      (2) Dyspnea.
      (3) Tachycardia.
      (4) Increased temperature.
      (5) CXR with platelike streaks.

Physical Therapy Intervention

See Table 3-14 for Preferred Cardiopulmonary Practice Patterns.

Manual Secretion Removal Techniques

1. Postural drainage.
   a. Placing the patient in varying positions for optimal gravity drainage of secretions and increased expansion of the involved segment (see Figure 4-5).
   b. Indications for use of postural drainage.
      (1) Increased pulmonary secretions.
      (2) Aspiration.
      (3) Atelectasis or collapse.
   c. Considerations prior to use of the postural drainage positions (see Table 4-5). These considerations are not intended to imply absolute danger, but rather a possible need for position modification.
   d. Procedure.
      (1) Explain procedure to the patient.
      (2) Place patient in appropriate postural drainage position.
      (3) Observe for signs of intolerance.
      (4) Duration of procedure can be up to 20 minutes per postural drainage position. Typically, duration equals the duration of other manual techniques used in conjunction with postural drainage.
2. Percussion.
   a. A force rhythmically applied with the therapist's cupped hands to the specific area of the chest wall that corresponds to the involved lung segment.
   b. Percussion is used to increase the amount of secretions cleared from the tracheobronchial tree; usually used in conjunction with postural drainage. Indications for use of percussion.
      (1) Excessive pulmonary secretions.
      (2) Aspiration.
      (3) Atelectasis or collapse due to mucous plugging obstructing the airways.
   c. Considerations to weigh possible benefits of percussion against possible detriments prior to the application of this technique are listed in Table 4-6. Modification of the technique may be necessary for patient tolerance.
   d. Procedure.
      (1) Explain procedure to the patient.
      (2) Place patient in the appropriate postural drainage position.
      (3) Cover the area to be percussed with a lightweight cloth to avoid erythema.
      (4) Percuss over area of thorax that corresponds to the involved lung segment. The duration of percussion depends on the patient's needs and tolerance. Three to five minutes of percussion per postural drainage position with clinically assessed improvement is a guideline.
      (5) The force of percussion causes the patient's voice to quiver.
3. Shaking (vibration).
   a. Following a deep inhalation, a bouncing maneuver is applied to the rib cage throughout exhalation; to hasten the removal of secretions from the tracheobronchial tree.
   b. Commonly used following percussion in the appropriate postural drainage position. Modification may be necessary for patient tolerance.
   c. Indications for the use of shaking.

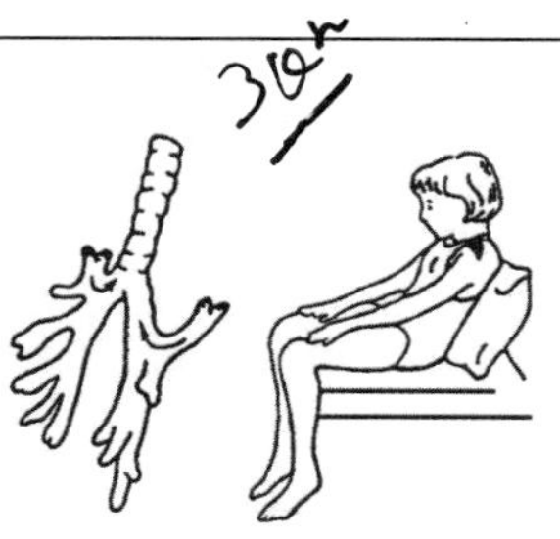

UPPER LOBES Apical Segments

Bed or drainage table flat.

Patient leans back on pillow at 30° angle against therapist.

Therapist claps with markedly cupped hand over area between clavicle and top of scapula on each side.

UPPER LOBES Posterior Segments

Bed or drainage table flat.

Patient leans over folded pillow at 30° angle.

Therapist stands behind and claps over upper back on both sides.

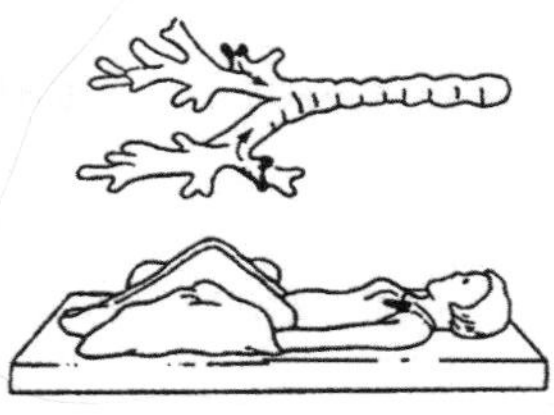

UPPER LOBES Anterior Segments

Bed or drainage table flat.

Patient lies on back with pillow under knees.

Therapist claps between clavicle and nipple on each side.

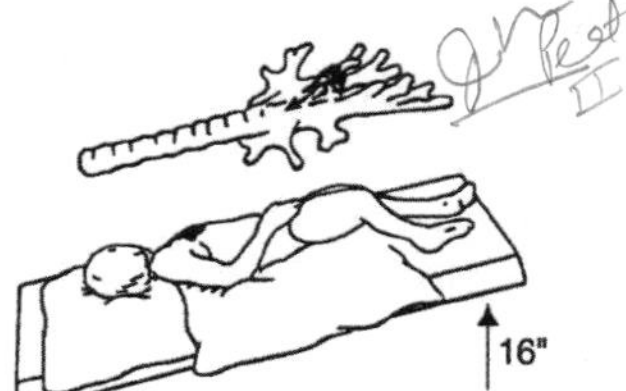

RIGHT MIDDLE LOBE

Foot of table or bed elevated 16 inches.

Patient lies head down on left side and rotates ¼ turn backward. Pillow may be placed behind from shoulder to hip. Knees should be flexed.

Therapist claps over right nipple area. In females with breast development or tenderness, use cupped hand with heel of hand under armpit and fingers extending forward beneath the breast.

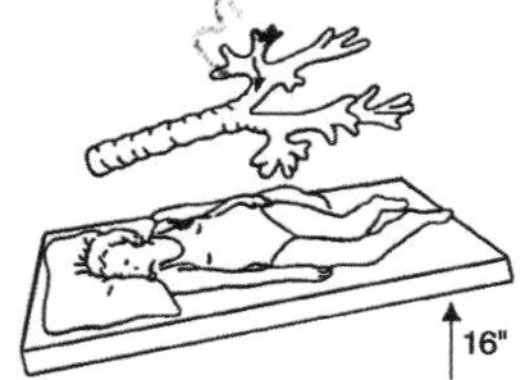

LEFT UPPER LOBE Lingular Segments

Foot of table or bed elevated 16 inches.

Patient lies head down on right side and rotates 1/4 turn backward. Pillow may be placed behind from shoulder to hip. Knees should be flexed.

Therapist claps with moderately cupped hand over left nipple area. In females with breast development or tenderness, use cupped hand with heel of hand under armpit and fingers extending forward beneath the breast.

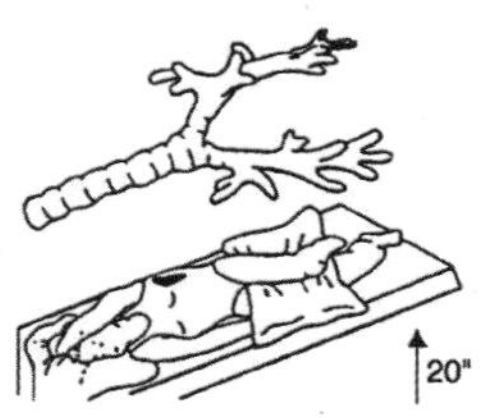

LOWER LOBE Anterior Basal Segments

Foot of table or bed elevated 20 inches.

Patient lies on side, head down, pillow under knees.

Therapist claps with slightly cupped hand over lower ribs. (Position shown is for drainage of left anterior basal segment. To drain the right anterior basal segment, patient should lie on the left side in same posture).

LOWER LOBES Lateral Basal Segments

Foot of table or bed elevated 20 inches.

Patient lies on abdomen, head down, then rotates ¼ turn upward. Upper leg is flexed over a pillow for support.

Therapist claps over uppermost portion of lower ribs. (Position shown is for drainage of right lateral basal segment. To drain the left lateral basal segment, patient should lie on the right side in the same posture).

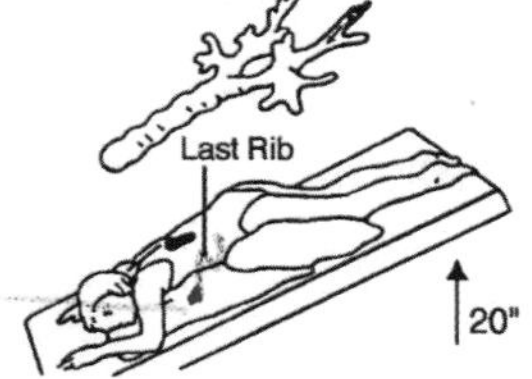

LOWER LOBES Posterior Basal Segments

Foot of table or bed elevated 20 inches.

Patient lies on abdomen, head down, with pillow under hips. Therapist claps over lower ribs close to spine on each side.

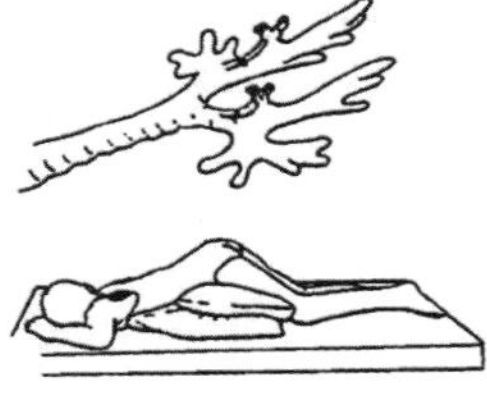

LOWER LOBES Superior Segments

Bed or table flat.

Patient lies on abdomen with two pillows under hips.

Therapist claps over middle of back at tip of scapula on either side of spine.

Figure 4-5 Bronchial drainage.

From Rothstein J, Roy S, and Wolf S: The Rehabilitation Specialist's Handbook, 3rd ed., FA Davis, 2005, p. 444, with permission.

(1) Excessive pulmonary secretions.
(2) Aspiration.
(3) Atelectasis or collapse of an airway from mucous plugging.

d. Considerations prior to the application of shaking are similar to those of percussion (see Table 4-6).

e. Procedure.
   (1) Explain procedure to the patient.

Table 4-5

Considerations Prior to the Use of Postural Drainage

Precautions to the use of Trendelenburg position (Head of bed tipped down 15° to 18°)	
Circulatory system	Pulmonary edema, congestive heart failure, hypertension.
Abdominal problems	Obesity, ascites, pregnancy, hiatal hernia, nausea and vomiting, recent food consumption.
Neurologic system	Recent neurosurgery, increased intracranial pressure, aneurysm precautions.
Pulmonary system	Shortness of breath.
Precautions to the use of sidelying position	
Circulatory system	Axillo-femoral bypass graft.
Musculoskeletal system	Humeral fractures, need for hip abduction brace, other situations that make sidelying uncomfortable, e.g., arthritis, shoulder bursitis.

Table 4-6

Considerations Prior to the Use of Percussion and Shaking

General guidelines	Pain made worse by the technique.
Circulatory system	Aneurysm precautions, hemoptysis.
Coagulation disorders	Increased partial thromboplastin time (PTT), increased prothrombin time (PT), decreased platelet count (below 50,000), or medications that interfere with coagulation.
Musculoskeletal system	Fractured rib, flail chest, degenerative bone disease, bone metastases.

(2) Place patient in appropriate postural drainage position.

(3) Perform percussion if appropriate.

(4) As patient inhales deeply, the therapist's hands are placed with fingers parallel to the ribs.

(5) As patient exhales, the therapist's hands provide a jarring, bouncing motion to the rib cage below.

(6) The duration of shaking depends on the patient's needs, tolerance, and clinical improvement. Five to 10 deep inhalations with the shaking technique is generally acceptable practice. Any more than 10 would risk hyperventilation (increased V_E resulting in decreased $PaCO_2$), and less than five may be ineffective.

4. Airway clearance techniques.

   a. Cough: patient should be asked to cough in the upright sitting position, if possible, after each area of lung has been treated. Coughing clears secretions from the major central airways.

   b. Huffing: more effective in patients with collapsible airways (e.g., chronic obstructive diseases), prevents the high intrathoracic pressure that causes premature airway closure.

   (1) Ask patient to inhale deeply.

   (2) Immediately, the patient forcibly expels the air, saying "Ha, ha."

   c. Assisted cough: the therapist's hand(s) or fist become the force behind the patient's exhaled air. Used when the patient's abdominal muscles cannot generate an effective cough (e.g., spinal cord injury). The amount of force by the therapist depends on patient tolerance and abdominal sensation.

   (1) Position the patient against a solid surface; supine with head of bed flat or in a Trendelenburg position, or sitting with wheelchair against the wall or against the therapist.

   (2) The therapist's hand is placed below the patient's subcostal angle (similar to hand placement for the Heimlich maneuver).

   (3) Patient inhales deeply.

   (4) As the patient attempts to cough, the therapist's hand pushes inward and upward, assisting the rapid exhalation of air.

   (5) Any secretions raised should be removed by a suction catheter if expectoration is problematic.

   d. Tracheal stimulation: used with patients who are unable to cough on command, such as infants or patients with brain injury or stroke.

   (1) The therapist's finger or thumb is placed just above the suprasternal notch, and a quick inward and downward pressure on the trachea elicits the cough reflex.

   e. Endotracheal suctioning: used only when the above airway clearance techniques fail to adequately remove secretions.

   (1) Standard precautions are employed, since contact with a patient's body fluid is expected.

   (2) Equipment: suction catheters come in sizes of 14 French gauge (Fr), usually for an adult, 10 Fr for older children, 8 and 5–6 Fr for young children and infants. Suction system set at approximately 120 mm Hg of suction. Sterile glove/clean glove.

   (3) Procedure: a catheter is fed through either an artificial airway, oral airway, or the nares

through the pharynx, larynx to the carina. When resistance is felt at the carina, the catheter is rotated and withdrawn. Suction is applied intermittently so as not to damage the inner lining of the trachea. The usual suctioning time is 10 to 15 seconds.

(4) Complications associated with suctioning: hypoxemia, bradycardia or tachycardia, hypotension or hypertension, increased intracranial pressure, atelectasis, tracheal damage, infections.

Independent Secretion Removal Techniques

1. Active cycle of breathing.
   a. An independent program to assist in the removal of more peripheral secretions that coughing may not clear.
   b. Breathe in a controlled, diaphragmatic fashion.
   c. Perform thoracic expansion exercises with or without percussion and shaking. These are deep inhalations with a hold at the top, if possible.
   d. Controlled, diaphragmatic breathing. The patient decides what is needed next. If no secretions seem to be mobilized the patient returns to step b, then c, and reassesses the situation. If the patient believes secretions can be cleared, the patient moves on to steps e and f.
   e. Inhale at a resting tidal volume. Contract the abdominal muscles to produce one or two forced expiratory huffs from mid to low lung volume to raise secretions.
   f. Huff from high lung volume or cough to clear.
   g. Controlled diaphragmatic breathing.
   h. Repeat these cycles until secretions are in large airways.
2. Autogenic drainage.
   a. An independent program used to sense peripheral secretions and clear them without the tracheobronchial irritation from coughing.
   b. Amount of time spent in each of the following phases is determined by where the patient feels the secretions.
      (1) Unstick phase: quiet breathing at low lung volumes to effect peripheral secretions.
      (2) Collect phase: breathing at mid lung volumes to affect secretions in the middle airways.
      (3) Evacuation phase: breathing from mid to high lung volumes to clear secretions from central airways; replaces coughing as the means to clear secretions.
      (4) Repeat the steps corresponding to the area of retained secretions until all secretions are removed from the airways.
3. FLUTTER or Acapella device.
   a. The patient uses an external device that vibrates the airways on exhalation to improve airway clearance with intermittent, positive expiratory pressure.
   b. Patient breathes in a normal tidal volume through the nose or around the mouthpiece of the FLUTTER device.
   c. Patient then exhales through the device, setting up a vibration within the airways. Experimentation in the tipped position of the device may provide the most vibration possible with exhalation.
   d. Repeat between 5 and 10 times.
   e. Patient then breathes in a full inhalation through the nose or around the mouthpiece.
   f. This is followed by a 3-second hold at the top of inhalation and rapid, forced exhalations through the FLUTTER device.
   g. Repeat 2 or 3 times.
   h. Huff or cough to clear secretions.
   i. Repeat steps a–h until all secretions are removed from the airways.
4. Low-pressure positive expiratory pressure (PEP) mask.
   a. The patient uses positive expiratory resistance via face mask to help remove airway secretions. Low-pressure PEP measures 10–20 cm H_2O.
   b. Seated patient breathes at tidal volumes with mask in place.
   c. After approximately 10 breaths, the mask is removed for coughing or huffing to clear secretions.
   d. The sequence is repeated until all secretions are removed from the airways.
5. High-pressure positive expiratory pressure (PEP) mask.
   a. The patient with an unstable airway uses high expiratory pressures via face mask to assist in the removal of airway secretions. High-pressure PEP uses the point of PEP between 50 and 120 cm H_2O, where the patient is able to exhale a larger FVC with the mask than without.
   b. Seated patient breathes at tidal volumes with mask in place.
   c. After approximately 10 breaths, huffing from high to low lung volumes is performed with the mask in place.
   d. The sequence is repeated until all secretions are removed from the airways.

Breathing Exercises

1. Diaphragmatic breathing.
   a. Used to increase ventilation, improve gas exchange, decrease work of breathing, facilitate relaxation, and maintain or improve mobility of chest wall.

b. Used with postoperative patients, posttrauma patients, and patients with obstructive or restrictive pulmonary lung diseases.
c. Procedure.
(1) Explain procedure to patient.
(2) Position patient in semireclined (e.g., semi-Fowler's position).
(3) Place therapist's hand gently over subcostal angle of the thorax.
(4) Apply gentle pressure throughout the exhalation phase.
(5) Increase to firm pressure at end of exhalation.
(6) Ask patient to inhale against resistance of the therapist's hand.
(7) Release pressure, allowing a full inhalation.
(8) Progress to independence of therapist's hand, in upright sitting, standing, walking, and stair climbing.

2. Segmental breathing.
a. Used to improve ventilation to hypoventilated lung segments, alter regional distribution of gas, maintain or restore functional residual capacity, maintain or improve mobility of chest wall, and prevent pulmonary compromise.
b. Used for patients with pleuritic, incisional, or posttrauma pain that causes decreased movement in a portion of the thorax (splinting), and those at risk of developing atelectasis.
c. Inappropriate for intractable hypoventilation until medical situation is resolved; palliative therapy to reduce bronchogenic tumor size or chest tube to reduce a pneumothorax.
d. Procedure.
(1) Explain procedure to patient.
(2) Position patient to facilitate inhalation to a certain segment, such as postural drainage positions, upright sitting.
(3) Apply gentle pressure to the thorax over area of hypoventilation during exhalation.
(4) Increase to firm pressure just prior to inspiration.
(5) Ask patient to breathe in against the resistance of therapist's hands.
(6) Release resistance, allowing a full inhalation.

3. Sustained maximal inspiration (SMI).
a. Used to increase inhaled volume, sustain or improve alveolar inflation, and maintain or restore functional residual capacity.
b. Used in acute situations; e.g., patients with posttrauma pain, postoperative pain, acute lobar collapse.
c. Procedure.
(1) Inspire slowly through nose or pursed lips to maximal inspiration.
(2) Hold maximal inspiration for 3 seconds.
(3) Passively exhale the volume.
(4) Incentive spirometers (devices used to measure and encourage deep inspiration) can help patient achieve maximal inspiration during SMI.

4. Pursed lip breathing.
a. Used to reduce respiratory rate, increase tidal volume, reduce dyspnea, decrease mechanical disadvantages of impaired ventilatory pump, improve gas mixing at rest for patients with COPD, and facilitate relaxation.
b. Primarily used for patients with obstructive disease who experience dyspnea at rest or with minimal activity/exercise, or with ineffective breathing patterns during activity/exercise.
c. Procedure.
(1) Slowly inhale through nose or mouth.
(2) Passively exhale through pursed lips (position mouth as if blowing out candles).
(3) Additional hand pressure from the therapist applied to abdomen can gently prolong expiration.
(4) Abdominal muscle contraction can be used judiciously to increase exhaled volume. Care must be taken not to increase intrathoracic pressure, which may cause airway collapse.

5. Abdominal strengthening.
a. Used when abdominal muscles are too weak to provide an effective cough. Abdominal splinting: used when the abdominal muscles cannot provide the necessary support needed for passive exhalation, e.g., in high thoracic and cervical spinal cord injuries. It is important to ensure that the binder does not restrict inspiration.
b. Glossopharyngeal breathing (air gulping) can also be taught to assist coughing.

Postsurgical Care

1. Postoperative physical therapy sessions.
a. Decrease the number and severity of pulmonary complications.
b. Prevent postoperative pulmonary complications.
(1) Remove residual secretions.
(2) Improve aeration.
(3) Gradually increase activity.
(4) Return to baseline pulmonary functioning.
c. Pertinent physical findings of postoperative pulmonary complications.
(1) Increased temperature.
(2) Increase in white blood cell count.
(3) Change in breath sounds from the preoperative evaluation.
(4) Abnormal chest x-ray.
(5) Decreased expansion of the thorax.
(6) Shortness of breath.
(7) Change in cough and sputum production.

d. Physical therapy considerations.
  (1) Determine need for pain management.
  (2) Choose appropriate intervention based on patient's needs.
    (a) Secretion removal techniques.
    (b) Breathing exercises to improve aeration, incentive spirometry.
    (c) Early mobilization.

Activities for Increasing Functional Abilities

1. General conditioning.
  a. A prescription for exercise can be written to improve cardiopulmonary fitness based on results of exercise tolerance test. (See Chapter 3 for discussion.) *Exercise and progressive physical activity regimens require monitoring of heart rate and blood pressure* (White N, et al. Phys Ther. 2015).
  b. Mode. Any aerobic activity that allows a graded workload; usually, a circuit program of multiple activities (e.g., bike, walking, arm ergometry) since patients with pulmonary disease may be deconditioned. Patient preference should be considered.
  c. Intensity. Patients with mild or moderate lung disease will likely reach their cardiovascular endpoint with an exercise test. Using the test data in Karvonen's formula ([maximum heart rate – resting heart rate] [40%–85%] + resting heart rate) results in safe range for exercise intensity. Patients with severe and very severe pulmonary disorders will likely reach a pulmonary endpoint before a cardiovascular endpoint. Intensity for these patients should be at or near maximum heart rate. Ratings of Perceived Exertion scale is used to monitor exercise intensity.
  d. Duration. With high-intensity exercise, the patient may need an intermittent exercise program with rest periods for tolerance. Progression is directed first toward a duration of 20–30 minutes of continuous exercise before an increase in intensity is considered.
  e. Frequency. The goal is 20–30 minutes of exercise three to five times per week. With durations of less than 20–30 minutes, exercise should occur more frequently (five to seven times per week).
2. Inspiratory muscle trainer (IMTs).
  a. Used to load muscles of inspiration by breathing through a series of graded aperture openings. By increasing strength and endurance of muscles of ventilation, the patient will develop more efficient ventilatory muscles, less effort in breathing, and decreased possibility of respiratory muscle fatigue. However, evidence is inconclusive for improved functional ability. Whether this translates into improved functional abilities has been cause for debate, and has yet to be conclusively proven.
  b. IMT is appropriate for patients with decreased compliance, decreased intrathoracic volume, resistance to airflow, alteration in length tension relationship of ventilatory muscles, decreased strength of the respiratory muscles.
  c. Procedure.
    (1) Explain procedure to patient with emphasis on maintenance of respiratory rate and tidal volume during training sessions.
    (2) Determine maximum inspiratory pressure (MIP).
    (3) Choose an aperture opening that requires 30%–50% of MIP (intensity) and allows 10–15 minutes of training per session.
    (4) Ask patient to inhale through device while maintaining their usual respiratory rate and tidal volume for at least 10–15 minutes.
    (5) Progression initially focuses on increasing duration to 30 minutes, then increasing intensity with smaller apertures.
3. Paced breathing (activity pacing).
  a. Used to spread out the metabolic demands of an activity over time by slowing its performance.
  b. Indications: patients who become dyspneic during the performance of an activity or exercise.
  c. Procedure.
    (1) Break down any activity into manageable components that can be performed within the patient's pulmonary system's abilities.
    (2) Inhale at rest.
    (3) Upon exhalation with pursed lips, complete the first component of the desired activity.
    (4) Stop the activity and inhale at rest.
    (5) Upon exhalation with pursed lips, complete next component of activity.
    (6) Repeat steps (4) and (5) until activity is accomplished in full without shortness of breath. For example, stair climbing can be done by ascending one or more stairs on exhalation, and then resting, inhaling at rest, then more stairs on exhalation, and so on.
4. Energy conservation.
  a. The energy consumption of many activities of daily living can be decreased with some careful thought and planning, making seemingly impossible tasks possible.
  b. For example, showering is difficult for the patient with pulmonary disease, given the activity and the hot, humid environment. With a shower seat, hand-held shower, and use of a terry cloth robe after showering, the patient does not have to stand, hold his or her breath as often or dry off in the humid environment, thus reducing the energy cost of the activity.

Medical and Surgical Management of Pulmonary Disease

Surgical Management

1. Types of surgeries to remove diseased lung portions.
   a. Pneumonectomy: removal of a lung.
   b. Lobectomy: removal of a lobe of a lung.
   c. Segmental resection: removal of a segment of a lobe.
   d. Wedge resection: removal of a portion of a lung without anatomical divisions.
   e. Lung volume reduction surgery (LVRS), or pneumectomy, removes large emphysematous, nonfunctioning areas of the lung to normalize thoracic mobility and improve gas exchange of the remaining lung.
2. Types of incisions.
   a. Midsternotomy: sternum is cut in half lengthwise and rib cage is retracted; used in most heart surgeries. The sternum is wired together at the close of surgery; therefore, physical therapy should encourage full upper-extremity range of motion postoperatively.
   b. Thoracotomy: used for most lung resections; incision follows the path of the fourth intercostal space; full range of motion should be encouraged postoperatively.

Medical Management

1. Rescue drugs.
   a. Used for immediate relief of breakthrough symptoms of tightness, wheezing, and shortness of breath.
   b. Short-acting beta-2 agonists (sympathomimetics): mimic the activity of the sympathetic nervous system that produce bronchodilation; can increase heart rate and blood pressure.
   c. Given topically through a metered-dose inhaler (MDI), unwanted systemic effects are reduced. Examples of rescue beta-2 agonists are Ventolin (albuterol), Alupent (metaproterenol), and Maxair (pirbuterol).
2. Maintenance drugs.
   a. Taken on a regular schedule to maintain optimal airway diameter.
   b. Long-acting beta-2 agonists (sympathomimetics): Mimic activity of sympathetic nervous system, allowing for bronchodilation; may decrease need for rescue drugs and inhaled anti-inflammatories. An example of this type of beta-2 maintenance drug is Serevent (salmeterol xinafoate).
   c. Anticholinergics: inhibit the parasympathetic nervous system; increase heart rate, blood pressure and bronchodilation. Side effects can include lack of sweating, dry mouth, and delusions. Administered by MDI with minimal side effects. Should be used on a regular schedule to maintain bronchodilation. An example of this category of drug is Atrovent (ipratropium).
   d. Methylxanthines: produce smooth muscle relaxation, but use is limited due to serious toxicity, increased blood pressure, increased heart rate, arrhythmias, gastrointestinal distress, nervousness, headache, and seizures. Blood levels should be drawn to ensure medication effect without toxicity. Examples are aminophylline and theophylline.
   e. Leukotriene receptor antagonists: block leukotrienes released in allergic reactions. Inhibit airway edema and smooth muscle contraction; additive benefits when used in conjunction with other anti-inflammatories. An example of this drug is montelukast (Singulair).
   f. Cromolyn sodium: antiallergic drug; prevents release of mast cells (i.e., histamine) after contact with allergens; used prophylactically to prevent exercise-induced bronchospasm and severe bronchial asthma via oral inhalation. Not to be used as a rescue drug during acute situations. Frequent inhalation can result in hoarseness, cough, dry mouth, and bronchial irritation. Symptoms of overdosage include paradoxical bronchospasm. Brand names include Intal.
   g. Anti-inflammatory agents: used to decrease mucosal edema, inflammation, and airway reactivity. Steroids can be administered systemically or topically (MDI). Side effects of systemic administration: increased blood pressure, sodium retention, muscle wasting, osteoporosis, gastrointestinal (GI) irritation, and hypercholesteremia. The main side effect of inhaled steroids is thrush, a fungal infection of the mouth and throat. Examples are Vanceril (beclomethasone, MDI), Azmacort (triamcinolone, MDI).
   h. Vaccinations. It is recommended that patients with pulmonary disorders routinely receive the influenza and the pneumonia vaccinations.
3. Crisis drugs.
   a. May be used in a crisis situation, such as in an emergency room. Often, drugs that might be given topically are given systemically, and potentially

in larger doses. For example, anti-inflammatory agents usually administered via MDI will now be prescribed as prednisone (oral) or SoluMedral (methylprednisolone, IV).

b. Antibiotics are not recommended for maintenance, but only for treatment of infection, such as an infectious exacerbation.
   (1) Categories: culture and sensitivity results are used to prescribe the most effective antibiotic.
      (a) Penicillins.
      (b) Erythromycins.
      (c) Tetracyclines.
      (d) Cephalosporins.
      (e) Aminoglycosides.
   (2) Side effects include allergic reactions, stomach cramps, nausea, vomiting, and diarrhea.

Intensive Care Unit Management

1. Physical therapy in the ICU.
   a. Employed for pulmonary care (secretion removal or improved aeration) and early mobility (range of motion, positioning, therapeutic exercise, transfers, ambulation). The following equipment is frequently encountered when treating patients in the ICU.
2. Mechanical ventilation.
   a. Maintains an adequate V_E for patients who cannot do so independently.
   b. Requires intubation with an endotracheal (oral), nasotracheal (nasal), or tracheal (through a tracheostomy directly into the trachea) tube. Endotracheal and nasotracheal tubes are taped in place, while tracheal tubes may be sutured in place.
   c. Tubes or mechanical ventilation pose no contraindications to physical therapy treatment. A patient who is intubated can ambulate using a mechanical resuscitator bag to maintain ventilation. It is sometimes easier to use a stationary device, e.g., peddler, to exercise a patient who needs a ventilator.
   d. When moving a patient who is intubated, avoid placing excessive tension on the tube. Alteration in the placement of the tube (either a drop inward or a pull outward) could reduce optimal ventilation. If tube movement is suspected, a nurse or respiratory therapist should check tube placement. If the tube is dislodged, a physician, often an anaesthesiologist, should replace the tube.
3. Chest tubes.
   a. Used to evacuate air or fluid trapped in the intrapleural space. Chest tubes are sutured in place to make them secure.
   b. There are no contraindications to physical therapy treatment with a chest tube. If the chest tube is connected to a suction device, mobility is limited only by the length of the tubing. Portable suction machines can be used for increased mobility.
   c. If the tube is dislodged during treatment, cover the defect and seek assistance.
4. IVs.
   a. Intravenous catheters used to deliver medications.
   b. There are no contraindications to physical therapy treatment with IV lines; however, the upper extremity should not be raised above the level of the IV medication for any length of time or backflow of blood may occur.
   c. Rolling IV poles allow for mobility. Most IV pumps have a battery backup system to allow patient mobility.
5. Arterial lines.
   a. Catheters that are placed within the arterial system, usually the radial artery. The tubing is connected to a pressure pack that exceeds arterial pressure so the line does not back up with blood.
   b. Caution to maintain patency during moving is warranted. These lines may be capped off by nursing for a short time to allow mobility. For out-bed activity for prolonged periods, mobility is limited only by the length of the tubing.
   c. If this line becomes dislodged, immediate, firm pressure must be applied to or above the arterial insertion site to stop bleeding.
6. Monitors/Oscilloscopes.
   a. Continuous electrocardiogram (ECG) with a reported heart rate.
   b. Blood pressure reading, either periodic using noninvasive cuff (NIBP), or continuous using a transducer attached to the arterial line (ABP).
   c. Continuous oxygen saturation (SaO_2) with pulse wave. SaO_2 is the percent saturation of oxygen in the arterial blood. This noninvasive measurement relates to the PaO_2 on an S-shaped curve, called the oxyhemoglobin desaturation curve. Normal levels are 98%–100% saturated. The pulse oximeter utilizes a finger sensor (or an ear sensor) to obtain a consistent reading.
7. Supplemental oxygen.
   a. Increases the FiO_2 (up to 1) of the patient's environment. A portable oxygen cylinder attached to the oxygen delivery device (cannula, mask, or manual resuscitator bag attached to the endotracheal tube) can be used during mobility training to provide supplemental oxygen for the patient.
   b. Supplemental oxygen is indicated if SaO_2 is $< 88\%$ or PaO_2 is < 55 mm Hg, regardless of activity level. Monitor the patient's SaO_2 to assure adequate oxygenation with increased activity.
   c. Oxygen must be prescribed by a physician, since it is considered a form of medication.

Review Questions

Pulmonary Physical Therapy

1. What are the PaO_2 and FiO_2 normal values in room air?

2. When auscultating the lungs, what are the main characteristics of crackles, wheezes, vesicular, and bronchial breath sounds?

3. What are the expected physical, imaging, PFT, and laboratory findings associated with moderate to severe asthma?

4. What are the precautions when using postural drainage in the Trendelenburg position?

5

Integumentary Physical Therapy

SUSAN B. O'SULLIVAN AND VINCENT LEPAK

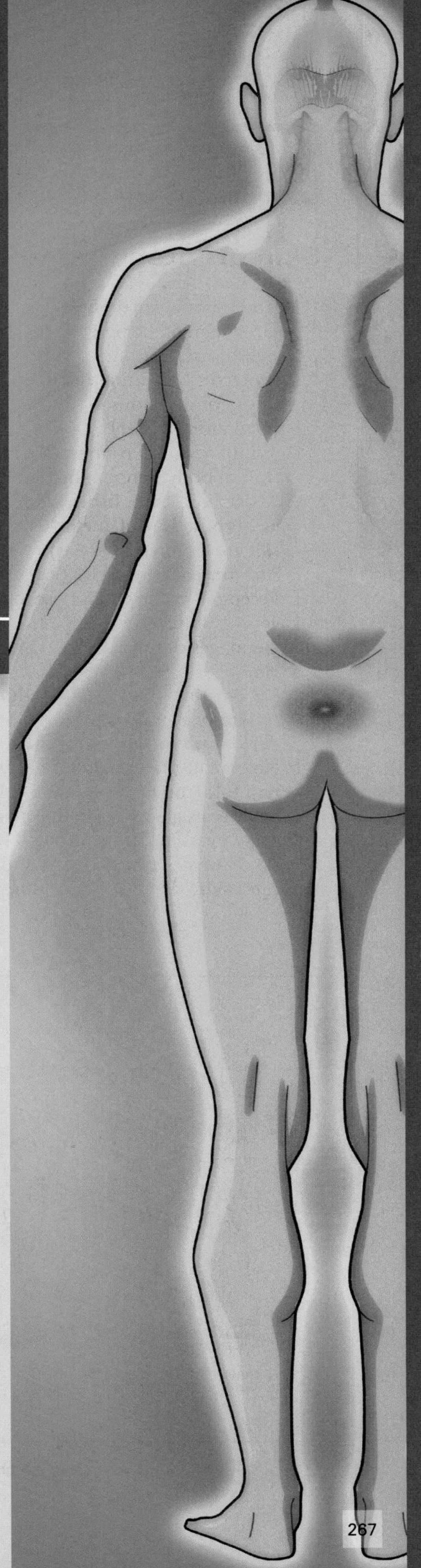

Chapter Outline

Integumentary System

Skin or Integument

1. External covering of the body (see Figure 5-1). The largest organ system of the body (15%–20% of body weight).
2. Functions of skin.
   a. Protection of underlying body structures against injury or invasion.
   b. Insulation of body.
   c. Maintenance of homeostasis: fluid balance, regulation of body temperature.
   d. Assists in metabolism: vitamin D production, aids in elimination of metabolic waste (e.g., urea and salt are excreted in sweat).
   e. Attachment of muscles (e.g., erector pili, frontalis).
   f. Receptors in dermis give rise to cutaneous sensations.
3. Layers of skin (see Table 5-1).
4. Appendages of the skin.
   a. Hair.
      (1) Terminal hair: coarse, thick, pigmented; e.g., scalp, eyebrows.
      (2) Vellus hair: short, fine; e.g., arms, chest.
   b. Nails: nail plate, lunula (whitish moon), proximal nail fold/cuticle, lateral nail folds.
   c. Sebaceous glands: exocrine glands that secrete fatty substance (sebum) through hair follicles; on all skin surfaces except palms and soles. Sebum lubricates skin, defends against bacteria and fungus.

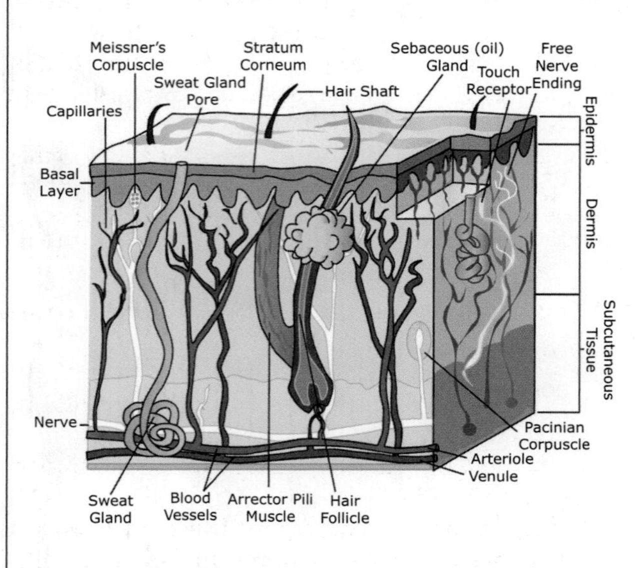

Figure 5-1 Cross-section of the skin.

Table 5-1

Layers of Skin	
Epidermis	Outer, most superficial layer; contains no blood vessels Composed of five layers: 1 Stratum corneum: outermost layer, shingle-like dead cells are filled with keratin 2 Stratum lucidum: formed from dead cells and only occurs in thick portions of the palms and soles of feet 3 Stratum granulosum: contains live keratinocytes (differentiate from epidermal stem cells in basal layer and eventually form outermost layer of epidermis) and Langerhans (immunity) cells 4 Stratum spinosum (spiny layer): also contain keratinocytes and Langerhans 5 Stratum basale (stratum germinativum): deepest layer of epidermis, contains epidermal cells, melanocytes (produce melanin), and Merkel cells (associated with light touch sensory discrimination)
Dermis (corium)	Inner layer composed primarily of collagen and elastin fibrous connective tissues Mucopolysaccharide matrix and elastin fibers provide elasticity, strength to skin Contains lymphatics, blood vessels, nerves and nerve endings, hair follicles, sebaceous and sweat glands Cells include: fibroblasts, macrophages, lymphocytes, and mast cells
Subcutaneous tissues (hypodermis)	Underneath dermis Consists of loose connective and fat tissues Provides insulation, support, and cushion for skin; stores energy for skin Muscles and fascia lie underneath subcutaneous layer

   d. Sweat glands.
      (1) Eccrine glands: widely distributed, open on skin; help control body temperature.
      (2) Apocrine glands: found in axillary and genital areas, open into hair follicles; stimulated by emotional stress.

Circulation

1. Blood flow to capillaries of the skin.
   a. Increased blood flow with an increase in oxyhemoglobin to skin capillaries causes reddening of the skin.
   b. Peripheral cyanosis is due to reduced blood flow to skin and loss of oxygen to tissues (changes to deoxyhemoglobin) and results in a darker, somewhat blue color.
   c. Central cyanosis is due to reduced oxygen level in the blood; causes include advanced lung disease, congenital heart disease, and abnormal hemoglobins.

Common Skin Disorders

Dermatitis (Eczema)

1. Inflammation. Causes itching, redness, skin lesions.
2. Causes.
   a. Allergic or contact dermatitis; e.g., poison ivy, harsh soaps, chemicals, adhesive tape.
   b. Actinic: photosensitivity, reaction to sunlight, ultraviolet.
   c. Atopic: etiology unknown, associated with allergic, hereditary, or psychological disorders.
3. Stages.
   a. Acute: red, oozing, crusting rash; extensive erosions, exudate, pruritic vesicles.
   b. Subacute: erythematous skin, scaling, scattered plaques.
   c. Chronic: thickened skin, increased skin marking secondary to scratching; fibrotic papules, and nodules; postinflammatory pigmentation changes. Course can be relapsing.
4. Precautions or contraindications.
   a. Some physical therapy modalities.
   b. Avoid use of alcohol.
5. Medical management aimed at inflammation. Topical or systemic therapy (e.g., corticosteroids, immunosuppressants, antihistamines).
6. Daily care includes hydration and lubrication of skin.

Bacterial Infections

1. Bacteria enter through portals in the skin (e.g., abrasions or puncture wounds).
2. Impetigo.
   a. Superficial skin infection caused by staphylococci or streptococci.
   b. Associated with inflammation, small pus-filled vesicles, itching.
   c. Contagious; common in children and the elderly.
3. Cellulitis.
   a. Suppurative inflammation of cellular or connective tissue in or close to the skin.
   b. Tends to be poorly defined and widespread.
   c. Streptococcal or staphylococcal infection common; can be contagious.
   d. Skin is hot, red, and edematous.
   e. Management: antibiotics; elevation of the part; cool, wet dressings.
   f. If untreated, lymphangitis, gangrene, abscess, and sepsis can occur.
   g. The elderly and individuals with diabetes, wounds, malnutrition, or on steroid therapy are at increased risk.
4. Abscess.
   a. A cavity containing pus and surrounded by inflamed tissue.
   b. The result of a localized infection.
   c. Commonly a staphylococcal infection.
   d. Healing typically facilitated by draining or incising the abscess.

Viral Infections

1. Herpes 1 (herpes simplex).
   a. Itching and soreness, followed by vesicular eruption of the skin on the face or mouth; a cold sore or fever blister.
2. Herpes 2.
   a. Common cause of vesicular genital eruption.
   b. Spread by sexual contact.
   c. In newborns, may cause meningoencephalitis; may be fatal.
3. Herpes zoster (shingles).
   a. Caused by varicella-zoster virus (chickenpox); reactivation of virus lying dormant in cerebral ganglia or ganglia of posterior nerve roots.
   b. Pain and tingling affecting spinal or cranial nerve dermatome; progresses to red papules along distribution of infected nerve; red papules progressing to vesicles develop along a dermatome.
   c. Usually accompanied by fever, chills, malaise, gastrointestinal (GI) disturbances.
   d. Ocular complications with cranial nerve (CN) III involvement: eye pain, corneal damage; loss of vision with CN V involvement.
   e. Postherpetic neuralgic pain: may be intermittent or constant; lasts weeks; occasionally, intractable pain lasts months or years.
   f. Management: no curative agent, antiviral drugs slow progression; symptomatic treatment for itching and pain; e.g., systemic corticosteroids.
   g. Contagious to individuals who have not had chickenpox.
   h. Heat or ultrasound contraindicated: can increase severity of symptoms.
4. Warts.
   a. Common, benign infection by human papilloma viruses (HPVs).
   b. Transmission is through direct contact; autoinoculation is possible.
   c. Common warts: on skin, especially hands and fingers.
   d. Plantar wart: on pressure points of feet.
   e. Management: cryotherapy, acids, electrodessication, and curettage; over-the-counter medications.

Fungal Infections

1. Ringworm (tinea corporis).
   a. Fungal infection involving the hair, skin, or nails.
   b. Forms ring-shaped patches with vesicles or scales.
   c. Itchy; transmission is through direct contact.
   d. Treated with topical or oral antifungal drugs (e.g., griseofulvin).
2. Athlete's foot (tinea pedis).
   a. Fungal infection of foot, typically between the toes.
   b. Causes erythema, inflammation, pruritus, itching, and pain.
   c. Treated with antifungal creams.
   d. Can progress to bacterial infections, cellulitis if untreated.
3. Transmission.
   a. Person-to-person or animal-to-person.
   b. Observe standard precautions.

Parasitic Infections

1. Caused by insect and animal contacts.
2. Scabies (mites).
   a. Burrow into skin, causing inflammation, itching, and possibly pruritus.
   b. Treated with scabicide.
3. Lice (pediculosis).
   a. A parasite that can affect head, body, genital area with bite marks, redness, and nits.
   b. Treatment with special soap or shampoo.
4. Transmission.
   a. Person-to-person or sexually transmitted.
   b. Avoid direct contact; observe standard precautions.

Immune Disorders of the Skin

1. Psoriasis.
   a. Chronic autoimmune disease of skin characterized by erythematous plaques covered with a silvery scale; common on ears, scalp, knees, elbows, and genitalia.
   b. Common complaints: itching and pain from dry, cracked lesions.
   c. Variable course: exacerbations and remissions are common.
   d. May be associated with psoriatic arthritis, joint pain, particularly of small distal joints.
   e. Etiological factors: hereditary, associated immune disorders, certain drugs.
   f. Precipitating factors: trauma, infection, pregnancy and endocrine changes; cold weather, smoking, anxiety, and stress.
   g. Management: no cure; topical preparations (corticosteroids, occlusive ointments, coal tar); immunosuppressive drugs (methotrexate).
   h. Physical therapy intervention: long-wave ultraviolet (UV) light; combination UV light with oral photosensitizing drugs (psoralens).
2. Lupus erythematosus.
   a. Chronic, progressive autoimmune inflammatory disorder of connective tissues; characteristic red rash with raised, red, scaly plaques.
   b. Discoid lupus erythematosus (DLE): affects only skin; flare-ups with sun exposure; lesions can resolve or cause atrophy, permanent scarring, hypopigmentation, or hyperpigmentation.
   c. Systemic lupus erythematosus (SLE): chronic, systemic inflammatory disorder affecting multiple organ systems, including skin, joints, kidneys, heart, nervous system, mucous membranes; can be fatal; commonly affects young women. Symptoms can include fever, malaise, characteristic butterfly rash across bridge of nose, skin lesions, chronic fatigue, arthralgia, arthritis, skin rashes, photosensitivity, anemia, hair loss, Raynaud's phenomenon.
   d. Management: no cure; topical treatment of skin lesions (corticosteroid creams); salicylates, or indomethacin with fever and joint pain; immunosuppressive agents (cytotoxic agents) with life-threatening disease.
   e. Observe for side effects of corticosteroids: edema, weight gain, acne, hypertension, bruising, purplish stretch marks; long-term use of corticosteroids is associated with increased susceptibility to infection (immunosuppressed patient); osteoporosis, myopathy, tendon rupture, diabetes, gastric irritation, low potassium.
3. Scleroderma.
   a. Chronic, autoimmune diffuse disease of connective tissues causing fibrosis of skin, joints, blood vessels, and internal organs (GI tract, lungs, heart, kidneys). Usually accompanied by Raynaud's phenomenon.
   b. Skin is taut, firm, edematous, firmly bound to subcutaneous tissues.
   c. Limited systemic sclerosis/scleroderma: symmetrical skin involvement of distal extremities and face; slow progression of skin changes; late visceral and pulmonary hypertension involvement. Associated with CREST syndrome (Calcinosis, Raynaud's phenomenon, Esophageal dysfunction, Sclerodactyly, Telangiectasias).
   d. Diffuse systemic sclerosis disease/scleroderma: symmetrical, widespread skin involvement of distal and proximal extremities, face, trunk; rapid progression of skin changes with early appearance of visceral involvement. Important internal organs

that are frequently involved include kidneys, heart, and lungs.

e. Management: no specific therapy; supportive therapy can include corticosteroids, vasodilators, analgesics, immunosuppressive agents.

f. Physical therapy slows development of contracture and deformity.

g. Precautions with sclerosed skin, sensitive to pressure; acute hypertension may occur, stress regular blood pressure checks and vital sign monitoring. Pulmonary hypertension can lead to right sided heart failure in severe cases.

4. Polymyositis (PM).

a. A disease of connective tissue characterized by edema, inflammation, and degeneration of the muscles; dermatitis is associated with some forms. Sclerodactyly and interstitial lung disease are commonly associated with this disease, but they are nonspecific to this disorder.

b. Affects primarily proximal muscles: shoulder and pelvic girdles, neck, pharynx; symmetrical distribution.

c. Etiology unknown; autoimmune reaction affecting muscle tissue with degeneration and regeneration, fiber atrophy; inflammatory infiltrates.

d. Rapid, severe onset: may require ventilatory assistance, tube feeding.

e. Cardiac involvement: may be fatal.

f. Management: medication (corticosteroids and immunosuppressants).

g. Precautions: additional muscle fiber damage with too much exercise; contractures and pressure ulcers from inactivity, prolonged bed rest.

h. Physical therapy includes fatigue management and conservation of energy principles, exercise (aerobic and resistance exercise at low levels are appropriate provided fatigue and overload are avoided; see precautions), and positioning to prevent contractures and pressure ulcers.

Skin Cancer

1. Benign tumors.

a. Seborrheic keratosis: proliferation of basal cells leading to raised lesions, typically multiple lesions on trunk of older individuals; untreated unless causing irritation, pain; can be removed with cryotherapy.

b. Actinic keratosis: flat, round or irregular lesions, covered by dry scale on sun-exposed skin. Precancerous: can lead to squamous cell carcinoma.

c. Common mole (benign nevus): proliferation of melanocytes, round or oval shape, sharply defined borders, uniform color, < 6 mm, flat or raised. Can change into melanoma: signs include new swelling, redness, scaling, oozing, or bleeding.

2. Malignant tumors.

a. Basal cell carcinoma: slow-growing epithelial basal cell tumor, characterized by raised patch with ivory appearance or as a reddened area of eczema; has rolled border with indented center or presents as a thickened area of skin. Rarely metastasizes, common on face in fair-skinned individuals. Associated primarily with prolonged sun exposure although can occur in non-sun exposed areas.

b. Squamous cell carcinoma (SCC): has poorly defined margins; presents as a flat red area, ulcer, or nodule. Grows more quickly, common on sun-exposed areas, face and neck, back of hand. Can be confined (in situ) or invasive to surrounding tissues; much higher risk than basal cell carcinoma to metastasize. Mucosal and lingual SCC are often related to alcohol and tobacco use. Marjolin's ulcer is an uncommon form of SCC that occurs in burns.

c. Malignant melanoma: tumor arising from melanocytes (cells that produce melanin); superficial spreading melanoma (SSM) most common type.

(1) Clinical manifestations of melanoma. (See Table 5-2.)

(2) Melanoma risk factors: family history, intense year-round sun exposure, fair skin and freckles, nevi that are changing or atypical, especially if > 50.

(3) Lesions may have swelling or redness beyond the border, oozing or bleeding, or sensations of itching, burning, or pain.

(4) Red Flags: Early detection requires skill and expertise since melanomas may look identical to a harmless mole. Suspicious lesions are referred immediately to a dermatologist for further evaluation and biopsy. Treatment includes surgical resection. Prognosis depends on early diagnosis and the extent of invasion.

d. Kaposi's sarcoma (KS): lesions of endothelial cell origin due to human herpes virus 8 with red or dark purple/blue macules that progress to nodules or ulcers; associated with itching and pain.

Table 5-2

Clinical Examination of Malignant Melanoma "ABCDEs"

Asymmetry	Uneven edges, lopsided
Border	Irregular, poorly defined edges, notching
Color	Variations, especially mixtures of black, blue, or red
Diameter	Larger than 6 mm
Elevation (or Evolving)	Usually elevated, but may be flat; moles that changed over time

(1) Common on lower extremities; may involve internal structures producing lymphatic obstruction.
(2) Increased incidence in individuals of central European descent and with AIDS-associated immunodeficiency.

Skin Trauma

1. Contusion.
   a. Injury in which skin is not broken; a bruise.
   b. Characterized by pain, swelling, and discoloration.
   c. Immediate application of cold may limit effects.
2. Ecchymosis.
   a. Bluish discoloration of skin caused by extravasation of blood into the subcutaneous tissues.
   b. The result of trauma to underlying blood vessels or fragile vessel walls.
3. Petechiae.
   a. Tiny red or purple hemorrhagic spots on the skin.
4. Abrasion.
   a. Scraping away of skin due to injury or mechanical abrasion (e.g., dermabrasion).
5. Laceration.
   a. An irregular tear of the skin that produces a torn, jagged wound.

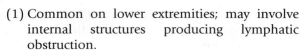

Examination of Integumentary Integrity

Patient/Client History

1. Complete history.
   a. Age, sex, race/ethnicity, social/health habits, work, living, general health status, medical/surgical.
2. Current condition(s)/chief complaint(s).
3. Functional status/activity level.
4. Medications.
5. Clinical tests.
6. Risk factor assessment.

Examination of Skin

1. Techniques. Observation, palpation, photographic assessment, and thermography.
2. Pruritus.
   a. Itching.
   b. Common in diabetes, drug hypersensitivity, hyperthyroidism.
3. Urticaria.
   a. Smooth, red, elevated patches of skin, hives.
   b. Indicative of an allergic response to drugs or infection.
4. Rash.
   a. Local redness and eruption on the skin, typically accompanied by itching.
   b. Seen in inflammation, skin diseases, chronic alcoholism, vasomotor disturbances, pyrexia, medications; e.g., diaper rash, heat rash, drug rash.
5. Xeroderma.
   a. Excessive dryness of skin with shedding of epithelium.
   b. Can indicate deficiency of thyroid function, diabetes.
6. Edema.
   a. Can indicate anemia, venous or lymphatic obstruction, inflammation; cardiac, circulatory, or renal decompensation.
   b. Determine activities and postures that aggravate or relieve edema.
   c. Palpation, volume, and girth measurements.
7. Changes in nails.
   a. Clubbing: thickened and rounded nail end with spongy proximal fold.
      (1) Indicative of Crohn's or cardiac/cyanosis, lung (cancer, chronic hypoxia), ulcerative colitis, biliary cirrhosis, neoplasm, GI involvement.
      (2) Present at birth (harmless).
      (3) Schamroth's window test is often positive (loss of diamond-shaped space when nails from opposite hands are placed back to back).
   b. White spots seen with trauma to nails.
   c. Splinter hemorrhages: small areas of bleeding under nails that look like splinters (potential cardiac or renal signs).
   d. Changes in nails (e.g., koilonychia, leukonychia) often indicate systemic issues unless it is congenital.
8. Changes in skin. Pigmentation, tissue mobility, skin turgor and texture.
   a. Wrinkling may be due to aging or prolonged immersion in water, dehydration.
   b. Blistering.
   c. Stemmer's sign. A thickened fold of skin at the base of the second toe or second finger that can be pinched or lifted; an early diagnostic indication of primary lymphedema.
9. Changes in skin color.
   a. Cherry red: palmar erythema could indicate liver or renal issues.

b. Cyanosis: slightly bluish, grayish, slate-colored discoloration.
  (1) Indicative of lack of oxygen (hemoglobin); can indicate congestive heart failure, advanced lung disease, congenital heart disease, venous obstruction.
  (2) Examine lips, oral mucosa, tongue for blue color (central causes) or nails, hands, feet (peripheral causes).

c. Pallor (lack of color, paleness).
  (1) Can indicate anemia, internal hemorrhage, lack of exposure to sunlight.
  (2) Temporary pallor seen with arterial insufficiency and syncope, chills, shock, vasomotor instability, or nervousness.

d. Yellow: indicates jaundice, liver disease; look for yellow color in sclera of eyes, lips, skin. Orange-yellow occurs with increased carotene intake (carotenemia), look for orange-yellow color of palms, soles, and face.

e. Liver spots: brownish yellow spots may be due to aging, uterine and liver malignancies, pregnancy.

f. Brown: increased pigmentation sometimes associated with venous insufficiency (i.e., hemosiderinosis).

10. Changes in skin temperature.
  a. Correlate with internal temperature, unless skin is exposed to local heat or cold.
  b. Examine with backs of fingers for generalized warmth or coolness.
    (1) Abnormal heat can indicate febrile condition, hyperthyroidism, mental excitement, excessive salt intake.
    (2) Abnormal cold can indicate poor circulation or obstruction; e.g., vasomotor spasm, venous or arterial thrombosis, hypothyroidism.
  c. Examine temperature of reddened areas: local warmth may indicate inflammation or cellulitis.

11. Hidrosis.
  a. Moist skin (hyperhidrosis), increased perspiration: can indicate fevers, pneumonic crisis, drugs, hot drinks, exercise.
  b. Dry skin (hypohidrosis): can indicate dehydration, ichthyosis, or hypothyroidism. Seen in later stages of diabetes mellitus.
  c. Cold sweats: can indicate great fear, anxiety, depression, or disease (AIDS).

12. Changes in hair.
  a. Examine quality, texture, distribution.
  b. Alopecia: hair loss.
  c. Hypothyroidism: thinning hair; hyperthyroidism sees silky hair.
  d. Hirsutism: male pattern hair growth (facial and body) in women; may indicate polycystic ovary syndrome, Cushing's, tumor, or an inherited trait.

13. Presence of lesions, unusual growths.
  a. Determine anatomical location and distribution; i.e., generalized or localized, exposed or non-exposed surface, symmetrical or asymmetrical.
  b. Type.
    (1) Flat spot: macule (small, up to 1 cm), patch (1 cm or greater).
    (2) Palpable elevated solid mass: papule (small, up to 1 cm), plaque (elevated, 1 cm or larger), nodule (marble-like lesion), wheal (irregular, localized skin edema; e.g., hives).
    (3) Elevated lesions with fluid cavities: vesicle (up to 1 cm, contains serous fluid; e.g., herpes simplex); bulla or blister (1 cm or larger, contains serous fluid; e.g., second-degree burn); pustule (contains pus; e.g., acne).
  c. Color.

Other Systems

1. Body composition.
  a. Height, weight.
  b. Body mass index; skinfold thickness.
2. Circulation (arterial, venous, lymphatic).
  a. Heart rate, rhythm, sounds.
  b. Blood pressures and flow.
  c. Superficial vascular responses.
3. Respiratory.
  a. Respiratory rate.
  b. Respiratory pattern.
4. Sensory.
  a. Superficial sensations: sharp/dull discrimination, temperature, light touch, pressure.
  b. Deep sensations: proprioception, kinesthesis.
  c. Pain and soreness.
5. Musculoskeletal.
  a. Gross range of motion (ROM) including muscle length.
  b. Gross strength.
6. Neuromuscular.
  a. Coordination.
  b. Gait, locomotion, balance.
7. Functional.
  a. Activities, positions, postures that produce or reduce trauma to skin.
  b. Safety during functional activities.
  c. Assistive, adaptive, protective, orthotic, or prosthetic devices that produce or reduce skin trauma.
  d. Likelihood of trauma to skin.

Physical Therapy Intervention for Impaired Integumentary Integrity

Interventions (see Table 5-3)

1. Patient/client-related instruction.
   a. Enhance disease awareness, healthy behaviors.
   b. Assist patient to avoid harsh soaps, known irritants, temperature extremes, exacerbating factors, or triggers.
   c. Enhance activities of daily living (ADLs), functional mobility, and safety.
   d. Enhance self-management of symptoms.
2. Infection control practices (see Box 6-1).
3. Therapeutic exercise, as indicated.
   a. Strengthening and ROM exercises.
   b. Aerobic conditioning.
   c. Body mechanics, postural awareness training.
   d. Gait, locomotion, and balance training.
4. Functional training.
   a. ADL training (basic and instrumental).
   b. Activity pacing and energy conservation; stress management.
   c. Skin and joint protection techniques.
   d. Instruction in safe use of assistive and adaptive devices.
5. Manual lymphatic drainage, therapeutic massage (see Chapter 3).
6. Dressings and topical agents (see Wound Care).

Table 5-3

Integumentary Practice Patterns	
PATTERN 7A	Primary Prevention/Risk Reduction for Integumentary Disorders
PATTERN 7B	Impaired Integumentary Integrity Associated with Superficial Skin Involvement
PATTERN 7C	Impaired Integumentary Integrity Associated with Partial-Thickness Skin Involvement and Scar Formation
PATTERN 7D	Impaired Integumentary Integrity Associated with Full-Thickness Skin Involvement and Scar Formation
PATTERN 7E	Impaired Integumentary Integrity Associated with Skin Involvement Extending into Fascia, Muscle, or Bone and Scar Formation

From Practice Patterns. American Physical Therapy Association, 2014. Note: On the APTA website each practice pattern includes:
- Inclusion criteria: risk factors or consequences of pathology/pathophysiology; impairments of body functions and structures, activity limitations, or participation restrictions
- Exclusion or Multiple-Pattern Classification
- Examination: relevant tests and measures
- Evaluation, Diagnosis, and Prognosis (including Plan of Care) factors
- Intervention categories

Burns

Pathophysiology

1. Burn injury. Results from thermal, chemical, electrical, or radioactive agents.
2. Burn wound, consists of three zones.
   a. Zone of coagulation: cells are irreversibly injured, cell death occurs.
   b. Zone of stasis: cells are injured; may die without specialized treatment, usually within 24–48 hours.
   c. Zone of hyperemia: minimal cell injury; cells should recover.
3. Degree of burn.
   a. Burns are classified by severity, layers of skin damaged (Table 5-4).
   b. Extent of burned area.
      (1) Rule of Nines for estimating burn area (estimates are for adult patients).
         - Head and neck: 9%.
         - Anterior trunk: 18%.
         - Posterior trunk: 18%.
         - Arms: 9% each.
         - Legs: 18% each.
         - Perineum: 1%.
      (2) Percentages vary by age (growth) for children: use Lund-Browder charts for estimating body areas.
   c. Classification by percentage of body area burned.
      (1) Critical: 10% of body with third-degree burns and 30% or more with second-degree burns; complications common (e.g., respiratory involvement, smoke inhalation).

Table 5-4

Burn Wound Classification

DEPTH OF BURN	CHARACTERISTICS	HEALING/SCARRING
Epidermal Burn (first degree)	Damage is to epidermis only Pink or red appearance; no blistering (dry surface) Minimal edema Tenderness, delayed pain	Spontaneous healing in 3–7 days No scarring
Superficial Partial-thickness Burn (second degree)	Epidermis and upper layers of dermis are damaged Bright pink or red appearance Blanching with brisk capillary refill Blisters, moist surface, weeping Moderate edema Painful, sensitive to touch, temperature changes	Spontaneous healing, typically in 7–21 days Minimal or no scarring; discoloration
Deep Partial-thickness Burn (second degree)	Severe damage to epidermis and dermis with injury to nerve endings, hair follicles, and sweat glands Mixed red or waxy white appearance Blanching with slow capillary refill Broken blisters, wet surface Marked edema Sensitive to pressure but insensitive to light touch or soft pin prick	Healing is slow and occurs through scar formation and reepithelialization Excessive scarring without preventive treatment
Full-thickness Burn (third degree)	Complete destruction of epidermis, dermis, and subcutaneous tissues; may extend into muscle White (ischemic), charred, tan, or black appearance No blanching; poor distal circulation Parchment-like, dry leathery surface; depressed area Little pain; nerve endings are destroyed	Removal of eschar and skin grafting are necessary due to destruction of dermal and epidermal tissue Risk of infection is increased Hypertrophic scarring and wound contracture are likely to develop without preventive measures
Subdermal Burn (fourth degree)	Complete destruction of epidermis, dermis, with involvement of subcutaneous tissues and muscle Charred appearance Destruction of vascular system, may lead to additional necrosis From electrical burns; prolonged contact with flame Additional complications likely with electrical burns: ventricular fibrillation, acute kidney damage, spinal cord damage	Heals with skin grafting and scarring Requires extensive surgery; amputation may be necessary

(2) Moderate: less than 10% with third-degree burns and 15%–30% with second-degree burns.

(3) Minor: less than 2% with third-degree burns and 15% with second-degree burns.

Complications of Burn Injury

1. Infection. Leading cause of death; gangrene may develop.
2. Shock.
3. Pulmonary complications.
   a. Smoke inhalation injury from inhalation of hot gases, smoke poisoning; results in pulmonary edema and airway obstruction; suspect with burns of the face, singed nose hairs.
   b. Restrictive lung disease from burns of the trunk.
   c. Pneumonia.
4. Metabolic complications. Increased metabolic and catabolic activity results in weight loss, negative nitrogen balance, and decreased energy.
5. Cardiac and circulatory complications. Fluid and plasma loss results in decreased cardiac output.
6. Integumentary scars (e.g., keloid management) and contractures.

Burn Healing

1. Epidermal healing. Retention of viable cells allows for epithelialization to occur (epithelial cells grow and proliferate, migrate to cover the wound).
   a. Protection of epithelial cells is critical.
   b. Loss of sebaceous glands can result in drying and cracking of wound; protection with moisturizing creams is important.
2. Dermal healing.
   a. Results in scar formation (injured tissue is replaced by connective tissue).
   b. Scars are initially red or purple, later become white.
3. Phases.
   a. Inflammatory phase: characterized by redness, edema, warmth, pain, decreased range of motion; lasts 3–5 days.
   b. Proliferative, granulation or fibroblastic phase (3 commonly used names).
      (1) Four primary events: angiogenesis, granulation formation, wound contraction, and epithelialization.

(2) Fibroblasts synthesize collagen, glycoaminoglycans, and elastin. Type III collagen is initially deposited and replaced later with Type I collagen and scar tissues.
(3) Myofibroblasts are responsible for wound contraction in dermal wounds.

c. Maturation phase: tissue remodeling lasts up to 2 years.
(1) Normal mature scar is soft, white, and flat (takes over a year to occur).
(2) At 6–12 weeks scar is immature (bright pink).
(3) Hypertrophic scar may result: a raised scar that stays within the boundaries of the burn wound and is characteristically red, raised, firm.
(4) Keloid scar may result: a raised scar that extends beyond the boundaries of the original burn wound and is red, raised, firm. More common in young women and those with dark skin.
(5) Hypotrophic scar: flat and depressed below the surrounding skin.

Burn Management

1. Emergency care.
   a. Immersion in cold water. If less than half the body is burned and injury is immediate; cold compresses may also be used.
   b. Cover burn with sterile bandage or clean cloth; no ointments or creams.
2. Medical management.
   a. Asepsis and wound care.
      (1) Removal of charred clothing.
      (2) Wound cleansing.
      (3) Topical medications (antibacterial agents): reapplied one to three times daily.
         (a) Ointments: Bacitracin, Polymyxin B, and Neomycin.
         (b) Silver sulfadiazine: common topical agent. Avoid at term pregnancy, on infants less than 2 months, and those with sulfa drug allergies.
         (c) Sulfamylon (mafenide acetate): penetrates through eschar. Avoid with sulfa drug allergies.
      (4) Dressings:
         (a) Prevents bacterial contamination, prevents fluid loss, and protects the wound.
         (b) May additionally limit ROM.
         (c) Dressings include: silver-impregnated, hydrogels, petroleum-impregnated, and gauze dressing.
   b. Establish and maintain airway, adequate oxygenation, and respiratory function.
   c. Monitor.
      (1) Arterial blood gases, serum electrolyte levels, urinary output, vital signs.
      (2) Gastrointestinal function: provide nutritional support.
   d. Pain relief; e.g., morphine sulfate.
   e. Prevention and control of infection.
      (1) Tetanus prophylaxis.
      (2) Antibiotics.
      (3) Standard Precautions (see Box 6-1).
   f. Fluid replacement therapy.
      (1) Prevention and control of shock.
      (2) Postshock fluid and blood replacement.
   g. Surgery.
      (1) Primary excision: escharotomies, fasciotomies may be required to prevent tourniquet effects. As the patient is stabilized, surgical removal of eschar begins.
      (2) Grafts: closure of the wound.
         (a) Allograft (homograft): use of other human skin; e.g., cadaver skin; temporary grafts for large burns, used until autograft is available.
         (b) Xenograft (heterograft): use of skin from other species; e.g., pigskin; a temporary graft.
         (c) Biosynthetic grafts: combination of collagen and synthetics.
         (d) Cultured skin: laboratory grown from patient's own skin.
         (e) Autograft: use of patient's own skin.
         (f) Split-thickness graft: contains epidermis and upper layers of dermis from donor site.
         (g) Full-thickness graft: contains epidermis and dermis from donor site.
      (3) Escharotomy and fasciotomy with circumferential burns of the extremities and compression due to increased tissue edema.
      (4) Surgical resection of scar contracture; e.g., Z-plasty (surgical incision in the form of the letter Z used to lengthen a burn scar).
3. Burn wound healing.
   a. Factors that affect healing include nutrition, infection, associated illnesses (e.g., diabetes, malignancy, vascular insufficiency), cytotoxic treatments.
   b. Significant burn injury more likely in very young or the elderly who have very thin skin.

Physical Therapy Goals, Outcomes, and Interventions

1. Burn wound cleansing and debridement.
   a. Use infection control techniques at all times.
   b. Maintain temperature of burn wound by warming cleansing solutions, maintaining ambient temperature, and avoiding lengthy exposure of wet wound surfaces.
   c. Cleansing with disinfectant soap and warm water.
      (1) Some wounds or dressings benefit from soaking, wet removal of dressings.
      (2) Excessive immersion is contraindicated. Risks include auto-contamination and electrolyte imbalance.

d. Wound debridement: removal of loose, charred, dead skin.
   (1) Autolytic dressings: use of moist dressings such as hydogels or hydrocolloids to help remove eschar.
   (2) Surgical or sharp debridement: excision of eschar using sterilized surgical instruments (forceps, scalpel, scissors).
   (3) Enzymatic: e.g., fibrinolysins.
   (4) Mechanical: wet to dry dressings, pulsed lavage, gentle washing.

2. Rehabilitation.
   a. Overall goals: limit loss of ROM, reduce edema, prevent predictable contractures through positioning and splinting, and prevent or reduce complications of immobilization.
   b. Typically includes twice-daily therapy sessions timed with planned pain medication.
   c. Exercises to promote deep breathing and chest expansion.
   d. Anti-contracture positioning and splinting: starts from day one and continues for many months.
      (1) Anterior neck: common deformity is flexion; stress hyperextension; position with firm (plastic) cervical orthosis.
      (2) Shoulder: common deformity is adduction and internal rotation; stress abduction, flexion, and external rotation; position with an axillary splint (airplane splint).
      (3) Elbow: common deformity is flexion and pronation; stress extension and supination; position in extension with posterior arm splint.
      (4) Hand: common deformity is a claw hand (intrinsic minus position); stress wrist extension (15°), MP flexion (70°), PIP, and DIP extension, thumb abduction (intrinsic plus position); position in intrinsic plus position with resting hand splint.
      (5) Hip: common deformity is flexion and adduction; stress hip extension and abduction; position in extension, abduction, neutral rotation.
      (6) Knee: common deformity is flexion; stress extension; position in extension with posterior knee splint.
      (7) Ankle: common deformity is plantar flexion; stress dorsiflexion; position with foot-ankle in neutral with splint or plastic ankle-foot orthosis.
   e. Edema control: elevation of extremities, active ROM.
   f. Stretching and early mobilization, taking all joints through full passive ROM.
      (1) Schedule therapy to coincide with optimal pain medication (30-45 minutes before session), and dressing changes/wound cleansing.
      (2) Postgrafting: discontinue exercise for 3–5 days to allow grafts to heal.

3. Rehabilitation (post-acute).
   a. Continued passive ROM, increasing active ROM.
   b. Progressive strengthening to correct loss of muscle mass and strength.
   c. Minimize edema. Elastic supports to control edema.
   d. Scar management.
      (1) Massage and application of moisturizer.
      (2) Regular massage and touching of scars to desensitize hypersensitive scars.
      (3) Pressure garments to help prevent hypertrophic scarring or keloid formation.
   e. Progressive ambulation to improve cardiovascular endurance and activity tolerance.
   f. Training in activities of daily living (ADL) and functional mobility skills.
   g. Preparation for home, work, play, or school.
   h. Management of chronic pain.
   i. Provide education and emotional support.

Skin Ulcers

Venous Ulcer

1. Etiology. Associated with chronic venous insufficiency; valvular incompetence, history of deep venous thrombosis (DVT), venous hypertension, calf muscle pump failure. Recurrence is high. Arterial insufficiency may coexist.
2. Clinical features.
   a. Can occur anywhere in lower leg; common over area of medial malleolus, sometimes lateral.
   b. Pulses: normal.
   c. Pain: none to aching pain in dependent position.
   d. Color: normal or cyanotic in dependent position. Dark pigmentation (hemosiderosis) may appear, liposclerosis (thick, tender, indurated, fibrosed tissue).
   e. Temperature: normal.
   f. Edema: present, often marked.
   g. Skin changes: pigmentation, stasis dermatitis may be present; thickening of skin as scarring develops.
   h. Ulceration: may develop, especially medial ankle; wet, with large amount of exudate.
   i. Gangrene: absent.
3. Staging for venous, arterial, and diabetic ulcers. Uses partial- and full-thickness classifications.

Table 5-5

Differential Diagnosis: Arterial versus Venous Ulcers		
	ARTERIAL	VENOUS
Etiology	Arteriosclerosis obliterans Atheroembolism	Valvular incompetance Venous hypertension
Appearance	Irregular, smooth edges Minimum to no granulation Usually deep	Irregular: dark pigmentation, sometimes fibrotic Good granulation Usually shallow
Location	Distal lower leg: toes, feet Lat. malleolus Ant. tibial area	Distal lower leg Med. malleolus
Pedal Pulses	Decreased or absent	Usually present
Pain	Painful, especially if legs elevated	Little pain, comfortable with legs elevated
Drainage	Not present	Moderate to large amounts of exudate
Associated Gangrene	May be present	Absent
Associated Signs	Trophic changes Pallor on foot elevation Dusky rubor on dependency	Edema Stasis dermatitis Possible cyanosis on dependency

4. Venous and arterial differential diagnosis chart (see Table 5-5).
5. Examination: DVT assessment (e.g., venogram [gold standard], ultrasonography, score of 3 or higher on clinical assessment guideline for DVT, cuff test and Homan's sign have low sensitivity and/or specificity), ABI, and venous filling time.
6. Interventions: see wound care, compression (contraindicated with ABI less than 0.7 or active DVT), exercise, patient education to prevent trauma and swelling. A compression wrap that remains in place during the day and preferable also at night is optimal.

Arterial Ulcer

1. Etiology. Associated with chronic arterial insufficiency; arteriosclerosis obliterans; atheroembolism; history of minor nonhealing trauma.
2. Clinical features.
   a. Can occur anywhere in lower leg; common on small toes, feet, bony areas of trauma (shin).
   b. Preceded by signs and symptoms of arterial insufficiency; pulses poor or absent, intermittent claudication.
   c. Pain: often severe, intermittent, progressing to pain at rest, exacerbated with limb elevation.
   d. Color: pale on elevation; dusky rubor on dependency.
   e. Temperature: cool.
   f. Skin changes: trophic changes (thin, shiny, atrophic skin); loss of hair on foot and toes; nails thickened.
   g. Ulceration: of toes or feet; can be deep.
   h. Gangrene: black, gangrenous skin adjacent to ulcer can develop.
3. Examination: pulses, temperature, ABI, segmental blood pressure measurements (greater than 20 mm Hg drop between segments is significant), capillary refill, $TcPO_2$, outcome measure (e.g., walking impairment questionnaire).
4. Interventions: see wound care, promote blood flow (medications, surgery, elevate head of bed to promote), exercise, patient education to prevent further trauma.

Diabetic Ulcer

1. Etiology.
   a. Diabetes is associated with arterial disease and peripheral neuropathy.
   b. Caused by repetitive trauma on insensitive skin.
2. Clinical features.
   a. Occurs where arterial ulcers usually appear; or where peripheral neuropathy appears (plantar aspect of foot).
   b. Pain: typically not painful; sensory loss usually present.
   c. Pulses: may be present or diminished.
   d. Absent ankle jerks with neuropathy.
   e. Sepsis common; gangrene may develop.
3. Examination: circulation, sensory integrity (e.g., monofilament testing), pain, integumentary.
4. Classification: use the Wagner Classification System and partial- and full-thickness scheme for diabetic foot ulcer classification.
5. Interventions: see wound care, off-loading neuropathic ulcer (e.g., total contact casting, removable walking boot), foot care guidelines, and exercise.

Pressure Ulcer (Decubitus Ulcer)

1. Etiology.
   a. Lesions caused by unrelieved pressure resulting in ischemic hypoxia and damage to underlying tissue.
2. Risk factors.
   a. Prolonged pressure, shear forces, friction, repetitive stress.
   b. Nutritional deficiency.
   c. Maceration (softening associated with excessive moisture).
   d. Common in:
      (1) Elderly, debilitated, or immobilized individuals.
      (2) Decrease blood flow from hypotension or microvascular disease: diabetes, atherosclerosis.
      (3) Neurologically impaired skin: decreased sensation.
      (4) Cognitive impairment.
3. Clinical features.
   a. Location: occurs over bony prominences; i.e., sacrum, heels, trochanter, lateral malleoli, ischial areas, elbows.
   b. Color: red, brown/black, or yellow.
   c. Localized infection.
   d. Pain: can be painful if sensation intact.
   e. Inflammatory response with necrotic tissue: hyperemia, fever, increased white blood cell count (WBC).
   f. If left untreated, will progress from superficial simple erosion to involvement of deep layers of skin and underlying muscle and bone.
4. Graded by stages of severity (tissue damage) (see Table 5-6 and Figure 5-2).
5. Examination: use a standardized pressure ulcer assessment instrument (e.g., Bates-Jensen wound assessment tool, pressure ulcer scale for healing, etc.), circulation, sensory integrity, pain, and integumentary. Risk assessment (e.g., Gosnell, Braden, or Norton) for pressure ulcers are done for those without pressure ulcers to examine risk.
6. Interventions: see wound care, patient education, and physical interventions include skin hygiene, incontinence management, seating, pressure relief, positioning, nutrition, exercise, and precautions.

Table 5-6

Staging of Pressure Ulcers

STAGE	CHARACTERISTICS
Stage I	Nonblanchable erythema of intact skin. May include changes in skin temperature (warm or cool), tissue consistency (firm or boggy), and/or sensation (pain, itching).
Stage II	Partial-thickness skin loss: involves epidermis, dermis, or both. Ulcer is superficial. Presents clinically as an abrasion, blister, or shallow crater.
Stage III	Full-thickness skin loss: involves damage to or necrosis of subcutaneous tissue. May extend down to, but not through, underlying fascia. Presents clinically as a deep crater.
Stage IV	Full-thickness skin loss: involves extensive destruction, tissue necrosis, or damage to muscle, bone, or supporting structures. Undermining and sinus tracts may be present.
Unstageable	Tissue depth is obscured due to slough or eschar and extent of damage cannot be determined.
Deep Tissue Injury	Discolored area of tissue (e.g., bruise) that is not reversible and will likely progress to a full-thickness injury.

Adapted from Consortium for Spinal Cord Medicine: Pressure Ulcer Prevention and Treatment Following Spinal Cord Injury, Paralyzed Veterans of America, August 2000; The National Pressure Ulcer Advisory Panel 2007 update to pressure ulcer stages and categories, www.npuap.org.

Examination of Wounds

1. Complete history, risk factor assessment.
2. Physical examination.
   a. Determine location of wound: use anatomical landmarks.
   b. Assess size: (length, width, depth, wound area).
      (1) Use clear film grid superimposed on wound for size.
      (2) Insert sterile cotton tip applicator into deepest part of wound for depth; indicate gradations of depth from shallow to deep.
   c. Examine for tunneling (rimming or undermining): underlying tissue destruction beneath intact skin.
      (1) Evaluate for sinus tracts (communication with deeper structures); associated with unusual or irregular borders.

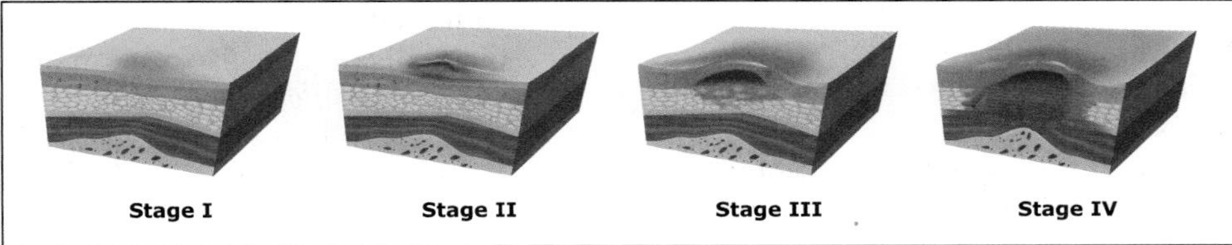

Figure 5-2 **Stages of Pressure Ulcers.**

d. Determine wound exudate (drainage).
   (1) Type: serous (watery serum), purulent (containing pus), sanguineous (containing blood).
   (2) Amount: dry, moderate, or high exudate.
   (3) Odor.
   (4) Consistency: e.g., macerated ulcer (softened tissues due to high fluid environment).
e. Identify color and tissues involved.
   (1) Clean red wounds: healthy granulating wounds (in need of protection); absence of necrotic tissue.
   (2) Yellow wounds: include slough (necrotic or dead tissue), fibrous tissue.
   (3) Black wounds: covered with eschar (dried necrotic tissue).
   (4) Indolent ulcer: ulcer that is slow to heal; is not painful.
   (5) Check to see if fascia, muscle, tendons, or bone involved.
   (6) Record if epithelialization or granulation is present.
f. Determine temperature: indicative of inflammation. Use temperature probe (thermistor) to detect surface temperature.
g. Determine girth.
   (1) Use circumferential measurements of both involved and noninvolved limbs; referenced to bony landmarks.
   (2) Use volumetric measurements: measure water displacement from filled volumeter. Reliable and valid for girth (edema) measurements, but unreliable for wound volume measurements.
h. Examine viability of periwound tissue.
   (1) Halo of erythema, warmth, and swelling may indicate infection (cellulitis).
   (2) Maceration of surrounding tissues due to moisture (urine, feces) or wound drainage increases risk for wound deterioration and enlargement.
   (3) Trophic changes may indicate poor arterial nutrition.
   (4) Cyanosis may indicate arterial insufficiency.
i. Determine sensory integrity, risk for trauma or pressure breakdown.
j. Examine for signs of infection.
   (1) Bacterial culture: to identify colonization and infection; culture wound site only.
   (2) Observations, palpation.
k. Wound scar tissue characteristics: banding, pliability, texture.
l. Photographic records of wound appearance aid narrative descriptions. Use marker pen to outline wound edges on transparent dressing with a calibrated grid to provide a measuring scale.
m. Pain: use a valid tool.
n. Selected imaging in wound care: arterial system; arteriogram, Doppler US, magnetic resonance angiography, CT angiography. Venous system: Doppler US, magnetic resonance venography, CT venography.

Wound Care

1. Infection control.
   a. Wounds are cultured; antibiotic treatment regimen prescribed.
      (1) Topical antimicrobial agents: e.g., silver nitrate, silver sulfadiazine, erythromycin, gentamicin, neomycin, triple antibiotic.
      (2) Anti-inflammatory agents: e.g., corticosteroids, hydrocortisone, ibuprofen, indomethacin.
      (3) Topical anesthetics and analgesics: e.g., lidocaine, lignocaine.
   b. Hand washing of health care practitioners.
   c. Sterile technique is most appropriate in acute care hospitals and with invasive procedures while clean technique is most appropriate for home care, long-term care facilities, outpatient, and routine procedures.
   d. Negative-pressure wound therapy (vacuum-assisted closure).
      (1) An open-cell foam dressing placed into the wound.
      (2) Controlled subatmospheric pressure (typically 125 mm Hg below ambient pressure) is applied via specialized device.
      (3) Helps to maintain a moist wound environment, control edema, increases localized blood flow, and reduces infectious material.
2. Surgical intervention.
   a. Indicated for excising of ulcer, enhancing vascularity and resurfacing wound (grafts), and preventing sepsis and osteomyelitis.
   b. May be indicated for stage III and IV ulcers.
3. Hyperbaric oxygen therapy (HBO).
   a. Patient breathes 100% oxygen in a sealed, full-body chamber with elevated atmospheric pressure (between 2.0 and 2.5 atmospheres absolute, ATA).
   b. Hyperoxygenation reverses tissue hypoxia and facilitates wound healing due to enhanced solubility of oxygen in the blood.
   c. Contraindicated in untreated pneumothorax and some antineoplastic medications (e.g., doxorubicin, disulfiram, cisplatin, mafenide acetate).
4. Wound cleansing.
   a. Removal of loose cellular debris, metabolic wastes, bacteria, and topical agents that retard wound healing.
   b. Cleanse wounds initially and at each dressing change.

c. Normal saline (0.9% NaCl) recommended for most ulcers; nontoxic effects in wound.
d. Cleansing topical agents: contain surfactants that lower surface tension. Limited use, may be toxic to healing tissues; e.g., povidone-iodine solution, sodium hypochlorite solution, Dakin's solution, acetic acid solution, hydrogen peroxide.
e. Mechanical delivery systems.
   (1) Minimal mechanical force: cleansing with gauze, cloth, or sponge.
   (2) Irrigation: recommend pressures range from 4–15 psi.
      (a) Squeeze bottle, bulb syringe, or piston syringe.
      (b) Pulsed lavage: delivery of irrigating solution under pressure that is produced by an electrically powered device. Pulsed lavage with vacuum (PLWV) assists in removal of wound debris.
   (3) Whirlpool therapy (WP) is not supported for wound care. Adverse events with WP can include contamination and infection associated with pathogens found in WP equipment, higher and unregulated pressures can damage granulation tissue, and limbs placed in a dependent position experience increased venous hypertension and vascular congestion. PLWV is a more effective treatment alternative.
f. Do not use harsh soaps, alcohol-based products, or harsh antiseptic agents; may erode skin.

5. Wound debridement.
   a. Removal of necrotic or infected tissue that interferes with wound healing. (See Table 5-7.)
   b. Allows examination of ulcer, determination of extent of wound.
   c. Decreases bacterial concentration in wound; improves wound healing.
   d. Decreases spread of infection; i.e., cellulitis or sepsis.
6. Wound dressings.
   a. Topical agents: used to manage nonhealing or infected wounds. Includes: wound cleanser and antiseptics (e.g., acetic acid, Dakin's solution, providone-iodine), antimicrobials (e.g., antifungals [nystatin] and antibacterials [Bacitracin, Neosporin, Polymyxin B]), anesthesia and analgesia agents (e.g., topical lidocaine), and enzymatic debridement (e.g., Santyl).
   b. Ideal wound dressings maintain a moist environment and controls excessive exudate, facilitate gaseous exchange (oxygen, carbon dioxide, water), insulates, prevents contamination from microorganisms, and non-traumatic to the wound. A moist wound environment facilitates autolytic debridement and promotes faster wound healing with less pain. (See Table 5-8.)
      (1) Alginate dressings: e.g., Sorbsan, Kaltostat.
      (2) Transparent film dressings: e.g., Bioclusive, OpSite, Tegaderm.
      (3) Foam dressings: e.g., LYOfoam, Flexzan.
      (4) Hydrogel dressings: e.g., Carrasyn gel, Vigilon, Second Skin, Clearsite.
      (5) Hydrocolloid dressings: e.g., DuoDerm, Curaderm, 3M Tegasorb.
      (6) Gauze dressings.
         a. Standard gauze (not impregnated): e.g., Kerlix, 4 × 4s, Nugauze, Telfa.
         b. Impregnated gauze: silver-, iodine-, or Vaseline (petroleum)-impregnated gauze. e.g., Adaptic, Xeroform.
      (7) Silver dressings: common antimicrobial agent found in foams, films, alginates, hydrocolloids, hydrogels, and other types of dressings.
      (8) Specialty dressings: Wound matrix dressings: provide a scaffolding for cellular deposit. Typically, collagen or hyluronan based dressings (e.g., Prisma); skin substitutes: epidermal, dermal, or both. e.g., Epicel, Dermagraft, Apligraf. Most are expensive and used when standard wound care has failed.
7. Edema management.
   a. Leg elevation and exercise (ankle pumps).
   b. Compression therapy: to facilitate movement of excess fluid from lower extremity.
      (1) Compression wraps: elastic or tubular bandages.
      (2) Paste bandages; e.g., Unna boot is a pliable, nonstretchable dressing impregnated with zinc or calamine and gelatin.
      (3) Compression stockings; e.g., Jobst.
      (4) Compression pump therapy.
8. Electrical stimulation for wound healing (see Chapter 10).
   a. Used to improve circulation, facilitate debridement, and enhance tissue repair.
   b. Continuous waveform application with direct current.
   c. High-voltage pulsed current.
   d. Pulsed biphasic current.
9. Nutritional considerations.
   a. Delayed wound healing associated with malnutrition and poor hydration.
      (1) Albumin: normal is 3.5–5.5 mg/dl; less than 3.5 = malnutrition.
      (2) BMI ≤ 21 with weight loss increased risk for pressure ulcer.
   b. Provide adequate hydration.
      (1) Individuals with wounds require approximately 3 or more liters of water a day.
      (2) Patients on air-fluidized beds require greater hydration (40–60 ml/Kg a day).
   c. Provide adequate nutrition: frequent high-calorie/high-protein meals; energy intake (25–35 kcal/kg/body weight) and protein (1.5–2.5 gm/kg body weight).
   d. Patients with trauma stress and burns require higher intakes.

Table 5-7

Methods of Debridement

METHOD	DEFINITION	INDICATIONS	CONTRAINDICATIONS
Autolytic	A selective method of natural debridement promoted under occlusive or semiocclusive moisture-retentive dressings that results in solubilization of necrotic tissue only by phagocytic cells and by proteolytic and collagenolytic enzymes inherent in the tissues.	• Individuals on anticoagulant therapy • Individuals who cannot tolerate other forms of debridement • All necrotic wounds in people who are medically stable	• Infected wounds • Wounds of immunosuppressed individuals • Dry gangrene or dry ischemic wounds
Enzymatic	A selective method of chemical debridement that promotes liquefication of necrotic tissue by applying topical preparation of collagenolytic enzymes to those tissues.	• All moist necrotic wounds • Eschar after cross-hatching • Homebound individuals • People who cannot tolerate surgical debridement	• Ischemic wounds unless adequate vascular status has been determined • Dry gangrene • Clean, granulated wounds
Mechanical	A nonselective method of debridement that removes foreign material and devitalized or contaminated tissue by physical forces (wet-to-dry gauze dressing, dextranomers, pulsatile lavage with suction), and may remove healthy tissue as well.	• Wounds with moist necrotic tissue or foreign material present	• Clean, granulated wounds
Sharp	A selective method of debridement using sterile instruments (scalpel, scissors, forceps, silver nitrate stick) that sequentially removes only necrotic wound tissue without anesthesia and with little or no bleeding induced in viable tissue.	• Scoring and/or excision of leathery eschar • Excision of moist necrotic tissue	• Clean wounds • Advancing cellulitis with sepsis • When infection threatens the individual's life • Individual on anticoagulant therapy or has coagulopathy
Surgical	For deep (stage III or IV) or complicated pressure ulcer, the most efficient method of debridement. It is selective and is performed by a physician or surgeon using sterile instruments (scalpel, scissors, forceps, hemostat, silver nitrate sticks) in a one-time operative procedure. The procedure usually removes most, if not all, necrotic tissue, but may also remove some healthy tissue in what is termed wide excision. Because there may be associated pain and/or bleeding, the individual may require anesthesia, and the procedure will likely require an operating or special procedures room.	• Advancing cellulitus with sepsis • Immunocompromised individuals • When infection threatens the individual's life • Clean wounds as a preliminary procedure to surgical wound closure line • Granulation and scar tissue may be excised	• Cardiac disease, pulmonary disease, or diabetes • Severe spasticity • Individuals who cannot tolerate surgery • Individuals with a short life expectancy • Quality of life cannot be improved
Kilohertz Ultrasound (e.g., MIST, Sonoca 180, Misonix devices)	This long-wave low frequency ultrasound typically operates between 20 and 50 kHz. This is a selective form of debridement. Autoclaving of contact probe is usually required (not all devices make direct contact with wound).	• Selective removal of necrotic tissue desired • Reduces bioburden • Increase angiogenesis • Wound bed preparation for grafting or flap closure	• Contraindications include: Vascular abnormalities (DVT, emboli, advanced PVD), irradiated areas, tumors, organs, or electrical devices. • Precautions over nerves, infections, anesthetic areas.
Biological (rarely used)	The use of maggots to debride nonviable tissue. They produce enzymes and phagocytize necrotic tissue and bacteria (e.g., MRSA, group A and B *streptococcus, Psuedomonas*). They may stimulate granulation formation and epithelialization.	• Individuals who cannot tolerate other forms of debridement • All non-healing necrotic wounds in people who are medically stable	• Psychological stress arises from having living creatures in wounds. • Reports of pain increasing.

Adapted from Consortium for Spinal Cord Medicine: Pressure Ulcer Prevention and Treatment Following Spinal Cord Injury, Paralyzed Veterans of America, August 2000.

Table 5-8

Characteristics of Some Major Dressing Categories

DRESSING CATEGORY AND DEFINITION	INDICATIONS	ADVANTAGES
Transparent Films Clear, adhesive, semipermeable membrane dressings. Permeable to atmospheric oxygen and moisture vapor yet impermeable to water, bacteria, and environmental contaminants.	• Stage I and II pressure ulcers • Secondary dressing in certain situations • For autolytic debridement • Skin donor sites • Cover for hydrophilic powder and paste preparations and hydrogels	• Visual evaluation of wound without removal • Impermeable to external fluids and bacteria • Transparent and comfortable • Promote autolytic debridement • Minimize friction
Hydrocolloids Adhesive wafers containing hydroactive/absorptive particles that interact with wound fluid to form a gelatinous mass over the wound bed. May be either occlusive or semi-occlusive. Available in paste form that can be used as a filler for shallow cavity wounds.	• Protection of partial-thickness wounds • Autolytic debridement of necrosis or slough • Wounds with mild exudate	• Maintain a moist wound environment • Nonadhesive to healing tissue • Conformable • Impermeable to external bacteria and contaminants • Support autolytic debridement • Minimal to moderate absorption • Waterproof • Reduce pain • Easy to apply • Time-saving • Thin forms diminish friction
Hydrogels Water- or glycerine-based gels. Insoluble in water. Available in solid sheets, amorphous gels, or impregnated gauze. Absorptive capacity varies.	• Partial- and full-thickness wounds • Wounds with necrosis and slough • Burns and tissue damaged by radiation	• Soothing and cooling • Fill dead space • Rehydrate dry wound beds • Promote autolytic debridement • Provide minimal to moderate absorption • Conform to wound bed • Transparent to translucent • Many are nonadherent • Amorphous form can be used when infection is present
Foams Semipermeable membranes that are either hydrophilic or hydrophobic. Vary in thickness, absorptive capacity, and adhesive properties.	• Partial- and full-thickness wounds with minimal to moderate exudate • Secondary dressing for wounds with packing to provide additional absorption • Provide protection and insulation	• Insulate wounds • Provide some padding • Most are nonadherent • Conformable • Manage minimal to heavy exudate • Easy to use • Some newer products are designed for deep cavities
Alginates Soft, absorbent, nonwoven dressings derived from seaweed that have a fluffy cottonlike appearance. React with wound exudate to form a viscous hydrophilic gel mass over the wound area. Available in ropes and pads.	• Wounds with moderate to large amounts of exudate • Wounds with combination exudate and necrosis • Wounds that require packing and absorption • Infected and noninfected exuding wounds	• Absorb up to 20 times their weight in drainage • Fill dead space • Support debridement in presence of exudate • Easy to apply
Gauze Dressings Made of cotton or synthetic fabric that is absorptive and permeable to water and oxygen. May be used wet, moist, dry, or impregnated with petrolatum, antiseptics, or other agents. Come in varying weaves and with different size interstices.	• Exudative wounds • Wounds with dead space, tunneling, or sinus tracts • Wounds with combination exudate or necrotic tissue WET TO DRY • Mechanical debridement of necrotic tissue and slough CONTINUOUS DRY • Heavily exudating wounds CONTINUOUS MOIST • Protection of clean wounds • Autolytic debridement of slough or eschar • Delivery of topical needs	• Readily available • Can be used with appropriate solutions such as gels, normal saline, or topical antimicrobials to keep wounds moist • Can be used on infected wounds • Good mechanical debridement if properly used • Cost-effective filler for large wounds • Effective delivery of topicals if kept moist

(*Continued*)

Table 5-8

Characteristics of Some Major Dressing Categories (*Continued*)

DISADVANTAGES	CONSIDERATIONS
Transparent Films • Nonabsorptive • Application can be difficult • Channeling or wrinkling occurs • Not to be used on wounds with fragile surrounding skin or infected wounds	• Allow 1- to 2-inch wound margin around bed • Shave surrounding hair • Secondary dressing not required • Dressing change varies with wound condition and location • Avoid in wounds with infection, copious drainage, or tracts
Hydrocolloids • Nontransparent • May soften and change shape with heat or friction • Odor and yellow drainage on removal (melted dressing material) • Not recommended for wounds with heavy exudate, sinus tracts, or infections; wounds that expose bone or tendon; or wounds with fragile surrounding skin • Dressing edges may curl	• Characteristic odor with yellow exudate similar to pus; normal when dressing is removed • Allow 1- to 1½-inch margin of healthy tissue around wound edges • Taping edges will help prevent curling • Frequency of changes depends on amount of exudate • Change every 3–7 days and as needed with leakage • Avoid in wounds with infection or tracts
Hydrogels • Most require a secondary dressing • Not used for heavily exudating wounds • May dry out and then adhere to wound bed • May macerate surrounding skin	• Sheet form works well on partial-thickness ulcers • Do not use sheet form on infected ulcers • Sheet form can promote growth of *Pseudomonas* and yeast • Dressing changes every 8–48 hours • Use skin barrier wipe on surrounding intact skin to decrease risk of maceration
Foams • Nontransparent • Nonadherent foams require secondary dressing, tape, or net to hold in place • Some newer foams have tape on edges • Poor conformability to deep wounds • Not for use with dry eschar or wounds with no exudate	• Change schedule varies from 1–5 days or as needed for leakage • Protect intact surrounding skin with skin sealant to prevent maceration
Alginates • Require secondary dressing • Not recommended for dry or lightly exudating wounds • Can dry wound bed	• May use dry gauze pad or transparent film as secondary dressing • Change schedule varies (with type of product used and amount of exudate) from every 8 hours to every 2–3 days
Gauze Dressings • Delayed healing if used improperly • Pain on removal (wet to dry) • Labor-intensive • Require secondary dressing • Avoid direct contact with granulating tissue	• Change schedule varies with amount of exudate • Pack loosely into wounds; tight packing compromises blood flow and delays wound closure • Use continuous roll of gauze for packing large wounds (ensures complete removal) • If too wet, dressings will macerate surrounding skin • Use wide mesh gauze for debridement and fine mesh gauze for protection • Protect surrounding skin with moisture barrier ointment or skin sealant as needed

Adapted from Consortium for Spinal Cord Medicine: Pressure Ulcer Prevention and Treatment Following Spinal Cord Injury, Paralyzed Veterans of America, August 2000.

10. Injury prevention or reduction.
    a. Daily, comprehensive skin inspection, paying particular attention to bony prominences (e.g., sacrum, coccyx, trochanter, ischial tuberosities, medial or lateral malleolus).
    b. Therapeutic positioning to relieve pressure and allow tissue reperfusion.
        (1) In bed: turning or repositioning every 2 hours during acute and rehabilitation phases.
        (2) In wheelchair: wheelchair push-ups every 15 minutes.
    c. Use techniques to ensure skin protection, avoid friction, shear, or abrasion injury.
        (1) Lifting, not dragging.
        (2) Use of turning and draw sheets; trapeze, manual, or electric lifts.
        (3) Use of cornstarch, lubricants, pad protectors, thin film dressings, or hydrocolloid dressings over friction risk sites.
        (4) Use of transfer boards for sliding wheelchair transfers.

d. Pressure-relieving devices (PRDs).
   (1) Reduce tissue interface pressures.
   (2) Static devices: use if patient can assume a variety of positions; examples include foam, air, or gel mattress overlays; water-filled mattresses; pillows or foam wedges, protective padding (heel relief boots).
   (3) Dynamic devices: use if patient cannot assume a variety of positions; examples include alternating pressure air mattresses, fluidized air or high-air-loss bed.
   (4) Seating supports: use for chair-bound or wheelchair-bound patients; examples include cushions made out of foam, gel, air, or some combination.

e. Avoid restrictive clothing, e.g., with rough textures, hard fasteners, and studs. Avoid tight-fitting shoes, socks, splints, and orthoses.

f. Avoid maceration injury.
   (1) Prevent moisture accumulation and temperature elevation where skin contacts support surface.
   (2) Incontinence management strategies: use of absorbent pads, brief, or panty pad; scheduled toileting and prompted voiding; ointments, creams, and skin barriers prophylactically in perineal and perianal areas.

g. Patient and caregiver education.
   (1) Mechanisms of pressure ulcer development.
   (2) Daily skin inspection and hygiene.
   (3) Avoidance of prolonged positions.
   (4) Repositioning, weight shifts, lifts.
   (5) Safety awareness during self-care.
   (6) Safety awareness with use of devices and equipment.
   (7) Importance of ongoing activity/exercise program.

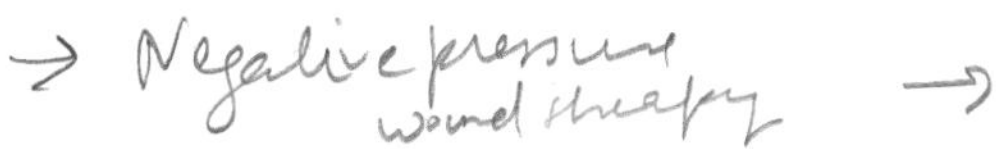

APPENDIX 5A

Selected Wound Related Assessment and Outcome Measures

Table 5A-1

MEASUREMENT TOOLS	TARGET POPULATION AND INTENDED USE	REFERENCES
Pressure Ulcer Scale for Healing	Primarily used to assess and monitor the healing of pressure ulcers. Valid to use for monitoring the healing of venous leg ulcers and diabetic foot ulcers.	Thomas DR, Rodeheaver GT, Bartolucci AA, et al. Pressure ulcer scale for healing: derivation and validation of the PUSH tool. The PUSH Task Force. *Adv Wound Care.* 1997; 10(5): 95–101.
Bates-Jensen Wound Assessment Tool (formerly, the Pressure Sore Status Tool)	Designed to assess and monitor healing rates in pressure ulcers and various other chronic wounds.	Harris C, Bates-Jensen B, Parslow N, Raizman R, Singh M, Ketchen R. Bates-Jensen wound assessment tool: pictorial guide validation project. *JWOCN.* 2010; 37(3): 253–259.
Pressure Sore Status Tool	Developed as both a research and clinical tool to assess and monitor tissue changes in pressure ulcers. In 2001, this tool was modified and formally renamed as the Bates-Jensen Wound Assessment Tool (see above).	Bates-Jensen BM, Vredevoe DL, Brecht ML. Validity and reliability of the Pressure Sore Status Tool. *Decubitus.* 1992; 5(6): 20–28.
Sussman Wound Healing Tool	Monitors tissue status, wound size, and phases of wound healing. Can be used with various wounds, but was primarily developed to monitor healing of pressure ulcers.	Sussman C, Swanson G. Utility of the Sussman Wound Healing Tool in predicting wound healing outcomes in physical therapy. *Adv Wound Care.* 1997; 10(5): 74–77.
Spinal Cord Impairment Pressure Ulcer Monitoring Tool	Used to monitor pressure ulcer healing in people with spinal cord injuries.	Thomason SS, Luther S, Nelson A, Palacios P, Harrow J. Pressure Ulcer Healing in SCI: A Novel Evidence-Based Tool: 2435. *JWOCN.* 2008; 35(3):S70.

Table 5A-1 (*Continued*)

MEASUREMENT TOOLS	TARGET POPULATION AND INTENDED USE	REFERENCES
Photographic Wound Assessment Tool	This tool was designed to examine the photograph of various wounds versus the actual wound. It is intended to be used when the expert clinician cannot be present to physically examine the wound (e.g., rural areas, home health, telemedicine).	Thompson N, Gordey L, Bowles H, Parslow N, Houghton P. Reliability and Validity of the Revised Photographic Wound Assessment Tool on Digital Images Taken of Various Types of Chronic Wounds. *Adv Skin Wound Care.* 2013; 26(8): 360–373.
The Wound Bed Score	Used to monitor wound bed preparation prior to the application of advance technologies. Does not monitor healing rates.	Falanga V, Saap LJ, Ozonoff A. Wound bed score and its correlation with healing of chronic wounds. *Dermatol Ther.* 2006; 19(6): 383–390.
Wagner Classification System	Designed to assess the depth and tissue involvement of diabetic foot ulcers.	Oyibo SO, Jude EB, Tarawneh I, Nguyen HC, Harkless LB, Boulton AJ. A comparison of two diabetic foot ulcer classification systems: the Wagner and the University of Texas wound classification systems. *Diabetes Care.* 2001; 24(1): 84–88.
University of Texas Wound Classification System	Designed to assess the depth and tissue involvement of diabetic foot ulcers. This scheme goes further than the Wagner Classification System by incorporating the presence or absence of infection and ischemia.	Armstrong DG, Lavery LA, Harkless LB. Validation of a diabetic wound classification system. The contribution of depth, infection, and ischemia to risk of amputation. *Diabetes Care.* 1998; 21(5): 855–859.
Braden	6-item pressure sore risk assessment scale (score range 6–23; 18 and lower scores indicate progressive risk).	Braden BJ, Bergstrom N. Clinical utility of the Braden scale for Predicting Pressure Sore Risk. *Decubitus.* 1989; 2(3): 44–46, 50–51.
Braden Q Scale (pediatric population)	Pressure sore risk assessment scale for the pediatric population (score range 7–28; 16 and lower scores indicate progressive risk).	Curley MA, Razmus IS, Roberts KE, Wypij D. Predicting pressure ulcer risk in pediatric patients: the Braden Q Scale. *Nursing Research.* 2003; 52(1): 22–33.
Norton	5-item pressure sore risk assessment scale (score range 5–20; 16 or lower indicate progressive risk).	Norton D. [Norton scale for decubitus prevention]. *Krankenpflege (Frankf).* 1980; 34(1): 16.
Gosnell	5-item pressure sore risk assessment scale (score range 5–20; *higher* score indicates progressive risk—opposite Braden and Norton).	Gosnell DJ. Pressure sore risk assessment: a critique. Part I. The Gosnell scale. *Decubitus.* 1989; 2(3): 32–38.
Rule of Nines	Estimates the size of burn injury using a percentage of total body surface area (TBSA) with partial- and full-thickness burns. Does not account for variations in age and body sizes.	Knaysi GA, Crikelair GF, Cosman B. The rule of nines: its history and accuracy. *Plast Reconstr Surg.* 1968; 41(6): 560–563.
Lund-Browder Charts (pediatric and adult population)	Estimates the size of burn injury using a percentage of TBSA with partial- and full-thickness burns. Designed for infants and adults to account for variations in age and body sizes. Preferred for the pediatric population.	Lund CC, Browder NC. The estimation of areas of burns. *Surg Gynecol Obstet.* 1944; 79: 352–358.
Palmar Method for TBSA	Size of a person's palm is approximately 1% of their TBSA.	Nagel TR, Schunk JE. Using the hand to estimate the surface area of a burn in children. *Pediatr Emerg Care.* 1997; 13(4): 254–255.
Walking Impairment Questionnaire	Self-reported tool to examine treatment effects on walking impairments and symptoms in patients with peripheral arterial disease with claudication. It examines pain, distance, walking speed, and stair climbing.	McDermott MM, Liu K, Guralnik JM, Martin GJ, Criqui MH, Greenland P. Measurement of walking endurance and walking velocity with questionnaire: validation of the walking impairment questionnaire in men and women with peripheral arterial disease. *J Vasc Surg.* 1998; 28(6): 1072–1081.

Review Questions

Integumentary Physical Therapy

1. Differentiate between the viral infections herpes simplex and herpes zoster in terms of expected symptoms.

2. When performing a physical examination of decubitus ulcer, what elements should be part of the physical therapist's examination?

3. Differentiate between a superficial partial-thickness burn and a full-thickness burn.

4. Differentiate between venous and arterial ulcers in terms of expected clinical presentation.

5. Which categories of wound dressings can be used for exudative wounds?

6. What are the important clinical changes affecting prognosis for a patient with diffuse systemic sclerosis?

6

Other Systems

SUSAN B. O'SULLIVAN

Chapter Outline

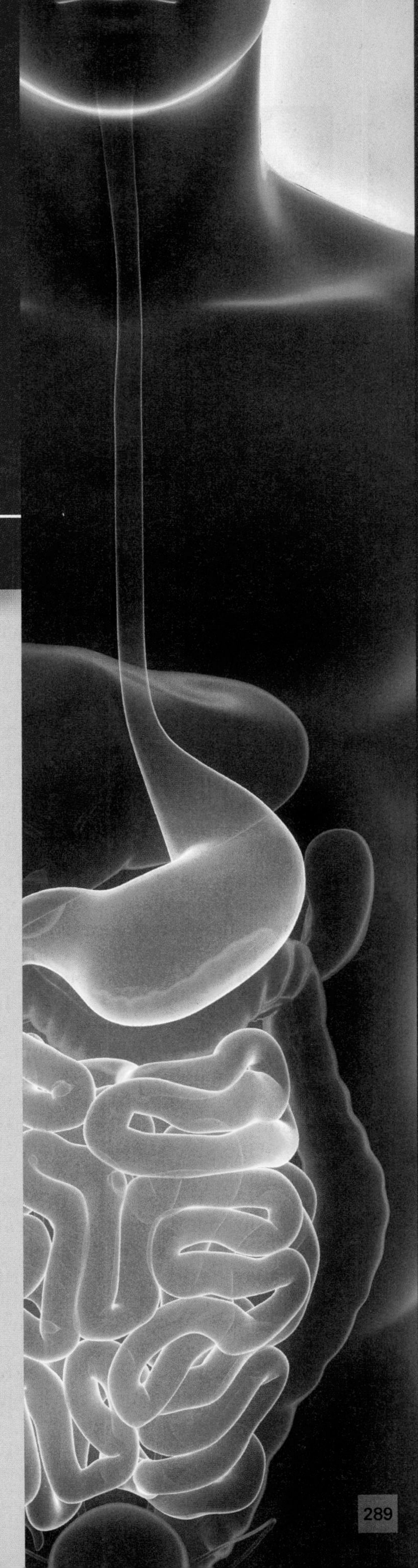

Immune System

Overview

1. Anatomy and physiology of the immune system.
   a. The immune system consists of immune cells, central immune structures where immune cells are produced (the bone marrow and thymus), and the peripheral immune structures (lymph nodes, spleen, and other accessory structures).
   b. There are several different types of immune cells.
      (1) An antigen (immunogen) is a foreign molecule that elicits the immune response. Antibodies or immunoglobulins are the proteins that are engaged to tag antigens.
      (2) Lymphocytes (T and B lymphocytes) are the primary cells of the immune system.
      (3) Macrophages are the accessory cells that process and present antigens to the lymphocytes.
      (4) Cytokines are molecules that link immune cells with other tissues and organs.
      (5) CD molecules (e.g., CD4 helper cells) serve as master regulators of the immune response by influencing the function of all other immune cells.
      (6) Recognition of foreign threat from self (autoimmune responses) is mediated by major histocompatibility complex (MHC) membrane molecules.
   c. The thymus is the primary central gland of the immune system. It is located behind the sternum above the heart and extends into the neck region to the lower edge of the thyroid gland.
      (1) It is fully developed at birth and reaches maximum size at puberty. It then decreases in size and is slowly replaced by adipose tissue.
      (2) It produces mature T lymphocytes.
   d. The lymph system is a vast network of capillaries, vessels, valves, ducts, nodes, and organs that function to produce, filter, and convey various lymph and blood cells. (See Figure 3-7.)
      (1) Lymph nodes are small areas of lymphoid tissue connected by lymphatic vessels throughout the body. High concentrations are found in the axillae, in the groin, and along the great vessels of the neck, thorax, and abdomen.
      (2) Lymph nodes function to filter the lymph and trap antigens. Lymphocytes, monocytes, and plasma cells are formed in lymph nodes.
   e. The spleen is a large lymphoid organ located in the upper left abdominal cavity between the stomach and the diaphragm.
      (1) It functions to filter antigens from the blood and produce leukocytes, monocytes, lymphocytes, and plasma cells in response to infection.
      (2) In the embryo, the spleen produces red and white blood cells; after birth, only lymphocytes are produced unless severe anemia exists.
2. The immune response.
   a. A coordinated response of the body's cells and molecules that provides protection from infectious disease (bacteria, viruses, fungi, parasites) and foreign substances (plant pollens, poison ivy resin, insect venom, transplanted organs). It also defends against abnormal cells produced by the body (cancer cells).
   b. Provides natural resistance to disease and consists of rapidly activated phagocytes (macrophages, neutrophils, natural killer cells, dendritic cells). Barriers also provide a natural defense (skin, mucous membranes) as do inflammation and fever (antimicrobial molecules).
   c. The adaptive immune response includes the slower acting defenses mediated by the lymphocytes.
   d. Repeat exposure activates immunological memory, producing more rapid and efficient responses.
   e. Excessive immune response causes allergies or autoimmune reactions.
3. Immunodeficiency diseases.
   a. Characterized by depressed or absent immune responses.
   b. Primary immunodeficiency disorders result from a defect in T cells, B cells, or lymphoid tissues.
      (1) Congenital disorders are a failure of organs to develop and produce mature lymphocytes.
      (2) Severe combined immunodeficiency disease (SCID).
   c. Secondary immunodeficiency disorders are caused by underlying pathology or treatment that depresses the immune system, resulting in failure of the immune response.
      (1) Diseases include leukemia, bone marrow tumor, chronic diabetes, renal failure, cirrhosis, cancer treatment (chemotherapy, radiation therapy).
      (2) Organ transplant, graft-versus-host disease.
4. Autoimmune diseases.
   a. Characterized by immune system responses directed against the body's normal tissues; self-destructive processes impair body function.
   b. Can be organ-specific: e.g., Hashimoto's thyroiditis.
   c. Can be systemic (non–organ specific): e.g., systemic lupus erythematosus (SLE), fibromyalgia.
   d. Etiology is unknown; possible factors include genetic predisposition, hormonal changes, environment, viral infection, and stress.

Human Immunodeficiency Virus (HIV) and Acquired Immunodeficiency Syndrome (AIDS)

1. Caused by a virus (HIV-1 or HIV-2) that weakens the immune system. Important cells that fight disease and infection are destroyed. About 50,000 people in the US get HIV each year and about 14,000 people with AIDS die each year.
2. Pathophysiology.
   a. Reduction of $CD4^+$ helper T cells, resulting in $CD4^+$ T lymphocytopenia; a major defect in the immune system.
   b. A retrovirus: replicates in reverse fashion; the RNA code is transcribed into DNA.
3. Stages of HIV.
   a. Stage 1 acute HIV infection: flu-like illness within 2–4 weeks after infection.
   b. Stage 2 clinical latency: asymptomatic HIV infection or chronic HIV infection; can last a decade or longer.
   c. Stage 3 AIDS: the most severe phase; over time, HIV destroys so many cells that the body can't fight off infections and disease, resulting in opportunistic illnesses.
4. Transmission.
   a. Through contact with certain body fluids (blood, semen, pre-seminal fluid, rectal fluids, vaginal fluids, and breast milk) from a person who has HIV. Fluid must come in contact with a mucous membrane, damaged tissue, or be directly injected into the blood stream (needle or syringe).
   b. High risk behaviors for HIV transmission.
      (1) Unprotected anal or vaginal sex with someone who has HIV.
      (2) Sharing needles or syringes, rinse water, or other equipment used to prepare drugs for injection with someone who has HIV.
      (3) Less commonly, HIV can be spread from mother to child during pregnancy, birth, or breastfeeding.
      (4) By being stuck with an HIV-contaminated needle or other sharp object (risk is mainly for health care workers).
   c. In rare cases HIV can be transmitted by:
      (1) Oral sex.
      (2) Receiving blood transfusions, blood products, or organ/tissue transplants contaminated with HIV.
      (3) Being bitten by a person with HIV.
      (4) Eating food that has been pre-chewed by an HIV-infected person.
      (5) Contact between broken skin, wounds, or mucous membranes with HIV-infected blood or bodily fluids.
      (6) Deep open-mouth kissing if both partners have sores or bleeding gums.
   d. HIV is not spread by saliva, tears, or sweat that is not mixed with the blood of an HIV-positive person; touching hugging; shaking hands; sharing toilets; sharing dishes; or closed-mouth "social" kissing.
   e. AIDS cannot be contacted through respiratory inhalation, skin contact, or human waste (urine, feces, sweat, or vomit).
5. Diagnosis of HIV. Requires positive results from two HIV tests.
   a. CD4 cell count: 500–1200 cells/mm.
   b. Testing with HIV-1/HIV-2 antigen/antibody combination immunoassays.
   c. Medical evaluation and laboratory evaluation including plasma HIV viral load, blood cell and CD4 count, antiretroviral resistance assay, drug-resistance testing, and testing for sexually transmitted infections (STDs).
6. Diagnosis of AIDS.
   a. CD4 cell count drops below 200 cells/mm or if they develop certain opportunistic illnesses. People with AIDs have a high viral load and are very infectious.
   b. AIDS-related complex (ARC): presence of acute symptoms secondary to immune system deficiency.
7. HIV symptoms.
   a. Includes flu-like symptoms: recurrent fever and chills, night sweats, swollen lymph glands, sore throat, rash, and muscle aches. Symptoms usually disappear after a few weeks.
   b. Getting tested is the only way to tell if HIV is present.
8. AIDS symptoms: exhibits some or all of the symptoms of HIV along with a general failure to thrive.
   a. Opportunistic infections: AIDS-defining conditions include pneumocystis pneumonia, candidiasis, cytomegalovirus, and toxoplasmosis.
   b. Malignancies: most common is Kaposi's sarcoma; also non-Hodgkin's lymphoma; primary brain lymphoma.
   c. Neurological conditions: focal encephalitis (central nervous system [CNS] toxoplasmosis); cryptococcal meningitis; AIDS dementia complex; herpes zoster.
   d. Deconditioning, anxiety, and depression are common.
9. Clinical course.
   a. May exhibit brief, early, nonspecific viral HIV infection, and then remain asymptomatic for many years.
   b. There is no cure for HIV infection. Without treatment nearly every person will progress to AIDS.
10. Medical interventions HIV.
    a. Antiretroviral therapies (ARTs): antiviral drugs (ARVs) are used to reduce the amount of virus (viral load) in the system and are always given in combination (usually three or more drugs); recommended for everyone infected with HIV, starting immediately.
    b. ART does not not cure HIV, but does keep people with HIV healthy for many years if taken consistently and correctly.

c. Red Flags: common adverse effects of ART include rash, nausea and vomiting, diarrhea, headaches, dizziness, fatigue, and pain.
d. Symptomatic treatment.
   (1) Education to prevent the spread of infection and disease.
   (2) Treat opportunistic infections; prophylactic vaccinations.
   (3) Maintain nutritional status.
   (4) Provide supportive care for management of fatigue, e.g., energy-conservation techniques, self-care.
   (5) Respiratory management as needed.
   (6) Provide skin care.
   (7) Maintain functional mobility and safety; prevent disability.
   (8) Provide supportive care, e.g., emotional support for patients and families.

11. Physical therapy goals, outcomes and interventions.
   a. Observe standard AIDS/HIV precautions for health care workers (see Box 6-1).
   b. Exercise has a positive effect on the immune system; reduces stress level and pain; improves cardiovascular endurance and strength (disuse effects common).
   c. Exercise: a moderate exercise program is recommended to improve body composition and minimize health risks (ACSM's Exercise Management for Persons with Chronic Diseases and Disabilities Human Kinetics, 2009).
      (1) Postpone exercise testing during acute infections.
      (2) Aerobic exercise: at least 20 minutes three times a week working up to 45 minutes to an hour, 3–4 times per week.
      (3) Resistance exercise: moderate levels—weights that can be lifted 8–10 times.
      (4) Avoid exhaustive exercise with symptomatic individuals. Possible immune suppression can occur with more intense exercise.
      (5) Day to day variations in health affect participation. During acute stages of opportunistic infections, reduce exercise to mild levels.
      (6) Avoid contact sports due to increased risk with bleeding.
   d. Teach activity pacing: balancing rest with activity; scheduling strenuous activities during periods of high energy.
   e. Teach energy conservation: analysis and modification of daily activities to reduce energy expenditure.
   f. Teach stress management, relaxation training (e.g., meditation and mindfulness, tai chi chuan, yoga).
   g. Neurological rehabilitation for patients with involvement of the CNS. (See Chapter 2.)

BOX 6-1 Standard Precautions*

Standard Precautions combine the major features of Universal Precautions (UP) and Body Substance Isolation (BSI) and are based on the principle that all blood, body fluids, secretions, excretions except sweat, nonintact skin, and mucous membranes may contain transmissible infectious agents. Standard Precautions include a group of infection prevention practices that apply to all patients, regardless of suspected or confirmed infection status, in any setting in which health care is delivered. These include hand hygiene; use of gloves, gown, mask, eye protection, or face shield, depending on the anticipated exposure; and safe injection practices. Also, equipment or items in the patient environment likely to have been contaminated with infectious body fluids must be handled in a manner to prevent transmission of infectious agents (e.g., wear gloves for direct contact, contain heavily soiled equipment, properly clean and disinfect or sterilize reusable equipment before use on another patient). The application of Standard Precautions during patient care is determined by the nature of the health care worker (HCW)–patient interaction and the extent of anticipated blood, body fluid, or pathogen exposure. For some interactions (e.g., performing venipuncture), only gloves may be needed; during other interactions (e.g., intubation), use of gloves, gown, and face shield or mask and goggles is necessary. Education and training on the principles and rationale for recommended practices are critical elements of Standard Precautions because they facilitate appropriate decision-making and promote adherence when HCWs are faced with new circumstances. An example of the importance of the use of Standard Precautions is intubation, especially under emergency circumstances when infectious agents may not be suspected, but later are identified (e.g., severe acute respiratory syndrome [SARS]–coronavirus [CoV], *Neisseria meningitidis*). Standard Precautions are also intended to protect patients by ensuring that health care personnel do not carry infectious agents to patients on their hands or via equipment used during patient care.

A.1. New Elements of Standard Precautions Infection control problems that are identified in the course of outbreak investigations often indicate the need for new recommendations or reinforcement of existing infection control recommendations to protect patients. Because such recommendations are considered a standard of care and may not be included in other guidelines, they are added here to Standard Precautions. Three such areas of practice that have been added are Respiratory Hygiene/Cough Etiquette, safe injection practices, and use of masks for insertion of catheters or injection of material into spinal or epidural spaces via lumbar puncture procedures (e.g., myelogram, spinal or epidural anesthesia). While most elements of Standard Precautions evolved from Universal Precautions that were developed for protection of health care personnel, these new elements of Standard Precautions focus on protection of patients.

A.1.a. Respiratory Hygiene/Cough Etiquette The transmission of SARS-CoV in emergency departments by patients and their family members during the widespread SARS outbreaks in 2003 highlighted the need for vigilance and prompt implementation of infection control measures at the first point of encounter within a health care setting (e.g., reception and triage areas

(Continued)

BOX 6-1 Standard Precautions* (*Continued*)

in emergency departments, outpatient clinics, and physician offices). The strategy proposed has been termed Respiratory Hygiene/Cough Etiquette and is intended to be incorporated into infection control practices as a new component of Standard Precautions. The strategy is targeted at patients and accompanying family members and friends with undiagnosed transmissible respiratory infections, and applies to any person with signs of illness including cough, congestion, rhinorrhea, or increased production of respiratory secretions when entering a health care facility. The term cough etiquette is derived from recommended source control measures for *Mycobacteria tuberculosis*. The elements of Respiratory Hygiene/Cough Etiquette include (1) education of health care facility staff, patients, and visitors; (2) posted signs, in language(s) appropriate to the population served, with instructions to patients and accompanying family members or friends; (3) source control measures (e.g., covering the mouth/nose with a tissue when coughing and prompt disposal of used tissues, using surgical masks on the coughing person when tolerated and appropriate); (4) hand hygiene after contact with respiratory secretions; and (5) spatial separation, ideally > 3 feet, of persons with respiratory infections in common waiting areas when possible. Covering sneezes and coughs and placing masks on coughing patients are proven means of source containment that prevent infected persons from dispersing respiratory secretions into the air. Masking may be difficult in some settings (e.g., pediatrics, in which case the emphasis by necessity may be on cough etiquette. Physical proximity of < 3 feet has been associated with an increased risk for transmission of infections via the droplet route (e.g., *N. meningitidis* and group A streptococcus) and therefore supports the practice of distancing infected persons from others who are not infected. The effectiveness of good hygiene practices, especially hand hygiene, in preventing transmission of viruses and reducing the incidence of respiratory infections both within and outside health care settings is summarized in several reviews.

These measures should be effective in decreasing the risk of transmission of pathogens contained in large respiratory droplets (e.g., influenza virus, adenovirus, *Bordetella pertussis*, and *Mycoplasma pneumoniae*. Although fever will be present in many respiratory infections, patients with pertussis and mild upper respiratory tract infections are often afebrile. Therefore, the absence of fever does not always exclude a respiratory infection. Patients who have asthma, allergic rhinitis, or chronic obstructive lung disease also may be coughing and sneezing. While these patients often are not infectious, cough etiquette measures are prudent.

Health care personnel are advised to observe Droplet Precautions (i.e., wear a mask) and hand hygiene when examining and caring for patients with signs and symptoms of a respiratory infection. Health care personnel who have a respiratory infection are advised to avoid direct patient contact, especially with high-risk patients. If this is not possible, then a mask should be worn while providing patient care.

Recommendations

IV. Standard Precautions

Assume that every person is potentially infected or colonized with an organism that could be transmitted in the health care setting and apply the following infection control practices during the delivery of health care.

IV.A. Hand Hygiene

IV.A.1. During the delivery of health care, avoid unnecessary touching of surfaces in close proximity to the patient to prevent both contamination of clean hands from environmental surfaces and transmission of pathogens from contaminated hands to surfaces.

IV.A.2. When hands are visibly dirty, contaminated with proteinaceous material, or visibly soiled with blood or body fluids, wash hands with either a nonantimicrobial soap and water or an antimicrobial soap and water.

IV.A.3. If hands are not visibly soiled, or after removing visible material with nonantimicrobial soap and water, decontaminate hands in the clinical situations described in IV.A.3.a–f. The preferred method of hand decontamination is with an alcohol-based hand rub. Alternatively, hands may be washed with an antimicrobial soap and water. Frequent use of an alcohol-based hand rub immediately following hand washing with nonantimicrobial soap may increase the frequency of dermatitis. Perform hand hygiene:

IV.A.3.a. Before having direct contact with patients.

IV.A.3.b. After contact with blood, body fluids or excretions, mucous membranes, nonintact skin, or wound dressings.

IV.A.3.c. After contact with a patient's intact skin (e.g., when taking a pulse or blood pressure or lifting a patient).

IV.A.3.d. If hands will be moving from a contaminated body site to a clean body site during patient care.

IV.A.3.e. After contact with inanimate objects (including medical equipment) in the immediate vicinity of the patient.

IV.A.3.f. After removing gloves.

IV.A.4. Wash hands with nonantimicrobial soap and water or with antimicrobial soap and water if in contact with spores (e.g., *Clostridium difficile* or *Bacillus anthracis*) is likely to have occurred. The physical action of washing and rinsing hands under such circumstances is recommended because alcohols, chlorhexidine, iodophors, and other antiseptic agents have poor activity against spores.

IV.A.5. Do not wear artificial fingernails or extenders if duties include direct contact with patients at high risk for infection and associated adverse outcomes (e.g., those in intensive care units [ICUs] or operating rooms).

IV.A.5.a. Develop an organizational policy on the wearing of nonnatural nails by health care personnel who have direct contact with patients outside of the groups specified above.

IV.B. Personal protective equipment (PPE)

IV.B.1. Observe the following principles of use:

IV.B.1.a. Wear PPE, as described in IV.B.2–4, when the nature of the anticipated patient interaction indicates that contact with blood or body fluids may occur.

(*Continued*)

BOX 6-1 ▶ Standard Precautions* (*Continued*)

IV.B.1.b. Prevent contamination of clothing and skin during the process of removing PPE.

IV.B.1.c. Before leaving the patient's room or cubicle, remove and discard PPE.

IV.B.2. Gloves.

IV.B.2.a. Wear gloves when it can be reasonably anticipated that contact with blood or other potentially infectious materials, mucous membranes, nonintact skin, or potentially contaminated intact skin (e.g., of a patient incontinent of stool or urine) could occur.

IV.B.2.b. Wear gloves with fit and durability appropriate to the task.

IV.B.2.b.i. Wear disposable medical examination gloves for providing direct patient care.

IV.B.2.b.ii. Wear disposable medical examination gloves or reusable utility gloves for cleaning the environment or medical equipment.

IV.B.2.c. Remove gloves after contact with a patient and/or the surrounding environment (including medical equipment) using proper technique to prevent hand contamination. Do not wear the same pair of gloves for the care of more than one patient. Do not wash gloves for the purpose of reuse since this practice has been associated with transmission of pathogens.

IV.B.2.d. Change gloves during patient care if the hands will move from a contaminated body site (e.g., perineal area) to a clean body site (e.g., face).

IV.B.3. Gowns.

IV.B.3.a. Wear a gown that is appropriate to the task to protect skin and prevent soiling or contamination of clothing during procedures and patient-care activities when contact with blood, body fluids, secretions, or excretions is anticipated.

IV.B.3.a.i. Wear a gown for direct patient contact if the patient has uncontained secretions or excretions.

IV.B.3.a.ii. Remove gown and perform hand hygiene before leaving the patient's environment.

IV.B.3.b. Do not reuse gowns, even for repeated contacts with the same patient.

IV.B.3.c. Routine donning of gowns upon entrance into a high-risk unit (e.g., ICU, neonatal intensive care unit [NICU], hematopoietic stem cell transplantation [HSCT] unit) is not indicated.

IV.B.4. Mouth, nose, eye protection.

IV.B.4.a. Use PPE to protect the mucous membranes of the eyes, nose, and mouth during procedures and patient-care activities that are likely to generate splashes or sprays of blood, body fluids, secretions, and excretions. Select masks, goggles, face shields, and combinations of each according to the need anticipated by the task performed.

IV.B.5. During aerosol-generating procedures (e.g., bronchoscopy, suctioning of the respiratory tract [if not using in-line suction catheters], endotracheal intubation) in patients who are not suspected of being infected with an agent for which respiratory protection is otherwise recommended (e.g., *M. tuberculosis*, SARS, or hemorrhagic fever viruses), wear one of the following: a face shield that fully covers the front and sides of the face, a mask with attached shield, or a mask and goggles (in addition to gloves and gown).

IV.C. Respiratory Hygiene/Cough Etiquette

IV.C.1. Educate health care personnel on the importance of source control measures to contain respiratory secretions to prevent droplet and fomite transmission of respiratory pathogens, especially during seasonal outbreaks of viral respiratory tract infections (e.g., influenza, respiratory syncytial virus [RSV], adenovirus, parainfluenza virus) in communities.

IV.C.2. Implement the following measures to contain respiratory secretions in patients and accompanying individuals who have signs and symptoms of a respiratory infection, beginning at the point of initial encounter in a health care setting (e.g., triage, reception, and waiting areas in emergency departments, outpatient clinics, and physician offices).

IV.C.2.a. Post signs at entrances and in strategic places (e.g., elevators, cafeterias) within ambulatory and inpatient settings with instructions to patients and other persons with symptoms of a respiratory infection to cover their mouths/noses when coughing or sneezing, use and dispose of tissues, and perform hand hygiene after hands have been in contact with respiratory secretions.

IV.C.2.b. Provide tissues and no-touch receptacles (e.g., foot pedal–operated lid or open, plastic-lined waste basket) for disposal of tissues.

IV.C.2.c. Provide resources and instructions for performing hand hygiene in or near waiting areas in ambulatory and inpatient settings; provide conveniently located dispensers of alcohol-based hand rubs and, where sinks are available, supplies for hand washing.

IV.C.2.d. During periods of increased prevalence of respiratory infections in the community (e.g., as indicated by increased school absenteeism, increased number of patients seeking care for a respiratory infection), offer masks to coughing patients and other symptomatic persons (e.g., persons who accompany ill patients) upon entry into the facility or medical office and encourage them to maintain special separation, ideally a distance of at least 3 feet, from others in common waiting areas.

IV.C.2.d.i. Some facilities may find it logistically easier to institute this recommendation year-round as a standard of practice.

IV.D. Patient placement

IV.D.1. Include the potential for transmission of infectious agents in patient placement decisions. Place patients who pose a risk for transmission to others (e.g., uncontained secretions, excretions or wound drainage, infants with suspected viral respiratory or gastrointestinal infections) in a single-patient room when available.

(*Continued*)

BOX 6-1 Standard Precautions* (*Continued*)

IV.D.2. Determine patient placement based on the following principles:

- Route(s) of transmission of the known or suspected infectious agent
- Risk factors for transmission in the infected patient
- Risk factors for adverse outcomes resulting from a hospital-acquired infection (HAI) in other patients in the area or room being considered for patient placement
- Availability of single-patient rooms
- Patient options for room sharing (e.g., cohorting patients with the same infection)

IV.E. Patient-care equipment and instruments/devices
IV.E.1. Establish policies and procedures for containing, transporting, and handling patient-care equipment and instruments/devices that may be contaminated with blood or body fluids.

IV.E.2. Remove organic material from critical and semicritical instruments/devices, using recommended cleaning agents before high-level disinfection and sterilization to enable effective disinfection and sterilization processes.

IV.E.3. Wear PPE (e.g., gloves, gown), according to the level of anticipated contamination, when handling patient-care equipment and instruments/devices that are visibly soiled or may have been in contact with blood or body fluids.

IV.F. Care of the environment
IV.F.1. Establish policies and procedures for routine and targeted cleaning of environmental surfaces as indicated by the level of patient contact and degree of soiling.

IV.F.2. Clean and disinfect surfaces that are likely to be contaminated with pathogens, including those that are in close proximity to the patient (e.g., bed rails, over-bed tables) and frequently touched surfaces in the patient-care environment (e.g., doorknobs, surfaces in and surrounding toilets in patients' rooms) on a more frequent schedule compared to that for other surfaces (e.g., horizontal surfaces in waiting rooms).

IV.F.3. Use Environmental Protection Agency (EPA)–registered disinfectants that have microbiocidal (i.e., killing) activity against the pathogens most likely to contaminate the patient-care environment. Use in accordance with manufacturer's instructions.

IV.F.3.a. Review the efficacy of in-use disinfectants when evidence of continuing transmission of an infectious agent (e.g., rotavirus, *C. difficile*, norovirus) may indicate resistance to the in-use product and change to a more effective disinfectant as indicated.

IV.F.4. In facilities that provide health care to pediatric patients or have waiting areas with child play toys (e.g., obstetric/gynecology offices and clinics), establish policies and procedures for cleaning and disinfecting toys at regular intervals.

Use the following principles in developing this policy and procedures:

- Select play toys that can be easily cleaned and disinfected.
- Do not permit use of stuffed furry toys if they will be shared.
- Clean and disinfect large stationary toys (e.g., climbing equipment) at least weekly and whenever visibly soiled.
- If toys are likely to be mouthed, rinse with water after disinfection; alternatively wash in a dishwasher.
- When a toy requires cleaning and disinfection, do so immediately or store in a designated labeled container separate from toys that are clean and ready for use.

IV.F.5. Include multiuse electronic equipment in policies and procedures for preventing contamination and for cleaning and disinfection, especially those items that are used by patients, those used during delivery of patient care, and mobile devices that are moved in and out of patient rooms frequently (e.g., daily).

IV.F.5.a. No recommendation for use of removable protective covers or washable keyboards. Unresolved issue.

IV.G. Textiles and laundry
IV.G.1. Handle used textiles and fabrics with minimum agitation to avoid contamination of air, surfaces, and persons.

IV.G.2. If laundry chutes are used, ensure that they are properly designed, maintained, and used in a manner to minimize dispersion of aerosols from contaminated laundry.

IV.H. Safe injection practices: see CDC website.

IV.I. Infection control practices for special lumbar puncture procedures: see CDC website.

IV.J. Worker safety. Adhere to federal and state requirements for protection of health care personnel from exposure to bloodborne pathogens.

***Date last modified:** October 12, 2007.

*Excerpt with modifications from Centers for Disease Control and Prevention, Guideline for Isolation Precautions: Preventing Transmission of Infectious Agents in Healthcare Settings, 2007. PDF (1.33MB/219 pages), downloaded 9.15.08. http://www.cdc.gov/ncidod/dhqp/gl_isolation_standard.html

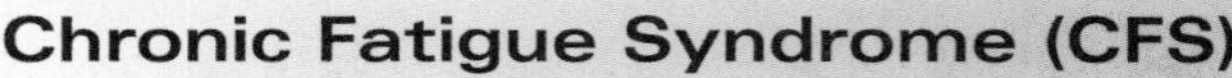

Chronic Fatigue Syndrome (CFS)

1. A complex, chronic syndrome characterized by overwhelming fatigue and other symptoms.
2. Pathophysiology.
   a. Etiology: unknown. Possible multiple triggers; viral infection, immune dysfunction.
   b. Immunological abnormalities present.
   c. Neuroendocrine changes.
3. Diagnosis by exclusion. No specific tests to diagnose CFS.
   a. Must have the two major criteria and four or more of the eight symptom criteria (CDC case definition).
   b. Major criteria.
      (1) New onset of persistent or relapsing fatigue; must be present for at least 6 months; does not resolve with bed rest and reduces daily activity by at least 50%.
      (2) Exclusion of other chronic conditions.
   c. Symptom criteria.
      (1) Profound or prolonged fatigue; post-exertional malaise lasting more than 24 hours.
      (2) Sore throat that is frequent or recurring.
      (3) Tender lymph nodes.
      (4) Muscle pain (myalgia).
      (5) Sleep that is not refreshing.
      (6) Headaches of a new type, pattern, or severity.
      (7) Multijoint pain (arthralgias) without swelling or redness.
      (8) Significant impairments of short-term memory or concentration.
   d. Deconditioning, anxiety, and depression are common.
   e. More common in women than men and in younger ages (20s and 30s).
   f. Limited recovery: only 5%–10% recover completely.
4. Medical interventions.
   a. No cure, no prescription drugs specifically for CFS.
   b. Supportive and symptomatic treatment; symptoms may persist for months or years.
      (1) Analgesics and anti-inflammatory nonsteroidal medications for myalgia and arthralgia.
      (2) Nutritional support.
      (3) Psychological support and counseling; antidepressants.
5. Physical therapy examination.
   a. Examine exercise tolerance levels. Vital signs may reveal fluctuations in heart rate (HR) and blood pressure (BP); orthostatic hypotension is common. If deconditioned, dyspnea with exercise.
   b. Examine posture. Postural stress syndrome (poor posture) and movement adaptation syndrome (inefficient movement patterns) may be present and can contribute to chronic pain and fatigue.
   c. Examine activity levels and degree of fatigue. Objective measure: Modified Fatigue Impact Scale.
   d. Examine for depression. Determine degree of emotional support present.
6. Physical therapy goals, outcomes, and interventions.
   a. Activities are reduced when fatigue is maximal; bed rest contraindicated other than for sleep.
   b. Exercise recommendations (ACSM's Exercise Management for Persons with Chronic Diseases and Disabilities Human Kinetics, 2009).
      (1) Overall goal to prevent deconditioning.
      (2) Aerobic exercise (e.g., walking).
         (a) Intensity: low to moderate levels of intensity (RPE 9-12/20), progress very gradually.
         (b) Frequency: 3–5 days/wk.
         (c) Duration: to tolerance, 5 min/session initially progressing to 40–60 min.
      (3) Maintain flexibility.
      (4) Maintain or improve muscle strength.
      (5) Maintain function: individualized activities.
   c. Avoid overexertion. Individuals should understand that they may experience increased fatigue in the first few weeks of an exercise program. Individuals should reduce exercise when symptoms are increased or not feeling well.
   d. Teach activity pacing: balancing rest with activity; scheduling strenuous activities during periods of high energy.
   e. Teach energy conservation: analysis and modification of daily activities to reduce energy expenditure.
   f. Teach stress management, relaxation training (e.g., meditation and mindfulness, tai chi chuan, yoga).
   g. Refer to support group.

Fibromyalgia Syndrome (FMS)

1. A disorder characterized by widespread musculoskeletal pain, fatigue with sleep, memory, and mood disturbances.
2. Pathophysiology.
   a. Etiology unknown; multifactoral; viral cause suspected. May develop after a triggering event: trauma, surgery, infection, or significant psychological stress.
   b. Immunological and neurohormonal abnormalities are present. More common in individuals with rheumatic disease.
   c. Genetic factor: tends to run in families.
   d. More common in women (75%–80% of cases) than men.
3. Characteristics.
   a. Myalgia (muscle pain).
   b. Generalized aching, persistent fatigue (mental and physical).
   c. Sleep disturbances with generalized morning stiffness.
   d. Multiple tender points (trigger points).
   e. Additional signs and symptoms: visual problems, mental and physical fatigue, spasm, cold intol-

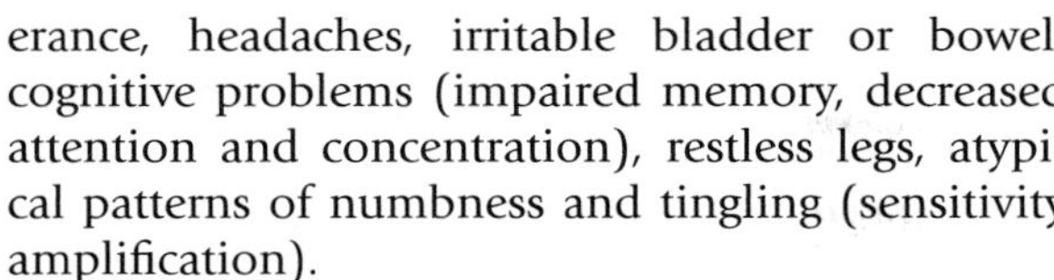

erance, headaches, irritable bladder or bowel, cognitive problems (impaired memory, decreased attention and concentration), restless legs, atypical patterns of numbness and tingling (sensitivity amplification).

f. Anxiety and depression are common.

4. Medical management.
   a. Diagnosis.
      (1) Two criteria for diagnosis: widespread pain lasting at least 3 months and presence of 11 positive tender points out of a total 18 (Copenhagen Fibromyalgia Syndrome definition).
   b. There is no cure for fibromyalgia.
   c. Symptomatic management: relief of pain from analgesics, antidepressants, and anti-seizure drugs.
   d. Nutritional support.
   e. Psychological support and counseling.
5. Physical therapy goals, outcomes, and interventions.
   a. See recommendations for chronic fatigue syndrome.
   b. Patient typically demonstrates exercise intolerance. Daily exercise is important. Focus is on aerobic training, mild to moderate intensities, 2–30 min duration progressing to 30–40 min, 2 times/wk.
   c. Teach protection strategies to avoid overuse syndromes.
   d. Aquatic therapy (warm water exercise) is ideal to decrease pain and increase cardiovascular conditioning and strength.
   e. Teach techniques for taking control and stress reduction: self-responsibility for own health, education, coping strategies, keeping a journal. Tai chi and yoga have been shown to be beneficial.
   f. Work and work environment adjustments.
   g. Refer to support group.

Infectious Diseases

Staphylococcal Infections

1. *Staphylococcus aureus* (SA).
   a. A common bacterial pathogen.
2. Pathophysiology.
   a. Typically begins as localized infection; entry is through skin portal, e.g., wounds, ulcers, burns.
   b. Bacterial invasion and spread is through bloodstream or lymphatic system to almost any body location, e.g., heart valves, bones (acute staphylococcal osteomyelitis), joints (bacterial arthritis), skin (cellulitis, furuncles and carbuncles, ulcers), respiratory tract (pneumonia), bowel (enterocolitis).
   c. Infection produces suppuration (pus formation) and abscess.
3. Medical interventions.
   a. Laboratory diagnosis to confirm pathogen.
   b. Antibiotic therapy; determine antibiotic sensitivity. Antibiotic resistance is common.
   c. Drainage of abscesses.
   d. Skin infections that are untreated can become systemic; sepsis can be lethal.
4. Methicillin-resistant *Staphylococcus aureus* (MRSA).
   a. An antibiotic-resistant strain.
   b. MRSA is resistant to all penicillins (especially methicillin) and cephalosporins.
   c. It is found in about 1% of the population.
   d. Hospitalized patients with MRSA infections are isolated and standard mask-gown-gloves precautions required.
5. Vancomycin-resistant *Staphylococcus aureus* (VRSA).
   a. Resistant to vancomycin.
   b. Can be a life-threatening infection.

Streptococcal Infections

1. Characteristics.
   a. A common bacterial pathogen.
   b. Types.
      (1) Group A streptococcus (*S. pyogenes*): pharyngitis, rheumatic fever, scarlet fever, impetigo, necrotizing fasciitis (gangrene), cellulitis, myositis.
      (2) Group B streptococcus (*S. agalactiae*): neonatal and adult streptococcal B infections.
      (3) Group C streptococcus (*S. pneumoniae*): pneumonia, otitis media, meningitis, endocarditis.
2. Medical interventions.
   a. Laboratory diagnosis to confirm pathogen.
   b. Antibiotic therapy; antibiotic resistance common.
   c. Skin infections that are untreated can become systemic.

Hepatitis

1. Characteristics.
   a. Inflammation of the liver; may be caused by viral or bacterial infection; chemical agents (alcohol, drugs, toxins).

b. Types.
(1) Hepatitis A virus (HAV, acute infectious hepatitis).
(a) Transmission is primarily through fecal-oral route; contracted through contaminated food or water, or person-to-person contact (infected food handlers).
(b) An acute illness (not chronic): can range in severity from mild to severe.
(c) Prevention: good personal hygiene, hand washing, sanitation; immunization (vaccine).
(2) Hepatitis B virus (HBV, serum hepatitis).
(a) Transmission from blood, body fluids, or body tissues, through blood transfusion, oral or sexual contact with a person infected with HBV or contaminated needles.
(b) Can range in severity from mild (acute, lasting a few weeks) to severe (chronic, lifelong).
(c) Prevention: education, use of disposable needles, screening of blood donors; precautions for health care workers; immunization (vaccine).
(3) Hepatitis C virus (HCV).
(a) Transmission is same as for HBV (post-transfusion or needle sharing are the most common routes).
(b) Can be acute or chronic.
(4) Hepatitis D (HDV).
(a) Similar to transmission of HBV.
(b) Rare in the US.
2. Clinical signs and symptoms.
a. Initial (preicteric phase): low-grade fever, anorexia, nausea, vomiting, fatigue, malaise, headache, abdominal tenderness, and pain.
b. Jaundice (icteric) phase: fever, jaundice, enlarged liver with tenderness; abatement of earlier symptoms.
c. Elevated lab values: hepatic transaminases and bilirubin.
d. Course: variable.
(1) Acute: may last from several weeks to months.
(2) Chronic: HBV and HCV may lead to chronic liver infection, including necrosis, cirrhosis, and liver failure.
3. Medical interventions.
a. No specific treatment for acute viral hepatitis; treatment is symptomatic, e.g., IV fluids, analgesics.
b. Chronic hepatitis: interferon is the main therapy.
c. Viral hepatitis is the leading cause of liver cancer and common reason for liver transplantation.

Tuberculosis (TB)

1. Characteristics.
a. An airborne infectious disease caused by the bacillus *Mycobacterium tuberculosis.*
b. Most commonly affects the respiratory system; may also affect the gastrointestinal and genitourinary systems, bones, joints, the nervous system, and skin.
c. Course: may be acute, generalized or chronic, localized.
2. Signs and symptoms.
a. Pulmonary: productive cough lasting 3 weeks or longer, rales, dyspnea, pain in the chest, and hemoptysis (coughing up blood or sputum).
b. Systemic: weakness or fatigue, low-grade fever, chills, night sweats, anorexia, and weight loss.
3. Diagnosis.
a. TB infection confirmed with positive TB skin test or TB blood test.
b. TB disease confirmed with chest x-ray, sputum sample, medical history, and physical examination.
4. Medical interventions.
a. Medications: a combination of daily drugs (e.g., isoniazid, rifampin, rafapentine) taken for 6–9 months.
b. Incidence of drug-resistant strains is increasing.
c. Isolation and bed rest (limited with advent of medications).
d. Adequate diet.
5. Pulmonary precautions.
a. Instruct patient in infection control measures.
b. Transmission is through:
(1) Respiratory droplets or sputum: use tissues to cover nose and mouth when coughing or sneezing; disposable containers for sputum, tissues.
(2) Soiled dressings.

Centers for Disease Control and Prevention (CDC) Standard Precautions

Standard Precautions

1. A group of infection prevention practices that apply to all patients, regardless of suspected or confirmed infection status (see Box 6-1).
2. Standard Precautions combine major features of:
a. Universal Precautions.
b. Body Substance Isolation.
c. Based on the principle that all blood, body fluids, secretions, excretions except sweat, nonintact skin, and mucous membranes may contain transmissible infectious agents.

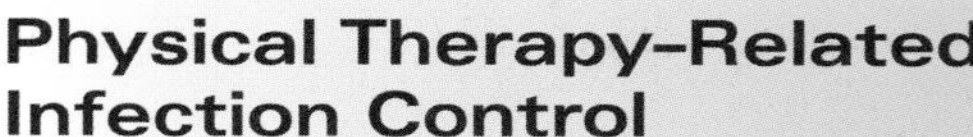

Physical Therapy–Related Infection Control

1. Purpose: to destroy bacteria, infectious organisms.
2. Sterilization.
   a. The total destruction of all microorganisms by exposure to chemical or physical agents; required for all objects introduced to the body; e.g., scalpels, catheters.
   b. Methods:
      (1) Autoclaving: sterilization of instruments by heat (250°F–270°F) and water pressure; contraindicated with heat-sensitive articles.
      (2) Boiling water (212°F): kills organisms that do not form spores.
      (3) Ionizing radiation: used to sterilize some medications, plastics, or sutures.
      (4) Dry heat: prolonged exposure to high heat in ovens.
      (5) Gaseous: ethylene oxide, formaldehyde gas.
3. Disinfection.
   a. The reduction of the number of microorganisms; typically used on surfaces or equipment, e.g., respiratory and hydrotherapy equipment.
   b. Methods:
      (1) Ultraviolet light: used for air and surface disinfection; harmful to unprotected skin and eyes.
      (2) Filtration: used for water or air purification.
      (3) Physical cleaning.
         (a) Ultrasonic: disinfects instruments.
         (b) Washing with an antimicrobial product: used to disinfect hands and surfaces.
      (4) Chemicals.
         (a) Chlorination: used for water disinfection, filtration systems; also used for food surface sanitizing.
         (b) Iodines: used in hydrotherapy when filtering system not possible; provides full bactericidal activity when organic matter (skin, feces, urine) is present.
         (c) Phenols: general disinfectants.
         (d) Quaternary ammonia compounds, e.g., benzalkonium chloride (Zephiran).
         (e) Formaldehyde (5%).
      (5) Hydrotherapy disinfection.
         (a) Drain and clean tanks after every patient.
         (b) Scrub pumps and equipment (e.g., drains, agitator unit) with a germicidal detergent, e.g., sodium hypochlorite (bleach), povidoneiodine, chloramine-T (Chlorazene).
         (c) Rinse before refilling.

Hematological System

Overview

1. Composition of blood (see Table 3-8 for normal values).
   a. Plasma makes up about 55% of total blood volume and is the liquid part of blood and lymph; it carries the cellular elements of blood through the circulation.
      (1) Plasma is composed of about 91% water, 7% proteins, and 2%–3% other small molecules.
      (2) Electrolytes in plasma determine osmotic pressure and pH balance and are important in the exchange of fluids between capillaries and tissues.
      (3) Carries nutrients, waste products, and hormones.
      (4) Plasma proteins include albumin, globulins, and fibrinogen.
      (5) Serum is plasma without the clotting factors.
   b. Erythrocytes or red blood cells (RBCs), make up about 45% of the total blood volume and contain the oxygen-carrying protein hemoglobin responsible for transporting oxygen.
      (1) RBCs are produced in the marrow of the long bones and controlled by hormones (erythropoietin). RBCs are time-limited, surviving for approximately 120 days.
      (2) RBC count varies with age, activity, and environmental conditions.
   c. Leukocytes, or white blood cells (WBCs), make up about 1% of total blood volume and circulate through the lymphoid tissues.
      (1) Leukocytes function in immune processes as phagocytes of bacteria, fungi, and viruses. They also aid in capturing toxic proteins resulting from allergic reactions and cellular injury.
      (2) Leukocytes are produced in the bone marrow.
      (3) There are five types of leukocytes: lymphocytes and monocytes (agranulocytes) and neutrophils, basophils, and eosinophils (granulocytes).
2. Hematopoiesis.
   a. The normal function and generation of blood cells in the bone marrow.
   b. Production, differentiation, and function of blood cells is regulated by cytokines and growth factors (chemical messengers) acting on blood-forming cells (pluripotent stem cells).
   c. Disorders of hematopoiesis include aplastic anemia and leukemias.
3. Blood screening tests.
   a. Complete blood count (CBC) determines the number of red blood cells, white blood cells, and platelets per unit of blood.

b. White cell differential count determines the relative percentages of individual white cell types.
c. Erythrocyte sedimentation rate (ESR) is the rate of red blood cells that settle out in a tube of unclotted blood; expressed in millimeters per hour.
  (1) Elevated ESR indicates the presence of inflammation.
  (2) Normal values (see Table 3-10).
4. Hemostasis.
  a. The termination or arrest of blood flow by mechanical or chemical processes. Mechanisms include vasospasm, platelet aggregation, and thrombin and fibrin synthesis.
  b. Blood clotting requires platelets produced in bone marrow, von Willebrand's factor produced by the endothelium of blood vessels and clotting factors produced by the liver using vitamin K.
  c. Fibrinolysis is clot dissolution that prevents excess clot formation.
5. Hypercoaguability disorders are caused by:
  a. Increased platelet function as seen in atherosclerosis, diabetes mellitus, elevated blood lipids, and cholesterol.
  b. Accelerated activity of the clotting system as seen in congestive heart failure, malignant diseases, pregnancy and use of oral contraceptives, immobility.
6. Hypocoagulopathy (bleeding) disorders are caused by:
  a. Platelet defects as seen in bone marrow dysfunction, thrombocytopenia, thrombocytopathia.
  b. Coagulation defects as seen in hemophilia and von Willebrand's disease.
  c. Vascular disorders as seen in hemorrhagic telangiectasia, vitamin C deficiency, Cushing's disease; senile purpura.
7. Shock.
  a. An abnormal condition of inadequate blood flow to the body tissues. It is associated with hypotension, inadequate cardiac output, and changes in peripheral blood flow resistance.
  b. Hypovolemic shock is caused by hemorrhage, vomiting, or diarrhea. Loss of body fluids also occurs with dehydration, Addison's disease, burns, pancreatitis, or peritonitis.
  c. Orthostatic changes may develop, characterized by a drop in systolic blood pressure of 10–20 mm Hg or more. Pulse and respiration increase.
  d. Progressive shock is associated with restlessness and anxiety, weakness, lethargy, pallor with cool, moist skin, and fall in body temperature.
  e. Vital functions must be carefully monitored and restored as quickly as possible. The patient should be placed supine or in a modified Trendelenburg position to aid venous return.
8. Signs and symptoms of hematological disorders.
  a. Easy bruising with spontaneous petechiae and purpura of the skin.
  b. External hematomas may also be present (e.g., thrombocytopenia).
9. Medications.
  a. Long-term use of certain drugs (steroids, nonsteroidal anti-inflammatory drugs [NSAIDs]) can lead to bleeding and anemia.
10. Red Flags: Physical therapy interventions.
  a. Use extreme caution with manual therapy and use of some modalities (e.g., mechanical compression).
  b. Strenuous exercise is contraindicated due to the risk of increased hemorrhage.

Anemia

1. Characteristics.
  a. Decrease in hemoglobin levels in the blood.
  b. Normal range. (See Table 3-10.)
2. Etiology.
  a. Decrease in RBC production: nutritional deficiency (iron, vitamin B, folic acid); cellular maturation defects, decreased bone marrow stimulation (hypothyroidism), bone marrow failure (leukemia, aplasia, neoplasm), and genetic defect.
  b. Destruction of RBCs: autoimmune hemolysis, sickle cell disease, enzyme defects, parasites (malaria), hypersplenism, chronic diseases (rheumatoid arthritis, tuberculosis, cancer).
  c. Loss of blood (hemorrhage): trauma, wound, bleeding, peptic ulcer, excessive menstruation.
3. Clinical symptoms.
  a. Fatigue and weakness with minimal exertion.
  b. Dyspnea on exertion.
  c. Pallor or yellow skin of the face, hands, nail beds, and lips.
  d. Tachycardia.
  e. Bleeding of gums, mucous membranes, or skin in the absence of trauma.
  f. Severe anemia can produce hypoxic damage to liver and kidney, heart failure.
4. Medical intervention.
  a. Variable, depends on causative factors.
  b. Transfusion.
  c. Nutritional supplements.
5. Physical therapy intervention.
  a. Red Flags: Patients with anemia exhibit decreased exercise tolerance.
    (1) Exercise should be instituted gradually with physician approval.
    (2) Perceived exertion levels should be used (rate of perceived exertion [RPE] ratings).

Sickle Cell Disease

1. Characteristics.
  a. Group of inherited, autosomal recessive red blood cell (RBC) disorders; erythrocytes, specifically

hemoglobin, are abnormal. RBCs are crescent or sickle-shaped instead of biconcave.

b. Types include HbSS (most severe); HbSC, HbS beta thalassemia, HbSD, HbSE, and HbSO.

c. Sickle cell trait: heterozygous form of sickle cell anemia characterized by abnormal red blood cells. Individuals are carriers and do not develop the disease. Counseling is important, especially if both parents have the trait.

d. Chronic hemolytic anemia (sickle cell anemia): hemoglobin is released into plasma with resultant reduced oxygen delivery to tissues; results from bone marrow aplasia, hemolysis, folate deficiency, or splenic involvement.

e. Vasoocclusion from misshapen erythrocytes: results in ischemia, occlusion, and infarction of adjacent tissue.

f. Chronic illness that can be fatal.

2. Sickle cell crisis.
   a. Acute episodic condition occurring in children with sickle cell anemia.
   b. Symptoms.
      (1) Pain: acute and severe from sickle cell clots formed in any organ, bone, or joint.
         (a) Acute abdominal pain from visceral hypoxia.
         (b) Painful swelling of soft tissue of the hands and feet (hand-foot syndrome).
         (c) Persistent headache.
      (2) Bone and joint crises: migratory, recurrent joint pain; extremity and back pain.
      (3) Neurological manifestations: dizziness, convulsions, coma, nystagmus.
      (4) Pulmonary (acute chest syndrome): chest pain, coughing, dyspnea, tachypnea may occur.
3. Complications.
   a. Vascular: stroke, chronic leg ulcers, bone infarcts, avascular necrosis of femoral head, hand-and-foot syndrome (dactylitis).
   b. Pulmonary hypertension.
   c. Neurologic: paresthesias, cranial nerve palsies, blindness, hemiplegia.
   d. Renal: enuresis, nocturia, hematuria, renal failure.
   e. Anemic crisis: characterized by rapid drop in hemoglobin levels.
   f. Aplastic crisis: characterized by severe anemia; associated with acute viral, bacterial, or fungal infection. Increased susceptibility to infection.
   g Splenic: liver and spleen enlargement, spleen atrophy.
4. Medical interventions.
   a. Exchange transfusions of packed red cells in acute anemic crisis or severe anemia.
   b. Medications that stimulate HbF production (e.g., hydrooxyurea).
   c. Analgesics or narcotics as needed for pain.
   d. Short-term oxygen therapy in severe anoxia.
   e. Hydration, electrolyte replacement.
   f. Antibiotics for infection control.
   g. Oral anticoagulants to relieve pain of vasoocclusion; associated with increased risk of bleeding.
   h. Splenectomy may be considered.
   i. Bone marrow transplant in severe cases.
   j. Uremia may require renal transplantation or hemodialysis.
   k. Stem cell transplant.
5. Physical therapy goals, outcomes, and interventions.
   a. During sickle cell event, pain control.
      (1) Application of warmth is soothing (e.g., hydrotherapy).
      (2) Relaxation techniques.
      (3) Red Flags: Cold is contraindicated, as it increases vasoconstriction and sickling.
   b. Exercise and activity training: appropriate for developmental level and patient status.
      (1) Exercise intolerance common: exaggerated heart rate response to exercise, limited peak performance in patients with anemia.
      (2) Low- to moderate-level exercise indicated.
      (3) Ensure adequate fluid intake.
      (4) High-level exercise and dehydration may increase risk of sickle cell crisis.
   c. Emotional support and counseling of family.
   d. Patient and family education: avoidance of stressors that can precipitate a crisis; teach joint protection strategies.

Hemophilia

1. Pathophysiology. A group of hereditary bleeding disorders.
   a. Inherited as a sex-linked recessive disorder of blood coagulation; affects males, females are carriers.
   b. Clotting factor VIII deficiency (hemophilia A) is most common; classic hemophilia.
   c. Clotting factor IX deficiency (hemophilia B or Christmas disease).
   d. Level of severity and rate of spontaneous bleeds varies by percentage of clotting factor in blood: mild, moderate, severe.
   e. Bleeding is spontaneous or a result of trauma; may result in internal hemorrhage and hematuria.
   f. Hemarthrosis (bleeding into joint spaces) most common in synovial joints: knees, ankles, elbows, hips.
      (1) Joint becomes swollen, warm, and painful with decreased range of motion (ROM).
      (2) Long-term results can include chronic synovitis and arthropathy leading to bone and cartilage destruction.
   g. Hemorrhage into muscles often affects forearm flexors, gastrocnemius/soleus, and iliopsoas; results in pain and decreased movement.

2. Medical interventions.
   a. Blood infusion, factor replacement therapy.
   b. Use of acetaminophen (Tylenol), not aspirin, for pain management.
   c. Rest, ice, elevation, functional splinting, and no weight-bearing during an acute bleed.
   d. HIV or hepatitis transmission was a possible transfusion result prior to current purification techniques.
3. Complications.
   a. Joint contractures.
      (1) Hip, knee, elbow flexion; ankle plantar flexion.
   b. Muscle weakness around affected joints.
   c. Leg length discrepancies.
   d. Postural scoliosis.
   e. Decreased aerobic fitness.
   f. Gait deviations.
      (1) Equinus gait.
      (2) Lack of knee extensor torque.
   g. Activities of daily living (ADL) deficiencies, e.g., elbow contractures could affect dressing ability.
4. Physical therapy examination.
   a. Clinical signs and symptoms of acute bleeding episodes: decreased ROM, stiffening, pain, swelling, tenderness, heat, prickling or tingling sensations.
   b. Goniometry.
   c. Joint deformities, e.g., genu valgum, rearfoot/forefoot.
   d. Muscle strength; girth.
   e. Functional mobility skills, gait.
   f. Pain.
   g. Activities of daily living.
5. Physical therapy interventions. Acute stage.
   a. RICE: rest, ice, compression, elevation.
   b. Maintain position, prevent deformity.
6. Physical therapy interventions. Subacute stage after hemostasis.
   a. Factor replacement best done just before treatment.
   b. Isometric exercise and aquatic therapy early.
   c. Pain management: transcutaneous electrical nerve stimulation (TENS), massage, relaxation techniques, ice, biofeedback.
   d. Active assistive exercise progressing to active, isokinetic, and open chain resistive exercises.
      (1) Passive ROM rarely, if ever, used.
      (2) Closed chain exercise may put too much compressive force through joint.
      (3) Important to strengthen hip, knee, elbow extensors, and ankle dorsiflexors.
   e. Contracture management.
      (1) Manual traction, mobilization techniques, serial casting, dynamic splinting during the day, resting splints at night.
      (2) Red Flags: Passive stretching is rarely used, due to risk of myositis ossificans.
   f. Functional and gait training as needed.
      (1) Protective use of helmets or pads for very young boys during ambulation and play.
      (2) Temporary use of ambulatory aids as needed.
      (3) Foot orthoses, shoe inserts, and adhesive taping for ankle or foot problems.
7. Physical therapy interventions. Chronic stage.
   a. Daily home exercise program to maintain or increase joint function, aerobic fitness, and strength.
   b. Outpatient physical therapy as necessary.
   c. Appropriate recreational activities or adaptive physical education if at school.
8. Emotional support for patients and families.

Cancer

Overview

1. Cancer is a broad group of diseases characterized by rapidly proliferating anaplastic cells.
2. Characteristics. Involves all body organs; invasive.
   a. Etiology: unknown; multiple factors are implicated.
      (1) Environmental: carcinogens (e.g., asbestos, smoking or oral tobacco), ionizing radiation (e.g., x-rays, sun exposure), petrochemicals or solvents and viral (e.g., herpes simplex, AIDS/immune system depression).
      (2) Genetic factors: hereditary.
      (3) Dietary factors: obesity, high-fat diet, diet low in vitamins A, C, E.
      (4) Psychological factors: chronic stress.
   b. Early warning signs.
      (1) Unusual bleeding or discharge.
      (2) A lump or thickening of any area, e.g., breast.
      (3) A sore that does not heal.
      (4) A change in bladder or bowel habits.
      (5) Hoarseness or persistent cough.
      (6) Indigestion or difficulty swallowing.
      (7) Change in size or appearance of a wart or mole.
      (8) Unexplained weight loss.
   c. Classification (staging): delineates extent and prognosis of disease.
   d. Incidence: second leading cause of death in United States.
   e. Prognosis: aggressive treatments have resulted in higher cure rates, increased survival times.
   f. Quality of life (maintaining normal function and lifestyle) is an important issue.

3. Pathophysiology.
   a. Tumor or neoplasm: an abnormal growth of new tissue that is nonfunctional and competes for vital blood supply and nutrients.
   b. Benign tumor (neoplasm): localized, slow-growing, usually encapsulated; not invasive.
   c. Malignant tumor (neoplasm): invasive, rapid growth giving rise to metastasis; can be life-threatening.
      (1) Carcinoma: a malignant tumor originating in epithelial tissues, e.g., skin, stomach, colon, breast, rectum. Carcinoma in situ is a premalignant neoplasm that has not invaded the basement membrane.
      (2) Sarcoma: a malignant tumor originating in connective and mesodermal tissues, e.g., muscle, bone, fat.
      (3) Lymphoma: affecting the lymphatic system, e.g., Hodgkin's disease, lymphatic leukemia.
      (4) Leukemias and myelomas: affecting the blood (unrestrained growth of leukocytes) and blood-forming organs (bone marrow).
   d. Metastasis: movement of cancer cells from one body part to another; spread is via lymphatic system or bloodstream.
4. Cancer staging: describes the extent or severity of a person's cancer. Based on primary tumor (T): regional lymph node involvement (N); and metastasis (M).
   a. Stage 0: carcinoma in situ.
   b. Stage I: tumor is localized, equal to or less than 2 cm; has not spread to lymph nodes.
   c. Stage II: tumor is locally advanced; 2 cm to 5 cm with or without lymph node involvement.
   d. Stage III: tumor is locally more advanced; spread to lymph nodes; cancer is designated stage II or III depending upon specific type of cancer.
   e. Stage IV: the tumor has metastasized, or spread to other organs throughout the body.
   f. Cancer grades.
      (1) Grade I (low-grade): cancer cells resemble normal cells (well differentiated) and are slow growing.
      (2) Grade II (intermediate-grade): cancer cells look more abnormal (moderately differentiated) and are slightly faster growing.
      (3) Grade III (high-grade): cancer cells are abnormal (poorly differentiated); grow or spread more aggressively.
      (4) Grade IV (high-grade): cancer cells are abnormal (undifferentiated).
5. Medical interventions.
   a. Curative versus palliative (relief of symptoms, e.g., pain); can be used singly or in combination. May be considered cured if patient does not have a reoccurrence within 5 years after treatment.
   b. Surgery.
      (1) Can be curative (tumor removal following biopsy) or palliative (to relieve pain, correct obstruction).
      (2) Often used in combination with chemotherapy or radiation therapy.
      (3) Can result in significant functional deficits and weakness; edema.
   c. Radiation therapy.
      (1) Destroys cancer cells, inhibits cell growth and division.
      (2) Can be used preoperatively to shrink tumors, prevent spread.
      (3) Can be used postoperatively to kill/prevent residual cancer cells from metastasizing.
   d. Chemotherapy.
      (1) Drugs can be given orally, subcutaneously, intramuscularly, intravenously, intrathecally (within the spinal canal).
      (2) Usually intermittent doses to allow for bone marrow recovery.
   e. Immunotherapy.
      (1) Strengthens host's ability to fight cancer cells.
      (2) Agents can include interferons, interleukin-2, and cytokines.
      (3) Bone marrow (stem cell) transplant; follows high doses of chemotherapy or radiation that destroys both cancer cells and bone marrow cells.
      (4) Monoclonal antibodies.
      (5) Hormonal therapy.
   f. Red Flags: Local and systemic effects of cancer therapy.
      (1) With radiation therapy, can see pain and fatigue, radiation sickness, immunosuppression, fibrosis, burns, delayed wound healing, edema, hair loss, CNS effects (radiation encephalopathy, demyelination).
      (2) With chemotherapy, can see fatigue, gastrointestinal symptoms (anorexia, nausea, vomiting, diarrhea, ulcers, hemorrhage), bone marrow suppression (anemia, leukopenia, thrombocytopenia), fatigue, skin rashes, neuropathies, phlebitis, and hair loss.
      (3) With immunotherapy, can see fatigue, weight loss, flu-like symptoms (fever, chills), nausea, vomiting, anorexia, fluid retention.
      (4) With hormonal therapy, can see gastrointestinal symptoms, hypertension, steroid-induced diabetes and myopathy, weight gain, hot flashes and sweating, altered mental status, impotence.
6. Hospice care. Institutional or home care for the terminally ill patient.
   a. Multidisciplinary focus.
   b. Palliative care provided at home or in a hospice center.
   c. Provision of supportive services: emotional, physical, social, spiritual, financial.

Physical Therapy Examination

1. Detailed systems assessment. Dependent upon cancer history.

2. Pain.
   a. Cancer pain syndrome: cancer-related pain is a common experience, e.g., nerve or nerve root compression, ischemic response to blockage of blood supply, bone pain. Sympathetic signs and symptoms may accompany moderate to severe pain, e.g., tachycardia, hypertension, tachypnea, nausea, vomiting.
   b. Pain at site distal to initial tumor site may suggest metastasis.
   c. Iatrogenic pain may result from surgery, radiation, or chemotherapy.
3. Cancer-related fatigue (CRF): most common symptom reported by patients with all cancers.
   a. Multiple causative factors: physical and emotional. Can use Brief Fatigue Inventory (BFI).
   b. Need to assess impact on Quality of Life (QOL).
4. Red Flags.
   a. Lung, breast, prostate, thyroid, and lymphatic cancers commonly metastasize to bone. Pathological fractures, pain, and muscle spasms may result.
   b. Paraneoplastic syndrome: signs and symptoms are produced at a site distant from the tumor or its metastasized sites, from ectopic hormone production by tumor cells or metabolic abnormalities from secretion of tumor-vasoactive products.
   c. Cushing's syndrome can result from small cell cancer of the lung.
   d. Symptoms can result from cancer stimulation of antibody production, e.g., anorexia, malaise, diarrhea, weight loss, fever, progressive muscle weakness (type II atrophy), diminished deep tendon reflexes (DTRs), myositis, joint pain.
   e. Neurological syndromes can include cerebellar degeneration, peripheral neuropathy, and myasthenia gravis.
5. Red Flags: Adverse side effects of cancer treatment.
   a. With immunosuppressed patient, monitor vital signs, physiological responses to exercise carefully; may see elevated HR and BP, dyspnea, pallor, sweating, fatigue. Patient is easily fatigued with minimal exertion.
   b. Muscle atrophy and weakness: secondary to high doses of steroids in many chemotherapy protocols; weakness may also result from disuse or tumor compression/invasion.
   c. ROM deficits: particularly with high-dose radiation around joints.
   d. Hematological disruptions.
      (1) White blood cell suppression (leukopenia); increased susceptibility to infection.
      (2) Platelet suppression (thrombocytopenia): increased bleeding.
      (3) Red blood cell suppression (anemia): diminished aerobic capacity.

Physical Therapy Goals, Outcomes, and Interventions

1. Educate patient and family about disease process, rehabilitation goals, process, and expected outcomes.
2. Identify and support patient and family.
   a. Assist in coping mechanisms.
   b. Assist through the grieving process.
3. Positioning.
   a. Provide for proper positioning to prevent or correct deformities, maintain skin integrity.
   b. Provide for overall patient comfort.
4. Edema control.
   a. Elevation of extremities, active ROM.
   b. Massage.
   c. Postoperative compression (elastic bandages, pressure garments).
5. Pain control.
   a. TENS stimulation: may not control deep cancer pain; effective for postoperative pain.
   b. Massage.
6. Maintain or correct loss of ROM.
   a. Active-assisted/stretching.
   b. Active ROM exercises.
7. Maintain or correct loss of muscle mass and strength.
   a. Isometric and lightweight isotonic strengthening exercises safe for most patients with cancer.
   b. Red Flags: Patients with significant bony metastases, osteoporosis, or low platelet counts (< 20,000).
      (1) AROM, ADL exercise only.
      (2) Weight bearing may be restricted; provide appropriate ambulatory aids, orthoses.
      (3) High risk of vertebral compression and other fractures with metastatic disease. Use light exercise only.
8. Improve aerobic capacity.
   a. Formal exercise testing should be individualized: based on history of diagnosis, treatment, adverse effects, and comorbidities.
   b. Exercise recommendations should be individualized, matched to patient's level of function (optimal level of exercise, ACSM's Guidelines for Exercise Testing and Prescription, 8th ed., 2010).
      (1) Generally low to moderate intensities (40%–< 60% oxygen uptake reserve or heart rate reserve; 11–13/20 Borg RPE scale; 3–5 days/wk, for 20–60 minutes/session.
      (2) Utilize a warm-up and cool-down before and after each session.
   c. Functional (activity) training includes activities of daily living and functional mobility skills, e.g., bed mobility, transfers, and ambulation.
   d. Monitor fatigue levels closely. Start slowly, progress incrementally, avoid exhaustion. Assess fatigue levels 12 hours later.
      (1) Encourage self-monitoring of fatigue level.

(2) Use activity pacing, carefully balance activity and rest periods; use short sessions throughout the day.
(3) Teach energy-conservation techniques.

9. Exercise Contraindications/Precautions.
   a. Exercise recommendations will vary based on individual patients and their past and present medical history.
   b. Review lab values prior to beginning each examination or treatment session. Table 6-1 includes recommendations for aerobic exercise.
   c. Exercise recommendations based on lab values (Table 6-1).
   d. Contraindications to exercise:
      (1) Day of intravenous chemotherapy or within 24 hours of treatment.
      (2) Severe reaction to radiation therapy.
      (3) Acute infection or febrile illness (temp. > 100 °F).
      (4) Severe nausea, vomiting, or diarrhea within 24–36 hours, dehydration, poor nutrition.
      (5) Unusual or extreme fatigue, muscular weakness, recent bone pain.
      (6) Chest pain, rapid or slow HR, elevated BP, swelling of ankles.
      (7) Severe dyspnea, pain on deep breath, cough/wheezing.
      (8) Dizziness/lightheadedness, disorientation, confusion, blurred vision, ataxia.
   e. Patients with low PLT may experience shortness of breath, excessive fatigue, possibly angina. Patients may develop petechiae, purpura, ecchymoses, hematuria, anemia, and hematochezia. Patients with critically low PLT (< 10,000/mm) may experience spontaneous bleeding.
   f. Patients with neutropenia (decreased neutrophils in blood) are at increased risk for infection. Adhere to infection control guidelines.
   g. Patients with bony metastases have increased risk of pathological fractures. Manual muscle testing, progressive resistive exercises, and high stress activities should be avoided.
   h. Recognize cancer-specific emergencies (sudden loss of limb function, spinal cord compression, fever in immune-compromised patients, superior vena cava syndrome). Initiate plan for emergency situation.

Table 6-1

Exercise Guidelines Based on Lab Values

NORMAL RANGE	ABNORMAL RANGE	EXERCISE RECOMMENDATIONS
Platelet count 150,000–450,000 cells/mm^3		Normal activity, unrestricted
	50,000–150,000	Some limitations
	30,000–50,000	Moderate exercise
	20,000–30,000	Light exercise
	< 20,000	ROM, ADLs, walking with physician approval
Complete Blood Count **White Blood Cell Count (WBC)** 4800–10,800 cells/mm^3		
	> 5000	Light or regular exercise
	< 5000 with fever	No exercise
	< 1000	No exercise; protective mask required
Hemoglobin (Hgb) Women 12–16 g/dL Men 13–18 g/dL		Normal activity, unrestricted
	> 10	Regular exercise
	< 8–10	Light exercise
	< 8	No exercise
Hemtocrit (HCT) % of RBC of whole blood Women 37%–48% Men 45%–52%		Normal activity, unrestricted
	> 25%	Light or regular exercise
	< 25%	No exercise

10. Specific considerations for exercise programs.
    a. Postmastectomy.
       (1) Focus is on restoration of pain-free full ROM of the shoulder, prevention/reduction of edema, restoration of function.
       (2) Early postoperative exercise is stressed: some protocols as early as Day 1.
    b. Post–bone marrow transplant.
       (1) Experience prolonged hospitalization and inactivity: average is 30 days; prolonged chemotherapy and radiotherapy, strict isolation.
       (2) Focus is on restoration of function, overcoming the effects of deconditioning.
       (3) Red Flags: Exercise is contraindicated in patients with platelet counts 20,000 or less; use caution with counts 20,000–50,000.

11. Physical agents (see Chapter 10).
    a. Thermal agents (hot packs, paraffin baths, fluidotherapy, infrared lamps) and deep heating agents (ultrasound, diathermy).
    Red Flags.
       (1) Do not use directly over tumor.
       (2) Do not use over dysvascular tissue: tissue exposed to radiation therapy.
       (3) Do not use with individuals with decreased sensitivity to temperature or pain in affected area.

(4) Do not use in areas of increased bleeding or hemorrhage, typically the result of corticosteroid therapy.
(5) Do not use with acute injury, inflammation, open wounds.

b. Cryotherapy.

 Red Flags.

(1) Do not use with patients with insensitivity to cold or delayed wound healing.
(2) Do not use over dysvascular tissue: tissue exposed to radiation therapy.

c. Hydrotherapy with agitation.

Red Flags.

(1) Do not use over dysvascular tissue: tissue exposed to radiation therapy.
(2) Do not use with individuals with decreased sensitivity to temperature or pain in affected area.
(3) Do not use in areas of increased bleeding or hemorrhage or open wounds.
(4) Risk of cross infection is high with immunosuppressed patients.

Gastrointestinal System

Overview

1. Anatomy/Physiology (see Figure 6-1).
   a. The gastrointestinal (GI) tract is a long hollow tube extending from the mouth to the anus. Ingested foods and fluids are broken down into molecules that are absorbed and used by the body, while waste products are eliminated.
      (1) The upper GI tract consists of the mouth, esophagus, and stomach and functions for ingestion and initial digestion of food.
      (2) The middle GI tract is the small intestine (duodenum, jejunum, and ileum). The major digestive and absorption processes occur here.
      (3) The lower GI tract consists of the large intestine (cecum, colon, and rectum), with primary functions that include absorption of water and electrolytes, storage and elimination of waste products.
      (4) Accessory organs aid in digestion by producing digestive secretions and include the salivary glands, liver, and pancreas.
   b. GI motility propels food and fluids through the GI system and is provided by rhythmic, intermittent contractions (peristaltic movements) of smooth muscle (except for pharynx and upper one-third of the esophagus).
   c. Neural control is achieved by the autonomic nervous system (ANS). Both sympathetic and parasympathetic plexuses extend along the length of the GI wall. Vagovagal (mediated by the vagus nerve) reflexes control the secretions and motility of the GI tract.
   d. Major GI hormones include cholecystokinin, gastrin, and secretin.
2. Signs and symptoms common to many types of GI disorders.
   a. Nausea and vomiting. Nausea is an unpleasant sensation that signals stimulation of medullary vomiting center and often precedes vomiting. Vomiting is the forceful oral expulsion of abdominal contents.

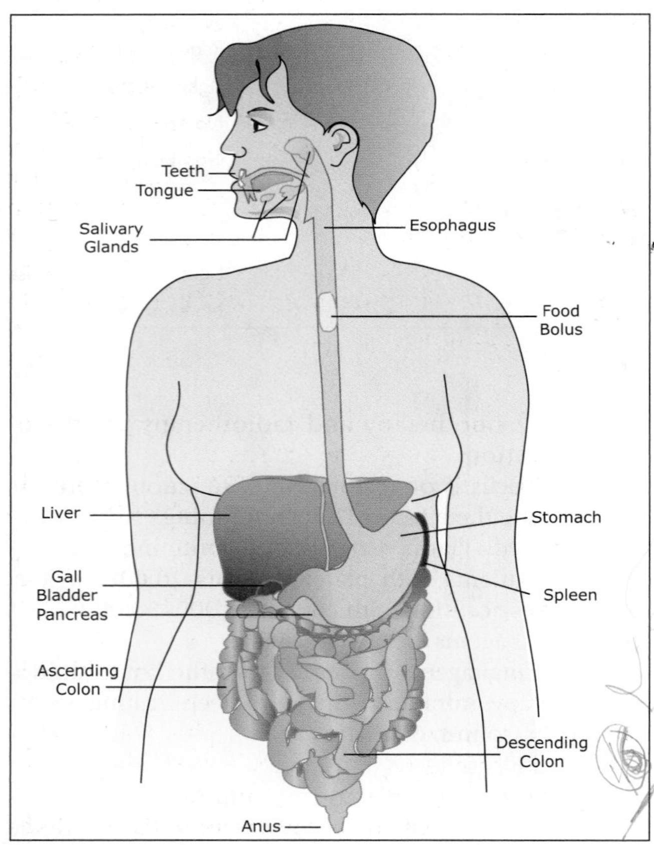

Figure 6-1 Gastrointestinal system anterior view.

(1) Nausea and vomiting can be triggered by many different causes including food, drugs, hypoxia, shock, inflammation of abdominal organs, distention, irritation of the GI tract, and motion sickness.

(2) Prolonged vomiting can produce fluid and electrolyte imbalance, and can result in pulmonary aspiration and mucosal or GI damage.

b. Diarrhea is the passage of frequent, watery, unformed stools. The amount of fluid loss determines the severity of the illness.

(1) Dehydration, electrolyte imbalance, dizziness, thirst, and weight loss are common complications of prolonged diarrhea.

(2) Numerous conditions can trigger diarrhea including infectious organisms (*Escherichia coli*, rotavirus, *Salmonella*), dysentery, diabetic enteropathy, irritable bowel syndrome, hyperthyroidism, neoplasm, and diverticulitis. Diet, medications, and strenuous exercise can also cause diarrhea.

c. Constipation is a decrease in normal elimination with excessively hard, dry stools and difficult elimination.

(1) Constipation causes increased bowel pressure and lower abdominal discomfort.

(2) Many different factors can trigger constipation, including a diet lacking in bulk and fiber, inadequate consumption of fluids, sedentary lifestyle, increasing age, and drugs (opiates, antidepressants, calcium channel blockers, anticholinergics).

(3) Numerous conditions can cause constipation including hypothyroidism, diverticular disease, irritable bowel syndrome, Parkinson's disease, spinal cord injury, tumors, bowel obstruction, and rectal lesions.

(4) Obstipation is intractable constipation with resulting fecal impaction, the retention of hard, dry stools in the rectum and colon. Impaction can cause partial or complete bowel obstruction. The patient may exhibit a history of watery diarrhea, fecal soiling, and fecal incontinence. Removal of the fecal mass is indicated.

(5) Red Flags: Constipation can cause abdominal pain and tenderness in the anterior hip, groin or thigh regions.

(6) Constipation may develop as a result of muscle guarding and splinting; e.g., in the patient with low back pain.

d. Anorexia is the loss of appetite with an inability to eat. It is associated with anxiety, fear, and depression along with a number of different disease states and drugs.

(1) Anorexia nervosa is a disorder characterized by prolonged loss of appetite and inability to eat. Individuals exhibit emaciation, emotional disturbance concerning body image, and fear of gaining weight. It is common in adolescent girls, who may also exhibit amenorrhea.

e. Dysphagia refers to difficulty in swallowing.

(1) Patients experience choking, coughing, or abnormal sensations of food sticking in the back of the throat or esophagus.

(2) Numerous conditions can cause dysphagia, including lesions of the CNS (stroke, Alzheimer's disease, Parkinson's disease), strictures and esophageal scarring, swelling, cancer, and scleroderma.

(3) Achalasia is a condition in which the lower esophageal sphincter fails to relax and food is trapped in the esophagus.

f. Heartburn is a painful burning sensation felt in the esophagus in the midepigastric area behind the sternum or in the throat.

(1) It is typically caused by reflux of gastric contents into the esophagus.

(2) Certain foods (fatty foods, citrus foods, chocolate, peppermint, alcohol, coffee, caffeine), increased abdominal pressure (food, tight clothing, back supports, pregnancy), and certain positions/movements (bending over or lying down after a large meal) can aggravate heartburn.

g. Abdominal pain is common in GI conditions. It is the result of inflammation, ischemia, and mechanical stretching. Visceral pain can occur in the epigastric region (T3–T5 sympathetic nerve distribution), the periumbilical region (T10 sympathetic nerve distribution), and the lower abdominal region (T10–L2 sympathetic nerve distribution).

h. Red Flags: Referred GI pain patterns.

(1) Visceral pain from the esophagus can refer to the midback.

(2) Midthoracic spine pain (nerve root pain) can appear as esophageal pain.

(3) Visceral pain from the liver, diaphragm, or pericardium can refer to the shoulder.

(4) Visceral pain from the gallbladder, stomach, pancreas, or small intestine can refer to the midback and scapular regions.

(5) Visceral pain from the colon, appendix, or pelvic viscera can refer to the pelvis, low back, or sacrum.

i. GI bleeding is evidenced by blood appearing in vomitus or feces.

(1) It can result from erosive gastritis, peptic ulcers, prolonged use of NSAIDs, and chronic alcohol use.

(2) Occult or hidden blood can be revealed only by stool testing.

j. Abdominal pain is generally aggravated by coughing, sneezing, or straining.

Esophagus

1. Gastroesophageal reflux disease (GERD).
   a. Caused by reflux or backward movement of gastric contents of the stomach into the esophagus, producing heartburn.
   b. Results from failure of the lower esophageal sphincter to regulate flow of food from the esophagus into the stomach and increased gastric pressure.
   c. The diaphragm that surrounds the esophagus and oblique muscles also contribute to antireflux function.
   d. Over time, acidic gastric fluids (pH < 4) damage the esophagus, producing reflux esophagitis.
   e. Heartburn commonly occurs 30–60 minutes after eating and at night when lying down (nocturnal reflux).
   f. Red Flags.
      (1) Atypical pain may present as head and neck pain.
      (2) Chest pain is sometimes mistaken for heart attack; it is unrelated to activity.
      (3) Respiratory symptoms can occur, including wheezing and chronic cough due to microaspiration, laryngeal injury, and vagus-mediated bronchospasm. Hoarseness can also result from chronic inflammation of the vocal cords.
   g. Complications include strictures and Barrett's esophagus (a precancerous state).
   h. Physical therapy interventions.
      (1) Positional changes from full supine to modified, more upright positions are indicated.
      (2) Valsalva's maneuver is contraindicated.
   i. Lifestyle modifications include avoiding large meals and certain foods; sleeping with head elevated; medications include acid-suppressing proton pump inhibitors (PPIs) (e.g., Prilosec), H_2 blockers (e.g., ranitidine [Zantac], cimetidine [Tagamet]), and antacids (e.g., Tums). In severe cases, surgery is an option.
2. Hiatal hernia.
   a. Protrusion of the stomach upward through the diaphragm (rolling hiatal hernia) or displacement of both the stomach and gastroesophageal junction upward into the thorax (sliding hiatal hernia).
   b. May be congenital or acquired.
   c. Symptoms include heartburn from GERD.
   d. Conservative or symptomatic treatment is the same as for GERD. Surgery may be indicated.

Stomach

1. Gastritis.
   a. Inflammation of the stomach mucosa. Gastritis can be acute or chronic.
   b. Acute gastritis is caused by severe burns, aspirin or other NSAIDs, corticosteroids, food allergies, or viral or bacterial infections. Hemorrhagic bleeding can occur.
   c. Symptoms include anorexia, nausea, vomiting, and pain.
   d. Chronic gastritis occurs with certain diseases such as peptic ulcer, bacterial infection caused by *Helicobacter pylori*, stomach cancer, pernicious anemia or with autoimmune disorders (thyroid disease, Addison's disease).
   e. Red Flags: Patients taking NSAIDs long term should be monitored carefully for stomach pain, bleeding, nausea, or vomiting.
   f. Management is symptomatic and includes avoiding irritating substances (caffeine, nicotine, alcohol), dietary modification, and medications that include acid-suppressing PPIs, H_2 blockers, and antacids.
2. Peptic ulcer disease.
   a. Refers to ulcerative lesions that occur in the upper GI tract in areas exposed to acid-pepsin secretions. It can affect one or all layers of the stomach or duodenum.
   b. Caused by a number of factors, including bacterial infection (*H. pylori*), acetylsalicylic acid (aspirin) and NSAIDs, excessive secretion of gastric acids, stress, and heredity.
   c. Symptoms include epigastric pain, which is described as a gnawing, burning, or cramp-like. Pain is aggravated by change in position and absence of food in the stomach and relieved by food or antacids.
   d. Complications include hemorrhage. Bleeding may be sudden and severe or insidious with blood in vomitus or stools. Symptoms can include weakness, dizziness, or other signs of circulatory shock.
   e. Management includes use of antibiotics for treatment of *H. pylori* along with acid-suppressing drugs (PPIs, H_2 blockers, and antacids). Dietary modification including avoidance of stomach irritants is indicated. Surgical intervention is indicated for perforation and uncontrolled bleeding.
   f. Red Flags.
      (1) Pain from peptic ulcers located on the posterior wall of the stomach can present as radiating back pain. Pain can also radiate to the right shoulder.
      (2) Stress and anxiety can increase gastric secretions and pain.

Intestines

1. Malabsorption syndrome.
   a. A complex of disorders characterized by problems in intestinal absorption of nutrients (fat, carbohydrates, proteins, vitamins, calcium, and iron).

b. Can be caused by gastric or small bowel resection (short-gut syndrome) or a number of different diseases including cystic fibrosis, celiac disease, Crohn's disease, chronic pancreatitis, and pernicious anemia. Malabsorption can also be drug-induced (NSAID gastroenteritis).

c. Deficiencies of enzymes (pancreatic lipase) and bile salts are contributing factors.

d. Symptoms can include anorexia, weight loss, abdominal bloating, pain and cramps, indigestion, and steatorrhea (abnormal amounts of fat in feces). Diarrhea can be chronic and explosive.

e. Red Flags.

(1) Iron-deficiency anemia.

(2) Easy bruising and bleeding due to lack of vitamin K.

(3) Muscle weakness and fatigue due to lack of protein, iron, folic acid, and vitamin B.

(4) Bone loss, pain, and predisposition to develop fractures from lack of calcium, phosphate, and vitamin D.

(5) Neuropathy including tetany, paresthesias, numbness and tingling from lack of calcium, vitamins B and D, magnesium, potassium.

(6) Muscle spasms from electrolyte imbalance and lack of calcium.

(7) Peripheral edema.

2. Inflammatory bowel disease (IBD).

a. Refers to two related chronic inflammatory intestinal disorders: Crohn's disease (CD) and ulcerative colitis (UC). Both diseases result in inflammation of the bowel and are characterized by remissions and exacerbations.

b. Symptoms include abdominal pain, frequent attacks of diarrhea, fecal urgency, and weight loss.

Red Flags.

(1) Joint pain (reactive arthritis) and skin rashes can occur. Pain can be referred to the low back.

(2) Complications can include intestinal obstruction and corticosteroid toxicity (low bone density, increased fracture risk).

(3) Intestinal absorption is disrupted and nutritional deficiencies are common.

(4) Chronic IBD can lead to anxiety and depression.

c. Crohn's disease involves a granulomatous type of inflammation that can occur anywhere in the GI tract. Areas of adjacent normal tissue called skip lesions are present.

d. Ulcerative colitis involves an ulcerative and exudative inflammation of the large intestine and rectum. It is characterized by varying amounts of bloody diarrhea, mucus, and pus. Skip lesions are absent.

3. Irritable bowel syndrome (IBS).

a. Characterized by abnormally increased motility of the small and large intestines. IBS is also known as spastic, nervous, or irritable colon.

b. IBS is associated with emotional stress and certain foods (high fat content or roughage, lactose intolerance). No structural or biochemical abnormalities have been identified.

c. Symptoms include persistent or recurrent abdominal pain that is relieved by defecation. Patients may experience constipation or diarrhea, bloating, abdominal cramps, flatulence, nausea, and anorexia.

d. Stress reduction and medications to reduce anxiety or depression are important components of treatment.

e. Regular physical activity is effective in reducing stress and improving bowel function.

4. Diverticular disease.

a. Characterized by pouch-like herniations (diverticula) of the mucosal layer of the colon through the muscularis layer.

b. Diverticulosis refers to pouch-like herniations of the colon, especially the sigmoid colon.

(1) Symptoms are minimal but can include rectal bleeding.

(2) Dietary factors (lack of dietary fiber), lack of physical activity, and poor bowel habits contribute to its development.

(3) Diverticulosis can lead to diverticulitis.

c. Diverticulitis refers to inflammation of one or more diverticula. Fecal matter penetrates diverticula and causes inflammation and abscess.

(1) Symptoms include pain and cramping in the lower left quadrant, nausea and vomiting, slight fever, and an elevated WBC.

(2) Complications include bowel obstruction, perforation with peritonitis, and hemorrhage.

d. Red Flags: Patients may complain of back pain.

e. Regular exercise is an important component of treatment.

5. Appendicitis.

a. An inflammation of the vermiform appendix. As the condition progresses, the appendix becomes swollen, gangrenous, and perforated. Perforation can be life threatening and lead to the development of peritonitis.

b. Pain is abrupt at onset, localized to the epigastric or periumbilical area, and increases in intensity over time.

c. Rebound tenderness (Blumberg's sign) is present in response to depression of the abdominal wall at a site distant from the painful area.

d. Point tenderness is located at McBurney's point, the site of the appendix located 1½–2 inches above

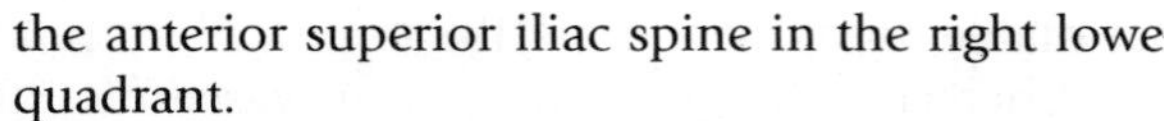

the anterior superior iliac spine in the right lower quadrant.

e. Red Flags: Immediate medical attention is required.

f. Elevations in WBC count (> 20,000/mm^3) are indicative of perforation. Surgery is indicated.

6. Peritonitis.
   a. Inflammation of the peritoneum, the serous membrane lining the walls of the abdominal cavity.
   b. Peritonitis results from bacterial invasion and infection of the peritoneum. Common agents include *E. coli, Bacteroides, Fusobacterium,* and streptococci.
   c. A number of different factors can introduce infecting agents, including penetrating wounds, surgery, perforated peptic ulcer, ruptured appendix, perforated diverticulum, gangrenous bowel, pelvic inflammatory disease, and gangrenous gallbladder.
   d. Symptoms include abdominal distension, severe abdominal pain, rigidity from reflex guarding, rebound tenderness, decreased or absent bowel sounds, nausea and vomiting, and tachycardia.
   e. Elevated WBC count, fever, electrolyte imbalance, and hypotension are common.
   f. Peritonitis can lead to toxemia and shock, circulatory failure, and respiratory distress.
   g. Treatment is aimed at controlling inflammation and infection and restoring fluid and electrolyte imbalances. Surgical intervention may be necessary to remove an inflamed appendix or close a perforation.

Rectum

1. Rectal fissure.
   a. A tear or ulceration of the lining of the anal canal.
   b. Constipation and large, hard stools are contributing factors.
2. Hemorrhoids (piles).
   a. Varicosities in the lower rectum or anus caused by congestion of the veins in the hemorrhoidal plexus.
   b. Hemorrhoids can be internal or external (protruding from the anus).
   c. Symptoms include local irritation, pain, rectal itching.
   d. Prolonged bleeding can result in anemia.
   e. Straining with defecation, constipation, and prolonged sitting contribute to discomfort.
   f. Pregnancy increases the risk of hemorrhoids.
   g. Treatment includes topical medications to shrink the hemorrhoid, dietary changes, sitz baths, local hot or cold compresses, and ligation or surgical excision.

Genital/Reproductive System

Overview: Female Reproductive System

1. Anatomy/Physiology (see Figure 6-2).
   a. External genitalia, located at the base of the pelvis, consist of the mons pubis, labia majora, labia minora, clitoris, and perineal body.
   b. The urethra and anus are in close proximity to the external genital structures, and cross-contamination is possible.
   c. The internal genitalia consist of the vagina, the uterus and cervix, the fallopian tubes, and paired ovaries.
2. Sexual and reproductive functions.
   a. The ovaries store female germ cells (ova) and produce female sex hormones (estrogens and progesterone) under control of the hypothalamus (gonadotropin-releasing hormone) and the anterior pituitary gland (gonadotropic follicle-stimulating and luteinizing hormones).
   b. Sex hormones influence the development of secondary sex characteristics, regulate the menstrual cycle (ovulation), maintain pregnancy (fertilization and implantation, gestation), and influence menopause (cessation of the menstrual cycle).
      (1) Estrogens decrease the rate of bone resorption.
      Red Flags: Osteoporosis and risk of bone fracture increase dramatically after menopause.
      (2) Estrogens increase production of the thyroid and increase high-density lipoproteins (a protective effect against heart disease).
      Red Flags: Heart disease and stroke risk increases after menopause.
3. Breasts.
   a. Mammary tissues located on the anterior chest wall between the 3rd and 7th ribs.

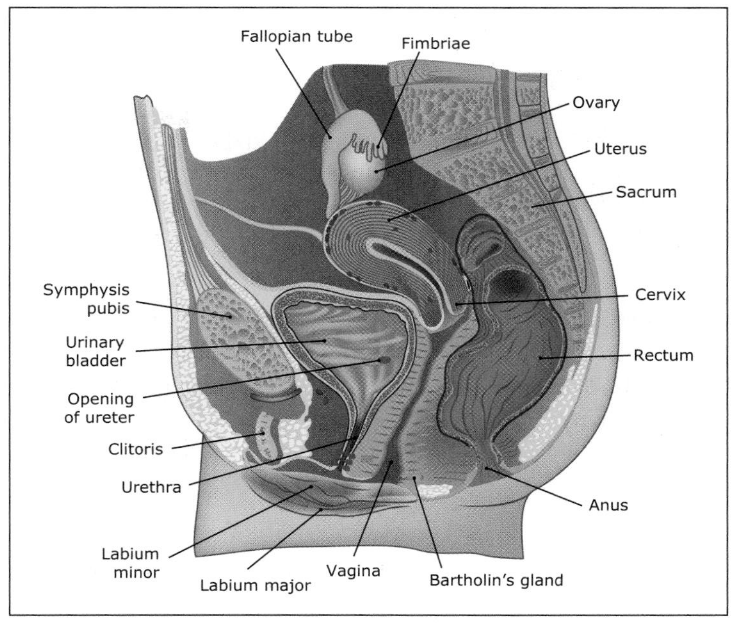

Figure 6-2 **Female Reproductive System.**

b. Breast function is related to production of sex hormones and pregnancy, producing milk for infant nourishment.

Pregnancy: Normal

1. Pregnancy weight gain. Average 20–30 lb.
2. Physical therapists teach childbirth education classes.
   a. Relaxation training: e.g., Jacobsen's progressive relaxation, relaxation response, mental imagery, yoga.
   b. Breathing management: slow, deep, diaphragmatic breathing; Lamaze techniques; avoidance of Valsalva's maneuver.
   c. Provide information about pregnancy and childbirth.
3. Common changes with pregnancy and physical therapy interventions.
   a. Postural changes: kyphosis with scapular protraction, cervical lordosis, and forward head; lumbar lordosis; postural stress may continue into postpartum phase with lifting and carrying the infant.
      (1) Postural evaluation.
      (2) Teach postural exercises to stretch, strengthen, and train postural muscles.
      (3) Teach pelvic stabilization exercises, e.g., posterior pelvic tilt.
      (4) Teach correct body mechanics, e.g., sitting, standing, lifting, ADLs.
      (5) Limit certain activities in the third trimester, e.g., supine position to avoid inferior vena cava compression, bridging.
   b. Balance changes: center of gravity shifts forward and upward as the fetus develops; with advanced pregnancy, there will be a wider base of support, increased difficulty with walking and stair climbing, rapid challenges to balance.
      (1) Teach safety strategies.
   c. Ligamentous laxity secondary to hormonal influences (relaxin).
      (1) Joint hypermobility (e.g., sacroiliac joint), pain.
      (2) Predisposition to injury especially in weight-bearing joints of lower extremities and pelvis.
      (3) May persist for some time after delivery; teach joint protection strategies.
   d. Muscle weakness: abdominal muscles are stretched and weakened as pregnancy develops; pelvic floor weakness with advanced pregnancy and childbirth. Stress incontinence secondary to pelvic floor dysfunction (experienced by 80% of women).
      (1) Teach exercises to improve control of pelvic floor, maintain abdominal function.
      (2) Stretching exercises to reduce muscle cramping.
      (3) Avoid Valsalva's maneuver: may exacerbate condition.
   e. Urinary changes: pressure on bladder causes frequent urination; increased incidence of reflux, urinary tract infections.

f. Respiratory changes: elevation of the diaphragm with widening of thoracic cage; hyperventilation, dyspnea may be experienced with mild exercise during late pregnancy.
g. Cardiovascular changes: increased blood volume; increased venous pressure in the lower extremities; increased heart rate and cardiac output, decreased blood pressure due to venous distensibility.
 (1) Teach safe progression of aerobic exercises.
  (a) Exercise in moderation, with frequent rests.
  (b) Stress use of familiar activities; avoidance of unfamiliar.
  (c) Postpartum: emphasize gradual return to previous level of activity.
 (2) Stress gentle stretching, adequate warm-ups and cool-downs.
 (3) Teach ankle pumps for lower extremity edema (late-stage pregnancy); elevate legs to assist in venous return.
 (4) Wear loose, comfortable clothing.
h. Altered thermoregulation: increased basal metabolic rate; increased heat production.

Pregnancy-Related Pathologies

1. Diastasis recti abdominis.
 a. Lateral separation or split of the rectus abdominis; separation from midline (linea alba) greater than 2 cm is significant; associated with loss of abdominal wall support, increased back pain.
 b. Physical therapy interventions.
  (1) Teach protection of abdominal musculature: avoid abdominal exercises, e.g., full sit-ups or bilateral straight leg raising.
  (2) Resume abdominal exercises when separation is less than 2 cm: teach safe abdominal strengthening exercises, e.g., partial sit-ups (knees bent), pelvic tilts; utilize hands to support abdominal wall.
2. Pelvic floor disorders.
 a. The result of weakening of pelvic floor muscles (pubococcygeal [PC] muscles).
 b. PC muscles normally function to support the vagina, urinary bladder, and rectum and help maintain continence of the urethra and rectum.
 c. Weakness or laxity of PC muscles typically results from overstretching during pregnancy and childbirth. Further loss of elasticity and muscle tone during later life can result in partial or total organ prolapse. Examples include:
  (1) Cystocele: the herniation of the bladder into the vagina.
  (2) Rectocele: the herniation of the rectum into the vagina.
  (3) Uterine prolapse: the bulging of the uterus into the vagina.
 d. PC muscles can also go into spasm.
 e. Symptoms include pelvic pain (perivaginal, perirectal, lower abdominal quadrant), urinary incontinence, and pain with sexual intercourse.
 Red Flags: Pain can radiate down the posterior thigh.
 f. Surgical correction is often required, depending on degree of prolapse.
 g. Physical therapy intervention (pelvic floor rehabilitation).
  (1) Observe for urinary frequency and urgency, painful urination, painful defecation; low back and perineal pain with prolapse.
  (2) Teach pelvic floor exercises (Kegel's exercises) to strengthen the PC muscles.
  (3) Postural education and muscle reeducation, pelvic mobilization, and stretching of tight lower extremity (LE) muscles are also important components.
3. Low back and pelvic pain.
 a. Physical therapy interventions.
  (1) Teach proper body mechanics.
  (2) Balance rest with activity.
  (3) Emphasize use of a firm mattress.
  (4) Massage, modalities for pain (no deep heat).
4. Sacroiliac dysfunction.
 a. Secondary to postural changes, ligamentous laxity.
 b. Symptoms include posterior pelvic pain; pain in buttocks, may radiate into posterior thigh or knee.
 c. Associated with prolonged sitting, standing, or walking.
 d. Physical therapy interventions.
  (1) External stabilization, e.g., sacroiliac support belt, may help reduce pain.
  (2) Avoid single-limb weight bearing: may aggravate sacroiliac dysfunction.
5. Varicose veins.
 a. Physical therapy interventions.
  (1) Elevate extremities; avoid crossing legs, which may press on veins.
  (2) Use of elastic support stockings may help.
6. Preeclampsia.
 a. Pregnancy-induced, acute hypertension after the 24th week of gestation.
 b. May be mild or severe.
 c. Evaluate for symptoms of hypertension, edema, sudden excessive weight gain, headache, visual disturbances, or hyperreflexia.
 d. Initiate prompt physician referral.

7. Cesarean childbirth.
   a. Surgical delivery of the fetus by an incision through the abdominal and uterine walls; indicated in pelvic disproportion, failure of the birth process to progress, fetal or maternal distress, or other complications.
   b. Physical therapy interventions.
      (1) Postoperative TENS can be used for incisional pain; electrodes are placed parallel to the incision.
      (2) Prevent postsurgical pulmonary complications: assist patient in breathing, coughing.
      (3) Postcesarean exercises.
         (a) Gentle abdominal exercises; provide incisional support with pillow.
         (b) Pelvic floor exercises: labor and pushing is typically present before surgery.
         (c) Postural exercises; precautions about heavy lifting for 4–6 weeks.
      (4) Ambulation.
      (5) Prevent incisional adhesions: friction massage.

Disorders of the Female Reproductive System

1. Endometriosis.
   a. Characterized by ectopic growth and function of endometrial tissue outside of the uterus. Common sites include ovaries, fallopian tubes, broad ligaments, uterosacral ligaments, pelvis, vagina, or intestines.
      (1) The ectopic tissue responds to hormonal influences but is not able to be shed as uterine tissue during menstruation.
      (2) Endometrial tissue can lead to cysts and rupture, producing peritonitis and adhesions as well as adhesions and obstruction.
   b. Symptoms include pain, dysmenorrhea, dyspareunia (abnormal pain during sexual intercourse), and infertility.
   c. Red Flags: Patients may complain of back pain. Endometrial implants on muscle (e.g., psoas major, pelvic floor muscles) may produce pain with palpation or contraction.
   d. Treatment involves pain management, endometrial suppression, and surgery.
2. Pelvic inflammatory disease (PID).
   a. An inflammation of the upper reproductive tract involving the uterus (endometritis), fallopian tubes (salpingitis), or ovaries (oophoritis).
   b. PID is caused by a polymicrobial agent that ascends through the endocervical canal.
   c. Symptoms include lower abdominal pain that typically starts after a menstrual cycle, purulent cervical discharge, and painful cervix. Fever, elevated WBC count, and increased ESR are present.
   d. Complications can include pelvic adhesions, infertility, ectopic pregnancy, chronic pain, and abscesses.
   e. Treatment involves antibiotic therapy to treat the infection and prevent complications.

Overview: Male Reproductive System

1. Anatomy/Physiology (see Figure 6-3).
   a. The male reproductive system is composed of paired testes, genital ducts, accessory glands, and penis.
   b. The testes, or male gonads, are located in the scrotum, paired egg-shaped sacs located outside the abdominal cavity. They produce male sex hormones (testosterone) and spermatozoa (male germ cells).
   c. The accessory glands (seminal vesicles, prostate gland, and bulbourethral glands) prepare sperm for ejaculation.
   d. The ductal system (epididymides, vas deferens, and ejaculatory ducts) stores and transports sperm.
   e. The urethra, enclosed in the penis, functions in the elimination of urine and semen.
   f. Sperm production requires an environment that is 2°C–3°C lower than body temperature.

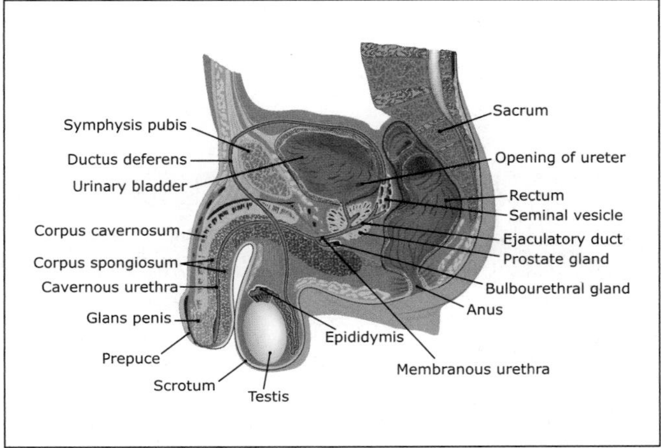

Figure 6-3 **Male Reproductive System.**

Chapter 6 OTH

g. Testosterone and other male sex hormones (androgens).
   (1) During development, induce differentiation of the male genital tract.
   (2) Stimulate development of primary and secondary sex characteristics during puberty and maintain them during life.
   (3) Promote protein metabolism, musculoskeletal growth, and subcutaneous fat distribution (anabolic effects).

h. The hypothalamus and anterior pituitary gland maintain endocrine via gonadotropic hormones (follicle-stimulating hormone [FSH] and luteinizing hormone [LH]).
   (1) FSH initiates spermatogenesis.
   (2) LH regulates testosterone production.

Disorders of the Male Reproductive System

1. Erectile dysfunction (ED) (impotence).
   a. The inability to achieve and maintain erection for sexual intercourse.
   b. Organic causes.
      (1) Neurogenic causes: stroke, cerebral trauma, spinal cord injury, multiple sclerosis, Parkinson's disease.
      (2) Hormonal causes: decreased androgen levels with hypogonadism, hypothyroidism, and hypopituitarism.
      (3) Vascular causes: hypertension, coronary heart disease, hyperlipidemia, cigarette smoking, diabetes mellitus, pelvic irradiation.
      (4) Drug-induced: antidepressants, antipsychotics, antiandrogens, antihypertensives, amphetamines, alcohol.
      (5) Aging increases risk of ED.
   c. Psychogenic causes.
      (1) Performance anxiety.
      (2) Depression and psychiatric disorders (schizophrenia).
   d. Surgical causes.
      (1) Transurethral procedures.
      (2) Radical prostatectomy.
      (3) Proctocolectomy.
      (4) Abdominoperineal resection.
   e. Treatment requires accurate identification and remediation of specific causes of ED.
   f. Medications are available to improve function (e.g., sildenafil [Viagra]).
2. Prostatitis.
   a. Infection and inflammation of the prostate gland.
   b. Types include acute bacterial, chronic prostatitis, and nonbacterial.
      (1) Acute bacterial prostatitis involves bacterial urinary tract infection (UTI) and is associated with catheterization and multiple sex partners. Symptoms include urinary frequency, urgency, nocturia, dysuria, urethral discharge, fever and chills, malaise, myalgia and arthralgia, and pain.

      Red Flags: Dull, aching pain may be found in the lower abdominal, rectal, lower back, sacral, or groin regions.

      (2) Chronic prostatitis can also be bacterial in origin and is associated with recurrent UTI. Symptoms include urinary frequency and urgency, myalgia and arthralgia, and pain in the low back or perineal region.
      (3) Nonbacterial inflammatory prostatitis produces pain in the penis, testicles, and scrotum; painful ejaculation; low back pain or pain in the inner thighs; urinary symptoms; decreased libido; and impotence.
   c. Because the prostate encircles the urethra, obstruction of urinary flow can result.

Renal and Urological Systems

Overview

1. Anatomy (see Figure 6-4).
   a. Kidneys are paired, bean-shaped organs located outside of the peritoneal cavity (retroperitoneal) in the posterior upper abdomen on each side of the vertebral column at the level of T12–L2.
   b. Each kidney is multilobular; each lobule is composed of more than 1 million nephrons (the functional units of the kidney).
   c. Each nephron consists of a glomerulus that filters the blood and nephron tubules. Water, electrolytes, and other substances vital for function are reabsorbed into the bloodstream, while other waste

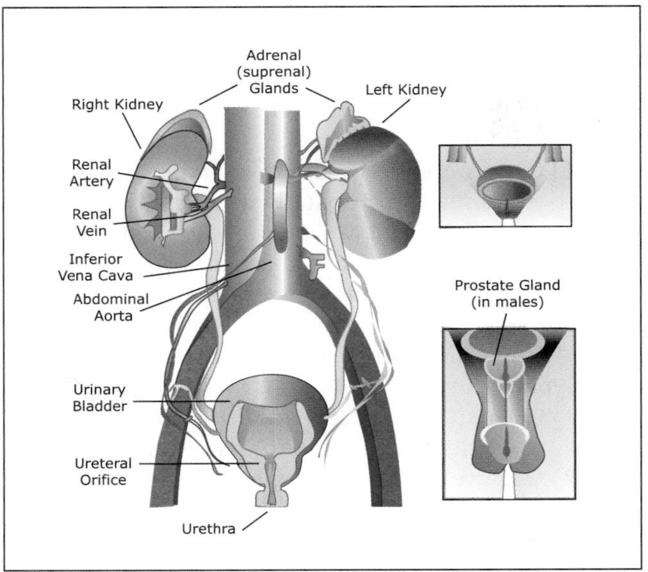

Figure 6-4 Renal and urological system anterior view.

products are secreted into the tubules for elimination.

d. The renal pelvis is a wide, funnel-shaped structure at the upper end of the urethra that drains the kidney into the lower urinary tract (bladder and urethra).
e. The bladder is a membranous sac that collects urine and is located behind the symphysis pubis.
f. The ureter extends from the renal pelvis to the bladder and moves urine via peristaltic action.
g. The urethra extends from the bladder to an external orifice for elimination of urine from the body.
h. In females, proximity of the urethra to vaginal and rectal openings increases the likelihood of UTI.

2. Functions of the kidney.
   a. Regulates the composition and pH of body fluids through reabsorption and elimination; controls mineral (sodium, potassium, hydrogen, chloride, and bicarbonate ions) and water balance.
   b. Eliminates metabolic wastes (urea, uric acid, creatinine) and drugs/drug metabolites.
   c. Assists in blood pressure regulation through rennin-angiotensin-aldosterone mechanisms and salt and water elimination.
   d. Contributes to bone metabolic function by activating vitamin D and regulating calcium and phosphate conservation and elimination.
   e. Controls the production of red blood cells in the bone marrow through the production of erythropoietin.
   f. The glomerular filtration rate (GFR) is the amount of filtrate that is formed each minute as blood moves through the glomeruli and serves as an important gauge of renal function.
      (1) Regulated by arterial blood pressure and renal blood flow.
      (2) Measured clinically by obtaining creatinine levels in blood and urine samples.
      (3) Normal creatinine clearance is 115–125 mL/min.
   g. Blood urea nitrogen (BUN) is urea produced in the liver as a by-product of protein metabolism that is eliminated by the kidneys.
      (1) BUN levels are elevated with increased protein intake, gastrointestinal bleeding, and dehydration.
      (2) BUN-creatinine ratio is abnormal in liver disease.
3. Normal values of urine (urinalysis findings).
   a. Color: yellow-amber.
   b. Clarity: clear.
   c. Specific gravity: 1.010–1.025 with normal fluid intake.
   d. pH: 4.6–8.0; average is 6 (acid).
   e. Protein: 0–8 mg/dL.
   f. Sugar: 0.

Urinary Regulation of Fluids and Electrolytes

1. Homeostasis. Regulated through thirst mechanisms and renal function via circulating antidiuretic hormone (ADH).
2. Fluid imbalances.
   a. Daily fluid requirements vary based on presence or absence of such factors as sweating, air temperature, and fever.
   b. Dehydration: excessive loss of body fluids; fluid output exceeds fluid intake.
      (1) Causes: poor intake; excess output: profuse sweating, vomiting, diarrhea, and diuretics; closely linked to sodium deficiency.
      (2) Observe for poor skin turgor, dry mucous membranes, headache, irritability, postural hypotension, incoordination, lethargy, disorientation.
      (3) May lead to uremia and hypovolemic shock (stupor and coma).
      (4) Decreased exercise capacity, especially in hot environments.
   c. Edema: an excess of body fluids with expansion of interstitial fluid volume.
      (1) Causes.
         (a) Increased capillary pressure: heart failure, kidney disease, premenstrual retention, pregnancy,

environmental heat stress; venous obstruction (liver disease, acute pulmonary edema, venous thrombosis).

(b) Decreased colloidal osmotic pressure: decreased production or loss of plasma proteins (protein-losing kidney disease, liver disease, starvation, malnutrition).

(c) Increased capillary permeability: inflammation, allergic reactions, malignancy, tissue injury, burns.

(d) Obstruction of lymphatic flow.

(2) Observe for swelling of the ankles and feet, weight gain; headache, blurred vision; muscle cramps and twitches.

(a) Edema can be restrictive, producing a tourniquet effect.

(b) Tissues are susceptible to injury and delayed healing.

(c) Pitting edema occurs when the amount of interstitial fluid exceeds the absorptive capacity of tissues.

3. Potassium.

a. Normal serum level is 3.5–5.5 mEq/L.

b. Hypokalemia.

(1) Causes: deficient potassium or excessive loss due to diarrhea, vomiting, metabolic acidosis, renal tubular disease, alkalosis.

(2) Observe for muscle weakness, aches, fatigue; cardiac arrhythmias; abdominal distention; nausea and vomiting.

c. Hyperkalemia.

(1) Causes: inadequate secretion with acute renal failure, kidney disease, metabolic acidosis, diabetic ketoacidosis, sickle cell anemia, SLE.

(2) Often symptomless until very high levels. Observe for muscle weakness, arrhythmias, electrocardiogram (ECG) changes (tall T wave, prolonged P-R interval, and QRS duration).

4. Sodium.

a. Normal serum level is 135–146 mEq/L.

b. Hyponatremia.

(1) Causes: water intoxication (excess extracellular water) associated with excess intake or excess ADH (tumors, endocrine disorders).

(2) Observe for confusion; decreased mental alertness can progress to convulsions; signs of increased intracerebral pressure; poor motor coordination; sleepiness; anorexia.

c. Hypernatremia.

(1) Causes: occurs with water deficits (not salt excesses) with dehydration, insufficient water intake.

(2) Observe for: circulatory congestion (pitting edema, excessive weight gain); pulmonary edema with dyspnea; hypertension, tachycardia; agitation, restlessness, convulsions.

5. Calcium.

a. Normal total calcium in blood is 8.4–10.4 mg/dL.

b. Hypocalcemia.

(1) Causes: reduced albumin levels, hyperphosphatemia, hypoparathyroidism, malabsorption of calcium and vitamin D, alkalosis, acute pancreatitis, vitamin D deficiency.

(2) Observe for muscle cramps, tetany, spasms; paresthesias; anxiety, irritability, twitching convulsion; arrhythmias, hypotension.

c. Hypercalcemia.

(1) Causes: hyperparathyroidism, tumors, hyperthyroidism, vitamin A intoxication.

(2) Observe for fatigue, depression, mental confusion, nausea/vomiting, increased urination, occasional cardiac arrhythmias.

6. Magnesium.

a. Normal serum level is 1.8–2.4 mg/dL.

b. Hypomagnesemia.

(1) Causes: hemodialysis, blood transfusions, chronic renal disease, hepatic cirrhosis (alcoholism), chronic pancreatitis, hypoparathyroidism, malabsorption syndromes, severe burns, excess loss of body fluid.

(2) Observe for hyperirritability, confusion; leg and foot cramps.

c. Hypermagnesemia.

(1) Causes: renal failure, diabetic acidosis, hypothyroidism, Addison's disease, with dehydration and with use of antacids.

(2) Observe for hyporeflexia, muscle weakness, drowsiness, lethargy, confusion, bradycardia, hypotension.

7. Acid-base balance.

a. Balance of acids and bases in the body (normally a ratio of 20 base to 1 acid; normal serum pH is 7.35–7.45 [slightly alkaline]); regulated by blood buffer systems (the lungs and the kidneys).

b. Metabolic acidosis: a depletion of bases or an accumulation of acids; blood pH falls below 7.35.

(1) Causes: diabetes, renal insufficiency or failure, diarrhea.

(2) Observe for hyperventilation (compensatory), deep respirations; weakness, muscular twitching; malaise, nausea, vomiting, and diarrhea; headache; dry skin and mucous membranes, poor skin turgor.

(3) May lead to stupor and coma (death).

c. Metabolic alkalosis: an increase in bases or a reduction of acids; blood pH rises above 7.45.

(1) Causes: excess vomiting, excess diuretics, hypokalemia; peptic ulcer, and excessive intake of antacids.

(2) Observe for hypoventilation (compensatory), depressed respirations; dysrhythmias; prolonged vomiting, diarrhea; weakness, muscle twitching; irritability, agitation, convulsions and coma (death).

d. Respiratory acidosis: CO_2 retention, impaired alveolar ventilation.

(1) Causes: hypoventilation, drugs/oversedation, chronic pulmonary disease (e.g., emphysema, asthma, bronchitis, pneumonia) or hypermetabolism (sepsis, burns).

(2) Observe for dyspnea, hyperventilation cyanosis; restlessness, headache.

(3) May lead to disorientation, stupor and coma, death.

e. Respiratory alkalosis: diminished CO_2, alveolar hyperventilation.

(1) Causes: anxiety attack with hyperventilation, hypoxia (emphysema, pneumonia), impaired lung expansion, congestive heart failure (CHF), pulmonary embolism, diffuse liver or CNS disease, salicylate poisoning, extreme stress (stimulation of respiratory center).

(2) Observe for tachypnea, dizziness, anxiety, difficulty concentrating, numbness and tingling, blurred vision, diaphoresis, muscle cramps, twitching or tetany, weakness, arrhythmias, convulsions.

Renal and Urological Disorders

1. Urinary tract infections (UTIs).

a. Infection of the urinary tract with microorganisms.

b. Lower UTI: cystitis (inflammation and infection of the bladder) or urethritis (inflammation and infection of the urethra).

(1) Usually secondary to ascending urinary tract infections; may also involve kidneys and ureters.

(2) Associated with symptoms of urinary frequency, urgency, burning sensation during urination. Urine may be cloudy and foul smelling. Pain is noted in suprapubic, lower abdominal, or groin area, depending on site of infection.

c. Upper UTI: pyelonephritis (inflammation and infection of one or both kidneys).

(1) Associated with symptoms of systemic involvement: fever, chills, malaise, headache, tenderness and pain over kidneys (back pain), tenderness over the costovertebal angle (Murphy's sign). Symptoms also include frequent and burning urination; nausea and vomiting may occur.

(2) Palpitation or percussion over the kidney typically causes pain.

(3) Can be acute or chronic; generally more serious than lower UTI.

d. Increased risk of UTI in persons with autoimmunity, urinary obstruction and reflux, neurogenic bladder and catheterization, diabetes, and kidney transplantation. Older adults and women are also at increased risk for UTI.

2. Renal cystic disease.

a. Renal cysts are fluid-filled cavities that form along the nephron and can lead to renal degeneration or obstruction.

b. Types include polycystic, medullary sponge, acquired, and simple renal cysts.

c. Symptoms can include pain, hematuria, and hypertension. Fever can occur with associated infection. Cysts can rupture producing hematuria. Simple cysts are generally asymptomatic.

3. Obstructive disorders.

a. Developmental defects, renal calculi, prostatic hyperplasia or cancer, scar tissue from inflammation, tumors, and infection.

b. Pressure build-up backward from site of obstruction; can result in kidney damage. Dilation of ureters and renal pelves may be used to reduce obstruction. Observe for pain, signs and symptoms of UTI and hypertension.

c. Renal calculi (kidney stones): crystalline structures formed from normal components of urine (calcium, magnesium ammonium phosphate, uric acid, and cystine).

(1) Etiological influences include concentration of stone components in urine and a urinary environment conducive to stone formation.

(2) Symptoms include renal colic pain (pain from a stone lodged in the ureter made worse by stretching the collecting system). Pain may radiate to the lower abdominal quadrant, bladder area and perineal area (scrotum in the male and labia in the female). Nausea and vomiting are common and the skin may be cool and clammy.

(3) Extracorporeal shock wave lithotripsy (ESWL) is used to break up stones into fragments to allow for easy passage.

(4) Treatment/prevention can also include increased fluid intake, thiazide diuretics, dietary restriction of foods high in oxalate, acidification or alkalinization of urine depending on type of stone.

4. Renal failure.

a. Acute renal failure: sudden loss of kidney function with resulting elevation in serum urea and creatinine.

(1) Etiology: may be due to circulatory disruption to kidneys, toxic substances, bacterial toxins, acute obstruction, or trauma.

b. Chronic renal failure: progressive loss of kidney function leading to end-stage failure.

(1) Etiology: may result from prolonged acute urinary tract obstruction and infection, diabetes, SLE, uncontrolled hypertension.

(2) Uremia: an end-stage toxic condition resulting from renal insufficiency and retention of nitrogenous wastes in blood; symptoms can include anorexia, nausea, and mental confusion.

(3) Red Flags: May lead to multisystem abnormalities and failure.

(a) Dizziness, headaches, anxiety, memory loss, inability to concentrate, convulsions, and coma.

(b) Hypertension, dyspnea on exertion, heart failure.

(c) Chronic pain: ischemic leg pain, painful cramps.

(d) Edema: peripheral edema, pulmonary edema.

(e) Muscle weakness: peripheral neuropathy, cramping, restless legs.

(f) Skeletal: osteomalacia, osteoporosis, bone pain, fracture.

(g) Skin: pallor, ecchymosis, pruritus, dry skin.

(h) Anemia, tendency to bleed easily.

(i) Decreased endurance; functional losses.

(j) Autonomic nervous system dysfunction: decreased heart rate, blood pressure; orthostatic hypotension.

c. Dialysis: process of diffusing blood across a semipermeable membrane for the purposes of removal of toxic substances; maintains fluid, electrolyte and acid-base balance in presence of renal failure; peritoneal, or renal (hemodialysis).

(1) Dialysis disequilibrium: symptoms of nausea, vomiting, drowsiness, headache, and seizures; the result of rapid changes after beginning dialysis.

(2) Dialysis dementia: signs of cerebral dysfunction (e.g., speech difficulties, mental confusion, myoclonus, seizures, eventually death); the result of long-standing years of dialysis treatment.

(3) Locate dialysis shunts: taking BP at the shunt site is contraindicated.

(4) Locate peritoneal catheters (if used): avoid trauma to area.

(5) Examine for multisystem dysfunction: vital signs, strength, sensation, ROM, function, and endurance.

d. Transplantation is a major treatment choice (renal allograft).

5. Urinary incontinence.

a. Inability to retain urine; the result of loss of sphincter control; may be acute (due to transient causes, e.g., cystitis) or persistent (e.g., stroke, dementia).

b. Types.

(1) Stress incontinence: sudden release of urine due to:

(a) Increases in intra-abdominal pressure, e.g., coughing, laughing, exercise, straining, obesity.

(b) Weakness and laxity of pelvic floor musculature, sphincter weakness, e.g., postpartum incontinence, menopause, damage to pudendal nerve.

(2) Urge incontinence: bladder begins contracting and urine is leaked after sensation of bladder fullness is perceived; an inability to delay voiding to reach toilet due to:

(a) Detrusor muscle instability or hyperreflexia, e.g., stroke.

(b) Sensory instability: hypersensitive bladder.

(3) Overflow incontinence: bladder continuously leaks secondary to urinary retention (an overdistended bladder or incomplete emptying of bladder) due to:

(a) Anatomical obstruction, e.g., prostate enlargement.

(b) Acontractile bladder, e.g., spinal cord injury, diabetes.

(c) Neurogenic bladder, e.g., multiple sclerosis, suprasacral spinal lesions.

(4) Functional incontinence: leakage associated with inability or unwillingness to toilet due to:

(a) Impaired cognition (dementia); depression, e.g., Alzheimer's type dementia.

(b) Impaired physical functioning, e.g., stroke.

(c) Environmental barriers.

c. Management.

(1) Dietary management: control of food and beverages that aggravate the bladder or incontinence (e.g., citrus fruit or juices, caffeine, chocolate); control fluid intake.

(2) Medical management.

(a) Identify and treat acute, reversible problems, e.g., cystometry.

(b) Drug therapy for urge, stress, and overflow incontinence, e.g., estrogen with phenylpropanolamine.

(c) Control of medications that may aggravate incontinence, e.g., diuretics for CHF, anticholinergic or psychotropic drugs.

(d) Catheterization: used for overflow incontinence and other types if unresponsive to other treatments and skin integrity is threatened; associated with high rates of urinary tract infection.

(e) Surgery: bladder neck suspension, removal of prostate obstructions; suprapubic cystostomy.

(3) Bladder training: prompted voiding to restore a pattern of voiding.

(a) Involves toileting schedule: taking patient to bathroom at regular intervals.

(b) May also include intermittent catheterization, e.g., for patients with overdistention, persistent retention (e.g., multiple sclerosis).

d. Examination.

(1) Symptoms of incontinence: onset and duration, urgency, frequency, timing of episodes/causative factors.

(2) Strength of pelvic floor muscles using a perineometer.

(3) Functional mobility, environmental factors.

e. Physical therapy goals, outcomes, and interventions for stress and urge incontinence.

(1) Teach pelvic floor muscle exercises (pubococcygeus muscle): used to treat stress incontinence.

(a) Kegel's exercises: active, strengthening exercises; type 1 works on holding contractions, progressing to 10-second holds, rest 10 seconds between contractions; type 2 works on quick contractions to shut off flow of urine, 10–80 repetitions a day. Avoid squeezing buttocks or contracting abdominals (bearing down).

(b) Functional electrical stimulation: for muscle reeducation if patient is unable to initiate active contractions.

(c) Biofeedback: uses pressure recordings to reinforce active contractions, relax bladder.

(d) Progressive strengthening: use of weighted vaginal cones for home exercises or pelvic floor exerciser.

(e) Incorporating Kegel's exercise into everyday life: e.g., with lifting, coughing, changing positions.

(2) Provide behavioral training.

(a) Record keeping: patients are asked to keep a history of their voiding (voiding diary).

(b) Education: regarding anatomy, physiology, reasons for muscle weakness, incontinence; avoidance of Valsalva's maneuver, heavy resistance exercises.

(3) Functional mobility training as needed. Ensure independence in sit-to-stand transitions, ambulation and safe toilet transfers.

(4) Environmental modifications as needed: e.g., toilet rails, raised toilet seat or commode.

(5) Maintain adequate skin condition.

(a) Teach appropriate skin care, maintain toileting schedule.

(b) Adequate protection: adult diapers, underpads.

(6) Provide psychological support: emotional and social consequences of incontinence are significant.

Endocrine and Metabolic Systems

Overview of the Endocrine System

1. Hormonal regulation (see Figure 6-5).

a. The endocrine system uses hormones (chemical messengers) to relay information to cells and organs and regulate many of the body functions (digestion, use of nutrients, growth and development, electrolyte and water balance, and reproductive functions).

b. The hypothalamus and pituitary gland, along with the nervous system, make up the central network that exerts control over many other glands in the body with wide-ranging functions. Endocrine functions are also closely linked with the immune system.

c. Hormones bind to specific receptor sites that are linked to specific systems and functions.

d. The hypothalamus controls release of pituitary hormones (corticotropin-releasing hormone [CRH], thyrotropin-releasing hormone [TRH], growth hormone–releasing hormone [GHRH], and somatostatin).

e. The anterior pituitary gland controls the release of growth hormone (GH), adrenocorticotropic hormone (ACTH), follicle-stimulating hormone (FSH), luteinizing hormone (LH), and prolactin.

f. The posterior pituitary gland controls the release of antidiuretic hormone (ADH) and oxytocin.

g. The adrenal cortex controls the release of mineral corticosteroids (aldosterone), glucocorticoids (cortisol), adrenal androgens (dehydroepiandrosterone [DHEA]), and androstenedione.

h. The adrenal medulla controls the release of epinephrine and norepinephrine.

i. The thyroid controls the release of triiodothyronine and thyroxine. Thyroid C cells control the release of calcitonin.

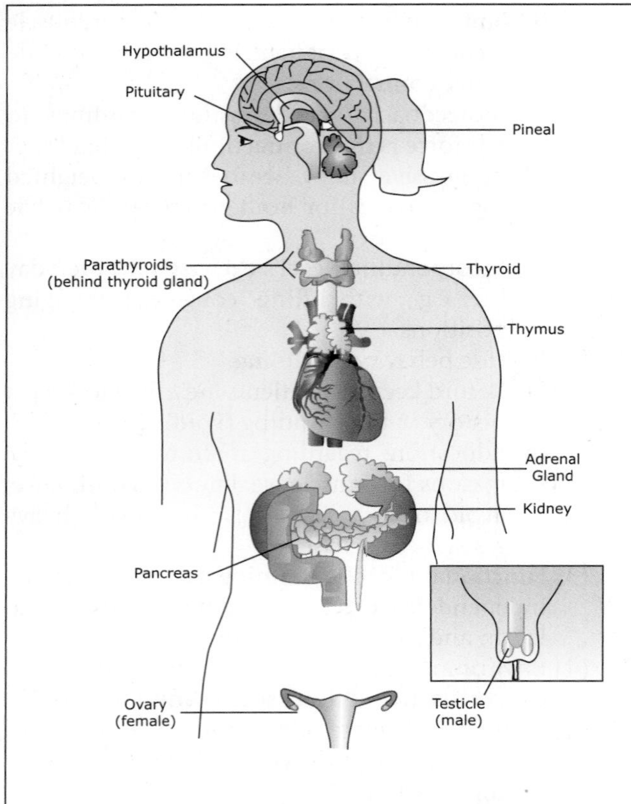

Figure 6-5 **Endocrine system anterior view.**

j. The parathyroid glands control the release of parathyroid hormone (PTH).
k. The pancreatic islet cells control the release of insulin, glucagons, and somatostatin.
l. The kidney controls the release of 1,25-dihydroxyvitamin D.
m. The ovaries control the release of estrogen and progesterone.
n. The testes control the release of androgens (testosterone).

Overview of the Metabolic System

1. Normal glucose control. The result of nutrient, neural, and hormonal regulation.
2. Hormones. Released by islets of Langerhans in pancreas.
   a. Insulin: allows uptake of glucose from the bloodstream; suppresses hepatic glucose production, lowering plasma glucose levels. Secreted by the beta cells.
   b. Glucagon: stimulates hepatic glucose production to raise glucose levels, especially in fasting state. Secreted by the alpha cells.
   c. Amylin: modulates rate of nutrient delivery (gastric emptying); suppresses release of glucagon. Secreted by the beta cells.
   d. Somatostatin: acts locally to depress secretion of both insulin and glycogen; decreases motility of stomach, duodenum, and gallbladder; decreases secretion and absorption of GI tract. Secreted by the delta cells.

Metabolic Syndrome (Syndrome X)

1. A cluster of risk factors that increase the likelihood of developing heart disease, stroke, and type 2 diabetes.
2. Criteria for diagnosis include three or more of the following:
   a. Abdominal obesity: large waist size: For men: 40 inches or larger; for women: 35 inches or larger.
   b. Cholesterol: elevated triglycerides: 150 mg/dL or higher or using a cholesterol medicine.
   c. Cholesterol: low HDL cholesterol; for men, less than 40 mg/dL; for women: less than 50 mg/dL or using a cholesterol medicine.
   d. High blood pressure: systolic BP 135 mm Hg or higher and/or diastolic pressure 85 mm Hg or higher.
   e. Blood sugar: fasting plasma glucose level 100 mg/dL or higher.
3. Etiology: No one cause, a collection of risk factors (listed above).
   a. Unhealthy lifestyle: diet high in fats; low levels of physical activity.
   b. Occurs with certain diseases and hormonal imbalance.
4. Incidence.
   a. May affect as many as one in four adults.
   b. More common in older adults and individuals prone to blood clots and inflammation.
   c. May run in families.
5. Treatment: management of risk factors.
   a. Lifestyle changes can reverse or reduce the chance of developing metabolic syndrome: healthy diet, weight loss, exercise, smoking cessation.
   b. Medications to control cholesterol, blood pressure, or diabetes (glucose intolerance).

Diabetes Mellitus (DM)

1. Characteristics.
   a. A complex disorder of carbohydrate, fat, and protein metabolism caused by deficiency or absence of insulin secretion by the beta cells of the pancreas or by defects of the insulin receptors. Causes an abnormally high level of sugar or glucose in the blood.

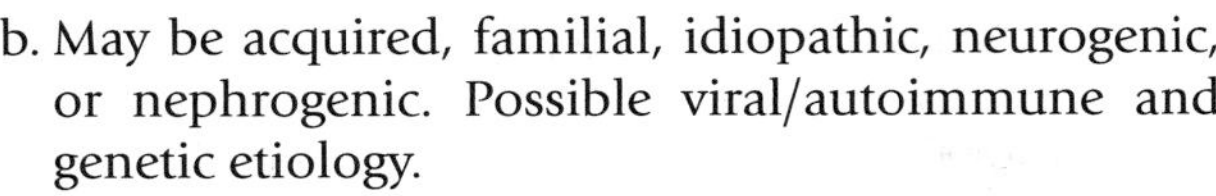

b. May be acquired, familial, idiopathic, neurogenic, or nephrogenic. Possible viral/autoimmune and genetic etiology.

2. Types.
   a. Type 1 diabetes mellitus (T1DM); also known as insulin-dependent, juvenile-onset diabetes. Affects about 1% of the population and 10% of all people with diabetes. Characteristics include:
      (1) Decrease in size and number of islet cells resulting in absolute deficiency in insulin secretion.
      (2) Usually occurs in children and young adults. Long preclinical period, often with abrupt onset of symptoms around the age of puberty.
      (3) Etiology: caused by autoimmune abnormalities, genetic causes or environmental causes.
      (4) Insulin-dependent: requires insulin delivery by injection, insulin pump, or inhalation.
      (5) Prone to ketoacidosis. Presence of ketone bodies in the urine, the by-products of fat metabolism (ketonuria).
   b. Type 2 diabetes mellitus (T2DM) results from inadequate utilization of insulin (insulin resistance) and progressive beta cell dysfunction; also known as non-insulin dependent or adult-onset diabetes. Represents 90%–95% of DM cases. Characteristics include:
      (1) Gradual onset.
      (2) Usually not insulin dependent.
      (3) Individual is not prone to ketoacidosis (may form ketones with stress).
      (4) Etiology: a progressive disease caused by a combination of factors, including:
         - Insulin resistance in muscle and adipose tissue.
         - Progressive decline in pancreatic insulin production.
         - Excessive hepatic glucose production.
         - Inappropriate glucagon secretion.
      (5) Risk factors.
         - Linked to obesity and older adults (significant risk factor over the age of 45). Increased incidence in obese children. Can occur in nonobese individuals with increased percentage of body fat in the abdominal region.
         - Family history of diabetes.
         - Unhealthy eating patterns.
         - Lack of physical activity.
   c. Secondary diabetes: associated with other conditions (pancreatic disease or removal of pancreatic tissue), endocrine disease (e.g., acromegaly, Cushing's syndrome, pheochromocytoma), drugs (e.g., some diuretics, diazoxide, glucocorticoids, levodopa), and chemical agents.
   d. Gestational diabetes mellitus (GDM): glucose intolerance (high blood sugar) associated with pregnancy; most likely in third trimester. Affects approximately 4% of pregnancies.
   e. Prediabetes: impaired glucose tolerance (IGT) with abnormal response to oral glucose test; 10%–15% of individuals will convert to type 2 diabetes within 10 years.

3. Classic signs and symptoms of DM.
   a. Elevated blood sugar (hyperglycemia).
   b. Elevated sugar in urine (glycosuria).
   c. Excessive excretion of urine (polyuria).
   d. Excessive thirst (polydipsia), dry mouth.
   e. Excessive hunger (polyphagia) especially after eating.
   f. Unexplained weight loss.
   g. Fatigue.
   h. Blurred vision, headaches.

4. Complications of DM.
   a. Microvascular disease.
      (1) Retinopathy.
      (2) Renal disease.
      (3) Polyneuropathy.
   b. Macrovascular disease: dyslipidemia (accelerated atherosclerosis).
      (1) Cerebrovascular accident (CVA, stroke).
      (2) Myocardial infarction (MI).
      (3) Peripheral arterial disease (PAD).
   c. Integumentary impairments: including degenerative connective tissue changes; slow healing of sores or cuts, anhidrosis; increased risk of ulcers and infections.
   d. Musculoskeletal impairments.
      (1) Joint stiffness and increased risk of contractures.
      (2) Increased risk of adhesive capsulitis of shoulder, tenosynovitis, plantar fasciitis.
      (3) Increased risk of osteoporosis.
   e. Neuromuscular impairments.
      (1) Diabetic polyneuropathy.
         (a) Symmetrical numbness and tingling of the hands and feet (stocking and glove distribution).
         (b) Distal (long nerves first) progressing to proximal.
         (c) Altered sensations; paresthesias, shooting pain; loss of protective sensations.
         (d) Motor weakness: foot/ankle weakness initially with balance and gait impairments.
      (2) Diabetic autonomic neuropathy (DAN).
         (a) Cardiovascular autonomic neuropathy (CAN): resting tachycardia; exercise intolerance with abnormal HR, BP, and cardiac output responses; exercise-induced hypoglycemia; postural hypotension.
         (b) Integumentary: anhidrosis, abnormal sweating, dry skin, heat intolerance.

(c) Gastrointestinal: gastroparesis, GERD, diarrhea, constipation.
(d) Metabolic: abnormal or delayed responses to hypoglycemia; lack of awareness of hypoglycemia.
(3) Mononeuropathies: focal nerve damage resulting from vasculitis with ischemia and infarction.
(4) Entrapment neuropathies: resulting from repetitive trauma to superficial nerves.
f. Kidney impairments, including kidney failure.
g. Vision impairments, including diabetic retinopathy (associated with chronic hyperglycemia) and diabetic macular edema.
h. Liver impairments, including fatty liver disease (steatosis).
5. Diagnostic criteria for DM.
a. Symptoms of diabetes plus casual plasma glucose concentration ≥ 200 mg/dL (11.1 mmol/L). Casual is defined as nonfasting any time of day, without regard to time since last meal.
b. Fasting plasma glucose (FPG) ≥ 126 mg/dL (7 mmol/L). Fasting is defined as no caloric intake for at least 8 hours.
c. 2-hour postload glucose ≥ 200 mg/dL (11.1 mmol/L) during an oral glucose tolerance test (OGTT). OGTT, as described by the World Health Organization, uses a glucose load containing the equivalent of 75 g anhydrous glucose dissolved in water.
6. Medical goals and interventions.
a. Maintain insulin glucose homeostasis.
(1) Frequent monitoring of blood glucose levels.
(2) Dietary control: weight reduction, control of carbohydrate, protein, fat, and calorie intake.
(3) Oral hypoglycemic agents to lower blood glucose; indicated for type 2 diabetes.
(4) Insulin to lower blood glucose via injections, infusion pump, or intraperitoneal dialysis for patients with renal failure. Indicated for type 1 diabetes or for more severe type 2 diabetes.
(5) Maintenance of normal lipid levels.
(6) Control of hypertension.
b. Exercise and physical fitness.
c. Health promotion.
7. Physical therapy goals, outcomes, and interventions.
a. Exercise.
(1) Outcomes of regular exercise include improved glucose tolerance, increased insulin sensitivity, decreased glycosylated hemoglobin, and decreased insulin requirements. Additional outcomes include improved lipid profiles, BP reduction, weight management, increased physical work capacity, and improved well-being.
(2) Response to exercise is dependent upon adequacy of disease control.
b. Exercise testing is recommended prior to exercise due to increased cardiovascular risk.
c. Exercise prescription—Cardiovascular training ACSM Guidelines, 2010).
(1) Intensity: 50%–80% of maximal oxygen uptake (VO_2 max) or heart rate reserve (HRR) corresponding to rating of perceived exertion (RPE) of 12–16 on the 6–20 Borg scale.
(2) Frequency: 3–7 days/week.
(3) Duration: 20–60 minutes.
(4) Type: rhythmic, large muscle activity: biking, treadmill walking, overground walking.
d. Exercise prescription: resistance training (ACSM Guidelines, 2010).
(1) Frequency: 2–3 days/week.
(2) Intensity: resistance 60%–80% of one repetition max, 2–3 sets of 8–12 repetitions.
(3) Type: multijoint exercises of major muscle groups.
(4) Proper technique: minimize sustained gripping, static work, and Valsalva's maneuver (essential to decrease risk of hypertensive response).
e. Flexibility exercises.
f. Balance exercises.
g. Red Flags: Exercise precautions.
(1) Monitor glucose levels prior to and following exercise.
(2) Hypoglycemia is the most common problem for patients with diabetes who exercise.
(a) Observe for signs and symptom of hypoglycemia (Box 6-2). Do not exercise if blood glucose is < 70 mg/dL. Provide carbohydrate snack initially (15 g of carbohydrate); have readily available during exercise (15 g carbohydrate for every hour of intense activity).
(b) Hypoglycemia associated with exercise may last as long as 48 hours after exercise. To prevent postexercise hypoglycemia, monitor plasma glucose levels and ingest carbohydrates as needed.
(3) Hyperglycemia: Do not exercise when blood glucose levels are high (fasting glucose > 300 mg/dL) or poorly controlled (ketosis is present with urine test) (Box 6-3).
(4) Do not exercise without eating at least 2 hours before exercise.
(5) Do not exercise without adequate hydration. Maintain hydration during exercise session.

BOX 6-2 Signs and Symptoms of Hypoglycemia (Low Blood Sugar)

Glucose is low: < 70 mg/dL or a rapid drop in glucose
Onset is rapid (minutes)

Early signs and symptoms:

Pallor
Shakiness/trembling
Sweating
Excessive hunger
Tachycardia and palpitations
Fainting or feeling faint
Dizziness
Fatigue and weakness
Poor coordination and unsteady gait

Late signs and symptoms:

Nervousness and irritability
Headache
Blurred or double vision
Slurred speech
Drowsiness
Inability to concentrate, confusion, delusions
Loss of consciousness and coma

Response: If patient is awake, provide sugar (juice, candy bar, glucose tablets, and gel).

If patient unresponsive, seek immediate medical treatment; glucagon injection or intravenous glucose is required.

BOX 6-3 Signs and Symptoms of Hyperglycemia (Abnormally High Blood Sugar)

Glucose is high: > 300 mg/dL. Gradual onset (days).
Weakness
Increased thirst
Dry mouth
Frequent, scant urination
Decreased appetite, nausea/vomiting, abdominal tenderness
Dulled senses, confusion, diminished reflexes, paresthesias
Flushed, signs of dehydration
Deep, rapid respirations
Pulse: rapid, weak
Fruity odor to the breath (acetone breath)
Hyperglycemic coma

Response: Seek immediate medical treatment.

(6) Do not exercise alone. Exercise with a partner or under supervision.
(7) Do not inject short-acting insulin in exercising muscles or sites close to exercising muscles as insulin is absorbed more quickly. Abdominal injection site is preferred.
(8) Use caution or do not exercise patients with poorly controlled complications.
  (a) Cardiovascular disease, hypertension. May see chronotropic incompetence, blunted HR and systolic BP response, blunted oxygen uptake, and anhidrosis. RPE may be used to regulate exercise intensity.
  (b) Retinopathy. Avoid activities that dramatically increase BP (> 170 mm Hg systolic BP); avoid pounding or jarring activities.
  (c) Neuropathy, nephropathy. Limit weight-bearing exercise for patients with significant neuropathy. There is increased fall risk with balance and gait abnormalities.
  (d) Autonomic neuropathy is associated with sudden death and silent ischemia. Monitor for signs and symptoms of silent ischemia due to patient's inability to perceive angina.
  (e) Nephropathy. Limit exercise to low to moderate intensities; discourage strenuous intensities.
(9) Do not exercise in extreme environmental temperatures (very hot or cold due to impaired thermoregulation).

h. With peripheral neuropathy emphasize proper diabetic foot care: good footwear, hygiene.
i. Patient and family education.
  (1) Control of risk factors (obesity, physical inactivity, prolonged stress, and smoking).
  (2) Dietary intervention strategies.
  (3) Injury prevention strategies.
  (4) Self-management strategies.

Obesity

1. Obesity.
  a. A condition characterized by excess body fat.
2. Body mass index (BMI).
  a. Formula for determining obesity.
  b. BMI is calculated by dividing an individual's weight in kilograms by the square of the person's height in meters.
  c. Criteria: World Health Organization classification (adopted by National Institutes of Health):
    (1) Overweight is defined as a BMI ranging from 25 to 29.9.

(2) Obesity is defined as a BMI ≥ 30.
(3) Morbid obesity is defined as a BMI > 40.

d. Measurement by skin calipers using a fold of skin and subcutaneous fat from various body locations (midbiceps, midtriceps, and subscapular or inguinal areas). Greater than 1 inch is indicative of excess body fat.

3. Scope of problem.
   a. A national health problem: 66% of Americans are overweight, 32% are obese, and 5% are morbidly obese.
   b. Health risks associated with obesity: hypertension, hyperlipidemia, type 2 diabetes, cardiovascular disease, stroke, glucose intolerance, gallbladder disease, menstrual irregularities and infertility, and cancer (endometrium, breast, prostate, colon).
   c. Waist circumference is used to determine distribution of body fat. Abdominal obesity (central accumulation of fat) is an independent predictor of morbidity and mortality.
   d. Childhood obesity: most prevalent nutritional disorder affecting children in United States with 14%–18% classified as overweight.
4. Causes.
   a. An imbalance when energy intake exceeds energy consumption. Excess calories are consumed, exceeding those expended through exercise and activity.
   b. Interaction of psychological and environmental factors (behavioral, cultural, social, economic factors). Observe for depression, smoking, yo-yo dieting with fluctuations in weight.
   c. Genetic factors (biochemical defects): may account for 30%–40% of BMI.
   d. Medical causes: endocrine and metabolic disorders (e.g., metabolic syndrome); hypothyroidism, Cushing's syndrome.
5. Prevention and management.
   a. Lifestyle modification: combination of dietary changes to reduce body weight combined with increased physical activity.
      (1) Personalized diet with reduced caloric intake: fat intake of < 30% of total energy intake, emphasis on fruits, vegetables, whole grains, and lean protein.
      (2) Personalized exercise program, including stretching exercises, resistance exercises, and aerobic exercises.
      (3) Instruction in self-monitoring of exercise responses (heart rate, perceived exertion).
   b. Behavior therapy: self-monitoring of eating habits and physical activity (use of a food and exercise diary); stress management, relapse prevention, and social support.
   c. Pharmacology: over-the-counter (OTC) and prescriptive weight loss therapy (e.g., sibutramine, orlistat).
   d. Surgery (bariatric surgery): usually limited to persons with BMI over 40 (or individuals with comorbid conditions and BMI over 35). Procedures include gastric banding and gastric bypass.
6. Exercise evaluation (ACSM Guidelines, 2010).
   a. Individuals are typically sedentary with low physical work capacities.
   b. Interviews should include goals, past exercise history, perceived barriers to exercise participation, and exercise likes and dislikes.
   c. Exercise testing: submaximal, low initial workload (typically 2–3 METs), small workload increments per test stage (0.5–1.0 METs).
   d. Use of leg or arm ergometry may enhance testing performance.
   e. Use of proper size equipment: wide seat ergometer, large-size BP cuff.
7. Exercise prescription (ACSM Guidelines, 2010).
   a. Start slowly, provide adequate warm-ups and cool-downs. Initial exercise intensity should be moderate (40%–60% oxygen uptake reserve [VO_2R] or HRR).
   b. Increase intensity gradually in order to prevent injury: moderate-intensity activity (50%–70% VO_2R or HRR).
   c. Frequency: 5–7 days/week.
   d. Duration: 30–60 minutes.
   e. Type: aerobic physical activities. Use of circuit training in order to combine resistive training with aerobic training activities. Provide with short rests between activities/exercise bouts.
   f. Involve the patient in activity selection, incorporating individual preferences.
   g. Select adequate footwear and orthotic devices as needed.
   h. Aquatic exercise programs can assist in reducing musculoskeletal strain and injury.
   i. Use of special bariatric equipment: wide seats on ergometers, bariatric lifts.
8. Red Flags: Exercise precautions and risks.
   a. Typically exhibit cardiopulmonary compromise: shortness of breath, elevated blood pressure, and angina.
   b. Typically exhibit altered biomechanics affecting hips, knees, ankle/foot; back and joint pain; and increased risk of orthopedic injury.
   c. Increased risk of skin breakdown due to shear forces.
   d. Increased heat intolerance, risk of hyperthermia and heat exhaustion.
   e. Increased risk of therapist injury: poor body mechanics, inadequate assistance during transfers and lifts.

Thyroid Disorders

1. Hypothyroidism. Decreased activity of the thyroid gland with deficient thyroid secretion.
   a. Metabolic processes are slowed.
   b. Etiology: decreased thyroid-releasing hormone secreted by the hypothalamus or by the pituitary gland; atrophy of the thyroid gland; chronic autoimmune thyroiditis (Hashimoto's disease); overdosage with antithyroid medication.
   c. Symptoms include weight gain, mental and physical lethargy, dry skin and hair, low blood pressure, constipation, intolerance to cold, and goiter.
   d. If untreated, leads to myxedema (severe hypothyroidism) with symptoms of swelling of hands, feet, face. Can lead to coma and death.
   e. Treatment: life-long thyroid replacement therapy.
   f. Red Flags: Can result in exercise intolerance, weakness, apathy; exercise-induced myalgia; reduced cardiac output.
2. Hyperthyroidism. Hyperactivity of the thyroid gland.
   a. Etiology unknown.
   b. Thyroid gland is typically enlarged and secretes greater than normal amounts of thyroid hormone (thyroxine), e.g., Graves' disease, thyroid storm, thyrotoxicosis.
   c. Metabolic processes are accelerated.
   d. Symptoms include nervousness, hyperreflexia, tremor, hunger, weight loss, fatigue, heat intolerance, palpitations, tachycardia, and diarrhea.
   e. Treatment: antithyroid drugs.
   f. Radioactive iodine may also be prescribed; surgical ablation may be necessary.

   g. Red Flags: Can result in exercise intolerance; fatigue is associated with hypermetabolic state.

Adrenal Disorders

1. Primary adrenal insufficiency (Addison's disease).
   a. Partial or complete failure of adrenocortical function; results in decreased production of cortisol and aldosterone.
   b. Etiology: autoimmune processes, infection, neoplasm, or hemorrhage.
   c. Signs and symptoms.
      (1) Increased bronze pigmentation of skin.
      (2) Weakness, decreased endurance.
      (3) Anorexia, dehydration, weight loss, gastrointestinal disturbances.
      (4) Anxiety, depression.
      (5) Decreased tolerance to cold.
      (6) Intolerance to stress.
   d. Medical interventions.
      (1) Replacement therapy: glucocorticoid, adrenal corticoids.
      (2) Adequate fluid intake, control of sodium and potassium.
      (3) Diet high in complex carbohydrates and protein.
2. Secondary adrenal insufficiency.
   a. Can result from prolonged steroid therapy (ACTH); rapid withdrawal of drugs; and hypothalamic or pituitary tumors.
3. Cushing's syndrome.
   a. Metabolic disorder resulting from chronic and excessive production of cortisol by the adrenal cortex.
   b. From drug toxicity (overadministration of glucocorticoids).
   c. Etiology: most common cause is a pituitary tumor with increased secretion of ACTH.
   d. Signs and symptoms.
      (1) Decreased glucose tolerance.
      (2) Round "moon" face.
      (3) Obesity: rapidly developing fat pads on chest and abdomen; buffalo hump.
      (4) Decreased testosterone levels or decreased menstrual periods.
      (5) Muscular atrophy.
      (6) Edema.
      (7) Hypokalemia.
      (8) Emotional changes.
   e. Medical interventions.
      (1) Goal is to decrease excess ACTH: irradiation or surgical excision of pituitary tumor or control of medication levels.
      (2) Monitor weight, electrolyte and fluid balance.

Psychiatric Conditions

Psychiatric States/Mechanisms

1. Anxiety.
   a. Feelings of apprehension, worry, uneasiness; a normal reaction to tension, conflict, or stress.
   b. Degree of anxiety is related to degree of perceived threat and capacity to engage behaviors that can reduce anxiety.
   c. Anxiety can be constructive, stimulate an individual toward purposeful activity or neurotic (pathological).

d. Sympathetic responses (fight or flight) generally accompany anxiety, e.g., increased heart rate, dyspnea, hyperventilation, dry mouth, GI symptoms (nausea, vomiting, diarrhea); palpitations.

2. Depression.
   a. Altered mood characterized by morbid sadness, dejection, sense of melancholy. Can be a chronic, relapsing disorder.
   b. Red Flags: Clinical manifestations.
      (1) Loss of interest in all usually pleasurable outlets, e.g., work, family.
      (2) Poor appetite, weight loss, or weight gain.
      (3) Insomnia or hypersomnia; decreased energy.
      (4) Psychomotor imbalance: agitation or excessive fatigue, irritability.
      (5) Feelings of worthlessness, self-reproach, guilt, hopelessness.
      (6) Impaired concentration, ability to think.
      (7) Recurrent thoughts of suicide or death.
   c. Management.
      (1) Treatment is pharmacological: tricyclic antidepressant drugs.
      Red Flags: Patients on these medications may exhibit disturbed balance, postural hypotension, falls and fractures, increased HR, dysrhythmias, ataxia, seizures.
      (2) Cognitive therapy may help.
   d. Physical therapy interventions.
      (1) Maintain a positive attitude, consistently demonstrate warmth and interest.
      (2) Acknowledge depression, provide hope.
      (3) Use positive reinforcement, build in successful treatment experiences.
      (4) Involve the patient in treatment decisions.
      (5) Avoid excessive cheerfulness.
      (6) Take all suicidal thoughts and acts seriously.
3. Coping and adapting mechanisms.
   a. Typically unconscious behaviors by which the individual resolves or conceals conflicts or anxieties.
   b. Compensation: covering up a weakness by stressing a desirable or strong trait, e.g., a learning disabled child becomes an outstanding athlete.
   c. Denial: refusal to recognize reality, e.g., refusal to acknowledge a fatal disease.
   d. Repression: refusal or inability to recall undesirable past thoughts or events.
   e. Displacement: the transferring of an emotion to a less dangerous substitute, e.g., yelling at your child instead of your boss.
   f. Reaction formation: a defensive reaction in which behavior is exactly opposite what is expected, e.g., a messy individual becomes neat.
   g. Projection: the attributing of your own undesirable behavior to another, e.g., "He made me do it."
   h. Rationalization: the justification of behaviors using reasons other than the real reason, e.g., presenting an attitude of not caring.
   i. Regression: resorting to an earlier, more immature pattern of functioning, e.g., in traumatic brain injury; common under high stress situations.
4. General adaptation syndrome (GAS).
   a. Total body coping/adaptation to a catastrophic event (illness, trauma).
   b. Alarm stage, or "fight-or-flight" response: activation of the sympathetic system.
   c. Sustained resistance.
   d. Chronic resistance, exhaustion leading to stress-related illnesses.

Pathologies

1. Anxiety disorders (anxiety neurosis).
   a. Excessive anxiety not associated with realistically threatening specific situations, e.g., generalized anxiety.
   b. Panic attacks: acute, intense anxiety or terror; may be uncontrollable, accompanied by sympathetic signs, loss of mental control, sense of impending death.
   c. Phobias: excessive and unreasonable fear leads to avoidance behaviors, e.g., agoraphobia (fear of being alone or in public places).
   d. Obsessive-compulsive behavior: persistent anxiety is manifested by repetitive, stereotypic acts; behaviors interfere with social functioning, e.g., hand washing, counting, and touching.
2. Posttraumatic stress disorder (PTSD).
   a. Exposure to a traumatic event produces a variety of stress-related symptoms.
   b. PTSD symptoms.
      (1) Reexperiencing the traumatic event.
      (2) Psychic numbing with reduced responsiveness.
      (3) Detachment from the external world; survival guilt.
      (4) Exaggerated autonomic arousal, hyperalertness.
      (5) Disturbed sleeping.
      (6) Ongoing irritability.
      (7) Impaired memory and concentration.
   c. PTSD can be acute (symptoms last < 3 months) or chronic (3 months or longer); onset can also be delayed.
   d. Symptoms should not be ignored. A mental health consultation is indicated.
3. Psychosomatic disorders (somatoform disorders).
   a. Physical signs or diseases that are related to emotional causes, e.g., psychosocial stress.
   b. Characteristics.
      (1) Cannot be explained by identifiable disease process or underlying pathology.

(2) Not under voluntary control; provides a means of coping with anxiety and stress.
(3) Patient is frequently indifferent to symptoms.

c. Types.
(1) Conversion disorder (hysterical paralysis): loss of or altered physical functioning representing psychosocial conflict or need, e.g., can result in paralysis, hemiplegia.
(2) Hypochondria: abnormal or heightened concerns about health or body functions; false beliefs about suffering from some disease or condition.

d. Management.
(1) Physical symptoms are real: treat the patient as you would any other patient with similar symptoms.
(2) Provide a supportive environment.
(3) Identify primary gain (internal conflicts); assist patient in learning new, alternative methods of stress management.
(4) Identify secondary gains (additional advantages, e.g., attention, sympathy); do not reinforce.
(5) Provide encouragement and support for the total person.

4. Schizophrenia.
a. A group of disorders characterized by disruptions in thought patterns; of unknown etiology; a biochemical imbalance in the brain.
b. Symptoms.
(1) Disordered thinking: fragmented thoughts, errors of logic, delusions, poor judgment, memory.
(2) Disordered speech: may be coherent but unintelligible, incoherent, or mute.
(3) Disordered perception: hallucinations and delusions.
(4) Inappropriateness of affect: withdrawal of interest from other people and from the outside world; loss of self-identity, self-direction; disordered interpersonal relations.
(5) Functional disturbances: inability to function in daily life, work.
(6) Little insight into problems and behavior.
c. Paranoia: a type of schizophrenic disorder characterized by feelings of extreme suspiciousness, persecution, grandiosity (feelings of power or great wealth), or jealousy; withdrawal of all emotional contact with others.
d. Catatonia: a type of schizophrenic disorder characterized by mutism or stupor; unresponsiveness; catatonic posturing (remains fixed, unable to move or talk for extended periods).

5. Bipolar disorder (manic-depressive illness).
a. A disorder characterized by mood swings from depression to mania; a biochemical dysfunction.
b. Often intense outbursts, high energy and activity, excessive euphoria, decreased need for sleep, unrealistic beliefs, distractibility, poor judgment, denial.
c. Followed by extreme depression (see depression symptoms).
d. Treatment is pharmacological, e.g., lithium carbonate.

6. Perseveration.
a. The continued repetition of a movement, word, or expression, e.g., patient gets stuck and repeats the same activity over and over again; often accompanies traumatic brain injury or stroke.

Grief Process

1. Emotional process. By which an individual deals with loss, e.g., of a significant loved one, body part, or function.
2. Characteristics.
a. Somatic symptoms: e.g., fatigue, sighing, hyperventilation, anorexia, insomnia.
b. Psychological symptoms: e.g., sorrow, discomfort, regret, guilt, anger, irritability, depression.
c. Resolution may take months or years.
3. Stages.
a. Shock and disbelief; inability to comprehend loss.
b. Increased awareness and anguish; crying or anger is common.
c. Mourning.
d. Resolution of loss.
e. Idealization of lost person or function.
4. Management.
a. Provide support and understanding of the grief process.
b. Encourage expression of feelings, memories.
c. Respect privacy, cultural or religious customs.

Death and Dying

1. Characteristics: decreasing physical and mental functioning, gradual loss of consciousness.
2. Stages (Kübler-Ross).
a. Denial: patients insist they are fine, joke about themselves, are not motivated to participate in treatment.
(1) Allow denial: denial is a protective compensatory mechanism necessary until such time as the patient is ready to face his/her illness.
(2) Provide opportunities for patient to question, confront illness and impending death.
b. Anger, resentment: patients may become disruptive, blame others.
(1) Be supportive: allow patient to express anger, frustration, resentment.

(2) Encourage focus on coping strategies.

c. Bargaining: patients bargain for time to complete life tasks; turn to religion or other individuals, make promises in return for function.

(1) Provide accurate information, honest, truthful answers.

d. Depression: patients acknowledge impending death, withdraw from life; demonstrate an overwhelming sense of loss, low motivation.

(1) Observe closely for suicidal ideation.

(2) Allay fears and anxieties, especially loneliness and isolation.

(3) Assist in providing for comfort of the patient.

e. Acceptance and preparation for death: acceptance of their condition; relate more to their family, make plans for the future.

3. Management.

a. Support patient and family during each stage.

b. Maintain hope without supporting unrealistic expectations.

Interventions

1. Physical therapist's role.

a. Motivate patients, manage the human side of rehabilitation.

b. Establish boundaries of the professional relationship: identify problems, expectations, purpose, roles, and responsibilities.

c. Provide empathic understanding: the capacity to understand what your patient is experiencing from that patient's perspective.

(1) Recognize losses; allow opportunity to mourn "old self."

(2) Ask open-ended questions that reflect what the patient is feeling.

(a) Empathetic response; e.g., "It sounds like you are worried and anxious about your pain and are trying your best."

(b) Nonempathetic response; e.g., "Don't worry about your pain" or "You're overreacting."

(3) Sympathy is not helpful or therapeutic; caregiver is closely affected by the patient's behaviors, e.g., therapist cries when the patient cries.

d. Set realistic, meaningful goals; involve the patient and family in the goal-setting process; self-determination is important.

e. Set realistic time frames for the rehabilitation program; recognize symptoms, stages of the grief process or death and dying and adjust accordingly.

f. Recognize and reinforce healthy, positive, socially appropriate behaviors; allow the patient to experience success.

g. Recognize secondary gains, unacceptable behaviors; do not reinforce (e.g., malingering behaviors such as avoidance of work).

h. Provide an environment conducive to the patient's emotional state, learning, and optimal function.

(1) Provide a message of hope tempered with realism.

(2) Keep patients informed.

(3) Lay adequate groundwork or preparation for expected changes or discharge.

(4) Help to reestablish personal dignity and self-worth; acknowledge whole person.

i. Help patients identify feelings, successful coping strategies, recognize successful conflict resolution and rehabilitation gains.

(1) Stress ability to overcome major obstacles.

(2) Stress that recovery is unique and highly individual.

Review Questions

Other Systems

1. What are the adverse side effects of cancer treatment that can impact physical therapy intervention?

2. What are the typical medications that may be prescribed for a patient diagnosed with GERD?

3. What are three possible interventions a physical therapist might use in the management of stress incontinence?

4. What are some of the long-term complications of diabetes that a physical therapist needs to consider during examination and treatment?

5. Differentiate between hypothyroidism and hyperthyroidism in terms of expected symptoms.

7

Pediatric Physical Therapy

SUZANNE M. GIUFFRE AND LINDA KAHN-D'ANGELO

Chapter Outline

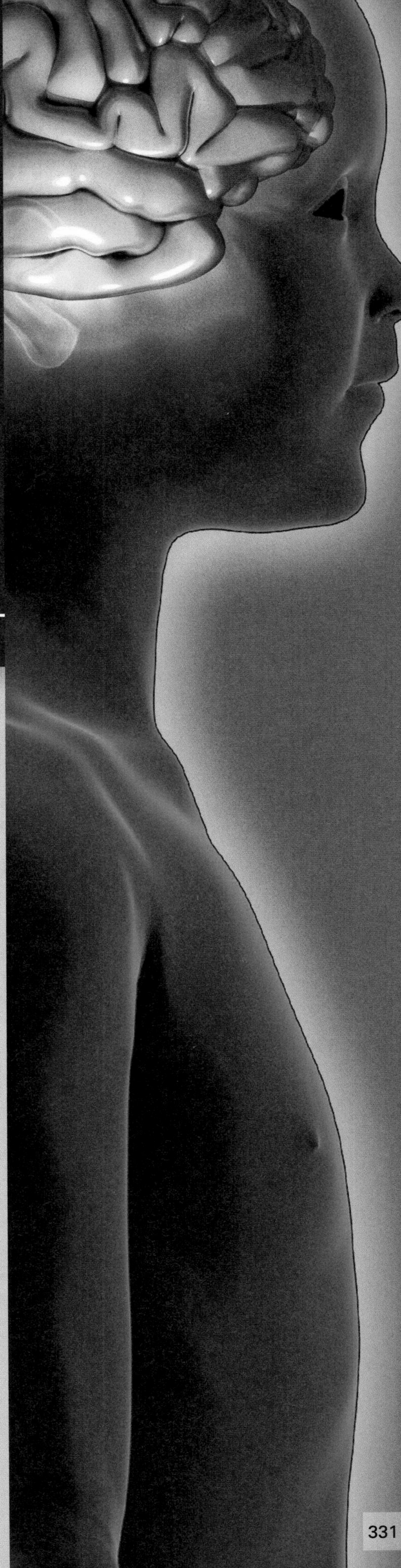

Theories of Development, Motor Control, and Motor Learning

Development

1. The sequence of events through which the individual grows, changes, evolves, and matures (see Tables 7-1 and 7-2).
2. Theories of development.
   a. Maturationist Hierarchical theory.
      (1) Individual genetically and biologically determined.
      (2) Aspects of human behavior are preformed and innate.
   b. Empiricist theory.
      (1) Source of human behavior is the environment.
   c. Behaviorist theory.
      (1) Environmental reinforcement motivates and shapes cognitive and motor behavior.
      (2) Used in behavior modification treatment where desired behaviors are positively reinforced and unwanted behaviors are ignored.

Table 7-1

Developmental Sequence Summary	
1 Month	• Decreased flexion • Momentary head elevation with minimal forearm support • Tracks a moving object with head rotation • Head usually to side • Reciprocal and symmetrical kicking • Positive support and primary walking reflexes in supported standing • Hands fisted with indwelling thumb most of the time • Neonatal reaching • Alert, brightening expression
2 Months	• Head elevation to 45° in prone, prone on elbows with elbows behind shoulders • Head bobs in supported sitting • Does not accept weight on lower extremities (astasia-abasia) • Responds to friendly handling
3 Months	• Prone on elbows, weight bearing on forearms • Elbows in line with shoulders, head elevated to 90° • Head in midline in supine, hands on chest • Increased back extension with scapular adduction in supported sitting • Takes some weight with toes curled in supported standing • Coos, chuckles • Optical and labyrinthine head-righting present
4 Months	• Rolls prone to side, supine to side • Sits with support • No head lag in pull-to-sit • Bilateral reaching with forearm pronated when trunk supported • Ulnar-palmar grasp • Laughs out loud
5 Months	• Rolls from prone to supine • Weight shifting from one forearm to the other in prone • Head control in supported sitting
6 Months	• Prone on hands with elbows extended, weight shifting from hand to hand • Rolls supine to prone • Independent sitting • Pulls-to-stand with hands held, bounces

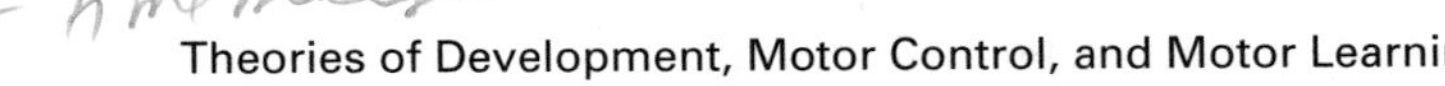

Table 7-1

Developmental Sequence Summary (Continued)	
7 Months	• Can maintain quadruped • Pivots on belly; moves body in circle while prone • Pivot prone (prone extension) position • Assumes sitting from quadruped • Trunk rotation in sitting • Recognizes tone of voice • May show fear of strangers
8–9 Months	• Belly crawls • Quadruped creeping • Moves quadruped to sitting • Side-sitting • Pulls-to-stand through kneeling at furniture • Cruises sideways, can stand alone • Reaches with closest arm, radial digital grasp, radial palmar, three-jaw chuck grasp, and inferior pincer grasp with thumb and forefinger • Can transfer objects from one hand to the other
10–15 Months	• Begins to walk unassisted • Transitions in/out of squatting • Creeps up/down steps • Transitions floor to stand • Begins self-feeding • Reaches with supination, neat pincer grasp, can release, build a tower of two cubes • Searches for hidden toys • Suspicious of strangers • Plays patty-cake and peekaboo • Imitates
20 Months	• Ascends stairs step-to pattern (2 feet on each step-non-reciprocal pattern) • Running more coordinated • Jumps off bottom step • Plays make-believe • Throws ball overhand a few feet
2 Years	• Runs well • Can go upstairs foot-over-foot (reciprocal stair climbing) • Active, restless, tantrums • Jumps with two feet • Catches large ball
3 Years	• Rides tricycle • Stands on one foot briefly • Jumps off step • Hops on one foot • Gallops • Kicks ball • Understands sharing • Climbs on playground equipment
4 years	• Hops on one foot several times • Stands on tiptoes • Relates to friends
5 years	• Skips • Kicks ball well • Dresses self • Swings self on playground swing (pumps legs independently)

Table 7-2

Development of Gait	
Birth–9 months	• Antigravity strength is obtained. Hip flexor strength by kicking, hip extensor strength by crawling on hands and knees and kneeling. Hip ABD strength by cruising. Extremities and trunk lengthen. Myelination of nerves completed.
9–15 months	• Fat decreases. Initial gait consists of: flexion, ABD and ER of hips, genu varum, eversion of the calcaneus, absent longitudinal arches, femoral anteversion, and internal tibial torsion.
18–24 months	• Gait characterized by: decreased base of support, heel remains everted, less co-contraction of muscles, genu varum resolved, and knee in neutral.
3–3.5 years	• More mature gait: genu valgum, heel eversion decreasing, consistent heel strike, femoral anteversion decreasing, arm swing noted.
6–7 years	• Fully mature gait: knees and heels in neutral position. Femoral anteversion almost resolved.

d. Interactionist theory.
   (1) Child is an active social being who contributes to his or her development.
e. Piagetian theory.
   (1) Interaction of environment and neural maturation results in spiraling of development, with equilibrium and disequilibrium resulting.

Motor Control

1. The study of postures and movement, and the parts of the mind and body that control them.
2. Theories of motor control.
   a. Neuromaturationist theory.
      (1) Cortex is command center, with descending control and inhibition of lower centers by higher one in central nervous system (CNS).
   b. Dynamic Systems theory.
      (1) Command center changes from cortex to other levels, depending on the task.
      (2) Stresses interaction between brain, body, and environment, including biomechanics and body geometry.
      (3) Sensory systems mature, become integrated and connected to muscle coordination patterns, starting with the visual system.
      (4) Immature postures involve cocontraction of agonists and antagonists; cocontraction decreases with maturation.
   c. Neuronal group selection theory.
      (1) Genetic code of species outlines limits of neural network formation.
      (2) Actual network formation results from individual experience.
      (3) Cell death of unexercised synaptic and strengthening of synaptic connections selectively activated.

Early Motor Learning

1. Motor skill. Any motor activity that becomes better organized, more effective, and more efficient as a result of practice.
2. Enhancement of early motor skills development.
   a. Use of goal-oriented tasks.
   b. Internal feedback via corollary discharge and effector organ feedback (i.e., visual, somatosensory vestibular feedback).
   c. External feedback through knowledge of results and knowledge of performance feedback from instructor; i.e., every other time and after a delay.
   d. Practice of high intensity and duration as tolerated.
3. Principles of motor development.
   a. Occurs in cephalocaudal and proximal to distal directions.
   b. Unrefined to refined movement.
   c. Stability to controlled mobility.
   d. Occurs in spiraling manner, with periods of equilibrium and disequilibrium.
   e. Sensitive periods occur when infant/child is especially affected by environmental input.

Fetal Sensorimotor Development

1. Gestational age (GA).
   a. Age of fetus or newborn, in weeks, from first day of mother's last normal menstrual period.
   b. Normal gestational period is 38–42 weeks. Infant considered premature if born at < 37 weeks GA.
   c. Gestational period is divided into three equal trimesters (see Table 7-3).
2. Conceptional age.
   a. Age of a fetus or newborn in weeks since conception.

Table 7-3

Fetal Sensorimotor Development

	FIRST TRIMESTER	SECOND TRIMESTER	THIRD TRIMESTER
Muscle Spindle	• Muscle starts to differentiate • Tissue becomes specialized	• Motor end plate forms • Clonus response to stretch	• Some muscles are mature and functional, others still maturing
Touch and Tactile System	• First sensory system to develop • Response to tactile stimulus	• Receptors differentiate	• Touch functional • Actual temperature discrimination at end of third trimester • Most mature sensory system at birth
Vestibular System	• Functioning at the end of the first trimester (not completely developed)		
Vision	• Eyelids fused • Optic nerve and cup being formed	• Startle to light • Visual processing occurs	• Fixation occurs • Able to focus (fixed focal length)
Auditory		• Turns to auditory sounds	• Debris in middle ear, loss of hearing
Olfactory			• Nasal plugs disappear, some olfactory perception
Taste	• Taste buds develop		• Responds to different tastes (sweet, sour, bitter, salt)
Movement	• Sucking, hiccupping • Fetal breathing • Quick, generalized limb movement • Positional changes • 7½ weeks: bends neck and trunk	• Quickening • Sleep states • Grasp reflex • Reciprocal and symmetrical limb movements	• 28 weeks: primitive motor reflexes • Rooting, sucking, swallowing • Palmar grasp • Plantar grasp • Moro away from perioral stroke • Crossed extension

Examination

Patient Interview

1. Mother's pregnancy and birth history. Prematurity, fetal distress, difficult labor, umbilical cord around neck.
2. Medical history. Special care unit admission, diagnoses, intubated or on ventilator, surgeries, medications.
3. Family history. Caretakers, current home situation, support to family, socioeconomic status.
4. Review of Systems.
5. Determine corrected age if premature. Example:
   a. If a child is 6 months-old the chronological age is 24 weeks.
   b. If that same child was born 8 weeks early, the corrected age is 16 weeks.

Preterm Infant Examination

1. Neurological assessment. Preterm and full-term newborn infants.
   a. Neurological items include newborn reflexes, infant states of alertness.
   b. Neurobehavioral items from Neonatal Behavioral Assessment Scale (NBAS).
   c. Assessment of gestational age by evaluation of muscle tone, physical characteristics.
2. Assessment of Premature Infant Behavior (APIB).
   a. Refinement and extension of NBAS.
   b. Assesses the organization and balance of infant's physiological, motor, and behavioral states.
   c. Test is lengthy, used mainly for research.
3. Newborn Individualized Developmental Care and Assessment of Progress (NIDCAP).
   a. Systematic behavioral observation of preterm or full-term infant in nursery or home during environmental input, caretaking, and treatments.
   b. Note what stresses, consoles infant.
4. Test of Infant Motor Performance (TIMP).
   a. Developed for infants from 32 weeks postconceptual age to 3½ months postterm.
   b. Evaluates spontaneous and elicited movements to analyze postural alignment and selective control for functional movements.

Full-Term Newborn, Infant, and Child Examination

1. Apgar screening test. Administered to newborn at 1, 5, 10 minutes after birth. Continues every 5 minutes if infant is having difficulties.
   a. Five items: heart rate, respiration, reflex irritability, muscle tone, color, each scored 0, 1, or 2.
   b. Score of 7 and above considered good.
2. Neurological examination of the newborn.
   a. Assigns states of consciousness.
   b. Tests newborn reflexes.
3. Neonatal Behavioral Assessment Scale.
   a. Tests interactive, self-organizational abilities and newborn reflexes and muscle tone.
4. Skeletal system examination.
   a. Fractured clavicle.
   b. Dislocated hip: asymmetrical gluteal folds, hip click.
   c. Spine: curved, inflexible, kyphosis, scoliosis; spina bifida occulta: dimple, patch of hair, pigmentation visible, and x-ray verification.
   d. Talipes equinovarus (clubfoot): ankle in plantar flexion, forefoot adduction and supination.
5. Range of motion (ROM).
   a. Newborn has decreased ROM into extension due to physiological flexion, but increased dorsiflexion of ankles and flexion at wrists.
6. Posture.
   a. Physiological flexion of all four limbs due to position in utero.
   b. Head to one side.
7. Movements.
   a. Spontaneous and reflexive.
   b. Occasional tremulousness normal.
8. Neonatal reflexes. Primary motor patterns and infant reflexes and reactions.
   a. Present at birth and become "integrated" or inhibited, or not evident later in development.
   b. In CNS lesions, they may persist and interfere with motor milestone attainment or cause deformities.
   c. Babinski reflex: stroke lateral aspect of the plantar surface of foot, get extension and fanning of toes (0–12 months).
   d. Flexor withdrawal: sharp, quick pressure stimulus to sole of foot or palm of hand causes withdrawal of stimulated extremity (0–2 months, although some sources say present throughout life).
   e. Crossed extension: sharp, quick pressure stimulus to sole of foot results in withdrawal of stimulated lower extremity and extension of opposite leg (0–2 months).
   f. Galant or trunk incurvation reaction: sharp stoke along paravertebral line from scapula to top of iliac crest results in lateral trunk flexion toward stimulated side (0–2 months).
   g. Moro reflex: sudden extension of neck results in flexion, abduction of shoulders, extension of elbows, followed by shoulder adduction and elbow flexion. Usually also results in crying, so test last! (0–4 months).
   h. Primary standing reaction: infant held in supported standing position supports some weight and extends lower extremities. If this reflex persists, will interfere with walking by causing extension of all joints of the lower extremity and preventing disassociation of flexion and extension.
   i. Primary walking: hold infant in supported standing, tilt trunk forward slightly, reciprocal stepping motions in lower extremities (0–2 months unless practiced).
   j. Neonatal neck righting (neck righting on body, NOB): turn head with infant in supine position; body log-rolls toward same side (0–6 months).
   k. Rooting: stroking of perioral region results in head turning to that side with mouth opening (0–3 months). Important feeding reflex.
   l. Sucking: touch to lips, tongue, palate results in automatic sucking (0–6 months). Important feeding reflex.
   m. Startle: loud noise, sudden light or cold stimulus causes a sudden jerking of whole body or extension and abduction of upper extremities, followed by adduction of shoulders (0–6 months).
   n. Tonic labyrinthine reflex (classic): prone position results in maximal flexor tone and supine position results in maximal extensor tone. If reflex persists and is strong, may block rolling from supine position, due to increased extensor tone (0–6 months).
   o. Asymmetrical tonic neck reflex: rotation of head results in extension of face side extremities and flexion of skull side extremities. Stronger in lower extremities of neonates (0–5 months). If reflex persists, may result in scoliosis or hip dislocation and interfere with grasping and hand-mouth activities.
   p. Palmar grasp: pressure stimulus against palm results in grasping of object with slow release (0–4 months).
   q. Plantar grasp: pressure stimulus to sole or lowering of feet to floor results in curling of toes. Must be integrated before walking occurs (0–9 months).
   r. Placing reactions: drag dorsum of foot or back of hand against edge of table, get placing of foot or hand onto table top (0–6 months).
   s. Traction or pull-to-sit: pull infant to sitting from supine position; upper extremities will flex, and head will lag until about 4–5 months.

t. Optical and labyrinthine righting: head orients to a vertical position when body is tilted. Test labyrinthine righting with the eyes blindfolded (1 month–throughout life).
u. Protective extension: quick displacement of trunk in downward direction while held or while sitting in forward, sideward, or backward direction results in extension of legs downward and extension of arms in sitting position to catch weight. Downward begins at 4 months, sideward sitting at 6 months, forward sitting at 7 months, backward sitting at 9 months; these reactions persist through life.
v. Body-righting reaction acting on the head (BOH): contact of body with solid surface results in head righting with respect to gravity, interacts with labyrinthine righting reaction on head to maintain orientation of head in space. Begins at 4–6 months and persists through life.
w. Body-righting reaction acting on the body (BOB): rotation of head or thorax results in rolling over, with rotation between trunk and pelvis. Begins at 6–8 months and persists.
x. Symmetrical tonic neck reflex: extension of cervical joints produces extension of upper extremities and flexion of lower extremities; flexion of cervical joints produces flexion of upper extremities and extension of lower extremities (6–8 months). If reflex persists, it may interfere with development of stable quadruped position and creeping.
y. Landau's reaction: infant held in ventral suspension will extend neck, trunk, and hips (4–18 months).
z. Tilting reactions: slow shifting of base of support or slow displacement of body in space will result in lateral flexion of spine toward elevated side of support, abduction of extremities on elevated side, and sometimes trunk rotation toward elevated side. Prone begins at 5 months; supine begins at 7 months; sitting at 8 months; quadruped at 12 months. These reactions persist throughout life.

9. Screening tests.
   a. Denver Developmental Screening Test II.
      (1) To screen for developmental delay.
      (2) Tests social, fine, gross motor, and language skills from birth to 6 years of age.
   b. Alberta Infant Motor Scale (AIMS): observational scale for assessing gross motor milestones in infants from birth through independent walking.
10. Standardized motor tests.
   a. Movement Assessment of Infants.
      (1) Identifies motor dysfunction and changes in the status of motor dysfunction and establishes an intervention program for infants from birth to 1 year.
      (2) Criterion-referenced exam of muscle tone, reflexes, automatic reactions, and volitional movements.
   b. Peabody Developmental Motor Scales.
      (1) Assesses gross and fine motor development from birth to 42 months.
      (2) Includes spontaneous, elicited reflexes and automatic reactions.
   c. Gross Motor Function Measure (GMFM-88).
      (1) Developed to measure change in gross motor function over time in children with cerebral palsy. Also valid to use with children with Down syndrome.
      (2) All items on the test could be accomplished by a 5-year-old with typical motor development.
      (3) Focuses on voluntary movement in five developmental dimensions: prone and supine, sitting, crawling and kneeling, standing, walking and jumping.
   d. Bruininks-Oseretsky Test of Motor Proficiency (BOT-2).
      (1) Developed to measure gross motor and fine motor abilities in children 4.5–21 years of age.
      (2) Norm-referenced on typical children.
      (3) Can use full battery or a short form for screening.
11. Sensory Integration and Praxis Test.
   a. Sensorimotor assessment for children between ages of 4 and 9 with mild to moderate learning impairment.
   b. Includes tests of balance, proprioceptive and tactile sensation and control of specific movements.
12. Comprehensive developmental assessments.
   a. Bayley Scales of Infant Development revision: norm-referenced motor and mental scales for children from birth to 42 months of age.
13. Pediatric functional assessments.
   a. Pediatric Evaluation of Disability Inventory (PEDI): interview or questionnaire scale of activities of daily living (ADL), with or without modification completed by caregiver.
   b. Functional Independence Measure for children (WeeFIM): assesses function in self-care, mobility, locomotion and communication and social cognition.
   c. School Functional Assessment (SFA): measures participation, task supports, activity performance, physical tasks, and cognitive/behavioral tasks within the school setting.
      (1) For children in grades K–6 (5–12 years of age).
      (2) Criterion-referenced.

Chapter 7 PED

Overview of Pediatric Physical Therapy Intervention

Roles of the Pediatric Physical Therapist

1. Direct care provider.
   a. In children's hospital settings.
   b. In special care nurseries, neonatal intensive care units.
   c. Pediatric rehabilitation settings.
   d. In Early Intervention Programs (EIPs) (0–3 years).
   e. In educational settings.
2. Consultant/indirect care provider.
   a. Pediatric PT may be consultant in educational settings, instructing teachers and teacher's assistants in facilitating attainment of educational goals.
   b. Pediatric PT may work with physical therapist assistant in delivery of care in many settings.
3. Parent education. Pediatric PT is always involved in parent/family or caretaker education.

Goals, Outcomes, and Intervention

1. Primary prevention of disability through education and treatment.
2. Prevention and/or improvement of secondary disabilities (e.g., contractures/deformities).
3. Attainment of maximal functional goals of child and family.

Pediatric Therapies

1. Developmental activities to facilitate development of functional motor skills. These activities use postures and movements from the developmental sequence to increase strength, ROM, coordination. Remember, play is the work of the child; make activities fun.
2. Neurodevelopmental Treatment (NDT).
   a. Sets anticipated outcomes and impairment goals in partnership with the family, the client, and the interdisciplinary team.
   b. Encourages active, goal-directed functional movements appropriate for the developmental level of the child.
   c. Utilizes therapeutic handling as the primary intervention strategy.
   d. Provides specific sensory input using careful grading of the intensity, rhythm, and duration of somatosensory inputs.
   e. Focuses on important components of motor learning.
      (1) Practice of task components as well as practice of the whole task.
      (2) Repetition.
      (3) Structuring an environment conducive to client participation and support.
3. Motor control/motor learning approaches. Utilize principles of motor control and early motor learning appropriate for individual child.
4. Sensory integration.
   a. Goal is to facilitate child's organization and processing of proprioceptive, tactile, and vestibular input.
   b. Facilitation will influence postural responses, environmental awareness, and motor planning.

Prematurity Physical Therapy Practice

1. A subspecialty of pediatrics. Requires advanced didactic and supervised practical experience.
2. Definition and categories.
   a. Birth of infant before 37 weeks gestation.
   b. Categorized by birth weight.
3. Preterm postural and movement profile.
   a. Preterm infant does not develop the physiological flexion of full-term newborn.
   b. May exhibit hyperextended neck and trunk (may be partially a result of supine and intubation positions).
   c. Shoulders may be elevated, abducted, extended with scapular retraction.
   d. Hips abducted and extended.
   e. Pelvis tipped anteriorly (increased lumbar lordosis).
   f. Decreased midline arm movement.
   g. May bear weight on toes when in supported standing position.

Conditions and Interventions

Premature Medical Complications

1. Complications depend on severity of prematurity and birth weight.
   a. Meconium Aspiration syndrome.
      (1) Due to bowel movement in utero (meconium) that mixes with amniotic fluid.
      (2) Near-term or term infant inhales substance and can develop respiratory distress.
      (3) Infants are hypersensitive to environmental stimuli—treat in quiet environment.
      (4) 20% present with developmental delays, some up until 3 years of age.
   b. Respiratory distress syndrome (RDS) or hyaline membrane disease.
      (1) Respiratory distress due to atelectasis caused by insufficient surfactant in premature lungs.
      (2) May lead to acute respiratory failure and death.
      (3) Treatment includes oxygen supplementation, assisted ventilation, and surfactant administration.
      (4) Chronic RDS may lead to bronchopulmonary dysplasia.
   c. Bronchopulmonary dysplasia.
      (1) Chronic lung disease as a result of damage to lungs from mechanical ventilation, oxygen administration, and chronic RDS.
      (2) Predisposes child to frequent respiratory infections and developmental disability.
      (3) Treatment includes respiratory support, infection control, and bronchodilator administration.
   d. Periventricular leukomalacia (PVL).
      (1) Necrosis of white matter adjacent to ventricles of brain due to systemic hypotension or ischemia.
      (2) May result in cerebral palsy.
   e. Periventricular-intraventricular hemorrhage.
      (1) Bleeding into immature vascular matrix.
      (2) Bleeds graded I–IV; grades II–IV may result in cerebral palsy.
   f. Retinopathy of prematurity (ROP).
      (1) Due to combination of low birth weight and high oxygen levels.
      (2) Sequelae may range from nonsignificant to detachment of retinas and blindness.
   g. Necrotizing enterocolitis.
      (1) Ischemia results in inflammatory, infected bowel.
   h. Patent Ductus Arteriosus (PDA).
      (1) Ductus arteriosus (temporary vessel between aorta and the pulmonary artery) should close soon after birth.
      (2) Non-oxygenated blood is circulated.
      (3) PT should monitor O_2 saturation, signs of cyanosis, shortness of breath, and respiratory rate.
   i. Failure to thrive.
      (1) Infant lacks adequate nutritional intake.
      (2) Infant can present with developmental delays.
   j. Increased fragility of skin.
   k. Thermoregulation problems.
   l. Feeding problems.
   m. Interaction/attachment problems with caregivers.
2. Physical therapy examination in prematurity.
   a. Medical history review.
   b. Autonomic functions.
   c. Neurobehavioral organization (interactive items after infant is 32 weeks conceptional age).
   d. Muscle tone.
   e. Postural control.
   f. Spontaneous movements.
   g. Reflexes including feeding.
   h. Musculoskeletal evaluation.
   i. Family needs.
3. Intervention/activities to teach parents.
   a. Play activities and positioning to facilitate shoulder protraction and adduction such as supported side-lying while doing visual (use black, white, and red objects 9 inches away) and auditory tracking, and reaching.
   b. Midline positioning of head.
   c. Encourage reaching for toys, parent's face if infant is over 32 weeks conceptional age.
   d. Supervised side-lying and prone positioning (tummy time) for periods during the day. Academy of Pediatrics recommends sleeping in the supine position to decrease possibility of sudden infant death syndrome (SIDS).
   e. Avoid activities that may increase extensor tone, such as use of infant jumpers and walkers.

Cerebral Palsy (CP)

1. Pathology.
   a. Group of disorders that are prenatal, perinatal, or postnatal in origin.
   b. Non-progressive encephalopathy: major causes include hemorrhage below lining of ventricles, hypoxic encephalopathy, malformations and trauma of CNS.
   c. Preterm birth associated with CP.
2. Classifications of CP.
   a. By area of body showing impairment.

(1) One limb: monoplegia.
(2) Two lower limbs: diplegia.
(3) Upper and lower limbs of one side of the body: hemiplegia.
(4) All four limbs: quadriplegia.
(5) Trunk can be involved in all types.

b. Movement disorders are the most obvious impairment.
(1) Spastic: increased tone, lesion of motor cortex, or projections from motor cortex.
(2) Athetosis: fluctuating muscle tone, involuntary slow writhing movements, lesion of basal ganglia.
(3) Ataxia: instability of movement, lesion of cerebellum.
(4) Dystonia: involuntary movements with sustained contractions.
(5) Hypotonia: decreased muscle tone.
(6) Mixed: can present with a multiple/mixture of movement disorders.

c. Gross motor function classification system for CP (see Table 7-4).

3. Impairments for all classifications of CP.
a. Insufficient force generation.
b. Tone abnormality.
c. Poor selective control of muscle activity.
d. Poor regulation of muscle activity in anticipation of postural changes.
e. Decreased ability to learn unique movements.
f. Abnormal patterns of movement in total flexion and extension.
g. Persistence of primitive reflexes.
(1) Interfere with normal posture and movement.
(2) May cause contractures and deformities.

4. Impairments by classification of CP.
a. Spastic cerebral palsy.
(1) Increased muscle tone in antigravity muscles.
(2) Abnormal postures and movements with mass patterns of flexion/extension.
(3) Imbalance of tone across joints may cause contractures and deformities, especially of hip flexors, adductors, internal rotators, and knee flexors, ankle plantarflexors in lower extremities; scapular retractors, glenohumeral extensors and adductors, elbow flexors, forearm pronators.
(4) Visual, auditory, cognitive, and oral motor deficits may be associated with spastic CP.
(5) "Crouched Gait": walks with hip flexion, hip internal rotation, and knee flexion. May also toe walk.

b. Athetoid cerebral palsy.
(1) Generalized decreased muscle tone, floppy baby syndrome.
(2) Poor functional stability especially in proximal joints.
(3) Ataxia and incoordination when child assumes upright position, with decreased base of support and muscle tone fluctuations.
(4) Poor visual tracking, speech delay, and oral motor problems.
(5) Tonic reflexes such as asymmetrical tonic neck reflex (ATNR), symmetrical tonic neck reflex (STNR), and tonic labyrinthine reflex (TLR) may be persistent, blocking functional postures and movement.

c. Ataxic cerebral palsy.
(1) Low postural tone with poor balance.
(2) Stance and gait are wide based.
(3) Intention tremor of hands.
(4) Uncoordinated movement.
(5) Ataxia follows initial hypotonia.
(6) Poor visual tracking, nystagmus.
(7) Speech articulation problems.
(8) May occur with spastic or athetoid CP.

5. Functional limitations.
a. Dependent on classification of CP.
b. Spasticity may lead to decreased ROM, which may limit mobility. Special attention to ROM needed during growth spurts.
c. Ambulation.
(1) Ambulation without use of assistive devices may be attained by children with hemiplegia, and by some with diplegia and ataxia.
(2) Ambulation may be attained with use of rollator walkers or crutches by some children with diplegia, athetosis and a few with mild quadriplegia.

Table 7-4

Gross Motor Classification for Cerebral Palsy	
Level I	• Walk without restrictions; limitations in more advanced gross motor skills.
Level II	• Walk without assistive devices; limitations walking outdoors and in the community.
Level III	• Walk with assistive mobility devices; limitations walking outdoors and in the community.
Level IV	• Self-mobility with limitations; children are transported or use power mobility outdoors and in the community.
Level V	• Self-mobility is severely limited, even with the use of assistive technology.

6. Interventions and goals in CP.
   a. Very individualized, depending on abilities, age, type of CP. Incorporate child and family in intervention planning, implementation, and goal-setting.
   b. Focus on prevention of disability by minimizing effects of impairment, preventing or limiting secondary impairment such as contractures, scoliosis.
      (1) Utilize static positioning and dynamic patterns of movement opposite to habitual abnormal spastic patterns.
      (2) Facilitate symmetry in postures.
      (3) Elongate spastic hamstrings and heel cords.
      (4) Serial casting may be used to increase length of muscle and decrease tone.
   c. Maximize the gross motor functional level.
      (1) Use principles of motor learning and motor control; facilitate functional motor skills, including voluntary movement, anticipatory and reactive postural adjustments. Use toys, fun activities, balls, and bolsters to facilitate postural control and developmental activities.
      (2) Use weight bearing and postural challenge to increase muscle tone and strength.
      (3) Incorporate orthoses as necessary.
         (a) Ankle-foot orthosis (AFO) most commonly used; may be rigid or with articulated ankle.
         (b) Submalleolar orthosis for forefoot and midfoot malalignment; e.g., pronated foot.
      (4) Utilize adaptive equipment as necessary.
         (a) Seating should maintain head in neutral position; trunk upright; hips, knees, and ankles at 90° flexion (hips in abduction if spastic adductors). Wheelchair or seat may be tilted posteriorly to decrease extensor tone and maintain hip flexion.
         (b) Prone or supine standers and parapodium will promote weight bearing through lower extremities and encourage bone mineralization (requires minimum of 5 hours/week in weight bearing), gastrointestinal function, tone, strengthening of lower extremity muscles, and social interaction. TLR will elicit more extensor tone in supine, more flexor tone in prone.
         (c) Side-lying will help decrease effect of TLR.
         (d) Rollator walkers often used. Posterior rollator walker helps child maintain upright position, and arm position helps decrease extensor tone.
7. Prognosis for CP.
   a. Prognosis depends on severity of brain lesion.
   b. Most children with spastic hemiplegia, mild to moderate spastic CP, and mild ataxia will be able to ambulate.
   c. Good prognosis for ambulation if child can sit independently by 2 years of age.
   d. If child is going to walk, most will walk by 8 years of age.
8. Medical-surgical, pharmacological interventions for CP.
   a. Management of spasticity (see Table 7-5).
      (1) Oral medications—presynaptic inhibition of acetylcholine release.
      (2) Intrathecal baclofen (ITB) pump.
         (a) GABA b-agonist; GABA is an inhibitory CNS neurotransmitter. Catheter delivers drug to the intrathecal (subarachnoid) space in the spinal cord, producing muscle relaxation with less medication. ITB is delivered to a specific segment of the spine and controls spasticity below that segment. Pump is implanted subcutaneously in abdomen with catheter to spinal cord. Programmable to allow for precise dosage and easily adjusted.
         (b) Pros: longer lasting, decrease spasticity/spasm, improves motor control, reversible, non-invasive dose, fewer side effects, reservoir holds 1–4-month supply.
         (c) Cons: side effects can include hypotonia, nausea, headaches, surgical complications, catheter kink/malfunction, overdose, and withdrawal. Refills needed approximately every 3 months.
         (d) Overdose signs and symptoms: drowsiness, dizziness, respiratory depression, seizures, hypotonia, loss of consciousness (can lead to coma). Call EMS!
         (e) Withdrawal signs and symptons: increased spasticity, itching without rash, tingling, headaches, hyperthermia, hypotension, seizures, hallucinations, altered mental state, autonomic dysreflexia. Call EMS!
      (3) Neurosurgery.
         (a) Neurectomy, anterior rhizotomy, selective dorsal rhizotomy, corectomy, thalmotomy, deep brain stimulation.
            - Selective dorsal rhizotomy (SDR).
               - Common procedure: dorsal sensory nerve rootles are stimulated, those responding abnormally are severed. Usually done between 4 and 10 years of age.
               - Pros: decrease spasticity, improved motor control, and not reversible.
               - Cons: Possible sensory loss, not reversible, not effective for dystonia, anesthesia risks.
         (b) Intensive strengthening program after surgery when ambulation is goal.

(4) Peripheral nerve block.
   (a) Injection of phenol/alcohol into peripheral nervous system from nerve root to motor endplate.
   (b) Lasts 3–6 months.
(5) Botox injections—minute amounts of botulinum toxin injected into muscle, paralyzing it for 4–6 months.

9. Orthopedic management of CP (see Table 7-6).
   a. Lengthening procedures.
      (1) Muscle/tendon lengthening to correct deformity or weak muscle prevents hip subluxation/dislocation.
      (2) Muscles most often lengthened include Achilles' tendon, hamstrings, iliopsoas, and hip adductors.

Table 7-5

Medical Treatment for Spasticity

ORAL MEDICATIONS

MOST COMMON	SITE OF ACTION	PROS OF ORAL MEDS	CONS OF ORAL MEDS
Baclofen (Lioresal)	CNS	Decreases spasticity and spasms	Decreased strength, may lose postural control
Diazepam (Valium)	CNS	Improves motor control	Difficult to maintain steady state
Tizanidine (Zanaflex)	CNS	Non-invasive, not permanent	Following dosage schedule may be difficult
Dantrolene Sodium (Dantrium)	Muscle	Can be effective for some patients	Side effects: drowsiness, hypotonia, weakness

*Oral meds are systemic and may be suggested for patients that have wide spread areas of spasticity.

INJECTION THERAPY

	PROS	CONS
Anesthetic/Diagnostic Nerve Blocks (Procaine, Lidocaine)	Decreases local spasticity and dystonia Not permanent Decreases contractures Improves motor control Not systemic	Not permanent
Neurolytic Nerve Blocks (Ethanol, Phenol)	Decreases local spasticity and dystonia Not permanent Decreases contractures Improves motor control Not systemic	Not permanent Ethanol and Phenol—great skill needed to inject; risk of paresthesias
Botulinum Toxin [Botox] (Clostridium Botulinum)—injected into muscles, interferes with release of acetylcholine at the neuromuscular junction. EMG used for guidance if needed.	Decreases local spasticity and dystonia Not permanent Decreases contractures Improves motor control No systemic effect Can be administered without anesthesia Lasts 3–6 months	Not permanent Expensive

*Injections are used for specific muscles and are better for patients with focal spasticity.

Table 7-6

Orthopedic Surgery

Soft tissue operations (tendon or muscle lengthening, muscle releases, tendon transfers). Bone-related (osteotomies, fusions).

PROS	CONS
Decrease contracture	Anesthesia risks
Decrease abnormal bony alignment	Non-weight bearing after bony procedures for several weeks
Improve motor control	Risk of weakness and decreased function
Effects last a few years or more	

b. Muscle transfers.
   (1) Muscle attachments moved to change direction of force in order to increase function and decrease spasticity.
   (2) Most often done with hip adductors transferred to hip abductor.
c. Osteotomies.
   (1) Cutting, removing, or repositioning bone to facilitate normal alignment, prevent subluxation/dislocation.
   (2) Most often performed in lower extremities (femoral, tibial, or pelvic osteotomy).

Myelodysplasia/Spina Bifida

1. Pathology.
   a. Neural tube defect resulting in vertebral and/or spinal cord malformation. Elevated serum or amniotic alpha-fetoprotein, amniotic acetylcholinesterase in prenatal period and sonogram are used for detection.
   b. Spina bifida occulta: no spinal cord involvement, may be indicated by a tuft of hair, dimple, or sinus.
   c. Spina bifida cystica: visible or open lesion.
      (1) Meningocele: cyst includes cerebrospinal fluid; cord intact.
      (2) Myelomeningocele: cyst includes cerebrospinal fluid (CSF) and herniated cord tissue.
   d. Neural tube defects linked to maternal decreased folic acid, infection, hot tub soaks, and exposure to teratogens such as alcohol and valproic acid.
   e. Hydrocephalus significantly related to closure of neural tube defect. Shunting relieves pressure of hydrocephalus. May develop Arnold-Chiari malformation Type II: cerebellum and brain stem are pushed through the foramen magnum.
   f. Meningitis common if defect not closed soon after birth.
   g. Foot deformities such as talipes equinovarus (clubfoot) common, especially with L4, L5 level.
   h. Tethered cord may lead to increased severity of problems as child grows.
   i. Latex sensitivity/allergy.
2. Impairments.
   a. Depends on level of lesion and amount of malformation of cord.
   b. Muscle paralysis and imbalance resulting from spinal and lower limb deformities and joint contractures.
      (1) Kyphoscoliosis.
      (2) Shortened hip flexors and adductors.
      (3) Flexed knees.
      (4) Pronated feet.
   c. L4, L5 lesion results in bowel and bladder dysfunction.
   d. Sensory loss.
   e. Developmental delays.
   f. Abnormal tone: may have low tone, leading to poor strength and/or spasticity in upper extremities.
   g. Osteoporosis.
   h. Cognitive impairments including mental retardation, learning and perceptual disabilities, language disorders.
3. Functional limitations.
   a. Highly variable, depending on level of lesion.
   b. Weakness or paralysis of hip flexors (high lumbar level lesion) makes ambulation possible only with reciprocating gait orthosis (RGO).
   c. Problems with learning, communication.
4. Medical-surgical management of spina bifida.
   a. If open defect, surgical closure within 24–48 hours.
   b. Ventriculoperitoneal (VP) shunt performed for hydrocephalus. Ventriculoatrial (AV) shunts can also be used.
   c. Orthopedic surgeries similar to cerebral palsy.
5. Physical therapy examination for spina bifida.
   a. Physiological homeostasis in infants, breathing, oxygenation.
   b. Gross and fine motor development including reflex and behavioral examination of infant.
   c. Communicate with parents, family members about concerns, goals for intervention.
   d. Functional abilities using PEDI or WeeFIM.
   e. Active and passive ROM.
   f. Muscle strength: may observe developmental abilities if child under 3 years of age.
   g. Sensation: stroke skin and note response; record by dermatome.
   h. Skin: check for skin breakdown, suture of closure, skin over shunt line.
6. Interventions, goals, and prognosis for spina bifida.
   a. Teach parents proper positioning, handling, and exercise, keeping physiological flexion of the newborn. Include prone positioning to avoid shortening of hip flexors, as well as hip ROM, low tone, and osteoporosis.
   b. Use adaptive equipment/orthoses, such as spinal orthoses for alignment, adaptive chairs for sitting (if needed), parapodium for early standing, lower extremity (LE) orthoses and ambulation assistive devices and/or wheelchair as needed.
   c. Facilitate functional motor development, including appropriate developmental activities, primary or voluntary movement as well as reactive and anticipatory postural adjustments.
   d. Educate parents regarding shunt malfunction. Signs include increased irritability, decreased muscle tone, seizures, vomiting, bulging fontanels, headache, and redness along shunt tract.
   e. See Table 7-7.

Table 7-7

Myelodysplasia Orthotics and Functional Prognosis

LEVEL	ORTHOSIS	FUNCTIONAL PROGNOSIS
Thoracic L2	THKAFO Parapodium	Wheelchair for all functional mobility, standing and walking for physiologic benefits.
L1–L3	Reciprocating Gait Orthosis (RGO) HKAFO	Wheelchair for most functional mobility, short household ambulation possible. Standing and walking for physiologic benefits.
L3–L4	KAFO	Wheelchair for community mobility. Household ambulation possible.
L4–S1	AFO Ground-Reaction AFO	Household or community ambulation (although may be limited).
S1	Foot Orthosis (FO) Supramalleolar Orthosis (SMO)	Community ambulation.

*Limited ambulation for all except S1 as a result of lack of muscle function and energy requirements to ambulate.

Brachial Plexus Injury

1. Pathology.
   a. Traction or compression injury to unilateral brachial plexus during birth process or due to cervical rib abnormality.
      (1) Erb's paralysis (also known as Erb-Duchenne paralysis) involves C5–6, upper arm paralysis, may involve rhomboids, levator scapulae, serratus anterior, deltoid, supraspinatus, infraspinatus, biceps brachii, brachioradialis, brachialis, supinator, and long extensors of wrist, fingers, and thumb.
      (2) Klumpke's paralysis involves C8–T1, lower arm paralysis, involves intrinsic muscles of hand, flexors and extensors of wrist and fingers.
      (3) Total or Whole Arm Paralysis (formerly known as Erb-Klumpke palsy), C5–T1.
   b. Nerve sheath is torn and nerve fibers compressed by hemorrhage and edema, although total avulsion of nerve is possible.
2. Impairments.
   a. Sensory deficits of upper extremity.
   b. Paralysis or paresis of upper extremity.
   c. Characteristic position for Erb's paralysis of upper extremity is adduction, internal rotation of shoulder with extension of elbow, pronation of forearm, and flexion of wrist. Waiter's tip deformity.
3. Functional limitations.
   a. Dependent on severity of injury.
      (1) Erb's paralysis results in decreased shoulder girdle function with 1:1 humeroscapular movement.
      (2) Klumpke's paralysis results in decreased wrist and hand function.
   b. Traction injuries resolve spontaneously.
   c. Avulsion injuries may require surgical nerve repair if not resolved within three months.
   d. Shoulder subluxation and contractures of muscles may develop.
4. Physical therapy examination for brachial plexus injury.
   a. Observe infant posture, as well as arm position and movement.
   b. Test reflexes: Moro, biceps, radial reflexes are not present; grasp is intact.
   c. Sensory testing of affected upper extremity (UE).
5. Physical therapy intervention and prognosis.
   a. Partial immobilization of limb across upper abdomen for 1–2 weeks to avoid further injury.
   b. Gentle ROM after initial immobilization to avoid contractures.
   c. Elicit muscle activity with age-appropriate functional movements of UE.
   d. May use gentle constraint of unaffected arm to facilitate use of affected UE. This can be done with positioning.
   e. Prognosis depends on severity of nerve injury, favorable in most instances. If recovery does not occur, surgery is indicated.

Down Syndrome (Trisomy 21)

1. Pathology.
   a. Chromosomal abnormality caused by breakage and translocation of a piece of chromosome onto normal chromosome. Two types: Standard (95% of cases) and Translocation.
   b. A third type is a milder form with some normal cells interspersed with abnormal cells, called mosaic.

These children can have normal cognition and will have less impairments and disability.
   c. Brain weight less than normal.
   d. Cerebellum and brain stem lighter than normal.
   e. Smaller convolutions of cortex.
2. Impairments.
   a. Hypotonia.
   b. Decreased force generation of muscles.
   c. Congenital heart defects especially septal defects.
   d. Visual and hearing losses.
   e. Atlantoaxial subluxation/dislocation could be due to laxity of transverse odontoid ligament.
      (1) Signs include decreased strength, decreased ROM, hyporeflexic deep tendon reflexes (DTRs) and decreased sensation in extremities, persistent head tilt and increase in muscle tone.
   f. Cognitive deficit.
3. Functional limitations.
   a. Gross motor developmental delay.
   b. Difficulties in eating and speech development due to low tone.
   c. Forceful neck flexion and rotation activities should be limited, due to atlantoaxial ligament laxity.
   d. Cognitive and perceptual deficits may result in delay of fine motor and psychosocial development.
4. Physical therapy examination for Down syndrome.
   a. Developmental test of gross and fine motor skills.
   b. Test of tone by passive ROM.
   c. Active and passive ROM.
   d. Muscle testing; may use observation of developmental postures and movements if child under 3 years of age.
   e. Functional level.
5. Physical therapy interventions, goals, and prognosis for Down syndrome.
   a. Minimize gross motor delay.
      (1) Facilitate gross and fine motor development through appropriate positioning, posture, and movement activities.
      (2) Increase strength and stability by manipulating gravity and resistance in a graded manner.
   b. Encourage oral motor function.
      (1) Facilitate lip closure and tongue retrusion.
      (2) Short, frequent feeding sessions for energy conservation.
   c. Avoid hyperextension of elbows and knees during weight-bearing activities.
   d. Avoid all traction on extremities or spine due to ligamentous laxity and low muscle tone.
   e. Prognosis may be correlated with tone: the lower the tone, the more significant the motor delay. Most children will walk by age 2 and all will walk by age 5.
6. Medical-surgical management of Down syndrome.
   a. Yearly radiographs to rule out atlantoaxial subluxation starts at age 3. X-ray is unable to detect subluxation prior to 3 years of age, so assume and treat as if child has AA instability.
   b. Medical-surgical correction of cardiac problems.

Traumatic Brain Injury (TBI)

1. Pathology.
   a. Primary brain injury due to mechanical forces of initial impact.
      (1) Acceleration-dependent injuries when force is applied to movable head such as coup-contrecoup and rotational injury.
      (2) Nonacceleration-dependent injuries include skull depression into brain tissue and vibration.
      (3) May be accidental or due to child abuse such as "shaken baby syndrome."
   b. Secondary brain injury due to processes initiated as a result of initial trauma.
      (1) Cerebral edema increases intracranial pressure and may lead to herniation, cerebral infarctions, brain stem injury, and coma.
      (2) Epidural hematoma due to bleeds of middle meningeal artery, vein or venous sinus bleeds into epidural space.
      (3) Subdural hematoma due to lacerated cortical blood vessels.
   c. Evaluation of traumatic brain injury.
      (1) Imaging such as computed tomography (CT) scan and magnetic resonance imaging (MRI) to determine extent of initial and secondary injury.
      (2) Monitoring intracranial pressure.
      (3) Behavioral scales such as the Glasgow Coma Scale and the Rancho Los Amigos Coma Scale assess the child's orientation to time and place and the ability to respond to various stimuli. Infant coma scale used for nonverbal infants.
2. Impairments.
   a. Depend on the severity and location of the initial and secondary injuries.
   b. Level of consciousness and cognitive level may be temporarily or permanently impaired.
   c. Spasticity, loss of functional ROM, contractures, and deformities.
   d. Weakness, balance and coordination problems.
   e. Heterotopic ossification—pathological bone formation around joint due to increased tone around joint, immobility and coma.
3. Functional limitations.
   a. Decreased mobility skills.
   b. Cognitive and perceptual difficulties.
   c. Developmental process may be affected, resulting in abnormal development or developmental delay.
4. Physical therapy examination of traumatic brain injury.

a. History, MRI, CT, electroencephalogram (EEG) results, current medications.
b. Level of consciousness (Children's Coma Scale, Rancho Los Amigos Coma Scale).
c. Active and passive ROM.
d. Muscle strength: observe spontaneous movements if manual muscle test (MMT) is not possible.
e. Sensory testing.
f. Balance and coordination testing, developmental testing if appropriate.
g. Determination of muscle tone (modified Ashworth Scale).
h. Cranial nerve testing.
i. Functional level testing.
j. Integumentary examination to check for pressure sores.

5. Interventions, goals, and prognosis.
a. Maintain or improve joint flexibility by positioning, serial casting, ROM.
b. Stimulate/arouse level of consciousness through sensory stimuli.
c. Minimize gross and fine motor delay.
(1) Facilitate gross and fine motor development through appropriate positioning, postures, and movement activities.
(2) Increase strength and stability by manipulating gravity and resistance in a graded manner.
d. Parent/family or caregiver education.
e. Prognosis depends on severity of injury, rate of recovery, social and physical supports available.

6. Medical-surgical management for TBI.
a. Mechanical ventilation, if needed.
b. Pharmacological agents to control intracranial pressure, including sedatives, paralytics, diuretics, and barbiturates.
c. Intracranial pressure monitored by intracranial pressure bolt.
d. Surgical evacuation of hematoma.

Duchenne's Muscular Dystrophy (DMD)* (Pseudohypertrophic Muscular Dystrophy)

1. Pathology.
a. X-linked recessive, inherited by boys, carried by recessive gene of mother. Diagnosis confirmed by clinical examination, EMG, muscle biopsy, DNA analysis, and blood enzyme levels.
b. Dystrophin gene missing results in increased permeability of sarcolemma and destruction of muscle cells.
c. Collagen, adipose laid down in muscle leading to pseudohypertrophic calf muscles.

2. Impairments.
a. Progressive weakness from proximal to distal beginning at 3 years of age to death in late adolescence or early adulthood.
b. Positive Gower's sign due to weak quadriceps and gluteal muscles; child must use upper extremities to "walk up legs" and rise from prone to standing.
c. Cardiac tissue also involved.
d. Contractures and deformities develop due to muscle imbalance, especially of heel cords and tensor fascia latae, as well as lumbar lordosis and kyphoscoliosis.

3. Functional limitations.
a. Developmental milestones may be delayed.
b. Ambulation ability will be lost, necessitating eventual use of wheelchair.
c. Progressive cardiopulmonary limitations.

4. Examination for muscular dystrophy.
a. Muscle strength—MMT, dynamometer.
b. Active and passive ROM.
c. Functional testing.
d. Skeletal alignment (check for lordosis, scoliosis, kyphosis).
e. Respiratory function, chest excursion during breathing or spirometer.
f. Assess need for adaptive equipment.

5. Interventions, goals, and prognosis.
a. Maintain mobility as long as possible by encouraging recreational and functional activities to maintain strength and cardiopulmonary function.
b. Maintain joint ROM with active and passive ROM exercises, and positioning devices, such as prone standers or standing frames. Gastrocnemius and tensor fascia lata shorten first. Night splints may be used.
c. Electrical stimulation of muscles for younger children may increase contractile ability.
d. Educate and support parents and family in a sensitive manner.
e. Do not exercise at maximal level; may injure muscle tissue (overwork injury).
f. Supervise use of adaptive equipment as needed.
g. Disease is progressive, leading to respiratory insufficiency and death in young adulthood.

6. Medical-surgical management.
a. Palliative and supportive, treating symptoms as they occur.

*See Chapter 1, Musculoskeletal Physical Therapy, for additional pediatric conditions, e.g., torticollis, arthrogryposis multiplex congenita, osteogenesis imperfecta, and other deformities; disorders of the hip, knee, ankle/foot, and spine.

b. Steroids (prednisone) increase life expectancy by decreasing pulmonary dysfunction. Antibiotics for pulmonary infections.
c. Orthopedic surgery for scoliosis (spinal instrumentation), muscle lengthening of gastrocnemius.

7. Becker's muscular dystrophy is a slower variant of DMD. Emerges in late childhood or adolescence. Cease walking around 27 years of age and death at approximately 42 years of age.

Autism Spectrum Disorder

1. Pathology.
   a. Developmental disorder that appears in the first 3 years of life and affects the brain's normal development of social and communication skills.
   b. Linked to abnormal biology and chemistry in the brain.
   c. Exact causes are unknown. It is probably a combination of factors that lead to autism. However, there seems to be a genetic link in some cases as it can "run in the family."
   d. Difficulties with verbal and nonverbal communication, social interaction, and atypical play skills.
   e. Sensory integration issues: hyposensitive (sensory-seekers) or hypersensitive (sensory-avoiders).
   f. Complex condition that varies greatly in severity. 40% have average to above average intelligence.
   g. Seen more in boys (1:54 boys versus 1:252 girl births).
   h. Diagnosis can now be made in some cases as early as 6 months of age.
2. Impairments.
   a. Decreased coordination.
   b. High level balance impairments.
   c. Occasional strength and ROM deficits.
   d. Sensory impairments.
3. Functional limitations.
   a. Delayed gross motor skills.
4. Physical therapy examination.
   a. Functional testing: age appropriate gross motor skills.
   b. Muscle strength: MMT, dynamometer.
   c. Coordination.
   d. High level balance activities.
   e. Active and passive ROM.
   f. Sensory exam.
5. Interventions, goals, and prognosis.
   a. Gross motor skill training to promote age appropriate abilities.
   b. Strengthening.
   c. Coordination training.
   d. Balance training.
   e. Sensory integration.
   f. Children tend to appear high functioning and age appropriate because they are independent ambulators. Many have delay in high level skills such as coordinated running, skipping, riding a bike, standing on one leg, etc. Some will demonstrate toe walking.
   g. Child with autism tends to have difficulty with new people and situations. They prefer a consistent routine and schedule.
   h. Aggressive behaviors or passive behaviors are seen.
6. Other interventions.
   a. Speech and occupational therapy is common.
   b. Medications for attention deficits and anxiety disorders that can exist.
   c. Some children are on special diets.

Pediatric Adaptive Equipment

1. Positioning equipment. Used to maintain skeletal alignment, prevent or reduce development of contractures and deformities, and facilitate functional abilities.
   a. Standers give the child weight-bearing experience, which maintains hips, knees, ankles, and trunk in optimal position, facilitates formation of acetabulum and aids bowel and bladder function.
   b. Side-lyers decrease effects of TLR, put hands in visual field.
   c. Adaptive seating is customized to meet the specific support and posture needs of the individual.
   d. Abductor pad at hips often used in positioning equipment to decrease scissoring extension pattern of hip extension, adduction, with knee extension and plantar flexion of ankles.
2. Equipment for therapeutic exercise.
   a. Balls of different sizes to promote strengthening, balance, and coordination, and make motor learning fun.
   b. Wedges to facilitate or increase muscle contraction needed, depending on position of wedge.
   c. Bolsters combine characteristics of ball and wedge.
   d. Swings to promote sensory integration.
   e. Scooter boards for prone stability/mobility work.
   f. Others include toys, modified tricycles, music, pets, and family members.
3. Lower extremity orthotics.
   a. AFOs to provide support to foot, ankle, and knee, to provide a stable base of support, and to reduce the effects of spasticity and hypoextensibility of muscles.
      (1) Ankle set at 5–10° dorsiflexion to decrease genu recurvatum.
      (2) Articulating-ankle AFO controls amount of dorsiflexion and plantar flexion.

(3) Tone-reducing AFO may be polypropylene or plaster cast, bivalved.
(a) Decreases effects of spasticity, including scissoring by maintained stretch.
(b) Stretches and maintains length of heel cord to prevent or lessen contracture.
(c) Provides good mechanical base of support for standing and ambulation.

b. Knee-ankle-foot orthosis (KAFO).
(1) For standing or ambulation.
(2) Reciprocal or swing-through gait.
(3) Knee may be solid at 0–5° flexion or hinged.
(4) Used by children with spina bifida or muscular dystrophy.

c. Hip-knee-ankle-foot orthosis (HKAFO).
(1) For standing and ambulation.
(2) Swing-through gait.
(3) Used by children with spina bifida or spinal cord injuries.

d. Reciprocating gait orthosis (RGO).
(1) HKAFO with molded body jacket.
(2) Cable system allows forward step with lateral weight shift.
(3) Used by children with thoracic level spinal bifida or spinal cord injuries.

e. Pavlik harness.
(1) For infants with congenital hip dysplasia.
(2) Hips held in flexion and abduction to maintain femoral head in acetabulum.

4. Mobility aids.

a. Wheelchairs.
(1) Must be the correct size for the child.
(2) Posture, movement, strength, endurance, abnormal tone, contractures are important in determining custom features of a wheelchair, including method of mobility, seating stability.
(3) Stroller-type chairs limit independence of child.
(4) Scooter/three wheelers require fair (3/5) sitting balance and upper extremity control.
(5) Power wheelchairs can be used as early as 18 months of age depending on the specific child.

b. Walkers.
(1) Rollator walkers with wheels usually used.
(2) Forward walker (anterior rollator walker).
(a) Encourages forward trunk leaning.
(b) Provides maximum anterior stability.
(3) Posterior walker (posture control walker).
(a) Encourages trunk extension.
(b) Encourages shoulder depression, elbow extension, neutral wrist, which may decrease scissoring in lower extremities.
(4) Gait trainers offer maximum support to upper extremities and trunk.

c. Crutches.
(1) Require more postural control than walkers.
(2) Axillary and Lofstrand crutches available.

Family, Early Intervention, and the Education Setting

1. Family. The single most important constant and environmental factor.

a. PT must collaborate with child and family.

b. Family-centered approach begins with child's and family's strengths, needs, and hopes, and results in a service plan that responds to the needs of the whole family. Role of PT is to support, encourage, and enhance the competence of parents or caretakers in their role as caregivers.

c. Parents of children with developmental disabilities often suffer from chronic sorrow due to the loss of the typical potential of their child.

2. Early Intervention Programs (EIPs).

a. Mandated by public law.
(1) To provide comprehensive, multidisciplinary EIP.
(2) For infants and children from birth to 3 years.
(3) Multidisciplinary assessment.
(4) Individual Family Service Plan (IFSP) developed.
(5) Family is a member of the team.

3. School System: Individual Education Plan (IEP).

a. Mandated by public law.
(1) Free and appropriate public education for all children with disabilities.
(2) For children 3 to 21 years.
(3) Multidisciplinary assessment.
(4) Right to related services such as PT is related to educational need.
(5) Least restrictive environment.

Review Questions

Pediatric Physical Therapy

1. In the developing infant, what are the differences in terms of age of onset and response between the asymmetrical tonic neck reflex (ATNR) and the symmetrical tonic neck reflex (STNR)?

2. When performing an examination of the skeletal system in a full-term neonate, what possible abnormal bony conditions should be part of the screening process?

3. What are the typical lower extremity contractures seen with the child with spastic cerebral palsy?

4. What is a realistic expectation for functional mobility in the community and in the household for a patient with myelodysplasia affecting the midlumbar levels (about L3)?

8

Geriatric Physical Therapy

SUSAN B. O'SULLIVAN

Chapter Outline

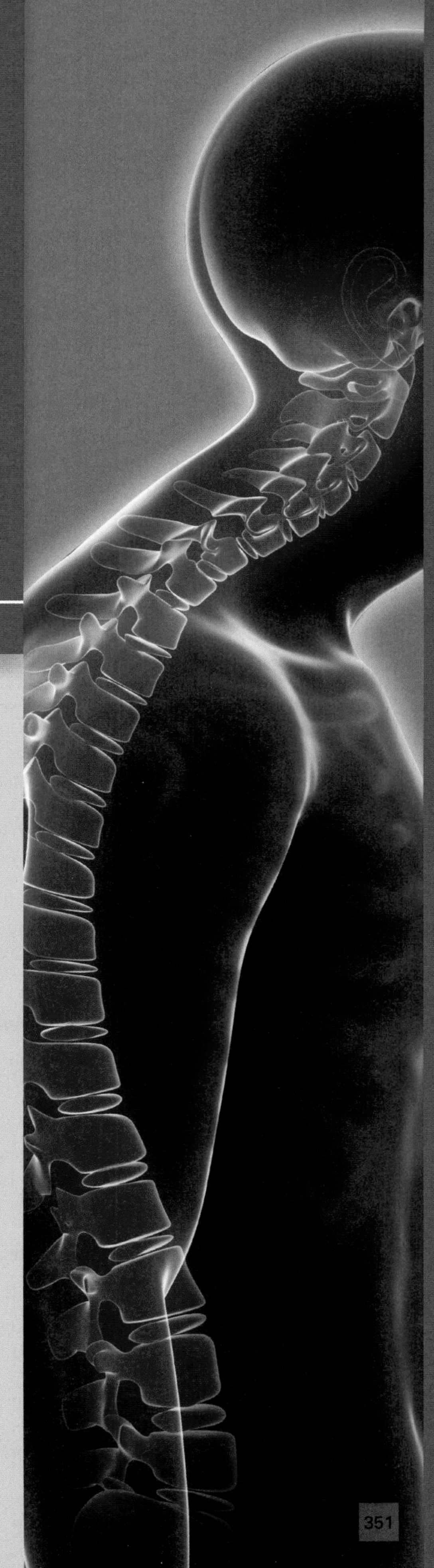

Foundations of Geriatric Physical Therapy

General Concepts and Definitions of Aging

1. Aging (senescence). The process of growing old.
   a. Common to all members of a given species.
   b. Progressive with time.
   c. Characterized by:
      (1) Declining ability to respond to stress and increasing homeostatic imbalance.
      (2) Increasing probability of disease with decreasing ability to successfully respond to insult.
   d. Varies among and within individuals.
2. Gerontology. The scientific study of the factors impacting the normal aging process and the effects of aging.
3. Geriatrics. The branch of medicine concerned with the illnesses of old age and their care.
4. Life span. Maximum survival potential, the inherent natural life of the species; in humans, 110–120 years.
5. Life expectancy. The number of years of life expectation from year of birth, 79.8 years in the United States, ranks 26th in the world (2013 WHO data); women live on average 6.6 years longer than men.
6. Categories of elderly.
   a. Young elderly: ages 65–74 (60% of elderly population).
   b. Old elderly: ages 75–84.
   c. Old, old elderly, or old and frail elderly: ages > 85.
7. Ageism. Discrimination and prejudice leveled against individuals on the basis of their age.

Demographics, Mortality, and Morbidity

1. Persons over 65.
   a. A rapidly growing segment of the population with lengthening of life expectancy; 13% of U.S. population in year 2010 (40 million people); by year 2030, expected to be 20% of U.S. population (72 million people).
   b. Older women outnumber older men; 145 women for every 100 men.
2. Increased life expectancy.
   a. Aging of the population due to:
      (1) Advances in health care, improved infectious disease control.
      (2) Advances in infant/child care, decreased mortality rates.
      (3) Improvements in nutrition and sanitation.
3. Leading causes of death (mortality) in persons over 65, in order of frequency (2012 U.S. Department of Health & Human Services).
   a. Coronary heart disease (CHD).
   b. Cancer.
   c. Stroke.
   d. Chronic pulmonary disease.
   e. Unintentional injuries, motor vehicle accident (MVA).
   f. Diabetes.
4. Leading causes of morbidity and risk factors in persons over 65, in order of frequency (2012 U.S. Department of Health & Human Services).
   a. Heart disease.
   b. Cancer.
   c. Hypertension.
   d. High serum cholesterol.
   e. Obesity.
   f. Cigarette smoking.
   g. Inactivity, lack of exercise.
   h. Persons over 65 reporting fair or poor health (26.9%).
5. Socioeconomic factors.
   a. Half of all older women are widows; older men are twice as likely to be married as older women.
   b. Most live on fixed incomes: social security is the major source of income; poverty rate for persons over 65 is 9%; another 26% of older persons have low annual incomes.
   c. About half of older persons have completed high school.
   d. Noninstitutionalized elderly: most live in family settings.
   e. Institutionalized elderly: about 5% of persons over 65 reside in nursing homes; percentage increases dramatically with age (22% of persons over 85).
6. Health care costs.
   a. Older persons account for 12% of population and 36% of total health care expenditures.
   b. Older persons account for 33% of all hospital stays, 44% of all hospital days of care.

Theories of Aging

1. Aging is a complex, multifactorial process.
   a. Aging occurs across molecular, cellular, and systemic levels.
   b. Processes interact simultaneously at many levels of functional organization.
   c. Both genetic and environmental factors contribute to shaping the life span.

2. Evolutionary theories.
   a. Aging results from a decline in the force of natural selection.
   b. Harmful late-acting mutations accumulate and lead to pathology and senescence.
3. Molecular theories.
   a. *Gene regulation theory*: senescence results from changes in gene expression.
   b. Exceptional longevity has a genetic component.
4. Cellular theories.
   a. *Cell senescence/telomere theory*: there are a limited number of cell divisions normal human cells can undergo.
   b. Replicative senescence: results from the loss of telomeres of a repeating DNA sequence. With each cell division, a small amount of DNA is lost.
   c. Stress-induced senescence: cells respond to a variety of stressors with DNA damage and modifications in structure.
   d. Damage accumulation theories include free radical damage, error catastrophe, and somatic mutation as a cause of cellular senescence.
5. Premature aging syndromes (progeria).
   a. Provides evidence of defective genetic programming and cellular damage.
   b. Individuals exhibit premature aging changes; i.e., atrophy and thinning of tissues, graying of hair, arteriosclerosis.
      (1) Hutchinson-Gilford syndrome: progeria of childhood.
      (2) Werner's syndrome: progeria of young adults.
6. System-based theories.
   a. Aging is related to a decline in organ systems. Nervous, endocrine, and immune systems play a key role in coordinating the responsiveness of body systems to external and internal stimuli.
   b. *Neuroendocrine theory*: neural and endocrine systems function to coordinate responsiveness of body systems to the external environment and maintain an optimal state for function and survival.
      (1) The hypothalamo-pituitary-adrenal axis is the master regulator for physiological adjustments necessary for preservation and maintenance of internal homeostasis (steady state).
      (2) Chronic exposure to stress may weaken or exhaust the capacity to adapt.
      (3) With aging there is a reduction in sympathetic responsiveness, feedback control, and hormonal adaptation.
   c. *Neuroendocrine-immuno theory*: stresses significant interaction and integration of the neuroendocrine and immune systems.
      (1) Immunosenescence is a decline in function of the immune system with aging.
      (2) Older adults demonstrate decreased resistance to infectious disease and protection against other diseases.
7. Environmental theories (stochastic or nongenetic theories).
   a. Aging is influenced by an accumulation of insults from the environment.
   b. Environmental toxins include ultraviolet, cross-linking agents (saturated fats), toxic chemicals (metal ions, Mg, Zn), radiation, and viruses.
   c. Can result in errors in protein synthesis and DNA synthesis/genetic sequences (error theory), cross-linkage of molecules, mutations.
8. Psychological theories.
   a. Stress theory: homeostatic imbalances alter structural and chemical composition.
      (1) Selye's *General Adaptation Syndrome*: initial alarm reaction, progressing to stage of resistance, progressing to stage of exhaustion.
      (2) Closely linked to hormonal theory.
   b. Erickson's *Bipolar Theory of Lifespan Development*; stages of later adulthood.
      (1) Integrity: individual exhibits full unification of personality; life is viewed with satisfaction (productive life), remains optimistic, continues to grow.
      (2) Despair: individual lacks ego integration; life is viewed with despair (fear of death, feelings of regret and disappointment, missed opportunities).
9. Sociological theories.
   a. Life experience/lifestyles influence aging process.
   b. *Activity theory*: older persons who are socially active exhibit improved adjustment to the aging process; allows continued role enactment essential for positive self-image and improved life satisfaction.
   c. *Disengagement theory*: distancing of an individual or withdrawal from society; reduction in social roles leads to further isolation and life dissatisfaction.
   d. Dependency: increasing reliance on others for meeting physical and emotional needs; focus is increasingly on self.
10. Mechanisms of successful aging.
   a. Persistence of normal function and plasticity.
   b. Compensatory responses to restore normal function (e.g., exercise, good nutrition, education).
   c. Interventions to restore normal function (e.g., modifying risk profile, successful disease management).
   d. Caloric restriction: diet restricted (by 30%–70%) in calories but containing all essential nutrients and vitamins. May promote longevity through metabolic reprogramming.
   e. Strengthening social interactions and support systems.

Physiological Changes and Adaptation in the Older Adult

Muscular

1. Age-related changes.
   a. Changes are due more to decreased activity levels (hypokinesis) and disuse than from aging process.
   b. Loss of muscle strength: peaks at age 30, remains fairly constant until age 50, after which there is an accelerating loss (20%–40% loss by age 65 in the nonexercising adult).
   c. Loss of power (force/unit time): significant declines due to losses in speed of contraction, changes in nerve conduction and synaptic transmission.
   d. Loss of skeletal muscle mass (atrophy): both size and number of muscle fibers decrease; by age 70, loss of 33% of skeletal muscle mass.
   e. Changes in muscle fiber composition: selective loss of type II, fast-twitch fibers, with increase in proportion of type I fibers.
   f. Changes in muscular endurance: muscles fatigue more readily.
      (1) Decreased muscle tissue oxidative capacity.
      (2) Decreased peripheral blood flow, oxygen delivery to muscles.
      (3) Altered chemical composition of muscle: decreased myosin adenosine triphosphatase (ATPase) activity, glycoproteins, and contractile protein.
      (4) Collagen changes: denser, irregular due to cross-linkages, loss of water content and elasticity; affects tendons, bone, cartilage.
2. Clinical implications.
   a. Movements become slower.
   b. Movements fatigue easier; increased complaints of fatigue.
   c. Connective tissue becomes denser and stiffer.
      (1) Increased risk of muscle sprains, strains, tendon tears.
      (2) Loss of range of motion (ROM): highly variable by joint and individual; activity level.
      (3) Increased tendency for fibrinous adhesions, contractures.
   d. Decreased functional mobility, limitations to movement.
   e. Gait changes.
      (1) Stiffer, fewer automatic movements.
      (2) Decreased amplitude and speed, slower cadence.
      (3) Shorter steps, wider stride, increased double support to ensure safety, compensate for decreased balance.
      (4) Decreased trunk rotation, arm swing.
      (5) Gait may become unsteady due to changes in balance, strength; increased need for assistive devices.
   f. Clinical risk of falls is evident in many older adults.
3. Interventions to slow or reverse changes.
   a. Improve health.
      (1) Correction of medical problems that may cause weakness: hyperthyroidism, excess adrenocortical steroids (e.g., Cushing's disease, steroids); hyponatremia (low sodium in blood).
      (2) Improve nutrition.
         (a) Correction of hyponatremia.
         (b) Increased fatigue associated with diarrhea, prolonged use of diuretics.
      (3) Address alcoholism.
   b. Increase levels of physical activity, stress functional activities and activity programs.
      (1) Gradual increase in intensity of activity to avoid injury.
      (2) Adequate warm-up and cool-down; appropriate pacing and rest periods.
   c. Provide strength training.
      (1) Significant increases in strength noted in older adults with isometric and progressive resistive exercise programs.
      (2) High-intensity training programs (70%–80% of one-repetition maximum) produce quicker and more predictable results than moderate-intensity programs; both have been successfully used with the elderly.
      (3) Age not a limiting factor: significant improvements noted in frail, institutionalized 80- and 90-year-olds.
      (4) Improvements in strength correlate to improved functional abilities.
   d. Provide flexibility, ROM exercises.
      (1) Utilize slow, prolonged stretching, maintained for 20–30 seconds.
      (2) Tissues heated prior to stretching are more distensible; e.g., warm pool.
      (3) Maintain newly gained range: incorporate into functional activities.
      (4) Mobility gains are slower with older adults.

Skeletal System

1. Age-related changes.
   a. Cartilage changes: decreased water content, becomes stiffer, fragments, and erodes; by age 60, more than 60% of adults have degenerative joint changes, cartilage abnormalities.

b. Loss of bone mass and density: peak bone mass at age 40; between ages 45 and 70, bone mass decreases (in women, by about 25%; in men, by 15%); decreases another 5% by age 90.
   (1) Loss of calcium and bone strength, especially trabecular bone.
   (2) See discussion of osteoporosis under Pathological Conditions Associated with the Elderly.
   (3) Decreased bone marrow red blood cell production.
c. Intervertebral discs: flatten, less resilient due to loss of water content (30% loss by age 65) and loss of collagen elasticity; trunk length, overall height decreases.
d. Senile postural changes.
   (1) Forward head.
   (2) Kyphosis of thoracic spine.
   (3) Flattening of lumbar spine.
   (4) With prolonged sitting, tendency to develop hip and knee flexion contractures.

2. Clinical implications.
   a. Maintenance of weight bearing is important for cartilage/joint health.
   b. Clinical risk of fractures.
3. Interventions to slow or reverse changes.
   a. Postural exercises: stress components of good posture.
   b. Weight-bearing (gravity-loading) exercise can decrease bone loss in older adults; e.g., walking, stair climbing, weight belts can increase load.
   c. Nutritional, hormonal, and medical therapies: see discussion of osteoporosis.

Neurological System

1. Age-related changes.
   a. Atrophy of nerve cells in cerebral cortex: overall loss of cerebral mass/brain weight of 6%–11% between ages of 20 and 90; accelerating loss after age 70.
   b. Changes in brain morphology.
      (1) Gyral atrophy: narrowing and flattening of gyri with widening of sulci.
      (2) Ventricular dilation.
      (3) Generalized cell loss in cerebral cortex: especially frontal and temporal lobes, association areas (prefrontal cortex, visual).
      (4) Presence of lipofuscins, senile or neuritic plaques, and neurofibrillary tangles (NFT): significant accumulations associated with pathology; e.g., Alzheimer's dementia.
      (5) More selective cell loss in basal ganglia (substantia nigra and putamen), cerebellum, hippocampus, locus coeruleus; brainstem minimally affected.
   c. Decreased cerebral blood flow and energy metabolism.
   d. Changes in synaptic transmission.
      (1) Decreased synthesis and metabolism of major neurotransmitters; e.g., acetylcholine, dopamine.
      (2) Slowing of many neural processes, especially in polysynaptic pathways.
   e. Changes in spinal cord/peripheral nerves.
      (1) Neuronal loss and atrophy: 30%–50% loss of anterior horn cells, 30% loss of posterior roots (sensory fibers) by age 90.
      (2) Loss of motoneurons results in increase in size of remaining motor units (development of macromotor units).
      (3) Slowed nerve conduction velocity: sensory greater than motor.
      (4) Loss of sympathetic fibers: may account for diminished, autonomic stability, increased incidence of postural hypotension in older adults.
   f. Age-related tremors (essential tremor, ET).
      (1) Occur as an isolated symptom, particularly in hands, head, and voice.
      (2) Characterized as postural or kinetic, rarely resting.
      (3) Benign, slowly progressive; in late stages, may limit function.
      (4) Exaggerated by movement and emotion.
2. Clinical implications.
   a. Effects on movement.
      (1) Overall speed and coordination are decreased; increased difficulty with fine motor control.
      (2) Slowed recruitment of motoneurons contributes to loss of strength.
      (3) Both reaction time and movement time increase.
      (4) Older adults are affected by the speed/accuracy tradeoff.
         (a) The simpler the movement, the less the change.
         (b) More complicated movements require more preparation, longer reaction and movement times.
         (c) Faster movements decrease accuracy, increase errors.
      (5) Older adults typically shift in motor control processing from open to closed loop; e.g., demonstrate increased reliance on visual feedback for movement.
      (6) Demonstrate increased cautionary behaviors, an indirect effect of decreased capacity.
   b. General slowing of neural processing: learning and memory may be affected.
   c. Problems in homeostatic regulation: stressors (heat, cold, excess exercise) can be harmful, even life-threatening.

3. Interventions to slow or reverse changes.
   a. Correction of medical problems: improve cerebral blood flow.
   b. Improve health: diet, smoking cessation.
   c. Increase levels of physical activity to encourage neuronal branching, slow rate of neural decline, improve cerebral circulation.
   d. Provide effective strategies to improve motor learning and control.
      (1) Allow for increased reaction and movement times to improve motivation, accuracy of movements.
      (2) Allow for limitations of memory by avoiding long sequences of movements.
      (3) Allow for increased cautionary behaviors: provide adequate explanation, demonstration when teaching new movement skills.
      (4) Stress familiar, well-learned skills and repetitive movements.

Sensory Systems

1. Age-related changes.
   a. May lead to sensory deprivation, isolation, disorientation, confusion, appearance of senility.
   b. May strain social interactions.
   c. May lead to decreased functional mobility, risk of injury.
2. Vision.
   a. Aging changes: there is a general decline in visual acuity; gradual prior to sixth decade, rapid decline between ages 60 and 90; visual loss as high as 80% by age 90.
      (1) Presbyopia: visual loss in middle and older ages characterized by inability to focus properly and blurred images due to loss of accommodation, elasticity of lens.
      (2) Decreased ability to adapt to dark and light.
      (3) Increased sensitivity to light and glare, increased difficulty with night driving.
      (4) Loss of color discrimination, especially for blues and greens.
      (5) Decreased pupillary responses, size of resting pupil increases.
      (6) Decreased sensitivity of corneal reflex: less sensitive to eye injury or infection.
      (7) Oculomotor responses diminished: restricted upward gaze, reduced pursuit eye movements; ptosis may develop.
   b. Additional vision loss with pathology.
      (1) Cataracts: opacity, clouding of lens due to changes in lens proteins; results in gradual loss of vision: central first, then peripheral; increased problems with glare; general darkening of vision; loss of acuity, distortion.
      (2) Glaucoma: increased intraocular pressure, with degeneration of optic disc, atrophy of optic nerve; results in early loss of peripheral vision (tunnel vision), progressing to total blindness.
      (3) Senile macular degeneration: loss of central vision associated with age-related degeneration of the macula, compromised by decreased blood supply or abnormal growth of blood vessels under the retina; initially, patients retain peripheral vision; may progress to total blindness.
      (4) Diabetic retinopathy: damage to retinal capillaries, growth of abnormal blood vessels and hemorrhage leads to retinal scarring and finally retinal detachment; central vision impairment; complete blindness is rare.
      (5) Cerebrovascular accident (CVA), homonymous hemianopsia: loss of half of visual field in each eye (nasal half of one eye and temporal half of other eye); produces an inability to receive information from right or left side; corresponds to side of sensorimotor deficit.
      (6) Medications: impaired or fuzzy vision may result with antihistamines, tranquilizers, antidepressants, steroids.
   c. Clinical implications/compensatory strategies.
      (1) Examine vision: acuity, peripheral vision, light and dark adaptation, depth perception, diplopia, eye fatigue, eye pain.
      (2) Maximize visual function: assess for use of glasses, cleanliness of glasses, need for environmental adaptations.
      (3) Sensory thresholds are increased: allow extra time for visual discrimination and response.
      (4) Work in adequate light, reduce glare; avoid abrupt changes in light; e.g., light to dark.
      (5) Decreased peripheral vision may limit social interactions, physical function: stand directly in front of patient at eye level when communicating with patient.
      (6) Assist in color discrimination: use warm colors (yellow, orange, red) for identification and color coding.
      (7) Provide other sensory cues when vision is limited; e.g., verbal descriptions to new environments, touching to communicate you are listening.
      (8) Provide safety education; reduce fall risk.
3. Hearing.
   a. Aging changes: occur as early as fourth decade; affect a significant number of elderly (23% of individuals aged 65–74 have hearing impairments and

40% over age 75 have hearing loss; rate of loss in men is twice the rate of women, also starts earlier).
(1) Outer ear: build-up of cerumen (earwax) may result in conductive hearing loss; common in older men.
(2) Middle ear: minimal degenerative changes of bony joints.
(3) Inner ear: significant changes in sound sensitivity, understanding of speech, and maintenance of equilibrium may result with degeneration and atrophy of cochlea and vestibular structures, loss of neurons.

b. Types of hearing loss.
(1) Conductive: mechanical hearing loss from damage to external auditory canal, tympanic membrane, or middle ear ossicles; results in hearing loss (all frequencies); tinnitus (ringing in the ears) may be present.
(2) Sensorineural: central or neural hearing loss from multiple factors; e.g., noise damage, trauma, disease, drugs, arteriosclerosis.
(3) Presbycusis: sensorineural hearing loss associated with middle and older ages; characterized by bilateral hearing loss, especially at high frequencies at first, then all frequencies; poor auditory discrimination and comprehension, especially with background noise; tinnitus.

c. Additional hearing loss with pathology.
(1) Otosclerosis: immobility of stapes results in profound conductive hearing loss.
(2) Paget's disease.
(3) Hypothyroidism.

d. Clinical implications/compensatory strategies.
(1) Examine hearing: acuity, speech discrimination/comprehension, tinnitus, dizziness, vertigo, pain.
(2) Measure air and bone conduction: Rinne's test, Weber's test. See Chapter 2.
(3) Determine use of hearing aids; check for proper functioning.
(4) Minimize auditory distractions: work in quiet environment.
(5) Speak slowly and clearly, directly in front of patient at eye level.
(6) Use nonverbal communication to reinforce your message; e.g., gesture, demonstration.
(7) Orient person to topics of conversation they cannot hear to reduce paranoia, isolation.

4. Vestibular/balance control.

a. Aging changes: degenerative changes in otoconia of utricle and saccule; loss of vestibular hair-cell receptors; decreased number of vestibular neurons; vestibular ocular reflex (VOR) gain decreases, begins at age 30, accelerated decline at ages 55–60 results in diminished vestibular sensation.
(1) Diminished acuity, delayed reaction times, longer response times.
(2) Reduced function of VOR; affects retinal image stability with head movements, produces blurred vision.
(3) Altered sensory organization: older adults more dependent on somatosensory inputs for balance.
(4) Less able to resolve sensory conflicts when presented with inappropriate visual or proprioceptive inputs due to vestibular losses.
(5) Postural response patterns for balance are disorganized: characterized by diminished ankle torque, increased hip torque, increased postural sway.

b. Additional loss of vestibular sensitivity with pathology.
(1) Ménière's disease: episodic attacks characterized by tinnitus, dizziness, and a sensation of fullness or pressure in the ears; may also experience sensorineural hearing loss.
(2) Benign paroxysmal positional vertigo (BPPV): brief episodes of vertigo (< 1 minute) associated with position change; the result of degeneration of the utricular otoconia that settle on the cupula of the posterior semicircular canal; common in older adults.
(3) Medications: antihypertensives (postural hypotension), anticonvulsants, tranquilizers, sleeping pills, aspirin, nonsteroidal anti-inflammatory drugs (NSAIDs).
(4) Cerebrovascular disease: vertebrobasilar artery insufficiency (transient ischemic attack [TIA], stroke); cerebellar artery stroke, lateral medullary stroke.
(5) Cerebellar dysfunction: hemorrhage, tumors (acoustic neuroma, meningioma); degenerative disease of brainstem and cerebellum; progressive supranuclear palsy.
(6) Migraine.
(7) Cardiac disease.

c. Clinical implications/compensatory strategies.
(1) Increased incidence of falls in older adults.
(2) Refer to section on falls and instability.

5. Somatosensory.

a. Aging changes.
(1) Decreased sensitivity of touch associated with decline of peripheral receptors, atrophy of afferent fibers; lower extremities more affected than upper.
(2) Proprioceptive losses, increased thresholds in vibratory sensibility, beginning around age 50: greater in lower than in upper extremities, greater in distal than proximal extremities.
(3) Loss of joint receptor sensitivity; losses in lower extremities, cervical joints may contribute to loss of balance.

(4) Cutaneous pain thresholds increased: greater changes in upper body areas (upper extremities, face) than in lower extremities.

b. Additional loss of sensation with pathology.
(1) Diabetes, peripheral neuropathy.
(2) CVA, central sensory losses.
(3) Peripheral vascular disease, peripheral ischemia.

c. Clinical implications/compensatory strategies.
(1) Examine sensation: check for increased thresholds to stimulation, sensory losses by modality, area of body.
(2) Allow extra time for responses with increased thresholds.
(3) Use touch to communicate: maximize physical contact; e.g., rubbing, stroking.
(4) Highlight, enhance naturally occurring intrinsic feedback during movements; e.g., stretch, tapping.
(5) Provide augmented feedback through appropriate sensory channels; e.g., walking on carpeted surfaces may be easier than on smooth floors.
(6) Teach compensatory strategies to prevent injury to anesthetic limbs; e.g., bathing.
(7) Provide assistive devices as needed to prevent falls.
(8) Provide biofeedback devices as appropriate (e.g., limb-load monitor).

6. Taste and smell.

a. Aging changes.
(1) Gradual decrease in taste sensitivity.
(2) Decreased smell sensitivity.

b. Additional loss of sensation.
(1) Smokers.
(2) Chronic allergies, respiratory infections.
(3) Dentures.
(4) CVA, involvement of hypoglossal nerve.

c. Clinical implications/compensatory strategies.
(1) Examine ability to identify odors, tastes (sweet, sour, bitter, salty); somatic sensations (temperature, touch).
(2) Decreased taste, enjoyment of food leads to poor diet and nutrition.
(3) Older adults frequently increase use of taste enhancers; e.g., salt or sugar.
(4) Decreased home safety; e.g., gas leaks, smoke.

Cognition

1. Age-related changes.

a. No uniform decline in intellectual abilities throughout adulthood.
(1) Changes do not typically show up until mid-60s; significant declines affecting everyday life do not show up until early 80s.
(2) Most significant decline in measures of intelligence occurs in the years immediately preceding death (termed terminal drop).

b. Tasks involving perceptual speed may show early declines (in some individuals by age 40); require longer times to complete tasks.

c. Numeric ability (tests of adding, subtracting, multiplying) and verbal abilities well-maintained in active individuals.

d. Memory.
(1) Impairments typically noted in short-term memory; long-term memory retained.
(2) Impairments are task-dependent; e.g., deficits primarily with novel conditions, new learning.

e. Learning. All age groups can learn; learning in older adults affected by:
(1) Increased cautiousness.
(2) Anxiety.
(3) Pace of learning: fast pace is problematic.
(4) Interference from prior learning.

2. Clinical implications.

a. Older adults utilize different strategies for memory (context-based strategies) than young adults (memorization).

b. Stress relationship, importance for function.

3. Interventions to slow or reverse changes.

a. Improve health.
(1) Correction of medical problems: imbalances between oxygen supply and demand to central nervous system (CNS); e.g., cardiovascular disease, hypertension, diabetes, hypothyroidism.
(2) Pharmacological changes: drug re-evaluation; decreased use of multiple drugs; monitor closely for drug toxicity.
(3) Reduction in chronic use of tobacco and alcohol.
(4) Correction of nutritional deficiencies.

b. Increase physical activity.

c. Increase mental activity.
(1) Keep mentally engaged—"Use it or Lose it"; e.g., chess, crossword puzzles, high level of reading.
(2) Engaged lifestyle: socially active; e.g., clubs, travel, work.
(3) Cognitive training activities.

d. If auditory processing is decreased, provide written instructions.

e. Provide stimulating, "enriching" environment; avoid environmental dislocation; e.g., hospitalization or institutionalization may produce disorientation and agitation in some elderly.

f. Stress support systems for remaining active: family and friends, senior groups supporting participation, activity, travel, and sports.

Cardiovascular System

1. Age-related changes.
   a. Changes due more to inactivity and disease than aging.
   b. Degeneration of heart muscle with accumulation of lipofuscins (characteristic brown heart); mild cardiac hypertrophy, left ventricular wall.
   c. Decreased coronary blood flow.
   d. Cardiac valves thicken and stiffen.
   e. Changes in conduction system: loss of pacemaker cells in sinoatrial node (SA) node.
   f. Changes in blood vessels: arteries thicken, less distensible; slowed exchange through capillary walls; increased peripheral resistance.
   g. Resting blood pressures rise: systolic greater than diastolic.
   h. Decline in neurohumoral control: decreased responsiveness of end-organs to beta-adrenergic stimulation of baroreceptors.
   i. Decreased blood volume, hemopoietic activity of bone.
   j. Increased blood coagulability.
2. Clinical implications.
   a. Changes at rest are minor: resting heart rate and cardiac output relatively unchanged; resting blood pressures increase.
   b. Cardiovascular responses to exercise: blunted; decreased heart rate acceleration, maximal oxygen uptake and heart rate; reduced exercise capacity; increased recovery time.
   c. Decreased stroke volume due to decreased myocardial contractility.
   d. Maximum heart rate declines with age (HR max = 220 – age).
   e. Cardiac output decreases 1% per year after age 20 due to decreased heart rate and stroke volume.
   f. Orthostatic hypotension: common problem in elderly due to reduced baroreceptor sensitivity and vascular elasticity.
   g. Increased fatigue; anemia common in elderly.
   h. Systolic ejection murmur common in elderly.
   i. Possible electrocardiographic (ECG) changes: loss of normal sinus rhythm; longer PR and QT intervals; wider QRS; increased arrhythmias.

Pulmonary System

1. Age-related changes.
   a. Chest wall stiffness. Declining strength of respiratory muscles results in increased work of breathing.
   b. Loss of lung elastic recoil, decreased lung compliance.
   c. Changes in lung parenchyma: alveoli enlarge, become thinner; fewer capillaries for delivery of blood.
   d. Changes in pulmonary blood vessels: thicken, less distensible.
   e. Decline in total lung capacity: residual volume increases, vital capacity decreases.
   f. Forced expiratory volume (airflow) decreases.
   g. Altered pulmonary gas exchange: oxygen tension falls with age, at a rate of 4 mm Hg/decade; PaO_2 at age 70 is 75, compared to 90 at age 20.
   h. Blunted ventilatory responses of chemoreceptors in response to respiratory acidosis: decreased homeostatic responses.
   i. Blunted defense/immune responses: decreased ciliary action to clear secretions, decreased secretory immunoglobulins, alveolar phagocytic function.
2. Clinical implications.
   a. Respiratory responses to exercise: similar to younger adults at low and moderate intensities; at higher intensities, responses include increased ventilatory cost of work, greater blood acidosis, increased likelihood of breathlessness, and increased perceived exertion.
   b. Clinical signs of hypoxia are blunted; changes in mentation and affect may provide important cues.
   c. Cough mechanism is impaired.
   d. Gag reflex is decreased, increased risk of aspiration.
   e. Recovery from respiratory illness: prolonged in the elderly.
   f. Significant changes in function with chronic smoking, exposure to environmental toxic inhalants.
3. Interventions.
   a. To slow or reverse changes in cardiopulmonary systems.
   b. Complete cardiopulmonary examination before beginning an exercise program is essential in older adults, due to the high incidence of cardiopulmonary pathologies.
      (1) Selection of appropriate exercise tolerance testing (ETT) protocol is important.
      (2) Absence of standardized test batteries and norms for elderly.
      (3) Many elderly cannot tolerate maximal testing; submaximal testing commonly used.
      (4) Testing and training modes should be similar.
   c. Individualized exercise prescription essential.
      (1) Choice of training program based on fitness level, presence or absence of cardiovascular disease, musculoskeletal limitations, individual's goals and interests.

(2) Prescriptive elements (frequency, intensity, duration, mode) are the same as for younger adults. See Chapter 3.
(3) Walking, chair and floor exercises, modified strength/flexibility calisthenics well tolerated by most elderly.
(4) Consider pool programs (exercises, walking, and swimming) with bone and joint impairments.
(5) Consider multiple modes of exercise (circuit training) on alternate days to reduce likelihood of muscle injury, joint overuse, pain, and fatigue.

d. Aerobic training programs can significantly improve cardiopulmonary function in the elderly.
(1) Decrease heart rate at a given submaximal power output.
(2) Improve maximal oxygen uptake (VO_2 max).
(3) Greater improvements in peripheral adaptation, muscle oxidative capacity than central changes; major difference from training effects in younger adults.
(4) Improves recovery heart rates.
(5) Decreases systolic blood pressure, may produce a small decrease in diastolic blood pressure.
(6) Increases maximum ventilatory capacity: vital capacity.
(7) Reduces breathlessness, lowers perceived exertion.
(8) Psychological gains: improved sense of well-being, self-image.
(9) Improves functional capacity.

e. Improve overall daily activity levels for independent living.
(1) Lack of exercise is an important risk factor in the development of cardiopulmonary diseases.
(2) Lack of exercise contributes to problems of immobility and disability in the elderly.

Integumentary System

1. Changes in skin composition.
   a. Dermis thins with loss of elastin.
   b. Decreased vascularity; vascular fragility results in easy bruising (senile purpura).
   c. Decreased sebaceous activity and decline in hydration.
   d. Appearance: skin appears dry, wrinkled, yellowed, and inelastic; age spots appear (clusters of melanocyte pigmentation); increase with sun exposure.
   e. General thinning and graying of hair due to vascular insufficiency and decreased melanin production.
   f. Nails grow more slowly, become brittle and thick.
2. Loss of effectiveness of skin as protective barrier.
   a. Skin grows and heals more slowly, less able to resist injury and infection.
   b. Inflammatory response is attenuated.
   c. Decreased sensitivity to touch, perception of pain and temperature; increased risk for injury from concentrated pressures or excess temperatures.
   d. Decreased sweat production with loss of sweat glands results in decreased temperature regulation and homeostasis.

Gastrointestinal System

1. Age-related changes.
   a. Decreased salivation, taste, and smell. Along with inadequate chewing (tooth loss, poorly fitting dentures), poor swallowing reflex may lead to poor dietary intake, nutritional deficiencies.
   b. Esophagus: reduced motility and control of lower esophageal sphincter; acid reflux and heartburn, hiatal hernia common.
   c. Stomach: reduced motility, delayed gastric emptying; decreased digestive enzymes and hydrochloric acid; decreased digestion and absorption; indigestion common.
   d. Decreased intestinal motility; constipation common.

Renal System

1. Age-related changes.
   a. Kidneys: loss of mass and total weight with nephron atrophy, decreased renal blood flow, decreased filtration.
   (1) Blood urea rises.
   (2) Decreased excretory and reabsorptive capacities.
   b. Bladder: muscle weakness; decreased capacity, causing urinary frequency; difficulty with emptying, causing increased retention.
   (1) Urinary incontinence common (affects over 10 million adults; over half of nursing home residents and one-third of community-dwelling elders); affects older women with pelvic floor weakness and older men with bladder or prostate disease.
   (2) Increased likelihood of urinary tract infections.

Pathological Conditions Associated with the Elderly

Musculoskeletal Disorders and Diseases

1. Osteoporosis.
   a. Disease process that results in reduction of bone mass; a failure of bone formation (osteoblast activity) to keep pace with bone reabsorption and destruction (osteoclast activity).
   b. World Health Organization diagnostic criteria.
      (1) Osteoporosis is defined by bone mineral density (BMD) at the hip or spine that is ≥ 2.5 standard deviations (SD) below the young, normal mean reference population.
      (2) Osteopenia is defined by a BMD between 1.0 and 2.5 SD below the young, normal mean reference population.
   c. Etiological factors.
      (1) Hormonal deficiency associated with menopause and hypogonadism: loss of estrogens or androgens.
      (2) Age-related deficiencies.
      (3) Nutritional deficiency: inadequate calcium, impaired absorption of calcium; excessive alcohol, caffeine consumption.
      (4) Decreased physical activity: inadequate mechanical loading.
      (5) Diseases that affect bone loss: hyperthyroidism, diabetes, hyperparathyroidism, rheumatic disease (lupus), celiac disease, gastric bypass, pancreatic disease, multiple myeloma, sickle cell disease, end-stage renal disease, Paget's disease, cancer, and chemotherapeutic drugs.
      (6) Medications that affect bone loss: corticosteroids, thyroid hormone, anticonvulsants, catabolic drugs, some estrogen antagonists, chemotherapy.
      (7) Additional risk factors: family history, Caucasian/Asian race, early menopause, thin/small build, smoking.
   d. Characteristics.
      (1) Estimated 10 million Americans with osteoporosis; additional 33.6 million with low bone density (osteopenia); 80% are women (will affect about one in two women); one-third will experience major orthopedic problems related to osteoporosis.
      (2) Bone loss is about 1% per year (starting at ages 30–35 in women and at ages 50–55 in men), accelerating loss in postmenopausal women, approximately 5% per year for 3–5 years.
      (3) Structural weakening of bone.
      (4) Decreased ability to support loads.
      (5) High risk of fractures.
      (6) Trabecular bone more involved than cortical bone; common areas affected:
         (a) Vertebral column.
         (b) Femoral neck.
         (c) Distal radius/wrist, humerus.
   e. Examination.
      (1) Medical record review.
         (a) History, physical exam, nutritional history.
         (b) BMD testing.
         (c) X-rays for known or suspected fractures.
         (d) Check for secondary causes.
      (2) Physical activity/fall history.
      (3) Assess dizziness: Dizziness Handicap Inventory.
      (4) Sensory integrity: vision, hearing, somatosensory, vestibular; sensory integration.
      (5) Motor function: strength, endurance, motor control.
      (6) ROM/flexibility.
      (7) Postural deformity.
         (a) Feet: hammer toes, bunions lead to antalgic gait.
         (b) Postural kyphosis, forward head position.
         (c) Hip and knee flexion contractures.
      (8) Postural hypotension.
      (9) Gait and balance assessment.
   f. Goals, outcomes, and interventions.
      (1) Medical therapy: initiated with BMD T-scores ≤ −2.5 at the femoral neck or spine by dual-energy x-ray absorptiometry (DXA) or individuals > 50 years with low bone mass (T-score between −1.0 and +2.5, osteopenia). Current Food and Drug Administration (FDA)–approved pharmacological options include:
         (a) Biphosphonates (alendronate, ibandronate, risedronate, and zoledronic acid).
         (b) Calcitonin.
         (c) Estrogens and/or hormone therapy.
         (d) Parathyroid hormone (teriparatide).
         (e) Estrogen agonist/antagonist (raloxifene).
      (2) Promote health; provide counseling on risk of osteoporosis and related fractures, health behaviors.
         (a) Daily calcium intake, individuals age 50 or older: 1200 mg per day.
         (b) Daily vitamin D intake, individuals age 50 or older: 800–1000 IU per day.

(c) Avoid tobacco smoking and excessive alcohol intake.
(d) Diet: low in salt; avoid excess protein, since it inhibits body's ability to absorb calcium.
(3) Maintain bone mass: regular weight-bearing exercise.
(a) Walking (30 minutes/day); stair-climbing; use of weight belts to increase loading.
(b) Muscle-strengthening (resistance) exercises to reduce risk of falls and fractures.
(4) Postural/balance training.
(a) Postural reeducation, postural exercises to reduce kyphosis, forward head position.
(b) Flexibility exercises.
(c) Functional balance exercises; e.g., chair rises, standing/kitchen sink exercises (e.g., toe raises, unilateral stance, hip extension, hip abduction, partial squats).
(d) Tai chi.
(e) Gait training.
(5) Safety education/fall prevention.
(a) Advise patients to avoid forward bending and exercising with trunk in flexion, especially in combination with twisting.
(b) Avoid long-term bed rest.
(c) Proper shoes: thin soles, flat shoes enhance balance abilities (no heels).
(d) Assistive device to decrease fall risk: cane; walker as needed.
(e) Fracture prevention: counselling on safe activities; avoid sudden forceful movements, twisting, standing, bending over, lifting, supine sit-ups.
(f) Hip protectors for patients with significant risk for falls or who have previously fractured a hip.
(g) Evaluate home environment for fall risk.

2. Fractures.
a. High risk of fractures in the elderly: associated with low bone density and multiple risk factors; e.g., age, comorbid diseases, dementia, psychotropic medications.
b. Hip fracture: common orthopedic problem of older adults, with more than 270,000 hip fractures annually in the United States; rate doubles each decade after age 50; by age 90, affects 32% of women and 17% of men.
(1) Mortality rate: 20%, associated with complications.
(2) About 50% will not resume their premorbid level of function; e.g., walk independently.
(3) May result in dependency; continued institutionalization occurs in as many as one-third of patients with hip fractures.
(4) Majority of hip fractures are treated surgically: 95% are femoral neck or intertrochanteric fractures; remaining 5% are subtrochanteric fractures.
(5) Intensive interdisciplinary rehabilitation program with early mobilization may improve outcome.
(6) Treatment protocols based on type of fracture and surgical procedure used: internal fixation versus prosthetic replacement.
c. Vertebral compression fractures.
(1) Usually occur in lower thoracic, lumbar regions (T8–L3).
(2) Typically result from routine activity: bending, lifting, rising from chair.
(3) Chief complaints: immediate, severe local spinal pain, increased with trunk flexion.
(4) Lead to shortening of spine, progressive loss of height, spinal deformity (kyphosis); can progress to respiratory compromise.
(5) Goals, outcomes, and interventions: acute phase.
(a) Horizontal bed rest, out of bed 10 minutes every hour.
(b) Emphasis on proper posture, extension in sleeping, sitting, and standing.
(c) Isometric extension exercises in bed.
(6) Goals, outcomes, and interventions: chronic phase.
(a) Teach patient extension exercises; avoid flexion activities.
(b) Postural training.
(c) Modalities for relief of pain.
(d) Safety education/modify environment.
(e) Decrease vertebral loading; e.g., use soft-soled shoes.
(f) Spinal orthotics: may provide pain relief; long-term use may lead to muscle weakness and further deconditioning.
(7) Red Flag: use caution with pain medications that can cause disorientation or sedation, increasing risk of falls.
(8) Surgery: Kyphoplasty or vertebroplasty can be performed for individuals with painful vertebral fractures.
d. Stress fractures: fine, hairline fracture (insufficiency fracture) without soft tissue injury.
(1) In elderly, common in pelvis, proximal tibia, distal fibula, metatarsal shafts, foot.
(2) May be unsuspected source of pain.
(3) Observe for signs of local tenderness and swelling; e.g., postexercise.
(4) Goals, outcomes, and interventions.
(a) Rest.
(b) Correction of exercise excesses or faulty exercise program.
(c) Reduction of vertical loading; e.g., soft-soled shoes.
e. Upper extremity fractures: humeral head, Colles' fractures common.

f. For discussion of fracture assessment and management, see Chapter 1.
g. Clinical implications of fracture management in the elderly.
  (1) Fractures heal more slowly.
  (2) Older adults are prone to complications; e.g., pneumonia, decubitus ulcers, mental status complications with hospitalization.
  (3) Rehabilitation may be complicated or prolonged by lack of support systems, comorbid conditions, decreased vision, poor balance.

3. Degenerative arthritis (osteoarthritis).
  a. A noninflammatory, progressive disorder of joints; typically affects hips, knees, fingers, and spine.
  b. Affects more than 16 million in the United States.
    (1) Incidence increases with age: at age 55, affects 57% of population; by age 75, affects 70% of population.
    (2) Prevalence higher in men up to age 45; by age 65, women five times more likely to be affected.
  c. Moderate to severe limitation in functional daily activities seen in 24% of individuals.
  d. Characteristics.
    (1) Pain, swelling, and stiffness, worse early morning or with overuse; e.g., knee pain, hip pain.
    (2) Muscle spasm.
    (3) Loss of ROM and mobility; crepitus.
    (4) Bony deformity.
    (5) Muscle weakness secondary to disuse.
  e. Goals, outcomes, and interventions.
    (1) Medical management: NSAIDs, corticosteroid injections, topical analgesics, joint replacements.
    (2) Reduction of pain and muscle spasm: modalities, relaxation training.
    (3) Exercises.
      (a) Maintain or improve ROM.
      (b) Correct muscle imbalances: strengthening exercises to support joints, improve balance and ambulation.
      (c) Aerobic conditioning: walking programs are associated with decreased joint symptoms, improved function, and sense of well-being.
      (d) Aquatic programs; e.g., pool walking, Arthritis Foundation program: produces beneficial effects similar to aerobic conditioning; enhances ease of movement.
    (4) Patient education and empowerment.
      (a) Teach patients about disease, taking an active role in care.
      (b) Teach joint protection, energy conservation strategies.
    (5) Provide assistive devices for ambulation and activities of daily living; e.g., canes, walkers, shoe inserts, reachers.
    (6) Promote healthy lifestyle: weight reduction to relieve stress on joints.

4. Cachexia.
  a. A multifactorial degenerative illness characterized by extreme weight loss and malnutrition, muscle atrophy, fatigue, and weakness.
  b. Loss of body mass that cannot be reversed nutritionally.
  c. Associated with severe chronic disease: e.g., cancer, HIV/AIDS, COPD, CHF, kidney failure, and so forth.

Neurological Disorders and Diseases

1. Stroke (CVA).
  a. Sudden, focal neurological deficit resulting from ischemic or hemorrhagic lesions in the brain.
  b. Most common cause of adult disability in the United States.
    (1) Incidence of stroke increases dramatically with age; most strokes (43%) occur in persons over the age of 74.
    (2) Approximately 30% die during the acute phase, and another 30%–40% will have severe disability.
  c. Clinical signs and symptoms; examination and intervention; see Chapter 2.

2. Degenerative diseases.
  a. Parkinson's disease: chronic, progressive disease of nervous system.
    (1) Parkinson's symptoms afflict about 20% of individuals over the age of 65; frequency of symptoms increases with age, affecting 50% of individuals over the age of 85.
    (2) Parkinson's disease affects about 1% of individuals over age 55, reaching proportions of 2.6% by age 85 in the United States. Affects approximately 1.5 million individuals, with 50,000 new cases annually; mean age of onset is between 59 and 62.
    (3) Clinical signs and symptoms; examination and intervention; see Chapter 2.

3. Clinical implications.
  a. Older adults are prone to complications/indirect impairments related to immobility and inactivity (e.g., contracture and deformity, decubitus ulcers).
  b. Rehabilitation may be complicated or prolonged by lack of support systems, comorbid conditions, decreased sensorimotor function, poor balance.
  c. With irreversible neurological disease, it is important to address the impairments and functional limitations responsive to interventions; overall focus should be on improved function and safety.
  d. Compensatory treatment strategies should be considered when disability is severe, there are multiple comorbidities, and impairments cannot be remediated; strategies can include environmental modifications, assistive devices, mobility devices, use of home health aides.

Table 8-1

Differential Diagnosis: Organic Brain Syndromes

	MULTI-INFARCT DEMENTIA	SENILE DEMENTIA ALZHEIMER'S TYPE (SDAT)	PRESENILE DEMENTIA ALZHEIMER'S TYPE (PDAT)
Age of Onset	55–70	60+	40–60
Gender Distribution	M:W = 3:1	M:W = 2:3	M:W = 2:3
Duration	Varies: days > years	Varies: months > years; mean survival 7–11 year	Rapid Mean survival: 4 years
Mode of Onset	Sudden	Gradual	Less gradual than SDAT
Course	Intermittent stepwise	Slowly or rapidly progressive	Rapidly progressive
Prognosis	Varies	Poor: mod. or severe cases	Very poor
Outcome	Death from CVA, CAD, or infection	Death from general system failure, infection	
Hereditary	Atherosclerosis	Multifactorial: age	
Precipitating Factors	Some familial tendency	Genetic: chromosome 21 abnormality; APOE4 gene; traumatic brain injury, Down syndrome	
Neuropathology	Small or large areas of infarction, secondary gliosis, senile plaques not common	Neuronal degeneration, neurofibrillary tangles, amyloid deposits, senile plaques, decreased cholinergic neuronal activity	
Clinical Signs of Brain Damage	Diffuse or focal, areas of preserved function	Diffuse, generalized	Diffuse, generalized, more severe than SDAT
Impairment of Higher Cortical Functions	Isolated impairments, focal signs, episodes of confusion with lucid intervals, some insight	Progressive dementia, progressive disorientation, memory loss, impaired cognition, judgment, abstract thinking, visuospatial deficits, apraxia, delusions, hallucinations; late stages: disorders of sleep, eating, sexual behavior, no insight	
Affect	Emotional lability, anxious, depressed	Variable: depressed, anxious, paranoid, hostile, restlessness, agitation, wandering, "sundowning" Late: apathy Personality changes: egocentricity, impulsivity, irritability, inappropriate social behaviors	
Neuromuscular	Focal signs: may see hemiparesis, hemisensory loss	Occasional tremors, generalized weakness, unsteady gait, increased tone: rigid postures, decreased postural reflexes, increased fall risk, repetitive behaviors	
Seizures	Yes	Rare	Occasional
Medical	TIAs, CVA, hypertension, headaches	Infections, contractures, fractures, decubitus ulcers, urinary and fecal incontinence	

Cognitive Disorders

1. Delirium
   a. Fluctuating attention state causing temporary confusion and loss of mental function; an acute disorder, potentially reversible.
   b. Etiology: drug toxicity and/or systemic illness, oxygen deprivation to brain; environmental changes and sensory deprivation; e.g., recent hospitalization, institutionalization.
   c. Characteristics.
      (1) Acute onset, often at night; fluctuating course with lucid intervals; worse at night.
      (2) Duration: hours to weeks.
      (3) May be hypoalert or hyperalert, distractible; fluctuates over course of day.
      (4) Orientation usually impaired.
      (5) Illusions/hallucinations, periods of agitation.
      (6) Memory deficits: immediate and recent.
      (7) Disorganized thinking, incoherent speech.
      (8) Sleep/wake cycles always disrupted.
2. Dementia.
   a. An acquired disorder of cognitive and behavioral impairment causing dysfunction in daily living (see Table 8-1).
   b. Characteristics of dementia.
      (1) Deterioration of intellectual functions: impoverished thinking, impaired judgment; disorientation, confusion; impaired social functioning.
      (2) Disturbances in higher cortical functions: language (aphasia), motor skills (apraxia), perception (agnosia).

(3) Memory impairment.
(4) Personality changes: alteration or accentuation of premorbid traits; behavioral changes.
(5) Alertness (consciousness) usually normal.
(6) Sleep often fragmented.

c. Reversible dementias: 10%–20% of dementias; multiple causes.
(1) Drugs: sedatives, hypnotics, antianxiety agents, antidepressants, antiarrhythmics, antihypertensives, anticonvulsants, antipsychotics, drugs with anticholinergic side effects.
(2) Nutritional disorders: vitamin B_6 deficiency, thiamine deficiency, vitamin B_{12} deficiency/pernicious anemia, folate deficiency.
(3) Metabolic disorders: hyper-/hypothyroidism, hypercalcemia, hyper-/hyponatremia, hypoglycemia, kidney or liver failure, Cushing's syndrome, Addison's disease, hypopituitarism, carcinoma.
(4) Psychiatric disorders: depression, anxiety, psychosis.
(5) Toxins: air pollution, alcohol.

d. Alzheimer's type dementia (Alzheimer's disease) (AD): 60%–80% of dementias.
(1) Most common cause of dementia; affects more than 5 million Americans; two-thirds are women primarily explained by the fact that women live longer than men and greatest risk is in the oldest age category.
(2) Costliest disease in United States; 6th leading cause of death.
(3) One in three seniors dies with AD or another dementia; leading cause of institutionalization; affects up to 50% of nursing home population.
(4) Etiology unknown.
(a) An incurable disease with a long and progressive preclinical course.
(b) Evidence of chromosomal abnormalities.
(c) Predisposing factors: family history, Down syndrome, traumatic brain injury, aluminum toxicity.
(5) Pathophysiological changes.
(a) Generalized atrophy of brain (hippocampus, entorhinal cortex, other cortical areas).
(b) Moderately enlarged ventricules.
(c) Decreased synthesis of neurotransmitters.
(c) Histopathological changes: accumulation of neurofibrillary tangles (protein tau) and beta-amyloid plaques eventually accompanied by damage and death of neurons.
(6) Risk factors for AD.
(a) Advanced age: 38% of 85+ years, 44% of 75–84 years, 15% of 65–74 years, and 4% of less than 65 years.
(b) Family history.
(c) Apolipoprotein E (APOE)-$_E$4 gene.
(d) Cardiovascular disease risk factors.
(e) Fewer years of formal education.
(f) Limited social and cognitive engagement.
(7) Types.
(a) Senile dementia, Alzheimer's type (SDAT): onset after the age of 60 (average age 75).
(b) Presenile dementia, Alzheimer's type (PDAT): onset between ages of 40–60.
(8) Diagnosis.
(a) Medical history and clinical examination: signs and symptoms.
(b) Cognitive tests.
(c) Biomarker tests: on lumbar puncture (CSF) see elevated levels of tau and phosphorylated tau; low amyloid levels.
(d) MRI scan to identify brain changes and rule out other causes of dementia (e.g., subdural hematoma, stroke, tumor, normal-pressure hydrocephalus).
(9) Stages of AD.
(a) AD is classified into stages (Box 8-1):
- Preclinical AD: individuals have measurable changes in brain CSF and blood biomarkers without noticeable symptoms.
- Mild AD (mild cognitive impairment): characterized by mild but measurable changes in cognitive abilities noticeable to person affected and family members; able to carry out everyday activities.
- Moderate AD: characterized by noticeable memory, thinking, and behavioral symptoms that impair a person's ability to function in daily life.
- Severe AD: characterized by loss of ability to communicate, recognize others, and complete dependence.

(b) Rate of progression varies from individual to individual.
(10) Signs and symptoms of AD (Box 8-1).
(a) Signs and symptoms vary by stage and presentation from patient to patient.
(11) Pharmacologic treatment.
(a) Disease-modifying therapies are not available to slow or stop disease progression.
(b) Limited number of drugs approved by FDA to temporarily improve AD symptoms.

e. Vascular dementia (multi-infarct dementias), 10% of dementias.
(1) Etiology: large and small vascular infarcts in both gray and white matter of brain, producing loss of brain function.
(2) Characteristics.
(a) Sudden onset rather than insidious; stepwise progression.
(b) Spotty and patchy distribution of deficits: areas of preserved ability along with impairments.

BOX 8-1 Signs and Symptoms of Alzheimer's Type Dementia (AD)

Preclinical AD:

- May appear normal on physical examination and mental status testing
- Memory loss is typically the first sign

Mild AD:

- Memory loss
- Confusion about the location of familiar places
- Taking longer to accomplish normal, daily tasks
- Trouble handling money and paying bills
- Compromised judgment, often leading to bad decisions
- Loss of spontaneity and sense of initiative
- Mood and personality changes; increased anxiety

Moderate AD:

- Increasing memory loss and confusion
- Shortened attention span
- Problems recognizing friends and family members
- Difficulty with language; problems with reading, writing, working with numbers
- Difficulty organizing thoughts and thinking logically
- Inability to learn new things
- Inability to cope with new or unexpected situations
- Restlessness, agitation, anxiety, tearfulness
- Wandering, especially in the late afternoon or at night (sundowning)
- Repetitive statements or movement; occasional muscle twitches
- Hallucinations, delusions, suspiciousness or paranoia, irritability
- Loss of impulse control: shown through behavior such as undressing at inappropriate times or places or vulgar language
- Perceptual-motor problems: such as trouble getting out of a chair or setting the table

Severe AD:

- Inability to communicate in any way
- Inability to recognize family or significant others
- Complete dependence on others for ADL and care
- Loss of sense of self

Other symptoms can include:

- Weight loss
- Seizures, skin infections, difficulty swallowing
- Groaning, moaning, or grunting
- Increased sleeping
- Lack of bladder and bowel control

End-stage AD, patients are restricted to bed; death results from other illnesses (e.g., aspiration pneumonia)

Adapted from Clinical Article: Alzheimer Disease. Medscape. Retrieved April 17, 2014 from http://emedicine.medscape.com/article/1134817-overview.

(c) Focal neurological signs and symptoms; e.g., gait and balance abnormalities, weakness, exaggerated deep tendon reflexes (DTRs).
(d) Pseudobulbar affect common.
(e) Associated with history of stroke, cardiovascular disease, hypertension.

f. Chronic traumatic encephalopathy (CTE).
(1) Acquired, progressive degenerative brain disease resulting from repetitive head trauma. Seen in boxers (i.e., dementia pugilistica) and athletes with a history of repeated head injury, multiple concussions.
(2) Pathophysiologic changes.
(a) Tau-positive neurofibrillary tangles (NFTs).
(b) Neurophil threads and neocortical diffuse amyloid plaques, with or without neuritic plaques.
(c) Hippocampus is spared (unlike AD).
(3) Signs and symptoms.
(a) Recurrent headaches and dizziness.
(b) Aggression, depression, anxiety, suicide.
(c) Impaired judgment and impulse control.
(d) Memory loss and confusion.
(e) Progressive dementia (late).
(f) Movement disorders (late).

g. Other types of dementia.
(1) Parkinson's disease (PD): symptoms include movement problems (slowness, rigidity, tremor, gait changes); dementia estimated in 10%–35% of cases, in late stages of the disease.
(2) Dementia with Lewy bodies (DLB): some symptoms of AD along with sleep disturbances, visual disturbances, slowness, and other PD movement features.
(3) Creutzfeldt-Jakob disease: rare and rapidly fatal disorder with memory, behavior changes, and incoordination; results from protein (prion) disorder.
(4) Normal pressure hydrocephalus: symptoms include memory loss, difficulty walking, inability to control urination; results from impaired reabsorption of CSF with build-up of fluid in the brain and increased brain pressures.
(5) Down syndrome: individuals demonstrate accelerated aging and AD; symptoms typically in late 40s or 50s.
(6) Chronic alcoholism with prolonged nutritional (vitamin B_{12}) deficiency; e.g., Korsakoff's psychosis.

h. Physical therapy examination.
(1) History: determine onset of symptoms, progression, triggering events, common problems, social history.
(2) Examine cognitive functions: orientation, attention, calculation, recall, language.
(3) Standardized tests for cognition: Mini-Mental State Examination (MMSE); score of < 24 out of possible 30 is indicative of mental decline/dementia.
(4) Examine for impairments in higher cortical functions: inability to communicate, perceptual dysfunction.
(5) Examine for behavioral changes: restless, agitated, distracted, paranoid, wandering, inappropriate social behaviors, repetitive behaviors.
(6) Examine self-care: ability to carry out activities of daily living; e.g., limitations in grooming and hygiene, continence.
(7) Examine motor function: dyspraxia, gait, balance instability.
(8) Examine environment for safety, optimal function.
(9) Standardized scales for AD: Blessed Performance of Everyday Activities; Alzheimer's Type Dementia Assessment Scale.

i. Goals, outcomes, and interventions.
(1) Environment.
(a) Provide safe environment: prevent falls, injury, or further dysfunction, safety from wandering; utilize safety monitoring devices as needed; e.g., alarm device.
(b) Provide soothing environment with reduced environmental distractions: reduces agitation, increases attention.
(c) Assistive and supportive devices to enhance self-care, effective positioning.
(2) Support individual's highest level of cognitive function.
(a) Approach the patient in a friendly, supportive manner; model calm behavior.
(b) Use consistent, simple commands; speak slowly.
(c) Use nonverbal communication as appropriate: sensory cues and demonstration.
(d) Provide reorienting information: use prompts; e.g., wall calendars, daily schedules, memory aids whenever possible.
(e) Avoid stressful tasks; emphasize familiar, well-learned skills; provide redirection.
(f) Approach learning in a simple, repetitious way; proceed slowly; and provide adequate rest time.
(g) Provide mental stimulation: utilize simple, well-liked activities, games.
(3) Provide regular physical activity, maintain physical fitness.
(a) Utilize functionally directed activities.
(b) Active assistive and passive ROM exercises to maintain ROM.
(c) Low intensity strengthening exercises.
(d) Safe daily walking program.
(e) Balance activities for fall prevention.

(f) Enhance body awareness and sensory stimulation; touch and light massage can be effective in promoting relaxation.
(4) Participate in restraint reduction program.
(5) Educate/support family, caregivers, significant others.
(6) Present a realistic, consistent team approach to management.

3. Depression.
   a. A disorder characterized by depressed mood and lack of interest or pleasure in all activities, and other associated symptoms, lasting for at least 2 weeks.
   b. Incidence.
      (1) Community-dwelling elderly: 5% have clinically diagnosed major depression (exhibit at least five symptoms); another 10%–20% have depressive symptoms.
      (2) Institutionalized elderly: 12% have major depression; another 15%–20% have depressive symptoms.
   c. Determine predisposing factors.
      (1) Family history, prior episodes of depression.
      (2) Illness, drug side effects; hormonal.
      (3) Chronic condition: loss of physical functions, pain; e.g., stroke.
      (4) Sensory deprivation (loss of vision or hearing).
      (5) History of losses: death of family and friends, job, income, independence.
      (6) Social isolation: lack of family support.
      (7) Psychological losses: memory, intellectual functions.
   d. Examine for depressive symptoms.
      (1) Nutritional problems: significant weight loss or weight gain; dehydration.
      (2) Sleep disturbances: insomnia or hypersomnia.
      (3) Psychomotor changes: inactivity with resultant functional impairments, weakness or agitation.
      (4) Fatigue or loss of energy.
      (5) Feelings of worthlessness, low self-esteem, guilt.
      (6) Inability to concentrate, slowed thinking, impaired memory, indecisiveness.
      (7) Withdrawal from family and friends, self-neglect.
      (8) Recurrent thoughts of death, suicidal ideation: document and immediately report all threats of suicide.
      (9) Decline in cognitive function; i.e., document with MMSE.
      (10) Standardized test: Geriatric Depression Scale; 30-item yes/no scale; score > 8 indicates depression.
   e. Goals, outcomes, and interventions.
      (1) Medical treatment.
         (a) Pharmacotherapy; tricyclic antidepressants (e.g., Chlorpromazine, fluoxetine [Prozac]) widely used.
         (b) Psychotherapy.
         (c) Electroconvulsive shock therapy (ECT) may be used if drug treatment is unsuccessful or contraindicated.
      (2) Avoid excessive cheerfulness; provide support and encouragement.
      (3) Assist patient in adjustment process to losses, coping strategies.
      (4) Encourage activities, exercise program: aerobic training is associated with increased feelings of well-being.
      (5) Assist in improving/maintaining independence; emphasize mastery by patient, achievement of short-term rather than long-term goals.

Cardiopulmonary and Integumentary Disorders and Diseases

1. Hypertension.
   a. Significant risk factor in cardiovascular disease, stroke, renal failure, and death.
2. Coronary artery disease (CAD).
   a. Affects 40% of individuals aged 65–74 and 50% over age 75.
   b. Angina.
      (1) Angina pain not always a consistent indicator of ischemia in elderly; shortness of breath, ECG ST segment depression may be more reliable indicators.
   c. Acute myocardial infarction.
      (1) Clinical presentation may vary from younger adults: may present with sudden dyspnea, acute confusion, syncope.
      (2) Clinical course often more complicated in the elderly, mortality rates twice that of younger adults.
   d. Congestive heart failure.
   e. Conduction system diseases: pacemaker dysfunction results in low cardiac output.
3. Peripheral vascular disease.
4. Clinical signs and symptoms.
   a. Examination and intervention. See Chapter 3.
5. Chronic bronchitis.
6. Chronic obstructive pulmonary disease (COPD).
7. Asthma.
8. Pneumonia.
   a. Initial symptoms may vary: instead of high fever and productive cough, may see altered mental status, tachypnea, dehydration.
9. Lung cancer.
10. Clinical signs and symptoms.
   a. Examination and intervention. See Chapter 4.
11. Pressure ulcers (decubitus ulcers).
   a. Characteristics.
      (1) Affects 10%–25% of hospitalized, ill elderly patients.

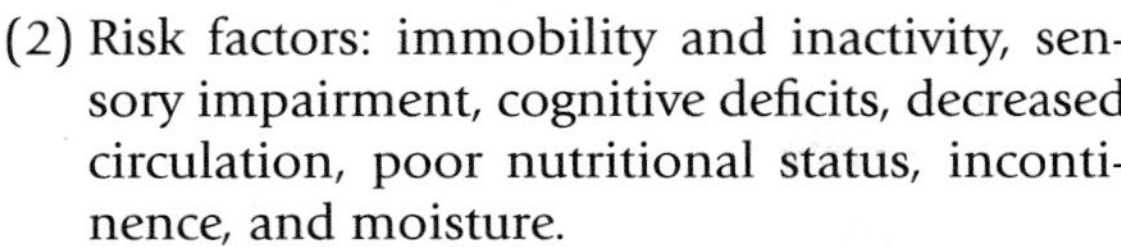

(2) Risk factors: immobility and inactivity, sensory impairment, cognitive deficits, decreased circulation, poor nutritional status, incontinence, and moisture.

(3) Common over bony prominences: ischial tuberosities, sacrum, greater trochanter, heels, ankles, elbows, and scapulae.

(4) If not treated promptly, can progress to damage of deep structures.

(5) Potentially fatal in frail elderly and chronically ill.

b. Clinical signs and symptoms; examination and intervention. See Chapter 5.

Metabolic Pathologies

1. Diabetes mellitus.
   a. Aging is associated with deteriorating glucose tolerance; type 2 diabetes affects as many as 10%–20% of individuals over age of 60.
   b. Associated with obesity and sedentary lifestyle.
   c. Clinical signs and symptoms; examination and intervention. See Chapter 6.

Patient Care Concepts

General Principles of Geriatric Rehabilitation

1. Recognize variability of older adults.
   a. Uniqueness of the individual.
   b. Developmental issues unique to the elderly.
2. Focus on careful and accurate clinical examination.
   a. Identify remediable problems.
   b. Determine capacity for safe function.
   c. Determine effects of inactivity versus activity.
   d. Determine effects of disease pathologies and inactivity versus normal aging.
3. Focus on functional goals.
   a. Determine priorities, remediable problems.
   b. Develop goals, plan of care in conjunction with patient/caregiver.
4. Promote optimal health.
   a. *Don't prescribe underdosed strength training programs for older adults. Instead, match the frequency, intensity, and duration of exercise to the individual's abilities and strengths* (White N, et al. Phys Ther. 2015).
   b. Monitor patient's heart rate and blood pressure during exercise or progressive physical activity regimens.
   c. Focus on increasing health-conducive behaviors, prevention of disability.
   d. Minimize and compensate for health-related losses and impairments of aging.
5. Restore/maintain.
   a. Individual's highest level of function and independence within the care environment.
   b. Determine how patient autonomy can be maximized by appropriate assistance and environmental manipulations.
   c. Empower elders: ensure they are in control of their own decisions whenever possible.
   d. Be sensitive to cultural and ethnicity issues; losses, fears, and insecurities; provide comfort and sustenance.
   e. Enhance coping skills.
   f. Recognize functional abilities, limitations of caregivers; enhance function and support caregivers.
6. Holism.
   a. Consider the whole person; integrate all facets of an individual's life.
   b. Determine social support systems, effects of social isolation.
   c. Determine effects of losses.
   d. Determine effects of depression, dementia.
7. Recognize demands.
   a. Enhance continuity of care, interactions in a complex health care delivery system.
   b. Advocate for needed services.
   c. Provide effective documentation.

Reimbursement Issues

1. Benefits from government programs.
   a. Cover about two-thirds (63%) of health care expenditures of older persons.
   b. Medicare: federal government–sponsored insurance for persons over age 65, disabled persons of all ages.
      (1) Part A (Hospital Insurance) covers inpatient hospital care, skilled nursing facility care, home health care provided by agencies, hospice care.
         (a) No premiums; eligibility under social security.
         (b) Must pay deductibles and coinsurance.

(2) Part B (Medical Insurance) covers physician services, eligible home health services, outpatient services, durable medical equipment.
(a) Must pay premiums to be eligible.
(b) Must pay deductibles and coinsurance.

c. Medicaid (federal-state funding): covers long-term care of frail and aged patients in nursing homes, impoverished adults, and children.
(1) Must spend down or exhaust income to qualify for low-income status.
(2) Administered by individual states that set qualification guidelines; specific requirements vary by state.

2. Supplemental insurance.
a. May be purchased from private insurance companies.
b. Copayments that elderly must pay under Medicare (Medex), termed Medigap policies.
c. Long-term care insurance.
d. Enrollment in health maintenance organizations (HMOs).

3. Documentation and reimbursement.
a. Requirements specific to type of insurance program.
(1) Medicare requirements for physical therapy services.
(a) Must be prescribed by a physician.
(b) Must include a determination of need: reasonable and necessary for individual's illness or injury according to acceptable standards of practice.
(c) Requires the skilled services of a licensed physical therapist.
- Condition must be expected to improve in a reasonable and generally predictable period of time.
- A skilled therapist is needed to safely and effectively establish the plan of care (POC) for a patient.
- A skilled therapist is needed to safely and effectively do maintenance therapy for a patient's condition (new Medicare wording for maintenance care based on *Jimma v. Sebelieus* Settlement Agreement, January/2013).

(d) The physician should review and sign and date the POC (certification). The POC should be certified for the first 30 days of treatment and recertified every 30 days (signed and dated).
(e) If the service is not covered under Medicare statutes (e.g., exceeding therapy cap, maintenance care, prevention and wellness), the patient can be billed directly.

(2) Private insurance requirements: vary by specific carrier; most adopt Medicare requirements (e.g., physician certification).

b. Baseline data must be described in functional and measurable terms.
c. Goals and outcomes should be measurable, objective, specific to patient, and indicate a predicted time frame.
d. Plan of care (POC).
(1) Address findings, relate impairments to functional performance.
(2) Include frequency and duration of treatment, projected end date, and disposition.

e. Progress report.
(1) Focuses on objective changes; subjective statements by patient.
(2) Documents remaining deficits, lack of progress, or declining status.
(3) Must be completed at least once during each Progress Report period.

Ethical and Legal Issues

1. Professional practice.
a. Affirms patient rights and dignity (professional ethical standards, APTA Code of Ethics).

2. Informed consent.
a. Respect for personal autonomy; competent patients have the right to refuse treatment; e.g., do not resuscitate (DNR) orders.
b. Legal right to self-determination. Information must be provided to patient that outlines:
(1) The nature and purpose of treatment.
(2) Treatment alternatives.
(3) Risks and consequences of treatment.
(4) Likelihood of success or failure of treatment.

c. Consent must be obtained from a legal guardian if the individual is judged incompetent.
(1) Older adults with fluctuating mental abilities must be carefully evaluated for periods of lucidity.
(2) Documentation with a mental status exam is essential.

3. Advance Care Medical Directive (Living Will).
a. Established by Federal Patient Self-Determination Act of 1990.
b. Health Care Proxy (Durable Power of Attorney): identifies a valid agent who is granted authority to make health care decisions for an individual, should that individual become incapacitated.
c. Requirements.
(1) Regulated by individual states; specific requirements vary by state.
(2) Must be in writing, signed by principal, witnessed by two adults.
(3) Empowers health care agent: includes specific guidelines on which treatment options will and will not be allowed; e.g., artificial life support, feeding tubes.
(4) Defines conditions/scope of agent's authority.

Common Problem Areas for Geriatric Clients

Immobility and Disability

1. Impaired mobility and disability.
   a. Can result from a host of diseases and problems.
2. Limitations in function.
   a. Increase with age in persons over age 65.
   b. 23% report difficulty with one or more personal care activities.
   c. 27% report difficulty with one or more home management activities.
3. Immobility.
   a. Can result in additional problems.
   b. Can lead to complications in almost every major organ system; e.g., pressure sores, contractures, bone loss, muscular atrophy, deconditioning.
   c. Metabolic changes can include negative nitrogen and calcium balance, impaired glucose tolerance, decreased plasma volume, altered drug pharmacokinetics.
   d. Psychological changes can include loss of positive self-image, depression.
   e. Behavioral changes can include confusion, dementia secondary to sensory deprivation, egocentricity.
   f. Loss of independence and dependency.
4. Examination.
   a. To identify the source of immobility or disability.
5. Goals, outcomes, and interventions.
   a. Establish a supportive relationship and promote self-determination of goals.
   b. Focus on optimal function, gradual progression of physical daily activities.
   c. Prevent further complications or injury.
   d. A team approach of health professionals to address all aspects of the patient's problems; patient participation in decision-making.

Falls and Instability

1. Falls and fall injury.
   a. Falls are a major public health concern for the elderly.
   b. Each year, approximately 30% of persons over the age of 65 fall.
   c. 24% of falls result in severe soft tissue injury and fractures.
      (1) Mortality rate associated with falls is 6%.
      (2) Falls are a factor in 40% of admissions to nursing homes.
   d. Fall results.
      (1) Increased caution and fear of falling.
      (2) Loss of confidence to function independently.
      (3) Reduced motivation and levels of activity.
      (4) Increased risk of recurrent falls.
2. Fall etiology.
   a. Most falls are multifactorial, the result of multiple intrinsic and extrinsic factors and their cumulative effects on mobility; e.g., disease states, age-related changes.
   b. Intrinsic/physiological factors.
      (1) Age: incidence of falls increases with age.
      (2) Sensory changes.
         (a) Reduced vision, hearing, cutaneous proprioceptive, and vestibular function.
         (b) Altered sensory organization for balance, reduced resolution of sensory conflict situations, increased dependence on support surface somatosensory inputs.
      (3) Musculoskeletal changes.
         (a) Weakness.
         (b) Decreased ROM.
         (c) Altered postural synergies.
      (4) Neuromotor changes.
         (a) Dizziness, vertigo common.
         (b) Timing and control problems: impaired reaction and movement times; slowed onset.
      (5) Cardiovascular changes.
         (a) Orthostatic hypotension.
         (b) Hyperventilation, coughing, arrhythmias.
      (6) Drugs.
         (a) Strong evidence linking psychotropic agents.
         (b) Some evidence linking certain cardiovascular agents, especially those that cause peripheral vasodilation.
         (c) Conflicting evidence linking analgesics, hypoglycemics.
   c. Intrinsic/psychosocial factors.
      (1) Mental status/cognitive impairment.
      (2) Depression.
      (3) Denial of physical limitations.
      (4) Fear of falling: associated with self-imposed activity restriction.
      (5) Relocation.
   d. Extrinsic/environmental factors.
      (1) Setting: three times as many falls for institutionalized or hospitalized elderly than for community-dwelling elderly.

(2) Consider ground surfaces, lighting, doors/doorways, stairs.
(3) At home, most falls occur in bedroom (42%); bathroom (34%).

e. Activity-related risk factors.
(1) Most falls occur during normal daily activity: getting up from bed/chair, turning head/body, bending, walking, climbing/descending stairs.
(2) Only a small percentage (5%) occur during clearly hazardous activities; e.g., climbing on ladder.
(3) Improper use of assistive device; e.g., walker, cane, wheelchair.

3. Fall prevention.
a. Examination.
(1) Accurate fall history: location, activity, time, symptoms, previous falls.
(2) Physical examination of patient: cognitive, sensory, neuromuscular, and cardiopulmonary.
(3) Standardized tests and measures for functional balance and instability; see Chapter 2.

b. Identify fall risk: determine all intrinsic and/or extrinsic factors.

c. Goals, outcomes, and interventions.
(1) Eliminate or minimize all fall risk factors; stabilize disease states, medications.
(2) Exercise to increase strength, flexibility.
(3) Sensory compensation strategies.
(4) Balance and gait training.
(5) Functional training.
(a) Focus on sit-to-stand transitions, turning, walking, and stairs.
(b) Modify activities of daily living for safety; provide assistive devices, adaptive equipment as appropriate.
(c) Allow adequate time for activities; instruct in gradual position changes.
(6) Safety education.
(a) Identify risks.
(b) Provide instructions in writing.
(c) Communicate with family and caregivers.
(7) Modify environment to reduce falls and instability: use environmental checklist.
(a) Ensure adequate lighting.
(b) Use contrasting colors to delineate hazardous areas, stairs.
(c) Simplify environment, reduce clutter.

d. When the patient falls.
(1) Check for fall injury.
(a) Hip fracture: complaints of pain in hip, especially on palpation; external rotation of leg; inability to bear weight on leg; changes in gait, weight-bearing.
(b) Head injury: loss of consciousness, mental confusion.
(c) Stroke, spinal cord injury: loss of sensation or voluntary movement.
(d) Cuts, bruises, painful swelling.
(2) Check for dizziness that may have preceded the fall.
(3) Provide reassurance.
(4) Do not attempt to lift patient by yourself; get help, provide first aid, and call emergency services if necessary.
(5) Solicit witnesses of fall event.

Medication Errors

1. Scope of the problem.
a. Most elderly (60%–85%) utilize prescription drugs to address a chronic medical problem.
b. One-third have three or more medical problems requiring multiple medications and complex dosage schedules.
c. Average older person takes between four and seven prescription drugs each day; takes an additional three over-the-counter drugs.
d. Adverse drug reactions.
(1) 4%–10% of hospital admissions in the elderly.
(a) Affects approximately 25% of all hospitalized patients over the age of 80.
(b) Adverse effects are potentially disabling or life-threatening.
(2) High incidence of falls/hip fractures; e.g., psychotropic agents.
(3) Motor vehicle accidents.

2. Older adults are at increased risk for drug toxicity.
a. Factors include age-related changes in pharmacokinetics.
(1) Alterations in drug absorption, distribution to tissues, oxidative metabolism.
(2) Alterations in excretion associated with a decline in hepatic and renal function: decreased clearance in certain drugs; e.g., digoxin, lithium.
(3) Altered sensitivity to the effects of drugs.
(a) Increased with certain drugs; e.g., narcotic analgesics, benzodiazepines.
(b) Decreased with certain drugs; e.g., drugs mediated by beta-adrenergic receptors, isoproterenol, propranolol.
(4) Drugs may interfere with brain function, cause confusion; e.g., psychoactive drugs: sedatives, hypnotics, antidepressants, anticonvulsants, antiparkinsonism agents.
(5) Older adults have less homeostatic reserve; e.g., are more susceptible to orthostatic hypotension with vasodilating drugs due to dampened compensatory baroreceptor response.

(6) Drug processing effects: multiple drugs compete for binding sites.
   (a) Drug-to-drug interactions; e.g., levodopa and monamine oxidase inhibitors (MAOIs) may result in hypertensive response.
   (b) Most drugs exert more than one specific action in the body (polypharmacological effects); e.g., prednisone prescribed for anti-inflammatory action may benefit arthritic symptoms but aggravate a coexisting diabetic state (augments blood glucose levels).

b. Physicians may prescribe inappropriate medications for elderly; estimated in 17.5% of Medicare prescriptions.
c. Most patients are not knowledgeable about drug actions, drug side effects.
d. Drug-food interactions can interfere with effectiveness of medications; e.g., efficacy of levodopa is compromised if ingested too close to a high-protein meal; potential vitamin/drug interactions.
e. Polypharmacy phenomena: multiple drug prescriptions.
   (1) Exacerbated by elderly who visit multiple physicians, use different pharmacies.
   (2) Lack integrated care; e.g., computerized system of drug monitoring.
f. Health status influences/socioeconomic factors.
   (1) Older adults have a high rate of medication dosage errors; associated with memory impairment, visual impairments, incoordination, and low literacy.
   (2) Older adults are targeted for aggressive marketing by drug companies: may result in self-administration of medications for uninvestigated symptoms.
   (3) Financial issues: due to high costs, fixed incomes, elderly may skip dosages, stop taking medications.
g. Common adverse effects.
   (1) Confusion/dementia; e.g., tranquilizers, barbiturates, digitalis, antihypertensives, anticholinergic drugs, analgesics, antiparkinsonians, diuretics, beta-blockers.
   (2) Sedation/immobility; e.g., psychotropic drugs, narcotic analgesics.
   (3) Weakness; e.g., antihypertensives, vasodilators, digitalis, diuretics, oral hypoglycemics.
   (4) Postural hypotension; e.g., antihypertensives, diuretics, tricyclic antidepressants, tranquilizers, nitrates, narcotic analgesics.
   (5) Depression; e.g., antihypertensives, anti-inflammatories, antimycobacterials, antiparkinsonians, diuretics, H_2 receptor antagonists, sedative-hypnotics, vasodilators.
   (6) Drug-induced movement disorders.
      (a) Dyskinesias (involuntary, stereotypic, and repetitive movements; i.e., lip smacking, hand movements, etc.) associated with long-term use of neuroleptic drugs and anticholinergic drugs, levodopa.
      (b) Akathisia (motor restlessness) associated with antipsychotic drugs.
      (c) Essential tremor associated with tricyclic antidepressants, adrenergic drugs.
      (d) Parkinsonism: associated with antipsychotics, sympatholytics.
   (7) Incontinence: caused or exacerbated by a variety of drugs; e.g., barbiturates, benzodiazepines, antipsychotic drugs, anticholinergic drugs.

3. Goals, outcomes, and interventions.
   a. Assist in adequate monitoring of drug therapy.
      (1) Recognize drug-related side effects, adverse reactions to drugs, potential drug interactions in the elderly.
      (2) Carefully document patient responses to medications, exercise, and activity.
   b. Assist in patient and family drug education/compliance; e.g., understanding of purpose of drugs, dosage, potential side effects.
   c. Encourage centralization of medications through one pharmacy.
   d. Assist in simplification of drug regimen and instructions.
      (1) Administration of drugs; e.g., daily pill box, drug calendar.
      (2) Check to see if patient is taking medications on schedule.
      (3) Time doses in conjunction with daily routine.
   e. Coordinate physical therapy with drug schedule/optimal dose; e.g., exercise during peak dose with individual on Parkinson's disease medications (levodopa).
   f. Recognize potentially harmful interaction effects: modalities that cause vasodilatation in combination with vasodilating drugs.

Nutritional Deficiency

1. Many older adults have primary nutritional problems.
   a. Nutritional problems in elderly are linked to health status and poverty rather than to age itself.
      (1) Chronic diseases alter the overall need for nutrients/energy demands, the ability to take in and utilize nutrients, and overall activity levels; e.g., AD, CVA, diabetes.
      (2) Limited, fixed incomes severely limit food choices and availability.

b. Both undernourishment and obesity exist in the elderly and contribute to decreased levels of vitality and fitness.
c. Contributing factors to poor dietary intake.
   (1) Decreased sense of taste and smell.
   (2) Poor teeth or poorly fitting dentures.
   (3) Reduced gastrointestinal function.
      (a) Decreased saliva.
      (b) Gastromucosal atrophy.
      (c) Reduced intestinal mobility; reflux.
   (4) Loss of interest in foods.
   (5) Lack of social support, socialization during meals.
   (6) Lack of mobility.
      (a) Inability to get to grocery store, shop.
      (b) Inability to prepare foods.
d. There is an age-related slowing in basal metabolic rate and a decline in total caloric intake; most of the decline is associated with a concurrent reduction in physical activity.
e. Dehydration is common in the elderly, resulting in fluid and electrolyte disturbances.
   (1) Thirst sensation is diminished.
   (2) May be physically unable to acquire/maintain fluids.
   (3) Environmental heat stresses may be life-threatening.
f. Diets are often deficient in nutrients, especially vitamins A, C, B_{12}, thiamine, protein, iron, calcium/vitamin D, folic acid, and zinc.
g. Increased use of taste enhancers; e.g., salt and sugar, or alcohol influences nutritional intake.
h. Drug/dietary interactions influence nutritional intake; e.g., reserpine, digoxin, antitumor agents, excessive use of antacids.

2. Examination.
   a. Dietary history: patterns of eating, types of foods.
   b. Psychosocial: mental status, desire to eat/depression, social isolation.
   c. Body composition.
      (1) Weight/height measures.
      (2) Skin fold measurements: triceps/subscapular skin fold thickness.
      (3) Upper arm circumference.
   d. Sensory function: taste and smell.
   e. Dental and periodontal disease; fit and use of dentures.
   f. Ability to feed self: mastication, swallowing, hand/mouth control, posture, physical weakness and fatigue.
   g. Integumentary: skin condition, edema.
   h. Compliance to special diets.
   i. Functional assessment: basic activities of daily living, feeding; overall exercise/activity levels.
3. Goals, outcomes, and interventions.
   a. Assist in monitoring adequate nutritional intake.
   b. Assist in health promotion.
      (1) Maintain adequate nutritional support.
         (a) Nutritional consults as necessary.
         (b) Nutritional educational programs.
         (c) Assistance in grocery shopping, meal preparation; e.g., recommendations for home health aides.
         (d) Elderly food programs: home-delivered/Meals on Wheels; congregate meals/senior center daily meal programs; federal food stamp programs.
      (2) Maintain physical function, adequate activity levels.

Review Questions

Geriatric Physical Therapy

1. What are the physiological changes that may occur in the visual system in older adults?

2. What risk factors are associated with development of osteoporosis?

3. What are the major side effects (red flags) of the use of pain medications in the geriatric population that can be a concern for physical therapists?

4. What are the most important components of the initial examination of a patient with dementia?

5. What are the major goals and interventions to minimize fall risk factors?

9 Therapeutic Exercise

THOMAS BIANCO and SUSAN B. O'SULLIVAN

Chapter Outline

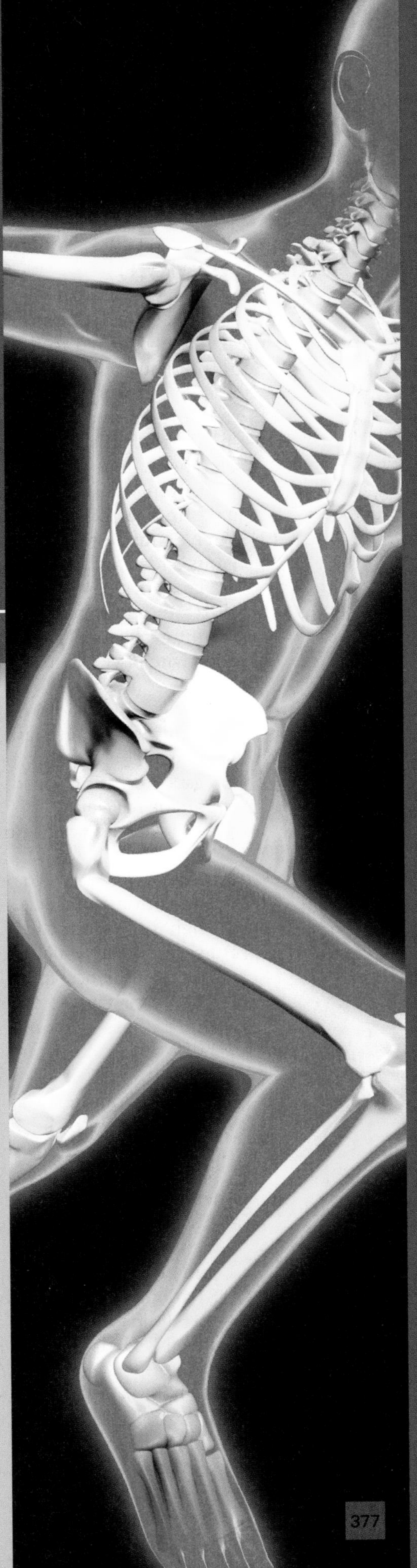

Strength Training

Concepts of Muscle Function and Strength

a. Strength is the force output of a contracting muscle and is directly related to the amount of tension a contracting muscle can produce.
b. Contractile elements of muscle.
  (1) Muscles are composed of fibers, which are made up of myofibrils. Myofibrils are composed of sarcomeres that are connected in series. The overlapping cross bridges of actin and myosin make up a sarcomere.
  (2) When a muscle contracts, the actin-myosin filaments slide together and the muscle shortens. The cross bridges slide apart when the muscle relaxes and returns to its resting length.
c. Motor unit nerve supply to the muscle.
  (1) Slow-twitch (ST) fibers (type I).
    (a) Slow contraction speed.
    (b) Low force (tension) production.
    (c) Highly resistant to fatigue.
  (2) Fast-twitch (FT) fibers (type IIa).
    (a) Fast contraction speed.
    (b) Fatigue resistant.
    (c) Characteristics can be influenced by the type of training.
  (3) Fast-twitch (FT) fibers (type IIb).
    (a) Fast contraction speed.
    (b) High force production.
    (c) Susceptible to quick fatigue.
  (4) Hereditary influences and fiber type distribution.
    (a) The percentage of either FT or ST fibers in the body is determined by genetics. This ratio cannot be changed via normal exercise.
    (b) Specific training can modify metabolic characteristics of all fiber types; e.g., high-intensity, anaerobic strength training will stimulate optimal FT adaptation.
  (5) Order of fiber type recruitment.
    (a) Recruitment order depends upon type of activity, force required, movement pattern, and position of the body.
    (b) ST motor units have the lowest functional thresholds and are recruited during lighter, slower efforts such as low-intensity, long-duration endurance activities.
    (c) Higher forces with greater velocity cause the activation of more powerful, higher threshold FT motor units.
    (d) Order of recruitment is ST, followed by FT IIa, and finally followed by FT IIb motor units.
d. Length tension.
  (1) As the muscle shortens or lengthens through the available range of motion (ROM), the tension it produces varies. Maximum tension is generated at some midpoint in the ROM; less tension is developed in either shortened or lengthened ROM.
  (2) The weight lifted or lowered cannot exceed that which the muscle is able to control at its weakest point in the ROM.
  (3) When a muscle is stretched beyond the resting length, there is a mechanical disruption of the cross bridges as the microfilaments slide apart and the sarcomeres lengthen. Releasing the stretch allows the sarcomeres to return to their resting length. This change in ratio of length to tension is called elasticity.
  (4) Once released, a muscle stretched into the elastic range will contract and produce a force or tension as the muscle returns to its original length.

Adaptations to Strength Training

a. Muscle.
  (1) Hypertrophy is an increase in muscle size as a result of resistance training and can be observed after at least 6–8 weeks of training.
  (2) Remodelling: individual muscle fibers are enlarged, contain more actin and myosin and have more, larger myofibrils; sarcomeres are increased.
  (3) An increase in motor unit recruitment and synchronization of firing facilitates contraction and maximizes force production.
  (4) The average person has a ratio of 50% fast- to slow-twitch motor units. Performing workloads of low intensity will challenge half of the body's muscle mass. High-intensity exercises for shorter durations (less than 20 repetitions) are needed to train the highly adaptable fast-twitch IIa fibers.
  (5) Disuse atrophy occurs when a muscle loses both size and strength from lack of use or when a limb is immobilized.
  (6) Cross-section area of a muscle highly correlates with strength gains. The larger the muscle, the greater the strength of that muscle.

b. Positive changes in impairments. Improvement in:
  (1) Strength.
  (2) Bone mass.
  (3) Body composition: fat to lean body composition.
  (4) Weight control and weight maintenance; decreased risk of adult-onset diabetes.
  (5) Reaction time.
  (6) Metabolism, calorie burning during and after exercise.
  (7) Cardiovascular status: reduction in resting blood pressure.
  (8) Immunological function.

c. Positive changes in function and quality of life.
  (1) Improved balance and coordination.
  (2) Improved gait and functional mobility.
  (3) Improved activities of daily living.
  (4) Improved job/recreational/athletic performance.
  (5) Improved sense of well-being, posture, and self-image.

Guidelines to Develop Strength

a. Overload principle: to increase strength, the muscle must be loaded or challenged beyond its current force capability. Higher levels of tension will cause hypertrophy and recruitment of muscle fibers. This level will change with each adaptation.

b. Specificity of training: adaptations in the metabolic and physiological systems of the body depending on the type of overload imposed. Specific modes of exercise elicit specific adaptations, creating specific training effects.

c. Reversibility: benefits of training are not sustained unless muscles are continuously challenged. Detraining effects include decreased muscle recruitment and muscle fiber atrophy.

d. Metabolic effects of strength training.
  (1) Muscle contraction to about 60% of its force-generating capacity causes a blockage of blood flow to the working muscle due to increased intramuscular pressure. The energy source for this level of muscle contraction is mainly anaerobic and does not improve with aerobic conditioning.
  (2) Strength training of specific muscles has a brief activation period and uses a relatively small muscle mass, producing less cardiovascular metabolic demands than vigorous exercise; e.g., walking, running, swimming.
  (3) Rhythmic activities increase blood flow to exercising muscles via a contraction and relaxation "milking action." The primary energy source is aerobic.
  (4) Circuit training (cross-training) with high repetitions and low weights incorporates all modes of training and provides more general conditioning to improve body composition, muscular strength, and some cardiovascular fitness.

e. Common errors associated with resistance or strength training.
  (1) Valsalva's maneuver: forcible exhalation with the glottis, nose, and mouth closed while contraction is being held. Valsalva's maneuver increases intrathoracic pressure, slows heart rate (HR), decreases return of blood to the heart, and increases venous pressure and cardiac work.
  (2) Inadequate rest after vigorous exercise. Three to four minutes are needed to return the muscle to 90%–95% of preexercise capacity. Most rapid recovery occurs in the first minute.
  (3) Increasing exercise progression too quickly (intensity, duration, frequency) can overwork muscles and cause injuries.
  (4) Substitute motions occur from too much resistance, incorrect stabilization, and when muscles are weak from fatigue, paralysis, or pain.

Exercises to Improve Strength and Range

a. Manual resistance: a type of active exercise in which another person provides resistance.
  (1) Advantages.
    (a) Useful in the early stages of an exercise program when the muscle is weak. The therapist can judge the capability of muscle to safely meet demands of exercise.
    (b) Can be modified for a painful arc in the joint range of motion.
    (c) Safe resistance exercise when the joint movement needs to be carefully controlled and the resistance is mild to moderate.
    (d) Can be easily changed to include diagonal or functional patterns of movement (e.g., proprioceptive neuromuscular facilitation [PNF]) or appropriate facilitation techniques (e.g., quick stretch).
  (2) Disadvantages.
    (a) The amount of resistance cannot be measured quantitatively.
    (b) It may be difficult to maintain the same resistance during the full joint ROM and to consistently repeat the same resistance.
    (c) The amount of resistance is limited by the strength of the therapist or caregiver.

b. Mechanical resistance: a type of active exercise in which resistance is applied through the use of equipment or mechanical apparatus.

(1) Advantages.
(a) The amount of resistance can be measured quantitatively and increased over time.
(b) Can be used when amounts of resistance are greater than the therapist can apply manually.
(2) Disadvantages.
(a) Not easily modified to exercise in diagonal or functional patterns.
(b) May not be safe if resistance needs to be carefully controlled or maintained at low levels.

c. Goals and indications for resistance exercise.
(1) Increase strength in a muscle group that lifts, lowers, or controls heavy loads for relatively low number of repetitions.
(2) Increase muscular endurance by performing low-intensity repetitive exercise over a prolonged period.
(3) Improve muscular performance related to strength and speed of movement.

d. Precautions.
(1) Local muscle fatigue is a normal response of the muscle from repeated dynamic or static contractions over a period of time. Fatigue is due to depleted energy stores, insufficient oxygen, and build-up of lactic acid. It is characterized by a decline in peak torque and increased muscle pain with occasional spasm and decreased active ROM (AROM).
(2) General muscular fatigue affects the whole body after prolonged activities such as walking or jogging; usually due to low blood sugar, decreased glycogen stores in muscle and liver, depletion of potassium.
(3) General or specific muscle fatigue may be associated with specific clinical diseases; e.g., multiple sclerosis, cardiac disease, peripheral vascular dysfunction, and pulmonary diseases. These patients fatigue more rapidly and require longer rest periods.
(4) Overwork or overtraining causes temporary or permanent loss of strength as a result of exercise. In normal individuals, fatigue causes discomfort, so overtraining and muscle weakness does not usually occur. Patients with lower motor neuron disease who participate in vigorous resistance exercise programs can have a deterioration of strength; e.g., postpolio syndrome, Duchenne muscular dystrophy. Overwork can be avoided with slow progression of the exercise intensity, duration, and progression.
(5) Osteoporosis makes the bone unable to withstand normal stresses and highly susceptible to pathological fracture. May develop as a result of prolonged immobilization, bed rest, inability to bear weight on an extremity, and nutritional or hormonal factors.
(6) Acute muscle soreness develops during or directly after strenuous anaerobic exercise performed to the point of fatigue. Decreased blood flow and reduced oxygen (ischemia) creates a temporary build-up of lactic acid and potassium. A cool-down period of low-intensity exercise can facilitate the return of oxygen to the muscle and reduce soreness.
(7) Delayed-onset muscle soreness (DOMS) can begin 12–24 hours after vigorous exercise or muscular overexertion. Peaks at 24–48 hours after exercise. Muscle tenderness and stiffness can last up to 5–7 days. Usually greater after muscle lengthening or eccentric exercise. Severity of soreness can be lessened by gradually increasing the intensity and duration of exercises.

e. Contraindications.
(1) Inflammation: resistance exercises can increase swelling and cause damage to muscles or joints.
(2) Pain: severe joint or muscle pain during exercise or for more than 24 hours after exercise requires elimination or reduction of the exercise.

f. Types of resistance exercise.
(1) Isometric exercise is static and occurs when a muscle contracts without a length change. Resistance is variable and accommodating. Contractions should be held for at least 6 seconds to obtain adaptive changes in the muscle.
(a) Strengthening of muscles is developed at a point in the ROM, not over the entire length of the muscle.
(b) This type of resistance exercise can increase blood pressure and should be used cautiously with the patient with a cardiac condition.
(c) Monitor for potential Valsalva's maneuver.
(2) Isotonic exercise is dynamic and can have a constant (free weights) or variable (machine) load as the muscle lengthens or shortens through the available ROM. Speed can be variable for this type of exercise.
(a) Weight-lifting machines have an oval-shaped cam or wheel that mimics the length-tension curve of the muscle; e.g., Nautilus or Cybex. These machines vary resistance as the muscle goes through the ROM, providing resistance that the muscle can safely complete at various points of the ROM.
(b) Free weights do not vary the resistance through the ROM of a muscle. The weakest point along the length-tension curve of each muscle limits the amount of weight lifted.

(c) Weight-lifting machines are safer than free weights; used early in a resistance exercise or rehabilitation program.

(3) Isokinetic exercise is dynamic and has a speed control for muscle shortening and lengthening. Resistance is accommodating and variable.

(a) Peak torque, the maximum force generated through the ROM, is inversely related to angular velocity (speed) as the body segment moves through ROM; e.g., increasing angular velocity decreases peak torque production.

(b) Concentric or eccentric resistance exercise can be performed on isokinetic equipment.

(c) Isokinetic exercise provides maximum resistance at all points in the ROM as the muscle contracts.

(d) During isokinetic testing, the weight of a body segment creates a torque output around the joint; e.g., the lower leg around the knee joint in sitting knee flexion. This gravity-produced torque adds to the force generated by the muscle when it contracts and gives a higher torque output than is actually created by the muscle. The higher value can affect the testing values of the muscle group and which muscle group needs to be strengthened. Software can correct for the effects of gravity.

(4) Eccentric (lengthening) versus concentric (shortening).

(a) Maximum eccentric contraction produces more force than maximal concentric contraction.

(b) Resistance training performed concentrically improves concentric muscle strength and eccentric training improves eccentric muscle strength (specificity of training).

(c) Eccentric contractions occur in a wide variety of functional activities, such as lowering the body against gravity; e.g., sitting down or descending stairs.

(d) Eccentric contractions provide a source of shock absorption during closed-chain functional activities.

(e) Eccentric contractions consume less oxygen and fewer energy stores than concentric contractions against similar loads.

g. Range of motion.

(1) Short-arc exercise: resistance exercise performed through a limited ROM; e.g., initial exercise post–knee surgery (anterior cruciate repair), painful full-range movement.

(2) Full-arc exercise: resistance exercise performed through full ROM.

h. Open-chain versus closed-chain exercises.

(1) Open-chain exercise occurs when the distal segment (hand or foot) moves freely in space; e.g., when an arm lifts or lowers a hand-held weight.

(2) Resistance exercises usually are open chain, which may be the only option if weight bearing is contraindicated.

(3) Open-chain exercise does not adequately prepare a patient for functional weight-bearing activities.

(4) Closed-chain exercise occurs when the body moves over a fixed distal segment; e.g., stair climbing or squatting activities.

(5) Closed-chain exercise loads muscles, bones, joints, and noncontractile soft tissues such as ligaments, tendons, and joint capsules.

(6) Mechanoreceptors are stimulated by closed-chain exercises, adding to joint stability, balance, coordination, and agility in functional weight-bearing postures.

Specific Exercise Regimens

a. Progressive resistive exercise (PRE): uses the repetition maximum (RM), or the greatest amount of weight a muscle can move through the ROM a specific number of times (e.g., DeLorme used 10 RM as baseline). Three sets of 10 repetitions are completed with brief rests (1–2 minutes) between sets. Progression (DeLorme): exercise begins with 10 repetitions at 50% RM, followed by 10 repetitions at 75% RM, and finally 10 repetitions at 100% RM (see Table 9-1).

Table 9-1

Resistance Training Specificity Chart

RELATIVE LOADING	OUTCOME	% 1 RM	REPETITION RANGE	# OF SETS	REST BETWEEN SETS
Light	Muscular Endurance	< 70	12–20	1–3	20–30 seconds
Moderate	Hypertrophy and Strength	70–80	8–12	1–6	30–120 seconds
Heavy	Maximum Strength	80–100	1–8	1–5+	2–5 minutes

b. Circuit weight training: a sequence of exercises for total-body conditioning. A rest period of usually 30 seconds to 1 minute is taken between each exercise. Exercises can be done with free weights or weight-training machines.

c. Plyometric training, or stretch-shortening activity: an isotonic exercise that combines speed, strength, and functional activities. Used in later stages of rehabilitation to achieve high level of performance; e.g., jumping off of a platform, then up onto the platform at a rapid pace to improve vertical jumping abilities.

d. Brief, repetitive isometric exercise: occurs with up to 20 maximum contractions held for 5–6 seconds and performed daily. A 20-second rest after each contraction is recommended to prevent increases in blood pressure. Strength gains occur in 6 weeks.

Endurance Training

Training Strategies to Develop Muscular Endurance

a. Muscular endurance: the ability of an isolated muscle group to perform repeated contractions over time.

b. Muscular endurance is improved by performing low-load resistance exercise for many repetitions. Exercise programs that increase strength also increase muscular endurance.

c. Muscular endurance programs are indicated after injuries to joints and soft tissues. Dynamic exercises at a high number of repetitions against light resistance are more comfortable and create less joint irritation than heavy resistance exercises.

d. Early in a strength-training program, high repetitions and low-load exercises cause less muscle soreness and reduce the risk of muscle injury.

Training Strategies to Develop Cardiovascular Endurance

a. Cardiovascular endurance: the ability to perform large-muscle, dynamic exercise, such as walking, swimming, and/or biking, for long periods of time.

b. Overload principle: used to enhance physiological improvement and bring about a training change. Specific exercise overload must be applied.
   (1) Training adaptation occurs by exercising at a level above normal.
   (2) The appropriate overload for each person can be achieved by manipulating combinations of training frequency, intensity, and duration.

c. Specificity principle: adaptations in the metabolic and physiological systems, depending on the type of overload imposed.
   (1) Specific exercise elicits specific adaptations, creating specific training effects; e.g., swim training will increase cardiovascular conditioning only when tested in swimming. There is no crossover for conditioning from swimming to running.

d. Individual differences principle: training benefits are optimized when programs are planned to meet the individual needs and capacities of the participants.

e. Reversibility principle: detraining occurs rapidly, after only 2 weeks, when a person stops exercising. Beneficial effects of exercise training are transient and reversible.

f. Exercise and progressive activity regimens require monitoring of heart rate, blood pressure, and other signs and symptoms of exertional intolerance (see Chapter 3).

g. FITT equation: includes factors that affect training; frequency, intensity, time, and type. Intensity is interrelated with both duration (time) and frequency.
   (1) Frequency is the number of exercise sessions per week. If training at a lower intensity, then more frequent exercise is indicated.
      (a) If the intensity is constant, the benefit from two versus four or three versus five times per week is the same.
      (b) For weight loss, 5–7 days per week increases the caloric expenditure more than 2 days per week.
      (c) Less than 2 days per week does not produce adequate changes in aerobic capacity or body composition.
   (2) Intensity (overload) is the primary way to improve cardiovascular endurance.
      (a) Relative intensity for an individual is calculated as a percentage of the maximum function; e.g. maximum oxygen consumption (VO_2 max) or maximum heart rate (HR_{max}).
      (b) The VO_2 max or HR_{max} can be measured directly or indirectly based on different methods; e.g., 3-minute step, 12-minute run, or 1-mile walk test.
      (c) HR_{max} can be estimated using 220 minus the age of individual. Training level or target

heart rate (THR) can be established at 70% of maximum to increase aerobic capacity.

(d) Karvonen's formula is used to predict heart rate reserve (HRR) or HR_{max} minus the resting heart rate (RHR) and correlates directly to VO_2 max. THR = (HR_{max} – RHR) × % of desired training intensity + RHR.

(e) Rating of perceived exertion (RPE) can be used to evaluate training at submaximal levels. A cardiorespiratory training effect can be achieved at a rating of "somewhat hard" or "hard" (13–16 on the original Borg scale of 6–19). An appropriate level of training should result in conversational exercise or "talk test"; moderate exercise that is not too strenuous and can improve endurance.

(3) Duration (time).

(a) Duration is increased when intensity is limited; e.g., by initial fitness level. Improvements in aerobic capacity, therefore, depend on increasing exercise duration and frequency; e.g., 3–5 minutes per day produces training effects in poorly conditioned individuals, whereas 20–30 minutes, three to five times per week is optimal for conditioned people.

(b) Multiple sessions of short durations are also indicated when intensity is limited by environmental conditions, such as heat and humidity or by medical conditions, such as intermittent claudication or congestive heart failure.

(c) Obese individuals should exercise at longer durations and lower intensities. At this exercise level, the person can speak without gasping and does not have muscle ache or burn from lactic acid accumulation.

(d) Obesity increases the mechanical work of the heart and can lead to cardiac and left ventricular dysfunction.

(4) Type of exercise needed to increase cardiovascular endurance should involve large muscle groups activated in rhythmic aerobic nature. Specificity of training should be considered.

(5) See Chapter 3.

Training Strategies to Develop Pulmonary Endurance

a. Pulmonary endurance is related to the ventilation of the lungs and oxygen consumption.

b. Ventilation is the process of air exchange in the lungs. The volume of air breathed each minute, or minute ventilation ($\dot{V}_E$), is 6 liters. $\dot{V}_E$ = breathing rate × tidal volume. In maximum exercise, increases in breathing rate and depth may produce ventilation as high as 200 liters per minute.

c. Energy is produced aerobically as oxygen is supplied to exercising muscles. Oxygen consumption rises rapidly during the first minutes of exercise, and then levels off as the aerobic metabolism supplies the energy required by the working muscles (steady state).

d. The more fit a person is, the more capable their respiratory system is of delivering oxygen to sustain aerobic energy production at increasingly higher levels of intensity.

(1) Obesity can impair pulmonary function because of the added effort to move the chest wall.

e. In severe pulmonary disease, the cost of breathing can reach 40% of the total exercise oxygen consumption. This decreases the oxygen available to the exercising nonrespiratory muscles and limits exercise capabilities. Obesity can significantly increase the level of impairments.

f. Exercise-induced asthma (EIA) can occur when the normal initial bronchodilation is followed by bronchoconstriction. The reduction in air-flow from airway obstruction affects the ability of the lungs to provide oxygen to exercising muscles.

(1) EIA is an acute, reversible airway obstruction that develops 5–15 minutes after strenuous exercise when a person does not breathe through the nose, which warms and humidifies the air.

(2) When a person mouth-breathes, the air is cold and dry, contributing to the bronchoconstriction.

(3) Lowering the intensity level and allowing the person to breathe through the nose can allow prolonged aerobic exercise to continue.

(4) The problem is rare in activities that require only short bursts of activity such as baseball, and is more likely to occur in endurance activities such as soccer.

(5) When exercising in humid versus dry environments, the exercise-induced asthmatic response is considerably reduced. See Chapter 4.

Aerobic Training

a. Aerobic training (cardiorespiratory endurance training) can result in higher fitness levels for healthy individuals, slow the decrease in functional capacity in the elderly, and recondition those with illness or chronic disease.

b. Positive effects of aerobic training on the cardiovascular and respiratory systems.
   (1) Improve breathing volumes and increase VO_2 max.
   (2) Increase heart weight and volume; cardiac hypertrophy is normal with long-term aerobic training.
   (3) Increase total hemoglobin and oxygen delivery capacity.
   (4) Decrease resting and submaximal exercise heart rates. Can be utilized to measure improvements from aerobic training.
   (5) Increase cardiac output and stroke volume.
   (6) Improve distribution of blood to working muscles and enhance capacity of trained muscles to extract and use oxygen.
   (7) Reduce resting blood pressure.

c. Continuous training at a submaximal energy requirement can be prolonged for 20–60 minutes without exhausting the oxygen transport system.
   (1) Work rate is increased progressively as training improvements are achieved; overload can be accomplished by increasing the exercise duration.
   (2) In healthy individuals, continuous training is the most effective way to improve endurance.

d. Circuit training uses a series of exercise activities that are repeated several times.
   (1) Several exercise modes can be utilized, involving large and small muscle groups both statically and dynamically.
   (2) Circuit training improves endurance and strength by stressing the aerobic and anaerobic energy systems.

e. Interval training includes an exercise period followed by a prescribed rest interval. It is perceived to be less demanding than continuous training, and tends to improve strength and power more than endurance.
   (1) The relief interval can be passive or active; its duration ranges from a few seconds to several minutes. Active or work recovery involves doing the exercise at a reduced level. During the relief period, a portion of the adenosine triphosphate (ATP) and oxygen used by the muscles during the work period is replenished by the aerobic system.
   (2) The longer the work interval, the more the aerobic system is stressed.
   (3) With appropriate spacing of work-relief intervals, a significant amount of high-intensity work can be achieved. The total amount of work completed with interval training is greater than the amount of work accomplished with continuous training.

f. Warm-up and cool-down periods: each exercise session includes a 5- to 15-minute warm-up and a 5- to 15-minute cool-down period.
   (1) The warm-up period prevents the heart and circulatory system from being suddenly taxed. It includes low-intensity cardiorespiratory activities and flexibility exercises.
   (2) The cool-down period also consists of exercising at a lower intensity. It reduces abrupt physiological alterations that can occur with sudden cessation of strenuous exercise; e.g., venous pooling in the lower extremities, which causes decreased venous return to the heart.
   (3) Longer warm-up and cool-down periods may be needed for deconditioned or older individuals.

Common Errors Associated with Muscular, Cardiovascular, and Pulmonary Endurance Training

a. Lack of exercise tolerance testing (ETT) before the exercise prescription is determined could result in a training program set too high or too low for that individual.
b. Starting out at too high a level can overly stress the cardiorespiratory and muscular systems and potentially cause injuries.
c. Increasing intensity too fast can create a problem for an individual during endurance training.
d. Exercising at too intense a level can use the anaerobic energy system, not the aerobic system; this increases strength and power, not endurance.
e. Insufficient warm-up or cool-down results in inadequate cardiorespiratory and muscular adaptation; there is inadequate time to prepare for or recover from higher intense activity.
f. Inconsistent training frequency, duration, or intensity does not properly stress or overload the aerobic system to create training effects.

Exercise at High Altitude

a. At altitudes of 6000 feet (1829 meters [m]) or higher there can be a noticeable drop in performance of aerobic activities.
b. The partial pressure of oxygen is reduced, resulting in poor oxygenation of hemoglobin.
c. This hypoxia at altitude can result in immediate compensatory hyperventilation (stimulation of the baroreceptors) and increased heart rate.
d. Reduction in CO_2 from hyperventilation results in more alkaline body fluids.

e. Adjustments or acclimatization to higher altitude.
   (1) Takes 2 weeks at 2300 m and an additional week for every additional 600 m in altitude.
   (2) There is a decrease in plasma volume (concentrating red blood cells) and an increase in total red blood cells and hemoglobin improving oxygenation.
   (3) Changes in local circulation may facilitate oxygen transport.
   (4) Adjustments do not fully compensate for altitude. VO_2 max is decreased 2% for every 300 m above 1500 m. Thus, there is a drop in performance for endurance activities.
   (5) Training at altitude does not provide any improvement in sea-level performance.

f. The air in mountainous regions tends to be cool and dry. Body fluids can be rapidly lost through evaporation and result in dehydration.
   (1) Ensure adequate hydration for those exercising or engaged in sports at altitude.

Exercise in Hot Weather

a. When exercising in the heat, muscles require oxygen to produce energy.

b. To decrease metabolic heat, blood is shunted to the periphery; thus, working muscles are deprived of needed oxygen.

c. Core temperature increases and sweating increases. Fluids must be continually replaced or core temperatures can rise to dangerous levels.

d. Hot, humid environments diminish the evaporative cooling component, even with profuse sweating. Excess fluid loss can compromise cardiovascular function.

e. Fluid replacement.
   (1) Maintain plasma volume.
   (2) Colder fluids are emptied from the stomach more rapidly than room-temperature fluids.
   (3) Concentrated carbohydrate drinks impair gastric emptying and slow fluid replacement.
   (4) Glucose-polymer drinks do not impair physiological functioning. They may also resupply lost electrolytes.

f. Repeated heat stress results in acclimatization in about 10 days of exposure.
   (1) Exercise capacity is increased.
   (2) Cardiac output is better regulated.
   (3) Sweating is more efficient.
   (4) Acclimatization to heat stress does not seriously deteriorate with age.

g. Men and women can adapt equally well to heat, even though the mechanisms of thermoregulation differ slightly. The menstrual cycle is not a factor.

h. Obesity is a major consideration when exercising in the heat.

i. Exercise recommendations for individuals with obesity. See Chapter 6.

Mobility and Flexibility Training

Flexibility

a. Flexibility refers to the ability to move a joint through an unrestricted, pain-free ROM; the musculotendinous unit elongates as the body segment moves through the ROM.

b. Dynamic flexibility refers to the active ROM of a joint and is dependent upon the amount of tissue resistance met during active movement.

c. Passive flexibility is the degree to which a joint can be passively moved through the available ROM and is dependent upon the extensibility of the muscle and connective tissue around the joint.

Stretching

a. Stretching involves any therapeutic technique that lengthens shortened soft-tissue structures and increases ROM.

b. Type of stretching is determined by the type of force applied, the intensity of stretch, and duration of stretch to contractile and noncontractile tissues.
   (1) Manual, passive stretching takes the structures beyond the free ROM to elongate tissues beyond their resting length.
      (a) The stretch force is applied for at least 15–30 seconds and repeated several times during a session.
      (b) Manual stretching is considered a short-duration stretch and is maintained statically for less time than mechanical stretching.
      (c) Intensity and duration depend on patient tolerance and therapist strength and endurance.
      (d) Low-intensity manual stretch, applied as long as possible, is better tolerated and results in optimal improvement in tissue length with minimal risk of injury to any weakened tissue.

(2) Ballistic stretching is a high-intensity, very short-duration "bouncing" stretch. By contracting the opposite muscle group, the patient uses body weight and momentum to elongate the tight muscle.
 (a) It is considered unsafe because of poor control and the potential of rupturing weakened tissues. It should not be performed after an injury or surgery.
 (b) Ballistic stretch facilitates the stretch reflex, causing an increase in tension in the muscle that is being stretched. It is contraindicated in spastic muscles.

(3) Prolonged low-intensity mechanical stretching.
 (a) An external force (5–15 lb to 10% of body weight) is applied by positioning a patient with weighted pulley and traction systems; e.g., to reduce knee flexion contractures in the patient who is bedridden. May be maintained for 20–30 minutes or as long as several hours.
 (b) A dynamic splint maintains the limb positioned at end range and is typically applied for 8–10 hours to increase ROM; e.g., to reduce wrist and finger flexion contractures.
 (c) A serial cast maintains the limb positioned at end range. Cast is typically applied for 5–7 days. Cast is then removed and a new cast reapplied with the limb positioned in the newly gained range; e.g., to reduce gastrocnemius/soleus contractures.
 (d) Low-intensity, prolonged stretching has been shown to be more effective than manual, passive stretching with long-standing flexion contractures.

(4) Active stretching occurs when voluntary, unassisted movement by the patient provides the stretch force to a joint. It requires strength and muscular contraction of the prime mover to actively stretch the antagonist muscle group.
 (a) The force is controlled by the patient and is considered low-intensity (to tolerance). The risk of tissue injury is low.
 (b) Duration is equal to passive, manual stretching or about 15–30 seconds and is limited by prime mover muscular endurance.

(5) Facilitated stretching (active inhibition) refers to techniques in which the patient reflexively relaxes the muscle to be elongated prior to or during the stretching technique; e.g., PNF (see Table 9-2).
 (a) Indications for active inhibition techniques include limitations in ROM caused by muscle tightness or muscle spasm; techniques are not effective with connective tissue changes.
 (b) Hold-relax (HR) is indicated for the patient with limited movement and pain.

c. Contractile tissue.
 (1) A muscle that is lengthened over a prolonged period will have an increase in the number of sarcomeres in series. The muscle will adjust its length over time.
 (2) A muscle immobilized in a shortened position will have a decrease in the number of sarcomeres and an increase in connective tissue.
 (3) The sarcomere adaptation is transient. A muscle allowed to resume its normal length will produce or absorb sarcomeres (lengthen or shorten).

d. Neurophysiological properties of contractile tissue.
 (1) The muscle spindle monitors the velocity and length changes in muscle.

Table 9-2

Facilitated Stretching Techniques

TECHNIQUE	DESCRIPTION	RATIONALE
Hold-relax (HR)	A relaxation technique usually performed at the point of limited ROM in the agonist pattern; an isometric contraction of the range-limiting antagonist is performed against slowly increasing resistance, followed by voluntary relaxation and passive movement by the therapist into the newly gained range of the agonist pattern.	The muscle relaxes as a result of autogenic inhibition, possibly from the Golgi tendon organ (GTO) firing and decreasing muscular tension.
Hold-relax-active contraction (HRAC)	Following hold-relax technique, active contraction into the newly gained range of the agonist pattern is performed.	Additional muscle relaxation is achieved through active contraction and reciprocal inhibition effects (a spindle response).
Contract-relax-active contraction (CRAC)	A relaxation technique usually performed at a point of limited ROM in the agonist pattern; isotonic movement in rotation is performed followed by an isometric hold of the range-limiting muscles in the antagonist pattern against slowly increasing resistance, voluntary relaxation and active movement into the new range of the agonist pattern.	Utilizes effects of both autogenic inhibition and reciprocal inhibition.

(2) A quick stretch to a muscle stimulates the alpha motoneurons and facilitates muscle contraction via the monosynaptic stretch reflex. This can increase tension in a contracting muscle and provide reciprocal inhibition to the tight muscle.
(3) The GTO inhibits contraction of the muscle. When excessive tension develops, the GTO fires, inhibiting alpha motoneuron activity and decreasing tension in the muscle.
(4) Slow stretching, especially applied at end range, causes the GTO to fire and inhibit the muscle (autogenic inhibition), allowing the muscle to lengthen (stretch-protection reflex).

e. Noncontractile connective tissue, including ligaments, tendons, joint capsules, fasciae, and skin, can affect joint flexibility and requires remodelling to increase length.
(1) Low-magnitude loads over long periods increase the deformation of noncontractile tissue, allowing a gradual rearrangement of collagen bonds (remodelling). This type of stretch is better tolerated by the patient.
(2) 15–20 minutes of low-intensity sustained stretch, repeated on 5 consecutive days, can cause a change in the length of muscles and connective tissue.
(3) Intensive stretching is usually not done every day in order to allow time for healing. Without healing time, a breakdown of tissue will occur, as in overuse syndromes and stress fractures.
(4) With aging, collagen loses its elasticity and tissue blood supply is decreased, reducing healing capability. Stretching in older adults should be performed cautiously.

f. Overstretch is a stretch well beyond the normal joint ROM, resulting in hypermobility. If the supporting structures of a joint are insufficient and weak, they cannot hold a joint in a stable, functional position during functional activities. This is known as stretch weakness.

g. Contracture is the adaptive shortening of muscle or other soft tissues that cross a joint; contracture results in decreased ROM.
(1) Myostatic contracture (pertaining to muscle) involves a musculotendinous unit that has adaptively shortened with loss of ROM. Usually occurs without specific tissue pathology and in two-joint muscles such as the hamstrings, rectus femoris, or gastrocnemius. Can typically be resolved in a short time with gentle stretching exercises and active inhibition techniques.
(2) Adhesions (an abnormal union of membranous tissue resulting from injury or inflammation) can occur if tissue is immobilized in a shortened position for extended periods of time, resulting in a loss of mobility.
(3) Scar tissue adhesions develop due to injury and the inflammatory response. Initially, new fibers develop in a disorganized pattern and will restrict motion unless remodelled along lines of stress; e.g., the patient with burns.
(4) Irreversible contracture: a permanent loss of soft tissue extensibility that cannot be released by nonsurgical treatment. Occurs when normal soft tissue is replaced by an excessive amount of nonextensible tissue, such as bone or fibrotic tissue.

Relaxation of Muscles

a. Local relaxation techniques can assist in the lengthening of contractile and noncontractile tissue.
b. Heat increases the extensibility of the shortened tissues. Warm muscles relax and lengthen more easily, reducing the discomfort of stretching. Connective tissue stretches with less force and shorter duration.
(1) GTO sensitivity is increased, making it more likely to fire and inhibit muscle tension.
(2) Low-intensity active exercise performed prior to stretching will increase circulation to soft tissue and warm the tissues to be stretched.
(3) Heat without stretching has little or no effect on long-term improvement in muscle flexibility. The combination of heat and stretching produces greater long-term gains in tissue length than stretching alone.
c. Massage increases local circulation to the muscle and reduces muscle spasm and stiffness.
d. Biofeedback helps the patient reduce the amount of tension in a muscle and improves flexibility while decreasing pain. Increased level of feedback signals (auditory, visual) assists the patient in recognizing tense muscles.

Common Errors Associated with Mobility and Flexibility Training

a. Passively forcing a joint beyond its normal ROM.
b. Aggressively stretching a patient with a newly united fracture or osteoporosis may result in fracture.
c. Using high-intensity, short-duration (ballistic) stretching procedures on muscles and connective tissues that have been immobilized over a long time or recovering from injury or surgery.
d. Stretching muscles around joints without using strengthening exercises to develop an appropriate balance between flexibility and strength.
e. Overstretching of weak muscles, especially postural muscles that support the body against gravity.

Postural Stability Training

Stability (Static Postural Control)

a. Refers to the synergistic coordination of the neuromuscular system that enables an individual to maintain a stable position in an antigravity, weight-bearing position.
b. Postural stability control involves prolonged holding of core trunk and lower extremity muscles. Postural sway is minimal.

Dynamic Stabilization, Controlled Mobility

a. Proximal segments and trunk provide a stable base for functional movements.
   (1) An individual maintains postural stability of the trunk while weight shifting.
   (2) Distal segments are fixed, while proximal segments are moving, e.g., weight shifts in sitting or standing.
   (3) Movement normally occurs through increments of range (small range to large range).
b. Patients with hyperkinetic movement disorders (e.g., ataxia) should be progressed from large range to small range movements, and finally to holding steady (stability control).

Dynamic Stabilization, Static-dynamic Control

a. An individual maintains postural stability of the trunk during dynamic extremity movements (e.g., reaching, kicking a ball).
b. Strength, endurance, flexibility, and coordination are needed for static and dynamic stabilization.

Guidelines to Develop Postural Stability

a. Consider exercise protocols that effectively challenge core muscle groups and create adequate stability to perform functional activities. Stability requires the recruitment of tonic, slow-twitch muscle fibers for sustained periods of time.
b. Start training by teaching safe spinal ROM in a variety of basic postures. Teach chin tucking with axial extension of the cervical spine and pelvic tilting with ROM of the lumbar spine.
c. Incorporate procedures to retrain kinesthetic awareness of postural position.
   (1) In sitting, teach the neutral pelvis position first to ensure a stable base. This is characterized by:
      (a) an anterior superior iliac spine (ASIS) that is level or slightly lower than the posterior superior iliac spine (PSIS) (sagittal plane) and
      (b) a level position of both ASIS (frontal plane).
   (2) Emphasis is placed on strength and endurance of back multifidi and oblique abdominals rather than erector spinae.
   (3) Focus patient's awareness on normal alignment of the spine and pelvis, and on muscles required to maintain that position.
   (4) Visual, verbal, and proprioceptive cues; e.g., resistance of elastic bands or light manual resistance, can be used to improve postural awareness.
d. To safely develop strength and endurance in the stabilizing muscles, practice maintained holding in a variety of postures. The higher the center of mass (COM) and smaller the base of support (BOS), the greater the degree of postural challenge; e.g., sitting versus standing.
e. Movements of the extremities challenge trunk and neck stabilization; functional position must be maintained as movements are carried out.
f. Resistance can be applied to the trunk or the moving extremities; functional position must be maintained as resistance is increased.
g. Alternating isometric contractions between antagonists can enhance stabilizing contractions and develop postural control; e.g., PNF techniques of stabilizing reversals and rhythmic stabilization.
   (1) Stabilizing reversals: isometric holding is facilitated first on one side of the joint, followed by alternate holding of the antagonist muscle groups. May be applied in a variety of directions; e.g., anterior-posterior, medial-lateral, diagonal.
   (2) Rhythmic stabilization (RS): simultaneous isometric contractions of both agonist and antagonist patterns performed without relaxation, using careful grading of resistance; results in cocontraction of opposing muscle groups; RS emphasizes rotational stability control.
h. During early training, emphasize muscles needed for trunk support in the upright posture, for performing basic body mechanics, and for upper extremity lifting.
i. Teach control of functional positions while moving from one position to another. This is called transitional stabilization and requires graded contractions

and adjustments between the trunk flexors and extensors. Consider moving out of a posture (eccentric control) before moving into a posture (concentric control).

j. Introduce simple patterns of motion that develop safe body mechanics and movement.
k. Closed-chain tasks are good choices to enhance postural stabilization (e.g., partial squats and controlled lunges); add arm motions and weights as tolerated.
l. More complex patterns of movement (e.g., rotation and diagonal motions) can be added (e.g., PNF trunk patterns of chop/reverse chop, or lift/reverse lift). Postures can be progressed to add difficulty (e.g., supine to sitting to standing).
m. Incorporate stretching into the postural exercise program. Adequate flexibility is necessary for postural muscles to hold body parts in proper alignment.

Common Errors Associated with Postural Stability Training

a. Inadequate stretching of tight muscles (e.g., tight hip flexors that hold the pelvis in an anterior pelvic tilt or tight hamstrings that hold the pelvis in a posterior tilt); both prevent a stable postural base (neutral pelvis and spine position).
b. Inadequate control of core muscles could place excessive stress on proximal structures during functional activities; e.g., the vertebrae and discs of the spine during sitting.
c. Progressing too quickly or starting at too high a functional level for the patient to maintain postural stability.
d. Exercising past the point of fatigue, which is determined by the inability of the trunk or postural muscles to stabilize in a functional position.
e. Attempting to force a patient into a general neutral position instead of finding the proper and safe position for each individual.

Stability Ball Training

a. Benefits/uses.
   (1) Promotes balance; provides an unstable base of support, requiring continuous adjustments in balance. Moving the feet and/or the ball changes the base of support and challenges balance. Allows safe practice of falling.
   (2) Works muscles in functional, synergistic patterns.
      (a) Recruits and retrains core muscles (deep spinal and abdominal muscles).
      (b) Promotes postural relearning; e.g., neutral position in sitting, cervical or trunk rotation.
      (c) Enhances coordination, movement combinations; e.g., arm and leg bilateral symmetrical, bilateral asymmetrical movements, four-limb Mexican hat dance.
   (3) Heightens proprioception and sensory perception, awareness of the body moving in space.
   (4) Improves range of motion, allows safe stretching; e.g., total body extension or flexion, upper or lower extremity stretches.
   (5) Allows relaxation training; e.g., gentle bouncing combined with deep breathing. Gentle rocking can be used to decrease tone in hypertonic patient.
   (6) Allows a safe, dynamic cardiovascular workout; e.g., dynamic bouncing with extremity movements.
   (7) Increases strength. Can be combined with resistance training (e.g., lifting a weighted ball), using hand weights or resistive bands while on the ball, or closed-chain exercises (e.g., partial squats using the ball).

b. Advantages: light, portable, durable, and inexpensive.
c. Determining appropriate ball size.
   (1) Sitting on ball with feet flat, the ball height should place the hips and knees at 90° angles.
   (2) Supine with ball under knees, the ball height should equal the distance between the greater trochanter and the knee.
   (3) Quadruped, the ball height should equal the distance between the shoulder and the wrist.

d. Firmness/inflation.
   (1) Ball should be comfortable and have some bounce.
   (2) A firm ball moves more quickly.
   (3) A soft ball moves more slowly, may make patient feel safer, more secure.
   (4) Surface affects movement of the ball: quicker on hard surface, slower on mat or soft surface.

e. Precautions.
   (1) Obese individuals, exceeding ball weight limits.
   (2) Avoid sharp belt buckles, zippers when over the ball; check surface for sharp objects.
   (3) Lack of foot traction, feet slipping: use bare feet, rubber-soled shoes, or yoga sticky mat.
   (4) Requires adequate space around exercising individual.
   (5) Watch for sensory overload: sympathetic signs (e.g., children, adults with traumatic brain injury).
   (6) Increased pain with mobility exercises and degenerative joint disease.
   (7) Muscle fatigue.

f. Contraindications.
   (1) Dizziness or nausea associated with movement, e.g., the patient with vestibular pathology.
   (2) Extreme anxiety or fear of being on the ball.

Coordination and Balance Training

Goals and Outcomes

a. Motor function (motor control and learning) is improved.
b. Postural control, biomechanical alignment, and symmetrical weight distribution are improved.
c. Strength, power, and endurance necessary for movement control and balance are improved.
d. Sensory control and integration of sensory systems (somatosensory, visual, and vestibular) necessary for movement control and balance are improved.
e. Performance, independence, and safety are improved in transfers, gait, and locomotion.
f. Performance, independence, and safety are improved in basic activities of daily living (BADL) and instrumental activities of daily living (IADL).
g. Aerobic capacity and endurance are improved.
h. Self-management of symptoms is improved.

Training Strategies to Improve Coordination and Balance

a. Motor learning strategies are important to assist the central nervous system (CNS) in adaptation for movement control.
   (1) Learning requires repetition. Practice schedules should be carefully organized.
   (2) Initial practice may feel threatening to patient; e.g., patient may feel in danger of losing control or balance. Progression should be gradual; the therapist should ensure patient confidence and safety, continuing motivation.
   (3) Sensory cues are used to enhance motor performance.
   (4) Feedback should stress knowledge of results (KR). Attention is drawn to the success of the outcome. It is important to establish a reference of correctness during early, cognitive learning.
   (5) Feedback should address knowledge of performance (KP). Attention is drawn to missing elements, how to recruit, correct responses, and sequence responses.
   (6) Feedback schedules: feedback given frequently (after every trial) improves initial performance. Feedback given less frequently (summed after a given number of trials or fading with decreasing frequency) improves retention of skills.
   (7) A variety of activities and environments should be used to promote adaptability and generalizability of skills. Practice should progress from a closed environment (fixed or controlled) to open variable environments.
   (8) Patient decision-making skills are promoted. Patients should be encouraged to self-analyze movements and develop strategies to ensure safety and function.
b. Remedial strategies focus on use of involved body segments (e.g., affected extremities in the patient with stroke).
   (1) Control is first developed in limited movements and progressed to more complex movements. Developmental postures/functional activities can be used to isolate body segments and focus on specific body skills; e.g., weight shifts to improve hip control are practiced first in kneeling before standing.
   (2) Postural control is first achieved in holding (stability) before moving in a posture (stability-dynamic control) and skill level function (e.g., gait).
   (3) Specific techniques can be used to remediate impairments (weakness, incoordination and adaptive shortening, abnormal tone); e.g., tapping to improve responses of a weak quadriceps in standing position.
   (4) As quality of movement improves, speed of movement and control are increased.
   (5) Active responses and active learning should be promoted; progression is to unassisted or nonfacilitated movements as soon as possible.
c. Compensatory strategies are utilized as appropriate to promote safety and early resumption of functional skills; e.g., the patient with delayed or absent recovery, multiple comorbidities. Compensatory training may lead to learned nonuse of impaired extremities and delay recovery in those patients with recovery potential; e.g., the patient with stroke.
   (1) Safety is improved by substitution: intact segments (sound limbs) for impaired segments; cognitive control for impaired motor control; e.g., the patient with ataxia.
   (2) Safety is improved by altering postural strategies; e.g., widening the BOS and lowering the COM.
   (3) Safety is improved by use of appropriate assistive devices and shoes; e.g., overhead support harness, walker, athletic shoes.
   (4) Safety is improved through environmental adaptations; e.g., handrails, adequate lighting, contrast tape on stairs, and removal of throw rugs.

Interventions to Improve Coordination

a. Functional training.
  (1) Initial focus is on postural stability activities: holding.
    (a) A number of different weight-bearing postures can be used; e.g., sitting, quadruped, kneeling, plantigrade, and standing. Progression is to gradually decrease BOS while raising height of COM.
    (b) Specific exercise techniques to enhance stability previously discussed.
  (2) Dynamic stability activities: patient practices moving in all directions while maintaining posture.
    (a) Progression is to increments of range (increasing ROM).
    (b) Moving in and out of postures (movement transitions); e.g., supine to/from sitting, sitting to/from standing.
    (c) Specific exercise techniques can include PNF dynamic reversals. Movements can also be resisted using dynamic tubing or resistance bands.
    (d) PNF patterns can be utilized to challenge dynamic stability control and enhance synergistic and reciprocal action of muscles; e.g., sitting, chop/reverse chop patterns; standing, lift/reverse lift patterns.
  (3) The patient with ataxia requires the opposite progression: from dynamic stability activities to stabilizing activities: weight shifting through decrements (decreasing) ROM progressing to stability (steady holding).
  (4) Aquatic exercises: water increases proprioceptive loading of muscles, slows down ataxic movements; provides buoyancy and light resistance assisting core muscles.
  (5) Stabilization devices; e.g., air splints, splints, soft neck collars, stabilize body segments and eliminate unwanted movement.
  (6) Environment: patients with ataxia do better in a low-stimulus environment; allows better utilization of cognitive strategies.

b. Sensory training.
  (1) Patients with proprioceptive losses.
    (a) Visual training strategies: patient guides movements and postures visually; e.g., use of a mirror and shirt with vertical line taped on it to achieve vertical sitting or standing posture.
    (b) Proprioceptive training strategies for patients with some residual proprioceptive sensations: use light weights: wrist cuffs, ankle cuffs, weighted walkers, elastic resistance bands, pool exercises to increase proprioceptive loading.
  (2) Patients with visual losses benefit from cognitive and proprioceptive training strategies.
  (3) Patients with vestibular losses benefit from visual and proprioceptive training strategies.
  (4) Patients with combined losses (two or more systems); e.g., the patient with proprioceptive losses (diabetic peripheral neuropathy) and visual losses (diabetic retinopathy) require compensatory training; e.g., use of environmental adaptations, assistive devices to promote safety.

Interventions to Improve Standing Balance

a. Exercises to improve ROM, strength, and synergistic responses in order to withstand challenges to balance.
  (1) "Kitchen sink exercises": heel-cord stretches, heel rises, toe-offs, partial wall squats, single-leg activities (side kicks, back kicks), marching in place, look-arounds (head and trunk rotation), and hip circles. Progression from bilateral upper extremity (UE) touch-down support to unilateral UE support to no UE support.
  (2) Postural awareness training: focus on control of body position, centering the COM within the limits of stability (LOS).
  (3) Weight shifts (postural sway): training of ankle strategies, hip strategies. Can include postural sway biofeedback; e.g., Balance Master.
  (4) Training of change-of-support strategies: stepping strategies (forward, backward, sideward, crossed-step); UE reaching and protective extension.

b. Functional training activities.
  (1) Sit-to-stand (STS) and sit-down (SIT) activities. Practice moving body mass forward over BOS, extending lower extremities (LEs), and raising body mass over feet and reverse. Focus on balance control while pivoting body mass over feet.
  (2) Floor-to-standing rises. Practice rising from floor to standing in the event of a fall; e.g., side-sit to quadruped to kneeling to half-kneeling to standing transitions.
  (3) Elevation activities: practice step-ups, lateral step-ups.

(4) Dual-task training. In standing, practice simultaneous UE activities (e.g., bouncing a ball, catching or throwing a ball); in standing, practice simultaneous UE activities (e.g., bouncing, catching/throwing a ball); LE activities (e.g., kicking a ball); cognitive activities (e.g., counting backwards from 100 by 7s).

c. Disturbed balance activities, including manual perturbations, use of moveable BOS devices (stability ball, wobble board, split foam roller, dense foam mat).
   (1) Carefully grade force of perturbations, range and speed of movements.
   (2) Stability ball training. Practice sitting, active weight shifts (e.g., pelvic clock), UE movements (e.g., arm circles, reaching), LE movements (e.g., stepping, marching), trunk movements (e.g., head and trunk turns).
   (3) Wobble board/equilibrium boards. Practice both self-initiated and therapist-initiated shifts in sitting or standing. Gradually increase range and speed of shifts.

d. Sensory training.
   (1) Visual changes. Practice standing with eyes open (EO) to eyes closed (EC); full lighting to reduced lighting.
   (2) Somatosensory changes. Practice standing and walking on tile floor to carpet (low pile to high), on and off dense foam, outside terrain.
   (3) Vestibular changes. Practice standing, walking, and moving head side-to-side, up-and-down; on a moving surface (e.g., escalator, elevator, bus).
   (4) Introduce sensory conflict situations (e.g., standing on foam cushion with eyes closed).

Interventions to Improve Locomotor Control

a. Functional gait activities.
   (1) Practice walking forward, backward, sideward.
   (2) Progress from slow speeds to normal walking speeds to fast walking speeds.
   (3) Progress from normal BOS to narrowed BOS.
   (4) Practice wide turns to small-based turns; to the right and left; 360° turns.
   (5) Practice head turns right and left, up and down.
   (6) Practice PNF braiding (grapevine steps).
   (7) Practice over and around obstacles, through doorways.
   (8) Practice elevation activities: practice step-ups, lateral step-ups, stair climbing, and ramps.
   (9) Practice dual-tasking. In walking, practice simultaneous UE activities (e.g., bouncing a ball, catching or throwing a ball). In walking, practice simultaneous cognitive activities (e.g., counting backwards from 100 by 7s).
   (10) Community activities. Practice walking in open (variable) environments; e.g., pushing or pulling doors, car transfers, grocery shopping.
   (11) Practice anticipatory timing activities; e.g., getting on/off elevator, escalator.

b. Treadmill walking: Focus on velocity control; progression is from slow to fast walking. Safety harness can be worn to provide partial body weight support (BWS) if patient is unstable; e.g., the patient with ataxia or stroke. Progression also achieved by increasing incline and distance walked (total time).

c. Ergometers. Pace pedalling on a cycle ergometer; progression is from slow to fast. Resistance and distance can also be modified. Can include both LE and UE training.

d. Strength training.
   (1) Active/active assistive exercise.
   (2) Manual resistance; PNF patterns can be used to promote synergistic control, improve timing.
   (3) Weights, pulleys, hydraulics, elastic resistance bands, mechanical or electromechanical devices.

e. Stretching exercises.

Teach Activity Pacing and Energy Conservation Strategies as Appropriate

a. The patient with debilitating fatigue (e.g., cerebellar ataxia, multiple sclerosis, chronic fatigue syndrome, fibromyalgia) will need to conserve energy.

b. Activity-based intervention refers to selection of activities and adaption of tasks so they will be easier and safer for the patient to complete (primary role of the occupational therapist).

c. Energy conservation refers to guidelines that allow for successful task completion, e.g., increased time for task completion; taking frequent, short rest breaks; avoiding complicated tasks; using energy-saving equipment.

Safety Education/Fall Prevention

a. Assist patient in identification of fall risk factors; e.g., effect of medications, postural hypotension.

b. Lifestyle counselling: assist patient in recognizing unsafe activities, harmful effects of a sedentary lifestyle.

Relaxation Training

Relaxation

a. Relaxation training refers to a conscious effort to relieve excess tension in muscles.
   (1) Excess muscle tension can cause pain leading to muscle spasm, which in turn produces more pain. To break the pain/spasm cycle, patients must learn to relax tense muscles.
   (2) Excess tension in tissues can result from maintaining a constant posture or sustaining muscle contractions for a period of time. Abnormal shortening or lengthening of muscles and ligaments is termed postural stress syndrome (PSS).
   (3) Habituation of compensatory movement patterns that contribute to the persistence of pain is termed movement adaptation syndrome (MAS).

b. Awareness of prolonged muscle tension is accompanied by techniques designed to promote relaxation, improve circulation, and maintain flexibility.

Training Strategies to Promote Relaxation

a. Start with the patient in a comfortable resting position, with all body parts well supported.

b. Jacobson's progressive relaxation technique includes a systematic distal to proximal progression of conscious contraction and relaxation of musculature.
   (1) A period of relaxation follows active contraction of muscle. The stronger the contraction, the greater the relaxation.
   (2) Breathing control: deep breathing coupled with the progressive relaxation to further promote relaxation. In diaphragmatic breathing, the patient breathes in slowly and deeply through the nose, allowing the abdomen to expand and then relax. This allows air to be expired through the relaxed, open mouth.

c. Cognitive strategies/guided imagery: the patient is instructed to focus on relaxing the body, visualizing calmness and relaxation.
   (1) Patient focuses on letting go of all muscular effort, letting tension melt away.
   (2) Patient focuses on a relaxing environment or pleasant images to promote relaxation; e.g., lying on a tropical beach in the warm sunshine.

d. Active range of motion: AROM can be used to reduce tension by moving body segments slowly.

e. Rhythmic rotation (RRo) involves slow, passive, rotational movements of the limbs or trunk, and can be very effective in relieving muscular tension and spasticity; e.g., hook-lying with both feet flat or with the LEs placed on a stability ball, gently rocking the knees from side-to-side for the patient with excess LE tone.

f. Slow vestibular stimulation: applied with gentle rocking techniques; can also be used to enhance relaxation; e.g., gentle rocking of the infant with colic.

g. Biofeedback training can be an effective modality to promote relaxation; e.g., training to reduce the level of tension in the frontalis muscle.

h. Stress management/lifestyle adaptation techniques.
   (1) Careful identification and evaluation of life stressors (e.g., Life Events Scale, Holmes-Rahe Social Readjustment Scale, and Hassles Scale) are critical in developing an appropriate plan of care to reduce chronic stress. Stress-control techniques include both cognitive and physical strategies.
   (2) Lifestyle modification reduces frequency of high-stress situations and events. It is important to ensure adequate rest, activity, and nutrition.
   (3) Enhance coping skills: ensure that the patient maintains some level of control and decision-making.
   (4) Maximize effective use of social support systems.

Common Errors Associated with Relaxation Training

a. Lack of awareness of the effects of the environment on an individual. Failure to have the patient in a low-stress environment and comfortably positioned.

b. Lack of awareness of stress factors affecting the patient. Failure to evaluate stressors carefully and incorporate stress-management techniques.

c. When using progressive relaxation techniques, progressing too fast from one body segment to another; e.g., distal to proximal body parts. Failure to combine slow deep breaths with each contraction and relaxation.

d. Lack of effective training of kinesthetic awareness. Patients do not recognize when their muscles are tense. They perceive the tense muscle as normal, not needing any relaxation intervention.

Aquatic Exercise

Goals and Outcomes

a. Motor function and motor learning are enhanced.
b. ROM and flexibility are improved.
c. Postural control, biomechanical alignment, and symmetrical weight distribution are improved.
d. Strength, power, and endurance are improved.
e. Sensory control and integration of sensory systems (somatosensory, visual, and vestibular) are improved.
f. Performance, independence, and safety in balance, gait, and locomotion are improved.
g. Aerobic capacity and endurance are improved.
h. Relaxation, reduction of pain, and decreased muscle spasm are enhanced.

Strategies

a. Immersion in pools or tanks is used to facilitate movement and exercise. Water buoyancy, buoyant devices, and various depths of immersion decrease body weight and enhance movement; similar movements on land may be more difficult or impossible to perform.
b. Allows greater freedom and range of movement than is permitted in smaller tanks; e.g., whirlpool or Hubbard tank.
c. Pools or tanks with a walking track, with or without a treadmill, are used to enhance gait and endurance.

Physics Related to Aquatic Exercise

a. Buoyancy: the upward force of water on an immersed or partially immersed body or body part. Equal to the weight of the water that it displaces (Archimedes' principle). This creates an apparent decrease in the weight and joint unloading of an immersed body part, allowing easier movement in water.
b. Cohesion: the tendency of water molecules to adhere to each other. The resistance encountered while moving through water is due to cohesion; some force is needed to separate water molecules.
c. Density: the mass per unit volume of a substance. The density of water is proportional to its depth; deeper water must support the water above it.
d. Hydrostatic pressure: the circumferential water pressure exerted on an immersed body part. A pressure gradient is established between the surface water and deeper water, due to the increase in water density at deeper levels.
   (1) Pascal's law states that the pressure exerted on an immersed body part is equal on all surfaces.
   (2) Increased pressure counteracts effusion and edema, and enhances peripheral blood flow.
e. Turbulence: movement of a body part through water creates circular motion of the water (eddy current) near the surface of the part, producing frictional drag.
   (1) As speed of movement increases, greater resistance is encountered.
   (2) Moving through turbulent water creates greater resistance as compared to calm water.
   (3) Use of equipment (e.g., paddle or boot) increases resistance and drag as the patient moves through water.

Thermodynamics

a. Water temperature affects body temperature and performance.
b. Water temperature is determined by specific needs of patient and intervention goals.
   (1) Cooler temperatures are used for higher intensity exercise.
   (2) Warmer temperatures are used to enhance mobility, flexibility, and relaxation; e.g., patients with arthritis.
   (3) Ambient air temperature should be close to water temperature (e.g., ±3 °C or ±4 °F).
c. There is decreased heat dissipation through sweating with immersion.
d. At temperatures > 37 °C (98.6 °F), patients have increased cardiovascular demands at rest and during exercise.
e. At temperatures < 25 °C (77 °F), patients have difficulty maintaining core temperature.

Special Equipment

a. Buoyancy assistance devices: inflatable cervical collar, flotation rings, buoyancy belt or vest, kickboard.
b. Buoyant dumbbells (swimmers): used for upright or horizontal support.

c. Webbed gloves and hand paddles: used to increase resistance to upper extremity movement.
d. Fins and boots: used to increase resistance to lower extremity movement.

Exercise Applications

a. Movement horizontal to or upward toward the water surface (active assistive exercise) is made easier due to the buoyancy of water. A flotation device may be needed to support very weak patients.
b. Movement downward into the water is more difficult because of the buoyancy of water.
   (1) A flotation device or hand-held paddle can be used to increase resistance.
   (2) A paddle turned to slice through the water decreases resistance.
c. Resistance exercise can be controlled by the speed of the movement.
   (1) Resistance increases with increased velocity of movement due to the cohesion and turbulence of the water.
   (2) Slower movements meet less resistance.
   (3) Ataxic movements are slower and more controlled against the resistance of water.
d. Stretching exercises can be assisted by the buoyancy of water.
e. The amount of weight bearing on the lower extremities is determined by the height of the water/level of immersion (buoyancy) relative to the upright patient.
   (1) The greater the water depth, the less the weight/loading on extremities.
   (2) Can be used for partial weight-bearing (PWB) gait training.
f. Lower extremity reciprocal movements are enhanced by use of a kickboard and using kicking movements.
g. Aerobic conditioning is enhanced with deep-water walking or running, high-step marching, or other calisthenics. Progresses to reduced water levels and then to land walking/running.
   (1) Immersed equipment (e.g., cycle ergometer, treadmill, or upper body ergometer) can be used to enhance conditioning. Hand floatation weights can be used to increased UE resistance.
   (2) Swimming is an excellent aerobic training activity.
   (3) Regular monitoring of exercise responses (e.g., ratings of perceived exertion) is required.
h. Treatment time varies with the type of activity, patient tolerance, and level of skill.

Contraindications

a. Bowel or bladder incontinence.
b. Severe kidney disease.
c. Severe epilepsy.
d. Severe cardiac or respiratory dysfunction; e.g., cardiac failure, unstable angina, severely reduced vital capacity, unstable blood pressure.
e. Severe peripheral vascular disease.
f. Large open wounds, skin infections, colostomy.
g. Bleeding or hemorrhage.
h. Water and airborne infections; e.g., influenza, gastrointestinal infections.

Precautions

a. Fear of water, inability to swim. Floatation supports can be used.
b. Patients with heat intolerance; e.g., patients with multiple sclerosis.
c. Use waterproof dressing on small open wounds.

Review Questions

Therapeutic Exercise Foundations

1. During strength training, what is the influence of the Valsalva maneuver regarding intrathoracic pressure, heart rate, venous pressure, and cardiac work?

2. What are the implications of the FITT equation in terms of strategies to develop cardiovascular endurance?

3. When exercising a patient in an aquatic environment, what are the factors that can make the activity easier to perform? More difficult to perform?

4. What is the main principle being employed when using the PNF-facilitated stretching technique of contract-relax?

5. What are the most common errors associated with training a patient to improve postural stability?

10

Biophysical Agents

JOHN CARLOS, JR. and ELIZABETH OAKLEY

Chapter Outline

Physical Agents

Superficial Thermotherapy

1. Physics related to heat transmission.
   a. Conduction: heat transfer from a warmer object to a cooler object by means of direct molecular interaction of objects in physical contact. Conductive modalities: hot packs, paraffin.
   b. Convection: heat transfer by movement of air or fluid from a warmer area to a cooler area or moving past a cooler body part. Convective modalities: whirlpool, fluidotherapy.
   c. Radiation: transfer of heat from a warmer object to a cooler object by means of transmission of electromagnetic energy without heating of an intervening medium. Infrared waves absorbed by cooler body. Radiation modality: infrared lamp.
2. Physiological effects of general heat application.
   a. Large areas of the body surface area are exposed to heat modality; e.g., whirlpool (hip and knee immersed) (Table 10-1).

Table 10-1

Physiological Effects of General Heat Application

INCREASED	DECREASED
Cardiac output	Blood pressure
Metabolic rate	Muscle activity (sedentary effect)
Pulse rate	Blood to internal organs
Respiratory rate	Blood flow to resting muscle
Vasodilation	Stroke volume

3. Physiological effects of small surface area heat application.
   a. Heat modality applied to discrete area of body; e.g., low back, hamstring, neck.
   b. Body tissue responses to superficial heat.
      (1) Skin temperature rises rapidly and exhibits greatest temperature change.
      (2) Subcutaneous tissue temperature rises less rapidly and exhibits smaller change.
      (3) Muscles and joints show least temperature change, depending on size of structure.
   c. Physiological effects on body systems and structures to small surface area heat modalities are listed in Tables 10-2 and 10-3.
4. Goals and indications for superficial thermotherapy.
   a. Modulate pain, increase connective tissue extensibility, reduce or eliminate soft-tissue inflammation and swelling, accelerate rate of tissue healing, reduce or eliminate soft tissue and joint restriction and muscle spasm.
   b. Preparation for electrical stimulation (ES), massage, passive and active exercise.
   c. *Don't use passive physical agents except when necessary to facilitate participation in an active treatment program* (White N, et al. Phys Ther 2015).
5. Precautions for use of superficial thermotherapy.
   a. Cardiac insufficiency, edema, impaired circulation, impaired thermal regulation, metal in treatment site, pregnancy, in areas where topical counterirritants have recently been applied, demyelinated nerves and open wounds.
6. Contraindications to the use of superficial thermotherapy.
   a. Acute and early subacute traumatic and inflammatory conditions, decreased circulation, decreased sensation, deep vein thrombophlebitis, impaired cognitive function, malignant tumors, tendency

Table 10-2

Increased Physiological Responses of Body Systems and Structures to Local Heat Application

SYSTEM/STRUCTURE	MECHANISM
Blood flow	Dilation of arteries and arterioles
Capillary permeability	Increased capillary pressure
Elasticity of nonelastic tissues	Increased extensibility of collagen tissue
Metabolism	For every 10°C increase in tissue temperature, the rate of cellular oxidation increases by two to three times (van't Hoff's law)
Vasodilation	Activation of axon reflex and spinal cord reflex, release of vasoactive agents (bradykinin, histamine, prostaglandin)
Edema	Increased capillary permeability

Table 10-3

Decreased Physiological Responses of Body Systems and Structures to Local Heat Application	
SYSTEM/STRUCTURE	MECHANISM
Joint stiffness	Increased extensibility of collagen tissue and decreased viscosity
Muscle strength	Decreased function of glycolytic process
Muscle spasm	Decreased firing of II afferents of muscle spindle and increased firing of Ib GTO fibers reduces alpha motor neuron activity, and thus decreases tonic extrafusal activity
Pain	Presynaptic inhibition of A delta and C fibers via activation of A beta fibers (gate theory), disruption of pain-spasm cycle

toward hemorrhage or edema, very young and very old patients. Additional contraindications are listed with each biophysical agent.

7. General treatment preparation for thermotherapy and cryotherapy.
   a. The application of physical agents must be performed by qualified physical therapy personnel. The treatment and expected sensations must be explained to the patient.
   b. Place patient in comfortable position.
   c. Expose treatment area and drape patient properly.
   d. Inspect skin and check temperature sensation prior to treatment.
   e. If patient has good cognitive function, a call bell or other signaling device can be given to the patient to alert personnel of any untoward effects of treatment. Check patient frequently during initial treatment.
   f. Dry and inspect skin at conclusion of treatment.
8. Superficial heating physical agents.
   a. Hot pack.
      (1) A canvas pack filled with silica gel, heated by immersion in water between 165°F and 170°F.
      (2) Method of heat transmission: conduction.
      (3) Method of application.
         (a) Add layers of towelling between the hot pack and the patient. This can be accomplished in the following ways:
         (b) Place pack on patient. If patient must be placed on pack, use additional towels to minimize excessive heating of treatment area caused by weight of patient on pack and to protect bony prominences.
         (c) The hot pack reaches peak heat within the first 5 minutes of application; during this time, the patient is at the greatest risk for a burn. Thus, the physical therapy personnel should check the skin within the first 5 minutes of treatment and periodically thereafter, especially if the patient is lying on top of the pack.
      (4) Treatment time: 20–30 minutes.
   b. Paraffin bath: therapeutic application of liquid paraffin to a body part for the transmission of heat. Paraffin bath is a thermostatically controlled unit that contains a paraffin wax and mineral oil mixture in a 6:1 or 7:1 ratio. The paraffin/mineral oil mixture melts between 118°F and 130°F and is normally self-sterilizing at temperatures of 175°F and 180°F. Paraffin is primarily applied to small, irregularly shaped areas such as the wrist, hand, and foot.
      (1) Method of heat transmission: conduction.
      (2) Procedure.
         (a) Glove method (dip and wrap with plastic wrap and towelling) or immersion (part remains in the bath after final dip).
      (3) Treatment time: 15–20 minutes.
      (4) Indications: painful joints caused by arthritis or other inflammatory conditions in the late subacute or chronic phase, joint stiffness. Most often used on wrists and hands.
      (5) Contraindications: allergic rash, open wounds, recent scars and sutures, skin infections.
   c. Fluidotherapy is no longer tested on the National Physical Therapy Exam (NPTE).
   d. Infrared lamp is no longer tested on the NPTE.
   e. Hydrotherapy (whirlpool): partial or total immersion baths in which the water is agitated and mixed with air to be directed against or around the affected part. Patients can move the extremities easily because of the buoyancy and therapeutic effect of the water.
      (1) Method of heat transmission: convection.
      (2) Method of application: whirlpool.
         (a) Turn on agitator and adjust the force, direction, depth, and aeration.
         (b) Monitor patient's response and tolerance to the whirlpool.
         (c) At end of treatment, dry and inspect.
      (3) Treatment temperature: varies with size and status of area treated.
         (a) 103°F–110°F: whirlpool.
         (b) 95°F–100°F: peripheral vascular disease.
      (4) Treatment time: 20 minutes.
      (5) Indications: subacute and chronic musculoskeletal conditions.

(6) Precautions.
(a) Local immersion: decreased temperature sensation, impaired cognition, recent skin graft, confusion/disorientation, deconditioned state.
(7) Contraindications.
(a) *Don't use whirlpool for wound management* (White N, et al. Phys Ther. 2015).
(8) Electrical safety: safety precautions must be taken with any modality that potentially exposes the patient to electrical hazards from faulty electrical connections.
(a) A ground fault circuit interrupter (GFI) should be installed at the circuit breaker of the receptacle of all whirlpools. The electrical circuit is broken if current is diverted to the patient (macroshock) who is grounded rather than to a grounded modality.
(b) All whirlpool turbines, tanks, and motors used to lift patients should be checked for current leakage (broken or frayed connections).

f. Nonimmersion irrigation device.
(1) Small, hand-held electric water pump that produces a water jet to create a shearing force to loosen tissue debris. Some devices produce a pulsed lavage and include suction to remove debris.
(2) Procedure.
(a) Treatment should take place in an enclosed area.
(b) Face and eye protection, gloves, and waterproof gown are required.
(c) Sterile, warm saline is used. Antimicrobials may be added.
(d) Select appropriate treatment pressure, usually 4–8 psi. Pressure may be increased in presence of large amounts of necrotic tissue or tough eschar. Pressure should be decreased with bleeding, near a major vessel, or if a patient complains of pain.
(e) Treatment time is usually 5–15 minutes, once a day. Wound size and amount of necrotic tissue may increase treatment parameters.

Cryotherapy

1. Physics related to cryotherapy energy transmission.
a. Abstraction: the removal of heat by means of conduction or evaporation.
(1) Conduction: transfer of heat from a warmer object to a cooler object by means of direct molecular interaction of objects in physical contact. Conductive modalities: cold pack, ice pack, ice massage, cold bath.

Table 10-4

Physiological Effects of General Cold Application

DECREASED	INCREASED
Metabolic rate	Blood flow to internal organs
Pulse rate	Cardiac output
Respiratory rate	Stroke volume
Venous blood pressure	Arterial blood pressure Shivering (occurs when core temperature drops)

(2) Evaporation (heat of vaporization): highly volatile liquids that evaporate rapidly on contact with warm object. Evaporative modality: vapocoolant sprays.

2. Physiological effects of large surface area cold application (see Table 10-4).
3. Physiological effects of small surface area cold application.
a. Effects of cold application on body tissues.
(1) Skin temperature falls rapidly and exhibits greatest temperature change.
(2) Subcutaneous temperature falls less rapidly and displays smaller temperature change.
(3) Muscles and joints show least temperature changes, requiring longer cold exposure.
b. Vasoconstriction of skin capillaries that results in blanching of skin in the center of contact area and hyperemia due to a decreased rate in oxyhemoglobin dissociation, around the edge of contact area in normal tissue.
c. Cold-induced vasodilation: cyclic vasoconstriction and vasodilation following prolonged cold exposure (> 15 minutes). Occurs mostly in hands, feet, and face, where arteriovenous anastomoses are found. Called the "hunting" reaction. Recent studies have questioned the clinical significance of this reaction.
d. Physiological effects on body systems and structures to small surface area cold modalities (Tables 10-5 and 10-6).
e. Adverse physiological effects of cold due to hypersensitivity.
(1) Cold urticaria: erythema of the skin with wheal formation, associated with severe itching due to histamine reaction.
(2) Facial flush, puffiness of eyelids, respiratory problems, and in severe cases, anaphylaxis (decreased blood pressure, increased heart rate) with syncope are also related to histamine release.

4. Goals and indications for cryotherapy.
a. Modulate pain; reduce or eliminate soft-tissue inflammation or swelling; reduce muscle spasm; reduce spasticity, cryokinetics, cryostretch; management of symptoms in multiple sclerosis.

Table 10-5

Decreased Physiological Responses of Body Systems and Structures to Local Cold Application	
SYSTEM/STRUCTURE	**MECHANISM**
Blood flow	Sympathetic adrenergic activity produces vasoconstriction of arteries, arterioles, and venules
Capillary permeability	Decreased fluids into interstitial tissue
Elasticity of nonelastic tissues	Decreased extensibility of collagen tissue
Metabolism	Decreased rate of cellular oxidation
Muscle spasm	Decreased firing of II afferents of muscle spindle, increased firing of Ib GTO fibers reduces alpha motor neuron activity and thus decreases tonic extrafusal activity
Muscle strength	Decreased blood flow, increased viscous properties of muscle (long duration: > 5–10 min)
Spasticity	Decreased muscle spindle discharge (afferents: primary, secondary), decreased gamma motor neuron activity
Vasoactive agents	Decreased blood flow

Table 10-6

Increased Physiological Responses of Body Systems and Structures to Local Cold Application	
SYSTEM/STRUCTURE	**MECHANISM**
Joint stiffness	Decreased extensibility of collagen tissue and increased tissue viscosity
Pain threshold	Inhibition of A delta and C fibers via activation of A beta fibers (gate theory), interruption of pain-spasm cycle, decreased sensory and motor conduction, synaptic transmission slowed or blocked
Increased blood viscosity	Decreased blood flow in small vessels facilitates red blood cells adhering to one another and vessel wall, impeding blood flow
Muscle strength	Facilitation of alpha motor neuron (short duration: 1–5 min)

5. Precautions.
   a. Hypertension, impaired temperature sensation, open wound, over superficial nerve, very old or young, cognitive changes.
6. Contraindications to use of cryotherapy.
   a. Cold hypersensitivity (urticaria), cold intolerance, cryoglobulinemia, peripheral vascular disease, impaired temperature sensation, Raynaud's disease, paroxysmal cold hemoglobinuria, over regenerating peripheral nerves.
7. Procedures.
   a. Cold packs: vinyl casing filled with silica gel or sand-slurry mixture.
      (1) Method of heat transmission: conduction.
      (2) Method of application.
         (a) Dampen a towel with warm water, wring out excess water, fold in half width-wise and place cold pack on towel.
         (b) Place pack on patient and cover with dry towel to retard warming.
      (3) Treatment temperature: packs are maintained in refrigerated unit at 0°F–10°F.
      (4) Treatment time: 10–20 minutes.
      (5) Indications/contraindications: see general information.
   b. Ice packs: crushed ice folded in moist towel or placed in plastic bag covered by moist towel.
      (1) Method of heat transmission: conduction (abstraction).
      (2) Method of application.
         (a) Apply the ice pack to body part.
      (3) Treatment time: 10–20 minutes.
   c. Ice massage: ice cylinder formed by freezing water in a paper or Styrofoam cup. Salt may be added to create a colder slush mixture. A lollipop stick or wooden tongue depressor may be placed in water during freezing process. During the application of ice massage, the patient will usually experience the following sequence of physiological response stages: cold, burning, aching, and numbness.
      (1) Method of heat transmission: conduction.
      (2) Method of application.
         (a) Apply the ice massage to an area no larger than 4 × 6 inches in slow (2 inches/second) overlapping circles or overlapping longitudinal strokes, each stroke covering one-half of previous circle or stroke. If treating a large area, divide into smaller areas.
         (b) Do not massage over bony area or superficial nerve (e.g., peroneal/fibular).
         (c) Continue treatment until anesthesia is achieved.
      (3) Treatment time: 5–10 minutes, or until analgesia occurs.

d. Vapocoolant spray: a nontoxic, nonflammable volatile liquid that produces rapid cooling when a fine spray is applied to the skin. Vapocoolant sprays are used primarily to reduce muscle spasm, desensitizing trigger points.
   (1) Method of heat transmission: evaporation.
   (2) Procedure (spray and stretch method).
      (a) Invert container, nozzle down, hold 18–24 inches from treatment area.
      (b) Spray at 30° angle and sweep spray over treatment at 4 inches/second.
      (c) Allow liquid to completely evaporate before applying next sweep. Caution! Do not frost skin.
      (d) The muscle should be passively stretched before and during application.
      (e) Cover the entire treatment area, starting at the pain site and moving to the area of referred pain.
      (f) Have patient perform active exercise after spraying.
   (3) Treatment time: 10–15 minutes.
   (4) Indications: myofascial referred pain, trigger points.
   (5) Contraindications: refer to Contraindications to use of cryotherapy section.

e. Contrast baths: the alternating immersion of a body part in warm and cold water to produce vascular exercise through active vasodilation and vasoconstriction of the blood vessels. The effectiveness of this method to raise deep tissue temperature via increased circulation of deep vessels has been questioned. It may be useful in promoting pain modulation.
   (1) Method of heat transmission: conduction.
   (2) Procedure.
      (a) Treatment usually begins in warm to hot water (100°F–111°F).
      (b) Place part in warm water for 4 minutes, and then transfer to cold water for 1 minute.
      (c) Immerse part in warm water for 4 minutes.
      (d) Continue sequence of 4:1, usually ending in warm water.
      (e) Patient's condition may determine the ending temperature. Ending in cold water may be more beneficial if reducing edema is the goal.
   (3) Treatment temperature.
      (a) Warm to hot water: 100°F–111°F.
      (b) Cold water: 55°F–65°F.
      (c) During initial treatment, you may wish to begin with the upper end of the cold range and the lower end of the hot range.
   (4) Treatment time: 20–30 minutes.
   (5) Indications: any condition requiring stimulation of peripheral circulation in limbs, peripheral vascular disease, sprains, strains, and trauma (after acute condition abates).
   (6) Contraindications: advanced arteriosclerosis, arterial insufficiency, loss of sensation to heat and cold.

Ultrasound (US)

1. Biophysics related to ultrasound.
   a. Spatial characteristics of US.
      (1) During continuous US, spatial characteristics of US are predominant.
      (2) Continuous US is applied to achieve thermal effects.
      (3) US energy (intensity) is not uniformly distributed over the surface of the transducer, because the energy is mechanically blocked by the adhesive bonding of the crystal in the transducer, and the pressure waves interfere with each other as they radiate from different areas of the crystal.
      (4) Uneven intensity produces a high level of energy in the center of the US beam relative to the surrounding areas. This effect produces a "hot spot" (peak spatial intensity) in the beam. Moving the soundhead or using pulsed US tends to reduce the effect of the hot spot.
      (5) Spatial average intensity. The total power (watts) divided by the area (cm^2) of the transducer head. This is typically the measurement used to document US treatments.
      (6) Beam nonuniformity ratio (BNR). The ratio of spatial peak intensity to spatial average intensity. The lower the BNR, the more uniform the energy distribution, and the less risk of tissue damage. BNR should be between 2:1 and 6:1. An ideal 1:1 ratio is not technically feasible.
   b. Temporal characteristics of US.
      (1) During pulsed US, temporal characteristics of the US are important.
      (2) Pulsed US is applied when nonthermal effects are desired (e.g., acute soft tissue injuries).
      (3) Duty cycle. The fraction of time the US energy is on over one pulse period (time on + time off). For example, a 20% duty cycle could have an on-time of 2 msec and an off-time of 8 msec. A duty cycle of ≤ 50% is considered pulsed US. A duty cycle of 51%–99% produces less acoustic energy and less heat than continuous US at 100% duty cycle.
      (4) Temporal peak intensity. The peak intensity of US during the on-time phase of the pulse period.

(5) Temporal average intensity. The US power averaged over one pulse period.

(6) Attenuation. The reduction of acoustical energy as it passes through soft tissue. Absorption, reflection, and refraction affect attenuation. Absorption is highest in tissues with high collagen and protein content (muscles, tendons, ligaments, capsules). The scattering of sound waves that result from reflection and refraction produces molecular friction that the sound wave must overcome to penetrate tissues.

c. Depth of penetration: 3–5 cm.

(1) At 3 MHz, greater heat production in superficial layers, caused by greater scatter (attenuation) of sound waves in superficial tissue; e.g., temporomandibular joint (TMJ).

(2) Increased heat production in deep layers at 1 MHz is caused by less scatter in superficial tissues; thus, more US energy is able to penetrate to deeper tissues.

2. Physiological effects of ultrasound.

a. Thermal: produced by continuous sound energy of sufficient intensity. Range: 0.5–3 w/cm². US intensity will vary depending upon tissue type and pathology.

(1) Increased tissue temperature, increased pain threshold, increased collagen tissue extensibility, alteration of nerve conduction velocity, increased enzymatic activity, and increased tissue perfusion.

(2) Increased temperature at tissue interfaces due to reflection and refraction. Tissue interfaces could be bone/ligament, bone/joint capsule, and bone/muscle.

(3) Excessively high temperatures may produce a sudden, strong ache caused by overheating of periosteal tissue (periosteal pain). Reduce intensity or increase surface area of treatment if periosteal pain is expressed by patient.

(4) Insufficient coupling agent may produce discomfort caused by a "hot spot," which is the uneven distribution of the acoustical energy through the sound head. However, this is a greater problem if the stationary technique is used.

b. Nonthermal: generated by very low intensity or pulsed (intermittent) sound energy. Pulsed US is related to duty cycle. Typical duty cycles are 20%–50% for nonthermal intervention.

(1) Cavitation: alternating compression (condensation phase) and expansion (rarefaction phase) of small gas bubbles in tissue fluids caused by mechanical pressure waves.

(a) Stable cavitation: gas bubbles resonate without tissue damage. Stable cavitation may be responsible for diffusional changes in cell membranes.

(b) Unstable cavitation: severe collapse of gas bubbles during compression phase of US can result in local tissue destruction due to high temperatures.

- Acoustic streaming: movement of fluids along the boundaries of cell membranes resulting from mechanical pressure wave. Acoustic streaming may produce alterations in cell membrane activity, increased cell wall permeability, increased intracellular calcium, increased macrophage response, and increased protein synthesis; may accelerate tissue healing.

3. Goals and indications.

a. Modulate pain, increase connective tissue extensibility, reduce or eliminate soft-tissue inflammation, accelerate rate of tissue healing, reduce or eliminate muscle spasm.

4. Precautions.

a. Acute inflammation, breast implants, open epiphyses, and US over healing fractures.

5. Contraindications.

a. Impaired circulation; impaired cognitive function; impaired sensation; malignant tumors; over or near an area with thrombophlebitis; joint cement; directly over plastic components; over vital areas such as brain, ear, eye, heart, cervical ganglia; carotid sinuses; reproductive organs; exposed or unprotected spinal cord; over or in the area of cardiac pacemakers or in the abdomen, low back, uterus, or pelvis during pregnancy.

b. *Don't use ultrasound to reduce swelling, promote joint healing, or achieve long-term pain relief for musculoskeletal conditions* (White N, et al. Phys Ther. 2015).

6. Procedures.

a. Direct contact (transducer/skin interface). Moving sound head in contact with relatively flat body surface.

(1) Apply generous amount of coupling medium (gel/cream) to skin.

(2) Select sound head size (ERA one-half the size of the treatment area). Place sound head at right angle to skin surface.

(3) Move sound head slowly (~1.5 inches/sec) in overlapping circles or longitudinal strokes, maintaining sound head to body surface angle.

(4) Each motion covers one-half of previous circle or stroke.

(5) Do not cover an area greater than two to three times the size of the effective radiating area (ERA) per 5 minutes of treatment. To cover an area greater than twice the ERA, apply US in two or more sections.

(6) While sound head is moving and in firm contact, turn up intensity to desired level.
(7) Treatment intensity: 0.5–2.5 w/cm², depending on treatment goal. Lower intensities for acute conditions or thin tissue (wrist joint); for chronic conditions or thick tissue (low back), higher intensities should be considered.
(8) Periosteal pain occurring during treatment may be caused by high intensity, momentary slowing, or cessation of moving head. If this occurs, stop treatment and readjust US intensity or add more coupling agent.
(9) Treatment time: 3–10 minutes, depending on size of area, intensity, condition, and frequency.

b. Indirect contact (water immersion). Use with irregular body parts.
(1) Fill container with water high enough to cover treatment area. A plastic container is preferred because it will reflect less acoustic energy than a metal container.
(2) Place body part and sound head in water, keeping it 1 cm from skin surface and at right angle to body part.
(3) Move sound head slowly, as in direct contact. If applying stationary technique, reduce intensity or use pulsed US.
(4) Turn up intensity to desired level.
(5) Periodically wipe off any air bubbles that may form on sound head or body part during treatment.

7. Phonophoresis.
a. The use of US to drive medications through the skin into the deeper tissues. Local analgesics (lidocaine) and anti-inflammatory drugs (dexamethasone, salicylates) are often used.
b. Method of application is similar to direct contact technique, except that a medicinal agent is used as part of coupling medium.
(1) Mode: pulsed 20%.
(2) Treatment time: 5–10 minutes.
(3) 0.5–0.75 w/cm², using a medication that is prepared in a medium that will allow transmission of the US. Gel mediums or transdermal patches have good transmissivity; avoid pastes and creams.
c. Goals and indications.
(1) Pain modulation; decrease inflammation in subacute and chronic musculoskeletal conditions.

Shortwave Diathermy (SWD)

1. Biophysics related to diathermy.
a. Electromagnetic energy produces deep heating within tissues.
b. Shortwave diathermy has a radiofrequency range of up to 300 MHz and a short wavelength of no more than 200m.
c. To avoid interfering with radio communications, SWD frequency is limited to three bands by the FCC. SWD devices generally use a frequency of 27.12 MHz.
d. Continuous SWD will increase tissue temperature in deeper structures. The tissue type determines the amount of energy absorption.
e. Pulsed shortwave diathermy (PSWD) allows dissipation of heat during the off cycle and can result in other physiological and therapeutic benefits.
f. Inductive coil.
(1) An alternating current in a coil produces a magnetic field. This results in electrical eddy currents in tissues, which causes charged particles in the tissue to vibrate. The vibration or oscillation causes tissue temperature to rise.
(2) The strength of the magnetic field and the distance of the applicator and conductivity of the tissues determine the heat generation when using SWD.
(3) Collagen, fat, and bone have low conductivity.
(4) Synovial tissue and muscle which are high in water and electrolyte content have high conductivity. The most heat is produced in these tissues.
(5) Applicators may be a single drum or two drums, which can be adjusted to conform to the shape of the body part. The drum is placed directly over the part to be treated. Actual coils wrapped around a body part are no longer used.
g. Capacitive plates.
(1) Carbon rubber or metal plates covered by felt pads and encased in plastic. They come in pairs.
(2) The plates are placed on opposite sides of the patient. A high frequency AC current flows from one plate to another through the patient.
(3) The patient becomes part of the circuit. Charged particles oscillate and tissue temperature increases. This is known as heating by electric field method. Inductive coils use magnetic field method.
(4) Capacitive heating produces more heat superficially under each plate. Inductive heating works better for deeper structures such as muscles.

2. Physiological effects of diathermy.
a. Thermal effects in continuous mode. Increased tissue temperature both deep and superficial, increased soft tissue extensibility, increased nerve conduction, increased pain threshold, vasodilation.
b. Nonthermal effects in pulsed mode. Increased microvascular perfusion, increased local tissue

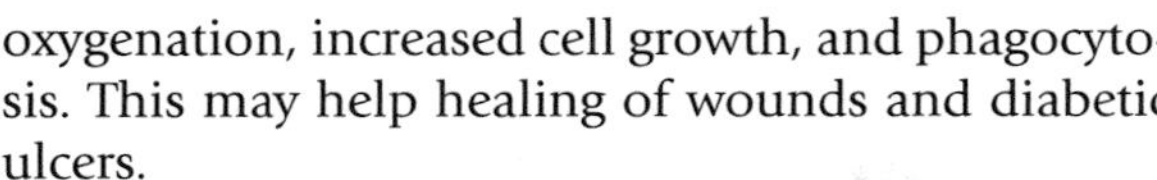

oxygenation, increased cell growth, and phagocytosis. This may help healing of wounds and diabetic ulcers.

3. Indications and goals.
   a. Thermal.
      (1) Increased joint ROM.
      (2) Pain management.
      (3) Increased tissue healing.
   b. Nonthermal.
      (1) Pain control.
      (2) Decreased edema.
      (3) Resolution of acute and chronic infections.
      (4) Wound control and soft tissue healing.
4. Contraindications.
   a. Pregnancy of patients.
   b. Cardiac pacemakers, neural stimulators, or any other implanted or transcutaneous device such as an insulin pump.
   c. Specific to thermal diathermy: open epiphyses, metal implants and jewelry, malignancy, near the testes or eyes.
   d. Specific to nonthermal diathermy: over diseased internal organs, over metal loops that secure plates or rods.
5. Precautions.
   a. Use of diathermy near other electronic or magnetic equipment; e.g., computers, cell phones.
   b. Very obese patients, since fat may be heated excessively.
   c. Patients or other nearby personnel using metal bearing intrauterine devices.
   d. Pregnancy of therapist or other personnel administering treatment.
6. Treatment considerations.
   a. Keep skin dry and cover with a layer of toweling for thermal diathermy.
   b. The patient should experience mild warmth for thermal diathermy.
   c. Use the manufacturer's suggested settings for nonthermal diathermy.
   d. Treatment time is 20 minutes for thermal and 30–60 minutes for nonthermal.

Mechanical Agents and Massage

Mechanical Spinal Traction (Intermittent Traction)

1. Description.
   a. A distraction force applied to the spine to separate articular surfaces between vertebral bodies and elongate spinal structures. This force is applied to multiple spinal segments in the cervical and lumbar region. Many types of spinal traction are presently used, such as manual, positional, gravity-assisted, inversion, continuous, and static traction. This section will focus on mechanical traction.
2. Effects of traction.
   a. Joint distraction: a separation of the facet joints occurs with sufficient force. This opens up the intervertebral foramen, relieves pressure on the nerve root, and decreases compressive forces on the facets. For the lumbar region, a force of 50% of the patient's body weight is required to cause separation. In the cervical region, 7% of the patient's body weight or about 20–30 lbs results in separation. In both instances, lower traction forces (lumbar: 30–40 lbs; cervical: 8–10 lbs) are recommended for initial treatment to decrease reactive muscle spasm and determine patient tolerance. In follow-up treatments, force can be gradually increased to achieve a maximal decrease in symptoms, but not to exceed 7% of body weight in the cervical region and 50% in the lumbar region.
   b. Reduction of disc protrusion: separation of vertebral bodies occurs at higher forces, causing a decrease in intradiscal pressure that creates a suction-like effect on the nucleus, drawing it back in centrally. The surrounding ligamentous structures are stretched taut, which also helps to push the disc in centrally. For the lumbar region, 60–120 lbs or up to 50% of a patient's body weight, and for the cervical region, 12–15 lbs is recommended to achieve these desired effects.
   c. Soft-tissue stretching: the surrounding spinal muscles, ligaments, tendons, and discs can be stretched, decreasing the pressure on the facet joints, nerve roots, vertebral bodies, and discs without achieving joint separation. Lower traction forces are sufficient to achieve this effect (lumbar region: 25% of body weight; cervical region: 12–15 lbs).
   d. Muscle relaxation: both intermittent and static traction can decrease muscle tone. Traction can interrupt the pain-muscle spasm cycle by stimulating mechanoreceptors through the motion caused by interrupted traction and by inhibiting motor neuron firing with static traction. The forces recommended for soft-tissue stretching are also used for muscle relaxation.

e. Joint mobilization: at lower forces, intermittent traction stimulates the mechanoreceptors to inhibit pain and decrease spasm, while high force traction causes decreased pressure on the joints and stretches the surrounding soft tissue. Unlike manual joint mobilization, traction cannot be isolated to a particular segment and provides general mobilization in the cervical or lumbar region.

3. Goals and indications.
   a. Decrease joint stiffness (hypomobility), decrease meniscoid blocking muscle spasm, degenerative disc, disc protrusion, joint disease, modulate discogenic pain, modulate subacute or chronic joint pain, reduce nerve root impingement.
   b. Summary evidence in recent systematic reviews and clinical practice guidelines concludes that mechanical lumbar traction is not effective for treating acute or chronic nonspecific low back pain. Activity/exercise is recommended although mechanical lumbar traction is neither detrimental nor beneficial (JOSPT, March 2016). Refer also to Appendix 1H Clinical Practice Guidelines: Low Back Pain.
4. Precautions.
   a. Claustrophobia, hiatal hernia, vascular compromise, pregnancy, and impaired cognition. Any disease or condition that can compromise the structure of the spine, such as: osteoporosis, tumor, infection, rheumatoid arthritis, or protracted steroid use; TMJ; problems with halter use; disc extrusion; medial disc protrusion; complete resolution of severe pain with traction.
5. Contraindications.
   a. Acute strains, sprains, and inflammation; spondylolisthesis, fractures, postop spinal surgery, spinal joint instability or hypermobility, and spinal cord compression; hypertension; increased peripheralization of pain, numbness or tingling, decreased myotomal strength, and decreased reflex response.
6. Procedure (intermittent traction).
   a. Cervical traction.
      (1) Can be seated or supine. Supine position is generally preferred.
      (2) Cervical halter.
         (a) Head halter is placed under the occiput and the mandible.
         (b) Head halter is attached to the traction cord directly or to the traction unit through the spreader bar.
         (c) Slack is removed from the traction cord. The neck should be maintained in 20°–30° of flexion; a pillow may be used to achieve this angle.
         (d) Some target area specificity may be achieved by varying the neck angle approximately 0°–5° of cervical flexion to increase intervertebral space and joint separation at C1 through C5; up to 25°–30° for C5 through C7; neutral spine (approximately 20° of flexion) for disc dysfunction.
         (e) Traction force should be applied to the occipital region and not on the chin. If patient expresses discomfort in the temporomandibular joint area, treatment should stop and head halter should be readjusted to ensure that the force is properly applied.
      (3) Cervical sliding device.
         (a) The head is placed on padded headrest, which positions the neck in 20°–30° of flexion.
         (b) Adjustable neck yoke is tightened to firmly grip just below the mastoid process.
         (c) Head strap is secured across the forehead.
         (d) Traction rope is then attached to the gliding platform of the device.
      (4) Traction force is determined by treatment goals and patient tolerance.
         (a) Acute phase.
            - Disc protrusion, elongation of soft tissue, muscle spasm, 10–15 pounds or 7%–10% of body weight.
            - Joint distraction 20–30 pounds.
      (5) Treatment time.
         (a) 5 to 10 minutes for acute conditions and disc protrusion, 15–30 minutes for other conditions.
      (6) Duty cycle.
         (a) Static traction is recommended for disc protrusions or when symptoms are aggravated by motion.
         (b) Intermittent traction can also be used for disc protrusions and joint distraction, but a 3:1 hold/rest ratio is recommended. A 1:1 ratio is recommended when mobility is desired; i.e., joint mobilization.
   b. Lumbar traction.
      (1) A split table is usually used to minimize friction between the body and the table.
      (2) Supine position, with pillow under the knee or small bench under lower leg, is recommended when the goal is to open up the intervertebral foramen, separate the facet joints, or elongate the muscles. The prone position may be preferable in the case of a posterior herniated lumbar disc. Some target area specificity may be achieved by varying the angle of pull (i.e., to increase intervertebral space at L5 to S1 up to 45°–60° of hip flexion, or at L3 to L4 up to 75°–90°).
      (3) Apply the pelvic harness so that the top edge is above the iliac crest.
      (4) Attach the thoracic harness so that the inferior margin is slightly below lower ribs.

(5) Secure the harness around the pelvis and attach it to the traction rope or spreader bar.
(6) Thoracic harness provides countertraction to the pull on the pelvis and is secured at the top of the table.
(7) Treatment force.
(a) Acute phase, 30–40 pounds.
(b) Disc protrusion, spasm; elongation of soft tissues, 25% of body weight.
(c) Joint distraction, 50 pounds or 50% of body weight.
(8) Treatment time: 5–10 minutes for herniated disc, 10–30 minutes for other conditions.

Intermittent Mechanical Compression

1. Description.
   a. Pneumatic device that applies external pressure to an extremity through an inflatable appliance (sleeve).
   b. Appliances are designed in a variety of sizes and lengths to fit either the upper or lower extremity (ankle, ankle and lower leg, or full extremity).
   c. The device is attached to an inflatable pneumatic sleeve by rubber tubing.
   d. The compression units and appliances are designed to inflate a single compartment to produce uniform, circumferential pressure on the extremity or multiple compartments by applying pressure in a sequential manner. Pressure is greater in the distal compartments and lesser in the proximal compartments.
   e. Cold can be applied simultaneously with intermittent compression in which a coolant (50°F–77°F) is pumped through an inflatable sleeve.
2. Physiological effects.
   a. External pressure on the extremity increases the pressure in the interstitial fluids, forcing the fluids to move into the lymphatic and venous return systems, thus reducing the fluid volume in the extremity. In addition to mechanical compression, some conditions may require the daily use of compression stockings to counteract the effect of gravity on the vascular and lymph systems in the lower extremities.
3. Goals and indications.
   a. Amputation, decrease chronic edema, postmastectomy lymphedema, stasis ulcer, venous insufficiency, subacute injuries such as ankle sprains with traumatic edema. Manual massage/drainage techniques have supplanted use of mechanical compression in many instances.
4. Precautions.
   a. Impaired sensation; malignancy; uncontrolled hypertension; over an area where there is a superficial peripheral nerve, such as the fibular nerve.
5. Contraindications.
   a. Acute inflammation, trauma, or fracture; acute deep venous thrombosis (DVT) and thrombophlebitis; obstructed lymph or venous return; arterial disease/insufficiency; arterial revascularization; acute pulmonary edema; diminished sensation; cancer; edema with cardiac or renal impairment; impaired cognition; infection in treatment area; hypoproteinemia (< 2 g/dL); very old or young patients.
6. Procedure.
   a. Check patient's blood pressure.
   b. Set the inflation and deflation ratio to ~3:1. Generally, for edema reduction, 45–90 seconds on/15–30 seconds off. To shape residual limb, a 4:1 ratio is often used.
   c. Turn the power on and slowly increase the pressure to the desired level.
      (1) The patient's blood pressure determines the setting of the device. Some manufacturers recommend that the setting never exceed the patient's diastolic blood pressure. Others advise that the pressure can fall between the diastolic and systolic pressure because the pressure is on for only a short period of time.
      (2) Numbness, tingling, pulse, or pain should not be felt by the patient during the treatment.
   d. Treatment time.
      (1) The duration may vary, depending on the patient's tolerance and condition.
         (a) Lymphedema: 2 hours progressing to two 3-hour sessions daily.
         (b) Traumatic edema: 2 hours daily.
         (c) Venous ulcers: 2.5 hours three times per week progressing to 2 hours daily.
         (d) Residual limb edema: 1 hour progressing to three 1-hour sessions daily.
         (e) Some conditions may warrant shorter treatment times initially.

Continuous Passive Motion (CPM)

1. Description.
   a. Uninterrupted passive motion of the joint through a controlled ROM. A mechanical device provides continuous movement for extended periods of time.
2. Physiological effects of CPM.
   a. Accelerate rate of interarticular cartilage regeneration, tendon and ligament healing.
   b. Decrease edema and joint effusion.
   c. Minimize contractures.
   d. Decrease postoperative pain.
   e. Increase synovial fluid lubrication of the joint.
   f. Improve circulation.
   g. Prevent adhesions.

h. Improve nutrition to articular cartilage and periarticular tissues.
i. Increase joint ROM.

3. Goals and indications.
   a. Postimmobilization fracture, tendon or ligament repair, especially ACL repairs/reconstruction.
   b. *Don't use continuous passive motion machines for the postoperative management of patients following uncomplicated total knee replacement* (White N, et al. Phys Ther. 2015).
4. Precautions.
   a. Intracompartmental hematoma from anticoagulant use.
5. Contraindications.
   a. Increases in pain, edema, or inflammation following treatment.

Tilt Table

1. Description.
   a. Mechanical or electrical table designed to elevate patient from horizontal (0°) to vertical (90°) position in a controlled, incremental manner.
2. Physiological effects of tilt table.
   a. Stimulate postural reflexes to counteract orthostatic hypotension.
   b. Facilitate postural drainage.
   c. Gradual loading of one or both lower extremities.
   d. Begin active head or trunk control.
   e. Provide positioning for stretch of hip flexors, knee flexors, and ankle plantar flexors.
3. Indications.
   a. Prolonged bed rest, immobilization, spinal cord injury, traumatic brain injury, orthostatic hypotension, spasticity.
4. Procedure.
   a. Patient is placed in supine position.
   b. Abdominal binder, long elastic stockings, or tensor bandaging to counteract orthostatic hypotension (venous pooling) may be used.
   c. Patient secured to table by straps.
   d. Take baseline vitals (blood pressure, heart rate, respiratory rate).
   e. Table raised gradually to given angle. Incremental rise to 30°, 45°, 60°, 80°, or 85°, or as tolerated. Position can be maintained for as long as 30–60 minutes.
   f. Vital signs (blood pressure, heart rate, respiratory rate) need to be monitored to assess the patient's tolerance to treatment. Cyanotic lips or fingernail beds may indicate compromised circulation.
   g. Treatment time.
      (1) Initially, the duration of treatment depends on the patient's tolerance, but should not exceed 45 minutes, once or twice daily.

Massage

1. Description.
   a. Mechanical manipulation of soft tissue by the hands. (Electrical, mechanical, or hydraulic methods will not be discussed. Alternate forms of massage such as acupressure, shiatsu, or reflexology are beyond the scope of this section).
   b. Note: Dry needling is currently not tested on the NPTE.
2. Physiological effects.
   a. Increased venous and lymphatic flow.
   b. Stretching and loosening of adhesions.
   c. Edema reduction.
   d. Sedation.
   e. Muscle relaxation.
   f. Modulate pain.
3. Description of selected techniques.
   a. Stroking (effleurage): gliding movements of hands over surface of skin. Superficial stroking: light contact. Deep stroking: heavy pressure.
   b. Kneading (petrissage): grasping and lifting of tissues. Similar to kneading bread.
   c. Friction: compression of tissue using small circular or long stroking movements, usually with the palmar surface of hand or fingers. Pressure may be light (superficial) initially, progressing to heavy (deep), moving superficial tissues over deeper tissues.
   d. Tapping (tapotement): rapid striking with palmar surface of hand and/or fingers, cupped hand (clapping, percussion), or ulnar edge of hand and fingers (hacking) in an alternating manner.
   e. Vibration: shaking of tissue using short, rapid quivering motion with hands in contact with the body part.
4. Procedure.
   a. Stroking: usually initiates and ends treatment. Hand is molded over body part and movement is usually distal to proximal. Stroking is used to move from one area to another and between other strokes. Superficial strokes make no attempt to move deep tissue. Some passive muscle stretching is performed with deep stroking.
   b. Kneading: milking effect of kneading aids in loosening adhesions and increasing venous return. Technique can be done with one or both hands, fingers, or the thumb and first finger. Wring and lift tissues to break down adhesions. Direction of strokes may vary, depending on body structure; however, to increase venous return, strokes should move from distal to proximal along the extremity.
   c. Friction: heavy compression over soft tissues will stretch scars and loosen adhesions. Ball of fingers or thumb should move in small circular or stroking

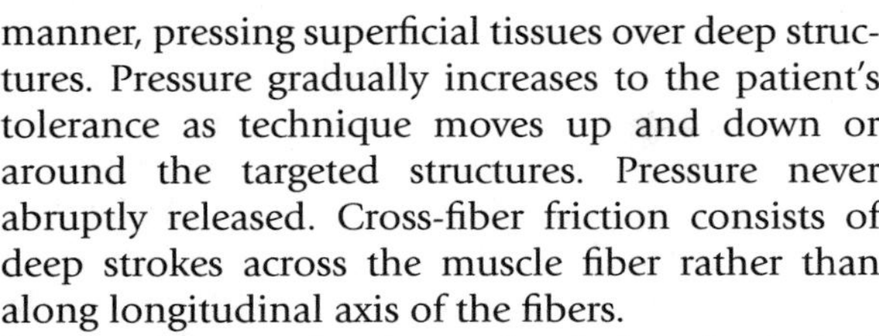

manner, pressing superficial tissues over deep structures. Pressure gradually increases to the patient's tolerance as technique moves up and down or around the targeted structures. Pressure never abruptly released. Cross-fiber friction consists of deep strokes across the muscle fiber rather than along longitudinal axis of the fibers.

d. Tapotement: used when stimulation is desired treatment effect.

e. Cupping: applied to the chest to mobilize bronchial secretions (postural drainage).

f. Vibration: often used in conjunction with cupping for postural drainage to loosen adherent secretions.

5. Contraindications.

a. Acute inflammation in area, acute febrile condition, severe atherosclerosis, severe varicose veins, phlebitis, areas of recent surgery, thrombophlebitis, cardiac arrhythmia, malignancy, hypersensitivity, severe rheumatoid arthritis, hemorrhage in area, edema secondary to kidney dysfunction, heart failure, and venous insufficiency.

Electrical Agents

Basic Concepts of Nerve and Muscle Physiology

1. Properties of electrically excitable cells (see Figure 10-1).

a. Resting membrane potential (RMP).

(1) The cell membrane is more permeable to potassium (K^+) compared to sodium (Na^+) and negatively charged proteins (anions).

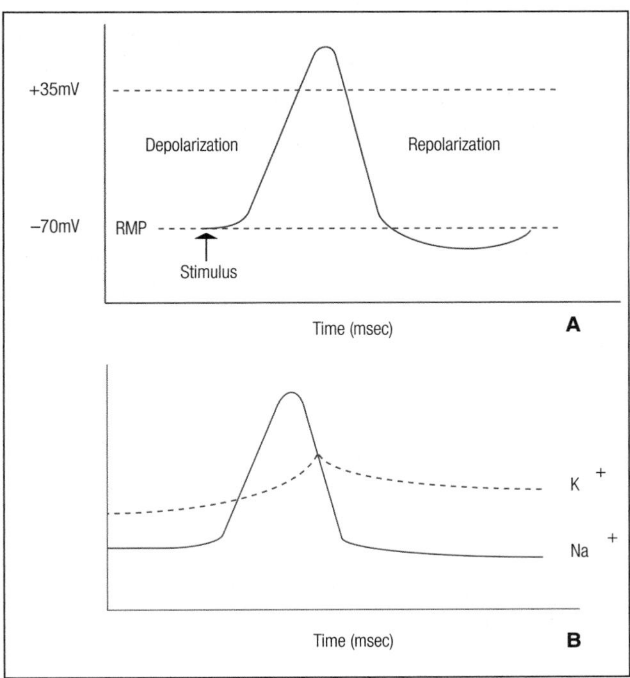

Figure 10-1 A. Changes in transmembrane potential. B. Changes in membrane permeability of sodium and potassium during an action potential.

(2) Electrical potential is generated across the cell membrane, due to the higher concentration of K^+ and anions on the inside of the cell relative to the concentration of Na^+ on the outside.

(3) A negative charge is produced within the cell, and a positive charge develops on the outside of the cell as the positively charged K^+ diffuses from the cell.

(4) RMP is –60 mV to –90 mV for excitable cells.

(5) RMP is maintained by an active sodium-potassium pump that takes in K^+ and extrudes Na^+.

b. Action potential (Figure 10-2).

(1) A stimulus (e.g., electrical) causes the cell membrane to become more permeable to Na^+ ions.

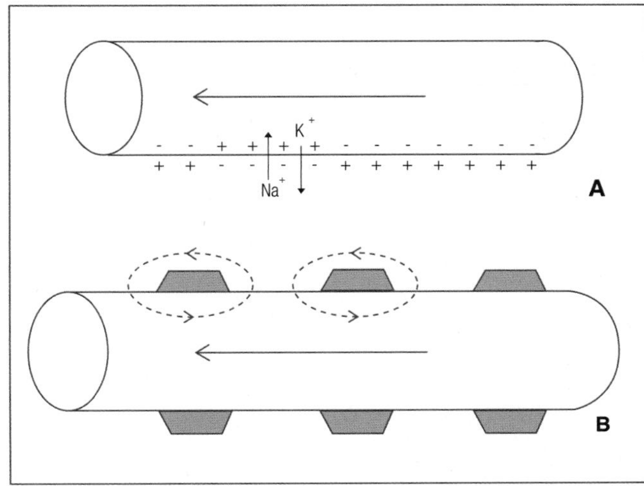

Figure 10-2 Propagation of action potential in A. unmyelinated axon and B. myelinated axon.

(2) An action potential (AP) is generated when the influx of Na^+ causes a reduction in RMP, which occurs slowly at first. Reduction in the RMP is called depolarization.

(3) When transmembrane potential reaches a critical threshold level (approximately −55 mV), the voltage-sensitive Na^+ and K^+ channels open widely. Permeability to Na^+ increases rapidly, whereas the permeability to K^+ increases slowly.

(4) During depolarization, transmembrane potential may rise as high as +35 mV. A positive charge is generated inside the cell, and a negative charge outside is produced, as a result of the flow of ions.

(5) The K^+ channels are fully open at about the time that the Na^+ are closed, and K^+ rushes rapidly out of the cell, making the transmembrane potential progressively more negative. This process is called repolarization.

(6) The K^+ channels remain open long enough to repolarize the membrane (10–20 mV < RMP). This is called hyperpolarization.

(7) The K^+ channels close and passive diffusion of the ions rapidly returns the RMP to its initial level.

c. Propagation of the action potential. See Figure 10-2.

(1) Opening of the Na^+ and K^+ channels and voltage changes that produce an AP at one segment of the membrane triggers successive depolarization in adjacent regions of the nerve, muscle, or membranes.

(2) AP movement occurs along the surface of the nerve or muscle cell.

(3) Movement of the AP along an unmyelinated nerve is generated via sequential depolarization (eddy currents) along neighboring sites in the nerve membrane. Speed of conduction in small diameter fibers is slow due to the greater internal resistance in the small fibers.

(4) In myelinated nerve fibers, saltatory conduction occurs at discrete junctures (nodes of Ranvier) in the myelin sheath that surrounds the nerve.

(5) Na^+ and K^+ ion exchange and current flow is concentrated at these points. The impulse jumps from node to node, conducting nerve impulses at greater rates compared to smaller, unmyelinated nerve fibers.

2. Electrical action of muscle and nerve.

a. Characteristics of ES necessary to initiate excitable cell depolarization.

(1) Amplitude or intensity of the stimulus must be great enough to cause the membrane potential to be lowered sufficiently to reach threshold levels.

(2) Duration of the individual stimulus must be long enough to produce depolarization of the cell membrane. A duration of ≤ 1 ms is sufficient to stimulate nerve cell membrane but is too short to stimulate muscle cell membrane.

(3) Rate of rise of the current to peak intensity must be rapid enough to prevent accommodation, which is the rapid adjustment of the membrane to stimuli to prevent depolarization. Square wave delivers instantaneous rise.

3. Strength-duration curve (Figure 10-3).

a. Rheobase is the intensity of the current, with a long duration stimulus, required to produce a minimum muscle contraction.

b. Chronaxie is the pulse duration of the stimulus at twice the rheobase intensity. Chronaxie of a denervated muscle is > 1 msec.

c. Very short pulse durations (< 0.05 msec) with low intensities can depolarize sensory nerves. Longer pulse durations (< 1 msec) are required to stimulate motor nerves. Long pulse durations (> 10 msec) with high intensities are needed to elicit a response from a denervated muscle.

d. Nerve conduction velocity and electromyography (EMG) have rendered strength-duration testing virtually obsolete.

4. Motor point.

a. An area of greatest excitability on the skin surface in which a small amount of current generates a muscle response.

b. In innervated muscle, the motor point is located at or near where the motor nerve enters the muscle, usually over the muscle belly.

c. In denervated muscle, the area of greatest excitability is located over the muscle distally toward the insertion.

5. Types of muscle contraction.

a. A low-frequency pulse (1–10 pulses/sec) produces a brief muscle twitch or muscle contraction with each stimulus.

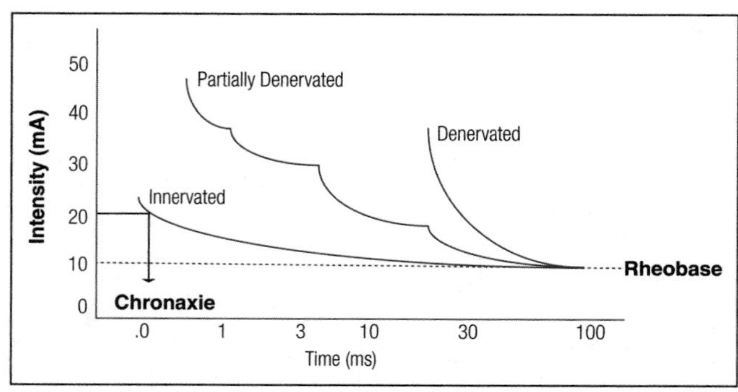

Figure 10-3 Strength-duration curves for normally innervated, partially denervated, and completely denervated muscle.

b. Increasing the number of stimuli (frequency) progressively fuses the individual muscle twitches to a point where individual twitches are not discernible. A tetanic contraction results.
c. An asynchronous or worm-like (vermicular) muscle response is noted in denervated muscle.

6. Basic concepts of electricity.
   a. Electrical current is the movement of electrons through a conducting medium.
   b. Amperage is the rate of flow of electrons.
   c. Voltage is the force that drives electrons through the conductive medium.
   d. Resistance is the property of a medium that opposes the flow of electrons. A substance with a high resistance (e.g., rubber) is an insulator, and a substance with a low resistance (e.g., metal) is a conductor.
   e. Ohm's law expresses the relationship between amperage, voltage, and resistance. The current is directly proportional to the voltage and inversely proportional to the resistance. The inverse of resistance is called conductance.

Electrical Stimulation (ES)

1. Characteristics.
   a. Wave forms (Figure 10-4).
      (1) Monophasic (direct or galvanic current): a unidirectional flow of charged particles. A current flow in one direction for a finite period of time is a phase (upward or downward deflection from and return to baseline). It has either a positive or negative charge.
      (2) Biphasic wave (alternating current): a bidirectional flow of charged particles. This type of wave form is illustrated as one-half of the cycle above the baseline and the second phase below the baseline. One complete cycle (two phases) equals a single pulse. It has a zero net charge if symmetrical.
      (3) Polyphasic wave: biphasic current modified to produce three or more phases in a single pulse. This waveform in medium frequency may be Russian or interferential current.

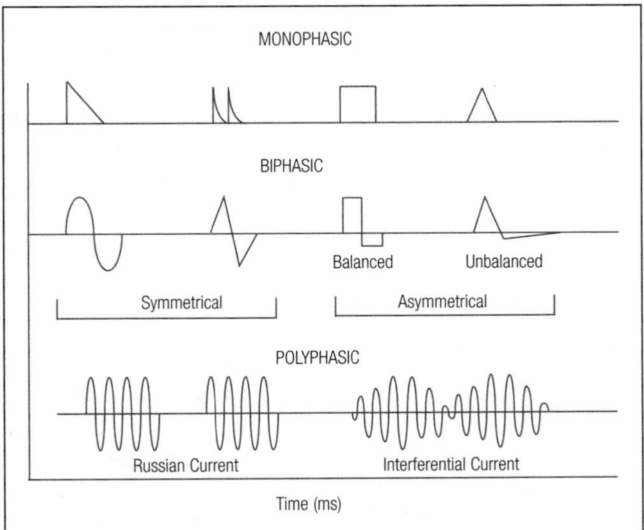

Figure 10-4 **Basic waveform characteristics.**

2. Current modulation.
   a. Continuous mode: uninterrupted flow of current.
   b. Interrupted mode: intermittent cessation of current flow for ≥ 1 second.
   c. Surge mode: a gradual increase and decrease in the current intensity over a finite period of time.
   d. Ramped mode: a time period with a gradual rise of the current intensity, which is maintained at a selected level for a given period of time, followed by a gradual or abrupt decline in intensity.
3. Goals and indications.
   a. Pain modulation.
      (1) Activation of gate mechanisms (gate theory).
      (2) Initiation of descending inhibition mechanisms (endogenous opiate production).
   b. Decrease muscle spasm.
      (1) Muscle fatigue: tetanic contraction sustained for several minutes by means of continuous modulation.
      (2) Muscle pump: interrupted or surge modulation producing rhythmic contraction and relaxation of the muscle to increase circulation.
      (3) Muscle pump and heat: combination of ES and US to increase tissue temperature and produce muscle pumping at the same time.
   c. Impaired ROM (increase in or maintenance of joint mobility).
      (1) Mechanical stretching of connective tissue and muscles associated with a joint. Used when muscle strength is deficient or neuromuscular dysfunction (e.g., spasticity) prevents adequate joint movement.
      (2) Decrease pain to encourage joint motion.
      (3) Decrease in edema if significant impediment to motion.
   d. Muscle reeducation (training muscles to respond appropriately to volitional effort).
      (1) Acts as active assistive exercise.
      (2) Provides proprioceptive feedback.
      (3) Assists in coordinated muscle movement.
   e. Disuse atrophy (muscle weakness).
      (1) Used as an adjunct to volitional movement.
   f. Soft-tissue repair (wound healing).
      (1) Pulsed currents (monophasic, biphasic, polyphasic) with interrupted modulations. Improved circulation via the muscle pump to improve tissue nutrition and hasten metabolic waste disposal.

(2) Monophasic currents (low-volt continuous modulations, high-volt pulsed currents).
   (a) Electrical potential theory. Restoration of electrical charges in wound area.
   (b) Bactericidal effect. Disruption of DNA, RNA synthesis, or cell transport system of microorganisms.
   (c) Biochemical effects. Increased adenosine triphosphate (ATP) concentration, amino acid uptake, and increased protein and DNA synthesis.
   (d) Galvanotaxic effect. Attraction of tissue repair cells via electrode polarity.
      - Inflammation phase: macrophages (positive), mast cells (negative), neutrophils (positive or negative).
      - Proliferation phase: fibroblasts (positive).
      - Wound contraction phase: alternating positive/negative.
      - Epithelialization phase: epithelial cells (positive).

(3) Both low-intensity, continuous nonpulsed low-volt direct current and high-volt pulsed current can be applied for wound healing. Though the current characteristics (continuous versus pulse) differ, the treatment protocols are similar (low amplitude current for 30–60 minutes).

g. Edema reduction.
   (1) Muscle pump to increase lymph and venous flow.
   (2) Electrical field phenomenon for acute edema. By electrostatic repulsion, a monophasic waveform with a negative polarity is set up to surround the injured area and repel the negatively charged proteins attempting to accumulate in the interstitium.

h. Spasticity (ES to reduce hypertonicity).
   (1) Fatigue of the agonist.
   (2) Reciprocal inhibition (stimulate antagonist/inhibit agonist).

i. Denervated muscle.
   (1) Controversy exists relative to the use of ES for denervated muscle. Previous animal and clinical studies indicated that denervated muscle can be stimulated by monophasic or biphasic currents with long pulse duration, producing a vermicular contraction. The goal of stimulation is to retard the effects of disuse atrophy and shorten recovery time.
   (2) Recent animal studies suggest that ES may be deleterious to denervated muscle by:
      (a) Interfering with regeneration of neuromuscular junction and subsequent re-innervation.
      (b) Traumatizing hypersensitive denervated muscle.
   (3) The financial cost and prolonged treatment time required until reinnervation occurs are additional factors for consideration of ES on denervated muscles.

4. Contraindications/Precautions.
   a. Contraindications.
      (1) Anywhere in the body for patients with demand-type pacemakers or other electronic devices such as insulin pumps, unstable arrhythmias, suspected epilepsy, or seizure disorder.
      (2) Over or in the area of the carotid sinus, thrombosis or thrombophlebitis, eyes, thoracic region, phrenic nerve, urinary bladder stimulators, and abdomen or low back during pregnancy.
      (3) Transcerebrally or transthoracically.
      (4) In the presence of active bleeding or infection.
      (5) Superficial metal implants.
      (6) Pharyngeal or laryngeal muscles.
      (7) Motor-level stimulation should not be applied in conditions that prohibit motion.
   b. Precautions.
      (1) Cardiac disease.
      (2) Impaired mentation.
      (3) In areas of impaired sensation, malignant tumors, skin irritation, or open wounds.
      (4) Applying iontophoresis in the area after the application of another physical agent.
      (5) In patients with hypotension or hypertension, excessive adipose tissue or edema.
      (6) Bleeding disorders.
      (7) Menstruating uterus.
      (8) Pregnancy: during labor and delivery.
   c. Procedural cautions.
      (1) Do not use any electrical modality if there is evidence of broken or frayed wires or if the unit is not connected to a ground fault circuit interrupter (see Hydrotherapy section).
      (2) Electrodes that are too small, have uneven contact, or are self-adhesive and no longer stick or conduct well can cause skin irritation or burns.
      (3) ES should not be used while playing sports, driving, operating heavy machinery, near a diathermy device, or in conjunction with other electronic monitoring equipment.

5. General guidelines for ES procedures.
   a. Electrode selection.
      (1) Electrode size.
         (a) Two electrodes (leads) are required to complete the current circuit. One electrode is generally called the active (stimulating) electrode and is often placed on the motor point; the second, larger electrode is called the dispersive or inactive electrode.
         (b) Current density (the amount of current that is dispersed under the electrode) is relative to the electrode size. A given current

intensity passing through the smaller active electrode produces high current density and thus a strong stimulus, while the same current is perceived as less intense under the larger dispersive electrode because of the lesser current density.

(c) Electrode size should be relative to the size of the treatment site. Large electrodes in a small treatment area (i.e., forearm) could result in current overflowing to surrounding muscles and produce undesired effects.

(d) Conversely, small electrodes applied to a large muscle (i.e., quadriceps) could result in high current density under the electrodes that make ES uncomfortable to the patient.

(2) The active electrode is usually placed over the treatment site (motor point) in order to produce a stimulation effect. The dispersive electrode may be placed on the treatment site or at a remote site (see Electrode placement).

(3) Unipolar/monopolar placement: one single electrode or multiple (bifurcated) active electrodes placed over treatment area. Usually larger dispersive electrode (inactive) placed ipsilaterally away from treatment area.

(4) Bipolar placement: equal-sized active and dispersive electrodes on same muscle group or in same treatment area. Smaller, bifurcated treatment electrodes may be used to better conform to small treatment areas.

(5) The space between the active and dispersive electrodes should be at least the diameter of the active electrode. The distance between the electrodes should be as great as is practicable. The greater the space between electrodes, the lesser the current density in the intervening superficial tissue, thus minimizing the risk of skin irritation and burns. If deep penetration causes contraction of undesired muscles, move the electrodes closer together.

(6) Inspect the patient's skin. Vigilant skin inspection and skin care is very important with long-term use of ES. This is especially important during home use of transcutaneous ES and other ES modalities. Long-term repetitive stimulation and electrode placement and removal can irritate the skin and initiate skin breakdown.

b. Muscle strengthening, muscle spasm or edema (muscle pump), ROM.

(1) Slowly increase intensity until a muscular response is observed.

(2) 10–25 muscle contractions may be sufficient to obtain treatment goal.

(3) Duty cycle.

(a) Interrupted/ramped modulation of current allows the muscle to recover between stimulation periods.

(b) It has been shown that stimulation on/off ratios of ≥ 1:3 minimize the fatigue effects of ES.

c. Muscle spasm (fatigue).

(1) Procedure as above for innervated muscle. Current applied in continuous mode or 1:1 on/off ratio.

d. Muscle reeducation.

(1) Parameters and procedure similar to muscle strengthening techniques.

(2) Stimulation for multiple sets of singular or multiple muscle repetitions.

(3) Treatment sessions of 10–30 minutes depending on patient's mental and physical tolerance.

Iontophoresis

1. Description.
   a. The application of a continuous direct current to transport medicinal agents through the skin or mucous membranes for therapeutic purposes.
2. Physics.
   a. Like charges repel like charges.
   b. Unlike charges attract unlike charges.
3. Electrochemical effects related to iontophoresis.
   a. Dissolved acids, bases, salts, or alkaloids in an aqueous solution dissociate into positively or negatively charged substances (ions) when electrical current flows through a substance.
   b. Polar effects.
      (1) Positive ions move toward the negative pole (cathode) where a secondary alkaline reaction (NaOH) occurs.
      (2) Negative ions move toward the positive pole (anode) where an acid is produced (HCl).
4. Ion transfer.
   a. The number of ions transferred through the skin is directly related to the:
      (1) Duration of treatment.
      (2) Current density.
      (3) Concentration of ions in the solution.
5. ES characteristics of iontophoresis.
   a. Direct current.
   b. Maximum intensity of 4–5 mA.
6. Indications (see Table 10-7).
7. Contraindications.
   a. Refer to general rules for ES.
   b. Impaired skin sensation.
   c. Allergy or sensitivity to medicinal agent or direct current.

Table 10-7

Indications for the Use of Iontophoresis and Ions Commonly Used			
INDICATIONS	**ION**	**POLARITY**	**SOURCE**
Analgesia	Lidocaine, Xylocaine Salicylate	Positive Negative	Lidocaine, Xylocaine Sodium salicylate
Calcium deposits	Acetate	Negative	Acetic acid
Dermal ulcers	Zinc	Positive	Zinc oxide
Edema reduction	Hyaluronidase	Positive	Wydase
Fungal infections	Copper	Positive	Copper sulfate
Hyperhidrosis	Water	Positive/Negative	Tap water
Muscle spasm	Calcium Magnesium	Positive Positive	Calcium chloride Magnesium sulfate
Musculoskeletal inflammatory conditions	Dexamethasone Hydrocortisone	Negative Positive	Dexamethasone phosphate Hydrocortisone sodium succinate

d. Denuded area or recent scars.
e. Cuts, bruises, or broken skin.
f. Metal in or near treatment area.

Transcutaneous Electrical Nerve Stimulation (TENS)

1. Description.
   a. TENS is designed to provide afferent stimulation for pain management.
2. Physiological effects.
   a. Pain modulation through activation of central inhibition of pain transmission (gate theory).
      (1) Large diameter A-beta fibers (Figure 10-5) activate inhibitory interneurons (substantia gelatinosa) located in the dorsal horn (primarily laminae II and III) of the spinal cord, producing inhibition of smaller A-delta and C-fibers (pain fibers).
      (2) Presynaptic inhibition of the T-cells closes the "gate" and modulates pain. The gating mechanism also includes release of enkephalins, which combine with opiate receptors to depress release of substance P from the A-delta and C-fibers.
   b. Pain modulation through descending pathways generating endogenous opiates (Figure 10-6).
      (1) Noxious stimuli generate endorphin production from the pituitary gland and other central nervous system (CNS) areas.
      (2) Endogenous opiate-rich nuclei, periaqueductal gray matter (PAG) in the midbrain and thalamus are also activated by strong stimuli.
      (3) Neurotransmitters from the PAG facilitate the cells of the nucleus raphe magnus (NRM) and reticularis gigantocellularis (RGC).
      (4) Efferents from these nuclei travel through the dorsal lateral funiculus, terminating on the

Figure 10-5 **Schematic of gate control theory.** (Adapted from Melzack and Wall.)

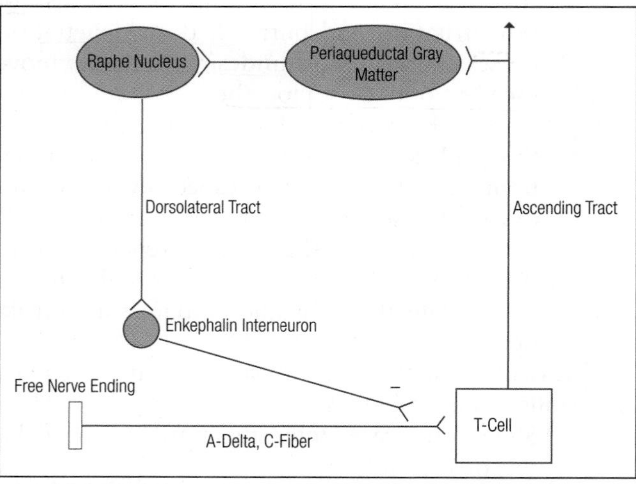

Figure 10-6 **Schematic of descending inhibition mechanisms.**

enkephalinergic interneurons in the spinal cord and presynaptically inhibit the release of substance P from the A-delta and C-fibers.

3. ES characteristics.
   a. Wave form: typically, asymmetrical biphasic with a zero net direct current component. Other variations including pulsed monophasic current have been used.
   b. Current: continuous pulsatile or burst.
4. Procedures.
   a. Conventional (high rate) TENS: this most common mode of TENS can be applied during the acute or chronic phase of pain. Modulation of pain via inhibition of pain fibers by large-diameter fiber activation (gate mechanism). Onset of pain relief is relatively fast and duration of relief is relatively short.
      (1) Amplitude: comfortable tingling sensation, paresthesia. No muscle response.
      (2) Pulse rate 50–80 pps.
      (3) Pulse duration 50–100 μsec.
      (4) Mode: continuous.
      (5) Duration of treatment: 20–60 minutes.
      (6) Duration of pain relief: temporary.
   b. Acupuncture-like (strong low rate) TENS can be applied during the chronic phase of pain. Analgesia produced through stimulation-evoked production of endogenous opiates. Onset of pain relief may be as long as 20–40 minutes. Duration of relief may be long-lasting (≥ 1 hour).
      (1) Amplitude: strong, but comfortable rhythmic muscle twitches.
      (2) Pulse rate: 1–5 pps.
      (3) Pulse duration: 150–300 μsec.
      (4) Mode: continuous.
      (5) Duration of treatment: 30–40 minutes.
      (6) Duration of pain relief: long-lasting.
   c. Brief intense TENS: this mode is used to provide rapid-onset, short-term pain relief during painful procedures (wound debridement, deep friction massage, joint mobilization, or passive stretching).
      (1) Amplitude: to patient's tolerance.
      (2) Pulse rate: 80–150 pps.
      (3) Pulse duration: 50–250 μsec.
      (4) Mode: continuous.
      (5) Duration of treatment: 15 minutes.
      (6) Duration of pain relief: temporary (30–60 minutes).
   d. Burst-mode (pulse trains) TENS: combines characteristics of both high- and low-rate TENS. Stimulation of endogenous opiates, but current is more tolerable to patient than low-rate TENS. Onset of analgesia similar to low-rate TENS.
      (1) Amplitude: comfortable, intermittent paresthesia.
      (2) Pulse rate: 50–100 pps delivered in packets or bursts of 1–4 pps.
      (3) Pulse duration: 50–200 μsec.
      (4) Mode: continuous.
      (5) Duration of treatment: 20–30 minutes.
      (6) Duration of pain relief: long-lasting (hours).
   e. Hyperstimulation (point stimulation) TENS: use of a small probe to locate and noxiously stimulate acupuncture or trigger points. Multiple sites may be stimulated per treatment. Onset of pain relief is similar to acupuncture-like TENS.
      (1) Amplitude: strong, to patient's tolerance.
      (2) Pulse rate: 1–5 pps.
      (3) Pulse duration: 150–300 μsec.
      (4) Duration of treatment: 15- to 30-second increments.
      (5) Duration of pain relief: long-lasting.
   f. Modulation mode TENS: a method of modulating the parameters of the above TENS modes to prevent neural or perceptual adaptation due to constant ES. Frequencies, intensities, or pulse durations can be altered by ≥ 10%, one or two times per second.
5. Electrode placement.
   a. Several options should be considered. Acupuncture site, dermatome distribution of involved nerve, over painful site, proximal or distal to pain site, segmentally related myotomes, or trigger points.
6. Goals and indications.
   a. Acute and chronic pain modulation.
7. Contraindications.
   a. Patient with demand-type pacemaker or over chest of patient with cardiac disease.
   b. TENS not applied over eyes, laryngeal or pharyngeal muscles, head, and neck of patient following cerebral vascular accident, or with epilepsy.
   c. TENS not applied to mucosal membranes.

High-Voltage Pulsed Galvanic Stimulation

1. Description.
   a. High-voltage pulsed current (HVPC): typically, monophasic, twin-peaked pulses of short duration.
2. Physics.
   a. Skin offers high resistance (impedance) to the flow of low-voltage current.
   b. Passage of HVPC decreases skin resistance caused by the current flowing toward the skin capacitors (little energy loss) rather than the skin resistors. Thermal effects are negligible (little resistance to current).
3. ES characteristics of HVPC.
   a. Wave form: paired monophasic, with instantaneous rise and exponential fall of current.
   b. Current: continuous, surged, or interrupted pulsatile current.

Chapter 10 BIO

4. Procedure.
 a. Muscle stimulation protocol: refer to general application procedure.
 b. Wound healing concept.
  (1) Intact skin surface negative with respect to deeper epidermal layers.
  (2) Injury to skin develops positive potentials initially and negative potentials during healing process.
  (3) Absent or insufficient positive potentials retard tissue regeneration.
  (4) Addition of positive potentials, initially through anode, may promote or accelerate healing.
 c. Wound healing parameters.
  (1) Amplitude: comfortable tingling sensation, paresthesia, no muscle response.
  (2) Pulse rate: 50–200 pps.
  (3) Pulse duration: 20–100 μsec.
  (4) Mode: continuous.
  (5) Duration of treatment: 20–60 min.
 d. Wound healing procedures.
  (1) Inspect wound area.
  (2) Position patient and support treatment area.
  (3) Clean and débride wound site. Pack with sterile saline-soaked gauze.
  (4) Both high-volt pulsed current and low-intensity continuous low-volt direct current can be used for wound healing. Although current characteristics differ, treatment parameters are similar in current intensity and treatment duration.
  (5) Place active electrode over gauze.
  (6) For bactericidal effect, active electrode should have negative polarity. For culture-free wound, active electrode should be positive.
5. Goals and indications.
 a. Inflammation phase: free from necrosis and exudates. Promote granulation.
 b. Proliferation phase: reduce wound size, including depth, diameter, and tunneling.
 c. Epithelialization phase: stimulate epidermal proliferation and capillary growth.
6. Contraindications.
 a. See general contraindications for ES.

Concept of Medium Frequency Currents in ES

1. Description.
 a. ES frequencies in the range of 2000–5000 pps that are modulated to produce physiologically applied frequencies. This concept is utilized in the Russian (time-modulated) and the interferential (amplitude-modulated) ES techniques.
2. Physics related to medium frequency.
 a. A decrease in the capacitive skin impedance of the skin is noted relative to the increase in current frequency (Figure 10-7).
 b. ES frequency categories:
  (1) Low frequency: 1–1000 pps.
  (2) Medium frequency: 1000–10,000 pps.
  (3) High frequency: > 10,000 pps.

Russian Current

1. Description.
 a. A 2500-Hz sine wave (carrier frequency), which is interrupted for 10 milliseconds at 10-millisecond intervals, producing fifty 10-millisecond bursts per second. This type of time interval interruption produces time-modulated current (Figure 10-8). Also known as medium frequency, burst-alternating current.

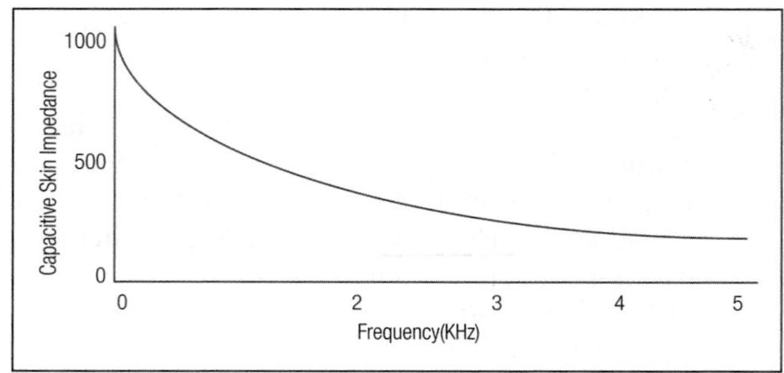

Figure 10-7 **Capacitive skin resistance decreases as current frequency increases.**

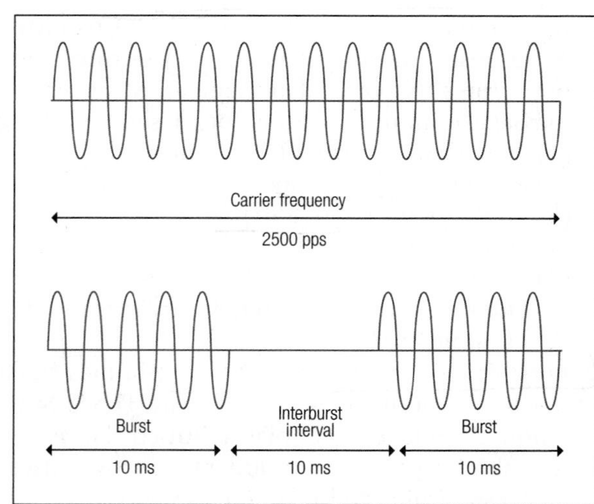

Figure 10-8 **Russian current. Time-modulated polyphasic waveform.**

2. ES characteristics of Russian current.
   a. Wave form: polyphasic sinusoidal burst.
   b. Current: time modulated to create a pulsatile burst current.
3. Method of application: muscle-strengthening protocol.
   a. Amplitude: tetanic muscle contraction.
   b. Pulse rate: 50–70 pps.
   c. Pulse duration: 150–200 μsec or 50% duty cycle.
   d. Mode: interrupted.
      (1) Ramp: 1–5 seconds, based on patient's tolerance.
      (2) Duty cycle: 1:5.
   e. Current applied to provide stimulation during the following volitional activities:
      (1) Isometric exercise at several points through ROM.
      (2) Slow isokinetic exercise; e.g., 5°–10°/sec.
      (3) Short arc joint movement when ROM is restricted.
4. Muscle spasm protocol.
   a. Muscle fatigue using continuous isometric contraction for several minutes to tolerance.
   b. If muscle pumping is goal, duty cycle is 1:1.
   c. If ROM is goal, duty cycle is 2:5.
5. Contraindications.
   a. See general contraindications for ES.

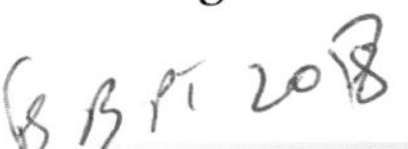

Interferential Current (IFC)

1. Description.
   a. This current is characterized by the crossing of two sinusoidal waves with similar amplitudes, but different carrier frequencies that interfere with one another to generate an amplitude-modulated beat frequency. The consequent beat frequency is the net difference between the two superimposed frequencies.
2. Physics related to IFC.
   a. Constructive interference: when the two waves are in phase, the sum of the superimposed wave is large (Figure 10-9A).
   b. Destructive interference: the sum of the two waves is zero when the waves are 180° out of phase (Figure 10-9B).
   c. Beat frequency (amplitude-modulated): resultant frequency produced by the two frequencies going into and out of phase (Figure 10-9C).
      (1) Constant. Both carrier frequencies are fixed. Beat frequency is net difference between both frequencies.
      (2) Variable. One carrier frequency is fixed and the other varies in frequency, generating a variable or sweep frequency. Sweep used to minimize accommodation.
   d. IFC produces a cloverleaf-like pattern, since the electrical stimulating effect is at a 45° angle to the flow of current in the two circuits as interference occurs at the targeted area of the body (Figure 10-10).
      (1) Static interferential fields are generated when four electrodes (two circuits) are used and the cloverleaf pattern is produced.
      (2) Dynamic (scan) interferential fields occur when the interferential fields are rotated 45°, caused by the vectoring effect of rhythmically unbalancing the IFC to change the position of the stimulation areas. This effect is purported to provide a greater area of stimulation in comparison with static interferential fields.
      (3) Full-field scanning produces a similar effect as dynamic interferential fields by bursting the current over the two circuits.
   e. Premodulated IFC occurs when two carrier frequencies are crossed in the ES unit. The interference occurs in the unit, and the current can then be delivered through one circuit. This is ideal for small areas that would be amply covered with two electrodes.
3. ES characteristics.
   a. Wave form: polyphasic, sinusoidal (amplitude-modulated) beats.

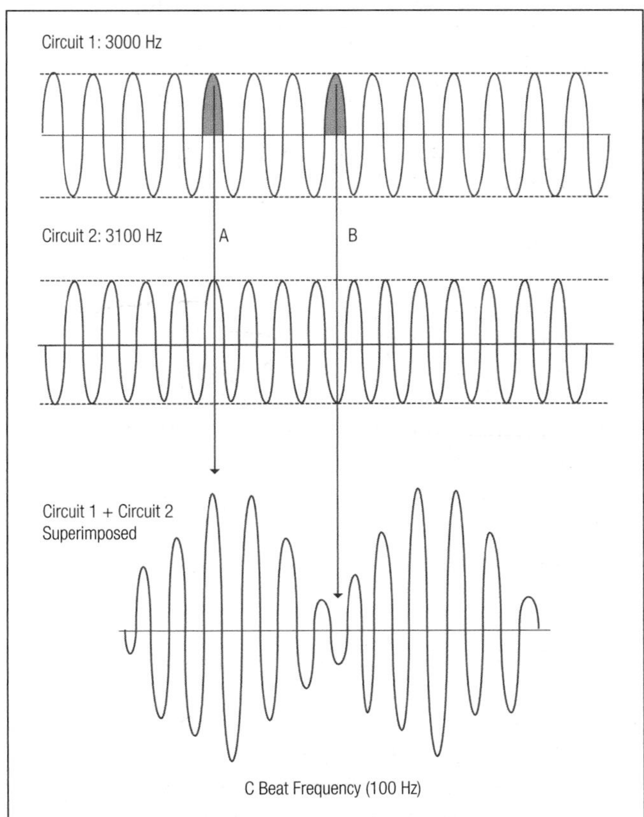

Figure 10-9 **Interferential current. Amplitude modulated polyphasic waveform.**

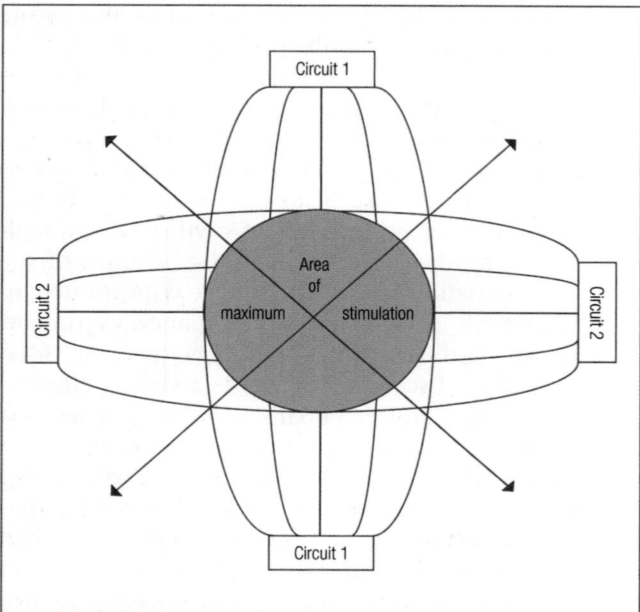

Figure 10-10 Static interference field depicting the area of maximum stimulation (circle) and the direction of maximal stimulation (arrows).

b. Current: amplitude-modulated continuous (pain); interrupted (muscle exercise).

4. Procedure.
   a. Electrode placement (pad or suction cup electrodes).
      (1) Bipolar (premodulated IFC). Active and dispersive electrodes placed over or around small area.
      (2) Quadripolar. Two sets of electrodes placed diagonally to one another over large area.
   b. Treatment parameters.
      (1) Pain protocol.
         (a) Similar to high- or low-rate TENS.
      (2) Muscle-strengthening protocol.
         (a) Similar to low- or medium-frequency ES.
5. Goals and indications.
   a. Modulate pain: increase muscle strength or ROM.
6. Contraindications.
   a. See general contraindications for ES.

Functional ES (FES)

1. Description.
   a. FES encompasses a wide range of stimulator units and techniques for disuse atrophy, impaired ROM, muscle spasm, muscle reeducation, and spasticity management. FES is also called neuromuscular electrical stimulation (NMES) and functional neuromuscular electrical stimulation. This section will describe FES as an alternative or supplement to the use of orthotic devices.
2. Shoulder subluxation.
   a. Patients with cerebrovascular accident (CVA) may initially exhibit weakness or flaccid paralysis of the muscles supporting the glenohumeral joint, especially the supraspinatus and posterior deltoid.
   b. The force of gravity acting on the unsupported upper extremity tends to stretch the ligamentous structures surrounding the glenohumeral joint, resulting in severe pain and decreased upper extremity function.
   c. ES characteristics of FES.
      (1) Wave form: asymmetrical biphasic square.
      (2) Current: interrupted pulsatile current.
   d. Procedure.
      (1) Electrode placement: bipolar. Electrodes on supraspinatus and posterior deltoid.
      (2) Treatment parameters.
         (a) Amplitude: tetanic muscle contraction to patient's tolerance.
         (b) Pulse rate: 12–25 pps.
         (c) Duration of treatment: 15–30 minutes. Three times daily, up to 6–7 hours. On/off ratio: 1:3 (2 sec: 6 sec) progressing to 12:1 (24 sec: 2 sec).
3. Dorsiflexion assist in gait training.
   a. Patients with hemiplegia sometimes exhibit paralyzed dorsiflexor and evertor muscles.
   b. FES controls foot drop, and facilitates dorsiflexors and evertors during swing phase.
   c. ES characteristics.
      (1) Wave form: asymmetric biphasic square.
      (2) Pulse duration: 20–250 µsec.
      (3) Mode: interrupted by foot switch.
   d. Procedure.
      (1) Electrode placement: bipolar. Peroneal (fibular) nerve near head of fibula or anterior tibialis muscle.
      (2) Treatment parameters.
         (a) Amplitude: tetanic muscle contraction sufficient to decrease plantar flexion.
         (b) Pulse rate: 30–300 pps.
         (c) Treatment mode: heel switch contains pressure-sensitive contact that stops stimulation during stance phase and activates stimulation during swing phase. Hand switch also allows therapist to control stimulation during gait.
4. Other gait-assisted protocol considerations.
   a. Placement of electrodes on appropriate muscles to control muscles during push-off (plantar flexors), late swing phase (hamstrings), quadriceps, and/or gluteals (stance phase).

b. ES characteristics: similar to dorsiflexion protocol.
c. Method of application: similar to dorsiflexion protocol, except for electrode placement.

Electromyographic (EMG) Biofeedback

1. Description.
   a. Electronic instrument used to measure motor unit action potentials (MUAP) generated by active muscles. The signals are detected, amplified, and converted into audiovisual signals that are used to reinforce voluntary control.
2. Principles of EMG biofeedback.
   a. Motor unit: the functional unit of the neuromuscular system that consists of the anterior horn cell, its axon, the neuromuscular junction, and all the muscle fibers innervated by the axon. Motor unit potentials (MUP) are measured in microvolts (μV). The signals generated by the MUP, which contain both positive and negative phases, are also called compound action potentials (CAP) because the sensors pick up signals from multiple motor units.
   b. The signal is processed through amplification, rectification (positive and negative components of the signal are made unidirectional), and integration (area under curve is computed). The integrated signal provides readings in microvolt-seconds and is displayed as the EMG biofeedback signal.
   c. The EMG biofeedback signals, in conjunction with the patient's voluntary effort, are used to either increase or decrease muscle activity to achieve a functional goal.
3. Recording electrodes.
   a. Surface electrodes.
      (1) Global detection: signals from more than one muscle.
      (2) Detection from mostly superficial muscles.
      (3) Advantages: easy to apply, acceptable to patient/client.
      (4) Disadvantages: detection from mostly superficial muscles, frequently from more than one muscle group.
   b. Types of surface electrodes/sensors.
      (1) Metal electrodes (silver/silver chloride): cup-shaped to accommodate conducting gel.
      (2) Disposable electrodes: pregelled center with surrounding adhesive backing.
      (3) Carbonized rubber electrodes (reusable): flexible to conform to body part.
   c. Needle electrodes/sensors.
      (1) Local detection: signals from specific muscle or muscle group.
      (2) Used primarily for EMG diagnosis or research. Rarely used for EMG biofeedback.
4. Electrode application.
   a. Electrode selection: select small electrodes (0.02 cm) for specific muscles (hand, forearm, face); large electrodes (1 cm) for large muscles or muscle groups.
   b. Electrode placement.
      (1) Bipolar technique: two active (positive and negative) and one reference (ground) electrode. The reference electrode may be placed between or adjacent to active electrodes. This minimizes or eliminates extraneous electrical activity (noise or cross-talk).
      (2) Active electrodes are placed on or near motor point of targeted muscle or muscle group.
      (3) Generally, active electrodes are placed 1–5 cm apart and parallel to muscle fibers. Reference electrode is placed near treatment site.
      (4) Active electrodes are placed close together; minimizes cross-talk, yields small, more precise signals.
      (5) Active electrodes are placed further apart; yields large signals, detection from more than one muscle.
5. Procedure.
   a. Protocol for increasing muscle activity (motor recruitment).
      (1) For weak muscles, begin with electrodes widely spaced and biofeedback instrument sensitivity high, to increase detection.
         (a) For a single weak muscle, begin with electrodes close together if a more precise signal is desired.
      (2) Instruct patient to try and contract muscle (isometrically for 6–10 sec) to produce an audiovisual signal.
      (3) As patient's motor recruitment ability improves, decrease the sensitivity, making it more difficult to produce an audiovisual signal.
      (4) Use facilitation techniques (tapping, cross-facilitation, vibration) to encourage motor unit recruitment, if necessary.
      (5) Progress from simple to more complex/functional movements as patient gains motor control.
      (6) Treatment sessions may be from 5–10 minutes to ≥ 30 minutes, depending on patient tolerance.
   b. Protocol for decreasing muscle activity (muscle relaxation).
      (1) Begin with electrodes closely spaced and biofeedback instrument sensitivity low to minimize cross-talk.
      (2) Instruct patient to relax, using deep breathing or visual imagery to help lower the audiovisual signal.

(3) Progress from low to high sensitivity as patient gains ability to relax muscle and perform functional activities.
(4) Treatment sessions may be from 5–10 minutes to ≥ 30 minutes, depending on patient tolerance.
(5) At end of session, clean patient's skin and electrodes.

6. Criteria for patient selection for biofeedback training.
   a. Good vision, hearing, and communication abilities.
   b. Good comprehension of simple commands, concentration.
   c. Good motor planning skills.
   d. No profound sensory or proprioceptive loss.

Review Questions

Biophysical Agents

1. What are the increased and decreased physiological responses to the local application of heat and cold?

2. Which characteristics of ultrasound application affect the depth of penetration and thermal effects?

3. Name at least five indications or goals for use of intermittent spinal mechanical traction.

4. What are the contraindications for use of electrical stimulation?

5. Which electrical stimulation characteristics are appropriate to use for wound healing?

11

Functional Training, Equipment, and Devices

SUSAN B. O'SULLIVAN

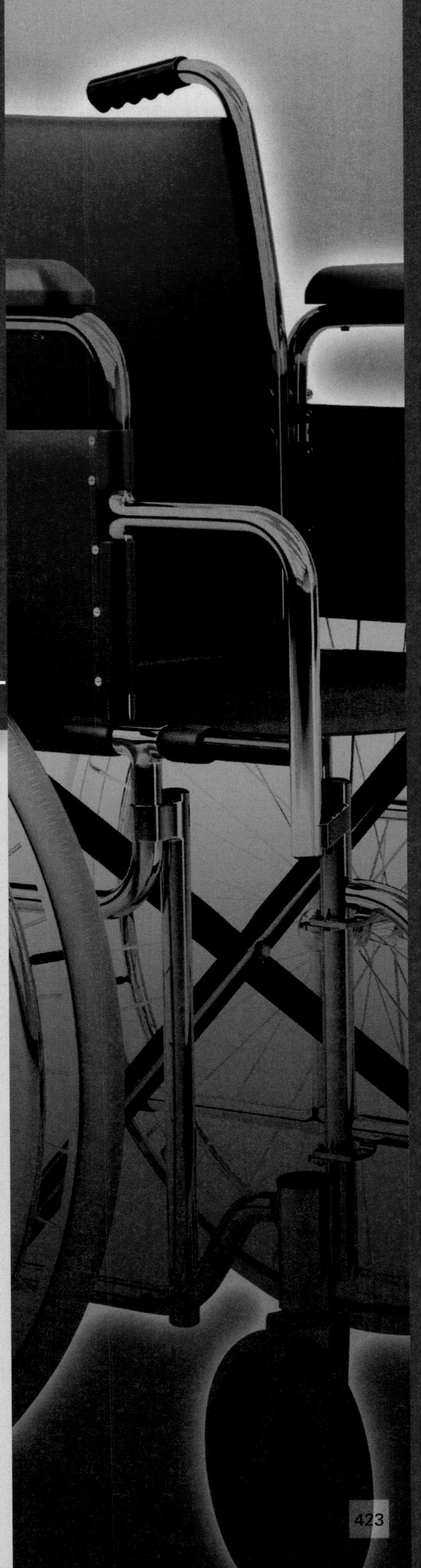

Chapter Outline

Gait

Phases of the Gait Cycle

Traditional terminology appears first and refers to points in time in the gait cycle; Rancho Los Amigos (RLA) terminology follows and refers to lengths of time in the gait cycle; as both are in clinical use, readers should be familiar with both.

1. Heel strike: the point when the heel of the reference or support limb contacts the ground at the beginning of stance phase.
   Initial contact (RLA): the instant that the foot of the lead extremity strikes the ground.
   Muscle activation patterns (see Figure 11-1): knee extensors (quadriceps) are active at heel strike through early stance to control small amount of knee flexion for shock absorption; ankle dorsiflexors (anterior tibialis, extensor hallucis longus, extensor digitorum longus) decelerate the foot, slowing the plantarflexion from heel strike to foot flat.
2. Foot flat: the point when the sole of the foot of the reference or support limb makes contact with the ground; occurs immediately after heel strike.
   Loading response (RLA): the first period of double support immediately after initial contact until the contralateral leg leaves the ground.
   Muscle activation patterns: gastrocnemius-soleus muscles are active from foot flat through midstance to eccentrically control forward tibial advancement.
3. Midstance: the point at which full body weight is taken by the reference or support limb.

Phase of gait
Stance phase
Swing phase
Double support
Single limb support
Double support
Single limb support (opposite side)

Pressure distribution
Heel strike
Foot flat
Mid-stance
Heel off
Toe off
Mid swing
Heel strike

Hip
Joint angle (extension = 0°): 45° 40° 30° 20° 5° 0° 20° 40° 50° 45°
Flexor muscles
Extensor muscles
Abductor muscles
Adductor muscles

Knee
Joint angle (extension = 0°): 5° 10° 15° 10° 5° 10° 65° 55° 30° 5°
Flexor muscles
Extensor muscles

Ankle foot
Joint angle (neutral = 0°): 5° plantar- 10° plantar- 0° 5° dorsi- 5° dorsi- 0° 5° plantar- 0° 5° plantar- 5° plantar-
Dorsiflexor muscles
Plantar flexor muscles
Inverter muscles
Everter muscles
Intrinsic muscles

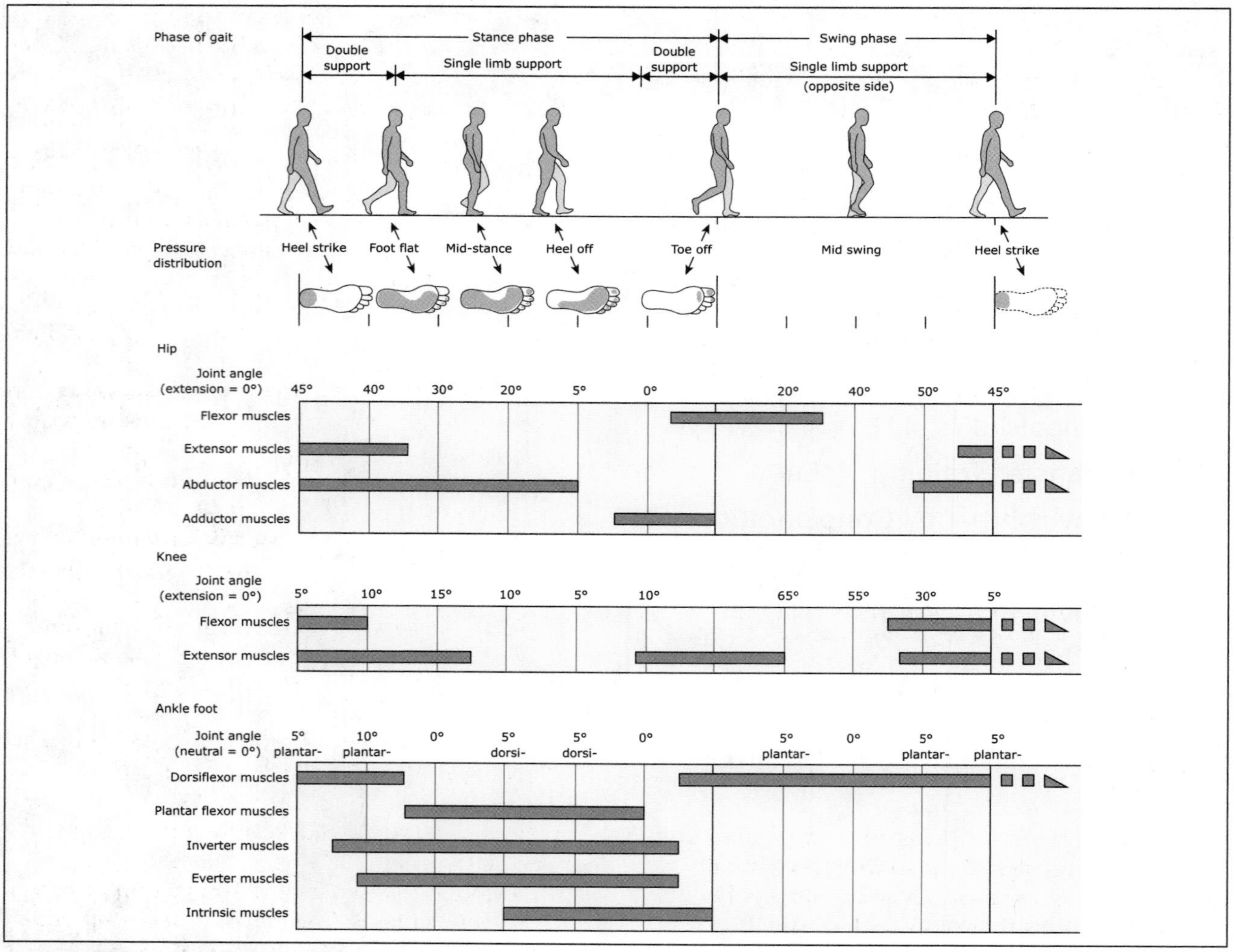

Figure 11-1 Phases of the gait cycle.
Adapted from Susan Standring (Editor-in-Chief). Gray's Anatomy. 39th ed. 2005. Page 1533. Elsevier Churchill Livingstone.

Midstance (RLA): the contralateral limb leaves the ground; body weight is taken and advanced over and ahead of the support limb; a period of single limb support.
Muscle activation patterns: hip, knee, and ankle extensors are active throughout stance to oppose antigravity forces and stabilize the limb; hip extensors control forward motion of the trunk; hip abductors stabilize the pelvis during unilateral stance.

4. Heel-off: occurs after midstance as the heel of the reference or support limb leaves the ground.
Terminal stance (RLA): the last period of single limb support that begins with heel rise and continues until the contralateral leg contacts the ground.
Muscle activation patterns: peak activity of plantarflexors occurs just after heel-off to push-off and generates forward propulsion of the body.
5. Toe-off: the last portion of stance following heel-off, when only the toe of the reference or support limb is in contact with the ground.
Preswing (RLA): the second period of double support from initial contact of the contralateral limb to lift-off of the support limb.
Muscle activation patterns: hip and knee extensors (hamstrings and quadriceps) may contribute to forward propulsion with a brief burst of activity.
6. Acceleration: the first portion of the swing phase from toe-off of the reference limb until midswing.
Initial swing (RLA): the first portion of the swing phase from toe-off of the reference limb until maximum knee flexion of the same extremity.
Muscle activation patterns: forward acceleration of the limb during early swing is achieved through the brief action of quadriceps; by midswing the quadriceps is silent and pendular motion is in effect; hip flexors (iliopsoas) aid in forward limb propulsion.
7. Midswing: the midportion of the swing phase when the reference extremity moves directly below the body.
Midswing (RLA): the portion of the swing phase from maximum knee flexion of the reference extremity to a vertical tibial position.
Muscle activation patterns: foot clearance is achieved by contraction of the hip, knee flexors, and ankle dorsiflexors.
8. Deceleration: the end portion of the swing phase when the reference extremity is slowing down in preparation for heel strike.
Terminal swing (RLA): the portion of the swing phase from a vertical tibial position of the reference extremity to just prior to initial contact.
Muscle activation patterns: hamstrings act during late swing to decelerate the limb in preparation for heel strike; quadriceps and ankle dorsiflexors become active in late swing to prepare for heel strike.
9. Pelvic motion.
   a. The pelvis moves forward and backward (transverse pelvic rotation).
      (1) Forward rotation occurs on the side of the unsupported or swing extremity; mean rotation is 4°.
      (2) Weight-bearing or stance extremity rotates 4° (a total of 8°).
   b. The pelvis moves up and down on the unsupported or swing side (lateral pelvic tilt): 5°; controlled by hip abductor muscles.
      (1) The high point is at midstance.
      (2) The low point is during the period of double support.
   c. The pelvis moves side to side 4 cm, follows the stance or support limb.
10. Cadence: the number of steps taken per unit of time.
    a. Mean cadence is 113 steps/minute.
    b. Increased cadence: shorter step length and decreased duration of period of double support.
    c. Running occurs when the period of double support disappears, typically at a cadence of 180 steps/minute.
11. Step.
    a. Step length: the linear distance between point of foot contact (preferably heel strike) of one extremity to the point of heel strike of the opposite extremity (in cm or m).
    b. Step time: the number of seconds that elapse during one step.
    c. Step width: the distance between feet (e.g., base of support); measured from one heel to the same point on the opposite heel (in cm or m).
       (1) Normal step width ranges between 2.54 and 12.7 cm (1 and 5 inches).
       (2) Increases as stability demands rise; e.g., wide-based gait in older adults or very small children.
12. Stride.
    a. Stride length: the linear distance between two consecutive contact points of the same extremity (in cm or m).
    b. Stride time: the number of seconds that elapse during one stride (one complete gait cycle).
13. Velocity (walking speed): the rate of motion in any direction; the distance is divided by the time (in cm/sec or m/min).
    a. Average walking speed is 82 m/min (3 mi/hour).
    b. Affected by physical characteristics: height, weight, gender.
    c. Decreased with age, physical disability, etc.
14. Acceleration: the rate of change of velocity in relation to time.
15. Energy cost of walking.
    a. Average oxygen rate for comfortable walking is 12 mL/kg × min.
    b. Metabolic cost of walking averages 5.5 kcal/min on level surfaces; energy costs may vary widely depending on speed of walking, stride length, body weight, type of surface, gradient, and activity (e.g., stair climbing).

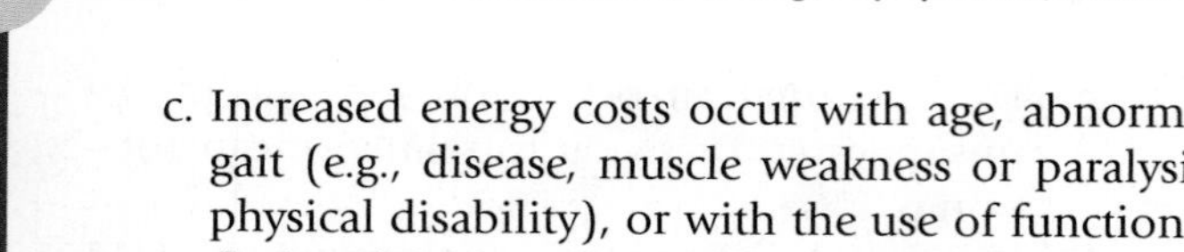

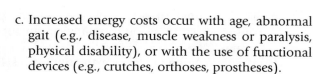

c. Increased energy costs occur with age, abnormal gait (e.g., disease, muscle weakness or paralysis, physical disability), or with the use of functional devices (e.g., crutches, orthoses, prostheses).

Common Gait Deviations: Stance Phase

1. Trunk and hip.
   a. Lateral trunk bending: the result of weak gluteus medius; will see bending to the same side as the weakness (Trendelenburg gait); also seen with pain in the hip.
   b. Backward trunk lean: the result of weak gluteus maximus; will also see difficulty going up stairs or ramps.
   c. Forward trunk lean: the result of weak quadriceps (decreases flexor movement at the knee), hip and knee flexion contractures.
   d. Excessive hip flexion: the result of weak hip extensors or tight hip and/or knee flexors.
   e. Limited hip extension: the result of tight or spastic hip flexors.
   f. Limited hip flexion: the result of weak hip flexors or tight extensors.
   g. Abnormal synergistic activity (e.g., stroke): excessive hip adduction combined with hip and knee extension, plantarflexion; scissoring or adducted gait pattern.
   h. Antalgic gait (painful gait): stance time is abbreviated on the painful limb that results in an uneven gait pattern; the uninvolved limb has a shortened step length since it must bear weight sooner than normal.
2. Knee.
   a. Excessive knee flexion: the result of weak quadriceps (knee wobbles or buckles) or knee flexor contracture.
      (1) Will also see difficulty going down stairs or ramps.
      (2) Forward trunk bending can compensate for weak quadriceps.
   b. Hyperextension: the result of a weak quadriceps, plantar flexion contracture, or extensor spasticity (quadriceps and/or plantar flexion).
3. Ankle/foot.
   a. Toe first: toes contact at heel strike; the result of weak dorsiflexors, spastic or tight plantarflexors; may also be caused by a shortened leg (leg length discrepancy); painful heel; or positive support reflex.
   b. Foot slap: the foot makes floor contact with an audible slap; the result of weak dorsiflexors or hypotonia; compensated for with steppage gait.
   c. Foot flat: entire foot contacts ground; the result of weak dorsiflexors, limited range of motion (ROM); immature gait pattern (neonatal).
   d. Excessive dorsiflexion with uncontrolled forward motion of the tibia (calcaneus gait): the result of weak plantarflexors.
   e. Excessive plantarflexion (equinus gait): heel does not touch the ground; the result of spasticity or contracture of the plantar flexors; will see poor eccentric contraction and advancement of the tibia.
   f. Supination: excessive lateral contact of foot during stance with varus position of calcaneus. May occur at initial contact and correct at footflat with weight acceptance or remain throughout stance. Possible causes: spastic invertors, weak evertors, pes varus, genu varum.
   g. Pronation: excessive medial contact of foot during stance with valgus position of calcaneus. Possible causes: weak invertors, spasticity, pes valgus, genu valgum.
   h. Toes claw: the result of spastic toe flexors, possibly a hyperactive plantar grasp reflex.
   i. Inadequate push-off: the result of weak plantar flexors, decreased ROM, or pain in the forefoot.

Common Gait Deviations: Swing Phase

1. Trunk and hip.
   a. Insufficient forward pelvic rotation (stiff pelvis, pelvic retraction): the result of weak abdominal muscles, weak flexor muscles (e.g., stroke).
   b. Insufficient hip and knee flexion: the result of weak hip and knee flexors; inability to lift the leg and move it forward.
   c. Circumduction: the leg swings out to the side (abduction/external rotation followed by adduction/internal rotation); the result of weak hip and knee flexors.
   d. Hip hiking (quadratus lumborum action): a compensatory response for weak hip and knee flexors, or extensor spasticity.
   e. Excessive hip and knee flexion (steppage gait): a compensatory response to shorten the leg; the result of weak dorsiflexors (e.g., diabetic neuropathy of the fibular nerve).
   f. Abnormal synergistic activity (e.g., stroke): excessive hip and knee flexion with abduction.
2. Knee.
   a. Insufficient knee flexion: the result of extensor spasticity, pain/decreased ROM, or weak hamstrings.
   b. Excessive knee flexion: the result of flexor spasticity; flexor withdrawal reflex.
3. Ankle/foot.
   a. Foot drop (equinus): the result of weak or delayed contraction of the dorsiflexors or spastic plantarflexors.
   b. Varus or inverted foot: the result of spastic invertors (anterior tibialis), weak peroneals, or abnormal synergistic pattern (e.g., stroke).
   c. Equinovarus: the result of spasticity of the posterior tibialis and/or gastrocnemius-soleus; developmental abnormality.

Ambulatory Aids

Canes

1. Indications.
   a. Widen base of support to improve balance; provide limited stability and unweighting (can unload forces on involved extremity by 30%); can be used to relieve pain, antalgic gait.
2. Cane measurement.
   a. 20°–30° of elbow flexion is desirable.
   b. Measure from the greater trochanter to a point 6 inches to the side of the toes.
3. Types.
   a. Wood or aluminum (adjustable with push pin lock).
   b. Standard, single point cane: handle and shaft may be standard (J-shaped) or offset.
   c. Quad cane: four contact points with the ground; provides increased stability but slows gait.
      (1) Small-based quad cane (SBQC): useful for stairs.
      (2) Wide-based quad cane (WBQC): does not fit on stairs.
4. Gait:
   a. Cane is held in the hand opposite to the involved extremity; cane and involved extremity are advanced together, followed by the uninvolved extremity.

Crutches

1. Indications.
   a. Used to increase the base of support, provide moderate degree of stability, or relieve weight bearing on the lower extremities.
2. Crutch measurement.
   a. 20°–30° of elbow flexion is desirable.
   b. For standing patients, subtract 16 inches from the patient's height or measure from a point 2 inches below the axilla to a point 6 inches in front and 2 inches lateral to the foot.
   c. For supine patients, measure from the axilla to a point 6–8 inches lateral to the heel.
   d. Forearm crutches: the cuff should cover the proximal third of the forearm, 1–1½ inches below the elbow.
3. Types.
   a. Axillary crutches: wood or aluminum designs; handgrip height and crutch height adjusted by wingnuts; push-button locks with telescoping legs on some aluminum crutches; axillary pads cushion the top of crutch.
      (1) Provide increased upper-extremity weight bearing over forearm crutches.
      (2) May be difficult to use in small areas.
      (3) Prolonged leaning on the axillary bar can result in vascular and/or nerve damage (axillary artery/radial nerve).
   b. Forearm (Lofstrand) crutches: have a forearm cuff and a hand grip; provide slightly less stability but increased ease of movement; frees hands for use without dropping the crutch (secured by cuff).
   c. Forearm platform crutches: allow weight bearing on the forearm; used for patients who are unable to bear weight through their hands; e.g., patients with arthritis; platforms can also be attached to walkers.
   d. Crutch tips: rubber ~1.5 inches in diameter; provide suction, minimize slippage.

Walkers

1. Indications.
   a. Widen base of support, provide increased lateral and anterior stability, can reduce weight bearing on one or both lower extremities; easy to use; frequently prescribed for patients with debilitating conditions, poor balance, or lower extremity injury when use of crutches is precluded; e.g., elderly patients. Negative features include no reciprocal arm swing and increased flexor posture.
2. Types of walkers.
   a. Folding (collapsible): facilitate mobility in the community, cars.
   b. Rolling (wheeled): available with either two or four wheels (four wheels require hand brake to provide added stability in stopping); facilitates walking as a continuous movement sequence (step-through gait pattern); allows for increased speed.
   c. Stair-climbing walker: has two posterior extensions and additional handgrips off the rear legs for use on stairs.
   d. Reciprocal walkers: hinged, allow advancement of one side of walker at a time; used with reciprocal gait patterns, reciprocating orthoses.
   e. Hemi walker: modified for use with one hand only.
   f. Attachments: fold-down seats, carrying baskets.
3. Measurement.
   a. Same as for cane.

Bariatric Equipment

1. See discussion of obesity in Chapter 6.
2. Selection: based on specific patient needs (patient safety, gait pattern, fatigue) and weight capacity.

3. Typical gait changes: include greater hip abduction and hip rotation, less knee flexion, difficulty rotating from side to side with increased girth.
4. Heavy duty mechanical lifts: used to help transfer patients (e.g., sit-to-stand).
5. Heavy duty, extra-wide walkers: used to assist ambulation.

Gait Patterns: Use of Assistive Devices

1. Weight-bearing status.
   a. Non–weight bearing: no weight bearing is permitted.
   b. Partial weight bearing: toes or ball of involved foot contacts with the floor; allows a limited amount of weight bearing.
   c. Full weight bearing: full weight is permitted on the involved extremity. Weight can be objectively controlled by means of a limb load monitor.
2. Two-point gait.
   a. One crutch and opposite extremity move together, followed by the opposite crutch and extremity; requires use of two assistive devices (canes or crutches).
   b. Allows for natural arm and leg motion during gait, good support and stability from two opposing points of contact.
3. Three-point gait.
   a. Both crutches and involved leg are advanced together, then uninvolved leg is advanced forward; requires use of two assistive devices (crutches or canes) or a walker.
   b. Indicated for use with involvement of one extremity; e.g., lower extremity fracture.
4. Four-point gait.
   a. A slow gait pattern in which one crutch is advanced forward and placed on the floor, followed by advancement of the opposite leg; then the remaining crutch is advanced forward, followed by the opposite remaining leg; requires the use of two assistive devices (crutches or canes).
   b. Provides maximum stability with three points of support while one limb is moving.
5. Swing-to gait.
   a. Both crutches are advanced forward together; weight is shifted onto hands for support and both legs are then swung forward to meet the crutches; requires the use of two crutches or a walker.
   b. Indicated for individuals with limited use of both lower extremities and trunk instability.
6. Swing-through gait.
   a. Both crutches are advanced forward together; weight is shifted onto hands and both legs, which are swung forward beyond the point of crutch placement; requires the use of two crutches.
   b. Both swing-to and swing-through gaits are used for bilateral lower extremity involvement, and trunk instability; e.g., patient with paraplegia, spina bifida. Not as safe as swing-to gait.
7. Stairs.
   a. Ascent: the uninvolved leg always goes up first, followed by the crutches (or cane) and the involved leg together.
   b. Descent: the crutches (or cane) and involved leg go down first, followed by the uninvolved leg.
   c. Mnemonic devices to teach patient: "The good go to heaven, the bad go to hell." "Up with the good, down with the bad."

Guarding

1. Indication: protects the patient from falling; requires the use of a gait belt for initial training for most patients.
2. Level surfaces: stand slightly behind and to one side, typically on the more involved side.
3. Stairs: therapist is positioned below the patient.
   a. Ascent: stand behind and slightly to the involved side.
   b. Descent: stand in front and slightly to the involved side.
4. Sit-to-stand transfers.
   a. Stand to one side and slightly behind the patient.
   b. Increased levels of assistance may require therapist to stand in front of patient.

Locomotor Training

1. Body weight support (BWS) and motorized treadmill.
   a. BWS: an overhead harness is used to support body weight.
      (1) Initially, support is high (e.g., 40% of body weight), progresses to less weight support (30%, 20%, 10%), to no body weight support.
      (2) BWS > 55% is contraindicated as it interferes with gait cycle (unable to achieve flat foot during stepping).
   b. Motorized treadmill training.
      (1) Progresses from treadmill walking with slow speeds (e.g., 0.6–0.8 mph) to faster, near-normal walking speeds (e.g., 2.6–2.8 mph).
      (2) Progresses from level walking to slight incline walking.
      (3) Progresses from treadmill walking to overground walking.

c. Manual assistance:
   (1) Level of assistance decreases as training progresses (maxA, to modA, to minA, to no assistance).
   (2) Assistance can include hands on pelvis (assisted pelvic motions) and hands on lower extremity (assisted stepping).

2. Robotic ambulation assistance.
   a. Can also be used to improve gait pattern and ambulatory status (e.g., Lokomat).
   b. Indications: Patients with paraparesis.
3. Conventional over-ground training.

Orthotics

General Concepts

1. Orthosis is a device used to:
   a. Correct malalignment and prevent deformity.
   b. Restrict or assist motion.
   c. Transfer load to improve function.
   d. Reduce pain.
2. Splint.
   a. A temporary device that may serve the same functions.
   b. Materials generally not as durable, able to withstand prolonged use.
3. Three-point pressure principle.
   a. Forms the mechanical basis for orthotic correction.
   b. A single force is placed at the area of deformity or angulation; two additional counterforces act in the opposing direction.
4. Alignment.
   a. Correct alignment permits effective function.
   b. Minimizes movement between limb and orthoses (pistoning).
   c. Minimizes compression on pressure-sensitive tissues.

Lower-Limb Orthoses: Components/Terminology

1. Shoes.
   a. The foundation for an orthosis; shoes can reduce areas of concentrated pressure on pressure-sensitive feet.
   b. Traditional leather orthopedic shoes or athletic sneakers can be worn with orthoses; attachments can be external (to the outer part of a leather shoe's sole) or internal (a molded shoe insert).
   c. Blucher opening: has vamps (the flaps contain the lace stays) that open wide apart from the anterior margin of the shoe for ease of application.
   d. Bal (Balmoral) opening: has stitched down vamps, not suitable for orthotic wear.
2. Foot orthosis (FO).
   a. May be attached to the interior of the shoe (e.g., an inserted pad) or the exterior of the shoe (e.g., Thomas heel).
   b. Soft inserts (i.e., viscoelastic plastic or rubber pads or relief cut-outs) reduce areas of high loading, restrict forces, and protect painful or sensitive areas of the feet.
      (1) Metatarsal pad: located posterior to metatarsal heads; moves pressure from the metatarsal heads to the metatarsal shafts; allows more push-off in weak or inflexible feet.
      (2) Cushion heel: cushions and absorbs forces at heel contact; used to relieve strain on plantar fascia in plantar fasciitis.
      (3) Heel-spur pad.
   c. Longitudinal arch supports: prevent depression of the subtalar joint and correct for pes planus (flat foot); flat foot can be flexible or rigid.
      (1) UCBL (University of California Biomechanics Laboratory) insert: a semirigid plastic molded insert to correct for flexible pes planus.
      (2) Scaphoid pad: used to support the longitudinal arch.
      (3) Thomas heel: a heel wedge with an extended anterior medial border used to support the longitudinal arch and correct for flexible pes valgus (pronated foot).
   d. Posting.
      (1) Rearfoot posting: alters the position of the subtalar joint (STJ), or rearfoot, from heel strike to footflat. Must be dynamic, control but not eliminate STJ motion.
         (a) Varus post (medial wedge): limits or controls eversion of the calcaneus and internal rotation of the tibia after heelstrike. Reduces calcaneal eversion during running.
         (b) Valgus post (lateral wedge): controls the calcaneus and subtalar joint that are excessively inverted and supinated at heel strike.
      (2) Forefoot posting: supports the forefoot.
         (a) Medial wedge prescribed for forefoot varus.
         (b) Lateral wedge prescribed for forefoot valgus.

(3) Contraindicated in the insensitive foot.

e. Heel lifts (or heel platform).

(1) Accommodates for leg length discrepancy; can be placed inside the shoe (up to 3/8 inch) or attached to the outer sole.

(2) Accommodates for limitation in ankle joint dorsiflexion.

f. Rocker bar: located proximal to metatarsal heads; improves weight shift onto metatarsals.

g. Rocker bottom: builds up the sole over the metatarsal heads and improves push-off in weak or inflexible feet. May also be used with insensitive feet.

3. Ankle-foot orthosis (AFO).

a. Consists of a shoe attachment, ankle control, uprights, and a proximal leg band.

b. Shoe attachments.

(1) Foot plate: a molded plastic shoe insert; allows application of the brace before insertion into the shoe, ease of changing shoes of same heel height.

(2) Stirrup: a metal attachment riveted to the sole of the shoe; split stirrups allow for shoe interchange; solid stirrups are fixed permanently to the shoe and provide for maximum stability.

c. Ankle controls.

(1) Free motion: provides mediolateral stability that allows free motion in dorsiflexion and plantar flexion.

(2) Solid ankle: allows no movement; indicated with severe pain or instability.

(3) Limited motion: allows motion to be restricted in one or both directions.

(a) Bichannel adjustable ankle lock (BiCAAL): an ankle joint with the anterior and posterior channels that can be fit with pins to reduce motion or springs to assist motion.

(b) Anterior stop (dorsiflexion stop): determines the limits of ankle dorsiflexion. In an AFO, if the stop is set to allow slight dorsiflexion (5°), knee flexion results; can be used to control for knee hyperextension; if the stop is set to allow too much dorsiflexion, knee buckling could result.

(c) Posterior stop (plantar flexion stop): determines the limits of ankle plantar flexion. In an AFO, if the stop is set to allow slight plantar flexion (5°), knee extension results; can be used to control for an unstable knee that buckles; if the stop is set to allow too much plantar flexion, recurvatum or knee hyperextension could result.

(d) Solid AFO: limits all foot and ankle motion.

(4) Dorsiflexion assistance.

(a) Spring assist (Klenzak housing): double upright metal AFO with a single anterior channel for a spring assist to aid dorsiflexion.

(b) Posterior leaf spring (PLS): a plastic AFO that inserts into the shoe; widely used to prevent drop foot.

(5) Varus or valgus correction straps (T straps): control for varus or valgus forces at the ankle. Medial strap buckles around the lateral upright and corrects for valgus; lateral strap buckles around the medial upright and corrects for varus.

d. Uprights and attachments (bands or shells).

(1) Conventional AFOs have metal uprights (aluminum, carbon graphite, or steel) and a hinged ankle joint allowing plantarflexion and dorsiflexion. Provides maximum support; if the patient's condition is changing (e.g., peripheral edema), conventional metal AFOs may be easier to alter to accommodate changes than molded AFOs.

(a) Double metal uprights extend upward from the ankle on both sides of the leg and attach to a calf band.

(b) Conventional AFO, calf band (metal with leather lining or plastic); provides for proximal stabilization on leg; anterior opening and buckle or Velcro closure.

(2) Molded AFOs are made of molded plastic and are lighter in weight and cosmetically more appealing; contraindicated for individuals with changing leg volume.

(a) Posterior leaf spring (PLS): has a flexible, narrow posterior shell; functions as dorsiflexion assist; holds foot at 90° angle during swing; displaced during stance; provides no medial-lateral stability.

(b) Modified AFO: has a wider posterior shell with trimlines just posterior to malleoli; foot plate includes more of medial and lateral borders of foot; provides more medial-lateral stability (control of calcaneal and forefoot inversion and eversion).

(c) Solid ankle AFO: has widest posterior shell with trimlines extending forward to malleoli; controls (prevents) dorsiflexion, plantarflexion, inversion, and eversion.

(d) Spiral AFO: a molded plastic AFO that winds (spirals) around the calf; provides limited control of motion in all planes.

(e) Hinged plastic AFOs are available.

(3) Specialized AFOs.

(a) Patellar-tendon-bearing brim: allows for weight distribution on the patellar shelf similar to patellar-tendon-bearing prosthetic socket; reduces weight-bearing forces through the foot.

(b) Tone-reducing orthosis: molded plastic AFO that applies constant pressure to spastic or hypertonic muscles (plantarflexors and invertors); snug fit is essential to achieve the benefits of reciprocal inhibition.

4. Knee-ankle-foot orthosis (KAFO).
   a. Consists of a shoe attachment, ankle control, uprights, knee control, and bands or shells for the calf and thigh.
   b. Knee controls.
      (1) Hinge joint: provides mediolateral and hyperextension control while allowing for flexion and extension.
         (a) Offset: the hinge is placed posterior to the weight-bearing line (trochanter-knee-ankle [TKA] line); assists extension, stabilizes knee during early stance; patients may have difficulty on ramps where knee may flex inadvertently.
      (2) Locks.
         (a) Drop ring lock: ring drops over joint when knee is in full extension to provide maximum stability; a retention button may be added to hold the ring lock up, permit gait training with the knee unlocked.
         (b) Pawl lock with bail release: the pawl is a spring-loaded posterior projection (lever or ring) that allows the patient to unlock the knee by pulling up or hooking the pawl on the back of a chair and pushing it up; adds bulk and may unlock inadvertently with posterior knee pressure.
      (3) Knee stability.
         (a) Sagittal stability achieved by bands or straps used to provide a posteriorly directed force.
            • Anterior band or strap (knee cap): attaches by four buckles to metal uprights; may restrict sitting, increases difficulty in putting on KAFO.
            • Anterior bands: pretibial or suprapatellar or both.
         (b) Frontal plane controls: for control of genu varum or genu valgum.
            • Posterior plastic shell.
            • Older braces utilize valgum (medial) or varum (lateral) correction straps, which buckle around the opposite metal upright; less effective as controls than plastic shell.
   c. Thigh bands.
      (1) Proximal thigh band.
      (2) Quadrilateral or ischial weight-bearing brim: reduces weight bearing through the limb.
         (a) Patten bottom: a distal attachment added to keep the foot off the floor; provides 100% unweighting of the limb; a lift is required on the opposite leg, e.g., used with Legg-Calvé-Perthes disease.
   d. Specialized KAFOs.
      (1) Craig-Scott KAFO: commonly used appliance for individuals with paraplegia; consists of shoe attachments with reinforced foot plates, BiCAAL ankle joints set in slight dorsiflexion, pretibial band, pawl knee locks with bail release, and single thigh bands.
      (2) Oregon orthotic system: a combination of plastic and metal components allows for triplanar control in three planes of motion (sagittal, frontal, and transverse).
      (3) Fracture braces: a KAFO device with a calf or thigh shell that encompasses the fracture site and provides support.
      (4) Functional electrical stimulation (FES) orthosis: orthotic use and functional ambulation is facilitated by the addition of electrical stimulation to specific muscles; the pattern and sequence of muscle activation by portable stimulators is controlled by an externally worn miniaturized computer pack; requires full passive range of motion (PROM); good functional endurance; in limited use with individuals with paraplegia, drop foot; also scoliosis.
   e. Standing frames.
      (1) Standing frames: allows for standing without crutch support; may be stationary or attached to a wheeled mobility base (e.g., used with some patients with [SCI]).
      (2) Parapodium: allows for standing without crutch support; also allows for ease in sitting with the addition of hip and knee joints that can be unlocked (e.g., used with children with myelodysplasia).

5. Specialized knee orthosis (KO).
   a. Articulated KO: controls knee motion and provides added stability.
      (1) Postsurgery KO protects repaired ligaments from overload.
      (2) Functional KO is worn long-term in lieu of surgery or during selected activities (sports competitions).
      (3) Examples include Lenox Hill, Pro-AM, Can-Am, Don Joy.
   b. Swedish knee cage: provides mild control for excessive hyperextension of the knee.
   c. Patellar stabilizing braces.
      (1) Improve patellar tracking; maintain alignment.
      (2) Lateral buttress (often made of felt) or strap positions patella medially.
      (3) A central patellar cutout may help positioning and minimizes compression.
   d. Neoprene sleeves.
      (1) Nylon-coated rubber material.
      (2) Provide compression, protection, and proprioceptive feedback.

(3) Provide little stabilization unless metal or plastic hinges are added.
(4) Retains body heat, which may increase local circulation.
(5) A central cutout minimizes patellar compression.
(6) Can be used in other areas of the body, such as elbow, thigh, and so on.

6. Hip-knee-ankle-foot orthosis (HKAFO).
   a. Contain a hip joint and pelvic band added to a KAFO.
   b. Hip joint: typically a metal hinge joint.
      (1) Controls for abduction, adduction, and rotation.
      (2) Controls for hip flexion when locked, typically with a drop ring lock; a locked hip restricts gait pattern to either swing-to or swing-through.
   c. Pelvic attachments: a leather-covered, metal pelvic band; attaches the HKAFO to the pelvis between the greater trochanter and iliac crest; adds to difficulty in donning and doffing; adds weight and increases overall energy expenditure during ambulation.
7. Specialized trunk-hip-knee-ankle-foot orthosis (THKAFO).
   a. Contains a trunk band added to a HKAFO.
   b. Reciprocating gait orthosis (RGO): utilizes plastic molded solid-ankle orthoses with locked knees, plastic thigh shells, a hip joint with pelvic and trunk bands; the hips are connected by steel cables, which allow for a reciprocal gait pattern (either four-point or two-point); when the patient leans on the supporting hip, it forces it into extension, while the opposite leg is pushed into flexion; allows limb advancement.
8. Specialized lower limb devices.
   a. Denis Browne splint: a bar connecting two shoes that can swivel; used for correction of club foot or pes equinovarus in young children.
   b. Frejka pillow: keeps hips abducted; used for hip dysplasia or other conditions with tight adductors in young children.
   c. Toronto hip abduction orthosis: abducts the hip; used in treatment of Legg-Calve-Perthes disease.

Spinal (Trunk) Orthoses: Components/Terminology

1. Corset.
   a. Provides abdominal compression, increases intra-abdominal pressure.
   b. Assists respiration in individuals with spinal cord injury.
   c. Relieves pain in low back disorders; sacroiliac support; e.g., pregnancy.
2. Lumbosacral orthosis (LSO).
   a. Controls or limits lumbosacral motions.
   b. Lumbosacral flexion, extension, lateral control orthoses (LS FEL) (Knight spinal): includes pelvic and thoracic bands to anchor the orthosis with two posterior uprights, two lateral uprights, and an anterior corset.
   c. Plastic lumbosacral jacket: provides maximum support by spreading forces over a larger area; more cosmetic, but hotter.
3. Thoracolumbosacral orthosis (TLSO).
   a. Controls or limits thoracic and lumbosacral motions.
   b. Thoracolumbosacral flexion, extension control orthosis (TLS FE) (Taylor brace): includes components of a LS FEL with the addition of axillary shoulder straps to limit upper trunk flexion.
   c. Plastic thoracolumbosacral jacket: provides maximum support and control of all motions; used in individuals recovering from spinal cord injury; allows for early mobilization out-of-bed and functional training.
   d. Jewett (TLSO): limits flexion, but encourages hyperextension (lordosis); used for compression fractures of the spine.
4. Cervical orthosis (CO).
   a. Controls or limits cervical motion.
   b. Soft collar: provides minimal levels of control of cervical motions; e.g., cervical pain, whiplash.
   c. Four-poster orthosis: has two plates (occipital and thoracic) with two anterior and two posterior posts to stabilize the head; used for moderate levels of control in individuals with cervical fracture/spinal cord injury.
   d. Halo orthosis: attaches to the skull with screws; four uprights connect from the halo to a thoracic band or plastic jacket; provides maximal control for patients with cervical fracture/spinal cord injury; allows for early mobilization out-of-bed and functional training.
   e. Minerva orthosis: a rigid plastic appliance that provides maximum control of cervical motion; uses a forehead band without screws.
5. Specialized trunk orthoses.
   a. Milwaukee orthosis: a cervical, thoracic, lumbosacral orthosis (CTLSO) used to control scoliosis; it has a molded plastic pelvic jacket with one anterior and two posterior uprights extended to a superior neck or chest ring; pads and straps are used to apply pressure to areas of convexity of spinal curves; bulky, less cosmetic; may be used for all kyphotic and scoliotic curves of $\leq 40°$.
   b. Boston orthosis (TLSO): a low-profile, molded plastic orthosis for scoliosis; more cosmetic, can be worn under clothing; used for midthoracic or lower scoliosis curves of $\leq 40°$; also used to treat spondylolisthesis and conditions of severe trunk weakness; e.g., muscular dystrophy.

Upper-Limb Orthoses: Components/Terminology

1. Functional considerations:
   a. Most upper limb (UL) orthoses are directed toward creating usable prehension, functional hand position.
2. Passive (static) positioning devices.
   a. Generally made out of a variety of low-temperature plastic; i.e., Orthoplast, Hexalite.
   b. Resting splint (cock-up splint): an anterior or palmar splint that positions the wrist and hand in a functional position.
      (1) Wrist can be held in neutral or in 12°–20° wrist extension.
      (2) Fingers supported, phalanges slightly flexed, with thumb in partial opposition and abduction.
      (3) Used for patients with rheumatoid arthritis, fractures of carpal bones, Colles' fracture, carpal tunnel syndrome, stroke with paralysis, etc.
   c. Dorsal wrist splint: frees the palm for feeling and grasping through the use of grips that curve around over the second and fifth metacarpal heads; allows for the attachment of dorsal devices (i.e., rubber bands) to form a dynamic device.
   d. Airplane splint: positions the patient's arm out to the side at 90° of abduction, with elbow flexed to 90°; the weight of the outstretched arm is borne on a padded lateral trunk bar and iliac crest band; a strap holds the device across the trunk; used to immobilize the shoulder following fracture or injury when strapping to the chest is not desirable, or with burns.
3. Dynamic devices.
   a. Wrist-driven prehension orthosis (flexor hinge orthosis): assists patients in use of wrist extensors to approximate the thumb and forefingers (grip) in the absence of active finger flexion; e.g., facilitates tenodesis grasp in patients with quadriplegia.
   b. Motor-driven flexor hinge orthosis: complex control systems that allow for grasp; not generally in widespread use.

Physical Therapy Intervention

1. Team: in the clinic, the physical therapist functions as a member of an orthotic clinic team that includes the physician, orthotist, and therapists.
2. Examination.
   a. Preorthotic assessment and prescription evaluate:
      (1) Joint mobility.
      (2) Sensation.
      (3) Strength and motor function.
      (4) Functional level.
      (5) Psychological status.
   b. Orthotic prescription: Considerations.
      (1) Patient's abilities and needs.
         (a) Level of impairments, functional limitations, disability.
         (b) Status: Consider whether the patient's condition is permanent or changing.
      (2) Level of function, current lifestyle.
         (a) Consider whether the patient is going to be a community ambulator versus a household ambulator.
         (b) Consider recreational and work-related needs.
      (3) Overall weight of orthotic devices, energy capabilities of patient. Some individuals abandon their orthoses quickly in favor of wheelchairs because of the high-energy demands of ambulating with orthoses; e.g., patients with high levels of paraplegia.
      (4) Manual dexterity, mental capacity of the individual. The donning and use of devices may be too difficult or complicated for some individuals.
      (5) Pressure tolerance of the skin and tissues.
      (6) Use of a temporary orthosis to assess likelihood of functional independence, reduce costs; e.g., patients with high levels of paraplegia.
   c. Orthotic check-out.
      (1) Ensure proper fit and function; construction of the orthosis.
      (2) Static assessment.
         (a) Examine alignments for lower limb orthoses: In midstance, foot should be flat on floor.
            - Orthotic hip joint: 0.8 cm (0.3 in) anterior and superior to greater trochanter.
            - Medial knee joint: ~2 cm (~0.8 in) above joint space, vertically midway between medial joint space and adductor tubercle.
            - Ankle joint: at tip of malleolus.
            - Plastic shells or metal uprights, thigh and calf bands: conform to contours of limb.
            - No undue tissue pressure or restriction of function.
      (3) Dynamic assessment.
         (a) Fit and function during activities of daily living (ADLs), functional mobility skills; e.g., sit-to-stand.
         (b) Fit and function during gait.
3. Orthotic training.
   a. Instruct the patient in procedures for orthotic maintenance: routine skin inspection and care.
   b. Ensure orthotic acceptance.
      (1) Patient should clearly understand functions, limitations of an orthosis.
      (2) Can use support groups to assist.

c. Teach proper application (donning/doffing) of the orthosis.
d. Teach proper use of the orthosis.
   (1) Balance training.
   (2) Gait training.
   (3) Functional activities training.
e. Reassess fit, function, and construction of the orthosis at periodic intervals; assess habitual use of the orthosis.

4. Selected orthotic gait deviations.
   a. Lateral trunk bending: patient leans toward the orthotic side during stance. Possible causes: KAFO medial upright too high; insufficient shoe lift; hip pain, weak or tight abductors on the orthotic side; short leg; poor balance.
   b. Circumduction: during swing, leg swings out to the side in an arc. Possible causes: locked knee; excessive plantar flexion (inadequate stop, plantar flexion contractures); weak hip flexors or dorsiflexors. All of these could also cause vaulting (rising up on the sound limb to advance the orthotic limb forward).
   c. Anterior trunk bending: patient leans forward during stance. Possible causes: inadequate knee lock; weak quadriceps; hip or knee flexion contracture.
   d. Posterior trunk bending: patient leans backward during stance. Possible causes: inadequate hip lock; weak gluteus maximus; knee ankylosis.
   e. Hyperextended knee: excessive extension during stance. Possible causes: inadequate plantar flexion stop; inadequate knee lock; poor fit of calf band (too deep); weak quadriceps; loose knee ligaments or extensor spasticity; pes equinus.
   f. Knee instability: excessive knee flexion during stance. Possible causes: inadequate dorsiflexion stop; inadequate knee lock; knee and/or hip flexion contracture; weak quadriceps or insufficient knee lock; knee pain.
   g. Foot slap: foot hits the ground during early stance. Possible causes: inadequate dorsiflexor assist; inadequate plantarflexor stop; weak dorsiflexors.
   h. Toes first: on-toes posture during stance. Possible causes: inadequate dorsiflexor assist; inadequate plantarflexor stop; inadequate heel lift; heel pain, extensor spasticity; pes equinus; short leg.
   i. Flat foot: contact with entire foot. Possible causes: inadequate longitudinal arch support; pes planus.
   j. Pronation: excessive medial foot contact during stance, valgus position of calcaneus. Possible causes: transverse plane malalignment; weak invertors; pes valgus; spasticity; genu valgum.
   k. Supination: excessive lateral foot contact during stance, varus position of the calcaneus. Possible causes: transverse plane malalignment; weak evertors; pes varus; genu varum.
   l. Excessive stance width: patient stands or walks with a wide base of support. Possible causes: KAFO height of medial upright too high; HKAFO hip joint aligned in excessive abduction; knee is locked; abduction contracture; poor balance; sound limb is too short.

Adhesive Taping

General Concepts

1. Purpose.
   a. Limit ROM of specific joints.
   b. Support injured body segment.
   c. Secure protective devices such as felt, foam, gel, or plastic padding, orthoplast or plastazote.
   d. Keep dressings and bandages in place and secure.
   e. Preventive support for a joint that is at risk.
   f. Realign position and reduce pain; e.g., McConnell treatment for patellofemoral pain.
   g. May enhance proprioception.
   h. Elastic therapeutic tape (e.g., Kinesio tape) is an acrylic adhesive backed with an elastic strip. It is used with athletes and others with impairments ostensibly to alleviate pain, enhance performance, relax muscles, support muscles, and reduce inflammation. Research has shown little evidence of benefit except for reducing pain.
2. Preparation.
   a. Part to be taped should be properly positioned and supported.
   b. Select appropriate type and width of tape.
   c. Body hair should be shaved, skin should be clean. Foam underwrap or stockinet may be used.
   d. Lubricated pads should be placed over areas of potential blister formation from friction. e.g.; heel and lace-area pads on the foot.
   e. Occlusive dressings should be applied over wounds or skin conditions to be covered by the tape.
   f. Skin adherent such as benzoin should be applied to increase adhesion of the tape and to aid in toughening the skin to decrease irritation.
3. Application.
   a. If the part has not been previously injured, it should be taped in a neutral position.
   b. Injured ligaments should be held in a shortened position.

(1) Lateral or inversion ankle sprains should be taped in an everted position.

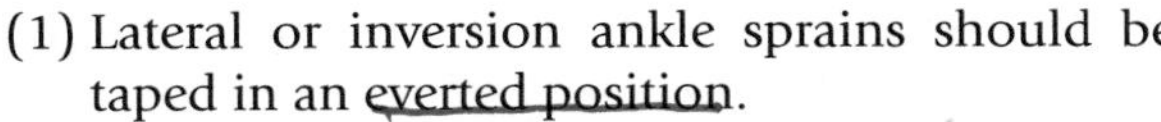

(2) Tape should follow body contours and be applied primarily from medial to lateral in the case of an inversion sprain.

c. Tape should be applied with even pressure, and with overlap of previous tape strip by one-half.

d. Circular strapping should be applied very cautiously due to potential circulatory compromise.

e. Avoid creases and folds.

f. If tape is too tight, adjust by removing or modifying strips or reapply.

g. Elastic therapeutic tape is applied in a variety of configurations according to manufacturer's specifications.

4. Complications.

a. Allergic reactions to the tape.

b. Skin irritation.

c. Reduced circulation.

d. If tape is too tight, it might compromise the ability of the patient to perform the skill intended.

e. Tape may lose its effectiveness in an hour or so, and may need to be reapplied.

Prosthetics

General Concepts

1. Prosthesis.
   a. A replacement of a body part with an artificial device; an artificial limb.
2. Levels of amputation.
   a. Transmetatarsal amputation: partial foot amputation.
   b. Ankle disarticulation (Syme's): amputation through the ankle joint; heel pad is preserved and attached to distal end of tibia for weight bearing.
   c. Transtibial amputation: below-knee (BK) amputation; ideally, 20%–50% of the tibial length is spared; short transtibial is < 20% of tibial length.
   d. Knee disarticulation: amputation through the knee joint; femur is intact.
   e. Transfemoral amputation: above-knee (AK) amputation; ideally 35%–60% of the femoral length is spared; short transfemoral is < 35% of femoral length.
   f. Hip disarticulation: amputation of entire lower limb, pelvis is preserved.
   g. Hemipelvectomy: amputation of entire lower limb, lower half of the pelvis is resected.
   h. Hemicorporectomy: amputation of both lower limbs and pelvis below L4, L5 level.
   i. Transradial amputation: below-elbow (BE) amputation.
   j. Elbow disarticulation: amputation through the elbow joint.
   k. Transhumeral amputation: above-elbow (AE) amputation.
   l. Shoulder disarticulation: amputation through the shoulder joint.
3. Components.
   a. All prosthetic devices contain a socket and terminal device with varying components in between.
   b. Sockets are custom-molded to the residual limb; total contact is desired, with the load distributed to all tissues; assists in circulation and provides maximal sensory feedback.
      (1) Functions to:
         (a) Contain the residual tissues.
         (b) Provide a means to suspend the prosthetic limb.
         (c) Transfer forces from the prosthesis to the residual limb.
      (2) Selective loading: pressure-tolerant areas are built up to increase loading (i.e., build-ups for tendon-bearing areas), while pressure-sensitive areas are relieved to decrease loading (i.e., relief for bony prominences, nerves, and tendons).
      (3) Types.
         (a) A socket made of hard plastic with a soft polyethylene foam liner is the most common type; removable liners aid in ease of prosthetic donning and adjustment.
         (b) Flexible sockets are made of soft, pliable thermoplastic material within a rigid frame; used for most AK sockets due to better suspension.
      (4) Socks.
         (a) Used in every suspension system except suction.
         (b) Provide a soft interface between the residual limb and the socket; minimize shear forces between socket and skin.
         (c) Changing sock thickness or adding more socks can assist in accommodating to changes in volume of residual limb, prevent pistoning.
         (d) Excessive thickness of socks (> 15 ply) can alter fit and weight-bearing ability of the socket.
   c. Terminal device (TD).
      (1) Provides an interface between the amputee's prosthesis with the external environment.
      (2) Lower-limb prosthesis: TD is a foot.
      (3) Upper-limb prosthesis: TD is a hook or hand.

Lower-Limb Prosthetics (LLPs)

1. Partial-foot prosthesis.
   a. Plastic foot replacement: restores foot length, protects amputated stump.
   b. Function may be assisted by the addition of a rocker bottom or plastic calf shell.
2. Transtibial (below knee) prosthesis.
   a. Foot-ankle assembly.
      (1) Functions to:
         (a) Absorb shock at heel strike.
         (b) Plantarflex in early stance, permits metatarsophalangeal hyperextension in late stance.
         (c) Cosmetic replacement of foot.
      (2) Solid ankle cushion heel (SACH) foot.
         (a) The most commonly prescribed foot; nonarticulated; contains an energy-absorbing cushion heel and internal wooden keel that limits sagittal plane motion, primarily to plantarflexion.
         (b) Permits a very small amount of mediolateral (frontal plane) and transverse plane motion.
         (c) Assists in hyperextension of knee (knee stability) during stance.
      (3) Solid ankle flexible endoskeleton (SAFE) foot: a flexible, nonarticulated foot (similar to SACH); permits more nonsagittal plane motions; prescribed for more active individuals.
      (4) Flex-foot: a leaf-spring shank (not a foot) used with an endoskeletal prosthesis; the long band of carbon fiber originates directly from the shank; stores energy in early stance for later use during push-off; prescribed for more active individuals.
      (5) Single axis foot: an articulated foot with the lower shank; motion is controlled by anterior and posterior rubber bumpers that limit dorsiflexion and plantarflexion; more stable (permits only sagittal plane motion); may be prescribed for individuals with bilateral transfemoral amputations.
   b. Shank.
      (1) Functions to:
         (a) Provide leg length and shape.
         (b) Connect and transmit weight from socket to foot.
      (2) Exoskeletal: conventional components, usually made of wood with a plastic laminated finish; colored for cosmesis; durable.
      (3) Endoskeletal: contains a central metal shank (aluminum, titanium, and other high-strength alloys), covered by soft foam and external stocking; offers improved cosmesis; modular components allows for increased ease of prosthetic adjustment.
   c. Socket.
      (1) PTB (patellar tendon-bearing) socket: a total contact socket that allows for moderate loading over the area of the patellar tendon.
      (2) Pressure-sensitive areas of the transtibial residual limb include:
         (a) Anterior tibia.
         (b) Anterior tibial crest.
         (c) Fibular head and neck.
         (d) Fibular nerve.
      (3) Pressure-tolerant areas of the typical transtibial residual limb include:
         (a) Patellar tendon.
         (b) Medial tibial plateau.
         (c) Tibial and fibular shafts.
         (d) Distal end (rarely, may be sensitive).
   d. Suspension.
      (1) Supracondylar leather cuff suspension: buckles over the femoral condyles; widely used, easily adjusted.
      (2) Supracondylar (SC) socket suspension: medial and lateral walls of the socket extend up and over the femoral condyles; a removable medial wedge assists in donning and removal; more cosmetic (no buckles or straps); provides increased mediolateral stability.
      (3) Supracondylar/suprapatellar (SC/SP) socket suspension: similar to SC but with a high anterior wall; assists in suspension of short residual limbs.
      (4) Thigh corset suspension: a hinged joint with metal uprights attached to a thigh corset; provides larger surface for weight bearing; prescribed for individuals with sensitive skin on the residual limb; the knee joint allows for knee control (locks); pistoning may be a problem.
3. Transfemoral (above-knee) prosthesis.
   a. Knee unit.
      (1) Axis.
         (a) Single axis: permits knee motions to occur around a fixed axis; knee flexion is needed during late stance and swing, sitting, and kneeling.
         (b) Polycentric systems (multiple axes): changing axis of motion allows for adjustments to the center of knee rotation; more stable than single axis joints; complex; not widely used.
      (2) Friction devices: control knee motions; provide resistance to pendular motion at the knee.
         (a) Constant friction: continuous resistance is provided by a clamp that acts on the knee mechanism; friction device can be easily adjusted by screws; usually prescribed for

older individuals who do not vary their gait speeds greatly.
   (b) Variable friction: resistance can be regulated to the demands of the gait cycle; at early swing, high resistance is needed to prevent excessive heel rise; during midswing when the leg swings forward, friction demands are minimal; at late swing, friction is increased to prevent terminal swing impact.
   (c) Hydraulic knee units (fluid-controlled) or pneumatic knee units (air-controlled): adjusts resistance dynamically to the individual's walking speed; prescribed for younger, more active individuals; heavier, more complicated; increased maintenance, cost.
  (3) Knee stabilization in extension achieved by:
   (a) Prosthetic alignment: the knee center is aligned posterior to the TKA line; a knee aligned farther posterior will be very stable (will not flex easily); may be prescribed for short residual limbs; an unstable knee may occur if the knee falls anterior to the TKA line.
   (b) Manual lock: prescribed for individuals who require a constantly locked knee; e.g., weakness of hip extensors; difficulty with clearance of the leg during swing can be controlled by shortening the total prosthetic limb length ~1 cm (~0.4 in).
   (c) Friction brake: a device that increases friction at midstance to prevent knee flexion, but permits smooth knee motion through the rest of the gait cycle.
   (d) Extension aid: an external elastic strap or internal coiled spring that assists in terminal knee extension during late swing.

b. Socket.
  (1) Quadrilateral socket: most commonly prescribed AK socket; quadrilateral in shape.
   (a) Contains a broad horizontal posterior shelf for seating of the ischial tuberosity and gluteals.
   (b) The medial wall is the same height as the posterior wall, while the anterior and lateral walls are 2½–3 inches higher.
   (c) A posterior directed force is provided by the anterior and lateral walls to ensure proper seating.
   (d) Scarpa's bulge: an area built up on the anterior wall to distribute forces across the femoral triangle.
   (e) Reliefs are provided for the adductor longus tendon, hamstring tendons, sciatic nerve, gluteus maximus, and rectus femoris.
  (2) Pressure-sensitive areas of the typical transfemoral residual limb.
   (a) Distolateral end of the femur.
   (b) Pubic symphysis.
   (c) Perineal area.
  (3) Pressure-tolerant areas of the typical transfemoral residual limb.
   (a) Ischial tuberosity.
   (b) Gluteals.
   (c) Lateral sides of residual limb.
   (d) Distal end (rarely, may be sensitive).

c. Suspension.
  (1) Suction suspension: suction is employed to maximize contact and suspension; air is pumped out through a one-way air release valve located at the socket's bottom; suction suspension can be total or partial (individual wears a sock).
  (2) Strap suspension: adjustable, readily accommodates to volume changes. Disadvantage: pistoning, when it is the sole type of suspension.
   (a) Silesian bandage: a strap that anchors the TKA prosthesis by reaching around the pelvis (below iliac crest); controls rotatory motions.
  (3) Hinge suspension: hinged hip joint attached to a metal/leather pelvic band, anchored around the pelvis.
   (a) Adds control for medial/lateral stability of hip (rotation, abduction/adduction).
   (b) Reduces Trendelenburg gait deviation.
   (c) Disadvantages: adds extra weight and bulk.

4. Knee disarticulation prosthesis.
 a. Functional, allows weight bearing on the distal end of the femur.
 b. Problems with cosmesis, added thigh length with the knee joint attached, especially noticeable in sitting.
 c. Lower shank is shortened to balance leg length in standing.

5. Hip disarticulation prosthesis.
 a. Socket is molded to accommodate the pelvis; weight bearing occurs on ischial seat, iliac crests.
 b. Endoskeletal components frequently used, decreases weight of prosthesis.
 c. Stability achieved with hip extension aid; posterior placement of knee joint with anterior placement of the hip joint to the weight-bearing line.

6. Immediate postoperative prosthesis (rigid dressing).
 a. Plaster of Paris socket is fabricated in the operating room with the capability to attach a foot and pylon.
 b. Advantages.
  (1) Allows early, limited weight-bearing ambulation within days of surgery.
  (2) Limits postoperative sequelae: edema, postoperative pain.

(3) Enhances wound healing.
(4) Allows for earlier fit of permanent prosthesis.
c. Limitations.
(1) Requires skilled application and close monitoring.
(2) Does not allow for daily wound inspection; contraindicated for older patients with cardiovascular compromise and increased risk for wounds.

Upper-Limb Prosthetics (ULPs)

1. Below elbow (BE) prosthesis: contains a terminal device (TD), wrist and forearm socket, harness system.
2. Above elbow (AE) prosthesis: in addition, contains an elbow and arm socket.
3. Conventional system.
a. Power for voluntary opening of the TD (hook or hand) is transmitted by a cable from a figure-of-eight shoulder harness to the TD.
b. Rubber bands are used for closure and prehensile strength.
c. Forearm rotation is done by manual prepositioning of the TD.
d. Movement control.
(1) BE prosthesis: bilateral scapular abduction or ipsilateral flexion of the humerus is used to pull on the cable and force opening of the hook.
(2) AE prosthesis (dual control system): the same motions can be used to flex the elbow in the AE prosthesis; when the elbow locks (by scapular depression and humeral extension), the forces are then transmitted to operate the TD.
4. Externally powered system.
a. Microswitches (myoelectric devices) are activated by the same motions as conventional power systems.
b. Small electric motors (battery-powered) are activated to operate the TD.
(1) Improves ease of function, prehensile strength.
(2) Adds weight, increased maintenance, cost.

Physical Therapy Intervention

1. Team: in the clinic, the physical therapist functions as a member of the prosthetic clinic team that includes physician, prosthetist, and therapist.
2. Preprosthetic management.
a. Preprescription examination.
(1) Skin: inspect incision for healing; scar tissue; other lesions.
(2) Residual limb.
(a) Circumference measurements: check for edema.
(b) Length: bone, soft tissue length.
(c) Shape: should be cylindrical or conical; check for abnormalities (i.e., bulbous end, dog ears, adductor roll).
(3) Vascular status of sound limb, residual limb: examine pulses, color, temperature, trophic changes, pain/intermittent claudication.
(4) AROM and PROM: examine for contractures that might interfere with prosthetic prescription (e.g., hip and knee flexion contractures).
(5) Sensation.
(a) Proprioception, visual, vestibular function, contributions to balance; loss of proprioception in the amputated limb will necessitate a compensatory shift to the other senses for balance control.
(b) Phantom limb sensation: a feeling of pressure or paresthesia as if coming from the amputated limb. Sensations are normal, not painful; may last for the lifetime of the individual.
(c) Phantom pain: an intense burning or cramping pain; disabling, frequently interferes with rehabilitation.
(6) Strength: examine strength of residual limb as tolerated; strength of the sound limb, trunk, and upper extremities needed for function.
(7) Functional status.
(a) Functional mobility skills: bed mobility, transfers, wheelchair use.
(b) Activities of daily living: basic, instrumental (use of telephone, shopping, etc.).
(8) Cardiopulmonary function, endurance.
(a) The shorter the amputation limb, the greater the energy demands; i.e., oxygen consumption is increased 65% over normal walking in the patient with transfemoral amputation; similar to fast walking in those without amputations for the patient with transtibial amputation.
(b) Functional capacity further limited by: concomitant diseases (e.g., cardiovascular disease, diabetes), individual fitness level, pain.
(9) Neurologic factors.
(a) Cognitive function.
(b) Check for neuropathy.
(c) Check for neuroma: an abnormal growth of nerve cells that occurs in the residual limb after amputation.
(10) Psychosocial factors: motivation, adjustment and acceptance, availability of support systems.
b. Preprosthetic training: goals and interventions.
(1) Ideally begins preoperatively and continues postoperatively.
(2) Facilitate psychological acceptance.
(3) Postoperative dressings: applied to the residual limb; helps to limit edema, accelerate healing,

reduce postoperative pain, and shape the residual limb.

(a) Elastic wraps: flexible, soft bandaging, inexpensive; requires frequent reapplication, with pressure greatest distal to proximal; if wraps are allowed to loosen, may have problems with edema control; avoid circular wrapping, which produces a tourniquet effect.

(b) Stump shrinkers: flexible, soft, inexpensive, readily available in different sizes.

(c) Semirigid dressings: Unna paste dressing (zinc oxide, gelatin, glycerin, and calamine); applied in the operating room.

(d) Rigid dressings: plaster of Paris dressing; applied in the operating room; a component of immediate postoperative fitting; allows for edema reduction and early ambulation with a temporary prosthesis (pylon and foot). Good for young patients who are good candidates for a permanent prosthesis.

(4) Desensitizing activities: pressure, rubbing, stroking, bandaging of the residual limb.

(5) Hygiene: inspection and care of the residual limb.

(6) Positioning for prevention of contracture; positions to avoid include:

(a) Transtibial: prolonged flexion and external rotation at the hip, knee flexion; counteract with use of a posterior board to keep knee straight while in wheelchair; regularly scheduled time in prone-lying.

(b) Transfemoral: flexion, abduction, external rotation of hip; counteract with regularly scheduled time in prone-lying time.

(7) Flexibility exercises.

(a) Full AROM and PROM, active stretching, especially in hip and knee extension.

(b) Flexibility of sound limb and trunk.

(8) Strengthening: utilize a general strengthening exercise program with special emphasis on:

(a) Hip extensors: especially for the patient with transfemoral amputation.

(b) Knee extensors: the patient with transtibial amputation.

(c) Hip abductors: for stance phase pelvic stability.

(d) Dynamic exercises: utilize gravity and body weight to provide resistance during functional mat activities.

(9) Functional mobility training.

(a) Sit-to-stand transitions, transfers, standing.

(b) Wheelchair independence.

(c) Hopping on the sound limb; mobility in the seated position; i.e., scooting for patients with bilateral transfemoral amputation.

(d) Early walking with crutches or walker; consider early ambulation with a temporary prosthesis.

(10) Bilateral lower-extremity amputation.

(a) Wheelchair training important. Will be primary means of locomotion.

(b) Prolonged wheelchair time increases likelihood of hip and knee flexion contractures; prone positioning program is important.

(c) Energy expenditure during prosthetic ambulation is increased dramatically; a trial period with temporary prostheses can be used to evaluate ambulation potential with permanent prostheses; especially useful with the elderly.

(d) Bilateral transfemoral amputation: ambulation usually requires walker; loss of lower-extremity proprioception increases balance difficulties; loss of knee extensor function will result in significant later difficulties with stair-climbing, curbs, stepping.

(e) Bilateral transfemoral amputation: patients can be fitted with shortened prostheses (stubbies) consisting of a socket and foot component (modified rocker feet) with no knee joints; increases ease of use and function; generally poor acceptance due to cosmesis.

3. Prosthetic management.

a. Prosthetic check-out.

(1) Prosthesis: delivered as ordered, proper functioning; inspect both on and off the patient.

(2) Static assessment.

(a) Alignment and comfort in standing, sitting.

(b) Leg length discrepancy: pelvis level.

(c) Fit and suspension: pistoning when pelvis is lifted.

(3) Dynamic assessment.

(a) Sit-to-stand transitions.

(b) Gait: smooth, safe gait, absence of gait deviations; gait speeds normally decrease to reduce high levels of energy expenditure.

(c) Stairs and inclines.

(4) Inspection of the residual limb with the prosthesis off.

(a) Proper loading: transient redness is to be expected in pressure-tolerant areas after prosthetic use.

(b) No redness should be seen in pressure-sensitive areas.

b. Prosthetic training: goals and interventions.

(1) Donning and doffing of the prosthesis: training specific to type of socket and type of suspension.

(2) Strengthening, flexibility exercises.

(a) Emphasis on hip extension and knee extension (transtibial) with the prosthesis on.

(3) Balance and coordination.
  (a) Symmetrical stance and weight bearing on prosthetic limb.
  (b) Weight shifting to limits of stability.
  (c) Dynamic balance control; e.g., stepping activities.
(4) Gait training.
  (a) Conventional training: focus on smooth weight transfer from sound limb to prosthetic limb, continuous movement sequence.
  (b) Biofeedback training: limb load devices to facilitate prosthetic weight acceptance.
  (c) Training with use of least restrictive assistive device; parallel bars may interfere with learning and independent ambulation in some patients.
(5) Functional activities training: including transfers, stairs, curbs, ramps, down and up from floor, recreational activities, etc.
(6) Regular inspection and maintenance of the prosthesis.
(7) Hygiene: care of stump socks, interior of the socket.
(8) Facilitate prosthetic acceptance.

4. Selected prosthetic gait deviations.
  a. Transfemoral amputation.
    (1) Circumduction: the prosthesis swings out to the side in an arc. Possible causes: a long prosthesis, locked knee, small or loose socket, inadequate suspension, foot plantar flexed, abduction contracture, poor knee control.
    (2) Abducted gait: prosthesis is laterally displaced to the side. Possible causes: crotch or medial wall discomfort, long prosthesis, low lateral wall or malalignment, tight hip abductors.
    (3) Vaulting: the patient rises up on the sound limb to swing the prosthesis through. Possible causes: prosthesis too long, inadequate suspension, socket too small, prosthetic foot set in too much plantarflexion, too little knee flexion.
    (4) Lateral trunk bending during stance: the trunk bends toward the prosthetic side. Possible causes: low lateral wall, short prosthesis, high medial wall; weak abductors, abductor contracture, hip pain, short amputation limb.
    (5) Forward flexion during stance: the trunk bends forward. Possible causes: unstable knee unit, short ambulatory aids, hip flexion contracture.
    (6) Lumbar lordosis during stance: exaggeration of the lumbar curve. Possible causes: insufficient support from anterior or posterior walls, painful ischial weight bearing, hip flexion contracture, weak hip extensors or abdominals.
    (7) High heel rise: during early swing, the heel rises excessively. Possible causes: inadequate knee friction, too little tension in the extension aid.
    (8) Terminal swing impact: the prosthesis comes to a sudden stop as the knee extends during late swing. Possible causes: insufficient knee friction or too much tension in the extension aid; patient fears that the knee will buckle; forceful hip flexion.
    (9) Swing phase whips: at toe-off, the heel moves either medially or laterally. Possible causes: socket is rotated, knee bolt is rotated, foot is malaligned.
    (10) Foot rotation at heel strike: as the heel contacts the ground, the foot rotates laterally, sometimes with vibratory motion. Possible causes: foot is malaligned, stiff heel cushion, or plantar flexion bumper.
    (11) Foot slap: excessive plantar flexion at heel strike. Possible cause: heel cushion or plantar flexion bumper is too soft.
    (12) Uneven step length: patient favors sound limb and limits weight-bearing time on the prosthetic limb. Possible causes: socket discomfort or poor alignment; hip flexion contracture or hip instability.
  b. Transtibial amputation.
    (1) Excessive knee flexion during stance. Possible causes: socket may be aligned too far forward or tilted anteriorly; plantar flexion bumper is too hard and limits plantar flexion; high heel shoes; knee flexion contracture or weak quadriceps.
    (2) Inadequate knee flexion during stance. Possible causes: socket may be aligned too far back or tilted posteriorly; plantar flexion bumper or heel cushion too soft; low heel shoes; anterodistal discomfort, weak quadriceps.
    (3) Lateral thrust at midstance. Possible causes: foot is inset too much.
    (4) Medial thrust at midstance. Possible causes: foot is outset too much.
    (5) Drop off or premature knee flexion in late stance. Possible causes: socket is set too far forward or excessively flexed; dorsiflexion bumper is too soft, resulting in excess dorsiflexion of the foot; prosthetic foot keel too short; knee flexion contracture.
    (6) Delayed knee flexion during late stance: patient feels as though walking "uphill." Possible causes: socket is set too far back or lacks sufficient flexion; dorsiflexion bumper is too stiff causing excess plantar flexion; prosthetic foot keel too long.

Wheelchairs

Components

1. Postural support system.
   a. Seating.
      (1) Sling seat: standard on wheelchairs. Hips tend to slide forward, thighs tend to adduct and internally rotate. Reinforces poor pelvic position (posterior pelvic tilt).
      (2) Insert or contour seat creates a stable, firm sitting surface; made of wood or plastic, padded with foam.
         (a) Improves pelvic position (neutral pelvic position).
         (b) Reduces the tendency for the patient to slide forward or sit with a posterior pelvic tilt (sacral sitting).
      (3) Seat cushion: distributes weight-bearing pressures. Assists in preventing decubitus ulcers in patients with decreased sensation, prolongs wheelchair sitting times.
         (a) Pressure-relieving, contoured foam cushion: uses dense, layered foam; accommodates moderate to severe postural deformity. Easy for caregivers to reposition patients, low maintenance. May interfere with slide transfers.
         (b) Pressure-relieving fluid/gel or combination cushion (fluid/gel plus foam). Can be custom-molded. Accommodates moderate to severe postural deformity. Easy for caregivers to reposition patients. Requires some maintenance, heavier, more expensive.
         (c) Pressure-relieving air cushion. Accommodates moderate to severe postural deformity. Lightweight, improved pressure distribution. Expensive, base may be unstable for some patients. Requires continuous maintenance.
      (4) Adds to measurements to determine back height.
      (5) Pressure relief push-ups are required, typically every 15–20 minutes (e.g., the patient with SCI).
   b. Back: support to the midscapular region is provided by most standard sling-back wheelchairs.
      (1) Lower back height may increase functional mobility, i.e., sports chairs; may also increase back strain.
      (2) High back height may be necessary for patients with poor trunk stability or with extensor spasms.
      (3) Insert or contour backs: improve trunk extension and overall upright alignment.
      (4) Lateral trunk supports: improve trunk alignment for patients with scoliosis, poor stability.
   c. Armrests.
      (1) Full-length or desk length; desk length facilitates use, proximity to a desk or table.
      (2) Fixed-height or adjustable height; adjustable-height arm rests can be raised to facilitate sit-to-stand transfers.
      (3) Removable armrests: facilitate transfers.
      (4) Wraparound (space saver) armrests: reduce the overall width of the chair by 1½ inches.
      (5) Upper extremity support surface (trays or troughs) can be secured to the armrests; provides additional postural assistance for patients with decreased use of upper extremities.
   d. Leg rests.
      (1) Fixed.
      (2) Swing-away, detachable: facilitates ease in transfers, front approach to wheelchair when ambulating.
      (3) Elevating: indicated for LE edema control, postural support; contraindicated for patients with knee flexor (hamstring) hypertonicity or tightness.
   e. Footrests.
      (1) Footplates: provide a resting base for feet, feet are neutral with knees flexed to 90°; footplates can be raised or removed to facilitate transfers.
      (2) Heel loops: help maintain foot position, prevent posterior sliding of the foot.
      (3) Straps (ankle, calf): can be added to stabilize the feet on the foot plates.
2. Wheeled mobility base.
   a. Frame.
      (1) Fixed or folding.
         (a) Folding facilitates mobility in the community, ease of storage.
         (b) Rigid frame facilitates stroke efficiency; increases distance per stroke.
      (2) Available in heavy-duty, standard, lightweight, active-duty lightweight, ultra-lightweight construction.
         (a) In general, the lighter the weight of the frame, the greater the ease of use.
         (b) Level of expected activity and environment should be taken into account when deciding on frame construction.

b. Wheels, handrims.
   (1) Casters: small front wheels, typically 8 inches in diameter; caster locks can be added to facilitate wheelchair stability during transfers.
   (2) Drive wheels: large rear wheels used for propulsion; outer rims allow for hand grip and propulsion.
      (a) Projections may be attached to the rims (vertical, oblique, or horizontal) to facilitate propulsion in patients with poor handgrip, e.g., quadriplegia; horizontal or oblique projections widen the chair and may limit maneuvering in the home.
      (b) Friction rims/leather gloves: increase handgrip friction, ease of propulsion in patients with poor handgrip.
      (c) Construction of drive wheels: standard spokes or spokeless wheels.

c. Tires.
   (1) Standard hard rubber tires: durable, low maintenance.
   (2) Pneumatic (air-filled) tires: provide a smoother ride, increased shock absorption; require more maintenance.

d. Brakes.
   (1) Most brakes consist of a lever system with a cam.
   (2) Brakes must be engaged for all transfers in and out of chair.
   (3) Extensions may be added to increase ease in both locking and unlocking; e.g., for upper extremity weakness, arthritis.

e. Additional attachments.
   (1) Seat belts (pelvic positioner): belt should grasp over the pelvis at a 45° angle to the seat.
   (2) Seat positioners: can add lateral positioners at hip and knee or medial positioner at knee (adductor pommel) to maintain alignment of lower extremities, control for spasticity; seat wedge or tilt-in-space seat can be used for extensor spasms or thrusting.
   (3) Seat back positioners: can add lateral trunk positioners to maintain alignment, control for scoliosis.
   (4) Antitipping device: a posterior extension attached to the lower horizontal supports, prevents tipping backward in the chair; also limits going up curbs or over door sills.
   (5) Hill-holder device: a mechanical brake that allows the chair to go forward, but automatically brakes when the chair goes in reverse; useful for patients who are not able to ascend a long ramp or hill without a rest.

3. Specialized wheelchairs.

a. Reclining back: indicated for patients who are unable to independently maintain upright sitting position.
   (1) Reclining wheelchairs include an extended back and typically elevating leg rests; head and trunk supports may also be added.
   (2) Electric reclining back helps to redistribute weight bearing if patient cannot do active pushups or pressure-relief maneuvers.

b. Tilt-in-space: motorized; entire seat and back may be tipped backward (normal seat to back angle is maintained); indicated for patients with extensor spasms that may throw the patient out of the chair, or for pressure relief.

c. One-arm drive: drive mechanisms are located on one wheel, usually with two outer rims (or by push lever); patient propels the wheelchair by pushing on both rims (or lever with one hand); difficult for some patients to use, e.g., patients with left hemiplegia, cognitive/perceptual impairments.

d. Hemiplegic chair (hemi chair): designed to be low to the ground, allowing propulsion with the noninvolved upper and lower extremities.

e. Amputee chair: wheelchair is modified by placing the drive wheels posterior to the vertical back supports (2 inches backward); increases the length of the base of support and posterior stability; prescribed for patients with bilateral lower-extremity amputations, whose center of gravity is now located more posterior when seated in the wheelchair.

f. Powered wheelchair: utilizes a power source (battery) to propel the wheelchair; prescribed for patients who are not capable of self-propulsion or who have very low endurance.
   (1) Microprocessors allow the control of the wheelchair to be adapted to various controls; i.e., joystick, head controls.
   (2) Proportional drives: changes in pressure on the control result in directly corresponding changes in speeds.
   (3) Microswitching systems: speed is preset; controls turn system on and off; i.e., puff-n-sip tubes for individuals with quadriplegia.

g. Bariatric wheelchair: heavy-duty, extra-wide wheelchair designed to assist mobility in individuals who are obese.
   (1) Selection based on patient characteristics, safety, and function.
   (2) The bariatric client has a center of body mass that is positioned several inches forward compared to the normal-sized person.
      (a) In order to ensure wheelchair stability, the rear axle is displaced forward compared to the standard wheelchair.
      (b) This forward position allows for a more efficient arm push (full-arm stroke with less wrist extension).

(3) Bariatric wheelchair can be ordered with special adaptations:
(a) Hard tires versus pneumatic tires for increased durability.
(b) Adjustable backrest to accommodate excessive posterior bulk.
(c) Reclining wheelchair to accommodate excessive anterior bulk, cardiorespiratory compromise (e.g., orthostatic hypotension).
(d) Power application attached to a heavy duty wheelchair to accommodate excessive fatigue.

h. Sports wheelchair: variable; generally includes lightweight, solid frame, low seat, low back, seat that accommodates a tucked position, leg straps, slanted drive wheels, small push rims.

Wheelchair Measurements

1. General concepts.
a. Overall the size of the wheelchair must be proportional to the size of the patient and take into account the demands of expected use and the environment in which the chair will be used.
b. Assessments should be taken with the patient on a firm surface (seated or supine).

2. Six key measurements.
a. Seat width.
(1) Measurement on the patient: width of the hips at the widest part.
(2) Chair measurement: add 2 inches to the patient's measurement.
(3) Potential problems.
(a) Excessive width of the wheelchair will result in added difficulties in reaching the drive wheels and propelling the chair.
(b) Wheelchair width should accommodate width of doorways; can use a narrowing device; requires coordination to turn the cranking device.
(c) A wheelchair that is too narrow will result in pressure/discomfort on the lateral pelvis and thighs; lateral space should allow for changes in the thickness of clothing.
(4) The bariatric client with a pear shape will have increased gluteal femoral weight distribution. Measurement should consider the widest portion of the seated position (e.g., at the forward edge of the seated position). Also consider room for weight-shifting maneuvers for pressure relief, and possible use of lift devices.

b. Seat depth.
(1) Measurement on the patient: posterior buttock to the posterior aspect of the lower leg in the popliteal fossa.
(2) Chair measurement: subtract 2–3 inches from the patient's measurement.
(3) Potential problems.
(a) Seat depth that is too short fails to support the thigh adequately.
(b) Seat depth that is too long may compromise posterior knee circulation or result in a kyphotic posture, posterior tilting of pelvis, and sacral sitting.

c. Leg length/seat to footplate length.
(1) Measurement on the patient: from the bottom of the shoe (customary footwear) to just below the thigh in the popliteal fossa; when a seat cushion is used, the height must be subtracted from the patient's measurement.
(2) Potential problems.
(a) Excessive leg length will encourage sacral sitting and sliding forward in the chair.
(b) Length that is too short will create uneven weight distribution on thigh and excessive weight on the ischial seat.

d. Seat height.
(1) No patient measurement.
(2) Chair measurement: minimum clearance between the floor and the footplate is 2 inches, measured from the lowest point on the bottom of the footplate.
(3) Add 2 inches to the patient's leg length measurement.

e. Arm rest height (hanging elbow height).
(1) Measurement on the patient: from the seat platform to just below the elbow held at 90° with the shoulder in neutral position.
(2) Chair measurement: add 1 inch to the patient's hanging elbow measurement.
(3) Potential problems.
(a) Armrests that are too high will cause shoulder elevation.
(b) Armrests that are too low will encourage leaning forward.

f. Back height: Height will vary depending upon the amount of support the patient needs.
(1) Measurement on the patient: from the seat platform to the lower angle of the scapula, midscapula, top of shoulder, based on the degree of support desired.
(2) If the patient plans to use a seat cushion, the height of the cushion must be added to the patient's measurement.
(3) Potential problems.
(a) Added back height may increase difficulty in getting the chair into a car or van.
(b) Added back height may also prevent the patient from hooking onto the push handle for stabilization and weight relief; e.g., the patient with quadriplegia.

Table 11-1

Standard Wheelchair Dimensions (in Inches)

CHAIR STYLE	SEAT WIDTH	SEAT DEPTH	SEAT HEIGHT
Adult	18	16	20
Narrow adult	16	16	20
Slim adult	14	16	20
Hemi/low seat			17.5
Junior	16	16	18.5
Child	14	11.5	18.75
Tiny tot	12	11.5	19.5

3. Standard dimensions (see Table 11-1).
   a. Custom-made wheelchairs add significantly to the cost of a wheelchair.
   b. Whenever possible, patients should be matched to standardized chairs.

Wheelchair Training

1. Purpose: many first-time users require instruction in use and care of the wheelchair.
2. Instruct in good sitting posture and pressure relief.
   a. Instruct in use of wheelchair cushion: care and maintenance, schedule of use (whenever sitting); limitations of cushion.
   b. Instruct in periodic pressure reliefs: arm push-ups; weight shifts—leaning to one side, then other.
3. Wheelchair propulsion.
   a. Instruct in manual wheelchair propulsion.
      (1) Both arms on drive (push) wheels, one arm on drive wheel/one foot pulls diagonally across floor under chair (e.g., the patient with hemiplegia), or one arm (one-arm drive, both outer rims located on one side).
      (2) Propulsion: forward/backward, flat surfaces, uneven surfaces.
      (3) Turning: pushing harder with one hand than other; sharp turning: pull one wheel backward while pushing other wheel forward.
      (4) Negotiation of obstacles.
   b. Power chair training: focus on driving skill and safety; instruct in use of switches (on/off, turns), joystick; maneuverability, safe stopping.
4. Wheelchair management.
   a. Instruct in use of wheel locks (brakes), foot supports (foot plate, leg rest), elevation of leg rests, and arm rests.
   b. Instruct in routine maintenance of wheelchair; normal cleaning and maintenance, power chair (battery) maintenance.
5. Community mobility.
   a. Ramps.
      (1) Ascending: forward lean of head and trunk, use shorter strokes; move hands quickly for propulsion.
      (2) Descending ramps: grip hand rims loosely, control chair's descent; or descend in wheelie position (steep ramp).
   b. Wheelies: instruct in how to "pop a wheelie" in order to negotiate curbs; the patient learns how to come up onto and balance on the rear wheels with the front casters off the ground (e.g., the patient with paraplegia).
      (1) Practice maintaining balance point in wheelie position (therapist tips chair back into position).
      (2) Practice moving into wheelie position: patient places hands well back on hand rims; then pulls (moves) them forward abruptly and forcefully. The head and trunk are moved forward to keep from going over backward. Use lightweight wheelchair to facilitate training.
      (3) Balancing in wheelie position: chair tips further back when wheels are pushed forward; chair tips toward upright when wheels are pulled back.
      (4) Practice curb ascent: place the front casters up on the curb, the patient then pushes rear wheels up curb; momentum used to assist.
      (5) Practice curb descent: descending backward with forward head and trunk lean; descending forward in wheelie position.
   c. Practice ascending/descending stairs: in wheelchair, on buttocks.
   d. Instruct in how to fall safely, return to wheelchair.
   e. Instruct in how to transfer into a car, place wheelchair inside car by pulling wheelchair behind the car seat, or to use a wheelchair lift (van-equipped).

Transfer Training

Dependent Transfers

1. General concepts: minimal or no active participation by patient.
2. Dependent lift transfer (football transfer).
   a. Wheelchair is positioned parallel to surface.
   b. Patient is flexed forward at hips in tucked position with hips and knees flexed.
   c. Therapist locks patient's tucked knees between legs; places one hand under buttocks and one hand on transfer belt.
   d. Patient is rocked forward and lifted using a backward weight shift with therapist in a semisquat position.
   e. Therapist then pivots using small steps and gently lowers patient to support surface.
3. Dependent stand-pivot transfer. Similar to above, but patient's lower extremities are extended and in contact with floor.
4. Hydraulic lift transfer. Positioning and widening of base of device is critical to stability.

Assisted Transfers

1. General concepts.
   a. Requires some participation by patient; levels of assistance include stand-by, minimal, moderate, or maximal assistance.
   b. Includes verbal cueing or manual assistance for lift, support, or balance control.
   c. Transfer belts, trapeze bars, overhead loops can be used to provide additional control.
2. Assisted stand-pivot transfer.
   a. Used for patients who are unable to stand independently and can bear some weight on lower extremities (e.g., patients with cerebrovascular accident [CVA], incomplete SCI, hip fracture/replacement).
   b. Wheelchair is placed parallel to surface (on the patient's sound or stronger side).
   c. Therapist can block out one or both of the patient's knees to provide stability; support can be added by placing both hands on the patient (on both buttocks, both on upper back, or one on buttock/ one on upper back).
   d. Patient rocks forward and pushes up into standing.
   e. Therapist assists patient with forward weight shift and standing, pivoting toward chair, and controlled lowering toward the support surface.
   f. Variation: assisted squat-pivot transfer for patients who are unable to stand fully; e.g., with marked weakness in both lower extremities.
3. Assisted transfer using a transfer (sliding) board.
   a. Used for patients with good sitting balance who can lift most but not all of weight of buttocks; e.g., patients with complete level C5 SCI.
   b. Wheelchair is placed parallel to surface.
   c. Patient moves forward in chair and board is placed well under buttocks.
   d. Patient performs transfer by doing a series of push-ups and lifts along board.
   e. Therapist assists in lift (hands on buttocks, on transfer belt, or one on buttock/one on belt).
   f. Care must be taken not to pinch fingers under board or drag/traumatize skin.
   g. Feet can remain on foot pedals or be positioned on the floor.
   h. Patients with complete level C6 SCI can be independent with transfer board on level surfaces.
4. Push-up transfer (pop-over transfer).
   a. Used for patients with good sitting balance who can lift buttocks clear of sitting surface; can be a progression in transfer training from using a transfer board.
   b. The patient with complete C7 SCI can be independent in transfers without a sliding board.
   c. The patient utilizes the head-hips relationship to successfully complete the transfer (movement of head in one direction results in movement of hips in the opposite direction/toward the support surface being transferred to).

Training

1. Practice.
   a. In and out of bed.
   b. In and out of wheelchair.
      (1) Level surfaces.
      (2) Unlevel surfaces: to floor.
   c. On and off toilet, tub seat.
   d. In and out of car.
2. Instructions.
   a. Inform patient about the transfer, as well as expectations for the patient.
   b. Synchronize actions using commands and counts.
   c. Reduce assistance as appropriate.

Environmental Considerations

Environmental Modification

1. Purpose.
   a. Assess degree of safety, function, and comfort of the patient in the home, community, and work environments.
   b. Provide recommendations to ensure a barrier-free environment, greatest level of functional independence.
2. Standard adult wheelchair dimensions for environmental access.
   a. Width: 24–26 inches from rim to rim.
   b. Length: 42–43 inches.
   c. Height (push handles to floor): 36 inches.
   d. Height (armrest to floor): 29–30 inches.
   e. Footrests may extend for very large people.
   f. 360° turning space = 60 inches × 60 inches.
   g. 90° turning space = minimum of 36 inches.
   h. Minimum clear width for doorways and halls = 32 inches; ideal is 36 inches.
   i. High forward reach = maximum of 48 inches from floor; low forward reach = a minimum of 15 inches from the floor.
   j. Side reach = maximum of 24 inches.
3. Home.
   a. Entrance: accessible; stairs with handrail, ramp, platform to allow for ease of door opening.
   b. Floors: nonskid surface, carpeting securely fastened; no scatter rugs.
   c. Furniture arrangement: should allow sufficient room to maneuver easily; e.g., with wheelchair or ambulation with assistive device.
   d. Doors: thresholds should be flush or level (no door-sills); standard door width is 32 inches; outside door swing area requires a minimum of 18 inches for walkers and 26 inches for wheelchairs.
   e. Stairs: uniform riser heights (7 inches high) with a tread depth (a minimum of 11 inches); handrails, recommended height is 32 inches, ½ to 2 inches in diameter; nonslip surface; well lighted; color code with warm colors (red, orange, yellow) if visual impairments exist.
   f. Bedroom: furniture arrangement for easy maneuverability; a minimum of 3 feet on side of bed for wheelchair transfers; firm mattress, stable bed, sufficient height to facilitate sit-to-stand transfers; phone accessibility; appropriate height for wall switches is 36–48 inches; outlets a minimum of 18 inches above the floorboard.
   g. Bathroom: optimal toilet seat height is 17–19 inches; tub seat, nonskid tub surface or mat; grab bars securely fastened; optimal height of horizontal grab bars is 33–36 inches.
   h. Kitchen: appropriate height of countertops, for wheelchair users no higher than 31 inches; counter depth of at least 24 inches; accessible equipment and storage areas.
4. Community/workplace.
   a. Steps: recommended height is 7–9 inches.
   b. Ramps: recommended ratio of slope to rise is 1:12 (for every inch of vertical rise, 12 inches of ramp is required); minimum of 36 inches wide, with nonslip surface; handrail waist high for ambulators (34–38 inches) and should extend 12 inches beyond the top and bottom of runs; ramp should have level landing at top and bottom.
   c. Parking (handicapped parking): parking space with adjacent 4-foot aisle for wheelchair maneuverability; accessible within a short distance of buildings; curb cutouts.
   d. Building entrance: accessible; accessible elevator.
   e. Access to public telephones, drinking fountains, bathrooms.
   f. Ergonomic assessment of immediate work area: appropriate lighting, temperature, seating surface, height and size of work counter.
   g. Public transportation: accessible.

APPENDIX 11A

Ergonomics

GERARD DYBEL AND THOMAS BIANCO

Ergonomics

1. Definitions.
   a. Ergonomics is the science of fitting workplace conditions and job demands to the capabilities of the working population.
   b. Work demands: determine the physical demands of work tasks including lifting weights, distances, tools used, production levels, and work schedules.
   c. Work capacity: objective assessment of worker's current level of ability to perform the physical demands of a specific identified job.
2. General concepts.
   a. Purpose of ergonomics is to assure high productivity, avoid injury and illness risks, and increase satisfaction among workforce.
   b. Ergonomics uses scientific and engineering principles to improve the safety, efficiency, and quality of movements involved in work.
   c. Ergonomics programs should focus on making the job fit the person.
3. Hazard control and prevention.
   a. General concepts: common risk factors for musculoskeletal disorders (MSDs) include awkward postures, forceful exertions, repetitive motions, duration, contact stresses, vibration, and workplace conditions (e.g., temperature, machine pace, insufficient breaks).
   b. Administrative controls: changes in the way that work is assigned or scheduled to reduce the magnitude, frequency, or duration of exposure to ergonomic risk factors (e.g., job rotation).
   c. Engineering controls: reduce the risk of injury by design or modifications of workstations, work methods, and tools to reduce exposure to ergonomic risk factors (e.g., adding lift tables to a workstation).
   d. Work style controls: train workers in the recognition of risk factors and instruct in work practices that decrease demands of work tasks.
   e. Personal protective equipment (PPE): wrist supports, back belts, or anti-vibration gloves may be effective at reducing risk of injury. Other PPE equipment include respirators, earplugs, safety goggles, hard hats, and safety shoes and are worn to provide a barrier between the worker and the hazard source.
   f. Evaluating control effectiveness: follow-up evaluation is needed to ensure that the controls reduced or eliminated the ergonomic risk factors and that no new risk factors were introduced.
4. Primary prevention of occupational injury.
   a. Evaluate tasks and workstations to determine biomechanical stresses.
   b. Redesign high-risk tasks to ensure that stresses on joints and muscles do not lead to injury.

c. Change workstation layouts to reduce postural stresses.
d. Assess awkward postures to eliminate fatigue and cumulative trauma.
e. Assess highly repetitive manual assembly operations to identify the risk of disorders such as tendinitis, epicondylitis, and carpal tunnel syndrome.
f. Educate workers and managers to increase their awareness of ergonomic prevention.

Role of Physical Therapist in Occupational Health

1. Examination of employees.
   a. Work-related injuries and impairments.
   b. Functional limitations of employee.
   c. Disability (if unable to find reasonable accommodations).
   d. Other health-related conditions that prevent individuals from performing work-related tasks.
   e. Determine diagnosis, prognosis, and intervention related to work injury and other medical conditions.
2. Integration of injury prevention and general health and wellness programs into the consultation, screening, and education of employees.
3. Management of the acutely injured worker.
   a. Manage lost time and minimize disability.
   b. Optimize work capacity while reducing risk of further injury.
   c. Assist employee participation in on-site productive light duty program that is appropriate for limitations.
   d. Encourage employers to make accommodations to normal duty or provide alternative or transitional duty work.
4. Management of work-related musculoskeletal disorders (WMSDs).
   a. Diagnose WMSDs and apply interventions to specific tissues affected by injury.
   b. Determine safe work activity that will not compromise medical condition.
   c. Design safe, progressive rehabilitation program based on worker job demands and within functional and medical limitations of worker.
   d. Minimize lost work time with aggressive clinical management and promotion of productive work.
5. Facilitation of timely and appropriate referrals.
   a. Monitor signs, symptoms, and medical progress to determine if necessary referrals should be facilitated.
   b. Work interdependently with occupational physicians and other health care providers to move worker through employer health care system.
6. Minimization of injury/re-injury incident rate.
   a. Make ergonomic recommendations for workstation design and worker training regarding specific WMSD.
   b. Early intervention for workers with potentially disabling WMSD (e.g., carpal tunnel surgery).
   c. Participate in a comprehensive team for the timely dissemination of information including physician, physical therapist, employer representative, safety management, and injured worker.
7. Phases of physical therapy intervention.
   a. Admission to a specific phase of care is based on the physical therapy examination, diagnosis, and prognosis of the worker's functional and medical status.
   b. Progression from one phase to the next is based on objective, functional tests, and measurements. Duration of treatment is influenced by the level of physical activity required by the job and if a reasonable accommodation is not available.
      (1) Acute phase: immediate post-trauma, focuses on control and reduction of localized inflammation, joint or soft tissue restriction, and stabilization of injury.
      (2) Post-acute: involve injured worker in functional activities and training to increase ability to perform work-related tasks.
      (3) Reconditioning phase: increase intensity of functional activities and exercises and emphasis on work-simulated activities to increase endurance.
      (4) Return to work phase: if worker is not capable of return to work due to physical, functional, behavioral, or vocational deficits then complete a functional capacity evaluation before entry into this phase.

Functional Capacity Evaluation (FCE)

1. Purpose.
   a. To objectively determine the intensity and duration of work that a patient is capable of safely performing.
2. Uses.
   a. Return to work and job placement decisions.
   b. Disability evaluation.
   c. Determination of work function with non-work-related and work-related injuries.
   d. Determination of functional level in nonoccupational settings.
   e. Intervention and treatment planning for work conditioning or work hardening.
   f. Determination of possible job modifications.
   g. Case management and case closure.

3. Definition.
   a. A detailed examination and evaluation that objectively measures the worker's current level of function within the context of competitive employment demands.
   b. Measurements of the FCE are compared to the physical demands of a job or other functional activity.
4. FCE protocols.
   a. Most common FCEs are 4–6 hours long and objectively measure work demands such as lifting, carrying, walking, bending, overhead work, and hand coordination.
   b. FCEs replicate work tasks in order to find realistic values for the return to work statement needed to conclude the rehabilitation process.
   c. Work Capacity Evaluations (WCEs) are job-specific tests and measures applied consistently to workers with reference to a specific job.
5. Definitions of work intensity.
   a. Sedentary: up to 10 lbs. of force occasionally, negligible weight frequently or constantly, 1.5–2.1 METS.
   b. Light: up to 20 lbs. occasionally, 10 lbs. frequently, negligible weight constantly, 2.2–3.5 METS.
   c. Medium: up to 50 lbs. occasionally, 20 lbs. frequently, 10 lbs. constantly, 3.6–6.3 METS.
   d. Heavy: up to 100 lbs. occasionally, 50 lbs. frequently, 20 lbs. constantly, 6.4–7.5 METS.
   e. Very heavy: > 100 lbs. occasionally, > 50 lbs. frequently, > 20 lbs. constantly, > 7.5 METS.
6. Definitions of work frequency.
   a. Never.
   b. Occasionally: up to one third of the work day.
   c. Frequently: from one third to two thirds of the work day.
   d. Constantly: greater than two thirds of the work day.

Work Conditioning and Work Hardening Programs

1. Definitions.
   a. Work conditioning programs.
      (1) Intensive, work-related, goal-oriented conditioning programs.
      (2) Designed specifically to restore systemic neuromusculoskeletal functions, muscle performance, motor function, ROM, and cardiovascular/pulmonary functions.
   b. Work hardening programs.
      (1) Highly structured, goal-oriented, individualized intervention programs designed to return the patient/client to work.
      (2) Multidisciplinary programs that use real and simulated work activities designed to restore physical, behavioral, and vocational functions.
2. Program content.
   a. Work conditioning.
      (1) Requires work conditioning examination and evaluation.
      (2) Utilizes work conditioning and functional activities related to work.
      (3) Provide multihour sessions of up to 4 hours/day, 5 days/week, 8 weeks.
      (4) Addresses physical and functional needs provided by one discipline.
   b. Work hardening.
      (1) Requires work hardening examination and evaluation.
      (2) Utilizes real or simulated work activities.
      (3) Provided in multihour sessions of up to 8 hours/day, 5 days/week, 8 weeks.
      (4) Addresses physical, functional, behavioral, and vocational needs within a multidisciplinary model.

Manual Material Handling and Lifting Limits

1. Factors affecting "safe" load lifting.
   a. Biomechanical factors.
      (1) Greatest biomechanical stressors and the largest moments during lifting occur in the lumbar spine, specifically the L5-S1 disc.
      (2) Disc compressive forces, shear forces, and torsional forces are believed to be largely responsible for vertebral end-plate fractures, disc herniations, and nerve root irritation.
      (3) The weight of the load and the distance from the load to the base of the spine are significant contributors to lumbosacral compressive and shear forces when using either a squat or stooped lifting posture.
   b. Physiological factors.
      (1) The worker's ability to perform dynamic, repetitive lifting is limited by his or her maximal aerobic capacity.
      (2) Repetitive lifting tasks could exceed the worker's normal energy capacities, which decrease strength and increase the risk of injury.
      (3) Age, gender, and physical conditioning may affect a worker's ability to perform repetitive lifting.
      (4) Lifting from floor to knuckle height requires greater whole-body work, although performing lifts above waist height requires greater shoulder and arm muscle work.
   c. Psychophysical factors.
      (1) The maximal acceptable weight of lift defines what a person can lift repeatedly for an extended period of time without excessive fatigue.

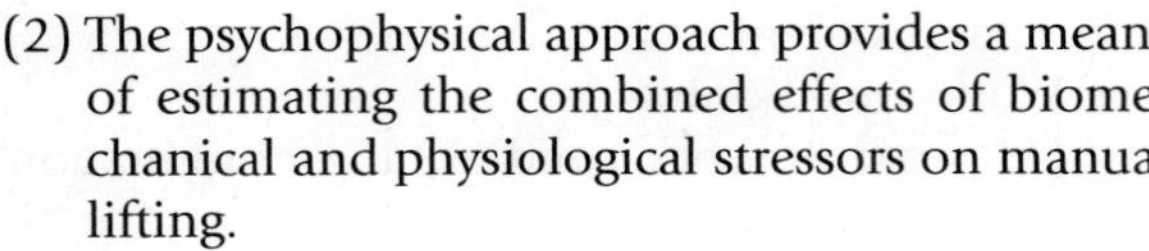

(2) The psychophysical approach provides a means of estimating the combined effects of biomechanical and physiological stressors on manual lifting.

Guidelines for Seated Work

1. Definition.
   a. Sitting transfers body weight to supporting areas.
      (1) Seat pan through ischial tuberosities.
      (2) Backrest through soft tissues.
      (3) Armrests through forearms.
      (4) Floor.
   b. Sitting posture varies with the design of the chair and the task being performed.
      (1) Lumbar spine posture during sitting.
      (2) Pelvis rotates posteriorly and lumbar spine flattens when moving from standing to unsupported sitting.
      (3) Knee and hip angles control spinal posture during sitting, caused by the insertion of various muscles on the pelvis and legs.
   c. Lumbar disc pressure during sitting.
      (1) Compression forces measured at L3 disc: pressures measured with the subject standing are about 35% lower than the pressure measured when the subject is sitting without support.
      (2) Use of a lumbar support decreases lumbar disc pressure.
      (3) Backward inclination of the backrest from 90°–110° results in decreased lumbar disc pressure.
      (4) Decreased disc pressure when arm rests were used.
   d. Chair dimensions for seated work.
      (1) Chair height: sufficient to allow the feet to be placed firmly on the floor or a foot support.
      (2) Knee flexion angle is 90° with the popliteal fold about 2–3 cm (0.8–1.2 in) above the seat surface. If too low, there is excessive knee flexion, the spine is flexed, and the pelvis is posteriorly rotated. If too high, the feet do not reach the floor and there is excessive pressure on the back of the thighs.
      (3) Chair length/depth: the seat pan should provide 10 cm clearance from the popliteal fossa to allow for leg movement and prevent pressure on the back of the knees.
      (4) Seat pan slope: a backward slope of 5° is suggested for normal, upright sitting.
      (5) Arm rest height: the elbow should be flexed to 90° and the shoulder should be in neutral position.

Review Questions

Functional Training, Equipment, and Devices

1. What are the muscle activation patterns during heel strike (initial contact) and heel-off (terminal stance) for the quadriceps, pretibial muscles, and plantar flexors?

2. What type of equipment and ambulatory aids might be needed to progress a morbidly obese patient from a sedentary bed-bound situation to independent ambulation?

3. How does rearfoot posting in a foot orthosis control for valgus or varus?

4. What are the pressure-tolerant areas in the typical transtibial residual limb that are suitable for a total contact socket?

5. What are two conditions that may warrant a therapist recommending a motorized tilt-in-space wheelchair for a patient?

12

Professional Responsibilities

LOIS SIEGELMAN AND WILLIAM FARINA

Chapter Outline

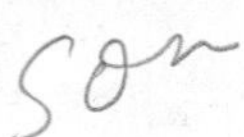

Chapter 12 PRO

Institutional Types

Practice Environments

1. Acute care (short-term hospital).
   a. Treatment for a short-term illness or health problem.
   b. Average patient length of stay is 4–5 days.
   c. Provider may be physician, physician assistant (PA), nurse, physical therapist (PT), etc.
   d. Rapid discharge for next level of care makes the PT's role in patient and family education and in discharge planning increasingly important.
2. Primary care.
   a. Basic or first-level health care.
   b. Provided by primary care physicians (PCPs), including family practice physicians, pediatricians, internists, and sometimes obstetric/gynecologic (OB/GYN) physician specialists.
   c. Provided on an outpatient basis.
   d. PTs support primary care teams through examination, evaluation, diagnosis, prognosis, and prevention of musculoskeletal and neuromuscular disorders.
   e. Often the PCP is the "gatekeeper" to other subspecialists, including physical therapy.
3. Secondary care (specialized care).
   a. Second-level medical services.
   b. Provided by medical specialists, such as cardiologists, urologists, and dermatologists, who do not have first contact with patients.
   c. This care often requires inpatient hospitalization or ambulatory same-day surgery such as hernia repair.
4. Tertiary care (tertiary health care).
   a. Highly specialized, technologically based medical services; e.g., heart, liver, or lung transplants, and other major surgical procedures.
   b. Provided by highly specialized physicians in a hospital setting.
   c. PTs respond to requests for consultation made by other health care practitioners.
5. Subacute care.
   a. An intermediate level of health care for medically fragile patients too ill to be cared for at home.
   b. Provided by medical and nursing services as well as rehabilitative services; e.g., PT, occupational therapy (OT), and speech therapy (ST) at a higher level than is offered in a skilled nursing facility (SNF) on a regular basis.
   c. Provided within the hospital or SNF setting.
6. Long term acute care hospital.
   a. Patients require complex medical intervention from specialized staff including 24 hour physician, nursing care, and therapy.
   b. Diagnoses treated include respiratory failure, ventilator dependency and weaning, septicemia with major complications, skin ulcers with major complications.
   c. Patients stays must be an average of 25 days or more.
7. Ambulatory care (outpatient care).
   a. Includes outpatient preventative, diagnostic, and treatment services.
   b. Provided at medical offices, surgery centers, or outpatient clinics.
   c. Providers may be physicians, PAs, nurse practitioners, PTs, or others.
   d. Less costly than inpatient care. Favored by managed-care plans.
   e. Outpatient rehabilitation centers, PT clinics, outpatient satellites of institutions, or privately owned outpatient clinics.
8. Skilled nursing facility.
   a. Free-standing or part of a hospital transitional care unit.
   b. Care provided by continuous nursing, rehabilitation, and other health care services on a daily basis.
   c. Medicare defines "daily" as 7 days a week of skilled nursing and 5 days a week of skilled therapy.
   d. Patients are not in an acute phase of illness, but require skilled care on an inpatient basis.
   e. SNFs must be certified by Medicare and meet qualifications, including 24-hour nursing coverage, availability of PT, OT, and ST.
9. Acute rehabilitation hospital.
   a. Facility that provides coordinated rehabilitation, social, and vocational services to disabled individuals to facilitate their return to maximal functional capacity.
   b. Patients must be able to participate in a minimum of 3 hours of daily therapy. Most common diagnoses treated are stroke, brain injury, other neurologic conditions (Parkinson's disease, multiple sclerosis), multiple trauma, general rehabilitation (spinal injury, amputation).
   c. Average length of stay is 15 days.
10. Nursing Home (long-term care facility).
    a. Long-term care facility provides services to patients for 60 days or more.

b. Medical services provided to patients with permanent or residual disability caused by a nonreversible pathological health condition.
c. May require specialized care/rehabilitation.

11. Custodial care facility.
    a. Patient care that is not medically required but necessary for the patient who is unable to care for him-/herself.
    b. Custodial care may involve medical or nonmedical services that do not seek a cure.
    c. This type of care is usually not covered under most health care plans.
    d. Daily care is delivered by nonmedical support staff.
12. Hospice care.
    a. Care available for dying patients and their families at home or inpatient settings.
    b. Hospice team includes: nurses, social workers, chaplains, volunteers, and physicians. PT and OT services are optional.
    c. Eligibility for reimbursement.
        (1) Medicare eligibility.
        (2) Certification by physician of terminal illness (≤ 6 months of life).
13. Home health care.
    a. Health care provided to individuals and their families in their homes.
    b. Provided by a home health agency (HHA), which may be governmental, voluntary, or private; nonprofit or for-profit.
    c. Eligible patients include those who:
        (1) Are homebound or have great difficulty leaving the home without assistance or an assistive device.
        (2) Would experience a health risk leaving the home.
        (3) Require skilled care from one of the following services: nursing, PT, OT, or ST.
        (4) Have physician certification.
        (5) Show potential for progress.
        (6) Have more than housekeeping deficits.
    d. Environmental safety is consideration of PT or OT; e.g., proper lighting; securing of scatter rugs, handrails, wheelchair ramps.
    e. Supplemental equipment may be necessary; e.g., raised toilet seats, grab bars, long-handled utensils, if delivered by a licensed durable medical equipment vendor to the home at the time of hospital discharge.
    f. Adaptive equipment ordered in the home is not reimbursable, except for items such as wheelchairs, commodes, and hospital beds.
    g. Substance abuse should be reported immediately to the physician.
    h. Physical abuse should be communicated immediately and directly to the proper authorities; e.g., Department of Social Services or equivalent should be notified if child abuse is suspected.
    i. The laws that mandate reporting of abuse of an elder, disabled individual, or minor may vary from state to state.
14. School system.
    a. The PT serves as a consultant to teachers who work with students with disabilities in the classroom.
    b. Major goal of PT treatment is the child's functioning in the school setting.
    c. Recommendations are made for adaptive equipment to facilitate improved posture, head control, and function; e.g., using a computer, viewing a blackboard, improving mobility from class to class.
15. Private practice.
    a. Entrepreneurial PTs who work for or own a free-standing, independent PT practice.
    b. May accept all insurances with provider numbers.
    c. Settings vary from sports physical therapy and orthopedic clinics, rehabilitation agencies, occupational health.
    d. Must document every visit and complete reevaluations at least every 30 days for reimbursement purposes.

The United States Health Care System

Organization

1. Overview.
    a. A group of decentralized subsystems that serve different populations.
    b. Most Americans have private health insurance via managed care plans (health maintenance organizations, preferred provider organizations), traditional fee-for-service plans, or participate in public programs, such as Medicare or Medicaid.
    c. Decentralization results in overlap in some areas and competition in others; therefore, health care is primarily a business that is market-driven, especially for patients covered by managed-care insurance.
        (1) Patients are viewed as consumers because of this economic focus.

(2) Cost containment while maintaining quality of service is a delicate balancing act that is not always achieved.

d. PCPs have increased significance as the first line for evaluation and intervention, and as the referral source for specialized and/or ancillary services.

2. Health care regulations.

a. Health care is a highly regulated industry, with most regulations mandated by law, at both the state and federal levels.

b. Legally mandated regulations are set forth by the Center for Medicare and Medicaid Services (CMS), a division of U.S. Department of Health and Human Services.

(1) CMS is the federal agency that develops rules and regulations pertaining to federal laws, specifically the Medicare and Medicaid programs.

(2) Facilities that participate in Medicare and/or Medicaid programs are monitored regularly for compliance with CMS guidelines by federal and state surveyors.

(3) Often, state departments of public health monitor Medicare/Medicaid compliance of inpatient institutions, and "fiscal intermediaries" are contracted to monitor compliance of Medicare Part B regulations.

(4) Facilities that repeatedly fail to meet CMS guidelines may lose their Medicare and/or Medicaid certification (e.g., "provider status").

c. Standards related to safety are set forth and enforced by the Occupational Safety and Health Administration (OSHA), a division of the U.S. Department of Labor.

(1) Structural standards and building codes are established and enforced by OSHA to ensure the safety of structures.

(2) The safety of employees and consumers is regulated by OSHA standards for handling infectious materials and blood products, controlling blood-borne pathogens, operating machinery, and handling hazardous substances.

(3) Material Safety Data Sheets are mandated by OSHA. These sheets give employees information about potentially hazardous materials in the workplace and how to protect themselves.

(4) The blood-borne pathogen standard requires institutions to have processes in place to reduce the risk of exposure to blood-borne pathogens. This includes a written safety plan, employee training, and proper disposal practices.

(5) Other OSHA standards cover x-ray safety, electrical and fire safety, and provide for the provision of personal protective equipment (PPE).

d. Individual states develop their own requirements with state agencies to enforce these regulations. State accreditation to obtain licensure for a health care facility is mandatory.

e. Local or county entities also develop regulations pertaining to health care institutions (i.e., physical plant safety features such as fire, elevator, and boiler regulations).

3. Voluntary accreditation.

a. Voluntary accreditation and self-imposed compliance with established standards is sought by most health care organizations.

b. Accreditation is a status awarded for compliance with standards and regulations, promulgated by the specific accrediting agency.

c. Accreditation ensures the public that a health care facility is adequately equipped, meets high standards for patient care, and has qualified professionals and competent staff.

d. Accreditation affirms the competence of practitioners and the quality of health care facilities and organizations.

e. Although national accreditation through an accrediting agency is voluntary, it is mandatory for most third-party reimbursement to meet eligibility requirements for federal government grants and contracts.

f. CMS and many states accept certain national accreditations as meeting their respective requirements for participation in the Medicare and Medicaid programs and for a license to operate.

4. Voluntary accrediting agencies.

a. Joint Commission on the Accreditation of Health Care Organizations (JCAHO).

(1) The voluntary agency that accredits health care facilities according to JCAHO-established standards and conditions.

(2) JCAHO accredits hospitals, SNFs, home health agencies, preferred provider organizations (PPOs), rehabilitation facilities, health maintenance organizations (HMOs), behavioral health (including mental health and chemical dependency facilities, ambulatory clinics, physician's networks, hospice care, long-term care facilities, and others).

b. Commission on Accreditation of Rehabilitation Facilities (CARF): the voluntary agency that accredits free-standing rehabilitation facilities and the rehabilitative programs of larger hospital systems in the areas of behavioral health, employment (work hardening) and community support services, and medical rehabilitation (spinal cord injury, chronic pain).

c. Accreditation Council for Services for Mentally Retarded and Other Developmentally Disabled Persons (AC-MRDD): a voluntary agency that accredits programs or agencies serving persons with developmental disabilities.

d. Outpatient centers for comprehensive rehabilitation can be accredited by JCAHO, CARF, and/or AC-MRDD.
e. National League for Nursing/American Public Health Association (NLN/APHA): a voluntary agency that accredits home health and community nursing agencies offering nursing and other health services outside hospitals, extended-care facilities, and nursing homes.
f. Some accreditation bodies may perform unannounced or unscheduled site surveys to ensure ongoing compliance.

5. Accreditation process.
a. Accreditation is initiated by the organization that submits an application for review, followed by a survey conducted by the accrediting agency.
b. A self-study or self-assessment is conducted to examine the organization based on the accrediting agency's standards.
c. An onsite review is conducted with an individual reviewer or surveyor, or a team that visits the organization.
d. The accreditation and reaccreditation processes involve all staff. Tasks include document preparation, hosting onsite visit teams, and interviews with accreditors.
e. Once accredited, the organization undergoes periodic review, typically every 3 years.

Reimbursement/Third-Party Payers for Health Care Services

1. Medicare.
a. Administered by federal government CMS, through the extension of Title XVIII of the Social Security Act, 1965.
b. Provides medical coverage and health care services to individuals:
(1) ≥ 65 years.
(2) With permanent kidney failure or other long-term disabilities at < 65 years.
c. Social Security Amendment of 1983.
(1) Established Medicare's prospective payment system.
(a) Based on diagnostic-related groups (DRGs).
- Classification system that places patients into disease categories or groups.
- Basis for Medicare's prospective payment system.
(b) Hospital paid a specific amount per diagnosis, regardless of the length of stay, number of services provided, or tests performed.
d. Medicare Part A benefits.
(1) Hospital insurance that covers:
(a) Inpatient hospital care.
- Limits number of hospital days.
(b) Skilled nursing facilities—first 100 days.
(c) Home Health Agencies.
(d) Hospice care.
(2) Provides basic protection against the cost of health care.
(3) Does not cover all medical expenses or the cost of long-term or custodial care.
(4) Provides coverage for patients that have been on Social Security disability for 24 months.
(5) Annual deductible fees paid by the patient.
e. Medicare Part B.
(1) Medical insurance that covers:
(a) Physician visits.
(b) Outpatient laboratory tests and x-rays.
(c) Ambulance transportation.
(d) Outpatient physical and occupational therapy services (hospital and private practice).
(e) Home health care provided by a PT in independent practice (PTIP).
(f) Durable medical equipment (e.g., wheelchairs, canes, walkers) determined to be "medically necessary."
(g) Medical supplies not covered by hospital insurance.
(h) Residents of long-term care facilities.
(2) Each patient must pay a monthly premium.
(3) PT treatment does not need to be given on a daily basis.
(4) The physician responsible for the care of the patient referred for PT must "certify" the plan of care.
(5) Only PT care that is considered to be "skilled," "necessary," and "certified" by the referring physician will be reimbursed by Medicare.
(6) Reimbursement mandates successfully reporting data using quality outcome measures.

2. Medicaid.
a. A joint state and federal program mandated by Title XIX of the Social Security Act.
b. Provides health care services to the poor, elderly, and disabled who do not receive Medicare, regardless of age.
c. Benefits vary from state to state.
d. Preauthorization is needed by a physician before treatment can begin.
e. Individual states can determine the scope, duration, and amount of services provided.

3. Workers' compensation.
a. Regulated by state statutes and administered by private insurers, self-insured employers, or other agencies in some states.
b. Provides health care for individuals injured on the job.

c. Some states limit the number of visits per diagnosis, and/or require a preapproval process for reimbursement.
d. Other states require that the total number of visits, total number of weeks (duration), and number of treatments per week (frequency) to be usual, customary, and reasonable.
e. Employers only contribute to the fund.
   (1) All large employers (≥ 10 employees) or high-risk employers must contribute to workers' compensation.

4. Private health insurance.
   a. Includes commercial insurance, fee-for-service or traditional indemnity plans, or employers who are self-insured.
   b. Patient has freedom to choose his/her providers.
   c. Preauthorization may not be needed.
   d. The number of PT visits should be usual, customary, and reasonable, which are often defined contractually in the insurance policy.
5. Managed health care systems.
   a. Third-party payers direct patients to certain providers and monitor services in order to avoid excessive and inappropriate treatment and limit access.
      (1) Third-party payers frequently use gatekeepers (usually the PCP) to manage access to certain providers, including PT.
      (2) Use techniques such as preadmission certification, concurrent reviews, financial incentives, or penalties.
      (3) Goal is to contain costs and ensure favorable patient outcomes.
   b. Health Maintenance Organization (HMO).
      (1) A form of managed care that provides a broad spectrum of health services to individuals and families for a preset amount of money.
      (2) Employers contract for these services as a benefit to their employees.
      (3) Employees may pay a small fee per visit (copay); e.g., $20/visit.
      (4) Patients are locked into use of the system of member health care providers and affiliating facilities.
      (5) Some HMOs allow patients to seek care "out of network," but at a higher or additional cost to the patient.
      (6) PCPs chosen by individuals act as gatekeepers for medical care beyond their scope of practice.
         (a) Must authorize PT services before they can be provided.
      (7) Total number of visits per diagnosis is limited.
      (8) Types of HMOs.
         (a) Individual Practice Associations (IPAs).
            - Physician groups contract independently with the HMO.
            - Physicians work out of their own offices instead of a central facility.
         (b) Prepaid Group Plan (PGP).
            - Physicians practice out of a central location.
   c. PPO.
      (1) A group of providers, usually physicians or hospitals, that offer health care services as an entity to employers.
      (2) Providers discount their fees to attract patients.
      (3) Patients are not locked into PPO providers, but receive financial incentives to use services through the PPO network.
      (4) An employer can offer its employees a traditional health care plan, HMO, or PPO.
      (5) Preauthorization is needed before services can be provided.
   d. Both HMOs and PPOs contain one or more of the following elements:
      (1) Capitation: a system whereby providers are paid a certain amount per case, no matter how many visits are rendered.
      (2) Copayment: insured's charge for the covered service.
         (a) Made at the time of service.
         (b) Predetermined amount.
      (3) Coinsurance: insured's share of the cost of the covered service.
         (a) Expressed as a percentage; e.g., 80% paid by insurance company and 20% paid by insured.
      (4) The provider is at financial risk if services are overutilized. This is called "shared risk."
6. Health savings accounts.
   a. Tax-free savings account that can be used to pay for health-related expenses and retiree health expenses.
   b. Must have a high-deductible health plan, which is an insurance product that covers catastrophic health occurrences.
7. Personal payment and free care.
   a. Individuals without health insurance must personally pay for all medical care.
   b. Individuals who cannot pay for health care can receive pro bono, or free, care through philanthropic donations and services.
   c. Many states have programs that offset some of the expense of providing free care by relying on other not-for-profit organizations.
8. Restructuring the health care system.
   a. Cost containment created incentives for health care providers and hospitals to control both cost and utilization of inpatient services by:
      (1) Reducing average length of hospital stay.
      (2) Reducing routine and/or unnecessary diagnostic testing and treatment.
      (3) Increasing use of outpatient diagnostic testing and treatment.

(4) Increasing utilization of home care and skilled long-term care.

9. Affordable Care Act.
   a. Because many Americans were uninsured due to finances and/or pre-existing conditions, the Affordable Care Act was enacted at the federal level. The overall goal is to provide quality affordable healthcare for all Americans. Some features include:
      (1) Patient bill of rights.
      (2) Increased cost-free preventive services.
      (3) Closing the gap in Medicare Part D prescription drug plan coverage or Medicare Advantage plan coverage where the Medicare plan member was 100% responsible for the cost of their prescription drugs (donut hole).
      (4) Mandatory affordable insurance options for small businesses and individuals.
      (5) Young adult coverage.
      (6) Prohibiting denial of coverage for pre-existing conditions in children.
      (7) Establishment of Accountable Care Organizations.
10. Accountable Care Organizations (ACOs).
   a. On October 20, 2011, the Centers for Medicare & Medicaid Services (CMS), an agency within the Department of Health and Human Services (HHS), finalized new rules under the Affordable Care Act to help physicians, hospitals, and other health care providers better coordinate care for Medicare patients through ACOs.
   b. Under the final rule, an ACO refers to a group of providers and suppliers of services (e.g., hospitals, physicians, and others involved in patient care) that will work together to coordinate care for the Medicare fee-for-service patients they serve. The goal of an ACO is to deliver seamless, high-quality care for Medicare beneficiaries, instead of the fragmented care that often results from a fee-for-service payment system in which different providers receive different, disconnected payments. The ACO will be a patient-centered organization where the patient and providers are partners in care decisions.
   c. An ACO can be based in physician practices, hospitals, or via networks comprised of partnerships or joint venture arrangements between hospitals and ACO professionals.

Defensible Documentation

1. The International Classification of Functioning, Disability, and Health Resources (ICF) model.
   a. Developed by the World Health Organization (WHO) and endorsed by the American Physical Therapy Association (APTA), the World Confederation for Physical Therapy, and other international organizations.
   b. The ICF model identifies dimensions of functioning (body functions and body structures, activities, participation) and dimensions of disability (impairments, activity limitations, participation restrictions). See Box 12-1 for complete definitions.
   c. The ICF model serves as a platform for communication among medical personnel, patients, and their family/caregivers.
   d. The ICF model serves as a platform for choosing and comparing interventions.
   e. The ICF model uses a unified, standard language and framework and permits documentation of functioning and disability as a multidimensional phenomena experienced at the level of the body, the person, and society.
   f. The ICF model represents a shift away from the medical model that focuses on the condition or the disease affecting the individual.
2. Outcome measures organized by the ICF categories.
   a. Physical therapists select tests and measures as a means to:
      (1) Identify and characterize signs and symptoms of pathology/pathophysiology, impairments, functioning, and disability.
      (2) Establish a diagnosis and prognosis, select interventions, and document changes in patient/client status.
      (3) Monitor outcomes, document end points of care, and ensure appropriate and timely discharge.
   b. Documentation is enhanced by using measurements with demonstrated reliability and validity.
3. Medical records.
   a. Complete, timely, and accurate documentation is essential for:
      (1) Patient safety.
      (2) Accurate communication between health care providers.
      (3) Compliance with federal and state regulations.
      (4) Appropriate utilization for third-party payers.
      (5) Historical record for potential legal situations.
   b. General guidelines for documentation.
      (1) All documentation must comply with all applicable state, federal, and regulatory agency laws and regulations.
      (2) All documentation must comply with Medicare guidelines and any other guidelines required by the local insurance carrier to ensure reimbursement.
      (3) Patient's right to privacy must always be respected and protected.
      (4) Release of any medical information must be authorized by the patient.

BOX 12-1 Terminology: Functioning, Disability, and Health

Health Condition is an umbrella term for disease, disorder, injury, or trauma, and may also include other circumstances, such as aging, stress, congenital anomaly, or genetic predisposition. It may also include information about pathogeneses and/or etiology.

Body Functions are physiological functions of body systems (including psychological functions).

Body Structures are anatomical parts of the body such as organs, limbs, and their components.

Impairments are the problems in body function or structure, such as a significant deviation or loss.

Activity is the execution of a task or action by an individual.

Participation is involvement in a life situation.

Activity Limitations are difficulties an individual may have in executing activities.

Participation Restrictions are problems an individual may experience in involvement in life situations.

Contextual Factors represent the entire background of an individual's life and living situation.

- **Environmental Factors** make up the physical, social, and attitudinal environment in which people live and conduct their lives, including social attitudes, architectural characteristics, and legal and social structures.
- **Personal Factors** are the particular background of an individual's life, including gender, age, coping styles, social background, education, profession, past and current experience, overall behavior pattern, character, and other factors that influence how disability is experienced by an individual.

Performance describes what an individual does in his or her current environment.

Capacity describes an individual's ability to execute a task or an action (highest probable level of functioning in a given domain at a given moment).

From The World Health Organization. International Classification of Functioning, Disability, and Health Resources (ICF). World Health Organization, Geneva, 2002. http://www.who.int/classifications/en/

(5) Records must be kept in a safe and secure place for a certain number of years (varies from state to state; usually 7 years).

c. Basic principles of documentation (see Guide to Physical Therapist Practice, APTA).
  (1) Documentation should be consistent with Guidelines for Physical Therapy Documentation, APTA.
  (2) All documents must be legible.
  (3) Only medically approved abbreviations or symbols can be used.
  (4) Mistakes should be crossed out with a single line through the error, and then initialed and dated by the therapist.
  (5) White-out material should never be used to correct text in a medical record.
  (6) Informed consent for treatment must be given only by a competent adult.
  (7) Noncompetent adults or minors must have a parent or legal guardian give written consent/proxy.
  (8) Document each episode of treatment.
  (9) Patient name and some other unique identifier should be on each page.
  (10) Date each entry (some payers require length of time per visit, particularly Medicare and Medicaid).
  (11) Sign each entry with first and last names and professional designation.
  (12) Record significant events; e.g., phone conversations with the physician or nurse.
  (13) Document treatment rendered in objective, measurable, and functional terms.
  (14) Document patient's response to treatment.
  (15) When goals and outcomes are reached, complete a discharge plan.
  (16) Electronic documentation systems must have both security and confidentiality provisions in place.
  (17) A computer signature is acceptable on a secured computer documentation system.
  (18) When correcting a charting error on an electronic medical record, it must be clearly indicated that a change was made without deletion of the original medical record.

d. Progress notes.
  (1) Document specific treatment, equipment provided; include signature of therapist who provides care.
  (2) Document patient response to treatment, functional progress, goals achieved, revision of goals, and treatment plan modifications.
  (3) Interim progress notes can be written by:
    (a) PT.
    (b) Physical therapist assistant (PTA).
    (c) Student (PT or PTA) notes must be cosigned by supervising therapist.

e. Reevaluation/summary progress report.
  (1) Completed minimally every 30 days for all Medicare patients; includes:
    (a) Restatement of initial problem.
    (b) Length of time patient has been treated.
    (c) Progress or regression since last summary or initial evaluation.
    (d) Rationale for continued care.
    (e) Revision of goals and outcomes.
    (f) Revision of plan of care.
    (g) Changes documented are stated in behavioral, objective, measurable, and functional terms; e.g., range of motion, strength, sitting tolerance.
  (2) Must be written by a PT.
    (a) PT students can complete if cosigned by supervising therapist.

f. Discharge summary includes:
  (1) Restatement of initial problem.
  (2) Length of time the patient has been treated.
  (3) Progress since initial evaluation.
  (4) Patient progress toward goal and outcome achievement.
  (5) Reason for discharge.
  (6) Must be written by a PT.
    (a) PT students can complete if cosigned by supervising therapist.

g. Discharge plan.
  (1) Referrals, written or verbal, related to patient's continued care.
    (a) Additional services.
    (b) Type of supervision the patient will require.
    (c) Home care.
    (d) Family intervention.
    (e) Patient and family education requirements.
    (f) Written home exercise program (HEP).
    (g) List of equipment ordered, vendor's name, and delivery date.
    (h) Social and community needs of the patient.
    (i) Date of discharge.
    (j) A PT should discharge a patient from PT treatment when maximum benefit is reached.
    (k) Identifies needs of patient after discharge from a facility.
      - Preferable setting for discharge.
  (2) Must be written by a PT.
    (a) PT students can complete if cosigned by supervising therapist.

h. Advance directives.
  (1) A legal document that delineates a patient's wishes for future medical care or no medical care.
  (2) Are implemented if the patient is cognitively impaired.
  (3) Can include living wills and durable power of attorney.

4. Common reasons for payment denials.
  a. Incomplete/insufficient documentation. Documentation that is submitted without required documentation elements may cause a denial of payment.
  b. Medically unnecessary. Poor documentation that does not fully explain the reasons for therapeutic interventions may result in denial of payment.
  c. Incorrect coding: Failure to document the proper CPT (Current Procedural Terminology), World Health Organization's International Classification of Diseases, 9th Revision, Clinical Modification (ICD-9-CM 2001) or other diagnosis or treatment codes can result in denial of payment.
  d. Pay for performance. As pay for performance programs (payment based on improved functional outcomes) grow, poor documentation may result in reduced payments for services.

Elements of Patient/Client Management

1. Initial examination/evaluation/diagnosis/prognosis.
  a. The PT performs an initial examination and evaluation to establish a diagnosis and prognosis prior to intervention.
  b. The PT examination:
    (1) Identifies the PT needs of the patient or client.
    (2) Incorporates appropriate tests and measures to facilitate outcome measurement.
    (3) Produces data that are sufficient to allow evaluation, diagnosis, prognosis, and the establishment of a plan of care.
    (4) May result in recommendations for additional services to meet the needs of the patient or client.
    (5) Used to determine proper diagnosis and treatment coding.
2. Examination.
  a. History.
    (1) Patient's name, age, race, and sex.
    (2) Chief complaint and risk factors, relevance for PT intervention, if applicable.
    (3) Referral source.
    (4) Pertinent diagnosis and medical history.
    (5) Demographic characteristics, including pertinent psychological, social, cultural, and environmental factors.
    (6) Concurrent medical services provided.
    (7) Pertinent problems.
    (8) Statement describing patient's understanding of problem.
    (9) Goals of the patient and/or patient's family.

b. Objective findings/systems review.
   (1) Physiologic and anatomic status.
      (a) Cognitive status, alertness, judgment, communication.
      (b) Neurological status: pain, sensation, reflexes, balance, motor function, etc.
      (c) Musculoskeletal: joint range of motion, strength, posture, etc.
      (d) Cardiovascular: vital signs, endurance, etc.
      (e) Integumentary.
   (2) Functional status: mobility, transfers, activities of daily living (ADLs), work, school, or athletic performance, etc.
   (3) Communication ability, affect, cognition, language, and learning style.

3. Evaluation.
   a. Analysis of current impairments and effect on function.
   b. Analysis of prolonged impairment, functional limitation, and disability.
   c. Analysis of living environment, potential discharge destination, and social supports.
4. Diagnosis.
   a. Encompasses a cluster of signs, symptoms, syndromes, or categories.
   b. Guides therapist in determining appropriate interventions strategy.
   c. Guides therapist in referring patient/client to an appropriate practitioner for services outside the scope of PT.
5. Prognosis.
   a. Includes predicted optimal level of improvement in function and amount of time needed to reach that level.
   b. Can also predict levels of improvement at various intervals during the course of therapy.
6. Plan of care.
   a. The PT establishes a plan of care for the patient/client based on the examination, evaluation, diagnosis, prognosis, anticipated goals, and expected outcomes of the planned interventions for identified impairments, functional limitations, and disabilities.
   b. The PT, in consultation with appropriate disciplines, plans for discharge of the patient/client, taking into consideration achievement of anticipated goals and expected outcomes, and provides for appropriate follow-up or referral.
   c. The PT also addresses risk reduction, prevention, impact on societal resources, and patient/client satisfaction.
   d. Identifies realistic long-term and short-term goals and expected functional outcomes.
      (1) Goals address impairment, functional limitations, and/or the prevention of additional problems.
      (2) Goals should address:
         (a) Who will participate in the activity?
         (b) A detailed description of the activity.
         (c) The connection of the activity to a specific function.
         (d) A specific measure for success.
         (e) A time measure.
7. Intervention.
   a. The PT provides, or directs, and supervises the PT intervention consistent with the results of the examination, evaluation, diagnosis, prognosis, and plan of care.
   b. The intervention is:
      (1) Provided under the ongoing direct care or supervision of the PT.
      (2) Provided in such a way that delegated responsibilities are commensurate with the qualifications and the legal limitations of the PT support and professional personnel involved in the intervention.
      (3) Altered in accordance with changes in response or status.
      (4) Provided at a level that is consistent with current PT practice.
      (5) Interdisciplinary when necessary to meet the needs of the patient or client.
   c. Documentation of the intervention is:
      (1) Dated and appropriately authenticated by the PT or, when permissible by law, by the PTA, or both.
8. Reexamination.
   a. The PT reexamines the patient/client as necessary during an episode of care to evaluate progress or change in patient/client status, and modifies the plan of care accordingly or discontinues PT services.
   b. The PT reexamination:
      (1) Identifies ongoing patient/client needs.
      (2) May result in recommendations for additional services, discharge, or discontinuation of PT needs.
9. Discharge/discontinuation of intervention.
   a. The PT discharges the patient/client from PT services when the anticipated goals or expected outcomes for the patient/client have been achieved.
   b. The PT discontinues intervention when the patient/client is unable to continue to progress toward goals or when the PT determines that the patient/client will no longer benefit from PT.
   c. Discharge:
      (1) Occurs at the end of an episode of care, and is the end of PT services provided during that episode.
   d. Discontinuation:
      (1) Also occurs when the patient/client, caregiver, or legal guardian declines to continue intervention.

10. Successful documentation practices.
    a. Incorporate evidence-based practice principles. Use standard tests and measures that are valid and reliable, and select interventions based on research and practice.
    b. Demonstrate progress in specific and functional terms.
    c. Document medical necessity and reasons for skilled care.
    d. Document to stand up in a court of law. Document fully, and limit the use of jargon and obscure abbreviations. Sign and date all entries. Be factual and objective.

Management and Legal Issues

Human Resources

1. Interview.
    a. Performed by supervisor, director, and also possibly a member of the human resources department.
    b. Purpose is to meet with prospective employee.
        (1) Exchange questions and answers to obtain enough information to make an informed decision.
        (2) Questions asked are informational to encourage discussion rather than questions that require "yes or no" answers.
        (3) No questions may be asked about a person's age, religion, race, marital status, politics, national origin, or number of children.
        (4) Information regarding academic record, educational program, or references cannot be obtained without consent.
        (5) Many employers will require a criminal background check (criminal offender record information referred to as CORI) that requires the consent of the applicant to pursue.
        (6) Interviewer provides information about:
            (a) Advantages and disadvantages of the organization.
            (b) Benefits available.
            (c) Work hours.
            (d) Vacation, sick, and personal time.
            (e) Salary range.
            (f) Job description.
    c. Employers look for the following information in an interview.
        (1) Decision-making style.
        (2) Communications skills.
        (3) Interpersonal skills: poise, tact, ability to work in groups.
        (4) Leadership.
        (5) Achievement record and relevant employment experience.
        (6) Sense of personal direction.
    d. Documents reviewed for employment:
        (1) Job application: completeness, attention to detail.
        (2) Previous employment experience.
        (3) Transcript from educational institution (especially for new graduates): grade point average and courses taken may be important in interview process.
        (4) Résumé: a brief written summary that highlights personal, educational, and professional qualifications and experience.
        (5) References.
            (a) Professional: former employers, clinical supervisors, faculty.
            (b) Character: family, friend, clergy.
2. Job descriptions.
    a. General summary of responsibilities.
        (1) Provides overview of position including supervisor relationships.
    b. Specific job responsibilities.
        (1) Identifies the specific responsibilities of the position.
        (2) Establishes performance standards.
        (3) Establishes skilled and nonskilled requirements of job.
        (4) Formalizes basic performance expectations by describing duties in detail.
        (5) Establishes degree of decision-making authority and autonomy.
        (6) Organizational and supervisory relationships of position.
            (a) Position title.
            (b) Department division.
            (c) Title of position's supervisor.
    c. Job specifications.
        (1) Educational requirements; e.g., graduate from accredited PT program.
        (2) State licensure.
        (3) Previous experience requirements.
        (4) Essential job functions or specific physical and mental demands of position.
            (a) Lifting requirements.
            (b) Transferring requirements.

(c) Ambulatory or positioning requirements.
(d) Proficiency in reading/writing/comprehension.
(e) Maintaining static postures: performing therapeutic procedures for several minutes.

(5) Ability to plan and organize time, and other work habits.

(6) Problem-solving skills.

3. Performance appraisal.
   a. Assesses an employee's performance in relation to performance expectations established with objective criteria.
   b. Written report and discussed verbally.
   c. Frequency can be 3–6 months or annually.
   d. Correlates to job description and goals of the organization.
   e. Improves communication between the employee and employer.
   f. Feedback should be immediate, specific, and communicated directly.
   g. Outcomes of performance appraisals can be motivational and used as a reward system; e.g., raises, bonuses, promotions. May also identify performance issues and areas for improvement.
   h. Examples of methods of review:
      (1) Essay appraisal: short paragraph on strengths and weaknesses.
      (2) Performance criteria-based method: based on functional job description using a weighted rating scale (most important task gets highest rating); e.g., patient evaluation, weighted average of 5, and personal appearance 2.
   i. Objective performance goals should be established for the next review.
4. Unions.
   a. Organized group of workers with the same goals and objectives.
   b. Provides collective bargaining when negotiating work contracts.
      (1) Salaries.
      (2) Fringe benefits.
      (3) Hours of work.
      (4) Conditions of work site.
   c. Mediates grievances due to labor disputes, disciplinary problems, etc.
5. Policy and procedure manual.
   a. Provides extensive information on what shall be done and how it shall be done in a PT department.
   b. Required by JCAHO, CARF, and other accrediting agencies. Often required by other state regulatory bodies, such as state boards of public health.
   c. Policies are broad statements that guide in decision-making. They may include:
      (1) Scope of service.
         (a) Mission and philosophy statement.
         (b) Identifies the types of services provided, hours available, referral requirements (if applicable), staffing, and other general information about the service.
      (2) Operational policies.
         (a) Billing policies.
         (b) Referral policies (if appropriate).
         (c) Medical record management.
         (d) Quality assurance and improvement activities.
         (e) Other applicable clinical policies.
      (3) Human resources policies.
         (a) Vacation: paid time off; varies according to length of employment, seniority, or other criteria.
         (b) Introductory period (also called probationary period).
         (c) Job descriptions and performance appraisal policies.
         (d) Time off, leave of absence, sabbaticals.
            - Military service.
            - Maternity leave.
            - Medical leave.
            - Jury duty.
         (e) Dress code.
   d. Procedures: specific guides to job behaviors for all departmental personnel, visitors, and patients that standardize activities with a high level of risk.
      (1) Safety and emergency procedures.
      (2) Equipment management, cleaning, maintaining, training requirements, safety inspections.
      (3) Hazardous waste management.
      (4) Disciplinary procedures.
         (a) Manager presents problem in clear and concise terms, and specifically references the problem to the job description and expectations.
         (b) Discussion is on performance discrepancy.
         (c) Employee is given chance to respond.
         (d) Manager presents action to be taken and why.
         (e) Follow-up date for reevaluation is set.
         (f) Consequences of noncompliance are established.
         (g) Documentation of meeting is objective.
6. Staff motivation.
   a. Sustains individual behavior toward attainment of an objective or goal by providing:
      (1) Challenging work, varied treatment assignments with opportunity to receive feedback regarding performance.
      (2) Good working conditions.
         (a) Essential equipment should be available for proper patient care.
      (3) Recognition of performance (praise or positive feedback, salary, bonuses, raises, and/or promotions).

(4) Enhanced opportunity to achieve job-related goals.
(a) Outline of policies.
(b) Development of a clear job description.
(c) Outline job responsibilities.
(5) Concern as a supervisor, in resolving work-related problems.
(6) Acknowledgment of the contributions of the staff toward realization of the mission, and scope of the service and/or institution.
(7) Fair compensation based on market factors and required qualifications, while ensuring equity among the staff of the department/service.
(8) Consultation with supervisor and involved staff member regarding problems that affect his or her employment.
(9) Realistic job expectations.
(a) Supervisor should avoid promising more than can be delivered; e.g., promising a promotion to a senior position when no budget has been approved.

7. Continuing education.
a. Ongoing educational activities to foster life-long learning.
(1) Enhances clinical knowledge.
(2) Exposes, instructs, and teaches therapists/assistants new techniques and technologies.
b. Educational programs can be delivered a variety of ways.
(1) On-site programs.
(a) In-services.
(b) Journal clubs.
(c) Case presentations.
(2) Off-site programs.
(a) Continuing education programs.
(b) National and state physical therapy meetings.
(c) Special interest group–sponsored courses.
c. Frequency can vary according to time and resources.
d. Employers should support and may subsidize staff member's attendance. Should promote professionalism, educational development, and continued competence.
e. Each state has its own requirements and expectations for licensee continuing education.

8. Sexual harassment.
a. All employees are protected through both state and federal laws through the EEOC (Equal Employment Opportunity Commission).
b. Sexual advances, requests for sexual favors, and verbal or physical conduct of a sexual nature.
(1) Submission to or rejection of such advances is made (explicitly or implicitly) a term or condition of employment and/or may affect promotions or other things such as vacations, etc.
(2) Such advances have the purpose or effect of unreasonably interfering with an individual's work performance by creating an intimidating, hostile, humiliating, or sexually offensive work environment.
c. Either sex may be the harasser.
d. Sexual harassment may occur regardless of the intentions of the harasser.
e. Harasser can be the victim's supervisor, a supervisor in another area, a coworker, or a nonemployee.
f. Harasser's conduct must be unwelcome.
g. Examples of sexual harassment.
(1) Sexual jokes.
(2) Leering, whistling, and brushing against the body.
(3) Display of sexually graphic art, cartoons, objects.
(4) Request for sexual favors in exchange for job benefits.
h. Employee education and prevention is the best tool against sexual harassment.
i. Individual can file a complaint through the human resources department.
j. Unlawful to retaliate against an individual for filing a complaint.

9. Non-discrimination laws.
a. Prevent a facility from discrimination against employees regarding race, color, religion, gender, or national origin.
b. Title VII of the Civil Rights Act of 1964 prohibits employment discrimination based on:
(1) Race.
(2) Color.
(3) Sex.
(4) Religion.
(5) National origin.
(6) Sexual harassment.
c. The Age Discrimination and Employment Act of 1967.
(1) Prohibits employers from discriminating against persons from 40–70 years of age in any area of employment.
d. 1973 Rehabilitation Act.
(1) Prohibits employment discrimination based on disability in:
(a) Federal executive agencies.
(b) All institutions receiving Medicare, Medicaid, and other federal support.
e. The Americans with Disabilities Act (ADA), 1990.
(1) Prevents discrimination against people with disabilities.
(2) Ensures their integration into mainstream American life.
(3) The definition of "disabilities" encompasses a wide range of physical and mental conditions.

(4) Requires businesses of ≥ 15 employees to accommodate needs of people with disabilities to facilitate their economic independence in both the public and private sectors.
(5) Equal Employment Opportunity Commission (EEOC) oversees issues and interprets regulations.
(6) Requires reasonable accommodation to the workplace by removing barriers unless this would cause "undue hardship" (an action requiring significant difficulty or expense).
   (a) Installing an elevator so the individual could access upper floors might be considered an undue hardship.
(7) PTs serve as consultants to:
   (a) Employers helping them meet their responsibilities.
   (b) Disabled, helping them achieve their rehabilitation potential and rights under law.

Departmental Operations Management

1. Meetings.
   a. Staff meeting.
      (1) Regularly held departmental meetings with a specific agenda set in advance.
      (2) Purpose is to discuss department or hospital/management business, state or national PT issues, and to educate staff members.
      (3) Agendas are predetermined to ensure that the objectives and purpose of the meeting are clear.
   b. Supervisory meeting.
      (1) Supervisor and staff meet regularly.
         (a) To discuss patient-care issues.
      (2) One-on-one meeting designed to meet the needs of the staff member.
   c. Team meeting.
      (1) Usually scheduled at least weekly.
      (2) Interdisciplinary (physicians, nurses, PTs, OTs, social services, etc.) to improve communication between all staff.
      (3) Purpose is to:
         (a) Discuss and coordinate patient care services.
         (b) Set goals and outcomes for individual patients.
         (c) Discuss goal/outcome achievement necessary for discharge.
         (d) Discuss discharge plans including destination, equipment needs, home-care services, etc.
2. Strategic planning.
   a. Organizational planning process for goal achievement and future goals.
      (1) Based on the organization's mission and philosophy statement.
      (2) Used for developing plans for implementation to achieve identified goals.
   b. Results of strategic planning process summarized in strategic plan.
      (1) Provides focused direction so goals of organization are achieved.
      (2) Identifies individuals responsible to develop and carry out the plan; e.g., staff members, department director sets the timeline, and the expected outcomes.
      (3) Informs external parties about organization.
      (4) Goals are time related; e.g., 1-year, 3-year, or 5-year plans.
      (5) Methodology for evaluating the progress of the plan should be developed as part of the plan.
      (6) Analysis of progress toward goals should be done by the director/manager at least quarterly.
   c. Strategic plans are always driven by and consistent with the organization's mission and philosophy.
3. Incident/occurrence and sentinel event reporting.
   a. Incident/occurrence report is used to document incidents that involve patients and/or staff and that result in harm and/or the potential for harm to the patient and/or staff.
      (1) Incident reports are not part of the medical record, nor are they referenced in the medical record.
      (2) Used to document additional information, circumstances, contributing factors that would not be appropriate to include in the medical record.
      (3) Used to evaluate systems and processes that may have contributed to the cause for the purpose of correcting and/or improving underlying causes or contributing factors.
      (4) Are part of an internal quality improvement program.
      (5) Can be used as a component of individual employee performance appraisal and improvement.
   b. Sentinel event: a specific, patient-related occurrence in which an unexpected finding or outcome can be analyzed to improve processes, systems, or therapist performance and reduce the likelihood of reoccurrence.
      (1) Part of a comprehensive quality assurance and improvement program.
      (2) When a sentinel event occurs, a "root cause" analysis is done to identify underlying problems with processes, systems, or performance that can be improved to reduce the likelihood of recurrence.
      (3) Many regulatory and accrediting agencies require sentinel event reporting and analysis, particularly on specific types of incidents.

4. Policy and procedure manual.
   a. Provides extensive information on what is to be accomplished and how it is to be accomplished in an organization, physical therapy department, and/or specific units or clinics.
   b. Policy and procedure manuals are required by:
      (1) The Joint Commission of Accreditation of Healthcare Organizations (JCAHO).
      (2) Commission on Accreditation of Rehabilitation Facilities (CARF).
   c. Policies are broad statements used as a guide in decision-making and may vary greatly depending on facility and its organizational structure.
      (1) Operational policies.
         (a) Billing policies.
         (b) Medical record management.
         (c) Quality assurance and improvement activities.
      (2) Human resources policies.
         (a) Vacation/time off.
         (b) Probationary period as a new employee.
         (c) Leave of absence/maternity leave.
         (d) Dress code.
      (3) Procedures.
         (a) Procedures are specific guides to job behaviors for all personnel.
            (1) Safety and emergency procedures.
            (2) Equipment management.
            (3) Hand washing.
            (4) Hazardous waste management.
            (5) Disciplinary action.
            (6) Reporting of abuse.
         (b) Policies outline specific procedures that all employees need to follow.
         (c) Disregard for policies and procedures can lead to disciplinary action and possible termination.
5. Health care marketing.
   a. Assess the true needs and wants of the patient/client (external factors).
   b. Analyze the strengths, weaknesses, opportunities, and threats (SWOT Analysis) of the organization to meet the needs of the customer.
   c. A needs assessment should be conducted, before providing a service or planning a new facility to determine:
      (1) Where is the market (consumer)?
      (2) Does a need for the service exist (environment)?
      (3) Who is the competition?
      (4) In-depth analysis of the marketplace, including demographical and epidemiological data.
      (5) Review of the literature.
      (6) Survey of colleagues and referral sources.
   d. Marketing methods:
      (1) Brochures, newsletters, educational pamphlets, newspaper articles, Internet.
      (2) Guest appearances on television, radio, and at local organizations.
      (3) Professional referral.
      (4) Word of mouth.
      (5) Direct marketing to managed-care groups; e.g., sport injuries, low back pain, and referral sources.
6. Service management.
   a. Management principles, functions, and strategies.
      (1) Management with a positive attitude about change and innovation fosters best practice.
      (2) Successful management supports open communication, team building, decentralization of resources, and the sharing of power.
      (3) Management that utilizes strategic thinking in a systems model can respond proactively to market demands and changes.
      (4) The use of different management styles (i.e., the manager's characteristic way of performing management tasks) has a significant impact on productivity, change, and growth.
      (5) Management's understanding and application of theories of motivation and behavior facilitates appropriate and effective responses to situations, fosters program efficacy, and promotes employee satisfaction.
      (6) Administrative functions of management include program development, fiscal and personnel management, and program evaluation.
      (7) Management by objective (MBO): a complete system of management based on a set of core goals to be accomplished by a program.
         (a) Mission and goals are established.
         (b) Measurable objectives are quantified.
         (c) Specific time frames for accomplishment of objectives are established.
         (d) Staff training needs and deterrents to progress are identified.
         (e) Program evaluation is instituted.
   b. Program development.
      (1) Purposes of developing specific programs.
         (a) To directly meet the needs of a specific population(s) or group(s).
         (b) To clearly focus evaluation and intervention efforts and activities.
         (c) To increase visibility and use of available services (e.g., offering an outpatient cardiac rehabilitation program is more visible than individual referrals, resulting in increased recognition and utilization of this service).
         (d) To convert an idea into a practice reality.

(2) Basic steps of program development.
(a) Needs assessment.
- Describe the community, its physical, social, cultural, and economic factors, and populations at risk.
- Describe the target population's demographics, disorder(s), functional level, and presenting problems.
- Identify specific needs of target population.
  - Perceived needs of the population as reported by others (e.g., family, physicians, and other professionals).
  - Perceived needs as stated by the individual members of the target population.
  - Real needs, which are the actual disabilities and functional limitations of the target population.
- Determine discrepancy between real and perceived needs.
- Determine unmet needs according to priority.
- Identify resources available for program implementation.
  - Formal or institutional resources such as staff, supplies, money, space.
  - Informal resources such as family, friends, cultural or religious figures, self-help/consumer groups.
- Needs assessment methods.
  - Survey, interview, or self-report of target population. A representative sample is required.
  - Key informant involves the surveying of specific individuals who are knowledgeable about the target population's needs.
  - Community forums to obtain information through public meetings or panels.
  - Service utilization review of records and reports.
  - Analysis of social indicators to identify social, cultural, environmental, and/or economic factors that can predict problems.

(b) Program planning.
- Define a focus for the program based on needs assessment results.
  - Problem areas, functional limitations, and unmet needs that are relevant to the majority of the target population are the priority focus.
  - Program level of difficulty as determined by the range of population's functional levels and the level required by the current and expected environment.
- Adopt a frame of reference that is most likely to successfully address and meet the needs that are the program's focus.
- Establish objectives and goals of the program specifically related to primary focus.
  - Set individual goals to be met by the program.
  - Determine programmatic goals to establish standards for program evaluation.
- Describe integration of program into existing system of care.
  - Establish realistic timetable for program implementation.
  - Define staff roles, responsibilities, and assignments.
  - Identify methods for professional collaboration.
  - Determine the physical setting and space requirements.
  - Consider potential barriers to program implementation.
  - Develop methods to deal effectively with identified obstacles before program implementation.
- Develop a referral system for entry into, completion of, and discharge from the program.
  - Evaluation protocols standardize information to be obtained from each person referred to the program and assess the type of program services needed.
  - Criteria for acceptance into the program and for movement through program levels are set.
  - Discharge criteria determine when an individual has achieved maximum gain from the program, usually defined as the achievement of program goals.
- Describe the fiscal implications of the program plan.
  - Determine projected volume or service demand to estimate revenue.
  - Identify resource utilization and projected expenses to estimate costs.
  - Directly compare estimated revenue and estimated expenses to determine financial viability of program.

(c) Program implementation.
- Initiate program according to timetable and steps set forth in the program plan.
- Document program activities, procedures, and use.
- Communicate and coordinate with other programs within the system.

- Promote program to ensure it reaches target population.

(d) Program evaluation.

- Determine whether program should continue, change, or be discontinued.

Fiscal Management

1. Budget.
   a. A financial plan, for a specific time period, of the amount of funds allotted to cover specific expenses of operating a PT department or private practice.
   b. An integral part of the planning process.
   c. Provides a mechanism of assessing the financial success of the practice, programs, or projects.
   d. Expresses anticipated income and expenditures over specific time periods in terms of:
      (1) Buildings.
      (2) Space.
      (3) Equipment.
      (4) Supplies.
   e. Operating budgets are usually planned for a one-year duration (e.g., the organization's fiscal year), and can be "flexible," changing according to volume and other factors.
   f. A budget is planned for capital expenses, including all major renovation expenses or the purchase of equipment that is reusable and will last a minimum of 3 years. Capital budgeting should be part of the strategic plan.
2. Expense budgets.
   a. Represent the amount of money spent by an organization to provide goods and services within a specific period of time.
   b. Two types of expense budgets:
      (1) Operating expense budgets.
         (a) Related to the day-to-day operation of the organization.
         (b) Include categories relating to: salaries, benefits (sick, vacation, etc.), supplies, utilities (telephone and electric), linen, housekeeping, maintenance, continuing education, etc.
      (2) Capital budgets.
         (a) Deal with the purchase of larger items that will be utilized for > 3 years, such as new equipment or new buildings.
         (b) Capital expense is equipment that is depreciable, and usually costs > $1000.
3. Costs.
   a. There are direct and indirect, fixed and variable, and discretionary costs associated with providing a PT service.
      (1) Direct costs are directly associated with the production of a service.
         (a) The cost of salaries for professional staff.
         (b) Treatment supplies (ultrasound gel, massage lotion).
         (c) Treatment equipment.
         (d) Continuing education.
      (2) Indirect costs are necessary to produce a service but are indirectly associated with that service.
         (a) Utilities (telephone and electric).
         (b) Housekeeping, laundry.
         (c) Marketing services, etc.
      (3) Fixed costs remain unchanged, even with changes in volume.
         (a) Air conditioning.
         (b) Rent.
      (4) Variable costs increase and decrease in direct proportion to the volume of activity.
         (a) Linen and labor costs increase as volume increases.
      (5) Discretionary expenses are those costs that are not essential for providing PT services. They may include budgeting for continuing education or recognition activities.
4. Accounts payable.
   a. Money owed to a creditor (individual who provides a service or equipment) for services rendered.
   b. A part of the budget where debts are listed.
5. Accounts receivable.
   a. Money owed to a company (hospital, PT practice) for providing a service; e.g., PT treatment on credit.
   b. An asset expected to benefit future operations.

Quality Assurance and Quality Improvement

1. Quality assurance (QA).
   a. Monitor quality.
   b. Monitor appropriateness of care.
   c. Resolve identified problems.
2. Continuous quality improvement.
   a. A systematic process that involves ongoing, deliberate, and continuous monitoring of the systems and processes that affect patient care to assure for the highest quality outcomes possible.
3. Utilization review (UR).
   a. Written plan to determine:
      (1) Appropriate use of resources.
      (2) Medical necessity of services provided.
      (3) Cost efficiency.
   b. Methods for UR.
      (1) Prospective review.
         (a) Evaluation of proposed treatment plan that specifies how care will be provided.
         (b) Used by third-party payers to approve proposed PT treatment program.

(2) Concurrent review.
   (a) Evaluation of ongoing treatment program during hospitalization or treatment.
   (b) Method to ensure that appropriate care is being delivered.
(3) Retrospective review.
   (a) Audits of medical records after treatment was rendered.
   (b) Method to ensure appropriate care was given.
   (c) Time-consuming, expensive method for third-party payers.
(4) Statistical utilization review (SUR).
   (a) Claims data, such as pricing and utilization, are analyzed.
   (b) Determines which providers offer the most efficient and cost-effective care.
(5) Peer review.
   (a) Performed by peer groups of health professionals.
   (b) Retrospective and concurrent review of clients' records to determine whether services provided are necessary, appropriate, and comprehensive in relation to the patient's needs.
      - Educational, not punitive.
      - Aim is improvement of quality of care.
      - Focuses on how well services are performed in the delivery of care under review.
      - Determines whether the patient's needs have been met.
   (c) May also be performed by peer review organization (PRO).
      - Reviews services provided to Medicare and Medicaid beneficiaries and some managed care plans.
      - Determines appropriateness of services delivered to patients.
(6) Audit or program evaluation.
   (a) Assessment of the management of patients with a specific diagnosis.
      - Objectives are established for patients; e.g., total hip replacements.
      - Outcomes are evaluated in terms of range of motion, strength, pain, function, gait level, ability to climb stairs, etc.
      - Comparisons made between treating therapists, other facilities, etc.
      - Programs can be modified or improved when indicated.

Professional Standards

1. See also Appendices 12A, 12B, 12C, and 12D.
2. Standards are developed by professional associations and are binding only on association members.
   a. Code of Ethics helps PTs and PTAs understand how to act morally and professionally (see Appendices 12A and 12C).
      (1) Code of Ethics (APTA) has been codified as law in many state practice/licensure law and regulations. It is often adopted by many institutions as the standard of behavior for PTs.
   b. Guide for Professional Conduct assists in the interpretation of the Code of Ethics (Appendix 12B).
   c. Guide for Conduct of PTAs determines the propriety of their conduct (Appendix 12C).

Caregiver Definitions and Roles

1. Physical therapist (PT).
   a. A skilled health professional with a minimum of a baccalaureate degree; current accreditation standards mandate a postbaccalaureate degree (doctorate).
   b. Licensed by each state or jurisdiction following successful performance on National Physical Therapy Examination.
   c. Examines patient, evaluates data, establishes diagnosis, prognosis, and plan of care, administers or supervises treatment.
   d. Delegates portions of plan of care to supportive personnel; e.g., PTA.
   e. Supervises and directs supportive staff (PTA, PT aide) in designated tasks.
   f. Reevaluates and adjusts plan of care as appropriate.
   g. Performs and documents final evaluation and establishes discharge and follow-up plans.
   h. Consultation by giving professional opinions to others to identify problems, recommend solutions, or produce a specific outcome.
      (1) May be patient-related consultation to evaluate the quality of PT services.
      (2) May be client-related consultation to a business, school, organization, or government agency.
         (a) Expert witness.
         (b) ADA compliance.
         (c) Work-related injury prevention.
         (d) Request for a second opinion.
2. Physical therapy director.
   a. Oversees function, responsibilities, and relationships of all personnel.
   b. Establishes, revises, and ensures that policies and procedures are carried out according to established policy and procedures.
   c. Acts as liaison with facility administration.
   d. Sets department goals and strategic plan.
3. Physical therapy supervisor.
   a. Qualified experienced PT with a variety of skills:
      (1) Professional knowledge and skill of tasks performed.

(2) Ability to motivate subordinates.
(3) Ability to evaluate staff and give oral and written feedback.
(4) Ability to interview new staff and help develop their skills.
(5) Delegate tasks to appropriate staff.

b. Patient care may or may not be primary responsibility of the supervisor.

4. Physical therapist assistant (PTA).
   a. Skilled physical therapy technologist, usually with a 2-year associate degree.
   b. Must work under the direction and supervision of a PT in all practice settings.
      (1) When the PT and PTA are not within the same physical setting, delegated functions by the PTA must be safe and legal physical therapy practice based on:
         (a) Complexity and acuity of the patient's needs.
         (b) Proximity and accessibility to the PT.
         (c) Supervision available in the event of emergencies.
         (d) Type of setting in which the service is provided.
      (2) In home health, regularly scheduled and documented supervisory meetings are established between the PT and PTA; the frequency is determined by the needs of the patient and the needs of the PTA, and include:
         (a) On-site reassessment of the patient.
         (b) On-site review of the plan of care with appropriate revision or termination.
         (c) Assessment and recommendation for utilization of outside resources.
   c. Able to adjust treatment procedure in accordance with changes in patient status within the scope of the established plan of care.
   d. May not evaluate, develop, or change plan of care, or write discharge plan or summary.
   e. May carry out routine operational functions, including supervision of the physical therapy aide and documentation of patient progress.
5. Physical therapy aide.
   a. A nonlicensed worker, specifically trained under the direction of a PT or PTA.
   b. Functions only with continuous on-site supervision by a PT or, where allowable by law or regulation, the PTA.
   c. Performs designated routine tasks related to the operation of a physical therapy service.
   d. Job responsibilities may include:
      (1) Functional and ambulation activities.
      (2) Application of specific heat, cold, and whirlpool treatments.
      (3) Equipment maintenance.
      (4) Patient transportation.
      (5) Secretarial or housekeeping duties.
   e. Aides are not licensed by the state and some state laws limit or prohibit treatment procedures by aides.
6. Physical therapy and physical therapist assistant student.
   a. Performs duties commensurate with level of education.
   b. PT clinical instructor (CI) is responsible for all actions and duties of affiliating student.
   c. PT may supervise both PT and PTA students.
   d. PTA may supervise only an assistant student.
7. Physical therapy volunteer.
   a. Member of the community.
      (1) Interested in assisting PTs with departmental activities.
      (2) Takes phone messages, does filing and other basic secretarial tasks.
      (3) May not provide or set up patient treatment, transfer patients, clean whirlpools, or maintain equipment.
8. Home health aide.
   a. A nonlicensed worker (e.g., nursing/rehabilitation assistant) specifically trained to:
      (1) Provide personal care and home-management services.
      (2) Assist patients to remain in the home environment.
   b. Supervised by a nurse, PT, or OT.
   c. Responsibilities include:
      (1) Bathing, grooming, light housework, shopping, or cooking in some circumstances.
      (2) Supervision of home exercise program (HEP) as directed by the PT; e.g., ambulation.
9. Occupational therapist (OT).
   a. A skilled health professional that holds a minimum of a baccalaureate degree (nowadays most have master's degrees and some clinical doctorates) and has passed a national certification examination [NBCOT exam]. OTs are licensed by some, but not all, states. The OT provides:
      (1) Education and training in ADLs.
      (2) Fabrication of orthoses (splints).
      (3) Guidance in selection and use of adaptive equipment.
      (4) Therapeutic activities to enhance functional performance, and cognitive/perceptual function.
      (5) Consultation concerning the adaptation of physical environments for the handicapped.
      (6) Creative activities in treatment of physically and emotionally disabled patients.
   b. Services are provided on an inpatient basis, outpatient basis, and in industrial environments.
10. Certified occupational therapist assistant (COTA).
   a. Skilled technician who holds an associate degree and has passed a national certification examination.

b. Works under the direction of an OT to carry out established treatment.
   (1) Cannot evaluate, establish, or revise a plan of care.
c. Performs duties in a rehabilitation or home setting.
   (1) Concerned with functional deficits in ADLs, including dressing, grooming, hygiene, housekeeping, etc.

11. Speech-language pathologist (SLP).
   a. A skilled health professional that holds a master's degree in communication disorders, has completed 1 year of field experience, and has passed a national examination to obtain the Certificate of Clinical Competence authorized by the American Speech and Hearing Association.
   b. Conducts remedial programs to restore or improve communication of patients with language and speech impairments.
      (1) May arise from physiological or neurological disturbances and defective articulation.
   c. Works with OT to correct swallowing problems and cognitive processing deficits; and with PT in the area of positioning and mobility.
12. Certified orthotist (CO).
   a. Designs, fabricates, and fits orthoses (braces, splints, collars, corsets) prescribed by physicians.
   b. Successfully completed the examination by the American Orthotic and Prosthetic Association.
   c. Provides these devices to patients with disabling conditions of limbs and spine.
   d. Works directly with physicians and physical and occupational therapists.
13. Certified prosthetist (CP).
   a. Designs, fabricates, and fits prostheses for patients with partial or total absence of a limb (amputation).
   b. Successfully completed the examination by the American Orthotic and Prosthetic Association.
   c. Works directly with physicians, PTs, and OTs.
   d. Individuals may be certified in both orthotics and prosthetics (CPO).
14. Certified respiratory therapy technician (CRTT).
   a. A skilled technician holding an associate degree from a 2-year training program accredited by the Committee in Allied Health Education and Accreditation.
      (1) Passes a national exam to become registered.
   b. Administers respiratory therapy as prescribed and supervised by a physician.
      (1) Performs pulmonary function tests.
      (2) Treatments consist of oxygen delivery, aerosols, and nebulizers.
      (3) Maintains all respiratory equipment and assists patients in their use; i.e., ventilators, oxygen, pressure machines, etc.
      (4) Coordinates care with pulmonary PT treatments.
15. Primary care physician (PCP).
   a. A practitioner, usually an internist, general practitioner, or family medicine physician, that provides primary care services and manages routine health care needs.
   b. Acts as the gatekeeper for patients covered by managed health care.
   c. May be an MD or DO (Doctor of Osteopathic Medicine).
      (1) Authorizes referrals to other specialty physicians or services, including PT.
16. Physician assistant (PA-C) and Nurse Practitioner (NP).
   a. Skilled health care professional, graduate of an accredited program at the graduate level.
      (1) Required to pass national certification examination.
      (2) Direct patient contact required during training in a variety of settings or specialty area.
   b. Under the supervision of a physician, performs routine diagnostic, therapeutic, preventative, and health maintenance services in any setting in which the physician renders care.
      (1) Specialties include family medicine, obstetrics, pediatrics, orthopedics, emergency medicine, and others.
   c. Able to write PT orders, order medical tests, and prescribe most medications.
   d. Often referred to as Physician Extenders.
   e. An NP must also be a registered nurse (RN).
17. Physiatrist.
   a. A physician specializing in physical medicine and rehabilitation.
      (1) Certified by the American Board of Physical Medicine and Rehabilitation.
      (2) Diagnoses and treats patients with disabilities involving musculoskeletal, neurological, cardiovascular, or other body systems.
   b. Primary focus on maximal restoration of physical, psychological, social, and vocational function, and alleviation of pain.
   c. May lead the rehabilitation team in coordination of patient care.
      (1) Works directly with PTs, OTs, and STs.
18. Chiropractor (DC).
   a. An alternative medical practitioner, usually licensed by a state board.
      (1) Deals with relationship of the nervous system and the spinal column in the restoration and maintenance of health.
   b. Services are covered for individuals in most group health plans.
   c. Patients may see a chiropractor and PT at the same time.
      (1) PT, with patient's permission, should contact chiropractor to coordinate care.

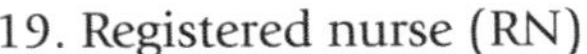

19. Registered nurse (RN).
    a. A skilled health professional that is a graduate of an accredited nursing program, and licensed by the state board following successful performance on licensure exam.
    b. Primary liaison between the patient and the physician.
        (1) Communicates to physician changes in patient's medical or social condition.
        (2) Educates the patient and family to facilitate recovery.
        (3) Makes referrals to other services under physician's direction.
        (4) Supervises other levels of nursing care (licensed practical nurse [LPN], home health aide).
        (5) Administers medication but cannot change drug dosages.
        (6) Carries out range of motion, bed exercises, transfers, and ambulation as instructed by the PT.
20. Rehabilitation counselor (vocational rehabilitation counselor).
    a. Counsels physically and mentally handicapped individuals.
        (1) Helps patients improve their ability to function optimally in society.
        (2) Administers vocational tests, procures vocational training, and provides occupational information for job placement.
21. Audiologist.
    a. A health professional with a graduate degree in audiology.
    b. A specialist in hearing disorders and evaluation who works to rehabilitate individuals with hearing loss.
        (1) Uses audiometric tests to assess sensitivity of sense of hearing.
        (2) Uses speech audiometric tests to assess ability to understand selected words.
        (3) Audiometrist is a technician trained to administer audiometric tests selected and evaluated by the audiologist.
22. Consultant.
    a. A person that, by training and experience, has acquired a special knowledge in a subject area that has been recognized by a peer group.
    b. A person that analyzes situations, offers advice and solutions to problems.
        (1) For example: physician referral for consultation or advice regarding diagnosis or treatment of a patient.
        (2) Consultant reviews history, examines patient, and writes opinion.
        (3) Responsibility of patient care not delegated to consultant.
23. Athletic trainer certified (ATC).
    a. A health professional with a minimum of a baccalaureate degree who is an integral part of the health care system associated with sports.
        (1) Usually works under supervision of a physician.
        (2) Provides injury prevention, recognition, treatment, and rehabilitation after athletic trauma.
    b. Settings for delivery of care:
        (1) Secondary schools, colleges and universities, professional athletic organizations, and private or hospital-based clinics.
24. Social worker (MSW).
    a. Usually completed a master's degree from a school of social work accredited by the Council on Social Work Education. After one year of practical field work, they are licensed or registered by the state.
    b. Acts as a resource director assisting patients and families with necessary applications for financial resources, appropriate discharge destinations (e.g., skilled nursing facility, custodial care facility), rental and loaner equipment, and support groups, etc.
    c. Acts as a personal or family counselor.
    d. Educates the patient and family about their medical problems. Also educates home health staff, helping them understand patient and family interaction, and crisis management.
    e. Acts as an advocate for the patient in dealing with outside agencies and procuring support services.
    f. Mediates between the patient and family by alleviating fears, developing realistic expectations of the patient to the family, and interpreting the patient and families' situation to outside relatives and the home health care team.
25. Alternative support staff: (e.g., massage therapists, exercise therapists, acupuncturists).
    a. May work within the supervision of a PT.
    b. Employed under their appropriate titles.
    c. Involvement in patient care activities should be within the limits of their education and in accordance with applicable laws and regulations and the discretion of the PT.
26. Team roles and principles of collaboration.
    a. Overview.
        (1) A team is a group of equally important individuals with common interests who collaborate to develop shared goals and build trusting relationships to achieve these shared goals.
        (2) Members of the team include the patient/client/consumer; his/her family, significant others, and/or caregivers, health care professionals; and the reimburser's gatekeepers.

(3) Professional members on the team will vary according to practice setting.
(4) The consumer, family, significant other, and/or caregiver role on the team has become increasing important. Collaboration with these individuals is even mandated by law (e.g., Omnibus Budget Reconciliation Act of 1990 [OBRA '90], Individuals with Disabilities Education Act [IDEA]).

b. Principles of collaboration.
(1) Factors that influence effective team functioning.
(a) Member skill and knowledge.
(b) Membership stability.
(c) Commitment to team goals.
(d) Good communication.
(e) Membership composition.
(f) Common language and goals.
(g) Effective leadership.

c. Types of teams.
(1) Multidisciplinary.
(a) A number of professionals from different disciplines conduct assessments and interventions independent from one another.
(b) Member's primary allegiance is to his/her discipline. Some formal communications occur between team members.
(c) Limited communications may result in lack of understanding of different perspectives.
(d) Resources and responsibilities are individually allocated between disciplines; therefore, competition among team members may develop.
(2) Interdisciplinary.
(a) All disciplines relevant to the case agree to collaborate for decision-making.
(b) Evaluation and intervention is still conducted independently within defined areas of each profession's expertise. However, there is a greater understanding of each discipline's perspective.
(c) Outcomes and goals are team-directed and not bound to discipline specific roles and functions.
(d) Members tend to use group process skills effectively (e.g., during team planning meetings).
(e) The exchange of information, prioritization of needs, allocation of resources, and responsibilities are based on members' expertise and skills, not on "turf" issues.
(f) Ongoing training, support, supervision, cooperation, and consultation among disciplines are important to this model to ensure that professional integrity and quality of care is maintained.
(3) Intradisciplinary.
(a) One or more members of one discipline evaluate, plan, and implement treatment of the individual; e.g., PT, PTA, PT consultant.
(b) Other disciplines are not involved; communication is limited, thereby limiting perspectives on the case.
(c) This "team" is at risk due to potential narrowness of perspective.
(d) Comprehensive, holistic care can be questionable.
(4) Team efficacy.
(a) Interdisciplinary teams are the most common and considered to be the most effective in today's health care system.

Statutory Laws

1. Health Insurance Portability and Accountability Act (HIPAA).
a. Elements of the act.
(1) Standards and safeguards to assure an individual's right to continuity in health care.
(2) Privacy and security of health care records.
(3) Portability of health insurance.
b. HIPAA privacy rule.
(1) Patient confidentiality is maintained in all oral, written, and electronic forms.
(2) Technical, administrative, and physical safeguards for privacy.
(3) All individuals must be informed of a facility's privacy policies.
(4) Written consent must be obtained before any personal health information is disclosed or used for other purposes.
(a) Exemptions to written consent may be made in emergencies or if delay will prevent timely care.
(b) If language barriers preclude signed consent in emergent or crucial situations, treatment may commence if the physician believes that consent is implied.
(5) Prior to discussion of a person's status with a family member or other providers, the person may grant permission or object.
(a) Providers can use clinical judgment to decide whether to discuss a case if the person cannot give permission, or even if there is an objection.
- Documentation for this decision is essential.
(6) All information disclosed must be the minimum needed for the immediate purpose.

c. Practice implications.
 (1) Physical identifiability of patients must be reduced.
 (2) Charts and other documentation must be stored out of public view and secured.
 (3) Any information stored or transmitted by computers must be safeguarded.
 (4) Faxes must be sent with cover sheets on dedicated lines to secure locations.
 (5) All e-mails should be password-protected.
 (6) All conversations regarding a person's health status must occur in private areas with minimal disclosure.
 (7) Cover sheets should be used on clipboards that contain patient paperwork.
 (8) Treatment may be provided in groups or open clinics. Discussions about these treatments should be done quietly and in a private space.
 (9) There is no guarantee of 100% confidentiality. Reasonable and vigilant safeguards are required.
 (10) HIPAA does not override state laws with more restrictive privacy policies, and defers to state laws regarding minors.

d. Patient's rights.
 (1) An individual can access all of their medical records.
  (a) Providers have 30–60 days to respond.
  (b) A reasonable charge can be imposed for copying.
 (2) An individual has the right to request that information in their record be amended.
  (a) The provider may refuse, but must provide a rationale.
  (b) The provider may comply and provide a reason for amending the record. Original documentation is not removed.

2. Professional licensing laws are enacted by all states.
 a. Protect the consumer against professional incompetence and exploitation by opportunists.
 b. Determine the minimal standards of education
  (1) Graduation from an accredited program or its equivalent in PT.
  (2) Successful completion of a national licensing examination.
  (3) Ethical and legal standards relating to continuing practice of PT.
  (4) All PTs must have a license to practice.
  (5) Each state determines criteria to practice and issue a license.
  (6) Licensure examination and related activities are the responsibility of the Federation of State Boards of Physical Therapy.
   - All states belong to this association.

3. Individuals with Disabilities Education Act (IDEA).
 a. Enacted in 1975 with the most recent revision in 2004. Ensures that children with disabilities receive appropriate, free public education.
 b. IDEA provides statutes and guidelines for states and school districts regarding the provision of special education and related services.
 c. Establishes Early Intervention Programs [EIP] including PT, OT, ST, and other services as needed.
  (1) Services are provided to children with developmental delays (physical, emotional, cognitive, or communicative).
  (2) Services provided to infants or toddlers "at risk" for developing delays.
  (3) Provision for necessary adaptive equipment.
 d. Requires creation of individualized education plans [IEPs].
  (1) Guides the team; however, child has the option of not attending planning meetings for the IEP.
  (2) Considers evaluation results and child's concerns.
   (a) Functional needs, strength, ROM.
   (b) Factors such as English proficiency, behavioral issues, vision, hearing, and communication needs.
   (c) Need for assistive devices.

Safety

1. Assuring patient safety.
 a. Risk management programs.
  (1) Identify, evaluate, and take corrective action against risk.
   (a) Potential patient, employee, and/or visitor injury.
   (b) Property loss or damage with resulting financial loss or legal liability.
  (2) Efforts taken to decrease risk in PT.
   (a) Equipment maintenance; e.g., biannual maintenance of electrical equipment.
   (b) Staff education; e.g., safety training for staff in use of equipment.
    - Regular check of essential safety equipment.
   (c) Policies to clean equipment and reduce the potential for spreading infection.
  (3) Patient and staff safety.
   (a) PTs must follow strict federal standards when using any form of patient restraint.
    - Restraint must be used for a specific reason, i.e., patient safety.
    - Restraints are considered temporary and may not be used for an indefinite amount of time.

- A patient in restraints must be checked on every 30 minutes.
- Restraints are not for punishment or to substitute proper staff supervision.
- Use proper patient identifiers, such as wrist bands, with patient date of birth, first and last names, or other unique patient identifiers.

(4) Identify risk factors in patient care or patient and therapist safety; e.g., more than three incidents of patient falls on the rehabilitation floor may require an in-service in transfer training.

(5) Proper and timely reporting of adverse patient occurrence or reactions as required by federal or state statute. These may include:
   (a) Adverse reactions to regulated medicines.
   (b) Incidents involving abuse or neglect of patient.
   (c) Outbreaks of disease that may affect public safety (i.e., influenza).
   (d) "Reportable" occurrences such as violence against patients where significant harm is caused to the patient (i.e., nursing home patient with a fall resulting in severe fracture or death).

(6) Annual certification/recertification of staff in cardiopulmonary resuscitation (CPR).

b. Abuse and neglect.
   (1) PTs and PTAs are mandated reporters of neglect and/or abuse of children, elders, and the disabled in all 50 states.
   (2) Each state may have specific reporting systems and requirements.
   (3) All 50 states have a hotline to report abuse/neglect.
   (4) Facilities will have specific protocols to report such findings.
   (5) States have varying levels of knowledge that trigger a report.
      (a) Some states may require only a "reasonable suspicion."
      (b) Other states may require a higher threshold of "know or suspect."
   (6) All states have legislation that provides for immunity from prosecution arising out of the reporting abuse/neglect.
   (7) In most states a person who reports suspected child abuse in "good faith" is immune from criminal and civil liability.
   (8) Victims are not likely to report abuse, as they are often dependent on the abuser.

c. Elder abuse/neglect.
   (1) Individuals 50 years of age or older.
   (2) Any action that constitutes the willful infliction of injury, unreasonable confinement, intimidation or cruel punishment with resulting physical harm, pain, or mental anguish.
   (3) Denial of goods or services (e.g., food, medical care) to an elder with the intent to cause physical harm, mental anguish, or mental illness.
   (4) Abuse/neglect can be physical, emotional, medical, financial, and/or sexual.
   (5) Signs of abuse/neglect.
      (a) Unexplained physical injuries.
      (b) Withdrawal.
      (c) Increased agitation.
      (d) Increased depression.
      (e) Malnutrition.
      (f) Substandard care or poor physical hygiene.

d. Sexual harassment/advances.
   (1) It is unlawful and unethical for a PT or PTA to have a sexual relationship with a patient/client.
   (2) Sexual harassment of patients/clients.
      (a) Sexual jokes.
      (b) Leering, whistling, rude and unwanted sexual comments.
      (c) Display of sexually graphic art, cartoons, objects.
      (d) Request for sexual favors in exchange for treatment.
      (e) Inappropriate touching or physical exam given diagnosis.
   (3) Even if contact is consensual, it is still unethical.
   (4) If patient/client makes advances to the PT/PTA the practitioner has to be clear that those actions are inappropriate.
      (a) Caution should be taken; work with those patients in an open area with others in the area.
         - If situation continues, care should be transferred to another therapist.
   (5) PTs and PTAs are obligated to report any caregivers who engage in sexual activity with their patients/clients.

Malpractice

1. Malpractice: PTs are personally responsible for negligence and other acts that result in harm to a patient through professional/patient relationships.
2. Negligence.
   a. Failure to do what reasonably competent practitioners would have done under similar circumstances.
   b. To find a practitioner negligent, harm must have occurred to the patient.
   c. Each individual (PT, PTA, student PT, or student PTA) is liable for his/her own negligence.
   d. Supervisors or superiors may also be found negligent due to the actions of their workers if they

provided faulty supervision or inappropriate delegation of responsibilities.

e. PT fails to perform a duty, thus causing harm.
f. Ethical principles are violated in caring for patients; e.g., acting without consent, breaking of confidentiality, lack of respect for patients.
g. Patients may also contribute to negligence if they do not follow directions of the therapist.
h. The institution is usually found negligent if a patient was harmed as a result of an environmental problem.
   (1) Slippery floor.
   (2) Fall in a poorly lit hall.
i. The institution is also liable if an employee was incompetent or not properly licensed.
j. PTs, PTAs, or students may be liable for:
   (1) Adverse reactions to treatment, such as burns (e.g., leaving a hot pack on too long), falls during gait training, injuries from therapeutic exercise, or harm caused by defective equipment.
   (2) Any action or inaction that is inconsistent with the Code of Ethics or the Standards of Practice that results in harm to a patient.
k. Patients, parents, or legal guardians can refuse treatment by a student practitioner.

3. PT may be asked to be an expert witness or testify in a malpractice case for:
   a. The plaintiff (victim).
   b. The defendant (accused).

Emergency Preparedness

1. PT's role in emergency preparedness and disaster management.
   a. PTs are taking on a larger role in an organization's emergency preparedness plan (EPP) and a more active role when an organization is faced with a disaster.
   b. Internal disaster.
      (1) Power or utility failures.
      (2) Telecom or equipment failure.
      (3) Fire/bomb scare.
      (4) Internal environmental conditions.
   c. External disaster.
      (1) Terrorism.
      (2) Weather-related: floods, hurricanes, etc.
      (3) Civil disturbances.
      (4) Hazmat incidents.
      (5) Large community casualty incidents.
   d. Possible PT roles.
      (1) Helping to triage casualties.
      (2) Assessing patients with musculoskeletal injuries, freeing up other providers.
      (3) Command and control functions/communications.
      (4) Patient transportation.
2. Emergency preparedness planning.
   a. Many state and federal agencies require that health organizations have some form of EPP ready.
   b. PTs can play key roles in developing EPPs.
      (1) Liaison with other local first responders, such as the fire and police departments.
      (2) Help develop and build the communication infrastructure to be used during a disaster.
      (3) Assist in determining which critical services are to be offered and which are secondary.
      (4) Help coordinate internal resources.
      (5) Participate in disaster drills.

Acknowledgement to Judith D. Hershberg, PT, DPT, MS; Catherine S. Lane, PT, DPT, MS; Linda Arslanian, PT, DPT, MS; and Rita P. Fleming-Castaldy, PhD, OTL, FAOTA for their original contributions in formulating this chapter.

APPENDIX 12A

Code of Ethics

Preamble

The Code of Ethics for the Physical Therapist (Code of Ethics) delineates the ethical obligations of all physical therapists as determined by the House of Delegates of the American Physical Therapy Association (APTA). The purposes of this Code of Ethics are to:

Define the ethical principles that form the foundation of physical therapist practice in patient/client management, consultation, education, research, and administration.

Provide standards of behavior and performance that form the basis of professional accountability to the public.

Provide guidance for physical therapists facing ethical challenges, regardless of their professional roles and responsibilities.

Educate physical therapists, students, other health care professionals, regulators, and the public regarding the core values, ethical principles, and standards that guide the professional conduct of the physical therapist.

Establish the standards by which the American Physical Therapy Association can determine if a physical therapist has engaged in unethical conduct.

No code of ethics is exhaustive nor can it address every situation. Physical therapists are encouraged to seek additional advice or consultation in instances where the guidance of the Code of Ethics may not be definitive.

This Code of Ethics is built upon the five roles of the physical therapist (management of patients/clients, consultation, education, research, and administration), the core values of the profession, and the multiple realms of ethical action (individual, organizational, and societal). Physical therapist practice is guided by a set of seven core values: accountability, altruism, compassion/caring, excellence, integrity, professional duty, and social responsibility. Throughout the document the primary core values that support specific principles are indicated in parentheses. Unless a specific role is indicated in the principle, the duties and obligations being delineated pertain to the five roles of the physical therapist. Fundamental to the Code of Ethics is the special obligation of physical therapists to empower, educate, and enable those with impairments, activity limitations, participation restrictions, and disabilities to facilitate greater independence, health, wellness, and enhanced quality of life.

Principle #1

Physical therapists shall respect the inherent dignity and rights of all individuals.

(Core Values: Compassion, Integrity)

1A. Physical therapists shall act in a respectful manner toward each person regardless of age, gender, race, nationality, religion, ethnicity, social or economic status, sexual orientation, health condition, or disability.

1B. Physical therapists shall recognize their personal biases and shall not discriminate against others in physical therapist practice, consultation, education, research, and administration.

Principle #2

Physical therapists shall be trustworthy and compassionate in addressing the rights and needs of patients/clients.

(Core Values: Altruism, Compassion, Professional Duty)

2A. Physical therapists shall adhere to the core values of the profession and shall act in the best interests of patients/clients over the interests of the physical therapist.

2B. Physical therapists shall provide physical therapy services with compassionate and caring behaviors that incorporate the individual and cultural differences of patients/clients.

2C. Physical therapists shall provide the information necessary to allow patients or their surrogates to make informed decisions about physical therapy care or participation in clinical research.

2D. Physical therapists shall collaborate with patients/clients to empower them in decisions about their health care.

2E. Physical therapists shall protect confidential patient/client information and may disclose confidential information to appropriate authorities only when allowed or as required by law.

Principle #3

Physical therapists shall be accountable for making sound professional judgments.

(Core Values: Excellence, Integrity)

3A. Physical therapists shall demonstrate independent and objective professional judgment in the patient's/client's best interest in all practice settings.

3B. Physical therapists shall demonstrate professional judgment informed by professional standards, evidence (including current literature and established best practice), practitioner experience, and patient/client values.

3C. Physical therapists shall make judgments within their scope of practice and level of expertise and shall communicate with, collaborate with, or refer to peers or other health care professionals when necessary.

3D. Physical therapists shall not engage in conflicts of interest that interfere with professional judgment.

3E. Physical therapists shall provide appropriate direction of and communication with physical therapist assistants and support personnel.

Principle #4

Physical therapists shall demonstrate integrity in their relationships with patients/clients, families, colleagues, students, research participants, other health care providers, employers, payers, and the public.

(Core Value: Integrity)

4A. Physical therapists shall provide truthful, accurate, and relevant information and shall not make misleading representations.

4B. Physical therapists shall not exploit persons over whom they have supervisory, evaluative, or other authority (e.g., patients/clients, students, supervisees, research participants, or employees).

4C. Physical therapists shall discourage misconduct by health care professionals and report illegal or unethical acts to the relevant authority, when appropriate.

4D. Physical therapists shall report suspected cases of abuse involving children or vulnerable adults to the appropriate authority, subject to law.

4E. Physical therapists shall not engage in any sexual relationship with any of their patients/clients, supervisees, or students.

4F. Physical therapists shall not harass anyone verbally, physically, emotionally, or sexually.

Principle #5

Physical therapists shall fulfill their legal and professional obligations.

(Core Values: Professional Duty, Accountability)

5A. Physical therapists shall comply with applicable local, state, and federal laws and regulations.

5B. Physical therapists shall have primary responsibility for supervision of physical therapist assistants and support personnel.

5C. Physical therapists involved in research shall abide by accepted standards governing protection of research participants.

5D. Physical therapists shall encourage colleagues with physical, psychological, or substance related impairments that may adversely impact their professional responsibilities to seek assistance or counsel.

5E. Physical therapists who have knowledge that a colleague is unable to perform their professional responsibilities with reasonable skill and safety shall report this information to the appropriate authority.

5F. Physical therapists shall provide notice and information about alternatives for obtaining care in the event the physical therapist terminates the provider relationship while the patient/client continues to need physical therapy services.

Principle #6

Physical therapists shall enhance their expertise through the life-long acquisition and refinement of knowledge, skills, abilities, and professional behaviors.

(Core Value: Excellence)

6A. Physical therapists shall achieve and maintain professional competence.
6B. Physical therapists shall take responsibility for their professional development based on critical self-assessment and reflection on changes in physical therapist practice, education, health care delivery, and technology.
6C. Physical therapists shall evaluate the strength of evidence and applicability of content presented during professional development activities before integrating the content or techniques into practice.
6D. Physical therapists shall cultivate practice environments that support professional development, life-long learning, and excellence.

Principle #7

Physical therapists shall promote organizational behaviors and business practices that benefit patients/clients and society.

(Core Values: Integrity, Accountability)

7A. Physical therapists shall promote practice environments that support autonomous and accountable professional judgments.
7B. Physical therapists shall seek remuneration as is deserved and reasonable for physical therapist services.
7C. Physical therapists shall not accept gifts or other considerations that influence or give an appearance of influencing their professional judgment.
7D. Physical therapists shall fully disclose any financial interest they have in products or services that they recommend to patients/clients.
7E. Physical therapists shall be aware of charges and shall ensure that documentation and coding for physical therapy services accurately reflect the nature and extent of the services provided.
7F. Physical therapists shall refrain from employment arrangements, or other arrangements, that prevent physical therapists from fulfilling professional obligations to patients/clients.

Principle #8

Physical therapists shall participate in efforts to meet the health needs of people locally, nationally, or globally.

(Core Values: Social Responsibility)

8A. Physical therapists shall provide *pro bono* physical therapy services or support organizations that meet the health needs of people who are economically disadvantaged, uninsured, and underinsured.
8B. Physical therapists shall advocate to reduce health disparities and health care inequities, improve access to health care services, and address the health, wellness, and preventive health care needs of people.
8C. Physical therapists shall be responsible stewards of health care resources and shall avoid over-utilization or under-utilization of physical therapy services.
8D. Physical therapists shall educate members of the public about the benefits of physical therapy and the unique role of the physical therapist.

American Physical Therapy Association, Core Documents, 2009 with permission

APPENDIX 12B

Guide for Professional Conduct

Purpose

This Guide for Professional Conduct (Guide) is intended to serve physical therapists in interpreting the Code of Ethics for the Physical Therapist (Code) of the American Physical Therapy Association (APTA) in matters of professional conduct. The APTA House of Delegates in June of 2009 adopted a revised Code, which became effective on July 1, 2010.

The Guide provides a framework by which physical therapists may determine the propriety of their conduct. It is also intended to guide the professional development of physical therapist students. The Code and the Guide apply to all physical therapists. These guidelines are subject to change as the dynamics of the profession change and as new patterns of health care delivery are developed and accepted by the professional community and the public.

Interpreting Ethical Principles

The interpretations expressed in this Guide reflect the opinions, decisions, and advice of the Ethics and Judicial Committee (EJC). The interpretations are set forth according to topic. These interpretations are intended to assist a physical therapist in applying general ethical principles to specific situations. They address some but not all topics addressed in the Principles and should not be considered inclusive of all situations that could evolve.

This Guide is subject to change, and the Ethics and Judicial Committee will monitor and timely revise the Guide to address additional topics and Principles when necessary and as needed.

Preamble to the Code

The Preamble states as follows:

The Code of Ethics for the Physical Therapist (Code of Ethics) delineates the ethical obligations of all physical therapists as determined by the House of Delegates of the American Physical Therapy Association (APTA). The purposes of this Code of Ethics are to:

1. Define the ethical principles that form the foundation of physical therapist practice in patient/client management, consultation, education, research, and administration.
2. Provide standards of behavior and performance that form the basis of professional accountability to the public.

3. Provide guidance for physical therapists facing ethical challenges, regardless of their professional roles and responsibilities.
4. Educate physical therapists, students, other health care professionals, regulators, and the public regarding the core values, ethical principles, and standards that guide the professional conduct of the physical therapist.
5. Establish the standards by which the American Physical Therapy Association can determine if a physical therapist has engaged in unethical conduct.

No code of ethics is exhaustive nor can it address every situation. Physical therapists are encouraged to seek additional advice or consultation in instances where the guidance of the Code of Ethics may not be definitive.

This Code of Ethics is built upon the five roles of the physical therapist (management of patients/clients, consultation, education, research, and administration), the core values of the profession, and the multiple realms of ethical action (individual, organizational, and societal). Physical therapist practice is guided by a set of seven core values: accountability, altruism, compassion/caring, excellence, integrity, professional duty, and social responsibility. Throughout the document the primary core values that support specific principles are indicated in parentheses. Unless a specific role is indicated in the principle, the duties and obligations being delineated pertain to the five roles of the physical therapist. Fundamental to the Code of Ethics is the special obligation of physical therapists to empower, educate, and enable those with impairments, activity limitations, participation restrictions, and disabilities to facilitate greater independence, health, wellness, and enhanced quality of life.

Interpretation

Upon the Code of Ethics for the Physical Therapist being amended effective July 1, 2010, all the lettered principles in the Code contain the word "shall" and are mandatory ethical obligations. The language contained in the Code is intended to better explain and further clarify existing ethical obligations. These ethical obligations predate the revised Code. Although various words have changed, many of the obligations are the same. Consequently, the addition of the word "shall" serves to reinforce and clarify existing ethical obligations. A significant reason that the Code was revised was to provide physical therapists with a document that was clear enough such that they can read it standing alone without the need to seek extensive additional interpretation.

The Preamble states that "[n]o Code of Ethics is exhaustive nor can it address every situation." The Preamble also states that physical therapists "are encouraged to seek additional advice or consultation in instances in which the guidance of the Code may not be definitive." Potential sources for advice and counsel include third parties and the myriad resources available on the APTA website. Inherent in a physical therapist's ethical decision-making process is the examination of his or her unique set of facts relative to the Code.

Topics

Respect

Principle 1A states as follows:

1A. Physical therapists shall act in a respectful manner toward each person regardless of age, gender, race, nationality, religion, ethnicity, social or economic status, sexual orientation, health condition, or disability.

Interpretation

Principle 1A addresses the display of respect toward others. Unfortunately, there is no universal consensus about what respect looks like in every situation. For example, direct eye contact is viewed as respectful and courteous in some cultures and inappropriate in others. It is up to the individual to assess the appropriateness of behavior in various situations.

Altruism

Principle 2A states as follows:

2A. Physical therapists shall adhere to the core values of the profession and shall act in the best interests of patients/clients over the interests of the physical therapist.

Interpretation

Principle 2A reminds physical therapists to adhere to the profession's core values and act in the best interest of patients/clients over the interests of the physical therapist. Often this is done without thought, but sometimes, especially at the end of the day when the physical therapist is fatigued and ready to go home, it is a conscious decision. For example, the physical therapist may need to make a decision between leaving on time and staying at work longer to see a patient who was 15 minutes late for an appointment.

Patient Autonomy

Principle 2C states as follows:

2C. Physical therapists shall provide the information necessary to allow patients or their surrogates to make informed decisions about physical therapy care or participation in clinical research.

Interpretation

The underlying purpose of Principle 2C is to require a physical therapist to respect patient autonomy. In order to do so, a physical therapist shall communicate to the patient/client the findings of his/her examination, evaluation, diagnosis, and prognosis. A physical therapist shall use sound professional judgment in informing the patient/client of any substantial risks of the recommended examination and intervention and shall collaborate with the patient/client to establish the goals of treatment and the plan of care. Ultimately, a physical therapist shall respect the patient's/client's right to make decisions regarding the recommended plan of care, including consent, modification, or refusal.

Professional Judgment

Principles 3, 3A, and 3B state as follows:

3: Physical therapists shall be accountable for making sound professional judgments. (Core Values: Excellence, Integrity)

3A. Physical therapists shall demonstrate independent and objective professional judgment in the patient's/client's best interest in all practice settings.

3B. Physical therapists shall demonstrate professional judgment informed by professional standards, evidence (including current literature and established best practice), practitioner experience, and patient/client values.

Interpretation

Principles 3, 3A, and 3B state that it is the physical therapist's obligation to exercise sound professional judgment, based upon his/her knowledge, skill, training, and experience. Principle 3B further describes the physical therapist's judgment as being informed by three elements of evidence-based practice.

With regard to the patient/client management role, once a physical therapist accepts an individual for physical therapy services he/she shall be responsible for: the examination, evaluation, and diagnosis of that individual; the prognosis and intervention; reexamination and modification of the plan of care; and the maintenance of adequate records, including progress reports. A physical therapist shall establish the plan of care and shall provide and/or supervise and direct the appropriate interventions. Regardless of practice setting, a physical therapist has primary responsibility for the physical therapy care of a patient and shall make independent judgments regarding that care consistent with accepted professional standards.

If the diagnostic process reveals findings that are outside the scope of the physical therapist's knowledge, experience, or expertise or that indicate the need for care outside the scope of physical therapy, the physical therapist shall so inform the patient/client and shall refer the patient/client to an appropriate practitioner.

A physical therapist shall determine when a patient/client will no longer benefit from physical therapy services. When a physical therapist's judgment is that a patient will receive negligible benefit from physical therapy services, the physical therapist shall not provide or continue to provide such services if the primary reason for doing so is to further the financial self-interest of the physical therapist or his/her employer. A physical therapist shall avoid over-utilization of physical therapy services. See Principle 8C.

Supervision

Principle 3E states as follows:

3E. Physical therapists shall provide appropriate direction of and communication with physical therapist assistants and support personnel.

Interpretation

Principle 3E describes an additional circumstance in which sound professional judgment is required; namely, through the appropriate direction of and communication with physical therapist assistants and support personnel. Further information on supervision via applicable local, state, and federal laws and regulations (including state practice acts and administrative codes) is available. Information on supervision via APTA policies and resources is also available on the APTA website. See Principles 5A and 5B.

Integrity in Relationships

Principle 4 states as follows:

4: Physical therapists shall demonstrate integrity in their relationships with patients/clients, families, colleagues, students, research participants, other health care providers, employers, payers, and the public. (Core Value: Integrity)

Interpretation

Principle 4 addresses the need for integrity in relationships. This is not limited to relationships with patients/clients, but includes everyone physical therapists come into contact with professionally. For example, demonstrating integrity could encompass working collaboratively with the health care team and taking responsibility for one's role as a member of that team.

Reporting

Principle 4C states as follows:

4C. Physical therapists shall discourage misconduct by health care professionals and report illegal or unethical acts to the relevant authority, when appropriate.

Interpretation

When considering the application of "when appropriate" under Principle 4C, keep in mind that not all allegedly illegal or unethical acts should be reported immediately to an agency/authority. The determination of when to do so depends upon each situation's unique set of facts, applicable laws, regulations, and policies.

Depending upon those facts, it might be appropriate to communicate with the individuals involved. Consider whether the action has been corrected, and in that case, not reporting may be the most appropriate action. Note, however, that when an agency/authority does examine a potential ethical issue, fact finding will be its first step. The determination of ethicality requires an understanding of all of the relevant facts, but may still be subject to interpretation.

The EJC Opinion titled: Topic: Preserving Confidences; Physical Therapist's Reporting Obligation With Respect to Unethical, Incompetent, or Illegal Acts provides further information on the complexities of reporting.

Exploitation

Principle 4E states as follows:

> 4E. Physical therapists shall not engage in any sexual relationship with any of their patient/clients, supervisees, or students.

Interpretation

The statement is fairly clear—sexual relationships with their patients/clients, supervisees, or students are prohibited. This component of Principle 4 is consistent with Principle 4B, which states:

> Physical therapists shall not exploit persons over whom they have supervisory, evaluative, or other authority (e.g. patients/clients, students, supervisees, research participants, or employees).

Next, consider this excerpt from the EJC Opinion titled Topic: Sexual Relationships With Patients/Former Patients:

> A physical therapist stands in a relationship of trust to each patient and has an ethical obligation to act in the patient's best interest and to avoid any exploitation or abuse of the patient. Thus, if a physical therapist has natural feelings of attraction toward a patient, he/she must sublimate those feelings in order to avoid sexual exploitation of the patient.
>
> One's ethical decision making process should focus on whether the patient/client, supervisee or student is being exploited. In this context, questions have been asked about whether one can have a sexual relationship once the patient/client relationship ends. To this question, the EJC has opined as follows:
>
>> The Committee does not believe it feasible to establish any bright-line rule for when, if ever, initiation of a romantic/sexual relationship with a former patient would be ethically permissible.
>>
>> ....
>>
>> The Committee imagines that in some cases a romantic/sexual relationship would not offend ... if initiated with a former patient soon after the termination of treatment, while in others such a relationship might never be appropriate.

Colleague Impairment

Principle 5D and 5E state as follows:

> 5D. Physical therapists shall encourage colleagues with physical, psychological, or substance-related impairments that may adversely impact their professional responsibilities to seek assistance or counsel.
>
> 5E. Physical therapists who have knowledge that a colleague is unable to perform their professional responsibilities with reasonable skill and safety shall report the information to the appropriate authority.

Interpretation

The central tenet of Principles 5D and 5E is that inaction is not an option for a physical therapist when faced with the circumstances described. Principle 5D states that a physical therapist shall encourage colleagues to seek assistance or counsel while Principle 5E addresses reporting information to the appropriate authority.

5D and 5E both require a factual determination on your part. This may be challenging in the sense that you might not know or it might be difficult for you to determine whether someone in fact has a physical, psychological, or substance-related impairment. In addition, it might be difficult to determine whether such impairment may be adversely affecting his or her professional responsibilities.

Moreover, once you do make these determinations, the obligation under 5D centers not on reporting, but on encouraging the colleague to seek assistance. However, the obligation under 5E does focus on reporting. But note that 5E discusses reporting when a colleague is unable to perform, whereas 5D discusses encouraging colleagues to seek assistance when the impairment may adversely affect his or her professional responsibilities. So, 5D discusses something that may be affecting performance, whereas 5E addresses a situation in which someone is clearly unable to perform. The 2 situations are distinct. In addition, it is important to note that 5E does not mandate to whom you report; it gives you discretion to determine the appropriate authority.

The EJC Opinion titled: Topic: Preserving Confidences; Physical Therapist's Reporting Obligation With Respect to Unethical, Incompetent, or Illegal Acts provides further information on the complexities of reporting.

Professional Competence

Principle 6A states as follows:

6A. Physical therapists shall achieve and maintain professional competence.

Interpretation

6A requires a physical therapist to maintain professional competence within one's scope of practice throughout one's career. Maintaining competence is an ongoing process of self-assessment, identification of strengths and weaknesses, acquisition of knowledge and skills based on that assessment, and reflection on and reassessment of performance, knowledge, and skills. Numerous factors including practice setting, types of patients/clients, personal interests and the addition of new evidence to practice will influence the depth and breadth of professional competence in a given area of practice. Additional resources on Continuing Competence are available on the APTA website.

Professional Growth

Principle 6D states as follows:

6D. Physical therapists shall cultivate practice environments that support professional development, life-long learning, and excellence.

Interpretation

6D elaborates on the physical therapist's obligations to foster an environment conducive to professional growth, even when not supported by the organization. The essential idea is that this is the physical therapist's responsibility, whether or not the employer provides support.

Charges and Coding

Principle 7E states as follows:

7E. Physical therapists shall be aware of charges and shall ensure that documentation and coding for physical therapy services accurately reflect the nature and extent of the services provided.

Interpretation

Principle 7E provides that the physical therapist must make sure that the process of documentation and coding accurately captures the charges for services performed. In this context, where charges cannot be determined because of payment methodology, physical therapists may review the House of Delegates policy titled Professional Fees for Physical Therapy Services. Additional resources on documentation and coding include the House of Delegates policy titled Documentation Authority for Physical Therapy Services and the Documentation and Coding and Billing information on the APTA website.

Pro Bono Services

Principle 8A states as follows:

8A. Physical therapists shall provide pro bono physical therapy services or support organizations that meet the health needs of people who are economically disadvantaged, uninsured, and underinsured.

Interpretation

The key word in Principle 8A is "or." If a physical therapist is unable to provide pro bono services he or she can fulfill ethical obligations by supporting organizations that meet the health needs of people who are economically disadvantaged, uninsured, and underinsured. In addition, physical therapists may review the House of Delegates guidelines titled Guidelines: Pro Bono Physical Therapy Services. Additional resources on pro bono physical therapy services are available on the APTA website.

8A also addresses supporting organizations to meet health needs. In terms of supporting organizations, the principle does not specify the type of support that is required. Physical therapists may express support through volunteerism, financial contributions, advocacy, education, or simply promoting their work in conversations with colleagues.

Issued by the Ethics and Judicial Committee
American Physical Therapy Association
October 1981
Last Amended November 2010

APPENDIX 12C

Guide for Conduct of the Physical Therapist Assistant

Purpose

This Guide for Conduct of the Physical Therapist Assistant (Guide) is intended to serve physical therapist assistants in interpreting the Standards of Ethical Conduct for the Physical Therapist Assistant (Standards) of the American Physical Therapy Association (APTA). The APTA House of Delegates in June of 2009 adopted the revised Standards, which became effective on July 1, 2010.

The Guide provides a framework by which physical therapist assistants may determine the propriety of their conduct. It is also intended to guide the development of physical therapist assistant students. The Standards and the Guide apply to all physical therapist assistants. These guidelines are subject to change as the dynamics of the profession change and as new patterns of health care delivery are developed and accepted by the professional community and the public.

Interpreting Ethical Standards

The interpretations expressed in this Guide reflect the opinions, decisions, and advice of the Ethics and Judicial Committee (EJC). The interpretations are set forth according to topic. These interpretations are intended to assist a physical therapist assistant in applying general ethical standards to specific situations. They address some but not all topics addressed in the Standards and should not be considered inclusive of all situations that could evolve.

This Guide is subject to change, and the Ethics and Judicial Committee will monitor and timely revise the Guide to address additional topics and Standards when necessary and as needed.

Preamble to the Standards

The Preamble states as follows:

> The Standards of Ethical Conduct for the Physical Therapist Assistant (Standards of Ethical Conduct) delineate the ethical obligations of all physical therapist assistants as determined by the House of Delegates of the American Physical Therapy Association (APTA). The Standards of Ethical Conduct provide a foundation for conduct to which all physical therapist assistants shall adhere. Fundamental to the Standards of Ethical Conduct is the special obligation of physical therapist assistants to enable patients/clients to achieve greater independence, health and wellness, and enhanced quality of life.
>
> No document that delineates ethical standards can address every situation. Physical therapist assistants are encouraged to seek additional advice or consultation in instances where the guidance of the Standards of Ethical Conduct may not be definitive.

Interpretation

Upon the Standards of Ethical Conduct for the Physical Therapist Assistant being amended effective July 1, 2010, all the lettered standards contain the word "shall" and are mandatory ethical obligations. The language contained in the Standards is intended to better explain and further clarify existing ethical obligations. These ethical obligations predate the revised Standards. Although various words have changed, many of the obligations are the same. Consequently, the addition of the word "shall" serves to reinforce and clarify existing ethical obligations. A significant reason that the Standards were revised was to provide physical therapist assistants with a document that was clear enough such that they can read it standing alone without the need to seek extensive additional interpretation.

The Preamble states that "[n]o document that delineates ethical standards can address every situation." The Preamble also states that physical therapist assistants "are encouraged to seek additional advice or consultation in instances where the guidance of the Standards of Ethical Conduct may not be definitive." Potential sources for advice or counsel include third parties and the myriad resources available on the APTA website. Inherent in a physical therapist assistant's ethical decision-making process is the examination of his or her unique set of facts relative to the Standards.

Standards

Respect

Standard 1A states as follows:

1A. Physical therapist assistants shall act in a respectful manner toward each person regardless of age, gender, race, nationality, religion, ethnicity, social or economic status, sexual orientation, health condition, or disability.

Interpretation

Standard 1A addresses the display of respect toward others. Unfortunately, there is no universal consensus about what respect looks like in every situation. For example, direct eye contact is viewed as respectful and courteous in some cultures and inappropriate in others. It is up to the individual to assess the appropriateness of behavior in various situations.

Altruism

Standard 2A states as follows:

2A. Physical therapist assistants shall act in the best interests of patients/clients over the interests of the physical therapist assistant.

Interpretation

Standard 2A addresses acting in the best interest of patients/clients over the interests of the physical therapist assistant. Often this is done without thought, but sometimes, especially at the end of the day when the clinician is fatigued and ready to go home, it is a conscious decision. For example, the physical therapist assistant may need to make a decision between leaving on time and staying at work longer to see a patient who was 15 minutes late for an appointment.

Sound Decisions

Standard 3C states as follows:

3C. Physical therapist assistants shall make decisions based upon their level of competence and consistent with patient/client values.

Interpretation

To fulfill 3C, the physical therapist assistant must be knowledgeable about his or her legal scope of work as well as level of competence. As a physical therapist assistant gains experience and additional knowledge, there may be areas of physical therapy interventions in which he or she displays advanced skills. At the same time, other previously gained knowledge and skill may be lost due to lack of use. To make sound decisions, the physical therapist assistant must be able to self-reflect on his or her current level of competence.

Supervision

Standard 3E states as follows:

3E. Physical therapist assistants shall provide physical therapy services under the direction and supervision of a physical therapist and shall communicate with the physical therapist when patient/client status requires modifications to the established plan of care.

Interpretation

Standard 3E goes beyond simply stating that the physical therapist assistant operates under the supervision of the physical therapist. Although a physical therapist retains responsibility for the patient/client throughout the episode of care, this standard requires the physical therapist assistant to take action by communicating with the supervising physical therapist when changes in the patient/client status indicate that modifications to the plan of care may be needed. Further information on supervision via APTA policies and resources is available on the APTA website.

Integrity in Relationships

Standard 4 states as follows:

4: Physical therapist assistants shall demonstrate integrity in their relationships with patients/clients, families, colleagues, students, other health care providers, employers, payers, and the public.

Interpretation

Standard 4 addresses the need for integrity in relationships. This is not limited to relationships with patients/clients, but includes everyone physical therapist assistants come into contact with in the normal provision of physical therapy services. For example, demonstrating integrity could encompass working collaboratively with the health care team and taking responsibility for one's role as a member of that team.

Reporting

Standard 4C states as follows:

4C. Physical therapist assistants shall discourage misconduct by health care professionals and report illegal or unethical acts to the relevant authority, when appropriate.

Interpretation

When considering the application of "when appropriate" under Standard 4C, keep in mind that not all allegedly illegal or unethical acts should be reported immediately to an agency/authority. The determination of when to do so depends upon each situation's unique set of facts, applicable laws, regulations, and policies.

Depending upon those facts, it might be appropriate to communicate with the individuals involved. Consider whether the action has been corrected, and in that case, not reporting may be the most appropriate action. Note, however, that when an agency/authority does examine a potential ethical issue, fact finding will be its first step. The determination of ethicality requires an understanding of all of the relevant facts, but may still be subject to interpretation.

The EJC Opinion titled: Topic: Preserving Confidences; Physical Therapist's Reporting Obligation With Respect to Unethical, Incompetent, or Illegal Acts provides further information on the complexities of reporting.

Exploitation

Standard 4E states as follows:

4E. Physical therapist assistants shall not engage in any sexual relationship with any of their patients/clients, supervisees, or students.

Interpretation

The statement is fairly clear—sexual relationships with their patients/clients, supervisees, or students are prohibited. This component of Standard 4 is consistent with Standard 4B, which states:

4B. Physical therapist assistants shall not exploit persons over whom they have supervisory, evaluative, or other authority (e.g., patients/clients, students, supervisees, research participants, or employees).

Next, consider this excerpt from the EJC Opinion titled Topic: Sexual Relationships With Patients/Former Patients (modified for physical therapist assistants):

> A physical therapist [assistant] stands in a relationship of trust to each patient and has an ethical obligation to act in the patient's best interest and to avoid any exploitation or abuse of the patient. Thus, if a physical therapist [assistant] has natural feelings of attraction toward a patient, he/she must sublimate those feelings in order to avoid sexual exploitation of the patient.
>
> One's ethical decision making process should focus on whether the patient/client, supervisee, or student is being exploited. In this context, questions have been asked about whether one can have a sexual relationship once the patient/client relationship ends. To this question, the EJC has opined as follows:
>
>> The Committee does not believe it feasible to establish any bright-line rule for when, if ever, initiation of a romantic/sexual relationship with a former patient would be ethically permissible.
>>
>> ....
>>
>> The Committee imagines that in some cases a romantic/sexual relationship would not offend ... if initiated with a former patient soon after the termination of treatment, while in others such a relationship might never be appropriate.

Colleague Impairment

Standard 5D and 5E state as follows:

5D. Physical therapist assistants shall encourage colleagues with physical, psychological, or substance-related impairments that may adversely impact their professional responsibilities to seek assistance or counsel.

5E. Physical therapist assistants who have knowledge that a colleague is unable to perform their professional responsibilities with reasonable skill and safety shall report this information to the appropriate authority.

Interpretation

The central tenet of Standard 5D and 5E is that inaction is not an option for a physical therapist assistant when faced with the circumstances described. Standard 5D states that a physical therapist assistant shall encourage colleagues to seek assistance or counsel while Standard 5E addresses reporting information to the appropriate authority.

5D and 5E both require a factual determination on the physical therapist assistant's part. This may be challenging in the sense that you might not know or it might be difficult for you to determine whether someone in fact has a physical, psychological, or substance-related impairment. In addition, it might be difficult to determine whether such impairment may be adversely affecting someone's work responsibilities.

Moreover, once you do make these determinations, the obligation under 5D centers not on reporting, but on encouraging the colleague to seek assistance. However, the obligation under 5E does focus on reporting. But note that 5E discusses reporting when a colleague is unable to perform, whereas 5D discusses encouraging colleagues to seek assistance when the impairment may adversely affect his or her professional responsibilities. So, 5D discusses something that may be affecting performance, whereas 5E addresses a situation in which someone is clearly unable to perform. The 2 situations are distinct. In addition, it is important to note that 5E does not mandate to whom you report; it gives you discretion to determine the appropriate authority.

The EJC Opinion titled Topic: Preserving Confidences; Physical Therapist's Reporting Obligation With Respect to Unethical, Incompetent, or Illegal Acts provides further information on the complexities of reporting.

Clinical Competence

Standard 6A states as follows:

6A. Physical therapist assistants shall achieve and maintain clinical competence.

Interpretation

6A should cause physical therapist assistants to reflect on their current level of clinical competence, to identify and address gaps in clinical competence, and to commit to the maintenance of clinical competence throughout their career. The supervising physical therapist can be a valuable partner in identifying areas of knowledge and skill that the physical therapist assistant needs for clinical competence and to meet the needs of the individual physical therapist, which may vary according to areas of interest and expertise. Further, the physical therapist assistant may request that the physical therapist serve as a mentor to assist him or her in acquiring the needed knowledge and skills. Additional resources on Continuing Competence are available on the APTA website.

Lifelong Learning

Standard 6C states as follows:

6C. Physical therapist assistants shall support practice environments that support career development and life-long learning.

Interpretation

6C points out the physical therapist assistant's obligation to support an environment conducive to career development and learning. The essential idea here is that the physical therapist assistant encourage and contribute to the career development and life-long learning of himself or herself and others, whether or not the employer provides support.

Organizational and Business Practices

Standard 7 states as follows:

7. Physical therapist assistants shall support organizational behaviors and business practices that benefit patients/clients and society.

Interpretation

Standard 7 reflects a shift in the Standards. One criticism of the former version was that it addressed primarily face-to-face clinical practice settings. Accordingly, Standard 7 addresses ethical obligations in organizational and business practices on a patient/client and societal level.

Documenting Interventions

Standard 7D states as follows:

7D. Physical therapist assistants shall ensure that documentation for their interventions accurately reflects the nature and extent of the services provided.

Interpretation

7D addresses the need for physical therapist assistants to make sure that they thoroughly and accurately document the interventions they provide to patients/clients and document related data collected from the patient/client. The focus of this Standard is on ensuring documentation of the services rendered, including the nature and extent of such services.

Support-Health Needs

Standard 8A states as follows:

8A. Physical therapist assistants shall support organizations that meet the health needs of people who are economically disadvantaged, uninsured, and underinsured.

Interpretation

8A addresses the issue of support for those least likely to be able to afford physical therapy services. The Standard does not specify the type of support that is required. Physical therapist assistants may express support through volunteerism, financial contributions, advocacy, education, or simply promoting their work in conversations with colleagues. When providing such services, including pro bono services, physical therapist assistants must comply with applicable laws, and as such work under the direction and supervision of a physical therapist. Additional resources on pro bono physical therapy services are available on the APTA website.

Issued by the Ethics and Judicial Committee
American Physical Therapy Association
October 1981
Last Amended November 2010

APPENDIX 12D

Standards of Practice for Physical Therapy

Standards of Practice for Physical Therapy June 2010 Preamble

The physical therapy profession's commitment to society is to promote optimal health and function in individuals by pursuing excellence in practice. The American Physical Therapy Association attests to this commitment by adopting and promoting the following *Standards of Practice for Physical Therapy*. These Standards are the profession's statement of conditions and performances that are essential for provision of high quality professional service to society and provide a foundation for assessment of physical therapist practice.

Ethical/Legal Considerations

1. Ethical Considerations.

   The physical therapist practices according to the *Code of Ethics* of the American Physical Therapy Association.

   The physical therapist assistant complies with the *Standards of Ethical Conduct for the Physical Therapist Assistant* of the American Physical Therapy Association.
2. Legal Considerations.

   The physical therapist complies with all the legal requirements of jurisdictions regulating the practice of physical therapy.

   The physical therapist assistant complies with all the legal requirements of jurisdictions regulating the work of the assistant.

Administration of the Physical Therapy Service

1. Statement of Mission, Purposes, and Goals.

   The physical therapy service has a statement of mission, purposes, and goals that reflects the needs and interests of the patients/clients served, the physical therapy personnel affiliated with the service and the community.
2. Organizational Plan.

   The physical therapy service has a written organizational plan.
3. Policies and Procedures.

   The physical therapy service has written policies and procedures that reflect the operation, mission, purposes, and goals of the service and are consistent with the Association's standards, policies, positions, guidelines, and *Code of Ethics*.

4. Administration.
A physical therapist is responsible for the direction of the physical therapy service.
5. Fiscal Management.
The director of the physical therapy service, in consultation with physical therapy staff and appropriate administrative personnel, participates in the planning for and allocation of resources. Fiscal planning and management of the service is based on sound accounting principles.
6. Improvement of Quality of Care and Performance.
The physical therapy service has a written plan for continuous improvement of quality of care and performance of services.
7. Staffing.
The physical therapy personnel affiliated with the physical therapy service have demonstrated competence and are sufficient to achieve the mission, purposes, and goals of the service.
8. Staff Development.
The physical therapy service has a written plan that provides for appropriate and ongoing staff development.
9. Physical Setting.
The physical setting is designed to provide a safe and accessible environment that facilitates fulfillment of the mission, purposes, and goals of the physical therapy service. The equipment is safe and sufficient to achieve the purposes and goals of physical therapy.
10. Collaboration.
The physical therapy service collaborates with all disciplines as appropriate.

Patient Client Management

1. Physical Therapist of Record.
The physical therapist of record is the therapist who assumes responsibility for patient/client management and is accountable for the coordination, continuation, and progression of the plan of care.
2. Patient/Client Collaboration.
Within the patient/client management process, the physical therapist and the patient/client establish and maintain an ongoing collaborative process of decision-making that exists throughout the provision of services.
3. Initial Examination/Evaluation/Diagnosis/Prognosis.
The physical therapist performs an initial examination and evaluation to establish a diagnosis and prognosis prior to intervention.
4. Plan of Care.
The physical therapist establishes a plan of care and manages the needs of the patient/client based on the examination, evaluation, diagnosis, prognosis, goals, and outcomes of the planned interventions for identified impairments, activity limitations, and participation restrictions.

   The physical therapist involves the patient/client and appropriate others in the planning, implementation, and assessment of the plan of care.

   The physical therapist, in consultation with appropriate disciplines, plans for discharge of the patient/client taking into consideration achievement of anticipated goals and expected outcomes and provides for appropriate follow-up or referral.
5. Intervention.
The physical therapist provides or directs and supervises the physical therapy intervention consistent with the results of the examination, evaluation, diagnosis, prognosis, and plan of care.
6. Reexamination.
The physical therapist reexamines the patient/client as necessary during an episode of care to evaluate progress or change in patient/client status and modifies the plan of care accordingly or discontinues physical therapy services.
7. Discharge/Discontinuation of Intervention.
The physical therapist discharges the patient/client from physical therapy services when the anticipated goals or expected outcomes for the patient/client have been achieved. The physical therapist discontinues intervention when the patient/client is unable to continue to progress toward goals or when the physical therapist determines that the patient/client will no longer benefit from physical therapy.
8. Communication/Coordination/Documentation.
The physical therapist communicates, coordinates, and documents all aspects of patient/client management including the results of the initial examination and evaluation, diagnosis, prognosis, plan of care, interventions, response to interventions, changes in patient/client status relative to the interventions, reexamination and discharge/discontinuation of intervention, and other patient/client management activities. The physical therapist of record is responsible for "hand off" communication.

Education

The physical therapist is responsible for individual professional development. The physical therapist assistant is responsible for individual career development.

The physical therapist and the physical therapist assistant, under the direction and supervision of the physical therapist, participate in the education of students.

The physical therapist educates and provides consultation to consumers and the general public regarding the purposes and benefits of physical therapy.

The physical therapist educates and provides consultation to consumers and the general public regarding the roles of the physical therapist and the physical therapist assistant.

Research

The physical therapist applies research findings to practice and encourages, participates in and promotes activities that establish the outcomes of patient/client management provided by the physical therapist.

Community Responsibility

The physical therapist demonstrates community responsibility by participating in community and community agency activities, educating the public, formulating public policy, or providing pro bono physical therapy services.

Review Questions

Professional Responsibilities

1. What are the main provisos of the Individuals with Disabilities Education Act (IDEA)?

2. What are the possible roles of the physical therapist in emergency preparedness/disaster planning?

3. What are the major components that constitute negligence by a physical therapist?

13

Teaching and Learning

SUSAN B. O'SULLIVAN

Chapter Outline

Physical Therapist Roles and Responsibilities

Patient/Client-Related Instruction

1. The process of: informing, educating, or training patients/clients, families, significant others, and caregivers in order to promote and optimize physical therapy services (APTA Guide to Physical Therapist Practice, 2nd ed. Phys Ther 81: 47, 2001).
2. Provided across all settings. For all patients/clients on promoting understanding of:
   a. Current condition, impairments, functional limitations and disabilities.
   b. Anticipated goals and expected outcomes, plan of care, specific intervention elements, and self-management strategies.
   c. Elements necessary for the smooth transition to home or an alternative setting, work and community.
   d. Individualized family service plans (IFSPs) or individualized education plans (IEPs).
   e. Safety awareness, and risk factor reduction and prevention.
   f. Health promotion, wellness, and fitness.

Educational Programs

1. Instruction and educational programs are provided for the following.
   a. Other therapists, health care providers, staff and/or students in academic and/or clinical settings. Programs can be formal or informal.
   b. Instruction and educational programs are provided for local, state, and federal agencies.
   c. The general public to increase awareness of health issues and roles of the physical therapist.
2. Frame of reference: Questions may address education of the patient/client/caregivers about current health status, rehabilitation plan of care, and healthy lifestyle. Education of the health care team and community groups about the role of physical therapy is also an important focus. Learning styles and theories provide a frame of reference for developing appropriate educational interventions.

Clinical Education of Students

1. Instruction and supervision of physical therapy or physical therapist assistant students.
   a. Provided by clinical instructors during scheduled clinical education experiences.
   b. Close communication and collaboration with the school and the academic coordinator of clinical education is necessary.

Educational Concepts

Learning Styles

1. Characteristic mode.
   a. Of gaining, processing, and storing information. Learning styles differ across dimensions.
2. Analytical versus intuitive learners.
   a. Analytical/objective learner.
      (1) Processes information in a step-by-step order.
      (2) Perceives information in an objective manner; is able to use facts and easily understand relationships between them.
      (3) Perceives information in an abstract, conceptual manner; information does not need to be related to personal experience.
      (4) Learns best with structure, step-by-step learning; may have difficulty comprehending the big picture.
   b. Intuitive/global learner.
      (1) Processes information all at once, in a simultaneous manner; not in an ordered sequence.
      (2) Perceives information in a subjective manner: reflects on personal experiences.
      (3) Perceives information in a concrete manner: information assimilated about practical, real-life experiences.
      (4) Learns best if information is connected to personal experiences and presented in a practical, real-life context. If not, knowledge may be disregarded. May have difficulty ordering steps and comprehending details.
3. Reasoning: inductive versus deductive.
   a. Inductive reasoner (assimilator): observes similarities, can develop theoretical models to explain relationships.

b. Deductive reasoner (converger): analyzes problems in depth; applies information, theoretical models to practical situations.

4. Initiative: active versus passive learner.
   a. Active/aggressive learner: exhibits initiative, actively seeks information; may reach conclusions quickly before all information is gathered.
   b. Passive learner: often exhibits little initiative; responds best to directed learning.

Learning Theories

1. Behaviorist (stimulus-response theory).
   a. Basic premises.
      (1) Behavior is modified in response to a given stimulus.
      (2) Behavior is determined by its consequences; the response of one behavior becomes the stimulus for the next response (chaining).
      (3) Learning occurs because the behavior is reinforced (learned association).
   b. Behavior can be controlled or shaped by operant conditioning (behavior modification techniques).
      (1) Desired or correct behaviors are identified.
      (2) Frequent and scheduled reinforcements are given to reinforce the desired behaviors; e.g., praise, encouragement, candy.
         (a) Accuracy of reinforcement is critical; e.g., use of rewards that are meaningful to the individual.
         (b) Timing of reinforcement is critical: immediate versus distant or delayed; e.g., use of a reinforcement schedule.
      (3) Negative behaviors are ignored; unreinforced behaviors are weakened and eventually extinguished.
      (4) Behavior that has aversive consequences (punishment) is less likely to occur again; aversive conditioning is less powerful as a tool for learning than positive reinforcements.
      (5) The environment is altered to promote correct responses; e.g., a closed environment with reduction of distractors.
      (6) Repetition is a necessary prerequisite for learning.
      (7) Clinical uses: limited; e.g., may be used when working with adults with impaired or limited cognitive abilities (traumatic brain injury, stroke) or young children.
   c. Prominent theorists: B.F. Skinner, G. Watson.
2. Cognitive theory.
   a. Basic premises.
      (1) Focus is on cognitive development of intellectual abilities and skills, from:
         (a) Symbolic function (ages 2–8).
         (b) Concrete mental operations (ages 8–12).
         (c) Conceptual thought (ages 12 and up).
      (2) Thinking emerges with language development.
      (3) Perceptual features are important conditions of learning; e.g., figure-ground, directional signs, sequence.
   b. Cognitive strategies are used; e.g., repeated challenges to thinking.
      (1) Knowledge is organized by the teacher; the teacher is the expert; a pedagogical approach (the art and science of teaching children).
      (2) Learning is culturally relative.
      (3) Cognitive feedback is used to confirm and correct knowledge.
      (4) Goal-setting by learner is important for motivation.
      (5) Both divergent and convergent theory is nurtured.
   c. Prominent theorists: J. Piaget, J.S. Bruner.
3. Humanist.
   a. Basic premises.
      (1) Personal freedom and dignity of the individual is emphasized in the learning process.
      (2) Understanding of the learner's needs and feelings is sought.
      (3) The learner experiences unconditional positive regard, acceptance, and understanding.
   b. Teaching is student-centered; e.g., self-discovery, self-appropriated learning, experiential learning.
      (1) Promotes active learning (self-initiated) rather than passive; e.g., knowledge is organized by the learner, not for the learner.
      (2) Learning addresses relevant problems and issues.
      (3) A positive learning climate is facilitated.
      (4) The teacher is a facilitator and resource-finder.
      (5) Learning is evaluated by the learner; e.g., self-assessment.
   c. Prominent theorists: Carl Rogers, A.H. Maslow.
4. Adult learning (andragogy).
   a. Basic characteristics of adult learners.
      (1) The learner is self-directed: goal-oriented, seeks knowledge for own sake.
      (2) Has a rich core of experience that serves as a broad base for learning.
      (3) Demonstrates a readiness to learn.
      (4) Demonstrates a problem-centered orientation to learning.
   b. Teaching is learner-centered.
      (1) The teacher interacts with the learner: helps to clarify the learning problem, structure the learning environment to enhance learning, provide resources.
      (2) Learners share the responsibility for planning the learning experience; actively participate in the learning process.
      (3) The learning process makes use of the experiences of the learner.
   c. Prominent theorists: M. Knowles, J.R. Kidd.

Domains of Learning

1. Cognitive: objectives concern mental processes and intellectual processes of recall of knowledge, comprehension, application, analysis, synthesis, and evaluation.
2. Affective: objectives concern feelings and emotions, including receiving (attending to phenomena and stimuli); awareness of environment (people and situations); responding (compliance, acceptance of responsibility, satisfaction); valuing (accepting and internalizing worth or value), organization of a value system; and characterization by a value or value complex (persistent and consistent behaviors influenced by a value system).
3. Psychomotor: objects concern motor skills (writing, speaking, performing motor skills safely, correctly, and independently).

Instruction

Instructional Process

1. Learner/needs assessment: identify relevant characteristics and needs of the learner prior to the educational experience; establish therapeutic relationship including active listening and positive verbal and nonverbal interactions.
   a. Determine what the learner needs to know.
      (1) Current level of knowledge.
      (2) Plans/needs for the future.
   b. Determine what the learner brings to the learning experience.
      (1) Educational background, previous knowledge and experiences, health beliefs, valued activities, and potential treatment barriers.
      (2) All instruction should take into account the influences of age, culture, race, gender, gender roles, sexual orientation, and socioeconomic status.
   c. Determine the learner's readiness to learn.
      (1) Learning style.
      (2) Capabilities, attentiveness, energy level.
   d. Identify impairments that may have impact on learning: e.g., perceptual deficits, visual impairments, communication impairments, confusion, memory loss, emotional dysregulation.
   e. Identify available resources; e.g., information about facilities, materials, time available for the instructional process.
2. Analysis of data, formulation of objectives of instruction.
   a. Specify what the learner should learn (goals and behavioral objectives).
      (1) Identify what the learner will do; e.g., describe, discuss, explain.
      (2) Identify what the criteria of performance are; e.g., given a list of risk factors that the learner will correctly identify.
      (3) Specify the conditions of the performance; e.g., 75% of the time.
      (4) Set goals that are attainable, mutually agreed upon by learner and instructor.
      (5) Use clear, unambiguous, and measurable terms; e.g., family/caregiver will demonstrate understanding of safety measures to prevent falls by correctly describing proper use of brakes and transfer sequence 100% of the time within 2 weeks.
   b. Set priorities.
      (1) Determine which educational goals are most important, what sequence is needed.
      (2) Ensure maximum utilization of available teaching time.
      (3) Avoid bombardment; e.g., too much, too soon.
      (4) Repetition is important for learning; build in experiences that reinforce instruction.
3. Analysis of instruction/planning: what, how, where, when.
   a. Select what materials to use; options include print, audiovisual media, computer-assisted instruction, models.
   b. Select what methods of teaching are appropriate; options include individual instruction, group discussion, organized classes/lecture, demonstration and modeling, tutorials. Also includes written or pictorial instruction; e.g., home exercise program.
      (1) Choice of method is dependent on:
         (a) The individual learner/unique characteristics; e.g., preferences for rate and style of learning, motivation.
         (b) Objectives of instruction.
      (2) A variety of teaching methods is typically helpful to reinforce the learning.
   c. Select what activities are likely to help the learner achieve the stated objectives.

4. Implementation: strategies to affect mastery of learning.
   a. Individuals learn best when:
      (1) They are actively involved in goal-setting and the learning process; learning is not dictated by the instructor.
      (2) Learners need to feel free to express their own ideas, beliefs, and concerns.
      (3) There is respect and trust between learner and instructor.
      (4) The instructor is supportive and nonjudgmental.
   b. Therapist/teacher should recognize that:
      (1) Individuals learn at different rates.
      (2) Trial and error and introspection are an essential part of the learning process.
      (3) Experiential learning is more effective than didactic learning.
      (4) Reinforcement is necessary to ensure a sense of competence and success.
   c. Therapist/teacher roles and responsibilities.
      (1) Gain the learner's attention, motivation, and active participation.
      (2) Provide an overview of the learning process: objectives, purposes, nature of the task, and procedures to follow.
      (3) Stimulate recall of previous learning; relate present learning to past and future learning.
      (4) Monitor and control the learning.
         (a) Organize learning units over a period of time.
         (b) Break down learning into a series of steps or units.
         (c) Determine the best sequence(s) of learning units and experiences; e.g., sequence from familiar to unfamiliar, simple to complex, concrete to abstract.
         (d) Provide ample opportunity for practice and repetition.
         (e) Progress at a comfortable pace for the learner.
         (f) Give timely feedback, provide accurate knowledge of results.
         (g) Reward successful behaviors.
      (5) Monitor and control the environment.
      (6) Reduce conditions that have a negative impact on learning; e.g., pain or discomfort, anxiety, fear, frustration, feelings of failure, humiliation or embarrassment, boredom, time pressures.
5. Evaluation.
   a. Initial evaluation.
      (1) Determine relevant previous achievement, learning skills.
      (2) Utilize diagnostic tests.
      (3) Determine aptitude/choice of learning approaches.
   b. Formative evaluation (diagnostic-progress assessment).
      (1) Analyze what learning has occurred, what must still be learned.
      (2) Institute appropriate changes/modifications in the teaching plan.
   c. Summative evaluation (outcome assessment).
      (1) Assess attainment of learning objectives and content/skills.
      (2) Determine effectiveness of teaching materials/methods.
   d. Sources: direct observation of behaviors, written and verbal feedback, formal checklists, questionnaires, pre- and post-tests.
6. Documentation: provide a complete record of activities and outcomes to assure accountability, continuity of care. Include:
   a. Educational plan: objectives and activities.
   b. Progression and modification of the educational plan; document the need for change.
   c. Outcomes: document the learner's progress and attainment of the learning objectives.

Interventions—Media

The selection of appropriate media can enrich the learning experience, clarify and support a presentation, and provide for self-instruction or individualized tutorial. Selection should be based on the needs assessment. Cost and availability are factors that may also enter into the decision-making process.

1. Media can include, but are not limited to:
   a. Print: written handouts.
      (1) Advantages: low cost.
      (2) Disadvantages: can be boring; inappropriate for educational level of individual; culturally biased.
   b. Computer-assisted instruction.
      (1) Advantages: can be individually paced; novel.
      (2) Disadvantages: higher cost; limited availability in clinical setting.
   c. Audiovisuals.
      (1) Slides (PowerPoint).
         (a) Advantages: easy to add color, realistic.
         (b) Disadvantages: no motion, cost, availability; lights must be low during presentation.
      (2) Audiotapes.
         (a) Advantages: self-paced.
         (b) Disadvantages: most learners are visually oriented.
      (3) Film/DVD/videotapes.
         (a) Advantages: demonstrates movement, 3-dimensional.
         (b) Disadvantages: can be time-consuming.
      (4) Models.
         (a) Advantages: can provide visual and "hands on" experience.
         (b) Disadvantages: limited choices, cost.

Motor Learning

"Motor learning is a set of internal processes associated with practice or experience leading to relatively permanent changes in the capability for skill" (Schmidt, 2011).

Phases of Motor Learning

1. Cognitive phase:
   a. The learner develops an understanding of the task; the process of cognitive mapping allows the learner to determine what to do.
2. Associative phase:
   a. The learner has determined a strategy, practices it and makes adjustments in how the motor skill is performed.
3. Autonomous phase:
   a. The learner has practiced the motor skill to the extent that the performance becomes largely automatic; characterized by high-level skilled performance with few adjustments needed.
4. See Table 2-16.

Motor Learning Evaluation

1. Performance:
   a. There is an acquired capability to perform the motor skill with practice.
      (1) Performance may not always present an accurate picture of learning since it can be affected by fatigue, motivation, or stress.
      (2) Determine efficiency (spatial and temporal organization or movement), level of effort, automaticity, and speed of decision-making.
2. Retention:
   a. The skill can be demonstrated after a period of no practice, called the retention interval.
      (1) Vary the retention interval: minutes, hours, or days.
      (2) Determine the capability to retain the skill, perform without decrement.
3. Generalizability:
   a. An acquired capability to adapt the skill to permit performance of other similar related tasks.
      (1) Vary the skill: have the patient perform the same skill in different postures; e.g., lower trunk rotation in side-lying, kneeling, standing.
      (2) Modify the skill: e.g., upper extremity PNF patterns with elbow straight, elbow flexing, or elbow extending.
4. Resistance to contextual change:
   a. There is an acquired capability to perform what is learned in other environments.
      (1) Vary the environment: in the clinic, on the nursing unit, at home, in the community.
      (2) Determine the capability to retain the skill, perform without decrement.

Motor Learning Strategies

1. Strategies vary by stage of motor learning (see Table 2-16).
2. Ensure learner readiness.
   a. Optimal arousal facilitates learning; high arousal and low arousal states interfere with learning (Inverted U theory).
   b. Optimal cognitive function: attention, concentration, memory ensures learning.
      (1) Vary strategies with specific cognitive impairments.
      (2) Avoid mental fatigue: give frequent rests.
   c. Communicate, encourage and support learner; reduce fear and apprehension.
3. Identify and describe the skill.
   a. Identify the reasons why the skill is important to learn; stress links to functional independence, patient goals.
   b. Promote insights into the relationship between parts of the task and the whole task, current learning and previous learning.
4. Demonstrate the skill.
   a. At ideal performance parameters (spatial and temporal organization).
   b. Provide the learner with an accurate reference of correctness.
5. Control the environment.
   a. A closed environment is important for early motor learning; reduce environmental distractors.
   b. Later learning will benefit from a shift toward a more open environment; vary the environment, introduce distractors.
6. Schedule appropriate practice sessions.
   a. Promote practice of variations of the task to promote generalizability, improved retention.
   b. Promote practice of the task in varying environments to promote resistance to contextual change.
   c. Use distributed practice with frequent rest periods for learners who demonstrate poor endurance, cognitive impairments (poor attention, concentration,

memory); or when the task is complex, long, and energy-intensive.

d. Vary practice schedules.
   (1) Variable practice (random or serial practice order of tasks) improves retention, enhances depth of cognitive processing and active learning.
   (2) Constant practice and blocked practice order improve performance, early learning.

e. Use mental practice: to cognitively rehearse task, preview movement, decrease apprehension.

f. Promote practice during off-therapy times.

7. Provide appropriate feedback.
   a. Maximize active learning: allow for trial and error learning; don't bombard with feedback. The learner needs to actively process intrinsic information, self-correct responses.
   b. Select appropriate (intact) sensory systems: visual, auditory, tactile, proprioceptive feedback.
   c. Include both knowledge of results (KR) and knowledge of performance (KP) information.
   d. Vary feedback schedules:
      (1) Summed, fading or bandwidth schedules improve retention, enhance depth of cognitive processing and active learning.
      (2) Feedback after every trial improves performance, early learning.
   e. Provide motivational feedback: reinforce desired skills, behaviors.

8. Demonstration and modeling.
   a. Useful to reduce errors, improve learning and performance by imitation.
   b. Use therapist demonstration, expert patients with similar disabilities, videotapes.

9. Guided movement (active assisted movement).
   a. Useful during early learning, not during associative or autonomous learning.
   b. Useful for slow positioning tasks; e.g., the therapist actively assists the patient in moving from supine to sitting or sitting to standing.
   c. Useful to reduce anxiety and inspire trust; ensure safety.

10. Transfer training as appropriate.
   a. Parts-to-whole transfer: for complex tasks with highly independent parts.
      (1) Demonstrate the integrated whole skill.
      (2) Break the skill down into component parts.
      (3) Practice the individual component parts.
      (4) Practice the integrated whole skill (each treatment session); delaying practice of the integrated whole skill may interfere with learning (parts to whole transfer).
   b. Bilateral transfer: practice movements with sound limb before practice with involved limb; e.g., the patient with stroke.

11. Evaluate outcomes.
   a. Level of independence, safety.
   b. Level of function, ease of movement effort.

Review Questions

Teaching and Learning

1. Differentiate between deductive and inductive reasoning.

2. How might operant conditioning be used to shape behavior in a noncompliant patient with TBI?

3. When teaching a patient to return to optimal functioning following trauma, how might the therapist provide appropriate feedback during the early treatment sessions?

14

Research and Evidence-Based Practice

SUSAN B. O'SULLIVAN

Chapter Outline

Physical Therapist Roles and Responsibilities

Physical Therapists Use Evidence-Based Practice (EBP)

1. Definition of EBP: The "conscientious, explicit, and judicious use of current best evidence in making decisions about the care of individual patients" (Sackett et al, 2000).
2. Clinical decisions are based on:
   a. Systematic review of research evidence: studies included are rigorous and clinically relevant, "best available external clinical evidence" (e.g., randomized trials and meta-analysis).
   b. Clinical expertise of the therapist; proficiency and judgment acquired through clinical practice, acquisition of clinical skills, and continued educational development. For example, the clinician accurately identifies the patient's health status and needs, the risks and benefits of possible interventions.
   c. Patient values: values and unique qualities (preferences, concerns, expectations) are identified and integrated into clinical decisions.
3. EBP is a four-step process (see Table 14-1).
4. Electronic medical databases (see Table 14-2).
5. APTA clinical research agenda. Support, explain, and enhance physical therapy clinical practice by facilitating research that is primarily useful to clinicians.
6. Clinical Practice Guidelines (CPGs). Systematically developed statements to assist the clinician and patient in decisions about appropriate courses of action.
   a. CPGs are developed through a combination of current best scientific evidence (e.g., systematic research and meta-analysis), expert judgment, and analysis of patient preferences combined with outcome-based guidelines.
   b. Guidelines issued by professional groups and governmental agencies are developed by expert consensus.
      (1) APTA currently has a program to assist CPG development, resources, and a submission/acceptance process.
      (2) Orthopedic CPGs developed by the Orthopaedic Section of the APTA are presented in Chapter 1 appendices.
      (3) Vascular CPG is presented in Chapter 3, Appendix 3B.
7. Physical Therapy Outcomes Registry (APTA): an organized system for collecting data to evaluate patient function.
   a. Includes clinically relevant measures for the population of patients receiving physical therapy services.
   b. Use of standardized outcome measures improves practice (patient outcomes, patient satisfaction, PT clinical decision-making), informs payment for physical therapy services, and promotes research.

Physical Therapists Conduct Research in Clinical and Academic Settings

1. Steps.
   a. The research question/proposal is developed and submitted for ethical approval and funding (Institutional Review Board).

Table 14-1

Steps in Evidence-Based Practice	
Step 1	A clinical problem is identified, and an answerable research question is formulated. • The question is clearly defined and related to a clinical decision (e.g., whether to use a therapeutic, preventive, or diagnostic intervention). • The question is focused to clarify the target of the literature search.
Step 2	A systematic literature review is conducted and best evidence is collected. • Sources of evidence include books, journals, clinical protocols, colleagues. • Stronger sources of evidence include a systematic review using an electronic search of the medical literature; see Electronic Medical Databases (Table 14-2). • Articles are selected that are most likely to provide valid results (e.g., randomized controlled trials [RCTs]).
Step 3	The research evidence is summarized and critically analyzed. • The type (design) of the study is identified. • Study methods are identified (e.g., Were all patients who entered the trial properly accounted for and attributed at the conclusion of the study? Were appropriate samples of patients used? What are the inclusion and exclusion criteria?). • Statistical methods and analysis are identified (e.g., Are results presented clearly? Statistically significant?).
Step 4	The research evidence is synthesized and applied to clinical practice. • Best evidence is available and applied to clinical practice using clinical decision analysis.

Table 14-2

Electronic Medical Databases
• PubMed—U.S. National Library of Medicine's search service to Medline and Pre-Medline (database of medical and biomedical research) http://www.ncbi.nlm.nih.gov/pubmed/
• APTA PTNow, www.ptnow.org (formerly Open Door at APTA.org) provides APTA members easy access to journals and other resources relevant to clinical practice at ArticleSearch@apta.org
• Cochrane Database of Systemic Reviews (Cochrane Reviews) (database of systematic reviews of RCTs; primary source for clinical effectiveness information) http://www.cochrane.org/reviews
• CINAHL (database of nursing and allied health research) http://www.cinahl.com
• Physiotherapy Evidence Database (PEDro) (database of physical therapy RCTs, systematic reviews, and evidence-based clinical practice guidelines) http://www.pedro.fhs.usyd.edu.au/index.html
• The Sheffield Evidence for Effectiveness and Knowledge http://www.shef.ac.uk/seek/infosearch.htm#guide
• The Centre for Health Evidence http://www.cche.net/
• ERIC (database of education research) http://www.eric.ed.gov/
• Ovid (database of health and lifescience research) http://www.ovid.com
• DARE (database of abstracts of reviews of evidence from medical journals) http://www.ovid.com/site/products/ovidguide/daredb.htm
• RehabDATA (database of disability and rehabilitation research) http://www.naric.com/research
• Center for International Rehabilitation Research Information and Exchange (database of rehabilitation research) http://www.cirrie.buffalo.edu

b. The research study is conducted.
c. The research data is analyzed and reported (i.e., presentation and written publication).

Physical Therapists Incorporate Research Evidence into Practice

1. Steps (see Table 14-1).
2. Sources: Evidence presented in publications, websites (Table 14-2), discussion groups, presentations.
3. Changes in clinical practice.
   a. Based on consultation with the patient, to arrive at a determination of which option best suits the patient (a client-centered approach).
   b. Physical therapists must exercise good clinical judgment in determining applicability of the research results to the specific patient (i.e., similarity to the research group).

Research Design

Methods

Common denominators include statement of the problem, formation of a research question, collection and analysis of data, results, and conclusions.

1. Historical research: involves investigation of a variety of data sources.
   a. Uses sources of data already available.
      (1) Primary sources: original documents, eyewitness accounts, direct recordings of events.
      (2) Secondary sources: description of an event by other than an eyewitness, summary information in textbooks, newspaper accounts.
   b. Investigates authenticity of the data (external criticism).
   c. Evaluates worth of the data (internal criticism).
      (1) Ensures that data are accurate (validity).
      (2) Ensures that data are reliable.
   d. Data synthesis: researcher determines relationships based on analyses and inferences; draws conclusions.
2. Descriptive research: involves collecting data about conditions, attitudes, or characteristics of subjects or groups of subjects.
   a. Determines and reports existing phenomena.
   b. Data collection: typically done through questionnaire survey, interview, or observation.
      (1) Permits classification, identification.
      (2) Data can be used for prediction, decision-making.

c. Examples of descriptive research.
   (1) Case studies or clinical reports: in-depth investigation of an individual, group, or institution.
   (2) Developmental research: studies of behaviors that differentiate individuals at different levels of age, growth, or maturation.
   (3) Longitudinal studies: differentiate changes in an individual or group of individuals over time; e.g., developmental sequences.
   (4) Normative research: investigates standards of behavior, standard values for given characteristics of a sample; e.g., gait characteristics.
   (5) Qualitative research: seeks facts or causes of social phenomena, complex human behavior.
      (a) Utilizes people's own written or spoken words, behaviors through interview or observation.
      (b) Develops concepts, insights, and understanding from patterns in the data; uses inductive reasoning.
      (c) Emphasis is on understanding of human experience, e.g., holistic view of people and settings.

3. Correlational research: attempts to determine whether a relationship exists between two or more quantifiable variables and to what degree.
   a. Describes relationships, predicts relationships among variables without active manipulation of the variables.
   b. Limitations.
      (1) Cannot establish cause-and-effect relationships; limits interpretation of results.
      (2) May fail to consider all variables that enter into a relationship.
   c. Degree of relationship is expressed as correlation coefficient, ranging from −1.00 to +1.00.
      (1) If the correlation is near +1.00, the variables are positively correlated.
      (2) If the correlation is near 0.00, the variables are not related.
      (3) If the correlation is near −1.00, the variables are inversely related.
   d. Examples of correlational research.
      (1) Retrospective: investigation of data collected in the past. Prospective: recording and investigation of present data.
      (2) Descriptive: investigation of several variables at once; determines existing relationships among variables.
      (3) Predictive: useful to develop predictive models.

4. Experimental research: attempts to define a cause and effect relationship through group comparisons.
   a. Alleged cause or treatment (the independent variable) is manipulated.
   b. Effect or difference (the dependent variable) is determined.
   c. Designs.
      (1) True experimental design: includes random assignment into experimental group (receives treatment) or control group (no treatment). All other experiences are held similar.
      (2) Cohort design: quasi-experimental design, subjects are identified and followed over time for changes/outcomes following exposure to an intervention; lacks randomization, may or may not have a control group.
      (3) Within-subject design (repeated measures): subjects serve as their own controls; randomly assigned to treatment or no treatment blocks.
      (4) Between-subject design: comparisons made between groups of subjects.
      (5) Single-subject experimental design: involves a sample of one with repeated measurements and design phases.
         (a) A-B design: involves two phases, a pretreatment or baseline phase followed by an intervention or treatment phase.
         (b) A-B-A design (multiple baseline design): involves three phases—a baseline phase and a treatment phase, followed by a second baseline phase.
         (c) A-B-A-B (multiple baseline, multiple treatment): includes baseline, treatment, and additional baseline and treatment phases.
      (6) Factorial design: refers to the number of independent variables utilized; e.g., single factor, multifactor.

5. Causal-comparative research: attempts to define a cause-and-effect relationship through group comparisons.
   a. Ex post facto research: the cause or independent variable has already occurred; cannot be manipulated (e.g., gender) or should not be manipulated (e.g., type of brain injury).
   b. Groups are compared based on the dependent variable.

6. Epidemiology: the study of disease frequency and distribution in a community; the science concerned with examining and determining the specific causes of health problems and interrelationships of factors.

Variables

1. Independent variable: the activity or factor believed to bring about a change in the dependent variable; the cause or treatment.
2. Dependent variable: the change or difference in behavior that results from the intervention (independent variable); the outcome that is being evaluated.

Hypothesis

1. Definition: a tentative and testable explanation of the relationship between variables; the results of an experiment determine whether the hypothesis is accepted or rejected.
   a. Directional hypothesis (research hypothesis): a generalization that predicts an expected relationship between variables.
   b. Null hypothesis: states that no relationship exists between variables, a statistical hypothesis; any relationship found is the result of chance or sampling error.
      (1) The null hypothesis is rejected; meaning that a significant difference was observed between groups or treatments.
      (2) The null hypothesis is accepted; meaning that no significant difference was observed between groups or treatments.

Data Types (Table 14-3)

1. Nominal scale: classifies variables or scores into two or more mutually exclusive categories based on a common set of characteristics; the lowest level of measurement; e.g., subjects are classified as male or female, tall or short, etc.
2. Ordinal scale: classifies and ranks variables or scores in terms of the degree to which they possess a common characteristic; intervals between ranks are not equal; e.g., subjects are ranked in a graduating class according to grade point average; manual muscle test grades (normal, good, fair, poor, trace, zero) are ranked as an ordinal scale.
3. Interval scale: classifies and ranks variables or scores based on predetermined equal intervals; does not have a true zero point; e.g., an IQ test with scores ranging from 0–200; temperature scales (Fahrenheit or Celsius).
4. Ratio scale: classifies and ranks variables or scores based on equal intervals and a true zero point; the highest, most precise level of measurement; e.g., goniometry, scales for height, weight, or force allow the use of precise physical measures (ratio data) for research.

Sampling

1. The selection of individuals (a sample) for a study from a population. The sample represents the larger group from which they were selected.
   a. Random: all individuals in a population have an equal chance of being chosen for a study.
   b. Systematic: individuals are selected from a population list by taking individuals at specified intervals; e.g., every 10th name.
   c. Stratified: individuals are selected from a population from identified subgroups based on some predetermined characteristic; e.g., by height, weight, or gender.

Table 14-3

Examples of Statistical Analyses According to the Study's Purpose and the Data's Level of Measurement

PURPOSES	LEVELS OF MEASUREMENT	STATISTICS
Describe the Variable	Nominal	Frequency, Percentage
	Ordinal	Median, Mode, Range
	Interval	Mean, Median, Mode, Range, Standard Deviation, Skew of the Distribution
Relationship	Nominal	Chi Square
	Ordinal	Spearman's Rank Order or Kendall's Tau Correlations
	Interval	Pearson's Product Moment Correlation, Partial Correlation, Multiple Correlation, Multiple Regression
Difference	Nominal	One group: Chi Square Two groups: Independent: Chi Square; Paired: McNemar Test More than two groups: Independent: Chi Square; Paired: Cochran's Q
	Ordinal	Two groups: Independent: Mann-Whitney U; Paired: Wilcoxon Signed Rank More than two groups: Independent: Kruskal-Wallis; Paired: Friedman ANOVA
	Interval	Two groups: Independent: t-test; Paired: Paired t-test; Statistical Control: ANCOVA More than two groups: Independent: ANOVA; Across time: Repeated ANOVA; Statistical Control: ANCOVA

Nominal: characteristics into categories
Ordinal: rank ordering, no specific intervals between ranks
Interval: values rank ordered on a scale that has equal distances (intervals) between points on that scale
Prepared by Nina Coppens, PhD, RN, University of Massachusetts, Lowell.

d. Double-blind study: an experiment in which the subject and the investigator are not aware of group assignment.
e. Effect size: the size (quantity, magnitude) of the differences between sample means; allows a statistical test to find a difference when one really does exist.
f. Generalizability: the degree to which a study's findings based on a sample apply to an entire population.

Instrumentation

1. Instrument selection: with established validity and reliability.
2. Gold standard: an instrument with established validity can be used as a standard for assessing other instruments.

Informed Consent

1. Definition: a document that includes consent of an individual prior to participation in a study with full disclosure of risks and benefits; ethical disclosure.
2. Components.
   a. Information about the general nature of what is to take place.
   b. Any risks to the individual and what will be done to minimize the risks.
   c. Possible benefits.
   d. An ethical disclosure.

Problems Related to Measurement

1. Control.
   a. The researcher attempts to remove the influence of any variable other than the independent variable in order to evaluate its effect on the dependent variable.
      (1) Control group: the group in a research study that resembles the experimental group but which does not receive the new or different treatment (e.g., treated as usual); provides a baseline for interpretation of results.
      (2) Experimental group: the group in a research study that receives a new or novel treatment that is under investigation.
      (3) Intervening variable: a variable that alters the relationship (intervenes) between the independent and dependent variable; may not be directly observable or easy to control (e.g., anxiety).
2. Validity.
   a. The degree to which a test, instrument, or procedure accurately measures what it is supposed to or intended to measure.
   b. Types.
      (1) Internal validity: the degree to which the observed differences on the dependent variable are the direct result of manipulation of the independent variable and not some other variable.
      (2) External validity: the degree to which the results are generalizable to individuals (general population) or environmental settings outside of the experimental study.
      (3) Face validity: the assumption of validity based on the appearance of an instrument as a reasonable measure of a variable; may be used for initial screening of a test instrument but psychometrically unsound.
      (4) Content validity: the degree to which an instrument measures an intended content area.
         (a) Determined by expert judgment.
         (b) Requires both item validity and sampling validity.
      (5) Concurrent validity: the degree to which the scores on one test are related to the scores on another criterion test with both tests being given at relatively similar times; usually involves comparison to the gold standard.
      (6) Predictive validity: the degree to which a test is able to predict future performance.
      (7) Construct validity: the degree to which a test measures an intended hypothetical abstract concept (nonobservable behaviors or ideas).
3. Threats to validity.
   a. Sampling bias (selection bias): the researcher introduces systematic sampling error; e.g., a sample of convenience (the use of volunteers or available groups) instead of random selection of subjects.
   b. Failure to exert rigid control over subjects and conditions: intervening variables interact with the dependent variable; e.g., in a longitudinal pediatric study, the outcome is due to the maturation of the child rather than the treatment intervention.
   c. The administration of the pretest influences scores on the posttest; e.g., a learning effect occurs as a result of taking a test.
   d. The measurement instrument is not accurate, the test does not measure the characteristic it purports to measure; e.g., muscle strength, not motor control.
   e. Pretest-treatment interaction: subjects respond differently to the treatment because of the pretest.
   f. Multiple treatment interference: more than one treatment is being given to the subjects at the same time; or carry-over effects from an earlier treatment influence the results of a later treatment, e.g., effects of ultrasound following application of a hot pack.
   g. Experimenter bias: expectations of the researcher about the expected outcomes of the study influence the results of a study.

h. Hawthorne effect: the subject's knowledge of participation in an experiment influences the results of a study.
i. Placebo effect: subjects respond to a sham treatment with positive effects; e.g., taking a sugar pill instead of an experimental drug results in a change.

4. Reliability.
   a. The degree to which a test consistently measures what it is intended to measure.
      (1) Interrater (intertester) reliability: the degree to which two or more independent raters can obtain the same rating for a given variable; the consistency of multiple raters.
      (2) Intrarater (intratester) reliability: the degree to which one rater can obtain the same rating for a given variable on multiple measurement trials; an individual's consistency of rating.
      (3) Test-retest reliability: the degree to which the scores on a test are stable or consistent over time; a measure of instrument stability.
      (4) Split-half reliability: the degree of agreement when a test is split in half and the reliability of first half is compared to the second half; a measure of internal consistency of an instrument.
5. Threats to reliability.
   a. Errors of measurement: random errors or systematic errors; e.g., repeat measurements of blood pressure may vary as a result of physiological changes (fear, anxiety).
6. Objectivity.
   a. Agreement among expert judges on what is observed or what is done; e.g., scoring of a perceptible sign or symptom is the same, regardless of who is observing the phenomena (e.g., licensure exam).
7. Subjectivity.
   a. Refers to a testing format that may differ depending upon the person grading the test (e.g., figure skating judging).
8. Sensitivity and specificity.
   a. Sensitivity: a test's ability to correctly identify the proportion of individuals who truly have a disease or condition (a true positive).
   b. Specificity: a test's ability to correctly identify the proportion of individuals who do not have a disease or condition (a true negative).
   c. Predictive value: a test's ability to estimate the likelihood that a person will test positive (or negative) for a target condition.
   d. True positive: individuals are correctly identified as having the target condition.
   e. True negative: individuals are correctly identified as not having the target condition.
   f. False positive: individuals are identified as having the target condition when they do not.
   g. False negative: individuals are identified as not having the target condition when they do.

Evaluating the Evidence: Levels of Evidence and Grades of Recommendation

Definitions

1. Systematic review (SR) including meta-analysis: a review in which the primary studies are summarized, critically appraised, and statistically combined; usually quantitative in nature with specific inclusion/exclusion criteria.
2. Randomized controlled trial (RCT): an experimental study in which participants are randomly assigned to either an experimental or control group to receive different interventions or a placebo.
3. Cohort study: a prospective (forward-in-time) study; a group of participants (cohort) with a similar condition is followed for a defined period of time; comparison is made to a matched group that does not have the condition.
4. Homogeneity: SR free of variations (heterogeneity) in the directions and degree of results between individual studies.
5. Case-control study: a retrospective (backward-in-time) study. A group of individuals with a similar condition (disease) is compared with a group that does not have the condition to determine factors that may have played a role in the condition.
6. Case report (study): type of descriptive research in which only one individual is studied in depth, often retrospectively.

Adapted from Centre for Evidence-based Medicine, (CEBM) www.cebm.net/

Levels of Evidence

1. Table 14-4 lists criteria used to determine the level of evidence and the accompanying grade of recommendation. Level I is based on the highest level of evidence and Level V is the lowest level of evidence. Grades are used when evaluating interventions and supporting action statements for best practice (CPGs).
2. See Appendix 1B for the summary table of Grades of Recommendation used in evaluating CPGs (Chapters 1 and 3).

Table 14-4

Levels of Evidence

LEVEL	DESCRIPTION	GRADE OF RECOMMENDATION
I	Evidence from high-quality studies: SR (with homogeneity) of multiple RCTs; randomization of large numbers of patients; multicenter; substantial agreement of size and direction of treatment effects. Individual RCT with narrow confidence level; treatment effects precisely defined. All-or-none case series. In absence of RCT, overwhelming evidence of substantial treatment effect following introduction of a new treatment (e.g., vaccine).	**A** Strong
II	Evidence from lesser-quality studies: SR (with homogeneity) of cohort studies (comparison groups). Prospective: patients are identified for study before outcomes achieved. Individual cohort study or low-quality RCT (small N). Quality study includes more than 80% follow-up of patients enrolled in study.	**B** Moderate
III	SR (with homogeneity) of case-control studies (case comparison). Individual case-control study. Retrospective: patients identified for study after outcomes have been achieved.	**B** Moderate
IV	Case-series and poor-quality cohort and case-control studies. Largely descriptive studies.	**C** Weak
V	Expert opinion without explicit critical appraisal, or based on physiology, bench research, or first principles. Observations not made on patients.	**D** Theoretical/foundational

Data Analysis and Interpretation

Descriptive Statistics

1. Purpose: summarize and describe data.
2. Measures of central tendency: a determination of average or typical scores.
   a. Mean: the arithmetic average of all scores (X).
      (1) Add all scores together and divide by the number of subjects (N).
      (2) The most frequently used measure of central tendency; appropriate for interval or ratio data.
   b. Median: the midpoint, 50% of scores are above the median and 50% of scores are below; appropriate for ordinal data.
   c. Mode: the most frequently occurring score; appropriate for nominal data.
3. Measures of variability: a determination of the spread of a group of scores.
   a. Range: the difference between the highest score and the lowest score.
   b. Standard deviation (SD): a determination of variability of scores (difference) from the mean.
      (1) Subtract each score from the mean, square each difference, add up all the squares, and divide by the number of scores.
      (2) The most frequently used measure of variability.
      (3) Appropriate with interval or ratio data.
   c. Normal distribution: a symmetrical bell-shaped curve indicating the distribution of scores; the mean, median, and mode will be similar.
      (1) Half the scores are above the mean and half the scores are below the mean.
      (2) Most scores are near the mean, within one standard deviation; approximately 68% of scores fall within −1 or +1 SD of the mean.
      (3) Frequency of scores decreases farther from the mean.
         (a) Approximately 95% of scores fall within −2 or +2 SD of the mean.
         (b) Approximately 99% of scores fall within −3 or +3 SD of the mean.
      (4) Distribution may be skewed (not symmetrical) rather than normal: scores are extreme, clustered at one end or the other; the mean, median, and mode are different.
   d. Percentiles and quartiles: describe a score's position within the distribution, relative to all other scores.
      (1) Percentiles: data are divided in 100 equal parts; position of score is determined.
      (2) Quartiles: data are divided into four equal parts and position of score is placed accordingly.

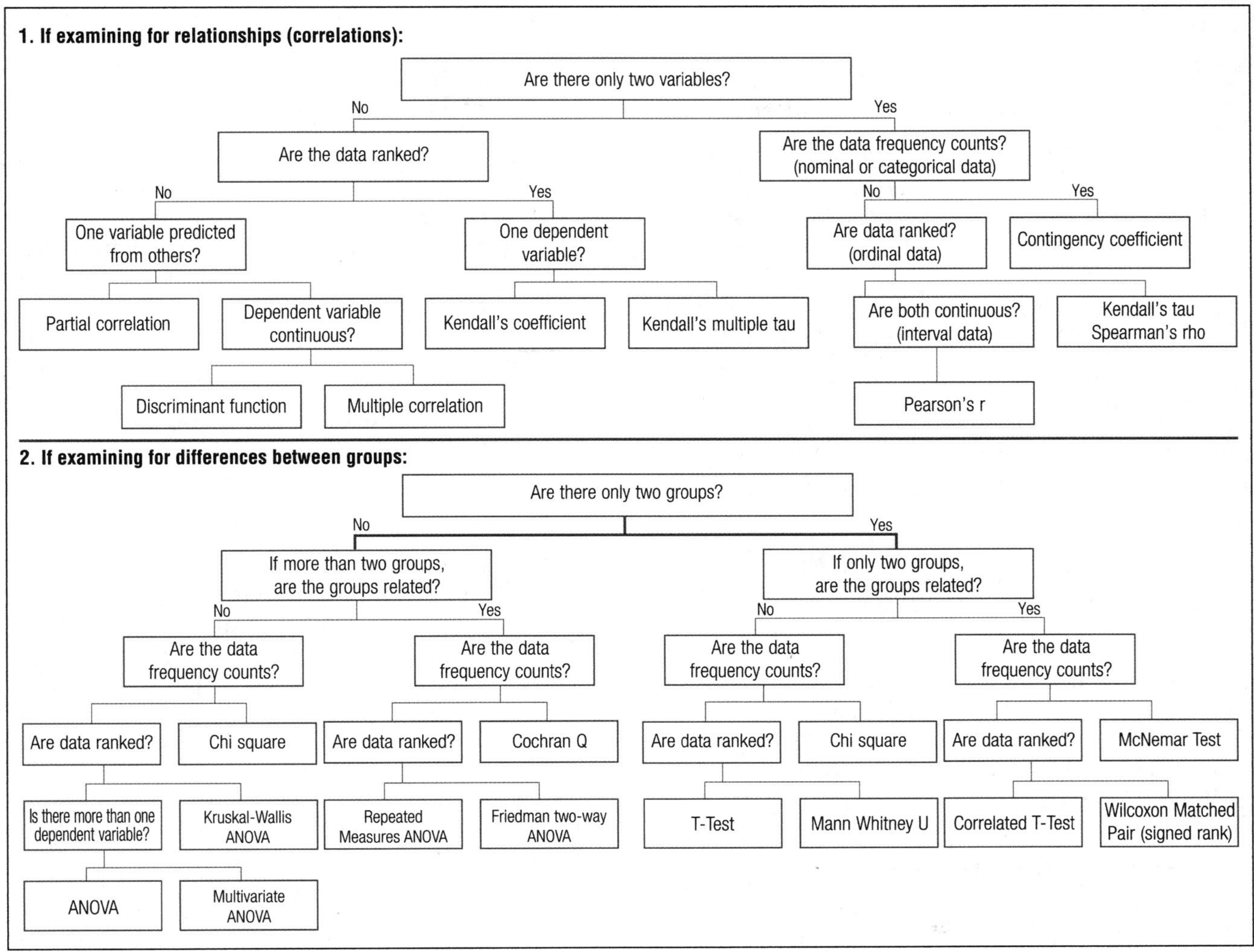

Figure 14-1 **Clinical decision-making: Flow diagram for determining appropriate statistics.**
Key: follow flow diagram to the right with yes answers; follow flow diagram to left with no answers.
Adapted from materials prepared by Dr. L Zaichkowsky, Boston University.

Inferential Statistics

1. Purpose.
   a. Help determine how likely the results of a study of a sample can be generalized to the whole population.
2. Concepts.
   a. Standard error of measurement: an estimate of expected errors in an individual's score; a measure of response stability or reliability.
   b. Tests of significance: an estimation of true differences, not due to chance; a rejection of the null hypothesis.
      (1) Probability levels are associated with inferential analyses. Alpha level: preselected level of statistical significance.
         (a) Most commonly set at 0.05 or 0.01; indicates that the expected difference is due to chance; e.g., at 0.05, only 5 times out of every 100 or a 5% chance, often expressed as a value of P.
         (b) Allows rejection of the null hypothesis: there are true differences on the measured dependent variable.
      (2) Degrees of freedom: based on number of subjects and number of groups; allows determination of level of significance based on consulting appropriate tables for each statistical test.
      (3) Errors.
         (a) Standard error: expected chance variation among the means, the result of sampling error.

(b) Type I error: the null hypothesis is rejected by the researcher when it is true; e.g., the means of scores are concluded to be truly different when the differences are due to chance.

(c) Type II error: the null hypothesis is not rejected by the researcher when it is false; e.g., the means of scores are concluded to be due to chance when the means are truly different.

(d) By increasing sample size, using random selection, and having valid measures, the chance of both Type I and II errors is decreased.

3. Parametric statistics: testing is based on population parameters; includes tests of significance based on interval or ratio data.
   a. Assumptions.
      (1) A normal distribution exists in the population studied of the variable measured, or distribution is known. In a large, representative sample, the assumption of normal distribution is probably met.
      (2) Random sampling is performed.
      (3) Variance in the groups is equal.
   b. T-test: a parametric test of significance used to compare two independent groups created by random assignment and identify a difference at a selected probability level (e.g., 0.05).
      (1) T-test for independent samples: compares the difference between two independent groups; e.g., a test to determine whether an intervention (a new hand splint) improves the function of patients with rheumatoid arthritis.
      (2) T-test for paired samples: compares the difference between two matched samples; e.g., Does therapy improve function in siblings with autism?
         (a) One-tailed t-test: based on a directional hypothesis; evaluates differences in data on only one end of a distribution, either negative or positive; e.g., patients who receive a certain treatment exhibit better rehabilitation outcomes than those who do not.
         (b) Two-tailed t-test: based on a nondirectional hypothesis; evaluates differences in data on both positive and negative ends of a distribution; tests of significance are almost always two-tailed; e.g., either group of patients (treatment or control) may exhibit better rehabilitation outcomes.
      (3) Inappropriate use of t-tests: use of a t-test to compare more than two means within a single sample; e.g., three modes of exercise are compared within a single sample.
   c. Analysis of variance (ANOVA): a parametric test used to compare three or more independent treatment groups or conditions at a selected probability level.
      (1) Simple (one-way) ANOVA: compares multiple groups on a single independent variable; e.g., three sets of posttest scores (balance scores from a Balance Master) are compared from three different categories of elderly: young elderly (65–74); old elderly (75–84); and old and frail elderly (> 85).
      (2) Factorial ANOVA (multifactorial) compares multiple groups on two or more independent variables; e.g., two groups of injured patients (those with severe ankle sprain and moderate ankle sprain) and a control group are compared for muscle activation patterns and sensory perception in each limb.
   d. Analysis of covariance (ANCOVA): a parametric test used to compare two or more treatment groups or conditions while also controlling for the effects of intervening variables (covariates), e.g., two groups of subjects are compared on the basis of gait parameters using two different types of assistive devices; subjects in one group are taller than subjects in the second group; height then becomes the covariate that must be controlled during statistical analysis.
4. Nonparametric statistics: testing not based on population parameters; includes tests of significance based on ordinal or nominal data.
   a. Used when above parametric assumptions cannot be met.
   b. Less powerful than parametric tests, more difficult to reject the null hypothesis; e.g., can be used with small sample and with ordinal or nominal level data.
   c. Chi square test: a nonparametric test of significance used to compare data in the form of frequency counts occurring in two or more mutually exclusive categories; e.g., subjects are asked to rate treatment preferences.
5. Correlational statistics: used to determine the relative strength of a relationship between two variables; e.g., compare progression of radiologically observed joint destruction in rheumatoid arthritis and its relationship to demographic variables (gender, age), disease severity, and exercise frequency.
   a. Pearson product-moment coefficient (r): used to correlate continuous data with underlying normal distribution on interval or ratio scales; e.g., the relationship between proximal and distal development in infants is examined.
   b. Spearman's rank correlation coefficient (r_s or Spearman's rho): a nonparametric test used to correlate

ordinal data; e.g., the relationship of verbal and reading comprehension scores is examined.

c. Point biserial correlation: one variable is dichotomous (nominal) and the other is ratio or interval; e.g., the relationship between elbow flexor spasticity and side of stroke (left or right) in stroke patients is examined.

d. Rank biserial correlation: one variable is dichotomous (nominal) and the other is ordinal; e.g., the relationship between gender and functional ability is examined.

e. Intraclass correlation coefficient (ICC): a reliability coefficient based on an analysis of variance.

f. Strength of relationships.
   (1) Positive correlations range from 0 to +1.00: indicates that as variable X increases, so does variable Y.
   - High correlations: > 0.76 to 1.00.
   - Moderate correlations: 0.51 to 0.75.
   - Fair correlations: 0.26 to 0.50.
   - Low correlations: 0.00 to 0.25.
   - 0 means no relationship between variables.

   (2) Negative correlations range from −1.0 to 0: indicates that as variable X increases, variable Y decreases; an inverse relationship.

g. Common variance: a representation of the degree that variation in one variable is attributable to another variable.
   (1) Determined by squaring the correlation coefficient, e.g., a correlation coefficient of 0.70 means that the common variance is 49%, i.e., the variation in one variable can be explained by the other 49% of the time.

6. Linear regression: used to establish the relationship between two variables as a basis for prediction.

a. An examination of two continuous variables that are linearly correlated. The variable designated X is the independent or predictor variable. The variable designated Y is the dependent or criterion variable.

b. The purpose is to generate an equation that relates X to Y, such that if given values of X, Y can be predicted, e.g., blood pressure (Y) is examined by age (X); answers the question, Can systolic blood pressure be predicted from age?

Review Questions

Research and Evidence-Based Practice

1. In experimental research, what is the difference between independent and dependent variables?

2. What is the significance of validity and reliability regarding a clinical test? What are the possible threats to each?

3. What is the significance of sensitivity and specificity regarding a clinical test?

4. From highest to lowest level of rigor, what is the hierarchy of evaluating and grading levels of evidence? Give an example of each.

15

Chapter Review Questions and Answers

Chapter Outline

Chapter 1 Review Questions

Musculoskeletal Physical Therapy

1. Which motion at the glenohumeral joint has the greatest limitation if the diagnosis is adhesive capsulitis?

External rotation (capsular pattern).

2. When considering the concave-convex rule, to which joints in the spine does the concave rule apply?

Every joint below the second vertebra. Only the atlanto-occipital joint is convex.

3. Which special test when applied to the ankle/foot is BEST used to identify ligamentous instability of the calcaneofibular ligament?

Talar tilt.

4. What are the major differences in diagnostic characteristics and pattern of joint dysfunction between osteoarthritis and rheumatoid arthritis?

Osteoarthritis is first manifested by changes in joint cartilage with eventual erosion to subchondral bone. All joints are not equally affected. The DIPs, PIPs, the CM of the thumb, cervical and lumbar spine, hips, knees, and MTPs are the primary sites.

Rheumatoid arthritis is an autoimmune disease that primarily affects the synovium. The synovium proliferates, dissolves collagen, and extends over the joint cartilage. There is persistent inflammation and systemic complaints such as morning stiffness, fever, and loss of appetite. Joints are affected in a bilateral symmetrical pattern. All joints including the spine and TMJ can be involved.

5. Based on Clinical Practice Guidelines for Knee Ligament Sprain, which intervention has the strongest overall evidence for effectiveness?

Therapeutic exercise, including NWB open-chain and WB closed-chain activities, is the most effective based on evidence when dealing with patients with knee instability and movement coordination impairments.

Other interventions, such as bracing, CPM, early intervention, etc., demonstrate moderate to weak evidence based on available studies.

6. Following a total hip replacement, in the acute phase, which positions should be avoided in bed positioning and activities involving bed mobility?

A wedge should be used in positioning to prevent hip adduction. Hip flexion should not exceed 90°. Adduction and internal rotation should be limited when moving in bed.

7. For an anteriorly displaced articular disc at the TMJ, what is the primary joint mobilization technique?

If TMJ restriction is present, primary glide is inferior, which gaps the joint, stretches the capsule and allows relocation of the disc.

Chapter 2 Review Questions

Neuromuscular Physical Therapy

1. Which cranial nerves may play any role in vision? What findings are normal or abnormal?

CN II (Optic)	Optic-visual acuity or visual fields, pupillary constriction
CN III (Oculomotor)	Pupillary size, extraocular movement
CN IV (Trochlear)	Extraocular movement
CN V (Trigeminal)	Corneal reflex
CN VI (Abducens)	Extraocular movement
CN VII (Facial)	Ability to close eyes tightly (may be absent in Bell's palsy)
CN VIII (Vestibulocochlear)	Nystagmus (secondary to brain dysfunction)

2. Following a CVA primarily affecting the occipital lobe, what are the major considerations when examining the patient for perceptual deficits?

Testing for visual field deficits such as homonymous or bitemporal hemianopsia.
Examine for body scheme or image such as unilateral neglect or somatognosia.
Examine for spatial relations such as figure-ground, depth perception, vertical disorientation, etc.
Examine for agnosia such as the inability to recognize familiar objects with an impaired sensory modality.
Examine for apraxias such as dressing apraxias, agraphia, etc.

3. When examining deep tendon reflexes, what is the score reported for an obligatory and sustained response?

0 = absent reflex
1+ = tone change but no movement
2+ = visible movement of extremity
3+ = exaggerated full movement of extremity
4+ = obligatory and sustained movement lasting > 30 seconds

4. What are the characteristics in terms of communication, gait, tone, balance, and respiratory function in a patient with late Parkinson's disease (Stage IV Hoehn and Yahr)?

Communication: dysarthria, hypophonia (low volume), masklike face, small writing.
Gait: poverty of movement, festinating gait possible.
Tone: cogwheel rigidity.
Balance: impaired postural reactions including trunk rigidity and lack of rotation.
Respiratory function: decreased chest expansion, decreased vital capacity.

5. What are the initial physical therapy goals and interventions upon receiving a referral for a patient recently diagnosed with a severe vestibular disorder?

Implement safety measures first. Teach sensory substitution (visual, tactile), and compensatory strategies and provide an ambulatory aid as indicated. Later on, habituation training, eye and head exercises, and postural stability activities can be implemented.

6. Following an MVA, a patient with a complete SCI at the C7 level has been admitted to a rehab facility after a lengthy stay at an acute care hospital. What are the components of the physical therapist's initial examination?

Vital signs, respiratory function, skin condition, muscle tone, DTRs, sensation, muscle strength, functional status, wheelchair skills, and administration of a standardized test such as the FIM.

7. What is the common pattern of fatigue in many patients with multiple sclerosis?

High energy in early morning, followed by early afternoon fatigue and exhaustion, and then some recovery by early evening. Thus, schedule these patients for morning intervention or consider this pattern for job or other ADL tasks.

Chapter 3 Review Questions

Cardiovascular and Lymphatic Physical Therapy

1. What risk factors contribute to the development of coronary artery disease?

   Risk factors include age, gender, family history, cigarette smoking, sedentary lifestyle, obesity (BMI > 30 kg/m or waist girth > 40 inches), hypertension, dyslipidemia, prediabetes, increased plasma glucose, diabetes.

2. What are the expected ST segment changes following an acute myocardial infarction and with impaired coronary perfusion?

   Following an acute MI the ST segment will be elevated.

   In case of impaired perfusion as in coronary artery disease, the ST segment becomes depressed and can be upsloping, horizontal, or downsloping.

3. How would you instruct your patient regarding possible circumstances that could elicit angina pectoris?

   Increased demands on the heart could elicit angina pectoris. These can include physical exertion, emotional stress, smoking, temperature extremes (especially cold), and overeating.

4. When exercising a patient with diabetes and coronary artery disease that is taking beta blockers, what is the best measure to monitor exercise performance?

   Borg's Ratings of Perceived Exertion scale (RPE scale or Modified RPE scale) can be used. RPE increases linearly with increasing exercise intensity and correlates closely with HR and work rate.

   Beta blockers blunt heart rate response to increasing exercise intensity. Thus, HR is not a reliable sign to monitor under these circumstances.

5. What are the goals of inpatient cardiac rehabilitation in the acute stage or Phase 1?

   The acute stage, lasting perhaps 3–5 days (sometimes longer), should focus on early return to independence in ADL, counteract effects of bed rest by reducing risk of thrombi, maintain muscle tone, reduce orthostatic hypotension, maintain joint mobility, help allay anxiety, provide patient and family education, and promote risk factor reduction.

6. When managing edema secondary to lymphatic dysfunction, use of manual lymph drainage (MLD) emphasizes which directional principles?

   Emphasis is on decongesting proximal segments first, then extremities. The flow within segments is distal to proximal.

Chapter 4 Review Questions

Pulmonary Physical Therapy

1. What are the PaO_2 and FiO_2 normal values in room air?

The partial pressure of oxygen in the arterial blood (PaO_2) is 95–100 mm Hg in young healthy individuals. It decreases with age.

The fraction of oxygen in inspired room air (FiO_2) is the percentage of oxygen in the air, which is 21% or written out as 0.21. Use of supplemental oxygen will increase FiO_2.

2. When auscultating the lungs, what are the main characteristics of crackles, wheezes, vesicular, and bronchial breath sounds?

Crackles (rales, crepitations) are crackling sounds heard during inspiration that indicate pathology such as pulmonary edema, fibrosis, or atelectasis.

Wheezes are musical sounds heard during expiration, especially with COPD.

Vesicular sounds (normal breath sounds) are soft, rustling sounds heard throughout inspiration and the beginning of expiration.

Bronchial sounds are hollow, echoing sounds usually heard over the right main stem bronchus during inspiration and expiration. They are normal sounds.

3. What are the expected physical, imaging, PFT, and laboratory findings associated with moderate to severe asthma?

Physical findings: productive cough, dyspnea, decreased breath sounds, wheezes, crackles, tachypnea, tachycardia, increased accessory muscle use, anxiety.

Imaging findings: hyperlucency and flattened diaphragms.

PFT findings: decreased FEV_1/FVC ratio, decreased FEV_1, lower flow rates.

Laboratory findings: ABG hypoxemia and hypercapnea with severe disease.

4. What are the precautions when using postural drainage in the Trendelenburg position?

Care should be exercised and use of the Trendelenburg (head down) position possibly limited or eliminated in situations involving congestive heart failure, significant hypertension, pulmonary edema, increased intracranial pressure, aneurysm, severe SOB, obesity, ascites, pregnancy, and hiatal hernia.

Chapter 5 Review Questions

Integumentary Physical Therapy

1. Differentiate between the viral infections herpes simplex and herpes zoster in terms of expected symptoms.

Herpes simplex is preceded by itching and soreness followed by vesicular eruptions. A good example is a cold sore.

Herpes zoster is the result of reactivation of the varicella-zoster virus (chickenpox). Often results in pain, tingling, and vesicle formation along dermatomes of spinal or cranial nerves. May last a long time. Superficial or deep heat contraindicated.

2. When performing a physical examination of decubitus ulcer, what elements should be part of the physical therapist's examination?

Determine the location of the wound; assess the length, width, girth, and depth of the wound; examine for tunneling; determine type, amount, color, and odor of exudates if any; determine presence of necrotic or granulation tissue; determine wound temperature using thermistor probe.

3. Differentiate between a superficial partial-thickness burn and a full-thickness burn.

Superficial partial-thickness: epidermis and upper dermis damage, bright pink or red, blisters, moderate edema, painful.

Full-thickness: complete destruction of epidermis, dermis, and subcutaneous tissues; white, gray, or charred appearance; poor circulation; dry, leathery surface; little pain as nerve endings destroyed.

4. Differentiate between venous and arterial ulcers in terms of expected clinical presentation.

Venous ulcers: irregular shape and dark appearance; shallow, often at medial malleolus; pulses present; little pain; fair amount of exudates.

Arterial ulcers: smooth edges; deep, often on toes, lateral malleoli and shin; pulses often absent; painful; no drainage.

5. Which categories of wound dressings can be used for exudative wounds?

Many modern dressings can be used for exudative wounds. Some are more suited for heavy exudation. Some are better if the exudate is moderate or mild.

Categories include hydrocolloids, hydrogels, foams, alginates, and gauze. The dressing category not used with exudates is transparent films.

6. What are the important clinical changes affecting the prognosis for a patient with diffuse systemic sclerosis?

Diffuse systemic sclerosis/scleroderma has a poorer prognosis than limited systemic sclerosis/scleroderma (LSS). The integumentary changes are more rapid and widespread, there is earlier involvement of visceral organs (e.g., kidneys, heart, and lungs), and mortality occurs sooner than someone with LSS and no organ involvement. Monitoring vital signs and blood pressure for acute hypertension is essential.

Chapter 6 Review Questions

Other Systems

1. What are the adverse side effects of cancer treatment that can impact physical therapy intervention?

   Chemotherapy affects the blood. Leukopenia can result in increased susceptibility to infection. Thrombocytopenia can result in increased bleeding. Anemia can decrease aerobic capacity.

   Use of steroids can result in muscle atrophy.

   Immunosuppression can result in fatigue with minimal exertion.

   Radiation can result in fibrosis.

2. What are the typical medications that may be prescribed for a patient diagnosed with GERD?

   Proton pump inhibitors (PPIs) such as Prilosec; H_2 blockers such as ranitidine (Zantac) or cimetidine (Tagamet) and antacids such as Tums.

3. What are three possible interventions a physical therapist might use in the management of stress incontinence?

   Use of Kegel's (pelvic floor) strengthening exercises, functional electrical stimulation, and biofeedback.

4. What are some of the long-term complications of diabetes that a physical therapist needs to consider during examination and treatment?

   There are many complications. A partial list includes retinopathy, renal disease, polyneuropathy, atherosclerosis, CVA, MI, peripheral arterial disease, joint stiffness, osteoporosis, gastroparesis, GERD, liver disease.

5. Differentiate between hypothyroidism and hyperthyroidism in terms of expected symptoms.

   Hypothyroidism: weight gain, lethargy, low blood pressure, constipation, intolerance to cold, dry skin, appearance of goiter (thyroid gland enlargement).

   Hyperthyroidism: nervousness, hyperreflexia, tremor, hunger, weight loss, fatigue, heat intolerance, tachycardia, diarrhea.

Chapter 7 Review Questions

Pediatric Physical Therapy

1. In the developing infant, what are the differences in terms of age of onset and response between the asymmetrical tonic neck reflex (ATNR) and the symmetrical tonic neck reflex (STNR)?

ATNR is normally present at birth. Rotation of the head to one side results in flexion of the skull-side limbs and extension of face-side limbs.

STNR usually appears between 4 and 6 months of age. Cervical flexion results in flexion of the arms and extension of the legs. Cervical extension results in extension of the arms and flexion of the legs.

2. When performing an examination of the skeletal system in a full-term neonate, what possible abnormal bony conditions should be part of the screening process?

Fractured clavicle, hip dysplasia, spinal curvature including kyphosis and scoliosis, spina bifida occulta (dimple or tuft of hair), and talipes equinovarus.

3. What are the typical lower extremity contractures seen with the child with spastic cerebral palsy?

Hip flexors, adductors, and internal rotators. Knee flexors and ankle plantar flexors.

4. What is a realistic expectation for functional mobility in the community and in the household for a patient with myelodysplasia affecting the midlumbar levels (about L3)?

Wheelchair for community mobility. Orthoses with walker or crutches for household ambulation.

Chapter 8 Review Questions

Geriatric Physical Therapy

1. What are the physiological changes that may occur in the visual system in older adults?

   May include general decline in visual acuity; presbyopia; decreased ability to adapt to light and dark; diminished oculomotor responses; cataracts; glaucoma.

2. What risk factors are associated with development of osteoporosis?

   Hormonal deficiency associated with menopause; nutritional deficiency of calcium, excessive alcohol and caffeine consumption; decreased physical activity; hyperthyroidism; diabetes; celiac disease; corticosteroids, thyroid hormone; family history, Caucasian and Asian races.

3. What are the major side effects (red flags) of the use of pain medications in the geriatric population that can be a concern for physical therapists?

   Increased fall risk, disorientation, and sedation.

4. What are the most important components of the initial examination of a patient with dementia?

   History including onset and progression of symptoms; cognitive function (e.g., Mini-Mental State Examination); impairments of communication and perception; behavioral changes; self-care; motor function including gait, balance, and dyspraxia; environmental safety.

5. What are the major goals and interventions to minimize fall risk factors?

   Based on examination findings, identify fall risk. Eliminate or minimize fall risk factors with consideration of disease and medications. Increase strength and flexibility. Balance and gait training. Compensate for sensory deficiencies. Functional training including sit-to-stand, stairs, walking, turning. Provide assistive devices as needed. Allow adequate time for activities. Safety education. Modify environment.

Chapter 9 Review Questions

Therapeutic Exercise

1. During strength training, what is the influence of the Valsalva maneuver regarding intrathoracic pressure, heart rate, venous pressure, and cardiac work?

The Valsalva maneuver (forced exhalation with a closed glottis) results in increased intrathoracic pressure, venous pressure, and cardiac work and decreased heart rate.

2. What are the implications of the FITT equation in terms of strategies to develop cardiovascular endurance?

The FITT equation includes the factors of frequency, intensity, time, and type of exercise. Intensity (overload) is the primary way to increase cardiovascular endurance. At least 2 days (frequency) of exercise a week or more is needed to increase endurance. Duration (time) of exercise depends on initial fitness level. The goal would be 20–30 minutes, 3–5 days a week for conditioned people. Initial time would be significantly curtailed for deconditioned or obese individuals. The type of exercise should involve large muscle groups.

3. When exercising a patient in an aquatic environment, what are the factors that can make the activity easier to perform? More difficult to perform?

Easier: movement horizontal to or upward to the water surface, use of a flotation device, a paddle turned to slice through the water, decreased speed of movement, exercising in deeper water increases buoyancy.

More difficult: increased speed of movement, use of fins, paddles, and boots to increase resistance, exercise in shallower water, movement downward in the water, increased speed of movement.

4. What is the main principle being employed when using the PNF facilitated stretching technique of contract-relax?

The muscle to be stretched relaxes as a result of autogenic inhibition possibly from Golgi tendon organ firing. The muscle can be further relaxed through the effects of reciprocal inhibition if active contraction is performed.

5. What are the most common errors associated with training a patient to improve postural stability?

Inadequate stretching of tight pelvic and hip musculature prior to training; inadequate core muscle control; starting at too high a functional level or progressing too rapidly; exercising past the point of fatigue.

Chapter 10 Review Questions

Biophysical Agents

1. What are the increased and decreased physiological responses to the local application of heat and cold?

   Increased heat: Blood flow, capillary permeability, elasticity, metabolism, edema.

   Increased cold: Joint stiffness, pain threshold, blood viscosity.

   Decreased heat: Joint stiffness, muscle strength, muscle spasm, pain.

   Decreased cold: Blood flow, capillary permeability, elasticity, metabolism, muscle spasm, muscle strength, spasticity.

2. Which characteristics of ultrasound application affect the depth of penetration and thermal effects?

   Frequency in MHz determines depth of penetration. Three MHz produces greater heat in superficial tissues. One MHz increases heat production in deep layers. Temporal characteristics are a major factor in determining thermal characteristics. Pulsed US (duty cycle < 50%) produces less acoustic energy and less heat and is considered nonthermal. Continuous US produces thermal effects and increases tissue temperature.

3. Name at least five indications or goals for use of intermittent spinal mechanical traction.

   Decrease joint stiffness; decrease muscle spasm; disc protrusion; degenerative disc; modulate discogenic pain; reduce nerve root impingement; modulate subacute or chronic joint pain.

4. What are the contraindications for use of electrical stimulation?

   Demand-type pacemakers; unstable arrhythmias; epilepsy; seizure disorder; active bleeding; near thrombophlebitis; superficial metal implants; over or near the carotid sinus, thoracic region, phrenic nerve, urinary bladder stimulators, low back during pregnancy; pharyngeal region.

5. Which electrical stimulation characteristics are appropriate to use for wound healing?

   High-volt pulsed galvanic current and low-intensity, low-volt continuous direct current can be used for wound healing.

Chapter 11 Review Questions

Functional Training, Equipment, and Devices

1. What are the muscle activation patterns during heel strike (initial contact) and heel-off (terminal stance) for the quadriceps, pretibial muscles, and plantar flexors?

Heel strike: Quadriceps is active for shock absorption and to control for knee flexion; pretibial muscles (anterior tibialis, extensor hallucis longus, and extensor digitorum longus) control plantar flexion by decelerating the foot.

Heel-off-peak activity of the plantar flexors to generate forward propulsion.

2. What type of equipment and ambulatory aids might be needed to progress a morbidly obese patient from a sedentary bed-bound situation to independent ambulation?

Heavy-duty mechanical lift (e.g., Hoyer lift) to help transfer a patient from sit-to-stand.

Body weight support system (BWS) with an overhead harness to unload some body weight in a progressive manner.

Heavy-duty, extra-wide walker.

3. How does rearfoot posting in a foot orthosis control for valgus or varus?

Rearfoot posting acts primarily on the subtalar joint from heel strike to foot flat.

A medial wedge (varus post) limits or controls calcaneal eversion and internal rotation of the tibia.

A lateral wedge (valgus post) controls an excessively inverted and supinated calcaneus and subtalar joint.

4. What are the pressure-tolerant areas in the typical transtibial residual limb that are suitable for a total contact socket?

The patellar tendon-bearing total contact socket (PTB) is ordinarily used for the transtibial amputation. The areas that can tolerate pressure are the patellar tendon, medial tibial plateau, tibial and fibular shafts, and the distal end of the residual limb. The distal end can be problematic if there are open wounds or sensitivity issues.

5. What are two conditions that may warrant a therapist recommending a motorized tilt-in-space wheelchair for a patient?

A tilt-in-space chair allows the seat and back to be tipped backward as a unit. It is indicated for patients with significant extensor spasms that could eject the patient from the chair.

Another indication would be for pressure relief. This situation is one in which the impairment prevents or limits the patient from changing positions and redistributing weight independently.

Chapter 12 Review Questions

Professional Responsibilities

1. What are the main provisos of the Individuals with Disabilities Education Act (IDEA)?

   Ensures that children with disabilities receive appropriate free public education. Establishes early intervention programs [EIP] including therapy services. Provides for necessary adaptive equipment. Requires the creation of an Individualized Education Plan [IEP].

2. What are the possible roles of the physical therapist in emergency preparedness/disaster planning?

   Liaison with local first responders including police and fire. Development of the communications infrastructure used during a disaster. Assist in prioritizing critical services during a disaster. Help coordinate internal resources. Participate in disaster drills. Serve as a resource for the needs of those with physical impairments.

3. What are the major components that constitute negligence by a physical therapist?

   The therapist owes a duty to the patient (i.e., a relationship exists). The therapist fails to perform at a level of what reasonably competent practitioners would have done under similar circumstances. The patient is harmed.

Chapter 13 Review Questions

Teaching and Learning

1. Differentiate between deductive and inductive reasoning.

Deductive reasoning is the process whereby conclusions are drawn based on information, theoretical models, laws, rules, or accepted principles.

Inductive reasoning is the process whereby conclusions are drawn by extrapolating specific situations to larger circumstances. It does not guarantee the conclusion in every case.

2. How might operant conditioning be used to shape behavior in a noncompliant patient with TBI?

Behavior modification uses operant conditioning techniques by identifying the desired behavior and reinforcing the desired behavior immediately in a meaningful way. Negative behaviors are ignored, aversive behavior (punishment) is minimized and a closed environment with few distractions is preferred.

3. When teaching a patient to return to optimal functioning following trauma, how might the therapist provide appropriate feedback during the early treatment sessions?

Maximize active learning; allow for trial and error learning and self-correction by the patient. Select appropriate sensory systems for feedback (visual, auditory, tactile, and proprioceptive). In early learning, the focus is on visual feedback. Include both Knowledge of Results (KR) and Knowledge of Performance (KP) information.

Begin with blocked practice and feedback after every trial to improve early learning and performance. Progress to variable practice (serial or random practice) and variable feedback (summed, fading, bandwidth) to improve retention of skills. Provide reinforcement as needed.

Chapter 14 Review Questions

Research and Evidence-Based Practice

1. In experimental research, what is the difference between independent and dependent variables?

   The independent variable is the treatment or cause believed to bring about a change. The dependent variable is the change, outcome or difference in behavior resulting from the independent variable.

2. What is the significance of validity and reliability regarding a clinical test? What are the possible threats to each?

   Validity is the degree to which an instrument or procedure accurately measures what it purports to measure. Threats to validity include sampling bias, lack of controls over the subjects, inaccurate measuring instrument, experimenter bias, variables in treatment administration, placebo effect, and Hawthorne effect (subject's knowledge of participation in an experiment).

   Reliability is the consistency with which a test measures what it purports to measure. Threats to reliability may deal with intrarater or interrater factors, errors of measurement, and systemic or environmental factors.

3. What is the significance of sensitivity and specificity regarding a clinical test?

   Sensitivity is a test's ability to correctly identify the proportion of those that truly have the condition, impairment, or disease. It is a measure of true positive.

   Specificity is a test's ability to correctly identify the proportion of those who do NOT have the condition, impairment, or disease. It is a measure of true negative.

4. From highest to lowest level of rigor, what is the hierarchy of evaluating and grading levels of evidence? Give an example of each.

   Level 1 (Grade A): systematic reviews including meta-analysis, individual randomized control trials

   Level 2 (Grade B): cohort studies

   Level 3 (Grade B): case-control studies, retrospective studies

   Level 4 (Grade C): case-series or poor quality cohort and case-control studies; descriptive studies

   Level 5 (Grade D): expert opinion or observations not made on patients

16

Computer Simulated Examinations

Examinations are on the flash drive. Follow the instructions. After completing each examination, your performance will be analyzed in terms of specific domains, categories and reasoning skills. The questions that follow are the ones that constitute the software examinations. Separate TEACHING POINTS for each question contain explanations of the correct answer, incorrect choices and reasoning subtype.

Domains of Knowledge

- Cardiovascular/Pulmonary and Lymphatic Systems
- Musculoskeletal System
- Neuromuscular and Nervous System
- Integumentary System
- Metabolic and Endocrine Systems
- Gastrointestinal System
- Genitourinary System
- System Interactions
- Nonsystem

Categories

- Examination
- Evaluation, Diagnosis
- Interventions
- Equipment, Devices, Biophysical Agents
- Safety, Professional Responsibilities, Research

Clinical Reasoning Strategies

 Inductive Reasoning

 Analysis

 Evaluation

 Deductive Reasoning

 Inference

Examination A

A1

Metabolic and Endocrine Systems | Evaluation, Diagnosis

An elderly patient with hypothyroidism is recovering from a fall and is referred to physical therapy to increase exercise tolerance and safety. The patient complains to the therapist of significant muscle pain in both lower extremities. What additional musculoskeletal effects should the therapist examine for?

Choices:

1. Distal muscle weakness.
2. Proximal muscle weakness.
3. Joint laxity.
4. Decreased deep tendon reflexes.

Teaching Points

Correct Answer: 2

Hypothyroidism can have numerous musculoskeletal effects, including myalgia (muscle pain) and proximal muscle weakness.

Incorrect Choices:

Additional musculoskeletal effects include stiffness (not joint laxity) and prolonged deep tendon reflexes (DTRs) (not decreased DTRs).

Type of Reasoning: Inferential

For this question, the test taker must determine what is most likely to be true based on knowledge of hypothyroidism. Questions of this nature, where one must infer information, require inferential reasoning skill. In this case, one should infer that proximal muscle weakness is most likely to be present. If answered incorrectly, review information on hypothyroidism.

A2

Genitourinary System | Examination

A patient is referred to a woman's health clinic with moderate to severe uterine prolapse. What symptoms should the therapist examine for?

Choices:

1. Absent perineal sensation.
2. Bowel leakage.
3. Low back pain and perineal discomfort aggravated by prolonged standing.
4. Low back pain and perineal discomfort aggravated by lying down.

Teaching Points

Correct Answer: 3

Low back pain and perineal discomfort aggravated by prolonged standing are common with uterine prolapse.

Incorrect Choices:

Perineal sensation is not decreased; patients typically experience a sensation of heaviness or pulling in the pelvis. Pain is often relieved by lying down (not aggravated). Constipation and painful bowel movement are common.

Type of Reasoning: Inferential

This question requires one to determine what is most likely to be true based on knowledge of uterine prolapse. Questions of this nature often require inferential reasoning skill. In this case, one should infer that back and perineal pain aggravated by prolonged standing are often associated with uterine prolapse. If answered incorrectly, review signs and symptoms of uterine prolapse.

A3

Integumentary System | Evaluation, Diagnosis

A child experienced a superficial partial-thickness burn from a scalding pot of water affecting 26% of the thorax and neck. On what should the therapist's **INITIAL** plan of care focus?

Choices:

1. Return to preburn function and activities of daily living.
2. Pain management.
3. Infection management.
4. Chest wall mobility and prevention of scar contracture.

Teaching Points

Correct Answer: 4

Prevention of scar contracture and preservation of chest wall mobility and normal neck range of motion (ROM) are the initial major goals to focus on with this patient.

Incorrect Choices:

Return to preburn function and ADLs is an important treatment goal but is not the initial focus. Pain and infection management are important goals of the medical team and are typically managed by the medical team.

Type of Reasoning: Inductive

For this question, the test taker must use clinical judgment to determine a best course of action, which necessitates inductive reasoning skill. Knowledge of effective treatment approaches for burns is paramount to arriving at a correct conclusion. In this case, chest wall mobility and prevention of scar contracture should be the initial focus of the therapist. Review treatment approaches for burns, especially in children, if answered incorrectly.

A4

Cardiovascular/Pulmonary and Lymphatic Systems | Evaluation, Diagnosis

A patient with coronary artery disease has been doing regular aerobic exercise on a treadmill. If the patient fails to comply in taking prescribed beta-blocker medication and continues to exercise, what potential rebound effect could result?

Choices:

1. Increase in blood pressure and decrease in heart rate during exercise.
2. Decrease in blood pressure and heart rate during exercise.
3. Increase in blood pressure and heart rate during exercise.
4. Decrease in blood pressure and increase in heart rate during exercise.

Teaching Points

Correct Answer: 3

Beta-blockers affect the beta-1 adrenergic receptors. Blocking these inhibits the sympathetic response. However, when abruptly terminated, they cause a reflexive opposite response. This patient will demonstrate increased contractility, blood pressure (BP), and heart rate (HR) as a result.

Incorrect Choices:

This patient's BP will increase, but the patient's HR will not decrease with exercise. The HR and BP will increase, not decrease with exercise on a beta-blocker or when it is quickly removed. The BP will increase, not decrease with activity due to the abrupt stopping of the medication.

Type of Reasoning: Inferential

This question requires one to determine the likely effects of exercise and not taking beta-blocker medication. Questions of this nature, where one must infer what is most likely to be true of a situation, require inferential reasoning skill. For this scenario, one should infer that the patient would have an increase in blood pressure and heart rate with exercise. If answered incorrectly, review information on effects of beta-blockers and exercise.

A5

Musculoskeletal | Examination

A patient has persistent midfoot pain with weight bearing. The injury occurred during a soccer match when an opposing player stepped on the patient's right foot when it was planted and cutting to the left. Patient locates the pain where laces are tied. Upon examination there is splaying of the first metatarsal and increased pain when passively stressing the foot with plantarflexion and rotation. What injury should the therapist suspect the patient has sustained?

Choices:

1. Lisfranc injury.
2. Turf toe.
3. Calcaneocuboid joint subluxation.
4. Hallux rigidus.

Teaching Points

Correct Answer: 1

The Lisfranc injury (also known as the Lisfranc fracture, tarsometatarsal injury, or simply midfoot injury) is an injury of the foot in which one or all of the metatarsal bones are displaced from the tarsus. Direct Lisfranc injuries are usually caused by a crush injury, such as when a heavy object falls onto the midfoot, or when landing on the foot after a fall from a significant height. The injury often occurs when an athlete has his or her foot plantar flexed and another player lands on his or her heel.

Incorrect Choices:

Turf toe is a sprain of the MTP joint of the first toe due to hyperextension, such as when pushing off into a sprint and having the toe get stuck flat on the ground. Calcaneocuboid joint subluxation (also known as cuboid syndrome) is defined as a minor disruption or subluxation of the structural congruity of the calcaneocuboid portion of the midtarsal joint. The disruption of the cuboid's position irritates the surrounding joint capsule, ligaments, and fibularis longus tendon. Hallux rigidus (stiff big toe) is a degenerative arthritis and stiffness due to bone spurs that affects the MTP joint at the base of the hallux. Symptoms include pain and stiffness in the joint at the base of the big toe during use (walking, standing, bending, etc.).

Type of Reasoning: Analytical

This question requires one to determine a type of injury sustained based on a description of mechanism of injury and symptoms. Questions that necessitate analyzing information to determine a reasonable conclusion often utilize analytical reasoning skill. For this situation, the symptoms are consistent with Lisfranc injury. Review signs and symptoms of Lisfranc injury if answered incorrectly.

A6

System Interactions | Evaluation, Diagnosis

A patient is referred to physical therapy with a 10-year history of rheumatoid arthritis (RA). What are possible extra-articular complications?

Choices:

1. Disc degeneration.
2. Psoriatic skin and nail changes.
3. Vasculitis.
4. Conjunctivitis and iritis.

Teaching Points

Correct Answer: 3

Rheumatoid arthritis is a progressive autoimmune disease affecting primarily joints and synovial tissue. Extra-articular complications of the disease can include vasculitis.

Incorrect Choices:

The other choices are not expected extra-articular complications in patients with RA. Disc degeneration is seen in degenerative disc disease. Psoriatic skin and nail changes and conjunctivitis and iritis can be seen in psoriatic arthritis.

Type of Reasoning: Inferential

For this question, the test taker must infer or determine what is most likely to be true for a patient with rheumatoid arthritis. This requires inferential reasoning skill. In this case, possible extra-articular complications include vasculitis. Review information on rheumatoid arthritis if answered incorrectly.

A7 

Integumentary System | Evaluation, Diagnosis

A physical therapist is instructing an elderly patient how to perform bed mobility following a total hip replacement. The therapist should carefully consider the effects of aging that relate to skin. What is one such effect?

Choices:

1. Increased perception of pain.
2. Impaired sensory integrity.
3. Increased skin elasticity.
4. Increased inflammatory responsiveness.

Teaching Points

Correct Answer: 2

Changes in skin composition associated with aging include decreased sensitivity to touch, decreased perception of pain and temperature, and increased risk of injury.

Incorrect Choices:

Perception of pain is decreased (not increased). The dermis thins, and elasticity is decreased (not increased). Inflammatory responses are attenuated (not increased).

Type of Reasoning: Inferential

For this question, the test taker must recall the effects of aging and then determine the most likely effect that relates to the skin. This requires inferential reasoning skill. For this situation, the most likely skin effect is impaired sensory integrity. Review effects of the aging process, especially those that affect the skin, if answered incorrectly.

A8 

Cardiovascular/Pulmonary and Lymphatic Systems | Examination

What would a therapist who is examining the breathing pattern of a patient with a complete (ASIA A) C5 spinal cord injury expect to observe?

Choices:

1. Asymmetric lateral costal expansion due to ASIA A injury.
2. An increased subcostal angle due to air trapping from muscle weakness.
3. No diaphragmatic motion since the diaphragm is below the level of the lesion.
4. Rising of the abdomen due to no abdominal muscle tone on the abdominal viscera.

Teaching Points

Correct Answer: 4

The abdominal musculature provides external stability to the abdominal viscera. Without this, the viscera are displaced with respiration.

Incorrect Choices:

With an ASIA A injury, the muscle weakness would be symmetric. The diaphragm is innervated by C3–5 nerve roots, so it will be functioning in this patient. Muscle weakness will cause a restrictive disorder (inability to generate negative pressure), not an obstructive disorder (air trapping).

Type of Reasoning: Inferential

One must determine what is most likely to be true for patients with cervical spinal cord injury in order to arrive at a correct conclusion. Questions that ask one to predict possible outcomes often necessitate inferential reasoning skill. For this case, the therapist should anticipate rising of the abdomen due to no abdominal muscle tone on the abdominal viscera. Review cervical spinal cord injury effects on respiration if answered incorrectly.

Metabolic and Endocrine Systems | Evaluation, Diagnosis

Men are at risk for development of metabolic syndrome if they exhibit which of the following symptoms?

Choices:

1. An HDL level lower than 45 mg/dL.
2. A waist size greater than 40 inches.
3. Triglyceride levels greater than 100 mg/dL.
4. Fasting blood glucose less than 100 mg/dL.

Teaching Points

Correct Answer: 2

Criteria for diagnosis of metabolic syndrome include abdominal obesity (waist circumference > 40 inches in men or > 35 inches in women).

Incorrect Choices:

Other criteria include elevated triglycerides (150 mg/dL or higher); low HDL levels (< 40 mg/dL in men or < 50 mg/dL in women); and a fasting plasma glucose level > 110 mg/dL.

Type of Reasoning: Deductive

This question requires the test taker to recall the guidelines for risk of developing metabolic syndrome. This is factual information, which is a deductive reasoning skill. For this situation, a waist size greater than 40 inches would be a risk factor. Review metabolic syndrome guidelines if answered incorrectly.

A10

Musculoskeletal System | Examination

During an examination, the limitations of ultrasound imaging include which of the following?

Choices:

1. Inability to clearly see cartilage in infants.
2. Disruption of cardiac pacemakers.
3. Difficulty penetrating bone and therefore visualizing internal structure of bones.
4. Inability to give a clear picture of tendons and therefore diagnose tendon tears.

Teaching Points

Correct Answer: 3

Ultrasound has difficulty penetrating bone. Ultrasound images are typically used to help diagnose tendon tears, such as tears of the rotator cuff in the shoulder or Achilles tendon in the ankle; abnormalities of the muscles, such as tears; bleeding or other fluid collections within the muscles, bursae, and joints; benign and malignant soft tissue tumors; early changes of rheumatoid arthritis; fluid in a painful hip joint in children; lumps in the neck muscles of infants; and soft tissue masses (lumps/bumps) in children.

Incorrect Choices:

The other choices are not limitations of diagnostic ultrasound.

Type of Reasoning: Deductive

One must recall the limitations of ultrasound in order to arrive at a correct conclusion. This necessitates factual recall of guidelines, which is a deductive reasoning skill. For this scenario, difficulty penetrating bone and visualizing internal structure of bones is a limitation of ultrasound. Review ultrasound guidelines and limitations if answered incorrectly.

A11 

Metabolic and Endocrine Systems | Evaluation, Diagnosis

A patient with a body mass index (BMI) of 37 is referred to physical therapy for exercise conditioning. What are additional clinical manifestations associated with the BMI that this patient might exhibit?

Choices:

1. Hyperpnea and hyperpituitarism.
2. Hypertension and hyperinsulinism.
3. Hormone-related cancer.
4. Hypolipoproteinemia and hypotension.

Teaching Points

Correct Answer: 2

Obesity is associated with hypertension, dyslipidemia, hyperinsulinemia (type 2 diabetes), and hyperglycemia. The presence of these comorbidities increases risk, resulting in the need for additional medical screening before exercise testing.

Incorrect Choices:

Hyperpituitarism, hormone-related cancer, and hypotension are not associated with obesity.

Type of Reasoning: Deductive

For this question, the test taker must recall the clinical manifestations associated with a high BMI (obesity). This is factual information, which necessitates deductive reasoning skill. In this case, the clinical manifestations include hypertension and hyperinsulinism. Review obesity guidelines if answered incorrectly.

A12 

Musculoskeletal System | Examination

When visually examining active abduction of the arm to 150 degrees, what is the normal composition of the motion a therapist would expect?

Choices:

1. 150 degrees of the glenohumeral motion and 0 degrees of scapulothoracic motion.
2. 110 degrees of the glenohumeral motion and 40 degrees of scapulothoracic motion.
3. 75 degrees of the glenohumeral motion and 75 degrees of scapulothoracic motion.
4. 100 degrees of the glenohumeral motion and 50 degrees of scapulothoracic motion.

Teaching Points

Correct Answer: 4

Elevation of the arm into abduction involves coordinated motions involving the scapulothoracic and glenohumeral joints (along with movements at the sternoclavicular and acromioclavicular joints). While there is some variability in the precise timing and amounts during the early, middle, and late phases, motion at the glenohumeral and scapulothoracic joints generally occurs at an overall 2 to 1 ratio. Given this ratio, 150 degrees of active abduction would be a result of 100 degrees of glenohumeral and 50 degrees of scapulothoracic motion.

Incorrect Choices:

The other ratios presented are not typical during normal active shoulder abduction.

Type of Reasoning: Deductive

One must recall the composition of motion with abduction of the arm in order to arrive at a correct conclusion. This necessitates recall of factual information, which is a deductive reasoning skill. For this case, the therapist should expect 100 degrees of glenohumeral motion and 50 degrees of scapulothoracic motion when abduction is 150 degrees. Review scapulothoracic and glenohumeral motion guidelines if answered incorrectly.

A13 

Neuromuscular and Nervous System | Interventions

To prepare a patient with a cauda equina lesion for ambulation with crutches, what upper-quadrant muscles would be the most important to strengthen?

Choices:

1. Upper trapezius, rhomboids, and levator scapulae.
2. Deltoid, coracobrachialis, and brachialis.
3. Middle trapezius, serratus anterior, and triceps.
4. Lower trapezius, latissimus dorsi, and pectoralis major.

Teaching Points

Correct Answer: 4

The muscles needed for crutch use include the shoulder depressors and extensors along with elbow extensors.

Incorrect Choices:

All other choices include muscles that enhance shoulder elevation or abduction.

Type of Reasoning: Inductive

For this question, one must utilize clinical judgment to determine the most important muscles to strengthen for crutch use. This requires inductive reasoning skill. For this scenario, the therapist should focus on strengthening the lower trapezius, latissimus dorsi, and pectoralis major. Review muscles needed for crutch use if answered incorrectly.

A14

Cardiovascular/Pulmonary and Lymphatic Systems | Examination

What will a patient with a significant right thoracic structural scoliosis demonstrate on examination?

Choices:

1. Decreased breath sounds on the right.
2. Decreased thoracic rib elevation on the right.
3. Increased lateral costal expansion on the right.
4. Shortened internal and external intercostals on the right.

Teaching Points

Correct Answer: 3

With a right thoracic scoliosis, the convex side is on the right. This would allow for increased aeration and mobility on that side.

Incorrect Choices:

The ribs would elevate normally or more on the right side. The remaining choices would be true on the contralateral or shortened side of the scoliosis. The left side would have shortened muscle length and decreased aeration.

Type of Reasoning: Deductive

This question requires the test taker to recall the structural changes that occur with thoracic scoliosis. This necessitates the recall of facts, which is a deductive reasoning skill. For this case, the therapist should anticipate that the patient will demonstrate an increased lateral costal expansion on the right. Review scoliosis information, especially thoracic scoliosis and structural changes, if answered incorrectly.

A15 

Musculoskeletal System | Interventions

A therapist has been treating a patient over a period of 4 months for decreased shoulder elevation and a loss of external rotation. Recovery has been good; however, the patient still complains of being unable to reach the upper shelves of kitchen cabinets and closets. To help the patient achieve this goal, what should be the focus of manual therapy?

Choices:

1. Superior glide.
2. Inferior glide.
3. Anterior glide.
4. Grade II oscillations.

Teaching Points

Correct Answer: 3

Anterior glide would help increase external rotation (ER), which is a component of full elevation. Performing anterior glides to improve ER and late flexion will help increase overhead reach since ER of humerus occurs with flexion.

Incorrect Choices:

Superior glide is not a joint mobilization for any pathology of the shoulder. Inferior glide would help increase shoulder abduction. Grade II mobilization would not improve motion.

Type of Reasoning: Inductive

One must utilize knowledge of joint mobilization techniques and benefits of specific mobilization approaches in order to arrive at a correct conclusion. This necessitates clinical judgment, which is an inductive reasoning skill. For this situation, the therapist should focus on anterior glides to improve ER and late flexion. Review joint mobilization techniques if answered incorrectly.

A16 

Neuromuscular and Nervous System | Interventions

Which activity would help break up obligatory lower extremity synergy patterns in a patient with hemiplegia?

Choices:

1. High kneeling position, ball throwing.
2. Standing, alternate marching in place with hip and knee flexion and hip abduction.
3. Sitting, alternate toe tapping.
4. Sitting, foot slides under the seat.

Teaching Points

Correct Answer: 1

Kneeling positions with the hip in extension and the knee flexed to 90 degrees, is an out-of-synergy position. Balance training activities (e.g., reaching, ball throwing) enhance postural control while engaging cognitive control on the added activity (ball throwing).

Incorrect Choices:

Marching with hip and knee flexion and hip abduction, toe tapping in sitting, and foot slides using knee flexors in sitting all utilize movement in synergy or a synergy-supported position.

Type of Reasoning: Inferential

For this question, the test taker must recall out-of-synergy positions and then use that knowledge to determine which described position would be most beneficial for breaking up lower limb synergy. This requires inferential reasoning skill. In this case, having the patient in a high kneeling position with ball throwing will accomplish this. Review out-of-synergy positions if answered incorrectly.

A17 

Neuromuscular and Nervous System | Examination

A patient recovering from stroke reports lack of feeling in the more-affected hand. Light touch testing reveals lack of ability to tell when the stimulus is being applied (only 1 correct response out of 10 tests). What additional sensory tests should the therapist perform?

Choices:

1. Test for pain and temperature.
2. Test for two-point discrimination.
3. Test for stereognosis.
4. Test for barognosis.

Teaching Points

Correct Answer: 1

Testing for pain and temperature can be performed as these sensations are carried in different pathways (anterolateral spinothalamic pathways); light touch is carried in dorsal column-lemniscal pathways.

Incorrect Choices:

All other choices test for discriminative sensations (two-point discrimination, stereognosis, barognosis) and require intact dorsal column–medial lemniscal pathways projecting to the somatic sensory cortex along with projection to the sensory association areas.

Type of Reasoning: Inductive

For this question, one must utilize knowledge of sensory testing and sensory pathways in order to determine the test that is best to perform next. This reasoning process requires inductive reasoning skill, where clinical judgment is paramount to arriving at a correct conclusion. For this case, the therapist should test for pain and temperature. Review the sensory pathways if answered incorrectly.

A18 

Musculoskeletal System | Evaluation, Diagnosis

In managing the residual limb of an elderly patient with a transfemoral amputation, what is the **MOST IMPORTANT** factor the therapist should consider?

Choices:

1. Contracture of hip musculature.
2. Residual limb shape.
3. Muscle atrophy.
4. Residual limb healing.

Teaching Points

Correct Answer: 4

All are important considerations. However, wound healing is most important to prevent infections and possible revision surgery or further amputation.

Incorrect Choices:

Contracture of hip muscles, especially the hip flexors, will lead to increased lordosis and affect standing posture and gait. Residual limb shape is important for preparing the limb to receive a prosthesis. Muscle atrophy of any of the lower extremity (LE) muscles will result in gait abnormalities. However, none of these are as important as preventing infections and the complications that could ensue.

Type of Reasoning: Inductive

This question requires the test taker to weigh the factors presented and determine which factor is of greatest importance. This requires clinical judgment coupled with knowledge of amputations and the recovery process in order to arrive at a correct conclusion, which is an inductive reasoning skill. In this case, the most important factor is residual limb healing. Review limb amputation information, especially the recovery process, if answered incorrectly.

A19

Musculoskeletal System | Interventions

Three months ago a patient experienced a traumatic injury to the hand that resulted in surgical tendon repair and fracture stabilization. The therapist is planning a treatment program to address tightness of the lumbricals. What exercises would be **BEST** in order to increase range of motion of the hand?

Choices:

1. Both the MCP and IP joints are moved into flexion.
2. Both the MCP and IP joints are moved into extension.
3. The MCP joints are extended and the IP joints are flexed.
4. The MCP joints are flexed and the IP joints are extended.

Teaching Points

Correct Answer: 3

Lumbrical action is extension of the interphalangeal (IP) joint and simultaneous flexion of the metacarpophalangeal (MCP) joint of the second through fifth digits. Therefore, the opposite motion of MCP joint extension and IP joint flexion would stretch the lumbricals.

Incorrect Choices:

None of the other combined motions would stretch the lumbricals.

Type of Reasoning: Inductive

One must determine the best exercise approach to most effectively increase range of motion of the lumbricals. Knowledge of the action of the lumbricals coupled with effective ways to stretch tight muscles is paramount to choosing a correct approach. This requires clinical judgment, which is an inductive reasoning skill. In this scenario, the therapist should extend the MCP joints and flex the IP joints during exercise. Review lumbrical action and exercise for the lumbricals if answered incorrectly.

A20

Cardiovascular/Pulmonary and Lymphatic Systems | Evaluation, Diagnosis

A patient with a long history of cigarette smoking has been admitted to the hospital and presents with tachycardia, signs of lung infection, abnormal breath sounds in both lower lobes, and dullness to percussion. What should the therapist's initial intervention focus on with this patient?

Choices:

1. Getting the patient to quit smoking.
2. Breathing reeducation to increase efficiency of ventilation.
3. Airway clearance and secretion removal.
4. Graded inspiratory muscle training.

Teaching Points

Correct Answer: 3

The patient has signs and symptoms consistent with pneumonia. It is most important to assist with secretions clearance to assist with recovery from the infection and to improve gas exchange.

Incorrect Choices:

Quitting smoking is an appropriate goal for this patient but would be best timed after the acute period has passed. It isn't stated that the patient's breathing pattern is impaired and therefore it is not imperative to address it at this time. If there is an increased work of breathing, it will be rectified by clearing the secretions. Patients with a history of chronic obstructive pulmonary disease (COPD), which is presumed in this case due to the long history of tobacco use, do benefit from inspiratory muscle training (IMT). However, this is best timed after the acute infection has resolved.

Type of Reasoning: Inductive

This question requires one to utilize clinical judgment to consider a best course of action for a patient with pneumonia. Knowledge of effective intervention approaches for pneumonia is paramount to arriving at a correct conclusion and requires inductive reasoning skill. For this case, the therapist should focus on airway clearance and secretion removal initially. Review intervention approaches for pneumonia if answered incorrectly.

A21

Musculoskeletal System I Evaluation, Diagnosis

A patient has adhesive capsulitis of the glenohumeral joint. What is the expected greatest limitation of motion when performing shoulder ROM?

Choices:

1. Flexion.
2. Abduction.
3. Medial rotation.
4. Lateral rotation.

Teaching Points

Correct Answer: 4

Adhesive capsulitis is diagnosed by numerous physical characteristics, including a thickening of the synovial capsule, adhesions within the subacromial or subdeltoid bursa, adhesions to the biceps tendon, and/ or obliteration of the axillary fold secondary to adhesions. Adhesive capsulitis is commonly associated with other systemic and nonsystemic conditions. By far the most common is the comorbid condition of diabetes mellitus. The common capsular pattern of limitation has historically been described as diminishing motions with external (lateral) shoulder rotation being the most limited, followed closely by shoulder flexion and internal rotation.

Incorrect Choices:

Adhesive capsulitis of the shoulder will present with loss of motion in abduction, flexion, internal rotation, and external rotation. The loss of motion is due to capsular restrictions of which there is a classical pattern of loss of motion (capsular pattern). The most severe loss of motion with a capsular pattern of the shoulder will be external (lateral) rotation.

Type of Reasoning: Deductive

For this question, the test taker must recall the limitations associated with adhesive capsulitis in order to arrive at a correct conclusion. This necessitates the recall of factual information, which is a deductive reasoning skill. For this case, the therapist should anticipate that lateral rotation will be most limited in ROM. Review adhesive capsulitis information and symptoms if answered incorrectly.

Nonsystem | Safety, Professional Responsibilities, Research

During a home visit an adult patient asks the physical therapist assistant to see the physical therapy progress notes in the medical record. What should the physical therapist assistant do?

Choices:

1. Refuse to let the patient see the record.
2. Allow the patient to see the notes.
3. Let the patient see the notes only with the permission of the physical therapist.
4. Contact the patient's physician and explain the situation.

Teaching Points

Correct Answer: 2

The law requires a health care provider, except in limited circumstances, to supply a patient, upon request, complete and current information the provider has about the patient's diagnosis, treatment, and prognosis. The provider must also notify a patient of any test results in the provider's possession or requested by the provider for purposes of diagnosis, treatment, or prognosis.

Incorrect Choices:

The law is pretty specific. The adult patient has access to the medical record and the physical therapist assistant (PTA) need not seek permission of the physical therapist (PT) or MD in this case.

Type of Reasoning: Evaluative

This question requires one to determine a best course of action based on knowledge of legal guidelines. Questions of this nature, where one must weigh potential options and determine which option will result in the best outcome often require evaluative reasoning skill. For this situation, the PTA should allow the patient to see the progress notes. Review legal guidelines for access to medical records if answered incorrectly.

Cardiovascular/Pulmonary and Lymphatic Systems | Evaluation, Diagnosis

A chest tube gets dislodged during physical therapy treatment. If the therapist fails to cover the defect, what could the patient develop?

Choices:

1. Pulmonary embolism.
2. Pulmonary edema.
3. Pneumothorax.
4. Aspiration pneumonia.

Teaching Points

Correct Answer: 3

With the removal of the chest tube, there is an increased positive pressure on the lung tissue. The lung is not able to inflate, and it succumbs to the pressure and therefore collapses.

Incorrect Choices:
Chest tube placement or removal has no effect on clotting and circulation. Pulmonary edema is caused by increased hydrostatic pressure within the pulmonary vascular system or by changes in the vascular membrane. A chest tube would have no effect on this. Aspiration pneumonia requires that a person inhales or has something travel into the trachea that was unintended. The removal of a chest tube would have no bearing on this.

Type of Reasoning: Inferential
For this question, one must determine what is likely to be true of a situation, which requires inferential reasoning skill. In order to arrive at a correct conclusion, one must draw from knowledge of chest tubes and risks associated with removal. In this case, if a chest tube becomes dislodged, the likely result is development of a pneumothorax. Review chest tube guidelines if answered incorrectly.

A24 

Cardiovascular/Pulmonary and Lymphatic Systems | Interventions

Following a motor vehicle accident, a patient with chest trauma developed atelectasis. What is the **LEAST** appropriate intervention to help with the immediate management of atelectasis?

Choices:
1. Pain reduction techniques.
2. Segmental breathing.
3. Incentive spirometry.
4. Paced breathing.

Teaching Points

Correct Answer: 4
In order to reverse atelectasis, the patient needs a technique to facilitate deep breathing. Paced breathing controls the rate of breathing, not the depth of breathing, and will therefore be ineffective.

Incorrect Choices:
Reducing the patient's pain associated with the trauma will allow the patient to take deeper breaths, which will decrease atelectasis. Segmental breathing will allow for prolonged inspiration with a breath hold. The long inspiration will facilitate deeper breathing, which can reverse the atelectasis. A breath hold will allow collateral ventilation via the pores of Kohn, which will result in increased pressures to inflate alveoli and therefore reverse atelectasis. Incentive spirometry will cause increased deep breathing with visual feedback, which can reverse atelectasis.

Type of Reasoning: Inductive
This question requires clinical judgment and knowledge of atelectasis in order to determine a best course of action. This necessitates inductive reasoning skill where clinical judgment is used to reach a sound conclusion. In this case, the least effective treatment would be paced breathing. Review atelectasis and treatment approaches if answered incorrectly.

Musculoskeletal System | Evaluation, Diagnosis

Following a reattachment of the flexor tendons of the fingers, the patient is in a splint. One physical therapy goal is to minimize adhesion formation. What should the physical therapist teach the patient to perform after 72 hours post-surgery?

Choices:

1. Passive extension and active flexion of the interphalangeal joints.
2. Active extension and flexion of the interphalangeal joints.
3. Active extension and passive flexion of the interphalangeal joints.
4. Gentle passive extension and flexion of the interphalangeal joints.

Teaching Points

Correct Answer: 3

Severe edema increases tendon drag and likelihood of rupture. Therefore, wait until 48 to 72 hours postop prior to initiating range of motion (ROM) therapy. This patient is a few days postop and can begin passive finger flexion with caution so as not to disrupt the repair. Begin by blocking the metacarpophalangeal (MCP) in full flexion and actively extend interphalangeal (IP) joints, followed by passive proximal interphalangeal (PIP) flexion and active extension.

Incorrect Choices:

Generally for weeks 1 through 3 there should be no active flexion of the involved digits, as this could damage and/or tear the repair. Passive extension of the fingers should not be done until there is adequate strength of the repair.

Type of Reasoning: Inductive

One must utilize clinical judgment coupled with knowledge of flexor tendon repairs in order to arrive at a correct conclusion. This requires inductive reasoning skill. For this scenario, the therapist should teach the patient to perform active extension and passive flexion of the interphalangeal joints. If answered incorrectly, review treatment approaches for flexor tendon repairs.

Musculoskeletal System | Evaluation, Diagnosis

A patient with a transtibial amputation of 2 months' duration complains of an intense burning pain that seems to emanate from the heel. This phantom pain mirrors the patient's preoperative pain. What is the most likely previous source of this pain?

Choices:

1. Dorsalis pedis artery obstruction.
2. Popliteal artery obstruction.
3. Damage to the superficial peroneal (fibular) nerve.
4. Damage to the tibial nerve.

Teaching Points

Correct Answer: 4

Although the limb is no longer there, the nerve endings at the site of the amputation continue to send pain signals to the brain that make the brain think the limb is still there. Sometimes, the brain memory of pain is retained and is interpreted as pain regardless of signals from injured nerves. In addition to pain in the phantom limb, some people experience other sensations such as tingling, cramping, heat, and cold in the portion of the limb that was removed. The question describes pain in the heel. Nerve supply to the heel is by the calcaneal branch of the tibial nerve.

Incorrect Choices:

Dorsalis pedis artery and popliteal artery are incorrect because phantom limb pain is the result of nerves being cut. The superficial peroneal (fibular) nerve ends above the ankle by dividing into the medial and lateral cutaneous branches. These nerves provide sensory innervations to the lateral and anterolateral skin of the distal leg and to the dorsum of the foot.

Type of Reasoning: Inferential

For this question, one must make a determination what is most likely to be true of a situation, while using knowledge of phantom limb pain. This requires inferential reasoning skill. For this case, because of the description of pain experienced, the source is most likely damage to the tibial nerve. Review phantom limb pain and tibial nerve innervation if answered incorrectly.

Nonsystem | Equipment, Devices, Biophysical Agents

A patient's plan of care includes use of iontophoresis for the management of calcific bursitis of the shoulder. To administer this treatment using the acetate ion, what current characteristics and polarity should be used?

Choices:

1. Monophasic twin-peaked pulses using the positive pole.
2. Monophasic twin-peaked pulses using the negative pole.
3. Direct current using the positive pole.
4. Direct current using the negative pole.

Teaching Points

Correct Answer: 4

The acetate ion has a negative charge, and thus a negative pole will be needed to repel the drug into the tissue. Direct current will continuously drive the acetate into the tissue during the treatment time.

Incorrect Choices:

While monophasic, twin-peaked current has polarity, it is a pulsed current and will not be able to continuously drive the acetate into the tissue resulting in less medication being delivered to the site. The positive pole will not repel the acetate ion.

Type of Reasoning: Deductive

For this question, one must recall the guidelines for application of iontophoresis and treatment using the acetate ion. This necessitates factual recall of information, which is a deductive reasoning skill. In this case, the therapist should use direct current using the negative pole. Review iontophoresis guidelines if answered incorrectly.

Musculoskeletal System | Evaluation, Diagnosis

A snowmobile left the trail and struck a tree. The driver's left knee was flexed approximately 90 degrees and the tibia impacted with the inside front of the snowmobile. What would this mechanism of injury **MOST LIKELY** result in?

Choices:

1. Dislocated patella.
2. Sprained or ruptured posterior cruciate ligament (PCL).
3. Sprained or ruptured anterior cruciate ligament (ACL).
4. Rupture of the popliteal artery.

Teaching Points

Correct Answer: 2

The above scenario describes one of the most common mechanisms of injury of the PCL, the "dashboard injury." This occurs when the knee is flexed, and an object forcefully strikes the proximal anterior tibia and displaces it posteriorly. It is called a "dashboard injury" because it can occur in automobile collisions when the tibia forcefully hits the dashboard. The PCL attaches from the lateral aspect of the medial femoral condyle to just posterior to the posterior horn of the medial meniscus. It is the primary restraint to posterior displacement of the tibia on the femur.

Incorrect Choices:

The usual mechanism of the ACL injury is in a noncontact deceleration that produces a valgus twisting injury (e.g., athlete quickly pivoting in the opposite direction). Other mechanisms of injury of the ACL can occur with hyperextension of the knee and severe medial tibial rotation.

The most common mechanism for patella dislocation is a powerful contraction of the quadriceps in combination with sudden flexion and external rotation of the tibia on the femur. This question describes trauma to the tibia, not the patella.

Rupture of the popliteal artery can occur from severe trauma resulting in a dislocation of the tibia on the femur. The most common mechanism of injury for a posterior knee dislocation is a direct force on the tibia while the knee is flexed, forcing the tibia posteriorly on the femur (e.g., dashboard injury). A tibial dislocation certainly could have occurred with the snowmobile injury, but it would not be the most likely.

Type of Reasoning: Inferential

For this question, the test taker must determine what is most likely to be true, based on a description of an injury. Questions of this nature, where one determines what is most likely to be true, require inferential reasoning skill. In this scenario, the mechanism of injury would most likely result in a sprained or ruptured posterior cruciate ligament (PCL). Review PCL injuries and dashboard injuries if answered incorrectly.

Musculoskeletal System | Evaluation, Diagnosis

The interview with an 18-year-old female cross-country runner elicits a history of stiffness and diffuse ache in her right knee that is aggravated by prolonged sitting. Going down stairs is also painful. Based on this information, what is the **LIKELY** diagnosis that should serve as a focus for the physical examination?

Choices:

1. Iliotibial band friction syndrome.
2. Osgood-Schlatter disease.
3. Meniscal tear.
4. Patellofemoral syndrome.

Exam A

Teaching Points

Correct Answer: 4

Patellofemoral syndrome ("runner's knee") is the most common overuse injury among runners. It occurs due to mistracking of the patella within the intercondylar groove. It generally occurs in younger, recreational runners and is more common in women. The main symptom of patellofemoral pain syndrome is knee pain, especially when sitting with knee flexion. This is known as the theater sign or movie-goer's knee. Squatting, jumping, or using the stairs (especially going down stairs) will also be painful. There may also be occasional buckling of the knee.

Incorrect Choices:

Iliotibial (IT) band friction syndrome also occurs in runners, but pain will be located over the lateral knee. It is the result of irritation of the distal portion of the IT band as it rubs against the lateral femoral condyle. This overuse injury occurs with repetitive flexion and extension of the knee. It is most common in athletes who participate in long-distance running.

Osgood-Schlatter disease occurs most often in children who participate in sports that involve running, jumping, and swift changes of direction such as soccer and basketball. The main symptom is painful swelling over the tibial tubercle. They may have leg or knee pain, which gets worse with running, jumping, and climbing stairs. The tibial tubercle is tender to palpation.

Pain from meniscal tears is usually deep within the knee, accompanied by swelling and symptoms of popping, catching, or locking.

Type of Reasoning: Analytical

This question provides a group of symptoms, and the test taker must determine the most likely diagnosis. This requires analytical reasoning skill, where pieces of information are analyzed in order to draw conclusions. For this case, the most likely diagnosis is patellofemoral syndrome. Review signs and symptoms of patellofemoral syndrome if answered incorrectly.

Cardiovascular/Pulmonary and Lymphatic Systems | Interventions

Following mastectomy with axillary lymph node dissection, a patient developed 4+ edema in the ipsilateral arm. A compression garment was ordered. What is the primary reason this garment decreases edema?

Choices:

1. It decreases the osmotic pressure of the capillaries.
2. It increases the capillary permeability.
3. It exceeds the internal tissue hydrostatic pressure.
4. It equals the fluid outflow from the capillaries.

Teaching Points

Correct Answer: 3

The external pressure caused by the compression garment essentially increases the amount of pressure on the tissue. This causes a relative increase in the hydrostatic pressure in the extravascular space compared with the intravascular space.

Incorrect Choices:

Osmotic pressure is most directly related to the protein content. Increases in external pressure will not modify this pressure gradient. An external pressure will have no effect on the vascular permeability. If the fluid outflow is equaled from the capillaries, then there is not a pressure gradient between two areas. Therefore, there will be no transfer of fluid from one area to the other.

Type of Reasoning: Deductive

This question requires the test taker to recall the therapeutic properties of pressure garments in order to arrive at a correct conclusion. This necessitates recall of factual guidelines, which is a deductive reasoning skill. For this situation, the garment decreases edema because it exceeds the internal tissue hydrostatic pressure. Review properties of pressure garments for edema if answered incorrectly.

A31 

Musculoskeletal System | Interventions

A patient presents with a chronic restriction of the temporomandibular joint (TMJ). The physical therapist observes the situation seen in the picture during mouth-opening range of motion (ROM) assessment. What is the **BEST** intervention if the patient has a classic TMJ unilateral capsular restriction?

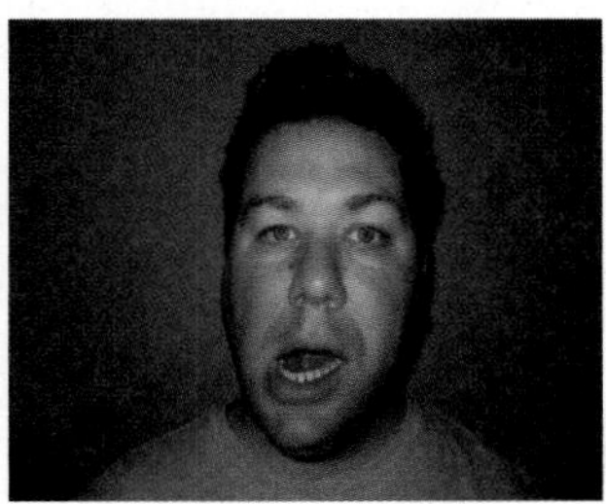

Choices:

1. Left TMJ, superior glide manipulation.
2. Left TMJ, inferior glide manipulation.
3. Right TMJ, superior glide manipulation.
4. Right TMJ, inferior glide manipulation.

Teaching Points

Correct Answer: 4

Right TMJ, inferior glide. In the photo, the chin has deviated to the right at terminal opening. The active range of motion (AROM) will be limited with ipsilateral opening and a lateral deviation to the side of restriction for patients with a TMJ capsular pattern of restriction.

Incorrect Choices:

The left TMJ incorrectly states the capsular pattern. Additionally, superior glide manipulation on the right would compress the joint, not affording a stretch to the capsule tightness.

Type of Reasoning: Inductive

This question requires clinical judgment in order to determine a best intervention approach for a patient with TMJ dysfunction. Knowledge of effective intervention approaches for the TMJ is paramount to arriving at a correct conclusion, necessitating inductive reasoning skill. For this case, the **BEST** intervention approach is right TMJ, inferior glide manipulation. Review intervention approaches for the TMJ if answered incorrectly.

A32 

Neuromuscular and Nervous System | Examination

A patient in the late stages of Parkinson's disease exhibits episodes of akinesia while walking. What should the therapist examine?

Choices:

1. Primary involvement of the head and trunk.
2. Associated dyskinesias.
3. Primary involvement of the hips and knees.
4. Triggers that precipitate the freezing episodes.

Teaching Points

Correct Answer: 4

Freezing of gait (episodes of akinesia) is typically associated with a trigger (e.g., turning, changing direction or speed, doorways). Identification of triggers is helpful in developing the plan of care.

Incorrect Choices:

Freezing is most often evident during gait and typically involves the entire body, not individual segments of the body. Associated dyskinesias may be present but do not typically influence freezing episodes.

Type of Reasoning: Inductive

For this question, one must utilize clinical judgment and knowledge of Parkinson's disease in order to arrive at a correct conclusion. This requires inductive reasoning skill. For this situation, the therapist should examine triggers that precipitate the freezing episodes. Review Parkinson's disease, especially examination of akinesia, if answered incorrectly.

 A33 

Metabolic and Endocrine Systems | Evaluation, Diagnosis

A patient is referred to physical therapy for balance and gait training following two falls in the home in the past month. The therapist notes in the medical record that the patient has adrenal insufficiency. What are the metabolic abnormalities associated with adrenal insufficiency?

Choices:

1. Hypokalemia.
2. Hyponatremia.
3. Hyperglycemia.
4. Alkalosis.

Teaching Points

Correct Answer: 2

Metabolic abnormalities seen in adrenal insufficiency include hyponatremia (decreased sodium concentration in the blood) secondary to renal loss of sodium ions. A decrease in cortisol results in an inability to regulate potassium and sodium.

Incorrect Choices:

Patients with adrenal insufficiency will be hyperkalemic, hypoglycemic, and may have acidosis.

Type of Reasoning: Deductive

For this question, the test taker must recall the metabolic abnormalities that are often associated with adrenal insufficiency in order to arrive at a correct conclusion. This necessitates the recall of factual information, which is a deductive reasoning skill. For this case, hyponatremia is often associated with adrenal insufficiency. Review signs and symptoms of adrenal insufficiency if answered incorrectly.

A34

Nonsystem | Safety, Professional Responsibilities, Research

A physical therapist is treating a patient with active infectious hepatitis B. In addition to wearing a protective gown when in the patient's room, what precautions should be taken to avoid transmission of the disease?

Choices:

1. Avoid direct contact with the patient's blood or blood-contaminated equipment by wearing gloves.
2. Avoid direct contact with any part of the patient.
3. Have the patient wear a mask to minimize droplet spread of the organisms from coughing.
4. Provide tissues and no-touch receptacles for disposal of tissues.

Teaching Points

Correct Answer: 1
Hepatitis B is transmitted in blood, body fluids, or body tissues. Precautions should include avoiding direct contact with blood or blood-contaminated equipment.

Incorrect Choices:
This is not an airborne infectious disease. The patient does not need to wear a mask or have specific no-touch tissue receptacles. Contact with body surfaces with no blood droplets or open wounds should also not be an issue.

Type of Reasoning: Deductive
For this question, one must recall the guidelines for standard precautions. This is factual information, which is a deductive reasoning skill. For this case, in addition to wearing a protective gown, the therapist should avoid direct contact with the patient's blood or blood-contaminated equipment by wearing gloves. Review standard precautions, especially for hepatitis B, if answered incorrectly.

A35

Musculoskeletal System | Examination

Idiopathic scoliosis is suspected in a 12-year-old girl. During the physical examination, what is the standard screening test for this condition?

Choices:

1. Longsitting, forward bend test.
2. Standing, Adam's forward bend test.
3. Sitting, rotation test to the right and left.
4. Standing, backward extension test.

Teaching Points

Correct Answer: 2
Screening is most commonly done on adolescents. Females achieve adolescence about two years before males and are afflicted with scoliosis requiring treatment three to four times more frequently than males. The Adam's forward bend test is the standard screening test for scoliosis. During the test, the child will bend forward with feet together, knees straight, and arms hanging free. The therapist observes child from the back, looking for a difference in the shape of the ribs on each side. A spinal deformity is most noticeable in this position.

Incorrect Choices:

All other choices are not appropriate for examining for scoliosis (e.g., backward extension, trunk rotation, forward bending in longsitting).

Type of Reasoning: Deductive

For this question, the test taker must recall the guidelines for conducting a scoliosis screening test in order to arrive at a correct conclusion. This necessitates factual recall of testing guidelines, which is a deductive reasoning skill. For this situation, the standard screening test is standing, Adam's forward bend test. Review scoliosis screening guidelines if answered incorrectly.

A36 

Musculoskeletal System | Interventions

A patient had anterior cruciate ligament (ACL) reconstructive surgery 2 weeks ago. During the initial examination, the physical therapist noticed marked edema around the knee and calf. Knee passive range of motion (PROM) was limited from –5 degrees extension to 90 degrees of flexion. Hip PROM was within normal limits. Ankle dorsiflexion was limited to 0 degrees because of pulling pain in the calf. Marked tenderness to superficial palpation to anterior knee and posterior calf and increased temperature were also noted. The patient is experiencing calf pain and discomfort when standing during partial weight-bearing ambulation. Upon completion of the examination, what is the **BEST** intervention at this time?

Choices:

1. Isometrics and PROM for the knee.
2. Massage to knee and calf to help alleviate the expected postsurgical edema.
3. Ice and interferential current to alleviate edema and facilitate movement.
4. Immediate referral to the surgeon.

Teaching Points

Correct Answer: 4

The patient may have a deep vein thrombosis (DVT) based on increased swelling, temperature, tenderness, and pain in the calf with weight bearing 2 weeks after surgery, so referral to the surgeon is the best intervention at this time.

Incorrect Choices:

All other answer choices are appropriate once DVT is ruled out.

Type of Reasoning: Inductive

This question requires one to determine a best course of action based on analysis of symptoms after an ACL reconstruction. Questions of this nature often require clinical judgment, which is an inductive reasoning skill. Based on the symptoms, the therapist should make an immediate referral to the surgeon, as the symptoms are indicative of a DVT. Review signs and symptoms of DVT if answered incorrectly.

Nonsystem I Equipment, Devices, Biophysical Agents

Use of continuous ultrasound at 1.5 watts/cm^2 can increase which of the following?

Choices:

1. Local metabolic rate.
2. Rate of muscle hypertrophy.
3. Stiffness of collagen tissue.
4. The resolution of acute inflammation.

Teaching Points

Correct Answer: 1

Continuous ultrasound (US) is used for its thermal effects, and the higher the intensity, the greater the probability of causing a tissue temperature rise that would result in an increased metabolic rate in the area applied.

Incorrect Choices:

US has no effect on muscle hypertrophy. Thermal US would decrease, not increase the stiffness of collagen tissue. Heat is contraindicated for acute inflammation. Thermal US would exacerbate the symptoms associated with acute inflammation.

Type of Reasoning: Deductive

For this question, the test taker must recall the effects of continuous ultrasound. This is factual information, which is a deductive reasoning skill. For this scenario, the effects of continuous ultrasound would include an increase in local metabolic rate. Review ultrasound guidelines, especially the use of continuous ultrasound, if answered incorrectly.

Musculoskeletal System I Examination

During observation of bilateral active straight leg raising in a supine position, the patient demonstrates progressively increasing lumbar lordosis during lowering of the limbs with each successive lift. What is the **MOST LIKELY** cause of the observed excessive lordosis during the bilateral straight leg activity?

Choices:

1. Muscle imbalance between the rectus femoris and the sartorius muscles.
2. Weakness of both quadratus lumborum muscles.
3. Fatigue weakness of the rectus abdominis and oblique muscle groups.
4. Excessive elastic shortening of the ipsilateral hamstring muscle group.

Teaching Points

Correct Answer: 3

During a dynamic activity such as the performance of a bilateral active straight leg raise, the weight of the limbs lifted produces an anterior torque on the pelvis. During this dynamic activity, excessive lordosis typically is associated with excessive anterior pelvic rotation. Normally muscles that control anterior pelvic rotation (posterior pelvic rotators) act to counter the anterior torques produced by the mass of the lower limbs lifted off the table, helping to prevent unwanted sagittal plane movements of the lumbar spine. Contractile activities of the anterior trunk muscles (rectus and obliques) provide a posterior rotation moment on the pelvis, helping to stabilize the pelvis. Fatigue weakness of the anterior trunk muscles in this patient could result in poor control of sagittal plane rotation of the pelvis, leading to the observed increasing lumbar lordosis.

Incorrect Choices:
The quadratus lumborum acts as a stabilizer and an extensor of the lumbar spine in the sagittal plane, and one would not suspect weakness as the cause of the observed excessive lordosis. Lack of hamstring lengthening could not directly produce the observed increasing lordosis. While the rectus femoris and sartorius are capable of anterior pelvic rotation when the lower limbs are fixed, they offer no direct force to produce unwanted anterior pelvic rotation and subsequent lordosis in this case in which the limbs have been lifted off the table.

Type of Reasoning: Inferential
For this question, one must infer, or draw a reasonable conclusion, for an increasing lumbar lordosis during bilateral straight leg raising. Questions that require one to determine what is most likely to be true often necessitate inferential reasoning skill. For this case, the cause is most likely fatigue weakness of the rectus abdominis and oblique muscle groups. Review causes of lumbar lordosis if answered incorrectly.

A39

System Interactions | Evaluation, Diagnosis

The therapist is treating a patient with chronic Lyme disease of more than 1 year's duration. What joints are likely to demonstrate more arthritic changes and therefore should be the focus of physical therapy interventions?

Choices:
1. Small joints of the hands and feet.
2. Large joints of the body, especially the knee.
3. Axial joints, especially the lumbrosacral spine.
4. Axial joints, especially the cervical and thoracic spine.

Teaching Points

Correct Answer: 2
Stage 3 Lyme disease (late or chronic Lyme disease) is characterized by intermittent arthritis with marked pain and swelling, especially in the large joints. Permanent joint damage can occur.

Incorrect Choices:
Other joints may be affected, though not with the same frequency as the large joints.

Type of Reasoning: Deductive
This question requires the test taker to recall the stages of Lyme disease and presenting symptoms in order to arrive at a correct conclusion. This necessitates the recall of facts and guidelines, which is a deductive reasoning skill. For this situation, the patient is likely to show arthritic changes of the large joints of the body, especially the knee. Review Lyme disease stages and symptoms if answered incorrectly.

A40

Cardiovascular/Pulmonary and Lymphatic Systems | Examination

During auscultation of the heart, the therapist hears S_1 and S_2 heart sounds. During early diastole the therapist also hears a low frequency sound of turbulence. What suspected abnormal sound should the therapist record this as?

Choices:

1. S_4 sound.
2. S_3 sound.
3. Heart murmur.
4. Pericardial friction rub.

Teaching Points

Correct Answer: 2

S_3 is an abnormal third heart sound due to poor ventricular compliance and turbulence. It is heard as a low-frequency sound during early diastole.

Incorrect Choices:

S_4 is an abnormal fourth heart sound due to exaggerated atrial contraction and subsequent turbulence. It is heard as a low-frequency sound in late diastole. Heart murmurs are heard as a swishing sound in systole, diastole, or both systole and diastole. Pericardial rub is heard as a leathery sound during systole.

Type of Reasoning: Analytical

This question provides a description of symptoms and the test taker must determine the most likely diagnosis. This requires analysis of symptoms to draw a conclusion, which is an analytical reasoning skill. For this case, the therapist should record the abnormal sound as an S_3 sound. Review heart auscultation information if answered incorrectly.

A41

Neuromuscular and Nervous System | Examination

A physical therapist observes a full-term infant in the neonatal intensive care unit (NICU) just after birth. In the supine position, the shoulders are abducted and externally rotated, elbows and fingers are flexed, hips are abducted and externally rotated, and knees are flexed. What would this posturing be an indication of?

Choices:

1. Upper extremity tone is abnormal.
2. Lower extremity tone is abnormal.
3. Tone is abnormal in both upper and lower extremities.
4. Tone is normal in both upper and lower extremities.

Teaching Points

Correct Answer: 4

A full-term infant in the NICU can have low Apgar scores, respiratory distress, or any one of a number of specific diagnoses (none listed in this case). Initial tone and posturing involve some flexion of the limbs. At 1 month, decreased flexion can be expected.

Incorrect Choices:

All other choices indicate that the flexor tone and posturing noted in a newborn's upper and lower limbs are abnormal.

Type of Reasoning: Analytical

For this question, one must analyze the description of posture in an infant and make a determination of what the posturing indicates. This requires analytical reasoning skill. For this case, the posturing indicates that tone is normal in both upper and lower extremities. Review posturing in infants if answered incorrectly.

A42 

Metabolic and Endocrine Systems | Interventions

A patient with type 1 diabetes mellitus has generalized osteoporosis. What is the **BEST** exercise to include in this patient's plan of care?

Choices:

1. Bilateral quadriceps presses against resistance in sitting.
2. Aquatic exercises.
3. Running on a treadmill.
4. Partial squats in standing.

Teaching Points

Correct Answer: 4

Extensor stabilization exercises in weight-bearing postures provide the best stimulus to bone (e.g., standing, holding against resistance, standing partial squats).

Incorrect Choices:

High-load, short-duration activities (jumping, running, weights) provide less stimulus to bone while posing increased risk of muscle strain and injury. The buoyancy of water limits the load on bone during aquatic exercises.

Type of Reasoning: Inductive

This question requires the test taker to utilize clinical judgment in order to determine a best course of action. Questions of this nature often require inductive reasoning skill. For this case, the best exercise to include for osteoporosis is partial squats in standing. Review exercise guidelines for osteoporosis if answered incorrectly.

A43 

Cardiovascular/Pulmonary and Lymphatic Systems | Interventions

A patient suddenly falls and lands on a piece of equipment left on the floor. A severe laceration with spurting blood is noted in the area of the lateral distal right thigh. To help control bleeding, where should the physical therapist apply pressure in addition to directly over the wound?

Choices:

1. Behind the knee at the popliteal fossa.
2. At the femoral triangle.
3. At the antecubital fossa.
4. At mid-thigh, directly over the profunda femoris artery.

Teaching Points

Correct Answer: 2

This patient is experiencing an arterial bleed most likely affecting the descending branch of the lateral circumflex femoral artery. Pressure should be applied over the wound and more proximally over the femoral artery, which is palpable in the femoral triangle just inferior to the inguinal ligament.

Incorrect Choices:

Applying pressure at the other sites would not reduce the bleeding. (The antecubital fossa is at the elbow!)

Type of Reasoning: Inductive

For this question, one must utilize knowledge of anatomy coupled with clinical decision making in order to arrive at a correct conclusion. This necessitates clinical judgment, which is an inductive reasoning skill. For this situation, the therapist should apply pressure at the femoral triangle to control bleeding. Review anatomy, especially arterial anatomy, if answered incorrectly.

A44 

Neuromuscular and Nervous System | Evaluation, Diagnosis

While gait training a patient following a stroke, the therapist observes the knee on the hemiparetic side going into recurvatum during stance phase. What is the **MOST LIKELY** cause of this deviation?

Choices:

1. Severe spasticity of the hamstrings or weakness of the gastrocnemius-soleus.
2. Weakness or severe spasticity of the quadriceps.
3. Weakness of the gastrocnemius-soleus or spasticity of the pretibial muscles.
4. Weakness of both the gastrocnemius-soleus and pretibial muscles.

Teaching Points

Correct Answer: 2

Weakness or severe spasticity of the quadriceps is the most likely cause of genu recurvatum.

Incorrect Choices:

Spasticity of the hamstrings or pretibial muscles is unlikely and would cause the knee to buckle. Weakness of the gastrocnemius-soleus would cause lack of push-off, while weakness of the pretibial muscles would cause a drop foot.

Type of Reasoning: Inferential

For this question, one must determine the most likely cause of genu recurvatum and use this knowledge to arrive at a correct conclusion. Questions of this nature often require inferential reasoning skill. For this case, the cause is most likely due to weakness or severe spasticity of the quadriceps. Review gait patterns, especially genu recurvatum, if answered incorrectly.

A45

Cardiovascular/Pulmonary and Lymphatic Systems | Examination

This picture depicts a clinician assessing for Stemmer's sign. The clinician is examining for what condition?

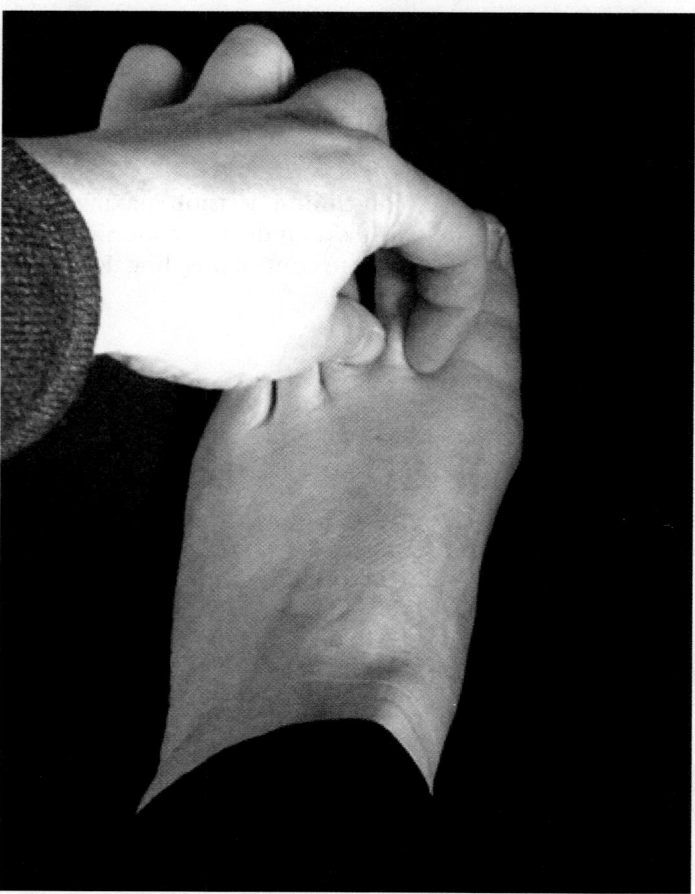

Choices:

1. Bunion.
2. Hammer toe.
3. Lymphedema.
4. Fracture of the second toe.

Teaching Points

Correct Answer: 3

Stemmer's sign is assessed by pulling up on the skin at the base of the second toe or finger, which the clinician is doing in this picture. If the skin is unable to be pulled up, then it is a sign of lymphedema, usually primary but also advanced secondary.

Incorrect Choices:

A bunion is diagnosed by the metacarpophalangeal (MCP) joint angle. A fracture is diagnosed by radiology. A hammer toe is usually diagnosed by visual inspection of the foot.

Type of Reasoning: Analytical

For this question, one must utilize knowledge of Stemmer's sign and analyze the information present in the picture in order to arrive at a correct conclusion. Questions that accompany pictures often necessitate analytical reasoning skill. For this situation, the picture depicts an examination for the presence of lymphedema. Review Stemmer's sign if answered incorrectly.

A46

Neuromuscular and Nervous System | Evaluation, Diagnosis

A child with spastic diplegia is becoming independent in using a walker. Additional goals desired by the physical therapist include improving posture and increasing the child's energy efficiency and velocity while ambulating. In this case, which walker is most likely to help improve these goals?

Choices:

1. A standard anterior walker with no wheels.
2. An anterior rollator walker with two wheels.
3. A posterior rollator walker with two wheels.
4. A posterior rollator walker with four wheels.

Teaching Points

Correct Answer: 4

A posterior rollator walker with four wheels is the best choice to improve upright posture, energy efficiency, and velocity.

Incorrect Choices:

An anterior walker enhances a forward lean posture (not upright). A two-wheeled device is not as energy efficient as a four-wheeled device. A walker with no wheels will be the most energy costly.

Type of Reasoning: Inferential

This question requires one to infer or determine what is most likely to be true of a situation, which requires inferential reasoning skill. In particular, one must utilize knowledge of walkers and benefits of the devices to arrive at a correct conclusion. For this scenario, a posterior rollator walker with four wheels is the best choice. Review benefits of walkers, especially for children, if answered incorrectly.

A47

Gastrointestinal System | Evaluation, Diagnosis

What is pain and tenderness with palpation over McBurney's point associated with?

Choices:

1. Acute appendicitis.
2. Hiatal hernia.
3. Acute cholecystitis.
4. GERD.

Teaching Points

Correct Answer: 1

Pain and tenderness with palpation over McBurney's point are associated with acute appendicitis. McBurney's point is located half the distance between the anterior superior iliac spine (ASIS) and the umbilicus in the right lower abdominal quadrant.

Incorrect Choices:

A positive Murphy's sign (pain and tenderness over the costovertebral angle) is associated with acute cholecystitis or acute pyelonephritis. Hiatal hernia pain is usually sharp and localizes to the lower esophagus/upper stomach area. Gastroesophageal reflux disease (GERD) produces persistent burning pain in the esophagus, throat, or chest.

Type of Reasoning: Deductive

This question requires factual recall of information in order to arrive at a correct conclusion. This is a deductive reasoning skill. One must recall what pain and tenderness of McBurney's point indicates. In this case, it is indicative of acute appendicitis. Review testing guidelines for acute appendicitis if answered incorrectly.

A48 

Cardiovascular/Pulmonary and Lymphatic Systems | Examination

What is the expected hemodynamic response for a patient on a beta-adrenergic blocking agent during exercise?

Choices:

1. Heart rate to be low at rest and rise minimally with exercise.
2. Heart rate to be low at rest and rise continuously to expected levels as exercise intensity increases.
3. Systolic blood pressure to be low at rest and not rise with exercise.
4. Systolic blood pressure to be within normal limits at rest and progressively fall as exercise intensity increases.

Teaching Points

Correct Answer: 1

A beta-blocker will decrease the sympathetic response to activity. This will decrease the heart rate at rest and will blunt the heart rate response to activity.

Incorrect Choices:

The heart rate response to exercise will be blunted. The blood pressure will rise with exercise, just not to the expected levels. The systolic blood pressure will be lowered at rest and will increase with activity, but not to normal levels.

Type of Reasoning: Inferential

For this question, one must determine what is most likely to be true of a situation, which is an inferential reasoning skill. One must utilize knowledge of beta-blockers and exercise with beta-blocker use in order to arrive at a correct conclusion. For this situation, one would expect heart rate to be low at rest and rise minimally with exercise. If answered incorrectly, review beta-blocker effects during exercise.

A49 

Neuromuscular and Nervous System | Examination

A neonate's Apgar score at 1 minute after birth is 8; at 5 minutes it is 9. Based on this score and expected heart rate, what can the therapist conclude about this infant?

Choices:

1. The infant would have a heart rate of less than 100 beats per minute with slow and irregular respirations and not require resuscitation.
2. The infant would require extensive resuscitation efforts including intubation.
3. The infant would require some resuscitation and administration of supplemental oxygen.
4. The infant would have a heart rate of greater than 100 beats per minute with good respiration and not require resuscitation.

Teaching Points

Correct Answer: 4

Early signs receiving the top Apgar score of 2 each include heart rate over 100 bpm, good respiration and crying, active movements, cough or sneeze, and pink color (total of 10). Apgar scores of 8 to 10 at 1 minute are considered normal.

Incorrect Choices:

All other choices indicate abnormal Apgar scores or extensive interventions, which are not needed in this case.

Type of Reasoning: Inferential

For this question, the test taker must determine what is likely to be true for an infant with an Apgar score of 8 one minute after birth and 9 five minutes after birth. Questions of this nature often require inferential reasoning skill, as one must infer likely conclusions based on information provided. For this case, one should conclude that the infant would have a heart rate of greater than 100 beats per minute with good respiration and not require resuscitation. Review Apgar guidelines if answered incorrectly.

A50

Neuromuscular and Nervous System | Evaluation, Diagnosis

With the patient supine, the vertebral artery test is performed by passively moving the head and neck into extension and side flexion, then rotation to the same side and holding for 30 seconds. Which of the following indicates a positive test?

Choices:

1. Sensory changes occur in the face along with visual changes.
2. Dizziness or nystagmus occurs, indicating that the opposite side artery is being compressed.
3. Hearing difficulties and facial paralysis occur.
4. Dizziness or nystagmus occurs, indicating that the same side artery is being compressed.

Teaching Points

Correct Answer: 2

The test is positive if dizziness or nystagmus occurs, indicating that the opposite side artery is affected. Current evidence demonstrates some limitations in use of this test; however, not performing it prior to cervical manual therapy could be considered a breach of the standard of care.

Incorrect Choices:

All other choices may indicate possible vertebral-basilar artery problems but are not indicative of a positive vertebral artery test.

Type of Reasoning: Deductive

One must recall the guidelines of the vertebral artery test in order to arrive at a correct conclusion. This necessitates the recall of factual guidelines, which is a deductive reasoning skill. Performing this test, one should see dizziness or nystagmus occur, indicating that the opposite side artery is being compressed in a positive test. Review the vertebral artery test if answered incorrectly.

A51

Neuromuscular and Nervous System | Evaluation, Diagnosis

A young adult who is comatose (Glasgow Coma Scale score of 3) is transferred to a long-term care facility for custodial care. On initial examination, the therapist determines the patient is demonstrating decerebrate posturing. Which limb or body position is indicative of this?

Choices:

1. The upper extremities in flexion and the lower extremities in extension.
2. Extreme hyperextension of the neck and spine with both lower extremities flexed and the heels touching the buttocks.
3. All four limbs in extension.
4. All four limbs in flexion.

Teaching Points

Correct Answer: 3

With decerebrate posturing (decerebrate rigidity), the upper and lower extremities are held rigidly in extension.

Incorrect Choices:

In decorticate posture, the upper extremities are held rigidly in flexion while the lower extremities are extended. With opisthotonos, extreme hyperextension of the neck and spine is evident, with both lower extremities flexed and the heels touching the buttocks. All limbs flexed is not typically found in the comatose patient.

Type of Reasoning: Deductive

This question requires the test taker to recall factual guidelines related to posturing with individuals who are comatose. Recall of facts and guidelines often necessitates deductive reasoning skill. For this case, decerebrate posturing would present as all four limbs in extension. Review various types of posturing with coma if answered incorrectly.

A52

Gastrointestinal System | Interventions

A patient is recovering from a mild stroke with trunk weakness and postural instability. The patient complains of severe heartburn. What is the **BEST** choice to maximize stroke recovery and improve trunk stabilization while minimizing heartburn?

Choices:

1. Perform trunk stabilization exercises with the patient in the semi-Fowler position.
2. Begin with bridging exercises progressing to sitting holding.
3. Perform resisted holding in sitting using rhythmic stabilization.
4. Take antacids before physical therapy.

Teaching Points

Correct Answer: 3

Heartburn is a common symptom of gastroesophageal reflux disease (GERD) and can be aggravated by positioning in supine, prone, or bridging. Modifying the patient's position to upright can alleviate the symptoms and demonstrate to the patient the therapist's concern.

Incorrect Choices:
Semi-Fowler position (supine, head and torso elevated 30 degrees) is not an effective position to work on trunk stabilization. Bridging will aggravate heartburn. Prophylactic use of antacids before therapy is not indicated. With severe heartburn, the patient will likely be on a proton pump inhibitor (PPI) such as Prilosec, Nexium, or Prevacid.

Type of Reasoning: Inductive
For this question, the test taker must utilize clinical judgment in order to arrive at a correct conclusion. This necessitates inductive reasoning skill. In this situation, the best choice for a patient with severe heartburn is to perform resisted holding in sitting using rhythmic stabilization. Review information regarding GERD and exercise approaches if answered incorrectly.

A53

Integumentary System | Interventions

To prevent contractures in a newly admitted patient with anterior neck burns, it would be best to position the neck in which of the following?

Choices:
1. Hyperflexion.
2. Slight flexion.
3. Neutral.
4. Slight extension.

Teaching Points

Correct Answer: 4
Positioning the head/neck in slight extension will counteract the expected pull of the head into flexion with contracture development.

Incorrect Choices:
Positioning in slight flexion or hyperflexion will enhance the expected development of an anterior neck flexion contracture. Neutral position does not provide enough lengthening of tissues.

Type of Reasoning: Deductive
This question requires one to recall the optimal positioning of the neck after burns. This necessitates the recall of factual information and guidelines, which is a deductive reasoning skill. For this scenario, the therapist should position the neck in slight extension to counteract the expected pull of the head into flexion. Review burn guidelines and positioning if answered incorrectly.

A54

Neuromuscular and Nervous System | Examination

A therapist wishes to examine the balance of an elderly patient with a history of falls. The Berg Balance Test is selected. Which area is **NOT** examined using this test?

Choices:
1. Sit-to-stand transitions.
2. Functional reach in standing.
3. Turning while walking.
4. Tandem standing.

Teaching Points

Correct Answer: 3

The Berg Balance Test (BBT) is a test of static and dynamic balance in sitting and standing. It includes transitional items of sit-to-stand and stand-to-sit. It does not include items on gait. Turning while walking is an item on both the Tinetti Performance-Oriented Mobility Assessment and the Dynamic Gait Index.

Incorrect Choices:

All other choices are items on the BBT.

Type of Reasoning: Deductive

For this question, the test taker must recall the features of the Berg Balance Test in order to arrive at a correct conclusion. This is factual recall of information, which is a deductive reasoning skill. In this case, the BBT does not examine turning while walking. Review the BBT if answered incorrectly.

A55 

Musculoskeletal System | Interventions

The physical therapist is instructing a new mother to perform range of motion and stretching for her newborn who has a clubfoot. In what directions should the therapist advise her to carefully stretch?

Choices:

1. Plantarflexion and inversion.
2. Plantarflexion and eversion.
3. Dorsiflexion and inversion.
4. Dorsiflexion and eversion.

Teaching Points

Correct Answer: 4

The term "clubfoot" (talipes equinovarus) refers to the way the foot is positioned at a sharp angle to the ankle, like the head of a golf club. It describes a range of foot abnormalities usually present at birth in which the infant's foot is twisted into an equinovarus deformity. Stretching should be opposite the direction of the deforming position; therefore, stretch is into dorsiflexion and eversion.

Incorrect Choices:

All other choices would not be beneficial when stretching a clubfoot.

Type of Reasoning: Inductive

This question requires one to determine a best course of action using clinical judgment, based on knowledge of clubfoot. Questions of this nature, where clinical judgment is utilized to reach a sound conclusion, often necessitate inductive reasoning skill. In this case, the therapist should recommend stretching in the opposite direction of the deforming position, which is dorsiflexion and eversion. Review clubfoot and treatment guidelines if answered incorrectly.

A56

Cardiovascular/Pulmonary and Lymphatic Systems | Interventions

Pursed lip breathing as part of the treatment regimen would be **MOST** appropriate for a patient with which condition?

Choices:

1. Circumferential thoracic burns.
2. Asbestosis.
3. Rib fracture.
4. Emphysema.

Teaching Points

Correct Answer: 4

Pursed lip breathing gives increased resistance to the airways on exhalation. The resistance causes increased pressure, which helps to prevent airway collapse (likely sequelae given the pathophysiology of emphysema). This occurs via collateral ventilation through pores of Kohn and canals of Lambert.

Incorrect Choices:

Circumferential thoracic burn is a restrictive disorder, and pursed lip breathing will not have any effect on this. Asbestosis is an interstitial lung disease where there are fibrotic changes within the lung tissue. Pursed lip breathing will have no effect on this patient's breathing pattern. Rib fractures are also a restrictive disorder. In order to improve the breathing pattern, it would be most beneficial to control pain. Pursed lip breathing will have little effect.

Type of Reasoning: Inferential

This question requires one to utilize knowledge of pursed lip breathing in order to determine a best course of action in choosing this approach for a specific diagnosis. This requires clinical judgment, which is an inductive reasoning skill. For this situation, pursed lip breathing is most appropriate for emphysema. If answered incorrectly, review pursed lip breathing guidelines and intervention approaches for emphysema.

A57

Musculoskeletal System | Examination

A patient has normal quadriceps strength but unilateral weakness (3/5) of the hamstring muscles on the right. What might the therapist observe during swing phase of gait?

Choices:

1. Excessive compensatory hip extension on the sound side.
2. Decreased hip flexion followed by increased knee flexion on the weak side.
3. Excessive hip extension followed by abrupt knee extension on the weak side.
4. Excessive hip flexion followed by abrupt knee extension on the weak side.

Teaching Points

Correct Answer: 4

The hamstring muscles primarily control the forward swing of the leg during terminal swing. Loss of function may result in abrupt knee extension and increased hip flexion.

Incorrect Choices:

Excessive compensatory hip extension on the sound side would help in pulling the weak side into flexion due to weak hip flexors. This is not the case. Decreased hip flexion followed by increased knee flexion on the weak side would be the result of weak hip flexors and knee extensors during terminal swing. There would be abrupt knee extension as the hamstrings need to decelerate the tibia at terminal swing; however, one would not have excessive hip extension.

Type of Reasoning: Inferential

This question asks one to determine what is likely to be true for a patient with unilateral weakness of the hamstring muscles during gait. This requires one to infer information and recall the effects of muscle weakness on gait, necessitating inferential reasoning skill. For this case, the therapist is likely to see excessive hip flexion followed by abrupt knee extension on the side with hamstring weakness. Review gait abnormalities associated with muscle weakness if answered incorrectly.

A58 

Musculoskeletal System | Interventions

Following cast immobilization for a now healed supracondylar fracture of the humerus, a patient's elbow lacks mobility. To increase elbow range of motion, joint mobilization in the maximum loose-packed position should be performed at what position?

Choices:

1. Full extension.
2. 90 degrees of flexion.
3. 70 degrees of flexion.
4. 30 degrees of flexion.

Teaching Points

Correct Answer: 3

The loose-packed position of the humeroulnar joint is 70 degrees of flexion. The loose-packed position for the radiohumeral joint is 70 degrees of flexion, 35 degrees of supination. The loose-packed position is basically the resting position where the joint capsule and ligaments are most relaxed.

Incorrect Choices:

Full extension is the close-packed position for the elbow. The close-packed position is where the surfaces are maximally congruent to one another and capsule and ligaments are taut. 90 degrees is near to but not the maximum loose-packed position. 30 degrees is much closer to the closed-pack position.

Type of Reasoning: Deductive

For this question, the test taker must recall the loose-packed position of the humeroulnar joint in order to arrive at a correct conclusion. This necessitates factual recall of guidelines, which is a deductive reasoning skill. In this scenario, the loose-packed position of the humeroulnar joint is 70 degrees of flexion. Review loose-packed positions of the upper extremity, especially the elbow, if answered incorrectly.

 A59

Neuromuscular and Nervous System | Interventions

A patient with a complete tetraplegia (ASIA A) at the C6 level is initially instructed to transfer using a transfer board. With shoulders externally rotated, how should the remaining upper extremity (UE) joints be positioned?

Choices:

1. Forearms pronated with wrists and fingers extended.
2. Forearms supinated with wrists extended and fingers flexed.
3. Forearms pronated with wrists and fingers flexed.
4. Forearms supinated with wrists and fingers extended.

Teaching Points

Correct Answer: 2

The patient with tetraplegia at the C6 level does not have triceps to assist in transfers. Independent transfers can be achieved using muscle substitution and positioning to lock the elbow. The hands are positioned anterior to the hips; the shoulders are externally rotated with the elbows and wrists extended, forearms supinated, and fingers flexed. Strong contraction of the anterior deltoid, shoulder external rotators, and clavicular portion of the pectoralis major flexes and adducts the humerus, causing the elbow to extend.

Incorrect Choices:

Fingers are always flexed (not extended) to preserve tenodesis grasp. Forearms are supinated (not pronated) and the wrist is extended (not flexed).

Type of Reasoning: Inductive

This question requires one to determine, through clinical judgment, what would be the best UE joint positioning for a patient with C6 tetraplegia in order to perform a transfer using a transfer board. This necessitates clinical judgment and use of knowledge of transfers with tetraplegia, which is an inductive reasoning skill. For this case, the therapist should ensure the forearms are supinated with wrists extended and fingers flexed. Review transfer guidelines for patients with tetraplegia if answered incorrectly.

 A60 

Integumentary System | Evaluation, Diagnosis

Upon removing the dressing covering a decubitus ulcer located on the heel of an elderly patient, the physical therapist observes copious amounts of a foul-smelling, yellow-green discharge. How should the therapist document this finding in the patient's medical record?

Choices:

1. There is likelihood of a *Staphylococcus aureus* infection.
2. Maceration of the wound is evident.
3. Wound exudate is purulent.
4. Wound exudate is serosanguinous.

Teaching Points

Correct Answer: 3

Wound exudate (drainage) is purulent (containing pus) on the basis of the yellow-green discharge.

Incorrect Choices:
Without a wound culture it is impossible to know the exact bacteria (cause) of the infection. Wound exudate was not serosanguinous (containing blood). Maceration refers to softening of the tissues. Macerated skin is drained of its pigment and has a white appearance.

Type of Reasoning: Analytical
This question requires one to analyze information regarding a wound and then make a determination of the finding for this situation. Questions that require one to analyze information in order to reach sound conclusions often necessitate analytical reasoning skill. For this situation, the findings are consistent with purulent wound exudate. Review wound guidelines if answered incorrectly.

A61 

Musculoskeletal System | Examination

During examination of the right shoulder of a teenager with anterior shoulder pain, the physical therapist notices an excessive amount of scapular abduction during both shoulder flexion and abduction. Full range of glenohumeral (GH) motion is achieved at the ends flexion and abduction. The axillary border of the scapula protrudes laterally beyond the thorax much more on the right as compared to the left. Which muscle(s) would be associated with excessive lengthening during the movements of shoulder flexion and abduction?

Choices:
1. Serratus anterior.
2. Rhomboids.
3. Teres major.
4. Levator scapula.

Teaching Points

Correct Answer: 2
During the motions of flexion and abduction, concentric muscle activity of the serratus anterior occurs, providing upward scapular rotation. However, concentric activity of the serratus anterior would also induce abduction of the scapula due to its line of action. Excessive scapular abduction can be controlled through muscle actions from those that can provide scapular adduction. The primary scapular adductors acting eccentrically to control excessive scapular abduction include the rhomboid and the trapezius muscle groups. Inadequately controlled lengthening of the rhomboids could contribute to hyperabduction of the scapula during the mid and later phases of shoulder flexion and abduction.

Incorrect Choices:
The other choices do not control scapular abduction.

Type of Reasoning: Analytical
For this question, the test taker must utilize knowledge of musculoskeletal anatomy in order to determine which muscle is associated with excessive lengthening during shoulder flexion and abduction. One must analyze the situation presented in order to draw the correct conclusion, which is an analytical reasoning skill. In this case, the rhomboids are associated with this issue. Review the actions of the rhomboids if answered incorrectly.

Musculoskeletal System | Evaluation, Diagnosis

A competitive gymnast is examined by the physical therapist. The chief complaint is nagging, localized pain in the anterior left lower leg that is consistently present at night and increases during activity with swelling. What are these complaints **MOST** characteristic of?

Choices:

1. Bone tumor.
2. Anterior compartment syndrome.
3. Shin splints.
4. Stress fracture.

Teaching Points

Correct Answer: 4

Symptoms of a stress fracture may include pain and swelling, particularly with weight bearing on the injured bone. Stress fractures should be considered in patients who present with tenderness or edema after a recent increase in activity or repeated activity with limited rest. The differential diagnosis varies based on location but commonly includes tendinopathy, compartment syndrome, and nerve or artery entrapment syndrome.

Incorrect Choices:

Bone tumor is a possibility but not the most characteristic in this scenario. Pain may be increased at night. In this case there was pain at night but not increased. Activity may also increase the amount of pain. There may also be swelling with a bone tumor. Imaging is required.

Compartment syndrome is a painful condition that occurs when pressure within the muscles builds to dangerous levels. This pressure can decrease blood flow, which prevents nourishment and oxygen from reaching nerve and muscle cells. Compartment syndrome can be either acute or chronic. Acute compartment syndrome is a medical emergency. It is usually caused by a severe injury. There may be pain, decreased pulses, paresthesias, pallor, and paralysis. Chronic compartment syndrome, also known as exertional compartment syndrome, is usually not a medical emergency. It is most often caused by athletic exertion. However, the patient usually complains of a bursting type of pressure and pain, and that was not the case here.

Shin splints (medial tibial stress syndrome) is a common condition that can be distinguished from tibial stress fractures by nonfocal tenderness (diffuse along the mid-distal, posteromedial tibia) and a lack of edema.

Type of Reasoning: Analytical

This question requires one to determine the most likely diagnosis based on a description of symptoms. Questions of this nature often necessitate analytical reasoning skill, where information is analyzed in order to draw reasonable conclusions. For this scenario, the symptoms are most consistent with a stress fracture. Review signs and symptoms of stress fractures if answered incorrectly.

A63 

Cardiovascular/Pulmonary and Lymphatic Systems | Evaluation, Diagnosis

Four days following open-heart surgery, a patient is ambulating with a physical therapist in the hallway. The patient complains of some chest discomfort during the activity and wishes to return to his or her room. What should the therapist do?

Choices:

1. Sit the patient down and call the physician immediately.
2. Complete the treatment and have an aide transport the patient to the room as some discomfort is expected.
3. Call the nurse and check to see if the discomfort is ongoing.
4. Sit the patient down, take vital signs, and inform nursing services of the patient's complaint.

Teaching Points

Correct Answer: 4

It is important to determine etiology of the pain. If it is anginal, having the patient stop will reduce the myocardial demand. Gathering timely vital signs will help determine if the patient was maintaining his or her cardiac output. If not, the demand of the activity may have been too great.

Incorrect Choices:

There is no need to call the physician immediately. The pain may be musculoskeletal in origin, which is not a medical emergency. Even if the pain is the anginal equivalent, then decreasing the intensity of exercise by sitting will stop the coronary ischemia. Having an aide transport the patient is inappropriate because the patient may be having angina, and failure to modify the intensity could result in increased ischemia and myocardial damage. As a physical therapist, it is important to be able to determine the etiology of the pain and determine if it is expected. The therapist should not have to rely on the nurse.

Type of Reasoning: Evaluative

One must determine the most prudent course of action based on a description of symptoms in order to arrive at a correct conclusion. This requires knowledge of the symptoms and appropriate responses that consider patient well-being. In this case, the therapist should sit the patient down, take vital signs, and inform nursing services of the patient's complaint. Review coronary therapy guidelines, especially responses to angina, if answered incorrectly.

A64 

Nonsystem | Safety, Professional Responsibilities, Research

A group of institutionalized elderly was examined for balance instability and fall risk using a standardized test, the Performance-Oriented Mobility Assessment (POMA). The test-retest reliability of total test (POMA-T) and the subtests, balance subtest (POMA-B) and gait subtest (POMA-G) varied between 0.77 and 0.86. The interrater reliability values ranged from 0.80 to 0.93. What is the therapist's correct interpretation of these findings?

Choices:

1. Overall, the test demonstrated moderate reliability.
2. The test demonstrated moderate reliability for test-retest and good reliability for interrater comparisons.
3. The test demonstrated poor reliability for test-retest and moderate reliability for interrater comparisons.
4. Overall, the test demonstrated good reliability.

Teaching Points

Correct Answer: 4

Reliability coefficients above 0.75 demonstrate good reliability. This test demonstrated good reliability both for test-retest and interrater comparisons.

Incorrect Choices:

Coefficients below 0.50 represent poor reliability, while coefficients from 0.50 to 0.75 demonstrate moderate reliability.

Type of Reasoning: Deductive

For this question, the test taker must recall the parameters of good reliability in order to arrive at a correct conclusion. This requires recall of facts and guidelines, which is a deductive reasoning skill. In this case, the coefficients indicate that the test demonstrates good reliability. Review research guidelines, including reliability information, if answered incorrectly.

A65 

Cardiovascular/Pulmonary and Lymphatic Systems | Evaluation, Diagnosis

A patient presents with hemosiderin changes and increased lower extremity edema. What diagnosis are these changes consistent with?

Choices:

1. Chronic venous insufficiency.
2. Acute venous insufficiency.
3. Acute arterial insufficiency.
4. Chronic arterial insufficiency.

Teaching Points

Correct Answer: 1

Lower extremity edema is usually due to incompetent valves, which causes the edema. Long-standing edema causes staining of the legs because of increased iron from pooling blood.

Incorrect Choices:

While lower extremity edema would be present in acute venous insufficiency, there is not any time for leg staining. Acute arterial insufficiency would cause significant pain, pale or cyanotic skin, and decreased or absent pulses. Chronic arterial insufficiency would cause pain, decreased or absent pulses, and dependent rubor along with trophic changes (nail changes, loss of hair, and pale, shiny skin).

Type of Reasoning: Analytical

For this question, one must analyze the symptoms presented and make a determination of the most likely diagnosis. This necessitates analytical reasoning skill, where symptoms are assessed to determine a sound conclusion. For this situation, the symptoms are consistent with chronic venous insufficiency. If answered incorrectly, review venous insufficiency information.

A66 

Neuromuscular and Nervous System | Evaluation, Diagnosis

A patient experienced a cerebrovascular accident (right CVA) 2 weeks ago. The patient has motor and sensory impairments primarily in the left lower extremity; the left upper extremity shows only mild impairment. There is some confusion and perseveration. Based on these findings, what type of stroke syndrome does this patient present with?

Choices:

1. Posterior cerebral artery stroke.
2. Internal carotid syndrome.
3. Anterior cerebral artery syndrome.
4. Middle cerebral artery syndrome.

Teaching Points

Correct Answer: 3

These signs and symptoms are characteristic of anterior cerebral artery (ACA) syndrome, with contralateral hemiplegia and lower extremities more affected than upper extremities.

Incorrect Choices:

Posterior cerebral artery (PCA) syndrome involving central territory typically results in central post-stroke pain and involuntary movements. Contralateral hemiplegia can occur. Middle cerebral artery (MCA) syndrome results in contralateral hemiplegia with greater involvement of the upper extremities than lower. Internal carotid lesions typically involve a massive infarction in the areas of the brain supplied by the MCA and ACA, producing significant edema with possible uncal herniation, coma, and death.

Type of Reasoning: Analytical

For this question, the test taker must analyze the symptoms presented and determine the specific type of stroke syndrome. Questions that require one to determine a diagnosis based on symptoms often necessitate analytical reasoning skill. In this case, the symptoms are consistent with anterior cerebral artery syndrome. Review types of stroke if answered incorrectly.

A67 

Cardiovascular/Pulmonary and Lymphatic Systems | Examination

A patient is walking on a motorized treadmill and is undergoing ECG monitoring. Based on viewing this cardiac rhythm strip, what action should the physical therapist take?

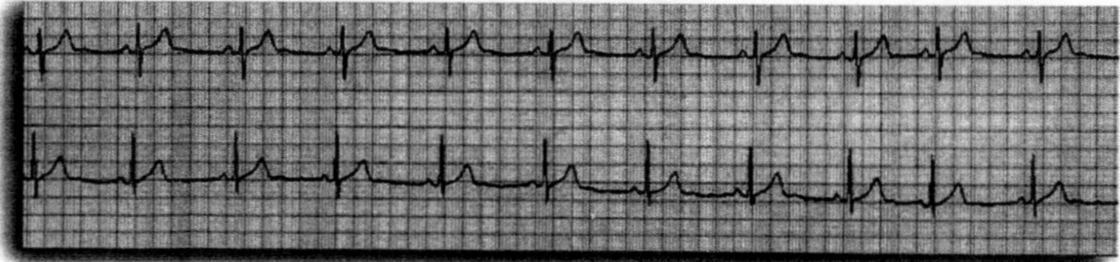

Choices:

1. Immediately call emergency medical services.
2. Modify the exercise based on past cardiac disease.
3. Modify the exercise based on current cardiac disease.
4. Exercise the patient/client without any cardiac restrictions.

Teaching Points

Correct Answer: 4

This is sinus bradycardia. There are no restrictions on proceeding with exercise in this patient.

Incorrect Choices:

This is a normal rhythm, so there is no need to alert emergency services. The past cardiac disease is irrelevant because this is a normal rhythm. This strip doesn't show any cardiac disease, as it is normal. There is no need for modifications.

Type of Reasoning: Analytical

This question requires one to apply knowledge of cardiac rhythms to the picture presented in order to determine a best course of action. Questions that require one to analyze information presented in pictures often necessitate analytical reasoning skill. For this scenario, the information should prompt the therapist to exercise the patient without any cardiac restrictions, since it is a normal rhythm. Review cardiac physiology and rhythms if answered incorrectly.

A68 

Cardiovascular/Pulmonary and Lymphatic Systems | Evaluation, Diagnosis

A therapist is planning to use percussion and shaking for assisting airway clearance with a patient diagnosed with chronic obstructive pulmonary disease (COPD). What major precaution might curtail selection of this form of intervention?

Choices:

1. A platelet count of 30,000.
2. Dyspnea when in the Trendelenburg position.
3. SaO_2 range of 88% to 94% on room air.
4. Functional Independence Measure (FIM) score of 4.

Teaching Points

Correct Answer: 1

A patient with a platelet count of 30,000 is at increased risk for bleeding. Percussion may cause microtraumas and increased bleeding risk.

Incorrect Choices:

While dyspnea in Trendelenburg is uncomfortable, the position could be modified so that percussion and vibration can be completed. While an SaO_2 range of 88% to 94% on room air is a consideration, it would not preclude this intervention. This should be monitored closely while considered positions maximize ventilation and perfusion. While this patient will require assistance for positioning, it doesn't eliminate this treatment intervention. The FIM score is nonspecific as to what function is impacted and whether a precaution is indicated.

Type of Reasoning: Inductive

This question requires the test taker to utilize clinical judgment in order to determine a best course of action. This requires inductive reasoning skill. In this case, a platelet count of 30,000 would curtail selection of the specific intervention approach. Review indications and contraindications for airway clearance techniques if answered incorrectly.

A69 

Musculoskeletal System | Examination

A patient with degenerative joint disease of the right hip complains of pain in the anterior hip and groin, which is aggravated by weight bearing. There is decreased range of motion and capsular restrictions. Right gluteus medius weakness is evident during ambulation, and there is decreased tolerance of functional activities including transfers and lower extremity dressing. In this case, a capsular pattern of joint motion should be evident by which of the following?

Choices:

1. Hip flexion, abduction, and internal rotation.
2. Hip flexion, adduction, and internal rotation.
3. Hip extension, abduction, and external rotation.
4. Hip flexion, abduction, and external rotation.

Teaching Points

Correct Answer: 1

The two classical capsular patterns at the hip are FAME and MEAL. FAME stands for loss of flexion, abduction, internal (medial) rotation, and extension. MEAL is loss of medial (internal) rotation, extension, and abduction. According to the American Physical Therapy Association (APTA) hip pain practice guidelines, patients were classified as having hip osteoarthritis (OA) if they (1) reported experiencing hip pain and (2) present with either one of the following clusters of clinical findings: (a) hip internal rotation less than 15 degrees, along with hip flexion less than or equal to 115 degrees and age greater than 50 years or (b) hip internal rotation greater than or equal to 15, along with pain with hip internal rotation, duration of morning stiffness of the hip less than or equal to 60 minutes, and age greater than 50 years.

Incorrect Choices:

The other patterns are not representative capsular patterns of the hip.

Type of Reasoning: Inferential

One must recall the capsular patterns of the hip in order to determine what is likely to be true for the patient in this question. This requires inferential reasoning skill, where one utilizes knowledge to determine likely symptoms or presentation of problems. In this case, the patient would likely show limitations in hip flexion, abduction, and internal rotation. Review capsular patterns of the hip if answered incorrectly.

A70 

Musculoskeletal System | Examination

Confirmation of a diagnosis of spondylolisthesis can be made when viewing an oblique radiograph of the spine. What is the relevant diagnostic finding?

Choices:

1. Posterior displacement of L5 over S1.
2. Bamboo appearance of the spine.
3. Compression of the vertebral bodies of L5 and S1.
4. Bilateral pars interarticularis defects.

Exam A

Teaching Points

Correct Answer: 4

Spondylolisthesis is defined as forward translation of a vertebral body with respect to the vertebra below. Spondylolysis, a break in the vertebra typically in the region of the pars interarticularis, may or may not be associated with a spondylolisthesis. If the pars defect is bilateral, it may allow slippage of the vertebra, typically L5 on S1, resulting in spondylolisthesis. Most cases are thought to result from minor overuse trauma, particularly repetitive hyperextension of the lumbar spine.

Incorrect Choices:

Posterior displacement of L5 over S1 is the wrong direction. Bamboo appearance of the spine would be found with ankylosing spondylitis. Compression of the vertebral bodies of L5 and S1 would be classified as compression fractures and generally would not result in forward slippage of a vertebra.

Type of Reasoning: Inferential

One must recall the typical diagnostic finding of spondylolisthesis in order to arrive at a correct conclusion. This requires the test taker to infer the likely symptoms based on knowledge of the diagnosis, which is an inferential reasoning skill. For this situation, one would expect to see bilateral pars interarticularis defects. If answered incorrectly, review radiograph findings of spondylolisthesis.

Nonsystem | Safety, Professional Responsibilities, Research

A physical therapist and physical therapist assistant are conducting a cardiac rehabilitation session for 20 patients. The therapist is suddenly called out of the room. The physical therapist assistant should do which of the following?

Choices:

1. Terminate the exercises and have the patients monitor their pulses until the therapist returns.
2. Have the patients continue with the same exercise until the therapist returns.
3. Have the patients switch to a less intense exercise until the therapist returns.
4. Continue with the outlined exercise progression for that session.

Teaching Points

Correct Answer: 4

The physical therapist provided an exercise program, and it is appropriate for the PTA to continue to follow it.

Incorrect Choices:

There is no need to terminate exercise since the patients have an established exercise program. It is within a PTA's scope of practice to progress a program, so there is no need to maintain the same intensity of exercise. There is no need to reduce the intensity of the program, as the PTA can monitor and progress a program.

Type of Reasoning: Evaluative

This question requires one to determine a best course of action based on knowledge of supervisory guidelines and scope of practice information. This requires evaluative reasoning skill, where one weighs the options presented and determines a best course of action. For this scenario, the PTA should continue with the outlined exercise progression for that session. Review scope of practice guidelines if answered incorrectly.

A72

Neuromuscular and Nervous System | Examination

A physical therapist is examining a patient who has a recent history of falls while ambulating on level surfaces. Interaction with the patient indicates that cognition is unaffected. Which tests should be performed next once it has been established that cognition is not impaired?

Choices:

1. Static balancing tests.
2. Locomotor tests.
3. Sensory testing.
4. Dynamic balance tests.

Teaching Points

Correct Answer: 3

Sensory testing should be performed next, including somatosensations from the feet and ankles, vision and visual proprioception, and vestibular sensations. Once the primary sensations have been tested, the Clinical Test for Sensory Interaction in Balance can reveal valuable information about the patient's ability to use sensory information under changing balance conditions.

Incorrect Choices:

Following sensory testing, static balance tests can then be performed, then dynamic balance tests, and finally locomotor tests. Primary impairments should always be identified before functional deficits.

Type of Reasoning: Inductive

This question requires clinical judgment in order to determine a best course of action for a patient with a history of falls. This necessitates inductive reasoning skill. For this case, the therapist should perform sensory testing as a first course of action before the others listed. Review fall examination guidelines if answered incorrectly.

A73

Nonsystem | Safety, Professional Responsibilities, Research

A therapist wishes to study the progress of patients with paraplegia who are discharged from a rehabilitation setting. Starting with the patients' discharge, and once a month for 3 years, the therapist will measure their joint range of motion of both hips and knees. Accurate analysis of this time series study is heavily dependent upon which of the following?

Choices:

1. Random sampling.
2. Interrater reliability.
3. Intrarater reliability.
4. Predictive validity of the measurements.

Teaching Points

Correct Answer: 3

Accurate analysis will depend on the therapist's ability to consistently measure ROM using standardized techniques on multiple measurement trials (intrarater reliability).

Incorrect Choices:
This is a cohort study, longitudinal in time (not a randomized controlled trial). Interrater reliability and predictive validity do not apply.

Type of Reasoning: Deductive
One must draw from knowledge of research guidelines in order to arrive at a correct conclusion for this question. Questions that require the application of facts and guidelines often necessitate deductive reasoning skill. For this situation, the study is heavily dependent on intrarater reliability. Review research guidelines if answered incorrectly.

A74 

Musculoskeletal System | Evaluation, Diagnosis

Which of these findings is characteristic of a boutonnière deformity of the finger?

Choices:
1. Flexion of the distal interphalangeal joint.
2. Contracture of the extensor digitorum communis tendon.
3. Rupture with volar slippage of the lateral bands.
4. Hyperextension of the proximal interphalangeal joint.

Teaching Points

Correct Answer: 3
Finger position marked by extension of the metacarpophalangeal (MCP) and distal interphalangeal (DIP) joints with flexion of the proximal interphalangeal (PIP) joints. Through injury or disease the central extensor tendon (extensor digitorum communis [EDC]) of the involved finger ruptures. The tendon then displaces palmarly relative to the PIP joint (volar slippage). The lateral bands become tight and are attached to the distal phalanx, extending it. The flexor digitorum profundus (FDP) is now unopposed, and it pulls the PIP joint into flexion. The result is a deformity that looks like a "buttonhole" or boutonnière in French.

Incorrect Choices:
The DIP joint will be in extension (not flexion) since the terminal tendon is intact. Contracture of the EDC tendon will not happen because the EDC becomes the central slip and the lateral bands. The lateral bands are still intact with a boutonnière deformity, and they come together to form the terminal tendon that is also intact. Hyperextension of the PIP is the opposite deformity of the boutonnière. The torn central slip can no longer extend the PIP joint and is therefore stuck in flexion.

Type of Reasoning: Deductive
For this question, one must recall the typical presentation of a boutonnière deformity in order to arrive at a correct conclusion. Recall of factual information requires deductive reasoning skill. For this case, the typical characteristic of this deformity is rupture with volar slippage of the lateral bands. Review boutonnière deformity characteristics if answered incorrectly.

A75 

Cardiovascular/Pulmonary and Lymphatic Systems | Evaluation, Diagnosis

A patient with chronic asthma has been admitted to the hospital for an acute exacerbation. What is the **MOST** important information the therapist needs in order to determine the patient's prognosis with physical therapy?

Choices:

1. A current medication list.
2. A previous history of the disease.
3. The most recent chest x-ray results.
4. The most recent pulmonary function test results.

Teaching Points

Correct Answer: 4

Recent pulmonary function test results will give the therapist information regarding the severity of the lung disease. This information will assist in determining how much the patient will progress.

Incorrect Choices:

While the current medication list will help determine how the patient is currently being managed, it doesn't give any information about his or her function. The previous history of the disease will not translate well into what the patient's function has been. It is possible that he or she has been quite functional despite terrible disease such that an acute exacerbation with little reserve will leave him or her quite limited. An acute asthma exacerbation will likely not appear on a chest x-ray, nor would chronic disease.

Type of Reasoning: Inductive

One must utilize clinical judgment in order to determine the most important information about a patient with asthma. Questions of this nature, where clinical judgment and knowledge are applied to patient cases, often necessitate inductive reasoning skill. For this situation, the most important information is the most recent pulmonary function test results. If answered incorrectly, review pulmonary rehab, including pulmonary testing information.

A76 

Nonsystem | Equipment, Devices, Biophysical Agents

A therapist is examining the gait of a patient with a transfemoral prosthesis. The patient circumducts the prosthetic limb during swing. The therapist needs to identify the cause of the gait deviation. What is the **MOST** likely prosthetic cause?

Choices:

1. Unstable knee unit.
2. Inadequate socket flexion.
3. Sharp or high medial wall or abducted hip joint.
4. Inadequate suspension or loose socket.

Teaching Points

Correct Answer: 4

Prosthetic causes of circumduction include a long prosthesis, locked knee unit, loose knee friction, inadequate suspension, small or loose socket, and plantar flexed foot.

Incorrect Choices:

An unstable knee unit will cause forward flexion during stance. Inadequate socket flexion will result in lordosis during stance. A sharp or high medial wall or abducted hip joint will result in an abducted gait.

Type of Reasoning: Inferential

For this question, one must determine the reason for a specific gait deviation in order to arrive at a correct conclusion. One must apply knowledge of prosthetics in order to infer the most likely reason, which necessitates inferential reasoning skill. For this situation, the most likely cause is inadequate suspension or loose socket. Review lower extremity prosthetics information if answered incorrectly.

A77 

Neuromuscular and Nervous System | Examination

A patient diagnosed with multiple sclerosis experiences sudden electric-like shocks spreading down the body elicited by the maneuver in the picture. This is known as which of the following?

Choices:

1. Head jolt test.
2. Kernig's sign.
3. Lhermitte's sign.
4. Tinel's test.

Teaching Points

Correct Answer: 3

Lhermitte's sign is sudden, transient, electric-like shocks spreading down the body when the head is flexed forward. It occurs chiefly in patients with multiple sclerosis but can also be seen in compression disorders of the cervical spine (tumor, cervical spondylitic myelopathy).

Incorrect Choices:

The head jolt test involves asking the patient to turn the head at a frequency of two to three times a second. A positive test is indicated by worsening of baseline headache and is indicative of meningeal irritation. Kernig's sign is also used to test for meningeal irritation. In supine, the lower extremity (LE) is flexed at the hip and knee; the knee is then straightened. Resistance to knee straightening is a positive Kernig's sign. Tinel's test involves percussion (tapping) of a nerve at the site of compression producing distal tingling sensations (often present in carpal tunnel syndrome).

Type of Reasoning: Analytical

This question requires one to analyze the information presented in the picture in order to determine the most likely test being performed. Questions of this nature, where information is assessed in pictures, necessitate analytical reasoning skill. For this scenario, the picture depicts testing for Lhermitte's sign. Review Lhermitte's sign and provocative testing if answered incorrectly.

Musculoskeletal System I Interventions

An elderly patient with degenerative joint disease is seen by a physical therapist 3 days following a total knee replacement. Which of these findings would be an indication for the therapist to contact the surgeon?

Choices:

1. Patient is noncompliant when learning to transfer properly.
2. Patient cannot ambulate at least 50 feet with a standard walker.
3. Patient fails to recognize the therapist on the third consecutive postoperative visit.
4. Patient complains of soreness at the incision site.

Teaching Points

Correct Answer: 3

Postoperative adverse effects on the cardiac, pulmonary, and neuromuscular systems and on cognitive function are the main concerns for elderly surgical patients who are at high risk. Postoperative delirium is characterized by incoherent thought and speech, disorientation, impaired memory, and attention. Elderly patients usually manifest delirium following a lucid interval of 1 postoperative day or more, a condition known as interval delirium. Symptoms are often worse at night. Alternatively, the condition can be silent and unnoticed, or misdiagnosed as depression. However, the effects of elderly postoperative delirium are evident in increased morbidity, delayed functional recovery, and prolonged hospital stay. Fortunately, the postoperative cognitive dysfunction is a reversible condition in the majority of elderly surgical patients. Preoperative risk factors of bilateral total knee arthroplasty are associated with a significantly higher incidence of acute delirium than unilateral total knee arthroplasty in patients over 80 years.

Failing to recognize the therapist after three visits is an indication of a declining mental condition. This would definitely be a safety consideration as the patient may not be able to follow all the precautions and may also put himself or herself in danger by walking without an ambulatory aid, etc. Wound infection is also a consideration. Contacting the surgeon is necessary.

Incorrect Choices:

Soreness at the incision site would be an expected common complaint. The patient being noncompliant could potentially be a safety issue; however, the therapist should first attempt behavior modification. If that failed, they could get advice from a co-worker and possibly counseling for the patient if deemed necessary. Not being able to ambulate 50 feet could be due to many problems including pain, weakness, and balance issues. None of these factors require consultation with the surgeon at this time.

Type of Reasoning: Evaluative

For this question, one must determine a best course of action based on presenting signs. Questions of this nature, where information is weighed to determine its significance, often necessitate evaluative reasoning skill. For this scenario, the patient failing to recognize the therapist on the third consecutive postoperative visit would be an indication to contact the surgeon. Review adverse postoperative effects, especially in older adults, if answered incorrectly.

A79 

Nonsystem | Safety, Professional Responsibilities, Research

The primary contribution of a physical therapist member of a facility emergency/disaster preparedness committee in formulating a disaster plan is describing the role of the physical therapists in providing which of the following?

Choices:

1. Triage and basic life support during the disaster.
2. Evaluation of soft tissue injuries and rendering appropriate care.
3. Unique preparedness concerns needed for people with disabilities or special needs.
4. Emotional distress management of victims or patients during crisis situations.

Teaching Points

Correct Answer: 3

The physical therapist's unique contribution to the team is in addressing the concerns of individuals with disabilities or special needs.

Incorrect Choices:

The physical therapist and the other team members may individually or collectively address the other needs listed.

Type of Reasoning: Evaluative

For this question, one must determine the unique contribution of a physical therapist in emergency/disaster preparedness situations in order to arrive at a correct conclusion. Specifically, one must weigh the information presented to make a sound conclusion, which necessitates evaluative reasoning skill. In this case, the unique contribution is in concerns needed for people with disabilities or special needs. Review emergency/disaster preparedness information if answered incorrectly.

A80 

Cardiovascular/Pulmonary and Lymphatic Systems | Examination

Following a hard tackle, a football player exhibits signs of fractured ribs and a pneumothorax. When auscultating during inhalation over the injured area, what would the physical therapist expect to hear?

Choices:

1. Soft, rustling sounds on inhalation.
2. Decreased or no breath sounds.
3. Crackles.
4. Wheezes.

Teaching Points

Correct Answer: 2

The fractured ribs will cause the patient to have pain and therefore not take deep breaths. More importantly, the pneumothorax will cause an increasing positive pressure on the lung, not allowing it to inflate. The result will be minimal air movement and decreased or absent breath sounds.

Incorrect Choices:

Soft, rustling sounds are normal, vesicular breath sounds. These would not be present with these injuries. Crackles would indicate atelectasis or secretions, but it would not be possible to hear these sounds with these injuries because there is minimal air movement. Likewise, wheezes wouldn't be possible to hear.

Type of Reasoning: Deductive

One must recall the auscultation sounds with a pneumothorax in order to arrive at a correct conclusion. This necessitates the recall of factual information, which is a deductive reasoning skill. For this case, one would expect to hear decreased or no breath sounds. Review auscultation guidelines, especially with pneumothorax, if answered incorrectly.

A81 

Cardiovascular/Pulmonary and Lymphatic Systems | Interventions

A patient with cystic fibrosis (CF) has been admitted to the hospital in acute respiratory failure as a result of an infection. What is the **BEST** choice for use of airway clearance techniques?

Choices:

1. Should not be administered since it is contraindicated in acute respiratory failure.
2. Should be administered two times a day to the patient's tolerance.
3. Should be administered according to the patient's current home regimen.
4. Should be administered vigorously once every 2 hours.

Teaching Points

Correct Answer: 4

Given the pathology of CF, it is important to clear all secretions as often as possible to assist with clearing the infection. It will also assist with maximizing gas exchange.

Incorrect Choices:

Airway clearance in the presence of CF with acute respiratory failure is not contraindicated. The other choices are not vigorous enough considering the patient's condition. The home program was not geared toward acute respiratory failure.

Type of Reasoning: Inductive

For this question, the test taker must utilize knowledge of CF and airway clearance techniques in order to arrive at a correct conclusion. This requires clinical judgment, which is an inductive reasoning skill. For this case, the therapist should administer airway clearance techniques vigorously once every 2 hours. Review CF guidelines and airway management techniques if answered incorrectly.

A82

Nonsystem | Safety, Professional Responsibilities, Research

While ambulating a patient in the parallel bars, a therapist loses control and the patient falls, hitting his or her head on the bar. The patient lies motionless on the floor between the bars bleeding heavily from a scalp laceration. What is the first thing the therapist should do?

Choices:

1. Apply a thick gauze and manual pressure to the scalp wound.
2. Check for responsiveness.
3. Call emergency medical services.
4. Immediately determine the patient's heart rate and blood pressure.

Teaching Points

Correct Answer: 2

The physical therapist's first course of action is to check for responsiveness.

Incorrect Choices:

The other steps listed may be considered but only after responsiveness is determined.

Type of Reasoning: Evaluative

For this question, the test taker must determine a best course of action by weighing the options presented and determining which action will have the best outcome. This requires evaluative reasoning skill. For this situation, the first thing the therapist should do is to check for responsiveness. Review emergency procedures if answered incorrectly.

A83

Integumentary System | Examination

A therapist is examining a patient with an ulcer in the lower leg/ankle and suspects it is an arterial rather than a venous ulcer. One of the factors the therapist uses to determine this is based on the location of the ulcer. What is the typical location of an arterial ulcer?

Choices:

1. Medial malleolus.
2. Posterior tibial area.
3. Lateral malleolus.
4. Medial distal tibia.

Teaching Points

Correct Answer: 3

The typical location of an arterial ulcer is the distal lower leg (toes, foot), the lateral malleolus, or the anterior tibial area.

Incorrect Choices:

The typical location of a venous ulcer is the distal lower leg and the medial malleolus.

Type of Reasoning: Inferential
One must determine what is likely to be true of a situation in order to arrive at a correct conclusion for this question. This necessitates inferential reasoning skill. The test taker must utilize knowledge of arterial ulcers to determine what is likely to be true. In this case, the typical location of an arterial ulcer is on the lateral malleolus. Review information on arterial ulcers if answered incorrectly.

A84 

Genitourinary System | Evaluation, Diagnosis

During pregnancy, the presence of the hormone relaxin can lead to abnormal movement and pain. Which joints are typically affected?

Choices:
1. Glenohumeral joints.
2. Hip joints.
3. Lumbrosacral joints.
4. Sacroiliac joints.

Teaching Points

Correct Answer: 4
The sacroiliac (SI) joints are most often affected in pregnancy, resulting in pain.

Incorrect Choices:
The other joints are not typically affected. Low back pain is common in pregnancy, largely resulting from the physical changes (added weight, poor muscle tone, increased lordosis, loose pelvic ligaments).

Type of Reasoning: Deductive
For this question, the test taker must recall the typical joints that are affected by pregnancy and may result in pain in order to arrive at a correct conclusion. This necessitates the recall of factual information, which is a deductive reasoning skill. For this scenario, the sacroiliac joints are typically affected by pregnancy. Review pregnancy and common physical changes if answered incorrectly.

A85 

Cardiovascular/Pulmonary and Lymphatic Systems | Evaluation, Diagnosis

A patient with angina pectoris has been instructed to use sublingual nitroglycerin in case of an acute anginal attack. What are the primary effects of this medication?

Choices:
1. Vasoconstriction of peripheral vessels.
2. Vasodilation of the coronary vessels.
3. Increasing myocardial oxygen consumption.
4. Increasing left ventricular end-diastolic pressure.

Teaching Points

Correct Answer: 2

Nitroglycerin increases coronary blood flow by dilating coronary arteries and improving flow to ischemic areas. In low doses it produces vasodilation (venous greater than arterial) and is used in the acute and long-term prophylactic management of angina pectoris.

Incorrect Choices:

Additional effects include decreasing left ventricular end-diastolic pressure (not increasing) and reducing myocardial oxygen consumption (not increasing).

Type of Reasoning: Deductive

One must recall the effects of nitroglycerin in order to arrive at a correct conclusion for this question. This requires the recall of facts and guidelines, which is a deductive reasoning skill. In this case, nitroglycerin will primarily cause vasodilation of the coronary vessels. Review information on nitroglycerin effects if answered incorrectly.

A86

Nonsystem | Equipment, Devices, Biophysical Agents

A patient has a body mass index (BMI) of 32 kg/m^2 with excessive tissue mass in the hip area. What accommodations are needed to the wheelchair prescription for this patient?

Choices:

1. Move the small front casters closer to the drive wheels to increase stability.
2. Add friction rims to increase handgrip function.
3. Add an antitipping device to prevent falls going up curbs.
4. Displace the rear axle forward for more efficient arm push.

Teaching Points

Correct Answer: 4

This patient is obese. A bariatric wheelchair with heavy-duty, extra-wide wheels is necessary. The rear axle is displaced forward compared to the standard wheelchair to allow for more efficient arm push.

Incorrect Choices:

Moving the front casters closer to the drive wheels would decrease stability (not increase). Friction rims and antitipping devices are adjustments that may be necessary for the patient with a spinal cord injury.

Type of Reasoning: Inductive

For this question, one must utilize knowledge of wheelchair prescription for patients with obesity in order to arrive at a correct conclusion. Clinical judgment coupled with knowledge of wheelchair prescription guidelines are required, which necessitates inductive reasoning skill. For this case, the therapist should recommend a wheelchair in which the rear axle is displaced forward for more efficient arm push. Review wheelchair prescription guidelines, especially for patient with obesity, if answered incorrectly.

A87

Neuromuscular and Nervous System | Interventions

A patient is diagnosed with benign paroxysmal positional vertigo (BPPV). What intervention should the plan of care for this patient emphasize?

Choices:

1. Gaze stability exercises using horizontal head rotation (X1 viewing).
2. Canalith repositioning treatment.
3. Postural stability exercises in sitting using a therapy ball.
4. Habituation exercises using provocative positions and movements.

Teaching Points

Correct Answer: 2

The goal of treatment is to remove the otoconia that have become dislodged and are free-floating in the semicircular canal (SCC), or canalithiasis. The patient's head is guided through a series of movements to move the debris out of the involved SCC and into the vestibule. Once moved, the symptoms should resolve. Canalith repositioning maneuver (modified Epley) is used for canalithiasis.

Incorrect Choices:

Gaze stability exercises and postural stability exercises (sitting on a ball) are treatments used for unilateral and bilateral vestibular hypofunction (UVH, BVH). Habituation training (motion sensitivity training) is used when a patient with UVH presents with continual complaints of dizziness. Patients with central vestibular lesions may also benefit from habituation exercises.

Type of Reasoning: Inductive

For this question, the test taker must recall intervention approaches for BPPV in order to arrive at a correct conclusion. Based on knowledge of effective approaches, one will utilize inductive reasoning skill to determine the intervention approach that is most effective. In this case, canalith repositioning treatment is the best approach. Review intervention approaches for BPPV if answered incorrectly.

A88

Neuromuscular and Nervous System | Interventions

Following a cerebral vascular accident (CVA), a patient is hospitalized. The therapist determines that a positioning schedule should be implemented. While in supine, what is the **BEST** position for the patient's affected upper extremity?

Choices:

1. Shoulder protracted and slightly abducted with external rotation, elbow extension, wrist neutral, and fingers extended.
2. Shoulder protracted and slightly abducted with internal rotation, elbow flexion, wrist neutral, and fingers extended.
3. Shoulder retracted and adducted with internal rotation and elbow, wrist, and fingers flexed.
4. Shoulder retracted and abducted with external rotation, elbow extension, wrist neutral, and fingers flexed.

Teaching Points

Correct Answer: 1

Positioning is opposite the expected posturing and spastic patterns of the more affected upper extremity (UE). This includes shoulder protraction with abduction and external rotation, elbow extension, wrist neutral, and fingers in extension.

Incorrect Choices:

Shoulder adductors and internal rotators, along with elbow and finger flexors, are typically spastic. The limb should be positioned in the opposite antagonistic pattern.

Type of Reasoning: Inductive

For this question, one must utilize clinical judgment, coupled with recall of positioning guidelines for patients with CVA in order to arrive at a correct conclusion. This requires inductive reasoning skill, where clinical judgment is paramount to drawing correct conclusions. In this case, the therapist should position the patient with the shoulder protracted and slightly abducted, with external rotation, elbow extension, wrist neutral, and fingers extended. Review bed positioning guidelines for patients with CVA if answered incorrectly.

A89

Cardiovascular/Pulmonary and Lymphatic Systems | Interventions

What is an acceptable modified position to drain the posterior basal segment of the left lower lobe in a patient with pulmonary congestion?

Choices:

1. Side-lying on the right, with a pillow under the right hip and the bed flat.
2. Prone, with a pillow under the hips and the bed flat.
3. Side-lying on the right, with a pillow between the legs and the foot of the bed elevated 18 inches.
4. Prone, with a pillow under the hips and the bed elevated 18 inches.

Teaching Points

Correct Answer: 2

Prone, with a pillow under the hips and the bed flat will raise the posterior basal segments up to facilitate drainage.

Incorrect Choices:

The side-lying position with the bed flat will drain the lingula more than the posterior basal segments. With the bed elevated in side-lying, the pillow position is just for comfort but will not facilitate drainage. Raising the bed up will cause drainage to go toward the base of the lungs, which would not be effective. Similarly, the bed is elevated up in prone, which will make it difficult for drainage to occur.

Type of Reasoning: Deductive

One must recall the proper positions for posterior basal segment drainage of the left lower lobe in order to arrive at a correct conclusion. This requires recall of facts and guidelines, which is a deductive reasoning skill. In this case, the therapist should position the patient in prone, with a pillow under the hips and the bed flat. Review postural drainage techniques if answered incorrectly.

A90

Musculoskeletal System | Evaluation, Diagnosis

When the ankle is forcibly inverted and plantar flexed, which ligament is **MOST FREQUENTLY** sprained?

Choices:

1. Deltoid.
2. Anterior talofibular.
3. Posterior talofibular.
4. Calcaneofibular.

Teaching Points

Correct Answer: 2

The anterior talofibular ligament is the most frequently injured ligament in the ankle, which occurs with an inversion sprain.

Incorrect Choices:

The deltoid is on the medial ankle and would be injured with eversion sprains. The posterior talofibular and calcaneofibular ligaments could also be injured with a more severe inversion sprain but would not be the most frequently injured of the ankle ligaments.

Type of Reasoning: Deductive

For this question, the test taker must recall the ligaments that are injured with ankle sprains, in order to arrive at a correct conclusion. This necessitates the recall of factual information, which is a deductive reasoning skill. In this case, the anterior talofibular ligament is most frequently sprained. Review ligaments of the ankle and ankle sprains if answered incorrectly.

A91

System Interactions | Evaluation, Diagnosis

A patient complains of excessive upper and lower extremity muscle aching, cramping, and right upper quadrant pain when exercising. The patient has a history of chronic alcoholism and was placed on atorvastatin (a statin drug) 2 months ago. The therapist should refer the patient to the primary care physician for which reason?

Choices:

1. For an exercise test to determine the right intensity for exercise.
2. To rule out cirrhosis of the liver.
3. To rule out liver and muscle dysfunction from statin.
4. To rule out gallstones that may be obstructing the bile duct.

Teaching Points

Correct Answer: 3

A small percentage of patients ($< 5\%$) who take statins (atorvastatin such as Lipitor, or others) can experience myalgia, cramps, stiffness, spasm, or weakness affecting exercise tolerance. The patient needs to see the primary care physician to have the dose or medication changed.

Incorrect Choices:

Determining the appropriate exercise intensity is within the scope of a physical therapist's practice. A physical therapist (PT) is the appropriate professional in this case, so no referral is needed. These signs and symptoms are not consistent with cirrhosis or gallbladder disorders. Exercise would not worsen this condition.

Type of Reasoning: Analytical

For this question, the test taker must analyze the symptoms presented and determine the likely reason for the symptoms. This necessitates analytical reasoning skill. In this case, the symptoms and current use of a statin drug should prompt the therapist to refer the patient to the physician to rule out liver and muscle dysfunction from statin use. Review side effects of statin use if answered incorrectly.

A92

Neuromuscular and Nervous System | Evaluation, Diagnosis

Following a period of spinal shock, a patient with a complete spinal cord injury (ASIA A) at the T5 level is placed on a bladder training program coordinated by the nurse. A realistic ultimate outcome for this program would be independent voiding by using which of the following?

Choices:

1. The Credé maneuver.
2. The Valsalva maneuver.
3. A timed voiding program.
4. Suprapubic stroking or tapping.

Teaching Points

Correct Answer: 4

A spastic or reflex (upper motor neuron [UMN]) bladder contracts and reflexively empties in response to a certain level of filling pressure. Reflex emptying can be triggered by manual stimulation techniques (e.g., stroking, kneading, or tapping the suprapubic area).

Incorrect Choices:

A flaccid or lower motor neuron (LMN) bladder does not have reflex action. It can be emptied by using the Credé maneuver (manually compressing the lower abdomen); increasing intra-abdominal pressure using a Valsalva maneuver; or using a timed voiding program.

Type of Reasoning: Inferential

For this question, one must utilize knowledge of spinal cord injury and effects on the bladder in order to determine the best voiding approach. This necessitates inferential reasoning skill. In this case, a patient with this type of injury would be independent using suprapubic stroking or tapping. Review spinal cord injury voiding techniques, especially for upper motor neuron injuries, if answered incorrectly.

A93 

Integumentary System | Evaluation, Diagnosis

A physical therapist is performing an examination of an elderly patient who is confined to bed in a custodial care facility. A large ulcer is observed on the right heel as shown in the picture. Based on the staging of pressure ulcers, how would this ulcer be classified?

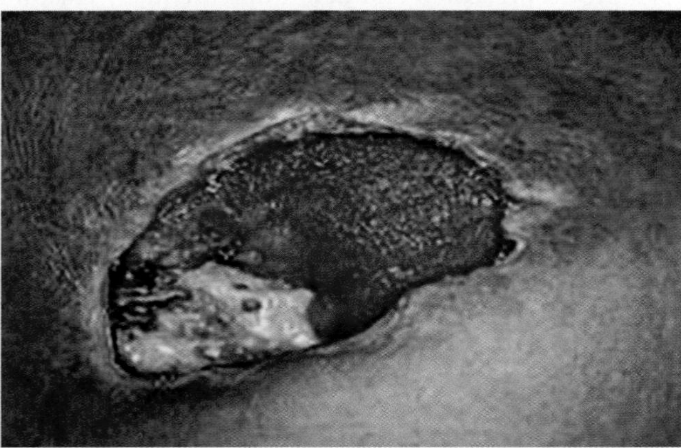

From: Perry, Potter, and Elkin, 2012/Courtesy Laurel Wiersma, RN, MSN, CNS, Barnes-Jewish Hospital.

Choices:

1. Stage I ulcer.
2. Stage II ulcer.
3. Stage III ulcer.
4. Stage IV ulcer.

Teaching Points

Correct Answer: 3

A stage III ulcer is characterized by full-thickness skin loss with damage to or necrosis of subcutaneous tissue. It presents clinically as a crater.

Incorrect Choices:

A stage I ulcer is characterized by nonblanchable erythema of intact skin. A stage II ulcer is characterized by partial-thickness skin loss involving the epidermis or dermis. The ulcer is superficial and presents clinically as an abrasion, blister, or shallow crater. A stage IV ulcer is characterized by full-thickness skin loss with extensive destruction, tissue necrosis, and damage to muscle, bone, or supporting structures. Undermining or sinus tracts may be present.

Type of Reasoning: Analytical

For this question, the test taker must examine the picture provided and determine the most likely stage of ulceration based on the picture. This requires analysis of information, which is an analytical reasoning skill. For this case, the picture represents a stage III ulcer. Review stages of ulcers if answered incorrectly.

A94 

Musculoskeletal System | Evaluation, Diagnosis

How would the clinical status of a patient with a posterior herniated nucleus pulposus be determined if there is improvement?

Choices:

1. Peripheral pain increases only when lumbar extension is attempted.
2. Peripheral pain occurs only with straight leg raising.
3. Pain centralizes with passive hyperextension of the spine.
4. There is flattening of the lumbar lordosis.

Teaching Points

Correct Answer: 3

Centralization describes the phenomenon by which distal limb pain, coming from the spine although not necessarily felt there, is immediately or eventually abolished in response to loading strategies. During centralization, the response to therapeutic loading strategies is assessed. Pain is progressively abolished in a distal to proximal direction with each progressive movement until all symptoms are abolished. In back pain only, the pain moves from a widespread to a more central location and then abolishes. Centralization has been proved to be a good indicator of a positive outcome in patients with low back pain.

Incorrect Choices:

Peripheral pain increasing only when lumbar extension is attempted would be an indication of worsening of symptoms as the disc could be pushed further onto the spinal nerve. Peripheral pain occurs only with straight leg raising (SLR). SLR is a neurodynamic test that produces movement in the sciatic nerve (L4, L5, S1, 2, 3). If during SLR the nerve is pressed against the disc bulge, it could produce pain. There is flattening of the lumbar lordosis. This leads to pressure on the anterior disc and could result in protrusion of the disc posteriorly if herniated.

Type of Reasoning: Inferential

One must make a determination of the likely clinical presentation for a patient with improvement in a posterior herniated nucleus pulposus. This requires one to infer what is likely to be true of a situation, which is an inferential reasoning skill. For this situation, it is likely that pain would centralize with passive hyperextension of the spine. Review symptoms of posterior herniated nucleus pulposus if answered incorrectly.

A95

Musculoskeletal System | Examination

The physical therapist is examining the muscle length of the patient's left hip and knee. How should the therapist interpret the muscle length test shown in the picture?

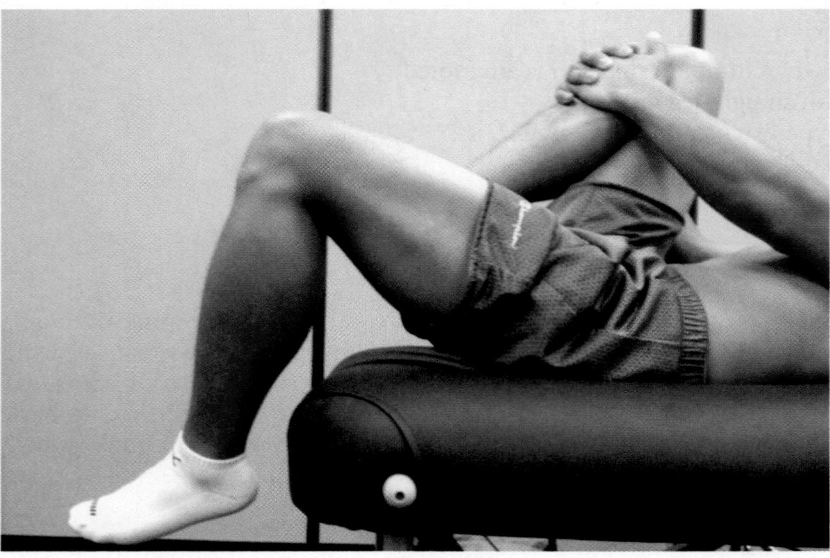

Choices:

1. Shortness of one joint and two joint hip flexors.
2. Shortness of one joint hip flexor with normal two joint hip flexors.
3. Normal one joint hip flexors with tightness of two joint hip flexors.
4. Normal one joint and two joint hip flexors.

Teaching Points

Correct Answer: 2

The posterior thigh does not touch the table, and the knee can be flexed as many degrees beyond 80 degrees as the hip is flexed. The Thomas test is utilized to test for hip flexor length and to distinguish between one joint and two joint hip flexor tightness. With low back and sacrum flat on the table, a normal one joint hip flexor length would be with thigh flat on the table. Normal two joint hip flexor length would be 80 degrees of knee flexion.

Incorrect Choices:

The other choices do not correctly interpret the test results.

Type of Reasoning: Analytical

For this question, one must analyze the information presented in the picture and make a determination of the likely outcome of the test conducted. This necessitates analytical reasoning skill, which is often used when analyzing information presented in pictures. For this situation, the therapist should interpret shortness of one joint hip flexor with normal two joint hip flexors. If answered incorrectly, review the Thomas test.

A96

Musculoskeletal System | Interventions

A therapist is instructing the family of a 9-year-old boy with Duchenne's muscular dystrophy (MD). What should be the main focus of the plan of care for maintaining function in the lower extremities?

Choices:

1. Strengthening the knee extensors and plantar flexors.
2. Strengthening the plantar flexors and stretching the hip extensors.
3. Stretching the hip flexors and plantar flexors.
4. Strengthening the hip flexors and knee extensors.

Teaching Points

Correct Answer: 3

Duchenne's MD is a rapidly progressive disorder characterized by muscle wasting and atrophy. Contractures of the hips, knees, plantar flexors, and iliotibial band are common. Scoliosis occurs at around age 11 or 12. The main focus is preventing contractures, maintaining activities of daily living (ADL), energy conservation, family education, and positioning.

Incorrect Choices:

Strenuous exercise and strengthening may cause breakdown of muscle fibers. Low repetition active range of motion (AROM) is safe but not strengthening.

Type of Reasoning: Inductive

This question requires the test taker to draw from knowledge of Duchenne's MD in order to determine a best course of action. This necessitates clinical judgment, which is an inductive reasoning skill. For this scenario, the therapist should focus on stretching the hip flexors and plantar flexors. Review Duchenne's MD if answered incorrectly.

A97

Nonsystem | Equipment, Devices, Biophysical Agents

A soccer player with a Q angle in excess of 30 degrees exhibits abnormal patellofemoral tracking. While playing soccer, what is the **MOST** often used device to address this problem?

Choices:

1. Patellar stabilizing brace with a lateral buttress.
2. Patellar stabilizing brace with a medial buttress.
3. Neoprene sleeve with a patellar cutout.
4. Derotation brace.

Teaching Points

Correct Answer: 1

An increased valgus deformity can result in a greater lateral displacement force on the patella, which can disrupt patella tracking and could even lead to subluxation. The theory behind the lateral buttress brace is that it provides support to help prevent subluxation and tries to maintain the normal patella tracking.

Incorrect Choices:

A medial buttress would be on the wrong side. A neoprene sleeve provides some increased warmth and could be beneficial to a painful arthritic knee but would be of no benefit in patella alignment problems. A derotation brace is designed for rotary instabilities secondary to cruciate injuries.

Type of Reasoning: Inferential

For this question, the test taker must utilize knowledge of abnormal patellofemoral tracking and devices used in order to arrive at a correct conclusion. One must infer what is most often used for the problem, which necessitates inferential reasoning skill. In this case, a patellar stabilizing brace with a lateral buttress is most often used. Review devices used in abnormal patellofemoral tracking if answered incorrectly.

A98 

Nonsystem | Equipment, Devices, Biophysical Agents

A patient with diabetes mellitus has had a stage III decubitus ulcer over the right ischial tuberosity for the past 5 months. The ulcer is infected with *Staphylococcus aureus*, and necrotic tissue covers much of the wound. What therapeutic modality is **CONTRAINDICATED** in this situation?

Choices:

1. Low-voltage, constant microamperage direct current.
2. High-voltage monophasic pulsed current.
3. Alternating/biphasic current.
4. Moist hot packs.

Teaching Points

Correct Answer: 4

Both a moist environment and heat can accelerate bacterial growth. Hot packs would be contraindicated in this case.

Incorrect Choices:

None of the other options are contraindicated for the treatment of this wound. They might aid in wound healing.

Type of Reasoning: Deductive

This question requires one to recall knowledge of wound treatment contraindications in order to arrive at a sound conclusion. This necessitates the recall of facts, which is a deductive reasoning skill. For this situation, moist hot packs are contraindicated. Review wound treatment guidelines and contraindications if answered incorrectly.

A99 

Neuromuscular and Nervous System | Interventions

A therapist is treating a child with spastic diplegia. What intervention can be used to promote relaxation?

Choices:

1. Rhythmic stabilization.
2. Slow rocking on a therapy ball.
3. Spinning in a hammock.
4. Rolling and spinning on a scooter board.

Teaching Points

Correct Answer: 2

Relaxation can be achieved using slow rocking (slow vestibular stimulation).

Incorrect Choices:

Rhythmic stabilization is a proprioceptive neuromuscular facilitation (PNF) technique used to improve postural stability. Spinning and rolling on a scooter board are interventions used to increase mobility based on fast vestibular stimulation.

Type of Reasoning: Deductive

For this question, the test taker must recall intervention approaches that promote relaxation for spastic musculature in order to arrive at a correct conclusion. This requires the recall of factual information, which is a deductive reasoning skill. For this case, slow rocking is an intervention approach that promotes relaxation. Review intervention approaches for relaxation of spastic muscles if answered incorrectly.

A100 

Musculoskeletal System | Interventions

Capsular tightness has limited a patient's ability to fully extend the left knee. What joint mobilization technique should be used to restore joint motion?

Choices:

1. Anterior glide and external rotation of the tibia.
2. Anterior glide and internal rotation of the tibia.
3. Posterior glide and external rotation of the tibia.
4. Posterior glide and internal rotation of the tibia.

Teaching Points

Correct Answer: 1

The concave-convex rule dictates roll and slide in the same direction. Joint mobilization to increase knee extension should emphasize anterior tibial glide. Anatomically, the medial femoral condyle is longer (has more articular surface) than the lateral; therefore, for the tibia to maintain maximum contact during the last 30 degrees (most evident during the last 5 degrees) of knee extension, external rotation of the tibia on the femur occurs in an open-chain movement. This happens because the shorter lateral tibial plateau/condyle pair completes its rolling and sliding motion before the longer medial articular surface does. The continued anterior motion of the medial tibial condyle results in external rotation of the tibia on the femur.

Incorrect Choices:

The other choices may assist in knee flexion or not be optimal for knee extension (e.g., anterior glide and internal tibial rotation).

Type of Reasoning: Inductive

For this question, one must draw from knowledge of joint mobilization guidelines in order to determine the best therapeutic approach to address capsular tightness of the knee into extension. This necessitates clinical judgment, which is an inductive reasoning skill. For this case, the therapist should perform anterior glide and external rotation of the tibia to address the tightness. Review joint mobilization techniques, especially of the knee, if answered incorrectly.

A101 

Nonsystem | Safety, Professional Roles, Research

A group of 37 adolescent girls ages 12 and 13 were recruited into a study on developmental changes in bone density. Bone mineral density (BMD) was measured on admission into the study and every 4 months thereafter for a period of 3 years. The investigators concluded that BMD peaked at the age of 14, with a standard deviation of 7 months. What is the category of this research?

Choices:

1. Randomized controlled trial.
2. Case control study.
3. Between-subject study.
4. Prospective cohort study.

Teaching Points

Correct Answer: 4

This is a prospective (forward-in-time) study. A group of participants (cohort) with a similar condition is followed for a defined period of time. This is a cohort study.

Incorrect Choices:

A randomized controlled trial (RCT) involves random assignment to either an experimental or a control group for the purposes of studying an intervention. It represents the highest level of scientific rigor. A case control study involves a retrospective (backward-in-time) study of a group of individuals with a similar condition compared with a group that does not have the condition. In a between-subject design, comparisons are made between groups of subjects.

Type of Reasoning: Deductive

For this question, one must recall research guidelines in order to arrive at a correct conclusion. This necessitates the recall of facts, which is a deductive reasoning skill. For this case, the category of research is a prospective cohort study. Review types of research studies if answered incorrectly.

A102 

Musculoskeletal System | Examination

The results of isokinetic dynamometry at 180 degrees per second indicate that a male patient can generate a peak torque of 120 ft lbs with the right quadriceps muscle and only 80 ft lbs with the right hamstring musculature. What situation is being described?

Choices:

1. Quadriceps torque generation is excessive.
2. Hamstring torque generation is insufficient.
3. Both quadriceps and hamstring torque generation is excessive.
4. Torque generation is proportionally correct.

Teaching Points

Correct Answer: 4

Hamstring/quadriceps torque generation at various speeds in 15- to 45-year-old males:

- 65% at 60 degrees/sec
- 69% at 180 degrees/sec
- 71% at 300 degrees/sec

Incorrect Choices:

Quadriceps torque generation is not used to describe function of the muscle relative to the hamstrings. Hamstring torque generation is not insufficient. At 180 degrees per second the hamstrings were 67% of the quadriceps (80/120), and 69% is considered normal. This patient exhibits 97% of the expected hamstring-to-quadriceps ratio and is therefore considered proportionally correct.

Type of Reasoning: Analytical

One must analyze the information presented about isokinetic dynamometry and draw upon knowledge of the subject in order to arrive at a sound conclusion. This necessitates the assessment of the significance of information, which is an analytical reasoning skill. For this situation, torque generation is proportionally correct. Review isokinetic dynamometry information if answered incorrectly.

A103 

Nonsystem | Equipment, Devices, Biophysical Agents

When using continuous ultrasound in treating the hip of an obese patient, the **GREATEST** benefit might occur if the ultrasound frequency and dosage are set at which parameters?

Choices:

1. 1 MHz and 1.5 watts/cm^2.
2. 1 MHz and 0.5 watts/cm^2.
3. 3 MHz and 1.5 watts/cm^2.
4. 3 MHz and 0.5 watts/cm^2.

Teaching Points

Correct Answer: 1

1 MHz frequency is recommended for target tissue deeper than 2 cm, and 1.5 watts/cm^2 would increase the rate of heating, allowing it to be treated in a reasonable time frame.

Incorrect Choices:

The frequency 3 MHz does not penetrate past 2 cm and would not be effective at the hip. A rate of heating of 0.5 watts/cm^2 intensity is very slow and would result in a prolonged treatment time.

Type of Reasoning: Inductive

For this question, one must utilize knowledge of ultrasound guidelines in order to determine which frequency and rate of heating would provide the greatest benefit. This requires clinical judgment, which is an inductive reasoning skill. For this scenario, 1 MHz and 1.5 watts/cm^2 would provide the greatest benefit. Review ultrasound guidelines, especially for the hip, if answered incorrectly.

A104 

Integumentary System | Interventions

A patient presents with a stage III pressure ulcer with a moist, necrotic wound. A hydrocolloidal dressing (DuoDERM) is being used. During the dressing change, the therapist detects a strong odor, and the wound drainage has a yellow color. What is the therapist's **BEST** course of action?

Choices:

1. Reapply a new gauze dressing instead of hydrocolloid and report the findings to the physician.
2. Speak to the nurse about changing to a hydrogel dressing.
3. Leave the dressing off the wound and report the findings immediately to the physician.
4. Reapply a new DuoDERM dressing and record the findings in the chart.

Teaching Points

Correct Answer: 4

Hydrocolloidal dressings are typically changed every 3 to 5 days or when drainage leaks out. An odor and yellowish color is to be expected as the dressing material melts.

Incorrect Choices:

The decision about what type of dressing to apply to a wound is the physician's in collaboration with the wound care team. This is not an emergency situation.

Type of Reasoning: Evaluative

For this question, the test taker must weigh the potential courses of action and determine which one will have the most beneficial outcome. This necessitates evaluative reasoning skill, where the value of information is weighed to make decisions on next steps. For this situation, the therapist should reapply a new DuoDERM dressing and record the findings in the chart. Review wound care guidelines, especially the use of hydrocolloidal dressings, if answered incorrectly.

A105 

Musculoskeletal System | Examination

During examination of a patient with degenerative osteoarthritic changes in the carpometacarpal (CMC) joint of the right thumb, the physical therapist notes a 20-degree loss of thumb palmar abduction. What translatory joint play motion (based on the traditional concave/convex rules of motion) is associated with thumb palmar abduction and should be examined?

Choices:

1. Dorsal translation of the metacarpal on the trapezium.
2. Palmar translation of the metacarpal on the trapezium.
3. Ulnar translation of the metacarpal on the trapezium.
4. Radial translation of the metacarpal on the trapezium.

Teaching Points

Correct Answer: 1

The carpometacarpal joint of the thumb is considered a saddle joint in which the articular surface geometry is generally concave in one plane and convex in a plane perpendicular to the other. The proximal joint surface of the first metacarpal is generally convex in the palmar to dorsal direction and concave in the medial to lateral direction. The articular surface of the base of the first metacarpal typically presents as the convex member of this joint when movement occurs in palmar abduction. Thumb palmar abduction thus involves a convex metacarpal surface moving on the concave surface of the trapezium. Following the traditional concave/convex rules of motion, one would expect a combination of palmar roll and dorsal translatory motion of the metacarpal on the trapezium during palmar abduction. In this case, a therapist would be sure to evaluate dorsal glide of the metacarpal on the trapezium.

Incorrect Choices:

The other examples of joint play motion are not congruent with palmar abduction of the thumb.

Type of Reasoning: Deductive

For this question, one must recall the translatory joint play motion of the CMC joint of the thumb in order to arrive at a correct conclusion. This necessitates the recall of facts, which is a deductive reasoning skill. For this case, the expected motion is dorsal translation of the metacarpal on the trapezium. Review joint play of the CMC joint of the thumb if answered incorrectly.

Neuromuscular and Nervous System | Evaluation, Diagnosis

Following a cerebrovascular accident involving the right hemisphere, a male patient is exhibiting unilateral neglect. What might he do as a result?

Choices:
1. Eat food only from the left side of a plate.
2. Bump his wheelchair into things on the right side.
3. Ignore or deny the existence of the right upper extremity.
4. Shave only on the right side of the face.

Teaching Points

Correct Answer: 4

A patient with a right hemisphere lesion (left hemiplegia) will tend to ignore items or body parts on the left side while favoring items or body parts on the right side.

Incorrect Choices:

All other choices do not match the above description and favor items or body parts on the left side.

Type of Reasoning: Inferential

One must infer, or determine what is likely to be true of a situation, in order to reach a sound conclusion. This necessitates inferential reasoning skill, where behavior in patients is predicted. In this case, one might expect the patient to shave only on the right side of the face. Review information on unilateral neglect if answered incorrectly.

A107 

Musculoskeletal System | Evaluation, Diagnosis

Damage as a result of Salter-Harris type IV supracondylar humeral epiphyseal fracture in a young athlete will **MOST LIKELY** result in what consequence?

Choices:
1. Refracture at a future time.
2. Nonunion.
3. Arrested growth.
4. Severing of the radial nerve.

Teaching Points

Correct Answer: 3

Supracondylar fractures are the most common pediatric elbow fracture, occurring most commonly between 3 and 10 years of age. Extension fractures account for about 95% of supracondylar fractures. The mechanism of injury is a fall on an outstretched hand with elbow hyperextended. Type I is a nondisplaced fracture across the growth plate. Type II supracondylar fractures are angulated and displaced fractures across the growth plate and continuing up through the shaft of the bone. Type III fractures may be displaced in three directions: posteromedial (the most common pattern), posterolateral, or anterolateral. A type III fracture also starts through the growth plate but turns and exits through the end of the bone and into the adjacent joint.

Type IV is a fracture through all three elements of the bone: the growth plate, metaphysis, and epiphysis (10% incidence). Type IV growth plate fractures start above the growth plate, cross the growth plate, and exit through the joint cartilage. These injuries can affect the joint cartilage and may impair normal growth. Complete growth retardation or partial growth arrest may result in progressive limb-length discrepancies. Complete growth arrest is uncommon and depends on when the injury to the physis occurs in relation to the remaining skeletal growth potential. The younger the patient, the greater is the potential for problems associated with growth. Premature partial growth arrest is far more common and can appear as peripheral or central closures.

Incorrect Choices:

Nonunion of pediatric fractures is a rare complication. However, in one study of nonunion fractures, 47% were about the elbow, with most of the nonunions at the lateral condyle. Refractures of the forearm have an incidence of about 5%. Overall, the incidence of supracondylar-associated neurovascular injury is 12% and increases with displacement to between 19% and 49%. The most commonly injured nerve is arguably the median (28%–60%), followed closely by the radial (26%–61%), and then the ulnar (11%–15%) nerves. Excessive swelling and ecchymosis are a significant risk factor for compartment syndrome, and a thorough neurovascular exam should be performed and should focus on the brachial artery as well as the median and radial nerves.

Type of Reasoning: Inferential

This question requires the test taker to determine the most likely consequence of a Salter-Harris type IV supracondylar humeral epiphyseal fracture. This requires knowledge of the Salter-Harris classification system in order to determine the most likely outcome. For this scenario, the most likely outcome is arrested growth. Review Salter-Harris fractures if answered incorrectly.

A108 

Cardiovascular/Pulmonary and Lymphatic Systems | Examination

What is the **BEST** way to monitor the intensity of exercise for a patient limited mostly by claudication?

Choices:

1. Assessing ankle-brachial index (ABI) during exercise.
2. Maintaining heart rate (HR) between 60% and 70% of age-predicted HR_{max} during exercise.
3. Sustaining pain levels of at least 2 out of 4 on the claudication scale during exercise.
4. Upholding rate of perceived exertion (RPE) levels of 11 to 13 out of 20 during exercise.

Teaching Points

Correct Answer: 3

It has been established that in order to generate collateral circulation in patients with ischemia (i.e., claudication), patients need to exercise with at least moderate claudication pain. This level of blood and oxygen deprivation over time initiates the generation of collateral circulation. This correlates to 2 out of 4 on the claudication scale.

Incorrect Choices:

The ABI is not practical to assess during exercise because the patient cannot be moving during this test. While the RPE and HR_{max} are at moderate levels, this may not be at an intensity that elicits claudication symptoms.

Type of Reasoning: Inductive

For this question, one must utilize clinical judgment in order to determine the best way to monitor the intensity of exercise for a patient with claudication. This requires knowledge of the effects of exercise on claudication, which is an inductive reasoning skill. For this case, the best way to monitor exercise is to sustain pain levels of at least 2 out of 4 on the claudication scale during exercise. Review information on claudication and exercise if answered incorrectly.

A109 

Musculoskeletal System | Evaluation, Diagnosis

A weightlifter with hypertrophy of the scalene muscles complains of pain and paresthesia in the right upper extremity when lifting weight overhead. What is the **MOST LIKELY** cause?

Choices:

1. Thoracic outlet syndrome.
2. Vertebral artery obstruction.
3. Cervical radiculopathy.
4. Complex regional pain syndrome type 1.

Teaching Points

Correct Answer: 1

Hypertrophied scalene muscles can result in thoracic outlet syndrome due to their close anatomical relationship to the neurovascular structures. The neurovascular bundle passes between the anterior and middle scalene muscles and could be under pressure from hypertrophied scalenes. The anterior and middle scalenes attach to the first rib, and tightness in these muscles could result in elevation of the first rib, thereby compressing the neurovascular bundle. Neurogenic (neurological) thoracic outlet syndrome is characterized by compression of the brachial plexus. In the majority of thoracic outlet syndrome cases, the symptoms are neurogenic. Signs and symptoms of neurological thoracic outlet syndrome often include wasting in the thenar area, numbness or tingling in the fingers, pain in the shoulder and neck, ache in the arm or hand, and weakening grip.

Incorrect Choices:

The clinical presentation of vertebral artery occlusion varies with the area of ischemia and cause of occlusion. Vertigo, dizziness, nausea, vomiting, and head or neck pain are the most common initial symptoms reported. Other common signs and symptoms include weakness, hemiparesis, ataxia, diplopia, pupillary abnormalities, speech difficulties, and altered mental status.

Cervical radiculopathy pain travels down the arm in the area of the involved nerve. Pain is usually described as sharp. There can also be a "pins and needles" sensation or even complete numbness. In addition, there may be a feeling of weakness with certain activities. Symptoms can be worsened with certain movements, like extending or straining the neck or turning the head.

Complex regional pain syndrome (CRPS) is a chronic pain condition that is believed to be the result of dysfunction in the central or peripheral nervous systems. Typical features include dramatic changes in the color and temperature of the skin over the affected limb or body part, accompanied by intense burning pain, skin sensitivity, sweating, and swelling. The key symptom of CRPS is continuous, intense pain out of proportion to the severity of the injury (if an injury has occurred), which gets worse rather than better over time. None of these are normally associated with hypertrophy of the scalene muscles.

Type of Reasoning: Analytical

This question provides a group of symptoms and the test taker must determine the most likely cause. Questions that require one to determine a diagnosis based on a description of symptoms often necessitate analytical reasoning skill. For this situation, the symptoms are indicative of thoracic outlet syndrome. Review thoracic outlet syndrome if answered incorrectly.

A110

Cardiovascular/Pulmonary and Lymphatic Systems | Evaluation, Diagnosis

A patient is immersed up to the neck in a therapeutic pool. While exercising this patient, the therapist should take into consideration the physiological effects of immersion. Which significant result might occur?

Choices:

1. Increased forced vital capacity.
2. Increased expiratory reserve volume.
3. Increased work of breathing.
4. Decreased pulmonary blood flow.

Teaching Points

Correct Answer: 3

Full chest immersion in a pool can result in increased work of breathing as a result of increased hydrostatic pressure.

Incorrect Choices:

The other choices are not consistent with the physiological effects resulting from full chest immersion in a pool.

Type of Reasoning: Inferential

This question requires one to determine what is most likely to be true for a patient who is immersed up to the neck in a therapeutic pool. Questions that require one to make a determination of what is true of a situation often necessitate inferential reasoning skill. For this scenario, full chest immersion would likely result in increased work of breathing. Review effects of immersion if answered incorrectly.

A111

Neuromuscular and Nervous System | Interventions

What intervention **BEST** illustrates selective stretching when working with a patient with a spinal cord injury (C6 complete)?

Choices:

1. Long finger flexors are fully ranged into extension with wrist extension.
2. Hamstrings are fully ranged to 110 degrees in supine.
3. Low back extensors are fully ranged in longsitting.
4. Hamstrings are fully ranged in longsitting.

Teaching Points

Correct Answer: 2

Hamstrings need to be fully ranged to 110 degrees in the supine position. This allows for function in the longsitting position (e.g., dressing, leg management during transfers).

Incorrect Choices:

Ranging the hamstrings or low back extensors in long sitting will result in overstretched low back extensors (needed for stability in sitting). The long finger flexors are ranged into full extension with wrist flexion (not wrist extension). This allows the hand to be used functionally for tenodesis grasp.

Type of Reasoning: Inductive

One must utilize knowledge of spinal cord injury and selective stretching techniques in order to arrive at a correct conclusion. This necessitates clinical judgment, which is an inductive reasoning skill. In this case, the intervention that best demonstrates this is when the hamstrings are fully ranged to 110 degrees in supine. Review stretching techniques for spinal cord injury if answered incorrectly.

A112 

Musculoskeletal System I Interventions

Strengthening of the lateral pterygoid, anterior head of the digastric muscle, and suprahyoid muscles would be the **MOST BENEFICIAL** intervention to improve which of the following?

Choices:

1. Mouth closing.
2. Mouth opening.
3. Mouth protrusion.
4. Mouth retrusion.

Teaching Points

Correct Answer: 2

The muscles involved in opening include the lateral pterygoid, anterior head of the digastric muscle, and suprahyoid muscles.

Incorrect Choices:

The muscles that assist with mouth closing are the masseter, temporalis, medial pterygoid, and lateral pterygoid. The muscles that assist with protrusion are the temporalis, medial pterygoid, and lateral pterygoid. The muscles that assist with retrusion are the temporalis and suprahyoid muscles.

Type of Reasoning: Inductive

For this question, one must utilize knowledge of musculoskeletal anatomy and muscle strengthening in order to determine the most beneficial intervention approach. This is an inductive reasoning skill. In this case, the approach improves mouth opening. If answered incorrectly, review lateral pterygoid and suprahyoid muscles.

A113 

Neuromuscular and Nervous System | Evaluation, Diagnosis

A physical therapist examined the deep tendon reflexes of a patient recently diagnosed with amyotrophic lateral sclerosis (ALS). The results are 2+ left and 4+ right. What is the correct interpretation of these findings regarding the reflexes?

Choices:
1. Abnormal on the left and normal on the right.
2. Normal on the left and brisker, possibly abnormal on the right.
3. Depressed, low normal on the left and normal on the right.
4. Normal on the left and abnormal on the right.

Teaching Points

Correct Answer: 4
Reflexes are average, normal (2+) on the left and very brisk, hyperactive, and abnormal (4+) on the right.

Incorrect Choices:
With a grade of 3+, reflexes are increased, brisker than average, possibly but not necessarily abnormal. With a grade of 1+, reflexes are present but depressed, low normal.

Type of Reasoning: Deductive
One must recall the reflex grades in order to arrive at a correct conclusion for this question. This requires the recall of facts and guidelines, which is a deductive reasoning skill. For this case, the therapist should interpret the findings as normal on the left and abnormal on the right. If answered incorrectly, review the reflex grading scale.

A114 

Nonsystem | Safety, Professional Responsibilities, Research

What is the **BEST** evidence to determine orthotic intervention to prevent inversion ankle sprains?

Choices:
1. Meta-analyses of cohort studies.
2. Systematic reviews of randomized controlled trials.
3. Meta-analyses of multiple case studies.
4. Randomized double-blind controlled trials.

Teaching Points

Correct Answer: 2
Systematic review including meta-analysis of randomized controlled trials (RCTs) provides the best research evidence of effectiveness of an intervention.

Incorrect Choices:
Meta-analysis is not applied to cohort studies or multiple case studies. While a RCT can provide strong evidence of the effectiveness of an intervention, evidence derived from a meta-analysis that combines multiple RCTs is stronger.

Type of Reasoning: Deductive

In order to arrive at a sound conclusion, the test taker must recall research designs, specifically which designs provide the strongest research evidence. This necessitates the recall of facts, which is a deductive reasoning skill. For this scenario, systematic reviews of randomized controlled trials provide the best evidence. Review research designs if answered incorrectly.

A115 

Musculoskeletal System | Interventions

A patient presents with insidious onset of low back pain that started 10 days ago. Examination reveals an Oswestry Disability Index score of 40%, a Fear Avoidance Belief Questionnaire for Physical Activity score of 16, hypomobility at L4–5 with posteroanterior (PA) glide, and pain that radiates into the right buttock. Lumbar active range of motion (AROM) is painful at 50% of expected range in all directions. Hip passive range of motion (PROM) is within normal limits. Abdominal strength is fair. Based on this data, what is the **BEST** intervention for this patient?

Choices:

1. Abdominal stabilization.
2. Manipulation.
3. Positional distraction.
4. Transcutaneous electrical nerve stimulation (TENS) and ice.

Teaching Points

Correct Answer: 2

If a patient presents with four out of five criteria listed in the examination findings, the patient has a 95% chance of benefiting from manipulation using the lumbopelvic regional thrust manipulation technique.

Incorrect Choices:

Abdominal stabilization is a good secondary intervention. Since the patient does not fit the clinical practice rules for abdominal stabilization, it should not be the first choice for intervention. Positional distraction would be appropriate for radicular pain; however, that is not the case here.

Type of Reasoning: Inductive

One must utilize clinical judgment in order to determine the best intervention approach for this patient. This requires one to have knowledge of the various intervention approaches and examination results, which necessitates inductive reasoning skill. For this situation, the best intervention approach is manipulation. Review intervention approaches for low back pain if answered incorrectly.

A116 

Gastrointestinal System | Evaluation, Diagnosis

Severe epigastric and abdominal pain that radiates to the middle back and may worsen when lying supine is **MOST** characteristic of which condition?

Choices:

1. Small intestine obstruction.
2. Irritable bowel syndrome.
3. Appendicitis.
4. Acute pancreatitis.

Teaching Points

Correct Answer: 4

Pancreatitis occurs midline or to the left of the epigastrium, just below the xiphoid process. Pain is referred to the middle or lower back and rarely to the upper back.

Incorrect Choices:

Small intestine pain is midabdominal, about the level of the umbilicus; pain is referred to the back if intense. Large intestine and colon pain (irritable bowel syndrome) is often poorly localized to the midabdominal area. Pain can be referred to the sacrum. Appendiceal pain is located in the right lower quadrant. Pain can be referred to the periumbilical area or right hip.

Type of Reasoning: Analytical

For this question, the test taker must analyze the symptoms presented in order to determine the most likely diagnosis. This necessitates analytical reasoning skill and is often used to determine diagnoses based on a group of symptoms. In this case, the symptoms are consistent with acute pancreatitis. Review symptoms of pancreatitis if answered incorrectly.

A117 

Neuromuscular and Nervous System | Examination

A physical therapist is working with a patient recovering from traumatic brain injury (Rancho Los Amigos Levels of Cognitive Functioning Scale level VII). The best test to determine if this patient demonstrates progression to open skills is to have the patient walk in which environment?

Choices:

1. In the hallway.
2. Across the busy hospital lobby.
3. In the patient's room.
4. In the patient's home.

Teaching Points

Correct Answer: 2

Open skills are motor skills (e.g., walking) that can be performed in a variable, changing environment (a busy hospital lobby).

Incorrect Choices:

Closed skills are motor skills that can only be performed in a constant, nonchanging environment (quiet hallway, patient's room, patient's home).

Type of Reasoning: Deductive

For this question, one must recall the guidelines for open skills in order to arrive at a correct conclusion. This requires the recall of facts, which is a deductive reasoning skill. For this situation, the best test for open skills is to have the patient walk across the busy hospital lobby. If answered incorrectly, review information on open skills.

A118

Neuromuscular and Nervous System | Examination

A patient with a 7-year history of Parkinson's disease is hospitalized. The patient is ambulatory but requires close supervision to prevent falls. What should be the focus of the physical therapist's plan of care?

Choices:

1. Manual balance perturbation training.
2. Transfer and wheelchair training.
3. Caregiver training for contact guarding during level walking and stairs.
4. Locomotor training using a rolling walker.

Teaching Points

Correct Answer: 3
Caregiver training with safety instruction in contact guarding during level walking and stairs is the best choice to keep this patient functional in the home environment.

Incorrect Choices:
Manual balance perturbation training will likely result in a rigid response, decreasing use of normal synergistic movements. This patient should be kept safe and ambulatory for as long as possible and not be relegated to a wheelchair. A rolling walker is contraindicated for patients with a forward, flexed posture (typical in patients with Parkinson's disease).

Type of Reasoning: Inductive
This question requires clinical judgment in order to determine a best course of action. Utilizing knowledge of Parkinson's disease and the current level of function, inductive reasoning skills are utilized to determine the focus for the plan of care. In this case, the focus should be on caregiver training for contact guarding during level walking and stairs. Review Parkinson's disease if answered incorrectly.

A119

Integumentary System | Examination

A patient is referred to physical therapy with a diagnosis of congestive heart failure. During the initial session, the physical therapist examines the skin for suspected changes. What appearance can be expected?

Choices:

1. Pale, washed-out color.
2. Yellowish discoloration.
3. Slightly bluish, slate-colored discoloration.
4. Cherry-red discoloration.

Teaching Points

Correct Answer: 3
Slightly bluish, grayish, slate-colored discoloration of the skin along with clubbing of the nails is characteristic of chronic hypoxia.

Incorrect Choices:
Pallor (lack of skin color, paleness) is indicative of anemia, internal hemorrhage, or lack of sunlight exposure. Yellowish discoloration of the skin is indicative of jaundice (liver disease). Cherry-red discoloration of the skin is indicative of carbon monoxide poisoning.

Type of Reasoning: Inferential

This question requires one to infer what is likely to be true of a situation in order to reach a sound conclusion. This necessitates inferential reasoning skill. For this situation, the patient with congestive heart failure is expected to show slightly bluish, slate-colored discoloration. Review congestive heart failure information if answered incorrectly.

A120 

Integumentary System | Interventions

A patient with a 10-year history of discoid lupus erythematosus presents with multiple discoid skin lesions that are raised and red and contain scaling plaques with central atrophy on the lower extremities. Topical corticosteroid creams are being used. What should be the focus of the therapist's initial plan of care?

Choices:

1. Range of motion (ROM) exercises and prevention of deformity.
2. Lightweight splints to provide joint protection.
3. Aerobic training using a treadmill.
4. Resistive training using weights at 60% to 80%, one repetition maximum.

Teaching Points

Correct Answer: 1

Range of motion (ROM) exercises and prevention of deformity are important elements of the plan of care.

Incorrect Choices:

Lightweight splints for joint protection can contribute to contracture development if worn too long. Furthermore, there are no reports of arthralgia in this case. Regular exercise is important but should not be aggressive (resistive training). Also, long-term use of corticosteroids puts this patient at risk for osteoporosis. Aerobic (treadmill) training might be indicated but is not an initial priority. Splints to provide joint protection are also not an initial priority.

Type of Reasoning: Inductive

This question requires one to determine a best course of action based on knowledge of discoid lupus erythematosus. This necessitates clinical judgment, which is an inductive reasoning skill. For this scenario, range of motion (ROM) exercises and prevention of deformity should be the initial focus. If answered incorrectly, review information on discoid lupus erythematosus.

A121 

Genitourinary System | Evaluation, Diagnosis

On the third day following a cesarean delivery, what should a physical therapist's interventions include?

Choices:

1. Gentle partial sit-ups and head lifts.
2. Breathing, coughing, and pelvic floor exercises.
3. Low-intensity aerobic conditioning.
4. Pelvic tilts on all fours.

Teaching Points

Correct Answer: 2

Initial postpartum interventions (days 1 to 3) should include breathing, coughing, and pelvic floor exercises.

Incorrect Choices:

All other choices can be part of the postpartum exercise program during later recovery.

Type of Reasoning: Inductive

This question requires one to utilize knowledge of postpartum intervention approaches in order to arrive at a correct conclusion. This necessitates clinical judgment, which is an inductive reasoning skill. For this case, the therapist should include breathing, coughing, and pelvic floor exercises. Review postpartum intervention approaches if answered incorrectly.

A122 

Cardiovascular/Pulmonary and Lymphatic Systems I Interventions

A patient with post–traumatic brain injury (Rancho Los Amigos Levels of Cognitive Functioning Scale level III) has evidence of retained secretions on auscultation and chest films. What is the **BEST** mode of airway clearance for this patient?

Choices:

1. Active cycle of breathing.
2. Autogenic drainage.
3. Use of the FLUTTER device.
4. Use of the Vest Airway Clearance System.

Teaching Points

Correct Answer: 4

The Vest Airway Clearance System provides high-frequency chest wall compression (HFCWC). It allows for control of inspiratory and expiratory flow rates. The device can be used in any position regardless of the patient's cognitive status.

Incorrect Choices:

The first two choices require a patient to consistently follow commands and potentially complete the activity alone, which would be difficult for a patient in this cognitive stage of recovery. Oscillatory positive expiratory pressure (PEP) using a FLUTTER device requires a patient to breathe through a mouthpiece with inspiration unimpeded and long exhalation against a back pressure, also impossible for this patient.

Type of Reasoning: Inductive

For this question, one must determine a best course of action for airway clearance, based on knowledge of effective airway clearance approaches. This necessitates inductive reasoning skill, where clinical judgment is paramount to arriving at a correct conclusion. For this situation, the best mode of airway clearance is the Vest Airway Clearance System. Review airway clearance approaches if answered incorrectly.

A123

Neuromuscular and Nervous System | Examination

A physical therapist is performing sensory tests on a patient diagnosed with C6 nerve root impingement. Where should the testing concentrate?

Choices:

1. Second, third, and fourth fingers, palmar surface.
2. Ulnar border of the hand (fifth finger).
3. Palmar surface of the thumb and distal, radial forearm.
4. Medial (ulnar) forearm.

Teaching Points

Correct Answer: 3

The C6 root supplies the palmar surface of the thumb and distal radial forearm.

Incorrect Choices:

The C7 root supplies the middle of the hand (second, third, and fourth fingers, palmar surface). The C8 root supplies the ulnar border of the hand (fifth finger). The T1 root supplies the medial surface of the forearm.

Type of Reasoning: Deductive

One must recall sensory testing guidelines in order to arrive at a correct conclusion for this question. This requires the recall of facts, which is a deductive reasoning skill. For this situation, the therapist should focus on the palmar surface of the thumb and distal, radial forearm. Review sensory testing for the upper extremity, especially the C6 distribution, if answered incorrectly.

A124

Neuromuscular and Nervous System | Evaluation, Diagnosis

A physical therapist is treating an elderly patient in the very early stages of amyotrophic lateral sclerosis (ALS). The patient lacks endurance to independently ambulate to and from the bathroom; however, she refuses to use a bedpan. This has caused added difficulties and stress for family members caring for her at home. What should the therapist do in this situation?

Choices:

1. Initiate ambulation endurance training with distance to and from the bathroom as the primary goal.
2. Recommend that the patient be transferred to a skilled nursing facility until she has sufficient endurance to get to and from the bathroom.
3. Recommend use of a commode chair for the bedroom.
4. Recommend use of a wheelchair and toilet grab rails.

Teaching Points

Correct Answer: 3

The bedside commode is the best choice to improve function.

Incorrect Choices:

ALS is a chronic progressive disorder. Ambulation endurance training will not likely produce significant gains. This patient is not a candidate for a nursing home or a wheelchair at this time. The patient should be kept functional in the home for as long as possible.

Type of Reasoning: Evaluative

For this question, one must determine a best course of action, weighing the options presented and determining which option will have the best therapeutic outcome. This requires evaluative reasoning skill. For this scenario, the therapist should recommend use of a commode chair for the bedroom. Review information on ALS and mobility modifications if answered incorrectly.

A125 

Musculoskeletal System | Evaluation, Diagnosis

If the sign indicated by the picture is positive, intervention should focus on strengthening which of the following?:

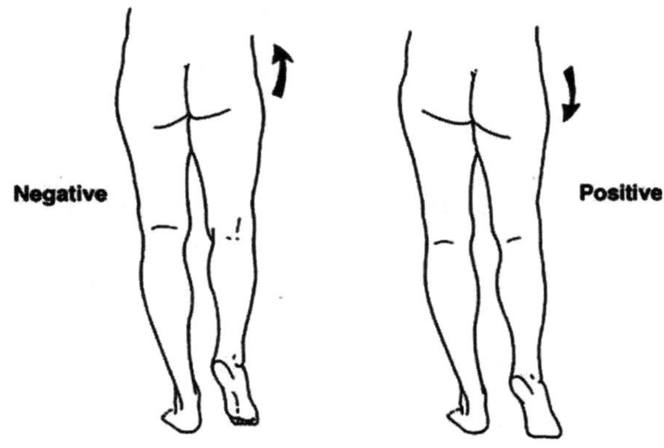

Choices:

1. Left gluteus medius.
2. Right gluteus medius.
3. Left quadratus lumborum.
4. Right quadratus lumborum.

Teaching Points

Correct Answer: 1

This picture depicts a positive Trendelenburg sign. Weakness of the left hip abductors (gluteus medius) results in dropping of the pelvis on the opposite side. A normal response would be no dropping of the pelvis during the standing test.

Incorrect Choices:

The right gluteus medius would not be active on the nonstance limb. The quadratus lumborum is the most ventral of the deep back muscles and forms part of the posterior wall of the abdomen. The action of the quadratus lumborum is lateral flexion of the vertebral column, with ipsilateral contraction, and extension of the lumbar vertebral column, with bilateral contraction.

Type of Reasoning: Analytical

One must analyze the information presented in the picture and draw from knowledge of the Trendelenburg sign in order to arrive at a correct conclusion. This necessitates analytical reasoning skill, which is often used to analyze information in pictures. For this case, the therapist should focus on strengthening the left gluteus medius. Review the Trendelenburg sign if answered incorrectly.

A126

Neuromuscular and Nervous System | Evaluation, Diagnosis

A physical therapist is working with a patient who exhibits fluent aphasia. What is a typical characteristic of this form of aphasia?

Choices:

1. Impaired auditory comprehension.
2. Slow, hesitant speech.
3. Good comprehension.
4. Impaired articulation.

Teaching Points

Correct Answer: 1

Fluent aphasia is characterized by impaired auditory comprehension and fluent speech that is of normal rate and melody (e.g., Wernicke's aphasia).

Incorrect Choices:

Nonfluent aphasia is characterized by speech that is slow, hesitant, awkward, interrupted, and produced with effort (e.g., Broca's aphasia). Patients tend to have good awareness of their deficit and comprehension. Impaired articulation characterizes the patient with dysarthria (a motor speech disorder).

Type of Reasoning: Deductive

One must recall the characteristics of fluent aphasia in order to arrive at a correct conclusion. This necessitates the recall of facts, which is a deductive reasoning skill. For this case, fluent aphasia is characterized by impaired auditory comprehension. Review types of aphasia, especially fluent aphasia, if answered incorrectly.

A127

Neuromuscular and Nervous System | Interventions

Three months following a left cerebrovascular stroke and a 4-week stay of inpatient rehabilitation, a patient is receiving home care physical therapy. The patient's movements in the right extremities show good recovery (out-of-synergy). Functional level is a 6 on the Functional Independence Measure (FIM). At this juncture, what should be the focus of motor learning strategies?

Choices:

1. Use of mental practice to improve performance.
2. Breaking down complex tasks into component parts.
3. Use of serial practice order of related skills.
4. Consistency of performance in variable environments.

Teaching Points

Correct Answer: 4

This patient demonstrates good functional recovery. Motor learning for the autonomous stage of motor learning should utilize variable practice in variable environments.

Incorrect Choices:

Mental practice and breaking down tasks into components can be helpful in the early cognitive stage of motor learning. Serial practice order is indicated for the middle, associative stage of motor learning.

Type of Reasoning: Inductive

One must utilize clinical judgment in order to determine a best intervention approach for a patient with CVA. Having knowledge of the stages of recovery, coupled with sound inductive reasoning skills, one should conclude that consistency of performance in variable environments is the best focus for intervention. Review motor learning strategies for CVA if answered incorrectly.

A128 

Musculoskeletal System | Examination

When performing neural tension testing to the lower limb, which ankle position when combined with a straight leg raise will **BEST** bias the peroneal (fibular) nerve?

Choices:

1. Dorsiflexion and eversion.
2. Dorsiflexion and inversion.
3. Plantarflexion and eversion.
4. Plantarflexion and inversion.

Teaching Points

Correct Answer: 4

Neural tension tests are used to determine neural mobility in relation to its surrounding tissue. It should be noted that patients will experience symptoms even when normal neural tissue is tensioned. It is paramount for the examiner to understand the expected normal responses with tension testing. A tension test can be considered positive if it reproduces the patient's symptoms, the test response can be altered by movement of distant body parts, and there are differences when comparing the left side to the right side.

Neural mobilization techniques including gliders/sliders and tensioners are interventions used to decrease adverse mechanical tension on nerves. A straight leg raise with plantarflexion and inversion is the optimal position for neural tissue provocation of the peroneal (fibular) nerve.

Incorrect Choices:

A straight leg raise with dorsiflexion and eversion and a straight leg raise with dorsiflexion and inversion will best bias the tibial and sural nerves, respectively. A straight leg raise with plantarflexion and eversion will not isolate a specific nerve.

Type of Reasoning: Inductive

One must utilize knowledge of neural tension testing in order to arrive at a sound conclusion. This necessitates clinical judgment to determine a best course of action, which is an inductive reasoning skill. For this situation, the best ankle position is plantarflexion and inversion. If answered incorrectly, review neural tension testing, especially for the peroneal (fibular) nerve.

A129

Neuromuscular and Nervous System | Examination

What is the most effective form of diagnostic imaging for patients with multiple sclerosis (MS) to help determine level of disease activity?

Choices:

1. Positron emission tomography (PET).
2. Magnetic resonance imaging (MRI).
3. Computed tomography (CT).
4. Transcranial sonography.

Teaching Points

Correct Answer: 2

MRI is highly sensitive for detecting MS plaques in the white matter of the brain and spinal cord. Lesions are seen as areas of increased signal intensity (bright spots). Contrast-enhanced scans are used for more long-term disease activity.

Incorrect Choices:

All other choices of diagnostic imaging techniques do not offer the same sensitivity and specificity for detecting plaques.

Type of Reasoning: Deductive

One must recall the most effective diagnostic tool for MS in order to arrive at a correct conclusion. This requires the recall of factual information, which is a deductive reasoning skill. For this scenario, the most effective test is magnetic resonance imaging (MRI). Review diagnostic imaging techniques, especially for MS, if answered incorrectly.

A130

System Interactions | Evaluation, Diagnosis

An elderly male patient is not able to participate in rehabilitation. He is lethargic, complains of nausea and painful urination, and seems to be feverish. The therapist should inform his primary care physician if which of the following is suspected?

Choices:

1. Bladder cancer.
2. Benign prostatic hyperplasia.
3. Urinary tract infection.
4. Renal calculi (kidney stones).

Teaching Points

Correct Answer: 3

These are signs and symptoms of urinary tract infection. Evidence of fever is especially significant. The physician should be informed.

Incorrect Choices:

The other choices do present with these same signs and symptoms. Fever is uncommon.

Type of Reasoning: Analytical

For this question, one must analyze the symptoms presented in order to determine the most likely diagnosis. Questions of this nature often necessitate analytical reasoning skill. For this situation, the symptoms are consistent with a urinary tract infection. Review signs and symptoms of urinary tract infection if answered incorrectly.

A131 

Musculoskeletal System | Evaluation, Diagnosis

The left phrenic nerve of a patient was accidentally severed during thoracic surgery. Which muscles should the physical therapist strengthen in order to provide substitute function?

Choices:

1. Tranversus abdominis.
2. Scalenes.
3. Internal obliques.
4. External obliques.

Teaching Points

Correct Answer: 2

The phrenic nerve arises from the neck (C3–5) and innervates the diaphragm. The diaphragm is responsible for 45% of the air that enters the lungs during quiet breathing. During quiet breathing, the predominant muscle of respiration is the diaphragm. As it contracts, pleural pressure drops, which lowers the alveolar pressure and draws in air down the pressure gradient from mouth to alveoli. Expiration during quiet breathing is predominantly a passive phenomenon; as the respiratory muscles relax, the elastic lung and chest wall return passively to their resting volume. With paralysis of the diaphragm, the accessory muscles of respiration should be strengthened. These include the scalenes and sternocleidomastoid.

Incorrect Choices:

During active expiration, the most important muscles are those of the abdominal wall (including the rectus abdominis, internal and external obliques, and transversus abdominis), which drive intra-abdominal pressure up when they contract and thus push up the diaphragm, raising pleural pressure, which raises alveolar pressure, which in turn drives air out. These muscles do not substitute for diaphragmatic function.

Type of Reasoning: Inductive

One must utilize knowledge of accessory muscles of respiration in order to arrive at a correct conclusion. Based on this knowledge, one can determine the best muscles to focus on for intervention, which is an inductive reasoning skill. In this case, the scalenes should be the focus. Review accessory muscles for respiration if answered incorrectly.

A132 

Neuromuscular and Nervous System | Interventions

A patient recovering from surgery to remove a cerebellar tumor presents with pronounced ataxia and problems with standing balance and postural stability. To help improve this situation, what would be **BEST** approach to incorporate in the intervention?

Choices:

1. Lower extremity splinting and light touch-down hand support.
2. Rhythmic stabilization during holding in kneeling.
3. Perturbed balance activities while standing on carpet.
4. Stabilizing reversals during holding in side-lying.

Teaching Points

Correct Answer: 2

Rhythmic stabilization is a proprioceptive neuromuscular facilitation (PNF) technique designed to improve stability. The high kneeling position is a good choice to begin with for the patient with pronounced ataxia. The posture is upright; while the center of mass (COM) is lowered, the degrees of freedom are reduced by kneeling (foot and ankle control not required) and the base of support (BOS) is increased over standing.

Incorrect Choices:

Splinting and touch-down support are compensatory interventions not likely to improve recovery. Perturbed balance activities are contraindicated for the patient with poor postural stability and pronounced ataxia. Stabilizing reversals in side-lying are also not indicated as the side-lying position does not require upright control.

Type of Reasoning: Inductive

One must utilize clinical judgment in order to determine the best intervention approach for this client. This necessitates inductive reasoning skill. For this scenario, the therapist should choose rhythmic stabilization during holding in kneeling to improve stability. Review intervention approaches for stability, especially rhythmic stabilization, if answered incorrectly.

Musculoskeletal System | Interventions

A patient with diabetes recently underwent a transtibial amputation. When instructing others in wrapping the residual limb to minimize edema and provide proper shape, it is important to stress which of the following?

Choices:

1. The greatest pressure should be provided distally.
2. The greatest pressure should be provided proximally.
3. The pressure should be evenly distributed.
4. An overlapping, circular, wrinkle-free pattern should be used.

Teaching Points

Correct Answer: 1

It is necessary to keep the residual limb wrapped to help shape it for possible prosthetic wear and to control swelling. It should be wrapped at all times except when bathing. Elastic wraps should be used initially. Wrap with the knee in as much extension as possible. Use two clean, rolled, bandages (4–6 inches wide). Use wraps that close with Velcro if possible or use tape to fasten rather than clips. Rewrap if the bandage is uncomfortable or if it slips. Make all turns diagonal, not circular. Circular turns could decrease circulation and produce discomfort. Make sure that the bandage is smooth, without wrinkles, and that all of the skin of the stump is covered and overlapped by ½ inch with each wrap. The pressure should be more at the bottom of the limb to help form the limb into a cylinder shape. To help prevent the wrap from slipping, continue the wrap above the knee one or two turns but finish the wrap on the residual limb.

Incorrect Choices:

Wrap with a pressure gradient from distal to proximal, not proximal to distal and not evenly distributed. Never use circular turns as this could decrease circulation and result in pain.

Type of Reasoning: Deductive

One must recall residual limb wrapping techniques in order to arrive at a sound conclusion. This necessitates the recall of facts and guidelines, which is a deductive reasoning skill. For this case, the therapist should stress that the greatest pressure should be provided distally when bandaging. Review residual limb wrapping techniques if answered incorrectly.

A134

Musculoskeletal System | Examination

A patient has worsening lateral knee pain that is exacerbated with running. Based on the history and symptoms, the therapist suspects iliotibial band friction syndrome. Which special test is performed that would help confirm this diagnosis?

Choices:

1. Stutter test.
2. Thessaly test.
3. Ely's test.
4. Noble compression test.

Teaching Points

Correct Answer: 4

The Noble compression test implicates iliotibial band friction syndrome. This test is performed with the patient supine. The examiner flexes the patient's knee and hip to 90 degrees and then applies pressure to the lateral femoral epicondyle with the thumb. While maintaining this position, the knee is passively extended. A positive test is reproduction of pain at approximately 30 degrees of knee flexion.

Incorrect Choices:

The Stutter test implicates a plica condition. This test is performed with the patient seated at the edge of the examination table with the knees flexed to 90 degrees. The examiner places a finger over the patella as the patient actively extends the knee. This motion should be a smooth movement. A positive test is noted when the patella jumps or stutters between 60 and 45 degrees of knee flexion.

The Thessaly test implicates a meniscal tear. The test is performed with the patient standing flat-footed on one leg with knee flexed to 20 degrees. The examiner supports the patient by holding the patient's outstretched hands. The patient rotates the knee and body, internally and externally, three times, keeping the knee flexed to 20 degrees. A positive test is reproduction of joint line pain.

Ely's test implicates decreased muscle length of the rectus femoris. This test is performed with the patient prone. The examiner passively flexes the patient's knee. A positive test is noted when the ipsilateral hip flexes during knee flexion.

Type of Reasoning: Deductive

One must recall the specific test to confirm iliotibial band friction syndrome in order to arrive at a correct conclusion. This requires the recall of factual information, which is a deductive reasoning skill. For this situation, the test to perform is the Noble compression test. If answered incorrectly, review the Noble compression test.

Musculoskeletal System | Examination

Six weeks following the conclusion of the football season, a therapist examines a player whose chief complaint is right thigh pain and decreased knee range of motion. Radiographic imaging of the area is shown in the picture. Intervention for this individual should be based on which diagnosis?

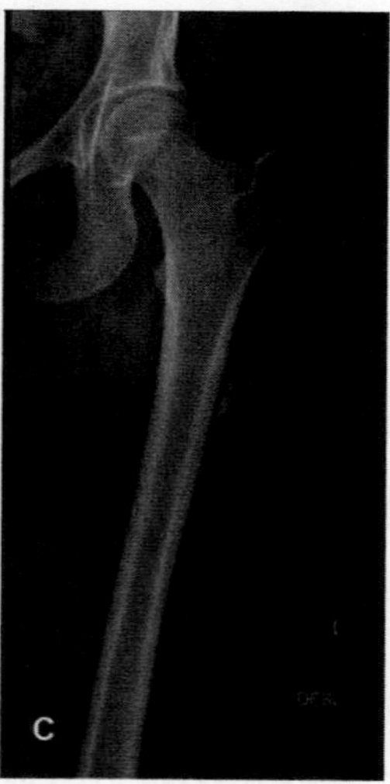

Choices:

1. Femoral stress fracture.
2. Neoplasm.
3. Quadriceps hematoma.
4. Myositis ossificans.

Teaching Points

Correct Answer: 4

Soft tissues that were injured in a traumatic event initially develop a hematoma and subsequently can develop into myositis ossificans. Myositis ossificans is a benign, ossifying soft-tissue lesion typically occurring within skeletal muscle. Patients are usually adolescents and young adults. Myositis ossificans is rare in children under 10 years of age. The most frequent symptoms and signs are pain and tenderness with a soft tissue mass. Approximately 80% of cases arise in the large muscles of the extremities.

The common concern when abnormal bone is seen on an x-ray is that there is a tumor within the soft tissues. Fortunately, myositis ossificans has some typical clues that usually make it easily differentiated from a tumor. Myositis ossificans appears on plain film at approximately 2 to 4 weeks after injury. The lesion begins to calcify at the periphery and works toward the center. At less than 3 weeks post trauma, bone scan demonstrates increased uptake in the area. Osteosarcoma calcifies at the center and continues to the periphery. Soft tissue ossification not attached to bone is common; x-rays show a round mass with a distinct peripheral margin of mature ossification and a radiolucent center of immature osteoid and primitive mesenchymal tissue; this peripheral maturation, the reverse of that seen in a malignant tumor, is characteristic of myositis ossificans.

Incorrect Choices:

A stress fracture is an overuse injury. Bone is constantly attempting to remodel and repair itself, especially when extraordinary stress is applied. When enough stress is placed on the bone, it causes an imbalance between osteoclastic and osteoblastic activity, and a stress fracture may appear. Insidious onset of pain and swelling over the affected region is the most important complaint, initially during the activity. With ongoing exposure, pain will last after the training, eventually causing the athlete to stop exercising. Finally pain is experienced at rest. Radiographs have a sensitivity of 15% to 35% for detecting stress fractures on initial examinations, increasing to 30% to 70% at follow-up due to more overt bone reaction. Stress fractures radiographically show the following signs:

- Osteal bone: endosteal or periosteal callus formation without fracture line. Circumferential periosteal reaction with fracture line through one cortex. Frank fracture.
- Cancellous bone: flake-like patches of new bone formation (2–3 weeks).
- Cloudlike area of mineralized bone. Focal linear area of sclerosis, perpendicular to the trabeculae. Differentiating between myositis ossificans and extraskeletal osteosarcoma is critical. The clinical features of myositis ossificans are rapid growth, often in athletes or laborers after trauma, associated with pain (sarcomas are more insidious and pain occurs late), with a diffuse, doughy swelling. Bone deposition in osteosarcoma is haphazard and disorganized, sometimes with a "reverse zoning effect," with bone formation in the center of the lesion and immature spindle cells toward the periphery.

Neoplasms, or cancer of bone, change the appearance of bone on an x-ray. Bone may look ragged or may appear to have a hole in it.

Hematomas look very different from tumors or bones on an x-ray because they are mostly fluid, and tumors and bones are solid.

Type of Reasoning: Analytical

For this question one must analyze the symptoms and information presented in the picture in order to determine the most likely diagnosis. This requires analytical reasoning skill, where assessing information from pictures is often used to reach sound conclusions. In this case, the symptoms presented and the picture depict myositis ossificans. Review signs and symptoms of myositis ossificans if answered incorrectly.

Neuromuscular and Nervous System | Examination

During a finger-to-nose test, a patient demonstrates hesitancy in getting started and is then unable to control the movement. The finger slams into the side of the face, missing the nose completely. How should the therapist document this finding?

Choices:

1. Dysmetria.
2. Dysdiadochokinesia.
3. Dyssynergia.
4. Intention tremor.

Teaching Points

Correct Answer: 1

Dysmetria is an inability to judge the distance or range of movement. It includes both overestimation (hypermetria) and underestimation (hypometria) of the required range needed to reach the goal.

Incorrect Choices:

Dysdiadochokinesia is an impaired ability to perform rapid alternating movements (RAM). Dyssynergia is an impairment in movement composition. Movements are typically performed in component parts rather than as a single, smooth activity. Intention (kinetic) tremor is an involuntary oscillatory movement that occurs during voluntary movement.

Type of Reasoning: Analytical

For this question, one must analyze the symptoms presented in order to determine the most likely cause. This requires analytical reasoning skill. For this situation, the symptoms are consistent with dysmetria. Review signs of dysmetria if answered incorrectly.

A137 

Cardiovascular/Pulmonary and Lymphatic Systems | Interventions

What is the primary reason a patient with advanced chronic obstructive pulmonary disease (COPD) has improved/increased aerobic capacity with bilateral upper extremity support during activity training?

Choices:

1. It facilitates reverse action latissimus dorsi function to maximize ventilation.
2. Holding on increases the resistance or workload.
3. It increases sensory input and decreases balance work.
4. It improves scalene recruitment to improve expiration.

Teaching Points

Correct Answer: 1

Stabilizing the upper extremities allows the latissimus dorsi to function such that it lifts the rib cage, thereby increasing negative pressure within the thorax and improving ventilation.

Incorrect Choices:

The workload is decreased, not increased, by holding on. While bilateral upper extremity assist will increase sensory input, there is no evidence that this patient has a balance deficit. Scalenes are not active during expiration.

Type of Reasoning: Inferential

One must infer or determine what is most likely to be true of a situation in order to arrive at a sound conclusion about a patient with COPD. This necessitates inferential reasoning skill. In this case, the primary reason is that bilateral upper extremity support facilitates reverse action latissimus dorsi function to maximize ventilation. Review information on COPD and improving aerobic capacity if answered incorrectly.

A138 

Nonsystem | Equipment, Devices, Biophysical Agents

A physician requests that a physical therapist perform hydrocortisone iontophoresis over the left shoulder of a patient with tendonitis. The therapist discovers that the patient has a pacemaker. In this case, what should the therapist do?

Choices:

1. Perform the treatment since there is no contraindication.
2. Refer the patient to another physical therapist who has greater expertise in using iontophoresis for patients with pacemakers.
3. Consult with the physician about alternative forms of therapy; do not perform the iontophoresis treatment.
4. Administer the iontophoresis but only on the top of the shoulder not near the chest wall.

Teaching Points

Correct Answer: 3

All applications of electrical stimulation are contraindicated in the presence of a pacemaker. Consultation with the referring physician is necessary.

Incorrect Choices:

All other options resulting in administration of iontophoresis in the presence of a pacemaker are contraindicated.

Type of Reasoning: Evaluative

This question requires the test taker to weigh the potential courses of action and determine which response will have the most beneficial outcome. This necessitates evaluative reasoning skill. For this scenario, the therapist should not perform the iontophoresis treatment and should instead consult with the physician about alternative forms of therapy. Review contraindications for iontophoresis treatment if answered incorrectly.

A139 

Metabolic and Endocrine Systems | Evaluation, Diagnosis

Normotensive overweight and obese adolescents are performing isometrics and weightlifting as part of an exercise program. What is an important factor for the physical therapist to consider?

Choices:

1. This type of exercise will decrease lean body mass and assist in weight loss.
2. Blood pressure will fall if participants continuously hold their breath at the beginning of these exercises.
3. This type of exercise will not affect cardiovascular conditioning.
4. Blood pressure will rise during exercise and fall below resting levels after exercise ceases.

Teaching Points

Correct Answer: 4

Blood pressure can be expected to rise during isometrics and weightlifting and fall below resting levels after exercise ceases. This is a normal hemodynamic response to exercise.

Incorrect Choices:

Resistive exercise can be expected to increase, not decrease, lean body mass. Breath holding can induce a Valsalva maneuver (forced expiratory effort), causing increased intrathoracic pressure, initial increase in blood pressure followed by a drop, slowing of the pulse, decreased return of blood to the heart, and increased (not decreased) venous pressure. Resistive exercise enhances muscular strength and physical function and increases the efficiency of O_2 extraction peripherally, which will assist with aerobic capacity.

Type of Reasoning: Inferential

One must determine what is likely to be true for this group of adolescents in order to arrive at a correct conclusion. This requires inferential reasoning skill, where one determines a likely outcome based on a course of action. For this situation, the therapist should expect that blood pressure will rise during exercise and fall below resting levels after exercise ceases. Review hemodynamic responses to exercise in overweight and obese individuals if answered incorrectly.

A140 

Musculoskeletal System | Evaluation, Diagnosis

During gait analysis, a therapist notes that a patient is lurching backward during stance phase. What is the cause of this compensatory motion?

Choices:

1. Gluteus medius weakness.
2. Hip and knee flexion contractures.
3. Quadriceps weakness.
4. Gluteus maximus weakness.

Teaching Points

Correct Answer: 4

Lurching backward during stance is a compensation for weak hip extensors, commonly called a gluteus maximus gait. Leaning backward during loading response inclines the ground reaction force vector posteriorly from its point of application at the hindfoot. Because the vector passes closer to the hip joint's lateral axis, its moment arm is shorter, and it produces a smaller hip flexor moment. If it falls behind the axis it can produce a hip extensor moment.

Incorrect Choices:

Gluteus medius weakness produces a Trendelenburg gait, or leaning to the side opposite the weakness.

When the quadriceps are weak, the person must compensate to preserve knee stability. Two of the common compensations will be hyperextension of the knee and forward trunk lean to put the center of gravity in front of the knee.

Hip and knee flexion contracture would produce a "short limb" during stance. This would result in the opposite extremity having to circumduct, hip hike, and steppage gait to get the lower extremity (LE) through swing. It will also lead to a shorter stride. Lumbar spine extension can effectively compensate for hip flexion contractures up to about 15 degrees. When hip flexion contractures exceed 15 degrees (a common occurrence) or there is limited lumbar spine extension range available (also common), the patient is forced to adopt a forward trunk tilt in terminal stance in order to complete the step. With a knee flexion contracture, it is more difficult to advance the ground reaction force vector anterior to the knee, its normal midstance position. This will force an increase in the muscular demands placed on the quadriceps muscle to maintain weight bearing through a flexed knee.

Type of Reasoning: Analytical

One must analyze the gait abnormality in order to determine the most likely cause for it. This requires analysis of specific deficits, which necessitates analytical reasoning skill. For this case, the lurching backward during gait is caused by gluteus maximus weakness. Review gait analysis guidelines and effects of gluteus maximus weakness if answered incorrectly.

A141 

Cardiovascular/Pulmonary and Lymphatic Systems | Evaluation, Diagnosis

What are some common adverse effects that patients taking nitrates, diuretics, beta-blockers, or calcium antagonists might experience?

Choices:

1. Hypotension and dizziness.
2. Arrhythmia and unstable blood pressure.
3. Extreme fatigue and arrhythmias.
4. Hypotension and decreased electrolytes.

Teaching Points

Correct Answer: 1

All of these medications lower blood pressure. If the dosage is too great for patients, they will be hypotensive and likely feel dizzy.

Incorrect Choices:

Beta-blockers and calcium antagonists control arrhythmias. All medications stabilize blood pressure. If the dose of all these medications is too great, then the patient might experience extreme fatigue.

Type of Reasoning: Deductive

One must recall the adverse effects of various medications in order to arrive at a correct conclusion. This necessitates the recall of facts, which is a deductive reasoning skill. For this case, all of the medications may cause hypotension and dizziness. Review adverse effects of cardiac medications if answered incorrectly.

A142 

Neuromuscular and Nervous System | Evaluation, Diagnosis

A 3-year-old child with Arnold-Chiari malformation has a ventriculoperitoneal shunt in place. During physical therapy treatment, the child becomes agitated and irritable, then drowsy and listless. What should the therapist do in this situation?

Choices:

1. Immediately place firm pressure over the fontanel.
2. Administer emergency oxygen.
3. Place the child in a head-down position.
4. Call for emergency medical services.

Teaching Points

Correct Answer: 4

These are all signs of shunt blockage. Emergency medical services are indicated.

Incorrect Choices:

All other choices are inappropriate given the emergency nature of this problem and they may also be harmful, exacerbating the developing pressure in the brain (especially the head-down position).

Type of Reasoning: Evaluative

For this question, the test taker must weigh the options presented and determine which option will most effectively address the problem at hand. This requires evaluative reasoning skill in order to reach a sound conclusion. For this situation, the therapist should call for emergency medical services. Review emergency procedures for shunt blockage if answered incorrectly.

A143 

Neuromuscular and Nervous System | Interventions

A patient with a 6-year history of Parkinson's disease (PD) has experienced two recent bouts of pneumonia and limited functional mobility in the home. The therapist's plan of care focuses on improving respiratory function and postural control. What is the **BEST** choice for intervention to address these issues at this time?

Choices:

1. Supine, UE PNF lift and reverse lift patterns using rhythmic initiation.
2. Quadruped, alternate arm and leg raises.
3. Sitting, bilateral symmetrical UE PNF D2 flexion patterns using rhythmic initiation.
4. Standing, bilateral symmetrical UE PNF D2 flexion patterns using dynamic reversals.

Teaching Points

Correct Answer: 3

Sitting, bilateral symmetrical UE PNF D2 flexion patterns using rhythmic initiation are the best choices to open up the chest and enhance lung function (restrictive lung function is common in patients with PD). The sitting posture is a good starting position for a patient with postural instability since the base of support (BOS) is wide and the center of mass (COM) is lowered compared to standing.

Incorrect Choices:

Progression can occur from sitting to standing postures, but beginning in standing is not a good choice. Supine, UE PNF lift, and reverse lift patterns using rhythmic initiation can be used to improve rolling in patients with PD. Quadruped, arm and leg raises do not address the problem of restrictive lung disease.

Type of Reasoning: Inductive

This question requires one to utilize clinical judgment coupled with knowledge of PNF approaches to determine a best course of action for a patient with PD. This necessitates inductive reasoning skill. For this situation, sitting, bilateral symmetrical UE PNF D2 flexion patterns using rhythmic initiation is best. Review PNF approaches and intervention approaches for PD if answered incorrectly.

A144 

System Interactions | Evaluation, Diagnosis

An elderly patient with diabetic peripheral neuropathy and retinopathy is having difficulty with balance when ambulating at home. The patient has fallen three times in the last month. What is the first priority of the home physical therapist's plan of care?

Choices:

1. Gait training with a cane to ensure safety.
2. Color-coding raised surfaces, such as steps, with a sharp color contrast.
3. Ambulation practice on changing floor to carpet surfaces in the home.
4. Installing nightlights in strategic areas throughout the house and keeping them lit continuously.

Teaching Points

Correct Answer: 1

The first priority of the home physical therapist should be gait training with a cane to ensure safety. This compensatory strategy is necessary as this patient is demonstrating complications of diabetes, which are chronic and progressive.

Incorrect Choices:

Color-coding steps and installing nightlights may also be necessary compensatory strategies to modify the home environment. However, they are not the first priority. Ambulation practice without a cane will not ensure the safety of this patient.

Type of Reasoning: Inductive

This question requires clinical judgment in order to determine a best course of action for an elderly patient with a history of falls. This necessitates inductive reasoning skill coupled with knowledge of effective approaches for home safety and fall prevention. For this scenario, the therapist should focus on gait training with a cane to ensure safety. Review fall prevention and home safety guidelines if answered incorrectly.

A145 Cardiovascular/Pulmonary and Lymphatic Systems | Interventions

What is the minimal recommended work interval duration for a nondeconditioned adult performing aerobic interval training?

Choices:

1. 5 minutes.
2. 10 minutes.
3. 20 minutes.
4. 30 minutes.

Teaching Points

Correct Answer: 2

Guidelines for interval training call for performance of intermittent exercise of at least 10 minutes of duration (American College of Sports Medicine).

Incorrect Choices:

Unless a person is extremely deconditioned, 5 minutes is too short of a work time to increase aerobic capacity. Twenty minutes is the lowest end of the acceptable amount of exercise time per day. Thirty minutes is the total recommended daily exercise time. It is still effective to break this up into three 10-minute bouts.

Type of Reasoning: Deductive

The key to arriving at the correct conclusion is in the recall of the acceptable guidelines for interval training. This is a deductive skill and helps shape our clinical judgment in situations such as this scenario.

A146 Cardiovascular/Pulmonary and Lymphatic Systems | Examination

A therapist is monitoring the blood pressure of a healthy athlete exercising on a treadmill. The speed and incline steadily increase during the exercise period. The therapist would expect the blood pressure response to demonstrate which of the following?

Choices:

1. Blunted rise in systolic pressure and a slight decrease in diastolic pressure.
2. Slight drop in systolic pressure and either a slight increase or decrease in diastolic pressure.
3. Steady increase in systolic pressure accompanied by a steady increase in diastolic pressure.
4. Steady increase in systolic pressure and either a slight increase or decrease in diastolic pressure.

Teaching Points

Correct Answer: 4

A steady increase in systolic pressure and either a slight increase or decrease in diastolic pressure is a normal response to ramp exercise protocol. With a continual, steady increase in exercise, the systolic blood pressure will continue to rise because the patient is not permitted to reach steady state.

Incorrect Choices:

In a healthy individual, there should not be a blunted systolic blood pressure response. This occurs most frequently in patients on a beta-blocker. In a normal patient who is not on medications, it is not a normal response to have a drop in blood pressure. A drop in blood pressure would indicate an inability to maintain cardiac output at that intensity of exercise. Diastolic blood pressure does not increase steadily with activity. The normal increase or decrease of diastolic blood pressure is 10 mm Hg.

Type of Reasoning: Deductive

One must recall the expected changes in blood pressure during treadmill exercise in order to reach a sound conclusion. This necessitates the recall of facts, which is a deductive reasoning skill. For this case, the therapist should expect a steady increase in systolic pressure and either a slight increase or decrease in diastolic pressure. Review responses to treadmill exercise if answered incorrectly.

A147 

Musculoskeletal System | Evaluation, Diagnosis

A therapist is examining a patient with a temporomandibular disorder. The patient had a history of jaw clicking upon opening and closing the mouth, but the noises are now gone. The current major complaint is inability to open the mouth wide and difficulty performing functional jaw movements such as chewing and yawning. What is the most likely cause of this current impairment?

Choices:

1. Capsular fibrosis.
2. Temporomandibular joint (TMJ) subluxation.
3. Chronic TMJ osteoarthritis.
4. Disc displacement without reduction.

Teaching Points

Correct Answer: 4

The mandible can open partway without clicking because the condyle is able to push the dislocated disc in front of it until the ligaments become taut. Further opening causes the chin to deviate off to the affected side because the affected condyle stops moving forward while the condyle of the other side keeps moving forward. Further jaw opening requires the affected side to jump over the back end of the dislocated disc and onto its thin center, causing a click or pop. Thus the opening click occurs near wide opening because it doesn't occur until the ligaments attached to the backs of the disc become taut; and the closing click is softer and occurs when the jaw is more nearly closed because the disc doesn't re-dislocate until the condyle reaches the depth of the socket where the disc can no longer fit. In later stages of forward disc dislocation, the disc usually stops going back into place during mouth opening, and the mandible cannot open past the point where it used to click.

Incorrect Choices:

With TMJ subluxation, the jaw locks in an open position and the patient cannot close the mouth. Although a capsular fibrosis would lead to decreased opening and chewing, it would not have clicking on opening and closing. Similarly, TMJ osteoarthritis (OA) would not have the characteristic clicking that is associated with disc displacement, but joint pain, stiffness, and crepitus can result from the articulation of irregular surfaces.

Type of Reasoning: Analytical

For this question, one must analyze the symptoms presented in order to determine the most likely cause for them. This necessitates analytical reasoning skill, where information is analyzed to reach sound conclusions. In this case, the symptoms are indicative of disc displacement without reduction. Review temporomandibular disorder if answered incorrectly.

A148 

Nonsystem | Safety, Professional Responsibilities, Research

A patient recovering from a total hip arthroplasty is seen by the physical therapist for early mobilization out of bed. While sitting on the edge of the bed, the patient experiences rapid onset of dyspnea, sudden chest pain, and cyanosis. What action should the therapist take?

Choices:

1. Return the patient to supine and monitor vital signs for the next 5 minutes.
2. Stabilize the patient and contact medical services immediately.
3. Allow the patient to rest for a few minutes and continue with the therapy session.
4. Return the patient to supine and reschedule the therapy session for later in the afternoon.

Teaching Points

Correct Answer: 2

This patient is exhibiting signs and symptoms of pulmonary embolism. This is an emergency medical situation and a cause of death in a substantial number of patients.

Incorrect Choices:

All other choices do not address the life-threatening and emergency nature of this situation.

Type of Reasoning: Evaluative

For this question, one must determine the best course of action by weighing the options presented. This requires analysis of the symptoms in order to determine the severity of the situation to reach a sound conclusion, which is an evaluative reasoning skill. In this case, the therapist should stabilize the patient and contact medical services immediately. Review emergency procedures for pulmonary embolism if answered incorrectly.

A149 

Neuromuscular and Nervous System | Examination

A patient with traumatic brain injury exhibits strong spasticity in both lower extremities (limbs are held rigid in extension). Using the Modified Ashworth Scale, the therapist gives this response which of the following grades?

Choices:

1. 1+.
2. 2.
3. 3.
4. 4.

Teaching Points

Correct Answer: 4

A grade of 4 is given for affected part(s) that are held rigid in flexion or extension.

Incorrect Choices:

A grade of 1+ is given when there is a slight increase in tone, manifested by a catch, followed by minimal resistance throughout the remainder (less than half) of the range of motion (ROM). A grade of 2 is given for more marked increase in muscle tone through most of the ROM, but the affected parts move easily. A grade of 3 is given when there is considerable increase in muscle tone and passive movement is difficult.

Type of Reasoning: Deductive

One must recall the Modified Ashworth Scale in order to arrive at a correct conclusion for this question. One must recall what each level of the scale indicates, which is a deductive reasoning skill. For this situation, a grade of 4 matches the description of the patient's spasticity. Review the Modified Ashworth Scale if answered incorrectly.

A150 

Neuromuscular and Nervous System | Interventions

When working with a child with Down syndrome and severe hypotonicity, how would it be best to activate the postural extensor muscles during early intervention?

Choices:

1. Slow, repetitive rocking movements with the child seated on a large gymnastic ball.
2. Prone positioning on a large gymnastic ball with the child looking up.
3. Quadruped, opposite arm and leg lifts.
4. Standing, weight shifts in modified plantigrade.

Teaching Points

Correct Answer: 2

The child with Down syndrome typically demonstrates hypotonia, developmental delay in postural stability, and poor use of proprioception for postural control. Prone positioning on a large gymnastic ball and having the child look up (neck extension) and/or reach up is a good early intervention to activate the postural extensors.

Incorrect Choices:

Slow, repetitive rocking on a large ball is relaxing and not indicated for patients with hypotonia. Quadruped opposite arm and leg lifts and standing, weight shifts in modified plantigrade are dynamic stability (controlled mobility) activities and are too advanced for this child who lacks basic stability.

Type of Reasoning: Inductive

One must utilize knowledge of effective intervention approaches to activate postural extensor muscles in order to arrive at a correct conclusion. This necessitates clinical judgment, which is an inductive reasoning skill. For this scenario, the therapist should place the child in prone on a large ball with the child looking up. Review intervention approaches for promoting extensor muscle activation if answered incorrectly.

A151 

Neuromuscular and Nervous System | Interventions

A patient recovering from stroke demonstrates dyspraxia. On what should physical therapy intervention optimally focus?

Choices:

1. Reeducation of weak muscles using isokinetics before activity practice.
2. Compensatory training strategies with maximum use of environmental cues.
3. Task-specific practice of familiar activities progressing from parts to whole.
4. Maximum use of manual facilitation of movements and new tasks.

Teaching Points

Correct Answer: 3

Dyspraxia is an impairment of skilled learned movement (a disconnect between the idea for movement and its motor execution). Task-specific practice using familiar activities and progression from parts to whole is the best choice to enhance learning.

Incorrect Choices:

Reeducation of weak muscles in isolated movements will not carry over to improved functional task performance. Compensatory techniques may be necessary if the dyspraxia is severe and the patient fails to benefit from a remedial intervention program (not evident in this case). Manual facilitation may benefit the patient during task practice, but both maximum use and practice of new tasks are not likely to benefit the patient.

Type of Reasoning: Inductive

For this question, the test taker must draw from knowledge of dyspraxia and effective intervention approaches for it in order to arrive at a correct conclusion. This necessitates clinical judgment, which is an inductive reasoning skill. In this case, the focus of intervention should be task-specific practice of familiar activities progressing from parts to whole. If answered incorrectly, review intervention approaches for dyspraxia.

Musculoskeletal System | Interventions

A patient presents with a limitation of wrist flexion. The joint manipulation technique that would **BEST** improve the patient's range of motion is which of the following Grade IV descriptions?

Choices:

1. Posterior to anterior glide of the proximal carpal row on distal radius and ulna.
2. Posterior to anterior glide of the lunate on capitates.
3. Anterior to posterior glide of the proximal carpal row on distal radius and ulna.
4. Anterior to posterior glide of lunate on capitates.

Teaching Points

Correct Answer: 3

A Grade IV anterior to posterior glide of proximal carpal row on distal radius and ulna is the correct choice because during wrist flexion, the proximal row moves dorsally on the distal radius and ulna.

Incorrect Choices:

Posterior to anterior glide of the proximal carpal row on distal radius and ulna is a component motion for wrist extension. Posterior to anterior glide of the lunate on capitates would likely improve wrist extension. Anterior to posterior glide of lunate on capitates may assist with flexion but does not address the primary area of motion during wrist flexion.

Type of Reasoning: Inferential

This question requires one to determine which intervention approach will have the optimal outcome in improving a wrist flexion limitation. This requires one to determine what is most likely to be true, which is an inferential reasoning skill. For this case, the best technique would be a Grade IV anterior to posterior glide of the proximal carpal row on distal radius and ulna. Review joint manipulation techniques, especially for the wrist, if answered incorrectly.

A153 

Neuromuscular and Nervous System I Examination

A therapist wishes to determine the fall risk of an elderly person in a long-term care facility. Which test of static balance would be most difficult for this person to perform?

Choices:

1. Standing unsupported with feet together, eyes open.
2. Standing unsupported with one foot in front, tandem position, eyes closed.
3. Standing unsupported with eyes closed.
4. Standing unsupported on one leg, eyes open.

Teaching Points

Correct Answer: 2

These are all measures of static standing balance found on the Berg Balance Scale (BBS). The most difficult test is tandem standing (reduced base of support [BOS]) with eyes closed (EC).

Incorrect Choices:

The other choices do not provide the same combination or level of difficulty. The BOS is reduced with feet together and on one leg but eyes remain open. The other item has EC but with a normal BOS.

Type of Reasoning: Inferential

This question requires one to determine what is most likely to be true of a situation, which requires inferential reasoning skill. Based on knowledge of static balance testing and greatest challenge in performing the various tests, one should conclude that standing unsupported with one foot in front, tandem position, eyes closed would be most difficult. Review static balance testing guidelines if answered incorrectly.

A154 

Metabolic and Endocrine Systems I Interventions

A patient with insulin-dependent diabetes is participating in an aerobic exercise class. The therapist recognizes that important dietary recommendations to prevent delayed hypoglycemia after exercise include intake of which of the following?

Choices:

1. Fruit juice or candy.
2. Crackers or bread.
3. Steak or chicken.
4. Salad or cooked vegetables.

Teaching Points

Correct Answer: 2

Slowly absorbed carbohydrates (crackers, bread, or pasta) can help prevent delayed-onset hypoglycemia.

Incorrect Choices:

Rapidly absorbed carbohydrates (e.g., fruit juice, candy, honey) are given during exercise to help prevent hypoglycemia. Foods with saturated fats (steaks) should be limited. Salads or vegetables do not have major effects in preventing hypoglycemia.

Type of Reasoning: Inferential

This question requires one to recall slowly absorbed carbohydrates in order to arrive at a correct conclusion. This necessitates the recall of factual information, which is a deductive reasoning skill. For this situation, crackers or bread should be chosen to prevent delayed hypoglycemia after exercise. Review dietary recommendations to prevent hypoglycemia if answered incorrectly.

A155 

Musculoskeletal System | Examination

A physical therapist is examining a patient who is complaining of pain in the left shoulder region. The examination of the shoulder elicits pain in the last 30 degrees of shoulder abduction range of motion. This finding is most congruent with which diagnosis?

Choices:

1. Calcific supraspinatus tendinitis.
2. Subacromial bursitis.
3. Acromioclavicular (AC) sprain.
4. Thoracic outlet syndrome.

Teaching Points

Correct Answer: 3

Typically, AC sprains will have pain at extremes of active range of motion (AROM), especially horizontal adduction and full elevation and pain on passive horizontal adduction and elevation. There are three special tests for AC joint:

- Acromioclavicular shear test: positive if abnormal movement of AC joint or pain at joint
- Passive cross-chest adduction
- O'Brien test

Incorrect Choices:

Calcific tendinitis may be found by an imaging study and causes no symptoms. If it is symptomatic, calcific tendinitis may present as (1) chronic, relatively mild pain similar to shoulder impingement syndrome; (2) large calcific deposit that may interfere with elevation of the arm; or (3) more severe acute pain attributed to the inflammatory response. The pain commonly radiates from the shoulder to the deltoid insertion and, less frequently, to the neck. It is often aggravated by elevation of the arm above shoulder level or by lying on the side. Other complaints may be stiffness, snapping, catching, or weakness of the shoulder. Supraspinatus tendinitis and subacromial bursitis will typically have a painful arc during 60 to 120 degrees of elevation and not at the extremes of motion. Thoracic outlet syndrome will usually manifest in symptoms of the arms and hands.

Type of Reasoning: Analytical

For this question, the test taker must analyze the symptoms presented in order to draw a sound conclusion about the likely diagnosis. This necessitates analytical reasoning skill, where pieces of information are analyzed to determine their relevance. In this case, the symptoms are consistent with acromioclavicular (AC) sprain. Review symptoms of AC sprain if answered incorrectly.

A156

Neuromuscular and Nervous System | Examination

Early intervention programs are usually required to use a standardized and comprehensive developmental test. What is the **BEST** test for use by a physical therapist?

Choices:
1. Functional Independence Measure for Children (WeeFIM).
2. Denver Developmental Screening Test (Denver II).
3. Peabody Developmental Motor Scales (PDMS-2).
4. Movement Assessment of Infants (MAI).

Teaching Points

Correct Answer: 3

The Peabody Developmental Motor Scales is a norm-referenced, standardized assessment of gross motor and fine motor skills divided into six subtests with an age range of 1 to 72 months.

Incorrect Choices:

The WeeFIM is a comprehensive, criterion-referenced assessment of 18 items in 6 subscales of functional performance (self-care, sphincter control transfers, locomotion, and cognitive function) with an age range of 6 months to 8 years. The Denver II is a norm-referenced, standardized test of development in personal-social, fine motor-adaptive, language, gross motor, and behavior categories and an age range of 1 week to 6½ years. The MAI is a criterion-referenced assessment of muscle tone, reflexes, automatic reactions, and volitional movement with an age range of birth to 12 months.

Type of Reasoning: Deductive

This question requires one to recall standardized tests of motor skills in children in order to arrive at a correct conclusion. Questions of this nature require the recall of facts, which is a deductive reasoning skill. For this case, the therapist should choose to administer the Peabody Developmental Motor Scales (PDMS-2). Review motor developmental tests, especially the PDMS-2, if answered incorrectly.

A157

Musculoskeletal System | Examination

A patient presents with an acquired flatfoot deformity. The therapist recognizes that this can result from injury to muscle tendon. Which structure should be examined?

Choices:
1. Anterior tibialis tendon.
2. Posterior tibialis tendon.
3. Fibularis longus tendon.
4. Achilles tendon.

Teaching Points

Correct Answer: 2

The posterior tibial tendon helps hold up the arch up and provides support when stepping off on the toes when walking. If this tendon becomes inflamed, overstretched, or torn, one may experience pain on the inner ankle and gradually lose the inner arch on the bottom of the foot, leading to flatfoot (posterior tibial tendon dysfunction [PTTD]).

Incorrect Choices:
The other choices are not associated with acquired flatfoot.

Type of Reasoning: Deductive
For this question, one must recall the tendon that is associated with flatfoot deformity. This necessitates the recall of factual information, which is a deductive reasoning skill. For this scenario, the tendon to be examined is the posterior tibialis tendon. Review flatfoot deformity if answered incorrectly.

A158 

Musculoskeletal System | Evaluation, Diagnosis

A 13-year-old girl has a structural right thoracic idiopathic scoliosis. The clinical features a physical therapist would expect to find include which of the following?

Choices:

1. A high right shoulder, a prominent right scapula, and a left hip that protrudes.
2. A high left shoulder, a prominent left scapula, and a right hip that protrudes.
3. A high right shoulder, a prominent left scapula, and a right hip that protrudes.
4. A high left shoulder, a prominent right scapula, and a left hip that protrudes.

Teaching Points

Correct Answer: 1
The Scoliosis Research Society defines scoliosis as a curvature of the spine measuring 10 degrees or greater on x-ray. The condition isn't rare. It mainly affects girls, many of whom have mild forms of scoliosis, are never even aware of it, and never need treatment. Three to five children out of every 1,000 develop spinal curves that are considered large enough to require treatment. "Idiopathic" simply means that there is no known cause. Common signs and symptoms of scoliosis may include:

- Uneven shoulder heights
- Head not centered with the rest of the body
- Uneven hip heights or positions
- Uneven shoulder blade heights or positions
- Prominent shoulder blade
- When standing straight, uneven arm lengths
- When bending forward, asymmetrical left and right sides of the back

A right thoracic scoliosis would result in a rib hump, which is an indicator of a rib cage deformity due to the rotation of the vertebrae. This happens because of coupled motion in the spine. Rotation rules: lumbar and thoracic spine rotation and side bending occur to the opposite side.

Incorrect Choices:
With a left scoliosis, one would expect a high left shoulder, a prominent left scapula, and a right hip that protrudes. The other two choices are not congruent with results of scoliosis.

Type of Reasoning: Inferential
One must recall the typical presentation of right thoracic idiopathic scoliosis in order to arrive at a correct conclusion. Specifically, one must infer what is likely to be the clinical features of this condition, which requires inferential reasoning skill. In this case, one should expect to see a high right shoulder, a prominent right scapula, and a left hip that protrudes. Review idiopathic scoliosis and clinical presentation if answered incorrectly.

A159 

Neuromuscular and Nervous System | Interventions

A patient with complete C7 spinal cord injury is receiving physical therapy in an inpatient rehabilitation setting to maintain joint mobility. What intervention is likely to produce the **GREATEST** risk of heterotopic ossification (HO)?

Choices:

1. Prolonged positioning with resting splints.
2. Forceful passive range of motion (PROM), especially if spasticity is present.
3. Prolonged stretching using tilt table standing.
4. Joint mobilization with PROM.

Teaching Points

Correct Answer: 2

Forceful PROM in the presence of spasticity increases the risk of developing HO (osteogenesis typically occurring in the soft tissues adjacent to large joints).

Incorrect Choices:

Joint mobility can usually be successfully maintained with all other choices.

Type of Reasoning: Inferential

For this question, the test taker is provided with a condition and must determine the greatest risk factor associated with the condition. This requires one to determine what is likely to be true of a situation, which necessitates inferential reasoning skill. For this scenario, forceful passive range of motion (PROM), especially with spasticity present, presents the greatest risk for developing HO. Review risk factors for development of HO if answered incorrectly.

A160 

Integumentary System | Examination

A patient complains of vascular changes in the hands usually experienced whenever it is cold. The therapist suspects Raynaud's disease. Which examination findings are consistent with this diagnosis?

Choices:

1. Hypersensitivity to tactile stimuli.
2. Loss of proprioception of the affected fingers.
3. Loss of two-point discrimination in the affected hands.
4. Temporary pallor and cyanosis of the digits.

Teaching Points

Correct Answer: 4

Raynaud's disease is a vasospastic disorder characterized by intermittent episodes of small artery constriction of the digits of the fingers (rarely the toes), causing temporary pallor and cyanosis.

Incorrect Choices:

The condition is most likely caused by hypersensitivity of the digital arteries to cold (not tactile stimulation). The condition is temporary and not associated with loss of proprioception or tactile discrimination.

Type of Reasoning: Deductive
This question provides a diagnosis and the test taker must infer the most likely examination findings. Questions of this nature often require inferential reasoning skill. For this situation, one would expect to see temporary pallor and cyanosis of the digits. Review signs and symptoms of Raynaud's disease if answered incorrectly.

A161

Nonsystem I Equipment, Devices, Biophysical Agents

A patient sustained a trimalleolar ankle fracture on the right and a fracture of the left distal radius. For partial weight bearing, it is **BEST** if the therapist has the patient use which device?

Choices:
1. Axillary crutches.
2. Forearm crutches.
3. Platform crutches.
4. Lofstrand crutches.

Teaching Points

Correct Answer: 3
Platform crutches allow weight bearing on the forearms and are used for patients who are unable to bear weight through their hands, as in this case.

Incorrect Choices:
All other choices allow weight bearing through the hands, placing stress on the distal radius.

Type of Reasoning: Inductive
For this question, one must determine the best assistive device for a patient with a trimalleolar ankle fracture on the right and a fracture of the left distal radius. This necessitates clinical judgment, which is an inductive reasoning skill. Based on the patient's injuries, platform crutches are the best choice. Review indications for platform crutches if answered incorrectly.

A162

Musculoskeletal System I Examination

Ten weeks after shoulder surgery, a patient develops capsular stiffness that is limiting glenohumeral internal rotation. The physical therapist chooses joint manipulation followed by a supportive exercise to correct this impairment. What is the **BEST** intervention?

Choices:
1. Anterior glide of the humerus and functional internal rotation stretch with arm up the back.
2. Anterior glide of the humerus and partial push-ups.
3. Posterior glide of the humerus and horizontal adduction stretch with arm across chest.
4. Posterior glide of the humerus and standing scapular retractions.

Teaching Points

Correct Answer: 3

The best intervention is posterior glide of the humerus and horizontal adduction stretch with arm across chest. During glenohumeral internal rotation, there is a posterior glide of the humerus in the glenoid fossa. The best way to self-stretch the posterior capsule is to adduct the arm, putting the posterior capsule and soft tissues on stretch.

Incorrect Choices:

The choices with anterior glide are incorrectly stated. Standing scapular retractions are helpful for posture and for strengthening scapular muscles but will not afford specific stretch to the posterior capsule.

Type of Reasoning: Inductive

For this question, one must utilize knowledge of joint manipulation techniques to arrive at a correct conclusion. This necessitates clinical judgment, which is an inductive reasoning skill. In this case, the therapist should perform posterior glide of the humerus and horizontal adduction stretch with arm across chest. Review joint manipulation guidelines for the humerus if answered incorrectly.

A163 

Neuromuscular and Nervous System | Interventions

A teenager is admitted to a skilled nursing facility with a severe traumatic brain injury and marked spasticity. Cognitive function is documented at Rancho Los Amigos Levels of Cognitive Functioning Scale level IV. Family members visit on a daily basis. In this situation, it would be **BEST** if passive range of motion (PROM) exercises are which of the following?

Choices:

1. Taught to family members in order for them to participate in the care of the patient.
2. Performed only by the physical therapist since the patient is unable to follow verbal commands.
3. Performed only by the physical therapist (PT) or physical therapist assistant (PTA) to minimize the possibility of pathological fractures.
4. Taught to all registered nurses (RNs) who might participate in the care for the patient.

Teaching Points

Correct Answer: 1

Passive range of motion (PROM) exercises can be taught to family members in order for them to participate in the care of the patient.

Incorrect Choices:

Other rehab staff, not only PTs or PTAs (e.g., rehabilitation aides, nursing assistants), can also be taught PROM techniques to maintain the joint mobility of the patient with marked spasticity. The RN is not typically engaged in this type of care of the patient.

Type of Reasoning: Evaluative

This question requires one to weigh the potential courses of action in order to determine which action will have the best therapeutic outcomes. This requires evaluative reasoning skill. For this situation, the therapist should teach family members PROM exercises so they can participate in the care of the patient. Review traumatic brain injury information and participation of family in the plan of care.

A164 Nonsystem | Equipment, Devices, Biophysical Agents

After gait training a patient with a transtibial prosthesis, a therapist notices redness along the patellar tendon and medial tibial flare. What would this indicate?

Choices:

1. The socket is too small and the residual limb is not seated properly.
2. The socket is too large and pistoning is occurring.
3. There is improper weight distribution during stance.
4. Pressure-tolerant weight bearing is occurring.

Teaching Points

Correct Answer: 4

Pressure-tolerant areas of the typical transtibial residual limb include the patellar tendon, the medial tibial plateau, the tibial and fibular shafts, and the distal end.

Incorrect Choices:

These are expected areas of redness. All other choices would not result in that pattern of redness.

Type of Reasoning: Inferential

For this question, one must infer what is likely to be true for a patient who is gait training with a transtibial prosthesis. This requires inferential reasoning skill. Using knowledge of prosthetics, one should conclude that pressure-tolerant weight bearing is occurring during stance. Review gait training guidelines with transtibial prosthetics if answered incorrectly.

A165 Neuromuscular and Nervous System | Examination

During the examination of a 2-year-old child with mild cerebral palsy, the therapist is encouraged because the normal developmental milestones for a child of this age have been achieved. This was demonstrated by the child's ability to perform which activity?

Choices:

1. Hop on one foot.
2. Stand on tiptoes.
3. Go up stairs foot-over-foot.
4. Jump with two feet.

Teaching Points

Correct Answer: 3

Going up stairs foot-over-foot (reciprocal stair climbing) is a developmental skill normally achieved by 2 years.

Incorrect Choices:

The ability to hop on one foot and stand on tiptoes is normally achieved by 4 years. The ability to jump with two feet is normally achieved by 3 years.

Type of Reasoning: Deductive

One must recall motor skill development in toddlers in order to arrive at a sound conclusion for this question. This necessitates the recall of factual information, which is a deductive reasoning skill. For this situation, going up stairs foot-over-foot is a normal developmental milestone for a 2-year-old child. Review motor skill milestones, especially stair negotiation, if answered incorrectly.

A166 

Cardiovascular/Pulmonary and Lymphatic Systems | Interventions

A therapist sees a patient in the intensive care unit with multiple trauma and severe traumatic brain injury. A chest tube is in place and it exits from the right thorax. The patient is in need of airway clearance. What action should be taken in this case?

Choices:

1. Percussion and shaking are contraindicated due to the traumatic brain injury.
2. Percussion and shaking can be done only in the right side-lying position.
3. Percussion and shaking can be done in the area surrounding the chest tube.
4. Percussion and shaking can be done only when the chest tube is removed.

Teaching Points

Correct Answer: 3

It is possible to complete manual techniques in the area of the chest tube. It is often the area in most need of airway clearance. It is important to consider pain management when doing this intervention.

Incorrect Choices:

Percussion and shaking are not contraindicated, but it is important to consider that this may be agitating to patients with a severe brain injury. Also, placing the patient in Trendelenburg should be avoided in the acute period to eliminate increases in intracranial pressure. Percussion and shaking can be completed bilaterally and with the chest tube in place. It is important to attend to patient comfort and chest tube positioning when in right side-lying.

Type of Reasoning: Inductive

This question requires one to determine a best course of action based on knowledge of airway clearance guidelines. This requires clinical judgment, which is an inductive reasoning skill. For this scenario, it is possible to perform percussion and shaking in the area surrounding the chest tube. Review airway clearance techniques, especially around chest tube sites, if answered incorrectly.

A167 

Musculoskeletal System | Interventions

To prevent maximal compressive forces being placed on the patella, a therapist should minimize placing the patient in which position?

Choices:

1. Prone and flexing the knee to 30 degrees.
2. In a sitting position with the knee flexed to 90 degrees.
3. Supine and flexing both the hip and knee to 110 degrees.
4. Prone and flexing the knee to 110 degrees with the hip extended.

Teaching Points

Correct Answer: 4

Extending the hip while flexing the knee will lengthen the rectus femoris and tensor fascia latae, resulting in increased compressive forces at the patellofemoral joint. This position should be avoided if the goal is to minimize this force. At 25 degrees, the force at the patellofemoral joint is equal to that passing through the tibiofemoral joints.

Incorrect Choices:

Prone and flexing the knee to 30 degrees will have minimum patella compressive forces. In a sitting position with the knee flexed to 90 degrees, and supine and flexing both the hip and knee to 110 degrees, will have similar contact forces and greater than at 30 degrees but less than prone because the two joint hip flexors are slack when the hip is flexed.

Type of Reasoning: Inductive

For this question, the test taker must utilize clinical judgment and knowledge of compressive forces of the patella to determine the position that should be minimized. This requires inductive reasoning skill, where clinical judgment is paramount to arriving at a correct conclusion. For this case, the therapist should minimize placing the patient in prone and flexing the knee to 110 degrees with the hip extended. Review compressive forces of the patella if answered incorrectly.

A168 

Nonsystem I Equipment, Devices, Biophysical Agents

To promote upright posture and higher walking speeds in a child with spastic diplegia, which ambulatory aid is **MOST** beneficial?

Choices:

1. A reciprocating gait orthosis.
2. An anterior rollator walker.
3. A posterior rollator walker.
4. A parapodium.

Teaching Points

Correct Answer: 3

A posterior rolling walker is used to promote an upright posture (eliminates the forward lean seen in use of the standard walker). The addition of wheels improves walking speed and reduces energy expenditure.

Incorrect Choices:

All other choices do not achieve these same goals. A parapodium is a standing frame with no mobility.

Type of Reasoning: Inductive

One must utilize knowledge of mobility devices in order to arrive at a sound conclusion for this question. This necessitates clinical knowledge and judgment, which is an inductive reasoning skill. For this scenario, the therapist should choose a posterior rollator walker to promote an upright posture and higher walking speeds. Review mobility devices, especially rolling walkers, if answered incorrectly.

A169

Cardiovascular/Pulmonary and Lymphatic Systems | Interventions

Following an exercise session for patients with heart failure in a Phase 3 cardiac rehabilitation program, what is prevented if the therapist employs a gradual and prolonged cool-down period?

Choices:

1. Exertional dyspnea.
2. Tachycardia.
3. Venous pooling.
4. Hypertension.

Teaching Points

Correct Answer: 3

There is vasodilation while exercising to increase oxygen supply to peripheral tissues. The return to normal arterial dilatation is delayed in patients with heart failure, and a prolonged, gradual cool down is recommended.

Incorrect Choices:

Exertional dyspnea is not a concern as the exercise intensity is reduced. Tachycardia is a concern as the intensity of exercise is increased but not as the exercise intensity is reduced. Hypertension is a concern while exercising. A normal cool-down or stopping exercise will avoid hypertensive episodes.

Type of Reasoning: Deductive

One must recall the reasons for a prolonged cool-down period for patients with heart failure in order to arrive at a correct conclusion. This requires the recall of factual information, which is a deductive reasoning skill. In this case, the prolonged cool-down period prevents venous pooling. Review cardiac exercise guidelines for heart failure if answered incorrectly.

A170

Neuromuscular and Nervous System | Examination

A therapist wishes to examine the effects of fatigue on physical, cognitive, and functional performance in a patient with a 7-year history of multiple sclerosis (MS). What is the **BEST** instrument to use?

Choices:

1. Functional Independence Measure (FIM).
2. Walking ability questionnaire (WAQ).
3. Outcome and Assessment Information Set (OASIS).
4. Modified fatigue impact scale (MFIS).

Teaching Points

Correct Answer: 4

The MFIS is an appropriate measure to examine the physical, cognitive, and psychosocial functional limitations of fatigue in patients with MS.

Incorrect Choices:

The FIM is a 7-level scale of functional performance and includes 18 items on self-care, sphincter control, transfers, locomotion, communication, and social cognition. The WAQ examines functional performance of walking skills. The OASIS is a measure of function in the home care setting and includes 79 core items, including sociodemographic characteristics, environmental factors, social support, health status, and functional status.

Type of Reasoning: Deductive

One must recall the instrument that would best measure the effects of fatigue on functional performance in order to arrive at a correct conclusion. Questions of this nature require the recall of facts, which is a deductive reasoning skill. For this scenario, the modified fatigue impact scale is the **BEST** choice. Review the MFIS if answered incorrectly.

A171

Neuromuscular and Nervous System I Interventions

As a result of diminished movement associated with rigidity in Parkinson's disease (PD), a physical therapist might employ rhythmic initiation (RI) primarily to help improve which of the following?

Choices:

1. Trunk stability and proximal tone.
2. Trunk rotation.
3. Upper extremity function.
4. Active and passive range of motion.

Teaching Points

Correct Answer: 2

RI is a proprioceptive neuromuscular facilitation (PNF) technique designed to improve mobility. Trunk rotation is particularly lacking in patients with PD and is a good activity to focus on in order to improve bed mobility.

Incorrect Choices:

Patients with PD demonstrate rigidity and excessive stability; also, RI is not used to enhance stability or improve ROM. Improving upper extremity function requires task-specific practice.

Type of Reasoning: Deductive

For this question, the test taker must recall the benefits of rhythmic initiation in order to arrive at a correct conclusion. This necessitates the recall of factual guidelines, which is a deductive reasoning skill. For this situation, RI will help improve trunk rotation. Review information on PNF, especially RI, if answered incorrectly.

A172 

Musculoskeletal System | Interventions

A physical therapist wishes to mobilize a patient's shoulder using an inferior glide technique. It would be **BEST** to initially use this technique by prepositioning the patient's arm in which position?

Choices:

1. 95 degrees of abduction with lateral rotation.
2. 125 degrees of abduction and internal rotation.
3. 35 degrees of abduction and neutral rotation.
4. 95 degrees of shoulder flexion and neutral rotation.

Teaching Points

Correct Answer: 3

Joint mobilization generally begins in the loose-pack position but with improvement can progress to more closed-pack positions of the joint. The loose-pack position of the glenohumeral joint is from 30 to 40 degrees in the scapular plane.

Incorrect Choices:

The closed-pack position for the glenohumeral joint is full abduction with full external rotation. The other choices approach a closed-pack position that is not suitable for initial mobilization.

Type of Reasoning: Inductive

One must recall joint mobilization guidelines and loose-pack positions of the shoulder in order to arrive at a correct conclusion. Based on this knowledge, one can then utilize clinical judgment to determine the best arm position, which is an inductive reasoning skill. In this case, the arm should be positioned in 35 degrees of abduction and neutral rotation. Review joint mobilization guidelines if answered incorrectly.

A173 

Musculoskeletal System | Examination

What is the Thompson test used to examine?

Choices:

1. Anterolateral rotational instability of the knee.
2. Iliopsoas tightness.
3. Rectus femoris tightness.
4. Achilles tendon rupture.

Teaching Points

Correct Answer: 4

The Thompson test is used to examine the integrity of the Achilles tendon. The patient lies prone with feet off the end of the plinth. The examiner squeezes the calf muscle. This should cause the toes to point downward as the Achilles pulls the foot. The foot will not move in a patient with a totally ruptured Achilles tendon (a positive Thompson test).

Incorrect Choices:

Iliopsoas and rectus femoris tightness can be evaluated with the Thomas test, not the Thompson test. To evaluate the knee for anterior lateral rotary instability, one could use the pivot shift test, the Slocum test, and variations of the anterior drawer. The Slocum test represents a modification of the anterior drawer test, which tests anteromedial rotary instability (AMRI) and anterolateral rotary instability (ALRI) of the knee. The anterior drawer test evaluates the anterior cruciate ligament. When adding an internal or external rotation to this test, anterolateral and anteromedial rotary instability can be evaluated.

Type of Reasoning: Deductive

For this question, one must recall the purpose of the Thompson test in order to arrive at a correct conclusion. This requires the recall of factual information, which is a deductive reasoning skill. In this case, the test is used to examine rupture of the Achilles tendon. Review the Thompson test if answered incorrectly.

A174 

System Interactions | Evaluation, Diagnosis

A physical therapist is treating a terminally ill patient with AIDS at home. What would be a major psychological focus or consideration when managing this patient?

Choices:

1. Discontinue treatment if the patient/therapist relationship becomes overly dependent.
2. Encourage expression of feelings and memories.
3. Keep the patient's friends and relatives up to date on the patient's treatment and state of mind.
4. Discontinue any activities that may cause the patient discomfort in order to keep anxiety levels low.

Teaching Points

Correct Answer: 2

When treating the patient with a terminal illness, the therapist should provide support and understanding of the grief process, encourage expression of feelings and memories, and respect privacy, cultural, or religious customs.

Incorrect Choices:

The therapist needs to maintain the boundaries of treatment and not discharge the patient. Keeping friends and relatives updated would violate the patient's privacy unless specific permission is given by the patient. The patient should be kept involved in the decision planning in order to reduce anxiety.

Type of Reasoning: Evaluative

One must weigh the options presented in order to determine the best course of action for a patient with AIDS. This necessitates evaluative reasoning skill, where one weighs the benefits of potential courses of action. For this scenario, the therapist should encourage expression of feelings and memories. Review the grief process for patients with terminal illness if answered incorrectly.

A175 

Neuromuscular and Nervous System | Evaluation, Diagnosis

A patient with a transverse spinal cord injury has total lack of hip flexion, abduction, and knee extension. This functional loss is consistent with a designation of a complete spinal cord lesion at which level?

Choices:

1. L1.
2. L3.
3. L4.
4. L5.

Teaching Points

Correct Answer: 1

Hip flexors are innervated and functional at the L2 (key muscle). Therefore, an L1 lesion would produce complete loss of this muscle function.

Incorrect Choices:

Key muscles innervated and therefore functional at the remaining lumbar segments include knee extensors at L3, ankle dorsiflexors at L4, and long toe extensors at L5.

Type of Reasoning: Deductive

For this question, the test taker must recall the innervation levels of the lumbar spine in order to arrive at a correct conclusion. This necessitates the recall of facts, which is a deductive reasoning skill. For this case, the lack of hip flexion, abduction, and knee extension are consistent with an L1 spinal cord lesion. Review innervation of the lumbar spine, especially L1, if answered incorrectly.

A176 

Nonsystem | Safety, Professional Responsibilities, Research

A physical therapist (PT) is substituting for an ill colleague and is unable to access the previous PT's notes in the medical record. In this case, what should the therapist do?

Choices:

1. Ask the patient what treatment had been administered in the last session.
2. Attempt to reach the ill therapist by phone before commencing the session.
3. See if other coworkers can figure out how to access the information in the medical record.
4. Briefly examine the patient and intervene appropriately.

Teaching Points

Correct Answer: 4

If a PT accepts an individual for physical therapy services, the PT will be responsible for the examination, evaluation, and intervention of a patient. At the least, a systems review and brief plan of care should be formulated before intervening. Electronic medical records help to minimize difficulties in handwriting interpretation; however, systems aren't perfect.

Incorrect Choices:

Asking the patient for information can be unreliable. Trying to reach the ill therapist by phone is inappropriate and may also be unreliable since the ill therapist may not have access to the medical record at home. It is not the co-worker's responsibility to interpret others' notes; no one should have access to patient information if not involved in the care of that patient.

Type of Reasoning: Evaluative

This question requires one to weigh the potential courses of action and determine which action will resolve the problem at hand. This necessitates evaluative reasoning skill, where potential courses of action are weighed to draw sound conclusions. For this situation, the therapist should briefly examine the patient and intervene appropriately. Review professional roles and responsibilities if answered incorrectly.

A177

System Interactions | Evaluation, Diagnosis

A physical therapist receives a referral to examine and treat an elderly patient in the early stage of amyotrophic lateral sclerosis (ALS). A confounding factor is the patient's mild Alzheimer's type dementia (AD). A significant factor in patient management at this time will **MOST LIKELY** be which impairment?

Choices:

1. Memory impairment.
2. Maintaining airway clearance.
3. Limited mobility.
4. Limited activities of daily living (ADL).

Teaching Points

Correct Answer: 1

The patient's memory impairment associated with AD will significantly impact management at this time. Significant others or home health aides will be necessary to maintain this patient's independence in the home.

Incorrect Choices:

Problems with airway clearance, ADLs, or limited patient mobility are not characteristic of the early stage of ALS or mild AD.

Type of Reasoning: Inferential

One must infer, or determine what is most likely to be true of a situation, in order to arrive at a sound conclusion. This necessitates inferential reasoning skill. For this situation, given the presence of mild dementia, memory impairment is a significant factor in patient management. Review information regarding ALS and AD memory impairment if answered incorrectly.

A178 

Musculoskeletal System | Examination

The physical therapist receives a referral to evaluate and treat a 6-month-old infant with right congenital muscular torticollis. On initial examination, the therapist would expect the head to be in which position?

Choices:

1. Tilted toward the noninvolved side, with the chin rotated toward the same side.
2. Tilted toward the involved side, with the chin rotated toward the opposite side.
3. Limited in ROM in lateral flexion toward the involved side.
4. Limited in ROM in neck flexion and extension.

Teaching Points

Correct Answer: 2

Congenital muscular torticollis involves a shortened sternocleidomastoid (SCM) muscle with a weakened contralateral SCM muscle, with a resulting posture of lateral flexion of the head to the involved (right) side, tight SCM muscle side and rotation of the head to the noninvolved (left) side.

Incorrect Choices:

The other choices do not correctly identify the impairments in head position and ROM seen with muscular torticollis.

Type of Reasoning: Inferential

For this question, the test taker must determine what is likely to be the clinical presentation for a child with torticollis. This requires one to recall the symptoms of congenital muscular torticollis in order to determine the likely clinical presentation, necessitating inferential reasoning skill. For this case, one would expect the head to be tilted toward the involved side with the chin rotated toward the opposite side. Review symptoms of congenital muscular torticollis if answered incorrectly.

A179 

System Interactions | Evaluation, Diagnosis

An elderly female patient is being evaluated for recurrent thoracic back pain. During the history, the patient reveals a smoking habit, and she drinks four to six cups of coffee a day. Activity level is low, consisting of daily trips to the local coffee shop to socialize with friends. Body weight and height are below normal. Medical history includes Graves' disease. The therapist decides to consult the primary physician for further workup. What is the suspected problem?

Choices:

1. Osteoporosis.
2. Osteoarthritis.
3. Gout.
4. Spinal stenosis.

Teaching Points

Correct Answer: 1

This patient is exhibiting several risk factors for osteoporosis: postmenopausal age, low body weight, loss of height, sedentary lifestyle, tobacco use, and hyperthyroidism (Graves' disease). Signs and symptoms include severe and localized thoracic-lumbar pain, increased pain with prolonged upright posture, decreased pain in hook-lying, loss of height, and kyphosis (dowager's hump). Her pain is most likely due to compression fractures, which can be confirmed on x-ray. Osteoporosis can be confirmed with a bone density scan.

Incorrect Choices:

Osteoarthritis produces asymmetrical pain with typical involvement of large weight-bearing joints. Gout pain is limited to only a few joints, typically affecting the first metatarsal, the knee, or the wrist. Spinal stenosis typically occurs in the lumbar spine and is accompanied by pain when standing and walking, extending into the buttocks and proximal thigh, nocturnal pain, and lower motor neuron (LMN) signs.

Type of Reasoning: Analytical

This question provides a group of symptoms, and the test taker must determine the most likely diagnosis based on a risk factor assessment. This requires analytical reasoning skill where symptoms are analyzed to reach sound conclusions. For this scenario, one would suspect the problem to be osteoporosis. Review risk factors for the development of osteoporosis if answered incorrectly.

Musculoskeletal System | Examination

A patient ambulates with excessive foot pronation. What will the therapist's examination likely reveal?

Choices:

1. Varus position of the heel.
2. Forefoot valgus.
3. Plantar fasciitis.
4. Valgus position of the heel.

Teaching Points

Correct Answer: 4

Excessive foot pronation is known as pes planus or pes valgus—a "flat foot deformity." The foot remains in pronation at the subtalar joint during weight bearing. The slight pronation of both the subtalar and transverse tarsal joints seen in normal stance is exaggerated.

Incorrect Choices:

The question asks what this observation during gait would reveal. Many patients have pronated feet without plantar fasciitis. Overpronation can cause stress or chronic inflammation on the planter fascia ligament (plantar fasciitis) and lead to numerous related foot and ankle injury conditions. Over time, the force of the impact is absorbed into the tissues, which can lead to conditions such as Achilles tendinitis, bunions, heel spurs, metatarsalgia, Morton's neuroma, plantar fasciitis (heel and arch pain), posttibial tendinitis, shin splints, and tarsal tunnel syndrome, as well as knee pain (chondromalacia, iliotibial band syndrome), hip pain, and lower back discomfort. Related conditions include corns, calluses, and hammertoes. Forefoot valgus and varus position of the heel are not congruent with foot pronation.

Type of Reasoning: Inferential

For this question, one must determine the likely clinical presentation based on the provided clinical observation. This necessitates inferential reasoning skill, where one determines what is likely to be true of a situation. In this case, one would expect valgus position of the heel to be present. If answered incorrectly, review flat foot deformity and clinical findings.

Musculoskeletal System | Interventions

A human bite injury resulted in laceration of the extensor tendons over the metacarpophalangeal (MCP) joints. Following surgical repair, the patient was placed in a dorsal dynamic extension splint (as pictured). Therapy is initiated in the first 24 to 48 hours, with the therapist instructing the patient to move in which way?

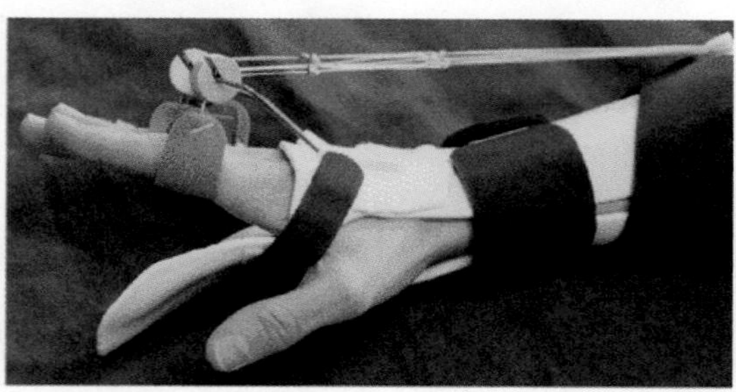
A

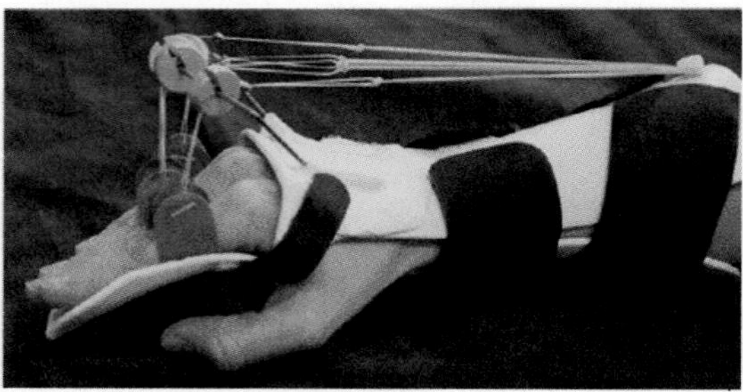
B

Choices:

1. Actively extend the wrist and passively flex the MCP joints.
2. Actively extend the wrist and MCP joints.
3. Passively extend the wrist and MCP joints.
4. Passively extend the wrist and actively flex the MCP joints.

Teaching Points

Correct Answer: 4

Goals during the first few weeks include preventing tendon rupture and promoting tendon healing as well as edema and pain control. For scar management, perform active range of motion (AROM) flexion, isolated joint and tendon gliding (hook and straight fist). Perform passive extension via elastic recoil of the dynamic splint, 10 to 20 reps hourly. Begin active MP flexion to 30 to 40 degrees (via flexion block on dynamic splint). Progress MP flexion as tolerated. Perform wrist and digit passive range of motion (PROM) in extension and tenodesis out of splint 10 repetitions hourly. Avoid making a full fist as this may place too much stress on the repair. The wrist is splinted in 40 to 45 degrees extension with 0 to 20 degrees of MP flexion and 0 degrees of IP flexion.

Incorrect Choices:

One would not want any active extension as this could disrupt the repair. There are many different protocols, but many avoid any active extension until 4 weeks postop. Passively extending the wrist and MCP joints would be safe but would not help with preventing contractures of the repaired extensor tendons.

Type of Reasoning: Deductive

For this question, one must recall the protocol for range of motion after extensor tendon repair. This requires the recall of protocol guidelines, which is factual information and necessitates a deductive reasoning skill. For this scenario, the therapist should instruct the patient to passively extend the wrist and actively flex the MCP joints. Review extensor tendon repair range of motion guidelines if answered incorrectly.

A182

Nonsystem | Equipment, Devices, Biophysical Agents

The patient has venous insufficiency in the right lower extremity resulting in fluid accumulation at the ankle. Which intervention would be most effective at reducing the edema?

Choices:

1. Crushed ice pack.
2. Intermittent compression pump.
3. Pulsed ultrasound.
4. Contrast bath.

Teaching Points

Correct Answer: 2

An intermittent compression pump provides external pressure, increasing the external hydrostatic pressure, which encourages reabsorption of the edema and minimizes fluid outflow from vessels.

Incorrect Choices:

The other physical agents are not effective for this type of edema. In addition, the target area is too large for ultrasound (US) to cover reasonably, and a contrast bath would require the patient to be treated in a dependent position, which would further contribute to edema formation.

Type of Reasoning: Inductive

For this question, one must utilize clinical judgment in order to determine the best intervention approach for a patient with venous insufficiency. This requires inductive reasoning skill. Having knowledge of effective edema reduction techniques for this diagnosis, the therapist should choose the intermittent compression pump to reduce edema. Review edema reduction techniques for venous insufficiency if answered incorrectly.

A183 

Musculoskeletal System | Interventions

Following serious trauma, a patient is casted as a result of multiple bilateral wrist and hand fractures. When would it be **BEST** for physical therapy intervention to begin?

Choices:

1. As early as possible to maintain or regain strength and range of motion in nonimmobilized joints of the upper extremities.
2. As soon as the casts are removed to regain strength of the wrists and hands.
3. About 2 weeks after the casts are removed so as not to damage vulnerable soft tissue.
4. After 6 weeks of immobilization to ensure that bone healing is almost complete.

Teaching Points

Correct Answer: 1

Rehab of the noninvolved joints should begin as early as possible to prevent circulatory stasis, atrophy, and contractures. In addition, exercise to the noninjured area will increase blood flow in the entire extremity and aid in healing and reducing edema. The benefits of range of motion (ROM) exercise include prevention of contracture, decreased pain, synovial fluid distribution, cartilage nutrition, stimulation healing along the lines of stress, prevention of thrombus formation, kinesthesia, increased bone activity, and patient participation.

Incorrect Choices:

Waiting until the casts are removed will not help prevent all the possible deleterious effects of immobilization. Unless specifically contraindicated, exercising the noninvolved joints will not have a deleterious effect on the immobilized fractures.

Type of Reasoning: Evaluative

This question requires one to weigh the options presented and determine which course of action will have the best therapeutic outcome. This necessitates evaluative reasoning skill. For this scenario, the therapist should begin intervention as early as possible to maintain or regain strength and range of motion in nonimmobilized joints of the upper extremities. Review intervention approaches for fractures if answered incorrectly.

A184

Cardiovascular/Pulmonary and Lymphatic Systems | Evaluation, Diagnosis

What is one of the most common early signs of right ventricular failure?

Choices:
1. Paroxysmal nocturnal dyspnea.
2. Exertional dyspnea.
3. Pulmonary edema.
4. Dependent edema.

Teaching Points

Correct Answer: 4

If the right ventricle fails, the increased fluid will back up. Traveling backward from the right ventricle, the edema goes into the right atrium and then the periphery. This causes dependent edema.

Incorrect Choices:

An inability to lie flat occurs when there is edema in the lungs. This doesn't occur in isolated right ventricular failure. Exertional dyspnea occurs in right ventricular failure as a result of deconditioning after a period of time. It is not an early indication. Pulmonary edema results from increased intravascular pulmonary pressures. This doesn't occur in right ventricular failure because there is a reduction in forward flow, and therefore there are lower pulmonary arterial pressures.

Type of Reasoning: Deductive

For this question, one must recall the early signs of right ventricular failure in order to arrive at a correct conclusion. This requires the recall of factual information, which is a deductive reasoning skill. In this case, an early sign is dependent edema. Review signs and symptoms of right ventricular failure if answered incorrectly.

A185 

Nonsystem | Equipment, Devices, Biophysical Agents

A patient with flaccid hemiplegia exhibits pain in the shoulder region secondary to inferior glenohumeral subluxation. Using electrical stimulation as orthotic substitution, where would it be **BEST** to place the electrodes?

Choices:
1. Posterior deltoid.
2. Supraspinatus.
3. Middle deltoid.
4. Anterior, middle, and posterior deltoid.

Teaching Points

Correct Answer: 2

Electromyography (EMG) studies confirm that the supraspinatus prevents downward migration of the humeral head. Shoulder alignment problems also influence subluxation (a downwardly rotated scapula, relative abduction, and internal rotation of the humerus).

Incorrect Choices:
The deltoid is not active during this function.

Type of Reasoning: Inductive
One must utilize clinical judgment in order to determine that the best course of action is treating inferior glenohumeral subluxation with electrical stimulation. This requires inductive reasoning skill. In this case, the therapist should place the electrodes over the supraspinatus muscle. Review electrical stimulation approaches for glenohumeral subluxation if answered incorrectly.

A186 

Musculoskeletal System | Examination

An ectomorphic adolescent patient presents at a physical therapy practice with a 6-month history of pain in both hands. Subjective complaints consist of pain that is worse in the morning but gradually improves throughout the day and overall fatigue. The only significant objective data from examination was mild edema and pain at end ranges of motion. What should the physical therapist do next in order to try to establish a diagnosis?

Choices:
1. Administer the Functional Independence Measure (FIM).
2. Examine for clubbing at the distal interphalangeal joints.
3. Examine for Dupuytren's contracture.
4. Refer the patient to a physician.

Teaching Points

Correct Answer: 4
This case represents the typical presentation for juvenile rheumatoid arthritis (JRA). The following are common symptoms of JRA: swollen, stiff, painful joints usually worse in the morning; fatigue; fever; swollen lymph nodes; and poor weight gain/slow growth. Additionally, the physical therapist was unable to identify specific impairments that would be potentially contributing to the patient's complaints, warranting referral to physician for additional testing.

Incorrect Choices:
The other choices do not address the findings of swollen, painful joints. The FIM evaluates functional performance (eating, dressing, grooming). Clubbing is seen with hypertrophic osteoarthropathy. Dupuytren's contracture involves flexion contractures of the fourth and fifth digits of the hand, MP, and proximal interphalangeal (PIP) joints.

Type of Reasoning: Evaluative
For this question, one must weigh the potential courses of action and determine which decision will best aid in establishing a diagnosis. This necessitates evaluative reasoning skill where one weighs the merits of each potential course of action to seek resolution. For this situation, the therapist should refer the patient to a physician. Review diagnostic approaches for JRA if answered incorrectly.

A187 

Nonsystem | Equipment, Devices, Biophysical Agents

A therapist has decided to use mechanical lumbar traction on a patient with posterior herniated nucleus pulposus at L2–3. If tolerated by the patient, what is the **BEST** positioning for this treatment?

Choices:

1. Prone, with no pillow under the hips or abdomen.
2. Prone, with a pillow under the hips and abdomen.
3. Supine, with the hips and knees flexed to 45 degrees.
4. Supine, with hips and knees flexed to 90 degrees.

Teaching Points

Correct Answer: 1

Neutral or extended position of the spine results in better separation of the disc space and should not exacerbate the posterior herniation.

Incorrect Choices:

The pillow could put the patient in more of a flexed-spine position and exacerbate the herniation. The supine position puts the patient in a flexed-spine position that is inadvisable with a posterior herniation.

Type of Reasoning: Inductive

For this question, one must utilize clinical judgment to determine the best positioning for lumbar traction. This requires inductive reasoning skill. For this case, the therapist should position the patient in prone, with no pillow under the hips or abdomen. Review lumbar traction techniques, especially for a posterior herniation, if answered incorrectly.

A188 

Musculoskeletal System | Interventions

A patient has osteophyte formation affecting the atlantoaxial joint with resultant cervical nerve root irritation. If the physical therapist elects to use gentle, static manual traction to help deal with this problem, what neck position would be best?

Choices:

1. 10 to 15 degrees of hyperextension.
2. Neutral or zero degrees of flexion.
3. 20 degrees of flexion.
4. 30 degrees of flexion.

Teaching Points

Correct Answer: 2

Manual techniques and angle of pull have been determined primarily by palpating where the separation is coming from. However, one should be aware that there is conflicting evidence on angle of pull and vertebral separation. Generally it is believed that C1–2 separation would best be treated with a neutral (0–5 degree) angle.

Incorrect Choices:
A position of 10 to 20 degrees would be appropriate for C3–4, and 25 to 30 degrees for C5–7. Traction in hyperextension has been shown to significantly decrease intervertebral separation posteriorly, especially at C6–7 (–50%), C5–6 (–37%), C4–5 (–26%), and C3–4 (–14%).

Type of Reasoning: Inductive
One must determine the best position of the neck for manual traction in order to arrive at a correct conclusion. This necessitates clinical judgment, which is an inductive reasoning skill. For this situation, the therapist should position the neck in neutral or zero degrees of flexion. Review manual traction techniques if answered incorrectly.

A189 

Cardiovascular/Pulmonary and Lymphatic Systems I Interventions

A patient with restrictive lung disease secondary to circumferential thoracic burns demonstrates decreased ability to expand the lower rib cage and push the abdominal wall anteriorly. The therapist should consider the use of facilitation techniques to enhance the function of which of the following?

Choices:
1. Rectus abdominis.
2. Anterior scalenes.
3. Internal intercostals.
4. Diaphragm.

Teaching Points

Correct Answer: 4
Contraction of the diaphragm causes the ribs to move outward, which is the desired motion in this case.

Incorrect Choices:
Facilitating the rectus abdominis will cause trunk flexion, which will not increase lower rib expansion. Anterior scalenes facilitation will assist with increasing the negative pressure on inspiration; however, it will not assist with expanding the lower rib cage. Facilitation of the internal intercostals will cause the opposite motion than the desired lower rib expansion.

Type of Reasoning: Inductive
One must determine, based on the deficits presented, which muscle to facilitate in order to improve function. This requires inductive reasoning skill, where clinical judgment is paramount to arriving at a correct conclusion. For this situation, the therapist should focus on facilitating the diaphragm. If answered incorrectly, review facilitation techniques of the rib cage.

A190

Musculoskeletal System | Examination

The picture shows the physical therapist examining the muscle length of the patient's right hip. How can the muscle length test be interpreted?

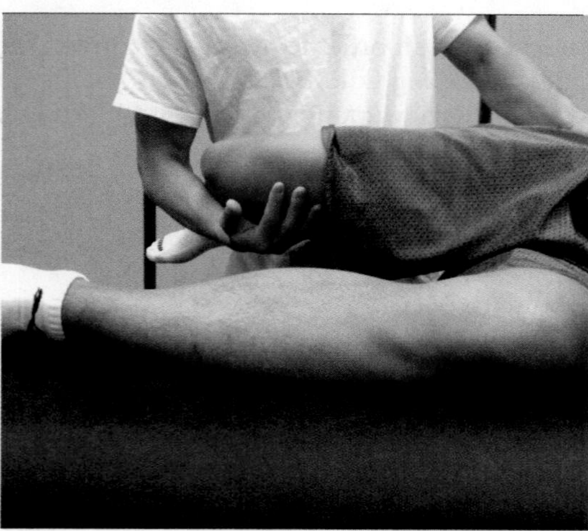

Choices:

1. Decreased length of the rectus femoris.
2. Decreased length of the tensor fascia latae.
3. Decreased length of the piriformis.
4. Normal muscle length of the tensor fascia latae.

Teaching Points

Correct Answer: 4

The Ober test is for tightness of the tensor fascia latae and iliotibial band. With the pelvis stabilized and the hip kept in neutral rotation, the Ober test would be considered normal if the thigh drops slightly below horizontal. Some sources say that the thigh should drop below the horizontal to the table.

Incorrect Choices:

The other choices incorrectly identify the muscle tested.

Type of Reasoning: Analytical

This question requires one to analyze the information depicted in the picture in order to determine the test being conducted. This requires analytical reasoning skill. For this scenario, the picture depicts normal muscle length of the tensor fascia latae. Review information regarding the Ober test if answered incorrectly.

A191

Neuromuscular and Nervous System | Interventions

A patient with postpolio syndrome (PPS) is referred to physical therapy for exercise training. The patient reports recent general fatigue and weakness along with muscle and joint pain. What is the **BEST** initial intervention?

Choices:

1. Treadmill training at 2 mph and a 10 degree slope, 3 days/week for 30 minutes.
2. Cycle ergometry at peak heart rate, 3 days/week for 40 minutes.
3. Therapeutic aquatics, 3 days/week for 20 minutes.
4. Strength training at 70% 1 RM, 2 days/week.

Teaching Points

Correct Answer: 3

A good choice for an initial intervention is therapeutic aquatics. The warmth of the water can ease muscle and joint pain, and the buoyancy can assist fatigued limbs. An initial exercise duration of up to 20 minutes per session in 2- to 4-minute intervals is recommended.

Incorrect Choices:

All other choices are too vigorous for this patient at this time. If weakness or symptoms are recent, exercise duration should be no more than 15 minutes per session.

Type of Reasoning: Inductive

For this question, the test taker must determine the best initial intervention approach for a patient with PPS. This necessitates clinical judgment, which is an inductive reasoning skill. For this case, the therapist should initiate intervention with therapeutic aquatics, 3 days/week for 20 minutes. Review intervention approaches for PPS if answered incorrectly.

Neuromuscular and Nervous System | Examination

A patient recovering from stroke walks with limited tibial advancement during stance on the more affected lower extremity. The therapist next examines the patient for a compensatory gait deviation. What is the **MOST LIKELY** deviation?

Choices:

1. Trendelenburg.
2. Circumduction.
3. Exaggerated flexion synergy.
4. Exaggerated extension synergy.

Teaching Points

Correct Answer: 2

Circumduction is the most likely compensatory gait deviation when tibial advancement is limited (e.g., spasticity of plantar flexors).

Incorrect Choices:

Trendelenburg gait is a lateral trunk lean that results from a weak or paralyzed gluteus medius on the stance side. An exaggerated flexion synergy results in flexion, abduction, and external rotation at the hip when the leg is lifted. An exaggerated extension synergy results in extension, adduction, and internal rotation (a scissoring pattern).

Type of Reasoning: Inferential

This question requires one to determine what is most likely to be true for a patient with a gait deviation. This requires inferential reasoning skill. Based on the description of symptoms, one should infer that circumduction would be the most likely gait deviation. Review gait deviations associated with limited tibial advancement.

A193 

Neuromuscular and Nervous System | Interventions

An elderly patient with a 5-year history of Parkinson's disease (PD) demonstrates frequent freezing of gait (FOG) episodes while ambulating. What is the **BEST** choice of intervention to improve gait and reduce FOG?

Choices:

1. Part-to-whole training in sequencing of required gait elements.
2. Walking using lightly resisted progression with elastic bands to facilitate forward progression.
3. Body weight support and treadmill training (BWSTT), 40% unweighting, 3% incline, at 2.7 mph.
4. Locomotor training using a personal listening device with 80 to 100 beats/min music.

Teaching Points

Correct Answer: 4

Locomotor training using a personal listening device and 80 to 100 beats/min music has been shown to improve rhythmicity and decrease FOG episodes in patients with PD.

Incorrect Choices:

Part-to-whole training is not effective for motor skills with highly integrated elements (gait). Light resistance will likely increase the patient's stiffness during gait (already a problem with PD). BWSTT might be helpful to improve the rhythmicity of gait, but 40% unweighting is too high and 2.7 mph is too fast for this patient.

Type of Reasoning: Inductive

For this question, one must utilize knowledge of Parkinson's disease and effective gait training approaches in order to arrive at a correct conclusion. This necessitates inductive reasoning skill, where clinical judgment is paramount to choosing sound conclusions. For this situation, the best intervention approach is locomotor training using a personal listening device with 80 to 100 beats/min music. Review gait training approaches for PD if answered incorrectly.

A194 

Musculoskeletal System | Interventions

A patient has limited motion in supination and calcaneal inversion at the subtalar joint. Using manual techniques, what is the accessory motion of the calcaneus that needs to be emphasized in order to increase the motions that are limited?

Choices:

1. Anterior glide.
2. Posterior glide.
3. Medial glide.
4. Lateral glide.

Teaching Points

Correct Answer: 4

Treatment direction is generally indicated by the convex-concave rule. The convex-concave rule states that when a convex surface moves on a concave surface, the mobilization force is applied opposite to the angular movement of the bone. If the moving surface is concave, the mobilization force occurs in the same direction as bone movement. The non-weight-bearing subtalar joint motion is described strictly by calcaneal movement. Pronation consists of calcaneal eversion, calcaneal dorsiflexion, and calcaneal abduction (medial tilt), whereas supination involves calcaneal inversion, calcaneal plantar flexion, and calcaneal adduction (lateral tilt).

Incorrect Choices:
Medial glide would improve eversion. Anterior to posterior talocrural joint mobilizations appear to increase ankle dorsiflexion ROM, while posterior to anterior would increase flexion.

Type of Reasoning: Inductive
This question requires one to recall effective manual techniques for the ankle based on knowledge of convex-concave theory. This necessitates clinical judgment, which is an inductive reasoning skill. For this case, the motion that should be emphasized is lateral glide. Review manual techniques for the ankle if answered incorrectly.

A195

Cardiovascular/Pulmonary and Lymphatic Systems | Interventions

A patient has a C5, ASIA A spinal cord injury. An effective coughing technique for this patient is which of the following?

Choices:
1. Should be facilitated by use of a phrenic nerve stimulator.
2. Should be facilitated by use of glossopharyngeal breathing.
3. Can be elicited with manual abdominal pressure provided with the assistance of a caregiver.
4. Can be elicited with manual abdominal pressure provided independently by the patient.

Teaching Points

Correct Answer: 3
The patient will need an external force to facilitate a cough and to clear secretions.

Incorrect Choices:
A phrenic nerve stimulator will facilitate diaphragm contraction. However, the diaphragm does not participate in a cough. Glossopharyngeal breathing technique forces air into the lungs but doesn't assist with coughing or forcing air out. The patient doesn't have the motor function at this spinal cord level to manually assist himself or herself. It is possible for the patient to use an arm of a chair or some other external pressure in order to be independent.

Type of Reasoning: Inductive
One must utilize knowledge of effective coughing techniques for patients with cervical spinal cord injury in order to arrive at a correct conclusion. This necessitates clinical judgment, which is an inductive reasoning skill. For this situation, the coughing technique for this patient can be elicited with manual abdominal pressure provided with the assistance of a caregiver. Review coughing techniques for spinal cord injury if answered incorrectly.

A196

Neuromuscular and Nervous System | Evaluation, Diagnosis

A patient with a crush injury to the foot appears to be developing complex regional pain syndrome (CRPS). What are some early signs of this clinical condition the therapist expects to see?

Choices:

1. Worsening pain with edema and atrophic skin and nail changes.
2. Cool, dry, and cyanotic skin with thickened fascia and developing contracture.
3. Hyperalgesia, allodynia, and hyperpathia.
4. Muscle atrophy, osteoporosis, and developing ankylosis.

Teaching Points

Correct Answer: 3

CRPS includes symptoms of pain, vascular changes, and atrophy. Early signs (stage 1) include hyperalgesia (increased sensitivity to pain), allodynia (all stimuli are perceived as painful), and hyperpathia (increased intensity) with edema, increased sweating, and thin, shiny skin.

Incorrect Choices:

Later signs and symptoms (stage 2) include increased pain with edema and atrophic skin and nail changes. Late stage changes (stage 3) include spreading pain, hardening of edema, cool, dry, and cyanotic skin, developing osteoporosis, and ankylosis.

Type of Reasoning: Inferential

One must infer what is likely to be true of a patient with early stage CRPS in order to arrive at a sound conclusion. This necessitates inferential reasoning skill, where one determines what is likely to be true of therapeutic situations. In this case, the early stage presentation is likely to be hyperalgesia, allodynia, and hyperpathia with edema, increased sweating, and thin, shiny skin. Review signs and symptoms of CRPS if answered incorrectly.

A197

Neuromuscular and Nervous System | Examination

A patient with long-standing diabetes mellitus is showing early signs of polyneuropathy. What is the **MOST** useful test to determine whether demyelination has taken place?

Choices:

1. Nerve conduction velocity (NCV) testing.
2. Electromyography (EMG).
3. Transcutaneous electrical nerve stimulation (TENS).
4. Motor point stimulation.

Teaching Points

Correct Answer: 1

NCV provides the most useful measurement of demyelinization in polyneuropathy. Conduction time is measured by recording the evoked potential from either a motor or sensory nerve. Speed of nerve transmission is directly related to level of myelination.

Incorrect Choices:
EMG is used to document (1) the role of muscle in physical activity, (2) the different types of peripheral nerve injury (e.g., neurapraxia, axonotmesis, neurotmesis), and (3) impairment of muscle recruitment in polyneuropathy. TENS is an electrical modality designed to provide afferent stimulation for pain management. Motor point stimulation is the area on the skin of greatest excitability to stimulate a muscle.

Type of Reasoning: Deductive
This question requires one to recall the benefits of each of the potential tests provided in order to choose the one that will be most useful in determining whether demyelination has taken place. This necessitates the recall of factual information, which is a deductive reasoning skill. For this situation, nerve conduction velocity (NCV) testing would be most useful. Review testing for demyelinization if answered incorrectly.

A198 

Musculoskeletal System | Evaluation, Diagnosis

During weight bearing, a soft tissue contracture resulting in supination of the forefoot will be compensated for by which of the following?

Choices:
1. Pronation of the forefoot.
2. Pronation of the rearfoot.
3. Supination of the rearfoot.
4. Pronation of the forefoot and rearfoot.

Teaching Points

Correct Answer: 2
When a forefoot is supinated, it can appear to be pronated because the body will get the forefoot onto the ground by pronating somewhere. The pronation that gets the foot on the ground actually occurs higher up the chain as at the rearfoot, ankle, knee, hip or pelvis, and lower back. When this occurs at the subtalar joint (STJ), for example, it is not uncommon to see the knees achieve a valgus position (knock knees). It is easy to confuse the appearance of pronation in the case of a forefoot varus, where the forefoot is effectively supinated.

Incorrect Choices:
If there is a forefoot supination contracture, then forefoot pronation, by definition, will not be possible. If there is also supination of the rearfoot, this would be an uncompensated forefoot varus. With an uncompensated forefoot varus the STJ is unable to fully evert for the forefoot varus deformity. The calcaneus does not evert past vertical, and the medial column of the foot is not stabilized. This foot is unable to absorb shock, rotate the limb, and adapt to uneven surfaces. The following are associated with uncompensated forefoot varus: stress fracture 5th, stress fracture of the fibula, and lateral ankle sprains.

Type of Reasoning: Inductive
For this question, one must determine through clinical judgment the likely compensatory pattern for supination of the forefoot. This requires inductive reasoning skill, where clinical judgment is paramount to arriving at a correct conclusion. In this case, one would expect pronation of the rearfoot to be the compensatory pattern. Review compensatory patterns of the ankle if answered incorrectly.

A199 

Cardiovascular/Pulmonary and Lymphatic Systems | Evaluation, Diagnosis

During a cardiac rehabilitation exercise session involving patients who experienced myocardial infarctions 6 to 8 weeks ago, what is the **MOST SIGNIFICANT** abnormal response requiring the immediate attention of the physical therapist?

Choices:

1. Decrease in systolic blood pressure.
2. Decrease in diastolic blood pressure.
3. Increase in diastolic pressure.
4. Increase in heart rate.

Teaching Points

Correct Answer: 1

A decrease in systolic blood pressure indicates an inability to maintain cardiac output. Exercise intensity should be immediately reduced or exercise stopped, depending upon the patient response.

Incorrect Choices:

Normal responses to exercise include a decrease in diastolic blood pressure, an increase in systolic blood pressure, and an increase in heart rate.

Type of Reasoning: Evaluative

This question requires one to determine a best course of action based on an understanding of cardiac rehabilitation guidelines. Evaluative reasoning is utilized whenever one must weigh potential courses of action and determine which action will have the best outcome. For this situation, the most significant abnormal response requiring the immediate attention of the therapist is a decrease in systolic blood pressure. Review cardiac rehabilitation guidelines and adverse responses requiring immediate attention if answered incorrectly.

A200 

Neuromuscular and Nervous System | Interventions

A patient with T8 paraplegia sustained 4 years ago is seen by a physical therapist at a routine outpatient clinic visit. The skin over the ischial tuberosities and sacral region is in perfect shape. The patient asks about the further need for pressure relief in the wheelchair, considering a new gel cushion is being used. What should the therapist advise the patient to do?

Choices:

1. Discontinue pressure relief as long as the gel cushion is used and visual inspection continues to reveal no skin breakdown.
2. Continue to perform push-ups in the chair at least once every 15 to 20 minutes.
3. Continue to perform push-ups in the chair at least once every 30 to 45 minutes.
4. Continue to perform push-ups in the chair once an hour.

Teaching Points

Correct Answer: 2

Current recommendations for prevention of pressure ulcers in patients with spinal cord injury who are wheelchair users include 10 to 15 seconds of pressure relief (push-ups) for every 15 to 20 minutes of sitting.

Incorrect Choices:

All other choices are inappropriate. Push-ups should be continued regardless of type of wheelchair cushion used. The other choices include time intervals that are too long between push-ups.

Type of Reasoning: Inductive

For this question, the test taker must utilize knowledge of spinal cord injury and effective pressure relief techniques to arrive at a correct conclusion. This requires inductive reasoning skill. For this scenario, the therapist should advise the patient to continue to perform push-ups in the chair at least once every 15 to 20 minutes. Review pressure relief techniques for spinal cord injury if answered incorrectly.

Examination B

B1

Neuromuscular | Evaluation, Diagnosis

A physical therapist is treating a child with spastic cerebral palsy who is 3 years old cognitively but at a 6-month-old gross developmental level. What is an appropriate treatment activity for this child?

Choices:

1. Reaching for a multicolored object while in an unsupported standing position.
2. Reaching for a multicolored object while in an unsupported, guarded sitting position.
3. Visually tracking a black and white object held 9 inches from his/her face.
4. Reaching for a black and white object while in the supine position.

Teaching Points

Correct Answer: 2

The appropriate task would include the 6-month-old gross developmental level activity of working on unsupported sitting. A multicolored object is appropriate for a 3-year-old cognitive level.

Incorrect Choices:

Standing and supine are not appropriate choices (too advanced or not advanced enough). The use of a multicolored object is more appropriate than a black and white object for a 3-year-old cognitive level.

Type of Reasoning: Analysis

In this question, the test taker must take into consideration the chronological, cognitive, and gross developmental levels of the child in order to arrive at the correct conclusion. In this scenario, the test taker must provide the appropriate physical challenge for a child developmentally functioning at 6 months in gross development, while providing activities that are appropriate for the 3-year-old cognitive level. If this question was answered incorrectly, review motor and cognitive developmental milestones.

B2

Musculoskeletal | Interventions

A patient is receiving mobilizations to regain normal mid thoracic extension. After three sessions, the patient complains of localized pain that persists for greater than 24 hours. What is the therapist's best option?

Choices:

1. Change mobilizations to gentle, low-amplitude oscillations to reduce the joint and soft tissue irritation.
2. Continue with current mobilizations, followed by a cold pack to the thoracic spine.
3. Place the physical therapy on hold and resume in 1 week.
4. Change to self-stretching activities, because the patient does not tolerate mobilization.

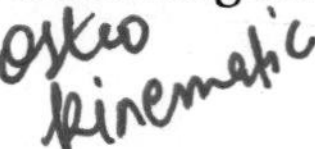

Teaching Points

Correct Answer: 1

Changing to low-amplitude oscillations will promote a decrease in the pain and tissue irritation. If pain persists for more than 24 hours, the soft tissue and joint irritation may progress.

Incorrect Choices:

Pain beyond 24 hours indicates possible tissue damage, so modification would be indicated. Placing the patient on hold would not be indicated or appropriate based on the patient's response. Self-stretching will improve the osteokinematic motion, but not the arthrokinematic motion, so this would not be an appropriate modification. It is not specific to the joint and may increase the irritation. It certainly would not decrease the pain and irritation.

Type of Reasoning: Inference

This question requires one to understand joint mobilization techniques, coupled with recognition of possible results that may occur when utilizing the techniques. In this scenario, the patient's symptoms indicate that the joint mobilization techniques resulted in soft tissue and joint irritation. Therefore, the therapist should consider less irritating mobilization for improved tolerance. If this question was answered incorrectly, refer to joint mobilization information.

Neuromuscular I Interventions

A therapist wishes to use behavior modification techniques as part of a plan of care to help shape the behavioral responses of a patient recovering from traumatic brain injury (TBI). What intervention is the **BEST** to use?

Choices:

1. Use frequent reinforcements for all desired behaviors.
2. Encourage the staff to tell the patient which behaviors are correct and which are not.
3. Reprimand the patient every time an undesirable behavior occurs.
4. Allow the patient enough time for self-correction of the behavior.

Teaching Points

Correct Answer: 1

Behavioral modification is best achieved through use of positive reinforcements for all desired behaviors.

Incorrect Choices:

Negative behaviors should be ignored, not reprimanded. Self-correction is not a form of behavior modification.

Type of Reasoning: Evaluation

The test taker utilizes knowledge of behavioral modification techniques to choose the correct answer in this scenario. Using evaluative skills, one determines the value of each of the four choices and which choice is most aligned with behavioral modification guidelines to promote positive behaviors via positive reinforcement techniques.

B4 

Neuromuscular | Interventions

A patient with multiple sclerosis (MS) presents with dysmetria in both upper extremities. Which of the following interventions is the **BEST** choice to deal with this problem?

Choices:

1. 3-lb weight cuffs to wrists during activities of daily living (ADL) training.
2. Isokinetic training using low resistance and fast movement speeds.
3. Pool exercises using water temperatures greater than 85°F.
4. Proprioceptive neuromuscular facilitation (PNF) patterns using dynamic reversals with carefully graded resistance.

Teaching Points

Correct Answer: 4

Dysmetria is a coordination problem in which the patient is unable to judge the distance or range of movement (overshoots or undershoots a target). Adding manual resistance with PNF can assist the patient in slowing down the movement and achieving better control.

Incorrect Choices:

The patient lacks speed control. Low-resistance, fast-speed isokinetic training is contraindicated. The resistance of water (pool therapy) could help control the speed of movements, but the temperature is too warm (patients with MS demonstrate heat intolerance). Weight cuffs could also help slow the movements down but would unnecessarily fatigue the patient (patients with MS demonstrate problems with excessive fatigue).

Type of Reasoning: Inference

One must understand the deficit of dysmetria in order to arrive at the correct conclusion. Using skills of inference, the test taker uses the knowledge of dysmetria to determine what course of action is useful to promote improved coordination and motor control. If this question was answered incorrectly, review information on dysmetria.

B5  

Musculoskeletal | Interventions

Knee capsular tightness has limited a patient's ability to attain full flexion. An **INITIAL** intervention a physical therapist can employ to restore joint motion should emphasize sustained mobilization in the loose-packed position. Which of the following is the **BEST** choice to use?

Choices:

1. Anterior glide and external rotation of the tibia.
2. Posterior glide and external rotation of the tibia.
3. Posterior glide and internal rotation of the tibia.
4. Anterior glide and internal rotation of the tibia.

Teaching Points

Correct Answer: 3

Posterior glide and internal rotation are accessory motions necessary to increase knee flexion. Initial treatment should not result in pain, soreness, or diminished range of motion.

Incorrect Choices:

Anterior glide and external rotation are motions necessary for knee extension.

Type of Reasoning: Inductive

For this question, one must utilize clinical judgment and reasoning to determine the most appropriate initial intervention approach for capsular tightness of the knee. This requires inductive reasoning skill. For this case, the appropriate joint motion should emphasize posterior glide and internal rotation of the tibia. Review joint mobilization techniques for the knee if answered incorrectly.

B6 

Cardiovascular/Pulmonary and Lymphatic | Interventions

A patient recovering from cardiac transplantation for end-stage heart failure is referred for exercise training. The patient is receiving immunosuppressive drug therapy (cyclosporine and prednisone). What guidelines should the therapist follow when implementing an exercise program for this patient?

Choices:

1. Require longer periods of warm-up and cool-down.
2. Require short bouts of exercise.
3. Eliminate all resistance training.
4. Require a frequency of 2–3 times/week.

Teaching Points

Correct Answer: 1

A patient recovering from cardiac transplantation will require longer periods of warm-up and cool-down because physiological responses to exercise and recovery take longer.

Incorrect Choices:

Low- to moderate-intensity resistance training can be performed. Aerobic exercise should be performed 4–6 times/week, while progressively increasing the duration of training from 15–60 minutes per session. (Source: *ACSM Guidelines for Exercise Testing and Prescription*)

Type of Reasoning: Inference

This question requires the test taker to infer what may be true of a patient, given the diagnosis of cardiac transplantation. Inferential reasoning skills are utilized whenever one must predict a best course of action or determine what may be true of a person or situation. In this case, the therapist should recognize that the patient will require longer periods of warm-up and cool-down. If this question was answered incorrectly, review exercise guidelines for patients with cardiac transplantation.

B7

Neuromuscular | Examination

A patient presents with weakness and atrophy of the biceps brachii resulting from an open fracture of the humerus. The therapist reads a report of needle electromyography (EMG) of the biceps. What is the anticipated muscle response after the needle is inserted and prior to active contraction?

Choices:

1. Polyphasic potentials.
2. Interference patterns.
3. Electrical silence.
4. Fibrillation potentials.

Teaching Points

Correct Answer: 3

Inserting an EMG needle into a normal muscle causes a burst of electrical activity (insertional activity) after which the muscle produces no sound (electrical silence).

Incorrect Choices:

Fibrillation potentials are spontaneous activity seen in relaxed denervated muscle, and polyphasic potentials are produced in the contracted muscle undergoing reorganization.

Type of Reasoning: Inference

One must understand the expected responses to EMG needle insertion in order to arrive at the correct conclusion. Inferential skills are used whenever one must determine what may occur based on facts and evidence. In this situation, the test taker must infer what happens after needle insertion and before muscle contraction.

B8 

Genitourinary | Evaluation, Diagnosis

A new staff physical therapist (PT) on the oncology unit of a large medical center receives a referral for strengthening and ambulation for a woman with ovarian cancer. She is undergoing radiation therapy after a surgical hysterectomy. Her current platelet count is 17,000. What intervention is indicated for this patient at this time?

Choices:

1. Active range-of-motion (AROM) exercises and activities of daily living (ADLs) exercises.
2. Aerobic exercise 3–5 days/week at 40–60% oxygen uptake reserve.
3. Resistance training at 60%, one repetition maximum.
4. Progressive stair climbing using a weighted waist belt.

Teaching Points

Correct Answer: 1

AROM and ADL exercises are beneficial and safe for this patient.

Incorrect Choices:

Exercise testing and training is contraindicated in patients with cancer whose platelets are <50,000, WBC <3,000, or Hemoglobin <10 g/dL. Additonal contraindications include significant bony metastases, severe cachexia, severe fatigue, or poor functional status.

Type of Reasoning: Evaluation

One must utilize knowledge of normal platelet counts and contraindications for resistive exercise in patients with cancer. In this situation, the patient's platelet count is low, which should alert the test taker that resistive exercise should be deferred. Questions such as these require one to review the merits of a situation, which is an evaluative skill. Knowledge of normal blood counts is very useful information.

Musculoskeletal | Interventions

A patient complains of increased pain and tingling in both hands after sitting at a desk for longer than 1 hour. The diagnosis is thoracic outlet syndrome (TOS). Which treatment would be the **MOST** effective physical therapy intervention?

Choices:

1. Cardiovascular training using cycle ergometry to reduce symptoms of TOS.
2. Stretching program for the pectoralis minor and scalenes.
3. Strengthening program for the scalenes and sternocleidomastoids.
4. Desensitization by maintaining the shoulder in abduction, extension, and external rotation with the head turned toward the ipsilateral shoulder.

Teaching Points

Correct Answer: 2

TOS is described as compression to the neurovascular structures in the scalene triangle, the area defined by the anterior and middle scalenes between the clavicle and the first rib. The compression is a result of a shortened pectoralis minor and scalene muscles. Therefore, a stretching program to these muscles to gain space in the scalene triangle is appropriate.

Incorrect Choices:

Shortening of the scalenes and sternocleidomastoids may be the culprit that caused TOS to develop. Strengthening these muscles would not improve the amount of space in the scalene triangle space. Cardiovascular training, especially performed in the posture using a cycle ergometer, would not improve the disorder. The problem in TOS is too much vascular volume in too small a space. Increasing the vascular volume through that space with cardiovascular exercise will not resolve the symptoms of TOS. Desensitization by putting the shoulder and neck in this position is likely to diminish the space in the scalene triangle and further compress the neurovascular structures that run through that triangle.

Type of Reasoning: Analysis

This requires analytical reasoning. If this question was answered incorrectly, review the causes and interventions for TOS.

B10 

Metabolic/Endocrine | Evaluation, Diagnosis

A patient with diabetes is exercising. The patient reports feeling weak, dizzy, and somewhat nauseous. The therapist notices that the patient is sweating profusely and is unsteady when standing. What is the therapist's **BEST** immediate course of action?

Choices:

1. Insist that the patient sit down until the orthostatic hypotension resolves.
2. Have a nurse administer an insulin injection for developing hyperglycemia.
3. Administer orange juice for developing hypoglycemia.
4. Call for emergency services; the patient is having an insulin reaction.

Teaching Points

Correct Answer: 3

Hypoglycemia, or abnormally low blood glucose, results from too much insulin (insulin reaction). It requires accurate assessment of symptoms and prompt intervention. Have the patient sit down and give an oral sugar (e.g., orange juice).

Incorrect Choices:

Once the patient is stabilized, the physician should be notified. Emergency services are generally not needed. Profuse sweating does not usually accompany orthostatic hypotension.

Type of Reasoning: Inductive

The test taker must first determine the cause of the patient's symptoms and then the appropriate course of action. Questions such as these utilize one's clinical judgment and diagnostic thinking, which is an inductive reasoning skill. One should recognize that these symptoms are indicative of hypoglycemia and require immediate administration of sugar to relieve symptoms.

B11 

Neuromuscular | Evaluation, Diagnosis

A patient with postpolio syndrome started attending a supervised outpatient exercise program. The patient failed to show up for follow-up sessions. The patient reported increased muscle pain and being too weak to get out of bed for the past 2 days. The patient is afraid to continue with the exercise class. What is the therapist's **BEST** course of action regarding the patient's exercise program?

Choices:

1. Discharge the patient from the program because exercise is counterproductive in postpolio syndrome.
2. Reschedule exercise workouts for early morning when there is less fatigue.
3. Decrease the intensity and duration, but maintain a frequency of 3 times/week.
4. Decrease the frequency to once a week for an hour session, keeping the intensity moderate.

Teaching Points

Correct Answer: 3

Clinical manifestations of postpolio syndrome include myalgias, new weakness as well as atrophy and excessive fatigue with minimal activity. Nonexhaustive exercise and general body conditioning are indicated. A change in the exercise prescription (intensity and duration) is warranted.

Incorrect Choices:

The patient should not exercise to the point of fatigue and exhaustion. A frequency of once a week is too little to be beneficial. Rescheduling exercise to early morning does not address the needed change in exercise prescription. Stopping exercise completely will not help this patient.

Type of Reasoning: Inference

This question requires the test taker first to understand the nature of postpolio syndrome and then determine the appropriate exercise regimen to prevent further exacerbation of symptoms. Therefore, one must infer, or draw conclusions, from the evidence presented to arrive at the correct decision. If this question was answered incorrectly, review information on postpolio syndrome.

B12

Nonsystem/Equipment, Devices, Biophysical Agents

A therapist has elected to use continuous inductive coil short wave diathermy (SWD) as one of the interventions in managing hip pain. Use of other thermal or electrical modalities were either ineffective or contraindicated. Which patient would be a candidate for use of short wave diathermy?

Choices:

1. A morbidly obese patient.
2. A patient with Type 1 diabetes who uses an insulin pump.
3. An 11 year-old boy with a slipped capital femoral epiphysis.
4. A patient with ankylosing spondylitis on high doses of NSAIDS and DMARDS.

Teaching Points

Correct Answer: 4

Ankylosing spondylitis is a form of arthritis that primarily affects the spine and other joints including the hip. Pain, stiffness, and inflammation can result. A physical therapy treatment plan can incorporate deep heating for muscle relaxation followed by stretching, posture management, and other exercises. Inductive SWD is preferred here as it penetrates more deeply than capacitive SWD. The use of the medications indicated will have no bearing on the application of SWD.

Incorrect Choices:

Collagen, fat, and bone have low conductivity. Synovial tissue and muscle have high conductivity and the most heat is produced in these tissues. Use of SWD with a morbidly obese patient with excessive amounts of fat in the hip region could result in selective overheating of adipose tissue because of poor conductivity of electromagnetic energy. The energy wouldn't effectively reach the joint and surrounding muscle.

SWD is contraindicated for patients that have implanted devices such as pacemakers, neural stimulators, or insulin pumps as diathermy can interfere with the functioning of the device. It is also contraindicated with those patients that have open, growing epiphyses as diathermy may alter the rate of epiphyseal closure.

Type of Reasoning: Deductive

This question requires knowledge of short wave diathermy indications and contraindications in order to arrive at a correct conclusion. Deductive reasoning skills are utilized for the recall of facts and guidelines, which is required for this question. For this case, a patient with ankylosing spondylitis on high doses of NSAIDS and DMARDS would be a candidate for SWD, as the use of medications will have no bearing on SWD treatment. If answered incorrectly, review SWD indications and contraindications.

B13

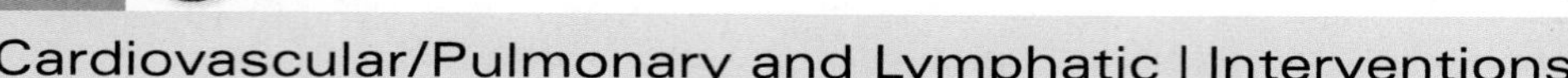

Cardiovascular/Pulmonary and Lymphatic | Interventions

A patient is recovering from open heart surgery (sternotomy and coronary artery bypass). The PT is supervising the patient's outpatient exercise program at 8 weeks postsurgery. What guidelines should be followed regarding the use of moderate to heavy weights during resistance training?

Choices:

1. Should include upper body exercises only.
2. Is contraindicated during the first two months.
3. Should be based on 60%–80%, one repetition maximum initially.
4. Can be included if resistance training is once a week.

Teaching Points

Correct Answer: 2

Resistive training after cardiothoracic surgery is restricted to 5 to 8 pounds for the first 5 to 8 weeks. Moderate to heavy resistance exercises are contraindicated.

Incorrect Choices:

Resistance training can begin 5 weeks postsurgery, including 4 weeks of consistent participation in a supervised cardiac rehabilitation endurance training program. Once cleared, initial loads for the upper body should be 30%–40%, one repetition max, and 50%–60% for hips and legs. (Source: *ACSM Guidelines for Exercise Testing and Prescription*)

Type of Reasoning: Deductive

One must recall the guidelines for cardiac exercise post-CABG in order to arrive at a correct conclusion. This requires recall of factual guidelines, which is a deductive reasoning skill. For this question, the key words are "8 weeks postsurgery," which should draw one to conclude that resistance training with moderate to heavy weights should be avoided during the first 3 months. If this question was answered incorrectly, review cardiac exercise guidelines, especially post-CABG.

B14

Cardiovascular/Pulmonary and Lymphatic | Evaluation, Diagnosis

A patient with asthma is taking a drug from the sympathomimetic group, albuterol (Ventolin). What is the MOST important effect of this medication?

Choices:

1. Increases airway resistance and decreases secretion production.
2. Reduces airway resistance by reducing bronchospasm.
3. Increases heart rate (HR) and BP to enhance a training effect during aerobic activity.
4. Reduces bronchial constriction and high blood pressure (BP) that accompanies exercise.

Teaching Points

Correct Answer: 2

Sympathomimetics are a class of drugs that mimics the effects of stimulation of body organs and structures by the sympathetic nervous system. Albuterol (Ventolin) has the primary action of reducing airway resistance by a decrease in bronchospasm.

Incorrect Choices:

Albuterol decreases airway resistance and has no effect on the volume or consistency of airway secretions. The primary effects of albuterol are on $\beta 2$ receptors in the bronchiole smooth muscle. It may also have an effect on $\beta 1$ receptors, producing cardiovascular adverse reactions of increased BP and tachycardia. These adverse effects can result in a patient monitoring exercise parameters at lower exercise workloads and reducing aerobic training effects.

Type of Reasoning: Inference

This question, while requiring knowledge of the effects and side effects of medication (a deductive skill), also requires one to determine the **MOST** important effects (not adverse effects). Therefore, this question utilizes inferential reasoning, in which the test taker must draw conclusions based on the information presented and determine what is most important, which encourages inferential deductive reasoning. If this question was answered incorrectly, refer to information on sympathomimetic medications.

B15 

Cardiovascular/Pulmonary and Lymphatic | Interventions

A PT decides to exercise a patient with lower extremity lymphedema using aquatic therapy. Hydrostatic pressure exerted by the water can be expected to do which of the following?

Choices:

1. Increase cardiovascular demands at rest and with exercise.
2. Reduce effusion and assist venous return.
3. Provide joint unloading and enhance ease of active movement.
4. Increase resistance as speed of movement increases.

Teaching Points

Correct Answer: 2

The pressure exerted by water on an immersed object is equal on all surfaces (Pascal's law). As the depth of immersion increases, so does hydrostatic pressure. Increased pressure limits effusion, assists venous return, and can induce bradycardia.

Incorrect Choices:

The other choices do not relate directly to hydrostatic pressure. Buoyancy of water provides an environment of relative weightlessness and assists in joint unloading and active movement. Hydromechanics, movement of water molecules, increases the resistance of water as speed of movement increases. Hot water immersion (> 35°C) can increase cardiovascular demands at rest and with exercise.

Type of Reasoning: Deductive

This question primarily requires recall of physics, including hydrostatic pressure and buoyancy. In order to arrive at the correct conclusion, one must apply knowledge of hydrostatic pressure to the patient in this case. If this question was answered incorrectly, refer to information on effects of hydrostatic pressure on cardiovascular function.

B16

Musculoskeletal | Interventions

A therapist determines that a patient is walking with a backward trunk lean with full weight on the right leg. The patient also demonstrates great difficulty going up ramps. What is the **BEST** intervention to remediate this problem?

Choices:

1. Strengthen hip extensors through bridging.
2. Stretch hip abductors through side-lying positioning.
3. Strengthen knee extensors with weights, using 80%, one repetition maximum.
4. Stretch hip flexors through prone-lying positioning.

Teaching Points

Correct Answer: 1

Backward trunk lean (gluteus maximus gait) is the result of a weak gluteus maximus. It causes increased difficulty going up stairs or ramps. Functional training exercises such as bridging are indicated.

Incorrect Choices:

The patient is able to perform a backward trunk lean in standing, indicating adequate range in hip flexors. Ability to take full weight on the limb without knee buckling indicates adequate strength of knee extensors. Tightness in hip abductors is rare and would result in the posture (lateral lean) being maintained during all phases of gait.

Type of Reasoning: Inference

In this question, the test taker must determine the cause of a backward trunk lean and difficulty ascending ramps and which muscle groups require strengthening. This type of question requires one to make inferences or draw conclusions from the evidence presented in order to make a clinical decision. If this question was answered incorrectly, review knowledge of gait deviations and their causes.

B17

Integumentary | Examination

A patient has developed a thick eschar secondary to a full-thickness burn. What is the antibacterial agent **MOST** effective for infection control for this type of burn?

Choices:

1. Sulfamylon.
2. Nitrofurazone.
3. Panafil.
4. Silver nitrate.

Teaching Points

Correct Answer: 1

Sulfamylon penetrates through eschar and provides antibacterial control.

Incorrect Choices:

Silver nitrate and nitrofurazone are superficial agents that attack surface organisms. Panafil is a keratolytic enzyme used for selective debridement.

Type of Reasoning: Analysis

This question requires recall of the properties of each agent in antibacterial control and then determination of which one would **MOST** effectively promote infection control. Therefore, the test taker must analyze each agent and rely on knowledge of these agents to arrive at the correct conclusion. If this question was answered incorrectly, review information on agents used after burns.

B18 

Neuromuscular | Evaluation, Diagnosis

An elderly person has lost significant functional vision over the past 4 years and complains of blurred vision and difficulty reading. The patient frequently mistakes images directly in front of her, especially in bright light. When walking across a room, the patient is able to locate items in the environment using peripheral vision when items are located to both sides. Based on these findings, what is the visual condition this patient is **MOST** likely experiencing?

Choices:

1. Glaucoma.
2. Cataracts.
3. Homonymous hemianopsia.
4. Bitemporal hemianopsia.

Teaching Points

Correct Answer: 2

Cataracts, which cause a clouding of the lens, result in a gradual loss of vision; central vision is lost first, then peripheral.

Incorrect Choices:

Glaucoma produces the reverse symptoms: loss of peripheral vision occurs first, then central vision, progressing to total blindness. Hemianopsia is a field defect in both eyes that often occurs following stroke. There was no mention of cerebrovascular accident (CVA) in the question.

Type of Reasoning: Analysis

In this question, symptoms are presented and one must make a determination of the most likely diagnosis. These types of questions require analysis of the meaning of information presented that utilizes analytical reasoning skill. If this question was answered incorrectly, refer to information on visual deficits associated with aging.

B19

Musculoskeletal | Examination

A patient presents with complaints of pain and difficulty with ADL that is consistent with carpal tunnel syndrome. What is the **BEST** test to identify the cause of symptoms in this patient?

Choices:

1. Pronator teres syndrome test.
2. Ulnar nerve tension test.
3. Allen's test.
4. Phalen's test.

Teaching Points

Correct Answer: 4

Phalen's test places stress on the compartment where the median nerve passes into the hand, so this test is typically positive for patients with carpal tunnel syndrome.

Incorrect Choices:

Allen's test is utilized to identify appropriate blood flow of the radial and ulnar arteries into the hand. The pronator teres syndrome test also involves the median nerve, but patients with median nerve involvement caused by an entrapment at the pronator teres will have signs and symptoms proximal to the hand as well. The ulnar nerve tension test (ULTT3) is utilized to determine an abnormal motion/glide for the ulnar nerve. None of these tests would duplicate the signs and symptoms of carpal tunnel syndrome.

Type of Reasoning: Deductive

For this question, the test taker must recall provocative testing guidelines in order to arrive at a correct conclusion. Specifically, one must recall the provocative test that is used to determine the cause for the patient's symptoms. This is factual recall of information, which is a deductive reasoning skill. For this scenario, Phalen's test is the best test to use. Review provocative tests of the hand and wrist, especially median nerve testing, if answered incorrectly.

B20

Neuromuscular | Interventions

A patient incurred a right CVA 1 month ago and demonstrates moderate spasticity in the left upper extremity (predominantly increased flexor tone). The major problem at this time is a lack of voluntary movement control. There is minimal active movement, with ¼ inch subluxation of the shoulder. What initial treatment activity is the **BEST** choice for this patient?

Choices:

1. Sitting, left active shoulder protraction with extended elbow and shoulder flexed to 90°.
2. Sitting, weight bearing on extended left upper extremity, weight shifting.
3. Quadruped, rocking from side to side.
4. PNF D2 flexion pattern, left upper extremity.

Teaching Points

Correct Answer: 2

Sitting, weight bearing, and rocking on an extended left upper extremity will help to decrease the flexor tone. It also provides joint compression (approximation) at the shoulder, which will help maintain shoulder position and stimulate stabilizing muscles.

Incorrect Choices:

Quadruped is too strenuous for this patient at this time (maximum weight bearing on a weak, unstable upper extremity). The other two activities demand more voluntary control than this patient currently demonstrates.

Type of Reasoning: Inductive

The test taker must make a determination of where the patient is currently functioning and match this knowledge to what the patient could most likely tolerate and achieve success in during interventions. In this situation, the patient would benefit the most from weight-bearing activities through the affected extremity with weight shifting. Questions such as these require clinical judgment, which is an inductive reasoning skill.

B21 Musculoskeletal | Examination

An older patient complains of pain in the right hip region. The therapist suspects hip osteoarthritis based on the patient's subjective symptoms. What clinical test is the **BEST** choice to confirm this diagnosis?

Choices:

1. Scouring test.
2. Thomas test.
3. Craig's test.
4. Posterior impingement test.

Teaching Points

Correct Answer: 1

A positive scouring test would be a consistent finding for a patient who has osteoarthrosis of the hip joint. It compresses the joint.

Incorrect Choices:

Craig's test is utilized to examine for increased or decreased anterior antetorsion angle. The Thomas test examines the flexibility of the hip flexor muscles. The posterior impingement test is utilized to examine for impingement of the posterior hip joint capsule and/or labrum. Therefore, none of these tests would produce positive findings consistent with hip osteoarthrosis.

Type of Reasoning: Deductive

This question requires one to recall the appropriate test for hip osteoarthrosis in order to arrive at a correct conclusion. This is factual recall of guidelines, which is a deductive reasoning skill. For this case, the scouring test is best. Review provocative testing of the hip, especially the scouring test if answered incorrectly.

B22

Musculoskeletal | Examination

The therapist in the photograph is testing which muscle?

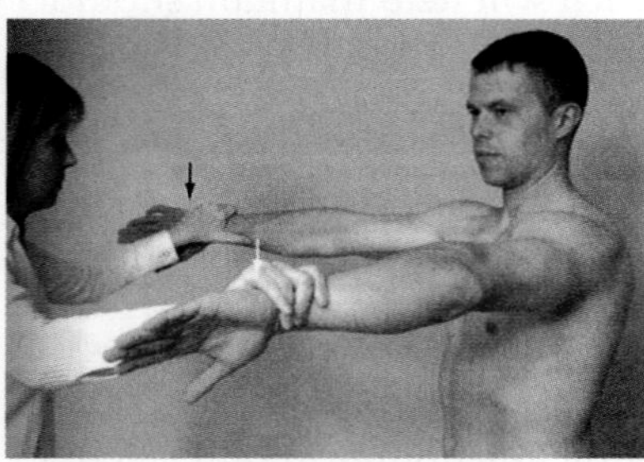

Choices:

1. Upper trapezius.
2. Middle deltoid.
3. Supraspinatus.
4. Anterior deltoid.

Teaching Points

Correct Answer: 3

The muscle being tested is the supraspinatus. The empty-can position puts the supraspinatus muscle in its most effective position for contraction. Weakness may be a result of inflammation, neuropathy of the suprascapular nerve, or a tendon tear.

Incorrect Choices:

The muscle test for the anterior deltoid would have the humerus and forearm in neutral rather than internal rotation of the humerus and pronation of the forearm shown in the picture. The muscle test for the middle deltoid would have the shoulder in abduction to 90°. The muscle test for the upper trapezius is the shoulder shrug.

Type of Reasoning: Analysis

In this situation, the test taker must recall knowledge of muscle testing of the supraspinatus to arrive at the correct conclusion. Whereas recall of muscle testing positions and procedures can be simple recall, the picture utilizes analysis of information coupled with recall, which becomes an analytical skill. If this question was answered incorrectly, refer to information on special tests of the shoulder complex.

B23 

Neuromuscular | Examination

During an examination, a patient demonstrates large-amplitude, sudden flailing motions of the arm and leg on one side of the body with primary involvement of axial and proximal joint muscles. What clinical term **BEST** describes the patient's behaviors?

Choices:

1. Chorea.
2. Intention tremor.
3. Hemiballismus.
4. Athetosis.

Teaching Points

Correct Answer: 3

Hemiballismus refers to sudden, jerky, forceful, and flailing involuntary movements on one side of the body. ("Hemi" was a clue).

Incorrect Choices:

Athetosis refers to slow, writhing, and twisting involuntary movements. Chorea refers to rapid, irregular, and jerky involuntary movements. Intention tremor refers to involuntary oscillatory movements that occur during voluntary movement. None of these are localized just to one side of the body.

Type of Reasoning: Analysis

In order to arrive at a correct conclusion, one must analyze the presenting symptoms and determine the most likely cause for those symptoms. This requires analytical reasoning skill. In this situation, the symptoms indicate hemiballismus. If answered incorrectly, review signs and symptoms of hemiballismus.

B24 

Musculoskeletal | Examination

A patient is referred to physical therapy after an antero-inferior dislocation of the right shoulder. What positive examination finding is expected as a result of this dislocation?

Choices:

1. Weak rhomboids.
2. Positive drop arm test.
3. Positive Neer's test.
4. Weak deltoids.

Teaching Points

Correct Answer: 4

Because of the anatomical position of the axillary nerve, it can be damaged by an antero-inferior dislocation at the glenohumeral joint. This results in weak deltoids.

Incorrect Choices:

A drop arm test evaluates the integrity of the rotator cuff. A Neer's test evaluates impingement of the shoulder. The rhomboids are innervated by the dorsal scapular nerve. Anatomically, the dorsal scapular nerve is medial and posterior to the shoulder joint.

Type of Reasoning: Analysis

This question requires one to recall musculoskeletal anatomy of the shoulder and the various tests that can be administered to determine dysfunction in the shoulder. For this case, the drop arm test and Neer's test are not administered to determine anterior shoulder dislocation, and rhomboids do not play a role in anterior shoulder stability. Through analysis of the information presented, the test taker should conclude that weak deltoids are the most likely result of the dislocation.

B25

Nonsystem | Safety, Professional Responsibilities, Research

A team of researchers investigates the use of constraint-induced movement therapy on patients with chronic stroke (> 1 year poststroke) using a multicenter randomized controlled trial (RCT). What are the specific characteristics of this type of research design?

Choices:

1. A sample of convenience for the intervention group.
2. Alternating experimental and control conditions for a subject.
3. Random assignment to an experimental or control group.
4. Random assignment to matched cohort groups.

Teaching Points

Correct Answer: 3

An RCT uses a randomization process to assign subjects to either an experimental group(s) or a control (comparison) group. Subjects in the experimental group receive the intervention and are then compared with subjects in the control group who do not receive the intervention. A large multicenter RCT study with large numbers of patients provides the highest level of scientific rigor and evidence.

Incorrect Choices:

Alternating experimental and control conditions for a subject is an A-B-A-B design typically used in single-subject design studies. A cohort design investigates a group of subjects without a control group (sample of convenience).

Type of Reasoning: Deductive

One must recall the guidelines for an RCT in order to arrive at a correct conclusion. Questions that require one to recall facts or guidelines often necessitate deductive reasoning skill. For this case, this type of research design provides the highest level of evidence due to the random assignment to an experimental or control group. If this question was answered incorrectly, review research guidelines, especially RCT study designs.

B26

Neuromuscular | Interventions

A therapist has been asked to give an in-service presentation to staff aides on safe guarding techniques in a nursing home. The patients are at risk for falls. How should the therapist **BEST** prepare for this talk?

Choices:

1. Provide a questionnaire to a random sampling of participants 1 week before the scheduled presentation.
2. Provide a questionnaire to all participants 2 weeks before the scheduled session.
3. Survey the audience a day before the scheduled session.
4. Survey the audience at the scheduled session.

Teaching Points

Correct Answer: 2

A questionnaire to all participants represents the best method of needs assessment in this situation.

Incorrect Choices:

Leaving the survey to the day of or day before the presentation does not allow for adequate advanced planning to meet the group's needs. Using a random sample of participants will not adequately represent the needs of the whole group.

Type of Reasoning: Evaluation

This question requires one to evaluate the merits of the statements presented, and the test taker must determine which course of action best meets the needs of the group. In a situation in which a therapist is preparing for an in-service, it is ideal to perform a needs assessment of the group as a basis for planning the manner in which to deliver information to the group. Evaluation questions can be challenging, because they require one to make a judgment call based on knowledge and experience.

B27 

Neuromuscular | Interventions

A therapist is treating a patient with left hemiplegia and profound visuospatial perceptual deficits. What is the **BEST** strategy to use initially to assist this patient in the relearning of motor tasks?

Choices:

1. Simplify and restructure the environment and minimize distractions.
2. Maximize use of demonstration and gesture.
3. Minimize use of verbal cues.
4. Encourage independent practice.

Teaching Points

Correct Answer: 1

Working in a closed environment in which clutter and distractions are minimized or eliminated is the best choice for this patient during initial training.

Incorrect Choices:

Patients with visuospatial deficits respond best to consistent, simplified verbal cues. Demonstration and gesture are likely to be confusing. Supervised practice is best initially because patients tend to be impulsive and unrealistic about their residual abilities.

Type of Reasoning: Inference

One must utilize knowledge of deficits related to right CVA (and, therefore, left hemiplegia) in order to arrive at the correct conclusion. It would be most beneficial to restructure and simplify the environment. The test taker must account for the key information in this question (patient with left hemiplegia) in order to infer the most effective intervention approach.

B28

Cardiovascular/Pulmonary and Lymphatic | Evaluation, Diagnosis

A 2-week-old infant born at 27 weeks gestation with hyaline membrane disease is referred for a physical therapy consult. Nursing reports that the child "desaturates to 84% with handling" and has minimal secretions at present. What is the therapist's **BEST** course of action?

Choices:

1. Provide suggestions to nursing for positioning for optimal motor development.
2. Put the PT consult on hold because the child is too ill to tolerate exercise.
3. Delegate to a physical therapy assistant (PTA) a maintenance program of manual techniques for secretion clearance.
4. Perform manual techniques for secretion clearance, 2–4 hours daily, to maintain airway patency.

Teaching Points

Correct Answer: 1

Excessive handling of a premature infant can cause oxygen desaturation. It is in the best interests of the infant to limit the number of handlers. The PT's role should be to assist nursing in developing positioning schedules, positions for feeding, infant stimulation activities, etc.

Incorrect Choices:

At present, there is little information provided that would necessitate the PT or PTA to be a direct caregiver to this child.

Type of Reasoning: Inductive

The test taker must utilize clinical judgment coupled with knowledge of neonatology physical therapy practice to arrive at the correct conclusion. One uses inductive reasoning skills whenever diagnostic thinking or clinical judgment is utilized. If this question was answered incorrectly, refer to information on neonatology practice.

B29

Musculoskeletal | Evaluation, Diagnosis

A patient sustained a valgus stress to the left knee while skiing. The orthopedist found a positive McMurray's test and a positive Lachman's stress test. The patient has been referred to physical therapy for conservative management of this problem. What is the **BEST** intervention for the subacute phase of rehabilitation?

Choices:

1. Open-chain exercises of the hip extensors and hamstrings to inhibit anterior translation of the femur on the tibia.
2. Closed-chain functional strengthening of the quadriceps femoris and hamstrings, emphasizing regaining terminal knee extension.
3. Closed-chain functional strengthening of the quadriceps femoris and hip abductors to promote regaining terminal knee extension.
4. Open-chain strengthening of the quadriceps femoris and hip adductors to inhibit anterior translation of the tibia on the femur.

Teaching Points

Correct Answer: 2

The evaluation is suggestive of an unhappy triad injury. Closed-chain exercises are emphasized during the **subacute phase** to enhance functional control of the muscles surrounding the knee. Terminal extension must be achieved during this stage if normal function is to occur.

Incorrect Choices:

Open-chain exercise does not promote regaining functional control for the muscle surrounding the knee. Focus on the hip abductors (rather than the hamstrings) will not promote regaining functional control of the knee joint.

Type of Reasoning: Analysis

The test taker must have knowledge of the patient's exact deficits and appropriate interventions in order to make the correct decision in this case. This requires knowledge of McMurray's test, Lachman's test, and rehabilitation strategies after an unhappy triad injury. In this type of question, the meaning of the information presented is analyzed to make the appropriate decision.

B30 

Musculoskeletal | Evaluation, Diagnosis

A patient with pain in the left lateral face and head is found to have limited active and passive mouth opening range of motion. However, passive lateral deviation is full to both sides. What is the likely reason for the limitation in mouth opening range of motion?

Choices:

1. An anteriorly displaced disc with reduction in the left temporomandibular joint.
2. Decreased flexibility in the muscles of mastication on the left.
3. Capsular restriction of the left temporomandibular joint.
4. An anteriorly displaced disc without reduction in the left temporomandibular joint.

Teaching Points

Correct Answer: 2

Mouth opening requires lengthening of the muscles of mastication as the body of the mandible moves away from the upper palate. Lateral deviation does not require a significant lengthening in the muscles of mastication, as the primary motion of the mandible is a slight anterior translation of the mandibular condyle without increasing the distance between the body of the mandible and the upper palate.

Incorrect Choices:

Unilateral capsular and interarticular restrictions of the temporomandibular joint would result in a deflection of the mandible toward the side of restriction with opening and would limit lateral deviation away from the side of restriction due to a decreased anterior translation of the mandibular condyle. An anterior disc displacement with reduction would not limit mouth opening.

Type of Reasoning: Analysis

This question requires an understanding of the basic biomechanics of the temporomandibular joint and the ability to analyze examination findings in order to arrive at a correct conclusion. The question tests the ability to relate various examination findings to normal and abnormal anatomy and biomechanics and make an appropriate clinical diagnosis, which is an analytical reasoning skill. For this case, the symptoms indicate decreased flexibility in the muscles of mastication on the left. Review temporomandibular joint function and dysfunction if answered incorrectly.

B31

Nonsystem | Safety, Professional Responsibilities, Research

A patient with TBI has a convulsive seizure during a therapy session. The patient has lost consciousness and presents with tonic-clonic convulsions of all extremities. What is the therapist's **BEST** response?

Choices:

1. Position in supine-lying with head supported with a pillow, and wait out the seizure.
2. Wrap the limbs with a sheet to prevent self-harm, position in supine-lying, and call for emergency assistance.
3. Position in side-lying, check for an open airway, and immediately call for emergency assistance.
4. Initiate rescue breathing immediately and call for help to restrain the patient.

Teaching Points

Correct Answer: 3

This is an emergency situation. In order to prevent aspiration, turn the head to the side or position in side-lying. Check to see whether the airway is open, and then call for emergency assistance. Wait for tonic-clonic activity to subside before initiating artificial ventilation, if needed.

Incorrect Choices:

Supine positioning can be life-threatening if the tongue falls backward to restrict the airway. Rescue breathing and restraining the patient are not indicated.

Type of Reasoning: Evaluation

This question requires one to make a value judgment of the most appropriate course of action in a treatment situation. In this case, the symptoms of the patient constitute an emergency, and the therapist should undertake first-aid actions and call for emergency assistance. If this question was answered incorrectly, refer to first-aid guidelines for patients with seizure disorders.

B32 

Nonsystem | Safety, Professional Responsibilities, Research

A therapist wants to know whether neurodevelopmental treatment (NDT) handling techniques produce an improvement in independent rolling that lasts longer than 30 minutes. In this study, rolling is what type of variable?

Choices:

1. Control variable.
2. Independent variable.
3. Dependent variable.
4. Intervening variable.

Teaching Points

Correct Answer: 3

The dependent variable is the change or difference in behavior (in this example, rolling) that results from the intervention.

Incorrect Choices:

NDT handling is the independent variable. The terms "intervening" and "control" are not used to correctly define the study.

Type of Reasoning: Deductive

Information related to research protocols and guidelines are often deductive reasoning–type questions. Here, the test taker must recall factual knowledge to make the correct decision. If this question was answered incorrectly, refer to terminology related to quantitative research, especially for types of variables.

B33

Cardiovascular/Pulmonary and Lymphatic | Evaluation, Diagnosis

An adult with no significant past medical history presents to the emergency room with complaints of fever, shaking chills, and a worsening productive cough. The patient has chest pains over the posterior base of the left thorax, which are made worse on inspiration. What would be an expected physical finding for this patient?

Choices:

1. Symmetrical breathing.
2. Crackles over the left thorax.
3. Increased chest excursion.
4. Slowed respiratory rate.

Teaching Points

Correct Answer: 2

Crackles are a typical finding over the area correlating with an infiltrate.

Incorrect Choices:

With a lower than normal tidal volume, a respiratory rate would have to be elevated, not slowed, to maintain an adequate minute ventilation (respiratory rate times tidal volume = minute ventilation). Because the patient is having pain, thoracic expansion would likely be limited and asymmetrical.

Type of Reasoning: Inference

In this question, one must draw conclusions from the evidence presented about the patient. In this situation, the patient's symptoms would **NOT** indicate the possibility of a slowed respiratory rate or symmetrical breathing. Therefore, to arrive at the correct conclusion, one must infer or make conclusions based on the evidence presented.

B34

Neuromuscular | Examination

A patient is referred to physical therapy for functional gait difficulties. The patient is unable to take a normal step and drags the left foot. Examination reveals muscle weakness with fasciculations in the left lower leg. For what should the therapist examine?

Choices:

1. Decreased tone and hyporeflexia.
2. Muscle spasms and positive Babinski.
3. Increased tone and hyperreflexia.
4. Dyssynergia and timing deficits.

Teaching Points

Correct Answer: 1

Muscle weakness with fasciculations is symptomatic of a lower motor neuron (LMN) lesion. Other signs and symptoms of a LMN lesion include hypotonia or flaccidity, hyporeflexia, or absent reflexes and neurogenic atrophy.

Incorrect Choices:

The other choices are all signs and symptoms of upper motor neuron (UMN) lesions.

Type of Reasoning: Inductive

This question requires the test taker to determine a best course of action based on signs and symptoms presented. This necessitates clinical judgment, which is an inductive reasoning skill. In this situation, the therapist should also examine for decreased tone and hyporeflexia. If answered incorrectly, review information on lower motor neuron lesions.

B35 

Metabolic/Endocrine | Evaluation, Diagnosis

An elderly patient with hyperthyroidism is referred to physical therapy following a period of prolonged bedrest. What should the therapist be alert for when monitoring exercise of this patient?

Choices:

1. Decreased heart rate and blood pressure.
2. Tachycardia and dyspnea.
3. Muscle weakness and joint pain.
4. Arrhythmias and bradycardia.

Teaching Points

Correct Answer: 2

Hyperthyroidism is a hypermetabolic state and is associated with exercise intolerance and impaired cardiopulmonary function. Symptoms include dyspnea, fatigue, tachycardia, and arrhythmia. In older people there is increased risk of aggravating preexisting heart disease (e.g., atrial fibrillation, angina, and myocardial infarction).

Incorrect Choices:

Heart rate is increased during exercise in hyperthyroidism. Muscle weakness (typically proximal) and fatigue are present while increased joint pain is not characteristic. Tachycardia, not bradycardia, is seen.

Type of Reasoning: Inference

This question provides a diagnosis and the test taker must determine the likely risk factors for it. This requires inferential reasoning skill, in which one determines what is most likely to be true of a diagnosis. For this case, the risk factors include tachycardia and dyspnea. Review risk factors for hyperthyroidism if answered incorrectly.

B36 

Nonsystem | Equipment, Devices, Biophysical Agents

A patient strained the lower back muscles 3 weeks ago, and now complains of pain (6/10). Upon examination, the therapist identifies bilateral muscle spasm from T10–L4. The therapist elects to apply interferential current to help reduce pain and spasm. What is the **BEST** electrode configuration in this case?

Choices:

1. Four electrodes, with current flow perpendicular to the spinal column.
2. Two electrodes, with current flow perpendicular to the spinal column.
3. Four electrodes, with current flow diagonal to the spinal column.
4. Two electrodes, with current flow parallel to the spinal column.

Exam B

Teaching Points

Correct Answer: 3

The crisscrossed electrode configuration allows: (1) a greater area to be treated and (2) current interference to occur between the frequencies of the two circuits because of the diagonal pattern.

Incorrect Choices:

A crisscrossed electrode configuration is needed to create interferential current. None of the other electrode configurations facilitates the flow of current diagonal to the spinal column, which would cause the frequencies to intersect.

Type of Reasoning: Deductive

This question requires recall of factual information related to the protocol for electrode placement when using interferential current. The test taker must refer to this knowledge to understand that four electrodes with current flowing diagonal to the spinal column are best for treating the patient's symptoms.

B37 

Neuromuscular | Examination

An infant is independent in sitting, including all protective extension reactions, and can pull-to-stand through kneeling, cruise sideways, and stand alone. The infant still demonstrates plantar grasp in standing. What is this infant's approximate chronological age?

Choices:

1. 6 months.
2. 5 months.
3. 8–9 months.
4. 10–15 months.

Teaching Points

Correct Answer: 3

The 8- to 9-month-old will be able to pull-to-stand, stand alone, and cruise sideways, but because he/she is not yet walking, may still exhibit plantar grasp in the standing position.

Incorrect Choices:

At 5 months, the infant can roll prone to supine and demonstrates head control in supported sitting. At 6 months, the infant can sit independently and pull-to-stand. At 10–15 months, the infant typically begins to walk unassisted.

Type of Reasoning: Deductive

In this question, one must recall the developmental milestones of an infant in order to arrive at the correct conclusion. This type of recall is factual and based on guidelines, which is a deductive reasoning skill. If this question was answered incorrectly, refer to the developmental milestones and reflexes of infants.

B38 

Musculoskeletal | Interventions

A retired bus driver has experienced increasing frequency of low back pain over the past 10 years. The patient states that nonsteroidal anti-inflammatory drugs (NSAIDs) help to relieve the symptoms, but there is always a nagging-type pain. The patient reports significant stiffness in the morning that dissipates by noon after exercising and walking. Pain is exacerbated with frequent lifting and bending activities, as well as sitting for long periods. What should the physical therapy plan of care emphasize?

Choices:

1. Modalities to reduce pain, postural reeducation, and dynamic stabilization exercises.
2. Postural reeducation, soft tissue mobilization, and dynamic stabilization.
3. Modalities to reduce pain, joint mobilization, and lumbar extension exercises.
4. Joint mobilization, soft tissue mobilization, and flexion exercises.

Teaching Points

Correct Answer: 2

This is a long-term degenerative and postural dysfunction that is manageable with medication and proper physical activity. Therefore, the most effective use of treatment time should emphasize regaining normal postural alignment and functional ADLs.

Incorrect Choices:

Whereas modalities and mobilization can relieve acute pain, this is a chronic problem that demands choices appropriate for long-term management of the problem.

Type of Reasoning: Inference

One must consider all of the patient's symptoms and determine what the likely cause(s) of the symptoms is (are) in order to make an appropriate decision for intervention. This requires the use of inferential reasoning, in which decisions are made after drawing conclusions from the evidence presented.

B39 

Musculoskeletal | Evaluation, Diagnosis

A patient presents to physical therapy with a primary complaint of low back pain and right lower extremity radicular symptoms extending distally to the calf of 2 weeks duration. Current pain intensity is rated as 2/10 with rest and 5/10 during lumbar extension movements. What is the strongest prognostic indicator that would affect the clinical outcome?

Choices:

1. 2/10 pain intensity with rest.
2. Current symptom duration (2 weeks).
3. Lower extremity radicular symptoms.
4. 5/10 pain intensity during lumbar extension.

Teaching Points

Correct Answer: 3

The presence of lower extremity radicular symptoms in patients experiencing low back pain is a strong negative prognostic indicator for achieving good clinical outcomes.

Incorrect Choices:

Pain intensity with rest in this case was fairly low (i.e., 2/10) and this pain intensity assessment alone may be limited because it does not consider pain intensity during activity. An increase in pain intensity with lumbar extension movements (i.e., 5/10) does provide important information relevant to activity; however, it does not necessarily indicate a poor prognosis alone and is not as strong a negative prognostic indicator when compared to lower extremity radicular symptoms. Symptom duration of 2 weeks is not considered a chronic state; therefore, it may not be viewed as a negative prognostic indicator for clinical outcomes.

Type of Reasoning: Evaluation

This question requires one to understand the concept of positive and negative prognostic indicators for good clinical outcomes. A positive prognostic indicator is one that is associated with achieving a good clinical outcome. A **negative prognostic indicator** (which was the focus of this question) is one that is associated with not achieving a good clinical outcome. In order to answer this question correctly, one must determine what provided information is associated with **NOT** achieving a good clinical outcome based on this clinical scenario.

B40

System Interactions | Evaluation, Diagnosis

An elderly patient with diabetes and bilateral lower extremity amputation is to be discharged from an acute care hospital 2 weeks postsurgery. The incisions on the residual limbs are not healed and continue to drain. The patient is unable to transfer because the venous graft sites in the upper extremities are painful and not fully healed. Endurance out-of-bed is limited. What is the **BEST** choice of discharge destination for this patient?

Choices:

1. Skilled nursing facility.
2. Custodial care facility.
3. Home.
4. Rehabilitation hospital.

Teaching Points

Correct Answer: 1

A skilled nursing facility is the best facility because the patient continues to require nursing care for the open wounds. Initiation of physical therapy when this patient is able is also available.

Incorrect Choices:

Discharge to home would be premature because the patient is unable to transfer. Custodial care involves medical or nonmedical care that does not seek a cure. A rehabilitation hospital is not appropriate at this time, because the patient cannot actively participate in rehabilitation 3 hours/day.

Type of Reasoning: Inductive

One must utilize clinical judgment in this situation to make an appropriate determination for the best discharge situation for this patient. The key is that the patient's current medical status requires continued nursing care, which can be managed at a skilled nursing facility. In addition, the patient can continue to receive rehabilitation at a duration that is most appropriate for the patient's current tolerance for functional activity. Questions that require clinical judgment often utilize inductive reasoning skill.

B41

Neuromuscular | Examination

A patient currently being seen for low back pain awoke one morning with drooping left facial muscles and excessive drooling. The patient was recovering from a cold and had experienced an earache in the left ear during the previous 2 days. The therapist suspects Bell's palsy. What cranial nerve test can confirm this diagnosis?

Choices:

1. Taste over the posterior tongue, and having the patient protrude the tongue.
2. Taste over the anterior tongue, and having the patient raise the eyebrows and puff the cheeks.
3. Corneal reflex and stretch reflexes of facial muscles.
4. Trigger points for pain, especially over the temporomandibular joint (TMJ).

Teaching Points

Correct Answer: 2

Bell's palsy is a lower motor neuron lesion affecting the branches of the facial nerve, CN VII. Examination of the motor function of the muscles of facial expression (i.e., raise eyebrows, show teeth, smile, close eyes tightly, puff cheeks) and taste over the anterior tongue will reveal deficits of CN VII function.

Incorrect Choices:

Taste over the posterior tongue is a function of CN IX (glossopharyngeal). Strength of tongue protrusion is a function of CN XII (hypoglossal). Pupillary reflexes are a function of CN II (optic).

Type of Reasoning: Inference

In this question, the suspected diagnosis and symptoms are provided, but the test taker must determine how to best confirm this diagnosis through testing of the cranial nerves. This question requires inferential critical reasoning, which uses clinical decision-making based on facts and evidence. If this question was answered incorrectly, refer to information on Bell's palsy.

B42

Neuromuscular | Examination

A PTA is assigned to ambulate a patient with a 10-year history of Parkinson's disease (PD). What should the PT instruct the PTA to watch for?

Choices:

1. Wider steps and increased double support time.
2. An abnormally wide base of support.
3. Decreased trunk rotation with shorter steps.
4. Unsteady, uneven gait with veering to one side.

Teaching Points

Correct Answer: 3

Gait changes characteristic of PD include loss of arm swing and reciprocal trunk movements, shuffling gait with shorter steps, and festinating gait (an abnormal and involuntary increase in the speed of walking).

Incorrect Choices:

Patients with PD take shorter steps (not longer). Veering to one side only is indicative of a unilateral peripheral vestibular deficiency (the patient veers to the side with the dysfunction). An abnormally wide base of support is indicative of gait unsteadiness but is not typical in the patient with PD.

Type of Reasoning: Deductive

This question essentially requires one to recall the typical gait pattern of patients with PD. This type of recall is factual and based on guidelines, thus utilizing deductive reasoning skills. If this question was answered incorrectly, refer to information of gait patterns in PD.

B43 

Cardiovascular/Pulmonary and Lymphatic | Evaluation, Diagnosis

A patient with congestive heart failure (CHF) is on a regimen of diuretics (chlorothiazide). What are the potential adverse effects of this medication that the PT should be alert for?

Choices:

1. Hyperkalemia and premature ventricular contractions (PVCs).
2. Myalgia and joint pains.
3. Orthostatic hypotension and dizziness.
4. Reflex tachycardia and unstable BP.

Teaching Points

Correct Answer: 3

Thiazide diuretics are used to manage mild to moderate hypertension. Adverse side effects include orthostatic hypotension and dizziness, along with drowsiness, lethargy, and weakness. These represent a safety risk during functional training and gait.

Incorrect Choices:

BP is lowered and is more stable, not less. Hypokalemia (not hyperkalemia) can occur, resulting in increased PVCs. Muscle cramps and weakness can occur. Joint pains are likely caused by a comorbid condition.

Type of Reasoning: Inference

The test taker utilizes factual knowledge of side effects of medications, coupled with knowledge of CHF to make the correct decision in this case, using inferential reasoning skills.

B44 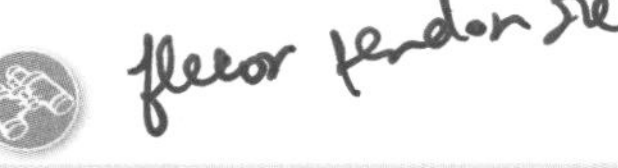

Musculoskeletal | Evaluation, Diagnosis

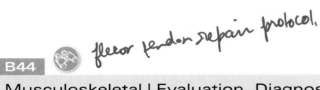

A patient with a traumatic injury to the right hand had a flexor tendon repair to the fingers. When should physical therapy intervention begin following this type of repair?

Choices:

1. After the splint is removed in 4–6 weeks to allow ample healing time for the repaired tendon.
2. After the splint is removed in 2–3 weeks to allow full AROM of all affected joints.
3. Within a few days after surgery to allow for early initiation of strengthening exercises.
4. Within a few days after surgery to preserve tendon gliding.

Teaching Points

Correct Answer: 4

Early passive and active assistive exercises promote collagen remodeling to allow free tendon gliding.

Incorrect Choices:

When rehabilitation is delayed by several weeks, adhesions form, which restrict free tendon gliding. Early initiation of strengthening exercises is contraindicated.

Type of Reasoning: Inductive

This question requires one to use clinical judgment to make a determination of the best intervention for a patient who has had a recent flexor tendon repair of the hand. One utilizes knowledge of hand therapy and early tendon repair protocols to arrive at the correct conclusion. If this question was answered incorrectly, review flexor tendon repair information and therapy protocols.

B45 

Musculoskeletal | Examination, Diagnosis

A female patient complains of intermittent pain in the right sacroiliac region. There was an insidious onset approximately 4 months ago. Pain has gradually worsened and is now fairly constant and does not vary much with activity or movement. Active motion assessment of the lumbar spine reveals no change in symptoms with movement. Sacroiliac provocation tests are negative. The patient is mildly tender over the right sacroiliac region. What is the **MOST** likely diagnosis for this patient?

Choices:

1. Sacroiliac joint sprain.
2. Multifidus muscle strain.
3. Ovarian cyst.
4. Right L5/S1 facet joint arthrosis.

Teaching Points

Correct Answer: 3

An ovarian cyst can refer pain to the sacroiliac region and is more likely to cause constant pain that does not vary much with activity. Symptoms are not likely to be reproduced with a musculoskeletal examination.

Incorrect Choices:

A sacroiliac joint strain, L5/S1 facet arthrosis, and multifidus muscle strain should cause reproduction of the patient's symptoms with active movements. The symptoms should be activity related. They will therefore vary in intensity depending on the particular activity in which the patient engages. In addition, a sacroiliac sprain would likely be symptomatic with SI provocation tests.

Type of Reasoning: Analysis

This question provides a group of symptoms and the test taker must determine the most likely cause for them. This is an analytical reasoning skill. For this situation, the symptoms are consistent with an ovarian cyst. Review signs and symptoms of an ovarian cyst if answered incorrectly.

B46

Neuromuscular | Examination

The therapist suspects that a patient recovering from a middle cerebral artery stroke is exhibiting a pure hemianopsia. What test should be used to confirm the hemianopsia?

Choices:

1. Penlight held approximately 12 inches from the eyes and moved to the extremes of gaze right and left.
2. Penlight held 6 inches from the eyes and moved inward toward the face.
3. Visual confrontation test with a moving finger.
4. Distance acuity chart placed on a well-lighted wall at patient's eye level 20 feet away.

Teaching Points

Correct Answer: 3

Visual field is examined using the confrontation test. The patient sits opposite the therapist and is instructed to maintain his/her gaze on the therapist's nose. The therapist slowly brings a target (moving finger or pen) in the patient's field of view alternately from the right or left sides. The patient indicates when and where he/she first sees the target.

Incorrect Choices:

Distance acuity vision is tested using a Snellen eye chart at a distance of 20 feet. Ocular pursuit is tested using a penlight moved in an H pattern to the extremes of gaze. Convergence is tested using a penlight and ruler; the patient keeps the penlight in focus as it moves inward from a distance of 4 or 6 inches.

Type of Reasoning: Inference

This question basically asks the test taker to recall the appropriate examination approach for hemianopsia. Questions such as these do require recall of factual knowledge (knowledge of the different tests), but then that knowledge must be applied to the specific patient presented in the question, which moves beyond factual recall to drawing a conclusion, which is an inferential reasoning skill.

B47

Musculoskeletal | Evaluation, Diagnosis

An overweight adult patient complains of right anterior hip and knee pain while walking, especially when weight bearing on the right. Lumbar AROM is normal and pain free. Right hip AROM and PROM are limited compared to the left. Right knee AROM and PROM are full and pain free. There is no pain with resisted testing at the right hip or right knee. The scouring test reproduces the patient's hip and knee symptoms. Hip joint distraction relieves these symptoms. Based on the above findings, what is the **MOST** likely diagnosis?

Choices:

1. Trochanteric bursitis.
2. Patellofemoral syndrome.
3. Piriformis strain.
4. Hip degenerative joint disease.

Exam B

Teaching Points

Correct Answer: 4

Scouring test or compression at the hip joint reproduces the patient's symptoms, suggesting a joint problem at the hip. The scouring test can also result in referred pain to the knee. Weight bearing that compressed the hip joint also reproduces the patient's symptoms. Distraction of the hip joint surfaces relieves symptoms, suggesting hip DJD. The anterior knee region is a common pain referral site for the hip joint. In addition, the overweight condition supports the diagnosis of hip DJD due to excessive compressive forces over an extended period of time.

Incorrect Choices:

There is no pain with resisted testing, which rules out a contractile problem. Knee AROM, PROM, and resisted testing are negative, ruling out patellofemoral syndrome. Pain from trochanteric bursitis is specifically localized to the greater trochanter on the lateral aspect of the hip.

Type of Reasoning: Analysis

For this question, a group of symptoms is presented and the test taker must analyze each in order to determine the most likely diagnosis. Questions of this type often require analytical reasoning skill, in which pieces of information are weighed to draw reasonable conclusions. For this case, the symptoms most likely indicate the presence of hip degenerative joint disease (DJD). If answered incorrectly, review hip DJD signs and symptoms.

B48 

Nonsystem | Safety, Professional Responsibilities, Research

A therapist investigated the accuracy of pulse oximetry estimates during exercise. Correlational analysis measured the strength of the relationship between two types of ear probe—equipped pulse oximeters during heavy cycle exercise under hypoxic conditions. The investigator found measured arterial oxyhemoglobin saturation (%HbO_2) levels to have a correlation of 0.89 at high saturation but only 0.68 at low saturation levels. How should the therapist interpret these results?

Choices:

1. During heavy exercise, oxygen saturation levels should be interpreted cautiously.
2. Both devices are highly accurate at all saturation levels.
3. Accuracy of the measurements increases at higher saturation levels.
4. Both devices are only moderately accurate.

Teaching Points

Correct Answer: 3

The result of the study indicates that the correlation between the two types of oximeters was high when oxygen saturation levels were high (0.89), but only moderate (0.68) at low oxygen saturation levels.

Incorrect Choices:

Accuracy was not the same at all saturation levels, and the high correlation during high saturation suggests that the devices are accurate during heavy exercise.

Type of Reasoning: Deductive

This type of question requires knowledge of guidelines in correlational research and parameters for high versus moderate correlation. This type of knowledge is factual recall using deductive reasoning skills. If this question was answered incorrectly, refer to correlational research guidelines.

B49

Musculoskeletal | Examination

A college soccer player sustained a hyperextension knee injury when kicking the ball. The patient was taken to the emergency room of a local hospital and was diagnosed with "knee sprain." The player was sent to physical therapy the next day for rehabilitation. As part of the examination to determine the type of treatment plan to implement, the therapist conducted the test shown in the figure. Based on the test picture, the therapist is examining the integrity of which structure?

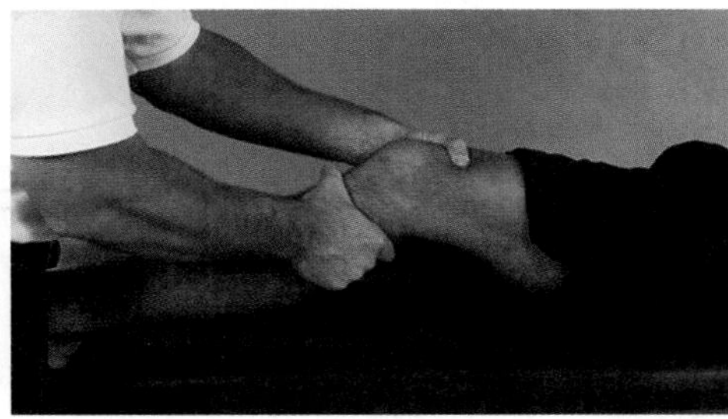

Choices:

1. Iliotibial band.
2. Posterior cruciate ligament.
3. Anterior cruciate ligament.
4. Medial meniscus.

Teaching Points

Correct Answer: 3

The test shown in the figure is Lachman's stress test to determine the integrity of the anterior cruciate ligament.

Incorrect Choices:

The posterior cruciate is examined using the posterior drawer and the reverse Lachman's stress test. The medial meniscus is examined using McMurray's and Apley tests. The iliotibial band is tested using the Noble compression test.

Type of Reasoning: Inference

The question requires the test taker to recall the visual information depicted as a test of integrity of the anterior cruciate ligament. This is factual recall of visual information, but also requires one to sort out other tests that may appear similar in order to arrive at the correct conclusion. This skill is therefore inferential, requiring one to draw conclusions based on visual information.

B50 

Musculoskeletal | Evaluation, Diagnosis

A patient is seen in physical therapy 2 days after a motor vehicle accident. The chief complaints are headaches, dizziness, neck pain with guarding, and a "sensation of a lump in the throat." Plain film x-rays were read as negative. The therapist should refer this patient for what type of imaging?

Choices:

1. Second series of plain film x-rays.
2. T2 magnetic resonance imaging (MRI).
3. Computed tomography (CT) scan.
4. Myelogram.

Teaching Points

Correct Answer: 3

The primary concern of the therapist is to rule out strong suspicions of an upper cervical spine fracture. CT scan is still preferred for assessing cortical bone, especially spinal fractures.

Incorrect Choices:

Plain films, already taken, did not show any fracture, which is not uncommon. A second series would not be expected to reveal any new information. The T2 MRI and myelogram are not as specific for assessing bony anatomy as the CT scan.

Type of Reasoning: Inductive

One must consider the symptoms of the patient and a possible cause to arrive at the conclusion that a CT would be the most appropriate next step in determining the cause for the symptoms. Inductive reasoning skills are utilized when one must use knowledge of symptoms plus diagnostic skills to make an appropriate decision. If this question was answered incorrectly, refer to information on indications for CT scans.

B51 

Neuromuscular | Examination

During a test of upper extremity rapid alternating movement (RAM), the movements of the hands and elbows become irregular with wider excursions than expected. As speed is increased, the movements become more disorganized. What are these findings indicative of?

Choices:

1. Brainstem dysfunction.
2. Lower motor neuron weakness.
3. Cerebellar dysfunction.
4. Upper motor neuron weakness.

Teaching Points

Correct Answer: 3

Cerebellar dysfunction is characterized by classic cerebellar movement disturbances of dyssynergia (in this case), dysmetria, and dysdiadochokinesia. Movement decomposition is velocity dependent, with greater disturbances in movement control at higher speeds.

Incorrect Choices:

UMN lesions can produce weakness and dyssynergia accompanied by spasticity. Spasticity is velocity dependent, with slowing of movements at faster speeds. LMN lesions produce weakness or paralysis, with hypotonia or flaccidity. Brainstem dysfunction produces a variety of deficits, with mixed sensory/motor symptoms. All of these findings are not reported in this case.

Type of Reasoning: Analysis

For this question, the test taker must analyze the symptoms presented and determine the likely cause for such symptoms. Questions of this nature require analytical reasoning skill. For this scenario, the symptoms indicate cerebellar dysfunction. Review symptoms of cerebellar dysfunction if answered incorrectly.

B52 

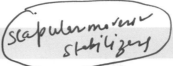

Musculoskeletal | Interventions

A patient presents with a persistently downwardly rotated and adducted scapula during humeral elevation. The plan of care includes stretching and strengthening to improve range of motion. What muscles should be stretched and strengthened?

Choices:

1. Stretching rhomboid muscles and strengthening serratus anterior muscle.
2. Stretching pectoralis major and strengthening rhomboid muscles.
3. Stretching pectoralis minor and strengthening trapezius muscles.
4. Stretching serratus anterior and strengthening levator scapula and lower trapezius.

Teaching Points

Correct Answer: 1

The rhomboids are scapular downward rotators, scapular adductors, and scapular elevators. Insufficient length of the rhomboids would limit upward scapular rotation, and stretching to restore proper length of these muscles would help to promote upward scapular rotation.

Incorrect Choices:

The serratus anterior muscle acts as an upward scapular rotator and scapular abductor. Weakness of the serratus anterior would impair active scapular upward rotation, and strengthening exercises would promote upward scapular rotation.

Type of Reasoning: Inductive

This question requires the test taker to determine a best course of action to improve a deficit. Questions of this nature require clinical judgment, which is an inductive reasoning skill. For this case, the deficit is best treated with stretching of the rhomboid muscles and strengthening of the serratus anterior muscle. If answered incorrectly, review muscle actions of the shoulder girdle, especially scapular movers and stabilizers.

B53 

Neuromuscular | Evaluation, Diagnosis

A patient is recovering from stroke and, at 4 months, is ambulating with a straight cane for household distances. During outpatient physical therapy, the therapist has the patient practice walking with no assistive device. Recurvatum is observed that worsens with continued walking. What is the therapist's **BEST** choice for intervention?

Choices:

1. Give the patient a small-based quad cane (SBQC) to improve stability and have him/her practice AROM in supine.
2. Exercise the quadriceps using isokinetic resistance at higher loads and increasing speeds.
3. Practice isolated small-range quadriceps eccentric control work in standing and continue with the straight cane.
4. Give the patient a KAFO to control the hyperextension and a hemi walker.

Teaching Points

Correct Answer: 3

Eccentric quadriceps control work (closed-chain exercises) is indicated in order to reduce recurvatum. The patient should continue with the straight cane until able to walk without the device and recurvatum.

Incorrect Choices:

Open-chain exercises (isokinetic resistance, AROM) do not adequately address the functional demands of gait. The use of SBQC or hemi walker will not correct the problem. A KAFO is inappropriate to stabilize the knee, which can be effectively stabilized using either an AFO or a Swedish knee cage. The use of an orthosis should be considered only as a last resort.

Type of Reasoning: Inductive

One must use clinical judgment and knowledge of recurvatum in ambulation to arrive at the correct conclusion. Inductive reasoning questions require use of knowledge combined with clinical judgment to determine the best course of action in clinical situations. In this situation, the test taker must recognize that the recurvatum indicates eccentric quadriceps control work.

B54 

Neuromuscular | Evaluation, Diagnosis

A patient recovering from an incomplete spinal cord injury at the L3 level (ASIA scale D) ambulates with bilateral Lofstrand crutches. The patient reports great difficulty going down ramps with unsteady, wobbly knees. What is the **BEST** intervention to use with this patient?

Choices:

1. Prolonged icing to reduce hamstring pain.
2. Stretching using a posterior resting splint for tight plantar flexors.
3. Progressive resistance training for the quadriceps.
4. Biofeedback training to reduce knee extensor spasticity.

Teaching Points

Correct Answer: 3

A spinal cord injury at the level of L3 affects knee extensors. ASIA scale D means the injury is incomplete, with at least half of the key muscles below the neurological level having a muscle grade of 3 or more. A weak knee will wobble or buckle going down stairs or ramps. It is the result of weak quadriceps or knee flexor contracture. Strengthening exercises using progressive resistance training for the quadriceps are indicated.

Incorrect Choices:

Biofeedback training may reduce knee extensor spasticity, but this may only increase knee instability and is not indicated in this case. There is no indication that hamstring pain or tight plantarflexors are present or precipitating causes of the patient's problem.

Type of Reasoning: Inference

In this question, the test taker must understand what impairments result from L3 spinal injury and what clinical interventions can be implemented to improve the patient's deficits. In this situation, the patient's deficits indicate weak knee extensors, which can be strengthened through a progressive resistive exercise program. If this question was answered incorrectly, refer to information on lumbar level spinal cord injury.

B55

Nonsystem | Safety, Professional Responsibilities, Research

Under HIPAA rules, to whom is it illegal to release protected health information (PHI) without a competent patient's consent?

Choices:

1. A State Agency responsible for investigating suspected abuse.
2. The insurance company that is paying for the patient's treatment.
3. Another health care provider involved in the care of the patient.
4. The patient's spouse.

Teaching Points

Correct Answer: 4

A spouse does not have the legal right to the patient's information without the patient's consent.

Incorrect Choices:

Those individuals involved in the care of the patient, a legal guardian with power of attorney in situations in which the patient is judged mentally incompetent, or the patient's payer have a legal right to information regarding a patient's care without obtaining the patient's consent for releasing information. The therapist has a positive legal obligation to report suspected abuse whether or not consent is granted.

Type of Reasoning: Evaluation

In this question, one must determine the strength of the statements presented as well as which statement adheres to legal guidelines related to HIPAA. Evaluation questions often require test takers to make value judgments and recall certain guidelines in order to make those judgments.

B56

Musculoskeletal | Interventions

With respect to a worker's sitting posture, which change provides the greatest reduction in lumbar spine compression forces?

Choices:

1. Eliminating armrests on the chair.
2. Decreasing the chair backrest–seat angle to 85°.
3. Increasing the chair backrest–seat angle to between 90° and 110°.
4. Using a 2-inch gel seat cushion.

Teaching Points

Correct Answer: 3

Maximal reduction of lumbar disc pressures can be achieved by increasing the angle between the seat pan and the chair backrest to between 90° and 110°, using armrests for support, or adding a lumbar support. Combining the effects of all three provides the best solution.

Incorrect Choices:

A gel seat cushion reduces pressures on the ischial seat. Eliminating armrests or decreasing the chair backrest–seat angle would only worsen the problem.

Type of Reasoning: Inference

This question requires one to make a clinical determination of the best course of action. Inferential questions require one to make sense of information presented and to draw conclusions from it. Therefore, one must draw conclusions about the sitting posture in order to determine which solution would most effectively reduce compression forces in the lumbar spine.

B57  

Musculoskeletal | Evaluation, Diagnosis

A baseball pitcher is referred to physical therapy with progressive posterior shoulder pain and weakness of the shoulder abductors and lateral rotators. The therapist notices muscle wasting superior and inferior to the scapular spine. Damage to which of the following structures is the **MOST** likely cause?

Choices:

1. Spinal accessory nerve.
2. Scalene muscles.
3. Suprascapular nerve.
4. Long head of the biceps brachii.

Teaching Points

Correct Answer: 3

Microtrauma to the suprascapular nerve can occur with repetitive activities involving shoulder "cocking" and follow-through resulting in inflammation and muscle weakness of the muscles supplied by the suprascapular nerve (the supraspinatus and infraspinatus muscles).

Incorrect Choices:

Damage to the spinal accessory nerve will promote weakness and atrophy of the upper trapezius muscle. Damage to the long head of the biceps brachii or scalene muscles will not present with posterior shoulder pain, weakness with shoulder abduction/external rotation, and/or atrophy of the supraspinatus and infraspinatus muscles.

Type of Reasoning: Analysis

This question requires one to rely on knowledge of shoulder neuroanatomy in order to choose the correct solution. This type of recall is factual in nature, with basic analysis or interpretation of the information presented. In this case, the patient's weakness of the shoulder abductors and lateral rotators is indicative of damage to the suprascapular nerve. If this question was answered incorrectly, refer to shoulder neuroanatomy and functional anatomy.

B58 

Cardiovascular/Pulmonary and Lymphatic | Examination

An elderly patient presents with severe COPD, GOLD stage 4. Which of the following physical examination findings would the therapist expect to find?

Choices:

1. Kyphosis with an increased thoracic excursion.
2. Barreled chest with a decreased thoracic excursion.
3. Pectus excavatum with an increased thoracic excursion.
4. Pectus carinatum with decreased thoracic excursion.

Teaching Points

Correct Answer: 2

A patient with severe COPD (GOLD 4) will have lost much of the elastic recoil properties of the lung. The usual elastic properties of the lung tissue help to pull the thorax into the normal chest wall configuration of health. Without these elastic recoil properties the patient's thorax will "barrel" in appearance, meaning it is larger and rounder than what you would normally expect. As the thorax has moved into an inspiratory position at rest, there is less movement available, so a decreased thoracic excursion would be expected.

Incorrect Choices:

Pectus excavatum (funnel chest) is not an acquired chest wall deformity that results in decreased thoracic excursion. Pectus carinatum (pigeon breast) is not an acquired chest wall deformity that results in a decreased thoracic excursion. While the barreling of the chest of COPD often has a kyphosis associated with it, the second hallmark to the chest wall deformity of COPD is a decrease in excursion.

Type of Reasoning: Deductive

This question provides a diagnosis and the test taker must recall the likely presentation of that diagnosis. This is a deductive reasoning skill, as one must recollect the signs and symptoms of COPD in order to arrive at a correct conclusion. For this case, one should expect a barreled chest with a decreased thoracic excursion. Review signs and symptoms of COPD if answered incorrectly.

B59 

Neuromuscular | Evaluation, Diagnosis

A patient is recovering from surgical resection of an acoustic neuroma and presents with symptoms of dizziness, vertigo, horizontal nystagmus, and postural instability. To address these problems, what should the physical therapy plan of care incorporate?

Choices:

1. Repetition of movements and positions that provoke dizziness and vertigo.
2. Hallpike's exercises to improve speed in movement transitions.
3. Strengthening exercises focusing on spinal extensors.
4. Prolonged bedrest to allow vestibular recovery to occur.

Teaching Points

Correct Answer: 1

In patients with unilateral vestibular pathology, habituation training (use of positions and movements that evoke symptoms) will encourage the vestibular system to recalibrate. Good recovery can generally be expected with gradual progression of exercises.

Incorrect Choices:

Prolonged bedrest will delay recovery and may result in incomplete recovery. Strengthening exercises for spinal extensors are not indicated in the case information. Hallpike-Dix maneuver is used for assessment and diagnosis of benign paroxysmal positional vertigo and is not a set of exercises.

Type of Reasoning: Inference

One must have knowledge of acoustic neuroma and expected symptomatology in order to choose the correct intervention approach. Inferential reasoning often requires the test taker to draw conclusions based on the evidence presented. Questions that ask what to expect from a diagnosis or a set of symptoms often require use of inferential reasoning. If this question was answered incorrectly, review intervention approaches for vestibular pathology.

B60 

Cardiovascular/Pulmonary and Lymphatic | Evaluation, Diagnosis

A physical therapist is treating a patient with diabetic peripheral neuropathy. The patient recently began taking Lyrica (pregabalin). During a monofilament exam of the feet the therapist notices circumferential marks bilaterally at the level of the malleoli after the socks are removed. The patient is complaining of increased difficulty ambulating long distances. In this situation, what is the therapist's **BEST** course of action?

Choices:

1. Contact the physician about possible development of congestive heart failure.
2. Begin manual lymphatic drainage for secondary lymphedema.
3. Complete the examination and instruct in proper skin care precautions.
4. Educate the patient about the risks of foot ulceration.

Teaching Points

Correct Answer: 1

It is important to recognize serious side effects of commonly used medications and to institute contact with the physician as appropriate. Lyrica is used to help treat diabetic neuropathy. Serious side effects include heart failure, greater difficulty walking long-distances, and lymphedema (marks from the sock).

Incorrect Choices:

Although patient education and manual lymphatic drainage can be important parts of treatment, they are not as important as recognizing the potential for heart failure.

Type of Reasoning: Inductive

This question requires clinical judgment in order to determine a best course of action for a patient with diabetic neuropathy. This necessitates inductive reasoning skill. For this case, the symptoms should alert the therapist to contact the physician about possible development of congestive heart failure. If answered incorrectly, review diabetic neuropathy guidelines and common medications for diabetes.

B61

Musculoskeletal I Examination

A patient presents to the clinic with pain and decreased function of the right shoulder. A full tear of the right rotator cuff musculature is suspected. Which special test will provide the most valid and reliable information confirming this diagnosis?

Choices:

1. Drop arm test.
2. Yergason's test.
3. Neer's impingement test.
4. Clunk test.

Teaching Points

Correct Answer: 1

The primary intent of the drop arm test is to assess if the rotator cuff is intact. If the rotator cuff is fully torn, the drop arm test will be positive, meaning that the arm will fall from a fully elevated position if it is unsupported. The Empty-can test is also a test for the rotator cuff muscles but is more specific for the supraspinatus.

Incorrect Choices:

Yergason's test assesses if the transverse ligament is intact. Neer's impingement test assesses for impingement of the rotator cuff, so once the tendon is torn this will no longer be positive. The clunk test is described as a test to assess for a glenoid labrum tear. None of these tests would be positive with a full tear of the rotator cuff.

Type of Reasoning: Deductive

This question requires the test taker to recall provocative testing guidelines for rotator cuff tears in order to arrive at a correct conclusion. This necessitates recall of facts, which is a deductive reasoning skill. For this case, the drop arm test should be performed to confirm the tear. Review provocative testing of the shoulder, especially rotator cuff injuries, if answered incorrectly.

B62

Cardiovascular/Pulmonary and Lymphatic I Interventions

A patient who is 5 weeks post-myocardial infarction (MI) is participating in a cardiac rehabilitation program. The therapist is monitoring responses to increasing exercise intensity. Which finding is an indication that exercise should be immediately terminated?

Choices:

1. 1.5 mm of downsloping ST segment depression.
2. Peak exercise HR > 140.
3. Appearance of a PVC on the electrocardiogram (ECG).
4. Systolic BP > 140 mm Hg or diastolic BP > 80 mm Hg.

Teaching Points

Correct Answer: 1

The upper limit for exercise intensity prescribed for patients post-MI is based on signs and symptoms. Of the choices, only ST segment depression (> 1.0 mm of horizontal or downsloping depression) is a significant finding, representative of myocardial ischemia.

Incorrect Choices:

Both HR and BP are expected to rise (the levels of 140 and 140/80 are not significant for most patients). The appearance of a single PVC is also not significant because single PVCs can occur in individuals without a cardiac history.

Type of Reasoning: Inference

When questions provide a diagnosis and the test taker must determine the symptoms to watch for, inferential reasoning is used. To answer this question correctly, the test taker must have knowledge of cardiac rehabilitation guidelines and indications for terminating exercise programs. If this question was answered incorrectly, refer to post-MI rehabilitation guidelines.

B63

Neuromuscular | Interventions

An infant who was 39 weeks gestational age at birth and is now 3 weeks chronological age demonstrates colic. In this case, what is the **BEST** intervention the PT should teach the mother?

Choices:

1. Stroking and tapping.
2. Neutral warmth.
3. Visual stimulation with a colored object.
4. Fast vestibular stimulation.

Teaching Points

Correct Answer: 2

Neutral warmth achieved through wrapping or bundling the infant is a calming stimulus.

Incorrect Choices:

All of the other choices would likely increase arousal of the infant. The infant is still too developmentally immature for any of the stimuli other than neutral warmth.

Type of Reasoning: Inductive

One utilizes clinical judgment, with combined knowledge of inhibitory and facilitatory stimuli in infants, in order to choose the best solution. In this scenario, the newborn is too developmentally immature to manage facilitatory stimuli and requires stimuli that are calming or inhibitory, especially if colic is demonstrated. If this question was answered incorrectly, refer to appropriate stimuli for newborns.

B64

Neuromuscular | Examination

A therapist is treating a patient with Brown-Séquard syndrome that resulted from a gunshot wound. Which of the following would the therapist expect to find during the examination?

Choices:

1. Sparing of tracts to sacral segments with preservation of perianal sensation and active toe flexion.
2. Loss of motor function and pain and temperature sensation with preservation of light touch and proprioception below the level of the lesion.
3. Loss of motor function below the level of the lesion primarily in the upper extremities.
4. Ipsilateral loss of motor function, ipsilateral loss of light touch and proprioception, and contralateral loss of pain and temperature.

Teaching Points

Correct Answer: 4

Brown-Séquard syndrome is a hemisection of the spinal cord characterized by ipsilateral loss of dorsal columns with loss of touch, pressure, vibration and proprioception; ipsilateral loss of corticospinal tracts with loss of motor function below level of lesion; contralateral loss of spinothalamic tract with loss of pain and temperature below level of lesion; at lesion level bilateral loss of pain and temperature.

Incorrect Choices:

Anterior cord syndrome: loss of lateral corticospinal tracts with bilateral loss of motor function; loss of spinothalamic tracts with bilateral loss of pain and temperature; preservation of dorsal columns (priopriocep-tion, vibratory sense).

Central cord syndrome: Loss of spinothalamic tracts with bilateral loss of pain and temperature; loss of ventral horn with bilateral loss of motor function (primarily the upper extremities); preservation of proprioception and discriminatory sensation.

Sacral sparing: sparing of tracts to sacral segments with preservation of perianal sensation, rectal sphincter tone, active toe flexion.

Type of Reasoning: Analysis

This question requires factual recall of neuroanatomy in order to arrive at the correct conclusion. One should recall the nature of Brown-Séquard syndrome as a hemisection of the spinal cord, which results in both ipsilateral and contralateral losses below the level of lesion. One also must separate out the symptoms of other spinal cord syndromes, which are different from this scenario. If this question was answered incorrectly, refer to spinal cord injuries and syndromes.

B65 

Neuromuscular | Interventions

A patient is recovering from stroke and presents with moderate impairments of the left upper and lower extremities. The PT's goal today is to instruct the patient in a stand-pivot transfer to the more affected side so the patient can go home on a weekend pass. The spouse is attending today's session and will be assisting the patient on the weekend. What is the **BEST** choice for teaching this task?

Choices:

1. Practice the task first with the patient then with the caregiver.
2. Demonstrate the task, then have the caregiver practice with the patient.
3. Practice the task first with the caregiver, then with the patient.
4. Demonstrate the task, and then practice with the patient.

Teaching Points

Correct Answer: 4

To ensure optimal motor learning, first demonstrate the task at ideal performance speeds. This provides the patient with an appropriate reference of correction (cognitive map) of the task. Then use guided practice with the patient to ensure safety and successful performance.

Incorrect Choices:

Caregivers should become involved only after initial practice of the task with the patient and after the safety of the patient can be assured.

Type of Reasoning: Inference

One must rely upon beliefs and assumptions about the clinical situation above in order to choose the best solution. This is a skill of inferential reasoning, in which the test taker must determine the best course of action to ensure optimal motor learning in educating a caregiver and a patient in transfer skills. Inferential reasoning combines clinical judgment with the need to draw conclusions from evidence presented.

B66

Musculoskeletal | Examination

A patient presents with low back pain of insidious onset. Based on the history and subjective complaints, the patient appears to have a dysfunction of a lumbar facet joint. What clinical test should be utilized to confirm this diagnosis?

Choices:

1. McKenzie's side glide test.
2. Stork standing test.
3. Slump test.
4. Lumbar quadrant test.

Teaching Points

Correct Answer: 4

The motion of the lumbar quadrant test places the lumbar facet joint in its maximally closed and therefore most provocative position, so if positive it is typically indicative of a lumbar facet dysfunction.

Incorrect Choices:

The slump test is utilized to assess the neurodynamics of the spinal and peripheral nerves. The stork standing test is utilized to identify a spondylolisthesis. McKenzie's side glide test is utilized to determine if a disc dysfunction with nerve root involvement is present versus a postural disorder.

Type of Reasoning: Deductive

This question requires the test taker to recall testing guidelines for lumbar facet dysfunction. This necessitates the recall of facts and guidelines, which is a deductive reasoning skill. For this situation, the lumbar quadrant test is best to confirm lumbar facet dysfunction. Review lumbar testing guidelines if answered incorrectly, especially the lumbar quadrant test.

B67 

Nonsystem | Equipment, Devices, Biophysical Agents

When using a patellar tendon-bearing (PTB) prosthesis, a patient experiences excessive knee flexion in early stance. What is the **MOST** likely cause of this problem?

Choices:

1. Socket is aligned too far back or tilted posteriorly.
2. Foot position is inset too much.
3. Socket is aligned too far forward or tilted anteriorly.
4. Foot position is outset too much.

Teaching Points

Correct Answer: 3

In a PTB prosthesis, the socket is normally aligned in slight flexion to enhance loading on the patellar tendon, prevent genu recurvatum and resist the tendency of the amputated limb to slide too deeply into the socket. If it is aligned incorrectly (too far anterior or excessively flexed), it will result in excessive knee flexion in early stance.

Incorrect Choices:
A socket aligned too posterior results in insufficient knee flexion. Excessive foot inset results in lateral thrust at midstance. Excessive foot outset results in medial thrust at midstance.

Type of Reasoning: Analysis
One must understand and analyze the properties and potential issues in using a PTB prosthesis in order to choose the best response. In this situation, excessive knee flexion in early stance is indicative of the socket aligned too far forward or anteriorly tilted. If this question was answered incorrectly, refer to information on PTB prosthetic alignment.

B68 

Integumentary | Evaluation, Diagnosis

A patient presents with bluish discoloration of the skin and nail beds of the fingers and toes. Palms are also cold and moist. What is the **MOST** likely cause of these changes?

Choices:
1. Carotenemia.
2. Hypothyroidism.
3. Cyanosis.
4. Liver disease.

Teaching Points

Correct Answer: 3
Bluish discoloration of the skin and nailbeds of fingers and toes, along with palms that are cold and moist, is indicative of cyanosis. It is caused by an excess of deoxygenated hemoglobin in the blood. It may be central (due to advanced lung disease, congenital heart disease, abnormal hemoglobin) or peripheral (decreased blood flow, venous obstruction).

Incorrect Choices:
Liver disease produces jaundice (diffusely yellow skin and sclerae). Carotenemia produces a yellow color, especially in the palms, soles, and face (does not affect the sclerae). Hypothyroidism produces dry and cool skin.

Type of Reasoning: Analysis
Questions that provide a group of symptoms and the test taker must determine the diagnosis often require analytical reasoning skill. In this situation, the symptoms described indicate the condition of cyanosis. Key words that help one to arrive at a correct conclusion are "bluish discoloration." If this question was answered incorrectly, review signs and symptoms of cyanosis.

B69

Musculoskeletal | Evaluation, Diagnosis

An outpatient physical therapist is examining a patient who underwent a total knee arthroplasty 2 weeks ago. The patient reports that the entire leg has started swelling in the past 2 days. On examination there is pitting edema throughout the lower leg and foot with tenderness throughout the mid calf. Girth measurements reveal a 3.5 cm increase in the size of the mid calf in the symptomatic leg. What recommendation should the physical therapist make to the patient?

Choices:

1. Rest, ice, and elevate the affected lower extremity.
2. Go home and monitor symptoms. Phone the physician if there is no improvement in 24 hours.
3. Go immediately to the emergency department.
4. Go to the physician's office after the therapy session for further assessment.

Teaching Points

Correct Answer: 3

The patient scores a 3 on Well's criteria for deep vein thrombosis, placing him/her in the high probability category. The most appropriate response for the physical therapist would be to send the patient to the emergency department for further assessment.

Incorrect Choices:

Any choice except sending the patient to the emergency department would place the patient at an unnecessary risk for developing a pulmonary embolism.

Type of Reasoning: Evaluation

This question requires one to be familiar with the signs and symptoms associated with deep vein thrombosis. To answer this question correctly one must evaluate the clinical presentation of the patient and weigh the merits of each approach, considering safety of the patient. This is an evaluative reasoning skill. For this situation, the therapist should recommend that the patient go immediately to the emergency department. Review signs and symptoms of deep vein thrombosis if answered incorrectly.

B70

Musculoskeletal | Examination

A patient complains of persistent wrist pain after painting a house 3 weeks ago. The patient demonstrates signs and symptoms consistent with de Quervain's tenosynovitis. What special test can be used to confirm the diagnosis?

Choices:

1. Finkelstein's test.
2. Phalen's test.
3. Froment's sign.
4. Craig's test.

Teaching Points

Correct Answer: 1

Finkelstein's test is specific for reproducing the pain associated with de Quervain's tenosynovitis of the abductor pollicis longus and extensor pollicis brevis.

Incorrect Choices:

Froment's sign is used to identify ulnar nerve dysfunction. Phalen's test identifies median nerve compression in the carpal tunnel. Craig's test identifies an abnormal femoral antetorsion angle, which you hopefully eliminated first.

Type of Reasoning: Deductive

This question requires factual recall of knowledge of provocative tests for de Quervain's tenosynovitis. In this case, the appropriate test is Finkelstein's test, which reproduces the pain of the abductor pollicics longus and extensor pollicis brevis tendons associated with de Quervain's. If this question was answered incorrectly, refer to provocative testing of the hand or wrist and de Quervain's tenosynovitis.

B71 

Cardiovascular/Pulmonary and Lymphatic I Examination

hyper inflated lungs

As part of the chart review, the physical therapist views the patient's most current chest film.

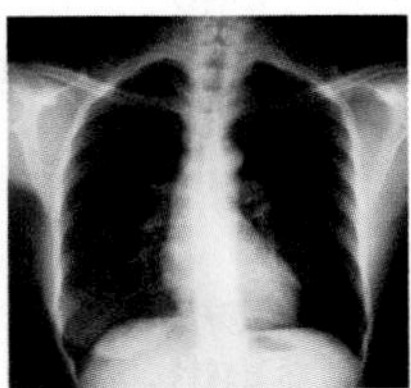

Based on this film, what is the **MOST** likely examination finding?

Choices:

1. Increased lateral costal expansion. ↓ se.
2. Increased subcostal angle.
3. Decreased inspiration:expiration (I:E) ratio.
4. Decreased mediate percussion.

Teaching Points

Correct Answer: 2

This film demonstrates a patient with hyperinflated lungs as evidenced by the flattened diaphragm, blunted costophrenic angle, and increased amount of air. This will cause the subcostal angle to increase significantly.

Incorrect Choices:

Hyperinflated lungs are indicative of obstructive disease. The I:E ratio will increase in this case as the patient has difficulty getting air out. There is no evidence of secretions in this film, which would alter the resonance of mediate percussion, so it can be assumed that this finding would be normal. Lateral costal expansion would be decreased in this patient due to the hyperinflated lungs.

Type of Reasoning: Analysis

This question requires the test taker to determine the **MOST** likely examination finding based on the x-ray. Questions that require analysis of pictures and graphs often necessitate analytical reasoning skill. If this question was answered incorrectly, review signs and symptoms of hyperinflated lungs.

B72

Neuromuscular | Examination

An elderly patient with persistent balance difficulty and a history of recent falls (two in the past 3 months) is referred for physical therapy examination and evaluation. During the initial examination, what should the therapist examine first?

Choices:

1. Level of dyspnea during functional transfers.
2. Cardiovascular endurance during a 6-minute walking test.
3. Sensory losses and sensory organization of balance.
4. Spinal musculoskeletal changes secondary to degenerative joint disease (DJD).

Teaching Points

Correct Answer: 3

A critical component of balance control is sensory input from somatosensory, visual and vestibular receptors, and overall sensory organization of inputs. Initial examination should address these elements before moving on to assess the motor components of balance (e.g., postural synergies). The Clinical Test for Sensory Integration in Balance (CTSIB) or modified CTSIB (Shumway-Cook, Horak) are appropriate instruments.

Incorrect Choices:

Cardiovascular endurance and level of dyspnea during functional transfers are appropriate elements to examine but should occur after key elements of balance are examined (sensory components and integration; motor and synergistic elements). In this case, DJD changes would not be crucial to examine initially.

Type of Reasoning: Inductive

This case scenario requires the test taker to combine knowledge of the somatosensory system and possible reasons for falls in order to arrive at the correct conclusion. A key facet of this question is in the terms "initial session" and "crucial." These words should cause the test taker to focus on what should come first in a sequence of intervention events and what is most important for the patient. This requires the use of clinical judgment, which is an inductive reasoning skill.

B73 

Musculoskeletal | Interventions

To reduce an elderly individual's chronic forward head posturing in standing and sitting, what muscles are likely shortened and should be stretched?

Choices:

1. Middle trapezius and rhomboid muscles.
2. Rectus capitis anterior muscles.
3. Longus capitis and longus colli muscles.
4. Rectus capitis posterior major and minor.

Teaching Points

Correct Answer: 4

Forward head posturing or forward translation of the occiput in relation to the neck and trunk is associated with extension of the occipital axial joint and flexion of the lower and mid cervical spines. Chronic extension of the occipital axial joint will lead to shortening of the suboccipital extensor muscles (rectus capitis posterior major and minor), and localized stretching of these muscles would be indicated as part of a therapeutic intervention to reduce forward head posturing.

Incorrect Choices:

Muscles anterior to the axis for mid and lower cervical flexion and extension will be chronically overlengthened, and therefore further stretching of these would not be indicated. Forward head posturing is also associated with forward scapular posturing, and therefore further stretching of scapular adductors (middle trapezius and rhomboid muscles) would not be indicated.

Type of Reasoning: Inductive

One must determine the best clinical course of action in order to arrive at a correct conclusion. Questions of this nature often require clinical judgment, which is an inductive reasoning skill. For this specific deficit, the therapist should consider exercises for the rectus capitis posterior minor and rectus capitis posterior major muscles. Review muscle actions of the cervical spine and upper trunk as well as exercises for forward head posturing if answered incorrectly.

Cardiovascular/Pulmonary and Lymphatic | Examination

What are the major benefits of using the 6-Minute Walk Test as an outcome measure?

Choices:

1. Accurately documents maximal exercise capacity.
2. Provides good correlation with functional abilities.
3. Allows determination of severity of lung disease.
4. Provides determination of peak oxygen uptake.

Teaching Points

Correct Answer: 2

The 6-Minute Walk Test (6MWT) shows a good correlation with function, as the 6MWT is a submax test, and function is performed at a submax work level.

Incorrect Choices:

The 6MWT does not correlate to lung disease severity.

The 6MWT has only about a 73% correlation with VO_{2max}. The 10-Meter Shuttle Walk Test would be a better test to use if correlation with VO_2 is desired.

As the 6MWT doesn't correlate with VO_{2max}, it cannot document maximal exercise capacity.

Type of Reasoning: Deductive

This question requires the test taker to recall the benefits of the 6MWT. This necessitates the recall of factual information, which is a deductive reasoning skill. For this situation, the 6MWT is a helpful measure, as it is correlated with functional abilities. Review benefits of the 6MWT if answered incorrectly.

B75 

Musculoskeletal | Examination

During a postural screen for a patient complaining of low back pain, the therapist notices that the knees are in genu recurvatum. What are the common contributory problems for which the therapist should examine?

Choices:

1. Ankle dorsiflexion and hip abduction.
2. Forefoot varus and posterior pelvic tilt.
3. Ankle plantarflexion and anterior pelvic tilt.
4. Lateral tibial torsion and anterior pelvic tilt.

Teaching Points

Correct Answer: 3

A common contributory problem or correlated motion for genu recurvatum is ankle plantarflexion due to shortened gastrocnemius muscles. Alterations occurring up the kinetic chain include anterior pelvic tilt to maintain the center of gravity over the feet.

Incorrect Choices:

Ankle dorsiflexion will lead to increased knee flexion. Forefoot varus may lead to tibial internal rotation, but not genu recurvatum. Tibial external rotation will lead to abnormal stresses at the knee joint, but not genu recurvatum.

Type of Reasoning: Inference

The test taker must understand the nature of genu recurvatum and contributory postures in order to choose the correct answer. This requires recall of lower extremity musculoskeletal pathology and biomechanics. Questions that require one to draw conclusions based on presented evidence often necessitate the use of inferential reasoning skills. If this question was answered incorrectly, refer to information on postural screening, kinetic chain, and genu recurvatum.

B76 

Musculoskeletal | Evaluation, Diagnosis

After treating a patient for trochanteric bursitis for 1 week, the patient has no resolution of pain and is complaining of problems with gait. After reexamination, the therapist finds weakness of the quadriceps femoris and altered sensation at the greater trochanter. What is the **MOST** likely cause of the problems?

Choices:

1. L5 nerve root compression.
2. Sacroiliac (SI) dysfunction.
3. L4 nerve root compression.
4. Degenerative joint disease (DJD) of the hip.

Teaching Points

Correct Answer: 3

The positive findings are consistent with an L4 nerve root compression.

Incorrect Choices:

Weakness of only one muscle group is not a common finding for DJD or SI dysfunction. L5 nerve root compression would result in hamstring weakness.

Type of Reasoning: Analysis

In this question, the symptoms are provided and the test taker must make a determination of the possible diagnosis. Questions such as these require analytical reasoning skill, using knowledge of neuroanatomy to determine that the most likely cause is L4 nerve root compression. If this question was answered incorrectly, review information on nerve compressions of the lumbar spine.

B77

Genitourinary | Examination

Dialysis PT care shunt

A patient in chronic renal failure is being seen in physical therapy for deconditioning and decreased gait endurance. The therapist needs to schedule the patient's sessions around dialysis, which is received three mornings a week. What guidelines should the therapist follow when taking the patient's blood pressure?

Choices:

1. Every minute during walking, using the nonshunt arm.
2. Pre- and postactivities, using the nonshunt arm.
3. In sitting when activity has ceased, using the shunt arm.
4. In the supine position, using the shunt arm.

Teaching Points

Correct Answer: 2

A dialysis shunt would interfere with taking BP. Use the nonshunt arm. Pre- and postexercise measurements are appropriate.

Incorrect Choices:

The shunt arm cannot be used to take BP. Taking BP in the shunt arm or during walking would result in inaccurate measurements.

Type of Reasoning: Inference

One must reason the best way to monitor a patient's BP using the appropriate guidelines when the patient has an atrioventricular shunt in the arm for dialysis. Guidelines dictate that you should not take BP on the arm where the shunt is located. Also, monitoring BP is best carried out pre- and postactivity to determine tolerance for activity. This type of reasoning is inferential because one must infer the best approach to patient care, considering the diagnosis and limitations of the patient.

B78

Integumentary | Evaluation, Diagnosis

A patient who is currently being treated for low back pain arrives for therapy complaining of pain across the middle of the right chest and back. When the therapist inspects the skin, clustered vesicles are apparent in a linear arc. The surrounding skin is hypersensitive. What is the **MOST** likely diagnosis?

Choices:

1. Herpes simplex infection.
2. Psoriasis.
3. Dermatitis.
4. Herpes zoster infection.

Teaching Points

Correct Answer: 4

Herpes zoster is an acute infection caused by reactivation of the latent varicella-zoster virus (shingles). It is characterized by painful vesicular skin eruptions that follow the underlying route of a spinal (in this case) or cranial nerve. Additional symptoms include fever, gastrointestinal disturbances, malaise, and headache.

Incorrect Choices:

Herpes simplex is an infection caused by the herpes simplex virus. These infections tend to occur on the face (around the mouth and nose). They are sometimes referred to as "cold sores." Psoriasis is a chronic skin condition characterized by red patches covered by dry, silvery scales. Dermatitis is an inflammatory condition of the skin characterized by eruptions (not associated with an underlying route of a nerve).

Type of Reasoning: Analysis

One must recall the signs and symptoms of herpes zoster infection in order to arrive at a correct conclusion. This requires analytical reasoning skill because one must weigh the symptoms provided in order to determine the most likely diagnosis. For this question, the key words of "vesicles" and "linear arc" help guide one toward the correct conclusion. If this question was answered incorrectly, review signs and symptoms of herpes zoster infection.

B79

Musculoskeletal | Examination

While providing sports coverage at a local high school, a physical therapist is asked to examine an athlete with a knee injury. Based on the mechanism of injury, the therapist suspects rupture of the anterior cruciate ligament (ACL). What test should be performed immediately to identify a torn ACL?

Choices:

1. McMurray's test.
2. Reverse Lachman's stress test.
3. Lachman's stress test.
4. Posterior sag test.

Teaching Points

Correct Answer: 3

Lachman's stress test is the primary clinical test utilized to identify if the anterior cruciate ligament is intact or ruptured.

Incorrect Choices:

McMurray's test is utilized to identify the integrity for the meniscus. The reverse Lachman's stress and posterior sag tests are both tests utilized to test the integrity of the posterior cruciate ligament.

Type of Reasoning: Deductive

For this question, the test taker must recall the testing guidelines to confirm the presence of an ACL tear. This requires factual recall of guidelines, which is a deductive reasoning skill. For this situation, Lachman's stress test is best to use. Review testing guidelines for knee injuries, especially Lachman's stress test if answered incorrectly.

Cardiovascular/Pulmonary and Lymphatic | Evaluation, Diagnosis

After a myocardial infarction (MI), a patient is a new admission to a phase 3 hospital-based cardiac rehabilitation program. During the initial exercise session, the patient's ECG responses are continuously monitored via radio telemetry. The therapist notices three PVCs occurring in a run with no P wave. What action should the therapist take?

Choices:

1. Modify the exercise prescription by decreasing the intensity.
2. Stop the exercise and notify the physician immediately.
3. Continue the exercise session, but monitor closely.
4. Have the patient sit down and rest for a few minutes before resuming exercise.

Teaching Points

Correct Answer: 2

A run of three or more PVCs occurring sequentially is ventricular tachycardia. The rate is very rapid, resulting in seriously compromised cardiac output. This is potentially an emergency situation that can deteriorate rapidly into ventricular fibrillation (no cardiac output) and cardiac arrest.

Incorrect Choices:

The other choices, which involve continuation of exercise, put the patient at serious risk for cardiac arrest.

Type of Reasoning: Inductive

This question requires the test taker to use diagnostic reasoning and clinical judgment to determine whether or not the PVCs and absence of P wave are significant enough to warrant physician notification. This type of reasoning is inductive, and the test taker is called to make a decision for the safety of the patient. In this case, physician notification is warranted, and exercise should be halted immediately. If this question was answered incorrectly, refer to cardiac rehabilitation guidelines and interpretation of ECGs.

B81 

Neuromuscular | Evaluation, Diagnosis

A patient with left hemiplegia is able to recognize his wife after she is with him for a while and talks to him but is unable to recognize the faces of his children when they come to visit. The children are naturally very upset by their father's behavior. What is the **BEST** explanation for his problem?

Choices:

1. Somatognosia.
2. Anosognosia.
3. Visual agnosia.
4. Ideational apraxia.

Teaching Points

Correct Answer: 3

All of the choices are indicative of perceptual dysfunction. This patient is most likely suffering from visual agnosia, which is an inability to recognize familiar objects despite normal function of the eyes and optic tracts. Once the wife talks with him, he is able to recognize her by her voice.

Incorrect Choices:

Ideational apraxia is the inability to perform a purposeful motor act, either automatically or upon command. Anosognosia is the frank denial, neglect, or lack of awareness of the presence or severity of one's paralysis. Somatognosia is an impairment in body scheme.

Type of Reasoning: Analysis

In this question, one must recall the meaning of the four choices provided and apply them to the patient's symptoms as described. This requires analytical reasoning, which often requires one to determine the meaning of statements or medical terminology. If this question was answered incorrectly, refer to information on the various perceptual problems after CVA.

B82 

Cardiovascular/Pulmonary and Lymphatic | Evaluation, Diagnosis

A home care PT receives a referral to evaluate the fall risk potential of an elderly community-dweller with chronic coronary artery disease (CAD). The patient has fallen three times in the past 4 months, with no history of fall injury except for minor bruising. The patient is currently taking a number of medications. What is the drug that is **MOST** likely to contribute to dizziness and increased fall risk?

Choices:

1. Colace.
2. Albuterol.
3. Nitroglycerin.
4. Coumadin sodium.

Teaching Points

Correct Answer: 3

Of the medications listed, nitroglycerin has the greatest risk of causing dizziness or weakness due to postural hypotension. Fall risk is increased even with small doses of nitroglycerin.

Incorrect Choices:

Colace (docusate sodium), an anticonstipation agent, can result in mild abdominal cramps and nausea. Coumadin (warfarin sodium) is an anticlotting medication. Adverse effects can include increased risk of hemorrhage, which indirectly can result in lightheadedness. Dosages are carefully monitored. Albuterol, a bronchodilator, can cause tremor, anxiety, nervousness, and weakness.

Type of Reasoning: Inference

One must infer information from the four medications provided in order to determine the one that is most likely to contribute to increased fall risk. In this circumstance, using inferential reasoning, one recalls the side effects of each medicine and determines that nitroglycerin is most likely to cause increased risk of falls because this is one of the common side effects.

B83 

Musculoskeletal | Interventions

A patient complains of foot pain when first arising that eases with ambulation. The therapist finds that symptoms can be reproduced in weight bearing and running on a treadmill. Examination reveals pes planus and pain with palpation at the distal aspect of the calcaneus. What is the **BEST** choice for early intervention?

Choices:

1. Prescription for a customized orthosis.
2. Strengthening of ankle dorsiflexors.
3. Modalities to reduce pain.
4. Use of a resting splint at night.

Teaching Points

Correct Answer: 4

The symptoms are suggestive of plantar fasciitis. The focus of patient management should be on decreasing the irritation to the plantar fascia. This is most effectively done with a resting night splint.

Incorrect Choices:

Modalities to reduce pain offer some symptomatic relief; however, the pain is not constant. Strengthening the dorsiflexors will not change irritation to the plantar fascia. A customized orthosis may be necessary at a later time if primary symptoms do not resolve after early management.

Type of Reasoning: Inductive

This question requires one to recognize the patient's symptoms as plantar fasciitis and then recall the common treatment strategies for this condition. This requires one to utilize clinical judgment, which is an inductive reasoning skill. If this question was answered incorrectly, refer to guidelines of treatment of plantar fasciitis.

B84 

Neuromuscular | Interventions

A patient with a T10 paraplegia (ASIA A) resulting from a spinal cord injury is ready to begin community wheelchair training. The therapist's goal is to teach the patient how to do a wheelie in order to manage curbs. What is the **BEST** training strategy to instruct the patient in performing a wheelie?

Choices:

1. Place a hand on the top of the handrims to steady the chair while throwing the head and trunk forward.
2. Throw the head and trunk backward to rise up on the large wheels.
3. Lean backward while moving the hands slowly backward on the rims.
4. Grasp the handrims posteriorly, and pull them forward abruptly and forcefully.

Teaching Points

Correct Answer: 4

A wheelie can be assumed by having the patient place his/her hands posterior on the handrims and pulling them abruptly and sharply forward. If the patient is unable to lift the casters in this manner, throwing the head back forcefully when pulling the handrims may work. An alternate technique is to grasp the handrims anteriorly, pull backward, then abruptly and forcefully reverse the direction of pull. The therapist can assist by steadying the chair at the patient's balance point until the patient learns to adjust the position through the use of handrim movements forward and backward.

Incorrect Choices:

Throwing the head and trunk backward alone or with moving the hands backward on the handrims will not result in a wheelie.

Type of Reasoning: Evaluation

This question requires one to evaluate the merits of each of the four possible solutions and to determine which solution seems most reasonable, which is an evaluative reasoning skill. One must recall knowledge of the strategies and techniques involved in performing a wheelie in order to arrive at the correct conclusion. If this question was answered incorrectly, refer to information on community wheelchair training, especially wheelie techniques.

B85 

Cardiovascular/Pulmonary and Lymphatic | Evaluation, Diagnosis

A PT should be alert to recognize the signs and symptoms associated with the onset of aspiration pneumonia. Which patient diagnosis is the **MOST** susceptible to develop this form of pneumonia?

Choices:

1. A circumferential burn of the thorax associated with significant pain.
2. Severe scoliosis with compression of internal organs, including the lungs.
3. Amyotrophic lateral sclerosis (ALS) with dysphagia and diminished gag reflex.
4. A complete spinal cord lesion at T2 with diminished coughing ability and forced vital capacity (FVC).

Teaching Points

Correct Answer: 3

Aspiration pneumonia results from an abnormal entry of fluids or matter (including food) into the airways. A patient with ALS with an inability to swallow (dysphagia) and diminished gag reflex is most susceptible to aspiration pneumonia.

Incorrect Choices:

Others listed may be susceptible to other forms of pneumonia or even, though less likely, aspiration pneumonia.

Type of Reasoning: Evaluation

In this question, the test taker must evaluate the four patient circumstances presented and determine which patient is most at risk for aspiration pneumonia. This requires one to determine the value of the information presented in each patient circumstance, which requires skills in evaluation. To arrive at the correct conclusion, one must understand each diagnosis and risks associated with those diagnoses, which should be reviewed if this question was answered incorrectly.

B86

Musculoskeletal | Interventions

A patient demonstrates quadriceps weakness (4/5) and difficulty descending stairs. What is the **MOST** appropriate intervention to regain functional strength in the quadriceps?

Choices:

1. Progressive resistance exercises, 70% 1 repetition maximum, three sets of 10.
2. Partial squats, progressing to lunges.
3. Maximum isometric exercise, at 45° and 90° of knee extension.
4. Isokinetic exercise, at 36°/sec.

Teaching Points

Correct Answer: 2

Closed-chain exercises are the most appropriate in this example because of the patient's difficulty descending stairs. Moving the body over a fixed distal segment provides loading to muscles, joints, and noncontractile soft tissues while stimulating the sensory receptors needed for stability and balance.

Incorrect Choices:

Open-chain exercise (all other choices), while improving strength, does not adequately prepare an individual for functional weight bearing and activities.

Type of Reasoning: Analysis

One must analyze the four choices presented in order to determine which activity is best to regain functional quadriceps strength. In this situation, a closed-chain activity is optimal because it is aligned most closely with the patient's functional challenge, which is descending stairs. This requires analytical reasoning skill to determine the precise meaning of the information presented in the four choices. If this question was answered incorrectly, review information on indications for closed-chain exercises.

B87

Neuromuscular | Evaluation, Diagnosis

Independent community ambulation as a primary means of functional mobility is a realistic functional expectation for some patients with complete spinal cord injury (ASIA A). What level of injury would allow for this?

Choices:

1. Low lumbar (L4–5).
2. Low thoracic (T9–10).
3. Midthoracic (T6–9).
4. High lumbar (T12–L1).

Teaching Points.

Correct Answer: 1

Patients with low lumbar lesions (L4–5) can become independent and functional ambulators providing that they exhibit adequate ROM, strength of residual muscles, and cardiovascular endurance. The locomotor training program emphasizes learning to use bilateral ankle-foot orthoses (AFOs) and canes.

Incorrect Choices:

Patients with complete higher lesions (all other choices) can learn to ambulate with KAFOs and crutches, but may demonstrate limited function and a high rate of orthotic rejection due to the high levels of energy expenditure required during ambulation. These patients typically choose wheelchair mobility as their primary means of locomotion.

Type of Reasoning: Inference

One must infer the abilities and limitations of each of the spinal injury levels presented in order to make an appropriate determination for the patient who can most realistically perform community ambulation as a primary means of mobility. This requires one to use knowledge of neuroanatomy and spinal innervation levels to determine how the intact musculature can realistically allow for community ambulation. If answered incorrectly, refer to spinal innervation levels and intact musculature for ambulation.

B88 

Nonsystem | Equipment, Devices, Biophysical Agents

A patient presents with multiple fractures of both hands and wrists as a result of a mountain bike accident. Now, 5 weeks later, the patient has limited wrist and finger motion and dry, scaly skin over the involved areas. What is the biophysical agent that would provide the **GREATEST** benefit?

Choices:

1. Contact ultrasound (US).
2. Hot packs.
3. Paraffin.
4. Functional electrical stimulation.

Teaching Points

Correct Answer: 3

Paraffin bath will provide circumferential heating of the hands and fingers and aid in softening the skin prior to exercise.

Incorrect Choices:

Active exercise, including functional electrical stimulation, would be more effective after the application of paraffin because tissue extensibility and pliability would be increased. Hot packs or US using direct contact would not completely cover the area to be treated.

Type of Reasoning: Inductive

This question requires one to use his/her clinical judgment to make the best determination for a physical agent to remedy the symptoms of the patient, which is an inductive reasoning skill. In this circumstance, paraffin is ideal for circumferential heating and skin softening. If this question was answered incorrectly, refer to indications for paraffin treatment.

B89 

Nonsystem | Equipment, Devices, Biophysical Agents

An elderly, frail patient demonstrates a history of recent falls (two in the past 2 months) and mild balance instability. The therapist's referral is to examine the patient and recommend an assistive device as needed. Based on the patient's history, what device would be of GREATEST benefit?

Choices:

1. Folding reciprocal walker.
2. Standard, fixed-frame walker.
3. Front wheel rolling walker that folds.
4. Hemi walker.

Teaching Points

Correct Answer: 3

A rolling walker will provide added stability, while maintaining gait as a continuous movement sequence. The additional benefit of a folding walker facilitates easy transport and mobility in the community.

Incorrect Choices:

A standard fixed-frame walker requires the patient to lift the walker and increases the energy expenditure. A hemi walker decreases the stability offered. A reciprocal walker requires increased motor control to use and also provides less stability.

Type of Reasoning: Inference

One must determine how each of the assistive devices will best aid stability for a patient with a history of falls and mild balance instability. Questions that require one to infer information and draw conclusions from that information encourage inferential reasoning skill.

B90 

Musculoskeletal | Interventions

After surgery, a patient develops a stiff pelvis and limited pelvic/lower trunk mobility. The therapist elects to use sitting exercises on a therapy ball to correct these impairments. In order to improve lower abdominal control, what direction should the patient move the ball?

Choices:

1. Backward, producing anterior tilting of the pelvis.
2. Forward, producing posterior tilting of the pelvis.
3. Forward, producing anterior tilting of the pelvis.
4. Backward, producing posterior tilting of the pelvis.

Teaching Points

Correct Answer: 2

Contraction of the lower abdominals results in posterior tilting of the pelvis and can be achieved with forward or anterior movement of the therapy ball.

Incorrect Choices:

The other choices incorrectly state the effects of pelvic control exercises while sitting on the ball. Backward or posterior motion of the ball produces anterior tilting of the pelvis.

Type of Reasoning: Analysis

One must link the motion of the therapy ball to the motion achieved at the pelvis in order to make a correct determination in this scenario. Using analytical reasoning skills, the test taker must determine the meaning of the information presented, and then link this information to improvement in lower abdominal control. In this case, forward motion of the ball will promote posterior pelvic tilt and contraction of the lower abdominals. If this question was answered incorrectly, review principles of therapy ball activities.

B91 

Neuromuscular | Evaluation, Diagnosis

A patient presents with weakness in the right lower leg 3 weeks after a motor vehicle accident. The patient complains of spontaneous twitching in the muscles of the lower leg. The therapist visually inspects both limbs and determines that muscle bulk is reduced on the involved right limb. Girth measurements confirm a 1-inch difference in the circumference of the right leg measured 4 inches below the patella. Deep tendon reflexes and tone are diminished. What is the **MOST** likely cause of the patient's weakness?

Choices:

1. Peripheral nerve injury.
2. Pyramidal tract dysfunction in the medulla.
3. Guillain-Barré syndrome.
4. Brainstem dysfunction affecting extrapyramidal pathways.

Teaching Points

Correct Answer: 1

This patient is exhibiting signs and symptoms of lower motor neuron injury (hypotonia, hyporeflexia, paresis, neurogenic atrophy). The presence of muscle fasciculations is a hallmark sign of lower motor neuron injury.

Incorrect Choices:

Upper motor neuron lesions (cortical or pyramidal tracts) would result in hypertonicity (hypotonicity initially during shock), hyperreflexia, generalized paresis, and variable disuse atrophy. Guillain-Barré syndrome is a lower motor neuron condition that produces symmetrical and ascending signs. Extrapyramidal signs (involuntary movements) are not evident in this case.

Type of Reasoning: Inductive

This question requires one to use diagnostic thinking and clinical judgment, which is an inductive reasoning skill. One should recognize that the hypotonia, hyporeflexia, paresis, and muscle fasciculations are indicative of a lower motor neuron injury and, therefore, a peripheral nerve injury. If this question was answered incorrectly, refer to information regarding lower motor neuron injuries and symptomatology.

B92 

Musculoskeletal | Examination

An elderly adult patient presents with a history of and subjective complaints consistent with lumbar central spinal stenosis. What is the **MOST** appropriate clinical test to differentiate spinal stenosis from intermittent vascular claudication?

Choices:

1. Femoral nerve traction test.
2. Bicycle (van Gelderen's) test.
3. Valsalva's maneuver.
4. Lumbar quadrant test.

Teaching Points

Correct Answer: 2

The bicycle (van Gelderen's) test is designed to differentiate between spinal stenosis and intermittent vascular claudication. Van Gelderen's bicycle test is designed to stress the LE vascular system without causing any central canal or foraminal stenosis that could be misinterpreted as intermittent neurogenic claudication.

Incorrect Choices:

The lumbar quadrant test is utilized to identify a lumbar facet dysfunction. The femoral nerve traction test is utilized to identify if there is an entrapment of the femoral nerve and thus it is not related to either of these two conditions directly. Valsalva's maneuver is utilized to identify a space-occupying lesion such as a disc herniation, a tumor, etc. This would not be sensitive in identifying a spinal stenosis.

Type of Reasoning: Deductive

One must recall the testing guidelines of the lumbar spine in order to reach a correct conclusion. This necessitates the recall of factual information, which is a deductive reasoning skill. Through the deductive process, one should recall that the bicycle (van Gelderen's) test is most appropriate to differentiate spinal stenosis from intermittent vascular claudication. Review lumbar testing guidelines if answered incorrectly, especially the bicycle test.

B93 

Cardiovascular/Pulmonary and Lymphatic | Interventions

A patient with bacterial pneumonia has crackles and wheezes in the left lateral basal segment and decreased breath sounds throughout. The patient is on 4 L of oxygen by nasal cannula with a resulting arterial oxygen saturation (SaO_2) of 90%. Respiratory rate is 28. What is the **MOST BENEFICIAL** intervention for this case?

Choices:

1. Postural drainage, percussion, and shaking over the appropriate area on the left lateral thorax for secretion removal.
2. Positioning in left side-lying to improve ventilation/perfusion ratios.
3. Postural drainage, percussion, and shaking to the right basilar segments in order to keep the right lung healthy.
4. Breathing exercises encouraging expansion of the right lateral basilar thorax, because the left side is not currently participating in gas exchange.

Teaching Points

Correct Answer: 1

A treatment of postural drainage, percussion, and shaking to the appropriate lung segments is advisable. The standard postural drainage position for the lateral basilar segment of the left lower lobe is in side-lying position with the head of bed tipped in full Trendelenburg position. Given the borderline SaO_2 values on 4 L of oxygen, modification of the position may be necessary for patient tolerance.

Incorrect Choices:

There is nothing that will ensure that the right lung stays healthy or makes it more functional. Therefore, positioning in left side-lying and focusing on left-sided breathing exercises are incorrect choices. In addition, placing the patient in the left side-lying position would increase blood flow to the left lateral base, an area that is getting little ventilation. This position would worsen ventilation/perfusion matching.

Type of Reasoning: Inductive

One must utilize clinical judgment to determine which intervention approach is most beneficial, given the patient's diagnosis and symptoms. This is an inductive reasoning skill, in which clinical judgment and diagnostic thinking are used to arrive at the correct conclusion. If this topic is not well understood, refer to indications for modified postural drainage procedures.

B94 

System Interactions | Evaluation, Diagnosis

A therapist receives a referral to see an elderly patient in the intensive care unit (ICU) recovering from a severe case of pneumonia. The patient is confused and disoriented. What criteria would allow the therapist to determine the disorientation is due to delirium rather than dementia?

Choices:

1. Hallucinations are present throughout the day.
2. Persistent personality changes are evident.
3. Symptoms are intermittent.
4. Level of arousal is significantly depressed.

Teaching Points

Correct Answer: 3

Acutely ill, hospitalized elderly patients frequently exhibit delirium, a fluctuating attention state. Patients demonstrate a fluctuating course with symptoms of confusion that alternate with lucid intervals. Sleep/wake cycles are disrupted and confusion is typically worse at night.

Incorrect Choices:

All other choices are signs of chronic dementia.

Type of Reasoning: Evaluation

One must evaluate the merits of each of the four statements in order to determine which statement most likely seems true for the patient's symptoms and diagnosis. In this case, the disorientation is due to delirium, because the symptoms are intermittent, whereas patients with dementia experience constant disorientation. Questions that require one to determine the value and merits of statements presented utilize evaluative reasoning skill, which can be challenging because of the need to make a judgment call.

B95 

Nonsystem | Safety, Professional Responsibilities, Research

A comparison of the effects of exercise in water, on land, or combined on the rehabilitation outcome of patients with intra-articular anterior cruciate ligament reconstructions revealed that less joint effusion was noted after 8 weeks in the water group. What is the appropriate statistical test to compare the girth measurements of the three groups?

Choices:

1. Analysis of covariance.
2. Spearman's rho.
3. Chi square.
4. ANOVA.

Teaching Points

Correct Answer: 4

ANOVA is a parametric statistical test used to compare three or more treatment groups (in this example, in water, on land, or combined exercise groups) on a measure of the dependent variable (joint effusion girth measurements) at a selected probability level.

Incorrect Choices:

Analysis of covariance compares two or more groups but also controls for the effects of an intervening variable. Chi square is a nonparametric statistical test used to compare data in the form of frequency counts. Spearman's rho (rank correlation coefficient) is a nonparametric test used to correlate ordinal data.

Type of Reasoning: Deductive

Questions that require one to recall factual information, especially information related to research protocols, require deductive reasoning skill. One must utilize knowledge of the indications for each statistical test in order to arrive at the correct conclusion. If this question was answered incorrectly, review information on guidelines for the use of ANOVA as well as parametric and nonparametric statistical tests.

B96 

Neuromuscular | Interventions

A patient has a recent history of strokes (two in the past 4 months) and demonstrates good return in the right lower extremity. The therapist is concentrating on improving balance and independence in gait. Unfortunately, speech recovery is lagging behind motor recovery. The patient demonstrates a severe fluent aphasia. What is the **BEST** strategy to use during physical therapy sessions?

Choices:

1. Demonstrate and gesture to get the idea of the task across.
2. Have the family present to help interpret during physical therapy sessions.
3. Utilize verbal cues, emphasizing consistency and repetition.
4. Consult with the speech pathologist to establish a communication board.

Teaching Points

Correct Answer: 1

Fluent aphasia (Wernicke's aphasia) is a central language disorder in which spontaneous speech is preserved and flows smoothly while auditory comprehension is impaired. Demonstration and gesture (visual modalities) offer the best means of communicating with this patient since the impairment is severe.

Incorrect Choices:

Verbal cues are best for patients with nonfluent aphasia (Broca's aphasia) in which understanding of verbal cues is intact but motor production of speech is not. A communication board is not needed. The family will also have difficulties communicating with the patient. Use of consistency and repetition is an appropriate motor learning strategy for all patients.

Type of Reasoning: Inductive

In this question, the patient requires gait training but has limitations in communication from Wernicke's aphasia. The test taker must determine the best way to communicate with a patient who has this severe deficit, which is to provide demonstrations and gestures, rather than verbal cues. Questions that elicit clinical judgment to determine a best course of action utilize inductive reasoning skills. If this question was answered incorrectly, refer to information on communication with patients who have Wernicke's aphasia.

B97 

Musculoskeletal/Examination

During a gait examination, a patient with a transfemoral prosthesis demonstrates terminal swing impact. What is the likely cause of this problem?

Choices:

1. Prosthesis has too little tension in the extension aid.
2. Hip flexors are weak.
3. Prosthesis is externally rotated.
4. Prosthesis has insufficient knee friction.

Teaching Points

Correct Answer: 4

Terminal swing impact refers to the sudden stopping of the prosthesis as the knee extends during late swing. Possible causes can include insufficient knee friction or too much tension in the extension aid. In addition, if the patient with an amputation fears the knee will buckle at heel strike, the patient can use forceful hip flexion to extend the knee.

Incorrect Choices:

Faulty socket contour results in an externally rotated prosthesis. The extension aid has too much tension (not too little). Weak hip flexors would result in decreased force to extend the knee.

Type of Reasoning: Inference

One must infer the reason for the terminal swing impact when walking with an above-knee prosthesis, which is an inferential reasoning skill (requiring one to draw conclusions based on presented evidence). Using knowledge of above-knee prostheses and proper tension of the extension aid, one can infer that the tension on the extension aid is too high. If this question was answered incorrectly, review information on above-knee prosthesis fit and functions.

B98

Integumentary | Interventions

A patient was burned over 40% of the body in an industrial accident and has full-thickness burns over the anterior trunk and neck and superficial partial-thickness burns over the shoulders. In order to stabilize this patient out of positions of common deformity, what orthotic device would be of GREATEST benefit?

Choices:

1. Soft cervical collar with an intrinsic plus hand splint.
2. A cervical thoracic lumbosacral orthosis (CTLSO) used during all upright activities.
3. Plastic cervical orthosis and axillary splints utilizing an airplane position.
4. Splints utilizing a flexed position for the shoulders and body jacket for the trunk.

Teaching Points

Correct Answer: 3

The common deformity for the anterior neck is flexion; the appropriate positioning device is a firm rigid plastic cervical collar that stresses extension. The common deformity of the shoulders is adduction and internal rotation; the appropriate position device is an axillary or airplane splint that stresses abduction, flexion, and external rotation.

Incorrect Choices:

Choices that involve hand splints should be ruled out immediately because there is no mention of burns to the hands. A CTLSO would prevent neck flexion but does not deal with the potential shoulder deformities. The CTLSO could also restrict breathing and enhance the risk of pneumonia.

Type of Reasoning: Inductive

This question requires one to recall common positioning techniques after burns to the anterior trunk and neck. Using knowledge of the typical deformity and contracture patterns with burns to this area, one can reason that the solution is to utilize axillary splints and cervical orthosis to bring about abduction, flexion, and external rotation of the shoulders and cervical extension. Questions that require one to make interpretations of clinical guidelines and make judgments from this utilize inductive reasoning skills.

B99 

Metabolic/Endocrine | Evaluation, Diagnosis

A patient with type 2 diabetes is referred to physical therapy for exercise conditioning. What is a pathophysiologic cause of type 2 diabetes?

Choices:

1. Metabolic syndrome.
2. Impaired ability of the tissues to use insulin and insulin deficiency.
3. Loss of beta-cell function and insulin deficiency.
4. Pancreatic tumor.

Teaching Points

Correct Answer: 2

Type 2 diabetes results from impaired ability of the tissues to use insulin (insulin resistance), accompanied by a relative lack of insulin or impaired release of insulin.

Incorrect Choices:

Type 1 diabetes results from loss of pancreatic beta-cell function and an absolute insulin deficiency. Metabolic syndrome is a precursor to type 2 diabetes and is evidenced by abdominal obesity, high triglycerides, low high-density lipoprotein (HDL), hypertension, and high fasting plasma glucose (> 110 mg/dL). Pancreatic tumor is not a causative factor in type 2 diabetes.

Type of Reasoning: Deductive

One must recall the factual guidelines of type 2 diabetes in order to arrive at a correct conclusion. This requires deductive reasoning skill. For this situation, type 2 diabetes is the result of an impaired ability of the tissues to use insulin and insulin deficiency. If this question was answered incorrectly, review type 2 diabetes information, especially causes of the condition.

B100 

Neuromuscular | Interventions

Which intervention is **BEST** to improve left-sided neglect in a patient with left hemiplegia?

Choices:

1. Hook-lying, holding, light resistance to both hip abductors.
2. Rolling, supine to side-lying on right, using a PNF lift pattern.
3. Sitting, with both arms extended, hands resting on support surface, active holding.
4. Bridging with both arms positioned in extension at the sides.

Teaching Points

Correct Answer: 2

Incorporating the involved left side into a crossing the midline activity (rolling, using PNF lift) is best.

Incorrect Choices:

All other choices involve symmetrical activity and do little to bring attention to the involved hemiplegic side.

Type of Reasoning: Inference

One must link the deficit of the patient (left-sided neglect) to the best treatment approach in order to arrive at the correct conclusion. This requires inferential reasoning skill, as one must infer the course of action that will have the best clinical outcome. In this circumstance, rolling supine to side-lying on the right using a PNF lift pattern is best because it incorporates use of the left side and promotes crossing the midline. If this question was answered incorrectly, review treatment strategies for hemiplegia, especially PNF.

B101 

Cardiovascular/Pulmonary and Lymphatic | Examination

A patient with no significant past medical history who now presents with a bacterial pneumonia in the right anterior base would present with which of the following exam findings?

Choices:

1. Decreased breath sounds throughout all lung fields, increased SaO_2, febrile.
2. Bronchial breath sounds at the right anterior base, increased SaO_2, febrile.
3. Crackles on inspiration only at right anterior base, decreased SaO_2 and productive cough × 3 days.
4. Wheezes on inspiration only throughout the right lung fields, decreased SaO_2, dry cough × 1 day.

Teaching Points

Correct Answer: 3

Bacterial pneumonia has a gradual onset of days with a productive cough. As pneumonia interferes with the transport of oxygen from the alveoli to the pulmonary capillaries, the PaO_2 and therefore the SaO_2 would be lower than expected, and crackles in the area of the pneumonia is a usual finding.

Incorrect Choices:

Wheezing may occur with a bacterial pneumonia and resound within that thorax, and a decrease in SaO_2, making this portion of the answer plausible. But a more abrupt onset with a dry cough is consistent with a viral infection, not bacterial infection.

An increased SaO_2 would not be seen, negating this answer as a possibility. Febrile (with fever) certainly would be plausible, but the overall decreased breath sounds don't fit with a pneumonia in a specific region of the lung.

An increased SaO_2 would not be seen, negating this answer as a possibility. Febrile (with fever) certainly would be plausible, as is a bronchial breath sound in the specific involved region of the lung.

Type of Reasoning: Inference

One must infer or draw a reasonable conclusion about what is likely to be true of a diagnosis in order to arrive at a correct conclusion. This necessitates inferential reasoning skill. For this case, a patient with bacterial pneumonia of the right anterior base would have crackles on inspiration at right anterior base, decreased SaO_2, and a productive cough for 3 days. Review signs and symptoms of bacterial pneumonia if answered incorrectly.

B102 

Cardiovascular/Pulmonary and Lymphatic | Evaluation, Diagnosis

A patient with chronic obstructive pulmonary disease (COPD) reports to the fourth outpatient pulmonary rehabilitation session complaining of nausea, gastric upset, and feeling jittery. The patient reports no change in pulmonary symptoms. The PT records the following set of vital signs: temperature 98.6°F, HR 110 beats/min and irregular, BP 150/86, respiratory rate 20. Breath sounds show no change from baseline. The therapist checks the medical record and finds that the patient has no history of gastric disease. The patient is presently taking theophylline, albuterol sulfate (Ventolin), and triamcinolone diacetate (Amcort). What action should the PT take?

Choices:

1. Call the patient's physician immediately and report signs of theophylline toxicity.
2. Have the patient increase use of Ventolin to improve respiratory status.
3. Have the patient stop use of Amcort until he/she schedules an appointment with the physician.
4. Send the patient home and notify the physician of current symptoms.

Teaching Points

Correct Answer: 1

Theophylline is a bronchodilator used to reverse airway obstruction. The combination of symptoms of irregular HR, feeling jittery, and gastric upset is consistent with theophylline toxicity. Because theophylline toxicity can cause arrhythmias and seizures, the patient's physician should be notified by the PT rather than wait for the patient to return home to call the physician. It is also likely that a blood test will be needed to check the theophylline toxicity level and this could be done at the facility.

Incorrect Choices:

Ventolin is a bronchodilator used in the treatment of asthma or COPD. Amcort is an anti-inflammatory agent used to manage bronchial asthma. Neither drug produces the same combination of symptoms described in the case. The therapist should not recommend increasing or stopping a prescribed medication. This is usually the physician's responsibility.

Type of Reasoning: Evaluation

This question requires one to make a judgment for the well-being of the patient as well as to make a determination of the reason for the patient's symptoms. Value judgments require the use of evaluative reasoning skill in order to determine the best course of action. If this question was answered incorrectly, review information on theophylline toxicity and adverse reactions/side effects of Ventolin and Amcort.

B103

Neuromuscular | Evaluation, Diagnosis

The therapist is treating a 1-year-old child with Down syndrome at home and notices decreasing strength in the extremities, with neck pain and limited neck motion. Upper extremity deep tendon reflexes (DTRs) are 3+. These signs and symptoms are a hallmark of what diagnosis?

Choices:

1. Lower motor neuron signs consistent with Down syndrome.
2. Atlanto-axial subluxation with lemniscal impingement.
3. Upper motor neuron signs consistent with Down syndrome.
4. Atlanto-axial subluxation with spinal cord impingement.

Teaching Points

Correct Answer: 4

Ligamentous laxity is a hallmark of Down syndrome and can lead to atlanto-axial instability (AAI) with spinal cord impingement. This is a medical emergency situation. Decreased muscle strength and increased DTRs are the signs of dislocation from loss of cord function. In this case, the increasing symptomatology (changes in strength, neck pain, limited neck motion, hyperreflexia) is significant for a developing subluxation. Other UMN signs (clonus, positive Babinski response) may also occur.

Incorrect Choices:

Children with Down syndrome often have low tone, not upper motor neuron or lower motor neuron signs. Lemniscal impingement would result primarily in sensory changes.

Type of Reasoning: Analysis

In this question, symptoms are provided and the test taker must determine the cause. This type of question requires analytical reasoning, in which the test taker must determine the meaning of the symptoms presented. In this situation, one should determine that the symptoms indicate atlanto-axial subluxation with spinal cord impingement, a medical emergency, which should be reviewed if this question was answered incorrectly.

B104

Neuromuscular I Evaluation, Diagnosis

Which of the following factors is likely to contribute to subluxation and shoulder pain in hemiplegia?

Choices:

1. Spastic paralysis of the biceps.
2. Traction acting on a depressed, downwardly rotated scapula.
3. PROM with normal scapulohumeral rhythm.
4. Spastic retraction with elevation of scapula.

Teaching Points

Correct Answer: 2

Shoulder pain and subluxation in hemiplegia may be caused by a number of different factors. One major cause is traction and gravitational forces acting on a depressed, downwardly rotated scapula.

Incorrect Choices:

An appropriate treatment intervention involves PROM with careful attention to maintaining scapulohumeral rhythm. This intervention if performed correctly is **NOT** likely to cause pain. Spastic biceps is likely but is not a contributing factor to subluxation and pain. Spastic retraction of the scapula is likely but with depression and downward rotation (not elevation).

Type of Reasoning: Inference

This question requires the test taker to determine which causative factor is unlikely to result in shoulder pain in hemiplegia. This requires one to draw conclusions from the information presented and to make assumptions about that information, which draws upon inferential reasoning skill. One must have knowledge of the factors that affect subluxation as well as those that do not in order to arrive at the correct conclusion.

B105

Neuromuscular I Examination

The therapist tests a patient's hearing by holding a vibrating tuning fork on the mastoid process and then in front of the ear. Comparison is made by asking the patient which is louder. What is the name of this test?

Choices:

1. Weber's test.
2. Rinne's test.
3. Hallpike-Dix test.
4. Caloric test.

Teaching Points

Correct Answer: 2

Rinne's test is used to compare bone conduction (BC) with air conduction (AC). If BC is greater than AC, the patient is experiencing conductive deafness. If AC is greater than BC, the patient is experiencing sensorineural deafness.

Incorrect Choices:

Weber's test involves holding a vibrating tuning fork on the vertex of the head. The patient is asked which ear is louder, differentiating the unimpaired ear from the deaf ear. Caloric testing involves placing cool or warm water in the ear and observing the pattern of nystagmus produced. Hallpike-Dix test is used to evaluate patients with positional vertigo.

Type of Reasoning: Analysis

For this question, the test taker must analyze the description of the testing procedure in order to determine which test correctly identifies the approach described. This requires analytical reasoning skill. In this case, the testing guidelines are consistent with a Rinne's test. If answered incorrectly, review hearing test guidelines, especially the Rinne's test.

B106 

Integumentary | Evaluation, Diagnosis

A patient with hemiplegia and a drop foot is referred for physical therapy gait training. Examination reveals a pressure ulcer on the patient's right heel (pictured). The ulcer has dry eschar without edema, erythema, fluctuance, or drainage. The patient is afebrile. What is the **BEST** choice for intervention?

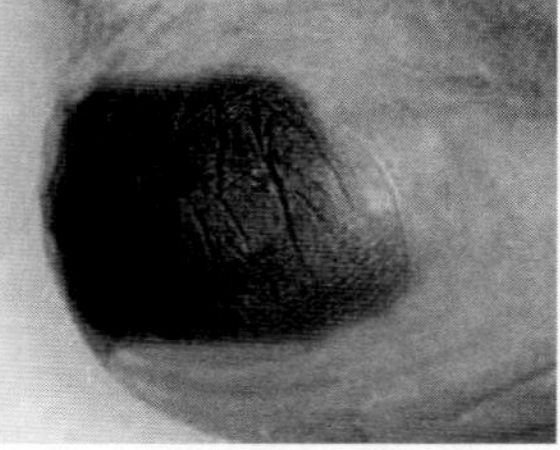

Choices:

1. Sharp debridement.
2. Refer for an arterial bypass graft.
3. Use an AFO with heel pressure relief.
4. Enzymatic debridement.

Teaching Points

Correct Answer: 3

The AFO helps to prevent plantarflexion contractures, while the heel pressure relief prevents further damage to the heel and promotes healing.

Incorrect Choices:

This pressure ulcer, based on the examination findings, is stable and needs to be monitored, not debrided. Arterial bypass grafts are needed if circulation is compromised. There is no indication that this is the case.

Type of Reasoning: Analysis

In this question, one must determine the best course of action for the patient with a pressure ulcer on the heel. When one must determine the meaning of visual information presented, such as the picture, analytical reasoning skills are utilized. If this question was answered incorrectly, review information on the treatment of pressure ulcers.

B107 

Musculoskeletal | Examination

A patient presents with an acute sprain of the right ankle. According to the patient, this has occurred fairly frequently over the past 5 years. What clinical test should the therapist use to examine the integrity of the anterior talofibular ligament?

Choices:

1. Anterior drawer test.
2. Morton's test.
3. Talar tilt.
4. Thompson's test.

Teaching Points

Correct Answer: 1

The anterior drawer test is specifically designed to assess the integrity of the anterior talofibular ligament.

Incorrect Choices:

The talar tilt assesses the integrity of the calcaneofibular ligament. Thompson's test assesses the integrity of the Achilles tendon. Morton's test assesses for the presence of a stress fracture or a neuroma in the forefoot.

Type of Reasoning: Deductive

This question provides a diagnosis and the test taker must recall the testing guidelines to confirm the diagnosis. This necessitates factual recall of information, which is a deductive reasoning skill. For this scenario, the test for laxity of the anterior talofibular ligament is confirmed via the anterior drawer test. Review testing guidelines for the ankle if answered incorrectly, especially the anterior drawer test.

B108 

Musculoskeletal | Evaluation, Diagnosis

A patient with left knee degenerative joint disease (DJD) complains of left-sided knee pain of 2 months' duration. The patient has been followed by outpatient physical therapy for 3 weeks and feels this condition is worsening. Pain has increased during weight-bearing activities, and the patient can no longer fully extend the left knee. Examination findings include increased swelling, decreased knee AROM into extension, and an antalgic gait. What action should the PT take?

Choices:

1. Tell the patient to see an orthopedic surgeon for possible immediate surgical intervention.
2. Immediately return the patient to the referring physician with documentation indicating that treatment was ineffective.
3. Continue physical therapy for another 2 weeks, because there is uncertainty whether the patient understands or is complying with the home exercise program.
4. Continue therapy for another week to ensure that all interventions have been attempted, and then return the patient to the referring physician.

Teaching Points

Correct Answer: 2

In this case, it would be best to send the patient back to the referring physician with an explanation of what was done, the ineffectiveness of the treatment, and any suggestions for further follow-up.

Incorrect Choices:

The therapist should not continue to treat a patient if the therapist feels no further benefit would be derived by continuing care because doing so contradicts the American Physical Therapy Association's (APTA's) Code of Ethics. Suggesting the patient needs immediate surgery is outside the scope of the PT's practice.

Type of Reasoning: Evaluation

One must rely on professional conduct principles and apply value judgments to the case situation described in order to arrive at the correct decision. This type of question, in which value judgments are needed to make a decision, necessitates the use of evaluative reasoning skill. In situations in which a patient demonstrates decline in status despite ongoing treatment, it is best to refer the patient back to the physician for follow-up and document the findings regarding this situation.

B109 

Genitourinary | Interventions

A postpartum patient with stress incontinence is referred for physical therapy. The therapist instructs the patient in pelvic floor exercises. What is the **BEST** choice for initial exercise?

Choices:

1. Supine, squeeze the sphincters and hold for 10 seconds.
2. Hooklying, bridge and hold for 5 seconds.
3. Sitting on toilet, stop and hold the flow of urine for 5 seconds during urination.
4. Supine, squeeze the sphincters and hold for 3 seconds.

Teaching Points

Correct Answer: 3

The stop exercise consists of sitting on the toilet and stopping and holding the flow of urine for 5 seconds before starting the flow again. This helps the patient identify the pelvic floor muscles. Once these muscles are identified, exercise can be progressed to tightening the muscles for 5 seconds and relaxing for 5 seconds with an empty bladder. Times are increased to 10 seconds each phase. The patient is instructed to repeat 3 sets of 10 at least 3 times a day.

Incorrect Choices:

While bridge and hold promotes lower trunk stability, it is not part of pelvic floor (Kegel's) exercises. Practicing sphincter control in supine is more difficult than practicing control in an upright position. Breath holding should be avoided.

Type of Reasoning: Inductive

One must recall the common intervention strategies for stress incontinence in order to arrive at a correct conclusion. This necessitates inductive reasoning skill, where clinical knowledge and judgment is paramount to drawing a correct conclusion. For this situation, sitting on toilet, stop and hold the flow of urine for 5 seconds during urination is a best initial approach. Review treatment strategies for stress incontinence if answered incorrectly.

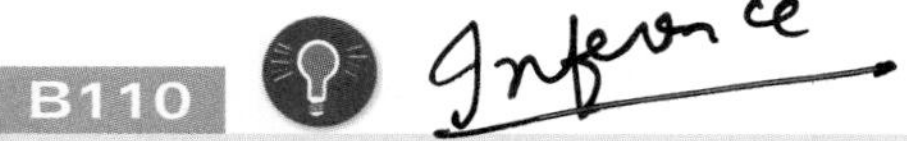

B110

Neuromuscular | Interventions

A patient with stroke demonstrates early recovery in the right upper extremity (RUE) with moderate spasticity in the biceps and finger flexors. Voluntary movement is evident in elbow flexors and shoulder abductors only (through ½ range). What is the **BEST** choice for initial exercise?

Choices:

1. Functional activities emphasizing ADL using the less-affected UE.
2. Facilitation of early movements in the flexor synergy pattern.
3. Weight bearing on an extended RUE with wrist and fingers extended.
4. Prolonged positioning of the RUE in a hemisling.

Teaching Points

Correct Answer: 3

Early intervention should focus on stretching and positioning the RUE into extension with the wrist and fingers extended. This helps decrease the developing flexor spasticity. Weight bearing on the limb promotes extensor activity in the triceps and shoulder stabilizers.

Incorrect Choices:

Obligatory synergistic patterns are never encouraged. Prolonged positioning is contraindicated because the patient may stiffen up with excess tone. Activities that utilize only the less-affected side are discouraged (compensatory training). Prolonged use of a sling can promote contractures.

Type of Reasoning: Inference

Effective intervention guidelines after stroke are based on the stage of recovery and presenting symptoms. This requires one to make assumptions based on facts, which is an inferential reasoning skill. If this question was answered incorrectly, review information on techniques and guidelines of stroke rehabilitation.

B111 

Nonsystem | Equipment, Devices, Biophysical Agents

A physical therapist and a physician are at odds regarding ordering a power wheelchair for a 3-year-old child. What is the **MOST** important factor to consider for not recommending a power wheelchair for this child?

Choices:

1. Age of the child.
2. Child has quadriplegic cerebral palsy.
3. Child is non-verbal.
4. Child has poor head and fine motor control.

Teaching Points

Correct Answer: 4

Most power wheelchairs require good head control to use a head rest control system or good fine motor skills to use a joy stick. Although there are other ways to propel a power chair, this is the best reason to NOT recommend a power chair.

Incorrect Choices:

Studies have found that children as young as 18 months of age can operate a power wheelchair, so age is not a factor here. Most children with power wheelchairs have quadriplegia and don't have a good prognosis for community ambulation. Without knowing any more about their abilities, it cannot be said that quadriplegia is a reason not to use a power chair. A child being non-verbal does not preclude them from using a power wheelchair. Just because a child is non-verbal does not mean that they cannot understand what is spoken to them or that they are cognitively impaired. Even if cognitive impairments were a factor, children with mild cognitive impairments can operate power mobility devices.

Type of Reasoning: Inductive

For this question, the test taker must determine the most important factor for not recommending a power wheelchair. This requires inductive reasoning skill where clinical judgment is paramount to arriving at a correct conclusion. In this case, poor head and fine motor control is the most important factor in not recommending a power wheelchair. Review power wheelchair prescription guidelines if answered incorrectly.

B112

Neuromuscular | Interventions

An ambulatory patient recovering from a left CVA is wearing a plastic AFO to stabilize the right foot. During gait analysis, the therapist observes lateral trunk bending toward the right as the patient bears weight on the right leg at midstance. What is the **BEST** intervention to correct this problem?

Choices:

1. Strengthen hip flexors on the right side.
2. Provide a lift on the shoe of the involved leg.
3. Strengthen the hip abductors on the right side.
4. Strengthen hamstrings on the right side.

Teaching Points

Correct Answer: 3

The lateral trunk bending (Trendelenburg gait) is the result of weak hip abductors on the right (a common problem for patients recovering from stroke). Strengthening of the abductors on the involved right side is indicated.

Incorrect Choices:

The other choices do not address the problem of lateral trunk bending. Weakness of the hip flexors or hamstrings would present as swing phase deficits (inability to shorten the leg so it can clear the floor). The patient is likely to compensate with circumduction. A lift on the left foot might be considered for patients with this problem but is not the intervention of choice.

Type of Reasoning: Inductive

This question requires one to utilize clinical judgment to determine the best choice to correct the Trendelenburg gait. Questions that encourage diagnostic thinking and clinical judgment utilize inductive reasoning skill. In this situation, the patient's gait pattern indicates weak hip abductors. If this question was answered incorrectly, review information on intervention approaches for Trendelenburg gait.

B113

Musculoskeletal | Interventions

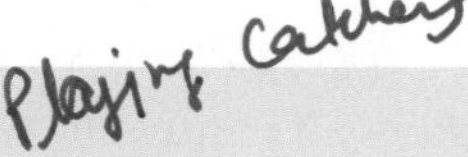

A 10-year-old boy who plays catcher on a baseball team complains of bilateral knee pain that is exacerbated with forceful quadriceps contraction. Examination reveals pain and swelling at the distal attachment of the patellar tendon. What is the **BEST** early intervention to use?

Choices:

1. Decreased loading of the knee by the quadriceps femoris muscle.
2. Strengthening exercises for the quadriceps femoris to prevent disuse atrophy.
3. Casting followed by decreased loading of the knee.
4. Ultrasound to decrease pain and inflammation.

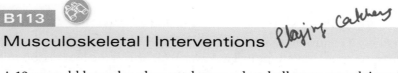

Teaching Points

Correct Answer: 1

Baseball catchers must make forceful contractions of the quadriceps muscles each time they stand up to throw the ball to the pitcher. This may precipitate Osgood-Schlatter disease in the adolescent or preadolescent boy. Early intervention of this condition focuses on reduction of the loading by the quadriceps, but still retaining normal lower extremity function.

Incorrect Choices:

Biophysical agents may provide temporary relief of pain; however, it will not improve the underlying condition. Use of ultrasound over open epiphyses (10-year-old boy) is also controversial. Strengthening may lead to continued excess loading of the structures. Casting may lead to restriction of normal movement.

Type of Reasoning: Inductive

In this question, the test taker must determine the best intervention approach for a child with bilateral knee pain related to playing catcher. This requires clinical judgment, which is an inductive reasoning skill. One must have an understanding of the nature of this activity on the quadriceps muscles, especially the need for forceful contractions each time the catcher stands up, to arrive at the correct conclusion.

B114 

Integumentary | Interventions

A patient presents with a decubitus ulcer of 3 months' duration on the lateral ankle. The ankle is swollen, red, and painful, with a moderate to high amount of wound drainage (exudate). What is the **BEST** choice of dressing for this wound?

Choices:

1. Hydrogel dressings.
2. Semipermeable film dressings.
3. Calcium alginate dressings. moderate to high exudate
4. Gauze dressings.

Teaching Points

Correct Answer: 3

Wounds with moderate to high exudate benefit from calcium alginate dressings. The dressings absorb large amounts of exudate (up to 20 times their weight) and form a gel, which maintains the moist wound environment while maintaining good permeability to oxygen.

Incorrect Choices:

Gauze and semipermeable film dressings require a secondary dressing and offer poor conformability to deep wounds. Hydrogel dressings are not recommended for wounds with heavy exudate.

Type of Reasoning: Inference

One must infer or draw conclusions based on the information presented in the patient's case, which draws upon inferential reasoning skill. In this situation, calcium alginate dressings are ideal for wounds with moderate to high exudate present. If this question was answered incorrectly, refer to information on wound dressings.

B115

Musculoskeletal | Examination

A patient was diagnosed with a bulging disc at the right L5–S1 spinal level without nerve root compression. What is the impairment **MOST** likely to be documented?

Choices:

1. Centralized gnawing pain with loss of postural control during lifting activities.
2. Centralized gnawing pain with uncompensated gluteus medius gait.
3. Radicular pain to the right great toe with a compensated gluteus medius gait.
4. Radicular pain to the right great toe with difficulty sitting for long periods.

Teaching Points

Correct Answer: 1

Discal degeneration without nerve root compression would likely be exhibited as a centralized gnawing pain with loss of proprioception.

Incorrect Choices:

Because there is no nerve compression, there will not be any type of radicular pain and/or decrease in specific muscle function (beyond the lumbar spine region), so one should not see a decrease in the function of the gluteus medius.

Type of Reasoning: Inference

This question provides the diagnosis, and the test taker must determine the most likely symptoms to be present. This type of question in which symptoms must be determined from a diagnosis draws upon inferential reasoning skill. To arrive at the correct answer, the test taker must have a good understanding of the nature of L5–S1 discal degeneration.

B116

Neuromuscular | Interventions

A patient recovering from traumatic brain injury (TBI) demonstrates impaired cognitive function (Rancho Cognitive Level VII). What training strategy should be the therapist's focus?

Choices:

1. Provide assistance as needed using guided movements during training.
2. Provide a high degree of environmental structure to ensure correct performance.
3. Involve the patient in decision-making and monitor for safety.
4. Provide maximum supervision as needed to ensure successful performance and safety.

Teaching Points

Correct Answer: 3

As patients with TBI recover, structure and guidance must be gradually reduced and patient involvement in decision-making increased. Safety must be maintained while increasing levels of independence are fostered. Patients at stage VII of recovery often exhibit rote movements (robot syndrome) indicative of the highly structured training utilized for patients during earlier stages of recovery.

Incorrect Choices:

A high degree of structure, assistance, and maximum supervision is not therapeutic at this stage of recovery.

Type of Reasoning: Deductive

Although this question does require one to utilize clinical judgment, the majority of skill required to answer this question correctly relies upon the recall of the Rancho Cognitive Function Levels and the guidelines for treatment provided within these levels. This is factual information and recall, which ultimately requires deductive reasoning ability to successfully choose the best type of training for the patient. If this question was answered incorrectly, refer to the Rancho Cognitive Function Levels.

B117 

Neuromuscular | Interventions

What is the **MOST** appropriate intervention to correct for the problem of a forward festinating gait in a patient with Parkinson's disease?

Choices:

1. Use of a heel wedge.
2. Use of a toe wedge.
3. Increase stride length using floor markers.
4. Increase cadence using a metronome.

Teaching Points

Correct Answer: 2

A festinating gait is an abnormal and involuntary increase in the speed of walking in an attempt to catch up with a displaced center of gravity due to the patient's forward lean. The most appropriate intervention would be to use a toe wedge, which would help to displace the patient's center of gravity backward.

Incorrect Choices:

Increasing cadence or stride length would serve only to increase, not decrease, the problem, as will the use of a heel wedge.

Type of Reasoning: Inductive

One must use clinical judgment to determine which approach would best decrease a forward festinating gait pattern in PD. The test taker must understand that forward festination results from forward displacement of center of gravity, which can be improved through the use of a toe wedge to displace the patient's gravity backward. The judgment in this case, utilizing one's knowledge of festinating gait pattern and the intervention approaches proposed, encourages use of inductive reasoning skill.

B118 

Musculoskeletal | Interventions

A patient presents with difficulty with fast movement speeds and fatigues easily. The therapist decides on a strength training program that specifically focuses on improving fast-twitch muscle fiber function. What is the optimal exercise prescription to achieve this goal?

Choices:

1. High-intensity workloads for short durations.
2. Low-intensity workloads for long durations.
3. Low-intensity workloads for short durations.
4. High-intensity workloads for long durations.

Teaching Points

Correct Answer: 1

High-intensity exercises at fast contraction speeds for shorter durations (< 20 repetitions) are needed to train the highly adaptable fast-twitch IIa fibers.

Incorrect Choices:

Performing workloads at low intensity and slow contraction speeds will challenge slow-twitch (type I) fibers. High-intensity workloads at long durations are contraindicated.

Type of Reasoning: Analysis

This question requires one to refer to knowledge of exercise physiology to recall the optimal method of improving fast-twitch fiber function. In order to arrive at the correct solution, one must analyze the information presented and determine its meaning, which is an analytical reasoning skill. If this question was answered incorrectly, refer to information on exercise physiology and fast-twitch fiber exercise.

B119 

Musculoskeletal | Examination

A cross-country runner presents with a complaint of pain in the proximal one-third of the right tibia with an insidious onset 4 weeks ago. The pain is present intermittently, and running exacerbates the symptoms. Ligamental testing and soft tissue examination of the knee and leg are unremarkable. Which imaging studies are recommended to be performed **INITIALLY** in order to help establish a diagnosis?

Choices:

1. Radiograph and if positive, then MRI.
2. CT scan and T2 MRI.
3. Bone scan and if positive, MRI.
4. Radiograph and if negative, a bone scan.

Teaching Points

Correct Answer: 4

This case represents the typical presentation of a stress fracture. Plain radiographs are an inexpensive and quick method to diagnose fractures and healing rates. Stress fractures may take 2–8 weeks before they can be visualized on plain films. If the plain films were negative, then a bone scan is performed (stress fracture, bone bruising).

Incorrect Choices:

If a bone scan is negative, then an MRI (meniscal, bone bruising, soft tissue) or CT scan (small, bony irregularities) is ordered. Both MRIs and CT scans are expensive and/or time-consuming. This is most likely a stress fracture and is best diagnosed by a radiograph and bone scan.

Type of Reasoning: Inductive

One must determine the most likely imaging studies to be initially recommended based on a patient's symptoms. This requires clinical judgment and knowledge of the diagnosis, which necessitate inductive reasoning skill. For this situation, it is likely that a radiograph and bone scan will be recommended, due to the patient's symptoms of stress fracture. If this question was answered incorrectly, review symptoms of stress fractures, especially imaging tests for stress fractures.

B120 

Neuromuscular | Evaluation, Diagnosis

What is the **MOST** appropriate functional goal for a 5-year-old child with a high lumbar lesion (myelomeningocele, L2 level) and minimal cognitive involvement?

Choices:

1. Household ambulation with KAFOs and rollator walker.
2. Community ambulation with an RGO and Lofstrand crutches.
3. Household ambulation with a reciprocating gait orthosis (RGO) and Lofstrand crutches.
4. Community ambulation with HKAFOs and Lofstrand crutches.

Teaching Points

Correct Answer: 3

A child with a high-level myelomeningocele will be able to ambulate for limited (household) distances with an RGO and Lofstrand crutches. Physiological benefits include improved cardiovascular and musculoskeletal functions.

Incorrect Choices:

The child will not be able to be a community ambulator because of the high-energy expenditure necessary with this level of lesion. An RGO is the best choice. The hips are joined by metal cables that prevent inadvertent hip flexion (possible using KAFOs) during a reciprocal two- or four-point gait.

Type of Reasoning: Inductive

This question requires the test taker to assess the value of each of the orthoses and assistive devices presented and then apply their value to the patient's specific diagnosis. This requires one to utilize clinical judgment, in which the test taker uses diagnostic reasoning to determine which solution will be most beneficial for the patient. In this case, an RGO and Lofstrand crutches are most beneficial for household ambulation.

B121 

Musculoskeletal | Examination

A patient with traumatic onset (motor vehicle accident) of neck pain presents with subjective complaints of frank upper cervical spine instability. Which test would safely assist in identifying the integrity of the C1–2 articulation?

Choices:

1. Transverse ligament stress test.
2. Vertebral artery test.
3. Maximum cervical compression test.
4. Hautant's test.

Teaching Points

Correct Answer: 1

The transverse ligament stress test is specifically designed to assess the integrity of the transverse ligament, which maintains the position of the dens of C2 with the anterior arch of C1.

Incorrect Choices:

The vertebral artery test is utilized to assess the status of the vertebrobasilar arterial system, and the maximum cervical compression test is utilized to identify dysfunction in the cervical facet joints. The motions associated with these two tests would be contraindicated for a patient who was suspected of having bony/joint instability. Hautant's test is utilized to differentiate between a vascular dysfunction in the vertebrobasilar system and a dysfunction of the vestibular system.

Type of Reasoning: Inductive

This question requires the test taker to utilize clinical judgment in order to determine the cervical test that would be safe for upper cervical spine instability. This necessitates clinical judgment, which is an inductive reasoning skill. For this situation, the therapist should perform the transverse ligament stress test. Review cervical testing guidelines, especially the transverse ligament stress test, if answered incorrectly.

B122 

Cardiovascular/Pulmonary and Lymphatic I Examination

The therapist is reading a recent report of arterial blood gas analysis with the following values:
Fraction of inspired oxygen (FiO_2) = 0.21
Arterial oxygen pressure (PaO_2) = 53 mm Hg
Arterial carbon dioxide pressure ($PaCO_2$) = 30 mm Hg
pH = 7.48
Bicarbonate ion = 24 mEq/L
What patient state do these findings indicate?

Choices:

1. Metabolic alkalosis.
2. Respiratory alkalosis.
3. Metabolic acidosis.
4. Respiratory acidosis.

Teaching Points

Correct Answer: 2

This arterial blood gas shows an increased pH, which is an alkalosis. When looking at arterial blood gas values, carbon dioxide can be viewed essentially as an acid. If the carbon dioxide level is low, then you have less acid, or a resulting alkalosis. This is, therefore, a respiratory alkalosis.

Incorrect Choices:

Because the blood pH is higher than normal (7.35–7.45), the condition is an alkalosis, not an acidosis. If the increased pH was due to a metabolic disorder, a high bicarbonate value would be anticipated. As the HCO_3 is normal (24 mEq/dL), the alkalosis is not from a metabolic cause.

Type of Reasoning: Analysis

One must make sense of the information presented in this question and recall the normal laboratory values. This requires analytical reasoning skill, in which one must make an interpretation of information. It is most beneficial to understand the values that indicate respiratory alkalosis to arrive at the correct conclusion. If this question was answered incorrectly, refer to information on arterial blood gas analysis.

B123

Metabolic/Endocrine I Evaluation, Diagnosis

A retired patient is referred to a cardiac exercise group after a mild MI. From the intake questionnaire, the therapist learns the patient has type 1 insulin-dependent diabetes mellitus (IDDM), controlled with twice-daily insulin injections. When initiating an exercise program, how should the therapist instruct the patient in order to minimize the risk of a hypoglycemic event?

Choices:

1. Exercise daily for 40–50 minutes to achieve proper glucose control.
2. Avoid exercise during periods of peak insulin activity.
3. Monitor blood glucose levels carefully every week during the rehabilitation program.
4. Decrease carbohydrate intake for 2 hours before the exercise session.

Teaching Points

Correct Answer: 2

The patient should monitor blood glucose levels frequently when initiating an exercise program and avoid exercise during periods of peak insulin activity (2–4 hours after injection). The therapist should use RPE in addition to HR to monitor exercise intensity.

Incorrect Choices:

A carbohydrate snack should be eaten before and during prolonged exercise bouts. Blood glucose levels should be monitored frequently throughout the day, not weekly. Exercise should begin with daily sessions, 20 minutes twice a day, not 40- to 50-minute sessions. (Source: *ACSM's Guidelines for Exercise Testing and Prescription,* 8th ed.)

Type of Reasoning: Inference

This question requires one to understand when peak insulin activity occurs in order to choose the best solution. For patients with IDDM, peak insulin activity occurs between 2 and 4 hours after injection, and therefore, exercise should be avoided during this time frame. One answers this question using inferential reasoning skill by drawing conclusions based on the information presented and making inferences about this information.

B124

Neuromuscular I Evaluation, Diagnosis

An elderly resident of a community nursing home is diagnosed with Alzheimer's type dementia. What patient behaviors should the therapist consider when formulating the plan of care?

Choices:

1. Can reliably perform wheelchair transfer activities.
2. Is more likely to remember current experiences than past ones.
3. Will likely be resistant to activity training if unfamiliar activities are used.
4. Can usually be trusted to be responsible for own daily care needs.

Teaching Points

Correct Answer: 3
Activity training is most likely to be successful if done with familiar activities.

Incorrect Choices:
A patient with Alzheimer's type dementia cannot be trusted to safely perform IADLs or functional mobility skills (wheelchair transfers). Memory for past events may be retained initially, but eventually all memory becomes impaired.

Type of Reasoning: Evaluation
This question requires one to make assumptions about the information presented and then determine the believability of the statements that are made. In this case, it is important to recall that patients with Alzheimer's disease can be resistant to trying unfamiliar activities and should, therefore, have training with familiar activities. When one needs to assess the value of statements made to choose the correct solution, evaluative reasoning skills are utilized.

B125 

Neuromuscular | Interventions

A patient with a spinal cord injury is having difficulty learning how to transfer from mat to wheelchair. The patient just cannot seem to get the idea of how to coordinate this movement. In this case, what is the **MOST** effective use of feedback during early motor learning?

Choices:
1. Focus on knowledge of performance and proprioceptive inputs.
2. Focus on guided movement and proprioceptive inputs.
3. Provide feedback only after a brief (5-sec) delay.
4. Focus on knowledge of results and visual inputs.

Teaching Points

Correct Answer: 4
During the early stage of motor learning (cognitive stage), learners benefit from seeing the whole task correctly performed. Dependence on visual inputs is high. Developing a reference of correctness (knowledge of results) is critical to ensure early skill acquisition (cognitive mapping).

Incorrect Choices:
Focus on proprioceptive inputs is important during the middle (associative) stage of motor learning. Delayed feedback may be used during later learning.

Type of Reasoning: Inference
One must infer information presented in this question, specifically, which approach is most effective during early motor learning. Visual inputs are key during early motor learning with a focus on knowledge of results. To answer this question successfully, one must recall effective teaching principles applied to early learning situations.

B126

Musculoskeletal | Interventions

A patient presents with pain and paresthesia over the first two metatarsal heads of her right foot. Pain is worse after prolonged periods of weight bearing. She typically wears shoes with 3-inch heels and pointed toes. What is the **BEST** intervention for this impairment?

Choices:

1. Pad placed proximal to the metatarsal heads.
2. Pad placed distal to the metatarsal heads.
3. Scaphoid pad to support the medial longitudinal arch.
4. Thomas heel to support the medial longitudinal arch.

Teaching Points

Correct Answer: 1

Compression of the digital nerves in the forefoot results in sensory symptoms of pain and paresthesia (metatarsalgia). It is typically the result of excessively tight shoes. The best intervention is to wear larger shoes, with a metatarsal pad placed proximal to the metatarsal heads to elevate the transverse (anterior) arch and separate the metatarsals. Custom orthotics can also be molded to decrease load. Wearing of high heels should be discouraged. Stretching of plantarflexors may also be helpful.

Incorrect Choices:

A pad placed distal to the metatarsal heads will not provide effective relief of pressure. A scaphoid pad and Thomas heel are used to support the longitudinal arch and prevent pes valgus, not metatarsalgia.

Type of Reasoning: Inference

The test taker must understand and infer what the cause is for the patient's symptoms and then understand the indications for each of the courses of action. In this case, the patient's tight high-heeled shoes are contributing to compression of the digital nerves in the forefoot. Having a thorough understanding of indications for using metatarsal pads, scaphoid pads, and a Thomas heel is key to arriving at the correct conclusion.

B127

Musculoskeletal | Evaluation, Diagnosis

A patient developed right throbbing shoulder pain after painting the kitchen. Passive and active glenohumeral motions increase pain. What is the suspected diagnosis and **BEST** initial intervention?

Choices:

1. Stretching of the pectoralis minor muscle after acromioclavicular joint inflammation.
2. Manual therapy techniques and biophysical agents to reduce pain as the result of subdeltoid bursitis.
3. Rotator cuff strengthening exercises to allow ADL function after biceps tendinitis.
4. Correction of muscle imbalances to allow healing of right shoulder supraspinatus tendinitis.

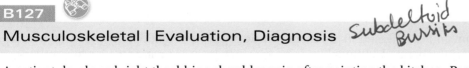

Teaching Points

Correct Answer: 2

Because pain occurs with both AROM and PROM, bursitis is the most likely cause of dysfunction. Initial interventions should focus on reducing pain and inflammation. Biophysical agents and manual therapy are the best choices.

Incorrect Choices:

Supraspinatus and/or bicipital tendonopathy would be most painful with AROM, not both AROM and PROM. An inflammatory condition of the acromioclavicular joint would not be improved by stretching the pectoralis minor muscle.

Type of Reasoning: Inductive

The test taker must determine the best initial intervention for the patient, given one's understanding of the diagnosis and typical intervention approaches. In order to choose the best solution, one must recognize the symptoms as indicative of subdeltoid bursitis and then recognize that biophysical agents and manual therapy techniques to reduce pain and inflammation are the best initial approaches. This decision-making process utilizes inductive reasoning skill, in which clinical judgment is paramount to finding the correct solution.

B128 

System Interactions | Evaluation, Diagnosis

A patient has a 5-year history of acquired immunodeficiency syndrome (AIDS) and poor compliance with taking medications. The physician has recently diagnosed the patient with HIV encephalopathy. What impairments should the therapist expect to find during the initial examination?

Choices:

1. Widespread sensory loss resulting in sensory ataxia.
2. Memory loss, confusion, and disorientation.
3. Progressive rigidity and akinesia with severe balance disturbances.
4. Emotional dysregulation and personality changes.

Teaching Points

Correct Answer: 2

Memory loss, confusion, and disorientation are characteristic of HIV encephalopathy (AIDS dementia) when the disease invades the brain. Additional impairments may include unsteadiness when walking, clumsiness, and shaky hands.

Incorrect Choices:

Widespread sensory loss with sensory ataxia or rigidity and akinesia are not seen. Patients may demonstrate personality changes, irritability, depression, or apathy, not emotional dysregulation.

Type of Reasoning: Evaluation

One must evaluate these statements and then recall knowledge of the neuromuscular changes associated with AIDS to arrive at the correct conclusion. This requires determination of the believability of the statements as true of someone with the diagnosis of AIDS, which is an evaluative reasoning skill. If this question was answered incorrectly, refer to information regarding neuromuscular changes associated with AIDS.

B129

Nonsystem | Safety, Professional Responsibilities, Research

A patient is referred by an orthopedist with a diagnosis of impingement syndrome of the shoulder. The initial PT examination reveals signs and symptoms that are not consistent with this diagnosis and are more consistent with thoracic spine pain and dysfunction. The therapist treats the patient consistent with PT findings without communicating with the referring physician. Months later, the therapist is sued by the patient's estate. The patient died of undiagnosed metastatic lung cancer. The therapist is:

Choices:

1. Not responsible for diagnosing metastatic cancer, therefore cannot be held responsible for the patient's death.
2. Responsible for communicating PT examination results to the referring physician.
3. Not responsible for the incorrect diagnosis because treatment was appropriate for the PT findings.
4. Responsible for making the diagnosis of possible cancer consistent with the PT examination of the patient.

Teaching Points

Correct Answer: 2

When a referral relationship exists with another health care professional, it is the PT's responsibility to communicate with the referring practitioner regarding the physical therapy examination, treatment plan, and management of the referred patient. This is particularly crucial when the findings are inconsistent with the referrer's diagnosis.

Incorrect Choices:

The therapist cannot diagnose metastatic cancer but can be held responsible for not communicating with the primary physician.

Type of Reasoning: Evaluation

This question encourages one to review the actions of the therapist, determine the value of those actions, and then decide whether they were appropriate, which necessitates evaluative reasoning. In this scenario, the therapist should have communicated the findings to the physician for follow-up, especially when they are inconsistent with the physician's findings. Questions that require value judgments are challenging because they move beyond factual knowledge to promote judgment, prudence, and ethical principles.

B130

Neuromuscular | Evaluation, Diagnosis

A PT is treating a 2-year-old child with Down syndrome who frequently uses a W sitting position. What impairments can prolonged W sitting cause in this child?

Choices:

1. Hip subluxation and lateral knee stress.
2. Femoral antetorsion and medial knee stress.
3. Abnormally low tone because of reflex activity.
4. Developmental delay of normal sitting.

Teaching Points

Correct Answer: 2

W sitting is a stable and functional position, but may cause later orthopedic problems of femoral antetorsion and knee stress. Low muscle tone and difficulty with achieving sitting are reasons why these children choose to sit in a stable W sit position. Children with Down syndrome typically exhibit low tone and hyperextensibility.

Incorrect Choices:

W sitting is not likely to affect low tone or reflex activity. It should also not promote delay of normal sitting. Hip subluxation is unlikely.

Type of Reasoning: Inference

One must infer the possible future occurrences from W sitting in order to arrive at the correct answer. First, one must have knowledge of what W sitting is and then understand the stresses that are placed upon the lower extremities, specifically the knees, from this sitting position. One infers these stresses, which utilizes inferential reasoning skill, to choose the correct answer. If this question was answered incorrectly, refer to information on W sitting and knee stresses.

Neuromuscular | Examination

A patient is being examined for impairments after stroke. When tested for two-point discrimination on the right hand, the patient is unable to tell whether the therapist is touching with one or two points. What areas of the CNS can be impaired with these findings?

Choices:

1. Spinotectal tract and somatosensory cortex.
2. Lateral spinothalamic tract and somatosensory cortex.
3. Dorsal column/lemniscal pathways and somatosensory cortex.
4. Anterior spinothalamic tract and thalamus.

Teaching Points

Correct Answer: 3

Discriminative touch, proprioceptive sensibility, and vibration sense are carried in the posterior white columns (fasciculus cuneatus for the upper extremity and fasciculus gracilis for the lower extremity). The long ascending tracts cross the medulla (sensory decussation) and form the medial lemniscus, which then travels to the thalamus (ventral posterolateral nucleus) and finally to the cortex (postcentral gyrus). Loss of two-point discrimination could result from an insult affecting any of these component parts. Parietal lobe or internal capsule lesions are the most common sites.

Incorrect Choices:

The anterolateral system pathways (spinothalamic tracts) convey pain and temperature. The spinotectal tract conveys information for spinovisual reflexes.

Type of Reasoning: Analysis

To answer this question, one must refer to knowledge of applied neuroanatomy, specifically spinal pathways that process discriminative touch of the upper extremity. This requires analysis of the information presented, utilizing analytical reasoning skill to arrive at the conclusion that the dorsal column/lemniscal pathways and somatosensory cortex is impaired. If this question was answered incorrectly, refer to discriminative touch processing of the upper extremity.

B132

Cardiovascular/Pulmonary and Lymphatic | Evaluation, Diagnosis

An elderly patient has a history of two myocardial infarctions (MIs) and one episode of recent congestive heart failure (CHF). The patient also has claudication pain in the right calf during an exercise tolerance test. Which of the following is the **BEST** initial exercise prescription for this patient?

Choices:

1. Daily walking, using interval training for 10- to 15-minute periods.
2. Walking five times a week using continuous training for 60 minutes.
3. Walking three times a week using continuous training for 40-minute sessions.
4. Walking three times a week using interval training for 30-minute periods.

Teaching Points

Correct Answer: 1

An appropriate initial exercise prescription for a patient with a history of CHF and claudication pain in the right calf should include low-intensity exercise (walking), low to moderate duration (10–15 min), and higher frequencies (daily). The exercise session should carefully balance activity with rest (interval or discontinuous training).

Incorrect Choices:

All other choices include durations that are too long (60, 40, or 30 min) and do not provide adequate rest periods.

Type of Reasoning: Inductive

One must utilize clinical judgment and diagnostic thinking (an inductive reasoning skill) to choose the best initial exercise prescription for this patient. This requires knowledge of CHF and claudication pain in order to arrive at the best solution. In this case, it is best to balance rest with activity because of the nature of CHF and limited tolerance to exercise.

B133

Musculoskeletal | Examination

A patient presents with signs and symptoms consistent with sacroiliac dysfunction. What cluster of special tests/findings provides the highest diagnostic accuracy for sacroiliac dysfunction?

Choices:

1. Thigh thrust test, Gillet's test, stork test, and Patrick's test.
2. Anterior superior iliac spine asymmetry, posterior iliac spine asymmetry, pubic symphysis pain with palpation, and sacral inferior lateral angle asymmetry.
3. Fortin finger test, torsion test, supine-to-sit test, and Gaenslen's test.
4. SI gapping, sacroiliac compression, thigh thrust test (P4), sacral thrust, and Gaenslen's test.

Teaching Points

Correct Answer: 4

It was found that if these 5 tests were clustered together as a group and at least 3/5 had a positive finding, they were found to have a high diagnostic accuracy.

Incorrect Choices:

There have been no outcome studies that support the grouping/clustering for any of these other choices as diagnostic for sacroiliac dysfunction.

Type of Reasoning: Inference

One must infer or draw a reasonable conclusion about the tests that are likely to have the highest diagnostic accuracy. This requires one to determine what is most likely to be true of a situation, which is an inferential reasoning skill. For this case, SI gapping, sacroiliac compression, thigh thrust test (P4), sacral thrust, and Gaenslen's test have the highest diagnostic accuracy. If answered incorrectly, review SI testing guidelines.

B134 

System Interactions | Evaluation, Diagnosis

A patient demonstrates postpartum sacral pain. The patient complains that pain is increased with prolonged walking, ascending or descending stairs, and rising from sit-to-stand. Which intervention would be the **MOST** beneficial for this patient?

Choices:

1. Manual therapy techniques of the SI joint to provide relief of symptoms and therapeutic exercise to restore normal function of the pelvic girdle.
2. Performing mobilization followed by cryotherapy to restore normal motion to the SI joint.
3. Cryotherapy and TENS to promote normal healing.
4. Increasing non–weight bearing with ambulation training and stabilization using a lumbosacral orthosis.

Teaching Points

Correct Answer: 1

Ligamentous laxity and pain during pregnancy secondary to hormonal influences (relaxin) most commonly affects the SI joint. This ligamentous laxity continues to occur for up to 3 months after pregnancy and leaves the pelvic area vulnerable to injury. SI pain is aggravated by prolonged weight bearing and stairs. Manual therapy techniques are effective for reducing pain and therapeutic exercise is beneficial to restore normal muscle function.

Incorrect Choices:

Modalities may provide temporary relief of pain, but will not promote any significant impact on healing. Promoting non–weight bearing does not allow the patient to return to normal function. Mobilization will further stretch joint structures that are already lax.

Type of Reasoning: Inference

One must infer the intervention that is most beneficial for a patient with postpartum sacral pain to arrive at the correct conclusion. Questions that encourage one to draw conclusions from evidence utilize inferential reasoning skill. One must understand the nature of postpartum sacral pain from ligamentous laxity and the intervention approach that is most effective in order to arrive at the correct conclusion.

B135

Musculoskeletal | Evaluation, Diagnosis

A patient complains of right shoulder pain since falling onto the right shoulder 3 weeks ago. There was no dislocation and x-rays were negative. AROM is 35° of flexion and abduction with scapular elevation noted. Passive ROM is nearly full with mild pain and muscle guarding at the end of range. Resisted abduction is weak with pain noted in the anterior and lateral deltoid region. There is no atrophy. What is the **MOST** likely diagnosis?

Choices:

1. Rotator cuff tear.
2. Axillary nerve palsy.
3. Supraspinatus tendinitis.
4. Adhesive capsulitis.

Teaching Points

Correct Answer: 1

A rotator cuff tear would be provoked by resisted testing because it is a contractile lesion. The patient would not be able to raise the arm over the head because of lack of force transmission secondary to the tear. Also, the mechanism of injury (trauma) could cause a tear.

Incorrect Choices:

A patient with supraspinatus tendinitis would likely be able to raise the arm overhead with a painful arc of motion or pain at end range. It is also more typically caused by overuse. An adhesive capsulitis would exhibit only a small amount of more passive range than active because the tight capsule is restricting ROM. An axillary nerve palsy is typically caused by a dislocation and would cause marked atrophy of the deltoid.

Type of Reasoning: Analysis

This question provides a group of symptoms and the test taker must determine the most likely diagnosis. This is an analytical reasoning skill, in which pieces of information are weighed in order to draw conclusions. For this situation, the symptoms are indicative of a rotator cuff tear. Review signs and symptoms of rotator cuff tear if answered incorrectly.

B136

Musculoskeletal | Examination

A patient presents with neck pain, which is a result of a motor vehicle accident (hit from behind while the car was at rest). To determine the function of the deep cervical flexors, the physical therapist decides to perform a muscle function test utilizing the cranio-cervical flexion test. What are the expected findings when the test is normal?

Choices:

1. When palpating the anterior cervical musculature during the active chin tuck, the sternocleidomastoid muscle activates prior to the longus colli muscle.
2. During active chin tuck, the patient is able to hold the head 1 inch above the table for 30 seconds.
3. During active chin tuck, the patient is able to maintain the normal cervical lordosis for 10 seconds.
4. During active chin tuck, the pressure in the stabilizer cuff increases to 22 and the patient can hold this position for 10 seconds.

Teaching Points

Correct Answer: 4

During an active chin tuck, the pressure in the stabilizer cuff increases to 22 and the patient can hold this position for 10 seconds.

Incorrect Choices:

Holding for 30 seconds is reflective for the endurance test, not the cranio-cervical flexion test. While performing this test the sternocleidomastoid muscle should remain inactive. During this procedure, the cervical spine should assume a flexed position so it loses its normal lordosis intentionally.

Type of Reasoning: Inference

This question requires one to infer the most likely findings from performing a cranio-cervical flexion test. Questions of this nature often necessitate one determining what is most likely to be true of a situation, which is an inferential reasoning skill. A normal finding during the cranio-cervical flexion test would show that during an active chin tuck the pressure in the stabilizer cuff increases to 22 and the patient can hold this position for 10 seconds. If answered incorrectly, review guidelines for performing cranio-cervical flexion testing.

B137 

Metabolic/Endocrine | Evaluation, Diagnosis

An elderly and frail older adult has low vision. The patient recently returned home from a 2-week hospitalization for stabilization of diabetes. The PT's goal is to mobilize the patient and increase ambulation level and safety. What is the **BEST** intervention strategy for this patient?

Choices:

1. Practice walking in areas of high illumination and low clutter.
2. Color-code stairs with pastel shades of blue and green to highlight steps.
3. Practice walking by having the patient look down at all times.
4. Keep window shades wide open to let in as much light as possible.

Teaching Points

Correct Answer: 1

Effective intervention strategies for the elderly patient with diabetes and low vision include ensuring adequate lighting. Vision and safety decrease dramatically in low lighting. Reducing clutter in the home is also an important strategy to improve safety during ambulation.

Incorrect Choices:

The patient should not continuously look down at the feet, because this poses a safety hazard. This restricts avoidance strategies for environmental objects. Visual acuity decreases dramatically with bright glare from sunlit windows. Color-coded stairs might help if they are well lit and if strong colors, not pastels, are used.

Type of Reasoning: Inference

This question requires one to recall the guidelines for intervention approaches with people who have low vision. Adequate lighting and low clutter are important to successful and safe navigation in the patient's living spaces. Using the skills of inferential reasoning, the test taker must draw conclusions from the evidence presented and make assumptions about that information.

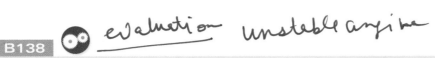

B138

Cardiovascular/Pulmonary and Lymphatic | Evaluation, Diagnosis

The patient has a history of angina pectoris and limited physical activity. As the patient participates in the second exercise class, the PT suspects that angina is unstable and may be indicative of a preinfarction state. What signs and symptoms would the therapist use to determine the presence of unstable angina?

Choices:

1. Prolonged cessation of pain following the administration of nitroglycerin for angina.
2. Angina that responds to rest and interval training but not to continuous training.
3. Arrhythmias of increasing frequency, especially atrial arrhythmias.
4. Angina of increasing intensity that is unresponsive to the nitroglycerin or rest.

Teaching Points

Correct Answer: 4

Preinfarction or unstable angina pectoris is unrelieved by rest or nitroglycerin (measures that typically reduce most angina). The pain is described as increasing in intensity. Unstable angina is an absolute contraindication to exercise.

Incorrect Choices:

Angina that decreases with rest and interval training along with nitroglycerin is considered stable. Increasing atrial arrhythmias may be a comorbidity, but is not expected with angina.

Type of Reasoning: Evaluation

In this question, the test taker must evaluate the merits of the statements presented and determine which statements seem most indicative of unstable angina. Relying on knowledge of angina pectoris and the indications for unstable angina, the test taker uses evaluative reasoning skill to arrive at the correct conclusion. If this question was answered incorrectly, review information on unstable angina.

B139

Neuromuscular | Interventions

A patient with a left CVA exhibits right hemiparesis and strong and dominant hemiplegic synergies in the lower extremity. Which activity would be **BEST** to break up these synergies?

Choices:

1. Foot tapping in a sitting position.
2. Supine, PNF D2F with knee flexing and D2E with knee extending.
3. Supine-lying, hip extension with adduction.
4. Bridging, pelvic elevation.

Teaching Points

Correct Answer: 4

The typical lower extremity synergies are effectively broken up using bridging (combines hip extension from the extensor synergy with knee flexion from the flexion synergy).

Incorrect Choices:

Supine hip extension with adduction and foot tapping in the sitting position are in-synergy activities (lower extremity flexion and extension synergies). Supine, lower extremity PNF D2F with knee flexing and D2E with knee extending moves the lower extremity in a pattern closely aligned with the typical flexion and extension synergies.

Type of Reasoning: Inference

This question requires one to determine what will best help a patient to break up a lower extremity synergy pattern after a stroke. Drawing conclusions based on the information presented, the test taker utilizes inferential reasoning to make the determination of which approach will benefit the patient. If this question was answered incorrectly, refer to information on limb synergy patterns and activities that promote this pattern.

B140 

Integumentary | Evaluation, Diagnosis

An elderly and frail resident of a nursing home has developed a stage III pressure ulcer. The wound is open with necrosis of the subcutaneous tissue down to the fascia. What are the age-related changes expected in this patient when compared to a younger patient?

Choices:

1. Decreased vascular and immune responses resulting in impaired healing.
2. Increased vascular responses with significant erythema.
3. Increased elasticity and eccrine sweating.
4. Increased scarring with healing.

Teaching Points

Correct Answer: 1

Age-associated changes in the integumentary system include decreased vascular and immune responses that result in impaired healing. Rate of healing is considerably slower.

Incorrect Choices:

In the elderly, scarring is typically less than in a younger individual. Both elasticity and eccrine sweating are decreased in the elderly. Vascular responses are typically decreased, not increased.

Type of Reasoning: Inference

One must infer or draw a reasonable conclusion about the likely healing abilities of an older adult with a pressure ulcer. This requires inferential reasoning skill. For this case, considering the patient's age as compared with a younger patient, one could expect decreased vascular and immune responses that impair healing. If this question was answered incorrectly, review age changes associated with changes in the integumentary system of older adults.

B141

Neuromuscular | Examination

The therapist is examining a patient recovering from stroke for the expected pattern of spastic hypertonia in the more involved upper extremity. What muscles are typically spastic in the hemiplegic upper extremity during early to middle recovery?

Choices:

1. Shoulder adductors, forearm pronators, and elbow extensors.
2. Shoulder retractors and abductors and flexors of the elbow, wrist, and hand.
3. Shoulder flexors and flexors of the elbow and hand.
4. Shoulder adductors; forearm pronators; and flexors of the elbow, wrist, and hand.

Teaching Points

Correct Answer: 4

The typical pattern of spasticity in the UE of the patient recovering from stroke is shoulder adductors; forearm pronators; and flexors of the elbow, wrist, and hand (antigravity muscles).

Incorrect Choices:

Spasticity is strong in shoulder adductors, not abductors. Spasticity is strong in elbow flexors, not extensors. Spasticity is not typically strong in shoulder flexors (the elbow is typically held in flexion, with arm adducted to the side).

Type of Reasoning: Inference

This question provides a diagnosis and the test taker must infer the typical pattern of spasticity. This requires one to determine what is likely to be true for a patient with a stroke, which is an inferential reasoning skill. In this situation, the patient is likely to display increased resistance to passive range of motion in the shoulder adductors; forearm pronators; and flexors of the elbow, wrist, and hand. Review information of spasticity patterns after stroke if answered incorrectly.

B142 

Gastrointestinal | Evaluation, Diagnosis

An elderly patient has been hospitalized for 3 weeks after a surgical resection of carcinoma of the colon. The patient is very weak and is currently receiving physical therapy to improve functional ambulation. During the initial sessions, the patient complains of pain in the left shoulder that is aggravated by weight bearing when using the walker. What action should the therapist take?

Choices:

1. Ambulate the patient in the parallel bars considering age and diagnosis.
2. Apply pulsed US to decrease pain.
3. Notify the physician immediately.
4. Apply heat in the form of a hot pack before ambulation.

Exam B

Teaching Points

Correct Answer: 3

The risk of metastatic disease is present; the therapist should notify the physician immediately.

Incorrect Choices:

Monitoring or modifying the plan of care to reduce pain should be considered only after consultation with the physician. If metastatic disease is present, the US would be contraindicated. Ambulating in the parallel bars exerts the same weight-bearing forces through the upper extremities as does a walker.

Type of Reasoning: Inductive

This question requires one to use clinical judgment and diagnostic thinking to make a determination of the cause for the patient's shoulder pain and then what is the best course of action based on this knowledge. In this situation, based on the patient's medical history, it is important to notify the physician immediately because of the risk of metastatic disease. Questions that require clinical judgment to make a determination of a best course of action utilize inductive reasoning skill.

B143 

Nonsystem | Equipment, Devices, Biophysical Agents

A patient sprained the left ankle 4 days ago. The patient complains of pain (4/10), and there is moderate swelling that is getting worse. At this time, which intervention would be **BEST** to use?

Choices:

1. Cold/intermittent compression combination with the limb elevated.
2. Cold whirlpool followed by massage.
3. Contrast baths followed by limb elevation.
4. Intermittent compression followed by elevation.

Teaching Points

Correct Answer: 1

The combination of RICE (rest, ice, compression, elevation) is best. Cold to decrease pain along with intermittent compression and elevation to facilitate fluid drainage provides the best intervention. Rest is required.

Incorrect Choices:

Contrast baths and whirlpool place the ankle in a dependent position, which might tend to increase edema. The interventions of intermittent compression and elevation should be combined, not sequential.

Type of Reasoning: Inference

In this question, the test taker must draw conclusions based on the information presented in the patient's case, which utilizes inferential reasoning skill. The patient's symptoms in this case indicate that cold and intermittent compression with limb elevation are best to relieve pain and facilitate fluid drainage. If this question was answered incorrectly, refer to information on intervention for acute ankle sprain.

Musculoskeletal | Examination

A patient diagnosed with left lateral epicondylitis has no resolution of symptoms after 2 weeks of treatment. The therapist decides to reexamine the patient. What location should be the focus of this reexamination?

Choices:

1. Cervicothoracic region.
2. Upper cervical region.
3. Cervicocranial region.
4. Mid cervical region.

Teaching Points

Correct Answer: 4

The patient has symptoms (diminished reflex) of a possible left C5 nerve root compression in the mid cervical spine. Any reflex change suggests nerve root irritation or compression. Lateral epicondylitis frequently involves the extensor carpi radialis brevis, which is innervated by spinal nerves emanating from the mid cervical region.

Incorrect Choices:

The presenting symptoms cannot be linked to involvement of the regions listed in the other choices.

Type of Reasoning: Analysis

This question provides the symptoms, and the test taker must determine the diagnosis or root cause, which relies primarily on analytical reasoning skill. The test taker must recall knowledge of neuroanatomy to recognize that a 1+ reflex in the left biceps is indicative of possible nerve root compression at the C5 level. If this question was answered incorrectly, refer to information on nerve root compressions of the cervical spine.

Cardiovascular/Pulmonary and Lymphatic | Examination

Which measure of aerobic capacity is supported as a reliable and valid functional capacity measure with reported minimal detectable change scores in patients with heart failure?

Choices:

1. 6-Minute Walk Test.
2. Bruce protocol treadmill test.
3. Canadian Aerobic Fitness Step test.
4. Lower extremity ergometer test.

Teaching Points

Correct Answer: 1

Only the 6-Minute Walk Test (6MWT) has minimal detectable change (MDC) scores associated with it.

Incorrect Choices:

All of these tests have literature to support that they are reliable (test-retest, intra-tester, and inter-tester reliability) and valid (concurrent, construct, and predictive validity), but cannot report minimal detectable changes.

Type of Reasoning: Deductive

For this question, the test taker must recall factual information about measures of aerobic capacity in order to arrive at a correct conclusion. This necessitates deductive reasoning skill, where facts are recalled to draw reasonable conclusions. For this scenario, the 6MWT is the only test that has minimal detectable change scores associated with it. Review measures of aerobic capacity, especially reliability and validity information, if answered incorrectly.

B146

Musculoskeletal | Examination

A patient underwent a right total hip replacement (THR) 4 months ago. The patient is now referred to physical therapy for gait evaluation. The patient demonstrates shortened stride length on the right. What is the **MOST** likely cause of this gait change?

Choices:

1. Weakened quadriceps.
2. Contracted hip flexors.
3. Weakened hip flexors.
4. Contracted hamstrings.

Teaching Points

Correct Answer: 2

Patients are less active after surgery and spend less time in standing and more time in sitting. The iliopsoas muscles become shortened with increased time in sitting. The contracted iliopsoas limits the patient's ability to extend the hip, which effectively shortens the stride length on the affected side.

Incorrect Choices:

Contracted hamstrings or weak quadriceps result in decreased knee extension during stance and an unstable knee. Weak hip flexors produce decreased limb shortening during swing, typically compensated by circumduction.

Type of Reasoning: Analysis

This question provides the symptoms and the test taker must determine the cause for the symptoms, which encourages analytical reasoning skill. In this case, the patient most likely has a contracted iliopsoas muscle, which will shorten the stride length on the right. One must recall reasons for decreased stride length, especially after THR surgery, in order to arrive at the correct conclusion.

Neuromuscular | Interventions

A child with spastic cerebral palsy is having difficulty releasing food from the hand to the mouth. Once the child has brought the food to the mouth, what should the caregiver be taught to do in order to assist the child?

Choices:

1. Slowly stroke the finger extensors in a proximal-to-distal direction.
2. Apply a quick stretch to the finger flexors.
3. Slowly stroke the finger flexors in a distal-to-proximal direction.
4. Passively extend the fingers.

Teaching Points

Correct Answer: 1

Slowly stroking the finger extensors will help to facilitate opening of the hand and allow the child to release the food into the mouth.

Incorrect Choices:

Stimulation of spastic finger flexors (slow stroking, quick stretch) is contraindicated. Passive extension of the fingers will not enhance the activity of feeding.

Type of Reasoning: Evaluation

One must evaluate the merits of the four statements presented to make a determination of the best approach to facilitate finger extension. Using knowledge of neurorehabilitation techniques, the test taker should conclude that stroking the fingers proximal to distal will be most effective in encouraging finger extension. Evaluative reasoning skill is used in this question because the test taker must evaluate the value of statements made to make a judgment for the best course of action.

Integumentary | Examination

During the examination of the cervical spine of a client for C5 radiculopathy, small groupings of nevi are noted near the superior angle of the left scapula. What is the NEXT action the therapist should take?

Choices:

1. Perform a vertebral artery examination.
2. Photograph the area in order to provide baseline documentation for the patient's record.
3. Ask the patient about any history of moles and examine them closely.
4. Contact the physician immediately.

Teaching Points

Correct Answer: 3

Nevi (moles) should be examined for asymmetry, border irregularities, color, and diameter (> 6 mm). It is not uncommon to have a group of moles, and they are usually benign, but if there is a transformation of a nevus (plural, nevi), then the primary care physician should be contacted. In this situation, the therapist needs to establish a baseline (history and physical examination) of the moles, and then determine whether there is an indication to contact the physician.

Incorrect Choices:

A photograph can be part of the examination, but this does not replace a thorough history and visual inspection. There are no indications for a vertebral artery examination. A vertebral artery examination is performed before manual or mechanical techniques of the cervical spine or if the client exhibits signs or symptoms of vertebral artery compromise.

Type of Reasoning: Evaluation

This question requires the test taker to determine the significance of nevi. In order to determine how significant they are (if at all), the next course of action (setting priorities) would be to ask the patient about any history of moles and then examine them closely. In order to arrive at a correct conclusion, one must evaluate the merits of each of the four possible courses of action presented and decide which action most adequately addresses patient well-being, while being prudent in approach.

B149 

Musculoskeletal | Examination

The figures below are lifting a constant load using either a stoop lift or a squat lift. In addition to the weight of the load, what is the **MOST** significant contributing factor for increasing lumbar spine compression forces?

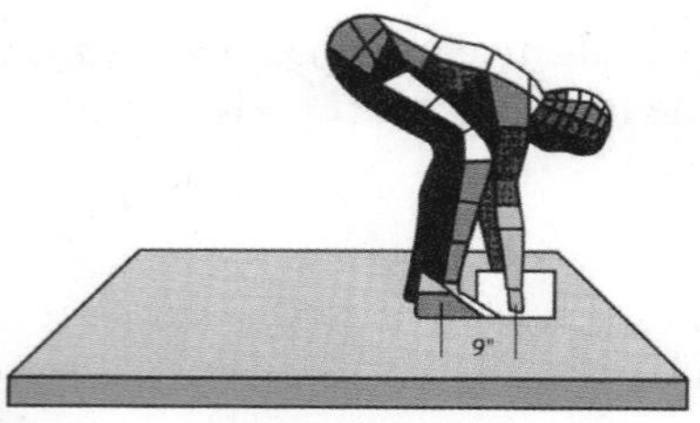

Stoop Lift

Deep Squat Lift

Musculoskeletal Disorders in the Workplace: Principles and Practice. Nordin M, Andersson G, Pope M (1997). St Louis, Inc., page 122, Figure 10-1, with permission.

Choices:

1. Performing the lift with the lumbar spine in a kyphotic posture.
2. Performing the lift with the lumbar spine in a neutral position rather than in a lordotic posture.
3. The height of the load from the ground.
4. The distance of the load from the base of the spine.

Teaching Points

Correct Answer: 4

Manual lifting biomechanical models have demonstrated high lumbar spine moments, especially when the load is not held close to the body.

Incorrect Choices:

The height of the load from the ground may decrease the overall work but is not the key factor in reducing lumbar compressive forces. The spine should be held in its normal position. A lumbar neutral position may change the biomechanics slightly but will not reduce lumbar compressive forces. Kyphosis occurs in the thoracic region, not lumbar.

Type of Reasoning: Analysis

Questions that require one to analyze information presented in pictures often encourage the use of analytical reasoning skill. In this question, one must analyze how the information presented in the picture best depicts how the distance of the load from the base of the spine is the most significant contributing factor for increasing lumbar spine compression forces. If this question was answered incorrectly, review information on biomechanics of lifting.

B150 

Musculoskeletal | Interventions

Nearly 2 months ago, a patient noticed left shoulder pain after walking the dog. This pain has progressively worsened. The patient now is unable to move the left upper extremity overhead while performing ADLs. An orthopedic surgeon diagnosed the problem as adhesive capsulitis. What is the **MOST** effective direction for glenohumeral mobilization for this patient?

Choices:

1. Posteroinferior translatory glides.
2. Anteroinferior translatory glides.
3. Anterosuperior translatory glides.
4. Posterosuperior translatory glides.

Teaching Points

Correct Answer: 1

The diagnosis is left shoulder adhesive capsulitis. Inferior glides will improve the abduction and flexion (overhead motion). Posterior glides have been shown to be the most effective glide to increase glenohumeral external rotation. This is an exception to the concave-convex rule.

Incorrect Choices:

Superior glides will improve extension, not elevation. Based on the concave-convex rule, it seems that anterior glides would be best to promote external rotation at the glenhohumeral joint. However, posteroinferior glides are more effective for this problem.

Type of Reasoning: Inference

This question requires one to determine the most effective treatment approach in glenohumeral mobilization techniques for adhesive capsulitis. This requires one to have a firm understanding of the nature of adhesive capsulitis, capsular patterns and joint mobilization techniques of the shoulder to arrive at the correct conclusion. This question utilizes inferential reasoning skill because the test taker must draw a conclusion based on the evidence presented for a best course of action.

B151 

System Interactions | Evaluation, Diagnosis

An elderly patient is referred to physical therapy for an examination of functional mobility skills and safety in the home environment. The family reports that the patient is demonstrating increasing forgetfulness and some memory deficits. During the examination, what would the therapist typically expect to find?

Choices:

1. Impairments in short-term memory.
2. Periods of fluctuating confusion.
3. Periods of agitation and wandering, especially in the late afternoon.
4. Significant impairments in long-term memory.

Teaching Points

Correct Answer: 1

Elderly patients with memory impairments typically demonstrate intact immediate recall (e.g., can repeat words); impairments are often noted in memory for recent events (e.g., Why did I come into this room? Who came to see me yesterday?). Long-term memory is usually intact.

Incorrect Choices:

Periods of fluctuating confusion are typically found in delirium, an acute state of disorientation and confusion. Hallucinations or delusions are common (not present in this case). Periods of agitation and wandering (sundowning) are seen in patients with Alzheimer's type dementia (AD). Whereas AD begins with mild memory loss (stage I), agitation and wandering typically do not occur until stage II.

Type of Reasoning: Analysis

In this situation, the test taker must analyze the patient's symptoms and make a determination of the root cause for them in order to decide what the therapist's findings may be. Analytical questions require one to interpret information and determine the precise meaning of that information. If this question was answered incorrectly, review information regarding age-related memory deficits.

B152 

Neuromuscular | Examination

A therapist is examining a patient with vestibular dysfunction. The patient is asked to assume a long sitting position with the head turned to the left side. The therapist then quickly moves the patient backward so that the head is extended over the end of the table approximately 30° below horizontal. This maneuver causes severe dizziness and vertigo. A repeat test with the head turned to the right produces no symptoms. What is the **BEST** way to document these results?

Choices:

1. Positive left Hallpike-Dix test.
2. Positive sharpened Romberg's test.
3. Positive right positional test.
4. Positive positional test.

Teaching Points

Correct Answer: 1

The test described is the Hallpike-Dix. It is a left positive test because, with the head turned to the left, the change in position produces the patient's symptoms.

Incorrect Choices:

The right Hallpike-Dix test with head turned to the right is negative. The sharpened Romberg's test is used to assess standing balance (disequilibrium) with the eyes closed and feet in a tandem (heel-toe) position. The Hallpike-Dix test is a positional test; a positive positional test.

Type of Reasoning: Deductive

This question requires one to determine which clinical test is represented by the information in the scenario. This requires factual recall of information related to protocols, which is a deductive reasoning skill. In this situation, the scenario describes administration of the Hallpike-Dix maneuver. If this question was answered incorrectly, review information on the Hallpike-Dix maneuver.

B153

Neuromuscular | Interventions

A therapist is instructing a patient with a stroke in gait training. The therapist determines that learning is going well because the patient's errors are decreasing and overall endurance is improving. What is the **BEST** strategy to promote continued motor learning at this point in the patient's rehabilitation?

Choices:

1. Have the patient practice walking in varying environments.
2. Intervene early whenever errors appear before bad habits become firmly entrenched.
3. Provide continuous feedback after every walking trial.
4. Have the patient continue to practice in the parallel bars until all errors are extinguished.

Teaching Points

Correct Answer: 1

This patient demonstrates the associative stage of motor learning (errors are decreasing and movements are becoming organized). It is appropriate to gradually progress this patient toward ambulating in a more open (varied) environment.

Incorrect Choices:

Continuous feedback may improve performance but delays motor learning. Practicing until errors are extinguished or intervening early whenever errors appear are also inappropriate strategies for the associative stage of learning. Some trial and error learning is the goal.

Type of Reasoning: Inductive

One must utilize clinical judgment to determine the best strategy to promote continued motor learning with the patient. Use of clinical judgment to make a determination of a best course of action is an inductive reasoning skill. It is important to know the stages of motor learning in order to arrive at the correct conclusion, which should be reviewed if this question was answered incorrectly.

B154

Cardiovascular/Pulmonary and Lymphatic | Interventions

A young child with newly diagnosed cystic fibrosis is being seen by a PT in the home. Which intervention should be considered for this patient?

Choices:

1. Teach the child use of the acapella device in postural drainage positions to be performed once or twice a day.
2. Teach the child autogenic drainage for secretion removal to be performed once or twice daily.
3. Teach the parents secretion removal techniques to all segments of all lobes of both lungs once or twice a day.
4. Teach the child active cycle of breathing technique (ACBT) to be done once or twice a day to clear retained secretions.

Teaching Points

Correct Answer: 3

For a young child, proper at-home interventions include secretion removal techniques including manual techniques performed by an adult once or twice a day.

Incorrect Choices:

The use of an acapella device, ACBT, and/or autogenic drainage can be helpful in clearing secretions in patients with cystic fibrosis; however, these three techniques are not appropriate for a young child, because they rely on independent use and an ability to self-monitor secretion clearance to know how long and how often to perform the techniques.

Type of Reasoning: Inference

The test taker must understand the nature of cystic fibrosis and home interventions for the condition to determine what is an acceptable intervention for a **YOUNG** child. Arriving at the correct conclusion requires inferential reasoning, which requires one to draw conclusions from information and form assumptions about the information. If this question was answered incorrectly, review home therapy interventions for young children with cystic fibrosis.

B155 

Genitourinary | Interventions

A middle-aged woman is referred to a women's clinic with problems of stress incontinence. She reports loss of control that began with coughing or laughing but now reports problems even when she exercises (aerobics 3 times/wk). What is the **BEST** intervention for this patient?

Choices:

1. Kegel's exercises several times a day.
2. Behavioral modification techniques to reward proper voiding on schedule.
3. Biofeedback 1 hour/wk to achieve appropriate sphincter control.
4. Functional electrical stimulation 3 times/wk.

Teaching Points

Correct Answer: 1

Symptoms of stress incontinence can be successfully managed through a variety of techniques. Pelvic floor exercises (Kegel's exercises) are the mainstay of treatment and must be performed daily, several times a day, in order to be effective.

Incorrect Choices:

Biofeedback and E-Stim offered weekly or 3 times/wk are not likely to be effective because of insufficient frequency. A voiding schedule does not address the primary impairment.

Type of Reasoning: Inductive

This question requires one to understand the nature of stress incontinence and the appropriate interventions for this condition in order to choose the best intervention approach. Using clinical judgment (an inductive reasoning skill), the test taker determines the best course of action for the patient. If this question was answered incorrectly, review intervention strategies for stress incontinence.

B156
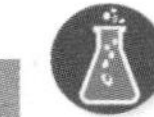

Neuromuscular | Evaluation, Diagnosis

An elderly patient suffered a cerebral thrombosis 4 days ago and presents with the following symptoms: decreased pain and temperature sensation of the ipsilateral face, nystagmus, vertigo, nausea, dysphagia, ipsilateral Horner's syndrome, and contralateral loss of pain and temperature sensation of the body. What is the **MOST** likely location of the thrombosis?

Choices:

1. Anterior cerebral artery.
2. Posterior inferior cerebellar artery.
3. Internal carotid artery.
4. Posterior cerebral artery.

Teaching Points

Correct Answer: 2

This patient presents with lateral medullary (Wallenberg's) syndrome, which can result from occlusion of the PICA, which is usually a branch of the vertebral artery. It involves the descending tract and nucleus of CN V, the vestibular nucleus and its connections, CN IX and CN X nuclei or nerve fibers, cuneate and gracile nuclei and spinothalamic tract.

Incorrect Choices:

The symptoms in this case clearly indicate brain stem (cranial nerve) involvement, not cortical involvement (anterior or posterior cerebral artery). An internal carotid artery stroke produces symptoms of combined middle cerebral and anterior cerebral artery strokes.

Type of Reasoning: Analysis

This question requires one to recall the symptoms that indicate involvement of the PICA. This requires the test taker to analyze the information presented and interpret it in order to determine that the symptoms are directly indicative of PICA thrombosis. It is important for one to recall applied neuroanatomy related to strokes in order to choose the best answer.

B157

Nonsystem | Equipment, Devices, Biophysical Agents

A patient with a 2-inch stage II decubitus ulcer over the left lateral malleolus is referred for physical therapy. The therapist notes a greenish, pungent exudate at the wound site. The therapist decides to use electrical stimulation. What is the **BEST** choice of polarity and electrode placement?

Choices:

1. Cathode placed in the wound.
2. Cathode placed proximal to wound.
3. Anode placed in the wound.
4. Anode placed proximal to wound.

Teaching Points

Correct Answer: 1

It is purported that the bactericidal effect produced by negative current is a result of substrate depletion or alteration of the internal processes of the microorganisms. Neutrophils are also attracted to the wound area by chemotaxis to purge the bacteria. The cathode should be placed directly in contact with the wound to cover as much treatment area as possible.

Incorrect Choices:

The anode is used to promote healing in clean uninfected wounds, and placement of an electrode in the wound ensures current will be delivered throughout the wound.

Type of Reasoning: Deductive

This question requires one to recall the protocol for electrical stimulation in treatment of infected decubitus ulcers. Questions that require one to recall protocols and guidelines require deductive reasoning skill. For this clinical situation, the cathode should be placed in the wound to promote healing. If this question was answered incorrectly, review protocols for electrical stimulation for wound healing.

B158 

Cardiovascular/Pulmonary and Lymphatic | Examination

A patient arrives for outpatient cardiac rehab 10 weeks after a coronary artery bypass graft. The postoperative course was complicated by atrial fibrillation, which has been controlled with medications prescribed by a cardiologist. The patient's resting vital signs are HR = 90 in atrial fibrillation, BP = 116/74, RR = 14, and SpO_2 = 99% on room air. Is a symptom-limited exercise test appropriate for this patient at this time?

Choices:

1. Yes, the patient is managed by a cardiologist and has no symptoms now.
2. Yes, the heart rate is well controlled and the cardiologist is aware of the arrhythmia.
3. No, the patient is tachycardic at rest and has an arrhythmia.
4. No, a patient in atrial fibrillation should not complete an exercise test.

Teaching Points

Correct Answer: 2

It is appropriate to perform an exercise test on a patient who is on medication to control his/her rate with atrial fibrillation (AF). A normal heart rate is between 60–100 beats per minute, which is where this patient's heart rate falls.

Incorrect Choices:

Patients can be asymptomatic with AF, so it is best to use objective measures to assess their response to activity. It is safe to exercise a patient who is in AF. It is a concern if the patient's heart rate is ≥ 115–120 beats per minute. This is the point at which diastolic filling time is decreased, which places a person in AF at risk of not maintaining his/her cardiac output with increased demand.

Type of Reasoning: Evaluation

This question provides symptoms, and the test taker must determine the best course of action for a client based on knowledge of cardiac exercise guidelines and safety in providing treatment. This is an evaluative reasoning skill, as the test taker must weigh the four options provided and determine what is prudent for the patient's current status and needs. In this case, the patient's rate is well controlled and the cardiologist is aware of the arrhythmia, so the therapist should proceed with symptom-limited exercise testing. Review cardiac exercise guidelines if the question was answered incorrectly.

B159 

System Interactions | Evaluation, Diagnosis

A patient presents with a complete T10 paraplegia. An extensive neurological workup has failed to reveal a specific cause for the paraplegia. The physician has determined a diagnosis of conversion disorder. What is the therapist's **BEST** choice of intervention?

Choices:

1. Initiate ROM and strength training after the patient receives psychological counseling.
2. Initiate functional training consistent with the level of injury.
3. Use functional electrical stimulation as a means of demonstrating to the patient that the muscles are functional.
4. Discuss possible underlying causes for the paralysis with the patient in an empathetic manner.

Teaching Points

Correct Answer: 2

A conversion disorder (hysterical paralysis) represents a real loss of function for the patient. The therapist should treat this patient the same as any patient with spinal cord injury with similar functional deficits. Early intervention is crucial.

Incorrect Choices:

A psychologist or psychiatrist is best able to help the patient understand the cause of the patient's paralysis. The therapist should be empathetic; however, counseling should not be the main focus of intervention in PT. Confrontation (using E-Stim to prove the patient has functioning muscles) is contraindicated.

Type of Reasoning: Evaluation

This question requires one to make a value judgment about the best course of action for this patient who has a conversion disorder. It is beneficial to understand what a conversion disorder is and the appropriate role for the PT in order to choose the best response. These types of questions, which require evaluative reasoning, are challenging because of the need to evaluate the believability of statements and make decisions based on values.

B160 

Nonsystem | Safety, Professional Responsibilities, Research

The director of a physical therapy department wants to fill a vacant PT position in the spinal cord injury program. Two résumés have been received. One candidate, a former employee, is a well-qualified and experienced 52-year-old female with a history of back pain that could impact her ability to do some heavy lifting at times. The other candidate is a newly licensed, very enthusiastic, 25-year-old male therapist for whom heavy lifting should not be a problem. In this case, what is the **BEST** hiring decision?

Choices:

1. As long as age and back pain history were NOT discussed during the interview process with the female candidate, the male candidate would best meet the caseload demands.
2. Hire the male candidate but ensure that age and back pain history were discussed with the female candidate as the rationale for hiring someone else.
3. Not have the female candidate partake in the interview process as issues with age and back pain would be justifiable grounds to rule her out based on the case load.
4. Hire the more qualified female and provide aide assistance or lift equipment when heavy lifting is required.

Teaching Points

Correct Answer: 4

The Age Discrimination and Employment Act of 1967 prohibits employers from discriminating against persons 40–70 years of age in any area of employment. The 1973 Rehabilitation Act prohibits employment discrimination based on disability and requires reasonable accommodation in the workplace by removing barriers unless there would be "undue hardship" for the employer. Title VII of the Civil Rights Act of 1964 might also come into play since one provision prohibits discrimination based on gender. The female candidate is clearly the more qualified and would be the best hire in this case.

Incorrect Choices:

Although asking about age is not permissible in the hiring process, familiarity with the candidate or a review of a résumé could unintentionally make the candidate's age obvious. Ruling out the female from the interview process with age and back pain as factors is clearly discriminatory. The male candidate may have potential; however, consideration of both age and back pain history, whether discussed or not, is discriminatory. The older candidate may be familiar with the caseload, department systems, and all other things being equal, is the stronger candidate if reasonable accommodations can be made.

Type of Reasoning: Evaluation

For this situation, the test taker must determine a best course of action from the information provided, while being mindful of employment regulations and guidelines. This requires evaluative reasoning skills, where one weighs various courses of action in order to arrive at a correct conclusion. In this situation, the director should hire the more qualified female and provide aide assistance or lift equipment when heavy lifting is required. If answered incorrectly, review the Age Discrimination and Employment Act of 1967 and the Rehabilitation Act of 1973 for employment guidelines.

B161 

Neuromuscular I Examination

Which is an abnormal finding during an examination of a newborn infant?

Choices:

1. Continuous tremulousness.
2. Response decrement to repetitive stimuli.
3. Dramatic skin color changes with change of state.
4. Symmetry in ROM.

Teaching Points

Correct Answer: 1

Continuous tremulousness is an abnormal finding, but occasional tremulousness is not.

Incorrect Choices:

All the other choices are normal findings in a newborn infant.

Type of Reasoning: Inference

This question requires one to understand normal activity and responses of infants in order to determine what is **NOT** a normal finding. The test taker must use inferential reasoning, which requires one to draw conclusions and make assumptions from the information presented. If this question was answered incorrectly, review information on abnormal findings in examinations of newborns.

B162

Neuromuscular | Evaluation, Diagnosis

A patient with long-standing traumatic brain injury (TBI) comes into an outpatient clinic using a standard wheelchair. The patient demonstrates sacral sitting with a rounded, kyphotic upper back. What is the **MOST** likely cause of this posture?

Choices:

1. Decreased floor to seat height.
2. Uneven weight distribution on the thighs and ischial seat.
3. Excessive leg length from seat to the foot plate.
4. Excessive seat width.

Teaching Points

Correct Answer: 3

Excessive leg length on a wheelchair can result in sliding forward in the wheelchair to reach the foot plate. This results in a posterior tilt of the pelvis and sacral sitting.

Incorrect Choices:

All other choices are not likely to produce these postural deficits.

Type of Reasoning: Inference

One must determine the most likely result of excessive leg length from the seat to the foot plate when sitting in a wheelchair. This requires inferential reasoning, in which the test taker must draw conclusions from the information presented. In this situation, the most likely result is sacral sitting and sliding forward in the chair.

B163

Integumentary | Examination

A patient presents with a large sacral decubitus ulcer that is purulent and draining. The therapist needs to take a representative sample of the infected material in order to obtain a laboratory culture. What is the **BEST** source to obtain a culture sample from this wound?

Choices:

1. Exudate in the wound and the surrounding tissues.
2. Dressing and exudate in the wound.
3. Exudate in the wound.
4. Dressing, exudate, and surrounding bed linen.

Teaching Points

Correct Answer: 3

The specimens must be collected from the wound site with a minimum of contamination by material from adjacent tissues. The exudate provides the best culture.

Incorrect Choices:
The margins of cutaneous lesions or pressure ulcers are usually contaminated with environmental bacteria. Using the dressing for a specimen sample would also contain contaminated tissues.

Type of Reasoning: Inductive
The test taker must use clinical judgment applied to a patient circumstance (an inductive reasoning skill) to determine the best method to obtain a sample culture of a wound. In this situation, it is best to minimize contamination by sampling the exudate in the wound. If this question was answered incorrectly, refer to information on methods for obtaining laboratory cultures.

B164 

Cardiovascular/Pulmonary and Lymphatic | Interventions

A phase 2 outpatient cardiac rehabilitation program uses circuit training with different exercise stations for the 50-minute program. One station uses arm ergometry. For arm exercise as compared with leg exercise, at a given workload, what can the therapist expect?

Choices:
1. Higher systolic and diastolic BP.
2. Higher HR and systolic/diastolic BP.
3. Higher HR and lower systolic BP.
4. Reduced exercise capacity owing to higher stroke volumes.

Teaching Points

Correct Answer: 2
Arm ergometry uses a smaller muscle mass than leg ergometry with resulting lower maximal oxygen uptake. In upper extremity exercise, both HR and BP will be higher than for the same level of work in the lower extremities.

Incorrect Choices:
The other choices do not correctly identify the expected changes with arm exercise.

Type of Reasoning: Inference
This question requires one to draw conclusions about arm ergometry and its impact on HR and BP, especially as it relates to leg ergometry. For this scenario, HR and systolic/diastolic BP will be higher with arm ergometry. To arrive at the correct conclusion, one must rely on knowledge of the impact of ergometry on cardiovascular activity, which should be reviewed if this question was answered incorrectly.

B165 

Nonsystem | Safety, Professional Responsibilities, Research

A therapist is working in a major medical center and is new to the acute care setting. An orientation session for new employees concerns infection control. What is the **MOST** common infection transmitted to health care workers?

Choices:
1. Tuberculosis.
2. Human immunodeficiency virus (HIV).
3. Hepatitis A.
4. Hepatitis B.

Teaching Points

Correct Answer: 4

Health care workers are most likely to contract hepatitis B (estimated incidence 300,000 new acute cases in the United States each year). Transmission is through exposure to blood and blood products and infected body fluids.

Incorrect Choices:

While the other three conditions listed require infection control, they are not the most common infections identified.

Type of Reasoning: Deductive

This question requires recall of the most common infection transmitted to health care workers. This is factual information, which necessitates deductive reasoning skill. Through recall of infection control information, one should conclude that hepatitis B is the most common infection to be transmitted. If answered incorrectly, refer to infection control guidelines, especially transmission of hepatitis B.

B166 

Gastrointestinal | Interventions

Before liver transplantation, a patient had a body mass index (BMI) of 17 and generalized muscle atrophy and completed the 6-minute walk with 65% of age-predicted distance. Surgery was 10 days ago, and the patient is able to complete bed mobility with an overhead trapeze, walk independently for short distances with a rolling walker, and complete deep breathing and lower extremity AROM exercises for two sets of 10 repetitions. The patient is being discharged home with family assistance today. Home care physical therapy is scheduled to begin in 1 week. What is the **BEST** choice for the patient's discharge home exercise program?

Choices:

1. Stationary cycling and lower extremity resistance exercises using a 5-lb weight cuff.
2. Independent bed mobility exercises, elastic resistance extremity exercise, and partial sit-ups.
3. Independent ambulation, elastic resistance lower extremity exercise, and active abdominal strengthening.
4. Breathing exercises, ambulation with walker, and AROM lower extremity exercises.

Teaching Points

Correct Answer: 4

The in-hospital program should be continued until the home care therapist can make his/her own assessment and plan of care. The postoperative goals of improved ventilation, assisted mobility, and AROM are appropriate for the 3-week postoperative time period, considering the debilitation before surgery and the abdominal surgery.

Incorrect Choices:

The other choices essentially change the exercise prescription and introduce unsupervised resistance exercises, which can be harmful to this debilitated patient.

Type of Reasoning: Inductive

This question requires one to consider the benefits of a home exercise program after liver transplantation. Given the patient's current status, the test taker must determine which exercise program will best address the patient's symptoms and result in functional improvement. This requires clinical judgment and prediction of what results will be yielded in the future, which is an inductive reasoning skill.

B167 

Neuromuscular | Examination

Based on the pictured CT scan, what impairments is this patient likely to demonstrate?

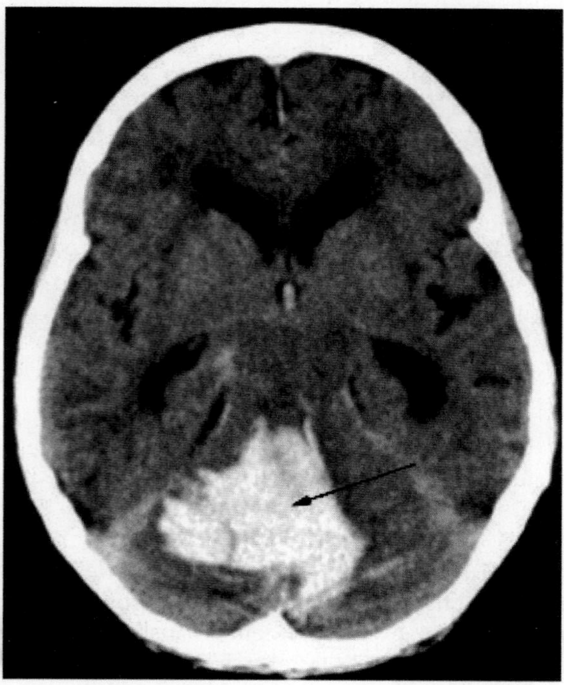

Image from: http://www.med-ed.virginia.edu/courses/rad/headct/index.html

Choices:

1. Ataxia.
2. Nonfluent aphasia.
3. Fluent aphasia.
4. Left-sided unilateral neglect.

Teaching Points

Correct Answer: 1

The arrow is pointing to a hemorrhage in the cerebellum. Damage to this area results in difficulty with movement, postural control, eye-movement disorders, and muscle tone. Ataxia is a common finding.

Incorrect Choices:

Aphasia is more typical of a left cerebral infarct, and left-sided unilateral neglect is typically due to a right cerebral injury. CT scans and MRIs can help the therapist predict clinical manifestations based on the area of injury.

Type of Reasoning: Analysis

This question requires the test taker to determine the most likely presentation of symptoms based on the CT image. Questions that require analysis of pictures and graphs often necessitate analytical reasoning skill. In this case, the patient has experienced a hemorrhage in the cerebellum and will most likely display ataxia. If this question was answered incorrectly, review signs and symptoms of cerebellar hemorrhages.

B168

Nonsystem | Safety, Protection, Professional Responsibilities, Research

A child with a developmental disability continues to be a no show for PT scheduled appointments. When the child does arrive to PT the family is usually late. It does not seem as though the home exercise program is being done and the child is regressing quickly. After the physical therapist discusses this with the parents they get angry and stop bringing the child for treatment. What is the therapist's **BEST** course of action in this situation?

Choices:

1. Report the family for neglect of the child.
2. Contact your supervisor with information that you are discharging this child.
3. Do nothing because it is the family's choice whether to continue or not.
4. Report the family for abuse of the child.

Teaching Points

Correct Answer: 1

Withholding necessary medical care from a child fits the definition of neglect. This is often a tough call, however, this child is regressing in ability and it seems that it is based on the parents' behavior.

Incorrect Choices:

Child abuse would require physical, sexual, or mental insult to the child. To do nothing is not in the best interest of the child and as health care providers it is the duty and often legal responsibility to protect those in our care. Discharging the child will be necessary since the parents have stopped bringing the child to PT, however, it does not help the child.

Type of Reasoning: Evaluation

For this case, the test taker must determine the significance of the information presented and then determine an appropriate course of action based on knowledge of guidelines of PT practice. This requires evaluative reasoning skill. In this situation, the PT must report the family for neglect of the child. If answered incorrectly, review guidelines on reporting cases of neglect and abuse.

B169

Musculoskeletal | Interventions

What is the **MOST** effective intervention to regain biceps brachii strength if the muscle is chronically inflamed and has a painful arc of motion?

Choices:

1. Active concentric contractions through partial ROM.
2. Active eccentric contractions in the pain-free range.
3. Isokinetic exercises through the full ROM.
4. Isometric exercises at the end range of movement only.

Teaching Points

Correct Answer: 2

For a muscle that is chronically inflamed, focus should be placed on eccentric contractions, because there is less effort and stress placed on the contractile units than with concentric contractions at the same level of work. The exercise should be performed in the pain-free portion of the range.

Incorrect Choices:

Isokinetic, isometric, and isotonic exercises do not allow for pain-free muscle contractions and can cause further inflammation of the muscle.

Type of Reasoning: Inductive

For this question, it is important to have knowledge of kinesiology, exercise physiology, and appropriate exercise for chronically inflamed muscles in order to choose the best exercise approach. This requires diagnostic thinking and clinical judgment, which is an inductive reasoning skill. For this situation, the most appropriate exercise is active eccentric contractions in the pain-free range to avoid further inflammation of the muscle. If this question was answered incorrectly, refer to information on appropriate exercises for various forms of muscle pathology.

B170 

Nonsystem | Equipment, Devices, Biophysical Agents

During an ultrasound (US) treatment, the patient flinches and states that a strong ache was felt in the treatment area. What is the therapist's **BEST** course of action?

Choices:

1. Decrease the US frequency.
2. Add more transmission medium.
3. Decrease the US intensity.
4. Increase the size of the treatment area.

Teaching Points

Correct Answer: 3

Acoustical energy is reflected from the bone into the bone-tissue interface, resulting in rapid tissue temperature elevation and stimulation of the highly sensitive periosteum of the bone. A reduction in intensity is indicated if a strong ache is felt.

Incorrect Choices:

The question assumes that the treatment size of the area is correct. Increasing the size of the treatment area would minimize the ability to elevate the tissue temperature. Thus, the patient would not experience a strong ache from rapid tissue temperature elevation. Adding more transmission medium would encourage transmission of acoustical energy and thus potentiate the rapid tissue temperature elevation, contributing to the patient's symptom. The frequency has to do with the depth of penetration of the US energy, not the rate/speed at which the tissue temperature is being elevated.

Type of Reasoning: Evaluation

This question requires one to determine the cause for the patient's discomfort during US treatment, and then to determine an appropriate course of action, which is an evaluative reasoning skill. For this patient, it is best to decrease the US intensity because the strong ache indicates it is a result of too high an intensity. If this question was answered incorrectly, review information on US guidelines and symptoms warranting change of protocol.

B171

Musculoskeletal | Interventions

A patient is referred for postoperative rehabilitation following a Type II SLAP repair performed 1 week ago. What is the therapist's **BEST** choice of intervention during early rehabilitation?

Choices:

1. Focus on biceps brachii stretching and strengthening.
2. Defer intervention during the maximum protection phase.
3. Perform careful ROM of the shoulder internal rotators.
4. Perform careful ROM of the shoulder external rotators.

Teaching Points

Correct Answer: 3

Internal rotation ROM does not create the peel back mechanism that increases stress to the repair. Given the nature of this repair, an understanding of the postoperative precautions is paramount to a successful surgical outcome. Early rehabilitation within the postoperative precautions correlates to a quicker overall recovery and improved outcomes.

Incorrect Choices:

Type II SLAP lesions are characterized by a detachment of the superior labrum and the origin of the tendon of the long head of the biceps brachii that results in instability of the biceps-labral anchor. The surgery requires reattachment of the labrum and biceps anchor. Given the repair of the biceps, contraction and stretching of the biceps should be avoided during the maximum protection phase. In addition, external rotation ROM/stretching should be avoided given the peel back mechanism and increased stress to the repair.

Type of Reasoning: Inductive

This question requires one to use clinical judgment to determine a best course of action. Questions of this nature often necessitate inductive reasoning skill. For this case, the therapist should choose to perform careful ROM to the internal rotators of the shoulder with a Type II SLAP repair. Review protocols for rehabilitation after SLAP lesions if answered incorrectly.

B172 

Integumentary | Interventions

A patient is recovering from deep partial-thickness burns over the posterior thigh and calf that are now healed. The therapist's examination reveals local tenderness with swelling and pain on movement in the hip area. While palpating the tissues, the therapist detects a mass. What is the therapist's **BEST** course of action?

Choices:

1. Use petrissage to work on this area of focal tenderness.
2. Report these findings promptly to the physician.
3. Continue with ROM exercises but proceed gently.
4. Use RICE to quiet down the inflammatory response.

Teaching Points

Correct Answer: 2

These signs and symptoms are characteristic of heterotopic ossification (HO), an abnormal bone growth typically around a joint. While the etiology is unknown, its presence can lead to serious ROM limitations. These findings should be reported promptly to the physician.

Incorrect Choices:

Petrissage and aggressive ROM exercises could exacerbate the condition. Ice does decrease metabolic activity; more in-depth medical management is required.

Type of Reasoning: Inductive

This question requires one to utilize clinical judgment to determine the reason for the patient's symptoms and then determine the best course of action, which is an inductive reasoning skill. In this situation, the findings indicate HO and the therapist should notify the physician promptly. If this question was answered incorrectly, review information on HO.

B173

Musculoskeletal | Examination

A patient presents with complaint of neck pain on the right. During the AROM examination, the physical therapist observes the following osteokinematic neck motions—full side-bending left, full rotation to the left, full forward flexion, limited and painful extension, limited and painful right side-bending, and limited and painful right rotation. Based on this pattern, what is the arthrokinematic restriction?

Choices:

1. Upglide of a facet on the left.
2. Upglide of a facet on the right.
3. Downglide of a facet on the left.
4. Downglide of a facet on the right.

Teaching Points

Correct Answer: 4

If a facet on the right was restricted with downgliding (arthrokinematic restriction), then the osteokinematic motions that would be limited would be rotation and side-bending to the right with limited extension. The fact that there is pain on the right supports that the restriction is on the right.

Incorrect Choices:

The osteokinematic limitation could also be seen with a facet restricted with upglide on the left, but the differentiator is the fact that the pain is on the right, indicating that the restriction is on the right. The arthrokinematic restrictions in the other choices do not correlate with the osteokinematic findings of the exam.

Type of Reasoning: Analysis

This question requires the test taker to analyze the symptoms presented in order to determine the most likely arthrokinematic restriction. Questions that require one to analyze pieces of information in order to draw conclusions often require analytical reasoning skill. For this situation, the arthrokinematic restriction is restriction with downglide of a facet on the right. Review arthrokinematics of the neck and restrictions if answered incorrectly.

B174 

Cardiovascular/Pulmonary and Lymphatic | Examination

What are the possible ECG changes with exercise that can occur in a patient with coronary artery disease (CAD) and prior myocardial infarction (MI)?

Choices:

1. Tachycardia at a relatively low intensity of exercise with ST segment depression.
2. Bradycardia with ST segment elevation.
3. Significant arrhythmias early on in exercise with a shortened QRS.
4. Bradycardia with ST segment depression > 3 mm below baseline.

Teaching Points

Correct Answer: 1

The typical exercise ECG changes in the patient with CAD include tachycardia at low levels of exercise intensity. The ST segment becomes depressed (> 1 mm is significant). In addition, complex ventricular arrhythmias (multifocal or runs of PVCs) may appear, and are associated with significant CAD and/or a poor prognosis.

Incorrect Choices:

The other choices do not accurately describe the expected ECG changes with exercise. Chronotropic incompetence is indicated by an HR that fails to rise; bradycardia (slowing of HR) is not expected. ST segment elevation with significant Q waves can occur and is indicative of aneurysm or wall motion abnormality.

Type of Reasoning: Inference

In order to answer the question correctly, the test taker must recall typical ECG changes for patients who have myocardial ischemia and CAD. Therefore, the test taker must draw conclusions about the patient's diagnosis, which is an inferential reasoning skill. For this patient, one would expect tachycardia and ST segment depression, which should be reviewed if this question was answered incorrectly.

Musculoskeletal | Interventions

A patient with long-term postural changes exhibits an excessive forward head and complains of pain and dizziness when looking upward. What is the **MOST** effective physical therapy intervention?

Choices:

1. Manual therapy techniques to provide pain relief and postural reeducation.
2. Postural reeducation to reduce compression of the cervical sympathetic ganglia.
3. Strengthening exercises to the posterior cervical musculature.
4. Anterior cervical muscle stretching and postural reeducation to relieve vertebral artery compression.

Teaching Points

Correct Answer: 1

Long-term postural changes with forward head posture include shortening of the posterior muscles, potential joint restrictions, with possible vertebral artery compromise at the occiput. Restoration of normal movement throughout the cervical region using manual therapy techniques and postural reeducation is the best choice for this condition.

Incorrect Choices:

The anterior cervical muscles are most likely already lengthened. Strengthening the posterior muscles will not provide full restoration to the movement restrictions. In addition, the anterior muscle will also benefit from the reconditioning exercises. Postural reeducation by itself will not promote restoration of normal function.

Type of Reasoning: Inference
This question provides symptoms, and the test taker must determine first what the diagnosis is in order to determine the most effective intervention to remedy the symptoms. Questions that require one to determine a most effective approach in therapy often utilize inferential reasoning skill. If this question was answered incorrectly, refer to information on treatment for vertebral artery compression.

B176 

Cardiovascular/Pulmonary and Lymphatic I Examination

A patient with idiopathic dilated cardiomyopathy is on the cardiac unit with telemetry ECG monitoring after a recent admission for decompensated heart failure. Figure 1 depicts this patient's resting telemetric ECG recording, and Figure 2 depicts the patient's exercise (ambulating 2.5 mph on a flat surface in the hallway) telemetric ECG recording. What is an accurate interpretation of the change between the two recordings?

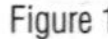
Figure 1

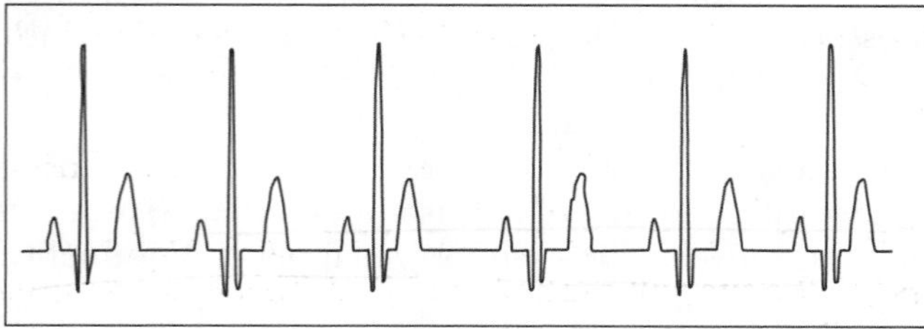

Figure 2

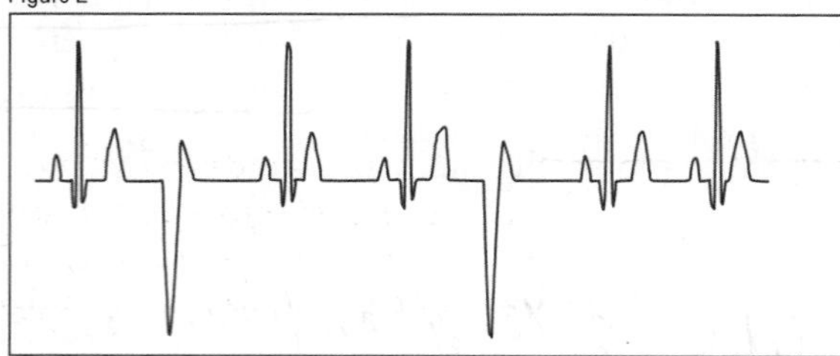

Choices:

1. Ventricular tachycardia, indicating abnormal response to increasing work demands and moderate risk.
2. Tachycardia, indicating normal response to increasing work demands and normal risk.
3. Bradycardia, indicating abnormal response to increasing work demands and high risk.
4. Preventricular contractions, indicating abnormal response to increasing work demands and high risk.

Teaching Points

Correct Answer: 4
New onset of preventricular contractions (wide complex, lack of a P or T wave) indicates an abnormal response to increasing work demands and indicates high risk for cardiac patients based on American College of Physicians and American Association of Cardiovascular and Pulmonary Rehabilitation risk stratification.

Incorrect Choices:
The rhythm in Figure 2 is not indicative of bradycardia, ventricular tachycardia, or tachycardia.

Type of Reasoning: Analysis
Questions that require the test taker to interpret information presented in the form of graphs or charts test analytical reasoning skill. In this situation, the ECG strip indicates PVCs or preventricular contractions with high risk. If this question was answered incorrectly, review information on ECG interpretation, especially PVCs.

B177

Nonsystem | Safety, Professional Responsibilities, Research

During the course of the physical therapy treatment in the ICU, a radial artery line gets pulled (comes out of the artery). What is the first action the PT should take?

Choices:

1. Push the code button in the patient's room, because this is a cardiac emergency.
2. Elevate the arm above heart level to stop the bleeding.
3. Place a BP cuff on the involved extremity and inflate the cuff until the bleeding stops.
4. Reinsert the arterial catheter into the radial artery and check the monitor for an accurate tracing.

Teaching Points

Correct Answer: 3

A radial arterial line is a catheter placed in the artery itself. If it becomes dislodged during treatment, the artery is now open to bleeding. This arterial bleeding needs to be stopped immediately, although it is not considered a cardiac emergency. Place a BP cuff above the site of bleeding and inflate the cuff to above systole to stop the bleeding or place enough manual pressure on the site to stop the bleeding. Then call for help.

Incorrect Choices:

Elevating the site of bleeding above heart level will not be as effective, because this is an arterial bleed. As long as the heart is pumping with adequate pressure, the site will continue to bleed. This is not a cardiac emergency. Never replace any line that has become disconnected. The line is no longer sterile and should not be reinserted into the patient. A new, sterile catheter will need to be used if the radial line is to be replaced.

Type of Reasoning: Evaluation

This question requires one to use judgment to evaluate the strength of the statements made in order to arrive at a decision for the first course of action with this patient. In this situation, it is important to stop the bleeding in the most effective manner possible, which is to inflate a BP cuff on the involved extremity until the bleeding stops. Questions such as these can be challenging because one must use a value judgment to make the best decision.

B178 

Metabolic/Endocrine | Evaluation, Diagnosis

A therapist working in an outpatient clinic examines a patient referred for exercise conditioning. During the initial examination, the therapist finds unusual swelling and enlargement in the anterior neck with mild tenderness. The patient does not have any hoarseness or difficulty swallowing. What is the therapist's **BEST** course of action?

Choices:

1. Notify the referring physician.
2. Document the findings in the medical record.
3. Take girth measurements of the neck.
4. Initiate the plan of care.

Teaching Points

Correct Answer: 1

This patient is likely exhibiting hyperthyroidism (Graves' disease) and should be referred to the physician of record. Additional manifestations of hyperthyroidism include cardiopulmonary changes (increased HR and respiratory rate, palpitations, dysrhythmias, breathlessness), CNS changes (tremors, hyperkinesias, nervousness, increased DTRs), musculoskeletal changes (weakness, fatigue, atrophy), and integumentary effects (heat intolerance).

Incorrect Choices:

Documenting the findings in the medical record without notifying the physician delays medical intervention. Taking girth measurements at this time is not useful information. This disorder should be treated before beginning an exercise program. The patient will exhibit exercise intolerance and reduced exercise capacity.

Type of Reasoning: Evaluation

This question requires the test taker to determine a best course of action based on the patient's symptoms. Questions such as these necessitate weighing of information to determine its significance and ultimately the best response. In this case, given the significance of the symptoms, the therapist should notify the patient's physician for follow-up. If this question was answered incorrectly, review symptoms of Graves' disease.

B179 

MRSA precaution

Nonsystem | Safety, Professional Responsibilities, Research

A patient with a methicillin-resistant *Staphylococcus aureus* (MRSA) infection has been discharged from an isolation setting with an open wound of the buttocks. The patient is now returning to physical therapy as an outpatient. The therapist should adhere to which precaution?

Choices:

1. An open wound must be contained within a dressing. 1st
2. Direct contact with the patient should be avoided. (Glove)
3. Gloves are needed only with dressing changes.
4. Treatment can be performed in the therapy gym if contact surfaces are covered. (inappropriate)

Teaching Points

Correct Answer: 1

Staphylococcal organisms are spread by contact. Open wounds must be well contained with a dressing. Standard germicidal cleaning measures (hand washing) should be followed. The therapist should be gloved for any direct contact with the patient's intact skin or surfaces or articles in close proximity to the patient. All equipment should be cleaned with an approved germicidal agent before and after use.

Incorrect Choices:

Isolation in a private room is not required; in ambulatory settings, the patient should be placed in an examination room or cubicle as soon as possible. Treatment in an open gym is inappropriate for patients with MRSA.

Type of Reasoning: Deductive

The test taker must recall standard precautions for MRSA infection in order to choose the best response. This type of recall is factual and dependent upon knowledge of protocols and guidelines, which is a deductive reasoning skill. If this question was answered incorrectly, review standard precaution guidelines for MRSA.

B180

Gastrointestinal | Evaluation, Diagnosis

After examining a patient who was referred to physical therapy for posterior thoracic pain, the therapist finds no musculoskeletal causes for the patient's symptoms. What anatomical structure may refer pain to this thoracic region?

Choices:

1. Heart.
2. Appendix.
3. Gallbladder.
4. Ovary.

Teaching Points

Correct Answer: 3

Dysfunction of the gallbladder often refers pain to the thorax.

Incorrect Choices:

The commonly observed referral pattern of the heart is to the chest and upper extremity, the ovaries to the low back, and the appendix to the right lower quadrant.

Type of Reasoning: Analysis

This question requires one to refer to knowledge of physiology and of common referred patterns of pain. The test taker must recognize that pain referred to the posterior thoracic region is typical of problems with the gallbladder. To arrive at the correct conclusion, the test taker must analyze the information presented and determine the meaning of that information, which is an analytical reasoning skill.

B181

Nonsystem | Equipment, Devices, Biophysical Agents

An elderly patient with a transfemoral amputation is being fitted with a temporary prosthesis containing a SACH (solid ankle cushion heel) prosthetic foot. Which of the following **BEST** characterizes the SACH foot?

Choices:

1. Is an articulated foot with multiplanar motion.
2. Allows full sagittal and frontal plane motion.
3. Absorbs energy through a series of bumpers, permitting sagittal plane motion only.
4. Allows limited sagittal plane motion with a small amount of mediolateral motion.

Teaching Points

Correct Answer: 4

The SACH foot is the most commonly prescribed type of prosthetic foot. It provides for sagittal plane motion (primarily plantarflexion) and very limited frontal plane motion (mediolateral motion).

Incorrect Choices:

Articulated feet (joined by a metal bolt or cable to the lower shank section) have rubber bumpers that absorb shock and control plantarflexion excursion. An anterior stop resists dorsiflexion. Full sagittal and frontal plane motions are not allowed.

Type of Reasoning: Analysis

One must recall the properties of a SACH foot in order to choose the correct solution. This requires knowledge of prostheses and their indications. The test taker must analyze the information presented and determine the meaning of that information, which is an analytical reasoning skill. If this question was answered incorrectly, refer to information on properties of prosthetic feet.

B182

Neuromuscular | Evaluation, Diagnosis

A physical therapist examines an adult patient that recently suffered a stroke that involved the right internal capsule. In addition to hemiparesis of the contralateral extremities, the patient also exhibits a facial palsy. Which facial muscles would **MOST** likely be affected?

Choices:

1. All muscles on the left side of the face.
2. All muscles on the right side of the face.
3. Only muscles on the lower half of the right side of the face.
4. Only muscles on the lower half of the left side of the face.

Teaching Points

Correct Answer: 4

A stroke that involves the internal capsule would result in a *supranuclear palsy*, which affects only the contralateral lower half of the face. The specific pathway that is affected is the corticobulbar tract, which contains upper motor neurons (UMN) that project from the motor cortex to the nucleus of the facial nerve (cranial nerve VII) in the brainstem. The muscles in the upper half of the face are spared because both the right and left cerebral cortex project to the lower motor neurons (LMNs) in the facial nucleus that the innervate muscles of the forehead. In contrast, the LMNs that innervate muscles of the lower half of the face receive input from the contralateral motor cortex only. Therefore, a stroke that affects the internal capsule (corticobulbar tract) prevents input from the motor cortex to the contralateral facial nucleus, causing paresis or paralysis of the muscles of the lower half of the face only.

Incorrect Choices:

A lesion that affects all muscles on the left side of the face is consistent with an LMN or peripheral nerve lesion, such as idiopathic Bell's palsy or trauma to the left facial nerve. A complete LMN lesion to the right CN VII would prevent motor commands from reaching all ipsilateral facial muscles, resulting in facial paralysis of those muscles. A lesion that affects the left internal capsule or corticobulbar tract would affect only muscles on the lower half of the right side of the face.

Type of Reasoning: Deductive

This question requires the test taker to recall guidelines for the muscles of the face that are most likely to be affected by a stroke involving the internal capsule. Questions that necessitate the recall of facts often utilize deductive reasoning skill. For this case, muscles on the lower half of the left side of the face are most likely to be affected. Review information regarding strokes impacting the internal capsule and facial palsy if answered incorrectly.

B183

Cardiovascular/Pulmonary and Lymphatic | Examination

A patient in the ICU is referred to physical therapy and presents with significant shortness of breath. Notable on physical examination is a deviated trachea to the left. Which of the following processes would account for such a finding?

Choices:

1. Right lung collapse.
2. Left pleural effusion.
3. Right hemothorax.
4. Left pneumothorax.

Teaching Points

Correct Answer: 3

A right hemothorax (blood was in the pleural space) takes up space in the right hemithorax, shifting the trachea to the left.

Incorrect Choices:

A left pneumothorax and a left pleural effusion take up space in the left thorax. The air (pneumothorax) or the sterile fluid (effusion) in the pleural space would push contents of the left hemithorax, including the trachea, to the right. A lung collapse, or a volume loss phenomenon, on the right would pull the trachea over toward the right.

Type of Reasoning: Inference

This question requires the test taker to make a determination for the patient's symptoms, which necessitates use of inferential reasoning. In this situation, the deviated trachea to the left is due to a right hemothorax. One must rely on knowledge of pulmonary pathology to arrive at a correct conclusion, which should be reviewed if this question was answered incorrectly.

B184 

Nonsystem | Equipment, Devices, Biophysical Agents

A patient complains of pain (7/10) in the shoulder region secondary to acute subdeltoid bursitis. As part of the plan of care during the acute phase, the therapist elects to use conventional TENS. Which of the following **BEST** identifies the modulating properties of this biophysical device?

Choices:

1. Stimulation of endorphins.
2. Gate control mechanisms.
3. Descending inhibition.
4. Ascending inhibition.

Teaching Points

Correct Answer: 2

The gate control mechanism is activated by the application of conventional (high-rate) TENS at the spinal cord level.

Incorrect Choices:

Ascending inhibition occurs after the gate control mechanism has been activated. Low-rate TENS, having a stronger stimulus and a longer pulse duration, activates the descending inhibition, stimulating endorphin production mechanisms.

Type of Reasoning: Deductive

This question requires one to recall the properties of conventional TENS and how pain is modulated. This primarily requires recall of the properties of conventional TENS, which is factual knowledge and encourages deductive reasoning skills. Review information on TENS properties and neurophysiological effects if this question was answered incorrectly.

B185

Musculoskeletal | Evaluation, Diagnosis

A patient described a sudden onset of back pain while trying to lift a heavy barrel. The patient described this pain as constant, unremitting at an intensity of 10/10 over the past 3 days, and unresponsive to pain medications. The patient is unable to work but is able to drive to the clinic for treatment unaided. There is no history of other back-related symptoms in the past. Which of the following is the **MOST** likely causative factor?

Choices:

1. Early degenerative osteoarthritis.
2. Herniated lumbar disc.
3. Neoplastic disease.
4. Secondary gain.

Teaching Points

Correct Answer: 4

A patient who is able to drive to the clinic for treatment and relates a pain level of 10/10 is not providing consistent subjective data. Secondary gain in this case, and not working, is a likely factor.

Incorrect Choices:

Pain from a disc pathology is typically worse in the morning and will decrease (at least slightly) when the patient gets out of bed and begins to walk around. The diagnosis is unlikely to be a neoplastic condition secondary to the acute, traumatic onset. Degenerative osteoarthritis is described as stiffness in the morning with worsening pain as the activity level increases throughout the day.

Type of Reasoning: Inductive

The test taker must utilize diagnostic thinking and clinical judgment to determine the most likely cause for the patient's symptoms, which is an inductive reasoning skill. In this case, the patient's inconsistency in engagement in activities (driving but not being able to work) most likely has secondary gain involved. If this question was answered incorrectly, review information on secondary gain in patient care.

B186

Cardiovascular/Pulmonary and Lymphatic | Evaluation, Diagnosis

After myocardial infraction (MI), a patient was placed on medications that included a beta-adrenergic blocking agent. When monitoring this patient's response to exercise, what changes in HR are expected?

Choices:

1. Increase proportionally to changes in diastolic BP.
2. Be low at rest and rise very little with exercise.
3. Increase proportionally to changes in systolic BP.
4. Be low at rest and rise linearly as a function of increasing workload.

Teaching Points

Correct Answer: 2

Beta-adrenergic blocking agents (e.g., propranolol [Inderal]) are used to treat hypertension, prevent angina pectoris, and prevent certain arrhythmias. In individuals taking these drugs, HR is low at rest and rises very little with exercise (blunted response). These changes, therefore, invalidate the use of HR to monitor exercise responses. A more sensitive measure would be RPE.

Incorrect Choices:

HR does not rise linearly with exercise in patients on propranolol. The medication is used for treatment of hypertension. Both resting and exercise BP are suppressed.

Type of Reasoning: Analysis

This question requires one to recall the indications for beta-adrenergic agents and effects on cardiovascular function. This requires one to interpret information and determine the meaning of that information, which necessitates analytical reasoning skill. If this question was answered incorrectly, review information on effects of beta-blockers on cardiovascular function.

B187 

Musculoskeletal | Interventions

An individual presents with chronic TMJ dysfunction. There is limited lateral movement of the mandible to the right as a result of muscular tightness. Which of the following muscles should be the focus of inhibitory or soft tissue lengthening techniques?

Choices:

1. Right temporalis muscle.
2. Right geniohyoid muscle.
3. Right medial pterygoid muscle.
4. Right digastric muscle.

Teaching Points

Correct Answer: 3

Lateral excursion of the mandible is produced by the contralateral medial and lateral pterygoids and ipsilateral temporalis muscles. Tightness of the ipsilateral pterygoids or contralateral temporalis muscles may need lengthening in order to allow full lateral mandibular excursion. The right medial pterygoid would be one of the muscles targeted for interventions restoring sufficient length.

Incorrect Choices:

The digastrics and geniohyoid muscles are mandibular depressors and would not be targets for muscle lengthening techniques. The left temporalis may need lengthening.

Type of Reasoning: Inductive

One must use clinical judgment to determine a best course of action in order to arrive at a correct conclusion. This often necessitates inductive reasoning skill. For this case, the therapist should focus treatment on the right medial pterygoid muscle to restore length. Review treatment approaches for TMJ dysfunction if answered incorrectly.

B188 

Metabolic/Endocrine | Interventions

A patient has a 20-year history of diabetes. Notable on the examination are the following: vascular insufficiency and diminished sensation of both feet with poor healing of a superficial skin lesion. It is important that the patient understand the precautions and guidelines on foot care for people with diabetes. Which recommendation is **CONTRAINDICATED** to include in patient care instructions?

Choices:

1. Inspect the skin daily for inflammation, swelling, redness, blisters, or wounds.
2. Wash the feet daily and hydrate with moisturizing lotion.
3. Wear flexible shoes that allow adequate room and change shoes frequently.
4. Use daily hot soaks and moisturize the skin.

Teaching Points

Correct Answer: 4

Daily hot soaks are contraindicated because of the increased risk of thermal injury. The patient with diabetes typically has loss of protective sensations.

Incorrect Choices:

All other instructions are correct and important to include in a well-balanced program of foot care.

Type of Reasoning: Inference

This question requires one to determine the recommendation to a patient with diabetes that is contraindicated. In this circumstance, one should **NOT** recommend hot soaks because of the risk of thermal injury from loss of protective sensations in the feet. Questions that require one to draw conclusions and formulate opinions based on information presented encourage use of inferential reasoning. If this question was answered incorrectly, refer to guidelines for diabetic foot care.

B189 

Musculoskeletal | Evaluation, Diagnosis

After completing an examination of a patient with shoulder pain, the PT concludes that the cause is subscapularis tendinitis. Which clinical finding is supportive of this conclusion?

Choices:

1. Tenderness at the greater tubercle of the humerus.
2. Painful resisted shoulder adduction.
3. Pain provoked with active glenohumeral external rotation.
4. Pain provoked with passive glenohumeral external rotation.

Teaching Points

Correct Answer: 4

The subscapularis is an internal rotator of the humerus. It will be painful if passively stretched into external rotation and irritated when contracting or being resisted when the shoulder internally rotates. The muscle inserts onto the lesser tubercle of the humerus and plays no role in shoulder adduction.

Incorrect Choices:

Active glenohumeral external rotation does not require activation of the subscapularis muscle. The subscapularis attaches to the lesser tuberosity. The subscapularis is not the primary mover for shoulder adduction, so is not likely to be painful with resisted shoulder adduction.

Type of Reasoning: Inductive

This question requires diagnostic reasoning and clinical judgment, which is an inductive reasoning skill. Knowledge of upper extremity orthopedics, especially rotator cuff impairments, is needed to answer this question. One must recall the typical positions and motions that will evoke pain for patients with subscapularis tendinitis in order to arrive at the correct conclusion, which should be reviewed if this question was answered incorrectly.

B190 

Musculoskeletal | Interventions

early treatment for inversion ankle sprain

A soccer player sustained a grade II inversion ankle sprain 2 weeks ago. What is the **BEST** intervention to use in the early subacute phase of rehabilitation?

Choices:

1. Mobilization at the talocrural and subtalar joints.
2. Closed-chain strengthening and proprioceptive exercises.
3. Plyometric-based exercise program.
4. Functional soccer-related drills.

Teaching Points

Correct Answer: 2

The most effective treatment for this athlete would involve closed-chain exercises and proprioceptive training, appropriate interventions for early subacute phase management.

Incorrect Choices:

The other choices are not appropriate or timely for early subacute phase management. These approaches may be useful later in the rehabilitation of this athlete.

Type of Reasoning: Inference

One must infer or draw conclusions for the best early intervention approach, given the injury and knowledge of rehabilitation techniques for this injury. This requires inferential reasoning skill, in which the test taker applies this knowledge and formulates conclusions about the patient for a best course of action. If this question was answered incorrectly, review information on early treatment for inversion ankle sprain.

B191 

Nonsystem | Equipment, Devices, Biophysical Agents

A patient is referred for outpatient care after a tendon transfer of the extensor carpi radialis longus. The muscle strength tests poor (2/5) in spite of previous intensive therapy. The therapist elects to apply biofeedback to assist in progressively increasing active motor recruitment. What is the **BEST** choice for the initial EMG protocol?

Choices:

1. High-detection sensitivity with recording electrodes placed far apart.
2. Low-detection sensitivity with recording electrodes placed close together.
3. High-detection sensitivity with recording electrodes placed close together.
4. Low-detection sensitivity with recording electrodes placed far apart.

Teaching Points

Correct Answer: 3

Initially, high-detection sensitivity is needed to detect low-amplitude signals generated by a small number of motor units such as in a weak extensor carpi radialis longus.

Incorrect Choices:

Wide electrode placement would pick up signals from more than one muscle and might invalidate the procedure. Low-detection sensitivity may not pick up the necessary motor unit signals.

Type of Reasoning: Deductive

This question requires application of knowledge of EMG biofeedback protocols in order to determine the best approach to early biofeedback intervention. This encourages deductive reasoning skill, which encourages recall of factual knowledge of protocols to apply information to a specific case situation of extensor carpi radialis longus tendon transfer. If this question was answered incorrectly, review information on EMG biofeedback guidelines.

B192 

System Interactions | Evaluation, Diagnosis

A PT receives a home care referral from the nurse case manager. An elderly man has lost functional independence after the recent death of his wife. His past medical history includes stroke with minimal residual disability. Currently, he no longer goes out of his house and rarely even gets out of his chair anymore. During the initial session, the therapist determines that depression may be the cause of his increasing inactivity. What clinical signs and symptoms would lead the therapist to reach this determination?

Choices:

1. Low scores on the Geriatric Depression Scale.
2. Weight loss and social withdrawal.
3. Complaints of increasing dizziness and palpitations.
4. Sleep apnea and weight gain.

Teaching Points

Correct Answer: 2

Depression is associated with symptoms of withdrawal, fatigue, and weight loss.

Incorrect Choices:
Sleep apnea is a potentially lethal disorder in which breathing stops for 10 seconds or more, many times a night. It is associated with obesity and anatomical obstruction. Increasing dizziness and palpitations are suggestive of cardiovascular problems. The Geriatric Depression Scale is a valid measure of depression in the elderly. High, not low, scores (> 8 of a possible 30) are indicative of depression.

Type of Reasoning: Inference
One must recall the typical symptoms associated with depression in the elderly to arrive at the correct conclusion. This requires one to draw conclusions and make assumptions based on the information presented, which is an inferential reasoning skill. If this question was answered incorrectly, review symptoms of depression, especially symptoms in the elderly.

B193 

Genitourinary/Interventions

Exercises, electrical stimulation and biofeedback methodology are **MOST OFTEN** employed by physical therapists in the management of which type of incontinence?

Choices:
1. Urge incontinence.
2. Functional incontinence.
3. Overflow incontinence.
4. Stress incontinence.

Teaching Points

Correct Answer: 4
Exercises (Kegel), electrical stimulation, and biofeedback are used to increase the strength and functionality of the levator ani and other pelvic muscles in cases where increased intra-abdominal pressure results or can result in a sudden release of urine. This is called stress incontinence. Urine leaks due to weakened pelvic floor muscles and tissues.

Incorrect Choices:
Urge incontinence is often referred to as an overactive bladder. Individuals with urge incontinence experience an urgent need to go to the bathroom and may not get there in time, leaking urine. This is often a result of hyperreflexia and may be seen in a number of neurologic disorders including stroke, Parkinson's, and multiple sclerosis. Exercises may be prescribed for these individuals but not as often as for patients with stress incontinence. Functional incontinence is the inability or unwillingness to go to the toilet because of impaired cognition, dementia, Alzheimer's, arthritis, or environmental impairments (e.g., distance to toilet). Overflow incontinence is the continuous leakage of urine that results from over distention of the bladder. Frequent "dribbling" of urine is a common symptom. This type of incontinence is seen more frequently in men and may be due to an enlarged prostate, weak bladder muscles, constipation, or a blockage of the urethra.

Type of Reasoning: Inductive
One must have knowledge of the different types of incontinence and their root causes in order to arrive at a correct conclusion. This requires clinical judgment, which is an inductive reasoning skill. For this case, because stress incontinence is often caused by weakened pelvic floor muscles and tissues, exercises, electrical stimulation, and biofeedback would be used in treatment of this condition. If answered incorrectly, review guidelines for treatment of stress incontinence.

B194 

Cardiovascular/Pulmonary and Lymphatic | Examination

A patient has been on bed rest for 4 days following complications after revascularization surgery involving a triple coronary artery bypass graft. During the first therapy session, the patient complains of tenderness and aching in the right calf. For what clinical signs should the therapist immediately examine?

Choices:

1. Lowered body temperature.
2. Bradycardia.
3. Swelling in the calf or ankle.
4. Homan's sign.

Teaching Points

Correct Answer: 3

Deep vein thrombophlebitis (DVT) is characterized by classic signs of inflammation (tenderness, aching, and swelling), typically in the calf. Rapid screening is possible with Doppler ultrasonography. Color flow venous duplex scanning is the primary diagnostic test for detection of DVT.

Incorrect Choices:

Tachycardia, not bradycardia, may be present. Slight fever can be present, as part of the inflammatory reaction, not lowered temperature. Homan's sign is pain in the calf perceived with squeezing the calf and dorsiflexion; this is not considered reliable and lacks specificity and sensitivity.

Type of Reasoning: Evaluation

This question requires one to evaluate the approaches presented and determine which approach has the most merit, given the patient's current symptoms. This requires evaluative reasoning skill, in which the test taker must weigh arguments and statements made and formulate a conclusion about the strength of these approaches. If this question was answered incorrectly, review symptomatology of DVT.

B195 

Musculoskeletal | Evaluation, Diagnosis

A patient is referred for physical therapy with jaw pain and dysfunction. The patient has experienced three episodes of jaw locking in an open position in the past week. What is the **MOST** likely cause of the patient's jaw locking?

Choices:

1. Entrapment of the retrodiscal lamina.
2. Lateral pterygoid muscle spasm.
3. Impingement of the temporomandibular ligament.
4. Disc displacement.

Teaching Points

Correct Answer: 4

This patient is experiencing temporomandibular joint dysfunction (TMJ). The jaw becomes locked in an open position when the disc is displaced. The muscles influence lateral deviation of the jaw with opening.

Incorrect Choices:

The temporomandibular ligament cannot become impinged. The lateral pterygoid muscle would not cause the mouth to be locked open if it experienced a spasm. Entrapment of the retrodiscal lamina is painful, but it is a consequence of a TMJ being locked open secondary to a disc displacement, not a cause.

Type of Reasoning: Analysis

This question requires knowledge of TMJ anatomy and typical dysfunction of the joint associated with TMJ disorder. The jaw locking in an open position most likely indicates that the disc has been displaced. Through analytical reasoning, one must interpret or analyze the information presented and determine which problem seems to be the most likely cause. If this question was answered incorrectly, review information on TMJ disorders.

B196 

System Interactions | Evaluation, Diagnosis

An elderly patient is referred to physical therapy after a fall and ORIF for a fracture of the right wrist. During the initial examination, the therapist observes that the patient's skin and eyes have a yellowish hue. What is the therapist's **BEST** course of action?

Choices:

1. Send a copy of the examination results to the referring surgeon, emphasizing the skin hue.
2. Treat the problem with whirlpool and massage and reevaluate skin color posttreatment.
3. Continue with the treatment; a yellowish hue is an expected finding 3–4 days post-ORIF.
4. Document the findings and consult with the surgeon immediately after treatment.

Teaching Points

Correct Answer: 4

This patient is most likely experiencing jaundice as a result of liver dysfunction. The therapist's best course of action is to document the findings and consult with the surgeon immediately, preferably by phone.

Incorrect Choices:

All other choices delay consulting with the primary physician. The symptoms indicate liver dysfunction and jaundice, which warrant immediate contact with the surgeon.

Type of Reasoning: Evaluation

The test taker must determine first what the patient's symptoms are indicative of and then determine what should be the appropriate course of action. Questions such as these, in which value judgments must be made, encourage evaluative reasoning skill.

B197

Musculoskeletal | Evaluation, Diagnosis

An older adult received a cemented total hip replacement (THR) 2 days ago. What is the therapist's initial priority?

Choices:

1. AROM exercises and early ambulation using a walker, non–weight bearing.
2. PROM exercises and gait training using crutches, weight bearing to tolerance.
3. Proper technique for transferring to the toilet.
4. Patient education regarding positions and movements to avoid.

Teaching Points

Correct Answer: 4

Education regarding positions and movements to avoid is the number one priority. Standard hip precautions stress avoiding excessive flexion, internal rotation, and adduction.

Incorrect Choices:

Patients with cemented THRs should initially be weight bearing to tolerance using a walker. Transfer training should occur, but it is not the first initial priority.

Type of Reasoning: Inductive

One must utilize clinical judgment and diagnostic thinking (an inductive reasoning skill) to determine the number one priority for this patient with a recent THR. In this situation, it is important to educate the patient regarding positions and movements to avoid, which if not followed could cause potential dislocation of the hip. If this question was answered incorrectly, refer to guidelines for early care of patients with THR.

B198

Musculoskeletal | Examination

A patient with recent trauma presents with restricted movement of the right hand. There is decreased motion at the third right MCP joint. To differentiate as to whether this is joint restriction or some other type of tightness (not joint), which examination procedure should be employed?

Choices:

1. Finkelstein's test.
2. Bunnel-Littler test.
3. Tight retinacular test.
4. Froment's sign.

Teaching Points

Correct Answer: 2

The Bunnel-Littler test is specifically utilized to determine if there is a joint restriction present at the MCP joints.

Incorrect Choices:

The retinacular test is used to determine if there is a restriction at the PIP joint. Finkelstein's test is used to assess for a tenosynovitis of the abductor pollicis longus and/or extensor pollicis brevis. Froment's sign is utilized to identify an ulnar nerve dysfunction.

Type of Reasoning: Deductive

This question provides a diagnosis and the test taker must recall the specific test that confirms the diagnosis. This necessitates factual recall of guidelines, which is a deductive reasoning skill. For this situation, the Bunnel-Littler test is the correct test to confirm joint restriction present at the MCP joints. Review differential testing for hand injuries if answered incorrectly, especially the Bunnel-Littler test.

B199 

Cardiovascular/Pulmonary and Lymphatic I Interventions

A patient with stage II primary lymphedema of the right lower extremity is referred for physical therapy. Examination reveals increased limb girth with skin folds/flaps evident. An important component of lymphedema management is manual lymphatic drainage. Which of the following describes a cardinal principle of manual lymphedema management?

Choices:

1. Deep tissue friction massage for several minutes on fibrotic areas.
2. Decongesting the proximal portions of the limb first and working distally.
3. Decongesting the trunk after the limb segments.
4. Decongesting the distal portions of the limb first and working proximally.

Teaching Points

Correct Answer: 2

Lymphedema is a swelling of the soft tissues that occurs with an accumulation of protein-rich fluid in the extracellular spaces. Causes of primary lymphedema include developmental abnormalities, heredity, surgery, or unknown etiology. Stage II lymphedema is characterized by nonpitting edema with connective scar tissue and clinical fibrosis. Lymphatic drainage is assisted by manual stroking (e.g., Vodder, Leduc's, Foldi's, Casley-Smith pressure techniques). All techniques use cardinal principles: proximal limb segments before distal, trunk segments before limb segments, and directing the flow of the lymphatics centrally toward the lymphatic ducts.

Incorrect Choices:

The other choices do not adhere to the cardinal principles of lymphatic drainage as explained.

Type of Reasoning: Deductive

This question requires one to recall factual knowledge—that of manual lymphatic drainage techniques for patients with primary lymphedema. This encourages deductive reasoning skill, in which the test taker must recall the protocols and guidelines for this technique. If this question was answered incorrectly, review information on manual lymphatic drainage techniques.

B200

Nonsystem | Equipment, Devices, Biophysical Agents

A patient with a 10-year history of multiple sclerosis (MS) demonstrates 3+ extensor tone in both lower extremities. The therapist needs to order a wheelchair. What is the **BEST** recommendation for this patient?

Choices:

1. Standard wheelchair with elevating legrests.
2. Tilt-in-space wheelchair with a pelvic belt.
3. Standard wheelchair with a 30° reclining back.
4. Electric wheelchair with toe loops.

Teaching Points

Correct Answer: 2

A patient with strong extensor tone needs controls over the hips (pelvic belt) to maintain the hips in flexion. The tilt-in-space design best assists in keeping the patient from coming out of the chair when extensor spasms are active.

Incorrect Choices

The other choices do not adequately address these problems. A reclining back would only increase extensor tone and extensor spasms. Elevating legrests assist circulatory flow in the lower extremities but may increase, not decrease, extensor tone. Toe loops function to keep the feet on the foot pedals. In the event of an extensor spasm, they would not control for proximal tone.

Type of Reasoning: Inductive

The test taker must utilize clinical judgment to determine the best recommendation for this patient, given the diagnosis and symptoms. For this patient, a tilt-in-space wheelchair with a pelvic belt would best address the patient's extensor tone in the lower extremities. If this question was answered incorrectly, review wheelchair prescription for patients with the presence of extensor tone.

Examination C

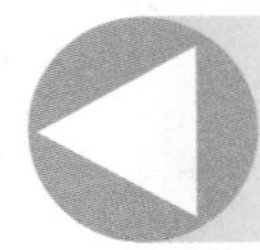

C1 

Cardiovascular/Pulmonary and Lymphatic | Examination

After an uncomplicated acute myocardial infarction (MI), under what circumstances should a patient be administered a graded exercise test (GXT) before hospital discharge?

Choices:

1. Symptom-limited GXT at 10 days post MI.
2. Low level GXT at 4 to 6 days post MI.
3. GXT to 85% age predicted maximum HR 3 to 5 days post MI.
4. GXT to 75% age predicted maximum HR 4 to 6 days post MI.

Teaching Points

Correct Answer: 2

Submaximal GXT can be administered before hospital discharge at 4 to 6 days post acute MI. Low-level exercise testing provides data for recommendations for ADL and early ambulatory exercise therapy. This amount of activity doesn't place too much demand on the healing myocardium (ACSM Guidelines for Exercise Testing and Prescription, 8th ed.).

Incorrect Choices:

An intensity higher than 70% can extend the zone of necrosis into the zone of injury and/or zone of ischemia. This will delay healing or, in the worst case, extend the MI. Using symptoms alone may allow the patient to exercise at too high or too low an intensity.

Type of Reasoning: Inductive

This question requires one to draw on clinical knowledge and judgment of cardiac exercise guidelines for patients with post–myocardial infarction in order to arrive at a correct conclusion. This is an inductive reasoning skill where clinical judgment is paramount to arriving at a correct conclusion. For this case, a submaximal GXT at 4 to 6 days is safe. Review cardiac exercise testing guidelines for patients with myocardial infarction if answered incorrectly.

C2 

Neuromuscular | Examination

A newborn is examined at birth using the APGAR test. Which of the following APGAR results is a likely indicator of potential neurological complications?

Choices:

1. 3 at 10 minutes.
2. 9 at 1 minute.
3. 8 at 1 minute.
4. 8 at 5 minutes.

Teaching Points

Correct Answer: 1

The APGAR score is based on heart rate (HR), respiration, muscle tone, reflex irritability (grimace), and color (appearance). APGAR scores are routinely assigned at 1 and 5 minutes and occasionally at 10 minutes postbirth.

Incorrect Choices:

Scores between 0 and 3 at 1 and 5 minutes are extremely low and indicative of the need for resuscitation. Neurological complications are likely with extremely low APGAR scores, particularly at 10 minutes.

Type of Reasoning: Inductive

The test taker must make a determination of the meaning of the APGAR score as likely to result in neurological complications. This requires one to rely on knowledge of what the scale measures and of score ranges that indicate possible neurological complications. This requires clinical judgment coupled with recall of the properties of the scale, which is an inductive reasoning skill. If this question was answered incorrectly, refer to information on the APGAR Scale.

C3 

Nonsystem | Safety, Professional Responsibilities, Research

A PT requested that a physical therapy assistant (PTA) perform ultrasound (US) to the shoulder of a patient. During the treatment session, the patient experienced an electrical shock. In which situation would the PT be responsible for any injury the patient might receive?

Choices:

1. Faulty circuitry.
2. The PTA failing to use a ground fault interrupter (GFI).
3. The patient touching the US device during treatment.
4. The PT having instructed the PTA to use a device that had malfunctioned on the previous day.

Teaching Points

Correct Answer: 4

The PT in this case correctly delegated the US treatment to the PTA. Every individual (PT, PTA) is liable for their own negligence; however, supervisors may assume liability of workers if they provide faulty supervision or inappropriate delegation of responsibilities (not evident in this case). PTs are liable for use of defective equipment if they contributed to its malfunction or continued to have it used in treatment without having it checked.

Incorrect Choices:

The institution may assume liability if the patient was harmed as a result of an environmental problem such as faulty circuitry or leakage current that would cause the patient to be shocked if they touched the US unit. The standard of practice is such that a GFI is used during administration of US, which would make the PTA primarily liable if a GFI was not used. The patient assumes no liability in this scenario.

Type of Reasoning: Evaluation

This question requires one to determine the value of the statements made in the question and then to determine the believability of these statements as applied to who should be assigned responsibility for the injury. This requires evaluative reasoning skill, in which beliefs and values must be weighed to arrive at a correct conclusion. In this situation, the PT should have taken the malfunctioning unit out of circulation to prevent anyone else from using it, thus making the PT primarily responsible.

C4 

Cardiovascular/Pulmonary and Lymphatic I Interventions

A patient with coronary artery disease received inpatient cardiac rehabilitation after a mild myocardial infarction (MI). The patient is now enrolled in an outpatient exercise class that utilizes intermittent training. What is the **BEST** initial spacing of exercise/rest intervals to safely stress the aerobic system?

Choices:

1. 5:1.
2. 1:1.
3. 10:1.
4. 2:1.

Teaching Points

Correct Answer: 4

Presuming that the exercise goals for inpatient cardiac rehabilitation are met, an exercise/rest ratio of 2:1 can be used with this patient to begin exercise in an outpatient setting in a safe manner.

Incorrect Choices:

An exercise/rest ratio of 1:1 is appropriate for an initial prescription for inpatient rehabilitation programs with a goal of achieving a 2:1 ratio. Ratios of 5:1 or 10:1 are too stressful to begin outpatient rehabilitation. A 5:1 ratio may be a goal for later exercise programming.

Type of Reasoning: Inductive

One must determine through clinical judgment which exercise/rest interval is **BEST**, given the patient's diagnosis and status. Questions that encourage clinical judgment to determine a best course of action require inductive reasoning skills. If this question was answered incorrectly, review information related to appropriate aerobic exercise and exercise/rest ratios for patients with coronary artery disease.

C5 

Musculoskeletal I Evaluation, Diagnosis

What is the **BEST** initial intervention to improve functional mobility in an individual with a stable humeral neck fracture?

Choices:

1. Isometrics for all shoulder musculature.
2. Heat modalities.
3. Active resistive range of motion (ROM).
4. Pendulum exercises.

Teaching Points

Correct Answer: 4

This individual will typically be immobilized with a sling for a period of 6 weeks. After 1 week, the sling should be removed to have the patient perform pendulum exercises to prevent shoulder stiffness.

Incorrect Choices:

Resistive exercises including isometrics are not indicated during this early period. Heat modalities may be effective in reducing pain but do not improve mobility.

Type of Reasoning: Inference

One must understand the nature of a stable humeral neck fracture and appropriate interventions in order to arrive at the correct conclusion. One must draw conclusions based on the patient's fracture status, which necessitates inferential reasoning skill. If this question was answered incorrectly, review information on appropriate exercises for stable humeral fractures.

C6 

Musculoskeletal | Interventions

A patient with unilateral spondylolysis at L4 is referred for physical therapy. The patient complains of generalized lower back pain when standing longer than 1 hour. Which strengthening exercise is **BEST** for the subacute phase of this patient's rehabilitation?

Choices:

1. Multifidi working from neutral to full extension.
2. Abdominals working from neutral to full flexion.
3. Multifidi working from full flexion back to neutral.
4. Abdominals working from full extension to full flexion.

Teaching Points

Correct Answer: 3

Performing strengthening exercises to the multifidi from flexion to neutral will not stress the pars defect.

Incorrect Choices:

Abdominal strengthening will not provide the segmental stability needed with this condition. Lumbar extension beyond neutral and rotation will tend to aggravate the condition in the early stages of rehabilitation.

Type of Reasoning: Analysis

One must understand the nature of unilateral spondylolysis, including symptomatology, in order to choose the best intervention approach. One must analyze the information presented and determine which intervention approach will provide the most benefit, while not stressing the pars defect. This requires analytical reasoning skill, in which the test taker weighs the information presented to choose the best solution.

C7 

Musculoskeletal | Examination

A patient has fixed forefoot varus malalignment. What possible compensatory motion or posture might occur?

Choices:

1. Excessive subtalar pronation.
2. Ipsilateral pelvic external rotation.
3. Hallux varus.
4. Genu recurvatum.

Teaching Points

Correct Answer: 1

Possible compensatory motions or postures for forefoot varus malalignment include excessive midtarsal or subtalar pronation or prolonged pronation; plantarflexed first ray; hallux valgus; or excessive tibial; tibial and femoral; tibial, femoral and pelvic internal rotation; and/or all with contralateral lumbar spine rotation.

Incorrect Choices:

The other compensatory motions or deformities are **NOT** typical of this problem.

Type of Reasoning: Inference

This question provides the diagnosis, and the test taker must determine what compensatory motions or postures are likely to occur. Questions that challenge one to determine possible symptoms from a given diagnosis require inferential reasoning skill. If this question was answered incorrectly, refer to information on forefoot varus malalignment.

C8

Integumentary | Evaluation, Diagnosis

A patient presents with fingertips that are rounded and bulbous. The nail plate is more convex than normal. These changes are the likely result of which condition?

Choices:

1. Psoriasis.
2. Chronic hypoxia from heart disease.
3. Inflammation of the proximal and lateral nail folds.
4. Trauma to the nail bed.

Teaching Points

Correct Answer: 2

Chronic hypoxia from heart disease or lung cancer and hepatic cirrhosis leads to clubbing of the fingers, characterized by fingertips that are rounded and bulbous and a nail plate that is more convex than normal.

Incorrect Choices:

Inflammation to the proximal and lateral nail folds (paronychia) is characterized by red, swollen, and tender folds. Trauma to the nail bed commonly results in white spots that grow out slowly with the nail. Psoriasis can result in small pits in the nails along with a circumscribed yellowish tan discoloration (oil spot lesion).

Type of Reasoning: Analysis

For this question, the test taker must analyze the symptoms and draw a conclusion regarding the likely diagnosis. This requires analytical reasoning skill. For this case, the symptoms are indicative of chronic hypoxia from heart disease. Review symptoms of chronic hypoxia if answered incorrectly.

C9 

Cardiovascular/Pulmonary and Lymphatic | Evaluation, Diagnosis

The PT is examining a patient for right neck pain and spasms. Several inflamed submandibular nodes are noted. The nodes are approximately 1.0 cm in size, tender, and erythematous. The patient has no known history of cancer or metabolic diseases. What is the **FIRST** action the therapist should take?

Choices:

1. Question the patient regarding impact of neck pain and emotional distress.
2. Question the patient regarding any recent dental or throat infections.
3. Have another therapist confirm the findings before implementing treatment.
4. Apply superficial heat and begin manual lymphatic drainage.

Teaching Points

Correct Answer: 2

Typically, lymph nodes are not palpable, but they can become palpable in the presence of infection or metastases. Past medical history is instrumental to identifying when follow-up is required by the physician. Recent infections (especially dental or pharyngeal) can make the lymph nodes swollen, tender, erythematous, and/or firm. Medical referral is necessary.

Incorrect Choices:

Treatment (manual lymph draining/superficial heat) should not be instituted. While questioning the patient regarding impact of neck pain and emotional distress is an important part of the examination, it will not influence the decision-making regarding enlarged lymph nodes. Having another therapist confirm the findings should not be necessary unless the therapist is inexperienced. In any case, treatment should not be implemented.

Type of Reasoning: Evaluation

This question requires the test taker to consider the symptoms presented and then determine the best course of action. Questions of this nature often require evaluative reasoning skill, as one must weigh information and its significance to determine a best course of action. For this situation, the **FIRST** action for the therapist is to question the patient regarding any recent dental or throat infections. Refer to examination guidelines for lymph nodes if answered incorrectly.

C10 

Neuromuscular | Evaluation, Diagnosis

A PT is reviewing a medical record prior to examining a patient for the first time. The suspected diagnosis is multiple sclerosis. On the neurologist's note, the therapist finds the following: deep tendon reflex (DTR); right quadriceps is 2+, left quadriceps is 4+. What is the correct interpretation of these findings?

Choices:

1. The right DTR is normal, the left is abnormal.
2. Both DTRs are abnormal and indicative of hyporeflexia.
3. The right DTR is exaggerated, the left is clearly abnormal.
4. Both DTRs are abnormal and indicative of upper motor neuron (UMN) syndrome.

Teaching Points

Correct Answer: 1

DTRs are graded on a 1–4 scale. Scores include 0 (no response); 1+ (present but depressed); 2+ (normal); 3+ (increased, brisker than average; possibly but not necessarily abnormal); and 4+ (very brisk, hyperactive, with clonus, abnormal). In this case, the right DTR is normal; the left is abnormal and consistent with strong hypertonicity.

Incorrect Choices:

The other choices do not correctly interpret these findings.

Type of Reasoning: Inference

This question requires one to draw conclusions about the information presented, which is an inferential reasoning skill. Here, the test taker must understand the meaning of 2+ and 4+ DTRs of the quadriceps in order to determine that the 2+ is normal and 4+ is abnormal. If this question was answered incorrectly, review information on measurement of DTRs.

C11 

Cardiovascular/Pulmonary and Lymphatic I Examination

A patient has an episode of syncope in the physical therapy clinic. The therapist attempts to rule out orthostatic hypotension as the cause of the fainting. What is the **BEST** test protocol to use?

Choices:

1. Palpate the carotid arteries and take resting HR and BP in the supine position.
2. Take resting HR and BP in supine, then in sitting, then in standing after 1 minute.
3. Take resting HR and BP in supine after 5 minutes, then in semi-Fowler position.
4. Take resting HR and BP in sitting and after 3 and 5 minutes of cycle ergometry exercise.

Teaching Points

Correct Answer: 2

Orthostatic hypotension is a fall in BP with elevation of position; thus responses to movements (HR and BP) are tested from supine to sitting or sitting to standing. A small increase or no increase in HR upon standing may suggest baroreflex impairment. An exaggerated increase in HR upon standing may indicate volume depletion.

Incorrect Choices:

The other choices do not challenge the system with adequate change of position (supine to semi-Fowler or remaining supine or sitting).

Type of Reasoning: Inductive

One must determine through clinical judgment the **BEST** method to rule out orthostatic hypotension. This requires knowledge of the nature of orthostatic hypotension and how it can be evaluated, which requires inductive reasoning skills. In this case, checking resting BP and HR in sitting and repeating after 1 minute of standing is the **BEST** way to rule out the diagnosis.

C12 

Integumentary | Evaluation, Diagnosis

An inpatient with a grade III diabetic foot ulcer is referred for physical therapy. Panafil has been applied to the necrotic tissue BID. The wound has no foul smell; however, the therapist notes a green tinge on the dressing. What is the **BEST** action for the therapist to take?

Choices:

1. Fit the patient with a total contact cast.
2. Document the finding and contact the physician immediately.
3. Begin a trial of acetic acid to the wound.
4. Document the finding and continue with treatment.

Teaching Points

Correct Answer: 4

In this case, the therapist should document the findings and continue with treatment. Panafil is a keratolytic enzyme used for selective debridement. A greenish or yellowish exudate can be expected.

Incorrect Choices:

If the exudate was green and had a foul smell, *Pseudomonas aeruginosa* should be suspected. The physician will most likely order a different topical agent. Acetic acid would not be the topical agent of choice. A total contact cast can be used only after the wound is free of necrotic tissue.

Type of Reasoning: Evaluation

The test taker must determine the significance of the information presented and evaluate the best course of action, given this information. This requires evaluative reasoning skill, in which one must assign value to the patient's wound status and judge how to proceed.

C13 

Neuromuscular | Evaluation, Diagnosis

A PT receives a referral to examine the fall risk of an elderly patient with Parkinson's disease who lives alone and has had two recent falls. Which activity is the **MOST** common reason for falls in the elderly?

Choices:

1. Walking with a roller walker with hand brakes.
2. Climbing on a step stool to reach overhead objects.
3. Turning around and sitting down in a chair.
4. Dressing while sitting on the edge of the bed.

Teaching Points

Correct Answer: 3

Most falls occur during normal daily activity. Getting up or down from a bed or chair, turning, bending, walking, and climbing/descending stairs are all high-risk activities.

Incorrect Choices:

Only a small percentage of individuals fall during clearly hazardous activities (e.g., climbing the step stool). Proper use of an assistive device reduces the risk of falls. Sitting does not typically present a fall risk.

Exam C

Type of Reasoning: Evaluation

One must reason out the **MOST** common risk factor for an elderly person with a history of falls. This requires the evaluation of the information presented and determining the believability of the statement, which encourages evaluative reasoning skill. In this question, most common risk factors for falls in the elderly are activities that are done during the normal daily mobility activities.

C14 

Metabolic/Endocrine | Evaluation, Diagnosis

A patient with Addison's disease is referred for physical therapy following a hip fracture. Which of the following is a cardinal symptom of Addison's disease?

Choices:

1. Weight gain.
2. Tremors.
3. Asthenia.
4. Diarrhea.

Teaching Points

Correct Answer: 3

The cardinal symptom of Addison's disease is asthenia. The weakness is slowly progressive and debilitating.

Incorrect Choices:

Other symptoms include anorexia, weight loss, nausea and vomiting, abdominal pain, and syncope. Other listed choices are not characteristic of Addison's disease.

Type of Reasoning: Inference

One must determine the cardinal symptom for Addison's disease in order to arrive at a correct conclusion. This requires one to determine whether it is likely to be true of a diagnosis, which is an inferential reasoning skill. For this situation, the cardinal symptom is asthenia. Review signs and symptoms of Addison's disease if answered incorrectly.

C15 

Musculoskeletal | Interventions

A 2-month-old child with bilateral hip dislocations is being discharged from an acute pediatric facility. The PT has developed a home exercise program and now needs to instruct the parents. What is the **MOST** important item for the therapist to assess before instructing the parents?

Choices:

1. Their degree of anxiety and attention.
2. Their knowledge of the etiology of the hip dislocations.
3. The home environment.
4. The financial reimbursement plan.

Teaching Points

Correct Answer: 1

A needs assessment should include a determination of the level of anxiety and ability to attend to the instructions given. If anxiety is high and the parents are unable to attend to the therapist's instructions, risk of failure to perform the home exercises correctly is high.

Incorrect Choices:

Although the other factors may also be considered in the development of a home exercise plan, they do not represent immediate priorities for instruction.

Type of Reasoning: Inference

This question requires one to draw conclusions about the diagnosis of the child and the **MOST** important item to assess before instructing the parents. This requires inferential reasoning skill, in which the test taker must make assumptions based on the information presented and determine the most appropriate course of action. In this case, it is most important to determine the parents' degree of anxiety and attention.

C16

Musculoskeletal | Examination

A PT receives a referral for a young child that had been swung around while being held from the wrists. The referral reads, "functional disuse following nursemaid's elbow." Which of the following commonly results from a forceful longitudinal pull of the forearm of a child?

Choices:

1. Superior subluxation of the radial head from the annular ligament.
2. Inferior subluxation of the ulna from the annular ligament.
3. Superior subluxation of the ulna from the annular ligament.
4. Inferior subluxation of the radial head from the annular ligament.

Teaching Points

Correct Answer: 4

The inferior subluxation of the radial head from the annular ligament typically occurs with a forceful longitudinal pull of the forearm in a child. It is also known as "baby sitter's elbow."

Incorrect Choices:

The ulna is not subluxed from the humerus with this condition, and the subluxation is not superior.

Type of Reasoning: Inference

In order to arrive at a correct conclusion, the test taker must recall the likely symptoms for nursemaid's elbow. This requires inferential reasoning skill. For this situation, the likely presentation for this injury includes inferior subluxation of the radial head from the annular ligament. Review symptoms of nursemaid's elbow if answered incorrectly.

Cardiovascular/Pulmonary and Lymphatic | Evaluation, Diagnosis

Which is a typical early clinical manifestation of cystic fibrosis (CF)?

Choices:
1. Increase in secretions of the endocrine system.
2. Frequent recurrent urinary tract infections.
3. Excessive appetite and weight loss.
4. Increased FEV_1 (forced expiratory volume in 1 sec) during pulmonary function testing.

Teaching Points

Correct Answer: 3

CF is an inherited disorder affecting the exocrine glands of the hepatic, digestive, and respiratory systems. The patient with CF is prone to chronic bacterial airway infections and progressive loss of pulmonary function from progressive obstructive lung disease. Early clinical manifestations include an inability to gain weight despite an excessive appetite and adequate caloric intake.

Incorrect Choices:

The pulmonary function test results in a patient with CF can have a mixed picture of both obstructive and restrictive disease components. It is typical to have a decrease in the FEV_1 value over time, not an increase. There will also be recurrent infections in patients with CF; however, these infections will be in the airways and lung parenchyma. Urinary tract infections, though quite possible, are no different in frequency than in any patient or nonpatient population. Finally, CF is a disorder of the exocrine glands, meaning those glands that excrete secretions. The endocrine system, including the hypothamus, pituitary, thyroid, etc., are not particularly involved in the disease of CF. The pancreas is both an exocrine and an endocrine gland. CF does affect the pancreas by *decreasing* the bicarbonate secretions, reducing the effectiveness of pancreatic enzymes and leading to pancreatic insufficiency.

Type of Reasoning: Inference

This question provides the diagnosis, and the test taker must determine the symptomatology that is expected. CF is a multisystem disorder, making the possible clinical manifestations quite varied. This question requires inferential reasoning skill, in which one infers knowledge of CF to arrive at the correct conclusion for what is expected, a gastrointestinal manifestation of poor weight gain despite adequate caloric intake.

Neuromuscular | Examination

Which of the following activities demonstrates an infant's integration of the asymmetrical tonic neck reflex?

Choices:
1. Turns head to one side and brings opposite hand to mouth.
2. Can turn head to either side with extended arms.
3. Turns head to one side and brings hand to mouth on the same side.
4. Turns head to one side and looks at the extended arm on that side.

Teaching Points

Correct Answer: 3

ATNR causes extension of upper extremity on the side the head is turned toward. Bringing the hand to the mouth would not be possible with an obligatory reflex.

Incorrect Choices:

The other choices do not correctly define actions that are limited with an obligatory ATNR. The ATNR is a total upper extremity response and not limited to hand opening or simply looking at the hand.

Type of Reasoning: Analysis

In this scenario, if the infant can turn the head and bring the hand to mouth on the same side, the reflex is no longer obligatory. Analytical reasoning skill is used in this question because the test taker must determine the meaning of the information presented and analyze what it means in relation to a correct solution.

C19 

Nonsystem | Safety, Professional Responsibilities, Research

A physical therapy aide is cleaning a mat table with a new product supplied by the housekeeping department. The spray from the cleaning agent contacted the skin resulting in irritation, redness, and some swelling. The symptoms were minor and abated within 20 minutes. Later, the aide informed the physical therapy supervisor of this situation. What action should the supervisor take?

Choices:

1. Initiate first aid by rinsing the affected area with a skin cleanser and applying cortisone cream for the inflammation.
2. Inform housekeeping to immediately cease using the cleaning agent.
3. Fill out an incident/occurrence report and have the aide examined by employee health or their own primary care physician.
4. Fill out an incident/occurrence report and review the Material Safety Data Sheet (MSDS) from Occupational Safety and Health Administration (OSHA) with the aide on how to properly handle the cleaning agent.

Teaching Points

Correct Answer: 4

Material Safety Data Sheets are mandated by OSHA of the U.S. Department of Labor. These sheets give employees information about potentially hazardous materials in the workplace and how to protect themselves. An incident/occurrence report is used to document situations that involve patients or staff that could have resulted in potential long-lasting or permanent harm and are part of an internal quality improvement program. The use of this cleaning agent may have some specific directions in method of application and precautions needed to be observed by the user. The MSDS would make this clear.

Incorrect Choices:

Application of first aid in this case seems unnecessary since the symptoms abated very soon. The aide may have used the cleaning agent inappropriately or not used proper precautions; therefore recommending that housekeeping cease using it immediately is premature. Filling out an incident report and having the aide seen by employee health is not a thorough enough response without going over the MSDS to prevent future problems.

Type of Reasoning: Evaluation

This question requires one to determine a best course of action based on the presenting issue and possible courses of action. This necessitates knowledge of OSHA guidelines coupled with sound reasoning for drawing an appropriate conclusion, which requires evaluative reasoning skill. In this case, the supervisor should fill out an incident/occurrence report and review the MSDS from OSHA with the aide. If answered incorrectly review OSHA and MSDS guidelines.

C20

Musculoskeletal | Interventions

During surgery to remove an apical lung tumor, the long thoracic nerve was injured. Muscle testing of the serratus anterior demonstrates its strength to be 3+/5. What is the **BEST** initial exercise for this patient?

Choices:

1. Standing wall push-ups.
2. Standing arm overhead lifts using hand weights.
3. Supine arm overhead lifts using weights.
4. Sitting arm overhead lifts using a pulley.

Teaching Points

Correct Answer: 1

The long thoracic nerve supplies the serratus anterior muscle. With a muscle grade of 3+/5, the patient can then begin functional strengthening using standing wall push-ups, with resistance provided by the patient's own body.

Incorrect Choices:

The other exercises would not be optimal or used **INITIALLY** for strengthening a fair plus serratus anterior. Performing overhead exercises with resistance (weights or pulleys) will overload the weakened serratus anterior muscle, causing the patient to compensate and potentially develop inappropriate movement patterns.

Type of Reasoning: Analysis

One must recall innervations for the long thoracic nerve in order to arrive at the correct conclusion. This requires analysis of the information presented and interpretation of that information, which requires analytical reasoning skill. Knowledge of neuropathology is helpful to arrive at the correct conclusion. If this question was answered incorrectly, review appropriate exercises for serratus anterior strengthening.

C21

Musculoskeletal | Evaluation, Diagnosis

A PT examination reveals posterior superior iliac spine (PSIS) is low on the left; anterior superior iliac spine (ASIS) is high on the left; standing flexion test shows that the left PSIS moves first and farthest superiorly; Gillet's test demonstrates that the left PSIS moves inferiorly and laterally less than right; long sitting test shows that the left malleolus moves short to long; and the sitting flexion test is negative. Based on these findings, what is the therapist's diagnosis?

Choices:

1. Left upslip.
2. Iliac inflare on the left.
3. Left posterior rotated innominate.
4. Left anterior rotated innominate.

Teaching Points

Correct Answer: 3

A posterior rotated innominate is a unilateral iliosacral dysfunction. The question outlines positive physical findings, both static and dynamic, found with this dysfunction. One of these positive findings alone does not confirm the diagnosis of left rotated posterior innominate.

Incorrect Choices:

The findings are opposite to what would be found with a left anterior ilial rotation. If the patient had an upslip, both the PSIS and the ASIS on the left would be elevated. If an inflare was present, the left PSIS would appear more lateral and the ASIS would appear more medial.

Type of Reasoning: Analysis

Questions provide the symptoms, and the therapist must determine the diagnosis; this requires the use of analytical reasoning skill. This is because of the high need to determine what the cluster of symptoms indicates in terms of deficits and functioning. For this patient, the symptoms indicate a left posterior rotated innominate, which should trigger a review of iliosacral dysfunction if this question was answered incorrectly.

C22 

Integumentary | Examination

A patient recovering from a burn on the back of the hand is referred to physical therapy for mobilization exercises. The therapist observes a 14-cm irregular area that is thick and pink. How should the therapist document this finding?

Choices:

1. Hypertrophic scarring.
2. An excoriation.
3. Atrophic scarring.
4. A scale.

Teaching Points

Correct Answer: 1

Hypertrophic scars are thick (raised) and pink (or red).

Incorrect Choices:

Atrophic scars are thin and white. Excoriation is an abrasion or scratch mark. A scale is a flake of exfoliated epidermis (e.g., dandruff, psoriasis, dry skin).

Type of Reasoning: Analysis

This question requires one to determine the clinical findings based on the observation of the patient's skin. This necessitates analytical reasoning skill because one must analyze the signs presented in order to determine the likely clinical finding. In this case, the therapist's observations are consistent with hypertrophic scarring. If this question was answered incorrectly, review signs and symptoms of hypertrophic scarring, especially in burns.

C23 

Nonsystem I Equipment, Devices, Biophysical Agents

A patient presents with partial- and full-thickness burns on the chest and neck regions. The therapist decides to apply transcutaneous electrical nerve stimulation (TENS) before debridement to modulate pain. Which TENS mode should provide the **BEST** relief?

Choices:
1. Acupuncture-like (low-rate) TENS.
2. Brief intense TENS.
3. Modulated TENS.
4. Conventional (high-rate) TENS.

Teaching Points

Correct Answer: 2
Brief intense TENS is used to provide rapid-onset, short-term relief during painful procedures. The pulse rate and pulse duration are similar to conventional TENS; however, the current intensity is increased to the patient's tolerance.

Incorrect Choices:
In this situation, intensity is the primary determinant of pain relief. Conventional TENS does not use as high of an intensity as brief intense TENS and the application time is longer. Acupuncture-like TENS does not give immediate relief of pain, because it has a long onset. Modulation is used to prevent accommodation, not to provide relief of pain.

Type of Reasoning: Deductive
One must recall the protocols for TENS use in order to determine the mode that would provide the **BEST** relief of pain for this patient. This requires factual recall of information, which necessitates deductive reasoning skill. In this case, brief intense TENS is **BEST** because it provides rapid-onset, short-term relief during painful procedures.

C24 

Neuromuscular I Interventions

A patient recovering from traumatic brain injury (TBI) demonstrates difficulties in feeding resulting from an unstable posture while sitting. The therapist determines that modification is necessary to ensure optimal function. What is the first body segment or segments that the therapist should align?

Choices:
1. Trunk.
2. Pelvis.
3. Head.
4. Lower extremities.

Teaching Points

Correct Answer: 2

Modification of the pelvic position in a neutral posture promotes good lumbar and trunk alignment. Many postural problems are correctable by aligning the pelvis first and achieving a stable base.

Incorrect Choices:

Modifying the position of the head, trunk, or lower extremities may be necessary but only after achieving a stable base.

Type of Reasoning: Inductive

The test taker must determine through clinical judgment the **FIRST** body segment(s) to align in order to promote good trunk alignment. This requires inductive reasoning skill, in which knowledge of biomechanics and neuropathology is beneficial for arriving at the correct conclusion.

C25 Neuromuscular | Interventions

A patient demonstrates some out-of-synergy movements in the right upper extremity indicative of stage 4 recovery after a left cerebrovascular accident (CVA). Which proprioceptive neuromuscular facilitation (PNF) pattern represents the **BEST** choice to promote continued recovery of the right upper extremity?

Choices:

1. Bilateral symmetrical D2F and D2E, elbows straight.
2. Chop, reverse chop with right arm leading.
3. Lift, reverse lift with right arm leading.
4. Bilateral symmetrical D1 thrust and reverse thrust.

Teaching Points

Correct Answer: 2

Both chop and reverse chop patterns move the affected arm out-of-synergy.

Incorrect Choices:

Thrust is an out-of-synergy pattern, and reverse thrust is in synergy. Lift is an out-of-synergy pattern, and reverse lift is in synergy. The same is true for bilateral symmetrical D2F (out of synergy) and D2E (in synergy).

Type of Reasoning: Inference

In order to arrive at the correct conclusion, one must recall the PNF patterns presented and then match these patterns to the stage of recovery of the patient. The chop, reverse chop with right arm leading encourages out-of-synergy movement, which is most beneficial during stage 4 of recovery. If this question was answered incorrectly, refer to PNF patterns and interventions for stage 4 of stroke recovery.

C26

Cardiovascular/Pulmonary and Lymphatic | Interventions

An elderly individual has limited endurance as a result of a sedentary lifestyle. There is no history of cardiorespiratory problems. An exercise tolerance test was negative for coronary heart disease. What is the **BEST** initial exercise prescription for this individual?

Choices:

1. 40%–50% HR_{max}.
2. 35%–50% of VO_{2max}.
3. 60%–90% HR_{max}.
4. 30%–50% HR_{max}.

Teaching Points

Correct Answer: 3

An appropriate **initial** exercise prescription for an asymptomatic elderly individual with general deconditioning is 60%–90% of HR_{max}, which is equivalent to 50%–85% of VO_{2max} or 50%–85% of HR reserve (Karvonen's formula). This is within the established intensity guidelines for adults for aerobic exercise training. Duration should be discontinuous, and exercise should be performed most days of the week (*ACSM Guidelines for Exercise Testing and Prescription,* 8th ed.).

Incorrect Choices:

All other choices are too conservative. The exercise tolerance test has ruled out coronary heart disease.

Type of Reasoning: Analysis

One must analyze the information presented and then determine, given the patient's health status, the **MOST** beneficial initial exercise prescription parameters. Analytical reasoning skill is utilized because the test taker must weigh the information presented and recall the typical prescription parameters for an asymptomatic individual.

C27

Cardiovascular/Pulmonary and Lymphatic | Interventions

A patient is admitted to a coronary care unit with a mild myocardial infarction (MI). After 2 days, the patient is referred to physical therapy for inpatient cardiac rehabilitation. During an initial exercise session on the unit, the patient reports chest pain, appears anxious and wants to go back to bed to rest. What is the therapist's **BEST** initial course of action?

Choices:

1. Assist the patient back to bed and contact the charge nurse on the floor.
2. Sit the patient down and monitor vital signs carefully during the rest period.
3. Assign the PTA to assist the patient back to bed and monitor vital signs carefully.
4. Terminate the exercise and contact the attending physician immediately.

Teaching Points

Correct Answer: 2

If the chest pain (angina) is exercise induced, this is an indication to stop the exercise session and provide a period of rest during which time the patient is closely monitored. Recovery is expected after a period of rest.

Incorrect Choices:

If the patient is still anxious after the rest, it is reasonable to return the patient to the room and inform the nurse. This should be done by the therapist personally in order to carefully monitor the patient's status. The PTA should not be expected to evaluate chest pain or reach a determination about its significance. This is not an emergency situation.

Type of Reasoning: Evaluation

One must make a judgment call for the **BEST** course of action for this patient, given the symptoms presented. Questions that require one to make value judgments necessitate evaluative reasoning skill and can be challenging to answer, because the key to finding the correct solution goes beyond factual knowledge. For this patient, it is best to have the patient sit down and monitor vital signs.

C28 

Integumentary | Evaluation, Diagnosis

A patient with a 10-year history of scleroderma is referred for physical therapy to improve functional status and endurance. The patient was recently treated with corticosteroids for a bout of myositis. Examination findings reveal limited ROM and fibrotic soft tissue along with hyperesthesia. What is the **BEST** choice for initial intervention?

Choices:

1. Treadmill walking using body weight support at an intensity of 40% HR_{max}.
2. Active range of motion (AROM) exercises and walking in a therapeutic pool.
3. Closed-chain and modified aerobic step exercises.
4. Soft tissue mobilization and stretching.

Teaching Points

Correct Answer: 2

Scleroderma (progressive systemic sclerosis) is a chronic, diffuse disease of connective tissues causing fibrosis of skin, joints, blood vessels, and internal organs. Patients typically demonstrate symmetrical skin thickening and visceral involvement of the gastrointestinal tract, lungs, heart, and kidneys along with hypersensitivity to touch. The **BEST** choice for initial intervention is to exercise in the pool. The warmth and buoyancy of the water will enhance the patient's movements and decrease pain.

Incorrect Choices:

The other choices are too aggressive at this time and risk increasing the patient's pain, thereby limiting any benefits in flexibility and endurance.

Type of Reasoning: Inductive

One must determine through clinical judgment the **BEST** initial intervention approach for this patient. Knowledge of the nature of scleroderma and expected symptomatology is key to arriving at the correct conclusion, which in this case is AROM exercises and walking in a therapeutic pool. If this question was answered incorrectly, refer to information on intervention approaches for patients with scleroderma.

C29

System Interactions I Evaluation, Diagnosis

A patient is referred to physical therapy after a fall injury (fractured left hip with operative reduction, internal fixation [ORIF]). Medical history reveals a diagnosis of mild Alzheimer's type dementia (AD). Given this stage of AD, which change should not be evident in this patient?

Choices:

1. Profound communication deficits.
2. Memory loss.
3. Anxiety and irritability.
4. Difficulty concentrating.

Teaching Points

Correct Answer: 1

Profound communication deficits (inability to speak), global deterioration of mental functions (delusions, hallucinations, fragmented memory), agitation, and pacing (sundowning) are all characteristic of later stages of AD.

Incorrect Choices:

Mild AD is characterized by memory loss, absentmindedness, anxiety and irritability, difficulty concentrating, and occasional word-finding problems.

Type of Reasoning: Inference

One must infer information from the diagnosis presented and the stage of the disease provided. This necessitates inferential reasoning skills, in which one must draw conclusions from the information presented to choose the best solution of what is **NOT** expected in early stage 1.

C30

Neuromuscular I Interventions

A patient recovering from stroke with minimal lower extremity weakness and spasticity is able to walk without an assistive device. The therapist observes that as the patient walks there is noticeable hip hiking on the more affected side during swing phase. What is the **BEST** initial intervention?

Choices:

1. Bridging exercises progressing to sit-to-stand training.
2. Marching while sitting on a therapy ball.
3. Standing and marching with manual pressure applied downward on the pelvis.
4. Partial wall squats using a small ball held between the knees.

Teaching Points

Correct Answer: 2

Hip hiking is a compensatory response for weak hip and knee flexors or extensor spasticity. Active exercises for the hip and knee flexors (marching) is the most appropriate intervention.

Incorrect Choices:

Downward manual pressure on the pelvis strengthens hip hikers. The other choices focus on strengthening hip and knee extensors.

Type of Reasoning: Inductive

The test taker must utilize clinical judgment to determine first what the patient's deficits are (related to the therapist's observation of the patient's gait) and then the **BEST** initial intervention for this patient. One must evaluate the four possible intervention choices given to determine which intervention is **BEST** for addressing the patient's deficits, which requires inductive reasoning skills. In this scenario, marching while sitting on a ball will **BEST** address the patient's weak hip and knee flexors or extensor spasticity.

C31

Neuromuscular | Interventions

The therapist is instructing a patient with traumatic brain injury (TBI) how to lock the brakes on a wheelchair. The patient is right-handed, and the right upper extremity is more affected than the left. What is the **BEST** motor learning strategy to use with this patient?

Choices:

1. Have the patient practice brake locking using the left hand to assist the right.
2. Guide the patient's right hand through the locking motions, then the left.
3. Verbally talk the patient through the locking motions, practicing with both hands simultaneously.
4. Have the patient practice locking the brakes first with the left hand and then with the right.

Teaching Points

Correct Answer: 4

Using the motor learning strategy of transfer of training is best to use with this patient. Practice is performed with the less affected extremity first and then progressed to use of the more affected extremity.

Incorrect Choices:

Guided movement (manual or verbal) represents a less active approach than the transfer of training approach. The more passive the performance, the slower the learning will take place. Bilateral tasks are more difficult than performing the task with one limb at a time.

Type of Reasoning: Inductive

The test taker must determine the **BEST** training strategy for a patient with traumatic brain injury, which necessitates inductive reasoning skill and, therefore, clinical judgment. For this patient, it is important to have him/her practice locking the brakes first with his/her left hand and then his/her right in order to encourage effective transfer of training. Knowledge of effective motor learning strategies for patients with brain injury is beneficial for arriving at the correct conclusion.

C32

Musculoskeletal | Examination

In neural tension testing, what position will **BEST** bias the tibial nerve?

Choices:

1. Straight leg raise with plantarflexion and eversion.
2. Straight leg raise with dorsiflexion and inversion.
3. Straight leg raise with plantarflexion and inversion.
4. Straight leg raise with dorsiflexion and eversion.

Teaching Points

Correct Answer: 4

A straight leg raise with dorsiflexion and eversion will best bias the tibial nerve. This is the optimal position for neural tissue provocation of the tibial nerve. Neural tension techniques are used to decrease adverse mechanical tension on the nerves. Peripheral nerves can often become trapped within the tissues, where there can be a pull on the nerve with movement. This technique frees up the nerve so that it can slide in its sheath.

Incorrect Choices:

Straight leg raise with dorsiflexion and inversion and straight leg raise with plantarflexion and inversion will best bias the sural nerve and peroneal (fibular) nerve, respectively. Straight leg raise with plantarflexion and eversion will not isolate a specific nerve.

Type of Reasoning: Inductive

This question requires the test taker to utilize clinical judgment in order to arrive at a correct conclusion. In this case, the test taker must draw upon knowledge of neural tension testing to determine the best position to bias the tibial nerve. This is an inductive reasoning skill. For this situation, the therapist should position the extremity in a straight leg raise with dorsiflexion and eversion to bias the tibial nerve. Review neural tension testing techniques if answered incorrectly.

C33

Cardiovascular/Pulmonary and Lymphatic | Evaluation, Diagnosis

A therapist is examining a patient with chronic obstructive pulmonary disease (COPD) GOLD stage III. What would be a clinical finding that the therapist would expect for this patient?

Choices:

1. Decreased anteroposterior-to-lateral chest ratio.
2. Muscle wasting.
3. Use of supplemental oxygen.
4. Weight gain.

Teaching Points

Correct Answer: 2

Muscle wasting is a common manifestation of COPD. The cause of muscle wasting is not clear, but it is not simply a malnutrition problem. The results of this muscle wasting are peripheral weakness, impaired functional abilities, poor quality of life, and a poor prognostic sign.

Incorrect Choices:

Supplemental oxygen is typically found in patients in stage IV of GOLD, not stage III. Weight loss is a common finding in patients with COPD, especially as the disease progresses. The energy demands of a person with COPD are higher than those of a person without COPD for the same activity. A usual finding is that persons with COPD are less active than their nondiseased counterparts. As the disease progresses, the person with COPD cannot maintain his/her independence with any further decrease in his/her activity and weight loss ensues. As lung destruction increases with worsening COPD, there are less elastic recoil properties of the lung to pull the thorax back into what we recognize as a usual thoracic configuration. A barreled chest, or an increased anteroposterior-to-lateral diameter of the chest, is a common finding in advanced, stage III COPD.

Type of Reasoning: Inference

One must infer from the symptoms presented what clinical finding would likely be found in a patient with severe (stage III) COPD. This requires knowledge of pulmonary disorders and the typical findings in order to determine, through the process of elimination, what finding is characteristic of that stage of COPD. If this question was answered incorrectly, refer to typical symptoms of COPD.

C34 

Musculoskeletal | Examination

What muscle length test for the tensor fascia lata is recommended in a patient with decreased muscle length of the rectus femoris?

Choices:

1. Modified Ober test (knee extended).
2. FAIR (flexion, adduction, internal rotation) test.
3. Ober test (knee flexed).
4. Ely's test.

Teaching Points

Correct Answer: 1

The modified Ober test is performed with the knee extended, which allows the patient to attain the necessary hip extension required to assess the tensor fascia lata.

Incorrect Choices:

The Ober test is performed with the knee in flexion. Given the decreased muscle length of the rectus femoris, the patient will not be able to attain the necessary hip extension required to assess the tensor fascia lata. Ely's test identifies tightness of the rectus femoris, which is a given. The modified Ober test will accommodate for the decreased muscle length of the rectus femoris. The FAIR test is performed to assess for piriformis syndrome.

Type of Reasoning: Inductive

This question requires clinical judgment in order to determine the best muscle length test for the tensor fascia lata tightness. Questions that draw on one's clinical knowledge and skill often require inductive reasoning skills. For this case, the modified Ober test is the best test, as it will accommodate for the decreased muscle length of the rectus femoris. Review muscle length tests, especially the modified Ober test, if answered incorrectly.

C35

Musculoskeletal | Interventions

During a postural screen for chronic shoulder pain, the therapist observes excessive internal rotation of the shoulders and winging of the scapula during overhead motion. What is the **BEST** choice for exercise intervention?

Choices:

1. Strengthening of rhomboids and stretching of upper trapezius.
2. Strengthening of pectoral muscles and stretching of upper trapezius.
3. Strengthening of upper trapezius and stretching of pectoral muscles.
4. Strengthening of middle and lower trapezius and stretching of pectoral muscles.

Teaching Points

Correct Answer: 4

Abnormal posture that produces excessive internal rotation of the shoulders may result in chronic shoulder impingement syndrome due to a loss of scapular stability with overhead motion. Shoulder pain is likely to continue until a balance between anterior and posterior trunk musculature is achieved. The anterior chest muscles (pectorals) are shortened and need stretching and posterior trunk muscles (middle and lower trapezius) are stretched and need strengthening.

Incorrect Choices:

The pectoralis major and minor need to be stretched not strengthened. Stretching of the upper trapezius will not change this condition.

Type of Reasoning: Analysis

Knowledge of shoulder kinesiology and pathology is beneficial to arriving at the correct conclusion for this answer. An understanding that excessive internal rotation of the shoulders and scapular winging could be caused by a weak middle and lower trapezius and shortened pectoral muscles results from a solid understanding of shoulder pathology and kinesiology. Through analytical reasoning, the test taker must determine which muscles are most likely to be affected and, therefore, produce these symptoms.

C36

Integumentary | Interventions

Examination of a patient with a dermal ulcer over the coccyx reveals a wound exposing the deep fascia. There is no necrotic tissue, exudate is minimal, and the borders of the ulcer are diffusely covered with granulation tissue. Previous treatment has included wet-to-dry dressings with normal saline. What is the **BEST** choice for intervention?

Choices:

1. Hydrogel dressings and whirlpool immersion.
2. Continuation of the same treatment.
3. Wound irrigation with pressures below 15 psi.
4. Calcium alginate dressings.

Teaching Points

Correct Answer: 3

Low-pressure wound irrigation helps to decrease colonization and prevent infection.

Incorrect Choices:

Wet-to-dry dressings help remove necrotic tissue. There is no necrotic tissue. Calcium alginate is used in the presence of heavy exudates, which is not the case here. Hydrogel would be best because it is nonadherent, keeps wounds moist, and protects granulation buds; however, whirlpool immersion is now contraindicated for all wound management.

Type of Reasoning: Inductive

One must utilize clinical judgment and knowledge of wound care approaches to determine the best intervention approach for this patient, which requires inductive reasoning skill. For this patient, wound irrigation with pressures below 15 psi is most appropriate for the type of wound described. If this question was answered incorrectly, review information on wound care procedures for this type of wound.

C37

Musculoskeletal | Evaluation, Diagnosis

Based on the spinal defect shown in the diagram, what lumbar spinal motion should be avoided?

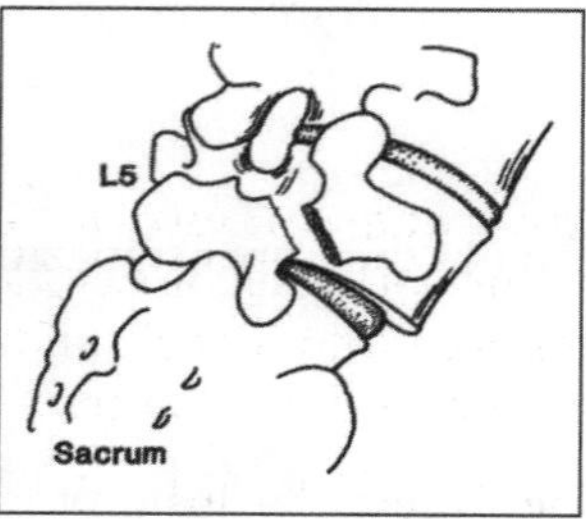

Choices:

1. Rotation.
2. Extension.
3. Lateral flexion.
4. Flexion.

Teaching Points

Correct Answer: 2

With spondylolisthesis, there is typically an anterior slippage of one vertebra on the vertebra below. Because of the anterior shearing forces acting at the vertebra caused by the wedge shape of the vertebra and gravity, spinal extension positions should be avoided.

Incorrect Choices:

Flexion, rotation, and lateral flexion will cause the bony structures to separate and will not cause any negative compressive loads to the damaged structures.

Type of Reasoning: Analysis

One must analyze the spinal defect displayed in the picture and determine the diagnosis in order to determine what lumbar position should be avoided. This requires analytical reasoning skill, in which the precise meaning of the spinal defect must be determined first, before determining the appropriate management of this patient. If this question was answered incorrectly, refer to intervention approaches for spondylolisthesis.

C38

Neuromuscular I Evaluation, Diagnosis

A computer specialist is unable to work because of weakness and altered sensation in the dominant right hand. The patient complains of pain and tingling of the thumb, index finger, long finger, and radial half of the ring finger. The therapist observes thenar weakness and atrophy. Strength, reflexes, and sensation are within normal limits throughout the remainder of the right upper extremity. These signs and symptoms are characteristic of what diagnosis?

Choices:

1. Ulnar nerve compression.
2. Carpal tunnel syndrome.
3. Pronator teres syndrome.
4. Cervical root compression.

Teaching Points

Correct Answer: 2

The pattern of motor and sensory loss corresponds to the median nerve distribution in the hand. The most likely cause is carpal tunnel syndrome.

Incorrect Choices:

Pronator teres syndrome (also a median nerve problem) produces similar deficits along with involvement of the flexors of the wrist and fingers. Cervical root compression would also produce proximal deficits in strength and sensation. Ulnar nerve compression (ulnar nerve palsy) would produce motor deficits of the flexor carpi ulnaris and medial half of the flexor digitorum profundus, resulting in claw hand. Sensory loss is to the ulnar side of the hand and/or arm.

Type of Reasoning: Analysis

This question provides the symptoms, and the test taker must determine the most likely diagnosis. This necessitates analytical reasoning skill, in which one must determine the exact meaning of the symptoms presented to arrive at the correct conclusion. If this question was answered incorrectly, review information on symptoms of carpal tunnel syndrome.

C39

Neuromuscular I Evaluation, Diagnosis

A patient presents with rapidly progressive symmetrical weakness that started in the distal lower extremity muscles but now has ascended to include proximal trunk and upper extremity muscles. The motor segments of the lower cranial nerves are also showing impairment. The patient complains of abnormal sensations of tingling and burning of the affected extremities. Consciousness, cognition, and communication are all normal. These signs and symptoms are characteristic of what diagnosis?

Choices:

1. Multiple sclerosis.
2. Guillain-Barré syndrome.
3. Amyotrophic lateral sclerosis.
4. Postpolio syndrome.

Teaching Points

Correct Answer: 2

These signs and symptoms are characteristic of Guillain-Barré syndrome, a peripheral neuropathy in which there is inflammation and demyelination of peripheral motor and sensory nerve fibers. Early in its progression, either upper or lower motor signs may predominate.

Incorrect Choices:

In almost all cases, patients with ALS show features of both UMN and lower motor neuron (LMN) dysfunction. Postpolio syndrome is an LMN syndrome that does not present with sensory paresthesias and is typically asymmetrical. MS will present with UMN signs: spasticity and hyperreflexia.

Type of Reasoning: Analysis

This question provides the symptoms, and the test taker must determine what the symptoms most likely indicate. This requires analytical reasoning skill, in which one evaluates the exact meaning of the symptoms presented to arrive at the correct conclusion. If this question was answered incorrectly, review information on symptoms of Guillain-Barré syndrome.

C40 

Cardiovascular/Pulmonary and Lymphatic I Interventions

A patient recovering from surgery for triple coronary artery bypass grafts is scheduled to begin a phase III cardiac rehabilitation program. During the resistance training portion of the circuit training program, the therapist instructs the patient to avoid the Valsalva maneuver. What are the expected adverse effects of the Valsalva maneuver?

Choices:

1. Slowing of pulse and increased venous pressure are possible.
2. The decreased return of blood to the heart can lead to pitting edema.
3. Heart rate (HR) and blood pressure are likely to be elevated.
4. A cholinergic or vagal response can occur.

Teaching Points

Correct Answer: 1

The Valsalva maneuver results from forcible exhalation with the glottis, nose, and mouth closed. It increases intrathoracic pressures and causes slowing of the pulse, decreased return of blood to the heart, and increased venous pressure. Although Valsalvas occur during normal daily activities (breath holding, straining), they can be dangerous for patients with cardiovascular disease. On relaxation, blood rushes to the heart and can overload the cardiac system, resulting in cardiac arrest.

Incorrect Choices:

HR is not elevated. A cholinergic or vagal response is the result of parasympathetic nervous system (PNS) stimulation providing inhibitory control of the vagus nerve over HR and atrioventricular conduction. Pitting edema is caused by long-term factors such as CHF.

Type of Reasoning: Evaluation

The test taker must determine the value and believability of the reasons presented to **AVOID** the Valsalva maneuver, which encourages evaluative reasoning skill. Having knowledge of the Valsalva maneuver and its effects on HR and venous pressure is important for arriving at the correct conclusion for this question. If this question was answered incorrectly, review information on the Valsalva maneuver.

C41

Cardiovascular/Pulmonary and Lymphatic | Evaluation, Diagnosis

A patient experiences color changes in the skin during position changes of the foot. During elevation, pallor develops. When the limb is then positioned in the seated hanging position, hyperemia develops. What do these changes indicate?

Choices:

1. Lymphedema.
2. Arterial insufficiency.
3. Deep vein thrombophlebitis.
4. Chronic venous insufficiency.

Teaching Points

Correct Answer: 2

Arterial insufficiency can be determined by skin color changes during position changes of the foot (termed rubor of dependency test).

Incorrect Choices:

Chronic venous insufficiency can be determined by the history, presence of aching calf pain with prolonged standing, a percussion test in standing, or Trendelenburg's test (retrograde filling test). With chronic venous insufficiency, skin will be dark and cyanotic. Acute deep vein thrombophlebitis (DVT) can be evident with aching calf pain, edema, and muscle tenderness. Lymphedema is evident with visual inspection (i.e., swelling, decreased ROM) and volumetric measurements.

Type of Reasoning: Inference

One must infer the exact meaning of the symptoms presented and then draw conclusions about what the diagnosis may be. Questions that inquire about a possible diagnosis for symptoms presented encourage inferential reasoning skill. If this question was answered incorrectly, refer to information on arterial insufficiency of the lower extremity.

C42

Neuromuscular | Examination

An elderly and frail adult is referred to physical therapy for an examination of balance. The patient has a recent history of falls (two in the last 6 months). Based on knowledge of balance changes in the elderly and scoring of standardized balance measures, which of the following test results **BEST** indicates increased fall risk?

Choices:

1. Tinetti Performance Oriented Mobility Assessment (POMA) score of 27.
2. Functional Reach of 7 inches.
3. Timed Get Up & Go (GUG) test result of 13 seconds.
4. Berg Balance score of 50.

Teaching Points

Correct Answer: 2

All of these instruments can be used to examine functional balance and fall risk. A Functional Reach score of < 10 is indicative of increased fall risk.

Incorrect Choices:

A POMA score of 27 out of a possible 28 is an excellent score. (Scores of < 19 indicate a high risk for falls, whereas scores between 19 and 24 indicate moderate risk for falls). A Berg score of 50 out of a possible 56 points also indicates low fall risk. A Timed GUG score of < 20 seconds for the 3-meter walk and turn test indicates low fall risk (scores > 30 second indicate increased risk).

Type of Reasoning: Deductive

This question requires one to recall factual information about the various tests described in the question and then determine the meaning of the scores (which also encourages some analytical reasoning). Factual knowledge recall often encourages deductive reasoning skill, in which recall of protocols and guidelines are pivotal to arriving at the correct conclusion. For this scenario, Functional Reach of 7 inches is the **BEST** indicator of increased fall risk. If this question was answered incorrectly, review standardized balance tests.

C43 

Gastrointestinal | Evaluation, Diagnosis

During an examination, a patient complains of right upper quadrant pain and tenderness. The PT percusses over the costal margin at the point where the lateral border of the rectus muscle intersects with the costal margin. The patient complains of acute pain and stops inspiratory effort. What does this patient's response indicate?

Choices:

1. Hernia.
2. Acute cholecystitis.
3. Irritation of the psoas muscle by an inflamed appendix.
4. Peritoneal inflammation.

Teaching Points

Correct Answer: 2

Percussion for costovertebral tenderness that reveals a sharp increase in tenderness with a sudden stop in inspiratory effort is a positive Murphy's sign and is indicative of acute cholecystitis.

Incorrect Choices:

An inflamed appendix results in pain in the right lower quadrant during left-sided pressure (positive Rovsing's sign) or right lower quadrant pain on quick withdrawal (referred rebound tenderness). A hernia produces a bulge in the abdominal wall (ventral hernias). Peritoneal inflammation presents with abdominal pain on coughing or with light percussion. Rebound tenderness is also present.

Type of Reasoning: Inference

In order to arrive at a correct conclusion, one must have knowledge of the indications for percussion of the costovertebral angle. This requires inferential reasoning skill, in which one draws conclusions based upon evidence and facts. In this situation, percussion is indicated to reveal acute cholecystitis. If this question was answered incorrectly, review indications for Murphy's percussion.

C44

Cardiovascular/Pulmonary and Lymphatic | Evaluation, Diagnosis

A 72-year-old patient is walking on a treadmill in the physical therapy department while vital signs and pulse oximetry are being monitored. It is noted that the patient's arterial oxygen saturation (SpO_2) drops from 95% to 92%. What is the therapist's **BEST** response to this change?

Choices:

1. Place a 40% O_2 face mask on the patient for the remainder of the exercise session.
2. Not use supplemental O_2.
3. Place 2 L of O_2 by nasal cannula on the patient for the remainder of the exercise session.
4. Place a 100% O_2 face mask on the patient for the remainder of the exercise session.

Teaching Points

Correct Answer: 2

A 72-year-old patient would likely have a resting SpO_2 of 95% from the changes associated with aging alone. There is no need to supplement oxygen in this case.

Incorrect Choices:

The guideline for using supplemental oxygen is a SpO_2 of < 88% or a PaO_2 of < 55 mm Hg. Therefore, the use of oxygen in this scenario is not justified (all other choices). Supplemental O_2 is by prescription only unless it is an emergency.

Type of Reasoning: Inference

One must infer the exact meaning of the symptoms presented from this patient in order to make a determination of the **BEST** course of action. For this situation, the patient's response is within normal parameters and does not require supplemental oxygen. Knowledge of oxygen saturation guidelines is key to arriving at the correct conclusion and should be reviewed if this question was answered incorrectly.

C45

Nonsystem | Equipment, Devices, Biophysical Agents

The therapist is evaluating the needs of a young child who is diagnosed with myelodysplasia at the T10 level. What is the therapist's **BEST** choice of mobility device for this child to use in the school environment?

Choices:

1. Bilateral knee-ankle-foot orthosis (KAFO).
2. Parapodium.
3. Bilateral hip-knee-ankle-foot orthosis (HKAFO).
4. Lightweight wheelchair.

Teaching Points

Correct Answer: 4

The lightweight wheelchair is the **MOST** beneficial choice for this child. It provides effective and efficient mobility.

Incorrect Choices:

Ambulation with orthotic devices at this level lesion requires too much energy and time to be functional. The parapodium permits standing but does not allow for sufficient mobility for the entire school day.

Type of Reasoning: Inductive

One must utilize clinical judgment to determine the **MOST** beneficial mobility device for this child. In order to arrive at the correct conclusion, the test taker must have a thorough understanding of the functional abilities of a child with myelodysplasia at the T10 level. In this case, a lightweight wheelchair is most appropriate because ambulation requires too much energy and time. If this question was answered incorrectly, review information on thoracic myelodysplasia.

C46 

Musculoskeletal | Interventions

A patient has limited right rotation caused by left thoracic facet joint capsular tightness at T6–7. What arthrokinematic glide would **MOST** effectively improve right rotation in sitting?

Choices:

1. Superior and anterior glide on the right T7 transverse process.
2. Superior and anterior glide on the left T7 transverse process.
3. Superior and anterior glide on the right T6 transverse process.
4. Superior and anterior glide on the left T6 transverse process.

Teaching Points

Correct Answer: 4

Because the left thoracic facet joint capsule is restricting movement, motion that would stretch the capsule would facilitate improved right rotation. With right rotation, the left superior facets move upward (opening the joint and stretching the capsule) and the right facets move downward (closing the joint and putting the capsule on relative slack).

Incorrect Choices:

Providing a superior and anterior glide on the right T6 transverse process would improve left rotation. Providing a superior and anterior glide on the left T7 transverse process would improve right rotation at T7–8. Providing a superior and anterior glide on the right T7 transverse process would improve left rotation between T7 and T8.

Type of Reasoning: Inductive

One must utilize clinical judgment to determine the **MOST** effective intervention approach for facilitating improved right rotation. In order to arrive at the correct conclusion, the test taker must have a thorough understanding of normal facet joint capsule motion with rotation. For this patient, a superior and anterior glide to the left T6 transverse process will **MOST** effectively stretch the joint capsule and improve right rotation.

C47

Musculoskeletal | Examination

Which muscles provide fairly continuous activity during quiet standing when measured by EMG?

Choices:

1. Quadriceps femoris and anterior tibialis.
2. Posterior tibialis and intrinsic foot muscles.
3. Anterior tibialis and peroneals.
4. Soleus and gastrocnemius.

Teaching Points

Correct Answer: 4

The soleus and gastrocnemius muscles oppose the dorsiflexion moment that exists at the ankle as a result of the line of gravity, which falls slightly anterior to the lateral malleolus. This fairly continuous activity is crucial for maintaining balance during quiet standing.

Incorrect Choices:

The anterior tibialis, peroneals, and tibialis posterior muscles are inconsistently active and provide transverse stability in the foot during postural sway. The quadriceps femoris and anterior tibialis are active during posterior sway.

Type of Reasoning: Analysis

One must recall the muscles that are active in the lower extremity during erect standing in order to arrive at the correct conclusion. This requires one to analyze the various muscles presented and make a determination of the correct solution, which encourages analytical reasoning skill. Knowledge of lower extremity kinesiology is beneficial to choosing the best solution.

C48

Nonsystem | Safety, Professional Responsibilities, Research

A patient falls while walking in the parallel bars. The therapist is required to fill out an incident report of the event. In addition to the names of those involved, what information is required in an incident report?

Choices:

1. A description of the event, where the patient was injured, and the corrective actions to be taken.
2. Witness reports and therapist's opinion as to the cause.
3. What occurred, when and where it occurred, and witness statements.
4. The cause of this fall and cross-references to others who have fallen in the parallel bars.

Teaching Points

Correct Answer: 3

The typical information included on an incident report are the names of those involved, inclusive of witnesses, what occurred, when it occurred, and where it occurred.

Incorrect Choices:

An incident report should avoid interpretive information such as cause of the occurrence or corrective actions that were taken. There is no presumption that someone was injured.

Type of Reasoning: Evaluation

One must weigh the information presented and determine which statement is most representative of the information that should appear in an incident report. This requires evaluative reasoning skill, in which one uses judgment to determine the most likely correct solution. If this question was answered incorrectly, review information on components of an incident report.

C49 

Cardiovascular/Pulmonary and Lymphatic I Interventions

A therapist is beginning manual lymphatic drainage for a patient recently diagnosed with secondary lymphedema in the left upper extremity following a radical mastectomy. What is the **BEST** choice for initial bandaging of the limb?

Choices:

1. Long-stretch compression wrap (Ace wrap).
2. Custom-made low-elastic garment.
3. Gauze wrap.
4. Short-stretch compression wrap (Comprilan®).

Teaching Points

Correct Answer: 4

A short-stretch wrap has a low resting pressure and high working pressure. This means it has enough pressure to enhance lymphatic return at rest, improve the activity of the lymphangion (contractile unit of the lymphatic system), and facilitate increased return during muscle pumping activities.

Incorrect Choices:

Long-stretch wraps have high resting pressures and low working pressure. The problem with long-stretch wraps (Ace wraps) is they can become like a tourniquet at rest and do not provide enough support during activities. Custom-made, low-elastic garments are not ordered until the limb reduction has reached a plateau, which may take 4–6 months. Gauze wraps provide no support.

Type of Reasoning: Deductive

This question requires the test taker to recall guidelines for lymphedema management in order to arrive at a correct conclusion. This is factual information, which is a deductive reasoning skill. For this scenario, short-stretch compression wrap is required. Refer to manual lymphatic drainage guidelines if answered incorrectly.

C50

Neuromuscular | Evaluation, Diagnosis

An elderly individual was found unconscious at home and was hospitalized with a diagnosis of cerebrovascular accident (CVA). Examination by the PT reveals normal sensation and movement on the right side of the body with impaired sensation (touch, pressure, proprioception) and paralysis on the left side of the body. The left side of the lower face and trunk are similarly impaired. What is the **MOST** likely location of the CVA?

Choices:

1. Left parietal lobe.
2. Right parietal lobe.
3. Left side of brain stem.
4. Spinal cord.

Teaching Points

Correct Answer: 2

This patient demonstrates involvement of the long tracts (sensory and motor) indicative of involvement of the contralateral cerebral cortex, parietal lobe.

Incorrect Choices:

Tracts cross in the medulla so it is the right brain that is involved, not the left. The involvement of the face indicates a lesion above the level of the midbrain. A lesion in the spinal cord would not affect the face. A lesion in the brain stem would produce facial signs contralateral to the limb signs.

Type of Reasoning: Analysis

The test taker must determine the precise location of the lesion given the symptoms presented. Questions that require one to draw conclusions based on symptoms often encourage analytical reasoning skill. For this patient, the symptoms indicate right parietal lobe damage, which should be reviewed if this question was answered incorrectly.

C51

Neuromuscular | Evaluation, Diagnosis

The loss of sensory function in peripheral neuropathy is often among the first noticeable symptoms. With large fiber damage, what is the typical pattern of the sensory loss?

Choices:

1. Allodynia of the feet accompanied by pronounced dorsiflexor weakness.
2. Band-like dysesthesias and paresthesias in the hips and thighs.
3. Paresthesias affecting primarily the proximal limb segments and trunk.
4. Stocking and glove loss of light touch and position sense.

Teaching Points

Correct Answer: 4

Symmetrical involvement of sensory fibers, progressing from distal to proximal, is the hallmark of polyneuropathy. It is termed "stocking and glove distribution" and is the result of the dying back of the longest fibers in all the nerves from distal to proximal. Sensory symptoms include decreased sensation and pain, paresthesias, and dysesthesias (abnormal sensations such as numbness, tingling, or prickling).

Incorrect Choices:

Proximal involvement (hips) can occur, but only after long-standing disease and distal involvement first. Involvement of the trunk is not typical. Allodynia refers to the perception of an ordinarily painless stimulus as painful and is not characteristic of polyneuropathy.

Type of Reasoning: Inference

This question requires one to determine the likely symptoms for polyneuropathy. This necessitates one to make inferences about the nature of polyneuropathy, which is an inferential reasoning skill. Through knowledge of neuropathology, the test taker should determine that polyneuropathy characteristically appears as a stocking-and-glove distribution of the hands and feet.

Cardiovascular/Pulmonary and Lymphatic | Interventions

The PT is supervising a phase II cardiac rehabilitation class of 10 patients. One of the patients, who is being monitored with radiotelemetry, is having difficulty. Which change would be a criterion for terminating this exercise session?

Choices:

1. An increase in systolic BP to 150 and diastolic BP to 90.
2. 1-mm ST segment depression, upsloping.
3. A second-degree atrioventricular (AV) heart block.
4. An increase in HR 20 beats/minute above resting.

Teaching Points

Correct Answer: 3

Criteria for reducing exercise intensity or termination according to the American College of Sports Medicine include (1) onset of angina and other symptoms of exertional intolerance; (2) systolic BP ≥ 240 mm Hg, diastolic BP ≥ 110 mm Hg; (3) > 1-mm ST segment depression, horizontal or downsloping; (4) increased frequency of ventricular arrhythmias; and (5) second-degree or third-degree AV block or other significant electrocardiogram (ECG) disturbances.

Incorrect Choices:

The other findings do not fall within the criteria listed. HR is expected to rise proportionally to workload intensity unless the patient is on beta-blockers. The rise in BP is not significant enough to stop exercise. 1-mm ST segment depression that is isoelectric or within 1 mm is within normal limits.

Type of Reasoning: Analysis

One must determine which symptoms warrant termination of the treatment session and which symptoms merely require monitoring. Through analytical reasoning, the person must interpret the symptoms presented and determine their significance. For this patient, second-degree AV heart block warrants termination of the treatment session. If this question was answered incorrectly, review cardiac rehabilitation guidelines for terminating exercise.

C53

Cardiovascular/Pulmonary and Lymphatic | Interventions

A patient presents with severe claudication that is evident when walking distances greater than 200 feet. The patient also exhibits muscle fatigue and cramping of both calf muscles. Upon examination, the PT finds the skin is pale and shiny with some trophic nail changes. What is the **BEST** choice for this patient's initial exercise program?

Choices:

1. Avoid any exercise stress until the patient has been on calcium channel blockers for at least 2 weeks.
2. Begin with an interval walking program, exercising just to the point of pain.
3. Utilize non–weight-bearing exercises such as cycle ergometry.
4. Utilize a walking program of moderate intensity, instructing the patient that some pain is expected and to be tolerated.

Teaching Points

Correct Answer: 2

This patient is exhibiting classic signs of peripheral artery disease (PAD). Rehabilitation guidelines for arterial disease include using an intermittent walking program of moderate intensity and duration, 2–3 times/day, 3–5 days/wk. The patient should be instructed to exercise to the point of claudication pain within 3–5 minutes, not beyond.

Incorrect Choices:

Exhaustive exercise and exercising with persistent pain are contraindicated. Calcium channel blockers may be used in vasospastic disease; exercise is not contraindicated. A cycle ergometry program is less desirable than a walking program (treadmill or track) to reduce claudication (*ACSM Guidelines for Exercise Testing and Prescription,* 8th ed.).

Type of Reasoning: Inductive

One must utilize clinical judgment to determine the **BEST** choice for intervention, which is an inductive reasoning skill. The test taker must understand what the symptoms are indicative of in order to arrive at the correct conclusion. If this question was answered incorrectly, refer to information on exercise for patients with PAD.

C54

Integumentary | Interventions

A patient is hospitalized with diabetes and a large stage II plantar ulcer located over the right heel. The patient has been non–weight-bearing for the past 2 weeks as a result of the ulcer. What is the **BEST** choice for this patient's initial intervention?

Choices:

1. Wash the foot and apply skin lubricants followed by a transparent film dressing.
2. Clean and bandage with a sterile gauze dressing.
3. Refer the patient for a surgical consult.
4. Clean and debride the wound and apply a hydrogel dressing.

Teaching Points

Correct Answer: 4

A stage II ulcer (deep ulcer) involves a partial-thickness skin loss with involvement of epidermis, dermis, or both; it is reversible. Intervention should be directed toward improving perfusion and relieving localized pressure. The wound should be cleaned with an antimicrobial agent, debrided of necrotic tissue, and covered with a sterile dressing. Hydrogel dressings maintain moisture in the wound bed, soften necrotic tissue, and support autolytic debridement. Pressure relief is also an important consideration. Techniques of protective foot care should be taught.

Incorrect Choices:

Application of a dry, sterile gauze dressing is contraindicated, as is the application of skin lubricants. A stage II ulcer has the potential to heal; a surgical consult is not needed at this time.

Type of Reasoning: Inference

One must utilize clinical judgment and knowledge of wound care approaches to determine the **BEST** intervention approach for this patient, which requires inductive reasoning skill. For this patient, cleaning and debriding of the wound with application of a hydrogel dressing is most appropriate for the type of wound described. If this question was answered incorrectly, review information on wound care procedures for stage II plantar ulcers.

C55 

Nonsystem | Equipment, Devices, Biophysical Agents

A PT is prescribing a wheelchair for a patient with left hemiplegia who is of average height (5 feet 7 inches). Which of the following is the **BEST** choice to improve the patient's function?

Choices:

1. Desk armrests.
2. A 20-inch seat height.
3. A 17.5-inch seat height.
4. Elevating leg rests.

Teaching Points

Correct Answer: 3

A hemi- or low-seat wheelchair has a seat height of 17.5 inches. The lower seat height permits the patient to propel and steer the wheelchair using the sound right upper and lower extremities.

Incorrect Choices:

A wheelchair with a standard seat height (20 inches) is too high to permit efficient use of the sound lower extremity for steering and propulsion. Elevating leg rests may be considered if the patient has problems with edema (not indicated in this case). Shorter-length desk arm rests are a useful option to allow an individual to get close to tables or work surfaces but they are not a priority in this example.

Type of Reasoning: Inference

This question requires one to determine the most beneficial feature in wheelchair prescription for a patient with hemiplegia. This requires knowledge of various wheelchair features and which patient populations derive the most benefit from these features.

C56

Nonsystem | Safety, Professional Responsibilities, Research

A patient who is participating in a cardiac rehabilitation program suddenly collapses and falls to the floor. The PT is the lone rescuer on site. The therapist checks for a response and finds the patient unresponsive. After activating the emergency response system (phone 911), what is the **BEST** action for the therapist to take?

Choices:

1. Use the automated external defibrillator (AED) to shock the patient after 3 minutes of cardiopulmonary resuscitation (CPR).
2. Begin CPR and attach and use the AED as soon as possible.
3. Give 100 chest compressions per minute.
4. Give two rescue breaths followed by 15 chest compressions, repeating the cycle for at least 2 minutes.

Teaching Points

Correct Answer: 2

Guidelines from the American Heart Association (2010) concerning Basic Life Support and CPR specify that the first responder call 911 for unresponsive adults, get an AED (if available), and return to the victim to provide CPR and defibrillation, if needed. Trained HCPs can use ventilations (1 breath every 8 seconds) with chest compressions (at least 100/minute).

Incorrect Choices:

The responder should use the AED as soon as possible after beginning CPR, and not wait 3 minutes. The compression rate for adult CPR is about 100/minute with a recommended compression-to-ventilation ratio of 30:2. The old ratio was 15:2. Untrained rescuers should use compressions only.

Type of Reasoning: Deductive

This question requires one to recall the proper and current Basic Life Support for health care provider guidelines. Questions that ask one to recall knowledge of protocols and guidelines necessitates deductive reasoning skill. If this question was answered incorrectly, refer to current guidelines for CPR.

C57

Musculoskeletal | Evaluation, Diagnosis

A patient who was casted for 3 weeks after a grade III right ankle sprain has been referred to physical therapy for mobility exercises. Examination shows a loss of 10° of dorsiflexion. Which activity will be the **MOST** difficult for the patient?

Choices:

1. Ambulating over rough surfaces.
2. Descending stairs.
3. Ambulating barefoot.
4. Descending a ramp.

Teaching Points

Correct Answer: 2

Loss of dorsiflexion will make descending stairs most difficult because the ankle must have dorsiflexion during the single-limb support phase during descent.

Incorrect Choices:

Although the activity may be changed, full range in dorsiflexion is not needed for the other choices.

Type of Reasoning: Inductive

The test taker must analyze all of the activities and then utilize clinical judgment to determine which activity requires the most ankle dorsiflexion range. This requires inductive reasoning skill, in which clinical judgment is paramount to finding the correct solution. For this patient, descending stairs would be **MOST** difficult because full-range dorsiflexion is required to complete the task successfully.

C58 

Musculoskeletal | Interventions

What is the torque output produced in the sitting position during isokinetic exercise involving the hamstring muscles?

Choices:

1. Higher than the torque actually generated by the contracting hamstrings.
2. Lower because of resistance of the quadriceps.
3. Higher because of eccentric assistance of the quadriceps.
4. Lower than the torque actually generated by the hamstrings.

Teaching Points

Correct Answer: 1

Gravity-produced torque adds to the force generated by the hamstrings when they contract, giving a higher torque output than is actually produced by the muscle (gravity-assisted exercise). Testing values may be misleading; software is available to correct for the effects of gravity.

Incorrect Choices:

Hamstring work is lower, not higher, during this activity. Eccentric assistance by the quadricps (effects of reciprocal inhibition) does not lower or significantly raise the work of the hamstrings but rather serves to smooth out contractions.

Type of Reasoning: Deductive

This question requires one to recall biomechanical guidelines of torque output in exercise. Recall of factual information and guidelines is a deductive reasoning skill. To arrive at the correct conclusion, one must recall that gravity-produced torque adds to the force generated by a contracting muscle, resulting in a higher torque output than what is produced by the muscle itself. If this question was answered incorrectly, review biomechanical guidelines of torque for isokinetic exercises.

C59

Musculoskeletal | Interventions

Which is the **BEST** choice of manual therapy technique to correct a closing restriction of T5 on T6?

Choices:

1. Unilateral posteroanterior (PA) pressure at a 60° angle on the left transverse process of T6 while stabilizing T5.
2. Central PA pressure at a 60° angle on the spinous process of T6 while stabilizing T5.
3. Unilateral PA pressure at a 45° angle on the right transverse process of T6 while stabilizing T5.
4. Central PA pressure at a 45° angle on the spinous process of T5 while stabilizing T6.

Teaching Points

Correct Answer: 2

In a closing restriction, the inferior facets of the superior vertebrae will not inferiorly glide on the superior facets of the inferior vertebra. Therefore, T5 inferior facets will not caudally glide on the superior facets of T6. Stabilizing T5 and application of pressure to T6 localizes the cephalad movement of the superior facets T6 on T5 bilaterally. The angle of the thoracic facets is 60°; therefore, the application of force should be at the same plane.

Incorrect Choices:

Providing the force at 45° does not match the anatomical orientation for the facets in that region so will not be as effective. The force should be a central PA glide because a unilateral glide will promote rotation and/or side-bending rather than extension.

Type of Reasoning: Analysis

Knowledge of anatomy and biomechanics is important for choosing the correct solution for this question. The test taker utilizes analytical reasoning skills, determining the meaning of the four choices and deciding which choice most accurately represents the correct manual therapy technique for a closing restriction of T5 on T6. If this question was answered incorrectly, refer to information on manual therapy for closing restriction of thoracic vertebrae.

C60

Neuromuscular | Evaluation, Diagnosis

A patient presents with an acute onset of vertigo overnight. Symptoms worsen with rapid change in head position. If the head is held still, symptoms subside usually within 30–60 seconds. What is the **MOST** likely cause of these symptoms?

Choices:

1. Ménière's disease.
2. Benign paroxysmal positional vertigo (BPPV).
3. Bilateral vestibular neuritis.
4. Acoustic neuroma.

Teaching Points

Correct Answer: 2

BPPV is characterized by acute onset of vertigo and is positional, related to the provoking stimulus of head movement.

Incorrect Choices:

Vestibular neuritis is an inflammation of the vestibular nerve caused by a virus and typically produces symptoms of dysequilibrium, nystagmus, nausea, and severe vertigo. Ménière's disease is characterized by a sensation of fullness in the ears associated with abnormal fluid buildup. Additional symptoms include tinnitus, vertigo, nausea, and hearing loss. Acoustic neuroma (vestibular schwannoma) produces unilateral sensorineural hearing loss along with vestibular symptoms.

Type of Reasoning: Analysis

One must analyze the symptoms and make a determination of the most likely cause for these symptoms, which requires analytical reasoning skill. For this case, the patient's symptom's **MOST LIKELY** cause is BPPV owing to the nature of an acute onset and being related to changing position of the head. Questions that inquire about a group of symptoms and whereby the test taker must determine the diagnosis often utilize analytical reasoning skill.

C61 

Cardiovascular/Pulmonary and Lymphatic | Evaluation, Diagnosis

A patient with a significant history of coronary artery disease is currently taking atropine. Based on knowledge of this medication, what are the expected effects?

Choices:

1. Increased HR and contractility at rest.
2. Increased myocardial ischemia.
3. Palpitations at rest and with exercise.
4. Orthostatic hypotension.

Teaching Points

Correct Answer: 1

Atropine is an anticholinergic agent (it blocks the action of acetylcholine at parasympathetic sites in smooth muscle, secretory glands, and the central nervous system). It produces an increase in HR and contractility and is used to treat symptomatic sinus bradycardia and exercise-induced bronchospasm.

Incorrect Choices:

The other choices are not expected effects of this medication but rather adverse cardiovascular reactions (not asked for in this question). These can include tachycardia, orthostatic hypotension, palpitations, ventricular fibrillation, and increased ischemia in patients with MI.

Type of Reasoning: Inference

This question requires one to infer the expected effects of atropine, thereby necessitating inferential reasoning skill. For this agent, atropine, one should anticipate possible increased HR and contractility at rest. Knowledge of anticholinergic agents and their effects are beneficial for arriving at the correct conclusion, which should be reviewed if this question was answered incorrectly.

C62

Neuromuscular | Interventions

A patient recovering from stroke is taking warfarin (Coumadin). What potential adverse reactions are associated with this medication?

Choices:

1. Hematuria and ecchymosis.
2. Palpitations and edema.
3. Edema and dermatitis.
4. Cellulitis and xeroderma.

Teaching Points

Correct Answer: 1

Warfarin sodium (Coumadin) is an anticoagulant indicated in the prophylaxis and treatment of venous thrombosis, pulmonary embolism, and thromboembolic disorders. Potential adverse reactions include hematuria and ecchymosis (skin discoloration and hemorrhaging). Serious bleeding is possible with drug toxicity.

Incorrect Choices:

Xeroderma (dry skin), cellulitis (inflammation of tissues), and palpitations (awareness of heart rhythm abnormalities) are not seen as adverse reactions with warfarin.

Type of Reasoning: Inference

One must infer the possible effects of warfarin therapy in order to arrive at the correct conclusion. This requires one to understand the common indications for the drug therapy and adverse side effects. For this medication, one should be watchful for hematuria and ecchymosis because of warfarin's properties of blood thinning. If this question was answered incorrectly, review information on warfarin therapy.

C63

Metabolic/Endocrine | Evaluation, Diagnosis

The PT reviews the laboratory results of a patient admitted to the acute care hospital yesterday: Hematocrit 45%, fasting blood glucose 180 mg/dL, and cholesterol 180 mg/dL. Based on these laboratory results, what condition is **MOST** likely?

Choices:

1. Polycythemia vera.
2. Hyperglycemia of diabetes.
3. Anemia.
4. Hyperlipidemia.

Teaching Points

Correct Answer: 2

Normal fasting blood glucose for adults is 65–99 mg/dL. A fasting blood glucose level of 180mg/dL is abnormal and indicative of hyperglycemia of diabetes.

Incorrect Choices:

The hematocrit and cholesterol readings are within normal limits. Hyperlipidemia (excessive level of lipids in the blood) and anemia (reduced circulating red blood cells [RBCs]) are not indicated. An elevated hematocrit could be indicative of polycythemia vera (proliferation or hyperplasia of all bone marrow cells with an increase of RBCs and hemoglobin concentration).

Type of Reasoning: Analysis

This question requires one to determine the precise meaning of the laboratory values as it relates to a diagnosis for the patient. In this situation, the patient's laboratory values indicate diabetes mellitus. Drawing conclusions based on a group of indicators or symptoms requires analytical reasoning skill. If this question was answered incorrectly, review information on blood glucose laboratory values.

C64 

Neuromuscular | Interventions

A patient recovering from a stroke is having difficulty with stair climbing. During ascent, the patient is able to position the more involved foot on the step above but is unable to transfer the weight up to the next stair level. What is the **BEST** exercise intervention to remediate this problem?

Choices:

1. Bridging, holding.
2. Standing, side steps.
3. Standing, partial wall squats.
4. Plantigrade, knee flexion with hip extension.

Teaching Points

Correct Answer: 3

The quadriceps muscle is responsible for most of the energy generation needed to transfer up stairs to the next level. Partial wall squats are the **BEST** choice to strengthen these muscles (closed-chain exercise). During forward continuance (corresponding to mid-stance), the ankle plantarflexors assist. Hip extensors are also active concentrically, assisting these actions.

Incorrect Choices:

The other choices might be good lead-up activities for gait but would not optimally strengthen the key muscles involved in ascending stairs.

Type of Reasoning: Analysis

This question requires one to analyze the described patient challenge and then determine the **BEST** intervention. The test taker must determine what the cause is for the patient who has difficulty transferring weight to ascend stairs, which necessitates analytical reasoning. After analyzing the situation, one should conclude that the quadriceps muscle is weak and that partial wall squats in standing would **BEST** address this issue.

C65

Cardiovascular/Pulmonary and Lymphatic I Evaluation, Diagnosis

An elderly patient has been hospitalized and on complete bed rest for 10 days. A physical therapy referral requests mobilization out of bed and ambulation. The patient complains of aching in the right calf. The therapist's examination reveals calf tenderness with slight swelling and warmth. What is the **BEST** course of action for the therapist?

Choices:

1. Begin with ankle pump exercises in bed and then ambulate.
2. Postpone ambulation and report the findings immediately.
3. Ambulate the patient with support stockings on.
4. Use only AROM exercises with the patient sitting at the edge of the bed.

Teaching Points

Correct Answer: 2

The patient is exhibiting early signs of acute deep vein thrombophlebitis (DVT). These findings should be reported immediately.

Incorrect Choices:

If DVT is present, the patient will be given anticoagulation therapy. After one dose of low molecular weight heparin, ambulation is encouraged. Compression stockings with a pressure gradient of 30–40 mm Hg can assist with pain and reduce the risk of post-thrombolytic syndrome.

Type of Reasoning: Evaluation

One must evaluate the patient's symptoms and determine the best course of action, given one's understanding of the symptoms. Here, the patient's symptoms are indicative of DVT, which necessitates immediate notification and postponement of ambulation. If this question was answered incorrectly, refer to information on DVT and appropriate actions.

C66

Neuromuscular I Examination

A 9-year-old boy with Duchenne's muscular dystrophy is referred for home care. How should the therapist begin the examination?

Choices:

1. Ask the parents to outline the boy's past rehabilitation successes.
2. Ask the child and his parents to describe the boy's most serious functional limitations.
3. Perform a complete motor examination.
4. Perform a functional examination using the weeFIM.

Teaching Points

Correct Answer: 2

The child and his parents/caretakers play an important part in determining impairments, functional limitations, disability, and future interventions. Taking a thorough initial history is important in determining what other components of the examination would be appropriate.

Incorrect Choices:

The other choices may indeed be appropriate; however, performing the interview first helps decide which examination tools are needed.

Type of Reasoning: Inductive

Questions such as these are difficult because one must determine what comes first in a process, especially when all the potential choices can be correct in the evaluation of a patient. For this question, the other choices are appropriate when conducting an examination, but the test taker must determine which one most logically should come first. This requires clinical judgment, an inductive reasoning skill.

C67 

Musculoskeletal | Evaluation, Diagnosis

During an examination of an adolescent female who complains of anterior knee pain, the PT observes that the lower extremity shows medial femoral torsion and toeing-in position of the feet. What pathology of the hip is commonly associated with medial femoral torsion and toeing-in?

Choices:

1. Retroversion.
2. Anteversion.
3. Medial/internal rotation.
4. Lateral/external rotation.

Teaching Points

Correct Answer: 2

The pathology commonly associated with medial femoral torsion and toeing-in is hip anteversion due to an increase in the antetorsion angle (> 15°) between the femoral condyles and the neck of the femur.

Incorrect Choices:

Excessive internal or external rotation of the hip would not force the patient to stand with toeing-in. Retroversion of the hips would cause the feet to toe-out.

Type of Reasoning: Analysis

This question provides the symptoms, and the test taker must determine the likely cause, which requires analytical reasoning skill. Here, the symptoms are analyzed in order to make a determination for the cause of this patient's medial femoral torsion and toeing-in position of the feet. The test taker should conclude that excessive hip anteversion is the cause, which should be reviewed if this question was answered incorrectly.

C68

Musculoskeletal | Interventions

A patient with osteoporosis and no fractures complains of increased middle and lower back pain during breathing and other functional activities. What is the **MOST** beneficial exercise intervention for this patient?

Choices:

1. Trunk flexion and rotation exercises.
2. Trunk flexion and extension exercises.
3. Trunk extension and abdominal stabilization exercises.
4. Trunk rotation and abdominal stabilization exercises.

Teaching Points

Correct Answer: 3

It is important to strengthen from the core to the floor as well as train in proprioception and balance enhancement techniques. Trunk extension and abdominal stabilization exercises are indicated.

Incorrect Choices:

Patients should avoid trunk flexion or rotation exercise because it can cause a compression fracture of the spine.

Type of Reasoning: Inference

One must determine first what may be the cause of the patient's pain and then determine the intervention approach that will **BEST** remedy the symptoms. If this question was answered incorrectly, refer to intervention approaches for osteoporosis.

C69

Nonsystem | Safety, Professional Responsibilities, Research

A single 22-year-old woman who is 3 months pregnant arrives at a therapist's private practice complaining of shoulder and leg pain. She has a black eye and some bruising at the wrists. The state in which the therapist practices has direct access. What is the **BEST** course of action for the therapist?

Choices:

1. Examine the patient, and if abuse is suspected, report the findings to the appropriate authorities.
2. Administer massage for bruising, TENS, and ice modalities for pain, as indicated by the examination findings.
3. Direct the patient to the nearest ambulatory care center for physician evaluation.
4. Refuse to examine the patient and send her to the nearest emergency room.

Teaching Points

Correct Answer: 1

According to the American Physical Therapy Association's (APTA's) Guidelines for Recognizing and Providing Care for Victims of Domestic Violence, this patient falls into a category of high risk. Women between the ages of 17 and 28 years and women who are single, separated, or divorced or who are planning a separation or divorce are at high risk. Battered women usually have more than one injury. Most injuries occur in the head, face, neck, breasts, and abdomen. According to the American Medical Association (AMA), battered women represent 23% of pregnant women who seek prenatal care. The victim may not volunteer information about her situation, but more often than not when asked will reveal it. It is important for the PT to examine the patient and, if abuse is suspected, report the findings to appropriate authorities. The therapist should be familiar with resources available for victims of domestic violence and their own state reporting laws.

Incorrect Choices:

In most state jurisdictions, a PT may be fined or indicted for failure to report (all other choices).

Type of Reasoning: Evaluation

This question requires one to make a judgment call for the **BEST** course of action, given the patient's symptoms. Questions that necessitate professional judgment in ethical situations often utilize evaluative reasoning skill, in which the merits of each potential choice are weighed. For this patient, it is important to do a comprehensive examination and then, if abuse is suspected, report it to the appropriate authorities.

C70

Nonsystem | Equipment, Devices, Biophysical Agents

An elderly patient presents with a stage III decubitus ulcer on the plantar surface of the right foot. After a series of conservative interventions with limited success, the therapist chooses to apply electrical stimulation for tissue repair. What is the **BEST** electrical current to administer in this case?

Choices:

1. Medium-frequency burst current.
2. High-volt monophasic pulsed current.
3. Medium-frequency beat current.
4. Low-volt biphasic pulsed current.

Teaching Points

Correct Answer: 2

Because high-volt pulsed current is a monophasic, unidirectional current, the unidirectional current would produce a therapeutic effect at the active (treatment) electrode. A negative charge (polarity) should be applied for a bactericidal effect or a positive charge given to promote wound healing.

Incorrect Choices:

A biphasic current, which alternates the polarity, would tend to negate the treatment effects. Russian (burst) and interferential (beat) are medium-frequency biphasic currents. Interrupted currents (> 0.5-second interruption) are also not used for tissue healing.

Type of Reasoning: Deductive

One must recall the appropriate electrical stimulation parameters to treat the patient's condition, which requires deductive reasoning skill. One must recall the differences between currents of differing low-, medium-, and high-volt currents, as well as pulsed, burst, and beat current, and the therapeutic effects on wound healing. If this question was answered incorrectly, review guidelines for electrical stimulation for wound healing.

C71

Nonsystem | Equipment, Devices, Biophysical Agents

A patient presents with pain radiating down the posterior hip and thigh as a result of a herniated disc in the lumbar spine. The therapist decides to apply mechanical traction. If the patient can tolerate it, what is the preferred patient position?

Choices:

1. Supine with one knee flexed.
2. Prone with pillow under the abdomen.
3. Supine with both knees flexed.
4. Prone with no pillow.

Teaching Points

Correct Answer: 4

Placing the patient in the prone position would better align the spine so that the pull of the traction would be along the axis of the vertebral bodies.

Incorrect Choices:

If the prone position is intolerable, then a pillow may be placed under the abdomen. Flexing the spine could exacerbate the disc herniation. A supine, knee-flexed position can be used for spinal stenosis.

Type of Reasoning: Inductive

The test taker must determine which patient position is **PREFERRED** for mechanical traction for a herniated lumbar disc. This requires recall of traction guidelines, but also clinical judgment to determine the correct solution, which necessitates inductive reasoning. Some other positions are acceptable but not preferred. If this question was answered incorrectly, review guidelines for mechanical traction for lumbar disk herniation.

C72

Neuromuscular | Interventions

A patient recovering from stroke demonstrates hemiparesis of the right upper extremity with moderate flexion and extension synergies (flexion stronger than extension). The therapist's goal is to strengthen the shoulder muscles first to promote elevation of the arm. What is the **BEST** exercise intervention to achieve this goal?

Choices:

1. Shoulder abduction with elbow flexion.
2. Shoulder flexion with elbow extension.
3. Shoulder horizontal adduction with elbow extension.
4. Shoulder horizontal adduction with elbow flexion.

Teaching Points

Correct Answer: 2

Obligatory hemiplegic synergies are present and should not be reinforced. Shoulder flexion with elbow extension is the correct choice. It is an out-of-synergy combination that strengthens the shoulder flexors needed to stabilize the shoulder in an elevated functional position. In sitting, bending forward with elbow straight and hand touching floor is a good example of an early activity to promote this.

Incorrect Choices:

Shoulder abduction with elbow flexion is part of the flexion synergy, whereas adduction with elbow extension is part of the extension synergy. Adduction with elbow flexion is an out-of-synergy combination but does not strengthen muscles needed to elevate and stabilize the upper extremity.

Type of Reasoning: Inference

One must evaluate the patient's symptoms and infer the **BEST** method for strengthening the shoulder muscles, thereby requiring inferential reasoning. Given the diagnosis and current status, shoulder flexion with elbow extension is **BEST** because hemiplegic synergies are discouraged using this approach. If this question was answered incorrectly, review limb synergies with stroke and out-of-synergy movement patterns.

C73 

Neuromuscular | Examination

A physical therapist shines a light into a patient's eye and observes the pupil of the eye. Constriction of the pupil results. Which cranial nerve is being tested?

Choices:

1. Abducens.
2. Trochlear.
3. Optic.
4. Oculomotor.

Teaching Points

Correct Answer: 4

The pupillary reflex (constriction of the pupil) is a function of the efferent portion of the oculomotor nerve (CN III).

Incorrect Choices:

The optic nerve (CN II) provides afferent signals to the brain and functions for visual acuity (interpretation of visual information). The trochlear nerve (CN IV) innervates the superior oblique muscles and helps to control extraocular eye movements (responsible for downward and lateral eye movements). The abducens nerve (CN VI) innervates the lateral rectus and helps to control extraocular eye movements (lateral eye movements).

Type of Reasoning: Deductive

This question necessitates factual recall of guidelines for testing the function of the cranial nerves in order to arrive at a correct conclusion. Questions of this nature often necessitate deductive reasoning skill, where recall of facts is used to make decisions. In this case, the description of the test performed is testing functioning of the oculomotor nerve (CN III). If answered incorrectly, review guidelines for testing the cranial nerves, especially CN III.

C74 

Cardiovascular/Pulmonary and Lymphatic | Examination

A patient is referred for physical therapy after a graded exercise test (GXT). The physician reports the test was positive and had to be terminated at 7 minutes. Which of the following criteria is an absolute indication for terminating exercise testing?

Choices:

1. Mild angina and dyspnea with progressive increases in the treadmill speed and grade.
2. A hypertensive response with blood pressure of at least 170/95.
3. ST segment depression from baseline of 3-mm horizontal or downsloping depression.
4. ECG changes from baseline of 1-mm ST segment elevation.

Teaching Points

Correct Answer: 3

A positive GXT indicates myocardial ischemia with increasing exercise intensities. The optimal test duration is 8–12 minutes but can be terminated if symptoms of exertional intolerance are evident. The American College of Sports Medicine (ACSM) indicates these include ECG changes from baseline (> 2 mm horizontal or downsloping; ST segment depression, or > 2 mm ST segment elevation).

Incorrect Choices:

Additional signs of exertional intolerance that indicate the test should be terminated include onset of moderate to severe angina (some angina is expected with increasing work), a drop in systolic BP with increasing workload, serious arrhythmias, signs of exertional intolerance (pallor, cyanosis, cold or clammy skin), unusual or severe shortness of breath (some shortness of breath is expected), CNS signs (ataxia, vertigo, visual or gait problems, confusion), and a hypertensive response equal to or greater than 260/115 (a BP of 170/95 is not a reason for stopping the test) (*ACSM Guidelines for Exercise Testing and Prescription*, 8th ed.).

Type of Reasoning: Inference

This question requires one to infer information based on the evidence presented. In this case, the test taker must infer what a positive GXT indicates an early termination of the test after 7 minutes. If this question was answered incorrectly, refer to information on exercise tolerance testing and ACSM guidelines for terminating the test.

..eletal | Evaluation, Diagnosis

..ege soccer player sustained a hyperextension knee injury when kicking the ball with the other lower ..xtremity. The patient was taken to the emergency room of a local hospital and was diagnosed with "knee sprain." The patient was sent to physical therapy the next day for rehabilitation. As part of the examination, the therapist conducts the test shown in the figure. Based on a positive test, what type of exercise intervention is indicated during the acute phase of treatment?

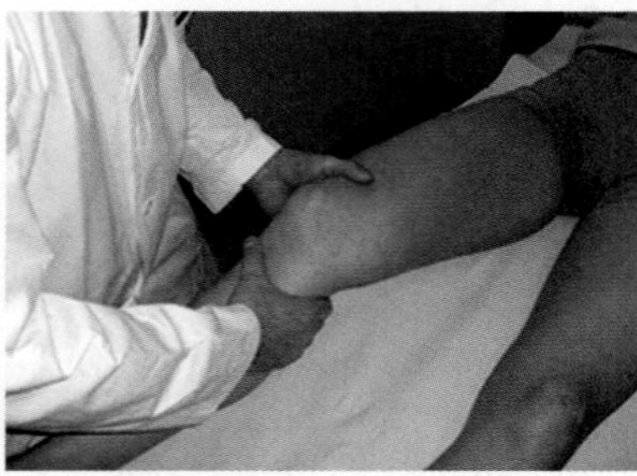

Choices:

1. Open-chain terminal knee extension exercises.
2. Closed-chain terminal knee extension exercises.
3. Plyometric functional exercises.
4. Agility exercises.

Teaching Points

Correct Answer: 2

The test that was conducted was a Lachman's test to determine integrity of the ACL. A positive test suggests laxity of the ACL. Closed-chain terminal knee extension exercises are safe and effective secondary to the dynamic stability inherent with this type of exercise.

Incorrect Choices:

Quick cutting/lateral movements that occur in agility training and heavy joint loading that occurs with plyometric exercise should be avoided until the muscular restraints that reduce excessive anterior translation of the affected tibiofemoral joint are strengthened. Open-chain knee extension may place excessive load on the ACL.

Type of Reasoning: Analysis

Questions that include analysis of information depicted in pictures often necessitate analytical reasoning skill. This question requires one to determine what type of test is being depicted in the picture and then determine, upon positive result, the best exercise approach. This picture depicts a Lachman's test for determining ACL integrity. The positive test indicates laxity of the ACL and that closed-chain terminal knee extension exercises are best.

C76

Integumentary | Interventions

A patient with a grade III diabetic ulcer is being treated with a calcium alginate wound dressing. What are the primary indications for this type of wound dressing?

Choices:

1. Provide semirigid support for the limb while maintaining a sterile field.
2. Facilitate autolytic debridement and absorb exudate.
3. Absorb exudate and allow rapid moisture evaporation.
4. Restrict bacteria from the wound while supporting the tissues.

Teaching Points

Correct Answer: 2

Moisture-retentive occlusive wound dressings such as calcium alginate are recommended for use on exudating wounds (grade III ulcer). They maintain a moist wound environment, absorb exudate, provide autolytic debridement, reduce pain at the wound site, or promote faster healing (reepithelialization).

Incorrect Choices:

Calcium alginate dressings do **NOT** allow rapid evaporation. A disadvantage is that the dressing is very permeable to bacteria, urine, and so forth. Unna's boot is a semi-rigid dressing that provides limb support.

Type of Reasoning: Deductive

This question requires one to recall the properties of a calcium alginate wound dressing. Recall of protocols and guidelines and other types of factual information often require deductive reasoning skill. For this question, calcium alginate dressings can be expected to facilitate autolytic debridement and absorption of exudate. If this question was answered incorrectly, review information on calcium alginate and other wound dressings.

C77

Nonsystem | Safety, Professional Responsibilities, Research

The PT receives a referral to treat a hospitalized patient with adhesive capsulitis. The patient is recovering from a recent hepatitis B infection. What precautions should the therapist observe?

Choices:

1. Use droplet transmission precautions.
2. Use contact precautions.
3. Ask the patient to wear gloves and avoid contact.
4. Wear personal protection equipment (PPE) when transporting the patient to therapy.

Teaching Points

Correct Answer: 2

Hepatitis B is a viral infection that is transmitted by close contact with the infected patient's body fluids (nasopharyngeal exudate, saliva, sweat, urine, feces, semen, vaginal secretions) and blood and blood products. Health care workers should be vaccinated against the possibility of infection because they are in a high-risk category. Contact precautions should be observed to reduce the risk of microorganism transmission by direct or indirect contact (refer to Box 6-1, Standard Precautions, Chapter 6).

Incorrect Choices:

Droplet precautions are used when microorganisms can be transmitted by the patient during coughing, sneezing, or talking. The therapist should wear PPE, gloves, and gowns when in direct contact with the patient. The patient does not wear the gloves.

Type of Reasoning: Deductive

This question causes one to recall the guidelines for standard precautions when working with a patient who has a history of cirrhosis and hepatitis B. The recall of guidelines is factual in nature and necessitates deductive reasoning skill. One must recall how hepatitis B is transmitted to arrive at the correct conclusion. For this patient, the therapist should avoid direct exposure to any blood or body fluids.

C78

Musculoskeletal | Evaluation, Diagnosis

A patient with a transtibial amputation is learning to walk using a patellar tendon-bearing (PTB) prosthesis and is having difficulty maintaining knee stability from heelstrike to foot-flat. Which muscles are **MOST** likely weak?

Choices:

1. Hip flexors.
2. Back extensors.
3. Knee extensors.
4. Knee flexors.

Teaching Points

Correct Answer: 3

The knee extensors (quadriceps) are maximally active at heelstrike (initial contact) to stabilize the knee and counteract the flexion moment.

Incorrect Choices:

Erector spinae, gluteus maximus, and hamstrings contribute to core stability (trunk and pelvis) and assist in counteracting the flexion moment from heelstrike to foot-flat. Hip flexors contribute to initiate swing (acceleration to midswing), whereas knee flexors (hamstrings) decelerate the momentum of the swinging leg (midswing to deceleration).

Type of Reasoning: Inference

One must infer the reason for the difficulty in maintaining prosthetic stability in order to choose the correct solution. This requires inferential reasoning, where one must determine the muscles that are **MOST LIKELY** weak.

C79 

Cardiovascular/Pulmonary and Lymphatic | Evaluation, Diagnosis

A patient with a history of coronary artery disease and recent myocardial infarction (MI) is exercising in an inpatient cardiac rehabilitation program. Because the patient is new, continuous ECG telemetry monitoring is being done. The therapist observes the following. What is the therapist's **BEST** course of action?

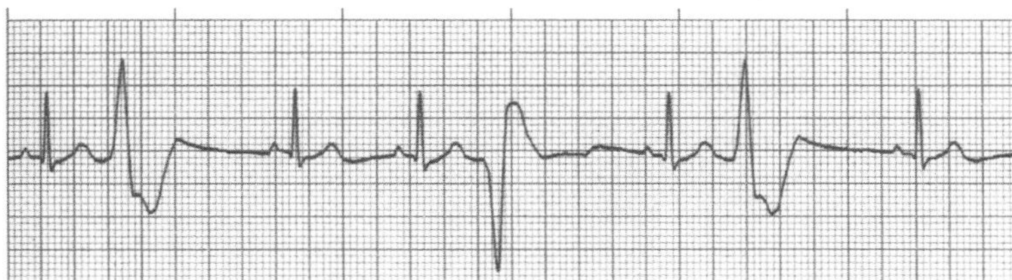

From: Jones, S (2005) ECG Notes. Philadelphia, F.A. Davis, p.51, with permission.

Choices:

1. Have the patient sit down, continue monitoring, and notify the physician immediately.
2. Activate the emergency medical response team.
3. Have the patient sit down, rest, and then resume the exercise at a lower intensity.
4. Have the patient sit down and send him/her back to the room after a brief rest period.

Teaching Points

Correct Answer: 1

This tracing shows premature ventricular contractions (PVCs) that are multifocal (originating from different irritable ventricular focus). These multiform PVCs pose a potential danger of deteriorating into ventricular tachycardia and ventricular fibrillation (cardiac standstill). Because the heart is demonstrating a high degree of irritability, the **BEST** course of action is to stop the exercise, have the patient sit down, continue monitoring carefully, and notify medical staff (attending physician) immediately.

Incorrect Choices:

Failure to report this finding by allowing the patient to rest or return to the room can be life-threatening. The patient has not arrested; therefore, the emergency medical response team should not be activated.

Type of Reasoning: Evaluation

This question actually couples two types of reasoning. First, analytical reasoning is used to evaluate the information depicted in the picture. However, ultimately, evaluative reasoning skills are used to determine the **BEST** course of action, given the information presented. For this patient, the information indicated multifocal PVCs and necessitates termination of exercise with careful monitoring and notification of the physician. If this question was answered incorrectly, refer to information on ECG interpretations and PVCs.

C80 

Neuromuscular | Interventions

A patient recovering from traumatic brain injury (TBI) is unable to bring the right foot up on the step during stair climbing training. What is the **BEST** choice to promote independent stair climbing for this patient?

Choices:

1. Practice marching in place.
2. Strengthen the hip flexors using an isokinetic training device before attempting stair climbing.
3. Passively bring the foot up and place it on the 7-inch step.
4. Practice stair climbing inside the parallel bars using a 3-inch step.

Teaching Points

Correct Answer: 4

The most appropriate lead-up activity to promote the skill of stair climbing is practice using a 3-inch step in the parallel bars.

Incorrect Choices:

Passive movements do not promote active learning. Marching in place and isokinetic training may improve the strength of the hip flexors but do not promote the same synergistic patterns of muscle activity as the desired skill.

Type of Reasoning: Inductive

One must determine through clinical judgment the **BEST** approach for promoting the skill of stair climbing. This question requires inductive reasoning skill, in which the test taker must first determine the problem and then judge which intervention approach leads up to improving stair climbing ability. If this question was answered incorrectly, review information on exercises to promote stair negotiation.

C81 

System Interactions | Evaluation, Diagnosis

The PT is completing general activity recommendations for a group home of young adults with emotional and behavioral issues. All patients are chemically controlled with either antipsychotic or antidepressant medications. Full-time supervision is available for any activity recommended. Which exercise precautions would be important for the therapist to include?

Choices:

1. Avoid games with throwing activities to prevent injuries.
2. Promote rhythmic movement to soothing music to avoid agitation.
3. Promote activities with sequential movements to improve memory.
4. Avoid aerobic exercises outdoors when temperature is over 90°F.

Teaching Points

Correct Answer: 4

Overheating is detrimental to individuals on antipsychotic or antidepressant medications.

Incorrect Choices:

Assumptions of agitation, memory deficits, or violence in such populations are discriminatory and inaccurate. Although an individual client may demonstrate these, it is inaccurate to suggest these for a group without further individual information.

Type of Reasoning: Inference

This question requires one to have knowledge of the adverse/side effects of antipsychotic and antidepressant medications in order to arrive at a correct conclusion. In this situation, the potential adverse effect is overheating; therefore, avoiding aerobic exercise outdoors in temperatures over 90°F is the **MOST** appropriate precaution. If this question was answered incorrectly, review information on adverse effects of antipsychotics and antidepressants.

Neuromuscular | Examination

Following an initial functional examination using the Functional Independence Measure (FIM), a patient is found to require minimal contact assistance in transferring from sit-to-stand and bed-to-wheelchair. Which of the following accurately documents these results?

Choices:

1. FIM level 4; completes activity with 75% or more of the effort.
2. FIM level 6; completes activity with extra time.
3. FIM level 5; completes activity with cueing.
4. FIM level 3; completes activity with 50% or more but less than 75% of the effort.

Teaching Points

Correct Answer: 1

This patient's performance is best categorized by FIM level 4 (completes activity with minimal contact assistance and 75% or more of the effort).

Incorrect Choices:

With FIM level 3 grades, the patient requires moderate assistance and completes activity with 50% or more but less than 75% of the effort. FIM level 5 grade specifies completes activity with cueing or standby assistance but no manual contact. FIM level 6 (modified independence) does not permit manual contact and allows for equipment or extra time.

Type of Reasoning: Deductive

This question requires one to recall the Functional Independence Measure (FIM) scale and to match the scale scores to the performance indicated with this patient. This is factual recall of knowledge, which is a deductive reasoning skill. In this case, the patient's performance indicates minimal assist (level 4). If answered incorrectly, review the FIM.

C83 

Neuromuscular | Interventions

The therapist is on a home visit, scheduled at lunchtime, visiting an 18-month-old child with moderate developmental delay. The therapist notices that the child and mother are experiencing difficulties with feeding. The child is slumped down in the highchair and is unsuccessfully attempting to use a raking grasp to lift cereal pieces to the mouth. Both the child and the mother are frustrated. Which intervention should the therapist work on **FIRST?**

Choices:

1. Recommend that the mother return to breastfeeding for a few more months.
2. Work on desensitizing the gag reflex.
3. Recommend that the mother feed the child baby food instead of cereal for a few more months.
4. Reposition the child in a proper sitting position using postural supports.

Teaching Points

Correct Answer: 4

Feeding can be successful only if the child is positioned in a stable sitting posture: Head upright, trunk erect with pelvis neutral and hips flexed to 90°, and feet resting flat. Correct positioning in sitting will facilitate upper extremity function (grasp and release) as well as swallowing.

Incorrect Choices:

The other choices fail to address the central problem in this case, lack of postural support. Changing the child's diet (baby food or breast milk) will not improve the functional skill of feeding.

Type of Reasoning: Inductive

One must determine what should happen **FIRST** when providing interventions for this child. This requires inductive reasoning skill, in which clinical judgment is utilized to determine a best course of action. For this child, the **FIRST** intervention should be to reposition the child in proper sitting and utilize postural supports.

C84 

Musculoskeletal | Interventions

A patient is referred to physical therapy with a diagnosis of "frozen shoulder." Which of the following is the **BEST** choice of technique to mobilize the shoulder?

Choices:

1. Lateral glide in neutral position.
2. Inferior glide at 55° of abduction.
3. Posterior glide at 10° of abduction.
4. Inferior glide at 95° of abduction.

Teaching Points

Correct Answer: 2

The convex-concave rule for mobilization applies. The **MOST** effective position to mobilize for improved shoulder abduction is in the resting position (55°). Because the convex humeral head is moving on the concave glenoid, an inferior glide would be **MOST** appropriate to improve shoulder abduction.

Incorrect Choices:

A posterior glide would improve external rotation. An inferior glide at 95° would be outside the normal glenohumeral joints resting position so this technique would not be optimal. A lateral glide (anatomical distraction) is a generic technique that is nonspecific for any one motion and is, therefore, not the best choice.

Type of Reasoning: Analysis

One must have knowledge of biomechanics and kinesiology in order to arrive at the correct conclusion. In addition, one should understand the diagnosis of frozen shoulder (adhesive capsulitis) and appropriate joint mobilization techniques. This necessitates analytical reasoning skill, in which one must interpret the information presented and determine its precise meaning. If this question was answered incorrectly, review joint mobilization guidelines for treatment of adhesive capsulitis.

C85 

Musculoskeletal | Evaluation, Diagnosis

A patient presents with insidious onset of pain in the jaw that is referred to the head and neck regions. As best as the patient can recall, it may be related to biting into something hard. Cervical ROM is limited in flexion by 20°, cervical lateral flexion limited to the left by 10°. Mandibular depression is 10 mm with deviation to the left, protrusion is 4 mm, and lateral deviation is 15 mm to the right and 6 mm to the left. What is the **MOST** likely diagnosis given this patient's symptoms?

Choices:

1. Weak lateral pterygoids on the right.
2. Weak lateral pterygoids on the left.
3. Capsule-ligamentous pattern of temporomandibular joint (TMJ) on the left.
4. Cervical spine and TMJ capsular restrictions on the left.

Teaching Points

Correct Answer: 3

The capsule-ligamentous pattern of the TMJ is limitation on opening, lateral deviation greater to the uninvolved side and deviation on opening to the involved side. Normal parameters for TMJ measures are 25–35 mm functional and 35–50 mm normal, normal protrusion is 3–6 mm and normal lateral deviation is 10–15 mm.

Incorrect Choices:

Weakness of the lateral pterygoids presents as deviation on protrusion to the opposite side of the muscle weakness. A capsular pattern of the cervical spine presents as side flexion and rotation, equally limited, and extension.

Type of Reasoning: Analysis

Questions that inquire about a potential diagnosis given a patient's symptoms necessitate analytical reasoning skill. This is because one must weigh the information and analyze the symptoms in order to reach a conclusion that the diagnosis is most likely capsule-ligamentous pattern of TMJ on the left. If this question was answered incorrectly, review information on symptoms of TMJ.

C86 

Neuromuscular | Evaluation, Diagnosis

A patient has been referred to physical therapy with a diagnosis of cervicogenic headaches. During the initial examination, the therapist notes clinical findings of a droopy eyelid, constricted pupil (a pinpoint pupil), and lack of sweating on the same side of the face. What is the **MOST** likely diagnosis based on this group of symptoms?

Choices:

1. Horner's syndrome.
2. Bell's palsy.
3. Trigeminal neuralgia.
4. Myasthenia gravis.

Teaching Points

Correct Answer: 1

The hallmark finding of Horner's syndrome is the clinical triad of ptosis (droopy eyelid), miosis (pupillary constriction), and anhydrosis (lack of sweating), all on the same side of the face and ipsilateral to the lesion. Skin vasodilation is also typically present. Horner's syndrome results from a lesion that affects the sympathetic pathway to the head. The syndrome may be caused by trauma, interruption of blood supply, tumors, or cluster headaches. Cranial nerve III, the oculomotor nerve, contains parasympathetic fibers that innervate the pupillary constrictor muscle. Therefore, loss of sympathetic innervation of the pupillary dilator muscle results in unopposed pupillary constriction.

Incorrect Choices:

Bell's palsy is an idiopathic lesion to CN VII, the facial nerve. This is a lower motor neuron or peripheral nerve lesion that results in paralysis or weakness of the muscles of facial expression on the same side as the lesion. Trigeminal neuralgia (tic douloureux) is a pain syndrome that involves CN V, the trigeminal nerve. The three branches (mandibular, maxillary, and ophthalmic) of CN V provide general sensation to the skin of the face, as well as the lips, corneas, and anterior one third of the tongue. Trigeminal neuralgia produces severe, sharp, stabbing pain in the distribution of one or more of the branches of the nerve. Common causes of the disorder include a peripheral lesion to the nerve, hyperexcitability of damaged fibers in the large trigeminal nerve ganglion, or pressure of a blood vessel on the nerve. Myasthenia gravis is an auto-immune disease of the neuromuscular junction resulting in severe muscle weakness, most notably with repeated contractions. While ptosis is a common finding in myasthenia gravis, none of the other findings in the scenario are consistent with the disorder.

Type of Reasoning: Analysis

This question provides a group of symptoms, and the test taker must determine the most likely diagnosis. This requires analytical reasoning skill, where pieces of information are analyzed in order to reach a sound conclusion about them. For this situation, the symptoms are indicative of Horner's syndrome. Review symptoms of Horner's syndrome if answered incorrectly.

C87 

Cardiovascular/Pulmonary and Lymphatic | Evaluation, Diagnosis

A patient with a recent history of rib fractures suddenly becomes short of breath during a bout of coughing. The patient looks panicked and complains of sharp pain in the left chest. A quick screen shows a deviated trachea to the right, among other signs and symptoms. What is the **MOST** likely diagnosis based on these symptoms?

Choices:

1. Pulmonary emboli.
2. Pneumothorax.
3. Angina.
4. Mucous plugging of an airway.

Teaching Points

Correct Answer: 2

The deviation of the trachea toward the right with the chest pain on the left is a match of symptoms for the occurrence of a pneumothorax on the left. The history of a rib fracture makes pneumothorax all the more likely.

Incorrect Choices:

Whereas all of the pathologies listed would cause panic on the part of the patient, mucous plugging of an airway would not cause pain. The deviation of the trachea would not result from angina or pulmonary emboli, but would happen with a pneumothorax and lung tissue collapse (which could result from mucous plugging).

Type of Reasoning: Analysis

This question provides symptoms, and the test taker must determine a cause for them. This necessitates analytical reasoning skill, in which one must produce the correct diagnosis based on the patient's symptoms. If this question was answered incorrectly, review information of symptoms of pneumothorax.

C88 

Musculoskeletal | Interventions

A patient presents with supraspinatus tendinitis. After the initial cryotherapy, the therapist decides to apply ultrasound (US). In what position should the therapist place the shoulder joint in order to effectively treat the supraspinatus tendon?

Choices:

1. Adduction and external rotation.
2. Slight abduction and internal rotation.
3. Adduction and internal rotation.
4. Slight abduction and external rotation.

Teaching Points

Correct Answer: 2

Abduction and internal rotation of the shoulder places the supraspinatus tendon in a good position to apply US by exposing the tendon from under the acromion process.

Incorrect Choices:

The other choices fail to position the supraspinatus tendon in optimal position.

Type of Reasoning: Inductive

One must utilize diagnostic and clinical judgment to determine the best course of action when providing US for supraspinatus tendinitis. Questions that require clinical and diagnostic reasoning utilize inductive reasoning skill.

C89 

Integumentary | Examination

A patient is referred for postmastectomy rehabilitation. During the initial examination, the therapist observes an irregular area of skin on the patient's shoulder about 7 mm in diameter. The patient reports that there has always been a mole there but is more prominent lately and that the color has changed, now ranging from black to red to blue. How should the therapist document this finding?

Choices:

1. Papule.
2. Wheal.
3. Atypical dysplastic nevus.
4. Benign nevus.

Teaching Points

Correct Answer: 3

A nevus is a common mole. A changing nevus (atypical dysplastic nevus) that presents with asymmetry (A), irregular borders (B), variations in color (C), diameter > 6 mm (D), and elevation (E) may be indicative of malignant melanoma (the "ABCDEs" from the American Cancer Society).

Incorrect Choices:

A benign nevus does not present with changes and variations in color. A papule is an elevated nevus. A wheal is an irregular, transient superficial area of localized skin edema (e.g., hive, mosquito bite).

Type of Reasoning: Analysis

Questions that provide an array of symptoms and require the test taker to determine the likely findings often require analytical reasoning skills. For this scenario, the key words including "irregular area" and "variations in color" should assist the test taker in concluding this finding as an atypical dysplastic nevus. If this question was answered incorrectly, review signs and symptoms of skin malignancies from the American Cancer Society.

Neuromuscular | Evaluation, Diagnosis

A patient is 2 days, post–left CVA and has just been moved from the intensive care unit to a stroke unit. When beginning the examination, the therapist finds the patient's speech slow and hesitant. The patient is limited to one- and two-word productions, and expressions are awkward and arduous. However, the patient demonstrates good comprehension. What type of speech disorder is this patient exhibiting?

Choices:

1. Fluent aphasia.
2. Global aphasia.
3. Nonfluent aphasia.
4. Dysarthria.

Teaching Points

Correct Answer: 3

This patient is demonstrating classic signs of nonfluent aphasia (Broca's motor or expressive aphasia). It is the result of a lesion involving the third frontal convolution of the left hemisphere. Nonfluent aphasia is characterized by slow and hesitant speech with limited vocabulary and labored articulation. There is relative preservation of auditory comprehension.

Incorrect Choices:

Fluent aphasia (Wernicke's or receptive aphasia) is characterized by impaired auditory comprehension and fluent speech. Global aphasia is a severe aphasia with marked dysfunction across all language modalities. Dysarthria is impairment in the motor production of speech.

Type of Reasoning: Analysis

This question provides symptoms, and the test taker must determine the diagnosis. This requires analytical reasoning skill, in which one must determine the cause for the symptoms. If this question was answered incorrectly, review symptoms of nonfluent (Broca's) aphasia.

C91

Neuromuscular | Examination

A patient recovering from traumatic brain injury (TBI) is functioning at level IV on the Rancho Los Amigos Levels of Cognitive Functioning Scale (LOCF). During the therapist's initial examination, the patient becomes agitated and tries to bite the therapist. What is the therapist's **BEST** course of action?

Choices:

1. Postpone the examination for 1 week and then try again.
2. Restructure the formal examination so the therapist can complete it in three very short sessions.
3. Document the behaviors and engage in a calming activity.
4. Postpone the examination until later in the day when the patient calms down.

Teaching Points

Correct Answer: 3

Patients with TBI in level IV of recovery are confused and agitated. Behavior is bizarre and nonpurposeful relative to the immediate environment. This patient is unable to cooperate directly with formal examination or treatment, lacking both selective attention and memory. The therapist needs to observe and document the behaviors closely and engage the patient in a calming activity such as slow rocking. A quiet, closed environment is critical.

Incorrect Choices:

Because the patient's symptoms are expected for a person in level IV of Rancho LOCF Scale, it is not appropriate to defer treatment or restructure the examination. The patient's immediate needs must be addressed.

Type of Reasoning: Evaluation

One must determine the **BEST** course of action based on evaluating the merits of the four possible CHOICES presented. One must ask, "Are these symptoms expected for this stage of recovery, and if so, what would be **BEST**?" If this question was answered incorrectly, review Rancho LOCF Scale.

C92

Cardiovascular/Pulmonary and Lymphatic | Evaluation, Diagnosis

A therapist is working on a cardiac care unit in an acute care facility. After exercising a patient recovering from a ventricular infarct, the therapist notices fatigue and dyspnea after mild activity. Later that day, on a return visit, the therapist notices the patient has a persistent spasmodic cough while lying in bed, heart rate is rapid (140), and slight edema is evident in both ankles. The patient appears anxious and agitated. What are these signs and symptoms characteristic of?

Choices:

1. Developing pericarditis.
2. Right ventricular failure.
3. Impending MI.
4. Left ventricular failure.

Teaching Points

Correct Answer: 4

Typical clinical manifestations of left ventricular failure (CHF) include those described in the case example along with an S3 heart gallop, paroxysmal nocturnal dyspnea, orthopnea, and signs and symptoms of pulmonary edema (marked dyspnea, pallor, cyanosis, diaphoresis, tachypnea, anxiety, and agitation).

Incorrect Choices:

Typical clinical manifestations of right ventricular failure include dependent edema of the ankles (usually pitting edema), weight gain, fatigue, right upper quadrant pain, anorexia, nausea, bloating, right-sided S3 or S4, cyanosis of nail beds, and decreased urine output. Impending MI may include anginal pain or discomfort in the chest, neck, jaw, or arms; palpitations; tachycardia; or unusual fatigue or dyspnea. Pericarditis produces substernal pain that may radiate to neck and upper back; difficulty swallowing; pain aggravated by movement or coughing and relieved by leaning forward or sitting upright; and a history of fever, chills, weakness, or heart disease.

Type of Reasoning: Analysis

This question provides symptoms of cardiac issues, and the test taker must determine the likely diagnosis. This necessitates analytical reasoning skills; one must determine the correct diagnosis based on the patient's symptoms. If this question was answered incorrectly, review symptoms of coronary artery disease.

C93 

Musculoskeletal | Examination

A patient with anterior knee pain has increased adduction and internal rotation at the hip when performing a squat. Which muscles are **MOST** likely weak, causing this compensatory movement?

Choices:

1. Knee flexors and extensors.
2. Hip adductors and internal rotators.
3. Hip and knee flexors.
4. Hip abductors and external rotators.

Teaching Points

Correct Answer: 4

Decreased strength of the hip abductors and external rotators are common findings in patients with anterior knee pain. Weakness is often demonstrated during a squat with increased hip adduction and internal rotation due to the poor eccentric control of these muscles.

Incorrect Choices:

Weakness of the knee flexors and extensors would not significantly affect hip mechanics during a squat. Weakness of the hip and knee flexors would not affect the squat as the hip and knee flexion are controlled eccentrically by the hip and knee extensors. Weakness of the hip adductors and internal rotators would not create this compensatory movement; rather, the opposite may occur.

Type of Reasoning: Inductive

This question requires the test taker to draw from clinical knowledge of knee pain and compensatory patterns of movement in order to arrive at a correct conclusion. This is an inductive reasoning skill. For this situation, a patient with anterior knee pain who demonstrates hip adduction and internal rotation during a squat is most likely compensating for weak hip abductors and external rotators. Review knee pain and compensatory movement strategies if answered incorrectly.

C94 

Metabolic/Endocrine | Evaluation, Diagnosis

A patient has been taking corticosteroids (hydrocortisone) for management of adrenocortical insufficiency and is referred to physical therapy for mobility training after a prolonged hospitalization. What are the potential adverse effects from prolonged use of this medication?

Choices:

1. Hypotension and myopathy.
2. Decreased appetite and weight loss.
3. Atrophy and osteoporosis.
4. Confusion and depression.

Teaching Points

Correct Answer: 3

Prolonged use of corticosteroids may result in muscle weakness, osteoporosis, fractures, and joint pain. Large doses are associated with cushingoid changes (e.g., moon face, central obesity, hypertension, myopathy, electrolyte and fluid imbalance). Common central nervous system changes include insomnia and nervousness.

Incorrect Choices:

The other choices are not expected potential adverse effects of corticosteroids.

Type of Reasoning: Inference

One must infer or draw conclusions about the expected symptoms of prolonged use of corticosteroids in order to arrive at the correct conclusion. For this patient, one could expect atrophy and osteoporosis to occur. If this question was answered incorrectly, review information on side effects of long-term corticosteroid use.

C95 

Integumentary | Evaluation, Diagnosis

A PT is treating a patient with deep partial-thickness burns over 35% of the body (chest and arms). Wound cultures reveal a bacterial count in excess of 105/g of tissue on the anterior left arm. What are the reasonable expectations for this type of burn wound?

Choices:

1. With antibiotics, spontaneous healing can be expected.
2. The risk of hypertrophic and keloid scars is low because there is no viable tissue.
3. The burn area is pain free because all nerve endings in the dermal tissue were destroyed.
4. The infected wound can convert the area to a full-thickness burn.

Teaching Points

Correct Answer: 4

A deep partial-thickness burn will heal in about 3–5 weeks if it does not become infected. An infection typically results in conversion of the wound to a full-thickness burn.

Incorrect Choices:

Full-thickness burns (not partial-thickness burns) are without sensation because the nerve endings are destroyed. However, the area is not pain free, because adjacent areas of partial-thickness burns have intact nerve endings and can be painful. The risk of hypertrophic and keloid scars is high (not low) with deep partial-thickness or full-thickness burns. With wound conversion, grafting will be necessary because all epithelial cells are destroyed with a full-thickness burn. With an infected wound, spontaneous healing is not expected.

Type of Reasoning: Inference

One must determine what a bacterial count of 105/g indicates in order to choose the correct solution. This requires one to draw conclusions about the information presented, which, when inferred correctly, indicates that the wound is infected and could convert the burned area to a full-thickness burn. If this question was answered incorrectly, refer to burn care guidelines, especially infected wounds.

C96 

Nonsystem | Equipment, Devices, Biophysical Agents

Recently, a 10-year-old patient has begun walking with supination of the right foot. With the shoe off, the therapist finds a new callus on the lateral side of the metatarsal head of the fifth toe. Which of the following is the **BEST** choice for orthotic prescription for this patient?

Choices:

1. Thomas heel.
2. Viscoelastic shoe insert with a forefoot medial wedge.
3. Viscoelastic shoe insert with forefoot lateral wedge.
4. Scaphoid pad.

Teaching Points

Correct Answer: 3

Supination of the foot (pes cavus) is accompanied by supination of the talocalcaneonavicular (TCN), subtalar and transversal tarsal joints. It is characterized by an abnormally high arch. The flexible cavus foot generally responds well to orthotic foot control, especially in a child. The best choice is a viscoelastic shoe insert with forefoot lateral wedge.

Incorrect Choices:

The other choices are used to control flexible pes valgus.

Type of Reasoning: Inductive

One must utilize clinical judgment in order to determine the **BEST** choice for orthotic prescription. This requires one to utilize inductive reasoning skill, which also includes diagnostic thinking, in order to determine a best course of action. If this question was answered incorrectly, review orthotic prescription approaches for children with foot supination.

C97 

Musculoskeletal | Interventions

A patient is recovering from a right total hip replacement (posterolateral incision, cementless fixation). During initial healing, what is the **MOST** appropriate type of bed-to-wheelchair transfer to teach this patient?

Choices:

1. Squat-pivot transfer to the surgical side.
2. Lateral slide transfer to the surgical side using a transfer board.
3. Stand-pivot transfer to the sound side.
4. Stand-pivot transfer to the surgical side.

Teaching Points

Correct Answer: 3
During initial healing, it is important to protect the hip from dislocation or subluxation of the prosthesis. With a posterolateral incision, excessive hip flexion and adduction past neutral are contraindicated. This is minimized by transferring to the sound side.

Incorrect Choices:
All other choices emphasize transfer to the surgical side, which can move the hip into adduction. In addition, the stand-pivot transfer with some hip extension is a better choice than transferring with the hip in full flexion.

Type of Reasoning: Deductive
This question requires one to recall the appropriate guidelines for bed-to-wheelchair transfers of patients with total hip replacements. The recall of guidelines necessitates deductive reasoning, in which factual recall of knowledge is expected. For patients with hip replacements, transfer toward the sound side helps to preserve hip precaution guidelines. If this question was answered incorrectly, review guidelines for transferring patients with hip replacements.

 C98 

Neuromuscular | Examination

During an initial interview and history, a patient with a right CVA seems unconcerned about obvious paralysis of the left arm and leg. When the therapist asks the patient to describe what happened, the patient says "I must have slept wrong and my arm and leg fell asleep." The patient further tells the therapist, "My family put me in this place so they could go on vacation." Which type of perceptual disorder **BEST** characterizes the patient's responses?

Choices:

1. Anosognosia.
2. Prosopagnosia.
3. Spatial relations disorder.
4. Somatoagnosia.

Teaching Points

Correct Answer: 1

Anosognosia is a perceptual disorder that is characterized by denial, neglect, and lack of awareness of the presence or severity of one's paralysis.

Incorrect Choices:

Somatoagnosia is a perceptual disorder characterized by an impairment in body scheme (a lack of awareness of body structure and the relationship of body parts of oneself or of others). Spatial relation disorders encompass a constellation of impairments characterized by difficulty in perceiving the relationship between self and two or more objects. Prosopagnosia is a perceptual disorder characterized by an inability to recognize faces (face blindness).

Type of Reasoning: Analysis

This question provides symptoms, and the test taker must determine the likely cause for such symptoms. Questions of this nature often require analytical reasoning skill, where pieces of information are analyzed to draw an appropriate conclusion. For this situation, the symptoms indicate anosognosia. Review symptoms of anosognosia if answered incorrectly.

C99 

Neuromuscular | Interventions

The therapist is treating a child with mild developmental delay secondary to 7 weeks prematurity at birth. The child is now 8 months old and is just learning to sit. Which is the **BEST** choice for a training activity?

Choices:

1. Sideward protective extension in sitting.
2. Supine tilting reactions.
3. Standing tilting reactions.
4. Prone tilting reactions.

Teaching Points

Correct Answer: 1

Sideward protective extension in sitting is a functional, protective reaction that normally occurs at about the same time as sitting begins.

Incorrect Choices:

The child who is starting to sit should already have prone and supine tilting reactions. It is too early to begin standing tilting reactions.

Type of Reasoning: Inference

One must recall the developmental milestones of infants and infer the **BEST** choice for training in order to choose the correct solution. If this question was answered incorrectly, review the motor developmental milestones of infants.

C100 

Cardiovascular/Pulmonary and Lymphatic | Examination

The picture depicts a patient who is learning to take her own pulse. What is the patient doing incorrectly?

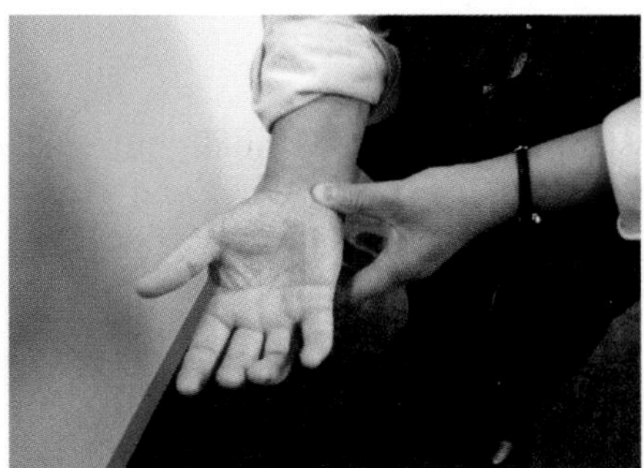

Choices:

1. Taking the pulse with the forearm supinated.
2. Palpating the ulnar artery.
3. Assessing the pulse with the thumb.
4. Palpating the right arm as opposed to the more accurate left arm.

Teaching Points

Correct Answer: 3

The thumb is pulsatile and cannot be used to assess a pulse.

Incorrect Choices:

A pulse can be assessed on any artery that can be palpated. While in some patients a pronated forearm can facilitate palpation of the pulse, any arm position is acceptable. The circulatory system is a closed system and therefore, in the absence of pathology, the pulse is the same in either upper limb.

Type of Reasoning: Inductive

This question requires the test taker to draw from clinical knowledge of taking a pulse in order to arrive at a correct conclusion. This is an inductive reasoning skill. If this question was answered incorrectly, review guidelines for taking the pulse.

C101 

Gastrointestinal | Interventions

A patient with complete spinal cord injury at the level of T11 is on a bowel program. Which of the following is the **MOST** effective bowel training program for this patient?

Choices:

1. Diet and medications to manage a flaccid bowel.
2. Digital stimulation of intact defecation reflexes.
3. Manual removal of stool from the rectum.
4. Medications such as laxatives for passive elimination.

Teaching Points

Correct Answer: 2

A SCI injury at the level of T11 produces an UMN or spastic bowel with intact spinal defecation reflexes. Bowel and anal sphincters respond to rectal/anal stimulation, enabling a planned bowel elimination program.

Incorrect Choices:

Medications such as laxatives and stool softeners can be used to assist the patient in manually stimulated elimination; however, the primary methodology is digital stimulation. A LMN or flaccid bowel occurs with lesions at T12 or below with loss of spinal defecation reflexes. Response to medications is less effective, and manual removal of stool may be required.

Type of Reasoning: Inductive

This question requires clinical judgment in order to determine a best course of action for a patient with a complete spinal cord injury. This necessitates inductive reasoning skills, where determining a best course of action is often used. For this case, the patient with a T11 injury would primarily use digital stimulation of intact defecation reflexes for bowel retraining. Refer to bowel retraining guidelines for patients with spinal cord injury, especially upper motor neuron injury, if answered incorrectly.

C102 

Musculoskeletal | Examination

When performing scoliosis screening in a school setting, what is the optimal age for girls to be screened?

Choices:

1. 12–14.
2. 6–8.
3. 9–11.
4. 15–17.

Teaching Points

Correct Answer: 3

The term adolescent describes children ranging in age from 10–18. The most effective age to screen girls for scoliosis is just before the pubescent growth spurt between 9 and 11 years, when the scoliotic curve can increase dramatically. Boys should be screened between 11 and 13 years of age because of differences in the age of onset of puberty between girls and boys.

Incorrect Choices:

Screening can occur at any age, but routine screening should be performed before the pubescent growth spurt. Large changes in abnormal spinal curves can occur during growth spurts.

Type of Reasoning: Analysis

One must analyze the merits of performing scoliosis screenings with each of the identified age groups in girls in order to determine the age at which it is optimal to complete the screening. This requires analytical reasoning skills, in which one interprets the various ages and how these ages are relevant to normal development and puberty. If this question was answered incorrectly, review information on scoliosis screening.

Musculoskeletal | Interventions

A patient with a confirmed left C6 nerve root compression due to foraminal encroachment complains of pain in the left thumb and index finger. What is the **MOST** effective cervical motion to alleviate this patient's pain?

Choices:

1. Lower cervical flexion.
2. Right rotation.
3. Lower cervical extension.
4. Left side bending.

Teaching Points

Correct Answer: 1

Lower cervical flexion increases the space at the intervertebral foramen, allowing the C6 nerve root to decompress and reduce or alleviate radicular pain.

Incorrect Choices:

Left side-bending, cervical extension, and/or right rotation all close down the foramen on the left hand side, which will increase the compression on the nerve.

Type of Reasoning: Inference

This requires the test taker to infer how various cervical positions will result in less pain from C6 nerve root compression. This requires knowledge of anatomy and the cervical position that will increase space at the intervertebral foramen to alleviate pain. Evaluative reasoning skills are utilized whenever one must make a judgment about a best course of action.

C104

Musculoskeletal | Examination

A patient is standing with excessive subtalar pronation. Which of the following indicates the obligatory motions that accompany this condition?

Choices:

1. Tibial, femoral, and pelvic external rotation.
2. Tibial and femoral internal rotation with pelvic external rotation.
3. Tibial and femoral external rotation with pelvic internal rotation.
4. Tibial, femoral, and pelvic internal rotation.

Teaching Points

Correct Answer: 4

With the patient standing, the calcaneus is fixed to the ground. Subtalar joint pronation will occur as the talus plantar flexes, adducts, and inverts. In response to subtalar joint pronation, obligatory internal rotation of the tibia, femur, and pelvis occurs.

Incorrect Choices:

External rotation of the tibia, femur, and pelvis would be associated with excessive subtalar supination. The pelvis must follow the rotation present in the lower limb (specifically the femur).

Type of Reasoning: Analysis

One must analyze these motions and postures in order to determine which solution is most likely correlated with the excessive subtalar pronation. Through analytical reasoning skill, one should determine that the tibial, femoral, and pelvic internal rotations are the possible obligatory motions as a result of the excessive subtalar pronation. If this question was answered incorrectly, refer to information on postures related to excessive subtalar pronation.

C105 

Genitourinary | Evaluation, Diagnosis

Which of the following conditions associated with pelvic floor muscle dysfunction may actually worsen when treated with Kegel exercises?

Choices:

1. Interstitial cystitis.
2. Stress incontinence.
3. Pelvic organ prolapse.
4. Chronic constipation.

Teaching Points

Correct Answer: 1

Kegel exercises are prescribed to strengthen weak pelvic floor muscles (levator ani) and to improve the motor control of these muscles. However, in individuals with interstitial cystitis (IC), the pelvic floor dysfunction is usually related to muscles that are too tense or in spasm in response to pain and chronic inflammation of the bladder. This is just the opposite of the too-relaxed state that leads to incontinence. Additionally, there are often tender points or nodules in the pelvic floor muscles of individuals with IC that can be treated with manual techniques. Therefore the goal of physical therapy in these patients is to relax and lengthen tight pelvic floor muscles and release trigger points.

Incorrect Choices:

Pelvic floor muscle weakness is a common cause of stress incontinence, and Kegel exercises are often prescribed to effectively treat this disorder. Similarly, strengthening of the pelvic floor muscles can be very beneficial in women who suffer from a prolapse of the uterus or vagina. Recent studies have shown that about half of all individuals with chronic constipation suffer from pelvic floor muscle dysfunction, and benefit from Kegel exercises combined with biofeedback to strengthen and coordinate the actions of the pelvic floor and abdominal muscles.

Type of Reasoning: Inductive

This question requires the test taker to utilize clinical judgment in order to determine which condition may worsen with Kegel exercises. This is an inductive reasoning skill, where knowledge of the diagnosis and intervention approach is paramount to arriving at a correct conclusion. For this case, interstitial cystitis would worsen with Kegel exercises. If answered incorrectly, review indications and guidelines for Kegel exercises.

C106 

Nonsystem | Equipment, Devices, Biophysical Agents

A therapist is applying a symmetrical biphasic pulsed current to the vastus medialis to improve patellar tracking during knee extension. The patient complains that the current is uncomfortable. To make the current more tolerable to the patient, yet maintain a good therapeutic effect, what should the therapist adjust?

Choices:

1. Current polarity.
2. Pulse duration.
3. Current intensity.
4. Pulse rate.

Teaching Points

Correct Answer: 2

Decreasing the pulse duration reduces the electrical charge of each pulse, making the current more comfortable by decreasing the total current applied while maintaining the full therapeutic effect.

Incorrect Choices:

The only other parameter that would have a direct effect on comfort would be the intensity. For motor level stimulation, decreasing the intensity would decrease the therapeutic effect by decreasing the quality of the contraction. For sensory level stimulation, decreasing the intensity would decrease the level of sensory input needed for the treatment of pain. The pulse rates used for pain management are typically modulated. For motor level stimulation, decreasing the pulse rate would decrease the quality of the contraction, and increasing the pulse rate could make it more uncomfortable or contribute to muscle fatigue. Changing the polarity would have no effect because a symmetrical biphasic waveform has no net polarity.

Type of Reasoning: Deductive

This question requires one to factually recall the correct parameters for high-volt pulsed current and how adjustments to the pulse or current results in alterations in therapeutic effect. Factual recall or protocols or guidelines is a deductive reasoning skill. If this question was answered incorrectly, review information on guidelines for high-volt pulsed current.

C107

Gastrointestinal | Evaluation, Diagnosis

Which of the following gastrointestinal sources of pain can refer to the shoulder?

Choices:

1. Esophageal pain.
2. Colon or appendix pain.
3. Spleen or diaphragmatic pain.
4. Gallbladder pain.

Teaching Points

Correct Answer: 3

Spleen or diaphragmatic pain can refer to the shoulder.

Incorrect Choices:

Esophageal pain can refer to the mid-back, head, or neck. Colon or appendix pain can refer to the lower back, pelvis, or sacrum. Gallbladder pain can refer to the mid-back and scapular regions.

Type of Reasoning: Deductive

One must recall the typical referral patterns for gastrointestinal pain in order to determine which refers to the shoulder. This requires deductive reasoning skills, because factual recall of guidelines is used to reach a conclusion. If this question was answered incorrectly, review gastrointestinal pain referral patterns.

C108

Neuromuscular | Evaluation, Diagnosis

A patient presents with symptoms of uncoordinated eye movements, profound gait and trunk ataxia, and difficulty with postural orientation to vertical. Balance deficits are pronounced in standing with eyes open and eyes closed. Examination of the extremities reveals little change in tone or coordination. What is the likely CNS location of the patient's dysfunction?

Choices:

1. Premotor cortex.
2. Vestibulocerebellum.
3. Spinocerebellum.
4. Basal ganglia.

Teaching Points

Correct Answer: 2

The symptoms are suggestive of cerebellar dysfunction. The vestibulocerebellum (archicerebellum) is concerned with adjustment of muscle tone in response to vestibular stimuli. It coordinates muscle actions to maintain postural coordination and balance control along with eye muscle control (all impaired in this example).

Incorrect Choices:

The spinocerebellum (paleocerebellum) controls muscle tone and synergistic movements of the extremities on the same side of the body. The basal ganglia's functions are complex. It contributes to motor planning and sequencing of voluntary movements. Deficits typically include rigidity, bradykinesia, and tremor along with postural instability. The premotor cortex (precentral area, frontal lobe) stores programs of motor activity assembled as the result of past experience and programs the motor cortex for voluntary movements. It assists the basal ganglia in control of coarse postural movements.

Type of Reasoning: Analysis

This question provides the symptoms, and the test taker must determine, through analytical reasoning, the cortical region responsible for the symptoms. If this question was answered incorrectly, review information on cerebellar dysfunction.

C109

System Interactions | Evaluation, Diagnosis

A patient with a 10-year history of diabetes complains of cramping, pain, and fatigue of the right buttock after walking 400 feet or climbing stairs. When the patient stops exercising, the pain goes away immediately. The skin of the involved leg is cool and pale. The therapist checks the record and finds no mention of this problem. Given this patient's symptoms, what is the likely diagnosis?

Choices:
1. Peripheral nerve injury.
2. Spinal root impingement.
3. Raynaud's phenomenon.
4. Peripheral arterial disease (PAD).

Teaching Points

Correct Answer: 4

Intermittent claudication, often the earliest indication of PAD, is manifested by cramping, pain, or fatigue in the muscles during exercise that is typically relieved by rest. The calf muscle is most commonly affected, but discomfort may also occur in the thigh, hip, or buttock. Cessation of pain immediately upon stopping the exercise is characteristic of intermittent claudication, not other spinal problems. With severe disease, however, pain may be present even at rest.

Incorrect Choices:

The pain associated with spinal root impingement (nerve pain) is often acute and becomes worse or aggravated by extension, side flexion, rotation, standing, walking, and exercise in general. It is relieved by lying down. Peripheral nerve injury presents with sensory and motor loss. Raynaud's phenomenon is an intermittent attack of pallor or cyanosis of the small arteries and arterioles of the fingers as a result of inadequate blood flow.

Type of Reasoning: Analysis

This is a question that provides the symptoms and one must determine the likely diagnosis. This requires analytical reasoning skill, in which the test taker utilizes knowledge of anatomy, physiology, and pathology to determine the cause. If this question was answered incorrectly, review information on symptoms of PAD.

C110 

Cardiovascular/Pulmonary and Lymphatic | Evaluation, Diagnosis

A patient with lower back pain has marked elevation of BP and complains of mild to severe mid-abdominal pain that increases upon exertion. Palpation reveals a pulsing mass in the lower abdomen. What is the therapist's **BEST** course of action?

Choices:

1. Discontinue treatment and notify the patient's physician immediately.
2. Provide hot packs to the abdomen to help relieve the muscle spasm.
3. Instruct the patient to contact his/her physician at the conclusion of therapy.
4. Instruct in relaxation exercises because a pulsating mass is not unusual with hypertension.

Teaching Points

Correct Answer: 1

This patient is demonstrating signs and symptoms of abdominal aortic aneurysm. Pain is intermittent or constant and can be felt in the mid-abdominal or lower back regions. The pulsating mass is highly significant, and the level of hypertension dramatically increases risk of rupture. This is a serious medical condition; the therapist should notify the physician immediately.

Incorrect Choices:

The therapist should not rely on the patient to contact the physician. All physical therapy intervention should cease.

Type of Reasoning: Evaluation

One must evaluate the significance of the information presented, determine the root cause of the symptoms, and then determine the best course of action. This requires evaluative reasoning skill, in which one evaluates the merits of the four possible choices and determines which approach is most appropriate and safe for the patient. In this case, it is important to discontinue treatment and immediately notify the physician.

C111 

Musculoskeletal | Examination

A patient presents for the initial examination with an acute and painful shoulder impingement. During the examination, the PT finds significantly increased muscle guarding around the shoulder girdle with difficulty in accurately assessing joint mobility. Which manual therapy technique is the **BEST** option to use to assist in performing a proper assessment?

Choices:

1. Maitland grade III posterior glide to the glenohumeral joint.
2. Maitland grade II oscillation to the glenohumeral joint.
3. Maitland grade III inferior glide to the glenohumeral joint.
4. Maitland grade IV inferior glide to the glenohumeral joint.

Teaching Points

Correct Answer: 2

Maitland grades I and II are used to improve joint lubrication/nutrition as well as to decrease pain and muscle guarding. A grade II oscillation will promote muscle relaxation, allowing a proper assessment of the patient's joint mobility.

Incorrect Choices:

Decreasing the muscle guarding is the first priority before more vigorous interventions are employed. Maitland grades III and IV are used to stretch tight muscles, capsule, and ligaments in order to improve motion.

Type of Reasoning: Inference

One needs to be aware of the indication for each of the five grades of Maitland's oscillatory techniques and determine the technique that will have the best outcome in order to arrive at a correct conclusion. This requires one to determine what is likely to be true of a situation, which is an inferential reasoning skill.

C112

System Interactions | Evaluation, Diagnosis

A frail, elderly wheelchair-dependent resident of a community nursing home has a diagnosis of organic brain syndrome, moderate Alzheimer's type dementia, During the therapist's initial interview, the patient demonstrates limited interaction and mild agitation and keeps trying to wheel the chair down the hall. Because it is late in the day, the therapist decides to resume the examination the next morning. How should the therapist document this in the medical record?

Choices:

1. Disorientation to time and date.
2. Inattention as a result of short-term memory loss.
3. Frustration because of an inability to communicate.
4. Sundowning behavior.

Teaching Points

Correct Answer: 4

A patient with moderate Alzheimer's type dementia can be expected to exhibit impaired cognition and abstract thinking, sundowning (defined as extreme restlessness, agitation, and wandering that typically occurs in the late afternoon), inability to carry out activities of daily living, impaired judgment, inappropriate social behavior, lack of insight, repetitive behavior, and a voracious appetite.

Incorrect Choices:

Inability to communicate is characteristic of severe Alzheimer's type dementia. Short-term memory loss and disorientation to time and date are early and persistent signs of the disease.

Type of Reasoning: Analysis

This question provides the symptoms, and the test taker must determine, through analytical reasoning, the most likely cause for the patient's behavior. In this situation, the symptoms suggest that the patient with moderate Alzheimer's type dementia is exhibiting sundowning behavior. If this question was answered incorrectly, review information on Alzheimer's type dementia and sundowning behavior.

C113 

Musculoskeletal | Interventions

A patient with a right transfemoral amputation is undergoing prosthetic training. What is the **BEST** technique to use to improve the patient's shortened step length on the right?

Choices:

1. Provide anterior-directed resistance to the right PSIS during swing.
2. Provide posterior-directed resistance to the left ASIS during swing.
3. Provide posterior-directed resistance to the right ASIS during stance.
4. Facilitate the gluteals with tapping over the muscle belly.

Teaching Points

Correct Answer: 3

Light resistance and stretch applied to the pelvis (right ASIS) in a posterior direction during mid-stance to late stance will facilitate forward pelvic rotation on that side and enhance forward movement of the limb during swing.

Incorrect Choices:

Anterior-directed resistance functions to pull the hip forward but does little to facilitate active forward limb movement. The gluteals function to stabilize the limb during stance (not advance the limb forward). Manual resistance applied to the pelvis during swing may interfere with stepping.

Type of Reasoning: Inference

One must infer the best approach to providing directed resistance for the patient with a transfemoral amputation. This requires knowledge of kinesiology and therapeutic exercise in order to arrive at the correct conclusion.

C114 

Gastrointestinal | Evaluation, Diagnosis

An elderly, frail resident of an extended care facility has intractable constipation. During a scheduled visit from the PT, the patient complains of abdominal pain and tenderness. Where may this patient experience referred pain?

Choices:

1. Buttock, thigh, and posterior leg.
2. Anterior hip, groin, or thigh region.
3. Low back and front of the thigh to the knee.
4. Medial thigh and leg.

Teaching Points

Correct Answer: 2

Intractable constipation (obstipation) can cause partial or complete bowel impaction, pain, and tenderness in the lower abdomen. Referred pain is to the anterior hip groin or thigh region.

Incorrect Choices:

Pain in the back and front of thigh to knee is characteristic of L2 nerve root compression. Pain in the buttock, thigh, and posterior leg is characteristic of S1 nerve root compression. Pain in the bladder can refer to the medial thigh and leg.

Type of Reasoning: Inference

One must infer or draw a reasonable conclusion about the symptoms a client is likely to experience given the diagnosis provided. Inferential reasoning skills are often utilized in cases in which one must determine what may be true of a patient. If this question was answered incorrectly, review signs and symptoms of intractable constipation and pain referral patterns from the viscera.

C115 

Musculoskeletal I Interventions

An adult patient is diagnosed with thoracic outlet syndrome. The patient presents with guarding in the upper trapezius and scalene muscles. Given this situation, which technique would be the **MOST** effective way to decrease the muscle guarding and provide pain relief?

Choices:

1. Maitland grade V manipulation of the C6–C7 joint.
2. Maitland grade II mobilization of the atlanto-axial joint.
3. Maitland grade III mobilization of the C6–C7 joint.
4. Maitland grade V manipulation of the first rib.

Teaching Points

Correct Answer: 4

One needs to be aware that the muscle guarding pattern present with this condition is increased tone of the scalene muscles. These muscles (anterior and middle portions) attach to the first rib. Grade V manipulation is used to decrease muscle guarding and pain in the target area.

Incorrect Choices:

The atlanto-axial and C6–C7 joints are not the target joints of most importance nor is the technique the most effective based on the pattern presented.

Type of Reasoning: Inference

One needs to be aware of the indication for each of the five grades of Maitland's oscillatory techniques in order to determine the correct conclusion. Questions that require one to infer what will result in a best clinical outcome often require inferential reasoning skill. For this scenario, Maitland grade V manipulation of the first rib is best. Review Maitland's oscillatory techniques if answered incorrectly.

C116 

Musculoskeletal I Interventions

A patient presents with decreased motion at the occipitoatlantal joint (OA). The PT wants to use the principles of coupled motions that occur in that area of the spine during manual therapy techniques. In order to improve OA mobility, when the occiput is side bent to the right, how should the therapist mobilize C1?

Choices:

1. Into rotation to the left.
2. Into rotation to the right.
3. Back into extension.
4. Forward into flexion.

Teaching Points

Correct Answer: 1

Given the rules of coupled movement in the upper cervical spine, when the occiput is sidebent into one direction, C1 rotates into the opposite direction. Side bending and rotation occur in the same direction from C2–C7 regardless if the spine is in flexion or extension.

Incorrect Choices:

The other choices do not represent opposite directions or coupled movement from a right side bend of the occiput at C1.

Type of Reasoning: Inductive

One must understand the coupled movements of the cervical spine in order to arrive at a correct conclusion. Questions of this nature often require inductive reasoning skill, as one must use clinical judgment to determine a best course of action. For this situation, the therapist should mobilize into rotation to the left when the occiput is side bent to the right. Review biomechanics and coupled movements of the cervical spine if answered incorrectly.

C117 

Cardiovascular/Pulmonary and Lymphatic | Examination

An apparently healthy individual has several risk factors for coronary artery disease. The client is interested in improving overall fitness and cardiac health. After a graded exercise test, which was asymptomatic, the client is referred for an exercise class. Which is the **BEST** measure of exercise intensity in a newly tested and exercising individual?

Choices:

1. Heart rate (HR).
2. Rating of perceived exertion (RPE).
3. MET level.
4. Respiratory rate.

Teaching Points

Correct Answer: 1

A graded exercise test should be performed before commencing an exercise program for all high-risk individuals. The best measurement of exercise intensity in a newly tested and exercising individual is HR.

Incorrect Choices:

RPE will become a valuable measurement tool once the patient becomes adept at using it, but it would not be reliable for the first exercise session. MET level is more of a measurement of workload, not an accurate measurement of an individual's response to exercise. Respiratory rate is not used to prescribe exercise intensity.

Type of Reasoning: Inductive

This question requires the test taker to recall the various measures of exercise intensity and determine, through clinical judgment, which measure will **MOST** accurately monitor the patient's exercise intensity, given his/her diagnosis and symptoms on the **FIRST** visit. Questions that require clinical judgment and diagnostic reasoning require inductive reasoning skill. If this question was answered incorrectly, review measures to monitor exercise intensity for at-risk individuals.

C118 

Neuromuscular I Examination

A mother brings her 8-week-old infant to be examined at early intervention clinic because she noticed that the infant was taking steps in supported standing at 2 weeks but is not able to do it now. What should the therapist do given the infant's symptoms and behaviors?

Choices:

1. Recommend that the mother bring the infant to a pediatric neurologist.
2. Explain that this was abnormal and it is a good sign that it has disappeared.
3. Recommend that a full developmental examination be performed by the early intervention team.
4. Explain that this is normal and that this early automatic walking is a newborn response.

Teaching Points

Correct Answer: 4

The mother probably saw the neonatal stepping reflex/automatic walking, which is normal in a newborn but is not exhibited in the older infant probably because of anthropomorphic factors and neural maturation. The age that this response typically disappears is 2–3 months of age.

Incorrect Choices:

In most infants, pull-to-stand emerges at 8–9 months, whereas unassisted standing and walking occurs at 10–15 months. Stepping at this age is not the result of a reflex (does not reemerge later on). A full developmental examination or referral to a neurologist is not indicated, and should be performed only after the child is older and is not walking. It is important to remember that these norms are averages, and that children may be more advanced or slower in reaching these milestones.

Type of Reasoning: Evaluation

One must have firm knowledge of the developmental milestones of infants in order to arrive at the correct conclusion. Using evaluative reasoning, one must evaluate the merits of the four possible choices and determine which solution seems most reasonable, given the infant's symptoms and behaviors. In this case, the behaviors are normal. If this question was answered incorrectly, review the neonatal stepping reflex and developmental milestones for walking.

C119 

Musculoskeletal I Examination

A patient complains of pain with mouth opening that makes it difficult to eat foods that require chewing. Which of the following provides the normal limits of mouth opening that should guide the therapist's examination?

Choices:

1. 15–24 mm.
2. 35–50 mm.
3. 51–65 mm.
4. 66–74 mm.

Teaching Points

Correct Answer: 2

Average AROM is approximately 35–50 mm. However, only 25–35 mm of opening between the teeth is required for normal everyday activity.

Incorrect Choices:

The TMJs are considered hypomobile if < 25 mm of opening is achieved. Hypermobility would include values > 50 mm.

Type of Reasoning: Analysis

One must recall normal AROM of the TMJ as well as functional AROM ranges in order to arrive at the correct conclusion. Through analytical reasoning, one must review each of the AROM parameters and determine which range seems most reasonable, given one's knowledge of normal ROM guidelines for the TMJ. If this question was answered incorrectly, review AROM guidelines for the TMJ.

C120

Musculoskeletal / Examination

The physical therapist is examining the muscle length of the patient's left hip and knee. What muscle length test is being shown in the picture below?

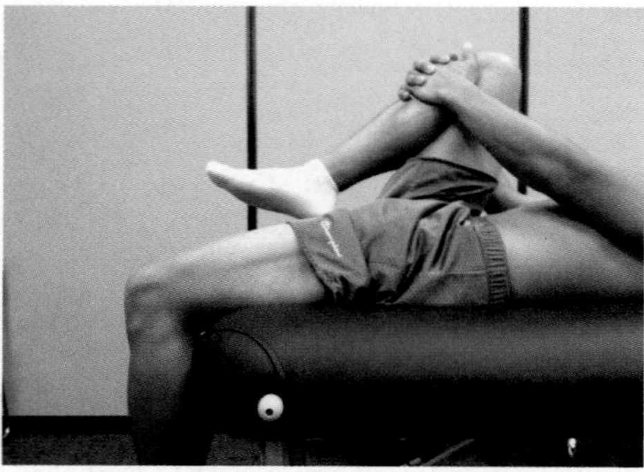

Choices:

1. FABER test.
2. Thomas test.
3. Noble test.
4. Ober test.

Teaching Points

Correct Answer: 2

The Thomas test is utilized to test for hip flexor length and to distinguish between one joint and two joint hip flexor tightness. With low back and sacrum flat on the table, a normal one joint hip flexor length would be with thigh flat on the table. Normal two joint hip flexor length would be 80° of knee flexion.

Incorrect Choices:

The Ober test is performed for tightness of the tensor fascia latae and iliotibial band. The Noble test is performed for iliotibial band friction syndrome. The FABER test is hip flexion, abduction, and external rotation and is to screen hip and SI pathology.

Type of Reasoning: Analysis

One must understand the tests described in the question in order to choose the correct one. Through analytical reasoning, the test taker must determine how each test is performed and for what purpose. If this question was answered incorrectly, review information on special tests.

C121

Musculoskeletal | Evaluation, Diagnosis

A patient presents with complaints of tingling and paresthesias in the median nerve distribution of the right forearm and hand. The following tests were found negative bilaterally: Adson's, hyperabduction, costoclavicular, Phalen's, and the ulnar nerve Tinel's sign. Based on this information, what is the likely diagnosis?

Choices:

1. Ulnar nerve entrapment.
2. Pronator teres syndrome.
3. Thoracic outlet syndrome (TOS).
4. Carpal tunnel syndrome.

Teaching Points

Correct Answer: 2

All of these special tests are used to determine neurological compromise of the lower trunk and brachial plexus. Special tests to rule out pronator teres syndrome are (1) passive supination to elongate the pronator, which is tight (this would compress the nerve at that level); and (2) active resistance of pronation, which would compress the nerve as it courses through the pronator muscle belly.

Incorrect Choices:

A negative Adson's test, hyperabduction test, and costoclavicular test will rule out TOS. A negative Phalen's test will rule out carpal tunnel syndrome. A negative ulnar nerve Tinel's sign will rule out ulnar nerve entrapment. By process of elimination, pronator teres syndrome is the only diagnosis remaining.

Type of Reasoning: Analysis

One must understand the tests described in the question in order to choose the correct solution. Through analytical reasoning, the test taker must determine what each test indicates (by a negative result) in order to determine the diagnosis that is likely. If this question was answered incorrectly, review information on provocative testing for pronator teres syndrome.

C122

Musculoskeletal | Evaluation, Diagnosis

A young adult patient is referred to outpatient physical therapy for an insidious onset of thoracic spine stiffness and mild pain. The patient reports a great deal of difficulty moving the mid-back region in the morning and states that this has become progressively worse over the past 6 months. The neurological exam is negative. Based on these symptoms, what is the likely diagnosis?

Choices:

1. Pneumothorax.
2. Thoracic compression fracture.
3. Ankylosing spondylitis.
4. Lyme disease.

Teaching Points

Correct Answer: 3

Ankylosing spondylitis is a rheumatic disease of the spine (spondyloarthropathy). Primary symptoms include back pain and back stiffness, especially in the morning. Chronic inflammation and irritation of the spinal joints results in stiffening of the joints and eventually abnormal fusion (anklyosis).

Incorrect Choices:

Lyme disease may be associated with flu-like and/or neurological signs and symptoms in early stages. Furthermore, there was no report of the common "red or bull's eye rash" frequently associated with Lyme disease. Pneumothorax is unlikely based on lack of reporting recent sickness, infection, or trauma, and onset was not insidious. Thoracic compression fracture is unlikely based on age of patient and lack of trauma.

Type of Reasoning: Analysis

This question requires the tester to critically evaluate key findings from the patient interview and determine the most likely differential diagnosis based on the information provided. Questions of this nature often require analytical reasoning skill, where pieces of information are analyzed to draw reasonable conclusions. For this case, the symptoms are indicative of ankylosing spondylitis. Review signs and symptoms of ankylosing spondylitis if answered incorrectly.

C123 

Cardiovascular/Pulmonary and Lymphatic | Interventions

A young patient presents with primary lymphedema of the right lower extremity. What is the **BEST** choice for initial exercise?

Choices:

1. Treadmill walking.
2. Treadmill jogging.
3. Exercising on a stair climbing machine.
4. Step aerobics.

Teaching Points

Correct Answer: 1

Initially, the patient should begin with beneficial low-risk activities (e.g., lymphedema exercise, walking, easy biking, swimming, water aerobics, or Tai Chi). Exercise should always be performed with a compression garment or compression bandages.

Incorrect Choices:

The patient should avoid medium-risk activities (e.g., jogging, running, or stair climbing machines) or sport activities that involve high risk of injury (e.g., soccer, tennis, golf volleyball, or karate). Eventually, patients can progress to certain higher-risk activities provided there is no exacerbation of their lymphedema.

Type of Reasoning: Inductive

This question requires one to use clinical judgment in order to draw a reasonable conclusion for a patient with primary lymphedema. For this case, it is best for the patient to begin exercise with a low-risk activity such as treadmill walking. If answered incorrectly, review exercise guidelines for patients with primary lymphedema.

C124

Neuromuscular | Interventions

An elderly patient is recovering from a right CVA and demonstrates strong spasticity in the left upper extremity. The therapist wants to reduce the expected negative effects of spasticity in the left upper extremity while the patient is working on sitting control. What is the **BEST** position for the upper extremity?

Choices:

1. Left elbow flexed with arm resting on supporting pillow, positioned on the patient's lap.
2. Affected upper extremity extended and internally rotated with the hand at the side.
3. Left shoulder abducted and externally rotated with elbow extended and weight supported on the palm of the hand.
4. Left shoulder adducted and internal rotation with arm extended and hand resting on the thigh.

Teaching Points

Correct Answer: 3

In the upper extremity, spasticity is typically strong in scapular retractors, shoulder adductors, depressors, and internal rotators; elbow flexors and forearm pronators; and wrist and finger flexors. The patient should be positioned opposite the expected pattern.

Incorrect Choices:

The other choices all emphasize one or more of the expected spastic muscles/pattern (i.e., internal rotation, elbow flexion, shoulder adduction, and internal rotation).

Type of Reasoning: Inference

One must recall the patterns of spasticity in the body after CVA in order to arrive at the correct solution. This requires inferential reasoning skill, in which the test taker must draw conclusions from the evidence presented and determine the possible outcomes from implementing the above positions for this patient. If this question was answered incorrectly, review spasticity after CVA and positioning strategies.

C125

Neuromuscular | Examination

During an initial examination, the therapist occludes vision by having the patient close the eyes. What can the therapist effectively examine?

Choices:

1. Discriminative touch and fast pain but not proprioception.
2. Vestibular/visual/somatosensory integration.
3. Conscious proprioception but not discriminative touch.
4. Somatosensory integrity.

Teaching Points

Correct Answer: 4

The term "somatosensation" refers to conscious relay pathways for discriminative touch, conscious proprioception, fast pain, and discriminative temperature. Sensory examination must rule out vision in order to establish the reliability of testing sensory integrity of these pathways.

Incorrect Choices:

Vestibular/visual/somatosensory integration can be established only by a series of tests that include both eyes open and eyes closed and by using flat and compliant (foam) or moving surfaces. The other choices exclude one of the sensory sensations that should be tested with the eyes closed.

Type of Reasoning: Inference

One must infer why blocking a subject's vision is important for certain testing protocols in order to arrive at the correct conclusion. Of all the named functions, somatosensory integrity requires the blocking of vision in order to effectively determine that the pathway is intact. Inferential reasoning is utilized because the test taker must infer why absence of vision is important to determining the functioning of each pathway.

C126 

Musculoskeletal | Examination

An adolescent felt a "clunk" in the lumbar spine 2 weeks ago while lifting weights. There was immediate right lumbar pain and spasm. Posteroanterior and bilateral radiographic views of the lumbar spine were normal except L4 was shifted approximately 1 mm anterior to L5 on the lateral views. Which of the following imaging techniques would give the PT the best information regarding a diagnosis and formulating a plan of care for this individual?

Choices:

1. Posteroanterior computed tomography (CT) scan.
2. Posteroanterior T1 magnetic resonance imaging (MRI).
3. Bilateral oblique radiographs.
4. Right oblique radiograph.

Teaching Points

Correct Answer: 3

The clinician should suspect a spondylolisthesis. A spondylolisthesis is a forward slippage of a vertebra due to a *bilateral* defect in the pars interarticularis. Causes include congenital, acute fracture, or degenerative conditions. The degree of forward slippage is graded on a 1–4 scale (4 being the most severe or a 75%–100% slippage) from the lateral view. It is unclear from the description whether there is an actual spondylolisthesis. Bilateral oblique views with a radiograph are needed to see whether there is a fracture at the pars interarticularis bilaterally. This is known as the "Scottie dog" defect (see Chapter 1 Appendix 1M for example).

Incorrect Choices:

A unilateral view would provide information only about one pars interarticularis. Although a CT scan and MRI might add some benefit, the posteroanterior view with these expensive techniques has no added benefit. Depending upon the pathology or presentation of a client, a PT should be able to recommend appropriate medical imaging to ensure accurate and effective patient/client treatment and management decisions.

Type of Reasoning: Inference

This question requires one to infer or draw a reasonable conclusion about imaging techniques that would provide the best information about a diagnosis and developing a plan of care. This requires inferential reasoning skill. For this scenario, the best imaging technique would be bilateral oblique radiographs for suspected spondylolisthesis. If this question was answered incorrectly, review symptoms of spondylolisthesis and radiographic imaging.

C127

Cardiovascular/Pulmonary and Lymphatic | Examination

A 28-year-old professional mountain bike rider presents to cardiac rehabilitation after suffering a myocardial infarction 8 weeks ago. Which graded exercise test would be **MOST** beneficial in order to assess aerobic capacity in this patient in order to create an aerobic conditioning program?

Choices:

1. Bruce protocol.
2. Step test.
3. Lower extremity ergometry.
4. 6-Minute Walk test.

Teaching Points

Correct Answer: 3

The patient is well-trained on a mountain bike and will benefit from LE ergometry testing and a bike training program to facilitate return to his role.

Incorrect Choices:

The Bruce Protocol and step test would provide an appropriate challenge for this patient, however would not appropriately assess his training effects. A 6-Minute Walk test will not allow the patient to exercise at an intensity appropriate enough to assess his aerobic capacity.

Type of Reasoning: Analysis

One must understand the exercise tests described in the question in order to choose the correct one. Through analytical reasoning, the test taker must determine how each test is performed and for what purpose. If this question was answered incorrectly, review information on modes and purposes of exercise tests.

C128 

Neuromuscular | Evaluation, Diagnosis

A patient with trigeminal nerve neuralgia (CN V) is referred to the physical therapist. What are the expected examination findings?

Choices:

1. Sudden severe pains in the ophthalmic division of CN V.
2. Paroxysmal and severe pain originating from the mandibular or maxillary divisions of CN V.
3. Unilateral sensory loss of the ophthalmic division of CN V.
4. Bilateral sensory loss of CN V in all three divisions.

Teaching Points

Correct Answer: 2

Trigeminal neuralgia (tic douloureux) is a condition characterized by sudden, severe pain occurring in the distribution of the trigeminal nerve (CN V). It typically occurs in the maxillary or mandibular division on one side of the face.

Incorrect Choices:

Symptoms are typically unilateral, not bilateral. It rarely affects the ophthalmic division.

Type of Reasoning: Inference

This question requires one to infer the common signs and symptoms of trigeminal nerve neuralgia. Questions that necessitate determining what is likely to be true of a diagnosis often require inferential reasoning skill. In this case, the physical therapist will likely find paroxysmal and severe pain originating from the mandibular or maxillary divisions of CN V. If this question was answered incorrectly, review signs and symptoms of trigeminal nerve neuralgia.

C129 

Metabolic/Endocrine | Interventions

A patient with hypothyroidism and poor drug compliance is referred to physical therapy following a fall. What symptoms might be evident during exercise based on this diagnosis?

Choices:

1. Paresthesias of the lower limbs.
2. Elevated cardiac output.
3. Sinus tachycardia and arrhythmias.
4. Myalgia and weakness.

Teaching Points

Correct Answer: 4

Hypothyroidism results in a decreased metabolic rate and is likely to produce exercised-induced myalgia and weakness (rhabdomyolysis).

Incorrect Choices:

Sinus bradycardia (not tachycardia) and decreased cardiac output (not increased) can occur. Sensory changes are not found.

Type of Reasoning: Inference

This question provides a diagnosis, and the test taker must determine the symptoms that could occur during exercise based on this diagnosis. This is an inferential reasoning skill. For this situation, the therapist should watch for signs of myalgia and weakness during exercise. If answered incorrectly, review exercise guidelines for patients with hypothyroidism.

C130 

Nonsystem | Safety, Professional Responsibilities, Research

A group of researchers utilized meta-analysis to identify the evidence for aerobic fitness exercises in the management of fibromyalgia. Thirteen randomized, controlled trials (RCTs) and three controlled clinical trials (cohort studies and case control studies) were selected. What is the main difference between the two types of trials?

Choices:

1. Duration of the studies.
2. Use of multiple centers versus single center trials.
3. Length of the studies.
4. Use of randomization of subjects.

Teaching Points

Correct Answer: 4

The main difference between the two types of trials is randomization of subjects into experimental and control groups (RCT).

Incorrect Choices:

Meta-analysis involves the combining of a series of independent, previously published studies of similar purpose to yield a larger target population. RCTs are used and can be either single-center or multiple-center trials. A cohort study is a prospective study involving a group of participants with a similar condition. Comparison is made with a matched group that does not have the condition. Duration and length of studies are not distinguishing factors between the two types of studies.

Type of Reasoning: Deductive

One must recall the guidelines for both RCTs and controlled clinical trials in order to arrive at a correct conclusion. Recalling such guidelines is factual information, which requires deductive reasoning skills. If this question was answered incorrectly, review types of research designs, especially RCTs and controlled clinical trials.

C131 

Neuromuscular | Interventions

A patient with a complete spinal cord injury at the level of T1 (ASIA A) is in the community phase of mobility training. In order for the patient to navigate a 4-inch-height curb with the wheelchair, what should the therapist tell the patient to do?

Choices:

1. Ascend backward with the large wheels first.
2. Descend backward with the trunk upright and arms hooked around the push handles.
3. Lift the front casters and ascend in a wheelie position.
4. Place the front casters down first during descent.

Teaching Points

Correct Answer: 3

Curbs are ascended in the wheelie position (front casters lifted with push forward on rear wheels). Individuals must learn to use momentum and a strong push to elevate the front casters of the chair and propel the wheelchair up the curb.

Incorrect Choices:

Patients can descend backward but must use a tucked forward lean position in order to prevent falling backward, or they can descend forward using a wheelie position, large wheels landing first. Curbs are not ascended backward or descended with the front casters touching first.

Type of Reasoning: Evaluation

Evaluative reasoning is important to arriving at the correct conclusion for this question, because the test taker must evaluate the merits of the four choices and then determine what is safe and appropriate for this patient. If this question was answered incorrectly, review curb negotiation guidelines for patients with paraplegia.

C132 

Cardiovascular/Pulmonary and Lymphatic | Interventions

A patient with a long history of systemic steroid use for asthma control is hospitalized with pneumonia. Which of the following is a contraindication to percussion?

Choices:

1. Barrel chest.
2. BP > 140/90.
3. Intercostal muscle wasting.
4. Decreased bone density.

Teaching Points

Correct Answer: 4

The only one that is a contraindication to percussion would be decreased bone density, because a rib fracture might be a possible result.

Incorrect Choices:

Although the other choices are sequelae to long-term systemic steroid use, they are not a contraindication for percussion. An increased BP higher than that reported in the scenario might be a contraindication to postural drainage. It is not a contraindication to percussion. Barrel chest is seen in patients with emphysema, not asthma.

Type of Reasoning: Inference

One must determine, given an understanding of the nature of long-term systemic steroid use for asthma, which condition would contraindicate percussion. It is beneficial to understand how percussion is performed, because it helps one to reason why decreased bone density would contraindicate the therapy. Inferential reasoning skill is used because one must infer the effects of long-term steroid use coupled with the nature of percussion therapy when used with patients who have asthma.

C133

Musculoskeletal / Examination

The physical therapist is examining the patient's left ankle. The test pictured below is testing the integrity of which structure?

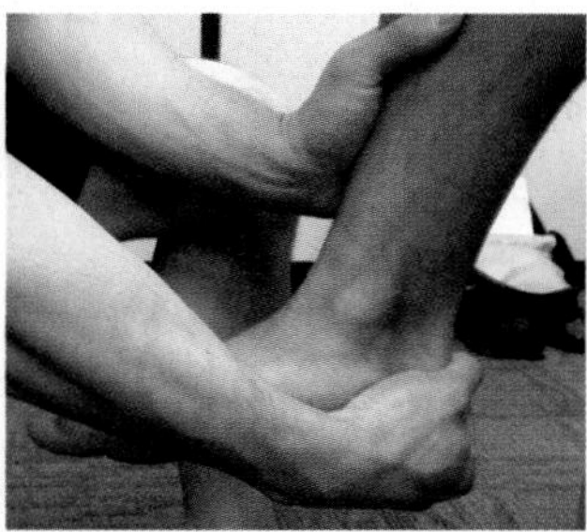

Choices:

1. Anterior tibiofibular ligament.
2. Tibiotalar ligament.
3. Calcaneofibular ligament.
4. Anterior talofibular ligament.

Teaching Points

Correct Answer: 4

The special test being performed is the anterior drawer test of the ankle. This test is designed primarily to test for injuries to the anterior talofibular ligament. This is the most frequently injured ligament in the ankle. When the foot is in slight plantarflexion position the anterior talofibular ligament is perpendicular to the long axis of the tibia. A positive anterior drawer test may be obtained with a tear of only the anterior talofibular ligament, but anterior translation is greater if the calcaneofibular ligament is also torn. Ideally, the knee should be placed in 90° of flexion to alleviate tension on the Achilles tendon.

Incorrect Choices:

The primary test for the calcaneofibular ligament is talar tilt. The tibiotalar and anterior tibiofibular ligament would not be stressed with the anterior drawer test.

Type of Reasoning: Analysis

One must understand the test described in the question in order to choose the correct solution. Through analytical reasoning, the test taker must determine how each ligament is tested. If this question was answered incorrectly, review information on provocative testing for ankle ligaments.

C134 

Musculoskeletal I Evaluation, Diagnosis

A patient with possible ligamentous injury of the knee presents with excessive tibial external rotation. Which ligament is **MOST LIKELY** to be injured?

Choices:

1. Posterior cruciate.
2. Medial patello-femoral.
3. Anterior cruciate.
4. Medial collateral.

Teaching Points

Correct Answer: 4

The medial collateral ligament prevents external rotation and provides stability to the knee. Excessive external rotation (ER) would represent injury to either the medial collateral ligament (MCL) or the lateral collateral ligament (LCL).

Incorrect Choices:

The anterior cruciate ligament (ACL) and posterior cruciate ligament (PCL) prevent internal rotation, and the medial patello-femoral ligament does not play a role in the prevention of tibial rotation.

Type of Reasoning: Inference

One needs to be aware of the anatomical attachment of both the cruciate and collateral ligaments in order to arrive at a correct conclusion. For this question, one must infer what is likely to be true of a case, which is an inferential reasoning skill. In this case, the medial collateral ligament is most likely injured. Review collateral and cruciate ligaments of the knee and stability if answered incorrectly.

C135 

Musculoskeletal | Interventions

A patient suffered a meniscus injury and underwent recent meniscal repair surgery. What is the earliest the patient will be allowed to weight bear after surgery?

Choices:

1. At the end of postsurgical week 1.
2. Immediately.
3. At the end of postsurgical week 3.
4. At the end of postsurgical week 2.

Teaching Points

Correct Answer: 3

After a meniscal repair, patients should be non-weight bearing for 3–6 weeks.

Incorrect Choices:

As the meniscus is still going through the healing process, it can be damaged if weight bearing occurs before 3 weeks.

Type of Reasoning: Deductive

One needs to know the difference in weight-bearing restrictions between a partial meniscectomy, which allows partial weight bearing as tolerated when full knee extension is obtained, and meniscus repair surgery, which requires 3–6 weeks of non-weight bearing for proper healing. This factual recall of guidelines is a deductive reasoning skill. For this situation, weight bearing can occur at the end of postsurgical week 3. Review postsurgical restrictions for meniscal repair if answered incorrectly.

C136

Musculoskeletal I Interventions

A therapist is treating a patient with a diagnosis of right shoulder rotator cuff tendinitis. The findings of a work site ergonomic assessment indicate that the worker is required to perform repetitive reaching activities above shoulder height. Which of the following is the **MOST** beneficial work site modification?

Choices:

1. Reposition the height of the shelf and items to below shoulder height.
2. Provide the worker with a taller, sit-stand chair.
3. Allow the worker to take more frequent rests to avoid overuse.
4. Provide the worker with a standing desk for daily activities.

Teaching Points

Correct Answer: 1

Work stations should be designed to accommodate the persons who actually work on the job. Work stations should be easily adjustable and designed to be comfortable for the worker. In this case, lowering the height of the shelf for frequent use is best.

Incorrect Choices:

Taking more frequent rests or providing a different chair does not eliminate the essential problem of repetitive overhead reach that is causing the shoulder tendinitis. Using a standing desk would eliminate overhead reach but is not as practical as lowering the shelf. In the workplace, individuals cannot be expected to stand all day long.

Type of Reasoning: Inference

One must infer the best solution to alleviate the patient's right shoulder rotator cuff tendinitis, given the nature of the patient's work environment. In this situation, one should infer that the overhead repetitive reaching is the cause for the diagnosis; therefore, reaching below shoulder height would help to alleviate the symptoms. If this question was answered incorrectly, refer to information on ergonomic workstation assessment.

C137

Musculoskeletal I Interventions

The patient has a fifth rib that is "stuck" in the position of maximal inspiration. Which technique is **BEST** to improve the rib mobility and assist it in returning to its resting position?

Choices:

1. Maitland grade IV mobilization of the head of the rib at the costovertebral joint in the superior direction.
2. Maitland grade II mobilization of the head of the rib at the costovertebral joint in the superior direction.
3. Maitland grade IV mobilization of the head of the rib at the costovertebral joint in the inferior direction.
4. Maitland grade II mobilization of the head of the rib at the costovertebral joint in the inferior direction.

Teaching Points

Correct Answer: 1

With inspiration, the lateral portion of the ribs moves up and the head moves down; to bring it back to a neutral position, the head needs to glide superiorly, allowing the lateral part of the rib to lower with expiration. Grade IV mobilizations are used to improve joint mobility.

Incorrect Choices:

All other choices have either the incorrect technique to improve joint mobility or incorrect direction.

Type of Reasoning: Inference

One needs to be knowledgeable of the different utilization of mobilization grades and of the biomechanics of the costovertebral joints during respiration in order to determine a correct conclusion. This necessitates inferring a best course of action for a successful clinical outcome, which is an inferential reasoning skill. For this situation, Maitland grade IV mobilization of the head of the rib at the costovertebral joint in the superior direction is best. Review Maitland's oscillatory techniques for the rib cage if answered incorrectly.

C138

Neuromuscular | Examination

A patient with a fibular fracture complains of weakness in the RLE following cast removal. Examination reveals measurable loss of muscle bulk (2-inch girth difference between the right and left legs). The therapist suspects neurogenic atrophy and next examines tone. Which finding is consistent with this diagnosis?

Choices:

1. Normal tone.
2. Hypotonia.
3. Dystonia.
4. Hypertonia.

Teaching Points

Correct Answer: 2

Hypotonia is one of a number of signs and symptoms of lower motor neuron (LMN) injury that also include neurogenic atrophy and weakness (as in this case), along with decreased or absent reflexes and fasciculations.

Incorrect Choices:

Hypertonia is seen with UMN lesion (corticospinal lesions). Dystonia is a CNS disorder characterized by prolonged involuntary muscular contractions and increased muscle tone. Tone should not be expected to be normal given the other findings.

Type of Reasoning: Inference

One must draw an appropriate conclusion of what is likely to be true in order to answer this question correctly. Questions that require one to determine what is likely to be true of a situation necessitate inferential reasoning. In this case, the most likely finding is hypotonia. Review hypotonia and typical features after cast removal if answered incorrectly.

Cardiovascular/Pulmonary and Lymphatic | Examination

A patient has a 10-year history of peripheral vascular disease (PVD) affecting the right lower extremity. During auscultation of the popliteal artery, what would the therapist expect to find?

Choices:

1. A positive Homan's sign.
2. Intense pain and cramping.
3. A bruit.
4. 4+ pulses.

Teaching Points

Correct Answer: 3

A bruit is a swishing sound that occurs in the presence of narrowing of an artery. It is a characteristic finding of PVD present on auscultation.

Incorrect Choices:

All other choices are not revealed on auscultation. Pulse palpation of the extremities will likely reveal a 0 (no pulse) or 1+ (diminished, barely perceptible), not 4+ (bounding, very strong). Homan's sign is pain in the calf when the foot is passively dorsiflexed. It is no longer considered an accurate test to detect DVT. Severe or intense pain with cramping is a likely response when the patient subjectively grades ambulatory ischemic pain. It is not auscultation.

Type of Reasoning: Inference

This question requires one to infer what a therapist should find with a patient who has a history of PVD. One must have a solid understanding of the nature of PVD and examination measures in order to choose the correct solution. If this question was answered incorrectly, review PVD examination.

Musculoskeletal | Examination

When performing the Thomas test, the patient's thigh does not touch the table, indicating limited hip extension. The amount of limited hip extension does not change when the ipsilateral knee is extended. What is the range-limiting muscle?

Choices:

1. Rectus femoris.
2. Tensor fascia lata.
3. Biceps femoris.
4. Iliopsoas.

Teaching Points

Correct Answer: 4

The iliopsoas is a one joint hip flexor muscle and will limit hip extension regardless of the amount of knee flexion.

Incorrect Choices:

The tensor fascia lata and rectus femoris are two joint muscles that flex the hip and extend the knee. Passive knee extension would allow for further hip extension in both of these muscles. The biceps femoris, a hamstring muscle, is a hip extensor and will not limit hip extension.

Type of Reasoning: Inference

One must infer the most likely muscle that is causing the limited hip extension, regardless of the amount of knee flexion present. This necessitates one to determine what is most likely to be true of a situation, which is an inferential reasoning skill. For this situation, the iliopsoas muscle is limiting the range. Review kinesiology of the hip and knee if answered incorrectly.

C141 

Musculoskeletal | Evaluation, Diagnosis

A teenager presents to the clinic with vague left hip and groin pain that worsens with weight bearing. The PT's examination reveals limited and painful hip internal rotation, antalgic gait, and a weak gluteus medius. Based upon this clinical presentation, what is the **MOST** likely diagnosis?

Choices:

1. Gluteus medius muscle strain.
2. Oligoarticular juvenile rheumatoid arthritis (JRA).
3. Slipped capital femoral epiphysis (SCFE).
4. Legg-Calvé-Perthes disease.

Teaching Points

Correct Answer: 3

The SCFE age range is 10–16 years of age, and the male to female ratio is 3:1. The incidence of left hip to right hip is 2:1, with 30% bilateral. The best examination findings include pain that worsens with weight bearing, limited and painful hip internal rotation, and weak hip abductors.

Incorrect Choices:

Legg-Calvé-Perthes disease is avascular necrosis of the femoral head with insidious onset between 3–12 years of age. The male to female ratio is 4:1. The clinical presentation is an antalgic gait, disuse atrophy of the hip and thigh muscles, and painful limitation of abduction and internal rotation. A gluteus medius muscle strain would present with more specific focal pain and pain with muscular contraction. The associated weakness in this case is secondary to an alteration of the length-tension relationship. Pauciarticular or oligoarticular JRA onset occurs in 40% of children with juvenile rheumatoid arthritis. In some combination, the knees, ankles, wrists, or elbows are the most frequently affected joints. The hips are usually spared.

Type of Reasoning: Inductive

This question provides a group of symptoms, and the test taker must determine the most likely diagnosis based on this information. Questions of this nature often require inductive reasoning skills. For this case, the symptoms most likely indicate slipped capital femoral epiphysis. If answered incorrectly, review signs and symptoms of SCFE.

C142 

Nonsystem | Equipment, Devices, Biophysical Agents

A patient with a transfemoral amputation and an above-knee prosthesis demonstrates knee instability while standing. The patient's knee buckles easily when performing weight shifts. What is the **MOST** likely cause of the problem?

Choices:

1. Weak gluteus medius.
2. Prosthetic knee set too far anterior to the TKA line.
3. Tight extension aid.
4. Prosthetic knee set too far posterior to the trochanter-knee-ankle (TKA) line.

Teaching Points

Correct Answer: 2

In order to increase stability of the knee, the prosthetic knee is normally aligned posterior to a line extending from the trochanter to the ankle (TKA line). A knee set anterior to the TKA line will buckle easily.

Incorrect Choices:

A prosthetic knee set too far posterior to the TKA would result in excessive knee stability and difficulty flexing the knee. The gluteus medius contributes to stability during stance, primarily lateral stability. Weak abductors can result in trunk lateral bend during stance. An extension aid assists knee extension during the latter part of swing phase. A tight extension aid will result in terminal swing impact during late swing.

Type of Reasoning: Inductive

Clinical judgment and diagnostic reasoning are utilized to determine the likely cause for the patient's knee instability while standing. Through inductive reasoning, the test taker should determine that the prosthetic knee is set too far anterior to the TKA line. If this question was answered incorrectly, review information on prosthetic adjustment/alignment for above-knee prostheses.

C143 

Neuromuscular | Examination

An older adult at risk for falls has undergone a structured home-based exercise program that consisted of standing balance training and strengthening exercises. Which measure is the **BEST** choice to document improvements?

Choices:

1. Timed Up & Go Test.
2. Berg Balance Test.
3. 6-Minute Walk Test.
4. Performance-Oriented Mobility Assessment (Tinetti).

Teaching Points

Correct Answer: 2

The Berg Balance Test is a 14-item test of static and dynamic balance in sitting and standing. It also examines sit-to-stand and stand-to-sit transitions. It does not include items examining gait. Gait was not part of this person's training program.

Incorrect Choices:

The TUG and Tinetti examine gait along with balance. The 6-Minute Walk Test is a measure of walking endurance.

Type of Reasoning: Inductive

This question requires clinical judgment to determine the **BEST** measurement tool for improvement in balance. This is an inductive reasoning skill, where clinical knowledge is applied to therapeutic situations to determine a best course of action. For this situation, the Berg Balance Test is best. If answered incorrectly, review balance tests, especially the Berg Balance Test.

C144 

Musculoskeletal | Evaluation, Diagnosis

A middle-aged patient complains of "throbbing pain" in the lumbar region with activities upon exertion, such as walking up a flight of steps or playing tennis. The patient expresses no complaints of pain with bending, twisting, sitting, standing, or walking any distance. Active movements of the lumbar spine are full and pain free. Provocation testing is negative. Neurological signs are unremarkable. There is no significant tenderness to palpation. What is the **MOST** likely diagnosis for this patient?

Choices:

1. Lumbar disc herniation.
2. Aortic aneurysm.
3. Quadratus lumborum muscle strain.
4. Sacroiliac joint sprain.

Teaching Points

Correct Answer: 2

Throbbing low back pain that occurs only with activities that increase the heart rate is a red flag for aortic aneurysm. Medical referral is indicated.

Incorrect Choices:

The fact that the patient reports no pain with activities such as bending, twisting, sitting, and walking reduces the odds that the problem is mechanical. In addition, the fact that the symptoms could not be reproduced during the physical therapy examination reduces the odds that it is a musculoskeletal condition.

Type of Reasoning: Analysis

This question provides a group of symptoms that the test taker must analyze to determine the most likely diagnosis. Questions of this nature often require analytical reasoning skill. For this situation, the most likely diagnosis is aortic aneurysm, given the symptoms presented. Review signs and symptoms of aortic aneurysm if answered incorrectly.

C145

Neuromuscular | Interventions

A patient who is undergoing spinal cord rehabilitation is viewed as uncooperative by staff. The patient refuses to complete the training activities outlined to promote independent functional mobility. A review of history reveals that previously the patient was the director of a company with a staff of 20. What is the **MOST** appropriate action the therapist can take?

Choices:

1. Have the patient work with a supervisor who is a person in authority.
2. Refer the patient to a support group before resuming rehabilitation.
3. Involve the patient in goal setting and structuring the training session.
4. Carefully structure the activities and slow down the pace of training.

Teaching Points

Correct Answer: 3

An andragogical approach is best. The patient is an adult learner who should be allowed to share in the responsibility for planning the learning experience and goal setting. The therapist should help clarify the problem, structure the learning environment, and provide necessary resources.

Incorrect Choices:

Passing the buck or transferring responsibility to a supervisor is not appropriate. Requiring participation in a support group before continuing rehabilitation or slowing down the pace of training would negatively impact rehabilitation and result in increased length of stay.

Type of Reasoning: Evaluation

One must evaluate the merits of each statement in order to make a best course determination for this patient. This question requires a judgment call and a value judgment, which necessitates evaluative reasoning skill. For this patient, it is **MOST** appropriate to involve the patient in goal setting and have him participate in structuring the training session.

Nonsystem | Safety, Professional Responsibilities, Research

A group of 10 patients is recruited into a study investigating the effects of relaxation training on blood pressure (BP). One group of patients is scheduled to participate in a supervised cardiac rehabilitation program that includes relaxation training three times a week for 12 weeks. The other group of patients is instructed to perform activities as usual. At the conclusion of the study, there was no significant difference between the groups; BP decreased significantly in both groups. What is the **MOST** accurate interpretation of this study?

Choices:

1. The rehabilitation group was not properly monitored.
2. Both groups had BPs initially so high that reductions should have been expected.
3. The activities of the nonrehabilitation group were not properly monitored and may account for these results.
4. Cardiac rehabilitation is not effective in reducing BP.

Teaching Points

Correct Answer: 3

To ensure adequate control, the researcher should attempt to remove the influence of any variable other than the independent variable in order to evaluate its effect on the dependent variable. In this study, the investigator did not adequately investigate the usual activities of the control group. The small number of subjects may also have contributed to lack of significance.

Incorrect Choices:

Accepting any statements concerning initial BP or changes in BP is not warranted because data on specific BPs were not provided. The rehabilitation group was closely supervised.

Type of Reasoning: Inference

Whereas research-related questions are typically factual in nature, requiring deductive reasoning skill, this question specifically asks for one to draw conclusions based on evidence and infer the reason for the research outcomes, which is an inferential reasoning skill.

C147 

Neuromuscular | Examination

A therapist is examining a patient newly diagnosed with multiple sclerosis. The patient experiences an intense shock-like pain throughout the body when the neck is passively flexed. What is the correct term for the therapist to use in order to document these findings?

Choices:

1. Lhermitte's sign.
2. Dysesthesias.
3. Paresthesias.
4. Uthoff's sign.

Teaching Points

Correct Answer: 1

Lhermitte's sign is a sign of posterior column damage in the spinal cord; flexion of the neck produces an electric shock-like painful sensation running down the spine and into the LEs. It can be seen in patients with MS.

Incorrect Choices:

Sensory disturbances are common in MS, although not described in this case. Paresthesias are abnormal sensations such as numbness, prickling, or tingling. Dyesthesias are abnormal and unpleasant sensations such as burning or pins and needles. Uthoff's sign is an adverse reaction to heat commonly seen in patients with MS.

Type of Reasoning: Analysis

One must analyze the presenting symptoms and determine the most likely cause for those symptoms. This necessitates analytical reasoning skill, where a cluster of symptoms must be weighed to draw a conclusion. For this case, the symptoms indicate the patient is demonstrating a Lhermitte's sign. If answered incorrectly, review common features of multiple sclerosis, especially Lhermitte's sign.

C148 

Cardiovascular/Pulmonary and Lymphatic | Examination

Which cluster of examination findings would indicate that a patient is in decompensated heart failure?

Choices:

1. S4 heart sound, wheezes on lung auscultation, decreased jugular vein distension.
2. S4 heart sound, crackles on lung auscultation, increased jugular vein distension.
3. S2 heart sound, crackles on lung auscultation, decreased jugular vein distension.
4. S2 heart sound, wheezes on lung auscultation, increased jugular vein distension.

Teaching Points

Correct Answer: 2

S4 indicates a pathology in the ventricle, as is present in a patient with heart failure. Crackles on auscultation are often heard in a patient with heart failure because they have compressive atelectasis due to pulmonary edema. When cued to take a deep breath, they can create enough pressure to open the alveoli, which causes the crackling sound. It is possible that a patient in heart failure will also have wheezes if there is significant pulmonary edema causing the alveoli to fill with fluid. With decompensated heart failure, there will be a back-up of fluid throughout the cardiac and pulmonary system, which can extend into the peripheral circulatory system. This will cause increased distension of the jugular veins.

Incorrect Choices:

An S2 heart sound is a normal sound, indicating the closure of the aortic and pulmonic valves. Decreased jugular vein distension occurs only when a patient has decreased volume or is dehydrated.

Type of Reasoning: Inductive

For this question, the test taker must utilize clinical judgment to determine the findings that best indicate decompensated heart failure. This is an inductive reasoning skill. For this situation, S4 heart sound, crackles on lung auscultation, and increased jugular vein distension are all indicative of decompensated heart failure. Review heart failure guidelines and signs and symptoms of decompensated heart failure if answered incorrectly.

C149 

Neuromuscular | Evaluation, Diagnosis

A physical therapist is observing a child who is typically developing and has just begun to walk within the last month. Which of the following is expected in a child just learning to walk?

Choices:

1. Neutral hip position.
2. Bilateral hip adduction.
3. Genu valgum.
4. External rotation of the hips.

Teaching Points

Correct Answer: 4

Children who have just begun to walk externally rotate their hips (toe out) for balance. This increases the base of support.

Incorrect Choices:

Children who have just learned to walk independently (12–15 months of age) typically display bowed legs (genu varum), flexion at the hips to keep the center of gravity forward, and have a wide base of support (hips in abduction). They also demonstrate "high guard" position of their upper extremities to help maintain balance.

Type of Reasoning: Inference

This question requires one to infer what is likely to be true of a therapeutic situation, which often necessitates inferential reasoning skill. One must also recall the developmental gait patterns of children. In this case, one would expect the child to demonstrate external rotation of the hips. If this question was answered incorrectly, review developmental gait patterns in children.

C150 

Musculoskeletal | Interventions

Where should a therapist's hand/fingers be located for posteroanterior mobilization to improve down-gliding/closure of the T7–8 facet joints?

Choices:

1. Spinous process of T6.
2. Transverse processes of T8.
3. Spinous process of T8.
4. Transverse processes of T7.

Teaching Points

Correct Answer: 2

The axis of motion for the mid-thoracic vertebrae is above the spinous processes and below the transverse processes. Therefore, if down-gliding/closure of T7–8 vertebral segment is required, the therapist's hand placement should be at the transverse process of T8 or the spinous process of T7.

Incorrect Choices:

PA pressures on the spinous process in this region of the thoracic spine will cause the spinous process to glide into and compress the spinous process of the segment below, so no arthrokinematic glide will occur. A PA central glide to the transverse process of T7 will increase extension between T6 and T7.

Type of Reasoning: Analysis

One must determine the correct mobilization techniques to improve down-gliding/closure of the T7–8 facet joints in order to arrive at the correct conclusion. This requires knowledge of appropriate mobilization techniques of the thoracic spine, including how to mobilize facet joints. Through analytical reasoning, one should conclude that the correct hand/finger placements should be located at the transverse processes of T8.

C151

Neuromuscular | Evaluation, Diagnosis

A patient complains of waking up several times at night from severe "pins and needles" in the right hand. On awakening, the hand feels numb for half an hour and fine hand movements are impaired. The therapist's examination reveals sensory loss and paresthesias in the thumb, index, middle, and lateral half of the ring finger, and reduced grip and pinch strength. Some thenar atrophy is present. Based on these examination findings, what is the **MOST** appropriate diagnosis?

Choices:

1. Pronator teres syndrome.
2. Ulnar nerve entrapment.
3. Thoracic outlet syndrome.
4. Carpal tunnel syndrome.

Teaching Points

Correct Answer: 4

Carpal tunnel syndrome is the result of compression of the median nerve under the flexor retinaculum at the wrist. It is characterized by thenar atrophy and sensory loss. Symptoms are worse at night and include burning, tingling, pins and needles, and numbness into the median nerve sensory distribution (palmar and dorsal thumb, index, middle, and lateral half of the ring finger).

Incorrect Choices:

Thoracic outlet syndrome is a neurovascular compression syndrome caused by compression of nerves and/or vessels in the neck. It is characterized by brachial neuritis with or without vascular and vasomotor disturbances in the upper extremity. Electrophysiological studies indicate proximal and not distal compression. Ulnar nerve entrapment typically presents with nocturnal numbness and sensory loss in the little finger and half of the ring finger. The palm is typically not affected. Pronator teres syndrome arises from compression of the median nerve at the elbow with radiation into the radial aspect of the hand. Pronation is possible but weak (not evident in this case). Numbness extends into the median nerve distribution. With passage of time, atrophy of the thenar muscles will occur.

Type of Reasoning: Analysis

One must analyze the symptoms presented in order to make a determination of the likely diagnosis. This requires analytical reasoning skills as one must determine the meaning of the symptoms in order to determine a diagnosis for the patient. In this case, the symptoms indicate carpal tunnel syndrome, which should be reviewed if this question was answered incorrectly.

C152

Musculoskeletal | Examination

A patient is referred for physical therapy with a diagnosis of degenerative joint disease (DJD) affecting C2 and C3. The patient complains of pain and stiffness in the cervical region and transient dizziness with some cervical motions. What is the **BEST** initial examination procedure?

Choices:

1. Vertebral artery test.
2. Adson's maneuver.
3. Lhermitte's test.
4. Oppenheim's test.

Teaching Points

Correct Answer: 1

The vertebral artery test checks the integrity of the blood flow through the artery in the cervical region. Because the patient is experiencing symptoms of circulatory disturbance and a unilateral pull could compress the left cervical structures, the vertebral artery test is an appropriate screening test. The test consists of passively placing the patient's head in extension and side flexion in a supine position. Then the head and neck are slowly rotated to the laterally flexed side and held for 30 seconds. Some of the positive signs may be syncope, lightheadedness, nystagmus, or visual disturbances. Though there are some doubts about the sensitivity/specificity of this test, the patient's initial complaint of dizziness with some cervical movements would indicate that it be applied in this case.

Incorrect Choices:

Lhermitte's sign is pain down the spine and into the upper or lower limbs with passive flexion of the neck. It is used to identify dysfunction of the spinal cord associated with upper motor neuron lesions and is typically positive in MS. Adson's maneuver is a test for thoracic outlet syndrome (TOS). Oppenheim's test involves running a fingernail along the crest of the tibia; a positive test is the same as a positive Babinski.

Type of Reasoning: Inference

One must first determine the meaning of each of the four possible tests and then infer which one is the **BEST** initial test, given the patient's diagnosis and symptoms. If this question was answered incorrectly, review the vertebral artery test.

C153 

Neuromuscular | Evaluation, Diagnosis

A young, otherwise healthy, adult is recovering from a complete spinal cord injury (ASIA A) at the level of L4. What are the functional expectations for this individual?

Choices:

1. Ambulation using bilateral AFOs and canes.
2. Ambulation using bilateral KAFOs, crutches, and a swing-through gait.
3. Ambulation using reciprocating gait orthoses and a reciprocating walker.
4. Ambulation using bilateral KAFOs and a reciprocating walker.

Teaching Points

Correct Answer: 1

A spinal cord lesion at the level of L4 is considered an LMN injury (cauda equina injury). Intact movements include hip flexion, hip adduction, and knee extension. The quadriceps become **FULLY** innervated at L4. This patient can be expected to be a functional ambulator using bilateral AFOs and crutches or canes.

Incorrect Choices:

All other choices include orthotic devices that offer control of joints that is not needed (orthotic bracing of knees and hips). Also crutches or walkers should not be needed.

Type of Reasoning: Analysis

One must recall past knowledge of neuroscience related to spinal cord injuries in order to determine the functional expectations for the patient with a complete L4 injury. In order to arrive at the correct conclusion, one must analyze the four possible choices and determine which choice is most aligned with one's knowledge of injury at this level. If this question was answered incorrectly, review functional expectations for patients with lumbar spinal cord injuries.

C154

Neuromuscular | Examination

To examine a patient with a suspected deficit in graphesthesia, what should the therapist ask the patient to identify with eyes closed?

Choices:

1. Different objects placed in the hand and manipulated.
2. The vibrations of a tuning fork when placed on a bony prominence.
3. A series of letters traced on the hand.
4. Differently weighted, identically shaped cylinders placed in the hand.

Teaching Points

Correct Answer: 3

Graphesthesia is the ability to recognize numbers, letters, or symbols traced on the skin.

Incorrect Choices:

Barognosis is the ability to recognize different weights placed in the hand using identically shaped objects. Pallesthesia is the ability to recognize vibratory stimuli (i.e., a vibrating tuning fork placed on a bony prominence). Stereognosis is the ability to recognize different objects placed in the hand and manipulated. During testing, vision is occluded.

Type of Reasoning: Deductive

This question requires factual recall of the definition of graphesthesia, which is a deductive reasoning skill. Using past knowledge of neuroscience is beneficial to arriving at the correct solution. If this question was answered incorrectly, review sensory testing procedures.

C155 

Neuromuscular | Interventions

A patient recovering from stroke is ambulatory without an assistive device and demonstrates a consistent problem with an elevated and retracted pelvis on the affected side. Which manual therapeutic exercise procedure is the **BEST** choice to remediate this problem?

Choices:

1. Provide downward compression during stance.
2. Utilize light resistance to posterior pelvic elevation during swing.
3. Provide anterior-directed pressure during swing.
4. Utilize light resistance to forward pelvic rotation during swing.

Teaching Points

Correct Answer: 4

An elevated and retracted pelvis is a common problem during gait for many patients recovering from a stroke. Providing light resistance to forward pelvic rotation actively engages those muscles and reciprocally inhibits the spastic retractors.

Incorrect Choices:

Providing anterior-directed pressure during swing or resistance to pelvic elevation may serve to only increase the problem. Downward compression during stance is also inappropriate as this is a swing phase deficit.

Type of Reasoning: Inductive

One must utilize clinical judgment in order to determine which therapeutic exercise procedure would **BEST** address the patient's problem. Using inductive reasoning skills, the test taker must analyze the four possible choices and then rely on knowledge of mobility challenges in a stroke in order to determine the **BEST** course of action for this patient.

C156 

Neuromuscular | Examination

A therapist suspects lower brain stem involvement in a patient with amyotrophic lateral sclerosis (ALS). Examination findings reveal motor impairments of the tongue with ipsilateral wasting and deviation on protrusion. These findings confirm involvement of which cranial nerve?

Choices:

1. Hypoglossal.
2. Glossopharyngeal.
3. Vagus.
4. Spinal accessory.

Teaching Points

Correct Answer: 1

The hypoglossal (CN XII) controls the movements of the tongue. Ipsilateral wasting and the deviation to the ipsilateral side on protrusion are indicative of damage.

Incorrect Choices:

Involvement of the glossopharyngeal (CN IX) results in slight dysphagia, loss of taste in the posterior third of the tongue, and loss of gag reflex. Involvement of the spinal accessory nerve (CN XI) results in minor problems in deglutition and phonation along with weakness in ipsilateral shoulder shrugging. Involvement of the vagus (CN X) results in dysphagia, hoarseness, and paralysis of the soft palate.

Type of Reasoning: Analysis

This question requires one to recall the functions of the 12 cranial nerves and then determine which nerve is most likely impaired in this situation. Questions that involve determining an impairment based on a group of symptoms require analytical reasoning skill. If this question was answered incorrectly, review examination of the 12 cranial nerves.

C157

Musculoskeletal | Evaluation, Diagnosis

A baseball pitcher reports insidious onset of symptoms characteristic of impingement, including catching and popping in the throwing arm. Examination reveals that glenohumeral passive internal rotation is painful and limited to 30°. External rotation is less symptomatic and has 130° of passive range. What is the **BEST** initial course of action for the therapist?

Choices:

1. Recommend an MRI.
2. Mobilize the glenohumeral joint to increase internal rotation ROM.
3. Begin elastic resistance exercises for impingement.
4. Recommend an anteroposterior radiograph.

Teaching Points

Correct Answer: 1

The therapist should suspect a labral tear. This is a common finding among pitchers and athletes who do a lot of throwing (especially those who present with abnormal ROM findings and instability symptoms of popping and catching). Although this athlete may present with impingement, an MRI is warranted to fully diagnose the condition and to develop an appropriate treatment plan.

Incorrect Choices:

Beginning treatment without definitive testing is contraindicated. Plain radiographs are inappropriate for suspected soft tissue lesions.

Type of Reasoning: Inductive

This question requires clinical judgment to determine a best course of action for a patient with painful passive internal rotation with limitations in range. Questions that require one to weigh a group of symptoms and determine a best course of action often necessitate inductive reasoning skills. If this question was answered incorrectly, review signs and symptoms of labral tear and diagnostic testing.

C158

System Interactions | Evaluation, Diagnosis

A woman is hospitalized in the intensive care unit with multiple closed and open fractures after a motor vehicle accident. A review of her medical record reveals the following laboratory values: hematocrit 28%, hemoglobin 10 g/100 mL and serum white blood cell (WBC) count 12,000/mm^3. What is the **MOST** accurate interpretation of these findings?

Choices:

1. Only serum WBC is abnormal.
2. Only hematocrit values are abnormal.
3. Hematocrit and hemoglobin values are abnormal; WBC is normal.
4. All values are abnormal.

Teaching Points

Correct Answer: 4

The hematocrit value is abnormally low; women average 42% with a normal range from 37%–47%. The hemoglobin value is also abnormally low; women average 12–16 g/100 mL of blood. The low values are most likely due to blood loss. The serum WBC (leukocytes) is abnormally high; normal values are 5,000 to 10,000/mm³. The elevated count (> 10,000) indicates acute infection.

Incorrect Choices:

The other choices present findings in which only some, not all, of the values are abnormal.

Type of Reasoning: Deductive

One must recall the normal laboratory values for female adults in order to arrive at the correct conclusion. This necessitates deductive reasoning, in which recall of factual knowledge and protocols is utilized to determine the correct solution. In this situation, all of the laboratory values are abnormal. If this question was answered incorrectly, review the parameters for these adult laboratory values.

C159 

Integumentary | Evaluation, Diagnosis

A patient with a transfemoral amputation is unable to wear a total contact prosthesis for the past 4 days. Examination of the residual limb reveals erythema and edema extending over most of the lower anterior limb. The patient tells the therapist that the limb is very itchy and painful. What is the **MOST** likely cause of these symptoms?

Choices:

1. Impetigo.
2. Herpes zoster.
3. Cellulitis.
4. Dermatitis.

Teaching Points

Correct Answer: 4

This patient is exhibiting symptoms of contact dermatitis. Primary treatment is removal of the offending agent (in this case, the total contact prosthesis) and treatment of the involved skin with lubricants, topical anesthetics, and/or steroids. The patient may require a thin sock if the problem does not resolve.

Incorrect Choices:

Cellulitis is a suppurative inflammation of the dermis and subcutaneous tissues frequently accompanied by infection. Impetigo is a staphylococcal infection with small macules (unraised spots) or vesicles (small blisters). Herpes zoster is a viral infection with red papules along the course of a nerve or dermatome.

Type of Reasoning: Analysis

This question requires the test taker to determine the **MOST LIKELY** cause for the patient's symptoms, which is an analytical reasoning skill. In order to arrive at the correct conclusion, one must analyze the four possible choices and determine which choice is most aligned with one's knowledge of skin irritations, inflammations, and infections. If this question was answered incorrectly, review symptoms and treatment approaches for dermatitis.

C160

Musculoskeletal | Examination

A PT is treating a patient who lacks wrist extension. The cause of the impairment is a problem at the radiocarpal joint with a lack of arthrokinematic motion necessary for proper wrist extension. What direction should the proximal aspect of the scaphoid/lunate glide?

Choices:

1. In a dorsal direction relative to the radius.
2. Radially.
3. Ulnarly.
4. In a palmar direction relative to the radius.

Teaching Points

Correct Answer: 4

The correct description of the arthrokinematic motion occurring at the radiocarpal joint lacking in this patient is the palmar glide. Due to the anatomical structure of the bones forming this joint, the convex scaphoid and lunate articulate with the concave radius, resulting in opposite roll and glide during extension.

Incorrect Choices:

Other choices describe movements occurring during ulnar and radial wrist deviation or of the glide occurring during flexion.

Type of Reasoning: Deductive

One needs to understand the convex-concave rules of joint movement to arrive at a correct conclusion. This requires recall of the anatomical structures of the wrist and proper rolls and glides, which is factual information and therefore a deductive reasoning skill. For this case, the therapist should glide the lunate/scaphoid palmarly relative to the radius. Review concave-convex rules of the wrist and mobilization techniques if answered incorrectly.

C161 

Musculoskeletal | Examination

Following a hip fracture that is now healed, a patient presents with weak hip flexors (2/5). All other muscles are within functional limits. Based on these findings, what should the therapist expect the patient may display during gait?

Choices:

1. Backward trunk lean.
2. Forward trunk lean.
3. A circumducted gait.
4. Excessive hip flexion.

Teaching Points

Correct Answer: 3

Circumduction is a compensation for weak hip flexors or an inability to shorten the leg (weak knee flexors and ankle dorsiflexors). Hip hiking can also compensate for an abnormally long leg (lack of knee flexion and dorsiflexion).

Incorrect Choices:

Excessive hip flexion is a compensation for footdrop. Forward trunk lean and backward trunk lean are stance phase deviations that compensate for quadriceps weakness and gluteus maximus weakness, respectively.

Type of Reasoning: Inference

This question requires the test taker to draw conclusions based on evidence presented, which is an inferential reasoning skill. Questions of this nature often provide a diagnosis, and the test taker must infer the likely symptoms. In this case, the test taker must determine that a patient with weak hip flexors will display a circumducted gait pattern during ambulation. If this question was answered incorrectly, review causes for a circumducted gait pattern.

C162 

Musculoskeletal | Interventions

An elderly patient with a left transfemoral amputation complains that when sitting, the left foot feels cramped and twisted. What is the therapist's **BEST** choice of intervention?

Choices:

1. Appropriate bed positioning with the residual limb in extension.
2. Iontophoresis to the distal residual limb using hyaluronidase.
3. Hot packs and continuous US to the residual limb.
4. Icing and massage to the residual limb.

Teaching Points

Correct Answer: 4

This patient is experiencing phantom pain, a common occurrence seen in as many as 70% of patients with lower limb amputations. Treatment interventions can include icing, pulsed US, TENS, or massage. Medical interventions for prolonged and intractable pain can include injections and surgical procedures (rhizotomy, neurectomy).

Incorrect Choices:

Prolonged inactivity and bed rest are contraindicated. Hyaluronidase is indicated for edema reduction. Continuous US is used to achieve thermal effects; heating is not indicated in this case.

Type of Reasoning: Inductive

This question asks the test taker to first consider what the cause for the symptoms is and then determine the **BEST** choice for intervention with this patient. This is an inductive reasoning skill, in which diagnostic reasoning is used to determine best approaches to clinical situations. For this patient, the symptoms clearly indicate phantom pain, and icing and massage to the residual limb are **BEST** to treat the symptoms.

C163

Nonsystem | Safety, Professional Responsibilities, Research

A researcher uses a group of volunteers (healthy college students) to study the effects of therapy ball exercises on ankle ROM and balance scores. Twenty volunteers participated in the 20-minute ball exercise class three times a week for 6 weeks. Measurements were taken at the beginning and end of the sessions. Significant differences were found in both sets of scores and reported at the local physical therapy meeting. What is the **MOST** accurate interpretation of this study and its results?

Choices:

1. The reliability of the study was threatened with the introduction of systematic error of measurement.
2. The Hawthorne effect may have influenced the outcomes of the study.
3. The validity of the study was threatened with the introduction of sampling bias.
4. Therapy ball exercises are an effective intervention to improve ankle stability after chronic ankle sprain.

Teaching Points

Correct Answer: 3

The investigator used a sample of convenience and therefore introduced systematic sampling error (a threat to validity). Random selection of subjects would improve the validity of this study.

Incorrect Choices:

Generalization to a group of patients with chronic ankle sprain cannot be made. There was no systematic error in measurement in this example. The Hawthorne effect refers to the influence that the subject's knowledge of participation in the experiment had on the results of the study.

Type of Reasoning: Inference

The test taker must determine what the most likely conclusion should be to this research study, given the protocol implemented. Questions that require one to draw conclusions based on evidence necessitate inferential reasoning skills to come to the correct conclusion. In this study, the validity has been threatened by convenience sampling. If this question was answered incorrectly, review guidelines to improve validity in research.

C164

Cardiovascular/Pulmonary and Lymphatic | Interventions

A patient has a very large right-sided bacterial pneumonia. Oxygen level is dangerously low. Which of the following body positions is the **MOST** likely to improve this patient's arterial oxygen pressure (PaO_2)?

Choices:

1. Prone-lying with the head of the bed in the Trendelenburg position.
2. Right side-lying with the head of the bed in the flat position.
3. Left side-lying with the head of the bed in the flat position.
4. Supine-lying with the head of the bed in the Trendelenburg position.

Teaching Points

Correct Answer: 3

In order to match perfusion and ventilation, the therapist needs to place the unaffected side in a gravity-dependent position or that of left side-lying.

Incorrect Choices:

Although prone and supine with the head of the bed in the flat position might be helpful, these positions would not be as likely to show as much improvement as left side-lying. The use of the Trendelenburg position (head lower than legs) is inappropriate.

Type of Reasoning: Inference

The test taker must infer the best body position in order to improve the patient's PaO_2 level. Knowledge of pulmonary rehabilitation guidelines is important in order to arrive at the correct conclusion. If this question was answered incorrectly, refer to pulmonary rehabilitation guidelines for patients with low PaO_2, especially body positions in bed.

C165 

Musculoskeletal | Evaluation, Diagnosis

An examination of a patient reveals drooping of the shoulder, rotary winging of the scapula, an inability to shrug the shoulder, and complaints of aching in the shoulder. Based on these findings, what is the **MOST** likely cause of these symptoms?

Choices:

1. Strain of the serratus anterior.
2. A lesion of the spinal accessory nerve.
3. A lesion of the long thoracic nerve.
4. Muscle imbalance.

Teaching Points

Correct Answer: 2

Rotary winging occurs when the inferior angle of one scapula is rotated farther from the spine than the inferior angle of the other scapula. The shoulder drooping and inability to shrug the shoulder are secondary to a lesion of the spinal accessory nerve (CN XI), which innervates the trapezius muscle.

Incorrect Choices:

Although this type of winging could be found with all of these answers, the findings of shoulder drooping and inability to shrug the shoulder clearly point to a lesion of CN XI.

Type of Reasoning: Analysis

This question requires the test taker to determine the diagnosis based on symptoms presented, which is an analytical reasoning skill. Knowledge of neuroscience and nerve innervations of the cervical spine is beneficial to arriving at the correct conclusion. If this question was answered incorrectly, refer to innervations of the spinal accessory nerve and symptoms of lesions associated with this nerve.

C166 

Nonsystem | Equipment, Devices, Biophysical Agents

A patient with spastic hemiplegia is referred to the therapist for ambulation training. The patient is having difficulty with standing up from a seated position as the result of co-contraction of the quadriceps and hamstrings during the knee and hip extension phase. The therapist wishes to use biofeedback beginning with simple knee extension exercise in the seated position. The plan is to progress to sit-to-stand training. What is the proper initial biofeedback protocol?

Choices:

1. Low-detection sensitivity with recording electrodes placed far apart.
2. High-detection sensitivity with recording electrodes placed closely together.
3. Low-detection sensitivity with recording electrodes placed closely together.
4. High-detection sensitivity with recording electrodes placed far apart.

Teaching Points

Correct Answer: 3

By initially placing the electrodes close together, the therapist decreases the likelihood of detecting undesired motor units from adjacent active muscles (crosstalk). By setting the biofeedback sensitivity (gain) low, the therapist would decrease the amplitude of the signals generated by the hypertonic muscles and keep the EMG output from exceeding a visual and/or auditory range (scale).

Incorrect Choices:

The other choices fail to use optimal placing of electrodes (electrodes placed far apart) or sensitivity (high-detection) to optimize outcomes. The wider the spacing of electrodes, the more volume of the muscle is monitored. Thus, when targeting a specific muscle, a narrow spacing should be used. When the focus is not on a specific muscle but rather to encourage a general motion such as shoulder elevation, then a wider spacing of electrodes can be used. In addition, when working with weakness of a muscle in which there is a decreased ability to recruit motor units or there is a decrease in the size and number of motor units, then a wider spacing and a high sensitivity would be used in order to create an adequate visible signal.

Type of Reasoning: Inductive

One must utilize clinical judgment and diagnostic reasoning in order to determine the most appropriate initial biofeedback protocol. This requires knowledge of biofeedback guidelines and benefits of using high- versus low-detection sensitivity and electrodes placed either closely together or far apart. If this question was answered incorrectly, review biofeedback guidelines of the lower extremity.

C167 

Neuromuscular | Examination

Examination of a patient recovering from stroke reveals a loss of pain and temperature sensation on the left side of the face along with loss of pain and temperature sensation on the right side of the body. All other sensations are normal. What is the likely location of the lesion?

Choices:

1. Right cerebral cortex or internal capsule.
2. Midbrain.
3. Left cerebral cortex or internal capsule.
4. Left posterolateral medulla.

Teaching Points

Correct Answer: 4

A lesion in the posterolateral medulla causes mixed sensory loss (described in this case). Pain and temperature are affected, whereas discriminative touch and proprioception are not (the medial lemniscus is not involved).

Incorrect Choices:

Sensory loss will be completely contralateral (not mixed) only after the discriminative sensory tracts (fasciculus gracilis and fasciculus cuneatus) cross in the upper medulla. Patients with lesions above the medulla (midbrain, cortex, or internal capsule) will present with contralateral sensory loss.

Type of Reasoning: Analysis

This question requires the test taker to determine the location of a lesion based on symptoms presented, which is an analytical reasoning skill. Knowledge of neuroscience and the discriminative sensory tracts is beneficial to arriving at the correct conclusion. If this question was answered incorrectly, refer to information regarding the discriminative sensory tracts and lesions.

C168

Neuromuscular | Evaluation, Diagnosis

A patient is taking the drug baclofen to control spasticity after a complete spinal cord injury at T10. This medication can be expected to decrease muscle tone and pain. What are the possible adverse effects of taking baclofen?

Choices:

1. Urinary retention and discomfort.
2. Drowsiness and muscle weakness.
3. Hypertension and palpitations.
4. Headache with visual auras.

Teaching Points

Correct Answer: 2

Baclofen, used in the management of spasticity, can produce CNS depression (drowsiness, fatigue, weakness, confusion, vertigo, dizziness, and insomnia), occurring in less than 10% of patients. Additional adverse effects can include hypotension and palpitations and urinary frequency. Vomiting, seizures, and coma are signs of overdosage.

Incorrect Choices:

Adverse effects include hypotension not hypertension. Headaches with visual auras are characteristic of migraines. Urinary frequency not retention is also an adverse effect.

Type of Reasoning: Deductive

One must recall the possible adverse effects of taking baclofen in order to arrive at the correct conclusion. This requires knowledge of guidelines and factual information, which is a deductive reasoning skill. If this question was answered incorrectly, refer to therapeutic uses of baclofen, including adverse effects.

C169 

Musculoskeletal / Examination

A teen-aged female distance runner presents a history of stress fractures and general leg pain. Her parents think it may be due to overtraining. Based on this subjective information, what should the physical therapist question the patient about next?

Choices:

1. Recent growth spurts.
2. Menses and eating habits.
3. Type of running shoe.
4. Participation in other sports.

Teaching Points

Correct Answer: 2

The female athlete triad is a syndrome common in females 14–20 years of age that consists of three related conditions: disordered eating habits, irregular or absent menstrual periods, and osteopenia (thinning of the bone density). It is imperative that the therapist inquire about menses and eating habits as they are two of the three hallmark signs of the female athlete triad. It would also be helpful for the physical therapist to inquire more about muscle pain, medications, and details of training regimen.

Incorrect Choices:

Recent growth spurts, participation in other sports, and type of shoes will not rule in/out the possibility of the runner having this serious condition.

Type of Reasoning: Evaluation

In this question, the therapist must determine the **BEST** course of questioning to determine the patient's likelihood of female athlete triad. This requires evaluative reasoning skill. If answered incorrectly, review symptoms and examination of female athlete triad.

C170 

Cardiovascular/Pulmonary and Lymphatic | Interventions

A patient is exercising in a phase 3 outpatient cardiac rehabilitation program that utilizes circuit training. One of the stations utilizes weights. The patient lifts a 5-lb weight, holds it for 20 seconds, and then lowers it slowly. The therapist corrects the activity and tells the patient to reduce the length of the static hold. Which of the following **BEST** describes the expected effects of isometric exercise?

Choices:

1. Reduced normal venous return to the heart and elevated BP.
2. Abnormal oxygen uptake.
3. Lower heart rate (HR) and arterial blood pressure (BP).
4. Higher HR and arterial BP.

Teaching Points

Correct Answer: 4

Dynamic exercise facilitates circulation, while isometric (static) exercise hinders blood flow, producing higher HRs and arterial BPs. Rise in BP is related to degree of intensity (effort).

Incorrect Choices:

Resistance exercise does little to increase oxygen uptake. HR and BP are higher (not lower). The Valsalva maneuver (forced expiration against a closed glottis) that accompanies breath holding produces increased intrathoracic pressure, which in turn hinders normal venous return to the heart. Breath holding is more likely with isometric exercise, but is not always present.

Type of Reasoning: Inference

One must infer the likely outcomes of static exercise on BP and HR in order to arrive at the correct conclusion. This requires one to draw conclusions based on the information presented, which is an inferential reasoning skill. In this case, one should expect an elevated HR and arterial BP as a result of isometric exercise, which should be reviewed if this question was answered incorrectly.

C171 

Musculoskeletal | Evaluation, Diagnosis

A patient complains of pain in the right lower aspect of the lateral rib cage. The chief complaint is intense pain, which also occurs at night. The pain lasts for approximately 15 minutes and then subsides. There was no mechanism of injury and no pain with activity during the day. Active and passive motion of the thoracic spine and costal cage is normal and pain free. Mild tenderness is present inferior to the right lateral ribcage. What is the **MOST** likely diagnosis for this patient?

Choices:

1. Intercostal muscle strain.
2. Costochondritis.
3. Systemic disease.
4. Abdominal muscle strain.

Teaching Points

Correct Answer: 3

This history is an insidious onset, with no injury and no pain with activity. There is no reproduction of symptoms with the physical exam. This is typically a red flag for a systemic condition that should be referred to a medical doctor.

Incorrect Choices:

Most musculoskeletal conditions have a mechanism of injury or repetitive stress that initially causes the symptoms. They are also activity related, so certain positions, activities, or movements aggravate or relieve the symptoms.

Type of Reasoning: Analysis

This question requires the test taker to analyze symptoms in order to determine the most likely cause for those symptoms. This requires analytical reasoning skill. For this case, the symptoms most likely indicate systemic disease, and the patient should be referred to a medical doctor. Review assessment of rib cage pain if answered incorrectly.

C172

System Interactions | Evaluation, Diagnosis

An elderly male patient recovering from a fractured hip repaired with ORIF has recently been discharged home. During a home visit, his wife tells the therapist that he woke up yesterday morning and told her he couldn't remember much. Upon examination, the therapist finds some mild motor loss in his right hand and anomia. The therapist affirms the presence of short-term memory loss. What is the therapist's **BEST** course of action?

Choices:

1. Advise the family to document and record any new problems that they notice over the next week and then report back to the therapist.
2. Ignore the findings because they are expected after surgical anesthesia.
3. Refer him to his physician immediately because the therapist suspects a stroke.
4. Refer him to his physician because the therapist suspects Alzheimer's type dementia.

Teaching Points

Correct Answer: 3

The presence of focal signs (incoordination, anomia) with cognitive signs (memory loss) is indicative of impaired brain function and may be the result of small strokes. This is the most likely choice given the spotty symptoms he presents with as well as their sudden onset.

Incorrect Choices:

Senile dementia, Alzheimer's type, can include some of the same symptoms but the onset is gradual and the course is typically slowly progressive. The reporting of these findings to the primary physician should not be delayed. Further diagnostic workup is indicated. Hospital admission and anesthesia can cause temporary cognitive difficulties (delirium), but these should not persist with discharge home.

Type of Reasoning: Evaluation

In this question, the test taker must determine the **BEST** course of action, given the nature of the patient's new symptoms. This requires evaluative reasoning skill, in which one evaluates the merits of each possible course of action in order to arrive at the correct conclusion. If this question was answered incorrectly, review symptoms of transient ischemic attack and stroke.

C173

Metabolic/Endocrine | Interventions

An adolescent with a 4-year history of type 2 diabetes is insulin dependent and wants to participate in cross-country running. The PT working with the school team advises the athlete to measure plasma glucose concentrations before and after running. What additional advice should the therapist give this student athlete?

Choices:

1. Increase insulin dosage immediately before running.
2. Consume a carbohydrate before or during practice to avoid hypoglycemia.
3. Avoid carbohydrate-rich snacks within 12 hours of a race.
4. Consume a carbohydrate after practice to avoid hyperglycemia.

Teaching Points

Correct Answer: 2

During exercise of increasing intensity and duration, plasma concentrations of insulin progressively decrease. Exercise-induced hypoglycemia (abnormally low levels of glucose in the blood) is common for exercising athletes with diabetes. Hypoglycemia associated with exercise can occur up to 48 hours after exercise. To counteract these effects, the individual may need to reduce his insulin dosage or increase carbohydrate intake before or after running. Consuming a carbohydrate product before or during the race will have a preventive modulating effect on hypoglycemia.

Incorrect Choices:

Hyperglycemia (abnormally high levels of glucose in the blood) is more a risk for individuals with uncontrolled type 1 diabetes. These patients should demonstrate glycemic control before starting an exercise program. Consuming carbohydrates will not lessen the likelihood of hyperglycemia.

Type of Reasoning: Evaluation

One must evaluate the merits of each of the four possible courses of action in order to arrive at the correct solution. This requires knowledge of the effects of exercise on glucose concentrations in athletes with diabetes. Through evaluative reasoning, one should conclude that the athlete should consume a carbohydrate snack before or during practice or a race to avoid hypoglycemia. If this question was answered incorrectly, review guidelines for exercise with athletes with diabetes and carbohydrate consumption.

C174 

Genitourinary | Evaluation, Diagnosis

A male patient is referred to outpatient physical therapy for lower back pain. During the patient interview, he describes a recent increased difficulty with urinating that does not affect his lower back pain symptoms. Neurological screening examination is normal and Murphy's sign is negative. Based on this clinical scenario, what may this patient's low back pain be associated with?

Choices:

1. Lower urinary tract.
2. First lumbar nerve root.
3. Kidney.
4. Sacro-iliac joint.

Teaching Points

Correct Answer: 1

The lower urinary tract can refer symptoms to the lumbar spine region, and the recent report of increased difficulty with urination is a key factor.

Incorrect Choices:

A negative Murphy's sign (percussion in the costovertebral area) decreases the likelihood of kidney symptoms. There was no information provided to specifically indicate the sacro-iliac joint as a source of current symptoms; moreover, the recent reports of increased difficulty with urination may indicate a potential systemic problem that may require immediate medical attention. Negative neurological findings would rule out the first lumbar nerve root as a source of symptoms.

Type of Reasoning: Analysis

This question requires the tester to critically evaluate key findings from the patient interview and determine the most likely differential diagnosis based on the information provided. This requires analytical reasoning skill, where symptoms are analyzed to draw reasonable conclusions about the diagnosis. For this scenario, the symptoms are consistent with the lower urinary tract. Review signs and symptoms of lower urinary tract problems if answered incorrectly.

C175 

Neuromuscular | Interventions

A PTA is ambulating a patient with a stroke using a walker. The patient is unsteady and fearful of falling. The patient does not appear to understand the correct gait sequence. What is the supervising PT's **BEST** course of action?

Choices:

1. Intervene and teach the correct sequence because the PTA is apparently unable to deal with this special situation.
2. Instruct the PTA to have the patient sit down and utilize mental practice of the task.
3. Tell the PTA and patient to stop the ambulation and work on dynamic balance activities instead.
4. Instruct the PTA to use a distributed practice schedule to ensure patient success.

Teaching Points

Correct Answer: 2

Mental rehearsal (mental practice) is the best strategy to have the patient learn the correct sequence. In the non–weight-bearing position, the patient's anxiety is lessened, leaving the patient free to concentrate on the task at hand.

Incorrect Choices:

The PT should provide appropriate guidance to the PTA but not necessarily take over care. Lack of understanding about the gait sequence rather than balance difficulties seems to be the major problem. Distributed practice with long rest times does not address the main difficulty.

Type of Reasoning: Evaluation

This question requires one to evaluate the value of each of the four possible solutions and then determine which solution is the **BEST** strategy, given the patient's challenges. Evaluative reasoning questions often require the test taker to make value judgments, which can be challenging for many test takers.

C176 

Musculoskeletal | Examination

A therapist is reviewing x-rays from a patient with a trimalleolar fracture. What are the **BEST** radiographic views to visualize this bony fracture?

Choices:

1. Oblique and lateral.
2. Anteroposterior and lateral.
3. Posteroanterior and lateral.
4. Lateral and coronal.

Teaching Points

Correct Answer: 2

A trimalleolar fracture includes fracture of both malleoli and the posterior rim of the tibia. Anteroposterior (AP) view of the ankle demonstrates the distal tibia and fibula, including the medial and lateral malleoli and the head of the talus. The fractures of both malleoli will be visible with this view. The lateral view provides evidence of the fracture at the posterior rim of the distal tibia.

Incorrect Choices:

An oblique view of the foot demonstrates the phalanges, the metatarsals, and the intermetatarsal joints. Posteroanterior (PA) view is not routine for the ankle. A coronal view is also not indicated for this type of fracture.

Type of Reasoning: Analysis

One must recall the nature of a trimalleolar fracture in order to make a determination of the **BEST** radiographic view for observation of this anomaly. This necessitates analytical reasoning skill, in which one must interpret the information presented in order to make a determination of a **BEST** course of action. If this question was answered incorrectly, review radiographic examination guidelines for trimalleolar fractures.

C177 

Nonsystem | Equipment, Devices, Biophysical Agents

A patient presents with pain and muscle spasm of the upper back (C7–T8) extending to the lateral border of the scapula. This encompasses a 10 × 10–cm area on both sides of the spine. If the US unit only has a 5-cm^2 sound head, how should the therapist treat the upper back area?

Choices:

1. Each side, allotting 5 minutes for each section.
2. The entire area in 5 minutes.
3. The entire area in 10 minutes.
4. Each side, allotting 2.5 minutes for each section.

Teaching Points

Correct Answer: 1

The total treatment area is too large for the 5-cm^2 sound head to produce adequate tissue heating. Sonating the two areas independently will allow more time for the tissue temperature to rise during the treatment time in each area.

Incorrect Choices:

Moving the transducer too fast to cover both sides adequately in the allotted time does not allow sufficient time for the acoustic energy to produce heat because the head is not in a given area long enough. Increasing the treatment time will not affect the rate of heat production. Two minutes is too brief to produce sufficient tissue heating.

Type of Reasoning: Inductive

This question requires clinical judgment and diagnostic reasoning in order to determine the best approach when providing US treatment for this patient. This requires recall of proper US treatment guidelines, including consideration of the size of the sound head and size of the area to be treated. If this question was answered incorrectly, review US treatment guidelines for larger treatment areas.

C178

Musculoskeletal | Examination

The physical therapist is examining the muscle length of the patient's right hip. What is the muscle length test pictured below?

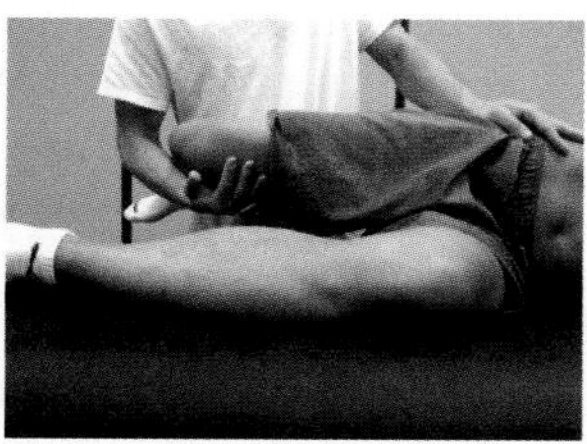

Choices:
1. Ober test.
2. FABER test.
3. Thomas test.
4. Noble test.

Teaching Points

Correct Answer: 1
The Ober test is for tightness of the tensor fascia latae and iliotibial band. With the pelvis stabilized and the hip kept in neutral rotation, the Ober test would be considered normal if the thigh drops slightly below horizontal.

Incorrect Choices:
The Thomas test is utilized to test for hip flexor length and to distinguish between one joint and two joint hip flexor tightness. The Noble test is for iliotibial band friction syndrome. The FABER test is hip flexion, abduction, and external rotation and is to screen hip and SI pathology.

Type of Reasoning: Analysis
One must understand the tests described in the question in order to choose the correct one. Through analytical reasoning, the test taker must determine how each test is performed and for what purpose. If this question was answered incorrectly, review information on special tests.

C179

Neuromuscular | Examination

A therapist is examining a patient's balance using posturography testing with the Clinical Test for Sensory Integration in Balance (CTSIB). The patient's sway increases with loss of balance under conditions with the eyes closed and platform moving (condition 5). During condition 6, with both the visual surround and platform moving, loss of balance is more immediate. Which of the following **BEST** identifies the source of the patient's problems?

Choices:
1. Vestibular deficiency.
2. Visual dependency.
3. Problems with sensory selection.
4. Somatosensory dependency.

Teaching Points

Correct Answer: 1

The CTSIB is positive for vestibular deficiency with loss of balance on conditions 5 and 6.

Incorrect Choices:

Patients who are surface dependent (somatosensory) have difficulties with conditions 4, 5, and 6. Patients who are visually dependent have difficulties with conditions 2, 3, and 6. Sensory selection problems are evident with loss of balance on conditions 3–6.

Type of Reasoning: Inference

One must first determine what conditions 5 and 6 are indicative of in CTSIB testing in order to arrive at the correct conclusion. This necessitates inferential reasoning, in which one must draw conclusions from the information presented in order to determine what the patient is likely to demonstrate. If this question was answered incorrectly, refer to posturography testing.

C180 

Neuromuscular I Examination

A patient presents with severe, frequent seizures originating in the medial temporal lobes. After bilateral surgical removal of these areas, the patient is unable to remember any new information from just prior to the surgery to the present. The patient cannot recall text read minutes ago or remember people previously met. How should this surgical outcome be characterized?

Choices:

1. Loss of integration of the temporal lobe with the basal ganglia and frontal cortex.
2. Loss of procedural memory and integration with frontal cortex.
3. Loss of the hippocampus and declarative memory function.
4. A primary deficit from the loss of the amygdala.

Teaching Points

Correct Answer: 3

Declarative memory refers to conscious, explicit, or cognitive memory. It is a function of the cerebral cortex and the hippocampus.

Incorrect Choices:

Procedural memory (unconscious memory or implicit memory) refers to the recall of skills and habits and emotional responses. It is the result of integrated action of the frontal cortex (neocortex), thalamus, and striatum of the basal ganglia. The amygdala is a collection of nuclei in the anteromedial temporal lobe, forming the core of the limbic circuits. It is important for triggering feelings and drive-related behaviors.

Type of Reasoning: Analysis

This question requires the test taker to determine the diagnosis based on symptoms presented, which is an analytical reasoning skill. In this situation, the symptoms are indicative of loss of the hippocampus and declarative memory function. Knowledge of neuroscience and the cortical structures responsible for declarative memory function are beneficial to arriving at the correct conclusion. If this question was answered incorrectly, refer to memory functions and structures.

C181

Metabolic/Endocrine I Evaluation, Diagnosis

A 14-year-old with a body mass index of 33 kg/m^2 and a history of limited participation in physical activities is referred for exercise training. The nutritionist has prescribed a diet limiting his caloric intake. What is the **BEST** initial exercise prescription for this patient?

Choices:

1. Three weekly sessions of 60 minutes at 50% VO_{2max}.
2. Three weekly sessions of 50 minutes at 75%–85% VO_{2max}.
3. Three weekly sessions of 30 minutes at 65%–70% VO_{2max}.
4. Two daily sessions of 30 minutes at 45%–70% VO_{2max}.

Teaching Points

Correct Answer: 4

This individual is obese (body mass index ≥ 30 kg/m^2) and will benefit from exercise to increase energy expenditure and diet to reduce caloric intake. The initial exercise prescription should utilize low-intensity with longer duration exercise. Splitting the training into two sessions each day is a good choice. The goal is to work toward bringing the target HR into a suitable range. Obese individuals are at increased risk of orthopedic injuries and require close monitoring.

Incorrect Choices:

Weekly sessions at high intensities (70%–85% VO_2max) and long duration (50 min) are contraindicated. Weekly sessions (two to three times/wk) are not as beneficial initially as are daily sessions at shorter durations and moderate intensities.

Type of Reasoning: Inductive

One must utilize clinical judgment and diagnostic reasoning to determine the **BEST** initial exercise prescription for this individual. This necessitates inductive reasoning skill, in which one must refer to knowledge of exercise for individuals with obesity to arrive at the correct conclusion. If this question was answered incorrectly, review exercise prescription guidelines for the obese.

C182

Metabolic/Endocrine I Evaluation, Diagnosis

A patient is admitted to a hospital after a fall. A review of the patient's medical chart reveals a blood pressure (BP) of 160/85, a triglyceride level of 160 mg/dL, and a fasting blood glucose level of 115 mg/dL. Weight is 310 lb. Examination of the patient reveals a rotund man with a 54-inch waistline. Which diagnosis is consistent with this patient's signs and symptoms?

Choices:

1. Type 1 diabetes.
2. Cushing's syndrome.
3. Metabolic syndrome.
4. Chronic heart disease.

Teaching Points

Correct Answer: 3

This patient is exhibiting four of the risk factors of metabolic syndrome (diagnosis is made if three or more are present). Risk factors include (1) abdominal obesity: waist circumference > 40 inches in men or > 35 inches in women; (2) elevated triglycerides: triglyceride level of 150 mg/dL or higher; (3) low high-density lipoprotein (HDL) cholesterol or being on medicine to treat low HDL: HDL level < 40 mg/dL in men or 50 mg/dL in women; (4) elevated BP: systolic BP ≥ 130 mm Hg and/or diastolic BP = 85 mm Hg; and (5) fasting plasma glucose level > 100 mg/dL. The therapist's plan of care should be reflective of the patient's increased risk for heart disease, stroke, and diabetes and should assist the patient in lifestyle changes that reduce these risk factors.

Incorrect Choices:

No mention is made of absolute insulin deficiency (type 1 diabetes). Although these are risk factors for heart disease, they do not specifically define or characterize chronic heart disease. Cushing's syndrome (glucocorticoid hormone excess) refers to the manifestations of hypercortisolism from any cause. Patients typically exhibit a round "moon face" with a protruding abdomen or "buffalo hump" on the back along with muscle weakness and wasting.

Type of Reasoning: Analysis

This question requires one to analyze all of the signs and symptoms presented and then draw a conclusion about a potential diagnosis. Questions of this nature require analytical reasoning skills. If this question was answered incorrectly, refer to signs and symptoms of metabolic syndrome.

C183 

System Interactions | Evaluation, Diagnosis

A patient in an exercise class develops muscle weakness and fatigue. Examination reveals leg cramps and hyporeflexia. The patient also experiences frequent episodes of postural hypotension and dizziness. Abnormalities on the ECG include a flat T wave, prolonged QT interval, and depressed ST segment. Which electrolyte imbalance is consistent with this patient's signs and symptoms?

Choices:

1. Hypocalcemia.
2. Hyperkalemia.
3. Hypokalemia.
4. Hyponatremia.

Teaching Points

Correct Answer: 3

Hypokalemia, decreased potassium in the blood, is characterized by these signs and symptoms. Other possible symptoms include respiratory distress, irritability, confusion or depression, and gastrointestinal disturbances.

Incorrect Choices:

Hyperkalemia is excess potassium in the blood. Hyponatremia is decreased sodium in the blood, and hypocalcemia is decreased calcium in the blood. These conditions cannot produce this battery of symptoms.

Type of Reasoning: Analysis

This question requires the test taker to determine the diagnosis based on the symptoms described, which is an analytical reasoning skill. The test taker must analyze the symptoms in order to determine the most likely cause for them. If this question was answered incorrectly, refer to signs and symptoms of the conditions listed (Chapter 6).

C184

Cardiovascular/Pulmonary and Lymphatic | Examination

A patient has experienced swelling in both lower legs (below the knees) since the age of 16 (10-year history). The referring diagnosis is bilateral lymphedema. Which test should the therapist include in the initial examination?

Choices:

1. Ankle-brachial index (ABI).
2. Systolic blood pressure before and after exercise.
3. Homan's sign.
4. Rubor of Dependency test.

Teaching Points

Correct Answer: 1

The ABI is helpful to determine the arterial patency or sufficiency. A value of 1.0 indicates normal arterial flow; values between 0.5 and 0.8 indicate moderate compromise while values below 0.5 indicate severe compromise of arterial flow. Adequate arterial blood flow is essential in considering application of compression for lymphedema.

Incorrect Choices:

Two tests (Rubor of Dependency test, systolic BP) are used in the examination of peripheral (sp) artery disease. Homan's sign was used in the examination of deep vein thrombophlebitis (DVT) though is no longer considered a reliable indicator of DVT.

Type of Reasoning: Analysis

One must understand the tests described in the question in order to choose the correct one. Through analytical reasoning, the test taker must determine how each test is performed and for what purpose. If this question was answered incorrectly, review information on special tests.

C185

Genitourinary | Interventions

A patient is referred to a woman's health specialist PT with a diagnosis of pelvic pain and uterine prolapse. Which of the following interventions is the **BEST** choice for this patient?

Choices:

1. External stabilization with a support belt.
2. Gentle abdominal exercises with incisional support.
3. Protective splinting of abdominal musculature.
4. Kegel's exercises.

Teaching Points

Correct Answer: 4

Intervention should focus on pelvic floor rehabilitation (Kegel's exercises to strengthen pubococcygeal muscles) along with postural education and muscle reeducation.

Incorrect Choices:

Diastasis recti abdominis requires protective splinting of abdominal musculature during initial separation (> 2 cm split of the rectus abdominis after pregnancy). External stabilization with a support belt may be required for sacroiliac dysfunction. Postcesarean interventions include gentle abdominal exercises with incisional support. There was no mention of pregnancy or postpregnancy complications.

Type of Reasoning: Inference

One must infer or draw a reasonable conclusion about the best intervention approach for a patient with pelvic pain and uterine prolapse. This requires inferential reasoning skills because one must determine which therapeutic approach will have the most effective outcome of improving function. If this question was answered incorrectly, review exercise guidelines for patients with uterine prolapse.

C186 

Neuromuscular | Interventions

A therapist is working with a patient recovering from traumatic brain injury, Rancho Los Amigos Levels of Cognitive Functioning (LOCF), level IV. This is the patient's first time in the physical therapy gym. While the therapist attempts to work with the patient on sitting control, the patient becomes agitated and combative. Which strategy is the **BEST** choice in this situation?

Choices:

1. Remove the patient to a quiet environment and provide support and calming stimuli.
2. Give the patient a 5-minute rest and resume the training activity.
3. Return the patient to his/her room and try the training activity later in the day.
4. Enlist the help of a PTA to support the patient while slowly instructing the patient again.

Teaching Points

Correct Answer: 1

The best choice is to remove the patient to a quiet room and provide calming stimuli and support. At level IV LOCF, the therapist can expect the patient to be confused, inappropriate, and highly distractable. The environment should be changed. Memory is severely impaired and the patient is unable to learn new information.

Incorrect Choices:

Enlisting the PTA or resuming training after a 5-minute rest does not change the environment nor calm the patient. Rescheduling for the afternoon similarly does not address the central problem of the patient's level IV behaviors.

Type of Reasoning: Inference

Questions that inquire about a **BEST** approach to a therapeutic situation often necessitate inferential reasoning skill. In this situation, the test taker must determine the **BEST** choice for a patient with a traumatic brain injury and Rancho Los Amigos Levels of Cognitive Functioning, level IV behaviors. Review Levels of Cognitive Function after traumatic brain injury and beneficial training strategies for each level.

C187

Neuromuscular I Interventions

A patient has a 10-year history of Parkinson's disease and has been on levodopa (Carbidopa) for the past 6 years. The patient has fallen three times in the past month, resulting in a Colles' fracture. The therapist decides to try postural biofeedback training using a platform balance training device. Which of the following is the **BEST** choice for a training protocol?

Choices:

1. Increase the limits of stability and improve anterior weight displacement.
2. Decrease the limits of stability and anterior weight displacement.
3. Increase the limits of stability and improve center of pressure alignment.
4. Decrease the limits of stability and improve posterior weight displacement.

Teaching Points

Correct Answer: 3

The patient with Parkinson's disease exhibits significant balance impairments including loss of postural reflexes; decreased limits of stability; flexed, stooped posture that alters the center of pressure in an anterior direction; freezing; and orthostatic hypotension. Platform balance training should work toward improving the limits of stability and center of pressure alignment (the patient should focus on reducing anterior displacement).

Incorrect Choices:

The patient is too unstable; decreasing limits of stability is contraindicated, as is promoting anterior weight displacement.

Type of Reasoning: Inference

One must infer the most appropriate training sequence for biofeedback postural training in order to arrive at the correct conclusion. This involves inferential reasoning, in which one must consider the patient's diagnosis and current limitations in order to choose the most appropriate training sequence. If this question was answered incorrectly, refer to balance deficits and training strategies for patients with Parkinson's disease.

C188 

Cardiovascular/Pulmonary and Lymphatic | Evaluation, Diagnosis

A patient is recovering from MI and is referred for supervised exercise training. While working out on a treadmill, the patient begins to develop mild shortness of breath. Continuous telemetry monitoring reveals the following ECG rhythm. What is the correct interpretation of this rhythm?

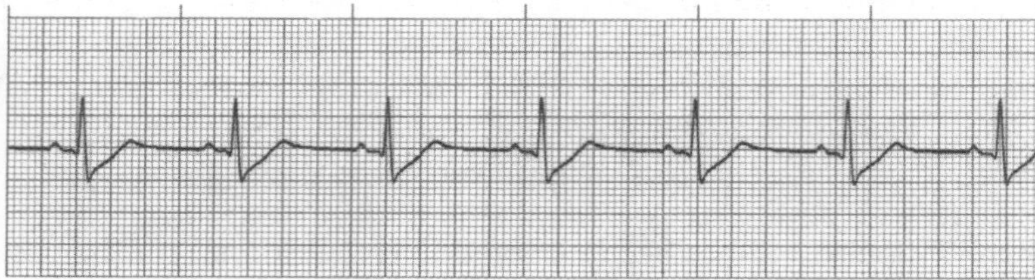

From: Jones S (2005) ECG Notes. Philadelphia, F.A. Davis, p. 162, with permission.

Choices:

1. Tachycardia with abnormal P waves.
2. Sinus rhythm with upsloping ST segment depression.
3. Sinus rhythm with sinoatrial blocks.
4. Sinus rhythm with downsloping ST segment depression.

Teaching Points

Correct Answer: 2

This patient is exhibiting sinus rhythm with upsloping ST segment depression. An abnormal ECG response is defined as ≥ 1 mm of horizontal or downsloping depression at 80 msec beyond the J point (*ACSM Guidelines for Exercise Testing and Prescription,* 8th ed.). Associated clinical signs suggestive of myocardial ischemia include dyspnea and angina. After a review of this patient's exercise responses coupled with the ECG findings, the therapist correctly determines that the exercise session does not have to be terminated. The therapist should continue to closely monitor the patient's responses.

Incorrect Choices:

This tracing does **NOT** indicate the other conditions listed (sinoatrial block, downsloping ST segment depression, or tachycardia with abnormal P waves).

Type of Reasoning: Analysis

Questions that require one to analyze visual information depicted in pictures, charts, etc., necessitate analytical reasoning skill. This question requires the test taker to appropriately interpret the ECG readout in order to determine the correct diagnosis. If this question was answered incorrectly, review ECG interpretation guidelines.

Exam C

C189

Musculoskeletal | Evaluation, Diagnosis

A female patient complains of right lumbosacral pain after giving natural childbirth to her first child 2 months ago. Pain has subsided somewhat, but remains high enough that she has to sit after walking more than 2 blocks. Pain is noted in the right lumbosacral region, buttock, and groin and is aggravated with weight bearing on the right. Active flexion, extension, and side bending reproduce the patient's symptoms. Hamstrings are slightly tight on the right, but no neural tension is noted. Neurological findings (reflexes, sensation, and motor) are unremarkable. SI provocation tests are positive. What is the **MOST** likely diagnosis for this patient?

Choices:

1. Lumbar disc protrusion at L5/S1.
2. Sacroiliac sprain.
3. Quadratus lumborum strain.
4. Piriformis syndrome.

Teaching Points

Correct Answer: 2

Child-bearing can place considerable stress on the sacroiliac joint, causing an overstretch of the ligaments. Pain is reproduced with active movement testing, which is characteristic of a musculoskeletal condition. Sacroiliac provocation tests are fairly valid as well, thus implicating the sacroiliac joint. The groin and buttock are common referral regions for the sacroiliac joint.

Incorrect Choices:

There is no neural tension or neurological signs that help to rule out disc dysfunction. There are no findings indicating specific strain of the piriformis or quadratus lumborum as SI provocation is positive.

Type of Reasoning: Analysis

For this question, the test taker must analyze the symptoms present and determine the most likely diagnosis. Questions of this nature often require analytical reasoning skill. For this scenario, given the symptoms presented, the most likely diagnosis is sacroiliac sprain. If answered incorrectly, review signs and symptoms of sacroiliac sprain/strain.

C190

Musculoskeletal | Evaluation, Diagnosis

A patient presents with a complaint of severe neck and shoulder pain of 2 days' duration. The patient reports falling asleep on the couch watching TV and has been stiff and sore since. There is tenderness of the cervical muscles on the right, with increased pain upon palpation. Passive ROM is most limited in flexion, then side-bending left, and then rotation left and active extension. Side-bending right and rotation right are also painful. What is the **MOST** likely diagnosis for this patient?

Choices:

1. Cervical strain.
2. Herniated disc.
3. Cervical radiculopathy.
4. Facet syndrome.

Exam C

Teaching Points

Correct Answer: 4

A facet syndrome presents with localized pain.

Incorrect Choices:

Cervical radiculopathy presents with arm pain in the dermatomal distribution and increased pain by extension and rotation or side flexion. Cervical strain presents with pain on activity or when the muscle is on stretch. Cervical disc herniation has a dermatomal pain distribution with an increase of pain on extension, and pain on flexion may either increase or decrease (most common).

Type of Reasoning: Analysis

This question requires the test taker to determine the diagnosis based on symptoms presented, which is an analytical reasoning skill. For this patient, the symptoms are indicative of facet syndrome. Knowledge of spinal disorders is required for arriving at the correct conclusion. If this question was answered incorrectly, refer to symptoms of facet syndrome.

C191

Musculoskeletal | Interventions

A postal worker (mail sorter) complains of numbness and tingling in the right hand. Examination reveals a median nerve distribution. When the therapist evaluates the patient's work tasks, the therapist notes that the patient is required to key in the zip codes of about 58 letters per minute. Which of the following is the **BEST** choice of administrative control to reduce this patient's problem?

Choices:

1. Require the worker to attend a cumulative trauma disorder educational class.
2. Provide the worker with a resting splint to support the wrist.
3. Provide a height adjustable chair to position the wrists and hands in a neutral alignment.
4. Use job rotation during the workday.

Teaching Points

Correct Answer: 4

Administrative controls reduce the duration, frequency, and severity of exposures to ergonomic stressors. Job rotation reduces fatigue and stress by rotating the worker to jobs that use different muscle-tendon groups during the workday.

Incorrect Choices:

The other choices represent either clinical, engineering, or educational interventions and do not address the essential question of an administrative control.

Type of Reasoning: Deductive

This question requires one to recall the parameters of an administrative control in ergonomic assessment. This is factual recall of ergonomic knowledge, which encourages the use of deductive reasoning skill. If this question was answered incorrectly, review administrative controls in ergonomic assessment.

C192

Nonsystem | Equipment, Devices, Biophysical Agents

A patient with a traumatic brain injury presents with hemiparesis. The examination reveals slight cutaneous and proprioceptive impairment, fair (3/5) strength of the shoulder muscles and triceps, and slight spasticity of the biceps. Voluntary control of the patient's left arm has not progressed since admission. The therapist decides to use functional electrical stimulation (FES), placing the active electrode on the triceps to facilitate active extension of the elbow. Which of the following is the **BEST** choice of timing sequence for FES in this case?

Choices:

1. No ramp up, 10-second stimulation, 2-second ramp down.
2. 2-second ramp up, 10-second stimulation, no ramp down.
3. 2-second ramp up, 5-second stimulation, 2-second ramp down.
4. 5-second ramp up, 5-second stimulation, 5-second ramp down.

Teaching Points

Correct Answer: 4

A relatively long ramp-up time over a 5-second period is used to minimize stimulating the muscle too quickly and increasing the spasticity. The ramp-down time has no effect on spasticity.

Incorrect Choices:

The other choices have too short or no ramp-up time, and this could increase the spasticity of the biceps.

Type of Reasoning: Inductive

This question requires one to predict the possible outcome of what will happen when each of the four possible approaches is applied. Via clinical judgment and the process of prediction, an inductive reasoning skill, one should determine that a 5-second ramp up, 5-second stimulation, and 5-second ramp down will be **MOST** beneficial for this patient. If this question was answered incorrectly, refer to guidelines for FES for spastic upper extremities.

C193

Neuromuscular | Interventions

After a traumatic brain injury, a patient presents with significant difficulties in learning how to use a wheelchair. Memory for new learning is present but limited (Rancho Los Amigos Levels of Cognitive Functioning, level VII). The patient is wheelchair dependent and needs to learn how to transfer from the wheelchair to the mat (a skill never done before). Which of the following is the **BEST** strategy to enhance this patient's motor learning?

Choices:

1. Use only guided movement to ensure correct performance.
2. Provide bandwidth feedback using a random practice schedule.
3. Provide consistent feedback using a blocked practice schedule.
4. Provide summed feedback after every few trials using a serial practice schedule.

Teaching Points

Correct Answer: 3

Early learning should focus on consistent feedback given after every trial to improve initial performance. A blocked practice schedule with repeated practice of the same skill will also reinforce early learning.

Incorrect Choices:

Variable feedback schedules (summed or bandwidth) and variable practice schedules (serial and random) are indicated for later learning to improve retention. Using only guided movement is contraindicated in this case because it minimizes active participation and active learning.

Type of Reasoning: Inference

One must infer the **BEST** strategy to enhance this patient's motor learning for transfer skills. Given the patient's current functional level, it is **BEST** to provide consistent feedback using a blocked practice schedule to reinforce early learning. Questions that require one to draw conclusions and infer strategies often utilize inferential reasoning skills. If this question was answered incorrectly, refer to strategies to enhance early learning after a traumatic brain injury.

C194 

Neuromuscular | Evaluation, Diagnosis

A patient recovering from stroke presents with predominant involvement of the contralateral lower extremity and lesser involvement of the contralateral upper extremity. These clinical manifestations are characteristic of which cerebral syndrome?

Choices:

1. Basilar artery syndrome.
2. Anterior cerebral artery syndrome.
3. Posterior cerebral artery syndrome.
4. Middle cerebral artery syndrome.

Teaching Points

Correct Answer: 2

These clinical manifestations are consistent with anterior cerebral artery syndrome (lower extremity is more involved than upper extremity).

Incorrect Choices:

Patients with middle cerebral artery syndrome demonstrate the opposite findings, greater involvement of the upper than the lower extremity. Patients with posterior cerebral artery syndrome demonstrate primary involvement of the visual cortex (contralateral homonymous hemianopsia) along with dyslexia (difficulty reading), prosopagnosia (difficulty naming people on sight), and memory defect (temporal lobe lesion). Patients with basilar artery syndrome demonstrate a combination of brain stem syndromes along with signs of posterior cerebral artery syndrome.

Type of Reasoning: Analysis

This question requires the test taker to determine the location of the patient's CVA based on symptoms presented, which is an analytical reasoning skill. Knowledge of neuroscience and the various arterial syndromes related to CVA are beneficial for arriving at the correct conclusion. If this question was answered incorrectly, refer to symptoms of cerebral artery syndromes.

C195 

Cardiovascular/Pulmonary and Lymphatic | Evaluation, Diagnosis

A patient presents with significant intermittent claudication with onset after 2 minutes of walking. Which of the following are likely findings for this patient, given the patient's symptoms in response to walking?

Choices:

1. Persistent local redness of the extremity in both gravity-dependent and -independent positions.
2. Elevation-induced pallor and dependent redness with the extremity in the gravity-dependent position.
3. Little or no changes in color with changes in extremity position.
4. A brownish color just above the ankle in both gravity-dependent and -independent positions.

Teaching Points

Correct Answer: 2

Intermittent claudication (episodic muscular ischemia induced by exercise) is due to obstruction of large- or middle-sized arteries by atherosclerosis. The Rubor of Dependency test is used to assess the adequacy of arterial circulation by evaluating the skin color changes that occur with first extremity elevation (pallor) and then lowering of the extremities (delayed color changes, redness).

Incorrect Choices:

Color changes are expected with change of position. A brownish color just above the ankle suggests chronic venous insufficiency. Persistent local redness is indicative of a thrombosed vein in the area.

Type of Reasoning: Inference

One must infer the likely findings for this patient, given that the patient's symptoms are in response to walking. It is beneficial to have prior knowledge of the Rubor of Dependency test in order to arrive at the correct conclusion. Through inferential reasoning, one should conclude that the patient would demonstrate elevation-induced pallor and dependent redness with the extremity in a gravity-dependent position. If this question was answered incorrectly, review examination of the patient with PVD.

C196 

Genitourinary | Evaluation, Diagnosis

After a recent cesarean, a patient tells the therapist that she is anxious to return to her prepregnancy level of physical activity (working out at the gym three days/wk and running 5 miles every other day). What is the **BEST** choice of activities for this patient at this time?

Choices:

1. Pelvic floor and gentle abdominal exercises for the first 4–6 weeks.
2. A walking program progressing to running after 4 weeks.
3. Pelvic floor exercises and refrain from all other exercise and running for at least 12 weeks.
4. Abdominal crunches with return to running after 5 weeks.

Exam C

Teaching Points

Correct Answer: 1

Postcesarean physical therapy can include postoperative TENS, assisted breathing and coughing techniques, and gentle abdominal exercises with incisional support provided by a pillow. Pelvic floor exercises are also important because hours of labor and pushing are typically present before surgery.

Incorrect Choices:

Vigorous exercise (abdominal crunches, running) is contraindicated for at least 6 weeks. Without complications, 12 weeks is too long to refrain from exercises and running.

Type of Reasoning: Evaluation

This question requires one to evaluate the merits of each of the four statements and then determine which response to the patient is **BEST** given her recent cesarean section. Evaluative reasoning skills are utilized whenever one must make value judgments and assess the worth of ideas presented. If this question was answered incorrectly, refer to guidelines on exercise for women postpartum.

C197

System Interactions | Evaluation, Diagnosis

A 26-year-old who was diagnosed with schizophrenia, disorganized type, at the age of 22 is referred for gait training after a compound fracture of the tibia. The therapist suspects the patient has recently experienced an exacerbation of schizophrenia. Which behaviors support this conclusion?

Choices:

1. Poor ability to perform multistep tasks requiring abstract problem-solving.
2. Sleep disturbances and flashbacks.
3. Increased fear of going out in public.
4. Frequent verbalizations of pervasive feelings of low self-esteem.

Teaching Points

Correct Answer: 1

Schizophrenia is characterized by disordered thinking (fragmented thoughts, errors of logic or abstract reasoning, delusions, poor judgment, and so forth).

Incorrect Choices:

Sleep disturbances and flashbacks are common with posttraumatic stress disorder. Increased fear of going out in public is agoraphobia. Pervasive feelings of low self-esteem can accompany depression or anxiety disorder.

Type of Reasoning: Inference

This question requires one to infer or draw a conclusion about the likely symptoms of disorganized schizophrenia. This necessitates inferential reasoning skills. For this situation, the therapist should expect behaviors of poor ability to perform multistep tasks requiring abstract problem-solving. If this question was answered incorrectly, review symptoms of schizophrenia, especially disorganized type.

C198

Nonsystem | Equipment, Devices, Biophysical Agents

The rehabilitation team is completing a home visit to recommend environmental modifications for a patient who is scheduled to be discharged next week. The patient is wheelchair dependent. The home has not been adapted. Which of the following recommendations is correct?

Choices:

1. Widening the door entrance to 28 inches.
2. Adding horizontal grab bars in the bathroom positioned at 34 inches.
3. Raising the toilet seat to 25 inches.
4. Installing an entry-way ramp with a running slope of 1:10.

Teaching Points

Correct Answer: 2

Horizontal grab bars should be positioned at an optimal height of 33–36 inches.

Incorrect Choices:

The minimum ramp grade (slope) is 1:12 (not 1:10, which would be too steep for functional use). The toilet seat should be raised to a height of 17–19 inches (not 25). Minimum clearance width for doorways is 32 inches (not 28); 36 inches is ideal.

Type of Reasoning: Inference

This question requires one to determine appropriate recommendations for patients utilizing wheelchairs for mobility in the home. This necessitates recall of factual knowledge and clinical judgment, which is an inferential reasoning skill. If this question was answered incorrectly, review guidelines for environmental (home) modifications for patients utilizing wheelchairs for mobility.

C199

Musculoskeletal | Examination

During an examination of gait, the therapist observes lateral pelvic tilt on the side of the swing leg during frontal plane analysis. What is the purpose of the lateral pelvic tilt on the side of the swing leg during gait?

Choices:

1. Reduce physiological valgum at the knee.
2. Reduce knee flexion at mid-stance.
3. Control forward and backward rotations of the pelvis.
4. Reduce peak rise of the pelvis.

Teaching Points

Correct Answer: 4

Lateral pelvic tilt in the frontal plane keeps the peak of the sinusoidal curve lower than it would have been if the pelvis did not drop. Lateral pelvic tilt to the right is controlled by the left hip abductors.

Incorrect Choices:

Forward and backward rotations of the pelvis assist the swing leg. The normal physiologic valgum at the knee reduces the width of the base of support. Knee flexion at midstance is another adjustment in keeping the center of gravity from rising too much. All are termed determinants of gait.

Type of Reasoning: Inference

One must infer the purpose of the lateral pelvic tilt on the side of the swing leg during gait in order to arrive at the correct conclusion. This necessitates inferential reasoning skills, where one must draw conclusions based on the evidence presented. If this question was answered incorrectly, review gait analysis guidelines.

C200

Nonsystem | Safety, Professional Responsibilities, Research

A group of researchers investigated the effect of tai chi on perceived health status in older, frail adults. The subjects were 269 women who were older than 70 years of age and recruited from five independent senior living facilities. Participants took part in a 48-week single-blind RCT. Perceived health status was measured by five pretrained testers using the Sickness Impact Profile (SIP). The researchers found significant perceived health benefits. Which of the following is an accurate conclusion regarding the design of this study?

Choices:

1. Generalizability to a larger population of elderly women.
2. Errors in reliability due to the number of testers.
3. Errors in validity due to the selection of the outcome measure.
4. Limited findings on the effects of tai chi exercise in the frail elderly.

Teaching Points

Correct Answer: 1

This study provides important findings on the effects of tai chi in elderly women. It is an RCT with a large number of subjects from multiple centers. Thus it has good generalizability to a population of elderly women. The SIP is a gold standard instrument with extensive testing and established validity and reliability.

Incorrect Choices:

Errors in reliability are not automatically inherent with multiple testers. Pretrial training reduces the likelihood of errors in reliability. There is no error in validity because of the use of the SIP. These findings are not limited in terms of frail, elderly women.

Type of Reasoning: Analysis

This question requires the test taker to analyze the design of the research study and then draw a conclusion about this design. This necessitates analysis of many factors, which is an analytical reasoning skill. For this scenario, the test taker should reasonably conclude that the study had good generalizability due to the number of subjects in the study and multiple centers involved in the study and good validity and reliability. If this question was answered incorrectly, review research design guidelines.

References

Adler S, Beckers D, Buck M (2008). *PNF in Practice,* 3rd ed. New York, Springer.

American College of Sports Medicine (2009). *ACSM's Guidelines for Exercise Testing and Prescription,* 8th ed. Philadelphia, Lippincott Williams & Wilkins.

American Physical Therapy Association (2014). *Guide to Physical Therapist Practice, Version 3.0.* Alexandria, VA, APTA.

American Physical Therapy Association. *Occupational Health Physical Therapy Guidelines: Prevention of Work-Related Injury/Illness.* Initial BOD11-99-25-71, APTA;

The Role of the Physical Therapist in Occupational Health. BOD 03-97-27-71, APTA;

Physical Therapist Management of the Acutely Injured Worker. BOD 03-01-17-56, APTA;

Evaluation Functional Capacity. BOD11-01-07-11, APTA;

Work Conditioning and Work Hardening Programs. BOD 03-01-17-58, APTA.

Baranoski S, Ayello E (2011). *Wound Care Essentials: Practice & Principles,* 3rd ed. Philadelphia, Lippincott Williams & Wilkins.

Bear M, Connors B, Paradiso M (2007). *Neuroscience—Exploring the Brain,* 3rd ed. Philadelphia, Lippincott Williams & Wilkins.

Belanger AY (2009). *Therapeutic Electrophysical Agents.* Philadelphia, Lippincott Williams & Wilkins.

Bickley L (2009). *Bates' Guide to Physical Examination and History Taking,* 10th ed. Philadelphia, Lippincott Williams & Wilkins.

Boissonnault W (2010). *Primary Care for the Physical Therapist—Examination and Triage,* 2nd ed. St Louis, Elsevier.

Brody L, Hall C (2010). *Therapeutic Exercise—Moving Toward Function.* Philadelphia, Lippincott Williams & Wilkins.

Cameron M (2013). *Physical Agents in Rehabilitation,* 4th ed. St Louis, Elsevier.

Campbell S (2012). *Physical Therapy for Children,* 4th ed. St Louis, Elsevier.

Carroll K, Edelstein J (2006). *Prosthetics and Patient Management: A Comprehensive Clinical Approach.* Thorofare NJ, Slack Inc.

Carter R, Lubinski J, Domholdt E (2011). *Rehabilitation Research,* 4th ed. St Louis, Elsevier.

Chaffin D, Andersson G, Martin B (2006). *Occupational Biomechanics,* 4th ed. New York, John Wiley & Sons.

Ciccone C (2013). *Davis Drug Guide for Rehabilitation Professionals,* Philadelphia, FA Davis.

Cleland J, Koppenhaver S (2010). *Netter's Orthopaedic Clinical Examination: An Evidence-based Approach,* 2nd ed. St Louis, Elsevier.

Cook C, Hegedus E (2012). *Orthopedic Physical Examination Tests: An Evidence-Based Approach,* 2nd ed. Upper Saddle River, NJ, Prentice Hall.

Davies P (2000). *Steps to Follow,* 3rd ed. New York, Springer.

Davis C (2006). *Patient Practitioner Interaction,* 4th ed. Thorofare, NJ, Slack.

Denegar C, Saliba E, Saliba S (2006). *Therapeutic Modalities for Musculoskeletal Injuries,* 2nd ed. Champaign, IL, Human Kinetics.

DeTurk W, Cahalin L (2010). *Cardiovascular and Pulmonary Physical Therapy,* 2nd ed. New York, McGraw-Hill.

DiFabio R (2013). *Essentials of Rehabilitation Research: A Statistical Guide to Clinical Practice.* Philadelphia, FA Davis.

Donatelli R (2007). *Sports-Specific Rehabilitation.* St Louis, Elsevier.

Donatelli R, Wooden M (2009). *Orthopedic Physical Therapy,* 4th ed. New York, Churchill Livingstone.

Drake R, Vogl A, Mitchell A (2010). *Gray's Anatomy for Students,* 2nd ed. Maryland Heights, MO, Elsevier.

Drench M, Noonan A, Sharby N, Ventura S (2012). *Psychosocial Aspects of Health Care,* 3rd ed. Upper Saddle River, NJ, Prentice Hall.

Durstine J, et al (2009). *ACSM's Exercise Management for Persons with Chronic Diseases and Disabilities,* 3rd ed. Champaign, IL, Human Kinetics.

Dutton M (2012). *Orthopaedic Examination, Evaluation, and Intervention,* 3rd ed. New York, McGraw-Hill.

Edelstein J, Moroz A (2010). *Lower-Limb Prosthetics and Orthotics: Clinical Concepts. Thorofare NJ, Slack Inc.*

Effgen S (2013). *Meeting the Physical Therapy Needs of Children,* 2nd ed. Philadelphia, FA Davis.

Erickson M, McKnight B, Utzman R (2008). *Physical Therapy Documentation: From Examination to Outcome.* Thorofare, NJ, Slack.

Field-Fote E (2009). *Spinal Cord Injury Rehabilitation.* Philadelphia, FA Davis.

Frontera W, Slovik D, Dawson D (eds) (2006). *Exercise in Rehabilitation Medicine,* 2nd ed. Champaign, IL, Human Kinetics.

Frownfelter D, Dean E (2006). *Cardiovascular and Pulmonary Physical Therapy: Evidence and Practice,* 4th ed. St Louis, Elsevier Mosby.

Goodman C, Fuller K (2009). *Pathology: Implications for the Physical Therapist,* 3rd ed. St Louis, Elsevier.

Goodman C, Snyder T (2013). *Differential Diagnosis in Physical Therapy: Screening for Referral,* 5th ed. St Louis, Elsevier.

Griffin L (2005). *Essentials of Musculoskeletal Care,* 3rd ed. Rosemont, IL, American Academy of Orthopedic Surgeons.

Guccione A, Wong R, Avers D (2012). *Geriatric Physical Therapy,* 3rd ed. St Louis, Elsevier.

Gutman S (2008). *Quick Reference Neuroscience for Rehabilitation Professionals: The Essential Neurological Principles Underlying Rehabilitation Professionals,* 2nd ed. Thorofare, NJ, Slack.

Guyton A, Hall J (2011). *Textbook of Medical Physiology,* 12th ed. St Louis, Elsevier.

Hack L, Gwyer J (2013). *Evidence into Practice: Integrating Judgment, Values, and Research.* Philidelphia, FA Davis.

Hengveld E, Banks K (2005). *Maitland's Peripheral Manipulation.* 4th ed. Philadelphia: Elsevier.

Hertling D, Kessler R (2006). *Management of Common Musculoskeletal Disorders: Physical Therapy Principles and Methods,* 4th ed. Philadelphia, Lippincott Williams & Wilkins.

Hillegass E (2011). *Essentials of Cardiopulmonary Physical Therapy,* 3rd ed. St Louis, Elsevier.

Hislop H, Montgomery J (2007). *Daniels and Worthingham's Muscle Testing: Techniques of Manual Examination,* 8th ed. St Louis, Elsevier.

Hoppenfeld S (1982). *Physical Evaluation of the Spine and Extremities.* New York, Appleton-Century-Crofts.

Hospital for Special Surgery (2008). *Handbook of Postsurgical Rehabilitation Guidelines for the Orthopedic Clinician.* St Louis, Elsevier.

Howle J (2002). *Neuro-Developmental Treatment Approach: Theoretical Foundations and Principles of Clinical Practice.* Laguna Beach, CA, Neuro-Developmental Treatment Association.

Huber F, Wells C (2006). *Therapeutic Exercise—Treatment Planning for Progression.* St Louis, Elsevier.

Irion G (2009). *Comprehensive Wound Management,* 2nd ed. Thorofare, NJ, Slack.

Irion J, Irion G (2009). *Women's Health in Physical Therapy.* Baltimore, Lippincott Williams & Wilkins.

Jenkins D (2009). *Hollinshead's Functional Anatomy of the Limbs and Back,* 9th ed. Maryland Heights, MO, Elsevier.

Jewell D (2008). *Guide to Evidence-Based Physical Therapy Practice.* Sudbury, MA, Jones & Bartlett.

Kaltenborn F (2003). *Manual Mobilization of the Joints.* The Spine, 4th ed. Oslo, Norway, Olaf Norlis Bokhandel.

Kaltenborn F (2007). *Manual Mobilization of the Joints. Vol 1.* The Extremities, 6th ed. Oslo, Norway, Olaf Norlis Bokhandel.

Kaltenborn FM (2003). *Manual Mobilization of the Joints: The Kaltenborn Method of Joint Examination and Treatment, Vol 2.* The Spine. 4th ed. Oslo, Norway: Norlis Bokhandel.

Kaltenborn FM (2007). *Manual Mobilization of the Joints: Joint Examination and Basic Treatment. Vol 1,* The Extremities. 6th ed. Oslo, Norway: Norlis Bokhandel.

Kandel E, Schwartz J, Jessell T, et al (2008). *Principles of Neural Science,* 4th ed. New York, McGraw-Hill.

Kauffman T, Barr J, Moran M (2007). *Geriatric Rehabilitation Manual,* 2nd ed. St Louis, Elsevier.

Kendall F, McCreary E, Provance P, et al (2005). *Muscle Testing and Function,* 5th ed. Philadelphia, Lippincott Williams & Wilkins.

Kiernan J (2006). *Barr's The Human Nervous System: An Anatomical Viewpoint,* 8th ed. Philadelphia, Lippincott Williams & Wilkins.

Kisner C, Colby L (2013). *Therapeutic Exercise Foundations and Techniques,* 6th ed. Philadelphia, FA Davis.

Kizior R, Hodgson B (2009). *Saunders Drug Handbook for Health Professionals.* St Louis, Elsevier.

Kolt G, Snyder-Mackler L (2007). *Physical Therapies in Sport and Exercise,* 2nd ed. St Louis, Elsevier Churchill Livingstone.

Law M, MacDermid J (2007). *Evidence-Based Rehabilitation: A Guide to Practice,* 2nd ed. Thorofare, NJ, Slack.

Levangie P, Norkin C (2011). *Joint Structure and Function: A Comprehensive Analysis,* 5th ed. Philadelphia, FA Davis.

LeVeau B (2010). *Biomechanics of Human Motion: Basics and Beyond for the Health Professions.* Thorofare NY, Slack Inc.

Lewis C, Bottomley J (2007). *Geriatric Rehabilitation—A Clinical Approach,* 3rd ed. Upper Saddle River, NJ, Pearson Education.

Long T, Toscana K (2001). *Handbook of Pediatric Physical Therapy,* 2nd ed. Baltimore, Lippincott Williams & Wilkins.

Lundy-Ekman L (2013). *Neuroscience,* 4th ed. St Louis, Elsevier.

Lusardi M, Jorge M, Nielsen C (eds) (2013). *Orthotics and Prosthetics in Rehabilitation,* 3rd ed. St Louis, Elsevier Butterworth-Heinemann.

Magee D (2007). *Orthopedic Physical Assessment,* 5th ed. St Louis, Elsevier.

Magee D, Zachazewski J, Quillen W (2007). *Scientific Foundations and Principles of Practice in Musculoskeletal Rehabilitation.* St Louis, Elsevier.

Magee D, Zachazewski J, Quillen W (2009). *Pathology and Intervention in Musculoskeletal Rehabilitation.* St Louis, Elsevier.

Maitland GD (2005). *Maitland's Peripheral Manipulation.* 4th ed. Philadelphia: Elsevier.

Maitland GD (2005). *Maitland's Vertebral Manipulation.* 7th ed. Philadelphia: Elsevier.

Malone D, Lindsay K (2006). *Physical Therapy in Acute Care: A Clinician's Guide.* Thorofare, NJ, Slack.

Malone, TR, Hazle, C, Grey, ML (2008). *Imaging in rehabilitation.* New York, McGraw-Hill.

Martin S, Kessler M (2007). *Neurologic Interventions for Physical Therapy,* 2nd ed. St Louis, Elsevier.

McArdle W, Katch F, Katch V (2006). *Exercise Physiology: Energy, Nutrition and Human Performance,* 5th ed. Philadelphia, Lippincott Williams & Wilkins.

McCulloch J, Kloth L (2010). *Wound Healing: Evidence-Based Management* (Contemporary Perspectives in Rehabilitation, 4th ed. Philadelphia, FA Davis.

McKinnis L, Mulligan M (2013). *Musculoskeletal Imaging Handbook: A Guide for Primary Practitioners.* Philadelphia, FA Davis.

McKinnis L (2010). *Fundamentals of Musculoskeletal Imaging,* 3rd ed. Philadelphia, FA Davis.

Michlovitz S, Bellew J (2012). *Modalities for Therapeutic Intervention,* 5th ed. Philadelphia, FA Davis.

Minor SM, Minor MS (2010). *Patient Care Skills,* 6th ed. Upper Saddle River, NJ, Prentice Hall Health.

Moore K, Agur A, Dalley A (2010). *Essential Clinical Anatomy,* Baltimore, Lippincott Williams & Wilkins.

Myers B (2012). *Wound Management: Principles and Practice,* 3rd ed. Upper Saddle River, NJ, Prentice Hall.

Netter FH (2010). *Atlas of Human Anatomy,* 5th ed. St Louis, Elsevier.

Neumann DA (2010). *Kinesiology of the Musculoskeletal System: Foundations for Physical Rehabilitation,* 2nd 3rd. St Louis, Elsevier.

Norkin C, White J (2009). *Measurement of Joint Motion: A Guide to Goniometry,* 4th ed. Philadelphia, FA Davis.

Nosse L, Friberg D (2009). *Managerial and Supervisory Principles for Physical Therapists,* 3rd ed. Philadelphia, Lippincott Willliams & Wilkins.

Oatis C (2008). *Kinesiology: The Mechanics & Pathomechanics of Human Movement.* Philadelphia, Lippincott Williams & Wilkins.

OConnell D, OConnell J, Hinman M (2011). Special Tests of Cardiopulmonary, Vascular and Gastrointestinal Systems. Thorofare NJ, Slack Inc.

Olson KA (2009). *Manual Physical Therapy of the Spine.* St Louis, Elsevier.

O'Sullivan S, Schmitz T (2014). *Physical Rehabilitation,* 6th ed. Philadelphia, FA Davis.

O'Sullivan S, Schmitz T (2016). *Improving Functional Outcomes in Physical Rehabilitation,* 2nd ed. Philadelphia, FA Davis.

Paz J, West M (2013). *Acute Care Handbook for Physical Therapists,* 4th ed. St Louis, Elsevier.

Perry J, Burnfield J (2010). *Gait Analysis—Normal and Pathological Function,* 2nd ed. Thorofare NJ, Slack Inc.

Pierson F, Fairchild S (2013). *Principles and Techniques of Patient Care,* 5th ed. St Louis, Elsevier.

Porth C (2008). *Pathophysiology,* 7th ed. Philadelphia, Lippincott Williams & Wilkins.

Portney L, Watkins M (2008). *Foundations of Clinical Research,* 3rd ed. Upper Saddle River, NJ, Prentice Hall Health.

Prentice W (2011). *Therapeutic Modalities for Allied Health Professionals,* 4th ed. New York, McGraw-Hill Medical.

Purtilo R, Doherty R (2011). *Ethical Dimensions in the Health Professions*, 5th ed. St Louis, Elsevier.

Purtilo R, Haddad A (2007). *Health Professional and Patient Interaction*, 7th ed. St Louis, Elsevier.

Quinn L, Gordon J (2010). *Documentation for Rehabilitation: A Guide for Clinical Decision-Making*, 2nd ed. St Louis, Elsevier.

Reese N (2011). *Muscle and Sensory Testing*, 3rd ed. St Louis, Elsevier.

Reese NB, Bandy WD (2009). *Joint Range of Motion and Muscle Length*, 2nd ed. St Louis, Elsevier.

Robinson A, Snyder-Mackler L (2008). *Clinical Electrophysiology—Electrotherapy and Electrophysiologic Testing*, 3rd ed. Philadelphia, Lippincott Williams & Wilkins.

Roy S, Wolf S, Scalzitti D (2013). *The Rehabilitation Specialist's Handbook*, 4th ed. Philadelphia, FA Davis.

Rubin M, Safdieh J (2007). *Netter's Concise Neuroanatomy*. St Louis, Elsevier.

Sahrmann S (2011). *Movement System Impairment Syndromes of the Extremities, Cervical and Thoracic Spines*. St Louis, Elsevier. Mosby.

Salter R (1999). *Textbook of Disorders and Injuries of the Musculoskeletal System*, 3rd ed. Baltimore, Williams & Wilkins.

Schmidt R, Lee T (2011). *Motor Control and Learning*, 5th ed. Champaign, IL, Human Kinetics.

Scifers J (2008). *Special Tests for Neurologic Examination*. Thorofare, NJ, Slack.

Scott R (2009). *Promoting Legal and Ethical Awareness: A Primer for Health Professionals and Patients*. St Louis, Elsevier.

Scott R, Petrosinol L (2008). *Physical Therapy Management*. St Louis, Elsevier.

Shumway-Cook A, Woollacott M (2012). *Motor Control—Theory and Practical Applications*, 4th ed. Philadelphia, Lippincott Williams & Wilkins.

Shurr D, Michael J (2001). *Prosthetics and Orthotics*, 2nd ed. Upper Saddle River, NJ, Prentice Hall.

Snell R (2009). *Clinical Neuroanatomy*, 7th ed. Philadelphia, Lippincott Williams & Wilkins.

Somers M (2009). *Spinal Cord Injury Rehabilitation*, 3rd ed. Upper Saddle River, NJ, Prentice Hall.

Starkey C, Ryan J (2009). *Evaluation of Orthopedic and Athletic Injuries*, 3rd ed. Philadelphia, FA Davis.

Starkey C (2013). *Therapeutic Modalities*, 4th ed. Philadelphia, FA Davis.

Stephenson R, O'Connor L (2000). *Obstetric and Gynecologic Care in Physical Therapy*, 2nd ed. Thorofare, NJ, Slack.

Straus S, Sackett, D, et al (2011). *Evidence-Based Medicine*, 4th ed. Philadelphia, Churchill Livingstone.

Sussman C, Bates-Jenson B (2011). *Wound Care: A Collaborative Practice Manual for Physical Therapists and Nurses*, 4th ed. Philadelphia, Lippincott Williams & Wilkins.

Swain J, Bush K, Brosing J (2009). *Diagnostic Imaging for Physical Therapists*. St Louis, Elsevier.

Tecklin J (2007). *Pediatric Physical Therapy*, 4th ed. Philadelphia, Lippincott Williams & Wilkins.

Umphred D (ed) (2013). *Neurological Rehabilitation*, 6th ed. St Louis, Elsevier Mosby.

Watchie J (2009). *Cardiovascular and Pulmonary Physical Therapy: A Clinical Manual*, 2nd ed. St Louis, MO, Elsevier.

Watson T (ed) (2008). *Electrotherapy: Evidenced-Based Practice*, 12th ed. St Louis, Elsevier.

Waxman S (2002). *Correlative Neuroanatomy*, 25th ed. New York, McGraw-Hill.

White N, Delitto A, Manal, T, et al (2015). *The American Physical Therapy Association's Top Five Choosing Wisely Recommendations*. Phys Ther 95:9-24.

Whittle M (2007). *Gait Analysis*, 4th ed. St Louis, Elsevier.

Wilmore J, Costill D, Kenney W (2007). *Physiology of Sport and Exercise*, 4th ed. Champaign, IL, Human Kinetics.

Young P, Young P, Tolbert D (2007). *Basic Clinical Neuroscience*. Philadelphia, Lippincott Williams & Wilkins.

Index

Note: *b* indicates box; *f*, figure; and *t*, table.

B

C

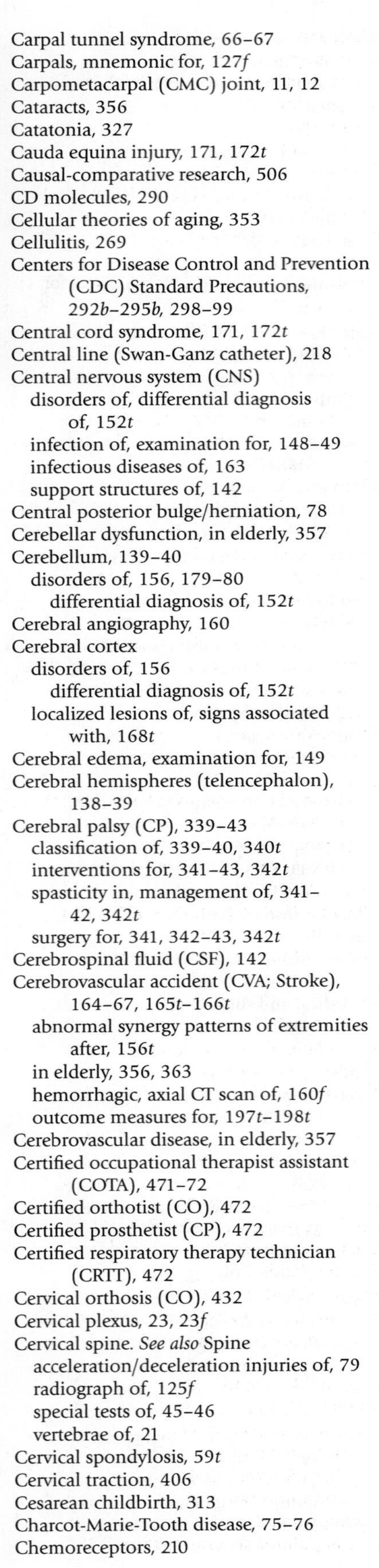

D

E

F

G

H

I

J

M

N

O

P

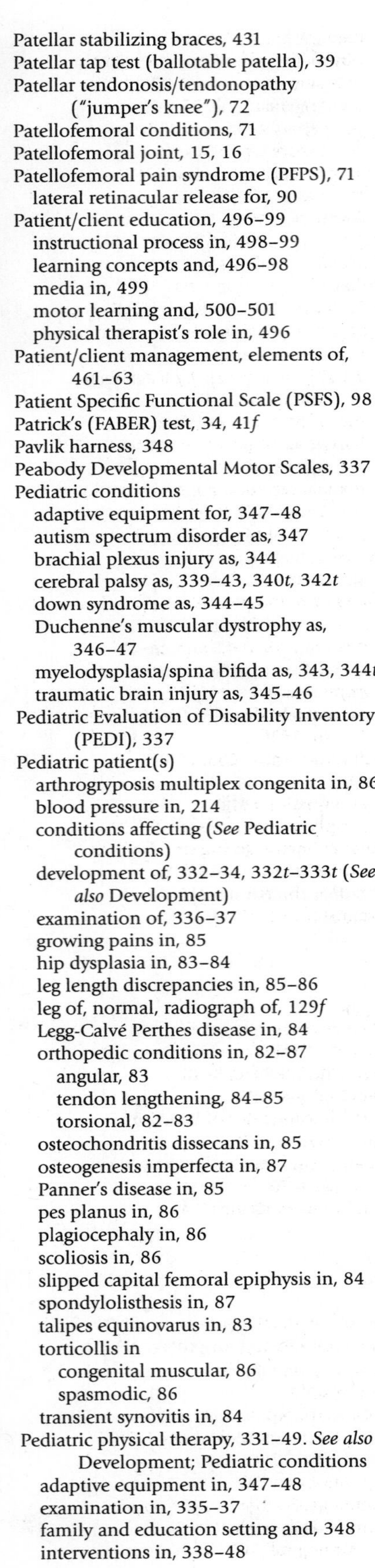

Index

S

T

U

V